AF767778

Advanced Mathematical Modeling and Numerical Solutions in Applied Mechanics and Engineering

Advanced Mathematical Modeling and Numerical Solutions in Applied Mechanics and Engineering

Editors

Shujin Laima
Yong Cao
Xiaowei Jin
Hehe Ren

MDPI

Basel • Beijing • Wuhan • Barcelona • Belgrade • Novi Sad • Cluj • Manchester

Editors
Shujin Laima
Harbin Institute of
Technology
Harbin
China

Yong Cao
Shanghai Jiao Tong
University
Shanghai
China

Xiaowei Jin
Harbin Institute of
Technology
Harbin
China

Hehe Ren
Nanjing University of
Aeronautics and Astronautics
Nanjing
China

Editorial Office
MDPI
St. Alban-Anlage 66
4052 Basel, Switzerland

This is a reprint of articles from the Special Issue published online in the open access journal *Mathematics* (ISSN 2227-7390) (available at: https://www.mdpi.com/si/mathematics/Mathematical_Model_Numerical_Solutions).

For citation purposes, cite each article independently as indicated on the article page online and as indicated below:

Lastname, A.A.; Lastname, B.B. Article Title. *Journal Name* **Year**, *Volume Number*, Page Range.

ISBN 978-3-7258-0219-7 (Hbk)
ISBN 978-3-7258-0220-3 (PDF)
doi.org/10.3390/books978-3-7258-0220-3

© 2024 by the authors. Articles in this book are Open Access and distributed under the Creative Commons Attribution (CC BY) license. The book as a whole is distributed by MDPI under the terms and conditions of the Creative Commons Attribution-NonCommercial-NoDerivs (CC BY-NC-ND) license.

Contents

About the Editors

Shujin Laima

Shujin Laima, a professor at the Civil Engineering School of Harbin Institute of Technology, has dedicated his career to bridge wind engineering. With a Ph.D. from Harbin Institute of Technology, his research focuses on fluid dynamics, fluid–structure interaction, and intelligent bridge wind engineering.

Dr. Laima's research interests cover a range of topics in fluid mechanics, wind engineering, and bridge engineering. His current projects include studying wind effects on bridge structures and developing advanced numerical simulation methods for fluid–structure interaction problems.

Yong Cao

Yong Cao, an associate professor at Shanghai Jiao Tong University, received his Ph.D. in December 2016 from the Tokyo Institute of Technology. His research interests include computational fluid dynamics, turbulence simulation, bluff body aerodynamics, separated flows, and wind engineering.

Xiaowei Jin

Xiaowei Jin, an associate professor in the Division of Intelligent Civil Infrastructure at Harbin Institute of Technology, received his Ph.D. from the same institution in January 2021. His primary research focus is on smart fluid mechanics, specifically fluid mechanics data modeling and the intelligent solution theory of nonlinear partial differential equations.

Hehe Ren

Hehe Ren, an associate professor at Nanjing University of Aeronautics and Astronautics, received his Ph.D. from Harbin Institute of Technology. His research interests span across multiple scales of wind field simulation methods, high-resolution typhoon numerical simulation, and physical mechanism analysis, as well as airport engineering and offshore wind turbine disaster prevention and reduction.

mathematics

MDPI

Article

A Parallel Approach of the Enhanced Craig–Bampton Method

Petr Pařík [1], Jin-Gyun Kim [2,*], Martin Isoz [1] and Chang-uk Ahn [2,3]

1 Department of Impact and Waves in Solids, Institute of Thermomechanics of the Czech Academy of Sciences, Dolejškova 5, 18200 Prague, Czech Republic; parik@it.cas.cz (P.P.); isozm@it.cas.cz (M.I.)
2 Department of Mechanical Engineering (Integrated Engineering), Kyung Hee University, Yongin-si 17104, Seoul 130-701, Korea; changuk.ahn@khu.ac.kr
3 Department of Robotics & Mechatronics Research, Korea Institute of Machinery and Materials, Daejeon 34103, Korea
* Correspondence: jingyun.kim@khu.ac.kr

Abstract: The enhanced Craig–Bampton (ECB) method is a novel extension of the original Craig–Bampton (CB) method, which has been widely used for component mode synthesis (CMS). The ECB method, using residual modal compensation that is neglected in the CB method, provides dramatic accuracy improvement of reduced matrices without an increasing number of eigenbasis. However, it also needs additional computational requirements to treat the residual flexibility. In this paper, an efficient parallelization of the ECB method is presented to handle this issue and accelerate the applicability for large-scale structural vibration problems. A new ECB formulation within a substructuring strategy is derived to achieve better scalability. The parallel implementation is based on OpenMP parallel architecture. METIS graph partitioning and Linear Algebra Package (LAPACK) are used to automated algebraic partitioning and computational linear algebra, respectively. Numerical examples are presented to evaluate the accuracy, scalability, and capability of the proposed parallel ECB method. Consequently, based on this work, one can expect effective computation of the ECB method as well as accuracy improvement.

Keywords: structural dynamics; model reduction; parallel computation; component mode synthesis; primal assembly

Citation: Pařík, P.; Kim, J.-G.; Isoz, M.; Ahn, C.-u. A Parallel Approach of the Enhanced Craig–Bampton Method. *Mathematics* **2021**, *9*, 3278. https://doi.org/10.3390/math9243278

Academic Editors: Shujin Laima, Yong Cao, Xiaowei Jin and Hehe Ren

Received: 10 November 2021
Accepted: 15 December 2021
Published: 16 December 2021

Publisher's Note: MDPI stays neutral with regard to jurisdictional claims in published maps and institutional affiliations.

Copyright: © 2021 by the authors. Licensee MDPI, Basel, Switzerland. This article is an open access article distributed under the terms and conditions of the Creative Commons Attribution (CC BY) license (https://creativecommons.org/licenses/by/4.0/).

1. Introduction

The Craig–Bampton (CB) method is one of the most successful component mode synthesis (CMS) techniques [1]. It has been implemented in various commercial software packages. The CB method was originally developed for structural vibration analysis in aerospace engineering, but it has been used in various engineering fields. The CB method is a standard coordinate reduction technique of elastic bodies (finite element model in general) in flexible multibody dynamics (FMBD) [2–5]. Recently, the CB method has been extended to structural vibration with uncertainties [6–8], and employed to multiphysics coupled problems, such as thermomechanical models [9] and vibro-acoustic interactions [10,11].

The CB method starts from substructuring (mathematically matrix partitioning). The original model is partitioned into substructures and the interface boundary. In the mode superposition manner, the substructural DOFs are presented by using few dominant modes that are substructural eigenvectors, and the constraint modes at the interface boundary are additionally employed to reassemble the substructural modes. Most eigenvectors of substructures, which are over 95% of the total DOFs in general, are neglected in the reduced matrix. It means that the accuracies of the CB-reduced matrices depend on the dominant and constraint modes. Thus, many researchers have sought to develop selection criteria of the important modes that well describe the substructural response [12–14]. Kim et al. investigated the performance of the various mode selection methods [15].

Conventionally, varying the numbers of retained dominant modes is one way to accuracy control of the reduced matrices. Using more modes provides better accuracy, but causes larger sizes of reduced matrices. Computational efficiency is then compromised in the desired accuracy level of the reduced matrices. The mode correction (or updating) techniques are alternatives of the mode selection methods. Considering residual flexibility to the dominant mode correction may be the most popular technique. The residual flexibility is natural in free interface CMS methods, which are the CMS methods with substructural interfaces, with classical and/or localized Lagrange multipliers [16–18]. However, the first trial using the residual flexibility of the CB method was proposed by Kim et al. [19], known as the enhanced CB (ECB) method. The ECB method considers the first order term of the residual flexibility in an infinite series expansion for dominant modal correction; nevertheless, it shows dramatic accuracy improvement, over (around) three or four digits, of the CB-reduced matrices, without increasing the number of the dominant modes. The ECB method has provided motives to many following works, such as iterative algorithms, considering higher order residual terms [20–22], precise stochastic model reduction [23], multiscale model reduction [24,25], eigenvalue problem solvers [26], etc. Kim et al. [27] generalized the model reduction with the residual flexibility, and summarized the relationship between the CMS and dynamic condensation methods. The accuracy improvement of the ECB families is clear, but treatments of the residual flexibility for the modal correction require additional computational costs. In particular, the ill-conditioned problems are severe through the higher iteration steps. Regularization may be considered to handle this problem. Go et al. [22] proposed a high fidelity iterative ECB method within a standard 16 digit computation, and compared the results with the other iterative techniques required over 32 digits to get stable numerical solutions. However, effective computation has been less investigated and, thus, the ECB family has been limited when applied into large-scale structural problems.

To overcome this issue, an efficient parallelization of the ECB method is presented. The original ECB formulation is then reorganized first for the parallel computation. In this numerical algorithm, the METIS library [28] is used to partition the structure automatically, then the reduced matrices are calculated directly by assembling blockwise contributions from substructures, exploiting the fact that substructures are independent and can be processed in parallel. The Intel MKL library [29] provides the necessary matrix operations. The blockwise ECB formulation for the applicability of the parallel computation is presented in Section 2. The details of the parallel implementation of the ECB method, including the algorithm, are described in Section 3. The performances of both accuracy and computational efficiency of the proposed algorithm are investigated in Section 4. Conclusions are presented in Section 5.

2. The Enhanced Craig–Bampton Method

The enhanced Craig–Bampton method [19] is presented in this section. In the substructuring manner, the original formulations are explicitly presented and modified for parallel implementation. The equations of the motion of structural dynamics can be written as

$$\mathbf{M}\ddot{\mathbf{u}} + \mathbf{K}\mathbf{u} = \mathbf{f}, \tag{1a}$$

$$\mathbf{M} = \begin{bmatrix} \mathbf{M}_s & \mathbf{M}_c \\ \mathbf{M}_c^T & \mathbf{M}_b \end{bmatrix}, \quad \mathbf{K} = \begin{bmatrix} \mathbf{K}_s & \mathbf{K}_c \\ \mathbf{K}_c^T & \mathbf{K}_b \end{bmatrix}, \tag{1b}$$

$$\mathbf{u} = \begin{bmatrix} \mathbf{u}_s \\ \mathbf{u}_b \end{bmatrix}, \quad \mathbf{f} = \begin{bmatrix} \mathbf{f}_s \\ \mathbf{f}_b \end{bmatrix}, \tag{1c}$$

where $\mathbf{M}$ and $\mathbf{K}$ are mass and stiffness matrices, respectively; $\mathbf{u}$ and $\mathbf{f}$ are displacement and force vectors, respectively. The subscripts s, b, and c denote substructure, interface boundary, and coupling matrices (or vectors), respectively. Here, the matrices and vectors with respect to substructures are

$$\mathbf{M}_s = diag\begin{bmatrix} \mathbf{M}_s^{(1)} & \dots & \mathbf{M}_s^{(i)} & \dots & \mathbf{M}_s^{(N_s)} \end{bmatrix}, \tag{2a}$$

$$\mathbf{K}_s = diag\begin{bmatrix} \mathbf{K}_s^{(1)} & \dots & \mathbf{K}_s^{(i)} & \dots & \mathbf{K}_s^{(N_s)} \end{bmatrix}, \tag{2b}$$

$$\mathbf{M}_c = \begin{bmatrix} \mathbf{M}_c^{(1)} \\ \vdots \\ \mathbf{M}_c^{(i)} \\ \vdots \\ \mathbf{M}_c^{(N_s)} \end{bmatrix}, \mathbf{K}_c = \begin{bmatrix} \mathbf{K}_c^{(1)} \\ \vdots \\ \mathbf{K}_c^{(i)} \\ \vdots \\ \mathbf{K}_c^{(N_s)} \end{bmatrix}, \mathbf{u}_s = \begin{bmatrix} \mathbf{u}_s^{(1)} \\ \vdots \\ \mathbf{u}_s^{(i)} \\ \vdots \\ \mathbf{u}_s^{(N_s)} \end{bmatrix}, \mathbf{f}_s = \begin{bmatrix} \mathbf{f}_s^{(1)} \\ \vdots \\ \mathbf{f}_s^{(i)} \\ \vdots \\ \mathbf{f}_s^{(N_s)} \end{bmatrix}, \tag{2c}$$

where $\mathbf{M}_s$ and $\mathbf{K}_s$ are block diagonal mass and stiffness matrices of substructures, respectively. N_s denotes number of substructures.

In the CB method [1], the original displacement vector $\mathbf{u}$ is approximated by combining the substructural eigenvectors and interface constraint modes as follows:

$$\mathbf{u} \approx \bar{\mathbf{u}} = \begin{bmatrix} \bar{\mathbf{u}}_s \\ \mathbf{u}_b \end{bmatrix} = \mathbf{T}\mathbf{p}, \mathbf{T} = \left[\begin{array}{c|c} \mathbf{\Phi}_s & \mathbf{C} \\ \mathbf{0} & \mathbf{I}_b \end{array} \right], \mathbf{p} = \begin{bmatrix} \mathbf{q}_s \\ \mathbf{u}_b \end{bmatrix}, \mathbf{C} = -\mathbf{K}_s^{-1}\mathbf{K}_c \tag{3}$$

where an overbar denotes an approximation. $\mathbf{T}$ is a transformation matrix, $\mathbf{q}_s$ is a generalized coordinate vector of substructures, $\mathbf{C}$ is a constraint matrix, and $\mathbf{I}_b$ is an identity matrix of interface boundary, respectively. $\mathbf{\Phi}_s$ is a substructural eigenvector matrix calculated from the following eigenvalue problems:

$$\mathbf{K}_s^{(k)}(\boldsymbol{\phi}^{(k)})_i = \lambda_i^{(k)}\mathbf{M}_s^{(k)}(\boldsymbol{\phi}^{(k)})_i, \text{ for } i = 1, 2, \dots, n_s^{(k)}, k = 1, 2, \dots, N_s, \tag{4}$$

where $n_s^{(k)}$ is the number of DOFs of the kth substructure. The number of total DOFs is defined as $n = n_b + n_s$ ($n_s = \sum n_s^{(k)}$), in which n_b is the number of interface boundary DOFs. The ith eigenvalue and its corresponding eigenvector of the kth substructure are denoted as $\lambda_i^{(k)}$ and $(\boldsymbol{\phi}^{(k)})_i$, respectively. Then, the component matrices and vectors of Equation (3) are

$$\mathbf{\Phi}_s = diag\begin{bmatrix} \mathbf{\Phi}_s^{(1)} & \dots & \mathbf{\Phi}_s^{(k)} & \dots & \mathbf{\Phi}_s^{(N_s)} \end{bmatrix}, \tag{5a}$$

$$\mathbf{\Phi}_s^{(k)} = \begin{bmatrix} \left(\boldsymbol{\phi}^{(k)}\right)_1 & \cdots & \left(\boldsymbol{\phi}^{(k)}\right)_i & \cdots & \left(\boldsymbol{\phi}^{(k)}\right)_{n_s^{(k)}} \end{bmatrix}, \tag{5b}$$

$$\mathbf{u}_s = \begin{bmatrix} \mathbf{u}_s^{(1)} \\ \vdots \\ \mathbf{u}_s^{(k)} \\ \vdots \\ \mathbf{u}_s^{(N_s)} \end{bmatrix}, \mathbf{f}_s = \begin{bmatrix} \mathbf{f}_s^{(1)} \\ \vdots \\ \mathbf{f}_s^{(k)} \\ \vdots \\ \mathbf{f}_s^{(N_s)} \end{bmatrix}, \mathbf{C} = \begin{bmatrix} \mathbf{C}^{(1)} \\ \vdots \\ \mathbf{C}^{(k)} \\ \vdots \\ \mathbf{C}^{(N_s)} \end{bmatrix}, \tag{5c}$$

$$\mathbf{C}^{(i)} = -\mathbf{K}_s^{(i)^{-1}}\mathbf{K}_c^{(i)}, \text{ for } i = 1, 2, \dots, n_s^{(k)}, k = 1, 2, \dots, N_s. \tag{5d}$$

Note that the eigenvectors in this paper are defined as *mass-orthonormal* vectors.

By decomposing dominant and residual eigenvectors, the approximated displacement vector in Equation (3) can be rewritten as

$$\bar{\mathbf{u}} = \mathbf{T}\mathbf{p},\ \mathbf{T} = \left[\begin{array}{cc|c} \mathbf{\Phi}_d & \mathbf{\Phi}_r & \mathbf{C} \\ \mathbf{0} & \mathbf{0} & \mathbf{I}_b \end{array}\right],\ \mathbf{p} = \left[\begin{array}{c} \mathbf{q}_d \\ \mathbf{q}_r \\ \mathbf{u}_b \end{array}\right], \tag{6a}$$

$$\mathbf{\Phi}_j = diag\left[\begin{array}{ccccc} \mathbf{\Phi}_j^{(1)} & \ldots & \mathbf{\Phi}_j^{(k)} & \ldots & \mathbf{\Phi}_j^{(N_s)} \end{array}\right], \tag{6b}$$

$$\mathbf{\Phi}_j^{(k)} = \left[\begin{array}{ccccc} \left(\boldsymbol{\phi}^{(k)}\right)_1 & \cdots & \left(\boldsymbol{\phi}^{(k)}\right)_i & \cdots & \left(\boldsymbol{\phi}^{(k)}\right)_{n_j^{(k)}} \end{array}\right], \tag{6c}$$

$$\text{for } i = 1, 2, \ldots, n_j^{(k)},\ j \in [d, r],\ k = 1, 2, \ldots, N_s, \tag{6d}$$

where $\mathbf{\Phi}_d$ and $\mathbf{\Phi}_r$ are dominant and residual substructural eigenvector matrices, respectively, and both are block diagonal matrices. $\mathbf{q}_d$ and $\mathbf{q}_r$ are the corresponding generalized coordinate vectors, respectively. The subscripts d and r denote the dominant and residual terms, respectively. Here, n_d and n_r denote numbers of the dominant and residual modes, which are defined as $n_d = \sum n_d^{(k)}$ and $n_r = \sum n_r^{(k)}$, respectively. The number of the dominant modes is much less than the number of the residual modes in general structural vibration ($n_d \ll n_r < n_s = n_d + n_r$).

Using Equations (6a)–(6d) in Equations (1a)–(1c), we obtain the equations of motion for the partitioned structure

$$\mathbf{T}^T\left[\frac{d^2}{dt^2}\mathbf{M} + \mathbf{K}\right]\mathbf{T}\mathbf{p} = \mathbf{T}^T\mathbf{f} \longrightarrow \tag{7a}$$

$$\left[\begin{array}{ccc} \hat{\mathbf{\Lambda}}_d & \mathbf{0} & \frac{d^2}{dt^2}\mathbf{\Phi}_d^T\hat{\mathbf{M}}_c \\ \mathbf{0}^T & \hat{\mathbf{\Lambda}}_r & \frac{d^2}{dt^2}\mathbf{\Phi}_r^T\hat{\mathbf{M}}_c \\ \frac{d^2}{dt^2}\hat{\mathbf{M}}_c^T\mathbf{\Phi}_d & \frac{d^2}{dt^2}\hat{\mathbf{M}}_c^T\mathbf{\Phi}_r & \hat{\mathbf{K}}_b + \frac{d^2}{dt^2}\hat{\mathbf{M}}_b \end{array}\right]\left[\begin{array}{c} \mathbf{q}_d \\ \mathbf{q}_r \\ \mathbf{u}_b \end{array}\right] = \left[\begin{array}{c} \mathbf{\Phi}_d^T\mathbf{f}_s \\ \mathbf{\Phi}_r^T\mathbf{f}_s \\ \mathbf{f}_b + \mathbf{C}^T\mathbf{f}_s \end{array}\right], \tag{7b}$$

and the component matrices are

$$\hat{\mathbf{\Lambda}}_d = \mathbf{\Lambda}_d + \frac{d^2}{dt^2}\mathbf{I}_d,\ \mathbf{\Lambda}_d = \mathbf{\Phi}_d^T\mathbf{K}_s\mathbf{\Phi}_d,\ \mathbf{I}_d = \mathbf{\Phi}_d^T\mathbf{M}_s\mathbf{\Phi}_d, \tag{8a}$$

$$\hat{\mathbf{\Lambda}}_r = \mathbf{\Lambda}_r + \frac{d^2}{dt^2}\mathbf{I}_r,\ \mathbf{\Lambda}_r = \mathbf{\Phi}_r^T\mathbf{K}_s\mathbf{\Phi}_r,\ \mathbf{I}_r = \mathbf{\Phi}_r^T\mathbf{M}_s\mathbf{\Phi}_r, \tag{8b}$$

$$\hat{\mathbf{M}}_c = \mathbf{M}_c + \mathbf{M}_s\mathbf{C},\quad \hat{\mathbf{K}}_b = \mathbf{K}_b + \mathbf{K}_c^T\mathbf{C}. \tag{8c}$$

$$\hat{\mathbf{M}}_b = \mathbf{M}_b + \mathbf{M}_c^T\mathbf{C} + \mathbf{C}^T\mathbf{M}_c + \mathbf{C}^T\mathbf{M}_s\mathbf{C}$$
$$\longrightarrow \hat{\mathbf{M}}_b = \mathbf{M}_b + \mathbf{M}_c^T\mathbf{C} + \mathbf{C}^T\hat{\mathbf{M}}_c. \tag{8d}$$

From the mass-orthonormal condition, $\mathbf{I}_d$ and $\mathbf{I}_r$ are identity matrices, and $\mathbf{\Lambda}_d$ and $\mathbf{\Lambda}_r$ are diagonal matrices with the dominant and residual eigenvalues computed from Equation (4), respectively.

The following reduced eigenvalue problem of the original CB method can be obtained by neglecting the terms of the generalized coordinates with respect to the residual modes from Equations (7a) and (7b):

$$\mathbf{K}_{\text{CB}}\left[\begin{array}{c} \mathbf{q}_d \\ \mathbf{u}_b \end{array}\right] = \omega^2\mathbf{M}_{\text{CB}}\left[\begin{array}{c} \mathbf{q}_d \\ \mathbf{u}_b \end{array}\right], \tag{9a}$$

$$\mathbf{K}_{\text{CB}} = \left[\begin{array}{cc} \mathbf{\Lambda}_d & \mathbf{0} \\ \mathbf{0} & \hat{\mathbf{K}}_b \end{array}\right],\ \mathbf{M}_{\text{CB}} = \left[\begin{array}{cc} \mathbf{I}_d & \mathbf{\Phi}_d^T\hat{\mathbf{M}}_c \\ \hat{\mathbf{M}}_c^T\mathbf{\Phi}_d & \hat{\mathbf{M}}_b \end{array}\right], \tag{9b}$$

$$\mathbf{\Lambda}_d = diag\left[\begin{array}{ccccc} \mathbf{\Lambda}_d^{(1)} & \ldots & \mathbf{\Lambda}_d^{(k)} & \ldots & \mathbf{\Lambda}_d^{(N_s)} \end{array}\right], \tag{9c}$$

in which ω is an angular frequency ($\lambda = \omega^2$). This is also derived by using the CB transformation matrix $\mathbf{T}_0$ from $\mathbf{T}$, neglecting the residual modes ($\mathbf{\Phi}_r$) in Equations (6a)–(6d) as

$$\mathbf{M}_{\text{CB}} = \mathbf{T}_0^T\mathbf{M}\mathbf{T}_0,\ \mathbf{K}_{\text{CB}} = \mathbf{T}_0^T\mathbf{K}\mathbf{T}_0,\ \mathbf{T}_0 = \left[\begin{array}{c|c} \mathbf{\Phi}_d & \mathbf{C} \\ \mathbf{0} & \mathbf{I}_b \end{array}\right]. \tag{10}$$

Equation (10) means that the residual mode are simply neglected in the original CB method, but considering the residual mode effect in the model reduction process provides a change to dramatic improvement. It is a main idea of the enhanced CB method. From the second row of Equations (7a) and (7b), assuming $\boldsymbol{\Phi}_r^T \mathbf{f}_s = \mathbf{0}$, the generalized coordinate vector of the residual modes, $\mathbf{q}_r$, can be expressed as

$$\mathbf{q}_r = -\hat{\boldsymbol{\Lambda}}_r^{-1} \boldsymbol{\Phi}_r^T \hat{\mathbf{M}}_c \left[\frac{d^2}{dt^2} \mathbf{u}_b \right]. \tag{11}$$

Using Equation (11) in Equations (7a) and (7b), $\mathbf{q}_d$ and $\mathbf{u}_b$ are redefined, and then the displacement vector in Equations (6a)–(6d) is modified as

$$\bar{\mathbf{u}} = \mathbf{T}_1 \begin{bmatrix} \mathbf{q}_d \\ \mathbf{u}_b \end{bmatrix}, \quad \mathbf{T}_1 = \mathbf{T}_0 + \mathbf{T}_r \boldsymbol{\Xi}, \tag{12a}$$

$$\mathbf{T}_r = \begin{bmatrix} \mathbf{0} & \mathbf{F}_r \hat{\mathbf{M}}_c \\ \mathbf{0} & \mathbf{0} \end{bmatrix}, \quad \boldsymbol{\Xi} := \mathbf{M}_{CB}^{-1} \mathbf{K}_{CB} = \begin{bmatrix} \boldsymbol{\Xi}_1 & \boldsymbol{\Xi}_2 \\ \boldsymbol{\Xi}_3 & \boldsymbol{\Xi}_4 \end{bmatrix}, \tag{12b}$$

$$\mathbf{F}_r = diag\begin{bmatrix} \mathbf{F}_r^{(1)} & \dots & \mathbf{F}_r^{(k)} & \dots & \mathbf{F}_r^{(N_s)} \end{bmatrix}, \tag{12c}$$

$$\mathbf{F}_r^{(k)} = \boldsymbol{\Phi}_r^{(k)} \boldsymbol{\Lambda}_r^{(k)^{-1}} \boldsymbol{\Phi}_r^{(k)^T} = \mathbf{K}_s^{(k)^{-1}} - \mathbf{F}_d^{(k)}, \; \mathbf{F}_d^{(k)} = \boldsymbol{\Phi}_d^{(k)} \boldsymbol{\Lambda}_d^{(k)^{-1}} \boldsymbol{\Phi}_d^{(k)^T}, \tag{12d}$$

where $\mathbf{F}_r^{(k)}$ is the residual flexibility of the kth substructure, which is simply computed by its full and dominant flexibilities. $\boldsymbol{\Xi}$ defined by using the CB-reduced matrices is an asymmetric matrix. The new transformation matrix $\mathbf{T}_1$ can be obtained by the original CB transformation matrix $\mathbf{T}_0$ and the additional transformation matrix $\mathbf{T}_r$, including the residual modal effect. The derivation details are well presented in Reference [19].

Using the enhanced transformation matrix $\mathbf{T}_1$ in Equation (10) instead of $\mathbf{T}_0$, the following enhanced reduced mass and stiffness matrices are defined

$$\mathbf{M}_{\text{ECB}} = \mathbf{T}_1^T \mathbf{M} \mathbf{T}_1 = \mathbf{M}_{\text{CB}} + \boldsymbol{\Xi}^T \mathbf{T}_r^T \mathbf{M} \mathbf{T}_0 + \mathbf{T}_0^T \mathbf{M} \mathbf{T}_r \boldsymbol{\Xi} + \boldsymbol{\Xi}^T \mathbf{T}_r^T \mathbf{M} \mathbf{T}_r \boldsymbol{\Xi}, \tag{13a}$$

$$\mathbf{K}_{\text{ECB}} = \mathbf{T}_1^T \mathbf{K} \mathbf{T}_1 = \mathbf{K}_{\text{CB}} + \boldsymbol{\Xi}^T \mathbf{T}_r^T \mathbf{K} \mathbf{T}_0 + \mathbf{T}_0^T \mathbf{K} \mathbf{T}_r \boldsymbol{\Xi} + \boldsymbol{\Xi}^T \mathbf{T}_r^T \mathbf{K} \mathbf{T}_r \boldsymbol{\Xi}. \tag{13b}$$

It clearly shows that the residual mode correction is additionally considered in the ECB-reduced matrices. Therefore, the ECB formulation provides more accurate reduced matrices than the original CB method.

Using the orthogonal condition and investigating the component matrix level in Equations (13a) and (13b), we obtain

$$\mathbf{A} := \mathbf{T}_r^T \mathbf{M} \mathbf{T}_0 = \mathbf{T}_r^T \mathbf{K} \mathbf{T}_r = \begin{bmatrix} \mathbf{0} & \mathbf{0} \\ \mathbf{0} & \mathbf{A}_{22} \end{bmatrix}, \mathbf{A}_{22} = \hat{\mathbf{M}}_c^T \mathbf{F}_r \hat{\mathbf{M}}_c, \tag{14a}$$

$$\mathbf{B} := \mathbf{T}_r^T \mathbf{M} \mathbf{T}_r = \begin{bmatrix} \mathbf{0} & \mathbf{0} \\ \mathbf{0} & \mathbf{B}_{22} \end{bmatrix}, \mathbf{B}_{22} = \hat{\mathbf{M}}_c^T \mathbf{F}_r \mathbf{M}_s \mathbf{F}_r \hat{\mathbf{M}}_c, \tag{14b}$$

$$\mathbf{T}_r^T \mathbf{K} \mathbf{T}_0 = \mathbf{0}. \tag{14c}$$

Using Equations (14a)–(14c), the reduced matrices in Equations (13a) and (13b) are rewritten as

$$\mathbf{M}_{\text{ECB}} = \mathbf{M}_{\text{CB}} + \boldsymbol{\Xi}^T \mathbf{A} + [\boldsymbol{\Xi}^T \mathbf{A}]^T + \boldsymbol{\Xi}^T \mathbf{B} \boldsymbol{\Xi}, \tag{15a}$$

$$\mathbf{K}_{\text{ECB}} = \mathbf{K}_{\text{CB}} + [\boldsymbol{\Xi}^T \mathbf{A}] \boldsymbol{\Xi}, \; \boldsymbol{\Xi}^T \mathbf{A} = \begin{bmatrix} \mathbf{0} & \boldsymbol{\Xi}_3^T \mathbf{A}_{22} \\ \mathbf{0} & \boldsymbol{\Xi}_4^T \mathbf{A}_{22} \end{bmatrix}, \tag{15b}$$

and then its eigenvalue problem is

$$\mathbf{K}_{\text{ECB}} \begin{bmatrix} \mathbf{q}_d \\ \mathbf{u}_b \end{bmatrix} = \omega^2 \mathbf{M}_{\text{ECB}} \begin{bmatrix} \mathbf{q}_d \\ \mathbf{u}_b \end{bmatrix}. \tag{16}$$

It clearly shows that the sizes of the ECB-reduced matrices are exactly the same as the sizes of the CB-reduced matrices.

After solving Equation (16), the original displacement vector can be obtained by back-transformation from the reduced unknown vector as

$$\mathbf{u} \approx \bar{\mathbf{u}} = \begin{bmatrix} \bar{\mathbf{u}}_s \\ \mathbf{u}_b \end{bmatrix} = \mathbf{T}_1 \begin{bmatrix} \mathbf{q}_d \\ \mathbf{u}_b \end{bmatrix}, \tag{17}$$

This is known as the *modal-displacement method* [30], which is a standard domain recovery technique. It also clearly shows that the substructural displacement vector $\bar{\mathbf{u}}_s$ is only approximated and needs to recover.

Considering Equations (12a)–(12d), the ECB transformation matrix is explicitly written as

$$\mathbf{T}_1 = \mathbf{T}_0 + \mathbf{T}_r \Xi = \left[\begin{array}{c|c} \mathbf{\Phi}_d + \mathbf{F}_r \hat{\mathbf{M}}_c \Xi_3 & \mathbf{C} + \mathbf{F}_r \hat{\mathbf{M}}_c \Xi_4 \\ \mathbf{0} & \mathbf{I}_b \end{array} \right], \tag{18}$$

and $\bar{\mathbf{u}}_s$ is then computed by

$$\bar{\mathbf{u}}_s = \left[\mathbf{\Phi}_d + \mathbf{F}_r \hat{\mathbf{M}}_c \Xi_3\right] \mathbf{q}_d + \left[\mathbf{C} + \mathbf{F}_r \hat{\mathbf{M}}_c \Xi_4\right] \mathbf{u}_b. \tag{19}$$

3. Parallel Implementation of the ECB Method

The implementation of the enhanced Craig–Bampton method is coded in Fortran, using OpenMP [31] for parallelization. The computation of matrix inversion and eigenproblem solution is done using the Intel Math Kernel Library [29], and the partitioning is done using the METIS library [28].

There are principally three levels of parallelization in the reduction algorithm:

1. All independent parts of the algorithm are executed in parallel (e.g., component matrices computation).
2. All 'inner' matrix operations (e.g., matrix-matrix multiplication) are explicitly parallelized and/or vectorized over matrix rows or columns.
3. At the lowest level, the code is optimized and auto-parallelized by the compiler. Library functions provided by METIS and Intel MKL are also optimized and parallelized.

3.1. Reduction Algorithm

Computing the reduced model matrices by multiplication with the transformation matrices

$$\mathbf{K}_{\mathrm{CB}} = \mathbf{T}_0^{\mathrm{T}} \mathbf{K} \mathbf{T}_0, \qquad \mathbf{M}_{\mathrm{CB}} = \mathbf{T}_0^{\mathrm{T}} \mathbf{M} \mathbf{T}_0 \tag{20}$$

and subsequently

$$\mathbf{K}_{\mathrm{ECB}} = \mathbf{T}_1^{\mathrm{T}} \mathbf{K} \mathbf{T}_1, \qquad \mathbf{M}_{\mathrm{ECB}} = \mathbf{T}_1^{\mathrm{T}} \mathbf{M} \mathbf{T}_1 \tag{21}$$

is not efficient in case of large structures. Therefore, our reduction algorithm closely follows the derivation given in Section 2. The properties of the involved matrices are carefully examined and exploited to calculate the reduced matrices directly and efficiently.

Our reduction algorithm, outlined in Figure 1, is described in the following subsections. The original model, represented by the sparse global stiffness matrix $\tilde{\mathbf{K}}$ and sparse global mass matrix $\tilde{\mathbf{M}}$, is supplied by the user, who also chooses the number of substructures N and the cutoff frequency f_{max}. The global matrices are *not* expected to contain any prescribed (fixed) DOFs.

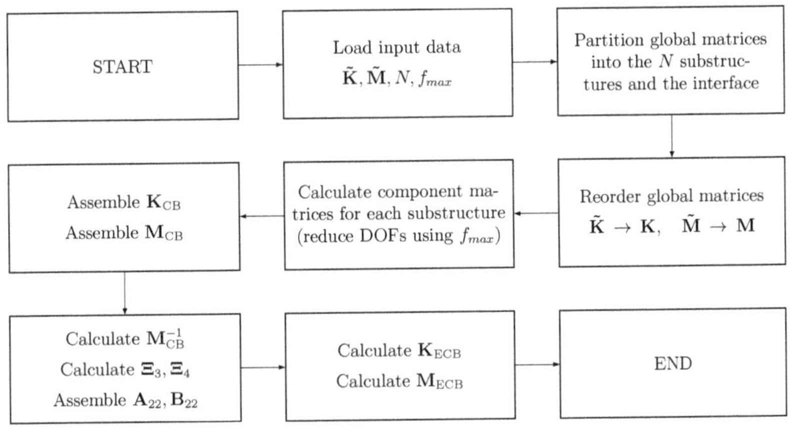

Figure 1. Parallel reduction algorithm.

3.1.1. Partitioning

The original model (structure) is partitioned into N partitions (substructures) using the METIS library routines. The obtained partitions, however, cannot be readily used, because they may contain interface DOFs. Therefore, an extra post-processing step is necessary to identify the interface DOFs, remove them from the substructures, and put them into the additional $(N+1)$-th 'interface' partition.

Finally, the original global stiffness and mass matrix are reordered so that their rows and columns correspond to the ordering of partitions

$$\mathbf{K} = \mathbf{P}\tilde{\mathbf{K}}\mathbf{P}, \qquad \mathbf{M} = \mathbf{P}\tilde{\mathbf{M}}\mathbf{P}, \tag{22}$$

where $\mathbf{P}$ represents the associated permutation matrix. Once again, it would not be efficient to form the permutation matrix explicitly and perform the double matrix multiplication. Consequently, the elements in the stiffness and mass matrices are widely distributed in the whole domain and, thus, those are inadequate for the sparse solver. To handle this issue, the matrices are reordered directly during a matrix copy operation. The reordering eliminates the need for complicated index-keeping and results in a significant simplification and speed-up of all subsequent matrix operations. The original global matrices are discarded after the reordering as they are no longer required.

3.1.2. Reduction

After the reordering, the substructural matrices $\mathbf{K}_s^{(i)}$, $\mathbf{K}_c^{(i)}$, $\mathbf{M}_s^{(i)}$ and $\mathbf{M}_c^{(i)}$ can be easily extracted for any i-th substructure, see Equations (2a)–(2c).

Each substructure $i = 1, \dots, N$ is independent and, therefore, can be processed in parallel to obtain the following 'substructural' component matrices using Equations (8a)–(8d):

$$\boldsymbol{\Lambda}_d^{(i)}, \tag{23}$$

$$\hat{\mathbf{D}}_K^{(i)} = (\mathbf{K}_c^{(i)})^{\mathrm{T}}\mathbf{C}^{(i)}, \tag{24}$$

$$\hat{\mathbf{C}}^{(i)} = (\boldsymbol{\Phi}_d^{(i)})^{\mathrm{T}}\hat{\mathbf{M}}_c^{(i)}, \tag{25}$$

$$\hat{\mathbf{D}}_M^{(i)} = (\mathbf{M}_c^{(i)})^{\mathrm{T}}\mathbf{C}^{(i)} + (\mathbf{C}^{(i)})^{\mathrm{T}}\hat{\mathbf{M}}_c^{(i)} \tag{26}$$

and the following 'interface' component matrices using Equations (14a)–(14c):

$$\hat{\mathbf{A}}^{(i)} = (\hat{\mathbf{M}}_c^{(i)})^{\mathrm{T}} \mathbf{F}_r^{(i)} \hat{\mathbf{M}}_c^{(i)}, \tag{27}$$

$$\hat{\mathbf{B}}^{(i)} = (\hat{\mathbf{M}}_c^{(i)})^{\mathrm{T}} \mathbf{F}_r^{(i)} \mathbf{M}_s^{(i)} \mathbf{F}_r^{(i)} \hat{\mathbf{M}}_c^{(i)}. \tag{28}$$

Although the interface component matrices will not be required until later, it is more efficient to include them here as their calculations are also independent for each substructure.

The number of reduced DOFs (i.e., dominant modes) of each substructure is determined automatically by examining the eigenvalues obtained from the eigenproblem

$$\mathbf{K}_s^{(i)} \mathbf{q}^{(i)} = \mathbf{\Lambda}_s^{(i)} \mathbf{M}_s^{(i)} \mathbf{q}^{(i)}$$

and considering only the eigenmodes that correspond to the eigenfrequencies that are lower than the user-chosen cutoff frequency f_{max}.

Finally, the substructural component matrices are assembled to directly obtain the reduced matrices as per Equation (9b):

$$\mathbf{K}_{\mathrm{CB}} = \begin{bmatrix} \sum \mathbf{\Lambda}_d^{(i)} & \mathbf{0} \\ \mathbf{0} & \mathbf{K}_b + \sum \hat{\mathbf{D}}_K^{(i)} \end{bmatrix}, \tag{29}$$

$$\mathbf{M}_{\mathrm{CB}} = \begin{bmatrix} \mathbf{I}_d & \sum \hat{\mathbf{C}}^{(i)} \\ \text{sym.} & \mathbf{M}_b + \sum \hat{\mathbf{D}}_M^{(i)} \end{bmatrix}. \tag{30}$$

3.1.3. Enhanced Reduction

To compute the enhanced reduced order matrices, we need the standard reduced order matrices and interface component matrices calculated earlier.

From the reduced model, the component matrices Ξ_3 and Ξ_4 are computed using Equation (12b):

$$\Xi = \mathbf{M}_{\mathrm{CB}}^{-1} \mathbf{K}_{\mathrm{CB}} = \begin{bmatrix} \Xi_1 & \Xi_2 \\ \Xi_3 & \Xi_4 \end{bmatrix}. \tag{31}$$

However, the full matrix multiplication is not necessary, because the component matrices Ξ_1 and Ξ_2 are never used.

Independently, the component matrices $\mathbf{A}_{22}$ and $\mathbf{B}_{22}$ are assembled using Equations (14a)–(14c):

$$\mathbf{A}_{22} = \sum \hat{\mathbf{A}}^{(i)}, \qquad \mathbf{B}_{22} = \sum \hat{\mathbf{B}}^{(i)}. \tag{32}$$

Finally, using the component matrices, the enhanced reduced matrices are computed directly using Equations (15a) and (15b):

$$\mathbf{K}_{\mathrm{ECB}} = \mathbf{K}_{\mathrm{CB}} + \begin{bmatrix} \Xi_3^{\mathrm{T}} \mathbf{A}_{22} \Xi_3 & \Xi_3^{\mathrm{T}} \mathbf{A}_{22} \Xi_4 \\ \text{sym.} & \Xi_4^{\mathrm{T}} \mathbf{A}_{22} \Xi_4 \end{bmatrix}, \tag{33}$$

$$\mathbf{M}_{\mathrm{ECB}} = \mathbf{M}_{\mathrm{CB}} + \begin{bmatrix} 0 & \Xi_3^{\mathrm{T}} \mathbf{A}_{22} \\ \text{sym.} & \Xi_4^{\mathrm{T}} \mathbf{A}_{22} + \mathbf{A}_{22} \Xi_4 \end{bmatrix} + \begin{bmatrix} \Xi_3^{\mathrm{T}} \mathbf{B}_{22} \Xi_3 & \Xi_3^{\mathrm{T}} \mathbf{B}_{22} \Xi_4 \\ \text{sym.} & \Xi_4^{\mathrm{T}} \mathbf{B}_{22} \Xi_4 \end{bmatrix}. \tag{34}$$

Equations (33) and (34) are independent and, therefore, computed in parallel.

4. Numerical Examples

To test the parallel reduction algorithm implementation, we used several example problems. The numerical tests were carried out on the 'Kraken' computing cluster at the Institute of Thermomechanics ASCR, Prague, Czechia. The used cluster nodes had the following basic hardware and software configuration: 2× Intel Xeon E5-2637 v4 processor at 3.5 GHz with 16 logical cores, 256 GiB local memory, 740 GiB local SSD disk, CentOS Linux 7, and Intel Fortran compiler 18.0.2.

The following sections present the obtained results. The example problems were partitioned to different numbers of substructures. The reduction was performed on each partitioned model to test the parallel algorithm, then performed again, restricted only to one processor core to simulate a serial algorithm.

To verify the parallel algorithm, and compare the accuracy of CB and ECB methods, the relative error for the first 100 eigenvalues is also shown for both the CB reduction and the ECB reduction. The relative eigenvalue errors are considered here:

$$\xi_i = \frac{\bar{\lambda}_i - \lambda_i}{\lambda_i}, \tag{35}$$

where ξ_i denotes the relative eigenvalue error for the i-th mode, and λ_i and $\bar{\lambda}_i$ are the exact and approximated eigenvalues, respectively.

It should be noted that the interface size significantly impacts the computational time; therefore, if an interface reduction technique could be devised and employed, it could have a considerable effect on the computational costs.

The used processor had 16 relatively powerful cores; thus, the obtained results show about 20% to 70% difference in computational times between the serial and the parallel algorithms. We expect that the superiority of the parallel algorithm will be more apparent on a processor with a large number of less-powerful cores (64, 128, etc.).

4.1. Cylindrical Shell

First, we implemented a cantilever cylinder problem, shown in Figure 2. The length L, thickness t, and radius d of the cantilever cylinder are 12, 0.06, and 0.5 m, respectively. Young's modulus, Poisson's ratio, and density are 69 GPa, 0.35, and 2700 kg/m^3, respectively. The finite element model was implemented by four-node quad elements. The model had 2880 DOFs and was partitioned to 2, 4, 8, 16, and 32 substructures. The used cutoff frequency was $f_{max} = 3400$ Hz.

To compare the accuracy for both the CB and the ECB methods, the relative error is also shown in Figure 3. The operation time at each step of the algorithm in Figure 1 is listed in Table 1. The obtained reduction times listed in Table 2 are small and the difference between the serial and the parallel algorithm is negligible, as expected. The quantities listed in Table 2 are the number of substructures N, minimum and maximum substructure sizes n_s, interface size n_{int}, reduced model size n_{red}, computational time for serial reduction t_s, and computational time for parallel reduction t_p.

Table 1. Operation time at each step of the algorithm in the cylindrical shell problem.

Step of Algorithm	**Operation Time [s]**				
	$N = 2$	$N = 4$	$N = 8$	$N = 16$	$N = 32$
Load input data	0.2	0.2	0.2	0.2	0.2
Partition global matrices	0.0	0.0	0.0	0.0	0.0
Reoder global matrices	0.0	0.0	0.0	0.0	0.0
Calculate component matrices	2.5	0.9	0.5	0.4	0.6
Assemble $\mathbf{M}_{\mathrm{CB}}$, $\mathbf{K}_{\mathrm{CB}}$	0.0	0.0	0.0	0.0	0.0
Calculate $\mathbf{M}_{\mathrm{CB}}^{-1}$, Ξ_3, Ξ_4, $\mathbf{A}_{22}$, $\mathbf{B}_{22}$	0.2	0.6	1.8	2.9	8.4
Calculate $\mathbf{M}_{\mathrm{ECB}}$, $\mathbf{K}_{\mathrm{ECB}}$	0.0	0.6	2.2	4.1	12.6
Write output data	1.1	2.2	3.7	5.3	9.2

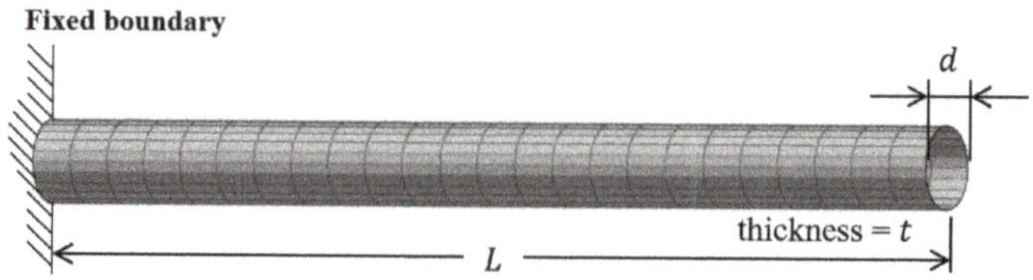

Figure 2. Example mesh, Cylindrical Shell.

Table 2. Reduction time [minute], Cylindrical Shell.

N	$\min(n_s)$	$\max(n_s)$	n_{int}	n_{red}	t_s	t_p
2	1320	1440	120	613	0.1	0.1
4	550	610	550	920	0.1	0.1
8	185	295	925	1195	0.2	0.1
16	60	135	1190	1397	0.3	0.2
32	10	65	1684	1795	0.6	0.5

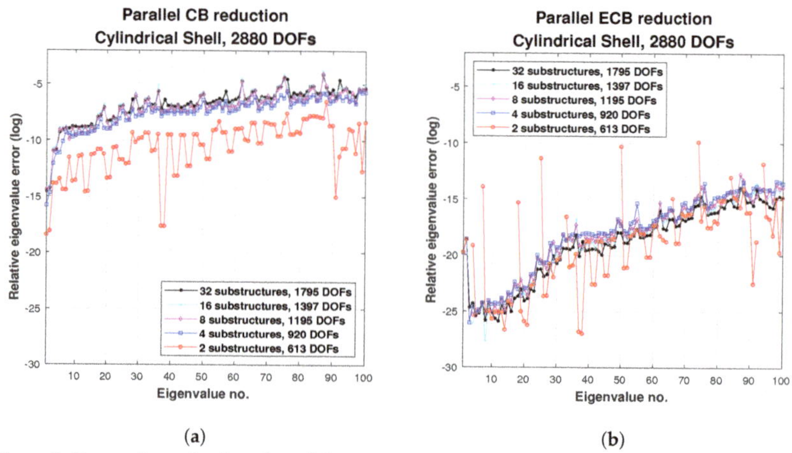

Figure 3. Comparison of reduced model accuracy, cylindrical shell. The results are obtained by (**a**) the CB method and (**b**) the ECB method, respectively.

4.2. Solid Ring

A solid ring problem was considered with a fixed boundary condition, which is illustrated in Figure 4. The height h, the inner radii d_{in}, and outer radii d_{out} are 0.2, 0.8, and 1.0 m, respectively. Young's modulus, Poisson's ratio, and density are 76 GPa, 0.3, and 2796 kg/m^3, respectively. The finite element model was implemented by eight-node hexahedral elements. The model has 34,062 DOFs and was partitioned to 2, 4, 8, 16, 32, 64, and 128 substructures. The used cutoff frequency was $f_{max} = 25{,}000$ Hz.

To compare the accuracy for both the CB and the ECB methods, the relative error is also shown in Figure 5. The operation time at each step of the algorithm in Figure 1 is listed in Table 3, and the obtained results listed in Table 4 indicate that the optimal partitioning for this problem is somewhere between 5 and 15 substructures. It can be seen that a higher number of substructures increases the interface size and, subsequently, the computational time, significantly. However, a lower number of substructures, while having a smaller interface, results in large substructures, which themselves take longer to analyze and, thus, negatively affect the overall computational time.

The parallel algorithm is about 70% faster than the serial algorithm in the most favorable case tested.

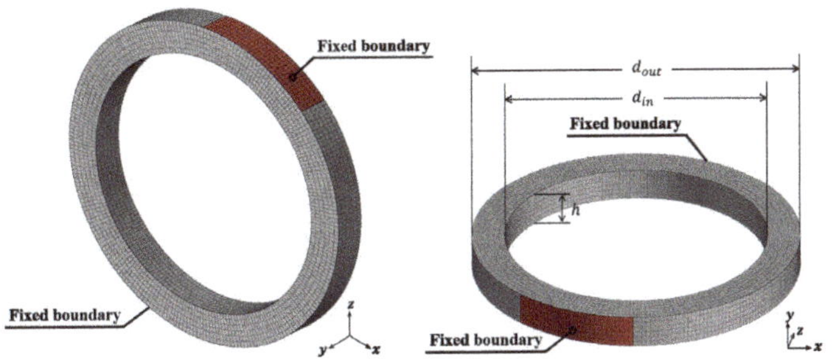

Figure 4. Example mesh, Solid Ring.

Table 3. Operation time at each step of the algorithm in the solid ring problem.

Step of Algorithm	Operation Time [s]				
	$N = 2$	$N = 4$	$N = 8$	$N = 16$	$N = 32$
Load input data	1.6	1.6	1.6	1.6	1.6
Partition global matrices	0.1	0.1	0.1	0.2	0.2
Reoder global matrices	0.0	0.0	0.0	0.0	0.0
Calculate component matrices	7148.2	1377.7	474.2	412.6	645.0
Assemble $\mathbf{M}_{\text{CB}}$, $\mathbf{K}_{\text{CB}}$	0.0	0.1	0.1	0.2	0.4
Calculate $\mathbf{M}_{\text{CB}}^{-1}$, Ξ_3, Ξ_4, $\mathbf{A}_{22}$, $\mathbf{B}_{22}$	35.3	104.5	316.4	782.2	5299.4
Calculate $\mathbf{M}_{\text{ECB}}$, $\mathbf{K}_{\text{ECB}}$	3.5	22.6	234.1	1255.4	8414.1
Write output data	56.8	74.9	105.8	176.8	388.3

Table 4. Reduction time [minute], Solid Ring.

N	$\min(n_s)$	$\max(n_s)$	n_{int}	n_{red}	t_s	t_p
2	16,785	16,785	492	4696	217.1	120.8
4	8223	8247	1137	5228	86.3	26.4
8	3924	3990	2367	6240	65.0	18.9
16	1803	1962	4644	8088	82.1	43.8
32	720	883	9425	11,994	365.1	245.8
64	180	364	17,982	19,113	1698.0	1288.2
128	18	198	22,030	22,721	2989.0	2382.0

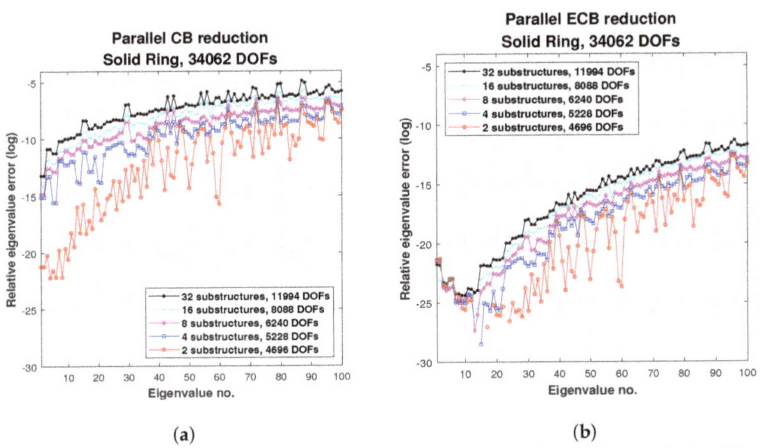

Figure 5. Comparison of reduced model accuracy, solid ring. The results are obtained by (**a**) the CB method and (**b**) the ECB method, respectively.

4.3. Shaft Assembly

We considered a shaft problem with a free boundary condition. The shaft model consisted of five components, and the detailed features are described in Figure 6. Young's modulus, Poisson's ratio, and density are 210 MPa, 0.3, and 7850 kg/m^3, respectively. The finite element model was implemented by four-node tetrahedral elements. The model had 64,086 DOFs and was partitioned to 2, 4, 8, 16, and 32 substructures. The used cutoff frequency was $f_{max} = 100{,}000$ Hz.

Figure 7 shows the conceptual reduction process. The first one on the left is a sparse matrix modeled by the general finite element method, and a compact reduced matrix can be obtained after the reduction process.

To compare the accuracy for both the CB and the ECB methods, the relative error is also shown in Figure 8. The operation time at each step of the algorithm in Figure 1 is listed in Table 5, and the obtained results listed in Table 6 indicate that the optimal partitioning for this problem is somewhere between three and seven substructures. In the most favorable case tested, the parallel algorithm is about 65% faster than the serial algorithm.

Note that the model is unconstrained, therefore, there is a gap in Figure 8 in place of the first six eigenvalues representing the free degrees of freedom.

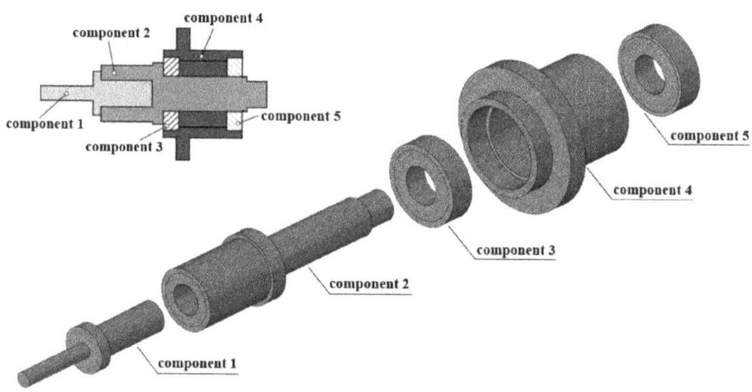

Figure 6. Example mesh, shaft assembly.

Table 5. Operation time at each step of the algorithm in the shaft problem.

Step of Algorithm	Operation Time [s]				
	$N = 2$	$N = 4$	$N = 8$	$N = 16$	$N = 32$
Load input data	3.1	3.0	3.2	3.1	3.1
Partition global matrices	0.1	0.2	0.3	0.3	0.5
Reoder global matrices	0.1	0.1	0.1	0.1	0.1
Calculate component matrices	56,310.5	17,074.7	8282.5	6210.4	6494.7
Assemble $\mathbf{M}_{\text{CB}}$, $\mathbf{K}_{\text{CB}}$	0.1	0.2	0.4	0.9	1.5
Calculate $\mathbf{M}_{\text{CB}}^{-1}$, Ξ_3, Ξ_4, $\mathbf{A}_{22}$, $\mathbf{B}_{22}$	174.7	1108.5	8680.3	26,534.1	61,743.2
Calculate $\mathbf{M}_{\text{ECB}}$, $\mathbf{K}_{\text{ECB}}$	92.8	1893.8	14,163.9	43,361.5	104,813.5
Write output data	72.4	195.2	483.8	936.4	1539.2

Table 6. Reduction time [minute], Shaft Assembly.

N	$\min(n_s)$	$\max(n_s)$	n_{int}	n_{red}	t_s	t_p
2	30,894	31,212	1980	5330	2556.3	944.2
4	14,052	15,201	5586	8573	1018.3	337.9
8	5964	7416	11,412	13,723	1204.1	526.9
16	2517	3618	16,998	18,746	2017.0	1284.1
32	1071	1677	22,912	24,186	3835.1	2909.9

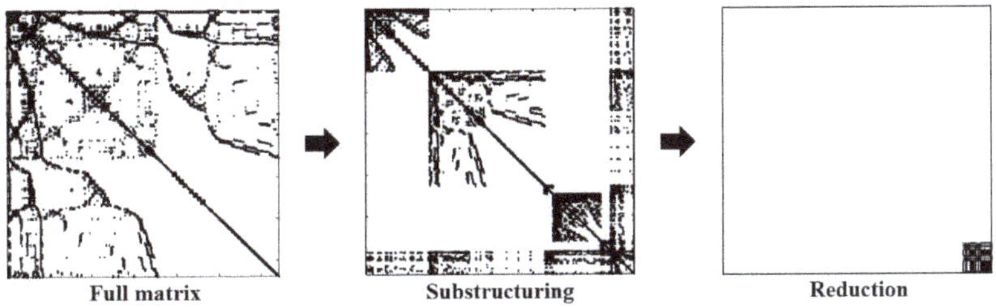

Figure 7. Illustration of reduction process of the shaft assembly.

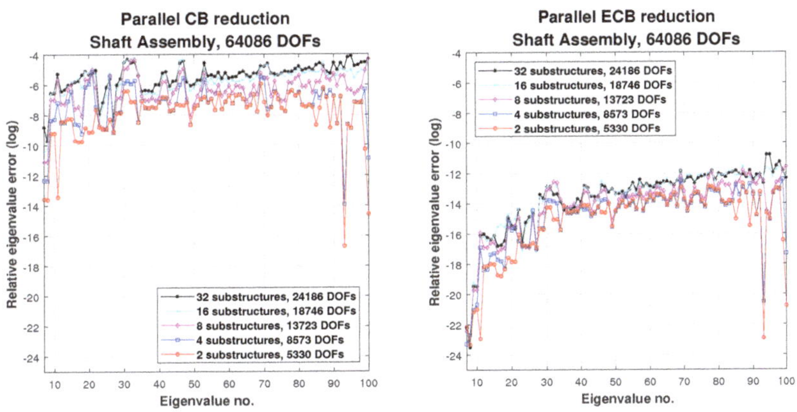

(a) (b)

Figure 8. Comparison of reduced model accuracy, shaft assembly. The results are obtained by (**a**) the CB method and (**b**) the ECB method, respectively.

5. Conclusions

The advanced residual modal compensation could offer dramatic accuracy improvements of the reduced matrices of the original CMS methods. However, the final reduced mass and stiffness matrices become fully populated and connected; thus, employing the parallel algorithm in the recent CMS methods with residual flexibility is difficult. To handle this issue, we introduce a component level parallel algorithm of the enhanced CB method. The reduced mass and stiffness matrices are obtained by assembling the blockwise component computation without direct transformation of the system level matrices. Automatic matrix partitioning and assembling procedures are achieved by the METIS library. Decoupling the original CB substructuring components and the ECB added matrices is essential in the proposed parallel algorithm.

The main idea of the proposed method can be extended to other iterative CMS methods with higher order residual flexibility, both primal and dual assemblies [22,32,33]. It should be noted that blockwise and decoupled formulations are prerequisites to achieve the parallel computations of iterative methods. In addition, many substructures are commonly adequate for parallel computations, but more substructures lead to larger interface DOFs in the proposed ECB formulation. Therefore, the interface reduction technique of the ECB method will be studied and considered for the high fidelity parallel ECB algorithm in the near future.

Author Contributions: Investigation, M.I. and C.-u.A.; methodology, J.-G.K.; resources, M.I.; supervision, J.-G.K.; validation, P.P.; visualization, C.-u.A.; writing—original draft preparation, P.P.; writing—review and editing, J.-G.K. and C.-u.A. All authors have read and agreed to the published version of the manuscript.

Funding: The work of Petr Pařík was supported by project no. 19-02288J of the Czech Science Foundation (CSF) within institutional support RVO:61388998. The work of Jin-Gyun Kim was supported by the Kyung Hee University in 2020 (KHU-20210488) and the National Research Foundation of Korea (NRF) grants funded by the Korean Government (2021R1A2C4087079). The work of Martin Isoz was supported by the Czech Centre of Excellence for Nonlinear Dynamic Behavior of Advanced Materials in Engineering CZ.02.1.01/0.0/0.0/15_003/0000493 (Excellent Research Teams) in the framework of Operational Programme Research, Development and Education.

Institutional Review Board Statement: Not applicable.

Informed Consent Statement: Not applicable.

Data Availability Statement: Not applicable.

Conflicts of Interest: The authors declare no conflict of interest.

References

1. Craig, R.R.; Bampton, B.C.C. Coupling of substructures for dynamic analysis. *AIAA J.* **1968**, *6*, 1313–1319. [CrossRef]
2. Shabana, A.A. *Dynamics of Multibody Systems*; Wiley: New York, NY, USA, 1989.
3. Kim, J.G.; Han, J.B.; Lee, H.; Kim, S.S. Flexible multibody dynamics using coordinate reduction improved by dynamic correction. *Multibody Syst. Dyn.* **2018**, *42*, 411–429. [CrossRef]
4. FunctionBay, Inc. *Recurdyn V9R3 User Manual*; FunctionBay, Inc.: Seongnam-si, Korea, 2019.
5. Cammarata, A.; Pappalardo, C.M. On the use of component mode synthesis methods for the model reduction of flexible multibody systems within the floating frame of reference formulation. *Mech. Syst. Signal Process.* **2020**, *142*, 106745. [CrossRef]
6. Sarsri, D.; Azrar, L.; Jebbouri, A.; El Hami, A. Component mode synthesis and polynomial chaos expansions for stochastic frequency functions of large linear FE models. *Comput. Struct.* **2011**, *89*, 346–356. [CrossRef]
7. Jensen, H.A.; Millas, E.; Kusanovic, D.; Papadimitriou, C. Model-reduction techniques for Bayesian finite element model updating using dynamic response data. *Comput. Methods Appl. Mech. Eng.* **2014**, *279*, 301–324. [CrossRef]
8. Yotov, V. Stochastic Finite Element Method for Vibroacoustic Loads Prediction. Ph.D. Thesis, University of Surrey, Guildford, UK, 2020.
9. Nachtergaele, P.; Rixen, D.J.; Steenhoek, A.M. Efficient weakly coupled projection basis for the reduction of thermomechanical models. *J. Comput. Appl. Math.* **2010**, *234*, 2272–2278. [CrossRef]
10. Kim, S.M.; Kim, J.G.; Chae, S.W.; Park, K.C. A strongly coupled model reduction of vibro-acoustic interaction. *Comput. Methods Appl. Mech. Eng.* **2019**, *347*, 495–516. [CrossRef]
11. Wang, X.; Wang, D.; Liu, B. Efficient Acoustic Topology Optimization Using Vibro-Acoustic Coupled Craig–Bampton Mode Synthesis. *Acoust. Aust.* **2020**, *48*, 407–418. [CrossRef]
12. Kammer, D.C.; Triller, M.J. Selection of Component Modes for Craig–Bampton Substructure Representations. *J. Vib. Acoust.* **1996**, *118*, 264–270. [CrossRef]
13. Bai, Z.; Liao, B.S. Towards an Optimal Substructuring Method for Model Reduction. In *PARA 2004: Applied Parallel Computing. State of the Art in Scientific Computing*; Springer: New York, NY, USA, 2004; pp. 276–285.
14. Kim, S.M.; Kim, J.G.; Park, K.C.; Chae, S.W. A Component Mode Selection Method Based on a Consistent Perturbation Expansion of Interface Displacement. *Comput. Methods Appl. Mech. Eng.* **2018**, *330*, 578–597. [CrossRef]
15. Kim, S.M.; Kim, J.G.; Chae, S.W.; Park, K.C. Evaluating Mode Selection Methods for Component Mode Synthesis. *AIAA J.* **2016**, *54*, 2852–2863. [CrossRef]
16. Park, K.C.; Park, Y.H. Partitioned component mode synthesis via a flexibility approach. *AIAA J.* **2004**, *42*, 1236–1245. [CrossRef]
17. Rixen, D.J. A dual Craig–Bampton method for dynamic substructuring. *J. Comput. Appl. Math.* **2004**, *168*, 383–391. [CrossRef]
18. Kim, J.G.; Markovic, D. High-fidelity flexibility based CMS method with interface degrees of freedom reduction. *AIAA J.* **2016**, *54*, 3619–3631. [CrossRef]
19. Kim, J.G.; Lee, P.S. An enhanced Craig–Bampton method. *Int. J. Numer. Methods Eng.* **2015**, *103*, 79–93. [CrossRef]

20. Boo, S.H.; Kim, J.H.; Lee, P.S. Towards improving the enhanced Craig–Bampton method. *Comput. Struct.* **2018**, *196*, 63–75. [CrossRef]
21. Tian, W.; Weng, S.; Xia, Y.; Zhu, H.; Gao, F.; Sun, Y.; Li, J. An iterative reduced-order substructuring approach to the calculation of eigensolutions and eigensensitivities. *Mech. Syst. Signal Process.* **2019**, *130*, 361–377. [CrossRef]
22. Go, M.S.; Lim, J.H.; Kim, J.G.; Hwang, K.R. A family of Craig–Bampton methods considering residual mode compensation. *Appl. Math. Comput.* **2020**, *369*, 124822. [CrossRef]
23. Jensen, H.A.; Muñoz, A.; Papadimitriou, C.; Vergara, C. An enhanced substructure coupling technique for dynamic re-analyses: Application to simulation-based problems. *Comput. Methods Appl. Mech. Eng.* **2016**, *307*, 215–234. [CrossRef]
24. Kim, J.; Kim, J.G.; Yun, G.; Lee, P.S.; Kim, D.N. Toward modular analysis of supramolecular protein assemblies. *J. Chem. Theory Comput.* **2015**, *11*, 4260–4272. [CrossRef]
25. Krattiger, D.; Hussein, M.I. Generalized Bloch mode synthesis for accelerated calculation of elastic band structures. *J. Comput. Phys.* **2018**, *357*, 183–205. [CrossRef]
26. Kim, J.G.; Boo, S.H.; Lee, P.S. An enhanced AMLS method and its performance. *Comput. Methods Appl. Mech. Eng.* **2015**, *287*, 90–111. [CrossRef]
27. Kim, J.G.; Park, Y.J.; Lee, G.H.; Kim, D.N. A general model reduction with primal assembly in structural dynamics. *Comput. Methods Appl. Mech. Eng.* **2017**, *324*, 1–28. [CrossRef]
28. Karypis, G.; Kumar, V. A fast and highly quality multilevel scheme for partitioning irregular graphs. *SIAM J. Sci. Comput.* **1999**, *20*, 359–392. [CrossRef]
29. Wang, E.; Zhang, Q.; Shen, B.; Zhang, G.; Lu, X.; Wu, Q.; Wang, Y. Intel Math Kernel Library. In *High-Performance Computing on the Intel® Xeon Phi™*; Springer: Cham, Switzerland, 2014. [CrossRef]
30. Kim, J.-G.; Seo, J.; Lim, J.H. Novel modal methods for transient analysis with a reduced order model based on enhanced Craig–Bampton formulation. *Appl. Math. Comput.* **2019**, *344*, 30–45. [CrossRef]
31. Dagum, L.; Menon, R. OpenMP: An industry standard API for shared-memory programming. *Comput. Sci. Eng.* **1998**, *1*, 46–55. [CrossRef]
32. Cui, J.; Xing, J.; Wang, X.; Wang, Y.; Zhu, S.; Zheng, G. A simultaneous iterative scheme for the Craig–Bampton reduction based substructuring. In *Dynamics of Coupled Structures*; Springer: Cham, Switzerland, 2017; Volume 4, pp. 103–114.
33. Chung, I.S.; Kim, J.G.; Chae, S.W.; Park, K.C. An iterative scheme of flexibility-based component mode synthesis with higher-order residual modal compensation. *Int. J. Numer. Methods Eng.* **2021**, *122*, 3171–3190. [CrossRef]

mathematics

Article

Theoretical Study of the Static and Dynamic Characteristics of a Slotted Adaptive Hydrostatic Thrust Bearing with a Regulator of the Lubricant Output Flow

Vladimir Kodnyanko *, Andrey Kurzakov, Alexey Surovtsev, Lilia Strok, Olga Grigorieva, Maxim Brungardt, Svetlana Belyakova and Ludmila Gogol

Polytechnic Institute, Siberian Federal University, 660079 Krasnoyarsk, Russia; AKurzakov@sfu-kras.ru (A.K.); ASurovtsev@sfu-kras.ru (A.S.); LStrok@sfu-kras.ru (L.S.); OGrigorieva@sfu-kras.ru (O.G.); MBrungardt@sfu-kras.ru (M.B.); SBelyakova@sfu-kras.ru (S.B.); LGogol@sfu-kras.ru (L.G.)
* Correspondence: VKodnyanko@sfu-kras.ru

Citation: Kodnyanko, V.; Kurzakov, A.; Surovtsev, A.; Strok, L.; Grigorieva, O.; Brungardt, M.; Belyakova, S.; Gogol, L. Theoretical Study of the Static and Dynamic Characteristics of a Slotted Adaptive Hydrostatic Thrust Bearing with a Regulator of the Lubricant Output Flow. *Mathematics* **2022**, *10*, 355. https://doi.org/10.3390/math10030355

Academic Editors: Shujin Laima, Yong Cao, Xiaowei Jin and Hehe Ren

Received: 6 January 2022
Accepted: 23 January 2022
Published: 24 January 2022

Publisher's Note: MDPI stays neutral with regard to jurisdictional claims in published maps and institutional affiliations.

Copyright: © 2022 by the authors. Licensee MDPI, Basel, Switzerland. This article is an open access article distributed under the terms and conditions of the Creative Commons Attribution (CC BY) license (https://creativecommons.org/licenses/by/4.0/).

Abstract: This manuscript considers the design of a slotted adaptive hydrostatic thrust bearing with a regulator of the lubricant output flow. A theoretical study of its static and dynamic characteristics was carried out. The aim of the study was to test the reliability of the hypothesis concerning the possibility of obtaining a stable-to-oscillation adaptive thrust bearing of negative compliance, avoiding the need for a complex system of external combined throttling by replacing it with a simple slotted throttle. Mathematical modeling of the thrust bearing movement was carried out. The possibility of reducing the compliance to negative values is shown, providing the bearing with an adaptive function, consisting of using the structure as a bearing and as an active deformation compensator of the elastic system of a metal-cutting machine in order to improve the quality of the metalwork. Analysis of load static characteristics showed that negative compliance is provided over a wide range of loads, which can be up to 75% or more of the range of permissible bearing loads. Based on the study of dynamic characteristics, it was concluded that with a targeted selection of parameters that have a major effect on the dynamics of the structure, the considered adaptive hydrostatic thrust bearing can attain a very high quality of dynamics. It is shown that the viscous damping of the lubricating film enclosed in the gaps and the damping of the material of the elastic ring of the regulator are important resources for ensuring the optimal dynamics of the thrust bearing.

Keywords: adaptive hydrostatic thrust bearing; adaptive function; regulator of the lubricant output flow; load capacity; compliance; dynamics quality

1. Introduction

Sliding bearings with hydrostatic lubrication (journal bearings, thrust bearings, and guides) used in modern metal-cutting machines usually work as passive supporting structures [1,2]. At the same time, these devices can act as adaptive units, which, in addition to their load-carrying function, are capable of performing the role of automatic deformation compensators of the technological system of the machine, thereby helping to reduce errors and, consequently, reduce the time of metalworking [3,4]. The adaptive function of such bearings arises only in those designs that are able to compensate for the positive compliance of the technological system of the machine, operating in the modes of negative compliance and thereby providing the total zero compliance of the machine [5,6]. In the latter cases, the direction of the reaction vector of the lubricating film under pressure is opposite to that of the cutting force.

The compliance of conventional hydrostatic bearings is always positive [7,8]. To reduce this, special devices are used; these are lubricant flow regulators or displacement compensators [9–12].

In hydrostatic and gas-static bearings with flow regulators, which are usually installed at the inlet of the lubricating flow, compliance reduction is obtained with the automatic supply of an additional volume of lubricant, which contributes to an additional increase in pressure in the bearing gap and, consequently, the desired compliance mode being achieved [13,14]. Studies have shown that the inflow of additional energy contributes to a significant deterioration in the dynamic quality of the structure up to the loss of stability [15,16]. It is possible to improve the dynamics of the bearings due to the complication of the design through the use of an external combined throttling system (ECTS) whereby an additional hydraulic resistance is installed between the bearing gap and the regulator, which makes it possible to put in place an inter-throttle chamber, the volume of lubrication of which acts as a viscous damper for energy dissipation [17,18].

Bearings with displacement compensators are divided into two types: those with full compensation and those with partial compensation [19,20]. In contrast to bearings with active compensation of the flow rate, passive throttles are installed at the inlet of the ECTS, which provides better dynamics for structures [11]. However, even such bearings with negative compliance have low dynamics; therefore, the ECTS is also used in these. In the first, the displacement compensator is installed between the input passive throttle and the bearing gap, which are separated by an intermediate throttle of low resistance and the ECTS chamber [21]. A decrease in compliance in such structures is achieved by adding the positive compliance of the bearing gap and the negative compliance of the compensator. Partial displacement compensation is the result of a combination of a displacement compensator and a lubricant output flow regulator (LOFR) [10,22]. The improvement in the dynamics of such structures is provided by the use of an ECTS.

In work [4], it is shown that the stability of a step hydrostatic thrust bearing with an LOFR can be provided without the use of an ECTS, which simplifies the design. The mathematical model of the bearing takes into account the compliance of the elastic displacement compensator, but what is not taken into account is that, at the same time, it can act as a damper, which improves the dynamics of the bearing.

In this paper, we consider the design of a slotted hydrostatic thrust bearing with an LOFR and study its static and dynamic characteristics, taking into account the compliance and damping of the regulator. Figure 1 shows a diagram of a slotted adaptive hydrostatic thrust bearing with LOFR.

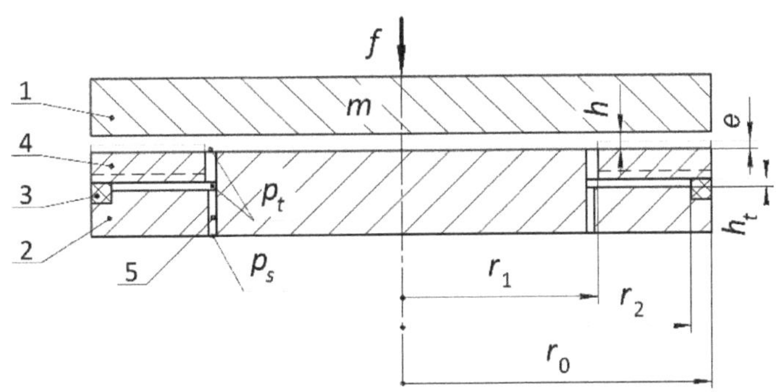

Figure 1. Design of slotted adaptive hydrostatic thrust bearing.

The structure contains a shaft, 1, and a base, 2, to which a rigid ring, 4, of an inner radius r_1 and an outer radius r_0 is hermetically connected by means of an elastic ring, 3, of an inner radius r_2. The thrust bearing is powered by a lubricant injection source supplied to the slotted throttle, 5, under pressure p_s. In working conditions, a lubricating gap of thickness h is created between the surfaces of ring 4 and shaft 1. Between base 2 and ring 4 there is a blind annular gap of thickness h_t, at the entrance to which the lubricant is under pressure $p_t < p_s$, formed as a result of overcoming the hydraulic resistance to the lubricant flow in slotted throttle 5. In the operating state, with increasing load f on the thrust bearing, the gap h decreases and its hydraulic resistance increases, as a result of which the pressure p_t increases. In this case, the force reactions w_t and w_e of the lubricant film (which is under pressure in the gaps h_t and h) both increase. At $w_t > w_e$, under the action of a force equal to the difference between these reactions, the axial deformation e of elastic ring 3 increases, limiting the gap h, again increasing its hydraulic resistance and pressure p_t, which brings about a decrease in the compliance of the thrust bearing

$$k = -\frac{\partial h_s}{\partial f}, \tag{1}$$

where

$$h_s = h + e \tag{2}$$

is the thickness of the lubricating gap enclosed between the working surfaces of base 2 and shaft 1, e is the deformation of ring 3. The force $w_t - w_e$ is balanced by the force of resistance to deformation of ring 3. By varying the size of the elastic ring and its axial compliance k_e, it is possible to reduce the compliance of the thrust bearing k to negative values.

The paper considers a mathematical model of the unsteady state of the thrust bearing; static and dynamic characteristics of the bearing are calculated and studied.

2. Mathematical Modeling

When studying the characteristics of the thrust bearing, we take a plane-parallel movement model of the working surfaces of the moving elements in which the thickness of the lubricant layer in the gaps does not depend on the radius. In addition, we assume that the loaded thrust bearing has reached a steady-state temperature regime at which the dynamic viscosity of the lubricant is constant.

It is convenient to study the characteristics of the thrust bearing in a dimensionless form. This allows us to significantly reduce the number of variable parameters that affect the characteristics of the thrust bearing. Following [4], we take the scales of values: p_s for pressures, r_0 for radii, t_0 for the current time, h_0 for gaps and deformation e, $\frac{\pi h_0^3 p_s}{6\mu}$ for volumetric lubricant flow rate, $2\pi r_0^2 p_s$ for axial forces, where h_0 corresponds to the gap h in the bearing that carries the design load f_0, and μ is the lubricant viscosity. Dimensionless quantities are signified by Greek and capital Latin letters.

The reactions of pressure forces in mentioned areas are determined by the general formula [4]

$$W_i = \int_{R_{i,1}}^{R_{i,2}} RPdR, \tag{3}$$

where $P(R,\tau)$ is a function of the pressure in the clearances of the thrust bearing.

The formula for the lubricant flow rate at the inlet and outlet of the corresponding gaps has the form [4]

$$Q_i = -H_i^3 \lim_{R \to R_1} \left(R \frac{dP}{dR} \right). \tag{4}$$

The pressure function satisfies the unsteady Reynolds equation for an incompressible fluid [22]

$$\frac{\partial}{\partial R} \left(R H_i^3 \frac{\partial P}{\partial R} \right) = \sigma R \dot{H}_i, \tag{5}$$

where $H_i(\tau)$ is the function of the gap, R is the current radius, $\sigma = \frac{12\mu r_0^2}{h_0^2 p_s t_0}$ is the so-called "compression number" of the film of the liquid in the gap, and τ is the dimensionless time.

On a circle, the $R \in [0, R_1]$ boundary conditions for the pressure function are of the form

$$\frac{\partial P}{\partial R}(0, \tau) = 0, P(R_1, \tau) = P_t(\tau). \tag{6}$$

On the ring $R \in [R_1, 1]$ in the gap H region, the boundary value problem for Equation (5) satisfies the boundary conditions

$$P(R_1, \tau) = P_t(\tau), P(1, \tau) = 0. \tag{7}$$

For the blind gap region, the boundary conditions for the boundary value problem with Equation (5) are

$$P(R_1, \tau) = P_t(\tau), \frac{\partial P}{\partial R}(R_2, \tau) = 0. \tag{8}$$

The solution of the boundary value problem (5), (6) is the function

$$P(R, \tau) = P_t + \frac{\sigma \dot{H}_s}{4H_s^3}\left(R^2 - R_1^2\right). \tag{9}$$

On the ring in the region of the gap H, for the boundary value problem (5), (7) has the solution

$$P(R, \tau) = P_t \frac{\ln R}{\ln R_1} + \frac{\sigma \dot{H}}{4H^3}\left[R^2 + \left(1 - R_1^2\right)\frac{\ln R}{\ln R_1} - 1\right]. \tag{10}$$

On the ring $R \in [R_1, R_2]$, in the region of the blind gap H_t, the solution to the boundary value problem (5), (8) is the function

$$P(R, \tau) = P_t + \frac{\sigma \dot{H}_t}{4H_t^3}\left(R^2 - R_1^2 - 2R_2^2 \ln \frac{R}{R_1}\right). \tag{11}$$

Substituting (8), (9), and (10) into (3), after integration, we find expressions for the force reactions

$$W_s = \int_0^{R_1} RPdR = A_0 P_t - B_0 \frac{\dot{H}_s}{H_s^3}, \tag{12}$$

$$W_e = \int_{R_1}^{1} RPdR = A_1 P_t - B_1 \frac{\dot{H}}{H^3}, \tag{13}$$

$$W_t = \int_{R_1}^{R_2} RPdR = A_3 P_t + B_2 \frac{\dot{H}_t}{H_t^3}, \tag{14}$$

where

$$A_0 = \frac{R_1^2}{2}, A_1 = \frac{1}{4}\left[\frac{R_1^2 - 1}{\ln R_1} - 2R_1^2\right], A_2 = A_0 + A_1, A_3 = \frac{R_2^2 - R_1^2}{2},$$

$$B_0 = \frac{\sigma R_1^4}{16}, B_1 = \frac{\sigma(1 - R_1^2)}{16}\left(\frac{1 - R_1^2}{\ln R_1} + 1 + R_1^2\right),$$

$$B_2 = \frac{\sigma}{16}\left[R_2^4\left(4\ln\frac{R_1}{R_2} + 3\right) + R_1^2\left(R_1^2 - 4R_2^2\right)\right].$$

The bearing capacity of the thrust bearing is determined by the expression

$$W = W_s + W_e = A_2 P_t - B_0 \frac{\dot{H}_s}{H_s^3} - B_1 \frac{\dot{H}}{H^3}. \tag{15}$$

The formula for the force equal to the difference between the reactions causing the deformation of ring 3 has the form

$$Q_s = -B_3 \dot{H}_s, \tag{16}$$

where $A_5 = A_3 - A_1 = \frac{1}{4}\left(2R_2^2 + \frac{1-R_1^2}{\ln R_1}\right)$.

The flow through the slotted throttle is determined by the formula

$$Q_c = A_s(1 - P_t), \tag{17}$$

where A_s is the criterion for the similarity of the throttle [12].

The flow rate at the outlet from the gap H_s in accordance with formula (4) has the form

$$Q_s = -B_3\dot{H}_s, \tag{18}$$

where $B_3 = \frac{\sigma R_1^2}{2}$.

At the entrance to the gap H, the flow rate is

$$Q = A_4 H^3 P_t + B_4\dot{H}, \tag{19}$$

where $A_4 = \frac{-1}{\ln R_1}$, $B_4 = \frac{\sigma}{4}\left(\frac{R_1^2-1}{\ln R_1} - 2R_1^2\right)$.

At the entrance to the gap H_t, the flow rate is determined by the formula

$$Q_t = B_5\dot{H}_t, \tag{20}$$

where $B_5 = \frac{\sigma}{2}(R_2^2 - R_1^2)$.

Formulae for hydrostatic forces and flow rates, derived from the analytical solutions to boundary value problems for the Reynolds equation, are verified using an alternative numerical finite difference method [23].

In a dynamic system, the force of inertia of the mass of shaft 1 acts as

$$F_{in} = M\ddot{H}_s, \tag{21}$$

where $M = \frac{mh_0}{2\pi r_0^2 p_s t_0^2}$, m is the mass of the shaft.

The bearing capacity of the thrust bearing is

$$W = W_s + W_e = A_2P_t - B_0\frac{\dot{H}_s}{H_s^3} - B_1\frac{\dot{H}}{H^3}. \tag{22}$$

Hydrostatic force acts on the working surfaces of ring 3

$$W_\varepsilon = W_t - W_e = A_5P_t + B_1\frac{\dot{H}}{H^3} + B_2\frac{\dot{H}_t}{H_t^3}. \tag{23}$$

The mathematical model of the thrust bearing dynamics includes two equations for the force balance of shaft 1 and ring 3, one equation for the balance of lubricant flow rate, and formulae for determining the gap H_t and the total gap H_s

$$W - F_{in} = F, \tag{24}$$

$$\varepsilon + D_e\dot{\varepsilon} - K_eW_\varepsilon = 0, \tag{25}$$

$$H_t = H_{t0} + \varepsilon, \tag{26}$$

$$Q_c - Q_s + Q_h - Q_t = 0, \tag{27}$$

$$H_s = H + \varepsilon, \tag{28}$$

where ε is the dimensionless axial deformation of ring 3, and H_{t0} is the thickness of the blind gap in the absence of load on ring 3. Formula (23) is obtained on the basis of Hooke's law [24] for small axial deformations of elastic ring 3, where K_e is the coefficient of its axial compliance (elasticity), and D_e is the damping coefficient of the elastic ring material.

Substituting (21)–(23) and (24) into (25), (26), and (28), and taking into account (27) and the fact that we represent the mathematical model of the thrust bearing dynamics in the form of the following combined system of nonlinear differential and algebraic equations

$$A_2P_t - B_1\frac{\dot{H}}{H^3} - B_0\frac{\dot{H}_s}{H_s^3} - M\ddot{H}_s = F, \tag{29}$$

$$A_d(1-P_t) - A_4H^3P_t + B_3\dot{H}_s - B_4\dot{H} - B_5\dot{\varepsilon} = 0, \tag{30}$$

$$\varepsilon + D_e\dot{\varepsilon} - K_e\left(A_5P_t + B_1\frac{\dot{H}}{H^3} + B_2\frac{\dot{\varepsilon}}{H_t^3}\right) = 0, \tag{31}$$

$$H_s - H - \varepsilon = 0. \tag{32}$$

The closed system of three nonlinear differential Equations (29)–(31) and one algebraic Equation (32) can be considered as a continuous automatic control system [25] containing an input-disturbing function of the external load F and four output-controlled functions H, H_s, ε, and P_t.

First, we conduct a study of the static characteristics of the thrust bearing in order to detect modes of negative compliance that provide the thrust bearing with an adaptive function. Then, we conduct a study of the stability criteria and the stability margin of the dynamic system, determine the optimal dynamic modes under which the structure has the maximum speed and stability margin in the negative compliance modes, and establish the particular parameters that have a decisive effect on the quality of the thrust bearing dynamics.

3. Static Characteristics of the Thrust Bearing

The mathematical model of the stationary state of the thrust bearing is a special case of the model of dynamics in the absence of oscillations, that is, with zero derivatives of the output functions H, H_s, ε, and P_t. The model can be represented as the following nonlinear system of four algebraic equations

$$A_2P_t = F, \tag{33}$$

$$\varepsilon - K_eA_5P_t = 0, \tag{34}$$

$$A_d(1-P_t) - A_4H^3P_t = 0, \tag{35}$$

$$H_s - H - \varepsilon = 0. \tag{36}$$

The study of the static characteristics is preceded by the adjustment of the thrust bearing parameters to the mode of the so-called "design point". This mode corresponds to a point on the load curve that in turn corresponds to a unit dimensionless gap $H = 1$, at which the dimensional gap is equal to the design gap $h = h_0$.

3.1. Calculation of the Parameters of the "Design Point" Mode

It is convenient to adjust the thrust bearing to this mode by setting the pressure at the outlet of slot 5 using the normalized pressure setting factor $\chi \in [0,1]$. At the "design point", the values of pressure P_t and this coefficient coincide so that $P_t = \chi$. We also set the radii R_1 and R_2 and the coefficient of elasticity K_e. Using Formulae (31)–(34), we calculate the deformation ε, the criterion for the similarity of the gap A_d, the gap H_s, the bearing capacity W, and the external force F

$$\varepsilon = K_eA_5\chi, A_d = \frac{A_4\chi}{1-\chi}, H_s = 1+\varepsilon, F = W = A_2\chi.$$

It was earlier mentioned that to ensure the adaptive function, it is necessary that the condition $W_e > 0$ be satisfied. It follows from (21) that this takes place at $A_5 > 0$. This condition allows us to find the smallest radius of elastic ring 3, at which can be ensured a decrease in the compliance of the thrust bearing

$$R_2 > R_{2,\min} = \sqrt{\frac{R_1^2 - 1}{2\ln R_1}}.$$

Let us find the value of the elasticity coefficient $K_e = K_{e0}$, at which the thrust bearing at the "design point" will have zero compliance $K = 0$.

The compliance of the structure is determined by the formula

$$K = -\frac{\partial H_s}{\partial F} = -\frac{\partial H_s}{\partial P_t} \cdot \frac{\partial P_t}{\partial F}.$$

Substituting (32) and (34) into (35), and performing the differentiation of this expression, taking into account (33) we obtain the formula for the compliance of the thrust bearing at the "design point"

$$K_0 = \frac{1}{A_2}\left[\frac{1}{3\chi(1-\chi)} - K_e A_5\right]. \tag{37}$$

It follows that the value of the elasticity coefficient $K_{e0} = K_e$, at which zero compliance of the thrust bearing $K_0 = 0$ is achieved at the "design point", can be calculated using the formula

$$K_{e0} = [3\chi(1-\chi)A_5]^{-1} = \frac{4}{3}\left[\left(2R_2^2 + \frac{1-R_1^2}{\ln R_1}\right)\chi(1-\chi)\right]^{-1}. \tag{38}$$

Formula (37) is convenient to use for calculating the static characteristics of bearing capacity, compliance, and lubricant flow rate, setting the elasticity coefficient K_e in proportion to the value of K_{e0}. With $K_e = K_{e0}$, the thrust bearing at the "design point" will have zero compliance $K = 0$, with $0 \leq K_e < K_{e0}$—positive and $K_e > K_{e0}$—negative.

3.2. Static Characteristics and Their Discussion

It is convenient to calculate the static characteristics of the thrust bearing in a parametric form, taking pressure as the parameter $P_t \in [0, 1]$. Using Formula (31), one can determine the external load F and the bearing capacity of the thrust bearing W, which are equal in the static mode. Equation (32) allows us to find the deformation of elastic ring 3 with the formula

$$\varepsilon = K_e A_5 P_t. \tag{39}$$

Transforming (33), we obtain the formula for calculating the gap

$$H = \sqrt[3]{\frac{\chi(1-P_t)}{(1-\chi)P_t}}. \tag{40}$$

Finally, using (34), we obtain a formula for calculating the total clearance

$$H_s = H + \varepsilon. \tag{41}$$

Taking into account (31), (32), and (39)–(41), we differentiate (30) and (33) with respect to the pressure P_t and substitute its results in (36). In this case, we obtain a formula for calculating the static compliance at any permissible load F on the thrust bearing

$$K = \frac{1}{3F}\left(\frac{H}{1-P_t} - 3\varepsilon\right). \tag{42}$$

Analysis of Formula (42) shows that, at extreme values of the load,

$$\lim_{F\to 0} K = \lim_{F\to F_{\max}} K = \infty.$$

Therefore, there are certain load values at which the compliance reaches a minimum. To find these values, let us determine the derivative of the compliance with respect to the load, which can be obtained by differentiating (42) with respect to the pressure P_t

$$G = -\frac{\partial^2 H_s}{\partial^2 F} = \frac{\partial K}{\partial F} = \frac{2H(3P_t - 2)}{[3A_2 P_t(1 - P_t)]^2}. \tag{43}$$

It can be easily observed that this function has a single zero $P_t = 2/3$, which is always constant and does not depend on the parameters of the thrust bearing, including the coefficient of elasticity K_e. Thus, the optimal mode of least compliance is achieved at $\chi = 2/3$, at which the minima of the dependences $K(F)$ and $K(\chi)$ coincide.

Figure 2 shows the graph of the load characteristics for various values of the coefficient of elasticity K_e. The adjustment factor is $\chi = 2/3$, radii $R_1 = 0.5$, $R_2 = 0.9 > R_{2,\min} = 0.736$, at which, according to (35), the adaptive function of the thrust bearing can be provided. The coefficient of elasticity of ring 3, according to (38), is $K_{e0} = 11.2$. With this value, the thrust bearing at the "design point" has zero compliance. For each curve in Figure 2, the coefficient of elasticity is set by the formula $K_e = i\, K_{e0}$.

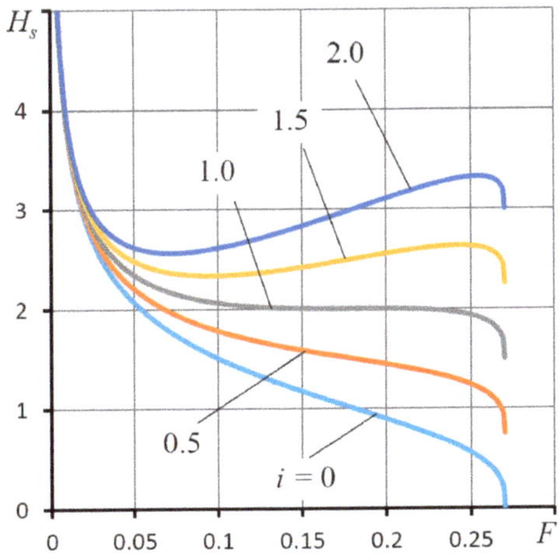

Figure 2. Load characteristics $H_s(F)$ of the thrust bearing for different values of the elasticity coefficient $K_e = i\, K_{e0}$.

The thrust bearing has a maximum permissible load $F_{\max} = 0.271$. The "design point" corresponds to the load $F_0 = \chi F_{\max} = 0.181$. The curve for $i = 0$ corresponds to the load characteristic of a conventional thrust bearing, for which the coefficient of elasticity is $K_e = 0$. The graph shows that with an increase in i and, consequently, an increase in the coefficient K_e, the nature of the curves changes. In this case, in the region of small and moderate values of the load F, the compliance K of the thrust bearing decreases, which can be determined by the change in the slope of the curves.

At $K_e = K_{e0}$ ($i = 1$), at the "design point", the thrust bearing acquires zero compliance $K = 0$. A further increase in the coefficient for $K_e > K_{e0}$ ($i > 1$) contributes to the establishment of a negative compliance mode. This mode is characterized by the presence of areas of simultaneous increases in load and clearance. It is in these areas that the thrust bearing acquires an adaptive function as it is able to perform not only the load bearing but also adaptive functions in order to actively compensate for the passive deformation of the elastic system of the machine due to the opposite direction of the force deformation of the lubricating gap of the thrust bearing.

The effect of negative compliance is illustrated by the curves of dependence of the compliance K on the external force F, which are shown in Figure 3. With an increase in the coefficient of elasticity K_e, the compliance K decreases in the range of working loads. At $K_e = K_{e0}$, the thrust bearing reaches zero compliance for $\chi = 2/3$ only at the "design point". At $K_e > K_{e0}$, the load range—where the thrust bearing has zero and negative compliance—becomes wider.

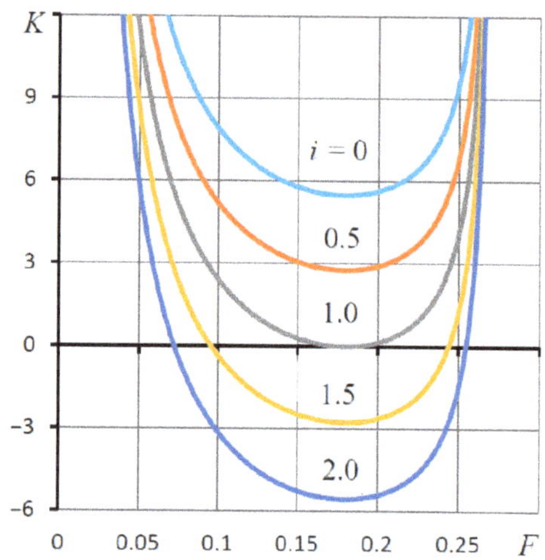

Figure 3. Dependences of compliance K on external force F for different values of the elasticity coefficient $K_e = i\,K_{e0}$.

In the range of loads F corresponding to negative compliance K, as mentioned above, the thrust bearing is able to carry the load and compensate for the elastic deformations of the machine, that is, it is able to perform an adaptive function. At $K_e = 2K_{e0}$, when at the "design point" the negative compliance in absolute value coincides with the compliance of a conventional thrust bearing ($K_e = 0$), the width of the adaptive load range in negative compliance modes is approximately 75% of the allowable load range width. With $K_e > 2K_{e0}$, the adaptive load range will be wider still.

The graph in Figure 4 shows the dependences $\varepsilon(F)$ of the deformation of elastic ring 4 on the external load on the bearing. These dependences are linear. To achieve negative compliance at the "design point", the deformation of elastic ring 3 must meet the condition $\varepsilon = K_e/K_{e0} > 1$.

It was mentioned above that as compliance decreases, the dynamic quality of the thrust bearing usually deteriorates, often to the point of loss of stability. Therefore, an important condition for the operability of an adaptive thrust bearing is its dynamic performance, which must meet certain criteria for response speed and stability margin. The speed of response is important so that, with a minimum duration of the transient response, the thrust bearing reaches the calculated negative compliance mode, and the stability margin is important from the point of view of guaranteeing the accident-free operation of the structure.

Thus, to ensure the operability of the adaptive thrust bearing, it is necessary to optimize its parameters based on the study of its dynamic characteristics in order to deliver the structure with sufficient dynamic quality.

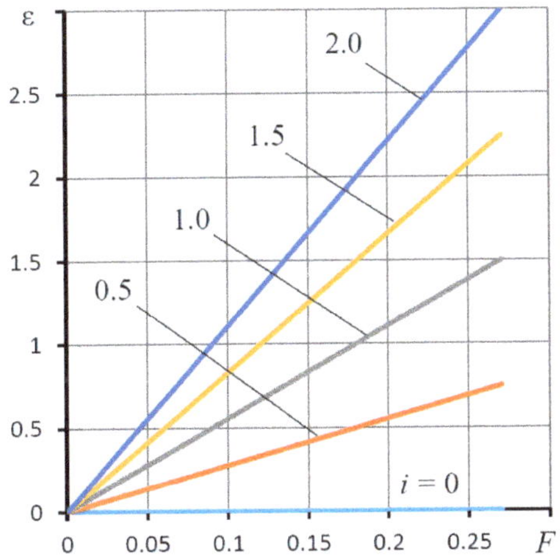

Figure 4. Characteristics of deformation $\varepsilon(F)$ of elastic ring 3 for different values of the elasticity coefficient $K_e = i\,K_{e0}$.

4. Dynamic Characteristics of the Thrust Bearing

Let us consider the dynamics of the thrust bearing, which, under the influence of small disturbances of the external load, bring about small fluctuations in the output values relative to their values in the steady (stationary) state. Let us take a unit dimensionless mass $M = 1$ of shaft 1. This allows us to determine the scale of the current time.

4.1. Linear Model of Thrust Bearing Dynamics

We represent dynamic quantities in the form

$$F + \Delta F(\tau), H + \Delta H(\tau), H_s + \Delta H_s(\tau), \varepsilon + \Delta\varepsilon(\tau), P_t + \Delta P_t(\tau), \quad (44)$$

where the first term in the expressions represents the static constituent and the second the small dynamic constituent. After substituting (44) into the nonlinear system of Equations (27)–(30), with its linearization and application to the resulting linear system of equations of the integral Laplace transform [25], we obtain a linear model of the dynamics of the studied thrust bearing in Laplace transforms. Eliminating ΔH, we obtain a system of three equations. The matrix form of this system is

$$\begin{bmatrix} -(B_6 s + M s^2) & B_7 s & A_{11} \\ -(A_6 + B_8 s) & (A_6 + B_9 s) & -A_7 \\ -B_{10} s & (1 + B_{11} s) & -A_8 \end{bmatrix} \begin{bmatrix} \overline{\Delta H_s}(s) \\ \overline{\Delta\varepsilon}(s) \\ \overline{\Delta P_t}(s) \end{bmatrix} = \begin{bmatrix} 1 \\ 0 \\ 0 \end{bmatrix} \overline{\Delta F}(s), \quad (45)$$

where $\overline{\Delta F}(s)$ is the Laplace transform of a small deviation of the disturbing external force, $\overline{\Delta H_s}(s), \overline{\Delta\varepsilon}(s), \overline{\Delta P_t}(s)$ are the transforms of small deviations of the corresponding output quantities, and s is the Laplace transform variable,

$$A_6 = 3A_4 H^3 P_t, A_7 = A_d + A_4 H^3, A_8 = A_5 K_e,$$

$$B_6 = \frac{B_0}{H_s^3} + \frac{B_1}{H^3}, B_7 = \frac{B_1}{H^3}, B_8 = B_4 - B_3,$$

$$B_9 = B_4 - B_5, B_{10} = \frac{K_e B_1}{H^3}, B_{11} = D_e + K_e\left(\frac{B_1}{H^3} - \frac{B_2}{H_t^3}\right).$$

Applying Cramer's rule [26] and the algorithm of symbolic expansion of the determinants of polynomial matrices to the solution of the system of linear Equation (45), we determined the transfer function (TF) of the dynamic compliance of the thrust bearing, which is a rational function of the variable s

$$K(s) = -\frac{\overline{\Delta H_s}}{\overline{\Delta F}} = \frac{b_0 + b_1 s}{a_0 + a_1 s + a_2 s^2 + a_3 s^3}, \tag{46}$$

where

$a_0 = -A_2 A_6,$
$a_1 = A_6[A_8(B_6 - B_7) + A_2(B_{10} - B_{11})] - A_7 B_6 - A_2 B_8,$
$a_2 = A_8(A_6 + B_6 B_9 - B_7 B_8) + A_7(B_7 B_{10} - 1 - B_6 B_{11}) + A_2(B_9 B_{10} - B_8 B_{11}),$
$a_3 = A_8 B_9 - A_7 B_{11},$
$b_0 = A_7 - A_6 A_8,$
$b_1 = A_7 B_{11} - A_8 B_9.$

The denominator of the TF (46) is the characteristic polynomial of the system, by which it is possible to judge the stability and quality of transients in a linear dynamic system that describes the dynamics of an adaptive hydrostatic thrust bearing for small deviations of non-stationary quantities from their stationary state.

4.2. Some Considerations Regarding the Methodology for Applying the Linear Dynamics Model to the Study of Sliding Bearings with Liquid and Gas Lubrication

When studying the quality of the dynamics of linear oscillatory systems, the model of the simplest damped harmonic oscillator (DHO) with a second-order characteristic equation is often used

$$j + cs + ms^2 = 0, \tag{47}$$

where j, c, and m refer to the stiffness, damping, and mass of the oscillator [27], respectively.

According to the Hurwitz conditions, such a system is stable if all the coefficients of Equation (47) are nonzero and have the same sign [28]. As the mass and damping of the generator are always positive, the stiffness should also be positive in stable systems. However, in slide bearings with regulators, which include the studied design, the stiffness, which is the opposite of the compliance, can be infinite or negative. On this basis, it could be assumed that the adaptive bearings of negative compliance are always unstable. However, this assumption is wrong.

In accordance with the basic provisions of the theory of automatic control, the characteristic polynomial of the control object is the denominator of the TF, which for DHO has the form [25]

$$\Phi(s) = \frac{b_0}{a_0 + a_1 s + a_2 s^2}. \tag{48}$$

The characteristic polynomial of the TF (48) can be reduced to the form of the polynomial (47) by multiplying the first by the constant b_0. Studies of adaptive slip bearings show that the sign of static compliance is determined by the coefficient b_0 [18,19]. In this case, the coefficients of the denominator polynomial for stable systems always remain positive, which indicates the stability of such dynamical systems. This also applies to the bearing under study. If we turn to TF (46), then only the coefficient b_0 depends on the compliance K_e of elastic ring 3, and the coefficient a_0 does not. Thus, an oscillator, which is an adaptive hydrostatic thrust bearing, can, like similar structures, have negative static compliance and still be stable.

Note that PFs of the form (48) and (46), which are the Laplace image of dynamic compliance, are rational functions; therefore, from the point of view of the theory of automatic control, the preferred term is "compliance" rather than "stiffness", the latter term often being used for the analysis of the characteristics of sliding bearings, including adaptive bearings. A particular case of a TF at $s = 0$ is the static compliance $K(0) = b_0/a_0$. Therefore, in this work and other works of the authors on the study of bearings with lubricant flow controllers and displacement compensators that provide the bearings with an adaptive function, the term "compliance" is used [4,5,10,11].

4.3. Dynamic Characteristics of the Thrust Bearing and Their Discussion

To assess the quality of the thrust bearing dynamics, we used the root criteria—the degree of stability and damping of oscillations over the period [25]. The degree of stability η characterizes the speed of the system, that is, the speed of damping of its free oscillations. By this criterion, one can determine the degree of stability of the system. For $\eta < 0$ the system is unstable, for $\eta > 0$ it is stable, and for $\eta = 0$ the system is on the boundary between stable and unstable. The criterion ξ of the damping of oscillations over a period can be applied to the assessment of the stability margin of the system. The smaller the value of ξ, the greater the oscillation of the transient response and the lower the stability margin of the dynamic system. It is considered that the system is well damped if $\xi \geq 90\%$ [25].

The calculation of the dynamic criteria was carried out for the same parameter values that were used to calculate the static characteristics of the thrust bearing. Three new parameters were added to the dynamics model:

- Unit mass of the shaft $M = 1$, taking into account the influence of the force of its inertia;
- "Compression number" σ, which is a measure of the viscous damping of the lubricant film under pressure;
- Damping coefficient D_e of the elastic ring material.

As the first parameter is constant, the other two parameters, as well as the parameter H_{t0}, are varied.

Calculations have shown that an increase in the parameter H_{t0} negatively affects the dynamics of the thrust bearing. The best value is $H_{t0} = 0.5$.

Let us consider the influence of the parameter σ on the dynamic characteristics of the structure. Figure 5 shows the curves of dependence of the degree of stability η on the parameter σ for different values of the elasticity coefficient K_e without taking into account the damping coefficient of elastic ring 3 ($D_e = 0$). The graph is constructed for the values of the elasticity coefficient K_e, which provide the thrust bearing negative static compliance in the "design point" mode.

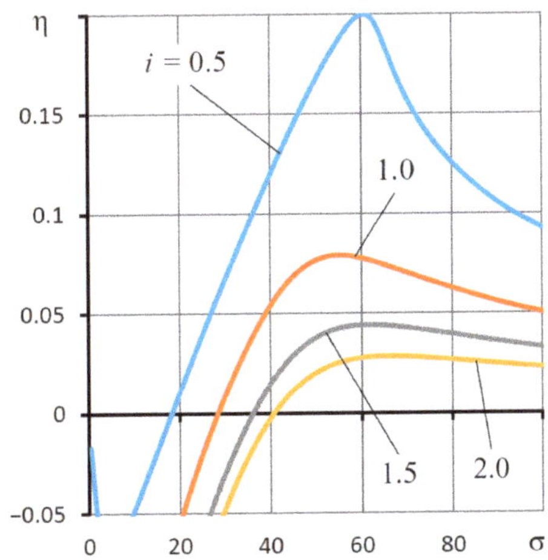

Figure 5. Dependences of the degree of stability η on the "compression number" σ for different values of the elasticity coefficient $K_e = i\,K_{e0}$.

Comparing the graphs of Figures 2 and 3 with Figure 5, we find that the stability ($\eta > 0$) of the thrust bearing of negative compliance is provided only for $\sigma > \sigma_{min}$, where σ_{min} is the value of the parameter σ at which the bearing reaches the stability boundary ($\eta = 0$). Therefore, for a bearing of negative compliance $K_e = 2K_{e0}$, the stability limit corresponds to $\sigma_{min} = 42$. At lower values of σ, the thrust bearing is unstable ($\eta < 0$). It can be seen that the larger the value of K_e, that is, the lower the compliance K, the larger the σ_{min} corresponding to the stability boundary. This result can be interpreted in such a way that the lower the compliance of the thrust bearing, the smaller the calculated dimensional clearance of the bearing lubricant gap must be to ensure the stability of the thrust bearing at the "design point".

It is also noteworthy that the dependences $\eta(\sigma)$ have a pronounced extreme character, which indicates the existence of an optimal value of the parameter $\sigma = \sigma_{opt}$. At this value, the dependence $\eta(\sigma)$ reaches a maximum, providing the thrust bearing with the maximum response rate, at which the fastest decay of transient processes is observed. For $K_e \geq K_{e0}$, the optimal performance takes place at approximately $\sigma_{opt} = 60$.

A comparison (presented in Figure 6) of the graph of the dependence of the damping criterion ξ of oscillations for the period on the parameter σ with the graph in Figure 5 shows that, in the stability region at $\sigma < \sigma_{opt}$, the transient response has a pronounced oscillatory character ($\xi < 80\%$). When approaching the point $\sigma = \sigma_{opt}$, the criterion ξ grows rapidly, which indicates a significant weakening of the oscillation of the transient characteristics and an increase in the stability margin of the thrust bearing. At the same time, for thrust bearings of low compliance ($K_e > 2K_{e0}$), the transient characteristics even at $\sigma > \sigma_{opt}$ remain somewhat oscillatory ($\xi < 90\%$).

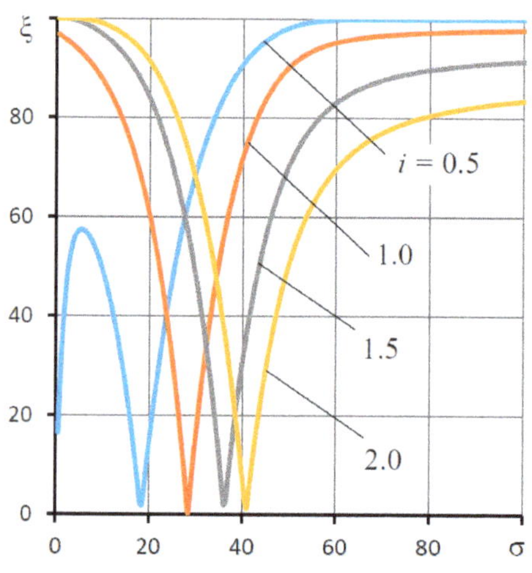

Figure 6. Dependences of the criterion ξ of damping of oscillations for a period on the "compression number" σ for different values of the elasticity coefficient $K_e = i\,K_{e0}$.

The graph in Figure 7 shows the dependences of the degree of stability η on the viscous damping coefficient D_e for different values of the elasticity coefficient K_e for a fixed value of $\sigma = 60$.

The graph shows that the damping of the elastic ring material 3 has a significant impact on the dynamics of the thrust bearing. This influence is especially noticeable with the thrust bearing operating in the modes of negative compliance when the performance at optimal D_e values can be increased several times. Therefore, for $K_e = 2K_{e0}$ without taking into account the coefficient D_e, the optimal criterion is $\eta = 0.03$. As can be seen from Figure 7, with the optimal $D_e = 11$, the criterion $\eta = 0.15$. That is, the choice of the elastic compensator material, which is optimal from the point of view of damping, enables the speed of the thrust bearing to be increased by a factor of 5.

As seen from Figure 8, the parameter D_e has a particularly significant effect on the criterion ξ of damping of oscillations over a period. For $D_e > 3$, the criterion is virtually equal to $\xi = 100\%$. This demonstrates that the corresponding transient processes are aperiodic in nature, indicating a minimum oscillation or even the complete absence of one. This result shows that the negative compliance thrust bearing, designed to take into account the optimal recommendations, has an absolute margin of stability to fluctuations.

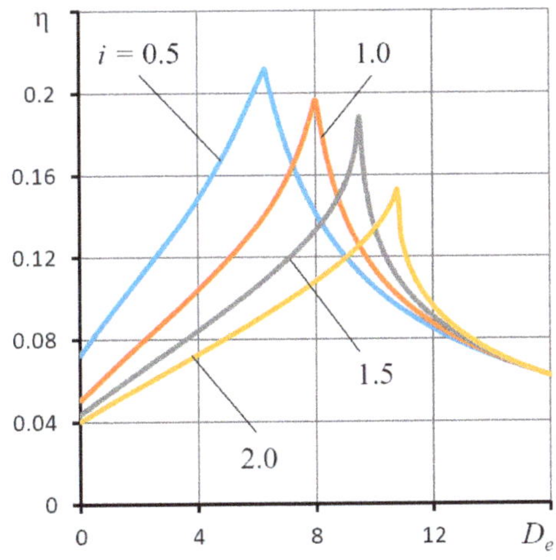

Figure 7. Dependences of the degree of stability η on the viscous damping coefficient D_e for different values of the elasticity coefficient $K_e = i\ K_{e0}$.

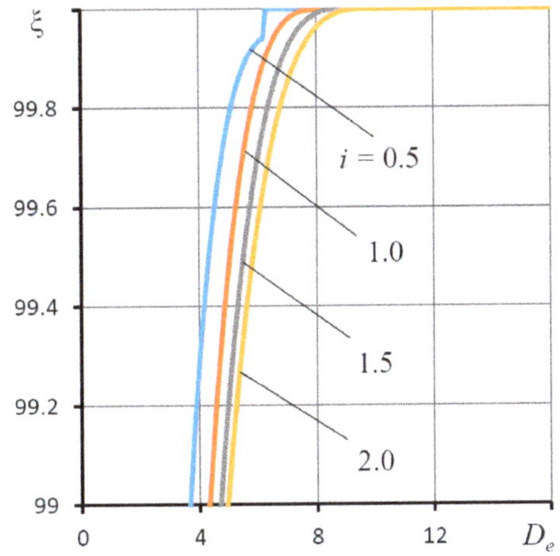

Figure 8. Dependences of the criterion ξ of damping of oscillations for the period of the viscous damping coefficient D_e for different values of the elasticity coefficient $K_e = i\ K_{e0}$.

It is interesting to consider the quality of the thrust bearing dynamics at various values of the load across the entire range of its variation. The graphs of Figures 9 and 10 show the curves of the degree of stability η and damping ξ of oscillations for the period on the load F for various values of the coefficient K_e at σ = 60 and D_e = 11.

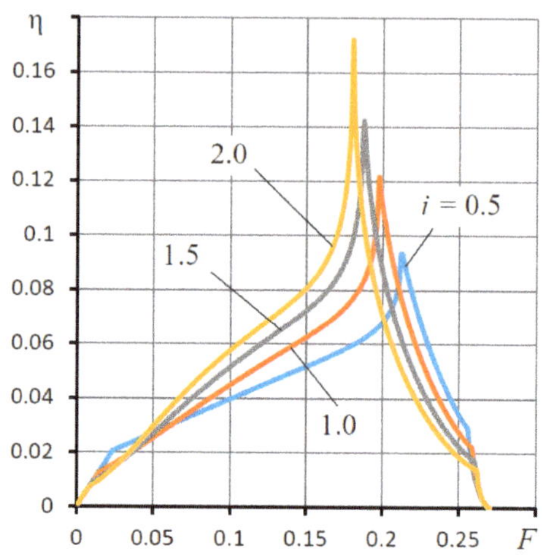

Figure 9. Dependences of the degree of stability η on the load F for different values of the coefficient of elasticity $K_e = i\,K_{e0}$.

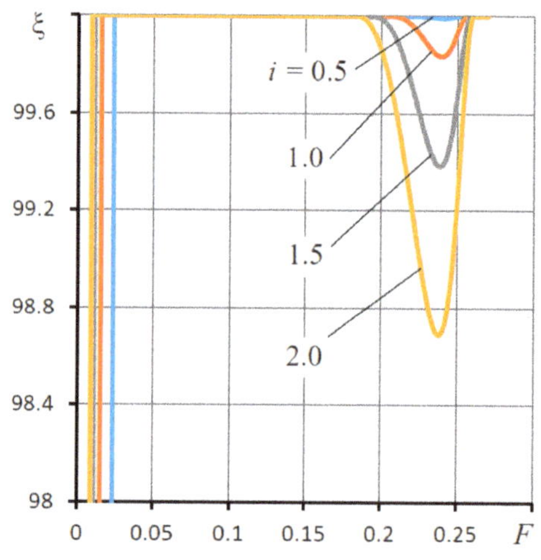

Figure 10. Dependences of the criterion ξ of damping of oscillations for a period on the load F for different values of the elasticity coefficient $K_e = i\,K_{e0}$.

The graph in Figure 9 shows that the thrust bearing remains stable for all values of the K_e coefficient over the entire range of load variation. In this case, the maximum speed at which the function η(F) reaches its maximum value falls on loads close to the calculated value ($F = 0.181$). On this basis, a significant conclusion can be reached—that the adaptive bearing can be operable not only in the "design point" mode but also, importantly, across the entire range of permissible loads.

The stability margin of the thrust bearing across the range of permissible loads is represented by the graph in Figure 10. As can be seen from the graph, the thrust bearing has an ideal stability margin over almost the entire range of permissible loads (ξ = 100%). A decrease in the values of the criterion ξ is observed only in the vicinity of the extreme points at which the thrust bearing loses its load-carrying function.

The study of the static and dynamic characteristics of the slotted adaptive hydrostatic thrust bearing shows that an almost ideal quality of its dynamics can be achieved without the use of an external combined throttling system that would over-complicate the design. Viscous damping of the pressurized lubricating film in the gaps of the structure and damping of the material of the elastic ring of the regulator are important resources for ensuring optimal dynamics of the thrust bearing.

5. Checking the Correctness of the Obtained Data

To confirm the correctness of the obtained data, they were compared with the theoretical and experimental data of other authors. The comparison was carried out for hydrostatic thrust bearings, in which ring 4 was motionless, which corresponds to the coefficient of elasticity of the compensator $K_e = 0$ (absolutely rigid ring 3). The data were compared with the theoretical data from [29] and the experimental results from [30].

Table 1 shows comparative theoretical data on the static load capacity of the thrust bearing for radii $r_1 = 30$ mm, $r_0 = 40$ mm for various values of external pressure p_s at $p_t = 0.5p_s$.

Table 1. Theoretical data comparison.

Performance Parameter	Supply Pressure (MPa)	Computational Data	Data [29]	Error (%)
Load capacity (N)	0.4	317	322	1.7
	0.8	634	644	1.7
	1.2	950	966	1.7
	1.6	1267	1288	1.7
	2.0	1584	1610	1.7

The presented theoretical results are in good agreement. A slight error is explained by the fact that in [29] a simplified method for calculating the bearing capacity was used, assuming that the pressure of the lubricating film on the surface of the outer ring is equal to half the pressure at the outlet of their supply gap.

Table 2 shows comparative theoretical and experimental data on the static bearing capacity of thrust bearings for radii $r_1 = 24$ mm and $r_0 = 32$ mm for different values of the gap h at an external pressure $p_s = 0.8$ MPa.

Table 2. Theoretical and experimental data comparison.

Performance Parameter	Bearing Gap (μm)	Computational Data	Data [30]	Error (%)
Load capacity (N)	10	386	320	17
	15	365	307	16
	20	343	295	14

A comparison of theoretical and experimental data provides a more significant difference. However, such a result can be considered quite satisfactory as the indicated data on the difference between theory and experiment can be explained by many reasons known to researchers, therefore the experiment as a whole confirms theoretical calculations. This allows us to conclude that for the considered particular case of the mathematical model of the thrust bearing, confirmation of its adequacy has been obtained.

As for the model of the movement of ring 4 on elastic suspension 3, for such a bearing the conduction of an experimental study is being planned, in the process of preparation and implementation of which several important practical problems will have to be solved, which are complex and beyond the scope of this paper. In this regard, the present theoretical study is fundamental to a certain extent, and the data obtained from the verification of a particular case provide reason to trust the calculated data and general conclusions about the performance of the considered design in the context of assessing its quantitative performance characteristics.

6. Conclusions

This paper considered the design of a slotted adaptive hydrostatic thrust bearing with a regulator of the lubricant output flow and conducted a theoretical study of its static and dynamic characteristics. The aim of the study was to test the reliability of the hypothesis that it is possible to obtain a vibration-resistant adaptive thrust bearing of negative compliance without having to use a complex system of external combined throttling by replacing it with a simple slotted throttle. Mathematical modeling of the movement of the thrust bearing and its structural elements was carried out. The paper presented the possibility of a significant decrease in the compliance of the structure, including negative compliance in order to provide an adaptive function, which consists of using the bearing not only as a support but also as an active compensator for the deformation of the elastic system of a metal-cutting machine in order to improve the quality of the metalwork. It was found that negative compliance is provided across a wide range of loads, which can be up to 75% or more of the range of permissible bearing loads. The study showed that with a purposeful selection of parameters that have the main influence on the dynamics of the structure, the considered adaptive hydrostatic thrust bearing can attain an almost ideal quality of its dynamics. Viscous damping of the lubricating film enclosed in the gaps and damping of the elastic ring material of the regulator are important resources for ensuring optimal thrust bearing dynamics.

Author Contributions: Conceptualization, V.K.; formal analysis, A.K.; investigation, S.B., A.S. and L.G.; data curation, O.G., M.B. and L.S.; writing—original draft preparation, V.K.; writing—review and editing, A.K.; project administration, A.K. All authors have read and agreed to the published version of the manuscript.

Funding: This research received no external funding.

Institutional Review Board Statement: Not applicable.

Informed Consent Statement: Not applicable.

Data Availability Statement: The data presented in this study are available on request from the corresponding author. The data are not publicly available due to privacy.

Conflicts of Interest: The authors declare no conflict of interest.

Nomenclature

H, h	dimensionless thickness, thickness of the gap
H_t	dimensionless thickness of the blind gap
H_s	dimensionless value of the total gap
ε	dimensionless deformation of elastic ring 3
K, K_e	dimensionless compliance of the bearing and elastic ring 3
$P(R,\tau)$	dimensionless dynamic pressure in the bearing gap
p_t	lubricant pressure at the outlet of the gap
p_s	supply pressure
Q_h	dimensionless flow rate through the gap
Q_t	dimensionless flow rate at the inlet to the gap H_t
Q_s	dimensionless flow rate at the outlet of the gap H_s
Q_c	dimensionless flow rate through the slotted throttle
r_0, r_1, r_2	bearing radii (Figure 1)
R	dimensionless radius
t_0	scale of current time
W	dimensionless load capacity

η degree of stability
μ coefficient of dynamic viscosity of the lubricant
ξ damping of oscillations over the period
χ normalized adjustment coefficient of the external throttling system
σ "compression number"
τ dimensionless time

References

1. Bouyer, J.; Wodtke, M.; Fillon, M. Experimental research on a hydrodynamic thrust bearing with hydrostatic lift pockets: Influence of lubrication modes on bearing performance. *Tribol. Int.* **2022**, *165*, 107253. [CrossRef]
2. Michalec, M.; Svoboda, P.; Křupka, I.; Hartl, M. A review of the design and optimization of large-scale hydrostatic bearing systems. *Eng. Sci. Technol. Int. J.* **2021**, *24*, 936–958. [CrossRef]
3. Yanqin, Z.; Yi, L.; Shiqian, N.; Zhiquan, Z. Heavy load characteristics of micro-beveled heavy-duty hydrostatic bearing lubricant oil film. *Proc. Inst. Mech. Eng. Part J J. Eng. Tribol.* **2020**, *235*, 738–747. [CrossRef]
4. Kodnyanko, V.; Kurzakov, A.; Grigorieva, O.; Brungardt, M.; Belyakova, S.; Gogol, L.; Surovtsev, A.; Strok, L. Theoretical disquisition on the static and dynamic characteristics of an adaptive stepped hydrostatic thrust bearing with a displacement compensator. *Mathematics* **2021**, *9*, 2949. [CrossRef]
5. Push, A. *Spindle Units: Quality and Reliability*; Mashinostroenie: Moscow, Russia, 1992; 288p.
6. Brzeski, L.; Kazimierski, Z. High stiffness bearing. *J. Lubr. Technol.* **1979**, *101*, 520–525. [CrossRef]
7. LaTray, N.; Kim, D.; Song, M. Static performance of a hydrostatic thrust foil bearing for large scale oil-free turbomachines. *J. Eng. Gas Turbines Power* **2021**, *143*, 041017. [CrossRef]
8. Brungardt, M.; Shatokhin, S. Spindles with multiply adaptive hydrostatic bearings. *Russ. Eng. Res.* **2021**, *41*, 10–15. [CrossRef]
9. Kurzakov, A. Adaptive gas-static spindle bearings. *Russ. Eng. Res.* **2013**, *33*, 389–391. [CrossRef]
10. Sawicki, J.; Capaldi, R.; Adams, M. Experimental and theoretical rotordynamic characteristics of a hybrid journal bearing. *J. Tribol.* **1997**, *119*, 132–141. [CrossRef]
11. Pourmehran, O.; Rahimi-Gorji, M.; Gorji-Bandpy, M.; Baou, M. Comparison between the volumetric flow rate and pressure distribution for different kinds of sliding thrust bearing. *Propuls. Power Res.* **2015**, *4*, 84–90. [CrossRef]
12. Shatokhin, S.; Shatokhin, S. Closed hydrostatic guides of metal-cutting machines. *Russ. Eng. Res.* **2014**, *34*, 326–329. [CrossRef]
13. Hesselbach, J.; Abel-Keilhack, C. Active hydrostatic bearing with magnetorheological fluid. *J. Appl. Phys.* **2003**, *93*, 8441–8443. [CrossRef]
14. Ow, D.S.; Lee, R.M.; Nissom, P.M.; Philp, R.; Oh, S.K.; Yap, M.G. Inactivating frur global regulator in plasmid-bearing escherichia coli alters metabolic gene expression and improves growth rate. *J. Biotechnol.* **2007**, *131*, 261–269. [CrossRef] [PubMed]
15. Lee, J.; Dixon, W.E.; Ziegert, J.C. Adaptive nonlinear contour coupling control for a machine tool system. In Proceedings of the 2005 IEEE/ASME International Conference on Advanced Intelligent Mechatronics, Monterey, CA, USA, 24–28 July 2005. [CrossRef]
16. Kodnyanko, V. Characteristics of a gas-static thrust bearing with an active displacement regulator. *Russ. J. STIN* **2005**, *9*, 32–34.
17. Kodnyanko, V.; Shatokhin, S. Theoretical study on dynamics quality of aerostatic thrust bearing with external combined throttling. *FME Trans.* **2020**, *48*, 342–350. [CrossRef]
18. Kodnyanko, V.; Shatokhin, S.; Kurzakov, A.; Pikalov, Y.; Strok, L.; Pikalov, I.; Grigorieva, O.; Brungardt, M. Theoretical efficiency study of output lubricant flow rate regulating principle on the example of a two-row aerostatic journal bearing with longitudinal microgrooves and a system of external combined throttling. *Mathematics* **2021**, *9*, 1689. [CrossRef]
19. Kodnyanko, V.; Kurzakov, A. Compliance of gas-dynamic bearing with elastic compensator of movement. *J. Sib. Fed. Univ. Eng. Technol.* **2017**, *10*, 657–663. [CrossRef]
20. Shatokhin, S.; Kodnyanko, V. Radial gasostatic bearing-seal with opposite internal gas flow compensation. *Sov. J. Frict. Wear* **1984**, *5*, 32–35.
21. Kodnyanko, V. Method for calculating the static characteristics of radial hydrostatic compensator of machine tool bearings deformation. *Period. Polytech. Transp. Eng.* **2021**, *49*, 114–119. [CrossRef]
22. Kazama, T.; Yamaguchi, A. Hydrostatic thrust bearing-theory and experiments. *Tribology* **1968**, *1*, 62. [CrossRef]
23. Demidovich, B.; Maron, I.; Shuvalova, E. Numerical methods of analysis. In *Approximation of Functions, Differential and Integral Equations*, 5th ed.; Lan: Moscow, Russia, 2010; 400p.
24. Wulandari, S.; Iswanto, B.; Sugihartono, I. Determination of springs constant by hooke's law and simple harmonic motion experiment. *J. Phys. Conf. Ser.* **2021**, *2019*, 012053. [CrossRef]
25. Besekersky, V.; Popov, E. *Theory of Automatic Control Systems*; Profession: Saint Petersburg, Russia, 2003; 752p.
26. Ricardo, H. *A modern Introduction to Linear Algebra*; CRC Press: New York, NY, USA, 2009; 670p.
27. Narendra, K.; Shorten, R. Hurwitz stability of metzler matrices. *IEEE Trans. Autom. Control* **2010**, *55*, 1484–1487. [CrossRef]
28. Baldiotti, M.; Fresneda, R.; Gitman, D. Quantization of the damped harmonic oscillator revisited. *Phys. Lett. A* **2011**, *375*, 1630–1636. [CrossRef]
29. Shatokhin, S.; Pikalov, I. Hydrostatic bearing. *Invent. Eng.* **2007**, *1*, 4.
30. Markhel, I. *Machine Parts*; Mashinostroenie: Moscow, Russia, 1986; 448p.

mathematics

MDPI

Article

Micropolar Dusty Fluid: Coriolis Force Effects on Dynamics of MHD Rotating Fluid When Lorentz Force Is Significant

Quanfu Lou [1], Bagh Ali [2], Saif Ur Rehman [3], Danial Habib [4], Sohaib Abdal [4], Nehad Ali Shah [5] and Jae Dong Chung [5,*]

1 College of Education, Nanchang Normal College of Applied Technology, Nanchang 330108, China; hhu2000@163.com
2 Faculty of Computer Science and Information Technology, Superior University, Lahore 54000, Pakistan; baghalisewag@gmail.com
3 Department of Mathematics, University of Management and Technology, Lahore 54770, Pakistan; saifurrehman8684@gmail.com
4 Department of Mathematics, Khwaja Fareed University of Engineering and Information Technology, Rheem Yar Khan 64200, Pakistan; danisheikh4006@gmail.com (D.H.); sohaibabdal8@gmail.com (S.A.)
5 Department of Mechanical Engineering, Sejong University, Seoul 05006, Korea; nehadali199@yahoo.com
* Correspondence: jdchung@sejong.ac.kr

Abstract: The main objective of this investigation to examine the momentum and thermal transportation of rotating dusty micropolar fluid flux with suspension of conducting dust particles across the stretched sheet. The novelty of the flow model is the exploration of the significance of boosting the volume concentration of dust particles in fluid dynamics. The governing PDEs of the problem for both phase models are transmuted into nonlinear coupled non-dimensional ODEs by utilizing suitable similarity modifications. The bvp4c technique was utilized in MATLAB script to acquire a graphical representation of the experimental results. This study illustrates the analysis of repercussions of pertinent parameters on non-Newtonian fluid and the dusty phase of fluid. By improving the volume concentration of dust particles and rotating parameters, the axial velocity for both phases depreciates, whereas temperature and transverse velocity for both phases have the opposite behavior. The micro-rotation distribution rises with higher contributions of rotating and material parameters, whereas it decreases against larger inputs of volume concentration of dust particles. The growing strength of the dust volume fraction (ϕ_d) caused the coefficient of skin friction to decrease along the x direction, and the skin friction coefficient is raised along the y direction.

Keywords: dusty micropolar fluid; non-Newtonian fluid; rotational flow

MSC: 76D05; 76W05; 76-10

Citation: Lou, Q.; Ali, B.; Rehman, S.U.; Habib, D.; Abdal, S.; Shah, N.A.; Chung, J.D. Micropolar Dusty Fluid: Coriolis Force Effects on Dynamics of MHD Rotating Fluid When Lorentz Force Is Significant. *Mathematics* **2022**, *10*, 2630. https://doi.org/10.3390/math10152630

Academic Editors: Shujin Laima, Yong Cao, Xiaowei Jin and Hehe Ren

Received: 4 July 2022
Accepted: 25 July 2022
Published: 27 July 2022

Publisher's Note: MDPI stays neutral with regard to jurisdictional claims in published maps and institutional affiliations.

Copyright: © 2022 by the authors. Licensee MDPI, Basel, Switzerland. This article is an open access article distributed under the terms and conditions of the Creative Commons Attribution (CC BY) license (https://creativecommons.org/licenses/by/4.0/).

1. Introduction

Eringen [1,2] proposed the theory of micropolar liquids, which is capable of explaining such fluids. The incorporation of novel kinematic variables is an important element to note in the development of Eringen's micro-continuum mechanics, such as the addition of the concept of body moments, gyration tensor, micro-inertia moment tensor, stress moments, and micro-stress averages to classical continuum mechanics. Nevertheless, substantial difficulties arise when this idea is implemented to real problems related to nontrivial flow; particularly in the case of linear theory, an issue involving basic micro-fluids must be expressed as a system of 19 PDEs with 19 unknowns. Moreover, the fundamental mathematical problem is challenging to solve. These unique characteristics for micropolar liquids were addressed in a comprehensive review of the subject and implications of micropolar liquid mechanics by Ariman et al. [3,4]. Early research in this area can be found in the review of [5], as well as in the more recent books, see [6,7]. Numerous investigators considered the non-Newtonian fluid due to wide scope of real life applications [8,9]; liquid-containing tiny particles are the most important variables in heat conduction processes in fluids [10,11]. Solid particle incorporation in the base fluid impacts the dynamics of the fluid and can influence the fluids' efficient thermal conductivity [11,12]. According to Ali et al. [13], MHD could have a noteworthy impact on the improvement of thermal conductivity of non-Newtonian fluids. More work on non-Newtonian fluid subject to various types of geometries and Lorentz force was carried out in [14–17].

Although classical Newtonian liquids cannot accurately represent the features of fluid flow with suspended particles, the concept of micropolar liquids has received significant attention in recent years due to their potential in a variety of industrial processes [18,19]. Extrusion of polymer liquids, cooling of a metallic surface in a bath, crystal, animal blood, solidification of liquid, colloidal, suspension solutions, and novel lubricants are a few examples of micropolar liquid use. The essence of the concept of a micropolar liquid flow lies in the extension of constitutive equations for Newtonian liquids, which allow this theory to represent more complicated fluids [20]. According to this idea, rigid elements trapped in a small fluid volume element can only rotate around the volume element's center, as specified by the microrotation vector. Furthermore, to the rigid body movement of the overall volume element, the particles rotate locally. The laws of classical continuum mechanics are supplemented in the micropolar fluid concept with extra equations that account for the conservation of micro-inertia moments and the balance of first stress moments that arise when the microstructure of a material is taken into account, as well as additional local constitutive parameters [21]. Actually, micropolar liquids can be defined as the non-Newtonian liquids containing short rigid cylindrical elements or dumb-bell molecules, polymer fluids, animal blood, fluid suspensions, etc. Micropolar fluid dynamics can also be used to represent the presence of dust or smoke, especially in a gas [22].

Rotational flux is significant due to its implementation in science, engineering, and manufacturing industries. For foundation and modeling capabilities, various manufacturing objects rely on rotating flow's physics such as whirlpools, tornadoes, vacuum pumps, jet engines, tropical cyclones, centrifugal pumps, etc., since the phenomena of rotational flux are complex and analysts are trying comprehend the underlying science. Abbasi et al. [23] estimated the activation energy attributes and thermal radiation in axisymmetric revolving stagnation point flux of hybrid nanoliquid. Bilal et al. [24] illustrated the hall current impact on time-dependent carbon nanotubes rotational flux with dust particles and nonlinearly thermal radiation in a porous medium. Ali et al. [25] investigated the time-dependent rotating flux of a fractional Maxwell liquid in a cylinder subject to shear stress on the boundary. Donghwan Kim et al. [26] deliberated the operating parameters' impacts on in-cylindrical flux features of an optical accessible engine in the presence of a spray-guided injector. Liu et al. [27] studied the rotational flux dynamics in the friction stir welding of aluminum alloys.

Dust consists of solid dry particles of matter that is found in the air; the less viscous fluid incorporated in the solid dust particles is called dusty fluid. The formulation of rain drops because of little solid dust particles is a typical illustration of dusty air [28]. It was pointed out by Fortov et al. [29] that there exists equality between the force exerted on the gas by the dust and force exerted on the dust by the gas. Bilal et al. [30] studied the viscoelastic fluid subject to dust particles; Jalil et al. [31] examined the exact solution of the boundary value fluid problem; Reena and Rana [32] considered the micropolar fluid subject to solid dust particles; Dasman et al. [33] analyzed the non-Newtonian fluid incorporation of dust particles. More work on dusty fluid subject to various types of geometries was carried out in [34–38].

By studying the above-mentioned literature, we concluded that research work on the two-phase dusty micropolar fluid subject to Coriolis and Lorentz forces has not yet been performed. Motivated by the aforementioned wide scope of non-Newtonian fluid and dusty fluid applications, we decided to evaluate the currently elaborated dusty fluid problem. The primary purpose of the present investigation was to analyze the outcomes of distinct parameters and volume concentrations of dust particles on the dynamics of micropolar dusty fluid across a stretching sheet. Very recently, research on non-Newtonian fluids has fascinated young researchers due to large-scale applications in different industries. By using similarity modifications, the relevant nonlinear PDEs are converted into a system of ODEs. The graphical outcomes of velocity, temperature, the skin friction factor, and the Nusselt number were investigated based on different inputs of physical parameters.

2. Mathematical Formulation

Let us analyze a incompressible time-independent 3D rotating laminar flux of dusty micropolar fluid across a stretching sheet. The sheet is stretched in xy-plane and fluid placed along the z-axis. Fluid revolves with constant velocity Ω around the z-axis. The feature of Coriolis forces in the primary momentum and secondary momentum equations are $+2\Omega v_1 \& -2\Omega v_2$, respectively. Although the first body force is positive, the velocity of secondary flow is negative, which creates an overall negative impact on the fluid primary velocity. The apparent and intended are two observable two paths in a rotatory frame of reference. The case of the intended/true path produces a trajectory that is easily deformed by some fictitious force, known as the Coriolis force, which influence the apparent path. Both fluid and dust particles were considered to be static at first. Dust particles are assumed to be evenly sized spheres with constant density all over the stream. Further, T_∞ and T_w are the liquid's ambient temperature and superficial temperature, respectively. Figure 1 displays the flux attributes and the coordinate system. For dusty phase flux, the model based on boundary layer approximation and physical assumptions and coupled with constraints is as follows [39–41].

$$\frac{\partial v_1}{\partial x} + \frac{\partial v_2}{\partial y} + \frac{\partial v_3}{\partial z} = 0, \tag{1}$$

$$(1-\phi_d)\left(v_1\frac{\partial v_1}{\partial x} + v_2\frac{\partial v_1}{\partial y} + v_3\frac{\partial v_1}{\partial z} - 2\Omega v_2\right) = (1-\phi_d)\left(\nu + \frac{k}{\rho}\right)\frac{\partial^2 v_1}{\partial z^2} + \frac{k}{\rho}\frac{\partial N_o}{\partial z} + \frac{KN}{\rho}(v_{1p} - v_1), \tag{2}$$

$$(1-\phi_d)\left(v_1\frac{\partial v_2}{\partial x} + v_2\frac{\partial v_2}{\partial y} + v_3\frac{\partial v_2}{\partial z} + 2\Omega v_1\right) = (1-\phi_d)\left(\nu + \frac{k}{\rho}\right)\frac{\partial^2 v_2}{\partial z^2} + \frac{KN}{\rho}(v_{2p} - v_2), \tag{3}$$

$$v_1\frac{\partial N_o}{\partial x} + v_2\frac{\partial N_o}{\partial y} + v_3\frac{\partial N_o}{\partial z} = \frac{\gamma}{\rho j}\frac{\partial^2 N_o}{\partial z^2} - \frac{k}{\rho j}\left(2N_o + \frac{\partial v_1}{\partial z}\right) \tag{4}$$

$$(\rho c_p)\left(v_1\frac{\partial T}{\partial x} + v_2\frac{\partial T}{\partial y} + v_3\frac{\partial T}{\partial z}\right) = k^*\left(\frac{\partial^2 T}{\partial z^2}\right) + \frac{\rho_p C_p}{\rho c_p \tau_T}(T_p - T). \tag{5}$$

For dusty particle flow

$$\frac{\partial v_{1p}}{\partial x} + \frac{\partial v_{2p}}{\partial y} + \frac{\partial v_{3p}}{\partial z} = 0, \tag{6}$$

$$v_{1p}\frac{\partial v_{1p}}{\partial x} + v_{2p}\frac{\partial v_{1p}}{\partial y} + v_{3p}\frac{\partial v_{1p}}{\partial z} = 2\Omega v_{2p} + \frac{KN}{\rho}(v_1 - v_{1p}), \tag{7}$$

$$v_{1p}\frac{\partial v_{2p}}{\partial x} + v_{2p}\frac{\hat{v_{2p}}}{\partial y} + v_{3p}\frac{\partial v_{2p}}{\partial z} + 2\Omega v_1 = \frac{KN}{\rho}(v_2 - v_{2p}), \tag{8}$$

$$v_1\frac{\partial T_p}{\partial x} + v_2\frac{\partial T_p}{\partial y} + v_3\frac{\partial T_p}{\partial z} = \frac{c_p}{c_m \tau_T}(T - T_p). \tag{9}$$

The relevant boundary conditions are [42–44]:

$$\left.\begin{array}{r} v_1 = v_{1w} = ax, v_2 = 0, v_3 = 0,\ N_o = -\beta\dfrac{\partial v_1}{\partial z}, T = T_w,\ at\ z = 0, \\ v_{1p} = v_{1w} = ax, v_{2p} = 0, v_3 = 0,\ T_p = T_w,\ at\ z = 0, \\ v_1 \to 0, v_2 \to 0, v_3 \to v_3,\ N_o \to 0,\ T \to T_\infty,\ as\ z \to \infty, \\ v_{1p} \to 0, v_{2p} \to 0, v_{3p} \to v_3,\ T_p \to T_\infty,\ as\ z \to \infty, \end{array}\right\} \quad (10)$$

where, v_1, v_2, and v_3 are velocity components in x, y, and z direction, respectively. v_{1p}, v_{2p}, and v_{3p} denote the velocity of the components of dust particles; Ω represents angular velocity and N_o, a is a constant of stretching rate ($a > 0$); v_{1w} is stretching velocity component along the a-axis; N stands for micro-rotation and dust particle's number density. ν shows kinematic viscosity, K signifies the Stoke's drag constant, ρ deputizes the density of fluid, c_p delegates the specific heat capacity of fluid, k^* demonstrates the thermal conductivity, T symbolizes liquid's temperature, ρ_p signifies the density of dust particles, τ_T constitutes the thermal equilibrium time, C_p represents concentration of dust particles, c_m denotes the specific heat of dust particles, T_p is the temperature of the dust particle, j, k, and γ are micro-inertia per unit mass.

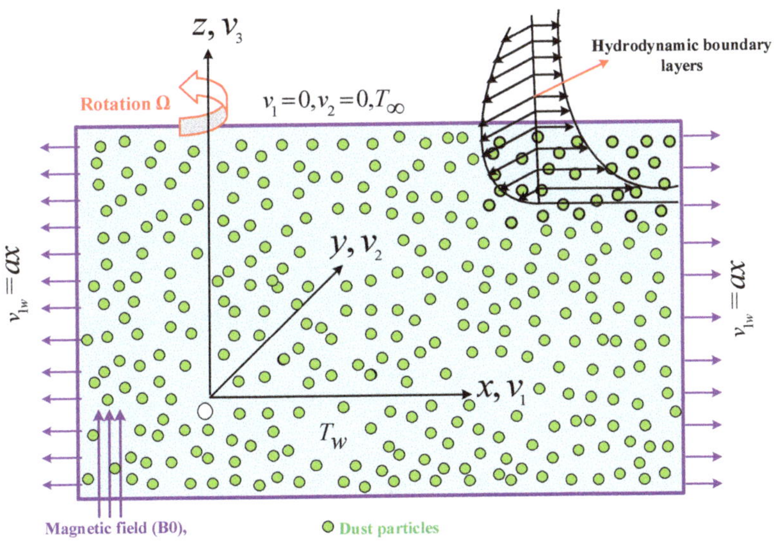

Figure 1. Schematic flow configuration.

The similarity transformation follows the work of [45,46]

$$\left.\begin{array}{r} v_1 = axG_1'(\eta),\ v_2 = axG_2(\eta),\ v_3 = -\sqrt{a\nu}G_1(\eta),\ N_o = ax\sqrt{\dfrac{a}{\nu}}H(\eta),\ \eta = \left(\dfrac{a}{\nu}\right)^{\frac{1}{2}}z, \\ \theta(\eta) = \dfrac{T - T_\infty}{T_w - T_\infty}, \\ v_{1p} = axG_1'(\eta),\ v_{2p} = axG_2(\eta),\ v_{3p} = -\sqrt{a\nu}G_1(\eta),\ \eta = \sqrt{\dfrac{a}{\nu}}z \\ \theta_p(\eta) = \dfrac{T_p - T_\infty}{T_w - T_\infty}, \end{array}\right\} \quad (11)$$

where η denotes the similarity variable. Equation (1) is satisfied identically. By using transformations, Equations (2)–(9) have the following structure:

$$(1-\phi_d)(1+\Lambda)G_1''' + (1-\phi_d)(G_1G_1''+2RG_2-G_1'^2)+\Lambda H'+\Gamma_v\gamma_v(G_{1p}'-G_1')=0, \quad (12)$$

$$(1-\phi_d)(1+\Lambda)G_2''+(1-\phi_d)(G_1G_2'-G_1'G_2-2RG_1')+\Gamma_v\gamma_v(G_{2p}-G_2)=0, \quad (13)$$

$$(1+\frac{\Lambda}{2})H''+G_1H'-G_1'H-(2H+G_1'')=0 \quad (14)$$

$$\theta''+Prf\theta'+Pr\gamma_t.\beta_t(\theta_p-\theta)=0, \quad (15)$$

For the dusty phase

$$G_{1p}'^2-G_{1p}G_{1p}''-2RG_{2p}+\gamma_v.\Gamma_v(G_{1p}'-G_1')=0, \quad (16)$$

$$G_{1p}'G_{2p}-G_{1p}G_{2p}'+2RG_{1p}'+\gamma_v.\Gamma_v(G_{2p}-G_2)=0, \quad (17)$$

$$G_{1p}\theta_p'+\gamma_t.\beta_t(\theta-\theta_p)=0, \quad (18)$$

with boundary constraints,

$$\left.\begin{array}{l} G_1(\eta)=0,\ G_2(\eta)=0,\ G_1'(\eta)=1, H=-\beta F_1'',\ \theta(\eta)=1,\ at\ \eta=0, \\ G_{1p}(\eta)=G_1(\eta),\ G_{2p}(\eta)=G_2(\eta),\ G_{1p}'(\eta)=1, \theta_p(\eta)=1,\ at\ \eta=0, \\ G_1'(\eta)\to 0, G_2'(\eta)\to 0,\ \theta(\eta)\to 0,\ H=0,\ at\ \eta\to\infty. \\ G_{1p}'(\eta)\to 0, G_{2p}'(\eta)\to 0,\ \theta_p(\eta)\to 0,\ at\ \eta\to\infty. \end{array}\right\} \quad (19)$$

where $Pr=\frac{\mu_f(cp)_f}{k_f}$ shows the Prandtl number, $\Lambda=\frac{k}{\mu}$ is the material parameter, $R=\frac{\Omega}{a}$ represents the rotational parameter, $\Gamma_v=\frac{1}{\tau_v c}$ denotes the fluid–particle interaction parameter for velocity, $\gamma_v=\frac{Nm}{\rho}$ is the mass concentration of dusty granules, $\gamma_t=\frac{c_p}{c_m}$ is the ratio of specific heat, and $\beta_t=\frac{1}{a\tau_T}$ is the fluid interaction parameter for temperature. This report is based upon the influence of volume fraction of dust particles subject to a small amount of dust $\phi_d=0.2$ and a large amount of dust particles $\phi_d=0.8$ when Coriolis and Lorentz forces are significant in the case of non-Newtonian fluid (micropolar fluid).

3. Physical Quantities

The important physical quantities of interest are discussed in this section. The Nusselt coefficients Nu_x and skin friction coefficients are given as [41,47]:

$$\left.\begin{array}{r} Cf_x=\dfrac{\tau_{xz}}{\rho(ax)^2} \\ Cf_y=\dfrac{\tau_{yz}}{\rho(ax)^2} \\ Nu=\dfrac{xq_w}{k_f(T-T_\infty)} \end{array}\right\} \quad (20)$$

with

$$q_w=-k\frac{\partial T}{\partial z}|_{z=0}\ldots, j_w=-D\frac{\partial C}{\partial z}|_{z=0} \quad (21)$$

Finally we have,

$$\left.\begin{array}{r} (Re_x)^{0.5}Cf_x=(1+\Lambda)G_1''(0) \\ (Re_x)^{0.5}Cf_y=(1+\Lambda)G_2'(0) \\ (Re_x)^{-0.5}Nu=-\theta'(0) \end{array}\right\} \quad (22)$$

$Re_x=\frac{u_w^2}{cv}$ stands for local Reynolds number.

4. Solution Procedure

A system of ordinary differential equations represents the flow model. The Equations (11)–(16) are numerically solved using the effectiveness and strength of numerical computing in the bvp4c approach using MATLAB. Ref. [48] provides more details on this solution approach (see Figure 2). The graphical and numerical results show the velocity and temperature fields as different physical factors. The bvp4c technique is used to transform the system of ODEs (11)–(16) into first-order ODEs for a solution:

$$\begin{aligned}
\lambda_1' &= \lambda_2, \\
\lambda_2' &= \lambda_3, \\
\lambda_3' &= \tfrac{(-1)}{(1-\phi_d)(1+\Lambda)}[(1-\phi_d)(\lambda_1\lambda_3 + 2R\lambda_4 - \lambda^2) + \Lambda\lambda_6 + \Gamma_v\gamma_v(\lambda_{11} - \lambda_2)], \\
\lambda_4' &= \lambda_5, \\
\lambda_5' &= \tfrac{(-1)}{(1-\phi_d)(1+\Lambda)}[(1-\phi_d)(\lambda_1\lambda_5 - \lambda_2\lambda_4 - 2R\lambda_2) + \Gamma_v\gamma_v(\lambda_{12} - \lambda_4)], \\
\lambda_6' &= \lambda_7, \\
\lambda_7' &= \frac{(-1)}{\left(1+\frac{\Lambda}{2}\right)}[\lambda_1\lambda_7 - \lambda_2\lambda_6 - (2\lambda_6 + \lambda_3)], \\
\lambda_8' &= \lambda_9 \\
\lambda_9' &= (-1)[\lambda_9\lambda_1 + Pr\Gamma_t\beta_t(\lambda_{14} - \lambda_8)], \\
\lambda_{11}' &= \tfrac{(1)}{\lambda_{10}}[\lambda_{11}^2 - 2R\lambda_{12} + \Gamma_v\gamma_v(\lambda_{11} - \lambda_2)], \\
\lambda_{12}' &= \tfrac{(1)}{\lambda_{10}}[\lambda_{11}\lambda_{12} + 2R\lambda_{11} + \Gamma_v\gamma_v(\lambda_{12} - \lambda_4)], \\
\lambda_{13}' &= \tfrac{(-1)}{\lambda_{10}}[\beta_t\gamma_t(\lambda_8 - \lambda_{13})].
\end{aligned}$$

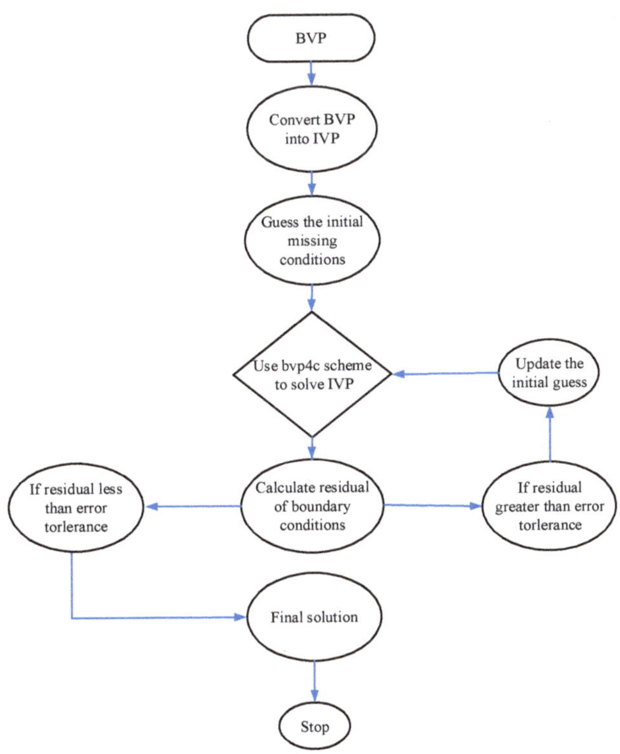

Figure 2. Numerical solution flow chart.

The corresponding boundary conditions are as follows:
$\lambda_1 = 0,\ \lambda_2 = 1,\ \lambda_4 = 0,\ \lambda_6 = -\beta\lambda_3,\ at\ \eta = 0,$
$\lambda_8 = 0,\ \lambda_9 = 1,\ \lambda_11 = 0,\ \lambda_{13} = 1,\ at\ \eta = 0,$
$\lambda_2 \to 0,\ \lambda_5 \to 0,\ \lambda_6 \to 0,\ as\ \eta \to \infty.$
$\lambda_9 \to 0,\ \lambda_{12} \to 0,\ \lambda_{13} \to 0,\ as\ \eta \to \infty.$

5. Results and Discussion

The main purpose of this investigation is to analyze the thermal transportation and flux of the micropolar fluid on a stretching surface with a suspension of dust particles. For solving highly nonlinear equations with related constraint, the bvp4c approach is applied and coded in MATLAB; graphical outcomes of the impacts of the variational behavior of different parameters on velocity and temperature and a micro-rotation distribution profile for both fluid and dusty phases were acquired. The outcomes for Nusselt number, skin friction factor, and couple stress were obtained graphically. Before plotting the results, we have justified our results with the already published research articles through Tables 1 and 2 subject to limited cases. An excellent correlation has been achieved which affirms the validity of numerical technique coded in MATLAB. The values of parameters that we used are as follows: $R = 0.5$, $Pr = 0.72$, $\phi_d = 0.1$ and 0.8, $\Gamma_v = 1$, $\beta_t = 0.1$, $\gamma_v = 0.2$, $\gamma_t = 0.2$, $\Lambda = 0.2$, and $\beta = 0.5$.

Table 1. Comparing the current numerical findings for M when and all others parameter are zero.

M	Rehman [49]	Bagh [50]	Present Results
0.0	1.00000130	1.0000080	1.000013
0.2	1.0954463	1.0954458	1.095446
0.5	1.2247454	1.2247446	1.224745
1.0	1.4142180	1.4142132	1.414218

Table 2. Comparing the current numerical findings for Pr when and all others parameter are zero.

Pr	Rehman [49]	Bagh [50]	Present Results
1.0	1.00000	1.0000	1.0000
3.0	1.92375	1.9236	1.9238
10.0	3.72061	3.7207	3.7210
100.0	12.29404	12.2940	1.2941

Figure 3a,b depicts the impact of rotating and dust particle volume concentration on axial and transverse velocity of fluid. It reveals that there is deceleration in G_1' with amplifying inputs of R and ϕ_d. This velocity acquires its maximum value in condition of $R = 0$ (pure stretching case). As a result of Coriolis forces, the motion of the fluid slows down; the transverse velocity G_2 has the opposite behavior, with incremented values of R and ϕ_d. Similarly, by increasing dust particle concentration, the fluid becomes thicker and offers resistance to motion, so G_1' reduced. Figure 4a,b demonstrate the influence of R and ϕ_d on the velocities of the dusty phase of fluid. Here, G_{1p} and G_{2p} signifies the momentum boundary layers for dusty phase in x and y direction, respectively. The axial velocity of the dusty phase of fluid recedes due to the growing strength of both dust particle concentration and rotating parameter; however, transverse velocity increases against these parameters. Figure 5a,b are plotted to see the effect of the material parameter and ϕ_d on G_1' and G_2. The axial velocities increased with amplified values of material parameter; however, transverse velocity decreased. Since the material parameter Λ is inversely proportional to the dynamic viscosity coefficients, its higher value indicates a reduction in viscous impacts, allowing the flow to move faster; for higher inputs of ϕ_d, both velocities are decreased.

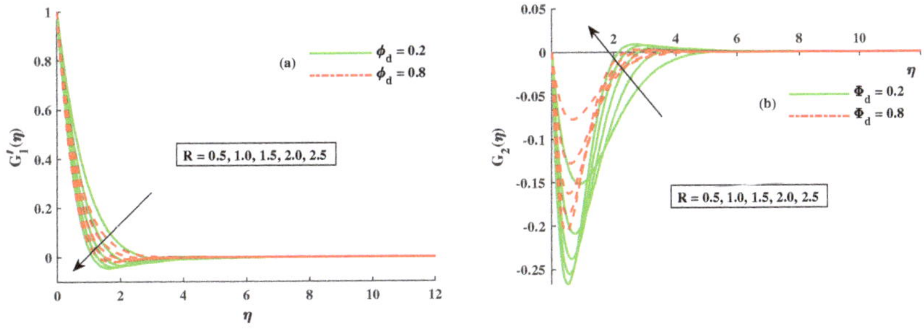

Figure 3. Fluctuation of R and ϕ_d on $G_1'(\eta)$ and $G_2(\eta)$.

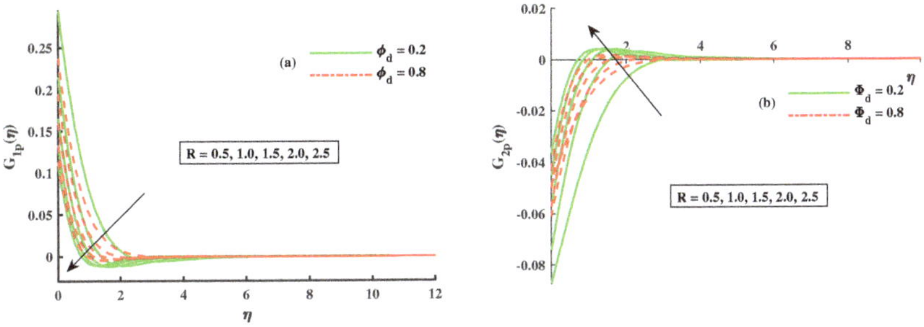

Figure 4. Fluctuation of R and ϕ_d on $G_{1p}(\eta)$ and $G_{2p}(\eta)$.

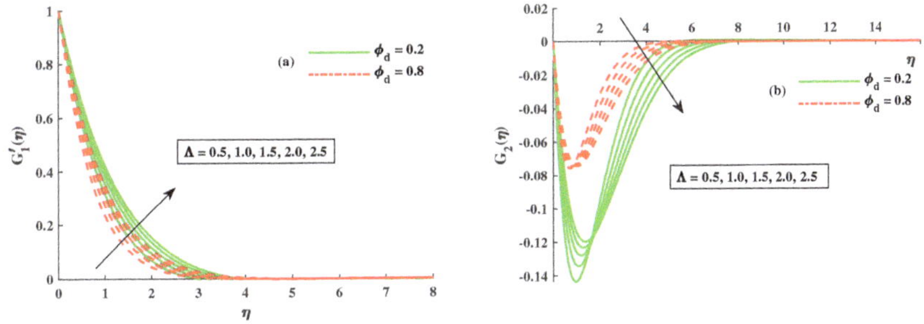

Figure 5. Fluctuation of Λ and ϕ_d on $G_1'(\eta)$ and $G_2(\eta)$.

Figure 6a,b demonstrate the affect of Λ and volume concentration of dust particles on dusty phase velocities G_{1p} and G_{2p}. It can be seen that G_{1p} velocity increased and G_{2p} velocity decreased with incremental values of material parameters; both velocities decreased with higher inputs of dust particle concentration. Figure 7a,b display the variation in micro-rotation distribution profile with varying inputs of rotational, material parameter, and concentration of dust particles. From Figure 7a, we can see that the micro-rotation profile was amplified with larger inputs of R, whereas it was reduced against higher inputs of dust particle concentration. Figure 7b reveals that micro-rotation was improved with increasing inputs of Λ parameters. Figure 8a,b illustrate the impact of R and ϕ_d on the temperature and dust phase of the fluid. It is obvious that the temperature of fluid and dusty phase increased with increasing inputs of R and ϕ_d. Basically, the development of heat is satisfied on the base of a higher diffusion process because of increased rotation. Figure 9a,b represent the fluctuation in θ and θ_p by different values of the material parameter and ϕ_d. The fluid temperature and dust phase temperature depreciate against magnified inputs of the material parameter; both phase temperatures rise with larger inputs of ϕ_d. Physically, the higher input of dust particles enhance the base fluid dust concentration, which causes the fluid velocity to decrease; however, the base fluid temperature increased due to the thermal conductivity of the additional dust particles.

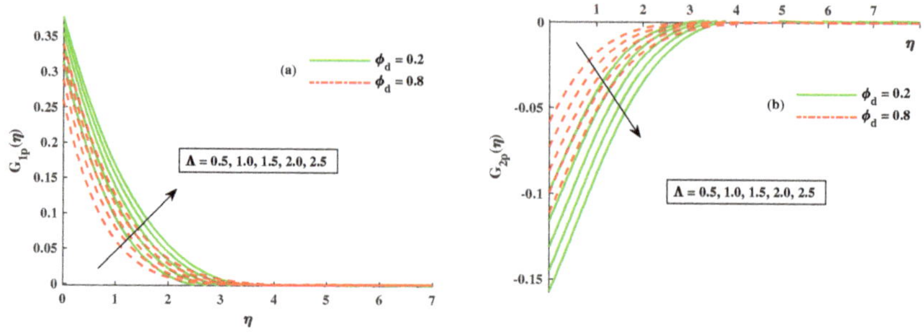

Figure 6. Fluctuation of Λ and ϕ_d on G_{1p} and G_{2p}.

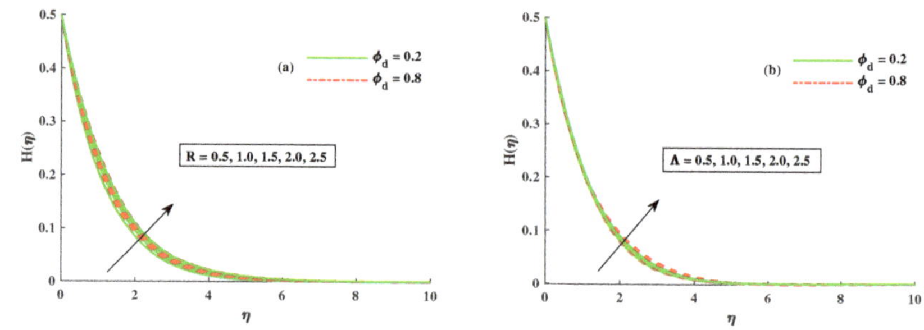

Figure 7. Fluctuation of R, Λ and ϕ_d on $H(\eta)$.

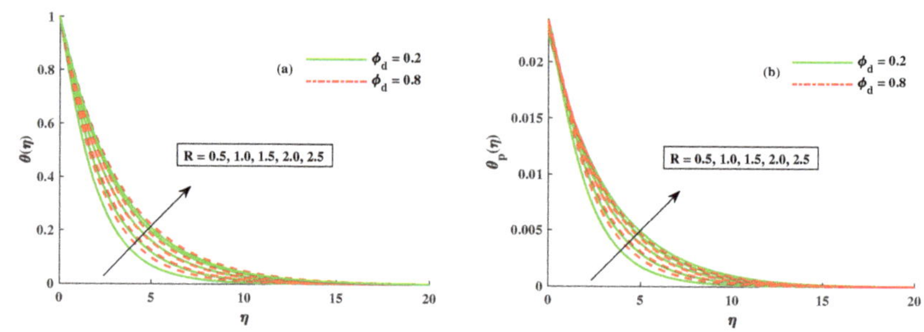

Figure 8. Fluctuation of R and ϕ_d on θ and θ_p.

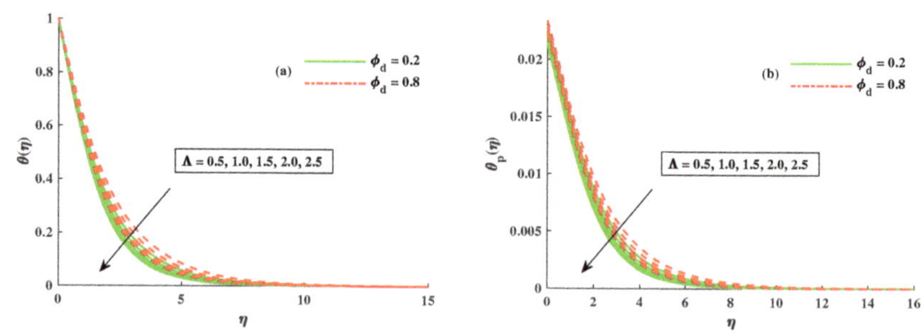

Figure 9. Fluctuation of Λ and ϕ_d on θ and θ_p.

Figure 10a,b portray the skin friction factor in x and y direction for different inputs of rotating parameter, material parameter, and dust particle concentration parameter. Figure 10a shows that the skin friction coefficient Cf_x was reduced against the enhanced values of Λ, R, and ϕ_d. Figure 10b reveals that the skin friction coefficient Cf_y depreciated against increasing values of the rotating parameter corresponding to the strong Coriolis force in the rotating system, but displayed the opposite behavior against Λ and ϕ_d. The larger strength of the rotating parameter generated the instability in the fluid flow, and this oscillation characteristic is reduced when low values of R are considered. We can infer that a critical rotating condition exists for which secondary flow is sustainable, and all the while, the fluid primary flow is stable. The excessive velocity of the rotational fluid system is not useful, and considering this, a reasonable choice of Ω is recommended for functional producing activities. The influence of different parameters on the Nusselt number are sketched in Figure 11a. From Figure 11a, we see that the Nusselt number reduced with rising values of rotation, material parameter, and volume concentration of dust particles. Figure 11b depicts the fluctuation of couple stress by rotation, material parameter, and volume concentration of dust particles. It displays an increasing behavior against the rising values of all parameters. The large values of R cause the fluid primary velocity to slow down, which is responsible for increasing the fluid temperature; a low Nusselt number implies a higher temperature.

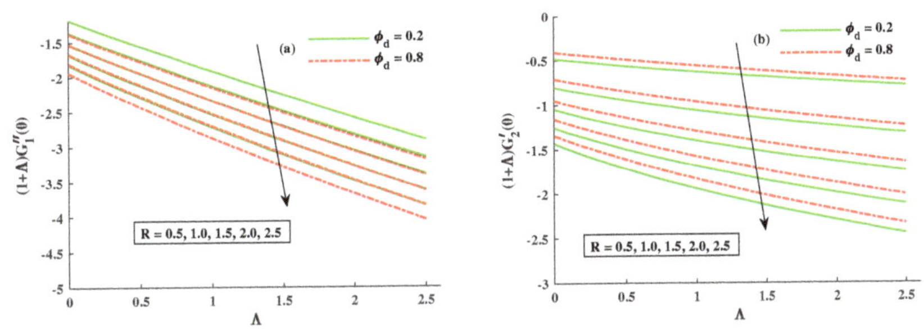

Figure 10. Fluctuation of R, Λ, and ϕ_d on $G_1''(0)$ and $G_2'(0)$.

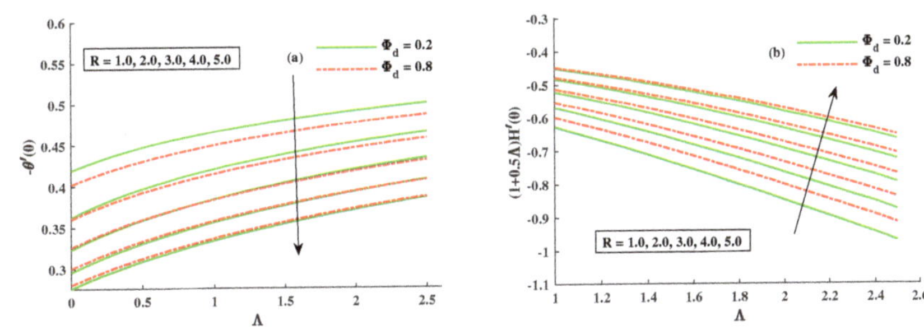

Figure 11. Fluctuation of R, Λ, and ϕ_d on Nusselt number and couple stress.

6. Conclusions

Efforts have been made to analyze the significance of micropolar dusty fluid and heat flux due to thermal boundary gradients across a stretching sheet. The non-dimensional problem is solved by using the bvp4c method developed in MATLAB script. Based on the consequences, it is reasonable to conclude that:

- $G_1'(\eta)$ and $G_{1p}(\eta)$ significantly decrease along with rising values of parameters ϕ_d, R and having increasing behavior against Λ, whereas $G_2(\eta)$ and $G_{2p}(\eta)$ have the opposite behavior against ϕ_d, R parameters while it decreased against Λ.
- The micro-rotation distribution profile depreciates by higher inputs of ϕ_d and amplified with larger inputs of rotation and material parameter.
- The temperature θ and θ_p aggrandize with higher inputs of volume concentration of dust particles and rotation parameter, whereas it declines against increasing inputs of Λ.
- Along the x direction, the coefficient of skin friction decreased with enhancing values of Λ, ϕ_d, and R. Along the y-direction, the skin friction coefficient is raised by enlarge-

ment in Λ and ϕ_d, but it has opposite behavior against increasing inputs of rotating parameter.

- The magnitude of the Nusselt number is reduced with a higher contribution of R, ϕ_d, and Λ, whereas couple stress exhibit rising behavior against these parameters.

Through this successful numerical computational effort, we have successfully elucidated the parametric impacts on the dynamics of micropolar dusty fluid. This study may be extended for Maxwell dusty nanofluid, Oldroyd-B dusty nanofluid, and viscoelastic Jeffrey's dusty nanofluid.

Author Contributions: Q.L. modeled the problem and wrote the manuscript. B.A. completed the formal analysis and revision. S.U.R. and D.H. thoroughly checked the mathematical modeling, English corrections, formal analysis, and revision. S.A. solved the problem using MATLAB software. N.A.S. and J.D.C.: writing—review and editing. All authors finalized the manuscript after its internal evaluation. Q.L. and N.A.S. contributed equally to this work and are co-first authors. All authors have read and agreed to the published version of the manuscript.

Funding: This work was supported by the Korean Institute of Energy Technology Evaluation and Planning (KETEP) grant funded by the Korean government (MOTIE) (No. 20192010107020, Development of hybrid adsorption chiller using unutilized heat source of low temperature).

Institutional Review Board Statement: Not applicable.

Informed Consent Statement: Not applicable.

Data Availability Statement: Not applicable.

Conflicts of Interest: The authors declare no conflict of interest.

References

1. Eringen, A.C. Theory of micropolar fluids. *J. Math. Mech.* **1966**, *16*, 1–18. [CrossRef]
2. Eringen, A.C. Theory of thermomicrofluids. *J. Math. Anal. Appl.* **1972**, *38*, 480–496. [CrossRef]
3. Ariman, T.; Turk, M.; Sylvester, N. Microcontinuum fluid mechanics—A review. *Int. J. Eng. Sci.* **1973**, *11*, 905–930. [CrossRef]
4. Ariman, T.; Turk, M.; Sylvester, N. Applications of microcontinuum fluid mechanics. *Int. J. Eng. Sci.* **1974**, *12*, 273–293. [CrossRef]
5. Peddieson, J. Boundary layer theory for a micropolar fluid. *Recent Adv. Eng. Sci.* **1970**, *5*, 405–426.
6. Lukaszewicz, G. *Micropolar Fluids: Theory and Application*; Birkhäuser: Boston, MA, USA, 1999.
7. Eringen, A.C. *Microcontinuum Field Theories: II. Fluent Media*; Springer Science & Business Media: New York, NY, USA, 2001; Volume 2.
8. Xia, W.F.; Animasaun, I.; Wakif, A.; Shah, N.A.; Yook, S.J. Gear-generalized differential quadrature analysis of oscillatory convective Taylor-Couette flows of second-grade fluids subject to Lorentz and Darcy-Forchheimer quadratic drag forces. *Int. Commun. Heat Mass Transf.* **2021**, *126*, 105395. [CrossRef]
9. Dawar, A.; Wakif, A.; Thumma, T.; Shah, N.A. Towards a new MHD non-homogeneous convective nanofluid flow model for simulating a rotating inclined thin layer of sodium alginate-based Iron oxide exposed to incident solar energy. *Int. Commun. Heat Mass Transf.* **2022**, *130*, 105800. [CrossRef]
10. Yu, C.J.; Richter, A.; Datta, A.; Durbin, M.; Dutta, P. Observation of molecular layering in thin liquid films using X-ray reflectivity. *Phys. Rev. Lett.* **1999**, *82*, 2326. [CrossRef]
11. Kim, S.H.; Choi, S.R.; Kim, D. Thermal conductivity of metal-oxide nanofluids: Particle size dependence and effect of laser irradiation. *J. Heat Transfer.* **2007**, *129*, 298–307. [CrossRef]
12. Prasannakumara, B.C.; Shashikumar, N.S.; Archana, M. Three-dimensional boundary layer flow and heat transfer of a dusty fluid towards a stretching sheet with convective boundary conditions. *J. Comput. Appl. Res. Mech. Eng.* **2018**, *8*, 25–38.
13. Ali, L.; Ali, B.; Liu, X.; Iqbal, T.; Zulqarnain, R.M.; Javid, M. A comparative study of unsteady MHD Falkner–Skan wedge flow for non-Newtonian nanofluids considering thermal radiation and activation energy. *Chin. J. Phys.* **2022**, *77*, 1625–1638. [CrossRef]
14. Wang, F.; Asjad, M.I.; Ur Rehman, S.; Ali, B.; Hussain, S.; Gia, T.N.; Muhammad, T. MHD Williamson Nanofluid Flow over a Slender Elastic Sheet of Irregular Thickness in the Presence of Bioconvection. *Nanomaterials* **2021**, *11*, 2297. [CrossRef] [PubMed]
15. Wang, F.; Rehman, S.; Bouslimi, J.; Khaliq, H.; Qureshi, M.I.; Kamran, M.; Alharbi, A.N.; Ahmad, H.; Farooq, A. Comparative study of heat and mass transfer of generalized MHD Oldroyd-B bio-nano fluid in a permeable medium with ramped conditions. *Sci. Rep.* **2021**, *11*, 23454. [CrossRef] [PubMed]
16. Fuzhang, W.; Akhtar, S.; Nadeem, S.; El-Shafay, A. Mathematical computations for the physiological flow of Casson fluid in a vertical elliptic duct with ciliated heated wavy walls. *Waves Random Complex Media* **2022**, *4*, 1–14. [CrossRef]
17. Anuar, N.S.; Bachok, N. Double solutions and stability analysis of micropolar hybrid nanofluid with thermal radiation impact on unsteady stagnation point flow. *Mathematics* **2021**, *9*, 276. [CrossRef]

18. Ali, L.; Ali, B.; Abd Allah, A.M.; Hammouch, Z.; Hussain, S.; Siddique, I.; Huang, Y. Insight into significance of thermal stratification and radiation on dynamics of micropolar water based TiO_2 nanoparticle via finite element simulation. *J. Mater. Res. Technol.* **2022**, *19*, 4209–4219. [CrossRef]
19. Wang, W.; Jaradat, M.M.; Siddique, I.; Mousa, A.A.A.; Abdal, S.; Mustafa, Z.; Ali, H.M. On Thermal Distribution for Darcy–Forchheimer Flow of Maxwell Sutterby Nanofluids over a Radiated Extending Surface. *Nanomaterials* **2022**, *12*, 1834. [CrossRef]
20. Ali, L.; Liu, X.; Ali, B.; Mujeed, S.; Abdal, S.; Mutahir, A. The impact of nanoparticles due to applied magnetic dipole in micropolar fluid flow using the finite element method. *Symmetry* **2020**, *12*, 520. [CrossRef]
21. Nabwey, H.A.; Rashad, A.M.; Mahdy, A.E.N.; Shaaban, S.M. Thermal Conductivity and Thermophoretic Impacts of Micropolar Fluid Flow by a Horizontal Absorbent Isothermal Porous Wall with Heat Source/Sink. *Mathematics* **2022**, *10*, 1514. [CrossRef]
22. Ghadikolaei, S.; Hosseinzadeh, K.; Hatami, M.; Ganji, D. MHD boundary layer analysis for micropolar dusty fluid containing Hybrid nanoparticles (Cu-Al2O3) over a porous medium. *J. Mol. Liq.* **2018**, *268*, 813–823. [CrossRef]
23. Abbasi, A.; Gulzar, S.; Mabood, F.; Farooq, W. Nonlinear thermal radiation and activation energy features in axisymmetric rotational stagnation point flow of hybrid nanofluid. *Int. Commun. Heat Mass Transf.* **2021**, *126*, 105335. [CrossRef]
24. Bilal, M.; Ramzan, M. Hall current effect on unsteady rotational flow of carbon nanotubes with dust particles and nonlinear thermal radiation in Darcy–Forchheimer porous media. *J. Therm. Anal. Calorim.* **2019**, *138*, 3127–3137. [CrossRef]
25. Ali Zafar, A.; Bilal Riaz, M.; Imran Asjad, M. Unsteady rotational flow of fractional Maxwell fluid in a cylinder subject to shear stress on the boundary. *Punjab Univ. J. Math.* **2020**, *50*, 21–32.
26. Kim, D.; Son, Y.; Park, S. Effects of operating parameters on in-cylinder flow characteristics of an optically accessible engine with a spray-guided injector. *Energy* **2022**, *245*, 123314. [CrossRef]
27. Liu, X.; Sun, Y.; Morisada, Y.; Fujii, H. Dynamics of rotational flow in friction stir welding of aluminium alloys. *J. Mater. Process. Technol.* **2018**, *252*, 643–651. [CrossRef]
28. Koriko, O.K.; Adegbie, K.S.; Shah, N.A.; Animasaun, I.L.; Olotu, M.A. Numerical solutions of the partial differential equations for investigating the significance of partial slip due to lateral velocity and viscous dissipation: The case of blood-gold Carreau nanofluid and dusty fluid. *Numer. Methods Part. Differ. Equ.* **2021**, *7*, 1–15. [CrossRef]
29. Fortov, V.; Vaulina, O.; Petrov, O.; Vasiliev, M.; Gavrikov, A.; Shakova, I.; Vorona, N.; Khrustalyov, Y.V.; Manohin, A.; Chernyshev, A. Experimental study of the heat transport processes in dusty plasma fluid. *Phys. Rev. E* **2007**, *75*, 026403. [CrossRef] [PubMed]
30. Bilal, M.; Khan, S.; Ali, F.; Arif, M.; Khan, I.; Nisar, K.S. Couette flow of viscoelastic dusty fluid in a rotating frame along with the heat transfer. *Sci. Rep.* **2021**, *11*, 1–16. [CrossRef]
31. Jalil, M.; Asghar, S.; Yasmeen, S. An exact solution of MHD boundary layer flow of dusty fluid over a stretching surface. *Math. Probl. Eng.* **2017**, *2017*, 1–5. [CrossRef]
32. Reena, R.; Rana, U. Effect of dust particles on rotating micropolar fluid heated from below saturating a porous medium. *Appl. Appl. Math. Int. J.* **2009**, *4*, 15.
33. Dasman, A.; Arifin, N.S.; Kasim, A.R.M.; Yacob, N.A. Formulation of dusty micropolar fluid mathematical model. *J. Phys. Conf. Ser.* **2019**, *1366*, 012032. [CrossRef]
34. Ramzan, M.; Shaheen, N.; Chung, J.D.; Kadry, S.; Chu, Y.M.; Howari, F. Impact of Newtonian heating and Fourier and Fick's laws on a magnetohydrodynamic dusty Casson nanofluid flow with variable heat source/sink over a stretching cylinder. *Sci. Rep.* **2021**, *11*, 2357. [CrossRef]
35. Ghadikolaei, S.; Hosseinzadeh, K.; Yassari, M.; Sadeghi, H.; Ganji, D. Boundary layer analysis of micropolar dusty fluid with TiO2 nanoparticles in a porous medium under the effect of magnetic field and thermal radiation over a stretching sheet. *J. Mol. Liq.* **2017**, *244*, 374–389. [CrossRef]
36. Varun Kumar, R.; Punith Gowda, R.; Naveen Kumar, R.; Radhika, M.; Prasannakumara, B. Two-phase flow of dusty fluid with suspended hybrid nanoparticles over a stretching cylinder with modified Fourier heat flux. *SN Appl. Sci.* **2021**, *3*, 384. [CrossRef]
37. Arifin, N.S.; Kasim, A.R.M.; Zokri, S.M.; Salleh, M.Z. Boundary Layer Flow of Dusty Williamson Fluid with Variable Viscosity Effect Over a Stretching Sheet. *J. Adv. Res. Fluid Mech. Therm. Sci.* **2021**, *86*, 164–175. [CrossRef]
38. Wang, F.; Khan, S.A.; Gouadria, S.; El-Zahar, E.R.; Khan, M.I.; Khan, S.U.; Yasir, M.; Li, Y.M. Entropy optimized flow of Darcy-Forchheimer viscous fluid with cubic autocatalysis chemical reactions. *Int. J. Hydrogen Energy* **2022**, *47*, 13911–13920. [CrossRef]
39. Rashid, S.; Hayat, T.; Qayyum, S.; Ayub, M.; Alsaedi, A. Three-dimensional rotating Darcy–Forchheimer flow with activation energy. *Int. J. Numer. Methods Heat Fluid Flow* **2019**, *29*, 935–948. [CrossRef]
40. Tayyab, M.; Siddique, I.; Jarad, F.; Ashraf, M.K.; Ali, B. Numerical solution of 3D rotating nanofluid flow subject to Darcy-Forchheimer law, bio-convection and activation energy. *S. Afr. J. Chem. Eng.* **2022**, *40*, 48–56. [CrossRef]
41. Ahmad, K.; Nazar, R.; Ishak, A.; Pop, I. Unsteady three-dimensional boundary layer flow due to a stretching surface in a micropolar fluid. *Int. J. Numer. Methods Fluids* **2012**, *68*, 1561–1573. [CrossRef]
42. Abbas, Z.; Javed, T.; Sajid, M.; Ali, N. Unsteady MHD flow and heat transfer on a stretching sheet in a rotating fluid. *J. Taiwan Inst. Chem. Eng.* **2010**, *41*, 644–650. [CrossRef]
43. Thumma, T.; Wakif, A.; Animasaun, I.L. Generalized differential quadrature analysis of unsteady three-dimensional MHD radiating dissipative Casson fluid conveying tiny particles. *Heat Transf.* **2020**, *49*, 2595–2626. [CrossRef]
44. Manghat, R.; Siddabasappa, S. MHD Boundary Layer Flow and Heat Transfer of Rotating Dusty Nanofluid over a Stretching Surface. *Kyungpook Math. J.* **2020**, *60*, 853–867.

45. Muhammad, S.; Ali, G.; Shah, Z.; Islam, S.; Hussain, S.A. The rotating flow of magneto hydrodynamic carbon nanotubes over a stretching sheet with the impact of non-linear thermal radiation and heat generation/absorption. *Appl. Sci.* **2018**, *8*, 482. [CrossRef]
46. Awan, A.U.; Ahammad, N.A.; Majeed, S.; Gamaoun, F.; Ali, B. Significance of hybrid nanoparticles, Lorentz and Coriolis forces on the dynamics of water based flow. *Int. Commun. Heat Mass Transf.* **2022**, *135*, 106084. [CrossRef]
47. Oyelakin, I.; Lalramneihmawii, P.; Mondal, S.; Sibanda, P. Analysis of double-diffusion convection on three-dimensional MHD stagnation point flow of a tangent hyperbolic Casson nanofluid. *Int. J. Ambient Energy* **2020**, *7*, 1–12. [CrossRef]
48. Habib, U.; Abdal, S.; Siddique, I.; Ali, R. A comparative study on micropolar, Williamson, Maxwell nanofluids flow due to a stretching surface in the presence of bioconvection, double diffusion and activation energy. *Int. Commun. Heat Mass Transf.* **2021**, *127*, 105551. [CrossRef]
49. Rehman, S.U.; Mariam, A.; Ullah, A.; Asjad, M.I.; Bajuri, M.Y.; Pansera, B.A.; Ahmadian, A. Numerical computation of buoyancy and radiation effects on MHD micropolar nanofluid flow over a stretching/shrinking sheet with heat source. *Case Stud. Therm. Eng.* **2021**, *25*, 100867. [CrossRef]
50. Ali, B.; Nie, Y.; Khan, S.A.; Sadiq, M.T.; Tariq, M. Finite element simulation of multiple slip effects on MHD unsteady maxwell nanofluid flow over a permeable stretching sheet with radiation and thermo-diffusion in the presence of chemical reaction. *Processes* **2019**, *7*, 628. [CrossRef]

mathematics MDPI

Article

Output Power Control and Load Mitigation of a Horizontal Axis Wind Turbine with a Fully Coupled Aeroelastic Model: Novel Sliding Mode Perspective

Hongfu Zhang [1], Jiahao Wen [1], Farshad Golnary [2,3] and Lei Zhou [2,*]

[1] School of Civil Engineering, Northeast Forestry University, Harbin 150040, China; zhanghongfu@nefu.edu.cn (H.Z.); wenjiahao@nefu.edu.cn (J.W.)
[2] Department of Civil Engineering, Hong Kong University of Science and Technology, Clear Water Bay, Kowloon, Hong Kong; fgaa@connect.ust.hk
[3] Department of Mechanical Engineering, Sharif University of Technology, Tehran 1458889694, Iran
* Correspondence: lzhouau@connect.ust.hk; Tel.: +852-95682550

Abstract: The power control of horizontal axis wind turbines can affect significantly the vibration loads and fatigue life of the tower and the blades. In this paper, we both consider the power control and vibration load mitigation of the tower fore-aft vibration. For this purpose, at first, we developed a fully coupled model of the NREL 5MW turbine. This model considers the full aeroelastic behaviour of the blades and tower and is validated by experiment results, comparing the time history data with the FAST (Fatigue, Aerodynamics, Structures, and Turbulence) code which is developed by NREL (National Renewable Energy Lab in the United States). In the next, novel sensorless control algorithms are developed based on the supper twisting sliding mode control theory and sliding mode observer for disturbance rejection. In region II (the wind speed is between the cut-in and rated wind velocity), the novel sensorless control algorithm increased the power coefficient in comparison to the conventional indirect speed control (ISC) method (the conventional method in the industry). In region III (the wind speed is between the rated and cut-out speed), an adaptive neural fuzzy inference system (ANFIS) is developed to estimate pitch sensitivity. The rotor speed, pitch angle, and effective wind velocity are inputs, and pitch sensitivity is the output. The designed novel pitch control performance is compared with the gain scheduled PI (GPI) method (the conventional approach in this region). The simulation results demonstrate that the flapwise blade displacement is reduced significantly. Finally, to reduce the fore-aft vibration of the tower, a tuned mass damper (TMD) was designed by using the genetic algorithm and the fully coupled model. In comparison to the literature body, we demonstrate that the fully coupled model provides much better accuracy in comparison to the uncoupled model to estimate the vibration loads.

Keywords: aeroelastic model; disturbance rejection; vibration control; tuned mass dampers; sliding mode observer

MSC: 74F10

Citation: Zhang, H.; Wen, J.; Golnary, F.; Zhou, L. Output Power Control and Load Mitigation of a Horizontal Axis Wind Turbine with a Fully Coupled Aeroelastic Model: Novel Sliding Mode Perspective. *Mathematics* **2022**, *10*, 2735. https://doi.org/10.3390/math10152735

Academic Editors: Shujin Laima, Yong Cao, Xiaowei Jin and Hehe Ren

Received: 21 June 2022
Accepted: 28 July 2022
Published: 2 August 2022

Publisher's Note: MDPI stays neutral with regard to jurisdictional claims in published maps and institutional affiliations.

Copyright: © 2022 by the authors. Licensee MDPI, Basel, Switzerland. This article is an open access article distributed under the terms and conditions of the Creative Commons Attribution (CC BY) license (https://creativecommons.org/licenses/by/4.0/).

1. Introduction

Wind energy generation has been growing at an unprecedented rate. For instance, the increase in wind energy capacity from 18 GW in 2000 to 590 GW in 2019 is solid evidence of the amazing growth in wind energy production [1,2]. Many countries have decided to produce energy through wind power because it is both clean and economical. According to the latest annual report from the World Wind Energy Association (WWEA), China is the largest wind energy harvester in the world with a capacity of 217 GW, following the USA with 96 GW, and Germany and India in third and fourth places with 59 GW and 39 GW, respectively [1].

A typical horizontal axis wind turbine has four main operational regions according to the incoming wind flow [3–6] (Figure 1). The wind turbine operates in region I if the wind velocity is lower than the cut-in wind velocity. Because of the low wind speed, a wind turbine that operates in the region I does not produce any energy. If the wind speed is between the cut-in wind velocity and the rated speed, then the wind turbine operates in region II and extracts as much energy from the wind as possible. Actuator control for this purpose is the generator. With the increase of wind speed from the rated wind velocity to the cut-out wind velocity, the wind turbine operates in region III with limited power output to its nominal value for the safety of machinery. Actuator control is the pitch angle mechanism for regulating the output power. Finally, in region IV, the wind turbine ceases to generate power to prevent any damage to the machinery due to the larger wind velocity than the cut-out wind velocity [3].

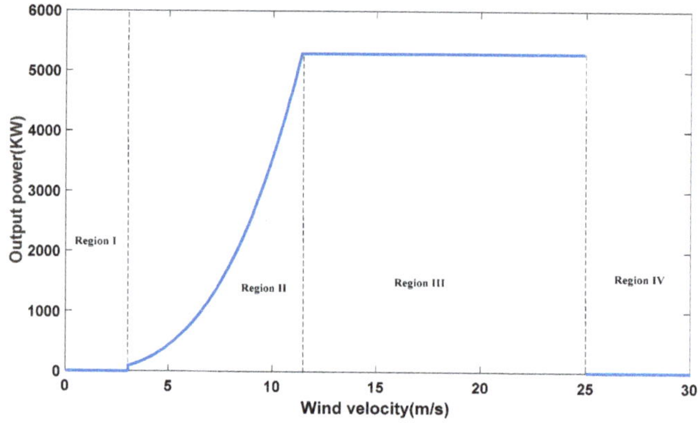

Figure 1. Different operational regions of a horizontal axis wind turbine [3].

There has been plenty of research studying the control problem in regions II and III. For region II, the maximum power point tracking algorithm (MPPT) has been extensively investigated and is the simplest method for achieving maximum power [5–7]. Its main problem, however, is that it has weak performance against the uncertainties in the model [7–10]. The gain schedule PI (GPI) control algorithm was first developed in [11] to limit the output power in region III. The gains of the algorithm were regulated by using pitch sensitivity, but its main obstacle was measurement noise due to the wind speed.

Control algorithms for bodies such as wind turbines can be categorizable, in literature, into model-based and non-model-based approaches [12–16]. Non-model-based approaches include fuzzy control systems [17,18] and PI or GPI control approaches [11]. The main part of each fuzzy system is the fuzzy rule base [19]. Designing the fuzzy rule base, most of the time is based on a trial-and-error process which makes it difficult to use. The model-based approaches are widely found in the literature [20–24]. Model-based predictive control (MPC), is widely used in many engineering applications [25–27]. MPC is a predictive approach based on the optimization of a cost function. The cost function must be defined to address the output power error and some sources of vibration loads. However, the main disadvantage of this approach is its inability to provide any analytical stability proof for the closed-loop system [25]. Most of the model-based approaches are based on non-linear control theory like sliding mode, adaptive control approach, and backstepping [22,23,28,29]. In these works, two simple models: one-mass and two-mass were considered for the whole wind turbine system. However, these models have not considered the aeroelastic behaviour of the blades and the tower. In addition, the control signal in these works contains unmeasurable (like the aerodynamic torque) and unknown state variables.

The above discussion demonstrates that in order to have a better understanding of the wind turbine loads, an aeroelastic model is necessary. Wind turbines are complex structures. The blades are like rotating beams that can vibrate in two directions that are perpendicular to each other [30]. The lateral vibration in the rotational plane is called edgewise and the lateral vibration perpendicular to the rotational plane is called flapwise vibration. The tower also cannot be considered a rigid body. Similar to the blades, the tower can vibrate in the rotational plane (i.e., "side-side" vibration), and also perpendicular to the rotational plane (i.e., "fore-aft" vibration) [30–32]. The mitigation of the vibration loads is a significant goal in increasing the life span of a wind turbine. Three main approaches, namely, passive, semi-active, and active have been proposed in the literature to reduce the vibration loads of the structure [33]. In particular, passive control has been widely studied. In [31], roller dampers were proposed to reduce the edgewise vibrations in the blades, in which, each blade of the wind turbine is considered as a two degree of freedom system and the roller damper is designed to minimize the edgewise vibration signal. In another research [34], tuned liquid dampers were used to mitigate vibrations in the edgewise direction. In [35], a 3D pendulum was suggested to reduce both fore-aft and side-side vibration of the tower. The results demonstrated that, with a 2% mass ratio (ratio between the mass of the pendulum with respect to the rotor), the pendulum can reduce the standard deviation (STD) of the vibration signals by around 10% in comparison to dual tuned mass dampers (TMDs). However, the main point of these studies is that the performance of the vibration absorber was designed by considering the constant rotor speed (12.1 rpm). In addition, the coupling dynamics between the drivetrain and the other parts were not investigated.

According to the above discussion, the following shortcomings in the literature body are addressed:

- In some of the previous research [22,23,28,36], the designed control signals contain unmeasurable or unknown terms. Any applicable control signal must estimate the unknown terms and uses the measurable terms.
- Pitch sensitivity is one of the key parameters in region III. In order to improve the computational time, it is better to estimate the pitch sensitivity rather than using look-up tables.
- Regarding the literature body, the passive vibration absorber is designed in the constant nominated rotor speed (which is 12.1 rpm) [31,32,34,35]. However, the rotor speed is not constant in region III. In addition, pitch control in region III has a significant effect on the tower vibration loads. Therefore, it is more accurate to estimate vibration loads by considering drivetrain dynamics.

To address these issues, our research considers both control and load mitigation of the NREL 5MW wind turbine. A complete aeroelastic model of this wind turbine is investigated. This model considers the continuous vibration of the blades in the edgewise and flapwise directions, the vibration of the tower in the fore-aft and side-side directions, and the flexibility of the drivetrain system. The interaction of the wind with the blades is obtained by the blade element momentum theory (BEM), Prandtl correction, dynamic stall, and wake modelling. This model is validated by the FAST numerical tool of NREL. The main contribution of this research is summarized as follows:

- The control problem in region II has been considered by a novel super twisting control approach. The main novelty and contribution of this part, in comparison to the literature body, is estimating the unknown terms by designing a novel nonlinear observer. The comparison of our results with the conventional ISC algorithm demonstrates that this approach can increase the mean value of the power coefficient by nearly 1%.
- In region III, we developed a novel sensorless pitch controller based on the previous research of the first author [37]. Similar to the previous part, we estimate the unknown terms (especially the aerodynamic torque derivatives) by a super twisting sliding mode observer. In order to fully design a sensorless approach, we estimate the pitch sensitivity by a novel ANFIS (adaptive neural fuzzy system) system. The inputs of this system are the effective wind velocity, pitch angle, and rotor speed. The simulation

results are compared with conventional GPI which demonstrates that the standard deviation of pitch angle, tower fore-aft vibration, and flapwise displacement of the blade is decreased significantly.

- Finally, unlike the previous literature, the passive vibration design is considered with the coupling effect of the drivetrain dynamic, the tower, and the blade. In the previous works, the drivetrain dynamic is ignored in the optimization process and the rotor speed is considered constant at the nominal value (12.1 rpm).

The remainder of this paper is organized as follows: The aeroelastic wind turbine modelling is investigated in Section 2. The model validation is considered in Section 3. The novel sliding mode control based on the sliding mode observer is studied in Section 4. Section 5 follows the TMD design procedure and compares the load mitigation with the fully coupled model and uncoupled model (without drivetrain dynamic). The simulation results are investigated in Section 6. Finally, Section 7 concludes this study and gives the future direction.

2. Obtaining the Multi-Body Model of a Fixed Bottom Wind Turbine

A brief description of the wind turbine model is given in this section. The model contains the mechanical subsystems of the blades, tower, and drivetrain system, as well as the aerodynamic modelling of wind profile and the wind-structure interactions. The following subsections describe how the proposed model integrates the dynamic model of the tower, the drivetrain model, and the dynamic equation of the blades. The modelling of the wind field and the aerodynamic modelling and the interaction of the wind and wind turbine are presented in the process of obtaining the dynamic equation of motion of the assembled system of a fixed-bottom wind turbine following the multi-body Euler-Lagrangian approach.

2.1. Dynamic Modeling of the Tower

The tower can be modelled as a flexible structure, with a nacelle mounted on top of it. The tower experiences lateral vibrations in the rotational plane, (called side-side vibrations), as well as perpendicular to the rotational plane, (called fore-aft vibrations). Therefore, two DOFs must be considered when modelling the tower.

$$\{q_{tower}\}_{2\times 1} = \left\{q_{fa}, q_{ss}\right\} \tag{1}$$

where q_{ss} is the displacement of the nacelle in the rotational plane and q_{fa} is the displacement of the nacelle perpendicular to the rotational plane. For obtaining the kinetic energy of the tower, only the first natural mode is considered for each side-side and fore-aft direction. Therefore, this leads to [30,32]:

$$T_{tower} = \frac{1}{2}\int_0^H (\rho A)_{tower}\left(\dot{q}_{fa}\varphi_{fa}\right)^2 dh + \frac{1}{2}\int_0^H (\rho A)_{tower}\left(\dot{q}_{ss}\varphi_{ss}\right)^2 dh + \frac{1}{2}M_{nac}\left(\dot{q}_{fa}^2 + \dot{q}_{ss}^2\right) \tag{2}$$

where T_{tower} is the kinetic energy of the tower, $(\rho A)_{tower}$ is the mass density of the tower, H is the height of the tower, φ_{fa} is the first fore-aft vibration mode of the tower, φ_{ss} is the first side-side vibration mode of the tower, and M_{nac} is the mass of the nacelle. According to the Euler-Bernoulli beam theory, the potential energy of the tower is given as [30]:

$$\pi_{tower} = \frac{1}{2}\int_0^H (EI)_{tower}\left(q_{fa}\frac{d^2\varphi_{fa}}{dh^2}\right)^2 dh + \frac{1}{2}\int_0^H (EI)_{tower}\left(q_{ss}\frac{d^2\varphi_{ss}}{dh^2}\right)^2 dh \tag{3}$$

where h is the position of each element along the tower from the bottom to the hub, π_{tower} is the potential energy of the tower, and $(EI)_{tower}$ is the bending stiffness of the tower. One should note that the aeroelastic properties (bending stiffness and mass density) are the same in both directions, fore-aft, and side-side. Thus the mode shapes in both directions are close to each other. Both $(EI)_{tower}$ and $(\rho A)_{tower}$ are a function of h from the bottom to the top of the tower.

2.2. Dynamic Modeling of the Drivetrain System

The drivetrain of a wind turbine is one of the most significant subsystems because the mechanical power passes through the drivetrain then transfers to the generator and finally produces electrical power [38]. A schematic view of the drivetrain is depicted in Figure 2. The main components of the drivetrain system are the rotor, low-speed shaft, gearbox, high-speed shaft, and generator. For the dynamic equation of the drivetrain system the generalized coordinates are given as:

$$\{q_{drivetrain}\}_{2\times1} = \{\theta_r, \theta_{ls}\} \tag{4}$$

where θ_r is the azimuth angle of the rotor and θ_{ls} is the low-speed shaft azimuth angle of the rotor. The kinetic energy of the generator is given as [28]:

$$T_{generator} = \frac{1}{2} j_g \omega_g^2 \tag{5}$$

where j_g is the generator inertia and ω_g is the generator speed ($\omega_g = \dot{\theta}_g = n_g\dot{\theta}_{ls}$) and n_g is the gearbox ratio. The kinetic energy of the rotor is considered in Section 2.3. The potential energy is related to the torsional stiffness of the low-speed shaft which can be computed as [23]:

$$\pi_{ls} = \frac{1}{2} K_{ls}(\theta_r - \theta_{ls})^2 \tag{6}$$

where π_{ls} and K_{ls} are the potential energy and torsional stiffness of the low-speed shaft.

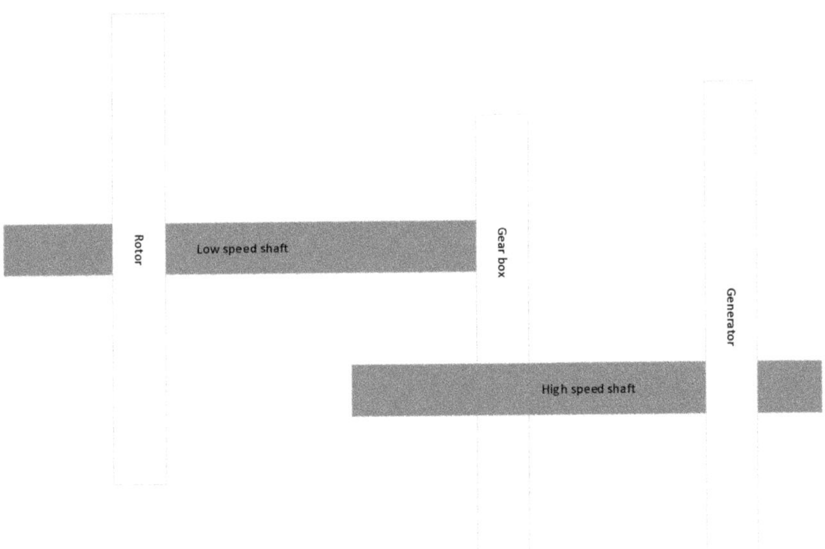

Figure 2. Schematic view of the drivetrain system.

2.3. Dynamic Modeling of the Blades

The blades of a wind turbine can be considered rotational beams. These structures may experience two sources of lateral vibrations, edgewise, and flapwise. By considering two DOFs for each blade (in the flapwise and edgewise directions), the generalized coordinates below are considered for describing the blades of the wind turbine [30,35,39,40]:

$$\{q_{blade}\}_{6\times 1} = \left\{q_{edg}^{b1}, q_{edg}^{b2}, q_{edg}^{b3}, q_{flp}^{b1}, q_{flp}^{b2}, q_{flp}^{b3}\right\} \quad (7)$$

where q_{edg}^{bi} describes the edgewise vibration displacement of the tip of the ith blade and q_{flp}^{bi} denotes the flapwise displacement of the ith blade. For obtaining the kinetic energy of each blade, the velocity profile of each infinitesimal element must be obtained then by integration along the blade, the total kinetic energy of the blades can be computed. For the velocity profile, it is convenient to express the velocity and also the position of each infinitesimal element in $\{x, y, z\}$ coordinates (Figure 3). This set of coordinates is attached to the hub of the turbine and also rotates with the rotational speed of the blades (the x-axis is along the blade, the y-axis is perpendicular to the x-axis in the rotational plane and the z-axis is determined by the right-hand rule law). The position of each element concerning the system $\{x, y, z\}$ is given as [32,35]:

$$\begin{aligned} x_{bi} &= -u_{ss}\sin\psi_i + r \\ y_{bi} &= -u_{ss}\cos\psi_i + u_{edg} \\ z_{bi} &= u_{fa} + u_{flp} \end{aligned} \quad (8)$$

where ψ_i is the azimuth angle of each blade, u_{ss} and u_{fa} denotes the side-side and fore-aft vibration of the nacelle, u_{edg} and u_{flp} denotes the edgewise and flapwise tip vibration of the blade, x_{bi}, y_{bi} and z_{bi} are the position of each element concerning the $\{x, y, z\}$ system and r is the radial position of each element in the non-deformable case of the blade (when there is no vibration displacement). The azimuth angles for each blade can be obtained as [39,40]:

$$\begin{aligned} \psi_i &= \psi_1 + \frac{2\pi}{3}(i-1), i = 1,2,3 \\ \psi_1 &= \int_0^t \omega_r dt \end{aligned} \quad (9)$$

where ψ_i is the azimuth angle of the ith blade and ω_r is the rotor speed. Also, the vibration displacements of the tip of blades can be obtained as [31,32,39]:

$$\begin{aligned} u_{edg} &= \varphi_{edg} q_{edg} \\ u_{flp} &= \varphi_{flp} q_{flp} \end{aligned} \quad (10)$$

Using the time derivative of Equation (8), the velocity of each infinitesimal element can be obtained for each blade:

$$\begin{bmatrix} V_{bi,x} \\ V_{bi,y} \\ V_{bi,z} \end{bmatrix} = \begin{bmatrix} \frac{dx_{bi}}{dt} \\ \frac{dy_{bi}}{dt} \\ \frac{dz_{bi}}{dt} \end{bmatrix} + \begin{bmatrix} 0 \\ 0 \\ \omega_r \end{bmatrix} \times \begin{bmatrix} -u_{ss}\sin\psi_i + r \\ -u_{ss}\cos\psi_i + u_{edg} \\ u_{fa} + u_{flp} \end{bmatrix} \quad (11)$$

Finally, the kinetic energy of blades can be obtained as the sum of the kinetic energy of each infinitesimal element [41]:

$$T_{blade} = \sum_{i=1}^{3} \int_0^R (\rho A)_{blade} V_{bi}^T V_{bi} dr \quad (12)$$

where R is the length of the blade, r is the radial position of each infinitesimal element along the non-deformed blade, T_{blade} and $(\rho A)_{blade}$ are the kinetic energy and mass density of the blade. For the potential energy, there are three sources for each edgewise and flapwise direction. The first source is related to the strain energy of the blade, and the second relates to the axial component of gravity which acts as an axial force. Finally, the third component is the centrifugal tension force which is related to the rotation of each blade. According to the Euler-Bernoulli beam theory, the strain energy of the beam is $\pi = \frac{1}{2}\int_0^R (EI)\left(\frac{\partial^2 u}{\partial r^2}\right)^2 dr$. By considering only one normal mode shape in each edgewise and flapwise direction, the strain energy term for each blade can be obtained as: ($u_{edg} \approx \varphi_{edg} q_{edg}, u_{flp} \approx \varphi_{flp} q_{flp}$):

$$
\begin{aligned}
\pi_{edg,strain} &= \frac{1}{2}\int_0^R (EI)_{edg}\left(\frac{d^2\phi_{edg}}{dr^2}\right)^2 dr \\
\pi_{flp,strain} &= \frac{1}{2}\int_0^R (EI)_{flp}\left(\frac{d^2\phi_{flp}}{dr^2}\right)^2 dr
\end{aligned}
\tag{13}
$$

where $\pi_{edg,strain}$ and $\pi_{flp,strain}$ are the strain energy of the blade in the edgewise and flapwise directions, ϕ_{edg} and ϕ_{flp} are the first natural mode shapes in the edgewise and flapwise directions, $(EI)_{edg}$ and $(EI)_{flp}$ are the bending stiffness in the edgewise and flapwise directions and R is the length of the blade. The axial gravity component and centrifugal force modelling are quite similar because both act like axial forces. According to [39,40] we have:

$$
\begin{aligned}
\pi_{edg,cen} &= \frac{1}{2}\omega_r^2 \int_0^R \int_r^R ((\rho A)_{blade}\xi d\xi)\left(\frac{d\phi_{edg}}{dr} q_{edg}\right)^2 dr \\
\pi_{flp,cen} &= \frac{1}{2}\omega_r^2 \int_0^R \int_r^R ((\rho A)_{blade}\xi d\xi)\left(\frac{d\phi_{flp}}{dr} q_{flp}\right)^2 dr \\
\pi_{edg,gravity,bladei} &= -\frac{1}{2} g \int_0^R \int_r^R ((\rho A)_{blade} d\xi)\left(\frac{d\phi_{edg}}{dr} q_{edg}\right)^2 \cos\psi_i dr \\
\pi_{flp,gravity,bladei} &= -\frac{1}{2} g \int_0^R \int_r^R ((\rho A)_{blade} d\xi)\left(\frac{d\phi_{flp}}{dr} q_{flp}\right)^2 \cos\psi_i dr
\end{aligned}
\tag{14}
$$

where $\pi_{edg,cen}$ and $\pi_{flp,cen}$ are the centrifugal terms of the potential energy for each blade in the edgewise and flapwise directions, $\pi_{edg,gravity,bladei}$ and $\pi_{flp,gravity,bladei}$ are the gravity term of the potential energy in the edgewise and flapwise directions of the ith blade.

Remark 1. *φ_{edg}, φ_{flp} φ_{fa} , and φ_{ss} are the first natural mode shapes of blade vibration in the edgewise and flapwise vibration and fore-aft and side-side vibration of the tower respectively. The mode shape of the blade of the NREL 5MW turbine is reported in [11] and can be found in Appendix B of this paper. φ_{edg}, φ_{flp} are a function of r and φ_{fa}, φ_{ss} are a function of h respectively.*

Remark 2. *The values $(\rho A)_{blade}$, $(EI)_{edg}$, and $(EI)_{flp}$ vary along the blade as a function of r. The whole structural properties of the blade can be found in [11] with 49 different sections with different structural properties. To compute the integrations in Equations (13) and (14), a linear pattern is considered between every two sections as a function of r.*

Remark 3. *Potential and kinetic energy are both scalar functions. it must be noted that total kinetic energy is the summation of the kinetic energy of the rotor, generator, and tower. The total potential energy is the summation of Equations (3), (6), (13) and (14).*

2.4. Aerodynamic Modeling

The conventional method for modelling the interaction between the wind and the wind turbine is called blade element momentum theory (BEM) [42]. The blade of each wind turbine consists of different airfoils, chord lines, and twist angles. By considering each section of the blade as a control volume, the magnitude of the relative velocity vector on each section can be obtained as shown in Figure 4 as:

$$V_{rel} = V_0\sqrt{(1-a)^2 + \left(\frac{r\omega_r}{V_0}(1+a')\right)^2} \tag{15}$$

where a and a' are the induction factors in the axial component and lateral component, V_0 is the wind velocity in each section, and V_{rel} is the relative velocity. In addition, it is easy to see that the angle of relative wind velocity with respect to the rotor plane is given as (Figure 4) [42]:

$$\tan(\phi) = \frac{V_0}{r\omega_r}\frac{1-a}{1+a'} \tag{16}$$

As can be seen in Figure 4, two components of the relative wind velocity (V_{rel}) are $V_0(1-a)$ normal to the rotational plane and $r\omega_r(1+a')$ in the rotational plane. α is the angle of attack and β is the pitch angle. In addition, the angle of attack of each airfoil can be easily obtained as $\alpha = \phi - \beta$. Furthermore, the normal (P_N) and tangential (P_T) aerodynamic forces can be obtained as a function of lift (f_L) and drag (f_D) forces (Figure 4):

$$\begin{aligned} P_N &= f_L \cos\phi + f_D \sin\phi \\ P_T &= f_L \sin\phi - f_D \cos\phi \end{aligned} \tag{17}$$

As can be seen from Equation (17), normal and tangential forces are a function of angle of attack, and angle of attack is a function of induction factors. The induction factors can be updated by modelling using the BEM approach. More details on the aerodynamic modelling and BEM approach more details are presented in Appendix A.

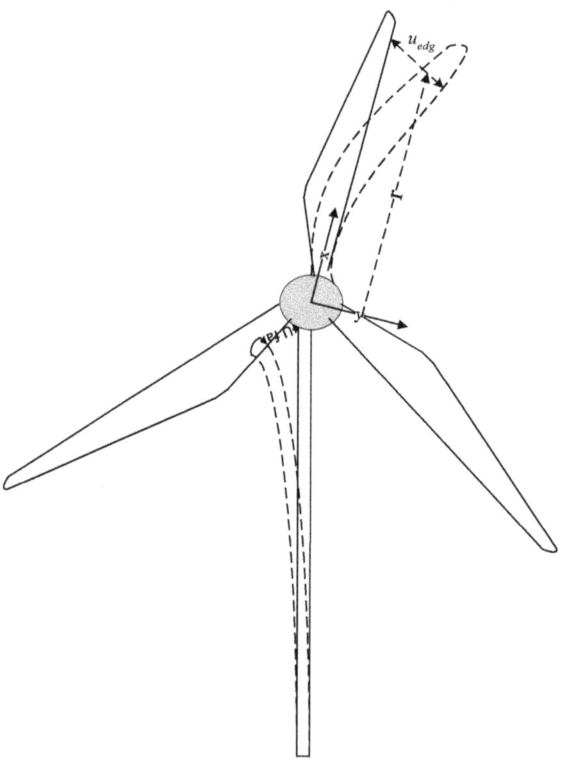

(a)

Figure 3. *Cont.*

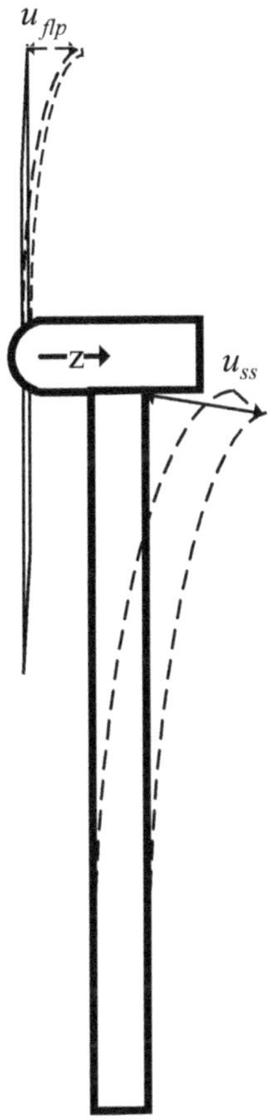

(**b**)

Figure 3. Schematic view of blade and tower. (**a**) front view of the wind turbine. (**b**) side view of the wind turbine.

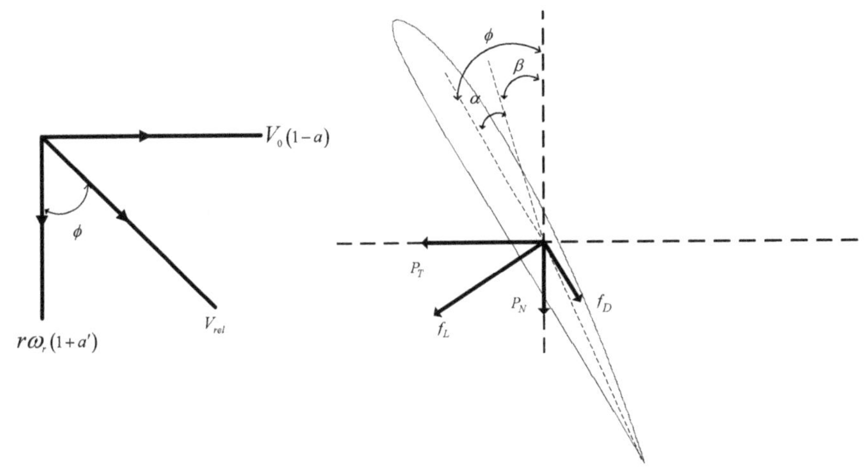

Figure 4. Lift, drag, thrust, and rotational forces produced by the wind interaction.

Remark 4. *There are 17 different sections along the blade with different chord lines, airfoil type, and twist angles. The above process must be investigated with each section along the blade.*

2.5. Wind Profile Modelling

Wind speeds are measured by anemometers at each point. The main concept in modelling wind velocity profiles is that the time history data must be consistent with the atmospheric boundary layer (ABL). It is common to assume that the flow is stationary and homogeneous, which means that the statistical properties of the wind (standard deviation, kurtosis, and other moments) do not change with time and space [43].

In Figure 5, the wind velocity at the hub (90 m above the ground for the NREL 5MW) has been depicted. The wind velocity for two points in the grid has been depicted in Figure 6. More details on generating the grid and rotational sampling approach can be found in [42,44].

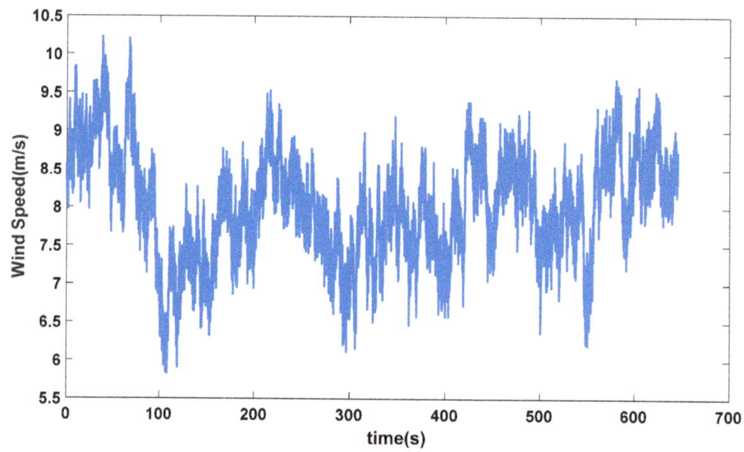

Figure 5. Wind speed at the hub height of the turbine.

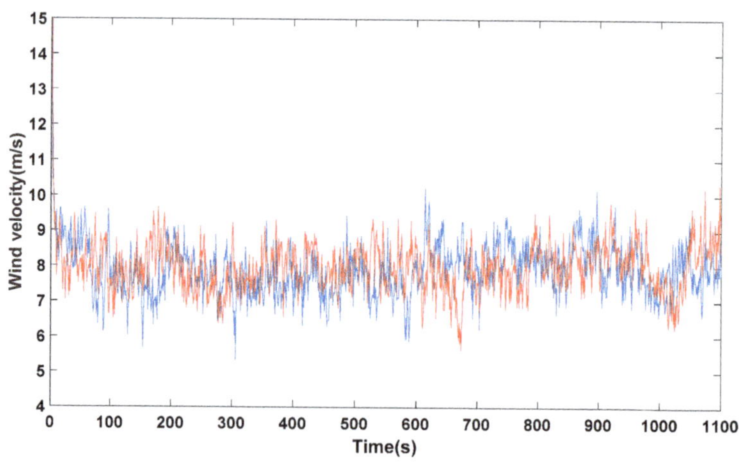

Figure 6. Wind speed at two different points in the grid with a distance of 10 m (blue and red are respectively the wind velocity at left and right points with the distance of 10 m).

2.6. Euler Lagrangian Approach for Modelling Multi-Body Systems

There are different ways of obtaining the governing equation of motion of a multi-body dynamic system. According to the literature, there include the Kane, Euler Lagrange, and the Gibbs-Appell method [45–47]. Sometimes, the generalized coordinates for describing the dynamic equation of a system are not independent of each other and they are related according to the constrained dynamics. These constrained dynamics can be integrable which in this case are called holonomic constraints and non-integrable which are called non-holonomic dynamic systems [45]. In these cases, the Kane method is an excellent approach for obtaining the governing equation of motion. Since the wind turbine system is not constrained (all the generalized coordinates are independent), the Lagrange method is quite acceptable. Furthermore, the Lagrange method uses energy functions that are easier to deal with in comparison to the vectors. According to the Lagrange approach, one can obtain:

$$\frac{d}{dt}\left(\frac{\partial L}{\partial\{\dot{q}\}_{10\times 1}}\right)-\frac{\partial L}{\partial\{q\}_{10\times 1}}=\{Q\}_{10\times 1} \tag{18}$$

where L is called the Lagrangian which can be obtained as the difference between the kinetic and the potential energy, such that $L = T - \pi$. $\{q\}_{10\times 1}$ is the vector of the generalized coordinates and $\{Q\}_{10\times 1}$ is the vector of generalized forces. The generalized coordinates can be described as:

$$\{q\}_{10\times 1}=\left\{\begin{array}{l}\{q_{drivetrain}\}_{2\times 1}\\ \{q_{blade}\}_{6\times 1}\\ \{q_{tower}\}_{2\times 1}\end{array}\right\} \tag{19}$$

For obtaining the generalized forces vector, virtual displacement must be considered in each positive direction of the generalized coordinates and the virtual work of each external force must be obtained. In general, the generalized force vector can be obtained as follows:

$$\{Q\}_{10\times 1}=\frac{\partial\delta W}{\partial\{q\}_{10\times 1}} \tag{20}$$

where δW is a total virtual work. Just like the generalized coordinates vector, the generalized forces is a 10×1 vector that can be defined as:

$$\{Q\}_{10\times 1}=\left\{\begin{array}{l}\{Q_{drivetrain}\}_{2\times 1}\\ \{Q_{blade}\}_{6\times 1}\\ \{Q_{tower}\}_{2\times 1}\end{array}\right\} \tag{21}$$

For the drivetrain, there are two-DOFs. the generalized force vector ($\{Q_{drivetrain}\}_{2\times 1}$) can be obtained as:

$$\begin{aligned}Q_{drivetrain,1}&=\frac{\partial\delta W}{\partial\theta_r}=T_a-D_{ls}(\omega_r-\omega_{ls})-D_r\omega_r\\ Q_{drivetrain,2}&=\frac{\partial\delta W}{\partial\theta_{ls}}=-T_e n_g+D_{ls}(\omega_r-\omega_{ls})-D_g n_g^2\omega_{ls}\end{aligned} \tag{22}$$

where D_{ls} is the low-speed shaft damper, D_r is the rotor damper, T_e is the generator torque, n_g is the gearbox ratio, D_g is the generator damping, and $Q_{drivetrain,i}$ is the i-th component of the vector $\{Q_{drivetrain}\}_{2\times 1}$. T_a is the aerodynamic torque for rotating the blade which can be obtained as:

$$T_a=\sum_{j=1}^{3}\int_0^R r p_{N,j}dr \tag{23}$$

where $p_{N,j}$ is the normal force for the jth blade. There are aerodynamic forces in both the edgewise and flapwise directions for each blade. Therefore, the generalized forces vector for the blade can be denoted as follows:

$$\{Q_{blade}\}_{6\times1} = \left\{ \begin{array}{c} \{Q_{blade,edg}\}_{3\times1} \\ \{Q_{blade,flp}\}_{3\times1} \end{array} \right\} \quad (24)$$

where $\{Q_{blade,edg}\}_{3\times1}$ is the generalized forces vector corresponding to the edgewise DOFs and $\{Q_{blade,flp}\}_{3\times1}$ is the generalized forces vector corresponding to the flapwise DOFs. In addition, structural damping must be considered external forces. Gravity has two components. The axial component is computed as the potential energy and the tangential component must be considered as an external force (Figure 7). By following the approach in [39], one can obtain:

$$\begin{aligned} \{Q_{blade,edg}\}_{3\times1} &= \frac{\partial \delta W}{\partial \{q\}_{edg}} = \left\{ \begin{array}{l} \left(\int_0^R p_{T,1}\varphi_{edg}dr\right) - c_{edg}\dot{q}_{edg,blade1} + \int_0^R (\rho A)_{blade}\varphi_{edg} g \sin\psi_1 dr \\ \left(\int_0^R p_{T,2}\varphi_{edg}dr\right) - c_{edg}\dot{q}_{edg,blade2} + \int_0^R (\rho A)_{blade}\varphi_{edg} g \sin\psi_2 dr \\ \left(\int_0^R p_{T,3}\varphi_{edg}dr\right) - c_{edg}\dot{q}_{edg,blade3} + \int_0^R (\rho A)_{blade}\varphi_{edg} g \sin\psi_3 dr \end{array} \right\} \\ \{Q_{blade,flp}\}_{3\times1} &= \frac{\partial \delta W}{\partial \{q\}_{flp}} = \left\{ \begin{array}{l} \left(\int_0^R p_{N,1}\varphi_{flp}dr\right) - c_{flp}\dot{q}_{flp,blade1} \\ \left(\int_0^R p_{N,2}\varphi_{flp}dr\right) - c_{flp}\dot{q}_{flp,blade2} \\ \left(\int_0^R p_{N,3}\varphi_{flp}dr\right) - c_{flp}\dot{q}_{flp,blade3} \end{array} \right\} \end{aligned} \quad (25)$$

where $\{q\}_{edg} = \left\{q_{edg}^{b1}, q_{edg}^{b2}, q_{edg}^{b3}\right\}$ and $\{q\}_{flp} = \left\{q_{flp}^{b1}, q_{flp}^{b2}, q_{flp}^{b3}\right\}$, c_{edg} is the damping coefficient in the edgewise vibration direction, c_{flp} is the damping coefficient in the flapwise direction, $P_{N,i}$ and $P_{T,i}$ are the normal and tangential aerodynamic forces of the ith blade. The damping coefficient in both these directions can be obtained as ($c = 2\zeta\sqrt{km}$) [30]:

$$\begin{aligned} c_{edg} &= 2\zeta_{edg}\sqrt{\left(\int_0^R EI_{edg}\left(\frac{d^2\varphi_{edg}}{dr^2}\right)^2 dr\right)\left(\int_0^R (\rho A)_{blade}\left(\varphi_{edg}\right)^2 dr\right)} \\ c_{flp} &= 2\zeta_{flp}\sqrt{\left(\int_0^R EI_{flp}\left(\frac{d^2\varphi_{flp}}{dr^2}\right)^2 dr\right)\left(\int_0^R (\rho A)_{blade}\left(\varphi_{flp}\right)^2 dr\right)} \end{aligned} \quad (26)$$

where ζ_{flp} and ζ_{edg} are the non-dimensional damping coefficients in the edgewise and flapwise directions. These values can be found in [11] (some general properties can be found in Appendix B).

Finally, the generalized force vector for the tower, which correspond to the fore-aft and side-side generalized coordinates can be modelled as [32]:

$$\begin{aligned} Q_{tower,1} &= \left\{\left(\sum_{i=1}^{3}\int_0^R p_{N,i}dr\right) - c_{fa}\dot{q}_{fa}\right\} \\ Q_{tower,2} &= \left\{\left(\sum_{i=1}^{3}\int_0^R p_{T,i}\cos\psi_i dr\right) - c_{ss}\dot{q}_{ss}\right\} \\ c_{fa} &= 2\zeta_{fa}\sqrt{\left(\int_0^H (EI)_{tower}\left(\frac{d^2\varphi_{fa}}{dh^2}\right)^2 dh\right)\left(\int_0^H (\rho A)_{tower}\left(\varphi_{fa}\right)^2 dh\right)} \\ c_{ss} &= 2\zeta_{ss}\sqrt{\left(\int_0^H (EI)_{tower}\left(\frac{d^2\varphi_{ss}}{dh^2}\right)^2 dh\right)\left(\int_0^H (\rho A)_{tower}(\varphi_{ss})^2 dh\right)} \end{aligned} \quad (27)$$

where $Q_{tower,i}$ is the ith component of the vector $\{Q_{tower}\}_{2\times1}$. For simplification, it is common to rewrite the Lagrange equation in the following form by using the chain derivation rule [45]:

$$\frac{d}{dt}\left(\frac{\partial L}{\partial\{\dot{q}\}_{10\times1}}\right)=\frac{\partial}{\partial t}\left(\frac{\partial L}{\partial\{\dot{q}\}_{10\times1}}\right)+\frac{\partial}{\partial\{q\}_{10\times1}}\left(\frac{\partial L}{\partial\{\dot{q}\}_{10\times1}}\right)\{\dot{q}\}_{10\times1}+\frac{\partial}{\partial\{\dot{q}\}_{10\times1}}\left(\frac{\partial L}{\partial\{\dot{q}\}_{10\times1}}\right)\{\ddot{q}\}_{10\times1} \quad (28)$$

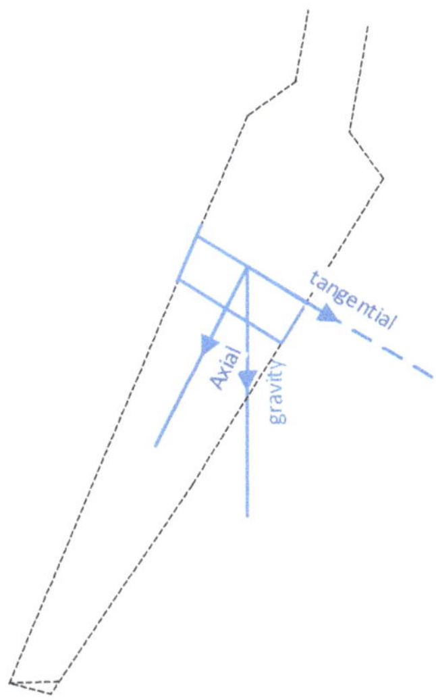

Figure 7. Schematic view of a very small component of the blade and two components of the gravity force.

By defining the following matrices, one can find the dynamic equation of motion by the Lagrange approach.

$$\begin{aligned}[M]_{10\times10}&=\frac{\partial}{\partial\{\dot{q}\}}\left(\frac{\partial L}{\partial\{\dot{q}\}}\right)\\ [N]_{10\times10}&=\frac{\partial}{\partial\{q\}}\left(\frac{\partial L}{\partial\{\dot{q}\}}\right)\\ \{K(q)\}_{10\times1}&=\frac{\partial}{\partial t}\left(\frac{\partial L}{\partial\{\dot{q}\}}\right)-\frac{\partial L}{\partial\{q\}}\end{aligned} \quad (29)$$

Finally, by applying the Lagrange equation, the following equation for the wind turbine dynamic equations is obtained:

$$[M]_{10\times10}\{\ddot{q}\}_{10\times1}+[N]_{10\times10}\{\dot{q}\}_{10\times1}+\{K(q)\}_{10\times1}=\{Q\}_{10\times1} \quad (30)$$

where $[M]$ and $[N]$ are 10×10 matrices and $\{K(q)\}$ is a 10×1 vector. The following governing equation can be solved by the Rang-Kutta approach in a numerical tool. For this purpose, the following state-space vector is defined:

$$\{z_{state}\}_{20\times1}=\left\{\begin{array}{c}\{q\}_{10\times1}\\ \{\dot{q}\}_{10\times1}\end{array}\right\} \quad (31)$$

where $\{z_{state}\}$ is a state-space vector. According to Equation (30), the time derivative of the state space vector can be obtained as follows:

$$\{\dot{z}_{state}\}_{20\times 1} = \left\{ \begin{array}{c} \{\dot{q}\}_{10\times 1} \\ \{\ddot{q}\}_{10\times 1} \end{array} \right\} = \left\{ \begin{array}{l} \{\dot{q}\}_{10\times 1} \\ [M]^{-1}_{10\times 10}(\{Q\}_{10\times 1} - [N]_{10\times 10}\{\dot{q}\} - \{K(q)\}_{10\times 1}) \end{array} \right\} \quad (32)$$

Equation (32) is in the standard form and can be solved easily by the Rang-Kutta method.

3. Validation of the Model by FAST

In this section, to ensure the compatibility of the obtained model, the results are compared to the numerical FAST aeroelastic code. FAST is an aeroelastic code which is developed by the national renewable energy lab in the USA [48,49]. The edgewise and flapwise displacement, as well as the nacelle vibrations, are compared with the FAST code. For extracting the wind field, the Turbsim code is used [50]. The results are obtained in the same mean wind speed and the same turbulence intensity situation in FAST and the proposed model in this research. Unlike the previous research [37], in which the uniform flow is simulated for simulation, the validation part in this research is presented by considering a fully 3D wind profile by considering the wind shear effect. The power control approaches in regions II and III are assumed as the baseline approaches which have been considered in [11]. The dynamic response of the proposed model is compared with FAST for two load cases. Load case I, has a mean wind velocity of 7 m/s and turbulence intensity of 10%(region II), whereas load case II has a mean wind speed of 20 m/s and turbulence intensity of 10% (region III) (Tables 1 and 2).

Table 1. Comparison with the performance of the aeroelastic model in this research with FAST. Mean wind speed 7 m/s and turbulence intensity 10% (region II).

	FAST Numerical Tool		Proposed Model	
Parameter	**Mean**	**STD**	**Mean**	**STD**
Rotor speed (rad/s)	0.7592	0.0404	0.7667	0.0414
Generator speed (rpm)	705.23	38.45	710.43	38.51
Flapwise tip deflection of blade 1 (m)	2.337	0.338	2.48	0.3574
Edgewise tip deflection of blade 1 (m)	−0.2482	0.3408	−0.2588	0.3378
Nacelle fore-aft deflection (m)	0.1437	0.0268	0.1329	0.02329
Nacelle side-side deflection (m)	−0.02105	0.01035	−0.02393	0.00840

Table 2. Comparison with the performance of the aeroelastic model in this research with FAST. Mean wind speed 18 m/s and turbulence intensity 10% (region III).

	FAST Numerical Tool		Proposed Model	
Parameter	**Mean**	**STD**	**Mean**	**STD**
Rotor speed (rad/s)	1.275	0.1448	1.272	0.1453
Generator speed (rpm)	1182	134.2	1178	134.62
Flapwise tip deflection of blade 1 (m)	1.349	1.632	1.416	1.509
Edgewise tip deflection of blade 1 (m)	−0.08809	0.3703	−0.1019	0.3507
Nacelle fore-aft deflection (m)	0.211	0.1163	0.216	0.1183
Nacelle side-side deflection (m)	−0.06475	0.02135	−0.0618	0.022s3

The power coefficient of the wind turbine is one of the most important characteristics that determine the ratio of mechanical convertible power to the kinetic energy of the wind. The power coefficient depends on the tip speed ratio (ratio between the tip velocity of the blade with respect to the hub height wind velocity) and the pitch angle. The tip speed ratio is defined as follows:

$$\lambda = \frac{R\omega_r}{V} \quad (33)$$

where V is the effective wind velocity and R is the length of the blade. The power coefficient can be modelled as follows:

$$C_p(\lambda, \beta) = \frac{P_a}{\frac{1}{2}\rho\pi R^2 V^3(t)} \tag{34}$$

where P_a is the aerodynamic power ($P_a = T_a\omega_r$), ρ is the air density, and $C_p(\lambda, \beta)$ is the power coefficient.

In Figure 8, the power coefficient is given as a function of tip speed ratio at different pitch angles (in degrees), and the results are compared with the FAST code. As can be seen, the results are compatible with the FAST simulations.

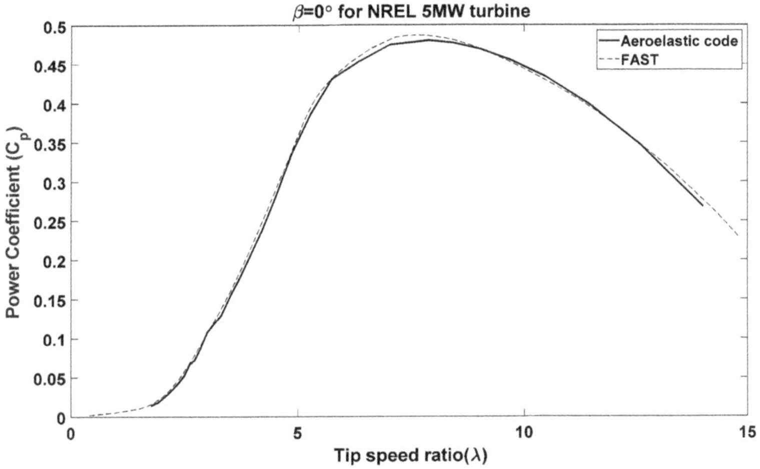

(a)

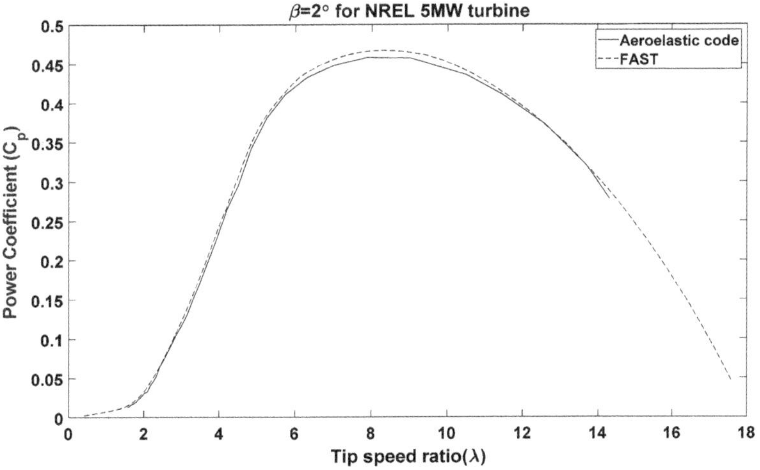

(b)

Figure 8. *Cont.*

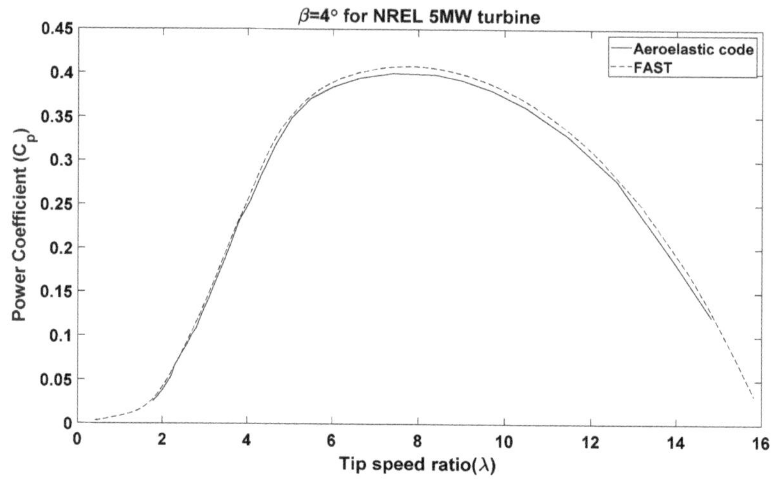

(c)

Figure 8. Power coefficient of the NREL 5MW wind turbine as a function of tip speed ratio in three different pitch angles. A comparison between the aeroelastic code and FAST (**a**) $\beta = 0°$. (**b**) $\beta = 2°$. (**c**) $\beta = 4°$.

Remark 5. *The source FAST code is compiled with the SIMULINK/MATLAB and it is possible to validate the performance of the control algorithm on the open loop model of the wind turbine and there is a module for designing the tuned mass damper. However, as far as we know, there is no place to both consider the effect of vibration absorbers and control algorithms on the power generation and dynamic loads. In addition, the aeroelastic code will be investigated in our future work for designing various types of vibration absorbers, besides tuned mass dampers.*

4. Designing the Sliding Mode Approach in the Low and High Values of Wind Speed

In this section, the power control problem for low and high values of wind speed is investigated from a load mitigation perspective. According to [3], the aeroelastic interaction of the blades and tower to the drivetrain is insignificant and can be ignored for control purposes. Therefore, the simplified model of the drivetrain can be obtained as [22,28]:

$$\begin{cases} \dot{\omega}_r = \dfrac{T_a - K_{ls}(\theta_r - \theta_{ls}) - D_{ls}(\omega_r - \omega_{ls}) - D_r\omega_r}{j_r} \\ \dot{\omega}_{ls} = \dfrac{-T_e n_g + K_{ls}(\theta_r - \theta_{ls}) + D_{ls}(\omega_r - \omega_{ls}) - D_g n_g^2 \omega_{ls}}{j_g n_g^2} \end{cases} \tag{35}$$

where j_r and j_g are rotor inertia (including the blades and rotor) and generator inertia respectively. ω_r and ω_{ls} are rotor speed and low-speed shaft speed ($\omega_{ls} = \dfrac{\omega_g}{n_g}$) respectively. All the parameters of the model for the NREL 5MW turbine can be found in [11].

Remark 6. *In Equation (35), the blade and rotor are assumed as a rigid disk. Therefore, this model does not give any sense regarding the vibration loads. For considering the vibration loads a full aeroelastic model is needed which are developed in the previous part.*

4.1. Control Problem in the Low-Speed Range of Wind Velocity

In region II, the main goal is to extract as much energy as possible from the wind. As stated before, the actuator is controlled by the torque from the generator. To achieve maximum energy, the power coefficient must be at its maximum value. For the NREL

5MW turbine, the optimum tip speed ratio (λ_{opt}) is 7 and the optimum pitch angle is 0 degrees [11]. Therefore, the optimum rotor speed (ω_{opt}) is obtained as:

$$\lambda_{opt} = \frac{R\omega_{opt}}{V} \Rightarrow \omega_{opt} = \frac{\lambda_{opt} V}{R} \tag{36}$$

where V is the effective wind velocity (EWV). In our previous research [23], we demonstrate how to estimate EWV, also, a detailed study can be found in [51]. Now, by defining the error signal as the difference between the optimum speed and the rotor speed, the generator's torque must be regulated in order to minimize the error signal. Next, we introduced a novel super twisting sliding mode control approach with an observer to estimate the unknown terms to achieve maximum power [52,53].

Theorem 1. *The following generator torque (T_e) is suitable for maximizing the power coefficient and output power.*

$$\begin{array}{l} T_e = -v_l \dfrac{j_r j_g n_g^2}{D_{ls}} \\ v_l = a_L \int_0^t e_l dt + b_L \dot{e}_l + c_L e_l - \ddot{\omega}_{opt} + \omega_{rej,l} \\ \omega_{rej,l} = \lambda_{0,l} |s_l|^{1/2} sign(s_l) + \eta_l \\ \dot{\eta}_L = \lambda_{1,l} |s_l|^{1/2} sign(s_l) \\ where \left\{ \begin{array}{l} s_l = \dot{e} + \zeta_l \\ \dot{\zeta}_l = -\ddot{\omega}_{opt} + v_l - \omega_{rej,l} \\ \lambda_{0,l} = 1.5\sqrt{L_1} \\ \lambda_{1,l} = 1.1\sqrt{L_1} \\ \left| \dfrac{d\Delta\psi_{unknown,l}}{dt} \right| < L_1 \end{array} \right. \end{array} \tag{37}$$

where T_e is the generator torque, v_l is the virtual controller in region II, $\omega_{rej,l}$ is the rejection term in region II (to reject uncertainties and unknown variables).

Proof. By defining the error signal as $e_l = \omega_r - \omega_{opt}$, and according to Equation (37), one can reach the following equation:

$$\begin{array}{l} \ddot{e}_l = \dfrac{\dot{T}_a - (D_{ls} + D_r)\dot{\omega}_r - K_{ls}(\omega_r - \omega_{ls})}{j_r} \\ + \dfrac{D_{ls}}{j_r j_g n_g^2} (D_{ls}(\omega_r - \omega_{ls}) + K_{ls}(\theta_r - \theta_{ls})) - \dfrac{D_{ls}}{j_r j_g n_g} \dot{T}_e - \ddot{\omega}_{opt} \end{array} \tag{38}$$

The generator torque (T_e) must be defined such that to stabilize the error signal. For this purpose, the generator torque must satisfy the following equation:

$$\ddot{e}_l + a_L \int_0^t e_l dt + b_L \dot{e}_l + c_L e_l = 0 \tag{39}$$

In Equation (39), aerodynamic torque, time derivation of the rotor speed, and low-speed shaft speed are not measurable. Therefore, these terms must be estimated. Now, by reorganizing Equation (40), we reach the following equation:

$$\begin{aligned}
&\ddot{e}_l = \psi_{known} + \Delta\psi_{unknown} - v_l \\
&where \\
&\Delta\psi_{unknown,l} = \frac{\dot{T}_a - (D_{ls} + D_r)\dot{\omega}_r - K_{ls}(\omega_r - \omega_{ls})}{j_r} \\
&+ \frac{D_{ls}}{j_r j_g n_g^2}(D_{ls}(\omega_r - \omega_{ls}) + K_{ls}(\theta_r - \theta_{ls})) \\
&\psi_{known,L} = -\ddot{\omega}_{opt} \\
&v_L = -\frac{D_{ls}}{j_r j_g n_g^2} T_e
\end{aligned} \tag{40}$$

One should note that the term $\psi_{known,l}$ defines the known terms of $\ddot{e}_l$ and $\Delta\psi_{unknown,l}$ denotes the unknown terms, which must be estimated and v_l is the virtual control signal. For designing the control signal v_l, we need to estimate the disturbance term $\Delta\psi_{unknown,l}$. For this purpose, a first-order dynamic system is introduced as follows [54]:

$$\begin{aligned}
s_l &= \dot{e}_l + \xi_l \\
\dot{\zeta}_l &= -\psi_{known,l} + v_l - \omega_{rej,l}
\end{aligned} \tag{41}$$

The Lyapunov function $V_l = \frac{1}{2}s_l^2$ is introduced, giving:

$$\dot{V}_l = s_l \dot{s}_l = s_l\left(\ddot{e}_l + \dot{\xi}_l\right) \tag{42}$$

The goal is to design the term $\omega_{rej,l}$ to reject the uncertainties. The rejection term must be designed in such a way $\dot{V}_l \leq -\eta|s_l|$ where η is a positive number. By a combination of Equations (42) and (49), one can reach:

$$\begin{aligned}
&\dot{V}_l = s_l \dot{s}_l = s_l\left(\Delta\psi_{unknown,l} - \omega_{rej,l}\right) \leq |||s_L|||||\Delta\psi_{unknown,L}|| - s_l\omega_{rej,l} \leq -\eta||s_l|| \\
&\Rightarrow \omega_{rej,l} \geq (\eta + L_{slide})sign(s_l)
\end{aligned} \tag{43}$$

where L_{slide} is a positive number which $||\Delta\psi_{unknown}|| \leq L_{slide}$. To reach origin asymptotically, we must have:

Finally, combining Equations (46) and (50) the control signal gives the control signal v_l $(\rho_L = (\eta + L_{slide}))$:

$$v_l = a_L \int_0^t e_l dt + b_L \dot{e}_l + c_L e_l - \ddot{\omega}_{opt} + \rho_L sign(s_l) \tag{44}$$

where a_L, b_L and c_L are positive coefficients which can be found in Appendix C. To design the rejection term, according to [51], the super twisting control method has a better performance in chattering rejection as well as better tracking ability. Therefore, the rejection term is defined as [54]:

$$\begin{aligned}
\omega_{rej,l} &= \lambda_{0,L}|s_l|^{1/2}sign(s_l) + \eta_l \\
\dot{\eta}_l &= \lambda_{1,L}sign(s_l)
\end{aligned} \tag{45}$$

In [54], a thorough discussion has been provided to select properly the parameters $\lambda_{0,L}$ and $\lambda_{1,L}$. Accordingly, two acceptable values for these two parameters are $\lambda_{1,L} = 1.1\sqrt{L_1}$ and $\lambda_{0,L} = 1.5\sqrt{L_1}$ where L_1 is the upper bound of $\dot{\psi}_{unknown,l}$.

Finally, by finding the virtual control signal v_l, the generator torque in each time step can be updated as follows:

$$T_e = -v_l \frac{j_r j_g n_g^2}{D_{ls}} \tag{46}$$

□

The whole structure of the designed control system is depicted in Figure 9.

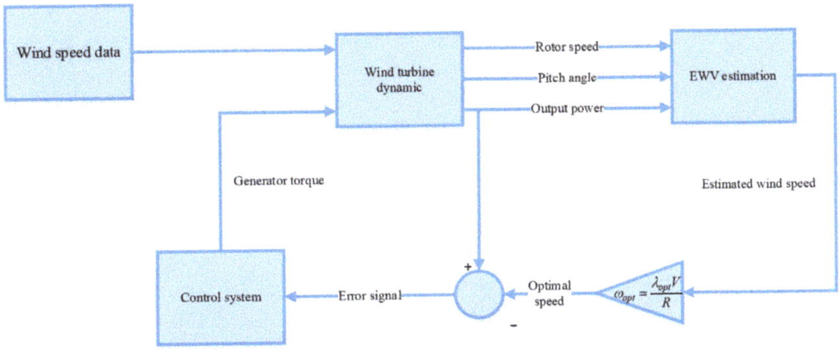

Figure 9. Schematic of the designed control system in region II.

Remark 7. *To obtain the value of $\ddot{\omega}_{opt}$, according to Equation (44), we need the second-time derivation of EWV. We used the following derivative estimation which is proposed in [54].*

$$\begin{aligned} v_{estimate,1} &= \dot{z}_0 = -2L_{estimate}{}^{1/3}|z_0 - V(t)|^{2/3} sign(z_0 - V(t)) + z_0 \\ v_{estimate,2} &= \dot{z}_1 = -1.5L_{estimate}{}^{1/2}|z_1 - v_{estimate,1}|^{1/2} sign(z_1 - v_{estimate,1}) + z_1 \\ \dot{z}_2 &= -1.1L_{estimate} sign(z_0 - v_{estimate,2}) \end{aligned} \tag{47}$$

where z_0 is the estimation of $V(t)$, z_1 is the estimation of $\dot{V}(t)$, and z_2 is the estimation of $\ddot{V}(t)$. $L_{estimate}$ is a positive number which must satisfy $\ddot{V}(t) \leq L_{estimate}$. In this research, we assumed $L_{estimate} = 10$. More details can be found in [54].

4.2. Control Problem Inregion III

The output power must be limited to the nominal power in region III to prevent any damage to the wind turbine due to high winds. For this purpose, the rotor speed must be compared to the reference rotor speed, which is 12.1 rpm for NREL 5MW. The difference between the rotor speed and the nominal value (12.1 rpm) can be communicated via an error signal in each time step. The pitch angle actuator system usually acts as a linear servo system. According to [9,24,55], the dynamic equation of the pitch system can be described as follows:

$$\dot{\beta} = -\frac{1}{\tau}(\beta - u) \tag{48}$$

where u is the input signal in region III. β is the 11th DOF in the fully coupled model of NREL 5MW. For the NREL 5MW wind turbine, the pitch angle dynamic can be changed in the range of 0 and 90 degrees ($\beta \in [0, 90]$), and the pitch rate cannot exceed 10 degrees per second ($\left|\dot{\beta}\right| < 10\text{deg/s}$) [11,56]. In the following, the pitch angle mechanism is described for limiting the output power without measuring the aerodynamic torque.

Theorem 2. *The following pitch regulator signal (u) can regulate the output power to its nominal value.*

$$u = -\frac{\tau v_h j_r}{\frac{\partial T_a}{\partial \beta}}$$
$$v_h = a_h \int_0^t e dt + b_h \dot{e} + c_h e - \frac{\partial T_a}{\partial \beta}\frac{\beta}{\tau j_r} + \omega_{rej,h}$$
$$\omega_{rej,h} = \lambda_{0,h}|s_h|^{1/2} sign(s_h) + \eta_h$$
$$\dot{\eta}_h = \lambda_{1,h} sign(s_h)$$
$$where \begin{cases} s_h = \dot{e}_h + \zeta_h \\ \dot{\zeta}_h = -\frac{\frac{\partial T_a}{\partial \beta}\beta}{\tau j_r} + v_h - \omega_{rej,h} \\ \lambda_{0,h} = 1.5\sqrt{L_2} \\ \lambda_{1,h} = 1.1 L_2 \\ \left|\frac{d\Delta\psi_{unknown,h}}{dt}\right| < L_2 \end{cases} \tag{49}$$

where u is the control signal, v_h is the virtual controller, β is the pitch angle, $\omega_{rej,h}$ is the rejection term in region III (to reject uncertainties and unknown variables), and $\frac{\partial T_a}{\partial \beta}$ is the pitch sensitivity.

Proof. By defining the error signal as $e_h = \omega_r - 12.1$, and according to Equation (35), the second derivative of the error signal can be computed as follows (We simplified $\dot{T}_a$ by the simple chain derivation rule, $\dot{T}_a(V, \omega_r, \beta) = \frac{\partial T_a}{\partial \omega_r}\dot{\omega}_r + \frac{\partial T_a}{\partial V}\dot{V} + \frac{\partial T_a}{\partial \beta}\dot{\beta}$):

$$\ddot{e}_h = \frac{\frac{\partial T_a}{\partial \omega_r}\dot{\omega}_r + \frac{\partial T_a}{\partial V}\dot{V} - \frac{\partial T_a}{\partial \beta}\frac{\beta}{\tau} - (D_{ls} + D_r)\dot{\omega}_r - K_{ls}(\omega_r - \omega_{ls}) + D_{ls}\dot{\omega}_{ls}}{j_r} + \frac{\partial T_a}{\partial \beta}\frac{u}{\tau j_r} \tag{50}$$

Just like the previous part, the pitch angle actuator must stabilize the rotor speed error. Therefore, the following equation must be satisfied [37]:

$$\ddot{e}_h + a_h \int_0^t e_h dt + b_h \dot{e}_h + c_h e_h = 0 \tag{51}$$

where, a_h, b_h, and c_h are some positive numbers. In addition, the time derivative of rotor speed, low-speed shaft speed, and wind velocity are unknown and must be estimated. To estimate the uncertainties, after simple calculations, the following equations are obtained:

$$\ddot{e}_h = \psi_{known,h} + \Delta\psi_{unknown,h} - v_h$$
$$where$$
$$\Delta\psi_{unknown,h} = \frac{\frac{\partial T_a}{\partial \omega_r}\dot{\omega}_r + \frac{\partial T_a}{\partial V}\dot{V} - (D_{ls} + D_r)\dot{\omega}_r - K_{ls}(\omega_r - \omega_{ls}) + D_{ls}\dot{\omega}_{ls}}{j_r}$$
$$\psi_{known} = -\frac{\partial T_a}{\partial \beta}\frac{\beta}{\tau j_r}$$
$$v_h = \frac{\partial T_a}{\partial \beta}\frac{u}{\tau j_r} \tag{52}$$

The term $\Delta\psi_{unknown,h}$ is unknown and must be estimated and v_h is the virtual controller in region III. For this purpose, the sliding mode approach is used similarly to the previous part. At the first, the sliding manifold is chosen as follows:

$$s_h = \dot{e}_h + \xi_h$$
$$\dot{\zeta}_h = -\psi_{known,h} + v_h - \omega_{rej,h} \tag{53}$$

By considering the Lyapunov function as $V_h = \frac{1}{2}s_h^2$ and doing the same process as the previous part:

$$v_h = a_h \int_0^t edt + b_h\dot{e} + c_h e - \frac{\partial T_a}{\partial \beta}\frac{\beta}{\tau j_r} + \rho_h sign(s_h) \tag{54}$$

Finally, by finding the virtual control signal v_h, the pitch controller can be obtained as follows:

$$u = -\frac{\tau v_h j_r}{\frac{\partial T_a}{\partial \beta}} \tag{55}$$

□

As stated before, the objective of this part is to design a novel sensorless controller in region III to both control the output power and reduce the vibration loads. According to Equation (55), $\frac{\partial T_a}{\partial \beta}$ is still unknown and must be estimated. The term $\frac{\partial T_a}{\partial \beta}$ is called pitch sensitivity and indicates how the aerodynamic torque or the aerodynamic power varies with pitch angle. Pitch sensitivity depends on EWV, pitch angle, and rotor speed. In this research, pitch sensitivity is estimated by using ANFIS (Adaptive Neuro-Fuzzy Inference System), which is a fuzzy inference system that is implanted into the neural network frame [57]. Fuzzy inference systems can be categorized into the Mamdani and Takagi-Sugeno (TS) systems [57]. The difference between these systems is the output of each If-Then fuzzy rule. In the TS fuzzy system, the output of each rule is a linear combination of the inputs, but in the regular Mamdani fuzzy system, each output is a linguistic variable that is described by membership functions. Pitch sensitivity depends on the rotor speed, pitch angle, and EWV. The training data for the estimation process is obtained by FAST. The grid partition method is used for generating the FIS (fuzzy inference system) and for training the ANFIS system, the hybrid method is considered. 70% of the extracted data is used for training and the other 30% is for testing the generated model (The details of extracting data can be found in [11]). For two inputs (EWV and pitch angle) five Gaussian membership functions are considered and for the third input (rotor speed) three membership functions are considered, therefore, for the whole system, 75 rules are required. Figure 10 shows the ANFIS surface as a function of pitch angle and effective wind velocity.

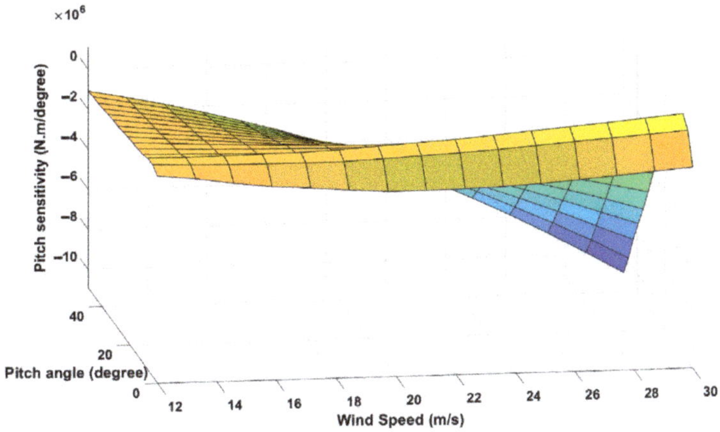

Figure 10. ANFIS surface for the pitch sensitivity as a function of effective wind velocity and pitch angle.

Figure 11 shows the pitch sensitivity at different mean wind velocities and a constant turbulent intensity of 10%. In order to consider the effect of turbulence on the estimation process, pitch sensitivity is investigated at a constant mean wind velocity of 20 m/s and different turbulence intensities (Figure 12). As can be observed, the proposed method has an excellent performance in the estimation of pitch sensitivity. The whole structure of the control system is shown in Figure 13.

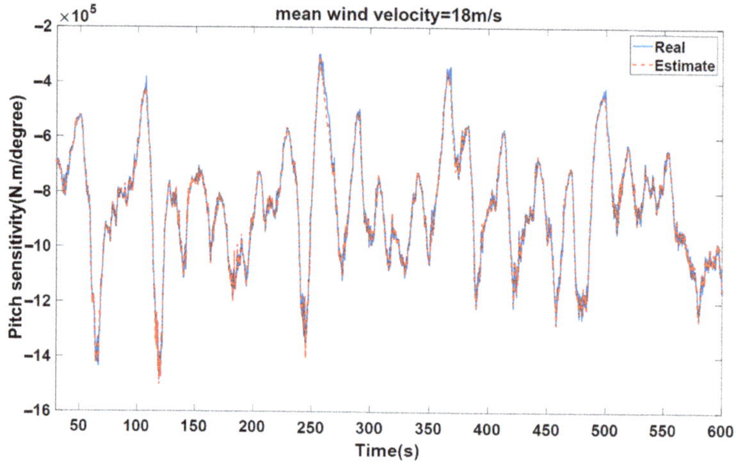

(a)

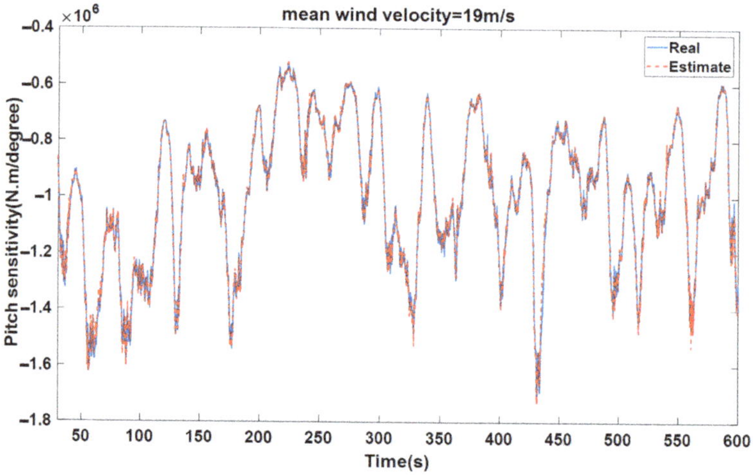

(b)

Figure 11. *Cont.*

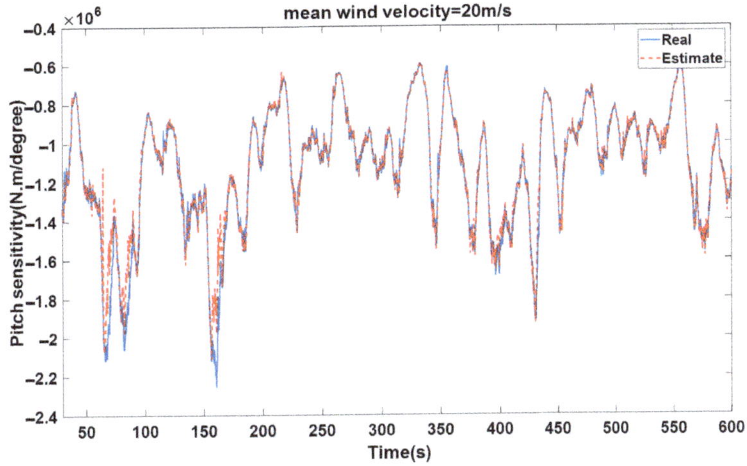

(c)

Figure 11. Pitch sensitivity estimation in different mean wind speed values by using the ANFIS system. (a) 18 m/s. (b) 19 m/s. (c) 20 m/s.

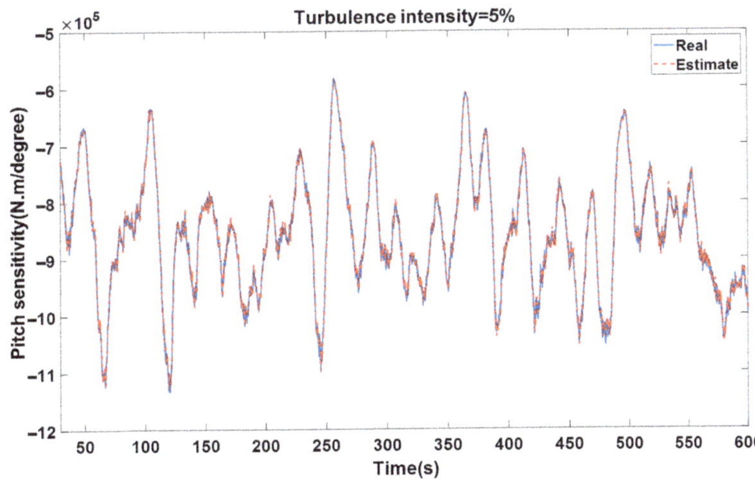

(a)

Figure 12. *Cont.*

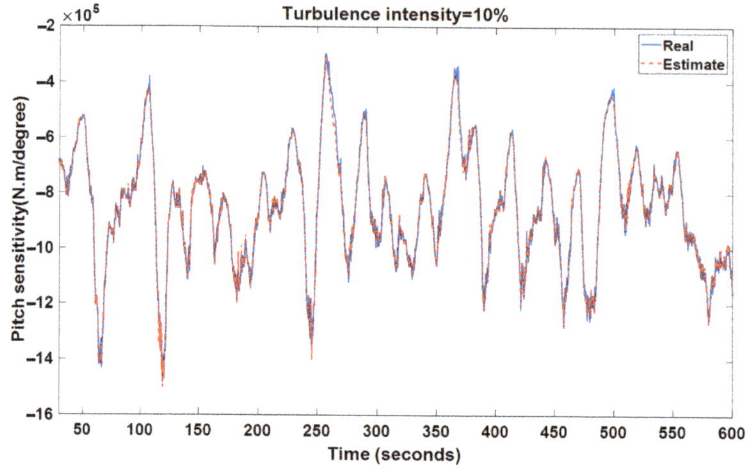

(b)

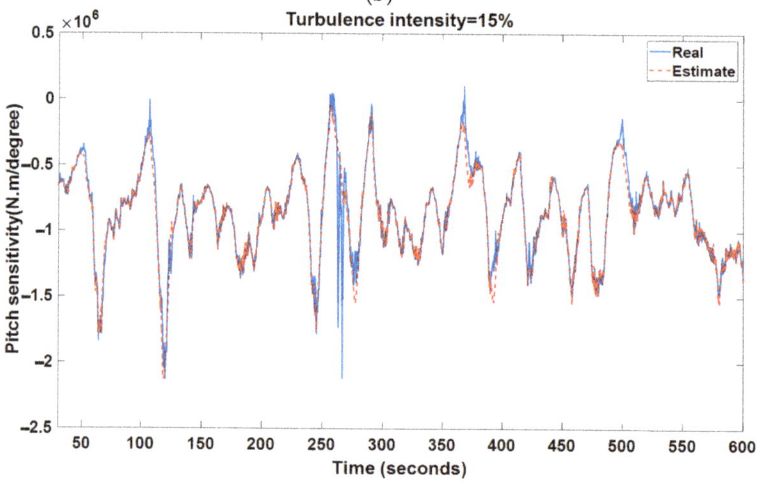

(c)

Figure 12. Pitch sensitivity estimation in different turbulence intensity and constant mean wind speed of 20 m/s by using the ANFIS system. (**a**) 5%. (**b**) 10%. (**c**) 15%.

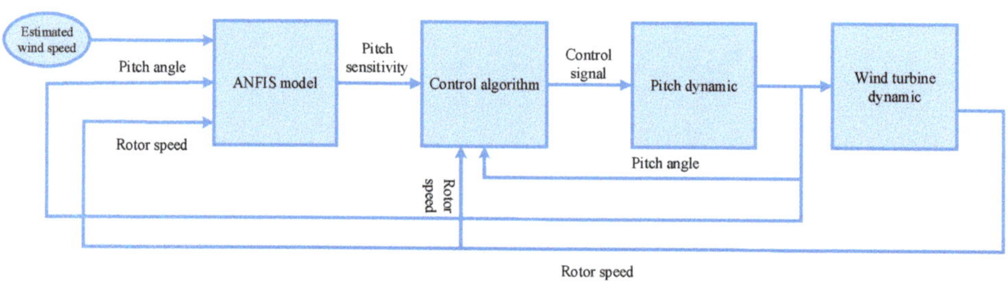

Figure 13. Schematic of the designed control system in region III.

The control parameters can be found in Appendix C.

5. Load Mitigation of the Tower Vibration Loads by Using TMD

In this section, the load mitigation of the tower of the NREL 5MW has been considered by using a vibration absorber. According to [32,34], load mitigation was considered at a constant rotor speed and ignoring the drivetrain system of a wind turbine. According to [58], the standard deviation of the pitch angle can significantly affect the vibration loads of the tower. The wind turbine's tower can be modelled as a beam that is fixed at the bottom with a concentrated mass (the nacelle) attached to the free end. This structure has two main sources of excitation:

- The vibration loads are transmitted from the blades to the hub and finally to the tower. These vibration loads can be influenced by the drivetrain control algorithms in the previous section.
- Aerodynamic loads from the wind.

According to [58], the aerodynamic loads of the tower are negligible in comparison to the first source of excitation; in other words, designing the vibration absorbers without considering the control algorithms would result in inaccuracies. To consider the effect of coupling between the drivetrain dynamic and the turbine on the load analysis, in Figure 14, the change between STD of nacelle fore-aft displacement and the two cases are considered in region III. The first case is the fully coupled model which is described in this research and is validated by FAST. The second case is the uncoupled model with constant rotor speed (12.1 rpm) and without considering the effect of the drivetrain and the pitch actuator. For this purpose, we defined the following parameter:

$$\gamma_{difference} = \frac{\sigma_{couple} - \sigma_{uncouple}}{\sigma_{couple}} \times 100 \quad (56)$$

where σ_{couple} is the STD of the parameter (nacelle fore-aft displacement and flapwise displacement of the blade) in the coupled model, $\sigma_{uncouple}$ is the STD of the parameter in the uncoupled model, and $\gamma_{difference}$ denotes the difference between the coupled and uncoupled model. As can be seen, the difference is significant and any load analysis and load mitigation perspective must consider the coupled model.

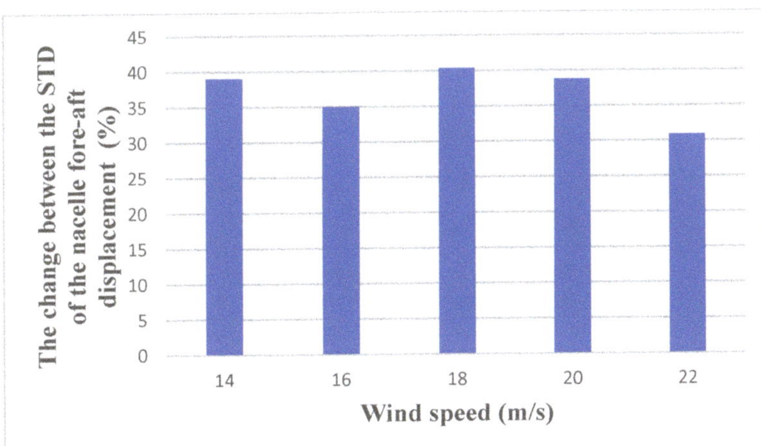

(a)

Figure 14. *Cont.*

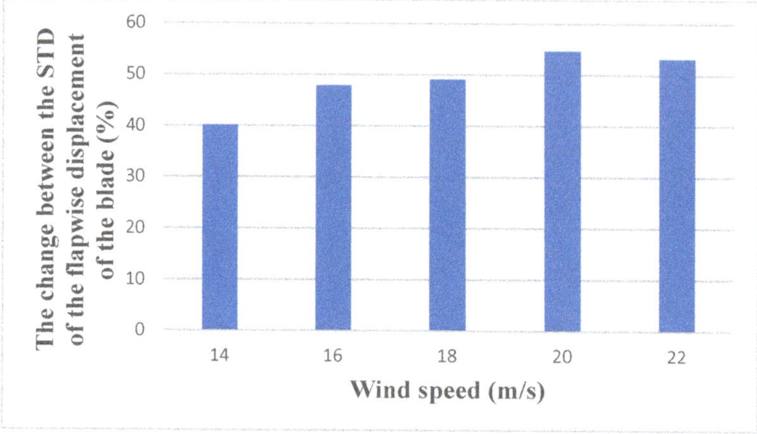

(**b**)

Figure 14. The difference between the STD of the vibration loads of the coupled model and the uncoupled model. (**a**) fore-aft displacement of the nacelle (**b**) flapwise tip displacement of the blade.

In this section, by considering the control algorithm in the previous section, a TMD system is designed to reduce the fore-aft vibration of the tower. In order to design the absorber, another DOF must be considered in the aeroelastic model.

$$\{q_{absorber}\} = \left\{q_{fa,abs}\right\} \tag{57}$$

Also, the kinetic energy, potential energy, and external work related to the damper of the absorber system can be calculated as [30]:

$$\begin{aligned} T_{absorber} &= \frac{1}{2} m_{fa,abs} \dot{q}^2_{fa,abs} \\ \pi_{absorber} &= \frac{1}{2} k_{fa,abs} \left(q_{fa,abs} - q_{fa}\right)^2 \\ \delta W_{absorber} &= -c_{fa,abs} \left(q_{fa,abs} - q_{fa}\right) \left(\delta q_{fa,abs} - \delta q_{fa}\right) \end{aligned} \tag{58}$$

where $m_{fa,abs}$, $k_{fa,abs}$ and $c_{fa,abs}$ are the mass, stiffness, and damping coefficient of the TMD in the fore-aft direction and $T_{absorber}$, $\pi_{absorber}$, and $\delta W_{absorber}$ are the kinetic energy, potential energy, and the virtual work of the damper respectively. The main goal is to design the parameters $\left\{m_{fa,abs}, k_{fa,abs}, c_{fa,abs}\right\}$ to minimize the fore-aft vibration signal.

Remark 8. *In Sections 2 and 3, we defined an 11 DOFs model. In this section, other DOFs (related to the TMD) must be considered. In other words, the new size of the matrices M and N in Equation (38) are 11 × 11 and the size of vector K is 11 × 1.*

6. Simulation Results

In this section, a complete aeroelastic simulation has been done by considering the control signal and the tuned mass damper in the nacelle of the wind turbine. These simulations considered 12 DOFs (6 DOFs for the blade, 2DOFs for the tower, 2DOFs for the drivetrain, 1 DOF for the pitch actuator, and 1 DOF for the absorber) of the wind turbine dynamic system. The simulation was run on MATLAB to investigate two load cases in region II and region III. The load case in region II was with a mean wind speed of 8 m/s and turbulence intensity of 10%, and the other load case in region III was with a mean wind speed of 20 m/s and turbulence intensity of 10%. The performance of the designed controllers in both regions was compared with conventional controllers (ISC control algorithm in region II and the GPI controller in region III) in terms of load mitigation. The following assumptions have been considered in the aeroelastic simulations:

- The optimum rotor speed in region II is smoothed by a low pass filter with a time constant = 1 s.
- The simulation time is considered as 10 min (according to the IEC standard [33]).
- In order to prevent chattering in the super twisting sliding mode approach, the rejection term is smoothed by a low pass filter with a time constant of 1 s.

In Figure 15, the performance of the super twisting control approach was compared with the ISC algorithm in absorbing wind energy, and also the vibration loads in region II. As Figure 15 shows, super twisting sliding mode control had a better performance in increasing power coefficient in region II. However, the performance of both approaches is very similar in the terms of vibration loads. More details of the simulation can be found in Table 3.

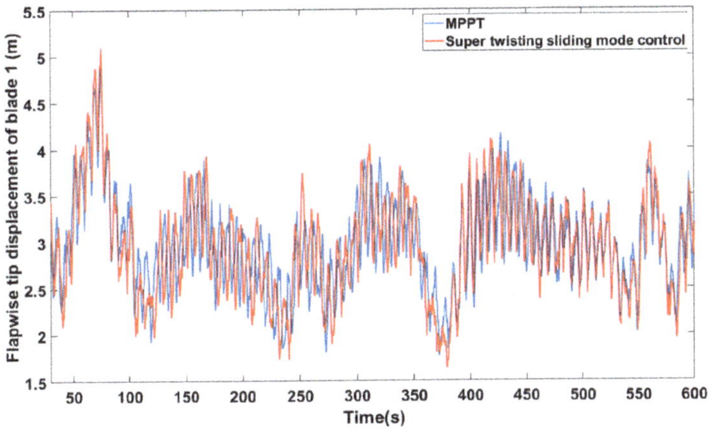

(a)

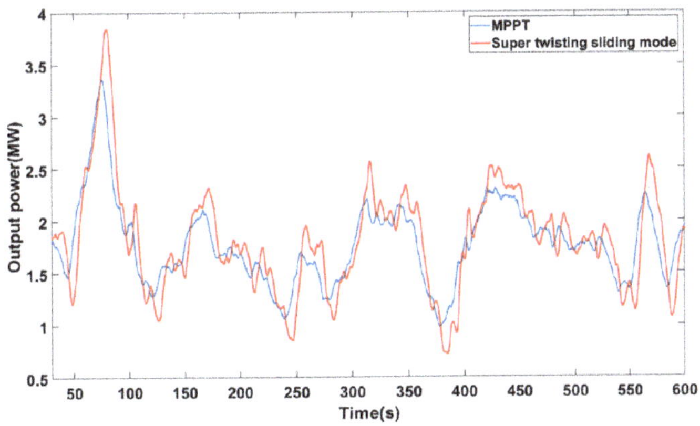

(b)

Figure 15. *Cont.*

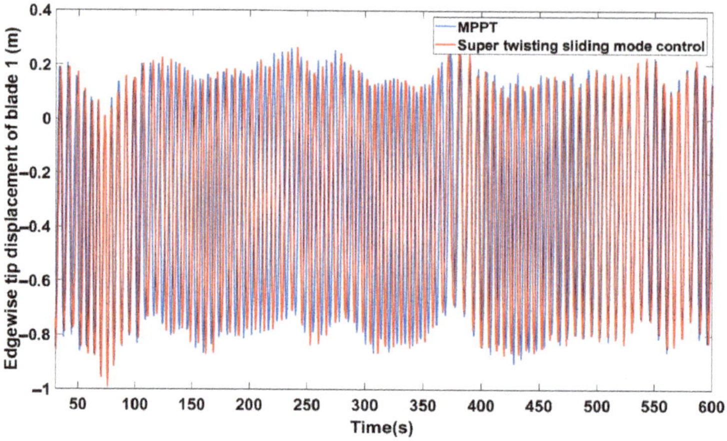

(**c**)

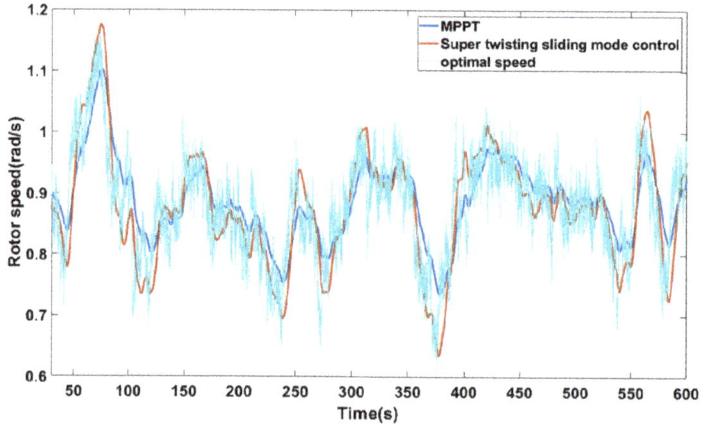

(**d**)

Figure 15. A comparison between the performance of the classical MPPT control approach (ISC) and Super twisting sliding mode control. (**a**) Flapwise tip deflection of blade 1. (**b**) Output power. (**c**) Edgewise tip deflection of blade 1. (**d**) Rotor speed of both approaches and the optimal value.

Table 3. Detailed simulation with mean wind speed 8 m/s and turbulence intensity 10%.

Control Approach	Edgewise (m)		Flapwise (m)		Output Power (kw)		Generator Torque (KN·m)	
	STD	Mean	STD	Mean	STD	Mean	STD	Mean
Super twisting sliding mode	0.3452	−0.3123	0.4823	2.958	368.3	1857	2.765	20.84
MPPT algorithm	0.3457	−0.3159	0.4369	3.023	320.06	1838	2.535	20.05

In Figure 16, the performance of these control approaches is compared in absorbing energy from the wind. As can be seen, the super twisting control approach can improve the absorbed energy in comparison to the conventional ISC algorithm by nearly 1%.

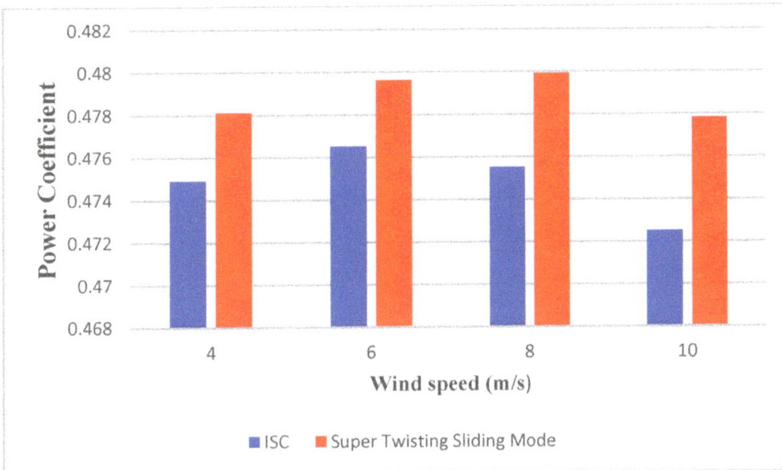

Figure 16. Comparison between ISC control approach and Super twisting sliding mode control in absorbing wind energy in different mean wind speed values with turbulence intensity 10%. Blue is the power coefficient of ISC and red is the power coefficient according to the super twisting sliding mode control approach.

Remark 9. *As sketched in Figure 15, the generated power of our novel approach in some regions is higher than the conventional MPPT method and in other regions, the MPPT approach generates more power. In order to have a justifiable comparison, in Figure 16 we compare the average value of the power coefficient. The averaged power coefficient has been calculated as follows:*

$$\overline{C}_p = \frac{1}{T}\int_0^T C_p dt \tag{59}$$

where C_p is the power coefficient as a function of time, T is the simulation time, which is 10 min in our work.

In Figure 17, the performance of the designed control system is compared with the GPI control system in region III. In Table 4, a complete comparison is investigated. As can be seen, the super twisting control approach has a very good ability to reduce the vibration loads of the blade in the flapwise and edgewise directions. In addition, according to Table 4, the super twisting approach has a better ability in tracking the nominal power and reducing vibration loads.

Table 4. Detailed simulation with mean wind speed = 20 m/s and turbulence intensity = 10%.

Control Approach	Edgewise (m)		Flapwise (m)		Output Power (MW)		Pitch Angle (Degree)	
	STD	Mean	STD	Mean	STD	Mean	STD	Mean
Super twisting sliding mode	0.3499	−0.07541	1.048	1.413	0.1382	5.294	2.007	17.63
GPI algorithm	0.355	−0.07803	1.062	1.612	0.1503	5.31	2.236	17.18

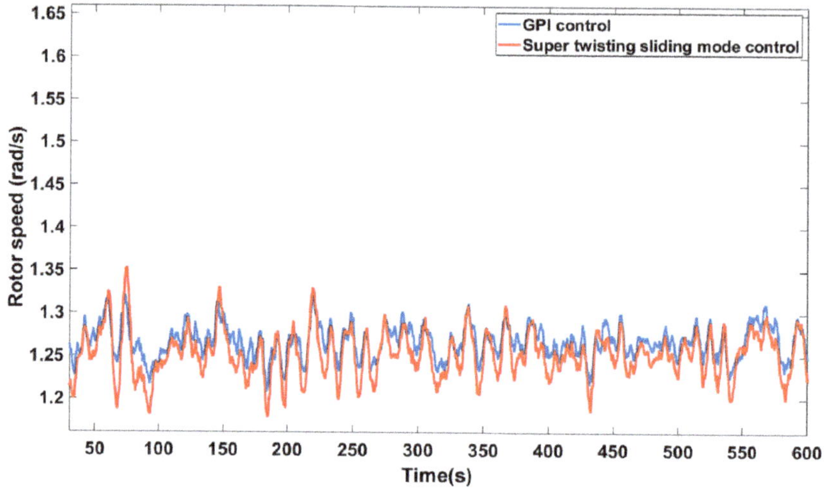

(a)

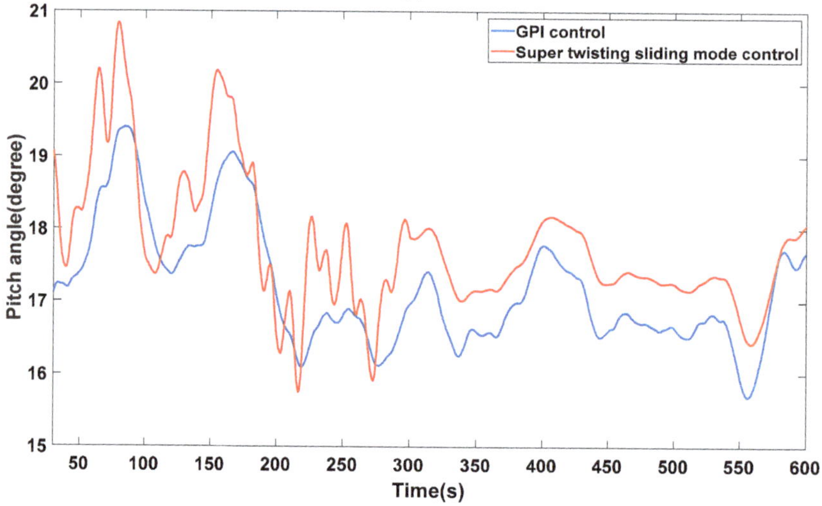

(b)

Figure 17. *Cont.*

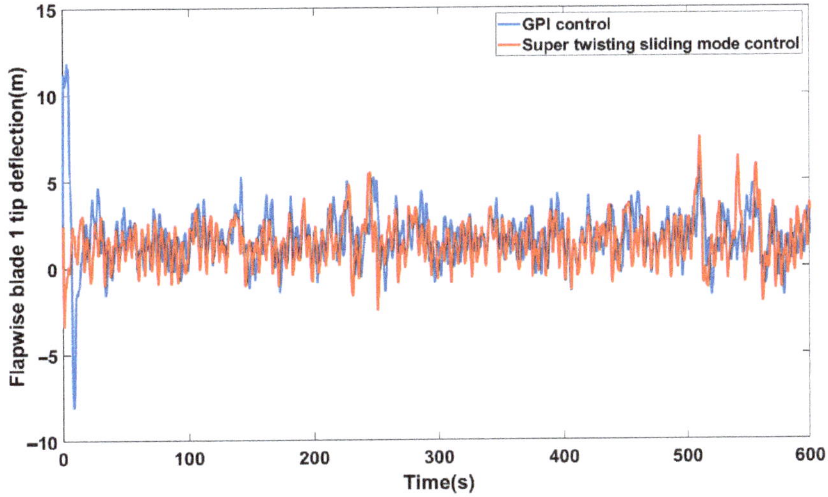

(c)

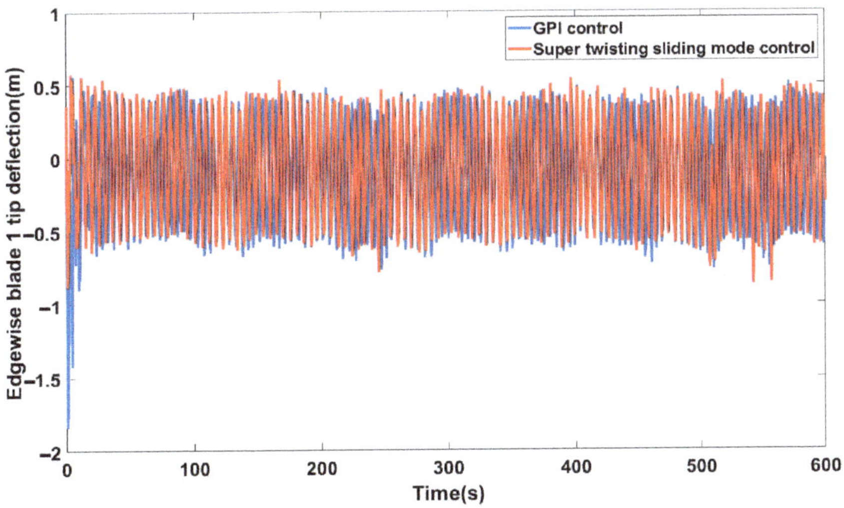

(d)

Figure 17. Comparison between the performance of the classical GPI control and Super twisting sliding mode control for (**a**) Rotor speed, (**b**) pitch angle, (**c**) Fdgewise blade 1 tip deflection, and (**d**) Edgewise tip deflection of blade 1.

In order to consider the performance of the super twisting sliding mode control, in Figure 18, the STD of pitch angle has been investigated. As can be seen, the proposed method can reduce the STD of pitch angle by approximately 12%. In Figure 19, the reduction in the mean value of flapwise vibration has been considered. As can be seen, the super twisting sliding mode can reduce the flapwise mean value by 7% to 12% in different mean wind velocities.

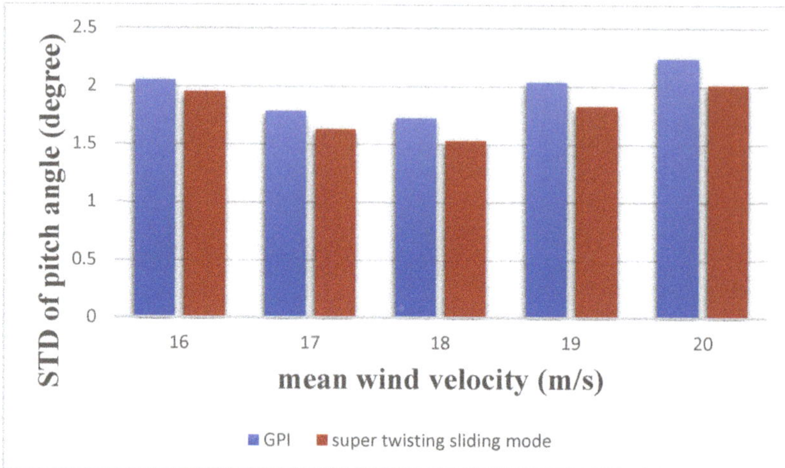

Figure 18. Comparison between the STD of pitch angle signal in gain schedule control approach and super twisting sliding mode control in different mean wind speed values with turbulence intensity 10%.

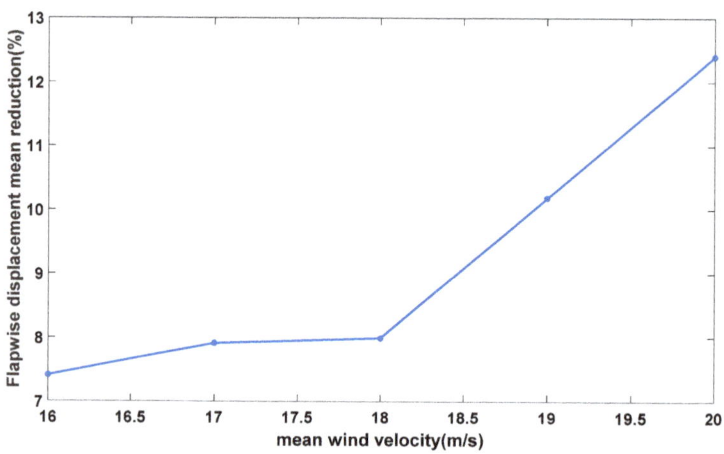

Figure 19. Flapwise displacement mean reduction in different mean wind velocities. The super twisting sliding mode can reduce the mean value of vibration signal by 7% to 12% in different mean wind velocities and turbulence intensity 10%.

For designing the TMD in the nacelle, the genetic algorithm was used for optimization with the root mean square (RMS) of the fore-aft vibration of the tower as the fitness function. For this purpose, the MATLAB optimization toolbox was used. One should note that the mass of the damper must not exceed 4% of the total mass of the rotor and nacelle [32]. Also, the stroke of the TMD in the nacelle is 8 m (because the length of the nacelle is 18 m. The best and mean individuals of the optimization process have been depicted in Figure 20. As is observed, the algorithm converges after 14 generations. The optimal results are:

$$m_{fa,abs} = 12060 \text{ kg},\ k_{fa,abs} = 54070 \text{ N/m},\ c_{fa,abs} = 8995 \text{ N·s/m} \quad (60)$$

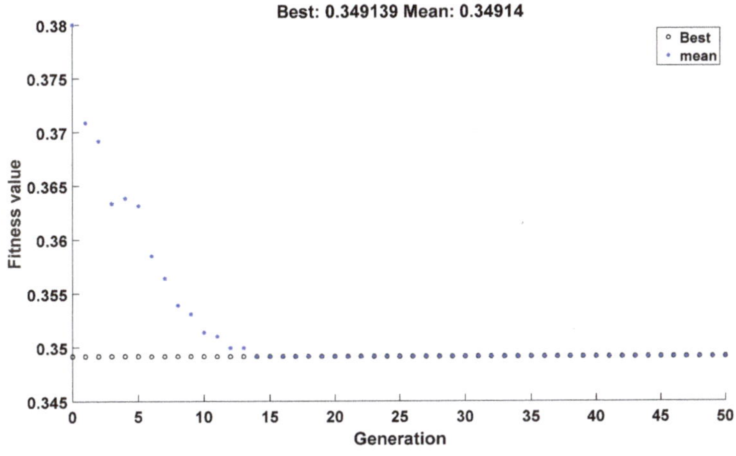

Figure 20. Iterations for finding optimal solutions. Best individuals and mean values are investigated.

The TMD strokes and fore-aft vibration signals are shown in Figure 21. The load reduction of the fore-aft vibration of the tower is given in Table 5 at different mean wind speeds with a constant turbulence intensity of 10%. The fore-aft vibration reduction of the tower at different turbulence intensities with a constant mean wind speed of 20 m/s has been investigated as seen in Table 6. The load reduction is defined as follows:

$$\eta_{red} = \frac{\sigma_{WTMD} - \sigma_{TMD}}{\sigma_{WTMD}} \times 100 \quad (61)$$

where η_{red} is the reduction rate, σ_{WTMD} is the STD of the tower fore-aft vibration without the TMD, and σ_{TMD} is the STD of the vibration signal by considering the TMD effect.

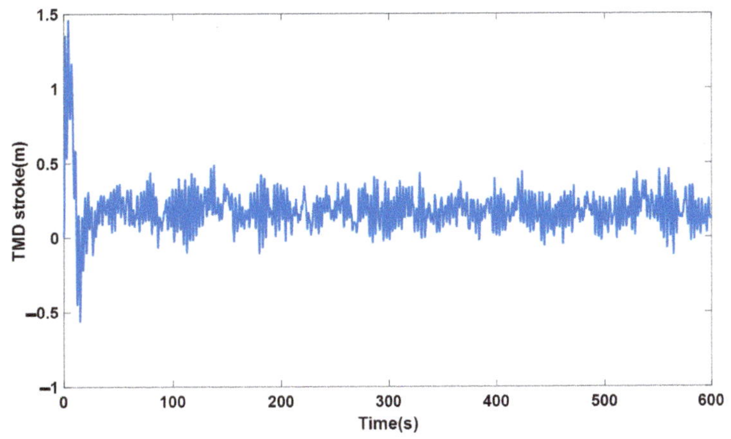

(a)

Figure 21. *Cont.*

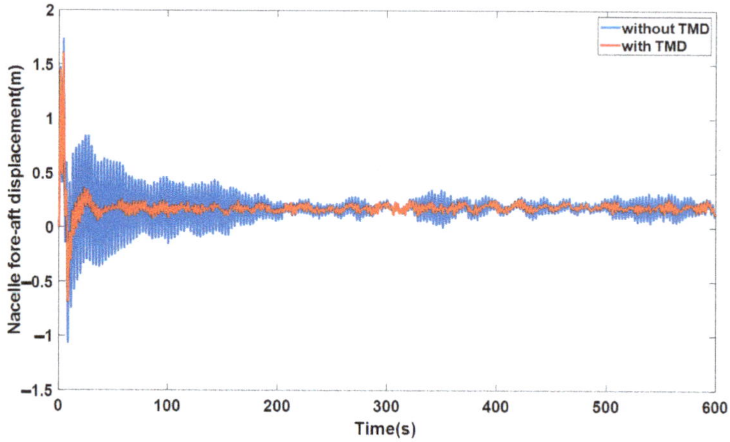

(**b**)

Figure 21. TMD performance in reducing tower fore-aft vibration. (**a**) TMD stroke. (**b**) fore-aft vibration of the tower with and without TMD.

Table 5. The reduction rate of fore-aft vibration in constant mean wind speed of 20 m/s and different turbulence intensities.

Turbulence Intensity (%)	Tower Fore-Aft Reduction (%)
5	51.65
10	45.65
15	32.73
20	37.21

Table 6. The reduction of fore-aft vibration in constant turbulence intensity of 10%, and different mean wind speed values.

Mean Wind Velocity (m/s)	Tower Fore-Aft Reduction (%)
6	40.00
8	58.46
18	33.49
20	45.65
22	35.44
24	38.27

Remark 10. *The main novelty of the TMD design procedure is considering the coupled dynamics of the wind turbine. Although it must be noted that the coupled model is completely available in the FAST and other similar aeroelastic codes. However, the accuracy of the constant speed model is the main concern of this part. As demonstrated in Figure 14, the coupled dynamics of the turbine and the drivetrain makes much better accuracy in the estimation of the dynamic loads. For doing this, we compare the standard deviation of the coupled model and the uncoupled model in comparison to the blades and the tower vibration. The difference between the coupled and uncoupled models in the estimation of the dynamic loads has been discussed in Figure 14.*

7. Conclusions

In this study, the wind turbine control problem has been investigated from the load reduction perspective. First, an aeroelastic model of the wind turbine was developed to consider the edgewise and flapwise vibration of the blade and also the fore-aft and side-side vibration of the tower. The blades were considered rotational beams and the tower is considered a beam with one fixed end and the other attached to a lumped mass. The Euler-Bernoulli beam theory was used to derive the dynamic behaviour of the blades and the tower. Based on the full-aeroelastic model, a reduced-order model was considered for control purposes. The control problem was investigated for both low and high wind velocities by the super twisting sliding mode control approach. In region III (high wind velocities), an adaptive neural fuzzy inference system (ANFIS) was used for estimating pitch sensitivity. The inputs of this system were pitch angle, effective wind velocity, and rotor speed. The training and test data were obtained by FAST aeroelastic code. Finally, to reduce the vibration loads of the tower, a TMD was used in the nacelle of the wind turbine to reduce the fore-aft vibration of the tower. The parameters of the TMD were chosen optimally by using the genetic algorithm. The results were compared to the baseline controllers in both operational regions which means the performance of the wind turbine system has been improved. Some findings about this research and future works are presented as follows:

- The simulation results demonstrate that the novel super twisting sliding mode approach proposed in this study can increase the power coefficient by approximately 1% (Figure 16) with no need to know state variables and aerodynamic torque (which is not measurable). In comparison with some recently published works [59,60], this work renders the stability proof of the proposed method.
- In region III, the power and rotor speed fluctuation is much smoother in comparison to the GPI control approach. This proposed method can reduce the STD of the pitch angle by 10% (Figure 19). Also, according to Figure 19, it can reduce the mean value of the flapwise vibration by 7–12% for different mean wind velocities.
- In comparison to the literature [31,32,34,35], we demonstrate that it is more accurate to consider the fully coupled model to estimate vibration loads and design vibration absorbers. In most of the previous works, the rotor speed is considered as a constant value (12.1 rpm) in region III and the drivetrain dynamic is ignored. In Figure 14, we compared the load estimation of the fully coupled model (by considering the drivetrain dynamic) and the uncoupled model (without drivetrain dynamic and constant rotor speed). As can be seen, the difference is significant in the wide range of wind velocity in region III (Figure 14).
- The TMD parameters are designed at the mean wind speed of 20 m/s in region III. Therefore, the results may be improved by considering a semi-active vibration absorber, which is optimal in both regions II and III.

Author Contributions: Data curation, H.Z.; Funding acquisition, H.Z.;Investigation, J.W.; Methodology, F.G.; Project administration, J.W.;Resources, L.Z.; Software, F.G.; Validation, F.G.; Writing—original draft, F.G.;Writing—review & editing, F.G. All authors have read and agreed to the published version of the manuscript.

Funding: The support for this work by the Natural Science Foundation of Heilongjiang Province China (Grant No. LH2020E010) is gratefully acknowledged.

Institutional Review Board Statement: Not applicable.

Informed Consent Statement: Not applicable.

Data Availability Statement: The data that support the findings of this study are available from the corresponding author upon reasonable request.

Conflicts of Interest: The authors declare no conflict of interest.

Appendix A

Appendix A.1. Aerodynamic Modelling and BEM Approach

It is convenient to non-dimensionalize these forces by the term $\frac{1}{2}\rho V_{rel}^2 c(r)$, which yields:

$$C_N = \frac{P_N}{\frac{1}{2}\rho V_{rel}^2 c(r)} \quad C_T = \frac{P_T}{\frac{1}{2}\rho V_{rel}^2 c(r)} \tag{A1}$$

where $c(r)$ is the chord length of each section. The classical BEM theory assumes an infinite number of blades. To correct this assumption, Prandtl suggests a correction factor F. According to [61], the values of induction factors (a and a') by considering Prandtl correction can be obtained as:

$$a = \frac{1}{1 + \frac{4F\sin^2\phi}{\sigma_{solid}C_N}} \quad a' = \frac{1}{\frac{4F\sin\phi\cos\phi}{\sigma_{solid}C_T} - 1} \quad \sigma_{solid} = \frac{c(r)N_{blade}}{2\pi r} \tag{A2}$$

where σ_{solid} is defined as the solidity, N_{blade} is the number of blades, and F is the Prandtl correction which is described as:

$$F = \frac{2}{\pi}\cos^{-1}\left(e^{-f}\right) \quad f = \frac{N_{blade}}{2}\frac{R - r}{r\sin\phi} \tag{A3}$$

when the axial induction factor (a) is larger than 0.4, simple BEM theory is not valid anymore. In this case, the Glauert correction is expressed as follows:

$$C_T = \begin{cases} 4a(1-a)F & a \le a_c \\ 4(a_c^2 + (1-2a_c)a)F & a > a_c \end{cases} \quad a_c \simeq 0.2 \tag{A4}$$

As well as the norm of the difference between a and a' with respect to their previous values is larger than an assumed small quantity, this algorithm continues. Otherwise, the algorithm converges, and we can obtain the aerodynamic force of each section. For more details on the dynamic wake model and dynamic stall, one can refer to [42]

Appendix A.2. Wind Profile Modelling

The wind profile is the summation of the mean wind velocity and the turbulence term. The mean wind velocity is a function of height and surface roughness. There are two models for describing the mean wind velocity profile, the power-law model, and the logarithmic law model [42]. The difference between these two models is that the logarithm law is scale-dependent but the power law is scale-independent. The logarithm law for modelling the wind time history data can be expressed as:

$$\frac{V_m(z)}{V_m\left(z_{ref}\right)} = \frac{\ln(z/z_{ref})}{\ln(z_{ref}/z_0)} \tag{A5}$$

where z is the height above the ground, z_{ref} is the reference height, z_0 is the surface roughness, and is the mean wind velocity. The turbulence of the incoming wind determines the degree of fluctuation in wind speed. The turbulence in the airflow can be described by the power density spectrum (PDS) which determines the energy of the vortices. There are various mathematical expressions for describing PDS and according to [42], one of the power spectrum models, the Kaimal spectrum function is as follows:

$$S(f) = \frac{I^2 V_m l}{\left(1 + 1.5\frac{f \cdot l}{V_m}\right)^{5/3}} \quad \text{(A6)}$$

where $I = \frac{\sigma_{wind}}{V_m}$ is called the turbulence intensity. σ_{wind} is the standard deviation of wind speed, and l is the turbulence length scale (l = 20H for $H < 30$ and l = 600 for $H > 30$ (H is the height of the tower)) [61].

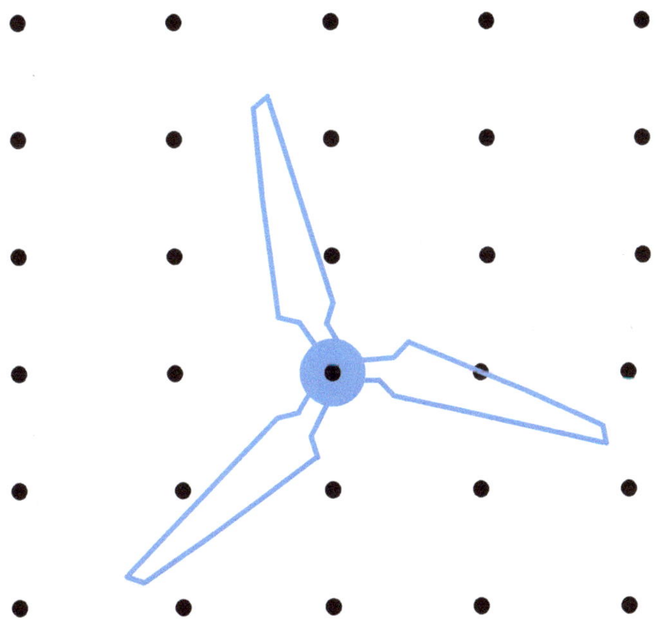

Figure A1. A schematic of the grid around the rotor of the wind turbine.

In order to obtain a 3D model of the wind field (in Figure A1, the grid around the rotor has been depicted), one should note that wind time histories at different points are not independent [45]. The coherence function between two points determines the correlation between different time history data in the grid. In general, the coherence function between two points j and k in the grid is defined below:

$$coh_{jk}(f) = \frac{\left|S_{jk}(f)\right|}{\sqrt{S_{jj}(f)S_{kk}(f)}} \approx \exp(-12fL_{jk}/V_m) \quad \text{(A7)}$$

where L_{jk} is the distance between two points j and k in the grid. To obtain the 3D time history of the wind, in this research we follow the rotational sampling concept which is introduced in [62].

Appendix B

Some important characteristics of the NREL 5MW turbine are given below.

Table A1. General characteristics of the NREL 5MW turbine [11].

Rating	5 MW
Rotor Orientation, Configuration	Upwind, 3 Blades
Control	Variable Speed, Collective Pitch
Drivetrain	High Speed, Multiple-Stage Gearbox
Rotor, Hub Diameter	126 m, 3 m
Cut-in, Rated, Cut-out Wind Speed	3, 11.4, 25 m/s
Rotor Mass	110,000 Kg
Nacelle Mass	240,000 Kg
Tower Mass	347,000 Kg

Also, the main mode shapes of the blade and tower of the wind turbine are:

$$\begin{aligned}
\varphi_{edg} &= -0.6952\bar{r}^6 + 2.376\bar{r}^5 - 3.5772\bar{r}^4 + 2.5337\bar{r}^3 + 0.3627\bar{r}^2 \\
\varphi_{flp} &= -2.2555\bar{r}^6 + 4.7131\bar{r}^5 - 3.2452\bar{r}^4 + 1.7254\bar{r}^3 + 0.0622\bar{r}^2 \\
\varphi_{fa} &= -2.504\bar{h}^6 + 6.2275\bar{h}^5 - 5.6202\bar{h}^4 + 2.1963\bar{h}^3 + 0.7004\bar{h}^2 \\
\varphi_{ss} &= 0.5357\bar{h}^6 - 2.2395\bar{h}^5 + 3.0871\bar{h}^4 - 1.7684\bar{h}^3 + 1.385\bar{h}^2
\end{aligned} \tag{A8}$$

where $\bar{r} = \frac{r}{61.7}$ and $\bar{h} = \frac{h}{87.2}$.

Appendix C

Table A2. Control parameters used in this research.

Parameter	Value
a_L	0.014
b_L	0.081
c_L	0.34
L_1	0.051
a_h	0.023
b_h	0.062
c_h	0.22
L_2	0.018

References

1. Dorrell, J.; Lee, K. The cost of wind: Negative economic effects of global wind energy development. *Energies* **2020**, *13*, 3667. [CrossRef]
2. Wiser, R.; Millstein, D. Evaluating the economic return to public wind energy research and development in the United States. *Appl. Energy* **2020**, *261*, 114449. [CrossRef]
3. Bianchi, F.D.; De Battista, H.; Mantz, R.J. *Wind Turbine Control Systems: Principles, Modelling and Gain Scheduling Design*; Springer Science & Business Media: London, UK, 2006.
4. Boukhezzar, B.; Lupu, L.; Siguerdidjane, H.; Hand, M. Multivariable control strategy for variable speed, variable pitch wind turbines. *Renew. Energy* **2007**, *32*, 1273–1287. [CrossRef]
5. Boukhezzar, B.; Siguerdidjane, H. Nonlinear control of a variable-speed wind turbine using a two-mass model. *IEEE Trans. Energy Convers.* **2010**, *26*, 149–162. [CrossRef]
6. Boukhezzar, B.; Siguerdidjane, H. Comparison between linear and nonlinear control strategies for variable speed wind turbines. *Control Eng. Pract.* **2010**, *18*, 1357–1368. [CrossRef]
7. Errami, Y.; Benchagra, M.; Hilal, M.; Maaroufi, M.; Ouassaid, M. Control strategy for PMSG wind farm based on MPPT and direct power control. In Proceedings of the 2012 International Conference on Multimedia Computing and Systems, Tangiers, Morocco, 10–12 May 2012.

8. Han, K.; Chen, G. A novel control strategy of wind turbine MPPT implementation for direct-drive PMSG wind generation imitation platform. In Proceedings of the 2009 IEEE 6th International Power Electronics and Motion Control Conference, Wuhan, China, 17–20 May 2009.
9. Pan, C.-T.; Juan, Y.-L. A novel sensorless MPPT controller for a high-efficiency microscale wind power generation system. *IEEE Trans. Energy Convers.* **2009**, *25*, 207–216.
10. Lin, W.-M.; Hong, C.-M.; Chen, C.-H. Neural-network-based MPPT control of a stand-alone hybrid power generation system. *IEEE Trans. Power Electron.* **2011**, *26*, 3571–3581. [CrossRef]
11. Jonkman, J.; Butterfield, S.; Musial, W.; Scott, G. *Definition of a 5-MW Reference Wind Turbine for Offshore System Development*; National Renewable Energy Lab (NREL): Golden, CO, USA, 2009.
12. Laima, S.; Li, H.; Chen, W.; Li, F. Investigation and control of vortex-induced vibration of twin box girders. *J. Fluids Struct.* **2013**, *39*, 205–221. [CrossRef]
13. Chen, W.L.; Zhang, Q.Q.; Li, H.; Hu, H. An experimental investigation on vortex induced vibration of a flexible inclined cable under a shear flow. *J. Fluids Struct.* **2015**, *54*, 297–311. [CrossRef]
14. Chen, W.L.; Xin, D.B.; Xu, F.; Li, H.; Ou, J.P.; Hu, H. Suppression of vortex-induced vibration of a circular cylinder using suction-based flow control. *J. Fluids Struct.* **2013**, *42*, 25–39. [CrossRef]
15. Jin, X.; Cheng, P.; Chen, W.L.; Li, H. Prediction model of velocity field around circular cylinder over various Reynolds numbers by fusion convolutional neural networks based on pressure on the cylinder. *Phys. Fluids* **2018**, *30*, 047105. [CrossRef]
16. Zhang, Q.; Xiang, X.; Hui, L.; Xiong, G.; Fisher, T.S. Mechanically robust honeycomb graphene aerogel multifunctional polymer composites. *Carbon* **2015**, *93*, 659–670. [CrossRef]
17. Pan, L.; Wang, X. Variable pitch control on direct-driven PMSG for offshore wind turbine using Repetitive-TS fuzzy PID control. *Renew. Energy* **2020**, *159*, 221–237. [CrossRef]
18. Dida, A.; Merahi, F.; Mekhilef, S. New grid synchronization and power control scheme of doubly-fed induction generator based wind turbine system using fuzzy logic control. *Comput. Electr. Eng.* **2020**, *84*, 106647. [CrossRef]
19. Zadeh, L.A.; Klir, G.J.; Yuan, B. *Fuzzy Sets, Fuzzy Logic, and Fuzzy Systems: Selected Papers*; World Scientific: Singapore, 1996.
20. Araghi, A.R.; Riahy, G.; Carlson, O.; Gros, S. Enhancing the net energy of wind turbine using wind prediction and economic NMPC with high-accuracy nonlinear WT models. *Renew. Energy* **2020**, *151*, 750–763. [CrossRef]
21. El-Baklish, S.K.; El-Badawy, A.A.; Frison, G.; Diehl, M. Nonlinear model predictive pitch control of aero-elastic wind turbine blades. *Renew. Energy* **2020**, *161*, 777–791. [CrossRef]
22. Golnary, F.; Moradi, H. Design and comparison of quasi continuous sliding mode control with feedback linearization for a large scale wind turbine with wind speed estimation. *Renew. Energy* **2018**, *127*, 495–508. [CrossRef]
23. Golnary, F.; Moradi, H. Dynamic modelling and design of various robust sliding mode controls for the wind turbine with estimation of wind speed. *Appl. Math. Model.* **2019**, *65*, 566–585. [CrossRef]
24. Ren, Y.; Li, L.; Brindley, J.; Jiang, L. Nonlinear PI control for variable pitch wind turbine. *Control Eng. Pract.* **2016**, *50*, 84–94. [CrossRef]
25. Garcia, C.E.; Prett, D.M.; Morari, M. Model predictive control: Theory and practice—A survey. *Automatica* **1989**, *25*, 335–348. [CrossRef]
26. Altan, A.; Hacıoğlu, R. Model predictive control of three-axis gimbal system mounted on UAV for real-time target tracking under external disturbances. *Mech. Syst. Signal Process.* **2020**, *138*, 106548. [CrossRef]
27. Huang, S.; Lin, Y.; Chinde, V.; Ma, X.; Lian, J. Simulation-based performance evaluation of model predictive control for building energy systems. *Appl. Energy* **2021**, *281*, 116027. [CrossRef]
28. Mérida, J.; Aguilar, L.T.; Dávila, J. Analysis and synthesis of sliding mode control for large scale variable speed wind turbine for power optimization. *Renew. Energy* **2014**, *71*, 715–728. [CrossRef]
29. Mérida, J.; Aguilar, L.T.; Dávila, J. Increasing Power Generation Efficiency in Horizontal Wind Turbines by Rejecting Electromechanical Uncertainties due to the Wind. *IEEE Control Syst. Lett.* **2021**, *6*, 217–222. [CrossRef]
30. Yang, J.; He, E. Coupled modeling and structural vibration control for floating offshore wind turbine. *Renew. Energy* **2020**, *157*, 678–694. [CrossRef]
31. Zhang, Z.; Li, J.; Nielsen, S.R.; Basu, B. Mitigation of edgewise vibrations in wind turbine blades by means of roller dampers. *J. Sound Vib.* **2014**, *333*, 5283–5298. [CrossRef]
32. Sun, C.; Jahangiri, V. Bi-directional vibration control of offshore wind turbines using a 3D pendulum tuned mass damper. *Mech. Syst. Signal Process.* **2018**, *105*, 338–360. [CrossRef]
33. Jalili, N. A comparative study and analysis of semi-active vibration-control systems. *J. Vib. Acoust.* **2002**, *124*, 593–605. [CrossRef]
34. Zhang, Z.; Nielsen, S.R.; Basu, B.; Li, J. Nonlinear modeling of tuned liquid dampers (TLDs) in rotating wind turbine blades for damping edgewise vibrations. *J. Fluids Struct.* **2015**, *59*, 252–269. [CrossRef]
35. Sun, C.; Jahangiri, V.; Sun, H. Performance of a 3D pendulum tuned mass damper in offshore wind turbines under multiple hazards and system variations. *Smart Struct. Syst.* **2019**, *24*, 53–65.
36. Saravanakumar, R.; Jena, D. Validation of an integral sliding mode control for optimal control of a three blade variable speed variable pitch wind turbine. *Int. J. Electr. Power Energy Syst.* **2015**, *69*, 421–429. [CrossRef]
37. Golnary, F.; Tse, K. Novel sensorless fault-tolerant pitch control of a horizontal axis wind turbine with a new hybrid approach for effective wind velocity estimation. *Renew. Energy* **2021**, *179*, 1291–1315. [CrossRef]

38. Tong, W. *Wind Power Generation and Wind Turbine Design*; WIT Press: Southampton, UK, 2010.
39. Fitzgerald, B.; Sarkar, S.; Staino, A. Improved reliability of wind turbine towers with active tuned mass dampers (ATMDs). *J. Sound Vib.* **2018**, *419*, 103–122. [CrossRef]
40. Sarkar, S.; Fitzgerald, B. Vibration control of spar-type floating offshore wind turbine towers using a tuned mass-damper-inerter. *Struct. Control. Health Monit.* **2020**, *27*, e2471. [CrossRef]
41. Zhang, R.; Zhao, Z.; Dai, K. Seismic response mitigation of a wind turbine tower using a tuned parallel inerter mass system. *Eng. Struct.* **2019**, *180*, 29–39. [CrossRef]
42. Hansen, M.O. *Aerodynamics of Wind Turbines*; Routledge: London, UK, 2015.
43. Sun, H.; Yang, H. Numerical investigation of the average wind speed of a single wind turbine and development of a novel three-dimensional multiple wind turbine wake model. *Renew. Energy* **2020**, *147*, 192–203. [CrossRef]
44. Hansen, M.O.L.; Sørensen, J.N.; Voutsinas, S.; Sørensen, N.; Madsen, H.A. State of the art in wind turbine aerodynamics and aeroelasticity. *Prog. Aerosp. Sci.* **2006**, *42*, 285–330. [CrossRef]
45. Greenwood, D.T. *Advanced Dynamics*; Cambridge University Press: Cambridge, UK, 2003.
46. Jazar, R.N. *Advanced Dynamics: Rigid Body, Multibody, and Aerospace Applications*; John Wiley & Sons: Hoboken, NJ, USA, 2011.
47. Roithmayr, C.M.; Hodges, D.H. Dynamics: Theory and Application of Kane's Method. *ASME J. Comput. Nonlinear Dyn.* **2016**, *11*, 11–066501. [CrossRef]
48. Jonkman, J.M.; Buhl, M.L., Jr. *FAST User's Guide*; National Renewable Energy Laboratory: Golden, CO, USA, 2005; p. 366.
49. Jonkman, J.M. Dynamics of offshore floating wind turbines—Model development and verification. *Wind Energy Int. J. Prog. Appl. Wind Power Convers. Technol.* **2009**, *12*, 459–492. [CrossRef]
50. Jonkman, B.J. *TurbSim User's Guide, Version 1.50*; National Renewable Energy Lab (NREL): Golden, CO, USA, 2009.
51. Soltani, M.N.; Knudsen, T.; Svenstrup, M.; Wisniewski, R.; Brath, P.; Ortega, R.; Johnson, K. Estimation of rotor effective wind speed: A comparison. *IEEE Trans. Control Syst. Technol.* **2013**, *21*, 1155–1167. [CrossRef]
52. Ding, S.; Hou, Q.; Wang, H. Disturbance-Observer-Based Second-Order Sliding Mode Controller for Speed Control of PMSM Drives. *IEEE Trans. Energy Convers.* **2022**, 1–10. [CrossRef]
53. Veysi, M.; Aghaei, J.; Soltanpour, M.R.; Shasadeghi, M.; Bahrani, B.; Ryan, D.J. Robust, Accurate and Fast Decentralized Power Sharing Mechanism for Isolated DC Microgrid Using Droop-Based Sliding Mode Control. *IEEE Trans. Smart Grid* **2022**. [CrossRef]
54. Shtessel, Y.; Edwards, C.; Fridman, L.; Levant, A. *Sliding Mode Control and Observation*; Springer: New York, NY, USA, 2014.
55. Lan, J.; Patton, R.J.; Zhu, X. Fault-tolerant wind turbine pitch control using adaptive sliding mode estimation. *Renew. Energy* **2018**, *116*, 219–231. [CrossRef]
56. Golnary, F.; Tse, K. Simultaneous active control of tower lateral vibration and power control of wind turbine: A novel multivariable approach. *Energy Rep.* **2022**, *8*, 4233–4251. [CrossRef]
57. Jang, J.-S. ANFIS: Adaptive-Network-based fuzzy inference system. *IEEE Trans. Syst. Man Cybern.* **1993**, *23*, 665–685. [CrossRef]
58. Lin, Z.; Chen, Z.; Liu, J.; Wu, Q. Coordinated mechanical loads and power optimization of wind energy conversion systems with variable-weight model predictive control strategy. *Appl. Energy* **2019**, *236*, 307–317. [CrossRef]
59. Song, D.; Liu, J.; Yang, Y.; Yang, J.; Su, M.; Wang, Y.; Gui, N.; Yang, X.; Huang, L.; Joo, Y.H. Maximum wind energy extraction of large-scale wind turbines using nonlinear model predictive control via Yin-Yang grey wolf optimization algorithm. *Energy* **2021**, *221*, 119866. [CrossRef]
60. Song, D.; Yang, Y.; Zheng, S.; Deng, X.; Yang, J.; Su, M.; Tang, W.; Yang, X.; Huang, L.; Joo, Y.H. New perspectives on maximum wind energy extraction of variable-speed wind turbines using previewed wind speeds. *Energy Convers. Manag.* **2020**, *206*, 112496. [CrossRef]
61. Moriarty, P.J.; Hansen, A.C. *AeroDyn Theory Manual*; National Renewable Energy Lab: Golden, CO, USA, 2005.
62. Veers, P.S. *Three-Dimensional Wind Simulation*; Sandia National Labs: Albuquerque, NM, USA, 1988.

mathematics

Article

A Hybrid Approach Based on Principal Component Analysis for Power Quality Event Classification Using Support Vector Machines

Akash Saxena [1], Ahmad M. Alshamrani [2], Adel Fahad Alrasheedi [2], Khalid Abdulaziz Alnowibet [2] and Ali Wagdy Mohamed [3,*]

1 Swami Keshvanand Institute of Technology, Management & Gramothan, Jaipur 302017, India
2 Statistics and Operations Research Department, College of Science, King Saud University, P.O. Box 2455, Riyadh 11451, Saudi Arabia
3 Operations Research Department, Faculty of Graduate Studies for Statistical Research, Cairo University, Giza 12613, Egypt
* Correspondence: aliwagdy@gmail.com

Abstract: Power quality has emerged as a sincere denominator in the planning and operation of a power system. Various events affect the quality of power at the distribution end of the system. Detection of these events has been a major thrust area in the last decade. This paper presents the application of Support Vector Machine (SVM) in classifying the power quality events. Well-known signal processing techniques, namely Hilbert transform and Wavelet transform, are employed to extract the potential features from the observation sets of voltages. Supervised architecture consisting of SVM has been constructed by tuning the parameters of SVM by various algorithms. It has been observed that Augmented Crow Search Algorithm (ACSA) yields the best accuracy compared to other contemporary optimizers. Further, Principal Component Analysis (PCA) is employed to choose the most significant features from the available features. On the basis of PCA, three different models of tuned SVMs are constructed. Comparative analysis of these three models, along with recently published approaches, is exhibited. Results are validated by the statistical one-way analysis of variance (ANOVA) method. It is observed that SVM, which contains attributes from both signal-processing techniques, gives satisfactory results.

Keywords: power quality; harmonics; Support Vector Machine (SVM); Augmented Crow Search Algorithm (ACSA)

MSC: 68T01; 68T05; 68T07; 68T09; 68T20; 68T30

Citation: Saxena, A.; Alshamrani, A.M.; Alrasheedi, A.F.; Alnowibet, K.A.; Mohamed, A.W. A Hybrid Approach Based on Principal Component Analysis for Power Quality Event Classification Using Support Vector Machines. *Mathematics* **2022**, *10*, 2780. https://doi.org/10.3390/math10152780

Academic Editors: Shujin Laima, Yong Cao, Xiaowei Jin and Hehe Ren

Received: 25 June 2022
Accepted: 28 July 2022
Published: 5 August 2022

Publisher's Note: MDPI stays neutral with regard to jurisdictional claims in published maps and institutional affiliations.

Copyright: © 2022 by the authors. Licensee MDPI, Basel, Switzerland. This article is an open access article distributed under the terms and conditions of the Creative Commons Attribution (CC BY) license (https://creativecommons.org/licenses/by/4.0/).

1. Introduction

In recent years, increasing demands and a competitive business environment have put a heavy burden on grid utilities. With modern power electronic devices, Power Quality (PQ) has become a major concern. In PQ problems, the deviation of voltage and current is observed from the ideal waveforms. Ideal voltage/current waveforms are sinusoidal signals of constant frequency and constant amplitudes [1]. Researchers have come forward with new approaches, designs, and hypotheses to improve the quality of power. Improvement of the quality refers to three common approaches namely identification, determination, and removal of the above said deviations from the voltage/current signals. Electromagnetic transients are the root cause of the PQ problems. These transients are occurred due to switching actions, lightning strokes, fault clearing mechanisms obtained by fuses, capacitor bank operation and end-user equipment switching [2]. Moreover the major causes of degradation in PQ are voltage sag, swell, flicker, notch, transients and harmonics [3–15]. PQ events recognition is an important issue for the development of the subsequent generation. This recognition can be done in two folds: firstly the employment of signal processing techniques like Wavelet transform [5,9,12,13] Discrete Fourier Transform (DFT) [4], Fast Fourier Transform (FFT) [5], Kalman filtering [3] and S-transforms [6–8,11] to extract few representative disturbance signals and secondly to use a supervised learning based paradigm for classification of the disturbances. Signal processing techniques are used for the separation of the disturbed signals into their frequency components. These processed frequency components with statistical attributes are characterized as features for classification. Traditionally Fourier transforms (FTs) are considered a powerful tool to analyze the frequency content of the signals. However, FTs are not efficient to extract the transient information from non-stationary signals [2]. Moreover, the non-stationary nature of PQ events also presents difficulty in the detection of disturbance waveforms. Recently, a Wavelet transform approach is applied by Yong et al. [9]. In this approach, one v/s and multiclass SVMs were employed. A three-stage algorithm namely preprocessing, feature extraction, and classification was employed in work [9]. Optimal feature selection by using k means aripori algorithm is performed in [13]. In the nine-level multiresolution analyses, Wavelet transform coefficients were obtained and a feature of having 90 dimensions is extracted from the signal data. SVM is used as a binary classifier to classify different events. Although Wavelet transforms are an efficient technique for feature extraction in the time and frequency domain, yet the excessive computation, vulnerability to the noise levels and dependency of the accuracy on the choice of mother wavelet make it less efficient for this recognition to be carried out. Another important methodology to detect PQ events is S-transform. Recently Biswal et al. [10] employed S-transform to extract the features from the disturbance signals by using a decision tree methodology. However, the decision tree methodology and several decision steps of the optimization algorithm caused time delay in classification. Short-Time Fourier Transform (STFT) was also employed in some approaches [4,5]. The quality of STFT is to divide the full time intervals into segments. However, the fixed window width of STFT is a significant limitation. The high-frequency signals, with multiple occurrences, pose a difficulty to detection. Recently, an interesting study of harmonic estimation with the application of a modified version of ACSA has been done in reference [16]. Till now various supervised learning models have been applied for the recognition of the PQ problems by researchers. These are namely Feed Forward Neural Network (FFNN), Radial Basis Function Neural Network (RBFNN) [15], Fuzzy classifiers [4,14], Modular Neural Networks [8], Probabilistic Neural Network [6] and Support Vector machines (SVMs) [9,10,12,13,17–20]. In some approaches Fuzzy classifiers are used along with Wavelet transforms [14], in which fuzzy classifier is advocated as a crisp classifier. The problem with fuzzy approaches is that there are no certain boundaries and a clear mathematical relationship between dependent and independent variables. For this reason, in many real classification problems, these approaches are not able to classify the events in an efficient manner. In the past, various approaches related to a single signal processing technique are observed and analyzed for PQ event classification problems. However, the combination of different signal processing techniques and statistical attributes of those remains unexplored. Further the reference [21], reports the application of optimized Bayesian convolutional neural networks for the classification of PQ events. The application of Variational Mode Decomposition and deep learning classifier (simple feed-forward neural network) has been employed for the classification of PQ events under the presence of distributed generation sources [22]. A Grey wolf Optimizer (GWO) based Extreme Learning Machine approach has been reported in reference [23]. The reference [24] reports the application of Discrete Wavelet Transform (DWT) on PQ data along with starting current data to identify the broken rotor bar and bearing fault in induction motors with a neural network for detection. A combined application of chirp mode pursuit and Grasshopper Optimization Algorithm has been reported in reference [25]. Real-time PQ analysis is conducted in reference [26].

The approaches pertaining to SVMs often employs optimization algorithms for tuning hyperparameters. As a parameter, tuning of the support vector machine always plays a critical role in the performance of classification accuracy. A hybrid algorithm-based approach has been proposed in reference to the identification of fault diagnosis of rotating machinery. The authors employed a hybrid algorithm called GWO and Sine Cosine Algorithm [27]. The GWO-based approach has been employed in the work for tuning the hyperparameter for the classification task [28]. In view of the above, the following literature review and objectives are formed for this work:

- To analyze two well-known signal processing techniques namely Hilbert and Wavelet transform for the PQ event classification problem.
- To perform the seven-level Multi-Resolution Analysis, in order to obtain the detailed and approximation coefficients of Wavelet transforms.
- To perform optimization with the help of a recently published advanced metaheuristic algorithm for hype parameter tuning of SVM and present a comparative analysis.
- To perform Principal Component Analysis (PCA) for choosing the efficient input features from the given 9 features.
- To build different modules of Support Vector Machines (SVMs) with the permutations of different efficient input features and present a comparison between these different modules on the basis of standard error indices.
- To test the efficacy of the proposed module by the statistical ANOVA test.

The remaining paper is organized as follows, In Section 2, system description along with preliminaries of PQ is discussed. The details of Hilbert and Wavelet transform are given in Section 3. Basics of SVM and tuning results are given in Section 4. In Section 5 PCA is discussed, following to this, results and conclusions are presented in Sections 6 and 7, respectively.

2. Materials and Methods

PQ disturbance classification is a potential area of research during the last decade. This section presents basic details for framing classification engine for PQ events.

2.1. *Power Quality Events*

PQ events are broadly classified into three categories namely short-term duration variations, e.g., sag, swell, interruptions [1]. Time durations of these events vary from a few cycles (5 cycles) to a minute. The second important category is the long duration, which consists of sustained interruptions, under voltage and overvoltages over a long time. The third category is transients. Description of the events along with the pictorial representation is exhibited in Table 1 and Figure 1 [29].

Table 1. Classification of power quality events.

S. No.	Categories	Duration	Voltage Magnitude
1.	Normal	-	Fundamental values
2.	Sag	Short term (up to 1 min)	0.1–0.9 p.u.
3.	Swell	Short term (up to 1 min)	1.1–1.4 p.u.
4.	Harmonic	Steady state THD > 5	
5.	Transients	<50 ns	0–4 p.u.

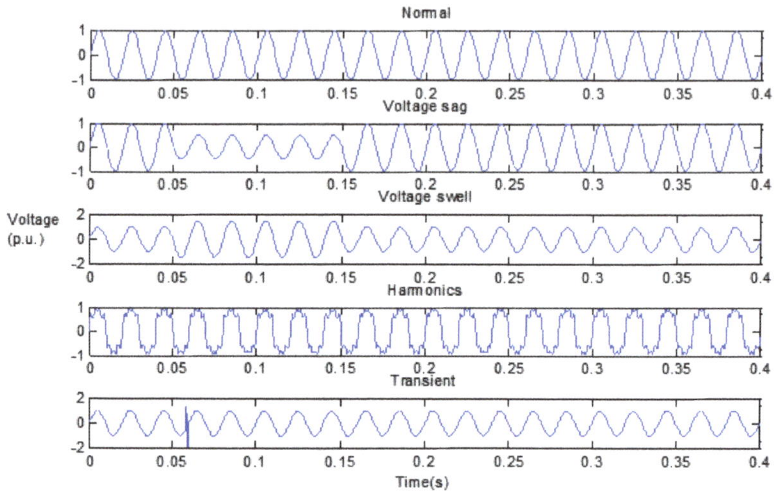

Figure 1. Different Power Quality Events.

2.2. System Description

To simulate this work a simple test network along with a laboratory setup, is shown in Figures 2 and 3. A three-phase power system (400 volts (line to line), 50 Hz) with a 100 km long transmission network terminated by an RL load of 10 ohms, 0.005 Henry is considered and simulated in Matlab Environment.

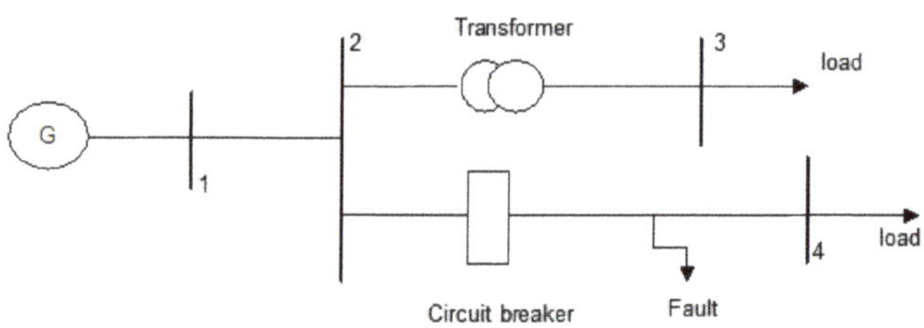

Figure 2. Test System.

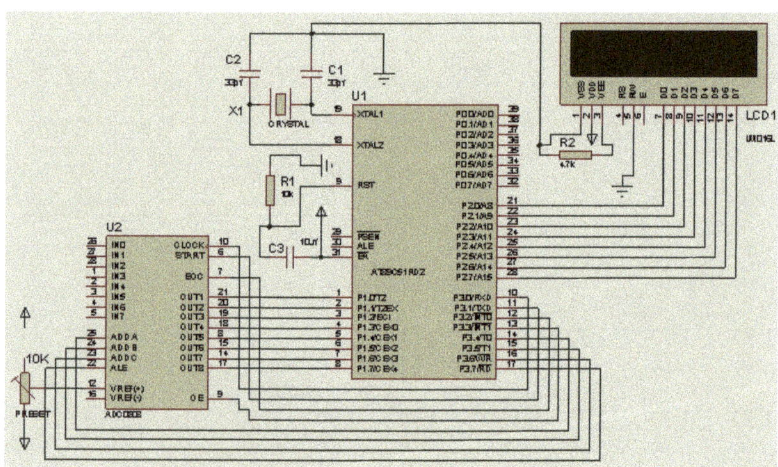

Figure 3. Laboratory Testing Module.

To analyze the system voltages, a potential transformer is employed with an Analog to Digital Converter IC-ADC 0808/0809. This chip is employed to convert analog signals into digital signals. This IC is an 8-bit IC; input three-phase voltages are given on input channels 0–2. The 8051 (Philips) P89V51RD2 microcontroller is the main processing unit for calculating the Hilbert and Wavelet transforms. The unit analyzes the output voltages along with the statistical attributes of features (standard deviations, mean, max, min, and norm values).

A seven-level Multi-Resolution Analysis (MRA) is processed for Wavelet transforms. The detailed coefficients window is shown in Figure 4a–d. Further, the digital to analog conversion is done with the help of DAC to show the status of waveforms. The responses under different operating conditions are analyzed by the controller and used for validation of the results of SVMs. The program for the micro-controller is written in C language. Liquid Crystal Display (LCD) 16 × 2 is used to display the results. In the first row, the initial five digits represent the target classes for all voltages. Target classes are shown in Table 2.

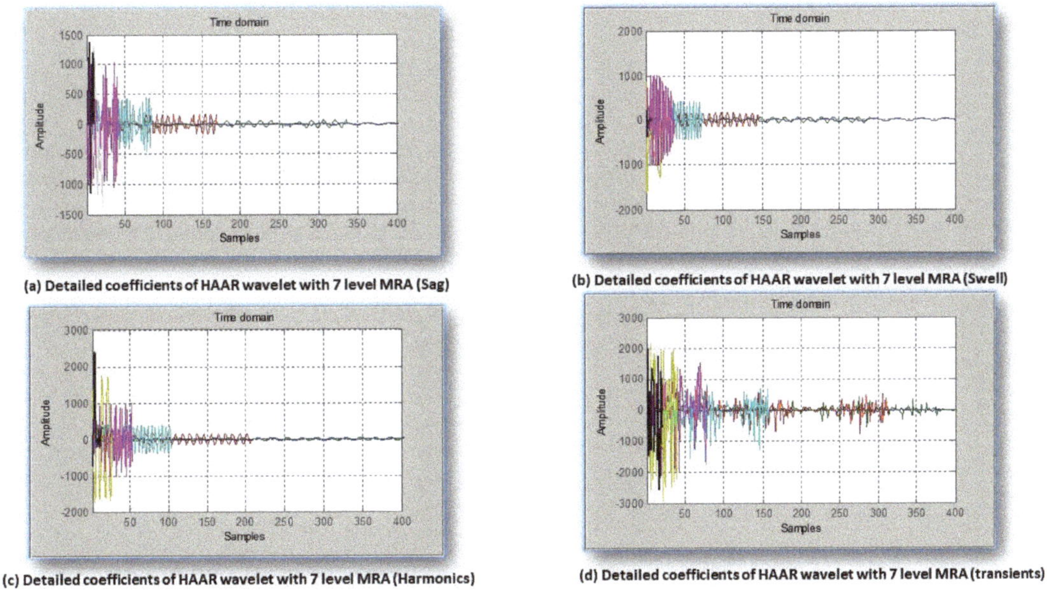

Figure 4. Analysis of detailed coefficients of HAAR Wavelet with different PQ events.

Table 2. Binary Classification for PQ event detection.

Sag	1	0	0	0	0
Swell	0	1	0	0	0
Normal	0	0	1	0	0
Transients	0	0	0	1	0
Harmonics	0	0	0	0	1

3. Signal Processing Techniques

In PQ events identification problems, the employment of an effective signal processing technique to extract significant features from the signals is the fulcrum of the module. In this section preliminaries pertaining to Wavelet and Hilbert transforms signal processing techniques are presented.

3.1. Wavelet Transform

In past, Wavelet transform shows the extraordinary capability to extract features in terms of detailed and approximate coefficients belonging to different event types. In reference [11], the coefficients associated with different levels along with statistical attributes of the coefficients are employed to train the neural networks. However, this procedure has a large number of input features according to different levels and incurs a heavy computational burden. Choice of mother Wavelet is also a critical issue in the Wavelet transforms. In this work "Haar" Wavelet is chosen for the feature extraction. "Haar" Wavelet is the simplest possible Wavelet and can be utilized for the analysis of signals with sudden transitions. A seven-level MRA is performed to extract detail and approximate coefficients. The detail and approximate coefficients alone are impractical to apply as inputs to the classifier. Hence, for each decomposition level, feature extraction methods are implemented. The energy at the decomposition level is given by the following equations:

$$E_i = \sum_{l=1}^{n} |D_{il}|^2 \quad i = 1,2,\ldots,7 \tag{1}$$

$$K_i = \sum_{l=1}^{n} |A_{il}|^2 \tag{2}$$

l is the decomposition level and n is the number of coefficients of detail or approximations at each decomposition level. Statistical attributes namely maximum, minimum, norm, mean values, and standard deviations of these coefficients at different decomposition levels are taken as the features. Figure 4a–d presents Detailed coefficients in a single window analyzer cumulatively for five events respectively. From this figure, it is empirical to judge that for complex events and with different multiple data sets, achieving higher classification rates from these features is a daunting task to perform. Windows for different events have been shown in Figure 4; it is empirical to judge that a clear distinction can be done by this transformation.

3.2. Hilbert Transform

Hilbert transform is a mathematical tool for the generation of an analytical signal from a real signal. It is obtained by convolving the real signal $g(t)$ with the function$(1/\pi t)$.

$$gH(t) = g(t)\left(\frac{1}{\pi t}\right) = \frac{1}{\pi}\int_{-\infty}^{\infty} g\left(\frac{\alpha}{t-\alpha}\right) d\alpha \tag{3}$$

A complex signal xc(k) consists of the original signal as a real part, and its Hilbert transform as an imaginary part. In this paper, the imaginary part of the complex voltage signal is captured for different types of events, and the statistical attributes are calculated of the transformed signals. Different statistical attributes of the Hilbert transform are employed as input features to SVM. Different statistical attributes for different events are shown in Figure 5. It is empirical to judge that for the events like sag, swell harmonics and transient this feature can be the source of important information to train the classifier. From Figures 4 and 5, it is judged that in many cases the performance of the classifier is based on the datasets.

Since no significant variations are observed in mean values, the following analysis will not include the mean of the signals as a potential feature. To compete with the pattern recognition-based classifiers, a hybrid approach, which employs features from both signal-processing techniques is more fruitful for such real problems. The motivation for this work hails from here only.

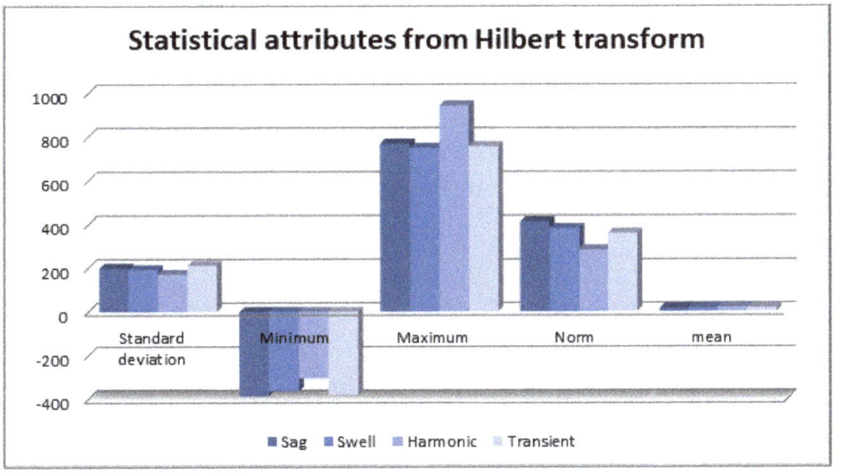

Figure 5. Values of different statistical attributes of Hilbert transforms for different events.

4. Support Vector Machines

In recent years, the applications of SVM in classification problems have increased due to its capability in the segregation of datasets by the best hyperplane. SVMs are applied for classification of PQ events [9,10,12,13,17–20], multi-dimensional data classification [17], classification of microarrays [18], wind speed prediction [19], voltage stability monitoring [20] and many more. The popularity of SVM is rising with every passing day because it can handle large feature space. Also, a large feature space cannot hinder the classification accuracy. In the case of other classifiers, the input feature space dimension is a very crucial design parameter [9].

Due to this virtue of SVM, its employment is a primary reason for large classification problems. SVM utilizes various kernel functions to transfer the input space of data to nonlinear high-dimensional data. A sparse prediction function is generated by choosing a selected number of points; these points are Support Vectors (SVs). SVMs possess two main features such as structural risk minimization and a tradeoff between empirical error and model complexity [19].

Let the n-dimensional inputs Xi (i = 1, 2, 3, …, m), where m is the number of samples belonging to class 1 and class 2. Associated labels are $K_{(i)} = 1$ and $K_{(i)} = -1$. SVM is an inherently two-class separator, hence, the linear hyperplane that separates the data can be determined by the following equation:

$$f(z) = W^T z + d = \sum_{k=1}^{n} W_k z_k + d \tag{4}$$

where W is an n-dimensional vector and d is scalar. These two parameters determine the location of the hyperplane. The constraints are $f(z) \geq 1$ if $K_{(i)} \geq 1$ and $f(z) \leq 1$ if $K_{(i)} \leq -1$. The separating data plane that generates the maximum distance between the nearest data and the plane, is called the optimal separating hyperplane. Geometric margin $\|w\|^{-2}$ and insensitive loss function ε are the most important parameters in SVM design. Let the error between predicted results and targets be visualized by ε, that is

$$|y - f(z)| = \left\{ \begin{array}{cc} 0 & |y - f(z)| \leqslant \varepsilon \\ |y - f(z) - \varepsilon| & |y - f(z)| \succ \varepsilon \end{array} \right\} \tag{5}$$

The optimization problem, which is convex in nature, is now converted to the minimization of geometric margin. This objective is subjected to the minimization of the error between predicted values and simulated values. The objective function I can be represented as:

$$I = min\frac{1}{2}||w||^2 \tag{6}$$

$$Subjectto(y - W.f(z) - d - \varepsilon) \leq 0 \tag{7}$$

$$(W.f(z) + d - y_i) \leq \varepsilon \;\; i = 1, 2, \ldots, m \tag{8}$$

Since the problems of PQ disturbance identification is data specific and also system specific, hence, it is necessary to add the non-negative slack variable χ. The convex optimization problem can be converted as follows:

$$I = min\frac{1}{2}||w||^2 + A\sum_{i=1}^{m}\chi_i \tag{9}$$

$$Subjectto(y - Wf(z) - d) \leq (\varepsilon + \chi_i), \;\; \chi_i \geqslant 0 \;\; i = 1, 2, \ldots, m \tag{10}$$

To find the optimal values, the problem (6) can be rearranged by the Langragian saddle point method, that is

$$L = \frac{1}{2}||w||^2 + A\sum_{i=1}^{m}\chi_i + \beta\sum_{1}^{m}(-y + Wf(z) + d + \varepsilon + \chi_i) - \sum_{1}^{m}\gamma\varepsilon_i \tag{11}$$

Hence, the classification-based optimization problem can be solved with respect to the primal variables W, d, ε, and χ. However, as per reported results in reference [30], we used a Radial Basis Function (RBF) kernel for the classification task. In general, also, the RBF function is the most common choice as the mercer kernel function because of its Gaussian function form. However, for tuning the parameters of SVM, we have experimented with 6 advanced algorithms. The detailed analysis of these algorithms and experimental results tuning are shown in the following subsection.

Choice of Algorithm for Parameter Tuning

In the past, various attempts have been made to tune the hyperparameters of the SVM in many approaches. Proper tuning of these parameters enhances the classification accuracy of the classifier. For constructing the optimization routine, an objective function that is based on the maximization of classification accuracy of the PQ events is considered here. For robustness of optimization, we have taken 2500 samples of different PQ events and classify according to the discussion presented in previous sections. For comparing the optimization performance, the search agents no. along with maximum iteration have been kept constant for all algorithms. Also, the parameter pertaining to algorithms are taken from the references. The following algorithms are considered for tuning tasks:

1. Augmented Crow Search Algorithm (ACSA): The author of the ACSA has developed a new variant of the Crow Search Algorithm. The author modified the algorithm by incorporating Opposition based learning and a gradient-based scheme for better exploration and exploitation.
2. Whale Optimization Algorithm (WOA): The recent application of WOA in the field of Demand Side Management (DSM) inspired authors to design and optimize the hyperparameter of SVM with the help of WOA.
3. Intelligent Grey Wolf Optimizer (IGWO): In a recent application of IGWO, the estimation of solar panel parameters attracted the interest of researchers, as well the authors of this paper for employing the algorithm for tuning task. The algorithm employs a sinusoidal bridging parameter and Opposition based learning.
4. Gaining Sharing Knowledge based Algorithm (GSK): The algorithm has previously been applied for classification tasks. The performance of the algorithm on various mathematical functions primarily became the criterion for choosing it.

5. Chaotic Marine Predator Algorithm (CMPA): A recently published chaotic version of the Marine Predator Algorithm and its performance on feature selection tasks inspired the authors to employ CMPA in tuning tasks. The algorithm embeds a chaotic function for position update in its intermediate stage.
6. Augmented Whale Optimization Algorithm (AWOA): This algorithm primarily works on Opposition based learning and updating of position based on the Cauchy mutation operator. The AWOA has been tested over a number of benchmark functions along with the real application.

The analysis of the results is shown in Table 3. For comparing the optimization performance, search agents no., maximum no. of iteration are kept constant. From the table, it has been observed the highest classification rate acquired with the help of ACSA that is 96.2%. Hence, for further analysis, ACSA has been taken for tuning the parameters of SVM. The following section presents the feature selection process based on PCA.

Table 3. Comparative analysis of different optimization algorithms for hyper-parameter tuning.

Size of Data Sets	Algorithm	Attribute of Algorithm	Regularization Parameter	Kernel Parameter	Classification
2500	ACSA [16]	Inculcation of OBL and bridging of the exploration and exploitation phase	10.523	0.325	96.2
2500	WOA [31]	hunting behavior of the whale	10.365	0.315	94.35
2500	IGWO [32]	OBL and Bridging through sinusoidal turncated function	10.245	0.369	92.65
2500	GSK [33]	Based on the behavior of gaining and sharing knowledge	10.362	0.354	91.25
2500	CMPA [34]	Chaotic algorithm that employs chaotic position update system	10.012	0.3257	94.21
2500	AWOA [35]	Cauchy mutation operator based position update	10.215	0.366	94.36

5. PCA-Based Feature Selection for PQ Event Classification

The efficiency of the supervised learning models is highly affected by the size of the features. To reduce the dimensionality of the input feature matrix, PCA is a well-known methodology. Recently PCA is used for wind speed prediction [19], building forecasting models for electricity consumption prediction [36] and for fault detection [37]. In PQ event detection problem, different statistical attributes of the output of signal processing techniques are chosen as input features. In this work, the dimension of the input feature size is 9. The first five attributes are from Wavelet transform and the last four are extracted from the Hilbert transform technique. It is necessary to select the major factors that contribute to the relevant information about the event using the well-known principal component analysis. The observation matrix (O) is first designed as:

$$O = \begin{bmatrix} k_1 & k_2 & k_3 & k_4 & k_5 & k_6 & k_7 & k_8 & k_9 \end{bmatrix} = \begin{bmatrix} k_{11} & k_{12} & k_{13} & k_{14} & k_{15} & k_{16} & k_{17} & k_{18} & k_{19} \\ \vdots & \vdots & \vdots & \vdots & \vdots & \vdots & \vdots & \vdots & \\ k_{s1} & k_{s2} & k_{s3} & k_{s4} & k_{s5} & k_{s6} & k_{s7} & k_{s8} & k_{s9} \end{bmatrix} \quad (12)$$

where s is the sample size (2500), the remaining variables are as follows:

$$k_1 = \frac{1}{s}\sum_{j=1}^{7} A_b(j) - \frac{1}{s}\sum_{j=1}^{7}\left(A_b(j)^2\right) \quad (13)$$

$$k_2 = min(A_b) \quad (14)$$

$$k_3 = norm(A_b) \quad (15)$$

$$k_4 = max(A_b) \quad (16)$$

$$k_5 = \frac{1}{s}\sum A_b \quad (17)$$

$$k_6 = \frac{1}{s}\sum_{j=1}^{j=s} X_h - \frac{1}{s}\sum_{j=1}^{j=s}(X_h)^2 \quad (18)$$

$$k_7 = minX_h \quad (19)$$

$$k_8 = normX_h \quad (20)$$

$$k_9 = maxX_h \quad (21)$$

Here $k_1 = \begin{bmatrix} k_{11} & k_{21} & \ldots & k_{s1} \end{bmatrix}$ and so on $k_9 = \begin{bmatrix} k_{19} & k_{29} & \ldots & k_{s9} \end{bmatrix}$ and A_b is the detailed coefficients of seven-level MRA of Wavelet transforms. X_h is the Hilbert transform of the voltage signals. Further, these features are normalized between 0.1 to 0.9 and the correlation coefficient matrix C_R is created as follows.

$$C_R = \begin{bmatrix} R_{11} & R_{12} & \ldots & R_{19} \\ R_{21} & R_{22} & \ldots & R_{29} \\ \vdots & \vdots & \vdots & \vdots \\ R_{91} & R_{92} & \ldots & R_{99} \end{bmatrix} \quad (22)$$

where

$$R_{ij} = \frac{\sum_{m=1}^{m=s} k^*_{mi} k^*_{mj}}{s-1} \quad (23)$$

and

$$k^*_{ij} = \frac{k_{ij} - k_j}{\sqrt{var(k_j)}}, k_j = \frac{\sum_1^s k_{ij}}{s} \quad (24)$$

Hence, the eigenvalue associated with this correlation matrix will be $(E_1 \ldots E_9)$. The contribution rate γ_i associated with each principal component can be calculated as:

$$\gamma_i = \frac{E_i}{\sum_{j=1}^{j=9} E_i} \quad (25)$$

The contribution rates of the different transforms are shown in Table 4. Based on the contribution rates various permutations of input features are constructed for SVM. Three modules are constructed with three different permutations of features; details and analysis of the results are given in the following sections.

Table 4. Results of Principal Component Analysis.

Signal Processing Technique	Principal Components	Eigenvalues	Contribution Rates (%)	Accumulative Contribution (%)
Hilbert Transform	Standard Deviation	3.1176	34.64	34.64
	Minimum Value	2.6355	29.28	63.92
	Norm Value	0.9305	10.34	74.26
	Maximum Value	0.8502	9.44	83.71
Wavelet Transform (Detailed Energy coefficients)	Standard Deviation	0.6518	7.24	90.95
	Minimum Value	0.4394	4.88	95.83
	Norm Value	0.2778	3.09	98.92
	Maximum Value	0.0969	1.08	100
	Mean Values	0.0001782	0.01	100

6. Results

This section presents a comparative analysis of the results obtained from the application of different combinations of SVMs obtained from PCA in the classification of different PQ events. The real power system model is simulated in Matlab. Different PQ events such as sag, swell, normal (without sag and swell), transients, and harmonics are simulated with the consideration of interruptions. Binary classification is used with five target classes namely sag, swell, transient, harmonics, and normal. Table 2 shows binary classification for PQ event detection. Total 2500 samples are generated for this classification task i.e., 500 for each event. Out of 2500 samples, 70% datasets are used for training purposes, the remaining 15% for testing, and 15% for validation. Signals are sampled at 256 points/cycle and the normal frequency is 50 Hz.

Hilbert transform and Wavelet transforms are applied to extract the information from the generated signals. Different statistical attributes of Hilbert transforms and Wavelet transforms namely minimum, maximum, standard deviation, and norm of the Hilbert coefficients and detailed energy coefficients are employed as an input feature for SVM. The nine significant features are extracted from this simulation process. The contribution rates and accumulative contribution rates are shown in Table 4. To carry out this analysis in a meaningful manner, different possible combinations of SVMs are employed and efficacy of the each module is tested.

The results of PCA are shown in Table 4. As per the datasets obtained from PCA, it is observed that the values of contribution rates for all statistical attributes of Hilbert coefficients along with standard deviations and minimum values of detailed energy coefficients of the Wavelet transform contribute around 95.82%. For this reason, these features are employed to construct the different architecture of SVMs.

Observation sets for SVM-1: In this observation set two extinct features of highest contribution rates (standard deviations and minimum values of Hilbert transform coefficients) are selected as input features. The confusion value for this module is 0.087. The confusion diagram for this classifier is exhibited in Figure 6a.

Observation sets for SVM-2: In this observation set all four features extracted from the statistical attributes of Hilbert transforms are employed. The confusion rate for this module is 0.043 and the confusion diagram for this classifier is shown in Figure 6b.

Observation sets for SVM-3: In this observation set all four features extracted from the statistical attributes of Hilbert transforms and two distinct features namely minimum values and standard deviations of detailed energy coefficients of Wavelet transforms are employed. The confusion rate for this module is 0.038 and the confusion diagram for this classifier is presented in Figure 6c.

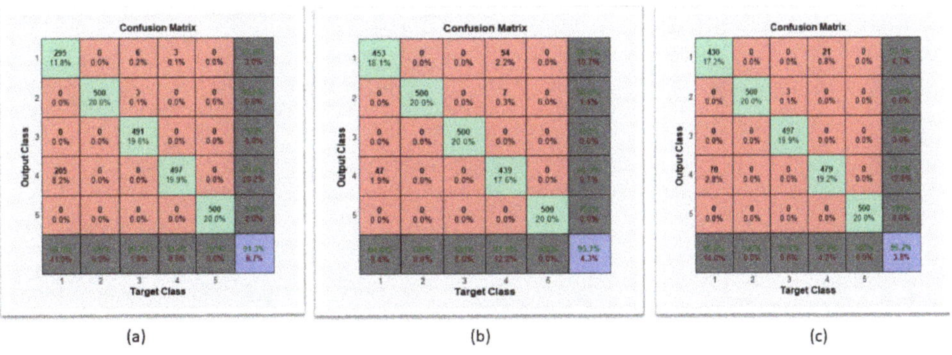

Figure 6. Comparative Analysis of Observation sets for SVM module 1 (**a**–**c**) to SVM module 3.

6.1. Discussions

Three standard error criteria are applied to measure the efficacy of these modules. These are Mean Square Error (MSE), Mean Absolute Error (MAE), and Root Mean Square Error (RMSE). Definitions of these indices are taken from [19]. From Figure 7, it is empirical to judge that the values for these error indices are minimum for SVM-3. Moreover, higher values are obtained for SVM-1 and RBFNN. The corresponding values of these error indices are shown in Table 5. In order to judge the classifier performance, confusion diagrams are utilized.

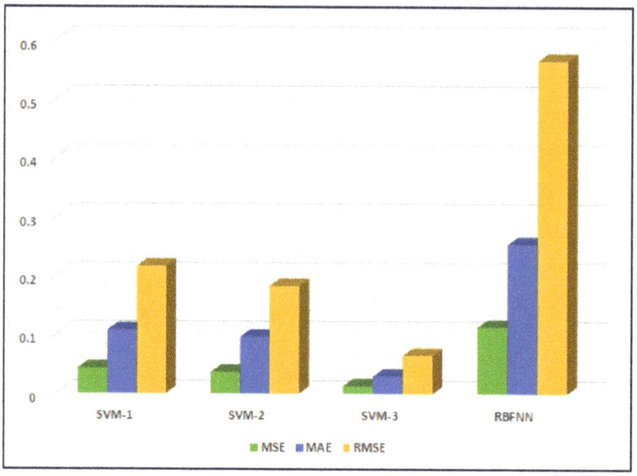

Figure 7. Error Indices.

Table 5. Comparison of Error Indices.

Supervised Learning Model	MSE	MAE	RMSE
SVM-1	0.0433	0.1076	0.2164
SVM-2	0.0365	0.0960	0.1824
SVM-3	0.0130	0.0297	0.0649
RBFNN	0.1131	0.2541	0.5655

The lower value of confusion indicates the higher classification efficacy of the classifier. As calculated, in this case, SVM-3 proves to be a better classifier. From Figure 6a it is empirical to judge that the classifier is able to judge the 91.3% events only. For class 1 the classification efficiency is 59% only. However, in classes 3 and 4, 98.2% and 99.4% efficiency are achieved by SVM-1 respectively. Figure 6b shows the classification accuracy of SVM module 2.

Similarly for SVM-3 as shown in Figure 6c the performance is 96.2%. Classification efficiencies for each class are indicated in the confusion diagrams and these are (86, 100, 99.4, 95.8, and 100%). It can be concluded that the statistical attributes of Hilbert coefficients and Wavelet energy coefficients provide a good combination as input features and SVM-3 gives a good performance as compared with the other two modules and RBFNN. To compare the performance of these classifiers few statistical tests are conducted here.

6.2. Statistical Analysis

The improved performance of SVM-3 over the existing method and other modules can be realized through statistical analysis. This module should be statistically significant in terms of error measures, classification accuracy, or any other classification problems. Implications of statistical tests and analytical measures in classification problems are discussed by Demsar [38]. In this paper one-way ANOVA test (fisher) [39,40] has been performed. The objective of ANOVA is to test the hypothesis to evaluate variability in the performance of the models. A null hypothesis can be constructed that all classifiers have the same classification accuracy. Rejection of this hypothesis can be based on error variability. To conduct this test, 5 fold cross validation technique is used. Classifier accuracies of different datasets of different capacities on all three SVMs are exhibited in Table 6. Datasets of different capacities are prepared and all three SVM models are applied. The simulation results are depicted in Figure 8.

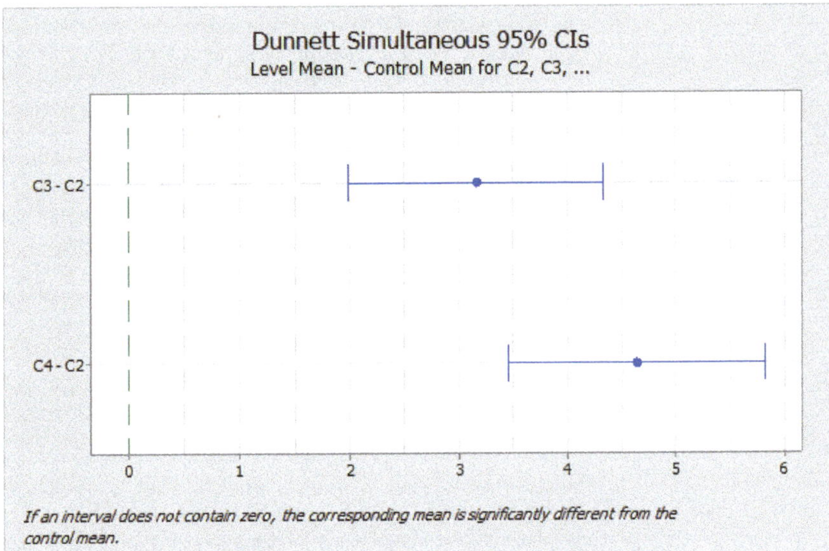

Figure 8. Test results for ANOVA—Dunnett simultaneous statistical test.

Table 6. Classification Accuracy of All SVM models for different datasets.

Model	Size of Datasets				
	500	1000	1500	2000	2500
SVM-1	90.89	91.01	90.49	90.36	91.3
SVM-2	93.14	92.98	93.75	94.29	95.7
SVM-3	94.9	95.4	94.76	95.78	96.2

6.3. Null Hypothesis

All means are equal (the classification efficiency of all classifiers is the same). This test has been carried out using one-way ANOVA in Duncan multiple test range [41] with 95% confidence interval, (0.05) significance level, and linear polynomial contrast and the results have been presented in Table 7 and Figure 8 shows the results of ANOVA test. In Duncan, multiple tests a control variable is considered, and the classification accuracy of SVM-2 (C2) is taken as a control variable.

Table 7. ANOVA results.

Model	Factor (N)	Mean	Standard Deviation	Confidence Interval for Mean	
				Upper Bound	Lower Bound
SVM-1	5	90.81	0.385	90.086	91.534
SVM-2	5	93.97	1.097	93.248	94.696
SVM-3	5	95.44	0.551	94.724	96.172

7. Conclusions

With the ever-rising concern of design engineers to attain a high quality of power, the focus is on PQ event classification and mitigation of unwanted signals. This paper had presented a combined application of SVM and signal processing techniques in PQ event classification. The salient features of this work are as follows:

1. Combined input features based on Wavelet and Hilbert transforms are employed to train, test, and validate the supervised learning module SVM for efficient detection of PQ events.

2. The tuning of SVM hyperparameters is carried out with the help of the latest developed versions of optimization algorithms. Some of the algorithms are developed by the authors, it has been concluded that ACSA yields the best classification accuracy.
3. Principal Component Analysis is carried out to detect efficient features from a large pool, based on different features; three models of SVMs are constructed. The comparison of these three modules is carried out based on the three-error criteria MSE, MAE, and RMSE.
4. Classification accuracy of these modules is tested based on confusion values and diagrams, it is concluded that SVM-3, possesses features from both transforms and gives the best results.
5. Last but not least, the validation of obtained results is carried out with a statistical ANOVA test. Rejection of the Null hypothesis is done based on obtained statistical values and the Dunnett test.

Application of these modules on a wind dominating system will be addressed in the future. Also, the application of deep learning models will be explored with the combined application of optimization, signal processing, and data mining.

Author Contributions: Formal analysis, K.A.A. and A.S.; Funding acquisition, K.A.A.; Investigation, K.A.A.; Methodology, A.F.A. and A.S.; Project administration, A.W.M.; Software, A.S.; Supervision, A.S. and A.W.M.; Validation, A.F.A. and A.W.M.; Visualization, A.F.A. and A.M.A.; Writing—original draft, A.S.; Writing—review & editing, A.M.A. and A.S. All authors have read and agreed to the published version of the manuscript.

Funding: The research is funded by Researchers Supporting Program at King Saud University, (RSP-2021/323).

Institutional Review Board Statement: Not applicable.

Informed Consent Statement: Not applicable.

Data Availability Statement: Not Applicable.

Acknowledgments: The authors present their appreciation to King Saud University for funding the publication of this research through the Researchers Supporting Program (RSP-2021/323), King Saud University, Riyadh, Saudi Arabia.

Conflicts of Interest: The authors declare no conflict of interest.

Abbreviations

The following abbreviations are used in this manuscript:

PQ	Power Quality
SVM	Support Vector Machine
ACSA	Augmented Crow Search Algorithm
PCA	Principal Component Analysis
FS	Feature Selection
MSE	Mean Square Error
MAE	Mean Absolute Error
RMSE	Root Mean Square Error

References

1. Acha, E.; Madrial, M. *Power System Harmonics: Computer Modeling and Analysis*; John Wiley and Sons Ltd.: London, UK, 2001.
2. Arrillaga, J.; Watson, N.R.; Chen, S. *Power System Quality Assessment*; John Wiley and Sons Ltd.: London, UK, 2000.
3. Dash, P.K.; Chilukuri, M.V. Hybrid S-transform and Kalman filtering approach for detection and measurement of short duration disturbances in power networks. *IEEE Trans. Instrum. Meas.* **2004**, *53*, 588–596. [CrossRef]
4. Dash, P.K.; Mishra, S.; Salama, M.M.A.; Liew, A.C. Classification of power system disturbances using a fuzzy expert system and a Fourier linear combiner. *IEEE Trans. Power Deliv.* **2000**, *15*, 472–477. [CrossRef]
5. Santoso, S.; Grady, W.M.; Powers, E.J.; Lamoree, J.; Bhatt, S.C. Characterization of disturbance power quality event with Fourier and wavelet transforms. *IEEE Trans. Power Deliv.* **2000**, *15*, 247–254. [CrossRef]

6. Mishra, S.; Bende, C.N.; Panigrahi, B.K. Detection and classification of power quality disturbances using S-transform and probabilistic neural networks. *IEEE Trans. Power Deliv.* **2008**, *23*, 280–287. [CrossRef]
7. Dash, P.K.; Panigrahi, B.K.; Panda, G. Power quality analysis using S-transform. *IEEE Trans. Power Deliv.* **2003**, *18*, 406–411. [CrossRef]
8. Bendhe, C.N.; Mishra, S.; Panigah, P.K.I. Detection and classification of power quality disturbances using S-transform and modular neural network. *Electr. Power Syst. Res.* **2008**, *78*, 122–128. [CrossRef]
9. Yong, D.D.; Bhowmik, S.; Magnago, F. An effective Power Quality classifier using Wavelet Transform and Support Vector Machines. *Expert Syst. Appl.* **2015**, *42*, 6075–6081. [CrossRef]
10. Biswal, B.; Biswal, M.K.; Dash, P.K.; Mishra, S. Power quality event characterization using support vector machine and optimization using advanced immune algorithm. *Neuro Comput.* **2013**, *103*, 75–86. [CrossRef]
11. Erişti, H.; Yıldırım, Ö.; Erişti, B.; Demir, Y. Automatic recognition system of underlying causes of power quality disturbances based on S-Transform and Extreme Learning Machine. *Int. J. Electr. Power Energy Syst.* **2014**, *61*, 553–562. [CrossRef]
12. Ekici, S. Classification of power system disturbances using support vector machines. *Expert Syst. Appl.* **2009**, *36*, 9859–9868. [CrossRef]
13. Erişti, H.; Demir, Y. A new algorithm for automatic classification of power quality events based on wavelet transform and SVM. *Expert Syst. Appl.* **2010**, *37*, 4094–4102. [CrossRef]
14. Meher, S.K.; Pradhan, A.K. Fuzzy classifiers for power quality events analysis. *Electr. Power Syst. Res.* **2010**, *80*, 71–76. [CrossRef]
15. Jayasree, T.; Devaraj, D.; Sukanesh, R. Power quality disturbance classification using Hilbert transform and RBF networks. *Neuro Comput.* **2010**, *73*, 1451–1456. [CrossRef]
16. Saxena, A. An efficient harmonic estimator design based on Augmented Crow Search Algorithm in noisy environment. *Expert Syst. Appl.* **2022**, *194*, 116470. [CrossRef]
17. Cyganek, B.; Krawczyk, B.; Woźniak, M. Multidimensional data classification with chordal distance based kernel and Support Vector Machines. *Eng. Appl. Artif. Intell.* **2015**, *46*, 10–22. [CrossRef]
18. Kumar, M.; Rath, S.K. Classification of microarray using Map Reduce based proximal support vector machine classifier. *Knowl. Based Syst.* **2015**, *89*, 584-602. [CrossRef]
19. Kong, X.; Liu, X.; Shi, R.; Lee, K.Y. Wind speed prediction using reduced support vector machines with feature selection. *Neuro Comput.* **2015**, *169*, 449–456. [CrossRef]
20. Sajan, K.S.; Kumar, V.; Tyagi, B. Genetic algorithm based support vector machine for on-line voltage stability monitoring. *Int. J. Electr. Power Energy Syst.* **2015**, *73*, 200–208. [CrossRef]
21. Ekici, S.; Ucar, F.; Dandil, B.; Arghandeh, R. Power quality event classification using optimized Bayesian convolutional neural networks. *Electr. Eng.* **2021**, *103*, 67–77. [CrossRef]
22. Subudhi, U.; Dash, S. Detection and classification of power quality disturbances using GWO ELM. *J. Ind. Inf. Integr.* **2021**, *22*, 100204. [CrossRef]
23. Cortes-Robles, O.; Barocio, E.; Obushevs, A.; Korba, P.; Sevilla, F.R.S. Fast-training feedforward neural network for multi-scale power quality monitoring in power systems with distributed generation sources. *Measurement* **2021**, *170*, 108690. [CrossRef]
24. Ganesan, S.; David, P.W.; Balachandran, P.K.; Samithas, D. Intelligent starting current-based fault identification of an induction motor operating under various power quality issues. *Energies* **2021**, *14*, 304. [CrossRef]
25. Motlagh, S.Z.; Foroud, A.A. Power quality disturbances recognition using adaptive chirp mode pursuit and grasshopper optimized support vector machines. *Measurement* **2021**, *168*, 108461. [CrossRef]
26. Bandla, P.B.; Vairavasundaram, I.; Teekaraman, Y.; Kuppusamy, R.; Nikolovski, S. Real Time Sustainable Power Quality Analysis of Non-Linear Load under Symmetrical Conditions. *Energies* **2021**, *15*, 57. [CrossRef]
27. Fu, W.; Tan, J.; Zhang, X.; Chen, T.; Wang, K. Blind parameter identification of MAR model and mutation hybrid GWO-SCA optimized SVM for fault diagnosis of rotating machinery. *Complexity* **2019**, *2019*, 3264969. [CrossRef]
28. Eswaramoorthy, S.; Sivakumaran, N.; Sekaran, S. Grey wolf optimization based parameter selection for support vector machines. *COMPEL* **2016**, 35, 1513–1523. [CrossRef]
29. Thakur, P.; Singh, A.K.; Bansal, R.C. A novel way for classification and type detection of voltage sag. *IET-Gener. Transm. Distrib.* **2013**, *7*, 398–404. [CrossRef]
30. Saxena, A.; Shekhawat, S. Ambient air quality classification by grey wolf optimizer based support vector machine. *J. Environ. Public Health* **2017**, *2017*, 3131083. [CrossRef]
31. Sharma, A.K.; Saxena, A. A demand side management control strategy using Whale optimization algorithm. *SN Appl. Sci.* **2019**, *1*, 870. [CrossRef]
32. Saxena, A.; Sharma, A.; Shekhawat, S. Parameter extraction of solar cell using intelligent grey wolf optimizer. *Evol. Intell.* **2020**, *15*, 167–183. [CrossRef]
33. Mohamed, A.W.; Hadi, A.A.; Mohamed, A.K.; Awad, N.H. Evaluating the performance of adaptive GainingSharing knowledge based algorithm on CEC 2020 benchmark problems. In Proceedings of the 2020 IEEE Congress on Evolutionary Computation (CEC), Glasgow, UK, 19–24 July 2020; pp. 1–8.
34. Alrasheedi, A.F.; Alnowibet, K.A.; Saxena, A.; Sallam, K.M.; Mohamed, A.W. Chaos Embed Marine Predator (CMPA) Algorithm for Feature Selection. *Mathematics* **2022**, *10*, 1411. [CrossRef]

35. Alnowibet, K.A.; Shekhawat, S.; Saxena, A.; Sallam, K.M.; Mohamed, A.W. Development and Applications of Augmented Whale Optimization Algorithm. *Mathematics* **2022**, *10*, 2076. [CrossRef]
36. Li, K.; Hu, C.; Liu, G.; Xue, W. Building's electricity consumption prediction using optimized artificial neural networks and principal component analysis. *Energy Build.* **2015**, *108*, 106–113. [CrossRef]
37. Huang, J.; Yan, X. Dynamic process fault detection and diagnosis based on dynamic principal component analysis, dynamic independent component analysis and Bayesian inference. *Chemom. Intell. Lab. Syst.* **2015**, *148*, 115–127. [CrossRef]
38. Demšar, J. Statistical comparisons of classifiers over multiple data sets. *J. Mach. Learn. Res.* **2006**, *7*, 1–30.
39. Fisher, R.A. *Statistical Methods and Scientific Inference*, 2nd ed.; Hafner Publishing Co.: New York, NY, USA, 1959.
40. Tukey, J.W. Comparing individual means in the analysis of variance. *Biometrics* **1949**, *5*, 99–114. [CrossRef] [PubMed]
41. Dunnett, C.W. A multiple comparison procedure for comparing several treatments with a control. *J. Am. Stat. Assoc.* **1980**, *50*, 1096–1121. [CrossRef]

mathematics

MDPI

Article

An Improved Blind Kriging Surrogate Model for Design Optimization Problems

Hau T. Mai [1,2], Jaewook Lee [1], Joowon Kang [3], H. Nguyen-Xuan [4] and Jaehong Lee [1,*]

1 Deep Learning Architectural Research Center, Sejong University, 209 Neungdong-ro, Gwangjin-gu, Seoul 05006, Korea
2 Faculty of Mechanical Technology, Industrial University of Ho Chi Minh City, Ho Chi Minh City 72308, Vietnam
3 School of Architecture, Yeungnam University, 280, Daehak-ro, Gyeongsan 38541, Korea
4 CIRTech Institute, HUTECH University, Ho Chi Minh City 72308, Vietnam
* Correspondence: jhlee@sejong.ac.kr; Tel.: +82-2-3408-3287; Fax: +82-2-3408-4331

Abstract: Surrogate modeling techniques are widely employed in solving constrained expensive black-box optimization problems. Therein, Kriging is among the most popular surrogates in which the trend function is considered as a constant mean. However, it also encounters several challenges related to capturing the overall trend with a relatively limited number of function evaluations as well as searching feasible points with complex or discontinuous feasible regions. To address this above issue, this paper presents an improved surrogate blind Kriging (IBK) and a combined infill strategy to find the optimal solution. According to enhancing the prediction accuracy of metamodels of objective and constraints, the high-order effects of regression function in the blind Kriging are identified by promising a variable selection technique. In addition, an infill strategy is developed based on the probability of feasibility, penalization, and constrained expected improvement for updating blind Kriging metamodels of the objective and constraints. At each iteration, two infill sample points are allocated at the positions to achieve improvement in optimality and feasibility. The IBK metamodels are updated by the newly-added infill sample points, which leads the proposed framework search to rapidly converge to the optimal solution. The performance and applicability of the proposed model are tested on several numerical benchmark problems via comparing with other metamodel-based constrained optimization methods. The obtained results indicate that IBK generally has a greater efficiency performance and outperforms the competitors in terms of a limited number of function evaluations. Finally, IBK is successfully applied to structural design optimization. The optimization results show that IBK is able to find the best feasible design with fewer evaluation functions compared with other studies, and this demonstrates the effectiveness and practicality of the proposed model for solving the constrained expensive black-box engineering design optimization problems.

Keywords: blind Kriging; surrogate model; black-box optimization; infill strategy

MSC: 65Kxx

Citation: Mai, T.H.; Lee, J.; Kang, J.; Nguyen-Xuan, H.; Lee, J. An Improved Blind Kriging Surrogate Model for Design Optimization Problems. *Mathematics* **2022**, *10*, 2906. https://doi.org/10.3390/math10162906

Academic Editors: Shujin Laima, Yong Cao, Xiaowei Jin and Hehe Ren

Received: 15 June 2022
Accepted: 10 August 2022
Published: 12 August 2022

Publisher's Note: MDPI stays neutral with regard to jurisdictional claims in published maps and institutional affiliations.

Copyright: © 2022 by the authors. Licensee MDPI, Basel, Switzerland. This article is an open access article distributed under the terms and conditions of the Creative Commons Attribution (CC BY) license (https://creativecommons.org/licenses/by/4.0/).

1. Introduction

The optimization process is critical in the engineering design, which requires lower computational cost, robustness, stability, and accuracy. However, most conventional optimization techniques face several challenges in solving the black-box global optimization problem, such as the unavailable expressions, gradient information of objective function or constraints, and the time-consuming effort. One way to circumvent these issues is based on the surrogate model (SM) [1,2]. Here, SM is an invaluable tool that is used to approximate the expensive computational models during the optimization process indirectly or directly. There are commonly used metamodels, such as response surface methodology [3,4], radial basis function (RBF) [5,6], Kriging [7,8], support vector regression

(SVR) [9], neural network (NN) [10–13], inverse distance weighting (IDW) [14], and so on. To achieve the optimal solution, the sampling technique and infill strategy are employed to build and iteratively refine the metamodel in order to ameliorate the solution found during the performance process. Therein, the sampling technique, which is also known as the design of the experiment, creates a set of points over the domain, and the initial metamodel is fitted to the observed points. Various sampling techniques for generating the sample points are developed, including Monte Carlo, random, and Latin hypercubic sampling (LHS) techniques. For more details, interested readers are suggested to refer to ref. [15].

In the past decade, variants of the metamodel-based optimization method have been successfully developed for solving the optimization problems with expensive simulations. For instance, Jones et al. [16] proposed an efficient global optimization (EGO) method where Kriging and expected improvement (EI) are introduced to find the solution. In addition, Huang et al. [17,18] extended the EGO algorithm by using the augmented EI function to determine the next sampling point. Additionally, a new infill strategy with adaptive radius and direction search is developed by Dong et al. [19] to indicate all local optimal values. To reduce the dimension of hyper-parameters, Zhao [20] incorporated the maximal information coefficient into Kriging. Gutmann [21] associated the measure of bumpiness in the RBF model to find the global minimum. Regis and Shoemaker [22–24] proposed a stochastic response surface to identify the promising points. More recently, Shepard [14] introduced the IDW, and then Joseph [25] added a linear regression function to improve accuracy. A conjugate between IDW and RBF is suggested by Bemporad [26].

The constrained black-box optimization problem is popular in many practical engineering designs. Hence, it has attracted the remarkable attention of researchers in recent years. They have been successfully applied to address this issue, such as ConstrLMSRBF [27], COBRA [28], RCGO [6], CARS [29], and so on. Among the surrogate models, Kriging has attracted more attention than other models due to estimating the prediction error and capacity to approximate the highly nonlinear functions. Therein, its regression function can be considered as the part trying to catch the general trend and thus the largest variations of the data. In recent times, Li et al. [30] proposed a new Kriging-based constrained global optimization algorithm in which the global optimal solution is obtained by two pivotal phases. An enhanced approach based on the modification of the probability of an improvement algorithm is presented by Carpio et al. Carpio et al. [31]. Additionally, Qian et al. [32] illustrated a new infill strategy, in which the position of the new sampling point is the intersection between the confidence interval and the constraint boundary. A combination of Kriging and the mixture of experts is proposed by Bartoli et al. [33] to improve the model's accuracy. In addition, Forrester and Keane [34] presented a constrained expected improvement criterion to attain a new sample for updating the surrogate model. Similarly, Shi et al. [35] developed a probability of constrained improvement based on filter technology. However, there are several challenges due to multimodal, nonlinear functions, limited sample size, and a strong overall trend exists. In addition, identifying the right regression function for a set of data with interactions between variables is a difficult task. To address the above issues, researchers have tried to improve the prediction accuracy of Kriging by adjusting either the regression function, the stochastic process, or both. A well-known author, Joseph et al. [36], presented the blind Kriging model, in which the optimal basis functions are estimated by the Bayesian variable selection technique. Additionally, Kersaudy et al. [37] introduced a combination of polynomial chaos expansions and universal Kriging. Zhang et al. [38,39] proposed the regularization method for constructing a trend function and the penalized blind likelihood Kriging. Nevertheless, the above-mentioned models are only established to solve the unconstrained optimization problem. Furthermore, to the best of our knowledge, it has still not been yet utilized for constrained optimization thus far.

In this study, an improved surrogate blind Kriging is first presented to handle computational expensive constrained optimization problems. In our work, the higher-order effects of the trend function are estimated by a Bayesian variable selection technique. Simultaneously, a new infill strategy is developed based on the probability of feasibility, penalization, and constrained expected improvement to refine the surrogate models and improve the solution found during the optimization process. According to this scheme, two sample points will be indicated corresponding to the exploration and exploitation stages for each iteration. It helps the IBK metamodel to learn the complex or discontinuous feasible domains. The performance and applicability of the proposed approach are demonstrated through several benchmark optimization problems. The outcomes of the proposed model are compared with other models to evaluate its efficiency and reliability. The obtained results showed that our work is able to find the best feasible design with fewer evaluation functions.

The rest of the paper is organized as follows. Section 2 introduces the IBK model. Next, an infill strategy based on the combination is presented in Section 3. Afterward, several numerical examples are investigated to demonstrate the efficiency of the proposed model in Section 4. Finally, the conclusions are outlined in Section 5.

2. Improved Blind Kriging

2.1. Basics

The primary objective of a metamodel is to search for the approximate function from a set of data points. A brief summary of Kriging and some basic formulas are described in this subsection.

Consider the function $y(x)$ as defined in the domain Ω. Let the n sample points $\mathbf{X} = \left\{\mathbf{x}^{(1)}, \mathbf{x}^{(2)}, ..., \mathbf{x}^{(n)}\right\}^T$ with $\mathbf{x} \in \mathbb{R}^d$ and the true response values $y = \left\{y^{(1)}, y^{(2)}, ..., y^{(n)}\right\}^T$ with $y \in \mathbb{R}$, respectively. The universal Kriging (UK) model postulates a combination of the regression function and a stochastic process, as demonstrated in Equation (1)

$$Y(\mathbf{x}) = f(\mathbf{x}) + Z(\mathbf{x}), \tag{1}$$

where $Y(\mathbf{x})$ represents a black-box function; $f(\mathbf{x}) = \boldsymbol{v}(\mathbf{x})^T \boldsymbol{\beta}_m$ denotes the regression function; $Z(\mathbf{x})$ is characterized by Gaussian process with zero mean and stationary covariance. For the blind Kriging, the trend function utilizes a regression function, as defined as Equation (2)

$$f(\mathbf{x}) = \boldsymbol{v}(\mathbf{x})^T \boldsymbol{\beta}_m, \tag{2}$$

in which $\boldsymbol{v}(\mathbf{x}) = \{1, v_1(\mathbf{x}), ..., v_m(\mathbf{x})\}^T$ is the vector that contains known basic functions; m is the number of basis functions, and $\boldsymbol{\beta}_m = \{\beta_0, \beta_1, ..., \beta_m\}^T$ denotes the unknown coefficients [40]. All of them are identified through the feature selection methods in Section 2.2.

Let $\boldsymbol{\Psi}$ be the correlation matrix of the samples, $\psi(\mathbf{x})$ the correlation vector between a point $\mathbf{x}$ and the sample point in the data set, and $\boldsymbol{F}_m$ the model matrix of the sample points. Then the predicted value at any point $\mathbf{x}$ by the blind Kriging model is given as,

$$\hat{y}(\mathbf{x}) = \boldsymbol{v}(\mathbf{x})^T \hat{\boldsymbol{\beta}}_m + \boldsymbol{\psi}(\mathbf{x})^T \boldsymbol{\Psi}^{-1}\left(\mathbf{y} - \boldsymbol{F}_m \hat{\boldsymbol{\beta}}_m\right), \tag{3}$$

where the variance $\hat{\sigma}_m^2$ and mean value $\hat{\boldsymbol{\beta}}_m$ of variance can be calculated as follows

$$\begin{aligned} \hat{\boldsymbol{\beta}}_m &= \frac{\boldsymbol{F}_m^T \boldsymbol{\Psi}^{-1} \boldsymbol{y}}{\boldsymbol{F}_m^T \boldsymbol{\Psi}^{-1} \boldsymbol{F}_m} \\ \hat{\sigma}_m^2 &= \frac{\left(\boldsymbol{y} - \boldsymbol{F}_m \hat{\boldsymbol{\beta}}_m\right)^T \boldsymbol{\Psi}^{-1}\left(\boldsymbol{y} - \boldsymbol{F}_m \hat{\boldsymbol{\beta}}_m\right)}{n} \end{aligned}. \tag{4}$$

To indicate the optimal hyper-parameters $\boldsymbol{\theta}$, in this paper, the differential evolution (DE) algorithm is employed to maximize the likelihood function. Their searching space is restricted to $(10^{-3}, 10^2)$ [34,41]. It should be noted that $\boldsymbol{\theta}$ is estimated two times. The first time, they are found at $m = 0$, and after choosing m, the hyper-parameters will be estimated again. The interested reader is referred to [36,39,40] for more details about deriving them.

Mean square error (MSE) at points in the design domain is given by [42]

$$\hat{s}^2(\mathbf{x}) = \hat{\sigma}_m^2\Big[1 - \boldsymbol{\psi}(\mathbf{x})^T\boldsymbol{\Psi}^{-1}\boldsymbol{\psi}(\mathbf{x}) + \Big(\boldsymbol{F}_m^T\boldsymbol{\Psi}^{-1}\boldsymbol{\psi}(\mathbf{x}) \\ -\boldsymbol{\nu}(\mathbf{x})\Big)^T\Big(\boldsymbol{F}_m^T\boldsymbol{\Psi}^{-1}\boldsymbol{F}_m\Big)^{-1}\Big(\boldsymbol{F}_m^T\boldsymbol{\Psi}^{-1}\boldsymbol{\psi}(\mathbf{x}) - \boldsymbol{\nu}(\mathbf{x})\Big). \tag{5}$$

To provide insight, a single variable test function from five initial samples, which is assumed as a black-box objective function, is investigated here, as shown in Figure 1. In which the solid black line represents the true function, the blue dashed line shows the prediction value, the red dots denote the set of sample points, and the solid red line shows the root mean squared error. It is easily seen that the predicted value at sample points is equal to the real value, and its MSE is zero. Note that MSE is used as the measure of uncertainty in each prediction and to estimate the approximate accuracy of the BK model.

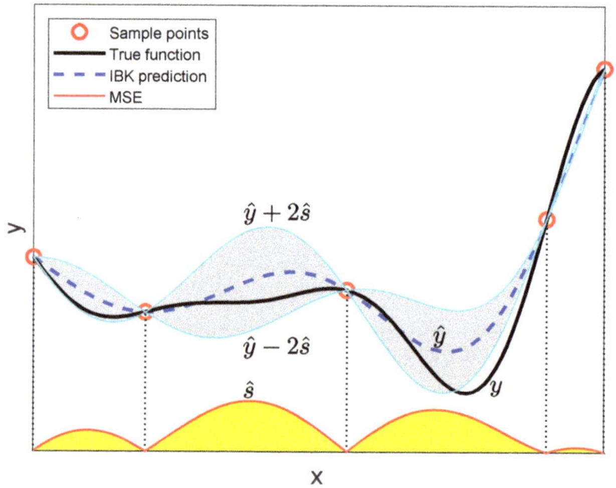

Figure 1. Mean square error of the IBK model.

2.2. Variable Selection

As mentioned by Couckuyt [40], BK can capture the most variance in the data set by data analysis methods. A collection of candidate functions is considered for selection by using cross-validation prediction error (CVPE). Now, we consider a trend function that combines the regression function with the set of candidate functions to fit the data in the following linear model

$$f(\mathbf{x}) = \sum_{i=0}^{m}\beta_i v_i(\mathbf{x}) + \sum_{i=0}^{t}\alpha_i u_i(\mathbf{x}), \tag{6}$$

where t is the number of potential functions; $u(\mathbf{x}) = \{1, u_1(\mathbf{x}), ..., u_t(\mathbf{x})\}$ denotes the set of candidate functions, and $\boldsymbol{\alpha}$ is the vector of corresponding coefficients. Note that β has already been determined independently $\boldsymbol{\alpha}$. When the transfer function f can be highly nonlinear, the number of candidate features to approximate are larger than the number of sample points. Therefore, we cannot determine all the coefficients α_i. In this study, a function prior to all parameters in the linear model is utilized to overcome this issue. Additionally, the trend function is improved by considering the high-order effect of the Bayesian variable selection technique, including linear, quadratic, cubic, quartic, and two-factor interaction effects. Consequently, the total of candidate variables and the mean term is $t = 4\left(d^2 + 2\sum_{i=1}^{d-1} i\right)$. Let us consider five-level, spaced factors with possible levels $l^{(1)}$, $l^{(2)}$, $l^{(3)}$, $l^{(4)}$, and $l^{(5)}$, which are defined as follows

$$\begin{aligned} l^{(1)} &= \min(\mathbf{X}) \quad , \\ l^{(2)} &= \frac{mean(\mathbf{X})}{2} \quad , \\ l^{(3)} &= mean(\mathbf{X}) \quad , \\ l^{(4)} &= \frac{3mean(\mathbf{X})}{2}, \\ l^{(5)} &= \max(\mathbf{X}) \quad . \end{aligned} \tag{7}$$

Therefore, the model matrix using orthogonal polynomial coding, which is the column lengths of $\sqrt{5}$, is

$$\boldsymbol{U}_j = \begin{bmatrix} 1 & -\sqrt{2} & \sqrt{\frac{10}{7}} & -\sqrt{\frac{1}{2}} & \sqrt{\frac{1}{14}} \\ 1 & -\sqrt{\frac{1}{2}} & -\sqrt{\frac{5}{14}} & \sqrt{2} & -\sqrt{\frac{8}{7}} \\ 1 & 0 & -\sqrt{\frac{10}{7}} & 0 & \sqrt{\frac{18}{7}} \\ 1 & \sqrt{\frac{1}{2}} & -\sqrt{\frac{5}{14}} & -\sqrt{2} & -\sqrt{\frac{8}{7}} \\ 1 & \sqrt{2} & \sqrt{\frac{10}{7}} & \sqrt{\frac{1}{2}} & \sqrt{\frac{1}{14}} \end{bmatrix}. \tag{8}$$

The corresponding correlation matrix is

$$\boldsymbol{\Psi}_j = \begin{bmatrix} 1 & \psi_j\left(l_j^{(2)}\right) & \psi_j\left(l_j^{(3)}\right) & \psi_j\left(l_j^{(4)}\right) & \psi_j\left(l_j^{(5)}\right) \\ \psi_j\left(l_j^{(2)}\right) & 1 & \psi_j\left(l_j^{(2)}\right) & \psi_j\left(l_j^{(3)}\right) & \psi_j\left(l_j^{(4)}\right) \\ \psi_j\left(l_j^{(3)}\right) & \psi_j\left(l_j^{(2)}\right) & 1 & \psi_j\left(l_j^{(2)}\right) & \psi_j\left(l_j^{(3)}\right) \\ \psi_j\left(l_j^{(4)}\right) & \psi_j\left(l_j^{(3)}\right) & \psi_j\left(l_j^{(2)}\right) & 1 & \psi_j\left(l_j^{(2)}\right) \\ \psi_j\left(l_j^{(5)}\right) & \psi_j\left(l_j^{(4)}\right) & \psi_j\left(l_j^{(3)}\right) & \psi_j\left(l_j^{(2)}\right) & 1 \end{bmatrix}, \tag{9}$$

and the $\boldsymbol{R}_j$ (5×5) variance-covariance matrix is calculated as follows

$$\boldsymbol{R}_j = \boldsymbol{U}_j^{-1}\boldsymbol{\Psi}_j\left(\boldsymbol{U}_j^{-1}\right)^T. \tag{10}$$

Note that we only use the diagonal elements of $\boldsymbol{R}_j$ [43]. Hence, the ith element of the diagonal matrix $\boldsymbol{R}((t+1) \times (t+1))$ can be written as

$$\boldsymbol{R}_{i,i} = \prod_{j=1}^{d} r_{jl}^{l_{ij}} r_{jq}^{q_{ij}} r_{jc}^{c_{ij}} r_{jq_r}^{q_{r_{ij}}}, \tag{11}$$

in which $l_{ij} = 1$ if α_i includes the factor's linear effect j and 0 otherwise. Similarly, q_{ij}, c_{ij}, $q_{r_{ij}}$ are assigned to the quadratic, cubic, and quartic effects, respectively.

$$\begin{aligned} r_{jl} &= \frac{\boldsymbol{R}_j(2,2)}{\boldsymbol{R}_j(1,1)}, \\ r_{jq} &= \frac{\boldsymbol{R}_j(3,3)}{\boldsymbol{R}_j(1,1)}, \\ r_{jc} &= \frac{\boldsymbol{R}_j(4,4)}{\boldsymbol{R}_j(1,1)}, \\ r_{jq_r} &= \frac{\boldsymbol{R}_j(5,5)}{\boldsymbol{R}_j(1,1)}, \\ 0 &\leqslant l_{ij} + q_{ij} + c_{ij} + q_{r_{ij}} \leqslant 2. \end{aligned} \tag{12}$$

The sample data will be normalized to the interval [0, 1]. The encoded samples for the linear, quadratic, cubic, and quartic effects are expressed as follows

$$\begin{aligned}
x_{j,l} &= \frac{1}{\sqrt{2}}\left(\frac{x_j}{l_j^{(5)}}\right), \\
x_{j,q} &= \sqrt{\frac{5}{14}}\left[\left(\frac{x_j}{l_j^{(5)}}\right)^2 - 2\right], \\
x_{j,c} &= \frac{5}{6\sqrt{2}}\left[\left(\frac{x_j}{l_j^{(5)}}\right)^3 - \frac{17}{5}\left(\frac{x_j}{l_j^{(5)}}\right)\right], \\
x_{j,q_r} &= \frac{35}{12\sqrt{14}}\left[\left(\frac{x_j}{l_j^{(5)}}\right)^4 - \frac{31}{7}\left(\frac{x_j}{l_j^{(5)}}\right)^2 + \frac{72}{35}\right],
\end{aligned} \tag{13}$$

where x_j defines the jth column $\mathbf{X}$. The two-factor interaction terms can be built from these basic effects. After the completion of the construction of $\mathbf{R}$ as shown above, the posterior mean of $\boldsymbol{\alpha}$ is defined as

$$\hat{\boldsymbol{\alpha}} = \left(\frac{\tau_m}{\sigma_m}\right)^2 \boldsymbol{R}\boldsymbol{F}_c{}'\boldsymbol{\Psi}^{-1}(\boldsymbol{y} - \boldsymbol{F}_m\boldsymbol{\beta}_m), \tag{14}$$

$$\mathrm{var}(\hat{\boldsymbol{\alpha}}) = \tau_m^2\left(\boldsymbol{R} - \left(\frac{\tau_m}{\sigma_m}\right)^2 \boldsymbol{R}\boldsymbol{F}_c{}'\boldsymbol{\Psi}^{-1}\boldsymbol{F}_c\boldsymbol{R}\right), \tag{15}$$

where $\boldsymbol{F}_c$ is the matrix of all candidate variables. As shown in refs. [36,40,43], the absolute of $\hat{\boldsymbol{\alpha}}$ is used instead of the standardized coefficient for variable selection. Hence, variables selected at each step correspond to the largest value $\hat{\boldsymbol{\alpha}}$. It should be noted that $\frac{\tau_m}{\sigma_m}$ is a constant, which is set to 1 for simplicity of the computation. To be specific, for the best value of m, the blind Kriging model has to go through five stages, which are described in detail as follows.

Step 1: The LHS technique is used to create initial sample points $\mathbf{X}$ and the obtained response values, respectively.

Step 2: Construct the ordinary Kriging surrogate model, and the leave-one-out cross-validation prediction error $\left(CVPE_{(m=0)}\right)$ is estimated to measure accuracy.

Step 3: Determine the coefficients $|\hat{\boldsymbol{\alpha}}|$ corresponding to each promising feature, and arrange $|\hat{\alpha}_i|$ from largest to smallest.

Step 4: If improving the accuracy of prediction has not been satisfied,

Step 4.1: Add a candidate function corresponding to each $|\hat{\alpha}_i|$ coefficient to the regression function.

Step 4.2: Construct the intermediate Kriging surrogate model with the new regression function.

Step 4.3: $CVPE_{(m)}$ is estimated to measure the accuracy of the model,

$$\begin{aligned}
CVPE_{(m)} &= \sqrt{\frac{\sum_{i=1}^{n} cv_i^2}{n}}, \\
cv_i &= y_i(\boldsymbol{x}_i) - \hat{y}_i(\boldsymbol{x}_i) \quad .
\end{aligned} \tag{16}$$

Step 5: The best set of features to minimize $\left(CVPE_{(m)}\right)$, will be chosen to build the final BK model. Finally, the new hyper-parameters are indicated for the new trend function [40] of the surrogate model.

3. Infill Strategy

The infill strategy is employed to iteratively refine the metamodel and guide the algorithm toward a promising region to improve the solution found. Its trade-off between exploration and exploitation decides the success of the implementation. Although there are several available infill strategies, such as expected improvement (EI), expected violation, probability of improvement function (PI), lower confidence bounding, etc., these procedures may be difficult to find feasible points or feasible disconnected regions [6,28]. In this section, a new combined infill strategy, which consists of the probability of feasibility, penalization, and a constrained expected improvement, is introduced to overcome the above limitations.

The mathematical formulation of the constrained expensive black-box global optimization problem

$$\begin{aligned} &\min_{\mathbf{x}\in\mathbb{R}^d} f(\mathbf{x}), \\ &s.t.\ g_j(\mathbf{x}) \le 0,\quad j = 1,\ 2, \ldots,\ m, \\ &\quad \mathbf{x}_{lb} \le \mathbf{x} \le \mathbf{x}_{ub}, \end{aligned} \tag{17}$$

where f and g_j denote the objective function and inequality constraints, respectively. Normally, if there is one equality constraint, it is converted to two inequality constraints using a very small relaxation factor. $\mathbf{x}_{ub}$ and $\mathbf{x}_{lb}$ are the upper and lower bounds of the design variables, respectively. It should be noted that the above problem belongs to the class of derivative-free optimization, so its derivatives are not available. In order to solve Equation (17), the constrained EI is usually employed as the infill criterion and expressed as follows

$$EI_C(\mathbf{x}) = EI_{C_i}(\mathbf{x}) + EI_{C_r}(\mathbf{x}), \tag{18}$$

with

$$\begin{aligned} EI_{C_i}(\mathbf{x}) &= (f(\mathbf{x}^*) - \mu_n(\mathbf{x}))\Phi\left(\frac{f(\mathbf{x}^*) - \mu_n(\mathbf{x})}{\sigma_n(\mathbf{x})}\right) PF(\mathbf{x}), \\ EI_{C_r}(\mathbf{x}) &= \sigma_n(\mathbf{x})\phi\left(\frac{f(\mathbf{x}^*) - \mu_n(\mathbf{x})}{\sigma_n(x)}\right) PF(\mathbf{x}), \\ PF(\mathbf{x}) &= \prod_{j=1}^{m} \Pr_j(g_j(\mathbf{x}) \le 0), \\ \Pr_j(g_j(\mathbf{x}) \le 0) &= \Phi\left(\frac{-\mu_{g_j}(\mathbf{x})}{\sigma_{g_j}(\mathbf{x})}\right), \end{aligned}$$

where $\mu_{g_j}(\mathbf{x})$ and $\sigma_{g_j}(\mathbf{x})$ are the posterior mean and covariance function of the jth constraint, respectively.

As indicated by Haftka et al. [44], $EI_{C_i}(\mathbf{x})$ indicates the exploitation sample points where the posterior mean of the objective function is small and has low uncertainty, and the constraints are likely to be near the boundaries of feasible operation. In contrast, $EI_{C_r}(\mathbf{x})$ aims to identify exploration sample points, which tend to be biased towards regions that are more likely to satisfy the constraints and high uncertainty of the objective function. However, the standard EI_C often fails when there is no initial feasible point in the data set [44]. To circumvent this, $PF(\mathbf{x})$ is one of the most used methods to favor the feasible region. Note that the value of $PF(\mathbf{x})$ is easy to be zero when one of the constraints violates the design specification [44]. Consequently, the high-priority data points are missed or overlooked.

To tackle these limitations, a combined computation strategy is first introduced in this study to achieve an initial feasible point as well as find the optimal solution. This scheme helps to reduce the number of constraint violations and explore other feasible regions, as follows:

$$PFC(\mathbf{x}) \ = \sigma_n(\mathbf{x})PF(\mathbf{x}), \tag{19}$$

$$PIC(\mathbf{x}) = -\sum_{j=1}^{m} \max\left(0, \mu_{g_j}(\mathbf{x})\right), \tag{20}$$

$$ISC_{14}(\mathbf{x}) = \prod_{j=1}^{m} \Pr_j\left(g_j(\mathbf{x}) \leq 0\right). D_j, \tag{21}$$

where $PFC(\mathbf{x})$ is combined by the covariance function and the probability of feasibility function; $PIC(\mathbf{x})$ is the penalization function corresponding to the constraint set; $ISC_{14}(\mathbf{x})$ is the infill sampling criterion for disconnected feasible regions; D is the distance to the nearest feasible point, and given by:

$$D = \min_{\mathbf{x}_{feas}} \left(\frac{\left\| \mathbf{x}_{feas} - \mathbf{x} \right\|}{range} \right), \tag{22}$$

in which *range* is the lag distance at which it reaches the sill from the variogram model.

According to the proposed strategy, if the feasible point is not found in the data, $PFC(\mathbf{x})$ and $PIC(\mathbf{x})$ will be used as an alternative for obtaining two infill sample points. In this case, providing that there exists a feasible region, two feasible sample points will be identified. More specifically, the first point is located in the sparsely sampled area by maximizing $PFC(\mathbf{x})$, so $\sigma_n(\mathbf{x})$ characterizes the sample density of the objective function in the design space. The other point indicates the corresponding minimum value of the total constraints $PIC(\mathbf{x})$. When the models fit poorly and do not have a feasible region, $PIC(\mathbf{x})$ is utilized to improve the locations that violated constraints. On the contrary, once an initial feasible point is found, Equations (18) and (21) are employed to determine infill sample points. $ISC_{14}(\mathbf{x})$ aims to effectively explore other feasible regions. The algorithm framework is provided in Algorithm 1.

Algorithm 1 The combined infill strategy for the expensive constrained optimization problem

Input: d : number of design variables
m : number of constraints
N_{max}: maximum expensive evaluation number
$[\mathbf{x}_{lb};\ \mathbf{x}_{ub}]$: design space
Output: $[\mathbf{x}_{best}, \mathbf{f}_{best}]$: the optimum solution

```
Generate n_0 sample points using LHS from the design space, evaluate the fitness values,
  and collect a set of initial observations D_{n_0} = {x_i, y_i, g_i} ∀i = 1, ..., n_0
Determine D^{fes} from D_{n_0}
Set n = n_0
while n ≤ N_max do
  Build surrogate models for the objective and each of the constraint functions
  if D_n^{fes} = ∅ then
    Find x_{n+1} by maximizing Equation (19)
    Find x_{n+2} by maximizing Equation (20)
  else
    Find x_{n+1} by maximizing Equation (18)
    Find x_{n+2} by maximizing Equation (21)
  end if
  Evaluate function values at x_{n+1,2}, append D_{n+2} = D_n ∪ {(x_{n+1,2}, y_{n+1,2}, G_{n+1,2})},
    and update D^{fes}_{n+1,2}
  n = n + 2
  Update [x_best, f_best]
end while
```

4. Numerical Examples

4.1. Study in High-Order Effects of the Trend Function

To evaluate the high-order efficiency of the trend function, a planar truss structure for maximum passive vibration isolation [45], as shown in Figure 2, is introduced. The authors of Keane and Bright [46] achieved results for this problem through analysis and experiment. The structures consist of 42 members with the same material properties. The right-hand end nodes are fixed. The unit force excitation is subjected to node 11 over a frequency range 100–200Hz. The x- and y-coordinates of nodes seventh) and eighteenth are considered as design variables, and the other nodes are fixed as per the regular structure. The objective function is stress at the left-hand end node. The interested reader is referred to [45,46] for more details. LHS is used to obtain data for building metamodels that differ in the number of sample points, and 100 validation runs were performed to validate the results. In this case, the average Euclidean error (AEE) is used to measure the prediction error using

$$AEE(\hat{y}, y) = \frac{1}{k} \sum_{i=1}^{k} \sqrt{(\hat{y} - y)^2}. \tag{23}$$

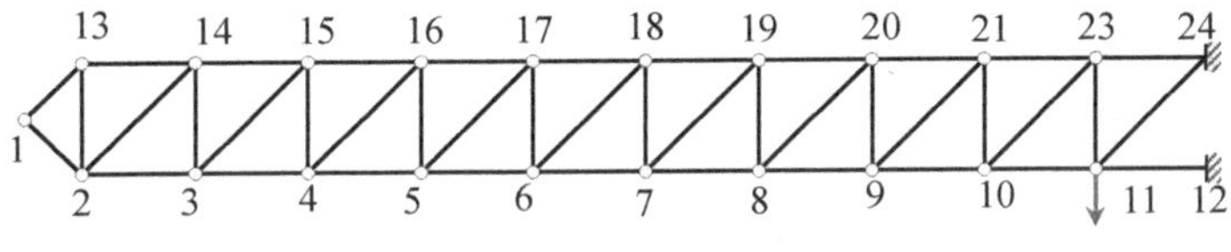

Figure 2. Planar truss structure. Adapted from [47].

As shown in Figure 3, it is easily seen that the BK model improves compared to the Kriging model. Clearly, the CVPE is smaller than the Kriging model. It is easy to explain that the linear, quadratic effect causes a significant rise in accuracy. On the other hand, the difference in AEE scores between the models was an insignificant amount with the number of sample points less than 30. This is explained by the fact that if the sample size is small, then the high-order effect of the regression function will not be much. However, the high-order BK model achieved a vast improvement over another model when the data size increased. Then, the regression function with the high-order effects is represented as Equations (24) and (25) for 100 and 200 sample points, respectively. Clearly, IBK can capture the overall trend to the largest variations of the data.

$$1 + x_1x_3 + x_1 + x_4 + x_1x_4 + x_3x_4 + x_2 + x_1x_2^3 + x_1^4x_2^4 + x_2x_4 + x_1^3x_2 + x_1^4x_3 + x_1^2x_3 + x_1^2x_4. \tag{24}$$

$$1 + x_1x_4 + x_1 + x_1x_3 + x_1^4x_3 + x_1x_2 + x_3x_4 + x_1^4x_2^4 + x_2 + x_1^4x_3^2 + x_2^4x_4 + x_1x_3^2 + x_2^4x_4^2. \tag{25}$$

4.2. Synthetic Test Problems

In this section, nine well-known benchmark problems, in which the number of variables, constraints, and the best know solutions are given Table 1, are investigated to evaluate the efficiency of the proposed model. More information about these problems can be seen in Appendix A and in ref. [28]. Although these optimization problems are not expensive to evaluate, they are treated as all computationally expensive functions to conduct meaningful comparisons of the performance of the alternative methods. The obtained results will be compared with the result of RCGO, FLT-AKM, COBRA-local, COBRA-global, and ConstrLMSRBF. Therein, the two algorithms RCGO and FLT-AKM are implemented by the authors following Wu et al. [6] and Shi et al. [35]. In the RCGO method, the distance coefficient in the first phase is $\Pi = [0.001, 0.005, 0.01, 0.05, 0.1]$, and $\Gamma = [0, 1, 2, 3, 4]$ is the value of the exponent in the second phase. In order to obtain a fair comparison between the different methods, all the tests are performed in a Matlab^{TM} environment using an Intel® Core(TM) i5-8500 CPU 3.0 GHz desktop machine (Microsoft, New York, NY, USA). Each metamodel is run ten times on each test problem to reduce the effect of random error.

Otherwise, the searching process of the model is terminated when either the maximum number of evaluation functions is reached or the best result does not improve after 10 iterations. LHS created ten different initial data sets. The differential evolution algorithm (DE) is employed to find hyper-parameters and the next points in the infill strategy.

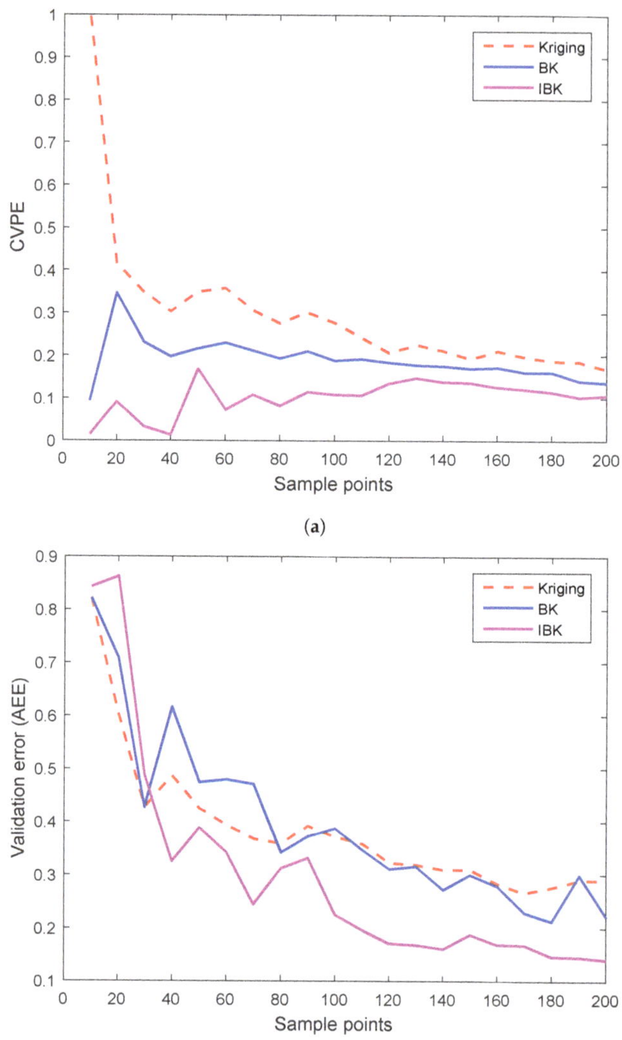

(**b**)

Figure 3. The relationship between flesh elements and thickness values. (**a**) Cross-validation prediction error of metamodels with different sample size. (**b**) Validation error of metamodels with different sample size.

Table 1. Constrained optimization benchmark problems.

Problems	Best Known Value	Dimensionality	No. Constraints
G24	−5.508	2	2
G8	−0.0958	2	2
Two_bars	0.0309	3	2
Four_bars	1400	4	1
Ibeam	0.0131	4	2
G5MOD	5126.5	4	5
G4	−30,665.539	5	6
Hesse	−310	6	6
SR	2994.42	7	11

The obtained results are summarized in Table 2, which provides the average number of evaluation functions (NEF), objective values of the best solution, median solutions, and mean solutions found by the six metamodels. Firstly, it is easily seen that RCGO has failed to indicate the feasible solution for G24, SR in all trials, and G5MOD in three trials. These are mainly due to the small feasible region, all the initial points are infeasible, or the incoherent distance coefficients. Clearly, IBK outperformed other algorithms for G24, G8, Two-bars, G4, Ibeam, and Hesse with the best solution. In addition, the IBK requires fewer evaluations than other metamodels. Figure 4 provides a graphical illustration of the overall process of identifying the infill samples of the G24 problem. Firstly, the feasible domain is discontinuous and includes one global and two local minimums corresponding to peaks of the feasible domain. All initial sample points are quite analogous to the metamodels for a fair comparison. Clearly, the infill samples obtained by IBK are distributed near the peaks of the feasible region as well as the boundary of the constraint set. On the contrary, the obtained result from FLT-AKM divided two groups of the infill samples, and the first group concentrates on the infeasible region far from the constrained boundary. This can easily be explained by the fact that the order of constraints is polynomials of degree four. Hence, IBK can easily capture the high-order effects compared with Kriging of the FLT-AKM. Furthermore, our infill strategy allows us to reduce the number of constraint violations and explore other feasible domains. More specifically, our model requires only 32 evaluation functions, while FLT-AKM requires 45 analyses for the convergence performance. This shows that the features of IBK and the combination infill strategy outperform other well-known existing algorithms.

For the Four-bars test, the obtained results of all these models are similar, and there are not many differences between the models. It is interesting that, among the problems, it requires few evaluation functions. Hence, IBK will not show much effect with small sample points or a simple, feasible domain. It can be observed that the optimal results found by the COBRA provide the best solution to the G5MOD and SR problems. However, IBK performs better than FLT-AKM and RCGO in terms of median, mean and best values of feasible optimum. Note that COBRA and RCGO require the initial data that contain the feasible points. However, it is difficult to find a feasible point for highly nonlinear problems, which then leads to failure. Clearly, RCGO could not find a feasible point in all trials for the SR problem. Although the result achieved from SR by IBK is close to FLT-AKM, IBK shows stability when the median and mean are close to the best value.

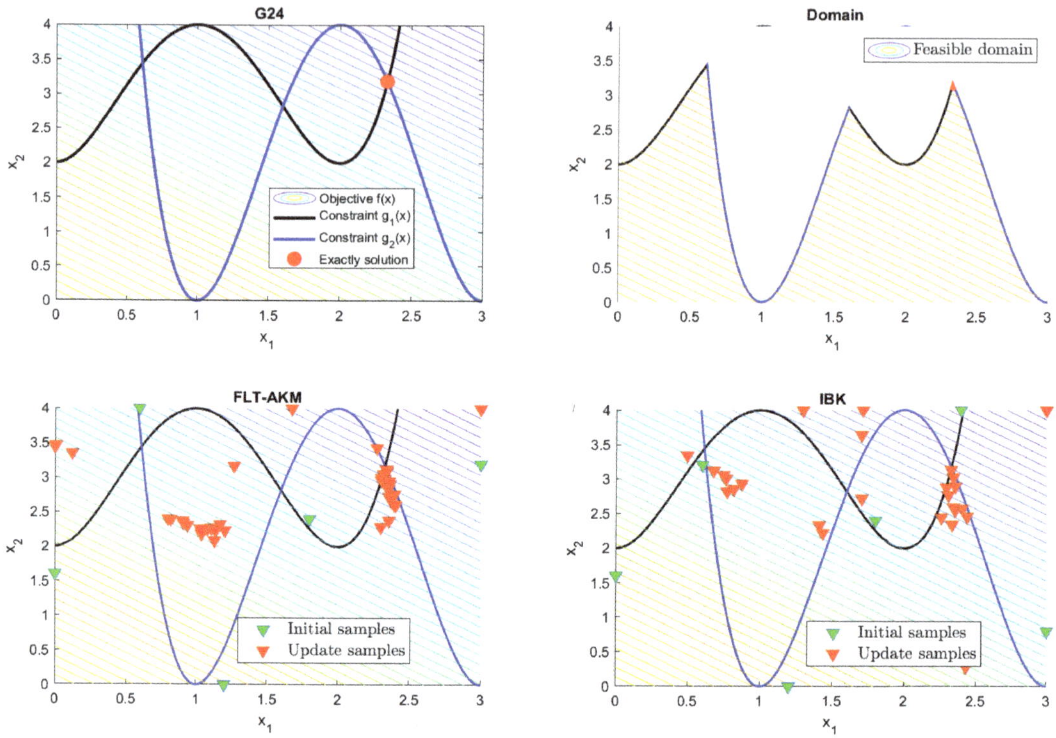

Figure 4. Optimization process-based infill strategy using IBK and FLT-AKM.

Table 2. Comparison of the obtained results for the test problems.

		Test Problems								
		G24	G8	Four Bars	Two Bars	Ibeam	G5MOD	G4	Hesse	SR
IBK	Best	−5.4669	−0.095	1400	0.031	0.013	5126.5	−30,665.5	−310	3042.2
	Median	−5.4075	−0.091	1400	0.031	0.014	5135.2	−30,665.5	−310	3051.3
	Mean	−5.3832	−0.089	1400	0.031	0.014	5167.1	−30,665.5	−310	3053.3
	NEF	33.2	46.8	17.4	36.2	60	74.0	24.2	38.6	68.4
FLT-AKM	Best	−5.46	−0.095	1400	0.031	0.013	5739.9	−30,611.7	−306.553	3024.4
	Median	−5.4173	−0.084	1400	0.031	0.015	6157.9	−30,416.8	−297.34	3061
	Mean	−5.415	−0.085	1400	0.031	0.018	6187.8	−30,411.2	−297.093	3058.5
	NEF	34	54.8	17.5	37.8	74.8	59.2	35.2	58.6	59.6
RCGO	Best		−0.096	1400	0.031	0.013	5323.5	−30,628.8	−306.428	
	Median		−0.096	1400	0.031	0.014	6099.8	−30,389.5	−294.812	
	Mean	N/A(10)	−0.073	1400	0.033	0.016	5992.9	−30,395.3	−296.239	N/A(10)
	NEF		51.7	17.2	40.4	67.8	65.4(3)	35	73.2	
COBRA-Local [28]	Best		−0.1				5126.5	−30,665.5	−309.94	2994.4
	Median	-	−0.1	-	-	-	5126.51	−30,665.2	−297.87	2994.7
	Mean		−0.09				5126.51	−30,665.1	−296.25	2994.7
	NEF		50				50	50	50	50
COBRA-Global [28]	Best		−0.1				5126.5	−30,665.4	−309.97	2994.7
	Median	-	−0.1	-	-	-	5126.51	−30,664.9	−297.87	2994.7
	Mean		−0.09				5126.62	−30,664.9	−296.25	2994.7
	NEF		50				50	50	50	50

4.3. Structural Design Optimization

Finally, the proposed model is applied to perform the shape optimization of truss structures. This benchmark problem has been previously analyzed by Shao [48] and Suprayitno [49] using the clustering-based surrogate model and Kriging, respectively. A 21-bars planar truss shown in Figure 5 is investigated for design optimization. Coordinates of all free nodes are treated as continuous design variables. The design aim is to maximize the truss performance, which is defined as the maximum load ratio ($F_{\max}$) that the truss can carry to the self-weight of the truss (W). The structure is subjected to stress and stability ratio constraints. The stress limitations of all members are the same for tension and compression and set to 200 MPa. The cross-sectional areas of all bars are 25 cm^2. The number of initial sample points is set at 14 [48]. Here, the critical buckling stress $S_{cr,i} = \pi^2 E/(L_{e,i}/\rho)^2$. Whereas E and ρ are Young's modulus of the truss material and the radius of gyration of the truss bar, respectively. It can be formulated as follows

$$\begin{aligned} &Maximize \quad \frac{F_{\max}}{W} = f(x_1, x_2, x_3, y_3, x_4, y_4, y_6), \\ &subjectedto \ \{\sigma_t, \sigma_c\} \leqslant \sigma_a, \\ &\qquad \frac{\sigma_{c,i}}{S_{cr,i}} \leqslant 1, \\ &\qquad 0.8 \leqslant x_1, x_3, y_3, y_4, y_6 \leqslant 3 \text{ m}, \\ &\qquad 3.3 \leqslant x_2, x_4 \leqslant 5.5 \text{ m}. \end{aligned} \tag{26}$$

The number of maximum evaluation functions is set to 100 for all models. The obtained optimal results are listed in Table 3 and Figure 6. It can easily be seen that IBK found the best feasible solution, where the objective value is 25.8541, while the maximum tensile stress and maximum compressive stress are 94.21 and -115.701 Mpa, respectively. In addition, IBK significantly decreased the number of simulations. These have demonstrated that IBK can solve expensive black-box structure design optimization problems effectively.

Table 3. Comparison of the obtained results for the 21-bars planar truss.

Design Variables	IBK	FLT-AKM	RCGO	CMLS [48]	EORKS [49]
x_1	3	3	2.98	2.37	3
x_2	4.31	4.251	4.19	4.174	4.209
x_3	1.907	1.91	1.91	1.877	1.902
y_3	2.267	2.275	2.278	1.721	2.285
x_4	4.218	4.218	4.237	4.024	4.222
y_4	1.706	1.708	1.705	1.438	1.709
y_6	2.723	2.702	2.624	2.186	2.644
Best	25.85	25.46	24.72	22.79	25.66
Median	25.27	25.21	23.46	-	-
Mean	25.36	25.33	23.75	-	-
NFE	55.6	65.7	72.3	95	87

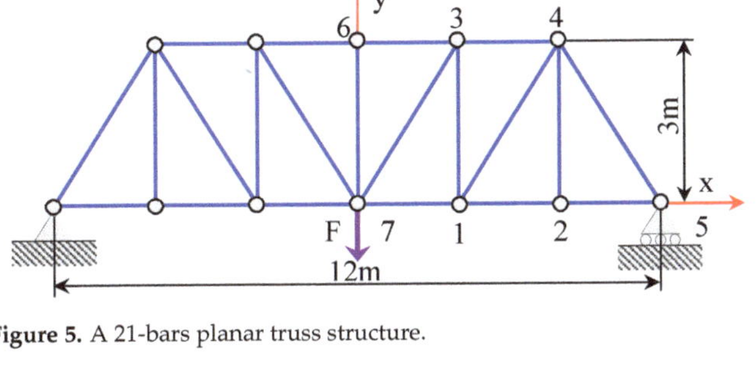

Figure 5. A 21-bars planar truss structure.

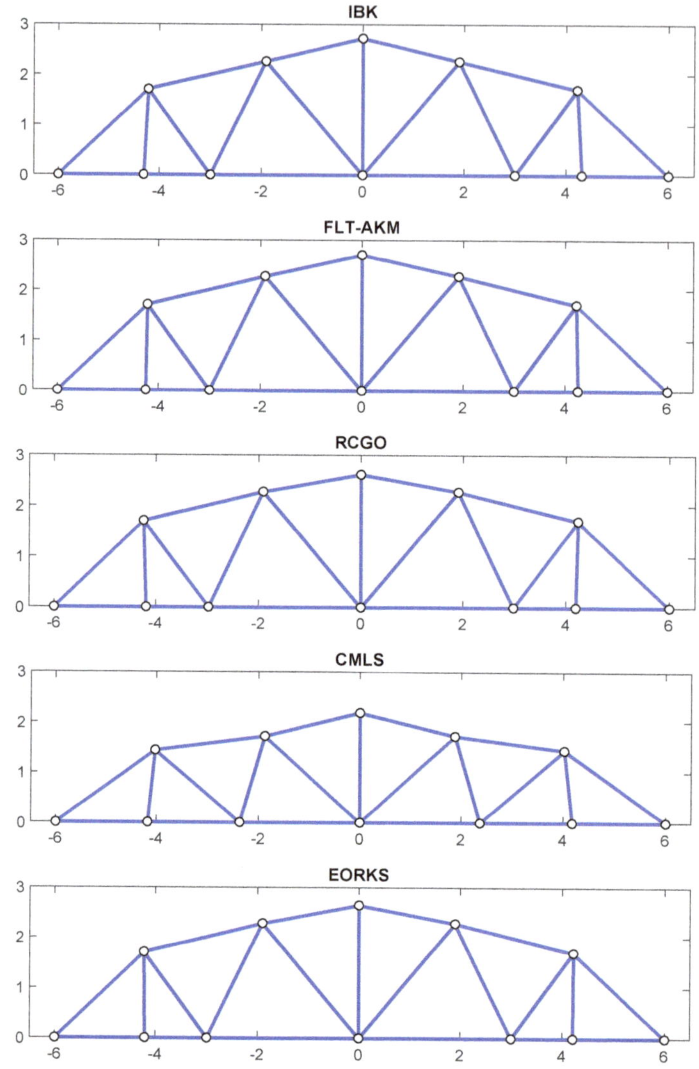

Figure 6. Comparison of optimal shapes of the 21-bars planar truss obtained by IBK.

5. Conclusions

In this study, an improved surrogate blind Kriging combined with the new infill strategy is introduced to solve the constrained expensive black-box optimization problems. According to that core idea, the high-order effects of the trend function are identified from the training data using the Bayesian variable selection method. Simultaneously, the novel infill strategy based on the probability of feasibility, penalization, and constrained expected improvement is constructed to reduce the number of constraint violations, explore other feasible domains, and handle the discontinuous design domain. The efficiency of the proposed approach is demonstrated through several numerical examples for synthetic test problems and shapes the optimization of the truss structure. The obtained results have indicated that the optimum solution obtained by this work is in good agreement with ten of the eleven tests. The proposed model saves a number of evaluation functions in almost all problems in comparison with other metamodels. In addition, it is also shown that the IBK predictor is simpler to interpret and is more robust than an ordinary Kriging predictor. This proved to be an efficient model for solving real-world engineering problems. Hence, it promises to be robust and effective at resolving complex problems in the expensive optimization of a complex design domain.

Author Contributions: H.T.M.: conceptualization, formal analysis, investigation, methodology, software, writing—original draft, visualization, writing—review and editing. J.L. (Jaewook Lee): data curation, validation. J.K.: data curation, validation. H.N.-X.: review, validation. J.L. (Jaehong Lee): conceptualization, methodology, supervision, funding acquisition. All authors have read and agreed to the published version of the manuscript.

Funding: This research was supported by a grant (NRF- 2020R1A4A2002855) from NRF (National Research Foundation of Korea) funded by MEST (Ministry of Education and Science Technology) of the Korean government.

Institutional Review Board Statement: Not applicable.

Informed Consent Statement: Not applicable.

Data Availability Statement: Not applicable.

Conflicts of Interest: The authors declare that they have no known competing financial interests or personal relationships that could have appeared to influence the work reported in this paper.

Appendix A

G5MOD [28]:

$$\begin{aligned}
\min f(x) &= 3x_1 + 10 - 6x_1^3 + 2x^2 + (2 \times 10^{-6}/3)x_2^3 \\
s.t.\ g_1(x) &= x_3 - x_4 - 0.55 \leqslant 0 \\
g_2(x) &= x_4 - x_3 - 0.55 \leqslant 0 \\
g_3(x) &= 1000sin(-x_3 - 0.25) + 894.8 - x_1 \\
&\quad +1000sin(-x_4 - 0.25) \leqslant 0 \\
g_4(x) &= 1000sin(x_3 - 0.25) + 894.8 - x_2 \\
&\quad +1000sin(x_3 - x_4 - 0.25) \leqslant 0 \\
g_5(x) &= 1000sin(x_4 - 0.25) + 1294.8 \\
&\quad + 1000sin(x_4 - x_3 - 0.25) \leqslant 0 \\
&0 \leqslant x_1, x_2 \leqslant 1200; \ -0.55 \leqslant x_3,\ x_4 \leqslant 0.55
\end{aligned}$$

Hesse [28]:

$$\begin{aligned}
\min f(x) &= -25(x_1 - 2)^2 - (x_2 - 2)^2 - (x_3 - 1)^2 \\
&\quad -(x_4 - 4)^2 - (x_5 - 1)^2 - (x_6 - 4)^2 \\
s.t.\ g_1(x) &= (2 - x_1 - x_2)/2 \leqslant 0 \\
g_2(x) &= (x_1 + x_2 - 6)/6 \leqslant 0 \\
g_3(x) &= (2 - x_1 + x_2)/2 \leqslant 0 \\
g_4(x) &= (x_1 - 3x_2 - 2)/2 \leqslant 0 \\
g_5(x) &= \left(4 - x_4 - (x_3 - 3)^2\right)/4 \leqslant 0 \\
g_6(x) &= \left(4 - x_6 - (x_5 - 3)^2\right)/4 \leqslant 0 \\
&0 \leqslant x_1 \leqslant 5; \ 0 \leqslant x_2 \leqslant 4; \ 1 \leqslant x_{3,5} \leqslant 5; \\
&0 \leqslant x_4 \leqslant 6; \ 0 \leqslant x_6 \leqslant 10
\end{aligned}$$

G4 [28]:

$$\begin{aligned}
\min f(x) &= 5.3578547x_3^2 + 0.8356891x_1x_5 \\
&\quad +37.293239x_1 - 40792.141
\end{aligned}$$

$$
\begin{aligned}
s.t.\, g_1(x) &= -u \leqslant 0; \\
g_2(x) &= u - 92 \leqslant 0 \\
g_3(x) &= -v + 90 \leqslant 0; \\
g_4(x) &= v - 110 \leqslant 0 \\
g_5(x) &= -w + 20 \leqslant 0; \\
g_6(x) &= w - 25 \leqslant 0 \\
u &= 85.334407 + 0.0056858 x_2 x_5 \\
&\quad + 0.0006262 x_1 x_4 - 0.0022053 x_3 x_5 \\
v &= 80.51249 + 0.0071317 x_2 x_5 \\
&\quad + 0.0029955 x_1 x_2 + 0.0021813 x_2^3 \\
w &= 9.300961 + 0.0047026 x_3 x_5 \\
&\quad + 0.0012547 x_1 x_3 + 0.0019085 x_3 x_4 \\
& 78 \leqslant x_1 \leqslant 102;\ 33 \leqslant x_2 \leqslant 45; \\
& 27 \leqslant x_i \leqslant 45\ \ for\ i = 3,4,5
\end{aligned}
$$

G24 [28]:

$$
\begin{aligned}
\min f(x) &= -x_1 - x_2 \\
s.t.\ g_1(x) &= -2x_1^4 + 8x_1^3 - 8x_1^2 + x_2 - 2 \leqslant 0 \\
g_2(x) &= -4x_1^4 + 32x_1^3 - 88x_1^2 + 96x_1 \\
&\quad + x_2 - 36 \leqslant 0 \\
& 0 \leqslant x_1 \leqslant 3; \quad 0 \leqslant x_2 \leqslant 4
\end{aligned}
$$

Ibeam [28]:

$$
\begin{aligned}
\min f(x) &= \frac{5000}{\frac{1}{12}x_3(x_1 - 2x_4)^3 + \frac{1}{6}x_2 x_4^3 + 2x_2 x_4\left(\frac{x_1 - x_4}{2}\right)^2} \\
s.t.\ g_1(x) &= 2x_2 x_4 + x_3(x_1 - 2x_4) \leqslant 300 \\
g_2(x) &= \frac{180000 x_1}{x_3(x_1 - 2x_4)^3 + 2x_2 x_4 (4x_4^2 + 3x_1(x_1 - 2x_4))} \\
&\quad + \frac{15000 x_2}{(x_1 - 2x_4)x_3^3 + 2x_2^3 x_4} \leqslant 6 \\
& 10 \leqslant x_1 \leqslant 80; \quad 10 \leqslant x_2 \leqslant 50; \quad 0.9 \leqslant x_{3,4} \leqslant 5
\end{aligned}
$$

SR [28]:

$$
\begin{aligned}
\min f(x) &= 0.7854 x_1 x_2^2 A - 1.508 x^1 B \\
&\quad + 7.477C + 0.7854D \\
s.t.\ g_1(x) &= (27 - x_1 x_2^2 x_3)/27 \leqslant 0 \\
g_2(x) &= (397.5 - x_1 x_2^2 x_3^2)/397.5 \leqslant 0 \\
g_3(x) &= (1.93 - (x_2 x_6^4 x_3)/x_4^2)/1.93 \leqslant 0 \\
g_4(x) &= (1.93 - (x_2 x_7^4 x_3)/x_5^3)/1.93 \leqslant 0 \\
g_5(x) &= ((A_1/B_1) - 1100)/1100 \leqslant 0 \\
g_6(x) &= ((A_2/B_2) - 850)/850 \leqslant 0 \\
g_7(x) &= (x_2 x_3 - 40)/40 \leqslant 0 \\
g_8(x) &= (5 - (x_1/x_2))/5 \leqslant 0 \\
g_9(x) &= ((x_1/x_2) - 12)/12 \leqslant 0 \\
g_{10}(x) &= (1.9 + 1.5x_6 - x_4)/1.9 \leqslant 0 \\
g_{11}(x) &= (1.9 + 1.1x_7 - x_5)/1.9 \leqslant 0
\end{aligned}
$$

$$A = 3.3333x_3^2 + 14.9334x_3 - 43.0934;$$
$$B = x_6^2 + x_7^2;\ C = x_6^3 + x_7^3;\ D = x_4x_6^2 + x_5x_7^2$$
$$A_1 = [(745x_4/(x_2x_3))^2 + (16.91 \times 10^6)]^{0.5}$$
$$A_2 = [(745x_5/(x_2x_3))^2 + (157.5 \times 10^6)]^{0.5}$$
$$B_1 = 0.1x_3;\ B_2 = 0.1x_3$$
$$2.6 \leqslant x_1 \leqslant 3.6;\quad 0.7 \leqslant x_2 \leqslant 0.8$$
$$17 \leqslant x_3 \leqslant 28;\quad 7.3 \leqslant x_4,\ x_5 \leqslant 8.3$$
$$2.9 \leqslant x_6 \leqslant 3.9;\quad 5.0 \leqslant x_7 \leqslant 5.5$$

G8 [28]:

$$\min f(x) = \frac{-sin^3(2\pi x_1)sin(2\pi x_2)}{x_1^3(x_1 + x_2)}$$
$$s.t.\ g_1(x) = x_1^2 - x_2 + 1 \leqslant 0$$
$$g_2(x) = 1 - x_1 + (x_2 - 4)^2 \leqslant 0$$
$$0 \leqslant x_1, x_2 \leqslant 10$$

Four-bar truss [50]:

The objective here is to minimize the total structural volume subject to the stress constraints on the members as in Figure A1.

$$\min\left(2a_1 + \sqrt{2}a_2 + \sqrt{2}a_3 + a_4\right)$$
$$s.t.\ \frac{FL}{E}\left(\frac{2}{a_1} + \frac{2\sqrt{2}}{a_2} - \frac{2\sqrt{2}}{a_3} + \frac{2}{a_4} \leqslant 0.04\right)$$
$$1 \leqslant a_{1,4} \leqslant 3;\quad \sqrt{2} \leqslant a_{2,3} \leqslant 3$$
$$L = 200\ \text{cm};\ F = 10\ \text{kN};\ E = 200{,}000\ \text{kN/cm}^2$$

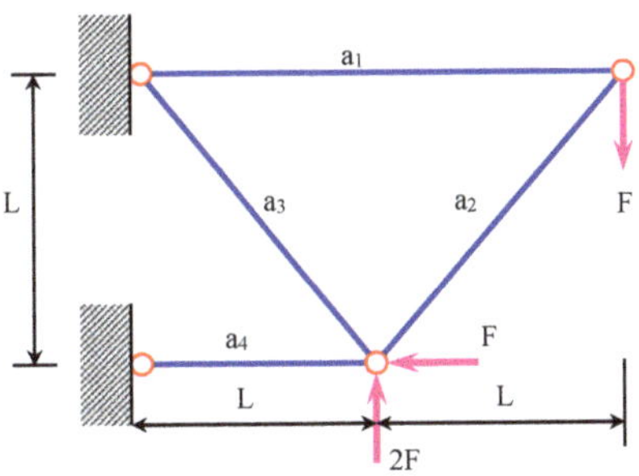

Figure A1. Four-bar truss.

Two-bar truss [50]:

The objective here is to minimize the total structural volume under stress constraints on member cross-sectional areas as in Figure A2.

$$\min\left(a_1\sqrt{b^2 + L^2} + a_2\sqrt{L^2 + (2L - b)^2}\right)$$
$$s.t.\ \frac{W_2b(2L - b) + W_1Lb}{2L^2a_1} \leqslant S_{\max}$$
$$\frac{(W_2b - W_1L)\sqrt{L^2 + (2L - b)^2}}{2L^2a_2} \leqslant S_{\max}$$
$$5.16 \leqslant a_{1,2} \leqslant 19.4\ \text{cm}^2;\quad 9.144 \leqslant b \leqslant 27.432\ \text{m}$$
$$W_1 = 445\ \text{kN};\ W_2 = 4450\ \text{kN}$$
$$L = 18.288\ \text{m};\ S_{\max} = 3.79 \times 10^6\ \text{kN/m}^2$$

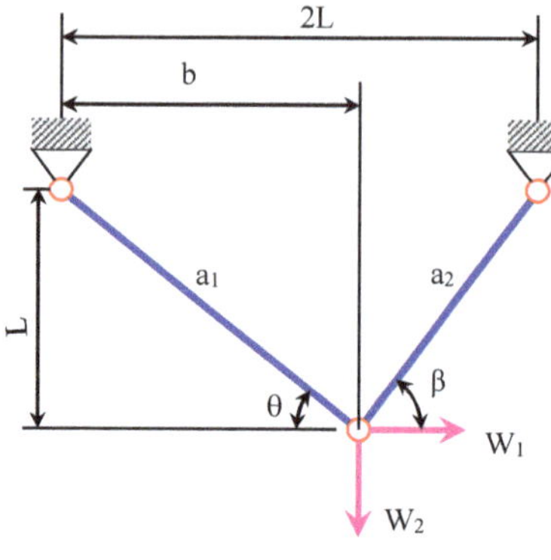

Figure A2. Two-bar truss.

References

1. Amine Bouhlel, M.; Bartoli, N.; Regis, R.G.; Otsmane, A.; Morlier, J. Efficient global optimization for high-dimensional constrained problems by using the Kriging models combined with the partial least squares method. *Eng. Optim.* **2018**, *50*, 2038–2053. [CrossRef]
2. Gu, J.; Zhang, H.; Zhong, X. Hybrid meta-model-based global optimum pursuing method for expensive problems. *Struct. Multidiscip. Optim.* **2019**, *61*, 543–554. [CrossRef]
3. Myers, R.H.; Montgomery, D.C.; Anderson-Cook, C.M. *Response Surface Methodology: Process and Product Optimization Using Designed Experiments*; John Wiley & Sons: Hoboken, NJ, USA, 2016.
4. Box, G.E.; Draper, N.R. *Empirical Model-Building and Response Surfaces*; Wiley: New York, NY, USA, 1987; Volume 424.
5. Powell, M. *The Theory of Radial Basis Function Approximation in 1990, Advances in Numerical Analysis II: Wavelets, Subdivision, and Radial Functions (WA Light, ed.)*; Oxford University Press: Oxford, UK, 1992; Volume 105, p. 210.
6. Wu, Y.; Yin, Q.; Jie, H.; Wang, B.; Zhao, J. A RBF-based constrained global optimization algorithm for problems with computationally expensive objective and constraints. *Struct. Multidiscip. Optim.* **2018**, *58*, 1633–1655. [CrossRef]
7. Sacks, J.; Welch, W.J.; Mitchell, T.J.; Wynn, H.P. Design and analysis of computer experiments. *Stat. Sci.* **1989**, *4*, 409–423. [CrossRef]
8. Sakata, S.; Ashida, F.; Zako, M. Structural optimization using Kriging approximation. *Comput. Methods Appl. Mech. Eng.* **2003**, *192*, 923–939. [CrossRef]
9. Clarke, S.M.; Griebsch, J.H.; Simpson, T.W. Analysis of support vector regression for approximation of complex engineering analyses. *J. Mech. Des.* **2005**, *127*, 1077–1087. [CrossRef]
10. Berke, L.; Hajela, P. Applications of artificial neural nets in structural mechanics. In *Shape and Layout Optimization of Structural Systems and Optimality Criteria Methods*; Springer: Berlin/Heidelberg, Germany, 1992; pp. 331–348.
11. Mai, H.T.; Kang, J.; Lee, J. A machine learning-based surrogate model for optimization of truss structures with geometrically nonlinear behavior. *Finite Elem. Anal. Des.* **2021**, *196*, 103572. [CrossRef]
12. Zhang, W.; Li, X.; Ma, H.; Luo, Z.; Li, X. Federated learning for machinery fault diagnosis with dynamic validation and self-supervision. *Knowl.-Based Syst.* **2021**, *213*, 106679. [CrossRef]
13. Zhang, W.; Li, X.; Ma, H.; Luo, Z.; Li, X. Universal domain adaptation in fault diagnostics with hybrid weighted deep adversarial learning. *IEEE Trans. Ind. Inform.* **2021**, *17*, 7957–7967. [CrossRef]
14. Shepard, D. A two-dimensional interpolation function for irregularly-spaced data. In Proceedings of the 1968 23rd ACM National Conference, New York, NY, USA, 27–29 August 1968; pp. 517–524.
15. Shields, M.D.; Zhang, J. The generalization of Latin hypercube sampling. *Reliab. Eng. Syst. Saf.* **2016**, *148*, 96–108. [CrossRef]
16. Jones, D.R.; Schonlau, M.; Welch, W.J. Efficient global optimization of expensive black-box functions. *J. Glob. Optim.* **1998**, *13*, 455–492. [CrossRef]
17. Huang, D.; Allen, T.T.; Notz, W.I.; Zeng, N. Global optimization of stochastic black-box systems via sequential kriging meta-models. *J. Glob. Optim.* **2006**, *34*, 441–466. [CrossRef]
18. Huang, D.; Allen, T.T.; Notz, W.I.; Miller, R.A. Sequential kriging optimization using multiple-fidelity evaluations. *Struct. Multidiscip. Optim.* **2006**, *32*, 369–382. [CrossRef]
19. Dong, H.; Song, B.; Wang, P.; Huang, S. A kind of balance between exploitation and exploration on kriging for global optimization of expensive functions. *J. Mech. Sci. Technol.* **2015**, *29*, 2121–2133. [CrossRef]
20. Zhao, L.; Wang, P.; Song, B.; Wang, X.; Dong, H. An efficient kriging modeling method for high-dimensional design problems based on maximal information coefficient. *Struct. Multidiscip. Optim.* **2019**, *61*, 39–57. [CrossRef]
21. Gutmann, H.M. A radial basis function method for global optimization. *J. Glob. Optim.* **2001**, *19*, 201–227. [CrossRef]

22. Regis, R.G.; Shoemaker, C.A. Improved strategies for radial basis function methods for global optimization. *J. Glob. Optim.* **2007**, *37*, 113–135. [CrossRef]
23. Regis, R.G.; Shoemaker, C.A. A stochastic radial basis function method for the global optimization of expensive functions. *INFORMS J. Comput.* **2007**, *19*, 497–509. [CrossRef]
24. Regis, R.G.; Shoemaker, C.A. Parallel stochastic global optimization using radial basis functions. *INFORMS J. Comput.* **2009**, *21*, 411–426. [CrossRef]
25. Joseph, V.R.; Kang, L. Regression-based inverse distance weighting with applications to computer experiments. *Technometrics* **2011**, *53*, 254–265. [CrossRef]
26. Bemporad, A. Global optimization via inverse distance weighting. *arXiv* **2019**, arXiv:1906.06498.
27. Regis, R.G. Stochastic radial basis function algorithms for large-scale optimization involving expensive black-box objective and constraint functions. *Comput. Oper. Res.* **2011**, *38*, 837–853. [CrossRef]
28. Regis, R.G. Constrained optimization by radial basis function interpolation for high-dimensional expensive black-box problems with infeasible initial points. *Eng. Optim.* **2014**, *46*, 218–243. [CrossRef]
29. Nuñez, L.; Regis, R.G.; Varela, K. Accelerated random search for constrained global optimization assisted by radial basis function surrogates. *J. Comput. Appl. Math.* **2018**, *340*, 276–295. [CrossRef]
30. Li, Y.; Wu, Y.; Zhao, J.; Chen, L. A Kriging-based constrained global optimization algorithm for expensive black-box functions with infeasible initial points. *J. Glob. Optim.* **2017**, *67*, 343–366. [CrossRef]
31. Carpio, R.R.; Giordano, R.C.; Secchi, A.R. Enhanced surrogate assisted framework for constrained global optimization of expensive black-box functions. *Comput. Chem. Eng.* **2018**, *118*, 91–102. [CrossRef]
32. Qian, J.; Yi, J.; Cheng, Y.; Liu, J.; Zhou, Q. A sequential constraints updating approach for Kriging surrogate model-assisted engineering optimization design problem. *Eng. Comput.* **2019**, *36*, 993–1009. [CrossRef]
33. Bartoli, N.; Lefebvre, T.; Dubreuil, S.; Olivanti, R.; Priem, R.; Bons, N.; Martins, J.R.; Morlier, J. Adaptive modeling strategy for constrained global optimization with application to aerodynamic wing design. *Aerosp. Sci. Technol.* **2019**, *90*, 85–102. [CrossRef]
34. Forrester, A.; Sobester, A.; Keane, A. *Engineering Design via Surrogate Modelling: A Practical Guide*; John Wiley & Sons: Hoboken, NJ, USA, 2008.
35. Shi, R.; Liu, L.; Long, T.; Wu, Y.; Tang, Y. Filter-based adaptive Kriging method for black-box optimization problems with expensive objective and constraints. *Comput. Methods Appl. Mech. Eng.* **2019**, *347*, 782–805. [CrossRef]
36. Joseph, V.R.; Hung, Y.; Sudjianto, A. Blind kriging: A new method for developing metamodels. *J. Mech. Des.* **2008**, *130*, 031102. [CrossRef]
37. Kersaudy, P.; Sudret, B.; Varsier, N.; Picon, O.; Wiart, J. A new surrogate modeling technique combining Kriging and polynomial chaos expansions–Application to uncertainty analysis in computational dosimetry. *J. Comput. Phys.* **2015**, *286*, 103–117. [CrossRef]
38. Zhang, Y.; Yao, W.; Ye, S.; Chen, X. A regularization method for constructing trend function in Kriging model. *Struct. Multidiscip. Optim.* **2019**, *59*, 1221–1239. [CrossRef]
39. Zhang, Y.; Yao, W.; Chen, X.; Ye, S. A penalized blind likelihood Kriging method for surrogate modeling. *Struct. Multidiscip. Optim.* **2019**, *61*, 457–474. [CrossRef]
40. Couckuyt, I.; Forrester, A.; Gorissen, D.; De Turck, F.; Dhaene, T. Blind Kriging: Implementation and performance analysis. *Adv. Eng. Softw.* **2012**, *49*, 1–13. [CrossRef]
41. Forrester, A.I.; Keane, A.J. Recent advances in surrogate-based optimization. *Prog. Aerosp. Sci.* **2009**, *45*, 50–79. [CrossRef]
42. Palar, P.S.; Shimoyama, K. On efficient global optimization via universal Kriging surrogate models. *Struct. Multidiscip. Optim.* **2018**, *57*, 2377–2397. [CrossRef]
43. Joseph, V.R.; Delaney, J.D. Functionally induced priors for the analysis of experiments. *Technometrics* **2007**, *49*, 1–11. [CrossRef]
44. Haftka, R.T.; Villanueva, D.; Chaudhuri, A. Parallel surrogate-assisted global optimization with expensive functions—A survey. *Struct. Multidiscip. Optim.* **2016**, *54*, 3–13. [CrossRef]
45. Forrester, A.; Jones, D. Global optimization of deceptive functions with sparse sampling. In Proceedings of the 12th AIAA/ISSMO Multidisciplinary Analysis and Optimization Conference, Victoria, BC, Canada, 10–12 September 2008; p. 5996.
46. Keane, A.; Bright, A. Passive vibration control via unusual geometries: Experiments on model aerospace structures. *J. Sound Vib.* **1996**, *190*, 713–719. [CrossRef]
47. Couckuyt, I.; De Turck, F.; Dhaene, T.; Gorissen, D. Automatic surrogate model type selection during the optimization of expensive black-box problems. In Proceedings of the 2011 Winter Simulation Conference (WSC), Phoenix, AZ, USA, 11–14 December 2011; IEEE: New York, NY, USA, 2011; pp. 4269–4279.
48. Suprayitno; Yu, J.C. Evolutionary reliable regional Kriging surrogate for expensive optimization. *Eng. Optim.* **2019**, *51*, 247–264. [CrossRef]
49. Shao, T.; Krishnamurty, S. A clustering-based surrogate model updating approach to simulation-based engineering design. *J. Mech. Des.* **2008**, *130*, 041101. [CrossRef]
50. Andrei, N.; Andrei, N. *Nonlinear Optimization Applications Using the GAMS Technology*; Springer: Berlin/Heidelberg, Germany, 2013.

mathematics

Article

Machine Learning-Based Models for Shear Strength Prediction of UHPFRC Beams

Xiangyong Ni [1,*] and Kangkang Duan [2]

1 Department of Disaster Mitigation for Structures, Tongji University, Shanghai 200092, China
2 Department of Civil Engineering, University of British Columbia, Vancouver, BC V6T 1Z4, Canada
* Correspondence: 20310091@tongji.edu.cn

Abstract: Estimating shear strength is a crucial aspect of beam design. The goal of this research is to develop a shear strength calculation technique for ultra-high performance fiber reinforced concrete (UHPFRC) beams. To begin, a shear test database of 200 UHPFRC beam specimens is established. Then, random forest (RF) is used to evaluate the importance of influence factors for the shear strength of UHPFRC beams. Subsequently, three machine learning (ML)-based models, including artificial neural network (ANN), support vector regression (SVR), and eXtreme-gradient boosting (XGBoost), are proposed to compute shear strength. Results demonstrate that the area of longitudinal reinforcement has the greatest influence on the shear capacity of UHPFRC beams, and ten parameters with high importance (e.g., the area of longitudinal reinforcement, the stirrup strength, the cross-section area, the shear span ratio, fiber volume fraction, etc.) are selected as input parameters. The models of ANN, SVR, and XGBoost have close accuracy, and their R^2 are 0.8825, 0.9016, and 0.8839, respectively, which are much larger than those of existing theoretical models. In addition, the average ratios of prediction values of ANN, SVR, and XGBoost models to experimental results are 1.08, 1.02, and 1.10, respectively; the coefficients of variation are 0.28, 0.21, and 0.28, respectively. The SVR model has the best accuracy and reliability. The accuracy and reliability of ML-based models are much better than those of existing models for calculating the shear strength of UHPFRC beams.

Keywords: ultra-high performance fiber reinforced concrete (UHPFRC); beams; machine learning-based models; shear strength

MSC: 62P30

Citation: Ni, X.; Duan, K. Machine Learning-Based Models for Shear Strength Prediction of UHPFRC Beams. *Mathematics* **2022**, *10*, 2918. https://doi.org/10.3390/math10162918

Academic Editors: Shujin Laima, Yong Cao, Xiaowei Jin and Hehe Ren

Received: 24 July 2022
Accepted: 11 August 2022
Published: 13 August 2022

Publisher's Note: MDPI stays neutral with regard to jurisdictional claims in published maps and institutional affiliations.

Copyright: © 2022 by the authors. Licensee MDPI, Basel, Switzerland. This article is an open access article distributed under the terms and conditions of the Creative Commons Attribution (CC BY) license (https://creativecommons.org/licenses/by/4.0/).

1. Introduction

High-performance materials play a significant advantage in improving the performance of structures, reducing self-weight and saving materials, and leading to the development of high-performance structures [1]. Ultra-high-performance fiber reinforced concrete (UHPFRC), a newly developed high-performance material in civil engineering, offers remarkable features such as ultra-high strength, high durability, and micro-crack solid self-healing capacity, which may help structures last longer and require less maintenance. The application of UHPFRC in concrete structures can significantly improve their mechanical performance and durability and reduce the size of the cross-section, saving concrete consumption. The research on the mechanical properties of UHFRPC members is the basis of the application of UHPFRC material in concrete structures, and the shear strength is an essential index for the evaluation and design of UHPFRC beams, so it is necessary to conduct in-depth discussion and research on the shear strength of UHPFRC beams.

The shear performance of UHPFRC beams has been experimentally investigated in depth. These shear tests have examined the effects of fiber volume fraction and type, shear-span ratio, stirrup configuration, longitudinal reinforcement configuration, and other parameters on the flexure and shear properties of UHPFRC beams. The experiment results show that the inclined cracks of the UHPFRC beam are dense and fine under shear force [2–5]. The bearing capacity and ductility of UHPFRC beams with fibers may be significantly increased compared to UHPC beams without fibers [3,6–10]. Brittle shear failure can be converted to ductile flexure failure thanks to the fibers [11–15]. The shear and flexural performance of UHPFRC beams may be significantly improved by increasing the fiber volume fraction [4,6,11,15–18]. The performance of UHPFRC beams is influenced by different kinds of fibers. Lowering the shear span ratio, which is similar to that of reinforced concrete beams, can improve the shear capacity of UHPFRC beams [5,12,17,19,20]. Shear experiments on UHPFRC beams reveal that fiber and stirrup can enhance beam shear strength, whereas fibers can lower the stirrup ratio [6,8,21,22]. As a result, numerous researchers have investigated the use of fibers to minimize the minimum stirrup ratio of UHPFRC beams [2,6,9,23–25]. The shear strength of UHPFRC beams without stirrups rises as concrete strength and fiber volume fraction increase, and the fibers aid in the shift from shear tension to shear compression failure mode [18,26–28].

However, there are limited theoretical studies on the strength calculation technique for UHPFRC beams. In general, the complex tensile stress distribution of UHPFRC in the tensile zone is equivalent to a rectangular distribution with the constant stress of kf_t, where f_t is the tensile strength of UHPFRC and k is a constant that indicates the stress reduction coefficient [29]. The existing theoretical models for the flexural strength of UHPFRC beams proposed by the above scholars are based on the assumption of a flat cross-section and take into account the tensile stress after cracking of the UHPFRC section. Qi et al. [30] proposed a method for calculating the shear strength of UHPFRC beams, which considers the influence of fibers, compressive UHPFRC, and stirrups. Shear tests of T-shaped UHPFRC beams confirmed the accuracy and dependability of the method. Ahmad et al. [31] combined UHPFRC with high-strength steel bars and applied them to beam members and conducted shear loading tests on ten beam specimens. Based on the test data of the ten beams, the formula for calculating the shear capacity of UHPFRC beams was fitted.

In recent years, the method based on computer machine learning has been widely used in the mechanical analysis of civil structures. This method can comprehensively consider the influence of various factors through computer algorithms and has high prediction accuracy. Roya et al. [32] collected UHPFRC beam test data from previous literature and used data-driven machine learning (ML) framework to predict the failure mode and strength of UHPFRC beams, and the methods included support vector machine (SVM), artificial neural networks (ANN), k-nearest neighbor (k-NN), and genetic programming (GP). The prediction accuracy was examined by the collected test data, and the research results showed that the proposed method has reasonable accuracy. Kim et al. [33] used the ML methods of CatBoost, eXtreme-gradient boosting, histogram gradient boosting, and random forest to predict the interfacial bonding strength of FRP–concrete, and the results indicate that the proposed models have high prediction accuracy. Yaseen et al. [34] used a new support vector regression algorithm coupled with particle swarm optimization to establish the method for the shear strength of fiber reinforced concrete beams, and the comparative analysis results show that this prediction method has reasonable accuracy and can provide a reference for the shear strength design of fiber reinforced concrete beams. Mangalathu et al. [35] collected the test data of the existing beam-column joint specimens and used these data to train the machine learning techniques and established the prediction model for failure modes and shear strength of beam-column joint members, and the prediction accuracy of the method was examined by the test data. The research results show that this prediction method has a good calculation efficiency and reasonable accuracy. Payam et al. [36] proposed three innovative ML-based models to calculate the shear strength of reinforced concrete (RC) walls, and the combination of the support vector regression with meta-heuristic optimization algorithms such as teaching–learning-based optimization (TLBO), particle swarm optimization (PSO), and Harris Hawks optimization (HHO) are used for establishing the models. The results indicate that the proposed ML-based models have better accuracy than the methods proposed by the design codes and the researchers. Chen et al. [37] utilized a hybrid intelligence algorithm including the artificial neural network and particle swarm (ANN-PSO) to propose an ML-based model to predict the shear strength of squat RC walls. A total of 139 test results of squat walls are collected and utilized to train and test the hybrid ANN–PSO model. The results show that the proposed ML-based model has good prediction accuracy of the shear strength of such RC walls. Keshtegar et al. [38] combined an artificial neural network (ANN) with adaptive harmony search optimization (AHS) algorithm to establish an ML-based model for the shear strength of RC walls, and the results indicate that the proposed ANN-AHS model has excellent prediction accuracy in modeling the shear strength of RC shear walls. Gondia et al. [39] utilized genetic programming (GP) to develop an elegant shear strength prediction expression using a dataset of 254 Squat reinforced concrete shear walls with boundary constraints. The results show that the proposed expression can better predict the shear strength of RC walls compared to other shear strength prediction methods in design codes and literature. Wu et al. [40] used a back-propagation (BP) neural network algorithm to predict the shear strength of discontinuities with different joint wall compressive strength (DDJCS), and the input parameters include the joint wall strength combination, normal stress, and joint roughness. The results indicate that the prediction accuracy of the developed ML-based model is better than the multivariate regression model. Nguyen et al. [41] utilized an artificial neural network (ANN) to establish an ML-based model for predicting the shear strength of squat flanged RC walls, and the test data of a total of squat flanged RC wall specimens were collected to train and test the ANN model. The results show that the developed ANN model has better prediction accuracy than the existing equations.

The above studies indicate that the ML-based models have high prediction accuracy for estimating the shear strength of RC members, while they are currently focused on the establishment of shear strength models of RC beams and walls, and little related research has been conducted on UHPFRC beams. Many parameters have a critical influence on the shear strength of RC members, and each parameter has different importance coefficients for the shear strength. The input parameters of the above ML-based models adopt the empirical critical parameters commonly used in theoretical models, such as stirrup strength, stirrup ratio, cross-section size, etc., while the other critical parameters may be not considered. In ML-based models, selecting the parameters with high importance as the input parameters can ensure the accuracy of the model prediction and improve computational efficiency. Therefore, it is necessary to evaluate the importance coefficient of each parameter to the shear capacity of RC members, while it is not considered in the previous ML-based models. The fibers in UHPFRC are distributed randomly in the beam specimens, and the direction and position of the fibers can affect the performance of the beam, but it cannot consider the effect of each individual fiber owing to a large number of fibers in the beams. In many theoretical models, an effective coefficient is used to consider the effect of fibers on average, and the coefficient is mostly a fixed value, and the empirical value obtained by the test is mostly used, but there is no uniform value for this value at present. In ML-based models, through machine learning, the complex mapping relationship between fibers and beam shear strength can be comprehensively established, and the effect of randomly distributed independent fibers on beam shear capacity can be accurately equivalent.

The method for shear strength of UHPFRC beams is an essential influencing parameter for its design, while the research on the shear bearing capacity of UHPFRC beams is relatively insufficient, so it is necessary to conduct in-depth research on the estimation for shear capacity to promote the application of UHPFRC in concrete structures. The existing theoretical methods have many assumptions, simplifications, and considered parameters, so their prediction accuracy may be not high. The ML-based method can accurately consider the influence of each parameter on the prediction targets, and it can address the gaps in the theoretical methods. To this end, this paper collects the test data of 200 UHPFRC beam specimens, and establishes three prediction models of the shear strength utilizing the machine learning (ML) methods, including ANN, SVR, and XGBoost. The accuracy and applicability of the proposed models are evaluated by comparing them to the existing theoretical methods.

2. Experimental Database

The shear tests of UHPFRC beam specimens in the previous literature are summarized, and the corresponding database is established to provide experimental verification for the subsequent research on the shear capacity of UHPFRC beams in this paper, as well as test data support for relevant theories and finite element research on UHPFRC beams. At present, the loading setup for shear tests of UHPFRC beams can be divided into four-point loading and three-point loading setups (Figure 1a,b), where a in the figure is shear span, and p is peak shear force of the beam specimens.

The experimental database contains 200 UHPFRC beam specimens failing in shear, as listed in Table A1 in Appendix A, which summarizes 24 parameters of the beam specimens, including dimension and reinforcement details. In Table A1, A_s is the longitudinal reinforcement area, f_{yw} is stirrup strength, A_{so} is the beam cross-section area, A is the total section area, λ is shear span ratio, A_s' is the area of compression longitudinal reinforcement, a is the shear span, V_f is the fiber volume fraction, ρ_w is the stirrup ratio, t_w is web thickness, f_y is longitudinal reinforcement yielding strength, UHPC-fc and ft are, respectively, compressive and tensile strength of UHPFRC, ρ_s is the ratio of longitudinal reinforcement, I is the depth of section moment of inertia, b_f is compressive flange width, h_o is the effective height of cross-section, ρ_s' is the ratio of compressive longitudinal reinforcement, h is the height of the cross-section, s is the stirrup spacing, t_f is the thickness of top flange, and t_b is the thickness of the bottom flange.

The purpose of this shear testing was to see how various conditions affected the shear performance of UHPFRC beams. According to the findings, the effects of the shear span ratio, longitudinal reinforcement ratio, and stirrup reinforcement ratio on the shear performance of UHPFRC beams are similar to those of reinforced concrete beams. Fibers in UHPFRC can ensure the integrity of the beams after the full development of inclined cracks, and it is conducive to enhancing the ductility of the components. The bridging effect of fibers at inclined fractures after UHPFRC cracking can produce tension stress, effectively increasing beam shear performance.

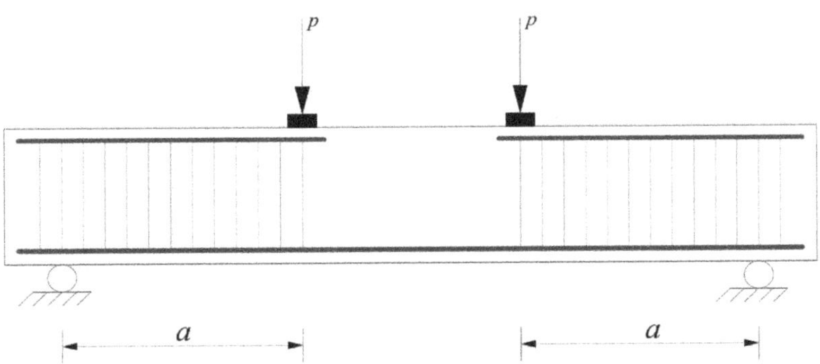

(a)

Figure 1. *Cont.*

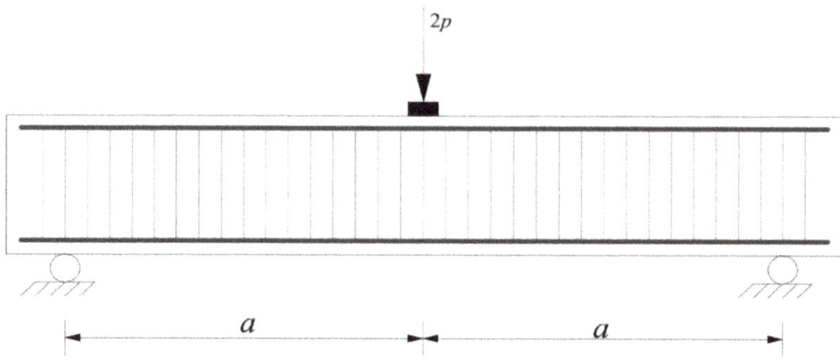

(b)

Figure 1. Shear loading tests of beams: (**a**) four-point loading setup; (**b**) three-point loading setup.

Figure 2 shows the key parameter distributions of the collected UHPFRC beam specimens. The cross-section forms of these beam specimens include rectangular (123 pieces), I-shaped (67 pieces), and T-shaped (10 pieces). The shear span ratios of the models range from 0.79 to 8.46, and most of them range from 1.38 to 3.74. The compressive strength values of UHPFRC used in the specimens are between 78 and 222 MPa, and most UHPFRC with a strength between 78 and 96 MPa do not have fibers or have a low volume fraction of fibers, which has relatively low compressive strength. In some literature, the data on the tensile strength of UHPFRC material is not given, and its tensile strength is calculated according to $0.6\sqrt{f_c}$. The fiber volume fractions of UHPFRC used in beam specimens are between 0 and 5%, and the yield strength of longitudinal bars is between 365 and 1835 MPa. The collected UHPFRC beam specimens include some illustrations without stirrups. The stirrup strength of the stirrups is between 284 and 568 MPa, and the stirrup ratio is between 0 and 1.7%. In conclusion, the dimensions of these beam specimens are various, and these UHPFRC beam specimens have investigated the influence of all critical parameters on the shear strength, so the research parameters are sufficient. Moreover, the variation range of the parameters is wide, and the parameter values of different beam specimens have obvious differences. The above features of the collected data allowing the ML-based model for the shear strength of UHPFRC beams to be effectively verified.

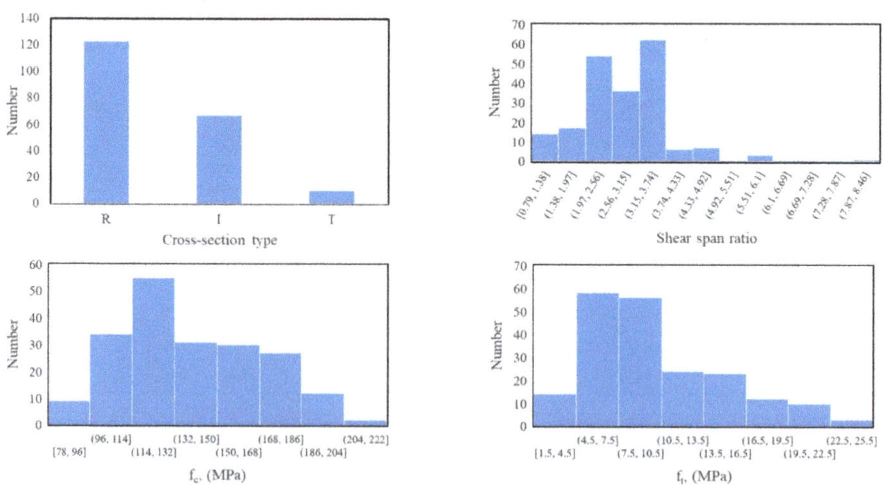

Figure 2. *Cont.*

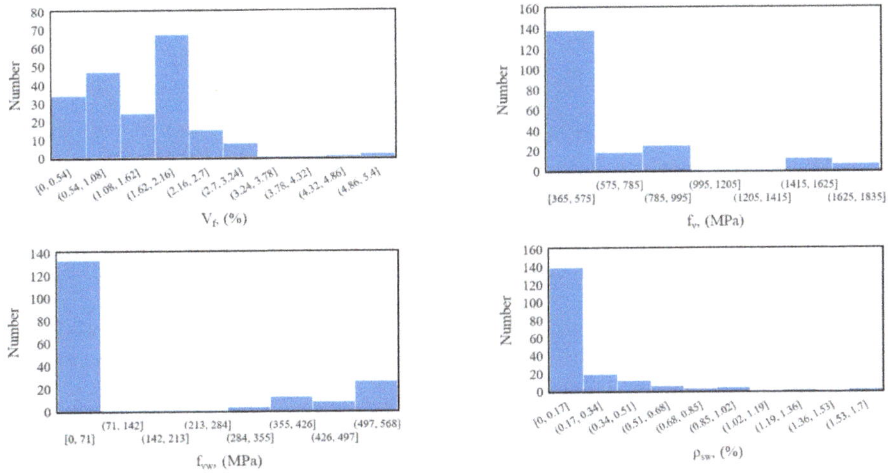

Figure 2. Parameter distributions of UHPFRC beam specimens.

3. Parameter Evaluation and Selection

3.1. Parameter Evaluation Method

The ML algorithm of random forest (RF) is used to evaluate the importance of the given parameters. RF combines the ensemble learning theory of Bagging with the random subspace method and introduces the random sampling of samples and random sampling of features to achieve a more accurate classification than the single algorithm. So, RF is composed of Bootstrap resampling, decision tree generation, and random forest formation, and the classification results are as follows:

$$h(x) = \arg\max_{y} \sum_{i=1}^{k} (Ih_i(x, \theta_i) = y) \tag{1}$$

where $h(x)$ represents the classification results determined by voting of multiple decision trees, h_i is the ith decision tree classification model; x is the vector of characteristic parameters to be identified, θ_i is the self-help training set for training the ith decision tree, k is the number of decision trees; $I(.)$ is an indicator function.

Gini coefficient (GC) is commonly utilized to split nodes during the generation of decision trees, and the parameter importance is obtained by calculating the average Gini coefficient change of feature f_i [42]. The GC can be defined as:

$$Gini(p) = \sum_{m=1}^{M} p_m(1 - p_m) \tag{2}$$

where p_m is the probability of a sample belonging to class m, and there is a total of M classes.

Analogously, the GC of Database D can be defined as:

$$Gini(D) = \sum_{m=1}^{M} \frac{|C_m|}{|D|}\left(1 - \frac{|C_m|}{|D|}\right) \tag{3}$$

where C_m is the subset of the samples in class m of Dataset D. On node n, feature f_i divides Dataset D into two parts, D_1 and D_2, so the changes in the *Gini* coefficient can be obtained by:

$$VIM_{i,n}^{gini} = Gini(D) - \frac{|D_1|}{|D|}Gini(D_1) - \frac{|D_1|}{|D|}Gini(D_2) \tag{4}$$

So, the importance of f_i in kth decision tree can be expressed as:

$$VIM_{i,k}^{gini} = \sum_{n=1}^{N_i} VIM_{i,k}^{gini} \tag{5}$$

where N_i is the node number divided by feature f_i. Therefore, f_i importance can be obtained by

$$VIM_i^{gini} = \frac{\sum_{k=1}^{K} VIM_{i,k}^{gini}}{\sum_{j=1}^{d}\sum_{k=1}^{K} VIM_{i,k}^{gini}} \quad (6)$$

where d is the feature number, and K is the decision tree number in the RF model.

3.2. Results and Discussions

Figure 3 shows the influence importance of various parameters on the shear strength of UHPFRC beams by the above ML methods. It can be seen that the sectional area of longitudinal reinforcement has the greatest influence on the shear capacity of the UHPFRC beam with the importance coefficient of 0.14, and the stirrup strength, the cross-section area, the shear span ratio, etc., all have significant influence of the shear strength of UHPFRC beams. According to the existing shear tests on the UHPFRC beams, these parameters have a significant impact on the shear capacity, indicating that the parameter evaluation is reasonable. The sum of the importance coefficients of the first 12 parameters has reached 0.96. To simplify the calculation and maintain a certain calculation accuracy, the first 10 parameters are selected as input parameters.

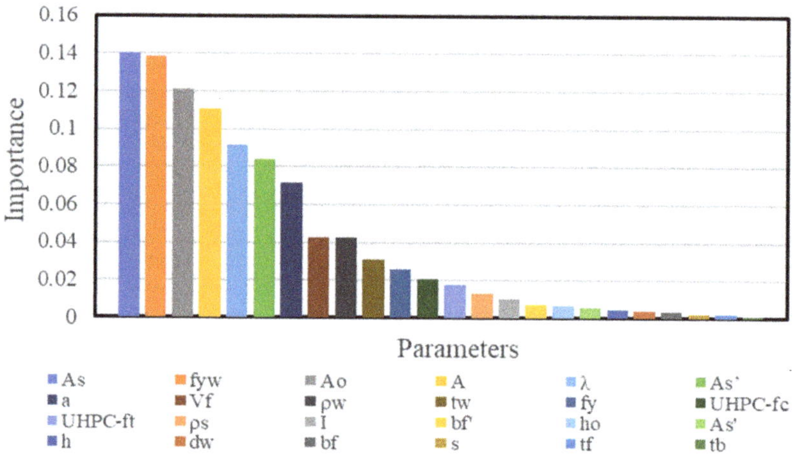

Figure 3. The influence importance of various parameters on the shear strength of UHPFRC beams.

4. ML Methods

Three commonly used ML algorithms were used to build the prediction models: ANN, SVR, and XGBoost. Based on statistical data, ML algorithms combine data and mathematical algorithms to find the relationships between the parameters and targets. After selecting appropriate parameters, the model usually achieves high accuracy, that is, ML methods are highly sensitive to parameter selection.

4.1. Prediction Steps

According to the workflow shown in Figure 4, the prediction models of shear capacity of UHPFRC beam based on ANN, SVR, and XGBoost are respectively established. The detailed prediction steps are as follows:

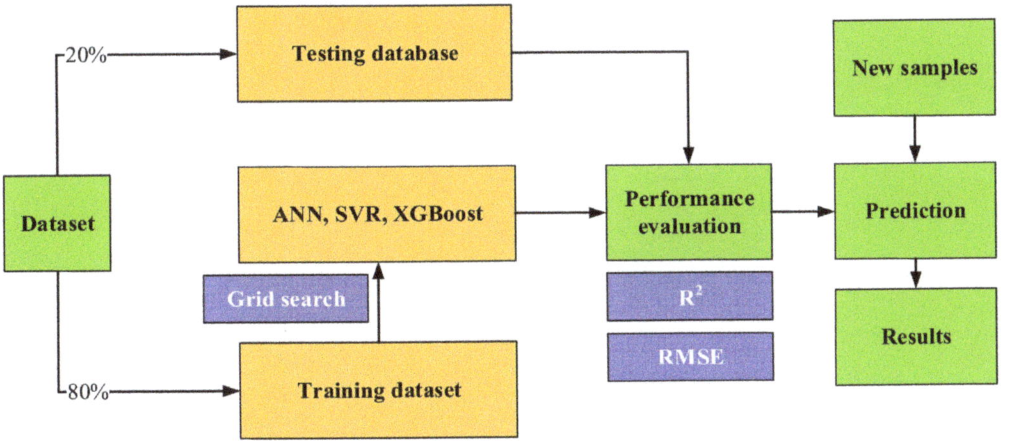

Figure 4. Flowchart of developing the ML model.

Step 1. Dividing the dataset. The dataset is divided into a training dataset and a testing dataset in the ratio of 8:2.

Step 2. Model training. ANN, SVR, and XGBoost are respectively used to establish the prediction models based on the training database. Cross-validation and grid search strategies were used to optimize the hyperparameters, and MSE (mean square error) was used as the loss function. Finally, the prediction model was obtained. During the training process, dropout and L2 regularization were used to avoid the overfitting of ANN models. Dropout randomly makes some neurons invalid at a probability of p during each epoch of training, and all neurons will be used for final models. Of course, to maintain the scale of predicted value, the weight of neurons in the final models will multiply p. In this study, $p = 0.2$. L2 regularization used a penalty coefficient to avoid the network becoming too complex. SVR used its regularized risk function to help it avoid overfitting. In XGBoost models, max depth and gamma were used to avoid overfitting. By and large, the smaller the maximum depth, the larger the gamma, and the more difficult the models are to overfit. Moreover, overfitting and underfitting can be prevented by controlling the MSE of the training set and the testing set.

Step 3. Prediction accuracy evaluation. The model obtained in Step 2 is evaluated by the testing dataset, and new samples are used for the prediction evaluation, which is verified by the fit goodness of R^2. R^2 represents the degree of fitting of regression results to measured values, and the closer it is to 1, the better fitting degree of regression results. The calculation formula is as follows:

$$R^2 = 1 - \frac{\sum_{i=1}^{n} (y_i - p_i)^2}{\sum_{i=1}^{n} (y_i - y_m)^2} \quad (7)$$

where y_i and p_i are, respectively, the measured and predicted results, and y_m is the mean value of measured results.

Meanwhile, the ratios of predicted to measured values are used to evaluate the accuracy of the prediction model, that is, the coefficient of variation (CoV) of the ratio is used for the evaluation. CoV is used for evaluating the reliability of the ML-based models.

$$CoV = \frac{\left[\sum_{i=1}^{n} \left(\frac{p_i}{y_i} - \sigma \right)^2 \Big/ n-1 \right]^{0.5}}{\sigma} \quad (8)$$

where σ is the mean value of p_i/y_i.

4.2. ML Methods

4.2.1. Artificial Neural Network (ANN)

ANN has three parts: the input layer, hidden layer, and output layer. Neurons in each layer can receive messages from all neurons in the previous layers, and generate signal output to the next layer, the signal from the input layer to the output layer does one-way propagation. For the training data in the input, each neuron in the first-layer network receives the input training data equally, and the training data received by each neuron should take into account the connection weight w and bias b between the input data. After processing by the activation function, the input value of this layer is generated and transferred to the next layer. After that, the output value of the neural network is finally obtained. In this way, a neural network resembles a composite function nested through layers of simple functions. In the training of the neural network model, the loss function to be optimized should be determined first, and in most cases, the mean square error function should be used as the loss function. The classification problem can also adopt the cross entropy function, where the loss function is assumed to be J, and then the model is trained by a gradient descent algorithm. As for the gradient derivative, it is easy to obtain the gradient of the jth node at the Nth layer to the last layer of the neural network, and it can be expressed as:

$$\delta_j^N = \frac{\partial J}{\partial w_j^N} = \frac{\partial J}{\partial y_j^N} \cdot \frac{\partial y_j^N}{\partial u_j^N} \cdot \frac{\partial u_j^N}{\partial w_j^N} \tag{9}$$

where y_j^N is the output value of the corresponding node. When the mean square error function is chosen, J can be expressed as:

$$J = \frac{1}{2}\left\|\bar{y}_j^N - y_j^N\right\|^2 \tag{10}$$

u_j^N is the input value of the function activated for the node:

$$u_j^N = w_j^N \cdot x_j^N + b_j^N \tag{11}$$

where w_j^N and b_j^N are, respectively, the weight and bias of the corresponding node, x_j^N is the input value of the node. When the node adopts the Sigmoid function as the activation function, the gradient can be obtained as follows:

$$\delta_j^N = -y_j^N(1 - y_j^N)(\bar{y}_j^N - y_j^N)x_j^N \tag{12}$$

After the gradient is obtained, the weight of this layer is updated according to the set step size, and the gradient of $N-1$ layer can be further obtained as:

$$\delta_j^{N-1} = \frac{\partial J}{\partial w_j^{N-1}} = \sum_k \frac{\partial J}{\partial u_j^N} \cdot \frac{\partial u_j^N}{\partial x_j^N} \cdot \frac{\partial x_j^N}{\partial w_j^{N-1}} \tag{13}$$

It can be seen that the gradient of $N-1$ layer is related to all nodes connected to N layer. Equation (13) can be regarded as the multiplication of three parts. The first part is the calculation content of the N layer, which is given in Equation (12). The middle reflects the content of the connection between the two layers, and the result of the derivative is the weight w_j^N. The last part is the derivation calculation of this layer, which can be referred to Equation (9). Repeat the above process until the weight of all layers is updated to complete a step of training, the above process is the back propagation algorithm.

We can refer to Equation (9) and repeat the above process until the weight of all layers is updated to complete a step of training, the above process is the back propagation algorithm.

4.2.2. Support Vector Regression (SVR)

SVR adopts statistical learning theory with the principle of structural risk minimization, and the sample generalization performance is very strong, avoiding the high dependence on sample data. The training set is given as:

$$T = \{(x_1, y_1), (x_2, y_2), \ldots, (x_n, y_n)\} \tag{14}$$

The regression function is assumed as:

$$y = f(x) = w^T(x) + b;\ i = 1, 2, \ldots, n \tag{15}$$

To improve the generalization ability, it is necessary to enlarge the ε pipeline. This minimizes the possibility of the unknown point going beyond the region. However, when the training set is nonlinear, the generalization performance of the regression function obtained is very poor even after the optimization is completed. Therefore, the kernel function $K(x_i.x_j)$ is introduced to transform the low-dimensional nonlinear problem into a high-dimensional linear problem, and finally, the regression problem is transformed into the following optimization problem:

$$\min \sum_{i,j=1}^{n} (\alpha_i - \alpha_i^*)(\alpha_j - \alpha_j^*)K(x_i, x_j) + \varepsilon \sum_{i=1}^{n} (\alpha_i + \alpha_i^*) - \sum_{i=1}^{n} (\alpha_i - \alpha_i^*) \tag{16}$$

where α_i and α_i^* are diagonal matrices for the undetermined coefficients. So we can get the optimal nonlinear regression function:

$$f(x) = \sum_{i=1}^{n} (\alpha_i - \alpha_i^*)K(x_i \cdot x_j) + b \tag{17}$$

The radial basis function is selected as the kernel function [43], which is expressed as:

$$K(x_i, x_j) = \exp\left(-\gamma \|x_i - x_j\|^2\right) \tag{18}$$

4.2.3. eXtreme-Gradient Boosting (XGBoost)

XGBoost is a promotion algorithm proposed by Chen et al. [44] of the University of Washington. The lifting algorithm is to train a large number of weak learners through certain strategies, for example, the shallow decision tree model, and then combine the prediction results of these weak classifiers through certain methods, and finally achieve the algorithm of greatly improving the prediction effect. XGBoost uses a shallow regression tree as the weak classifier. For the first shallow regression tree model obtained by training, assuming that it is represented as $F_0(\boldsymbol{t})$ and $\boldsymbol{t}$ represents the instance vector in the feature space, let the classifier obtained in the first step be $y;_0{}'$. On this basis, train the 1, 2, 3, etc. M shallow regression tree model $F_m(\boldsymbol{t})$. XGBoost first calculates and obtains the first and second derivatives h_i and g_i of the loss function of the error between the classifier and the predicted value obtained in the previous step, namely $m-1$, then the objective function of $F_m(\boldsymbol{t})$ can be obtained according to the second-order expansion of Taylor function:

$$obj^{(m)} = \sum_{i=1}^{N} \left[g_i F_m(t_i) + \frac{1}{2} h_i F_m^2(t_i) \right] + \Omega(F_m) \tag{19}$$

$\Omega(F_m)$ is the regularization term, which can prevent the algorithm from blindly increasing the model complexity to improve the accuracy, thus leading to overfitting. $\Omega(F_m)$ can be expressed as:

$$\Omega(F_m) = \gamma T + 1/2\lambda ||w||^2 \tag{20}$$

where γ and λ are both penalty coefficients, T is the number of regression leaf nodes, and $||w||^2$ expresses the influence of the weight of regression leaf nodes on model complexity. It can be seen from Equation (17) that the fitting object in the iteration of XGBoost objective function is the residual between the predicted value and the observed value of the sample. The training process is to make $obj^{(m)}$ reach the minimum value, and the regression tree node splitting can adopt the mean square error to select the splitting feature. Finally, a new shallow tree model $F_m(t)$ can be obtained and the classifier is updated as:

$$y'_m(t) = y'_{m-1}(t) + F_m(t) \tag{21}$$

Figure 5 represents the XGBoost regression mechanism.

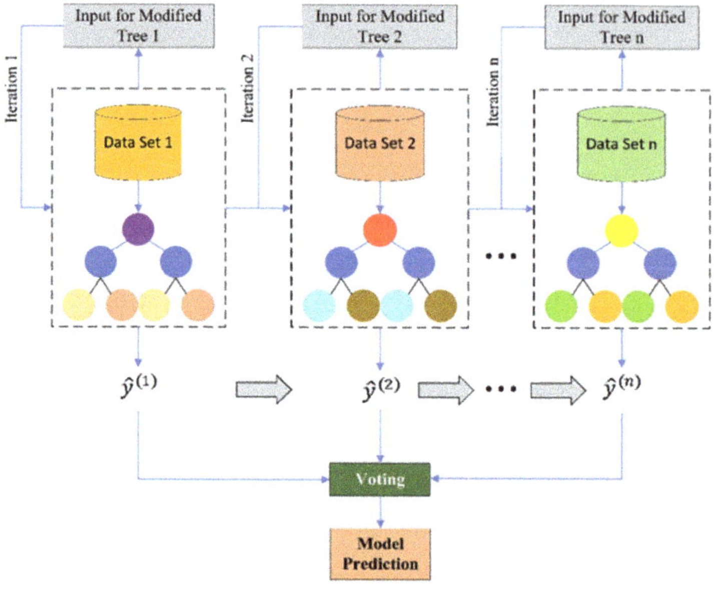

Figure 5. XGBoost regression mechanism.

4.3. Parameter Settings

(1) The number of hidden layers and neurons n was optimized by using the grid search method and cross-validation strategy. Figure 6 shows the variation in the goodness of fit with the number of hidden layers and neurons. As mentioned in Alavi et al.'s work [45], different metrics have different preferences. In this study, we used R^2 to perform a grid search and find the optimal values of hyperparameters since traditional models usually R^2 use to depict the performance. Moreover, we used mean absolute error as the index to explore the performance of parameter tuning. Results showed that the hyperparameters obtained by using R^2 also made models have lower mean absolute errors, i.e., in this study, the selection of metrics does not cause a big difference. Finally, one hidden layer containing 20 units was selected as the final ANN model structure. The activation function dropout was 0.2, and the regularized parameter L2 was 0.001.

(2) SVR uses the kernel function to nonlinearly map low-dimensional data to high-dimensional feature space and then obtains regression function in high-dimensional feature space. The same grid search method and cross-validation strategy were used to optimize the hyperparameters in SVR: penalty coefficient C and kernel function parameter γ. Finally, the hyperparameters C = 3500 and γ = 0.8 were selected.

(3) In XGBoost, at each boosting iteration, the 1st and 2nd order gradient for the objective function "squared error" was calculated for each training case. The model was built using XGBoost's scikit-learn compatibility. The best results were achieved using tree-based learners in XGBoost, and the parameters are listed in Table 1.

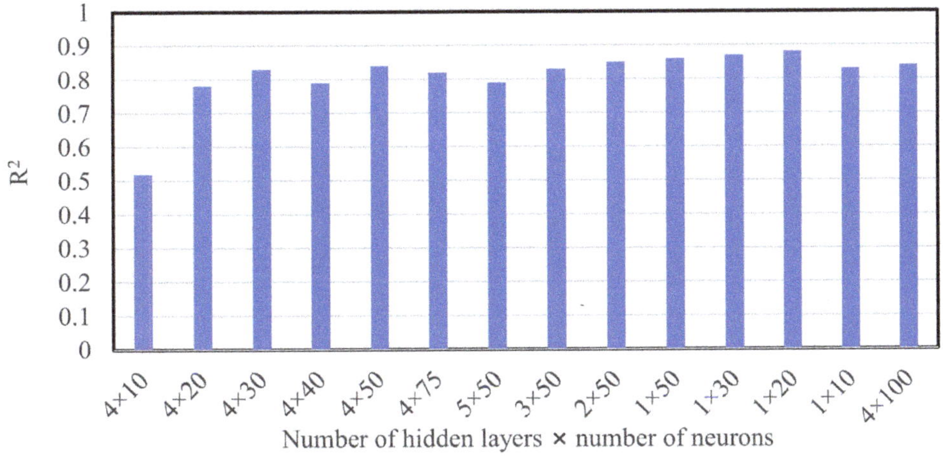

Figure 6. Goodness of fit with different numbers of hidden layers and neurons.

Table 1. Parameters of XGBoost.

Parameters	Values
Number of estimators	30
Learning rate	0.2
Max depth	3
Min child weight	2
Gamma	2000
Subsample	0.3
Colsample bytree	0.4
Scale pos weight	0.7

5. Comparative Analysis

5.1. Existing Models for Calculating Shear Strength of Fiber Reinforced Concrete Beams

(1) Qi et al. model for UHPFRC beams [30]

Qi et al. [30] suggested a calculating model for UHPFRC beam shear strength. The shear strength of UHPFRC beams is made up of three aspects: the shear capacity (V_c) provided by the shear-compression zone of the cross-section, the shear capacity supplied by the stirrups (V_s), the shear strength (V_{fi}) provided by the fibers, and the expression of the shear strength is shown as Equations (29) and (30). V_s is calculated using the truss model. The angle of the inclined crack is assumed to be 45°, and the shear strength provided by the fiber is calculated using the Mesoscale Fiber-Matrix Discrete (MFMD) Model.

$$V_{u1} = V_c + V_s + V_{fi} \tag{22}$$

$$\begin{cases} V_c = \frac{2}{3}bc\sqrt{f_t(f_t + 0.425f_c)} \\ V_s = \rho_v f_{vy} bd\cot(\varphi) \\ V_{fi} = \frac{1.28V_f bdl_f \tau_b \cot\varphi}{\pi d_f} \end{cases} \tag{23}$$

where c is the height of the compression zone of the cross-section, τ_b is the bond strength between a single fiber and the matrix.

(2) Ahmad et al. model for UHPFRC beams [31]

Based on the shear test data of UHPFRC beams, Ahmad et al. [31] fitted the formula of shear strength, which is expressed as Equation (31).

$$\begin{cases} V_{u2} = \left[0.35\sqrt{f_c} + 132\rho_l\frac{d}{a} + 14F_1^{5.8}\left(\frac{d}{a}\right)^{1.1}\right]\cdot b\cdot h + \frac{A_{sv}\cdot f_{vy}\cdot d}{s} \\ F_1 = (l_f/d_f)\cdot V_f\cdot \alpha \end{cases} \quad (24)$$

where α is a bond factor (for straight steel fibers = 0.5), a is the shear span, ρ is the ratio of longitudinal reinforcement, and h is the overall depth of the beam.

(3) The method for shear strength of fiber reinforced concrete (FRC) beams in China Association for Engineering Construction Standardization (CECS) 38:2004 [46]

This formula (Equation (32)) is suitable for calculating the shear strength of FRC beams. In this paper, the above test data is used to explore its applicability to the shear capacity of UHPFRC beams.

$$V_{u3} = 0.7f_t bd(1+\beta_v\lambda_f) + f_{vy}\frac{A_{sv}}{s}d \quad (25)$$

where β_v is the fiber shape coefficient, the straight shape is 0.7, the irregular shape is 0.5, and λ_f is the fiber characteristic value, $\lambda_f = \frac{V_f l_f}{d_f}$.

(4) Sharma et al. [47] model for shear strength of FRC beams

Sharma et al. [47] developed an equation for shear strength, which is illustrated in Equation (33). The aforesaid test data is utilized in this research to investigate its application to the shear strength of UHPFRC beams.

$$V_{u4} = V_c + V_f = \left[\frac{2}{3}f_t'\left(\frac{d}{a}\right)^{0.25}\right]bd,\ f_t' = 0.79\sqrt{f_c} \quad (26)$$

5.2. Comparison and Analysis

The values of shear strength of each UHPFRC beam specimen are derived using the above ML models and compared to the corresponding experimental data, as shown in Figure 7, to examine the correctness and reliability of the aforementioned methodologies. It compares the experimental and calculated values obtained by the models proposed in this paper. They appear to be in accord. The models of ANN, SVR, and XGBoost have close goodness of fit, and their R^2 are, respectively, 0.8825, 0.9016, and 0.8839, and the mean value is 0.8893. Figure 7d compares the experimental and calculated shear strength obtained by the model proposed by Qi et al. [30], and the R^2 is 0.6427, which is much smaller than those obtained by the ML-based models. The model may underestimate the shear strength of the UHPFRC beams. In the experimental and estimated shear strengths of UHPFRC specimens obtained by Ahmad et al. [31], the R^2 is 0.7026. The actual and predicted shear strength of UHPFRC specimens produced using the shear strength equations for FRC beams are shown in Figure 7f,g, and it can be observed that the discreteness is rather substantial. The goodness of fit of the prediction results obtained by the ML models are much larger than those of the existing models for calculating the shear strength of UHPFRC beams, and the ML models can better predict the shear strength of UHPFRC beams.

By analyzing and comparing the ratios (V_{pre}/V_{exp}) of the calculated values of shear capacity (V_{pre}) to the experimental values (V_{exp}) obtained by the above methods, the prediction accuracy and reliability of the above models are further analyzed and evaluated. The V_{pre}/V_{exp} ratios of each model are shown in Figure 8. The CoV is a parameter used to evaluate the calculation reliability of the model. The lower the value, the higher the reliability of the model. This value is very important for the engineering application of theoretical models. The average values of the ratio (V_{pre}/V_{exp}) obtained by the above three ML models (ANN, SVR, XGBoost) in this paper are, respectively, 1.08, 1.02, and 1.10, and the coefficients of variation are, respectively, 0.28, 0.21, and 0.28, so the SVR prediction model shows better accuracy and reliability. Figure 8c shows the distribution of the ratio (V_{pre}/V_{exp}) obtained by the model proposed by Qi et al. [30]. The average value is 0.72 and the coefficient of variation is 0.36. This model underestimates the shear strength of UHPFRC beams and shows reasonable reliability. Figure 8e presents the distribution of the ratios (V_{pre}/V_{exp}) obtained by the method proposed by Ahmad et al. [31]. The average value is 1.10 and the coefficient of variation is 0.41. The fitted calculation formula is fairly accurate, and the accuracy and reliability may be enhanced further by increasing the amount of fitted data. Figure 8f,g shows the distribution diagrams of the ratios (V_{pre}/V_{exp}) obtained by the methods of the shear strength of FRC beams, and it can be seen that the methods have a lot of discreteness and need to be improved for estimating shear strength of UHPFRC beams. The CoV obtained by the SVR prediction model is much smaller than those obtained by the exciting theoretical models, and the average value of the ratios (V_{pre}/V_{exp}) obtained by the SVR prediction model is also closer to 1, so the SVR prediction model has better prediction accuracy and reliability.

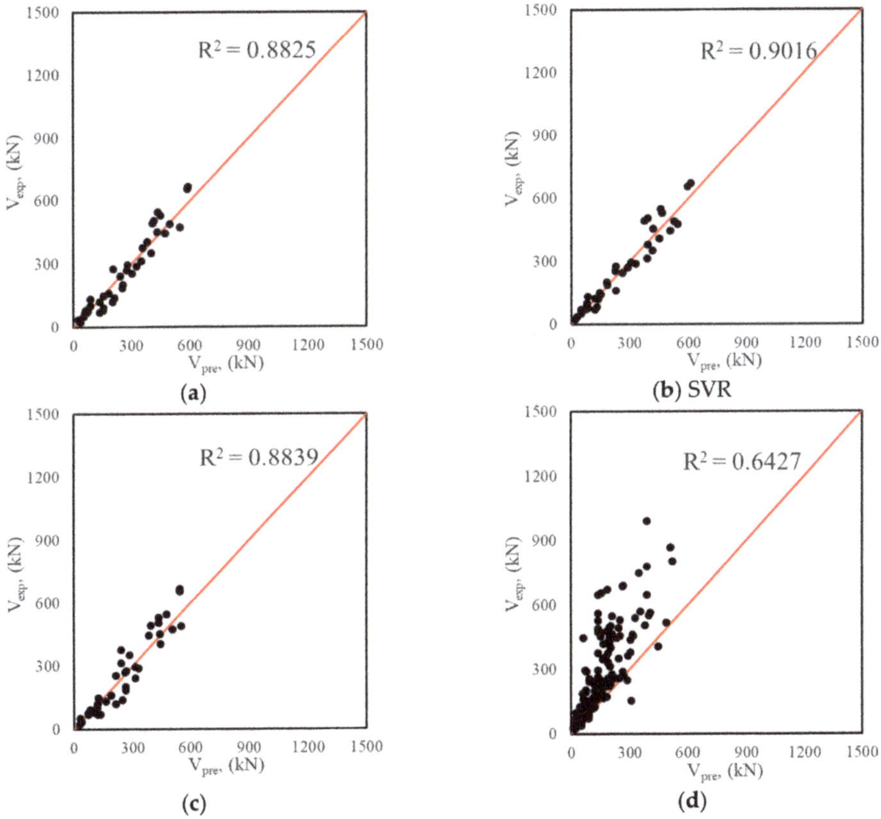

Figure 7. *Cont.*

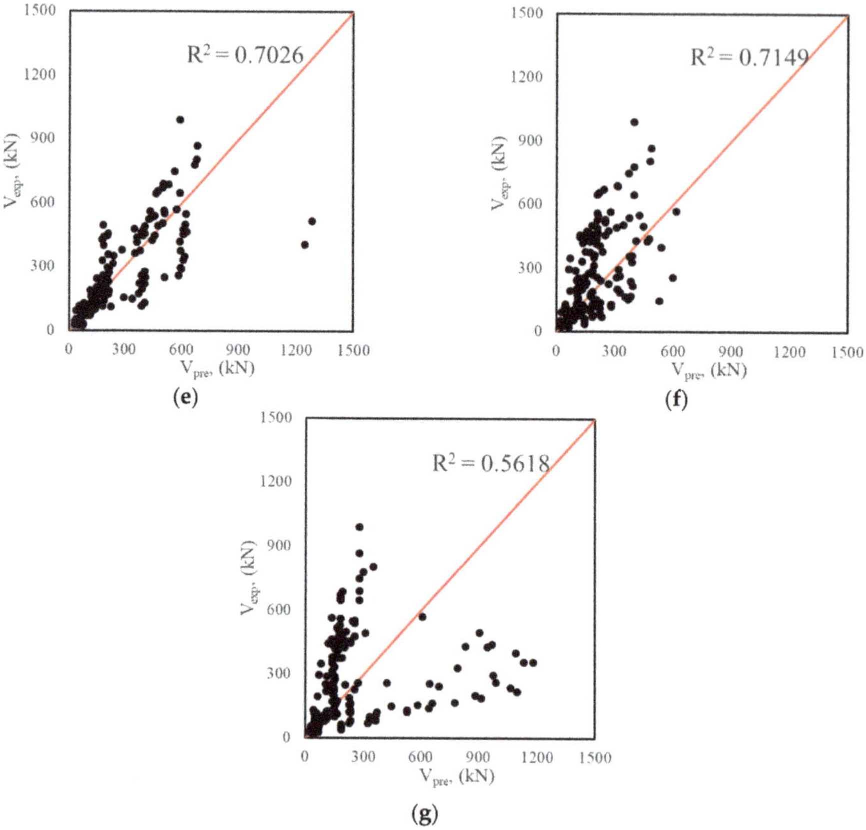

Figure 7. Comparison between predicted and experimental values of shear strength. (**a**) ANN; (**b**) SVR; (**c**) XGBoost; (**d**) Qi et al.; (**e**) Ahmad et al.; (**f**) CECS 38:2004; (**g**) Sharma et al.

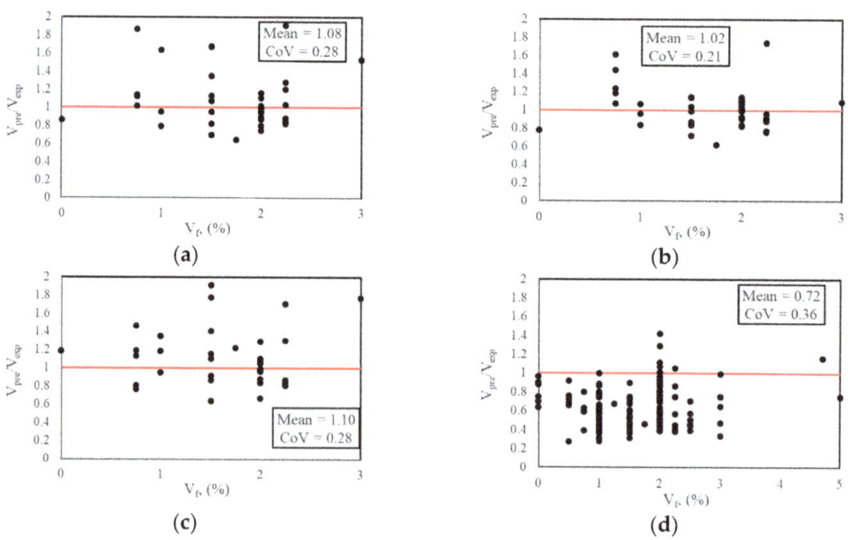

Figure 8. *Cont.*

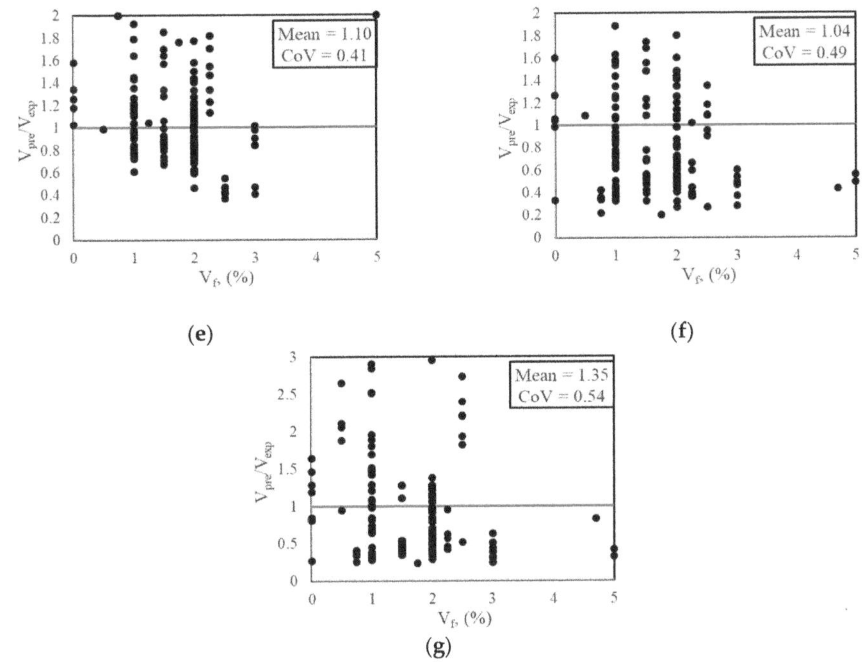

Figure 8. Distribution of the ratios (V_{pre}/V_{exp}) obtained by different methods. (**a**) ANN; (**b**) SVR; (**c**) XGBoost; (**d**) Qi et al.; (**e**) Ahmad et al.; (**f**) CECS 38:2004; (**g**) Sharma et al.

The R^2, maximum, minimum, mean, and coefficients of variation of the ratios (V_{pre}/V_{exp}) obtained by the above models are all summarized in Table 2.

Table 2. Accuracy evaluation details of the above prediction methods.

Methods	R^2	V_{pre}/V_{exp}			
		Max	Min	Mean	CoV
ANN	0.8825	1.91	0.64	1.08	0.28
SVR	0.9016	1.74	0.62	1.02	0.21
XGBBOOST	0.8839	1.91	0.63	1.1	0.28
Qi et al.	0.6427	2	0.27	0.72	0.36
Ahmad et al.	0.7026	2.05	0.25	1.1	0.41
CECS 38:2004	0.7149	1.95	0.37	1.04	0.49
Sharma et al.	0.5618	3	0.21	1.35	0.54

6. Conclusions

In this study, ML-based models (ANN, SVR, and XGBoost) for the shear strength of UHPFRC beams are developed and their accuracy is also compared with existing analytical models. The correctness of the suggested model is studied and assessed using primary shear test data of UHPFRC beam specimens. The following are the results:

(1) The ML algorithm of random forest (RF) is used to evaluate the importance of the given parameters for the shear strength of UHPFRC beams, and the studies show that the area of longitudinal reinforcement has the greatest influence on the shear capacity of UHPFRC beam, and its importance coefficient is 0.14. To simplify the calculation and maintain certain calculation accuracy, the first 12 parameters of the

area of longitudinal reinforcement, the stirrup strength, the cross-section area, the shear span ratio, fiber volume fraction, etc., are selected as input parameters.

(2) The suggested approach is evaluated for accuracy and reliability using a shear test database, and it is also compared to existing methods for shear strength of UHPFRC and FRC beams. The models of ANN, SVR, and XGBoost have close goodness of fit, and their R^2 are, respectively, 0.8825, 0.9016, and 0.8839, the mean value is 0.8893, and it is much larger than those obtained by the existing models for calculating shear strength of UHPFRC beams. The computed to experimental shear strength ratios generated by the suggested ML models (ANN, SVR, XGBoost), respectively, have the average values of 1.08, 1.02, and 1.10, and the coefficients of variation are, respectively, 0.28, 0.21, and 0.28, so the SVR prediction model has better accuracy and reliability. The accuracy and reliability of ML-based models are much better than those of existing models for calculating the shear strength of UHPFRC beams, and the existing analytical methods for determining the shear strength of FRC beams are not applicable for UHPFRC beams.

Author Contributions: Data curation, K.D.; Methodology, X.N.; Writing—original draft, X.N.; Writing—review & editing, K.D. All authors have read and agreed to the published version of the manuscript.

Funding: This work was supported by the National Postdoctoral Program for Innovative Talents (Grant No. BX20200246).

Data Availability Statement: The data used to support the findings of this study are included within the article.

Conflicts of Interest: The authors declare no conflict of interest.

Abbreviations

UHPFRC	Ultra-high performance fiber reinforced concrete
RF	Random forest
ANN	Artificial neural network
SVR	Support vector regression
XGBoost	eXtreme-gradient boosting
RC	Reinforced concrete
ML	Machine Learning
SVM	Support vector machine
k-NN	k-nearest neighbor
GP	Genetic programming
TLBO	Teaching–learning-based optimization
PSO	Particle swarm optimization
AHS	Harmony search optimization
BP	Back-propagation
GC	Gini coefficient
CoV	Coefficient of variation
MFMD	Mesoscale Fiber-Matrix Discrete
FRC	Fiber reinforced concrete
CECS	China Association for Engineering Construction Standardization

Appendix A

Table A1. Test data of UHPFRC beam specimens.

Ref.	C	lo	ho	λ	l	hw	tw	bf′	tf′	bf	tf	Aw	Awo	I	fc	ft	Vf	fy	As	ϱs	fy′	As′	ϱs′	fyw	dsw	s	ϱsw	Fv
[2]	I	760	305	2.5	2000	380	65	270	45	230	105	51,250	34,000	887,612,083	203	8.5	2.5	551	2061	6.06	551	314	0.92	0	0	0	0	455
	I	760	305	2.5	2000	380	65	270	45	230	105	51,250	34,000	887,612,083	205	8.6	2	551	2061	6.06	551	314	0.92	0	0	0	0	448
	I	760	305	2.5	2000	380	65	270	45	230	105	51,250	34,000	887,612,083	187	8.2	0	551	2061	6.06	551	314	0.92	0	0	0	0	181
	I	760	305	2.5	2000	380	65	270	45	230	105	51,250	34,000	887,612,083	157	7.5	4.7	551	2061	6.06	551	314	0.92	0	0	0	0	249
[3]	I	1100	320	3.4	3000	350	60	200	60	200	60	37,800	31,800	572,635,000	185	8.2	2	900	2198	5.1	550	251	0.79	550	10	125	0.63	270
	I	1100	320	3.4	3000	350	60	200	60	200	60	37,800	31,800	572,635,000	184	8.1	2	900	2198	5.1	550	251	0.79	550	10	125	0.63	289
	I	1000	320	3.1	3000	350	60	200	60	200	60	37,800	31,800	572,635,000	154	7.5	0	900	2198	5.1	550	251	0.79	550	10	125	0.63	169
	I	1000	320	3.1	3000	350	60	200	60	200	60	37,800	31,800	572,635,000	173	7.9	0	900	2198	5.1	550	251	0.79	550	10	125	0.63	185
	I	1000	320	3.1	3000	350	60	200	60	200	60	37,800	31,800	572,635,000	170	7.8	2	900	2198	5.1	550	251	0.79	550	10	200	0.39	222
	I	1000	320	3.1	3000	350	60	200	60	200	60	37,800	31,800	572,635,000	163	7.7	2	900	2198	5.1	550	251	0.79	550	10	200	0.39	258
	I	1000	320	3.1	3000	350	60	200	60	200	60	37,800	31,800	572,635,000	169	7.8	1	900	2198	5.1	550	251	0.79	550	10	200	0.39	223
	I	1000	320	3.1	3000	350	60	200	60	200	60	37,800	31,800	572,635,000	168	7.8	0	900	2198	5.1	550	251	0.79	550	10	200	0.39	150
	I	1000	320	3.1	3000	350	60	200	60	200	60	37,800	31,800	572,635,000	170	7.8	2	900	2198	5.1	550	251	0.79	550	10	300	0.26	223
	I	1000	320	3.1	3000	350	60	200	60	200	60	37,800	31,800	572,635,000	166	7.7	1	900	2198	5.1	550	251	0.79	550	10	300	0.26	199
	I	1000	320	3.1	3000	350	60	200	60	200	60	37,800	31,800	572,635,000	175	7.9	0	900	2198	5.1	550	251	0.79	550	10	300	0.26	127
	I	1000	320	3.1	3000	350	60	200	60	200	60	37,800	31,800	572,635,000	160	7.6	2	900	2198	5.1	550	251	0.79	0	0	0	0	126
	I	1000	320	3.1	3000	350	60	200	60	200	60	37,800	31,800	572,635,000	188	8.2	2	900	2198	5.1	550	251	0.79	0	0	0	0	160
	I	1000	320	3.1	3000	350	60	200	60	200	60	37,800	31,800	572,635,000	178	8	2	900	2198	5.1	550	251	0.79	0	0	0	0	179
	I	1000	320	3.1	3000	350	60	200	60	200	60	37,800	31,800	572,635,000	162	7.6	1	900	2198	5.1	550	251	0.79	0	0	0	0	133
	I	1000	320	3.1	3000	350	60	200	60	200	60	37,800	31,800	572,635,000	175	7.9	1	900	2198	5.1	550	251	0.79	0	0	0	0	99.5
	I	1000	320	3.1	3000	350	60	200	60	200	60	37,800	31,800	572,635,000	187	8.2	1	900	2198	5.1	550	251	0.79	0	0	0	0	154
	I	1000	320	3.1	3000	350	60	200	60	200	60	37,800	31,800	572,635,000	161	7.6	0	900	2198	5.1	550	251	0.79	0	0	0	0	41
	I	1000	320	3.1	3000	350	60	200	60	200	60	37,800	31,800	572,635,000	170	7.8	0	900	2198	5.1	550	251	0.79	0	0	0	0	31.5
	I	1000	320	3.1	3000	350	60	200	60	200	60	37,800	31,800	572,635,000	167	7.7	0	900	2198	5.1	550	251	0.79	0	0	0	0	25.5
[4]	R	1397	235	5.9	3658	270	180					48,600	42,300	295,245,000	167	15		436	398	0.94	0	0	0	0	0	0	0	63.3
	R	610	235	2.6	3658	270	180					48,600	42,300	295,245,000	167	15		436	531	1.26	0	0	0	0	0	0	0	88.6

Table A1. *Cont.*

Ref.	C	lo	ho	λ	l	hw	tw	bf′	tf′	bf	tf	Aw	Awo	I	fc	ft	Vf	fy	As	ϱs	fy′	As′	ϱs′	fyw	dsw	s	ϱsw	Fv
[5]	I	504	180	2.8		200	20	200	20	110	40	11,200	9000	65,853,333	150	10	3	500	785	8.72	0	0	0	500			0.94	115
	I	504	180	2.8		200	20	200	20	110	40	11,200	9000	65,853,333	150	10	3	500	785	8.72	0	0	0	0	0	0	0	92
	I	1120	320	3.5		350	58	200	58	200	58	36,772	30,772	562,963,969	166	7.7	2	900	2200	7.15	0	0	0	550			1.35	379
	I	1120	320	3.5		350	58	200	58	200	58	36,772	30,772	562,963,969	170	7.8	2	900	2200	7.15	0	0	0	550			0.9	352
	I	1120	320	3.5		350	58	200	58	200	58	36,772	30,772	562,963,969	170	8	2	900	2200	7.15	0	0	0	0	0	0	0	244
	I	1120	320	3.5		350	58	200	58	200	58	36,772	30,772	562,963,969	166	7.7	1	900	2200	7.15	0	0	0	550			0.9	314
	I	1120	320	3.5		350	58	200	58	200	58	36,772	30,772	562,963,969	174	7.9	1	900	2200	7.15	0	0	0	0	0	0	0	204
	R	436	218	2		300	150					45,000	32,700	337,500,000	156	7.5	2	474	2000	6.12	0	0	0	0	0	0	0	375
	R	327	218	1.5		300	150					45,000	32,700	337,500,000	152	7.4	2	474	2000	6.12	0	0	0	0	0	0	0	425
	R	660	220	3		290	150					43,500	33,000	304,862,500	167	12	1.5	618	2640	8	0	0	0	0	0	0	0	476
	R	660	220	3		290	150					43,500	33,000	304,862,500	167	12	1.5	618	2640	8	0	0	0	538			0.6	538
	R	660	220	3		290	150					43,500	33,000	304,862,500	167	12	1.5	618	2640	8	0	0	0	538			0.9	552
[6]	I	900	360	2.5	4000	400	60	140	60	140	80	35,200	29,600	625,853,333	138	12	1	365	380	1.28	0	0	0	0	0	0	0	121
	I	828	360	2.3	4000	400	60	140	60	140	80	35,200	29,600	625,853,333	138	12	1	365	380	1.28	0	0	0	0	0	0	0	160
	I	900	360	2.5	4000	400	60	140	60	140	80	35,200	29,600	625,853,333	138	12	1	365	380	1.28	0	0	0	0	0	0	0	70
	I	828	360	2.3	4000	400	60	140	60	140	80	35,200	29,600	625,853,333	138	12	1	365	380	1.28	0	0	0	0	0	0	0	129
	I	828	360	2.3	4000	400	60	140	60	140	80	35,200	29,600	625,853,333	138	12	1	365	380	1.28	0	0	0	0	0	0	0	119
	I	900	360	2.5	4000	400	60	140	60	140	80	35,200	29,600	625,853,333	138	12	1	365	380	1.28	0	0	0	0	0	0	0	189
	I	828	360	2.3	4000	400	60	140	60	140	80	35,200	29,600	625,853,333	138	12	1	365	380	1.28	0	0	0	0	0	0	0	80
	I	900	360	2.5	4000	400	60	140	60	140	80	35,200	29,600	625,853,333	138	12	1	365	380	1.28	0	0	0	502	8	100	1.67	154
[7]	R	300	130	2	900	150	100					15,000	13,000	28,125,000	127	6.8	0	550	157	1.2	0	0	0	0	0	0	0	18.2
	R	300	130	2	900	150	100					15,000	13,000	28,125,000	127	6.8	0	550	226	1.7	0	0	0	0	0	0	0	22.1
	R	300	130	2	900	150	100					15,000	13,000	28,125,000	130	6.8	0.5	550	157	1.2	0	0	0	0	0	0	0	21
	R	300	130	2	900	150	100					15,000	13,000	28,125,000	130	6.8	0.5	550	226	1.7	0	0	0	0	0	0	0	27
	R	300	130	2	900	150	100					15,000	13,000	28,125,000	135	7	0.5	550	157	1.2	0	0	0	0	0	0	0	26.9
	R	300	130	2	900	150	100					15,000	13,000	28,125,000	135	7	0.5	550	226	1.7	0	0	0	0	0	0	0	30.2
[8]	R	277	350	0.8	750	400	80					32,000	28,000	426,666,667	173	7.9	1.5	491	1017	3.63	408	314	1.12	400	6	150	0.47	445
	R	277	350	0.8	750	400	80					32,000	28,000	426,666,667	173	7.9	1.5	491	1017	3.63	408	314	1.12	400	8	150	0.84	530
	R	329	350	0.9	750	400	80					32,000	28,000	426,666,667	173	7.9	1.5	491	1017	3.63	408	314	1.12	400	6	150	0.47	415
	R	329	350	0.9	750	400	80					32,000	28,000	426,666,667	173	7.9	1.5	491	1017	3.63	408	314	1.12	400	8	150	0.84	455
	R	329	350	0.9	750	400	80					32,000	28,000	426,666,667	173	7.9	1.5	491	1017	3.63	408	314	1.12	400	8	75	1.68	505

Table A1. *Cont.*

Ref.	C	lo	ho	λ	l	hw	tw	bf′	tf′	bf	tf	Aw	Awo	I	fc	ft	Vf	fy	As	ϱs	fy′	As′	ϱs′	fyw	dsw	s	ϱsw	Fv
	R	392	112	3.5	1200	140	100					14,000	11,200	22,866,667	78	5.5	0	520	401	3.4	0	0	0	0	0	0	0	35.5
	R	392	112	3.5	1200	140	100					14,000	11,200	22,866,667	94	9.2	0.5	520	401	3.4	0	0	0	0	0	0	0	66.5
	R	392	112	3.5	1200	140	100					14,000	11,200	22,866,667	98	11	1	520	401	3.4	0	0	0	0	0	0	0	70
	R	392	112	3.5	1200	140	100					14,000	11,200	22,866,667	103	15	1.5	520	401	3.4	0	0	0	0	0	0	0	77.5
	R	392	112	3.5	1200	140	100					14,000	11,200	22,866,667	110	15	2	520	401	3.4	0	0	0	0	0	0	0	82.5
	R	392	112	3.5	1200	140	100					14,000	11,200	22,866,667	110	15	2	589	559	4.9	0	0	0	0	0	0	0	108
	R	392	112	3.5	1200	140	100					14,000	11,200	22,866,667	110	15	2	609	628	5.9	0	0	0	0	0	0	0	113
[9]	R	392	112	3.5	1200	140	100					14,000	11,200	22,866,667	101	14	2	520	401	3.4	0	0	0	0	0	0	0	77.5
	R	392	112	3.5	1200	140	100					14,000	11,200	22,866,667	93	13	2	520	401	3.4	0	0	0	0	0	0	0	75
	R	280	112	2.5	1200	140	100					14,000	11,200	22,866,667	110	15	2	520	401	3.4	0	0	0	0	0	0	0	125
	R	336	112	3	1200	140	100					14,000	11,200	22,866,667	110	15	2	520	401	3.4	0	0	0	0	0	0	0	97.5
	R	280	112	2.5	1200	140	100					14,000	11,200	22,866,667	98	11	1	520	401	3.4	0	0	0	0	0	0	0	100
	R	504	112	4.5	1200	140	100					14,000	11,200	22,866,667	98	11	1	520	401	3.4	0	0	0	0	0	0	0	55
	R	392	112	3.5	1200	140	100					14,000	11,200	22,866,667	125	17	2	520	401	3.4	0	0	0	0	0	0	0	94
	I	2000	600	3.3	4000	650	50	400	100	250	100	87,500	75,000	5,349,479,167	161	19	2.5	1750	1716	2.29	0	0	0	0	0	0	0	430
	I	2000	600	3.3	4000	650	50	400	100	250	100	87,500	75,000	5,349,479,167	160	21	2.5	1750	1716	2.29	0	0	0	0	0	0	0	497
	I	2000	600	3.3	4000	650	50	400	100	250	100	87,500	75,000	5,349,479,167	149	22	2.5	1750	1716	2.29	0	0	0	0	0	0	0	428
[10]	I	2000	600	3.3	4000	650	50	400	100	250	100	87,500	75,000	5,349,479,167	164	18	1.3	1750	1716	2.29	0	0	0	0	0	0	0	337
	I	2000	600	3.3	4000	650	50	400	100	250	100	87,500	75,000	5,349,479,167	171	22	2.5	1750	1716	2.29	0	0	0	0	0	0	0	440
	I	2000	600	3.3	4000	650	50	400	100	250	100	87,500	75,000	5,349,479,167	157	18	2.5	1750	1716	2.29	0	0	0	0	0	0	0	330
	I	2000	600	3.3	4000	650	50	400	100	250	100	87,500	75,000	5,349,479,167	169	25	2.5	1750	1716	2.29	0	0	0	0	0	0	0	400
	I	1000	230	4.3	2300	250	40	150	40	150	40	18,800	15,800	150,276,667	148	7.3	0	471	157	0.8	0	0	0	0	0	100	0	15.8
	I	1000	230	4.3	2300	250	40	150	40	150	40	18,800	15,800	150,276,667	163	7.7	1	472	157	0.8	0	0	0	0	0	100	0	26.4
[11]	I	1000	230	4.3	2300	250	40	150	40	150	40	18,800	15,800	150,276,667	163	7.7	1	472	226	1.2	0	0	0	0	0	100	0	46.9
	I	1000	230	4.3	2300	250	40	150	40	150	40	18,800	15,800	150,276,667	163	7.7	1	468	308	1.7	0	0	0	0	0	100	0	39.4
	I	1000	230	4.3	2300	250	40	150	40	150	40	18,800	15,800	150,276,667	163	7.7	1	467	402	2.2	0	0	0	0	0	100	0	55.3
[12]	R	750	380	2	2300	400	200					80,000	76,000	1,066,666,667	107	9.9	0.5	475	760	1	0	0	0	0	0	0	0	147

Table A1. *Cont.*

Ref.	C	lo	ho	λ	l	hw	tw	bf′	tf′	bf	tf	Aw	Awo	I	fc	ft	Vf	fy	As	ϱs	fy′	As′	ϱs′	fyw	dsw	s	ϱsw	Fv
[13]	R	952	280	3.4		350	200					70,000	56,000	714,583,333	198	12	0	445	2453	4.38	0	0	0	0	0	0	0	120
	R	952	280	3.4		350	200					70,000	56,000	714,583,333	198	12	0	445	2453	4.38	0	0	0	422	9.5	150	0.47	258
	R	952	280	3.4		350	200					70,000	56,000	714,583,333	117	7.8	2	445	2453	4.38	0	0	0	0	0	0	0	259
	R	560	280	2		350	200					70,000	56,000	714,583,333	198	12	0	445	2453	4.38	0	0	0	0	0	0	0	236
	R	560	280	2		350	200					70,000	56,000	714,583,333	217	15	2	445	2453	4.38	0	0	0	0	0	0	0	568
	R	560	280	2		350	200					70,000	56,000	714,583,333	117	7.8	2	445	2453	4.38	0	0	0	0	0	0	0	493
[14]	I	1588	397	4		460	50	230	70	220	120	56,000	42,140	1,495,429,167	148	20	2	450	2280	5.41	0	0	0	0	0	0	0	130
	I	1588	397	4		460	50	230	70	220	120	56,000	42,140	1,495,429,167	144	14	1	450	3040	7.21	0	0	0	0	0	0	0	120
	I	1588	397	4		460	50	230	70	220	120	56,000	42,140	1,495,429,167	146	20	2	450	3040	7.21	0	0	0	0	0	0	0	120
	I	1588	397	4		460	50	230	70	220	120	56,000	42,140	1,495,429,167	152	25	3	450	3040	7.21	0	0	0	0	0	0	0	165
	I	1890	315	6		380	50	170	60	165	110	38,850	28,125	651,852,500	147	20	2	450	1700	6.05	0	0	0	0	0	0	0	80
	I	2520	315	8		380	50	170	60	165	110	38,850	28,125	651,852,500	149	21	2	450	1700	6.05	0	0	0	0	0	0	0	70
	I	1260	315	4		380	50	170	60	165	110	38,850	28,125	651,852,500	146	20	2	450	1963	6.98	0	0	0	0	0	0	0	110
	I	1890	315	6		380	50	170	60	165	110	38,850	28,125	651,852,500	147	20	2	450	1963	6.98	0	0	0	0	0	0	0	90
[15]	R	660	220	3	1320	290	150					43,500	33,000	304,862,500	167	12	1.5	618	2641	0.78	0	0	0	0	0	0	0	229
[16]	R	1600	640	2.5	3200	700	50	500	100	500	110	129500	99,500	9,873,704,167	175	10	1	1600	2176	2.19	0	0	0	0	0	0	0	244
	R	1600	640	2.5	3200	700	50	500	100	500	110	129,500	99,500	9,873,704,167	181	9.4	1	1600	2176	2.19	0	0	0	0	0	0	0	257
	R	1600	640	2.5	3200	700	50	500	100	500	110	129,500	99,500	9,873,704,167	188	14	1.5	1600	2176	2.19	0	0	0	0	0	0	0	264
	R	1600	640	2.5	3200	700	50	500	100	500	110	129,500	99,500	9,873,704,167	184	14	1.5	1600	2176	2.19	0	0	0	0	0	0	0	295
	R	1600	640	2.5	3200	700	50	500	100	500	110	129,500	99,500	9,873,704,167	186	17	2	1600	2176	2.19	0	0	0	0	0	0	0	356
	R	1600	640	2.5	3200	700	50	500	100	500	110	129,500	99,500	9,873,704,167	190	17	2	1600	2176	2.19	0	0	0	0	0	0	0	359
	R	2200	640	3.4	4400	700	50	500	100	500	110	129,500	99,500	9,873,704,167	169	10	1	1600	2176	2.19	0	0	0	0	0	0	0	140
	R	2200	640	3.4	4400	700	50	500	100	500	110	129,500	99,500	9,873,704,167	167	9.2	1	1600	2176	2.19	0	0	0	0	0	0	0	154
	R	2200	640	3.4	4400	700	50	500	100	500	110	129,500	99,500	9,873,704,167	193	14	1.5	1600	2176	2.19	0	0	0	0	0	0	0	202
	R	2200	640	3.4	4400	700	50	500	100	500	110	129,500	99,500	9,873,704,167	189	14	1.5	1600	2176	2.19	0	0	0	0	0	0	0	187
	R	2200	640	3.4	4400	700	50	500	100	500	110	129,500	99,500	9,873,704,167	189	17	2	1600	2176	2.19	0	0	0	0	0	0	0	219
	R	2200	640	3.4	4400	700	50	500	100	500	110	129,500	99,500	9,873,704,167	182	17	2	1600	2176	2.19	0	0	0	0	0	0	0	239
[17]	I	700	230	3	2300	250	50	150	40	150	40	20,500	17,500	154,370,833	121	10	0	470	402	2.3	0	0	0	0	0	0	0	33.4
	I	700	230	3	2300	250	50	150	40	150	40	20,500	17,500	154,370,833	143	18	2	470	157	0.9	0	0	0	0	0	0	0	36.8
	I	700	230	3	2300	250	50	150	40	150	40	20,500	17,500	154,370,833	143	18	2	470	226	1.29	0	0	0	0	0	0	0	49.9
	I	700	230	3	2300	250	50	150	40	150	40	20,500	17,500	154,370,833	143	18	2	470	308	1.76	0	0	0	0	0	0	0	62.7
	I	700	230	3	2300	250	50	150	40	150	40	20,500	17,500	154,370,833	143	18	2	470	402	2.3	0	0	0	0	0	0	0	60.1

Table A1. *Cont.*

Ref.	C	lo	ho	λ	l	hw	tw	bf′	tf′	bf	tf	Aw	Awo	I	fc	ft	Vf	fy	As	ρs	fy′	As′	ρs′	fyw	dsw	s	ρsw	Fv
[18]	R	279	223	1.3	1400	240	50	120	90	120	90	24,600	22,560	136,980,000	136	21	1.5	512	308	1.37	512	155	0.69	0	0	0	0	100
	R	279	223	1.3	1400	240	50	120	90	120	90	24,600	22,560	136,980,000	138	24	1.5	512	308	1.37	512	155	0.69	0	0	0	0	80
	R	390	260	1.5	1350	350	165					57,750	42,900	589,531,250	119	2.5	0	474	3215	7.5	490	760	1.77	0	0	0	0	245
	R	390	260	1.5	1350	350	165					57,750	42,900	589,531,250	115	3.2	0.8	474	3215	7.49	490	760	1.77	0	0	0	0	288
	R	390	260	1.5	1350	350	165					57,750	42,900	589,531,250	124	6.3	1.5	474	3215	7.49	490	760	1.77	0	0	0	0	454
	R	390	260	1.5	1350	350	165					57,750	42,900	589,531,250	112	2.1	0.8	474	3215	7.49	490	760	1.77	0	0	0	0	296
	R	390	260	1.5	1350	350	165					57,750	42,900	589,531,250	105	4.3	2.3	474	3215	7.49	490	760	1.77	0	0	0	0	334
	R	390	260	1.5	1350	350	165					57,750	42,900	589,531,250	126	2.3	0.8	474	3215	7.49	490	760	1.77	0	0	0	0	347
	R	390	260	1.5	1350	350	165					57,750	42,900	589,531,250	107	4.9	1.5	474	3215	7.49	490	760	1.77	0	0	0	0	377
	R	390	260	1.5	1350	350	165					57,750	42,900	589,531,250	124	5.6	2.3	474	3215	7.49	490	760	1.77	0	0	0	0	466
	R	390	260	1.5	1350	350	165					57,750	42,900	589,531,250	123	5.1	1.5	474	3215	7.49	490	760	1.77	0	0	0	0	474
	R	390	260	1.5	1350	350	165					57,750	42,900	589,531,250	119	7	2.3	474	3215	7.49	490	760	1.77	0	0	0	0	547
[19]	R	390	260	1.5	1350	350	165					57,750	42,900	589,531,250	114	6	2.3	474	3215	7.49	490	760	1.77	0	0	0	0	500
	R	390	260	1.5	1350	350	165					57,750	42,900	589,531,250	98	4.4	2	474	3215	7.49	490	760	1.77	0	0	0	0	419
	R	858	260	3.3	1900	350	165					57,750	42,900	589,531,250	95	2.6	0	474	3215	7.49	490	760	1.77	0	0	0	0	70.2
	R	858	260	3.3	1900	350	165					57,750	42,900	589,531,250	117	2.3	0.8	474	3215	7.49	490	760	1.77	0	0	0	0	193
	R	858	260	3.3	1900	350	165					57,750	42,900	589,531,250	103	3.9	1.5	474	3215	7.49	490	760	1.77	0	0	0	0	223
	R	858	260	3.3	1900	350	165					57,750	42,900	589,531,250	115	1.6	0.8	474	3215	7.49	490	760	1.77	0	0	0	0	115
	R	858	260	3.3	1900	350	165					57,750	42,900	589,531,250	94	5.8	2.3	474	3215	7.49	490	760	1.77	0	0	0	0	174
	R	858	260	3.3	1900	350	165					57,750	42,900	589,531,250	134	1.5	0.8	474	3215	7.49	490	760	1.77	0	0	0	0	130
	R	858	260	3.3	1900	350	165					57,750	42,900	589,531,250	132	3.8	1.5	474	3215	7.49	490	760	1.77	0	0	0	0	219
	R	858	260	3.3	1900	350	165					57,750	42,900	589,531,250	117	5.1	2.3	474	3215	7.49	490	760	1.77	0	0	0	0	234
	R	858	260	3.3	1900	350	165					57,750	42,900	589,531,250	110	3.7	2.3	474	3215	7.49	490	760	1.77	0	0	0	0	254
	R	858	260	3.3	1900	350	165					57,750	42,900	589,531,250	124	5.4	2.3	474	3215	7.49	490	760	1.77	0	0	0	0	277
	R	858	260	3.3	1900	350	165					57,750	42,900	589,531,250	113	4.6	2	474	3215	7.49	490	760	1.77	0	0	0	0	221
	T	1000	300	3.3	3000	350	100	300	50		142	45,000	40,000	53,4375,000	152	7.4	0	557	1256	3.58	557	1256	3.58	552	6	380	0.15	113

Table A1. *Cont.*

Ref.	C	lo	ho	λ	l	hw	tw	bf′	tf′	bf	tf	Aw	Awo	I	fc	ft	Vf	fy	As	ϱs	fy′	As′	ϱs′	fyw	dsw	s	ϱsw	Fv
	T	361	114	3.2	1140	140	40	120	35		53	8400	7360	14,577,500	116	7.1	2	761	226	4.96	0	0	0	0	0	0	0	38
	T	361	114	3.2	1140	140	40	120	35		53	8400	7360	14,577,500	96	5.2	0.5	761	226	4.96	0	0	0	0	0	0	0	26.1
	T	361	114	3.2	1140	140	40	120	35		53	8400	7360	14,577,500	94	6.1	1	761	226	4.96	0	0	0	0	0	0	0	26.3
	T	285	114	2.5	1140	140	40	120	35		53	8400	7360	14,577,500	116	7.1	2	761	226	4.96	0	0	0	0	0	0	0	52
[20]	T	428	114	3.8	1140	140	40	120	35		53	8400	7360	14,577,500	116	7.1	2	761	226	4.96	0	0	0	0	0	0	0	44
	T	361	114	3.2	1140	140	40	120	35		53	8400	7360	14,577,500	121	7.7	2	761	226	4.96	0	0	0	0	0	0	0	34.5
	T	361	114	3.2	1140	140	40	120	35		53	8400	7360	14,577,500	113	6.5	2	761	226	4.96	0	0	0	0	0	0	0	33.1
	T	361	114	3.2	1140	140	40	120	35		53	8400	7360	14,577,500	121	7.7	2	761	226	4.96	0	0	0	0	0	0	0	23.6
	T	361	114	3.2	1140	140	40	120	35		53	8400	7360	14,577,500	113	6.5	2	761	226	4.96	0	0	0	0	0	0	0	38.5
	R	620	310	2	2000	350	200					70,000	62,000	714,583,333	125	7.1	2	474	2944	4.75	474	981	1.58	568	8	200	0.25	991
	R	465	310	1.5	2000	350	200					70,000	62,000	714,583,333	125	7.1	2	474	2943	4.75	474	981	1.58	568	8	200	0.25	778
	R	620	310	2	2000	350	200					70,000	62,000	714,583,333	125	7.1	2	474	2943	4.75	474	981	1.58	568	8	200	0.25	646
	R	775	310	2.5	2000	350	200					70,000	62,000	714,583,333	119	5.2	1	474	2943	4.75	474	981	1.58	568	8	200	0.25	687
[21]	R	620	310	2	2000	350	200					70,000	62,000	714,583,333	132	8.9	3	474	2943	4.75	474	981	1.58	568	8	200	0.25	805
	R	620	310	2	2000	350	200					70,000	62,000	714,583,333	125	7.1	2	474	2943	4.75	474	981	1.58	0	0	0	0	689
	R	620	310	2	2000	350	200					70,000	62,000	714,583,333	125	7.1	2	474	2943	4.75	474	981	1.58	568	8	100	0.5	867
	R	620	310	2	2000	350	200					70,000	62,000	714,583,333	125	7.1	2	474	2943	4.75	474	981	1.58	568	8	300	0.17	748
	R	313	125	2.5	1300	150	100					15,000	12,500	28,125,000	118	6.5	2	570	509	4.1	340	57	0.45	0	0	0	0	85.5
	R	313	125	2.5	1300	150	100					15,000	12,500	28,125,000	118	6.5	2	570	509	4.1	340	57	0.46	340	6	200	0.28	87.5
	R	313	125	2.5	1300	150	100					15,000	12,500	28,125,000	118	6.5	2	570	509	4.1	340	57	0.46	340	6	150	0.38	91.5
[22]	R	313	125	2.5	1300	150	100					15,000	12,500	28,125,000	118	6.5	2	570	509	4.1	340	57	0.46	340	6	100	0.56	93.5
	R	313	125	2.5	1300	150	100					15,000	12,500	28,125,000	110	6.3	1	570	509	4.1	340	57	0.46	0	0	0	0	79
	R	313	125	2.5	1300	150	100					15,000	12,500	28,125,000	100	6	0.5	570	509	4.1	340	57	0.46	0	0	0	0	71
	R	313	125	2.5	1300	150	100					15,000	12,500	28,125,000	129	6.8	2	570	509	4.1	340	57	0.46	0	0	0	0	89

Table A1. *Cont.*

Ref.	C	lo	ho	λ	l	hw	tw	bf′	tf′	bf	tf	Aw	Awo	I	fc	ft	Vf	fy	As	ϱs	fy′	As′	ϱs′	fyw	dsw	s	ϱsw	Fv
	R	312	260	1.2	1000	300	150					45,000	39,000	337,500,000	108	4.1	0	526	1963	5.23	476	226	0.58	466	6	200	0.19	445
	R	312	260	1.2	1000	300	150					45,000	39,000	337,500,000	118	6.4	1	526	1963	5.23	476	226	0.58	466	6	200	0.19	645
	R	312	260	1.2	1000	300	150					45,000	39,000	337,500,000	118	6.4	1	526	1963	5.23	476	226	0.58	0	0	0	0	580
	R	312	260	1.2	1000	300	150					45,000	39,000	337,500,000	118	6.4	1	526	1963	5.23	476	226	0.58	466	6	100	0.38	670
[23]	R	312	260	1.2	1000	300	150					45,000	39,000	337,500,000	118	6.4	1	526	1963	5.23	476	226	0.58	466	6	150	0.25	655
	R	312	260	1.2	1000	300	150					45,000	39,000	337,500,000	118	6.4	1	520	1741	4.65	476	226	0.58	466	6	200	0.19	560
	R	312	260	1.2	1000	300	150					45,000	39,000	337,500,000	118	6.4	1	519	1520	4.06	476	226	0.58	466	6	200	0.19	490
	R	364	260	1.4	1000	300	150					45,000	39,000	337,500,000	118	6.4	1	526	1963	5.23	476	226	0.58	466	6	200	0.19	525
	R	416	260	1.6	1000	300	150					45,000	39,000	337,500,000	118	6.4	1	526	1963	5.23	476	226	0.58	466	6	200	0.19	475
[25]	R	203	124	1.6	610	152	152					23,104	18,848	44,482,901	121	4.9	0	406	603	3.2	485	85	0.45				0	103
	R	601	258	2.3	1200	300	150					45,000	38,700	337,500,000	125	5.6	3	543	2454	6.34	540	226	0.58	423	6	50	0.75	565
	R	599	255	2.4	1200	300	150					45,000	38,250	337,500,000	125	5.6	3	543	1610	4.21	540	226	0.59	423	6	100	0.38	463
[26]	R	601	272	2.2	1200	300	150					45,000	40,800	337,500,000	125	5.6	3	543	1473	3.61	540	226	0.55	423	6	150	0.25	436
	R	601	272	2.2	1200	300	150					45,000	40,800	337,500,000	125	5.6	3	543	1473	3.61	540	226	0.55	423	6	200	0.19	364
	R	601	259	2.3	1200	300	150					45,000	38,850	337,500,000	138	6.8	5	543	1884	4.85	540	226	0.58	423	6	100	0.38	518
	R	600	262	2.3	1200	300	150					45,000	39,300	337,500,000	138	6.8	5	543	1572	4	540	226	0.58	423	6	200	0.19	406

References

1. Ni, X.; Qiang, Z.; Li, Y. Cyclic test and numerical analysis of the seismic performance of concrete columns reinforced by HRB600 steel bars. *J. Build. Eng.* **2022**, *50*, 104211. [CrossRef]
2. Baby, F.; Marchand, P.; Toutlemonde, F. Shear behavior of ultrahigh performance fiber-reinforced concrete beams. I: Experimental investigation. *J. Struct. Eng.* **2014**, *140*, 04013111. [CrossRef]
3. Mészöly, T.; Randl, N. Shear behavior of fiber-reinforced ultra-high performance concrete beams. *Eng. Struct.* **2018**, *168*, 119–127. [CrossRef]
4. Kodur, V.; Solhmirzaei, R.; Agrawal, A.; Aziz, E.M.; Soroushian, P. Analysis of flexural and shear resistance of ultra high performance fiber reinforced concrete beams without stirrups. *Eng. Struct.* **2018**, *174*, 873–884. [CrossRef]
5. Franssen, R.; Guner, S.; Courard, L.; Mihaylov, B.I. Numerical modeling approach for UHPFRC members including crack spacing formulations. *Eng. Struct.* **2021**, *238*, 112179. [CrossRef]
6. Zagon, R.; Matthys, S.; Kiss, Z. Shear behaviour of SFR-UHPC I-shaped beams. *Constr. Build. Mater.* **2016**, *124*, 258–268. [CrossRef]
7. Kamal, M.M.; Safan, M.A.; Etman, Z.A.; Salama, R.A. Behavior and strength of beams cast with ultra high strength concrete containing different types of fibers. *HBRC J.* **2014**, *10*, 55–63. [CrossRef]
8. Yousef, A.M.; Tahwia, A.M.; Marami, N.A. Minimum shear reinforcement for ultra-high performance fiber reinforced concrete deep beams. *Constr. Build. Mater.* **2018**, *184*, 177–185. [CrossRef]
9. Ridha, M.M.; Sarsam, K.F.; Al-Shaarbaf, I.A. Experimental study and shear strength prediction for reactive powder concrete beams. *Case Stud. Constr. Mater.* **2018**, *8*, 434–446. [CrossRef]
10. Voo, Y.L.; Foster, S.J.; Gilbert, R.I. Shear strength of fiber reinforced reactive powder concrete prestressed girders without stirrups. *J. Adv. Concr. Technol.* **2006**, *4*, 123–132. [CrossRef]
11. Türker, K.; Yavaş, A.; Birol, T.; Gültekin, C. Evaluation of using ultra-high performance fiber reinforced concrete in I-section RC beam. *J. Fac. Eng. Archit. Gazi Univ.* **2021**, *36*, 1431–1448.
12. Smarzewski, P. Hybrid fibres as shear reinforcement in high-performance concrete beams with and without openings. *Appl. Sci.* **2018**, *8*, 2070. [CrossRef]
13. Bae, B.I.; Lee, M.S.; Choi, C.S.; Jung, H.S.; Choi, H.K. Evaluation of the ultimate strength of the ultra-high-performance fiber-reinforced concrete beams. *Appl. Sci.* **2021**, *11*, 2951. [CrossRef]
14. Wu, X.; Han, S.M. First diagonal cracking and ultimate shear of I-shaped reinforced girders of ultra high performance fiber reinforced concrete without stirrup. *Int. J. Concr. Struct. Mater.* **2009**, *3*, 47–56. [CrossRef]
15. Ţibea, C.; Bompa, D.V. Ultimate shear response of ultra-high-performance steel fibre-reinforced concrete elements. *Arch. Civ. Mech. Eng.* **2020**, *20*, 1–16. [CrossRef]
16. Lim, W.Y.; Hong, S.G. Shear tests for ultra-high performance fiber reinforced concrete (UHPFRC) beams with shear reinforcement. *Int. J. Concr. Struct. Mater.* **2016**, *10*, 177–188. [CrossRef]
17. Yang, I.H.; Joh, C.; Kim, B.S. Shear behaviour of ultra-high-performance fibre-reinforced concrete beams without stirrups. *Mag. Concr. Res.* **2012**, *64*, 979–993. [CrossRef]
18. Yavas, A.; Goker, C.O. Impact of reinforcement ratio on shear behavior of I-shaped UHPC beams with and without fiber shear reinforcement. *Materials* **2020**, *13*, 1525. [CrossRef]
19. Bermudez, M.; Hung, C.C. Shear behavior of ultra-high performance hybrid fiber reinforced concrete beams. In *International Interactive Symposium on Ultra-High Performance Concrete*; Iowa State University Digital Press: Ames, IA, USA, 2019; Volume 2.
20. Zhengdong, Z. Experimental and Numerical Research on Mechanical Performance of UHPC-T Beam. Master's Thesis, Beijing Jiaotong University, Beijing, China, 2021.
21. Qi, J.; Wang, J.; Zhou, K.; Liu, J.; Li, W. Experimental and theoretical investigations on shear strength of UHPC beams. *China J. Highw. Transp.* **2020**, *33*, 95.
22. Kaize, M.; Yudong, M.; Guohua, X.; Boquan, L. Study on shear behavior of ultra-high performance concrete beams. *J. Build. Struct.* **2021**, 1–13. [CrossRef]
23. Min, L.; Pengzhen, L.; Zijiang, Y.; Yinglong, L. Analysis of shear capacity and mechanical performance of R-Uhpc beam. *Bridge. Constr.* **2021**, *51*, 53–60.
24. Chen, B.; Wu, Q.; Huang, Q.; Ma, X.; Su, J. Experimental study on shear behavior of reinforced ultra-high performance concrete beams. *J. Fuzhou Univ.* **2018**, *46*, 512–517.
25. Xinyue, W. Research on Mechanical Properties of Reinforced Ultra-High Performance Concrete Beams. Master's Thesis, Xi'an University of Architecture and Technology, Xi'an, China, 2021.
26. Liang, X.; Wang, Z.; Yu, J.; Li, L. Study on shear behavior and shear bearing capacity of UHPC beams with stirrups. *China Civ. Eng. J.* **2018**, *51*, 56–67.
27. Deng, Z.; Wang, Y.; Xiao, R. Flexural test and theoretical analysis of UHPC beams with high strength rebars. *J. Basic Sci. Eng.* **2015**, *23*, 68–78.
28. Kahanji, C.; Ali, F.; Nadjai, A. Structural performance of ultra-high-performance fiber-reinforced concrete beams. *Struct. Concr.* **2007**, *18*, 249–258. [CrossRef]
29. Xu, M.; Liang, X.; Wang, P.; Wang, Z. Theoretical investigation on normal section flexural capacity of UHPC beams. *Eng. Mech.* **2019**, *36*, 70–78.

30. Qi, J.; Ma, Z.J.; Wang, J. Shear strength of UHPFRC beams: Mesoscale fiber-matrix discrete model. *J. Struct. Eng.* **2017**, *143*, 04016209. [CrossRef]
31. Ahmad, S.; Bahij, S.; Al-Osta, M.A.; Adekunle, S.K.; Al-Dulaijan, S.U. Shear behavior of ultra-high-performance concrete beams reinforced with high-strength steel bars. *ACI Struct. J.* **2019**, *116*, 3–14. [CrossRef]
32. Solhmirzaei, R.; Salehi, H.; Kodur, V.; Naser, M.Z. Machine learning framework for predicting failure mode and shear capacity of ultra high performance concrete beams. *Eng. Struct.* **2020**, *224*, 111221. [CrossRef]
33. Kim, B.; Lee, D.E.; Hu, G.; Natarajan, Y.; Preethaa, S.; Rathinakumar, A.P. Ensemble Machine Learning-Based Approach for Predicting of FRP–Concrete Interfacial Bonding. *Mathematics* **2022**, *10*, 231. [CrossRef]
34. Yaseen, Z.M.; Tran, M.T.; Kim, S.; Bakhshpoori, T.; Deo, R.C. Shear strength prediction of steel fiber reinforced concrete beam using hybrid intelligence models: A new approach. *Eng. Struct.* **2018**, *177*, 244–255. [CrossRef]
35. Mangalathu, S.; Jeon, J.S. Classification of failure mode and prediction of shear strength for reinforced concrete beam-column joints using machine learning techniques. *Eng. Struct.* **2018**, *160*, 85–94. [CrossRef]
36. Parsa, P.; Naderpour, H. Shear strength estimation of reinforced concrete walls using support vector regression improved by Teaching–learning-based optimization, Particle Swarm optimization, and Harris Hawks Optimization algorithm. *J. Build. Eng.* **2021**, *44*, 102593. [CrossRef]
37. Chen, X.L.; Fu, J.P.; Yao, J.L.; Gan, J.F. Prediction of shear strength for squat RC walls using a hybrid ANN–PSO model. *Eng. Comput.* **2018**, *34*, 367–383. [CrossRef]
38. Keshtegar, B.; Nehdi, M.L.; Kolahchi, R.; Trung, N.T.; Bagheri, M. Novel hybrid machine leaning model for predicting shear strength of reinforced concrete shear walls. *Eng. Comput.* **2021**, 1–12. [CrossRef]
39. Gondia, A.; Ezzeldin, M.; El-Dakhakhni, W. Mechanics-guided genetic programming expression for shear-strength prediction of squat reinforced concrete walls with boundary elements. *J. Struct. Eng.* **2020**, *146*, 04020223. [CrossRef]
40. Wu, Q.; Xu, Y.; Tang, H.; Fang, K.; Jiang, Y.; Liu, C.; Wang, X. Peak shear strength prediction for discontinuities between two different rock types using a neural network approach. Bulletin of Engineering. *Geol. Environ.* **2019**, *78*, 2315–2329. [CrossRef]
41. Nguyen, D.D.; Tran, V.L.; Ha, D.H.; Nguyen, V.Q.; Lee, T.H. A machine learning-based formulation for predicting shear capacity of squat flanged RC walls. *Structures* **2021**, *29*, 1734–1747. [CrossRef]
42. Duan, K.; Cao, S.; Li, J.; Xu, C. Prediction of neutralization depth of RC bridges using machine learning methods. *Crystals* **2021**, *11*, 210. [CrossRef]
43. Yongmei, X.; Guiguo, Y.; He, L. GA optimization method based on Gauss kernel function parameters. *Electr. Power Autom. Equip.* **2008**, *28*, 52–54.
44. Chen, T.; Guestrin, C. *XGBoost: A Scalable Tree Boosting System*; Association for Computing Machinery: San Francisco, CA, USA, 2016.
45. Naser, M.Z.; Alavi, A.H. Error Metrics and Performance Fitness Indicators for Artificial Intelligence and Machine Learning in Engineering and Sciences. *Archit. Struct. Constr.* **2021**, 1–19. [CrossRef]
46. Dalian University of Technology. *Technical Specification for Fiber Reinforced Concrete Structures: CECS 38: 2004*; China Planning Press: Beijing, China, 2004.
47. Sharma, A.K. Shear strength of steel fiber reinforced concrete beams. *J. Proc.* **1986**, *83*, 624–628.

mathematics

MDPI

Article

Characterization of Blast Wave Parameters in the Detonation Locus and Near Field for Shaped Charges

Nestor Mejía [1,*], Rodrigo Mejía [2] and Theofilos Toulkeridis [1]

1 Department of Earth Sciences and Construction, University of the Armed Forces ESPE, Av. General Rumiñahui S/N, Sangolquí 171103, Ecuador
2 The Ecuadorian Army Corps of Engineers, Av. Rodrigo de Chávez, Quito 170111, Ecuador
* Correspondence: daweimejia1984@icloud.com or ndmejia1@espe.edu.ec; Tel.: +593-987-424-443

Abstract: Understanding physical phenomena such as blast shock waves produced by controlled explosions are relevant for issues appearing in the fields of military and civilian activities. The current study analyzes detonations of cylindrical and 3D cone-shaped charges through experimental trials and numerical simulations. In order to accomplish such goals, the work is divided into three sections, which include (a) numerical studies on spherical charges to define an accurate model; (b) numerical and experimental studies to assess the influence of cylindrical and 3D cone-shaped charges on incident peak pressure and the shape of shock wave propagation; and (c) numerical studies to define the magnitude of incident peak pressure as a function of orientation, L/D aspect ratio and scaled distance. Validation studies proved that the applied model was reasonably accurate. Furthermore, relevant findings included the observation that when the L/D aspect ratio decreases, more release energy is concentrated in the axial direction for a 3D cone-shaped charge, while as the aspect ratio increases, more release energy is concentrated in the radial direction for a cylindrical-shaped charge. Additionally, the blast shock wave produced a great quantity of energy for the explosive charge with the largest surface. Finally, the orientation has less influence than the L/D aspect ratio on the incident pressure contours. Therefore, cylindrical charges have the potential of inflicting great damage when used as confined charges, and 3D charges are able to cut solid materials in case of a direct contact.

Keywords: shaped charges; shape of shock wave; incident peak pressure; Multimaterial-Euler

MSC: 76L05

Citation: Mejía, N.; Mejía, R.; Toulkeridis, T. Characterization of Blast Wave Parameters in the Detonation Locus and Near Field for Shaped Charges. *Mathematics* **2022**, *10*, 3261. https://doi.org/10.3390/math10183261

Academic Editors: Shujin Laima, Yong Cao, Xiaowei Jin and Hehe Ren

Received: 15 August 2022
Accepted: 6 September 2022
Published: 8 September 2022

Publisher's Note: MDPI stays neutral with regard to jurisdictional claims in published maps and institutional affiliations.

Copyright: © 2022 by the authors. Licensee MDPI, Basel, Switzerland. This article is an open access article distributed under the terms and conditions of the Creative Commons Attribution (CC BY) license (https://creativecommons.org/licenses/by/4.0/).

1. Introduction

A prison break recently occurred in the Ecuadorian coastal city of Guayaquil, as reported by a variety of mass media and the proper government [1–3]. This escape occurred due to the planting of explosive charges placed on drones, which detonated with a considerable magnitude. The explosion caused severe damage to the structure elements, breaching walls and roofs. Additionally, organized crime performed a terrorist attack on government facilities using a non-spherical type of explosive charge. Non-spherical-shaped charges release a large quantity of energy on a specific area, subsequently inflicting a great amount of damage on it. The affectations that were caused by the non-spherical explosive charge at the near-field include the cracking, spalling and fragmentation of concrete, large deformations or shears in the transversal and longitudinal steel bars, loss of concrete strength, breaching walls and in some cases, the demolition of structural elements, which may lead to a collapse of a given structure. Consequently, the national Bureau of Prisons demanded a guidance for improving the structural performance to be better prepared for further eventual attacks based on a variety of explosive materials. Therefore, in order to develop and design a sophisticated protective guidance, it is mandatory to characterize the blast shock wave in terms of incident peak pressure and net impulse as well as the determination of dynamic response of such structures and the subsequent impact on its final state of damage.

In this sense, the current study is the first of a set of studies that are part of an official national research project, which intends to provide information and design concepts for the improvement of the aforementioned structural performances of state facilities of strikes with explosive materials involved. Therefore, this initial research has been focused on the characterization of the blast shock waves generated by the detonation of cylindrical- and 3D cone-shaped charges, the results of which may be a constructive technical and blast engineering support through the understanding of the mathematical model that describes how the shock wave is propagated through the surrounding air.

2. Theory and Technical Context of Blast Shock Waves

An explosive is defined as a chemical substance with the capacity to react readily and subsequently release chemical energy stored in its molecular structure. The science of explosives comprises four specific events: ignition, the growth of deflagration (burning), the deflagration to detonation transition, and the propagation of detonation [4]. The intensity of the first three events depends on the stoichiometry and thermochemistry of the explosives. On the other hand, the fourth effect depends on fluid dynamics. A vast collection of observations regarding the analytical expressions of blast shock wave propagation has led to an advanced degree of documentation upon this issue.

Mespoulet et al. [5] and Hryciow et al. [6] exposed that a blast shock wave could be characterized if the explosive type, explosive weight, standoff distance, and explosive shape are known. The explosive type defines the chemical properties, while the weight infers the quantity of release energy. Furthermore, the standoff distance is directly related to the magnitude of the incident pressure and impulse, whereas the explosive shape is defined as a shock wave which is propagated through the surrounding air receding from the source of the explosion.

The present study commences the research with a literature review of existing methods of characterization of blast shock waves. In recent years, an immensely vast ssemblage of studies regarding the analytical methods for the characterization of blast shock waves produced by the detonation of spherical- (Figure 1a) and hemispherical-shaped explosive charges have been well documented and have been presented in manuals, codes, articles, and reports such as [7–10]. The theories and models developed in such a scenario are not applicable to characterize the blast shock waves generated by the detonation of non-spherical explosive shaped charges. This happens because the detonation and blast wave propagation of shaped charges are non-axisymmetric problems of thermochemistry and fluid dynamics [11].

Regarding cylindrical-shaped charges, Figure 1b, ref. [12] defined the incident peak pressure as a function of R/a, where a is the radius of the cylinder and R is the distance from the axis. The results demonstrated that such a shape concentrates the effect of the explosive's energy at the axial axis. Therefore, the incident peak pressure is higher for a cylindrical charge that an equivalent spherical charge at the near-field. However, it gradually adopts the values of a spherical charge when the shock wave moves away from detonation point. Some researchers have stated some empirical equations which define the incident peak pressure in terms of scaled distance Z and charge aspect ratio L/D, e.g., ref. [13] $P = 11.34Z^{-1} - 185.9Z^{-2} + 19210Z^{-3}$; ref. [14] $P = 2127\frac{1}{Z^3} + 305\frac{1}{Z^3}$ for $Z > 4\,[\frac{\mathrm{m}}{\mathrm{kg}^{1/3}}]$; $P = 2565\frac{M}{Z^3}$ for $Z < 3\,[\frac{\mathrm{m}}{\mathrm{kg}^{1/3}}]$; ref. [15] ($L/D = 0.25, 0.5, 1, 2, 3, 4$ and 6), where $\frac{P_{cylinder}}{P_{sphere}} = 5.53\,\frac{L/D^{0.308}}{z^{0.998}}$. Through graphs, Plooster et al. [16] depicted the incident pressure fluctuations for $2.7 \leq Z \leq 12.28\,[\frac{\mathrm{m}}{\mathrm{kg}^{1/3}}]$ as function L/D (0.25, 0.5, 1, 2, 3, 4 and 6) and angle orientation $0° \leq \theta \leq 180°$ with intervals every 22.5°. The results indicated that the method is only able to be applied at the far-field. Fan et al. [17] characterized the blast shock wave considering the influences of charge aspect ratio, orientation, and detonation configuration. The outcomes (incident peak pressure and impulse) are expressed as a function of scaled distance. Such research quantitatively reported the distribution of incident pressure, which was mainly concentrated along the axial axis direction. Additionally, the results yielded that the effects of a shaped charge have no influence for scaled distances greater than $2\ [\frac{\mathrm{m}}{\mathrm{kg}^{1/3}}]$ at 45° orientation relative to the axial axis direction, while the effects of an aspect ratio less than 2 have a significant impact on the incident peak pressure at 90° orientation. Gao et al. [18] stated the propagation of a blast shock wave in terms of pressure contours using the hydrocode AUTODYN. The contours are categorized into patterns and are analyzed in detail. Hereby, some three regions are identified, which are called axial, vertex and radial. The research introduces a term known as a bridge wave. This is the connection medium for linking the front waves produced by the flat and curved surfaces of a charge. The interaction of three waves leads to another wave and subsequently causes superposition effects. Therefore, an accurate mathematical model which comprises all effects is a significant challenge. However, it will certainly have an enormous contribution in blast engineering.

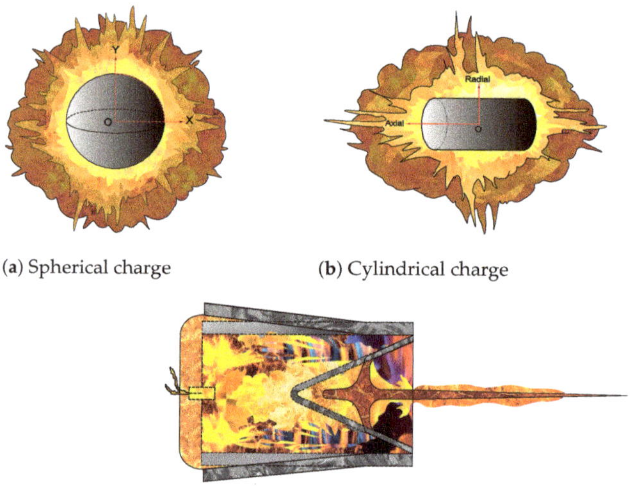

(**a**) Spherical charge (**b**) Cylindrical charge

(**c**) Conical-shaped charge

Figure 1. Sketch of shapes of shock wave propagation.

Rigby et al. [19] graphically represents a mass equivalence model between spherical and cylindrical-shaped charges through logarithmic interpolations of kinetic energy at the same scaled distance. The verification indicates that the accuracy of the model ranges between 4% and 10%. This is due to the condition of non-sphericity of a charge. The aforementioned studies shared a common criterion in that the pressure produced by cylindrical charges presents asymmetrical effects that are relatively more significant in the axial axis direction than in the radial axis direction and therefore are significantly higher for the widest surface area.

Furthermore, a conical-shaped charge is defined in geometrical terms as a 3D solid with rectangular or cylinder shapes with a negative conical cavity at one face [20,21]. Liu et al. [22] numerically characterized the blast effects produced by the detonation of a shaped charge with a conic and semi-elliptical cavity; see Figure 1c. The results allowed to observe that the explosive gases form a high-velocity jet. The jet formation is composed by two stages, of which the former appears when the release energy converges into the cavity, while the latter emerges when the energy gradually diverge as the jet moves away from the detonation point. Additionally, different cavity shapes lead jets to adopt different velocity distributions. Pyka et al. [23] studied the physical principles behind the mechanism of jet formation of a shaped charge. The morphology of the jet was stated through photo sequences. They demonstrated that the difference in velocity between the head and tail of the jet is directly related to the lengthening of the jet and consequently to the kinetic energy. Some studies have described the equations that govern the physical mechanism that describe the morphology of jet formation and how this may be solved mathematically in a variety of forms. Subsequently, the Jones–Wilkins–Lee (JWL) equation of state (EOS) of explosives is used for calculating the pressure of detonation products [24]. The Mie–Grüneisen equation of state (EOS) is often used for modeling condensed materials at high pressure [25]. The Johnson–Cook model is used for computing the material flow stress as a function of strain hardening, strain-rate hardening, and thermal softening [26]. Geum et al. [27] numerically dealt with the discontinuous interface of multiphase flow through the ghost fluid method. Additionally, sequence images captured the detonation wave propagation and also the interaction between the detonation wave and liner (metallic material), as well as the evolution of a metal jet. The most relevant finding is the emergence of a slug in the rear part on the liner.

Overall, numerical simulations have been developed using hydrocodes with the capability of simulating blast shock wave propagation. The most common commercial hydrocodes include Epic Dynamic Finite Element Code, LS-DYNA, Explicit Dynamic, Autodyn, Dytran, Nastran, Europlexus and Apollo Blast Simulator [28]. They have incorporated some discretization methods such as the Lagrange solver, Euler solver, arbitrary Lagrange–Euler (ALE) solver, multi-material ALE formulation (MM-ALE), computational fluid dynamics (CFD) and smooth particle hydrodynamic (SPH) solver [29]. Each one has certain advantages and also limitations. Several studies have been conducted in the field of shock wave propagation and the effects on materials using the different discretization methods such as performing numerical simulations of free-air explosion using the MM-ALE solver [30]. Furthermore, there are numerical and experimental validations of the dynamic pressure of a shock wave under a free-field blast loading ALE solver [31], using CFD solver for blast wave propagation under a structure [32], and shock wave propagation using the Euler solver [28,33,34].

According to a generalized view in given studies, there is still a strong lack of information about the characterization of blast shock wave propagation for a non-spherical charge at the near-field. In fact, the blast shock wave propagation for 3D cone-shaped charges (different from conical shaped charges) has not yet been characterized and is poorly understood.

3. Materials and Methods

The characterization of blast shock waves produced by cylindrical and 3D cone-shaped charges are studied experimentally and numerically. The former is conducted by the detonations of such charges on a blasting zone and recording the events by high-speed camera, while the latter is carried out using hydrocodes that are normally used on the prediction of fluctuation of incident peak pressure and impulse produced on shock wave propagation. Hereby, different parameters, such as type and weight of the explosive, orientation, scale distance, L/D aspect ratio and mesh size, need to be considered.

3.1. Experimental Study

The conducted experimental test site's blasting zone was formed from a crater with a depth of five meters and having a diameter of 18 m. Some fence posts were cemented into the ground, while additionally, a rope spider web was tightened. The explosive charge was positioned into a ceiling mount and subsequently positioned into the rope spider web. Finally, the priming charge was initiated.

Later, filmmaking equipment (Phantom v2512) was installed some thirty meters distant to the explosive charge. The set up was established with parameters such as an area field of view of 400 m^2, a resolution of 512 $\times$ 512 pixels, 4 K video recording at 75,000 fps, an interval of 13.32 and 32.41 mm of focal length. The explosive charge was detonated and subsequently recorded. Finally, digital images of each trial were processed. Due to the large amount of data generated, images were processed with specialized commercial software at two stages. Initially, images were processed using the Phantom Camera Control (PCC) commercial software, and then, the Phantom System Developer Kit (SDK) was used to create an interface between PCC and Matlab software. Finally, a code based on the artificial vision technique was developed to customize, track, analyze the movement as well as present the results of the output variable. The explosive used was a pentolite 50/50 ($C_{2.33}H_{2.37}N_{1.29}O_{3.22}$), which is a mixture of 50% pentaerythritol tetranitrate (PETN) and 50% trinitrotoluene (TNT) [35]. The charges used were spherical by validation of a mathematical model and cylindrical and 3D cone-shaped charges by characterization of the shock wave, as seen in Figure 2.

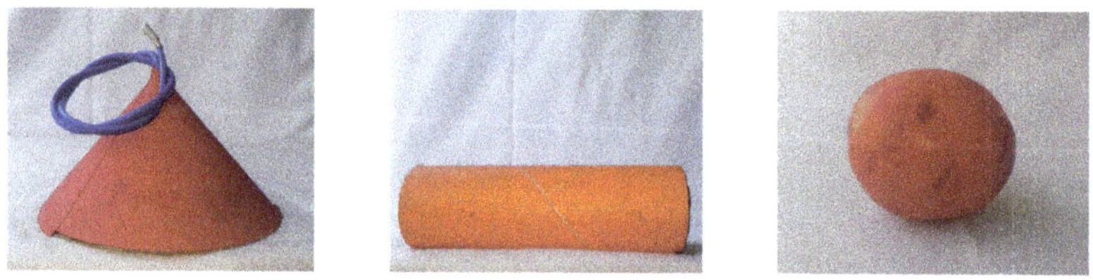

(**a**) 3D cone charge (**b**) Cylindrical charge (**c**) Spherical charge

Figure 2. Types of explosive charges.

3.2. Numerical Study

The fluid dynamic equations correspond to the Navier–Stokes equation and conservation of energy, which describe the space-time evolution of a blast wave and are extremely extensive to be solved in detail. Therefore, instead, two assumptions were realized: the blast wave should be considered as an axisymmetric problem, and the principle of superposition of waves should be avoided. The assumption that the shock front grows radially and symmetrically is only applicable on spherical charges, as illustrated in Figure 1a. Figure 1b,c indicates the evolution process of a shock wave for non-spherical-shaped charges after detonation. The waves adopt irregular forms in which the radius of the shock wave is a vector-valued function that directly depends on the orientation, aspect ratio L/D and time. Subsequently, flow properties such as density, velocity, temperature, and pressure are described by fluid dynamic equations, which are expressed in terms of radius of shock wave and orientation. The other assumption has been previously extensively discussed. While the shock wave is moving, it almost always undergoes non-linear effects such as reflection, refraction, and diffraction. Therefore, the equations that govern the oblique regime need to be included to capture the non-linear effects.

The present research used a commercial hydrocode (Ansys-Autodyn). This selection was based on four parts. First, it includes the conservation equations (mass, momentum, and energy) that describe the dynamic of a continuous media in terms of displacement, velocity, and acceleration. Secondly, it contains the thermochemistry of explosives, which is modeled with the Jones–Wilkins–Lee (JWL) equation of state (2) and relates pressure to the density and internal energy [36]. Furthermore, it counts with the ideal-gas equation of state for air (3) and finally with the constitutive model (4), which relates stress to a combination of strain ϵ_{ij}, strain rate effects $\dot{\epsilon}_{ij}$, internal energy I, and damage D.

$$\text{Conservation of momentum}: \frac{Dv_i}{Dt} = f_i + \frac{1}{\rho}\frac{\partial \sigma_{ji}}{\partial x_j} \quad (1a)$$

$$\text{Conservation of mass}: \frac{D\rho}{Dt} + \rho\frac{\partial v_i}{\partial x_i} = 0 \quad (1b)$$

$$\text{Conservation of energy}: \frac{DI}{Dt} = -\frac{p}{\rho}\frac{\partial v_i}{\partial x_j} + \frac{1}{\rho}\Pi ij \dot{\epsilon_{ij}} \quad (1c)$$

where ρ is the material density, v_i is the velocity, I is the specific internal energy, σ_{ij} is the stress tensor, p is the pressure, a deviatoric part Π_{ij}, f_i is the external body forces per unit mass, and $\dot{\epsilon_{ij}}$ is the deviatoric strain rate [36].

$$p = A\left(1 - \frac{\omega}{R_1 V}\right)e^{-R_1 V} + B\left(1 - \frac{\omega}{R_2 V}\right)e^{-R_2 V} + \frac{\omega E_0}{V} \quad (2)$$

In Equation (2), A, B, R_1, R_2 and ω represent the input parameters, E_0 represents the initial ratio of the internal energy, and V represents the initial relative volume of the detonation products [37]. The characteristics of the TNT and pentolite 50/50 are listed in Table 1.

Table 1. Characteristics of the explosives [38].

Parameter	Unit	Pentolite 50/50	TNT
Density	g/cm^3	1.6	1.56
Heat of Explosion	kcal/kg	1300	1080
Velocity of Detonation	m/s	7418	6900
Pressure of Detonation	kbar	220	210
Temperature of Explosion	°K	4497	3500

The air is treated as an ideal gas. The terms of Equation (3) are defined as: the ratio of the specific heat ($\gamma = 1.4$), density (ρ), initial density ($\rho_o = 1.29$ (kg/m^3)) and internal energy at ambient pressure, which is 2.068×10^5 (mJ/mm^3).

$$p = (\omega - 1)\frac{\rho}{\rho_o}E \quad (3)$$

The constitutive model is defined by Equation (4).

$$\sigma_{ij} = g\left(\epsilon_{ij}, \dot{\epsilon_{ij}}, I, D\right) \quad (4)$$

The solution of Equations (1)–(4) needs to be solved in both space and time domains. The former is defined by different spatial discretizations, while the latter is achieved by an explicit time integration method. The present research uses the multimaterial Euler discretization method. This mainly consists of modelling materials as grids, in which individual elements can contain multiple materials of the hydrodynamic type. As time progresses, the properties of these flows, such as velocity, pressure, density, etc., are computed at the fixed points of the grid, whereas mass, momentum, and energy flow across cell boundaries to subsequently compute the new mass, pressure, velocity, energy, etc., of that cell. The mathematical procedure has been previously described in [39].

The explicit time integration method needs to ensure the stability and accuracy of the solution. Therefore, the hydrocode has to satisfy the Courant–Friedrichs–Lewy (CFL) condition (5). It implies that the shock wave must not travel further than the minimum distance between grid elements in a single time step.

$$C = u\frac{\Delta t}{\Delta x} \leq 1 \quad (5)$$

The flow out boundary condition is also necessary in the code because it prevents the blast wave reflection at the border of the grid.

The numerical study is divided in three sections. The first is a set of 1D and 2D numerical studies on spherical charges to define an accurate model, which is validated through mesh refinement, empirical methods, and numerical uncertainty studies. The second section comprises numerical studies to assess the influence of cylindrical and 3D cone-shaped charges on the incident pressure, arrival time and shape of shock wave propagation. The third part includes numerical studies to define the magnitude incident pressure as a function of angle orientation, L/D aspect radio and scaled distance.

Methodology

A set of six 1D simulations were extended with different mesh sizes of 2, 1, 0.5, 0.25, 0.1 and 0.067 mm to reach a high confidence level. The computational domain was based on a 1D wedge using a radial symmetric model (Figure 3a). The explosive charge was the spherical type. It had a radius of 33.57 mm, which is equivalent to 225 g of TNT. Flow properties were measured through the set of gauges, which were placed every 40 mm. Next, a set of six 2D simulations were performed. Subsequently, a comparison set of incident peak pressure histories between 1D and 2D model was extended to define a 2D numerical model with high convergence and optimal mesh size. The air domain used was a square of 200 × 200 mm (Figure 3b). All the other parameters were equivalent to the previous analysis.

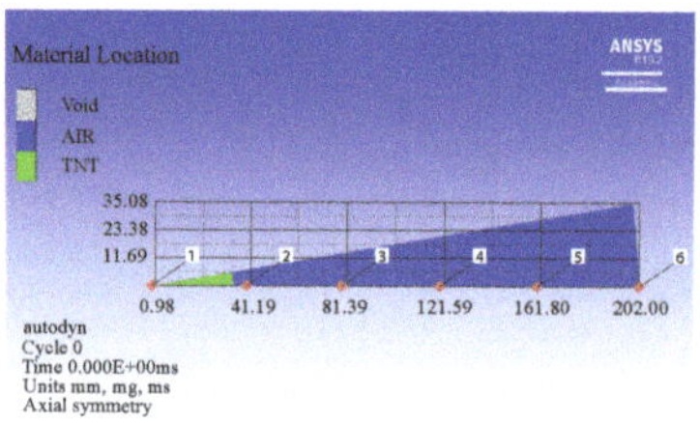

(**a**) 1D wedge

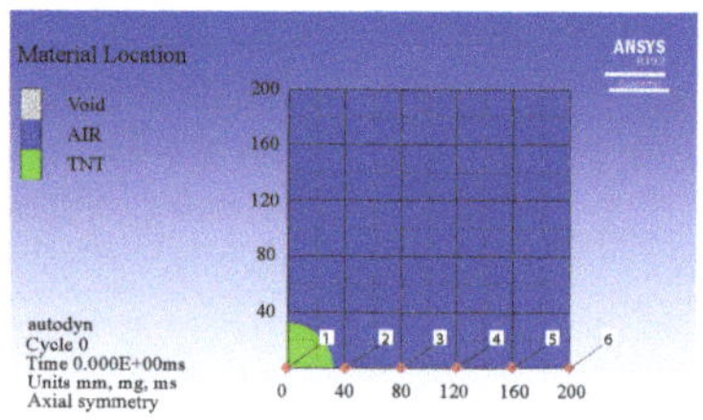

(**b**) 2D square

Figure 3. 1D and 2D numerical models.

Later, a set of three 2D simulations were performed with pentolite 50/50 charges of 450 g. The computational domain was based on a 2D square using an axially symmetric model and with a mesh size of 0.1 mm. The explosive charges were the spherical, cylindrical, and 3D cone types. Figure 4 illustrates the dimensions for each shape. Flow properties were measured through a set of gauges, which were placed every 120 mm at the abscissa and ordinate.

Finally, a set of 2D simulations for spherical, cylindrical, and 3D cone charges were extended with a mass of 0.25, 0.5, 0.75, 1, 1.5, 2, 2.5, 3, 3.5, 4, 4.5 and 5 kg. They were conducted to collect pressure data in both space and time domains to trace the fluctuation of incident pressure as a function of angle orientation, L/D aspect ratio, scaled distance, and shape of shock wave. Hereby, twelve simulations for spherical shaped charge were performed using TNT, while a total of thirty-six simulations for cylindrical (L/D = 3), (L/D = 5) and 3D cone (L/D = 0.625) shapes were performed using pentolite 50/50. Flow properties were measured through a set of gauges which were placed every fifteen degrees and every 50 mm (Figure 5).

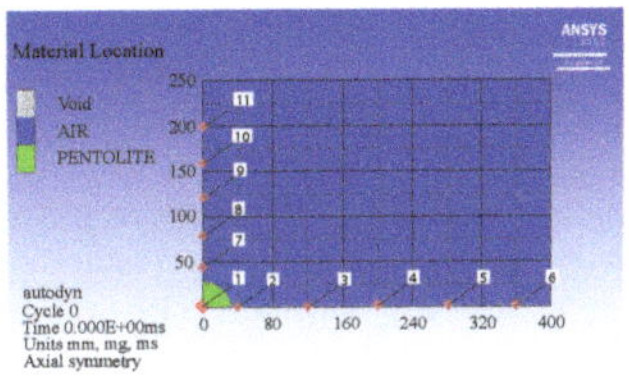

(**a**) Spherical charge

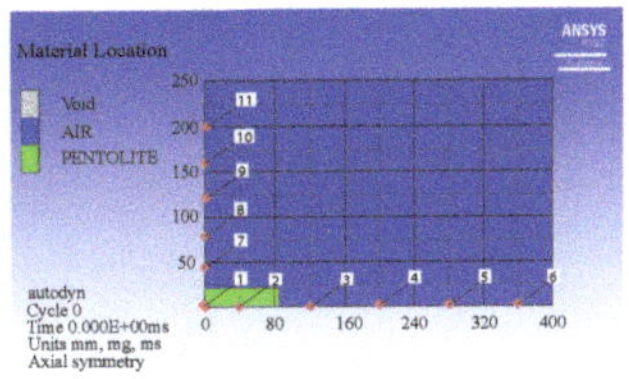

(**b**) Cylindrical charge

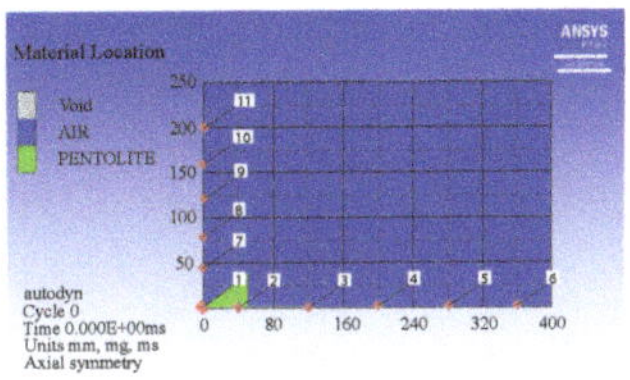

(**c**) 3D cone charge

Figure 4. 2D Axially symmetric model.

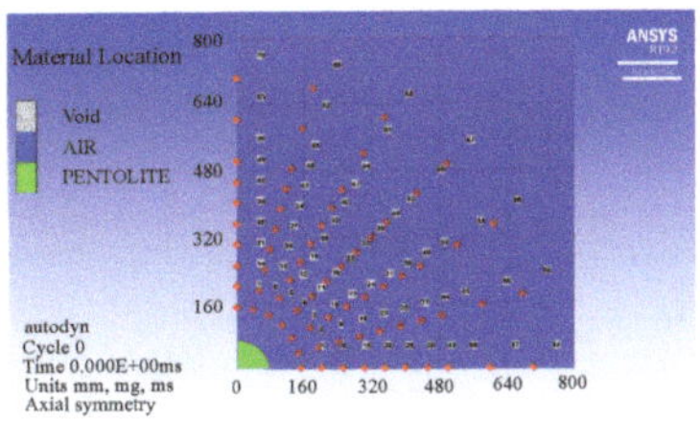

(**a**) Spherical charge

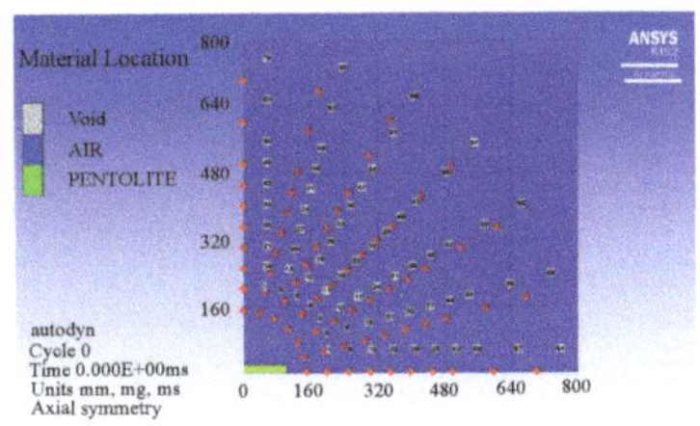

(**b**) Cylindrical charge

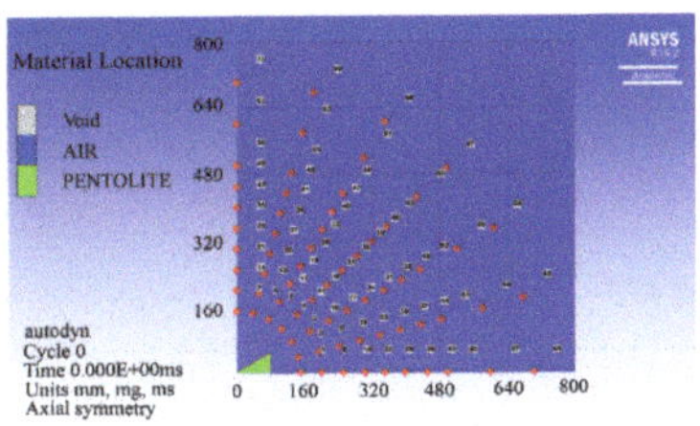

(**c**) 3D cone-shaped charge

Figure 5. 2D numerical models.

3.3. *Convergence Criteria*

The quantification of numerical uncertainty is popular among studies in computational simulations journals [40–42].

The uncertainty of a CFD model is an estimation error involved in the numerical results. There is a consistent method called the grid convergence index that applies the generalized Richardson extrapolation theory. It uses the finest three meshes per size (fine, medium, and coarse) to determine a relative error. If its value is below 4%, it infers that the solutions calculated for the finest mesh slightly differ from the asymptotic value [43].

Equation (6) allows us to relate the mesh refinement ratio r with the fine and medium mesh size h_i.

$$r = \frac{h_{i+1}}{h_i} \quad (6)$$

The order of convergence p could be obtained by Equation (7). The term f is the solution value of the numerical simulation for each mesh size. Refer to Table 2.

Table 2. Pressure results of autodyn calculation for the near-field.

Mesh	h [mm]	Pressure f [kPa]			
		Gauge (2) at 40 (mm)	**Gauge (3) at 80 (mm)**	**Gauge (4) at 120 (mm)**	**Gauge (5) at 160 (mm)**
1	0.075	1.35×10^5	2.41×10^4	1.52×10^4	1.07×10^4
2	0.1	1.46×10^5	2.40×10^4	1.51×10^4	1.06×10^4
3	0.25	1.88×10^5	2.26×10^4	1.47×10^4	1.03×10^4
4	0.5	2.58×10^5	2.01×10^4	1.39×10^4	9.94×10^3
5	1	3.29×10^5	1.70×10^4	1.23×10^4	9.20×10^3
6	2	4.71×10^5	1.59×10^4	1.05×10^4	8.14×10^3

$$p = \frac{ln\left(\frac{f_3 - f_2}{f_2 - f_1}\right)}{ln(r)} \quad (7)$$

Equation (8) calculates the asymptotic solution for h approaching 0.

$$f_{h=0} \cong f_1 + \frac{f_1 - f_2}{r^p - 1} \quad (8)$$

The GCI error is defined by Equation (9). Where F_s is defined as the safety factor. It is 1.25 for three or more meshes [43], and ϵ is the relative error.

$$GCI = \frac{F_s\,|\epsilon|}{r^p - 1}\,100\% \quad (9)$$

Equation (10) relates the GCI from fine to intermediate GCI_{12} and from intermediate to coarse grid GCI_{23} to define the asymptotic range [40].

$$GCI_{23} = r^p\,GCI_{12} \quad (10)$$

4. Results and Discussion

4.1. *1D Analysis for Spherical Charge*

Figure 6 illustrates incident pressure histories for 1D analysis and gives important remarks. Hereby, the empirical method (Kingery–Bulmash equation) can only be used for distances over 160 mm. The highlighted results in Table 2 lists that the convergence order at the vicinity of detonation requires a tiny mesh size due to its sensitivity. Therefore, it is necessary to use a mesh size of 0.1 mm to capture the blast wave for distances below 40 mm. It infers directly with high computational requirements.

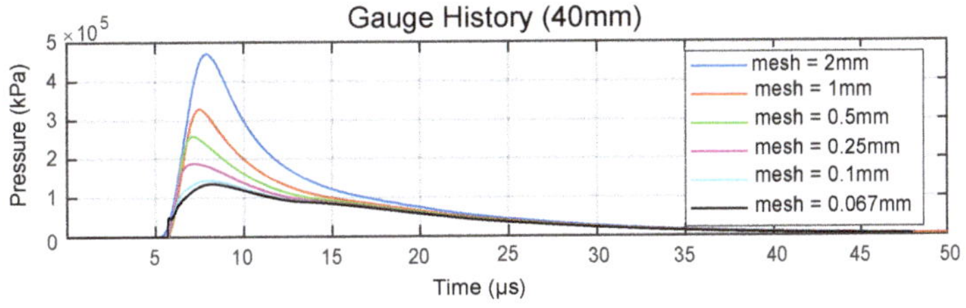

(**a**) Incident pressure histories at 40 mm

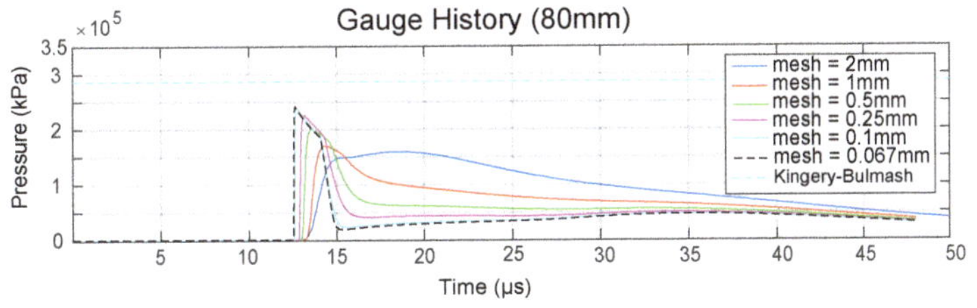

(**b**) Incident pressure histories at 80 mm

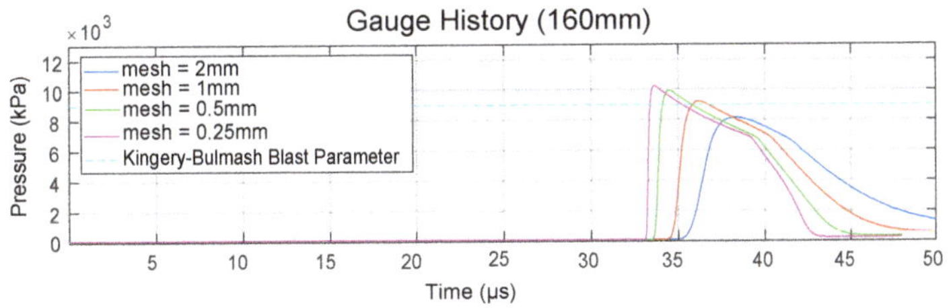

(**c**) Incident pressure histories at 160 mm

Figure 6. Near-field incident pressure histories for a spherical charge of 225 g of TNT.

4.2. Convergence Criteria

The GCI method was developed from the pressure values obtained from the numerical simulations for the three finest mesh sizes, which are 0.25, 0.1 and 0.067 mm (Figure 7). This lists the asymptotic solution and the asymptotic range. The abscissa of Figure 7 is formed by the mesh size as it approaches zero and the other mesh sizes. The ordinate of Figure 7 represents the asymptotic solution and the pressure values obtained from the three mesh sizes. Additionally, this analysis was performed for distances of 40, 80, 120 and 160 mm from the detonation point. Hereafter, these distances are referred to as gauge 2, gauge 3, gauge 4, and gauge 5, respectively. The GCI represents a relative error bound. Figure 7 lists $GCI_{12} < GCI_{23}$, where GCI_{12} reaches a percentage of less than 0.6% and the asymptotic range approaches 1 for gauge 2, 3 and 4. This means that the numerical analysis has reached a high convergence for mesh sizes of less than 0.067 mm. Even though the system corresponds to a chaotic type of system at the vicinity of the detonation point, gauge 1 has reached an acceptable convergence. This conclusion considers that the asymptotic range is 0.925 and GCI_{12} is 3.61%. This can be confirmed through the slope of the first two points illustrated in Figure 6, which represents the difference between the finest solutions and the solution with a mesh size of 0.

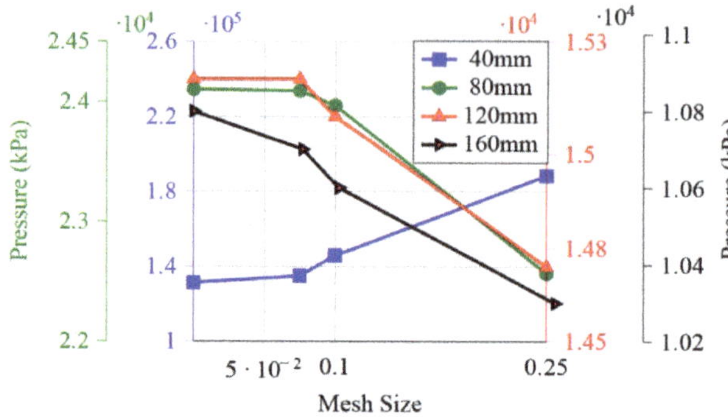

Figure 7. Calculation of grid convergence index for near-field.

4.3. 2D Analysis for Spherical Charge

The study compared incident pressure histories between 1D and 2D analysis (Figure 8). As per the criterion of superposition of curves drawn, the 2D model appears to be accurate. Thus, the mesh size for 2D model is 0.1 mm for distances lower than 40 mm and 1 mm for distances higher than 40 mm.

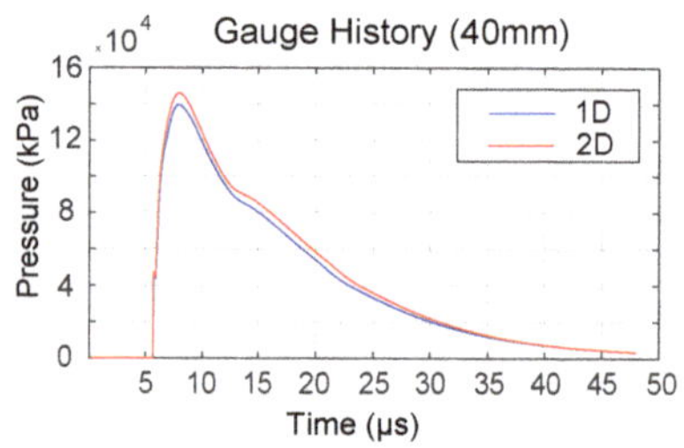

(**a**)

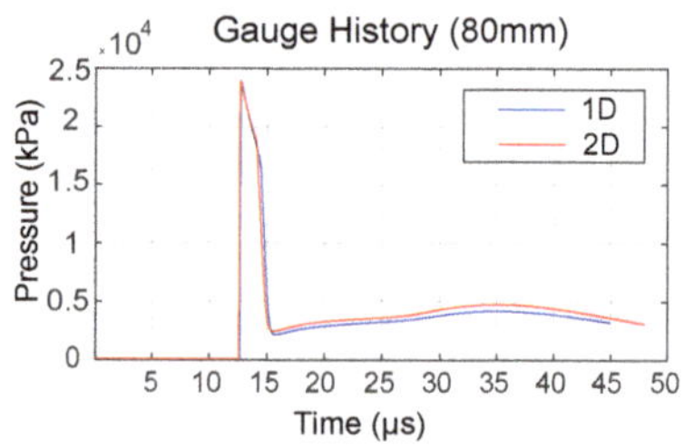

(**b**)

Figure 8. Convergence analysis between 1D and 2D. (**a**) Incident pressure histories at 40 mm [44], (**b**) Incident pressure histories at 80 mm.

4.4. Shaped Charge Analysis

Figure 9 depicts the results of image processing in terms of change of light area and exposition time. They illustrate that the exposition time is the fastest for 3D conic-shaped charges and slowest for spherical charges, while the area of combustion behind the shock wave reaches higher values for spherical charges and lower values for 3D conic-shaped charges. Therefore, the geometrical propagation of combustion behind the shock wave may be directly related to the shock wave propagation, as indicated in the numerical results.

The images obtained from high-speed cameras (Figures 10–12) contain a type of disturbances called noise. Noise is generated due to blasting zone environment conditions such as dust as well as wind effects. Therefore, some noise filters were developed through algorithms to improve image quality and accuracy.

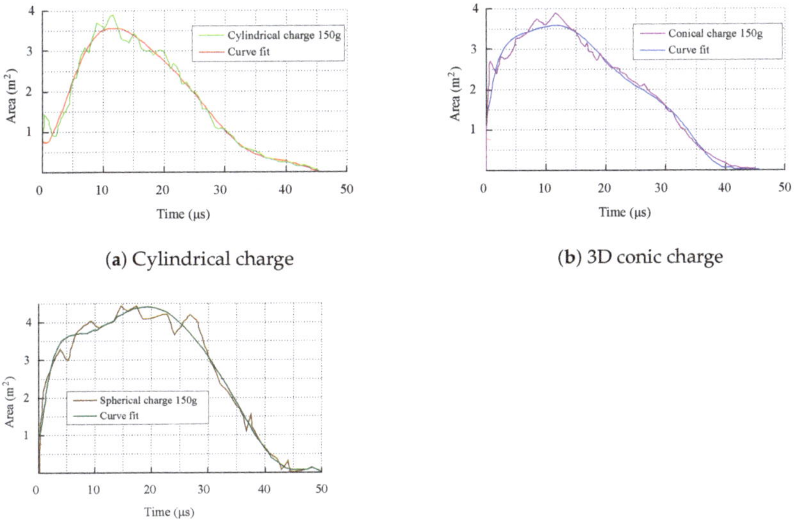

(**a**) Cylindrical charge

(**b**) 3D conic charge

(**c**) Spherical charge

Figure 9. Area of combustion behind the shock wave.

4.4.1. Spherical Charge

Numerical calculations indicate that the incident pressure at the front of the shock wave is a function of the radial distance. The shock wave expands uniformly through the surrounding air in the form of concentric circles, whereas the schlieren and shadowgraph images obtained demonstrate that the shock wave expands as a shadow ball (Figure 10). Other fundamental findings include that the incident peak pressure at the front of the shock wave in the radial direction reaches its highest magnitude at 20.10 μs, which then gradually diminishes (Figure 13). Furthermore, we encountered that spherical-shaped charges produce the fastest-travelling shock waves in the radial axis.

Figure 10b demonstrates the ignition process, while Figure 10d,f indicate the growth of deflagration (burning). The detonation close-ups clearly illustrate that it expands in form of concentric circles. Therefore, a combustion model can further be proposed, which should include equation of state, equations for sphere and dimensional analysis based on the images obtained.

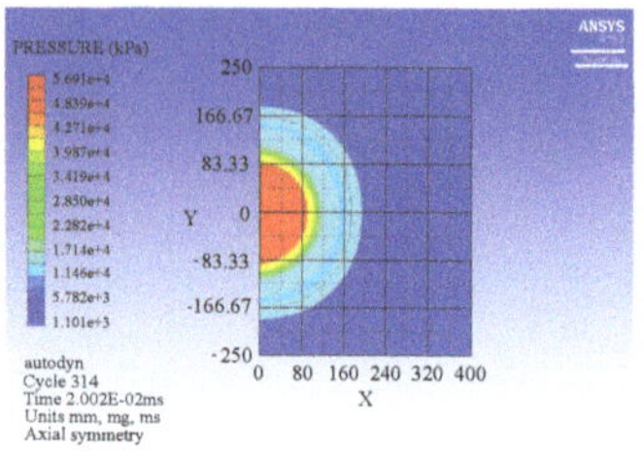

(**a**) t = 20 µs

(**b**) t = 26.5 µs

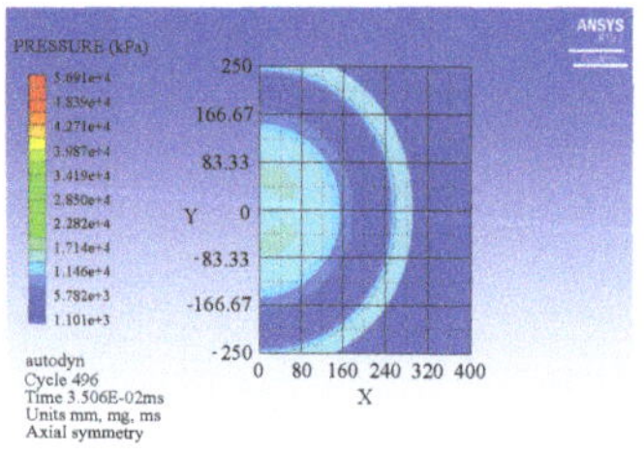

(**c**) t = 35.06 µs

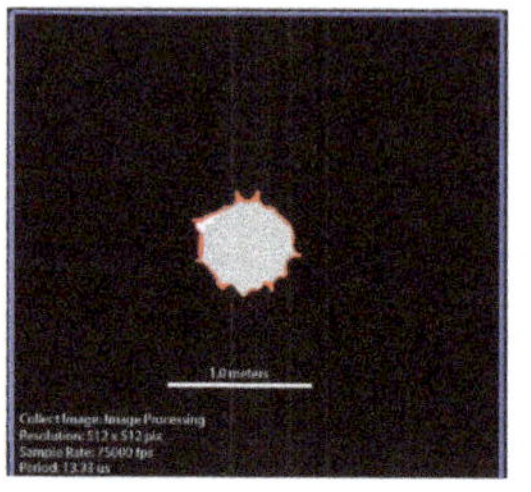

(**d**) t = 39.97 µs

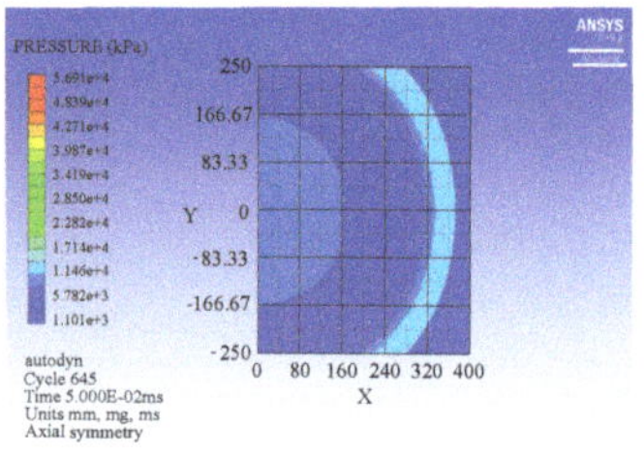

(**e**) t = 50.00 µs

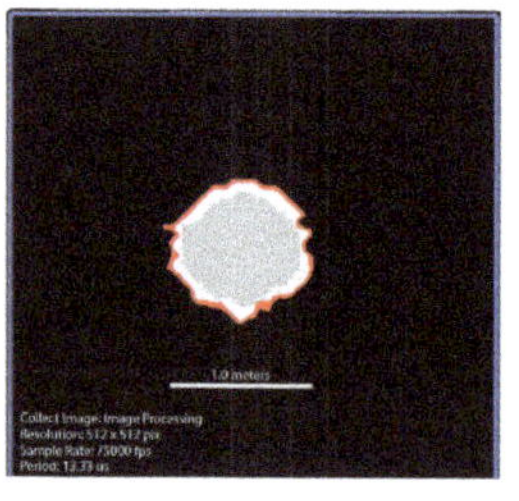

(**f**) t = 52.39 µs

Figure 10. Numerical and experimental results for spherical charge of 150 g of pentolite.

4.4.2. Cylindrical Charge

Numerical calculations yielded that the shock wave non-uniformly expands through the surrounding air. Such a shock wave adopts two well defined forms, an oblate spheroid, which is formed at the rear, and a bullet, which is formed at the front. Within the given experimental results, the schlieren and shadowgraph images indicate that the shock wave expands as a shadow ball until 26.65 µs. After this time, it tends to adopt an elliptical shape (Figure 11). Similarly, the incident peak pressure in the axial direction $(-x,\ +x)$ is greater than in the radial direction $(-y,\ +y)$, while the release energy is more concentrated in the axial direction. Additionally, we have realized that the shock wave travels faster in the axial direction and that the history at 200 mm demonstrates the presence of a secondary shock in the radial direction at approximately 50 µs (Figure 13).

Shadowgraph images depict the morphology of the combustion process. First, the energy is released in the form of heat. Later, it expands as function of the shape of the charge. In other words, as the curved face of the charge is greater than the planar face, the heat distribution is greater in the curve face than the planar face (Figure 11b,d,f). Therefore, it has a direct relationship with the shock wave propagation as the hydrodynamic regime completely predominates just after deflagration, and its initial boundaries are taken from the combustion process.

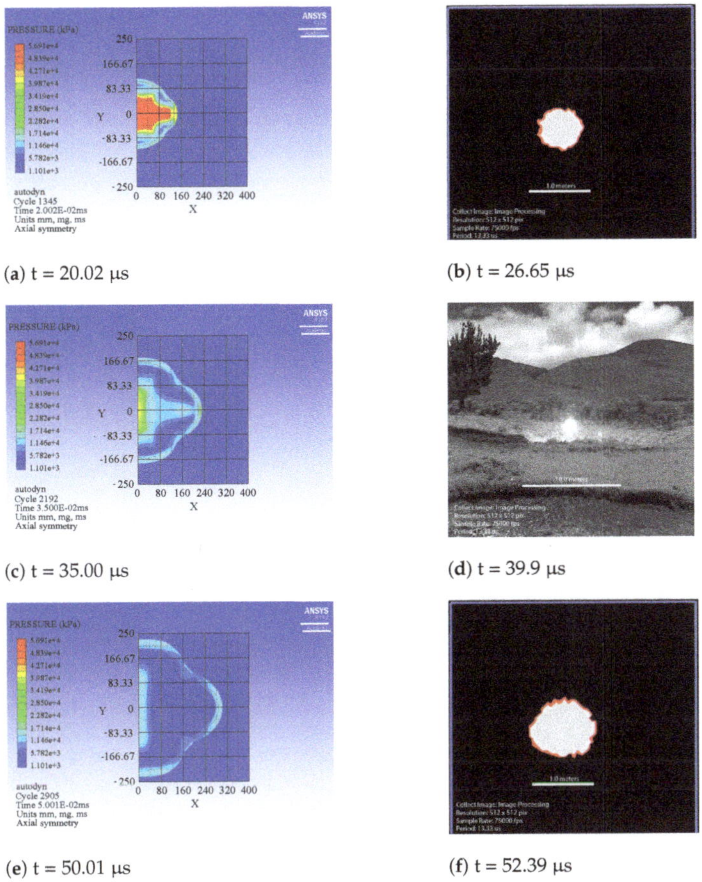

(a) t = 20.02 μs (b) t = 26.65 μs

(c) t = 35.00 μs (d) t = 39.9 μs

(e) t = 50.01 μs (f) t = 52.39 μs

Figure 11. Numerical and experimental results for a cylindrical charge of 150 g of pentolite.

4.4.3. 3D Conic Charge

Numerical calculations yielded that the shock wave non-uniformly expands through the surrounding air. The shock wave first adopts a vertical ellipse contour until 20 μs (Figure 12). After this time, it adopts a symmetric jellyfish dome-type profile. Other essential findings include that the incident peak pressure in the axial direction is greater than in the radial direction, while both axes present secondary shocks. Furthermore, the shadowgraphs (Figure 12b,d,f) must rotate 90 degrees clockwise to allow a comparison.

On the other hand, the schlieren and shadowgraph images obtained from the experimental results generated a shadow ellipse that later adopts a domed shape, equivalent to those of the numerical results. The lightest gray color refers to how the evolution of pressure distributes, while the darkest gray color refers to the combustion process (Figure 12b,d,f). Therefore, such a distribution, being sharp-shaped at the corner. infers that the release energy is mostly concentrated in the axial direction.

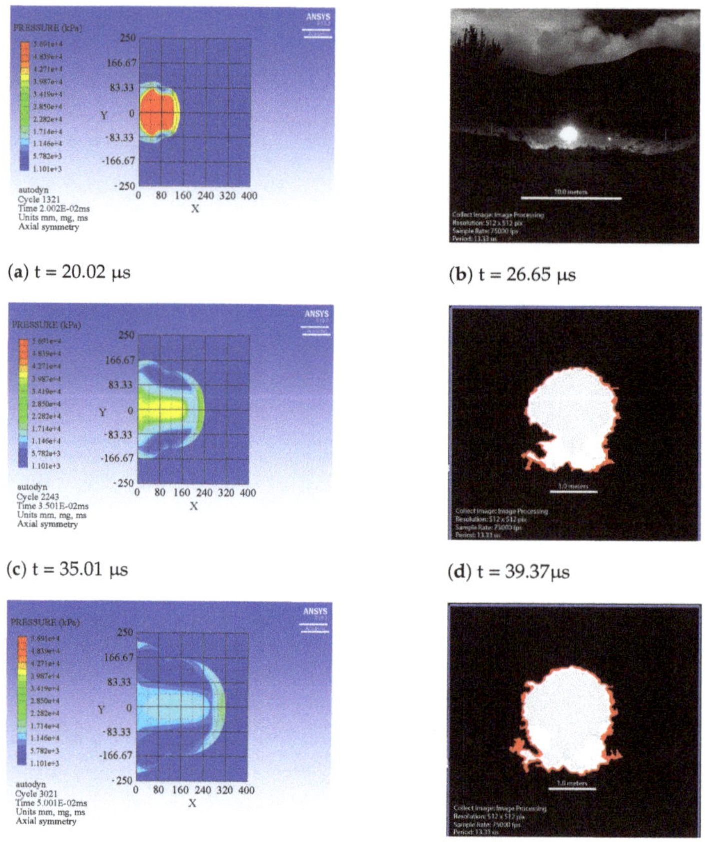

(a) t = 20.02 μs

(b) t = 26.65 μs

(c) t = 35.01 μs

(d) t = 39.37μs

(e) t = 50.01 μs

(f) t = 52.39 μs

Figure 12. Numerical and experimental results for 3D cone charge of 150 g of pentolite [44].

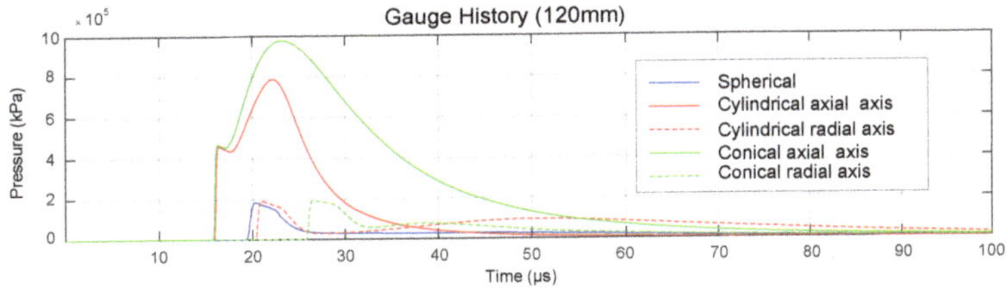

(**a**) t = 30 μs

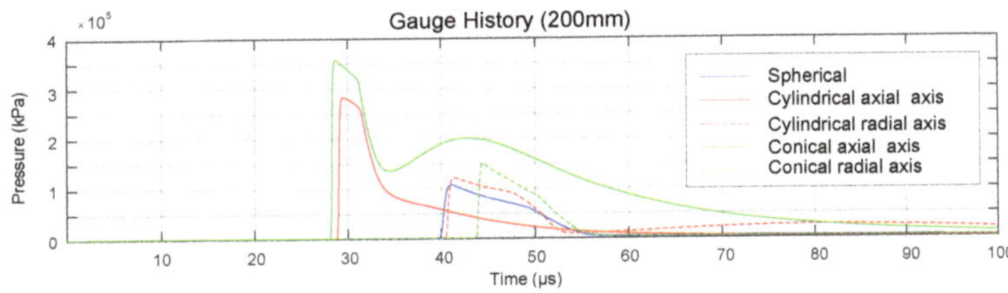

(**b**) t = 50 μs

Figure 13. Incident peak pressure histories for 150 g of pentolite.

4.5. Blast Parameters for the Positive Phase

The present study allowed us to realize that there is a superposition of the curve depicted in the Kingery–Bulmash blast parameters and the results obtained from the numerical simulation (Figure 14). This indicates that both curves keep the same tendency of the incident pressure as a function of the scaled distance. However, the Kingery-Bulmash blast parameters are more conservative with an increase by a factor of 1.67, as also indicated by previous studies where a factor of 1.65 was obtained [43]. This demonstrates that this study's computational model provides an acceptable confidence, and subsequently, it can be applied to other shaped charges.

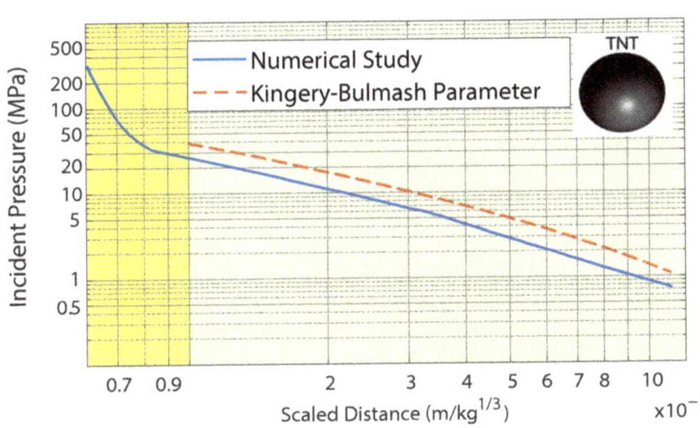

Figure 14. Comparison between Kingery–Bulmash blast parameters and numerical simulations for TNT spherical free-air charges.

4.6. Influence of the L/D Aspect Ratio, Scaled Distance and Orientation

The propagation of a blast shock wave for a cylindrical-shaped charge with an $L/D = 3$ and $L/D = 5$ and a 3D conic-shaped charge with an $L/D = 0.625$ is illustrated (Figure 15). Hereby, the incident peak pressure at the axial axis reaches the highest magnitudes for cylindrical charges with $L/D = 3$ and the lowest for cylindrical charges with $L/D = 5$ (Figure 15a). The incident peak pressure at the axial axis reaches the highest magnitude for 3D conic charges and the lowest for cylindrical charges with $L/D = 3$ (Figure 15b,c). The L/D for cylindrical charges has no effect for distances over 500 mm at the axial axis. The incident peak pressure at the radial axis at all distances is higher for cylindrical charges with $L/D = 3$ and lower for 3D conic charges. Additionally, results indicate that the incident peak pressure at the axial axis is concentrated at 0 to 5 degrees for cylindrical charges and at 0 to 15 degrees for 3D conic charges.

With the characterization of a blast wave for pentolite 50/50 for cylindrical and 3D conic-shaped charges, the current study demonstrates the change of incident peak pressure on cylindrical-shaped charges as a function of angle orientation and scaled distance for cylinder ratios of $L/D = 3$ and 5 (Figure 16a,b) and for a 3D conic ratio of $L/D = 0.625$ (Figure 17). Results for cylindrical-shaped charges yielded that the incident peak pressure reaches its highest magnitude at 0 degrees for both ratios. However, the principal limitation is that the incident peak pressure could not be obtained for a scale distance of less than 0.17 for $L/D = 3$ and 0.15 for $L/D = 5$. This limitation is related to the inaccuracy of incident peak pressure at that range. The effect of L/D over incident peak pressure can only be observed at 0 and 15 degrees, whereas the incident peak pressure at 45, 60, 75 and 90 degrees has its own tendency against the scaled distance, while the angle orientation does not have much influence on the incident peak pressure. Regarding 3D conic shaped charges, the incident peak pressure reaches its highest magnitude at 30 degrees. However, the incident peak pressure for 0, 15 and 30 degrees could not be obtained for a scale distance of less than 0.1. Lastly, the effect of 3D conic geometry over incident peak pressure can only be observed at 0, 15 and 30 degrees.

In general terms, the shaped charge and L/D aspect ratio utterly define the inception and evolution of the blast wave because it defines the vector-valued function of the radius of the shock wave at the near-field. The Schlieren and shadowgraph images evidence that such a function is directly related to energy concentration, and it depends on the face area of charge, being predominant within the largest area.

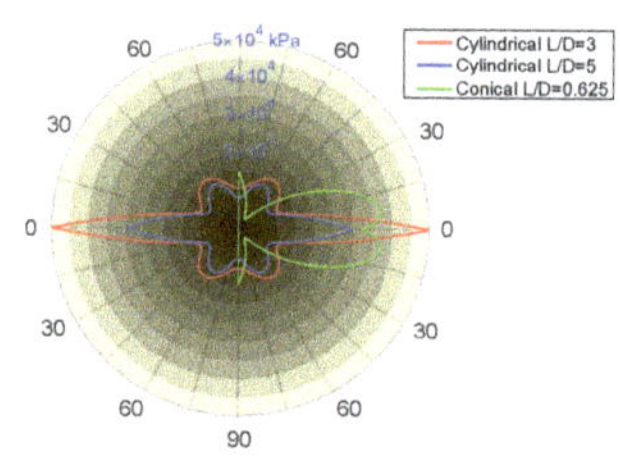

(**a**) at 200 mm

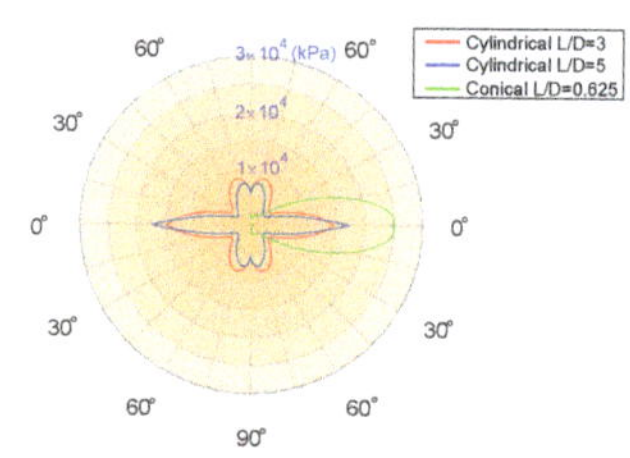

(**b**) at 350 mm

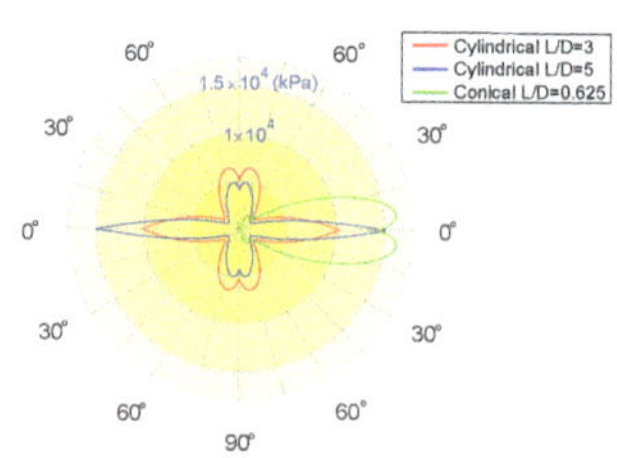

(**c**) at 450 mm

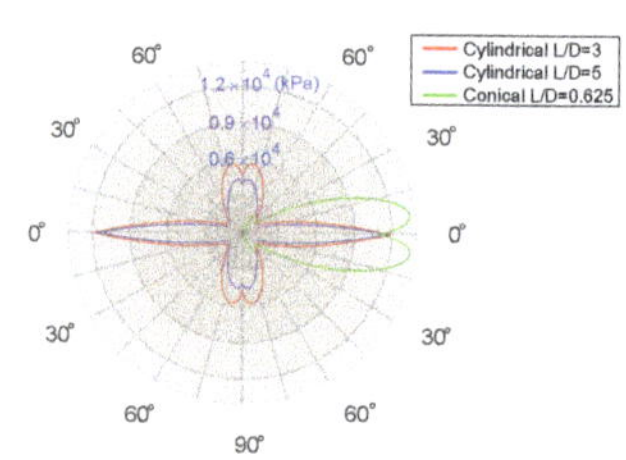

(**d**) at 500 mm

Figure 15. The incident pressure vs. angle orientation for 0.5 kg of pentolite 50/50.

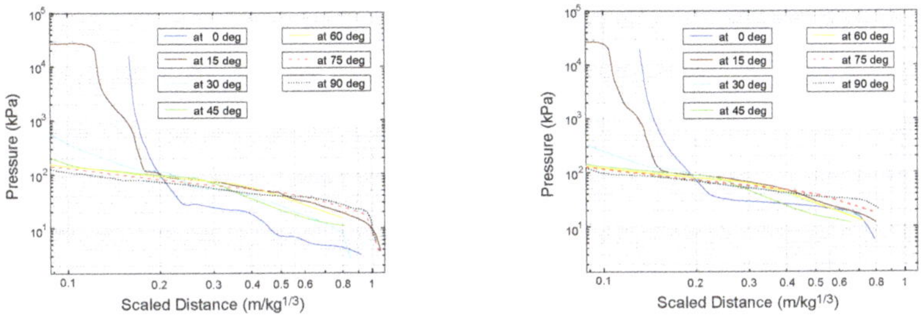

(**a**) Cylindrical charge $L/D = 3$ (**b**) Cylindrical charge $L/D = 5$

Figure 16. Comparison of incident pressure vs. scaled distance for cylindrical charges.

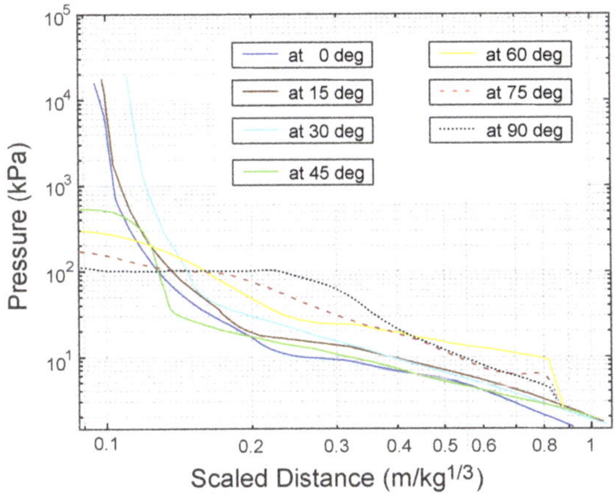

Figure 17. Comparison of incident pressure vs. scaled distance for 3D conic charge $L/D = 0.625$.

5. Conclusions

The predominant objective of the present research was to predict the effects generated by the detonation of cylindrical and 3D cone-shaped charges of pentolite 50/50 to define the fluctuation of incident peak pressure as a function of orientation, L/D aspect ratio, scaled distance, and shape of shock wave. For this purpose, a set of two-dimensional numerical models were used to compare the incident peak pressure from 3D cone explosives from cylindrical explosives with different aspect ratios. Subsequently, a set of experimental trials were conducted at a blasting zone. Moreover, the multimaterial Euler method was verified by comparing with the test results. Then, the shape of shock wave caused by 3D cone and cylindrical explosives with different L/D ratios were compared and discussed. This has led to several conclusions:

1. The L/D aspect ratio of the cylindrical and 3D cone-shaped charge have a significant effect on the inception, evolution, shape, propagation of the blast shock wave and incident peak pressure. As the L/D aspect ratio decreases, more release energy is concentrated in the axial direction for a 3D cone-shaped charge, while as the aspect ratio increases, more release energy is concentrated in the radial direction for a cylindrical-shaped charge. The incident peak pressure follows the same previous analysis, but it decreases in the other direction. At an equivalent weight, the incident peak pressure caused by a 3D conic-shaped charge reaches higher values than a cylindrical charge. Therefore, the effect of a cylindrical-shaped charge could be

considered for confined areas, while 3D conic shaped-charges could be considered for cutting purposes in the axial direction.

2. From the experimental and numerical results, we realized that the orientation has less influence than the L/D aspect ratio on the incident pressure contours. However, it defines the vector-valued function of the radius of ashock wave in its early stage. The influence range on the incident pressure contours is from 0 to 5 degrees for cylindrical charges and from 0 to 30 degrees for 3D cone charges. In other words, cylindrical and 3D conic charges amplify their damage effect for such ranges, respectively.
3. One of the challenges in the numerical simulation was to determine the effects caused by released energy in heat form. Typically, these data are simulated through an afterburn energy model which must be associated with chemistry. Unfortunately, this model is not available in the Autodyn hydrocode. Therefore, some non-linear effects caused by afterburn energy could not be simulated by numerical studies.
4. The quantification of the magnitude of non-linear effects such as the reflection, refraction, and diffraction is an essential stage for providing full understanding of inception and evolution of a blast shock wave caused by cylindrical and 3D cone-shaped charges. Hereby, the results presented, which are mostly based on the hydrodynamic regime where radiation becomes less important, capture the superposition of waves. The image sequences indicate the presence of bridge waves which rarely emerge following a pattern. Subsequently, the results also yield the interaction between bridge waves and primary waves. It leads to a secondary shock wave. These facts allow the characterization of a blast shock wave for non-spherical charges significantly more complex than those by spherical charges. Therefore, compressible multiphase flows should be developed and incorporated into the Autodyn hydrocode in order to deal with discontinuous interfaces.

Author Contributions: N.M.: Conception and design of study, Acquisition of data, Analysis and/or interpretation of data, Writing—original draft, Writing—review & editing. R.M.: Acquisition of data, Analysis and/or interpretation of data, Writing—original draft. T.T.: Writing—review & editing. All authors have read and agreed to the published version of the manuscript.

Funding: This research received no external funding.

Institutional Review Board Statement: Not applicable.

Informed Consent Statement: Not applicable.

Data Availability Statement: All the data and models employed and/or generated during the study appear in the submitted article.

Acknowledgments: We gratefully acknowledge the financial support provided by our university and the valuable support received from ESPE's Innovative Public Company, the Operations Department of the Defense High Command, and the Scientific and Technological Research Center of Army (CICTE). We are grateful to Fernando Olmedo, Julio Ortiz, Edison Morales, Patricio Navia, Esteban Vasconez, Tatiana Almeida, Andres Sarango, Rodrigo Tapia, Klever Madrid, David Zapata, Rashid Salazar, Mireya Paredes and Sebastian Cajas for their contribution during the experimental phase of the current study.

Conflicts of Interest: In the case of the submitted manuscript entitled "Characterization of Blast Wave Parameters for Cylindrical and Conical Explosive Charges Close to the Detonation Point" authored by Nestor Mejía, Rodrigo Mejía, Theofilos Toulkeridis, we declare that we ensure that our manuscript has not been submitted simultaneously for publication anywhere else, containing original data and a paper with all its content (not even partially) not presented previously in any journal, symposium or congress. Additionally, we do not have any material (figures, images or tables) included in the manuscript that may require to obtain a permission to reproduce copyrighted material from other sources. There is no conflict of interest with any party and there is no problem with the ethical standards of any kind. Therefore, we are able and willing to sign an agreement for transfer of copyright to the publisher the moment our manuscript is accepted for publication.

References

1. Ataque Con Drones en la Penitenciaría de Guayaquil. Available online: https://www.expreso.ec/actualidad/explosiones-posible-drones-carcel-maxima-seguridad-guayaquil-111763.html (accessed on 13 September 2021).
2. Reportan Ataque con Drones a cáRcel en Guayaquil, Ecuador. Available online: https://www.telesurtv.net/news/ecuador-reportan-ataque-drones-carcel-guayaquil-20210913-0016.html (accessed on 13 September 2021).
3. Drones Atacan Penal de máXima Seguridad de Ecuador. Available online: https://www.vozdeamerica.com/a/drones-atacan-penal-maxima-seguridad-ecuador/6225705.html (accessed on 13 September 2021).
4. Zhao, Y.; Cao, W.; Huang, F.; Han, Y.; Long, X. Evaluation of detonation performance and working capacity of explosives by optimized VLW EOS. *Combust. Flame* **2022**, *235*, 111734. [CrossRef]
5. Mespoulet, J.; Plassard, F.; Hereil, P.; Lefrançois, A. Influence of HE shape on blast profile. In Proceedings of the 8th European LS-DYNA Users Conference, Strasbourg, France, 24 May 2011.
6. Hryciow, Z.; Borkowski, W.; Rybak, P.; Wysockiois, Z. Influence of the shape of the explosive charge on blast profile. *J. KONES* **2014**, *4*, 169–176. [CrossRef]
7. Castellano, A.; Caltagirone, J. TM5-1300, Structures to Resist Accidental Explosions. In *Contents of Structures to Resist the Effects of Accidental Explosions (TM 5-1300, NAVFAC P-397, AFM 22)*; Department of Army Navy NAVFAC (Naval Facilities) P-397, Air Force Regulation 88-2; Department of Defense Explosives Safety Board: Alexandria, VA, USA, 1990; pp. 369–388.
8. Castellano, A.; Caltagirone, J. Design and Analysis of Hardened Structures to Conventional Weapons Effects. In *Contents of Structures to Resist the Effects of Accidental Explosions (TM 5-1300, NAVFAC P-397, AFM 22)*; U.S. Army Corps of Engineers, UNIFIED FACILITIES CRITERIA (UFC): Washington, DC, USA, 2002; pp. 254–268.
9. Department of Army Navy. Structures to Resist the Effects of the Accidental Explosions. *Int. J. Trend Sci. Res. Dev.* **2019**, *3*, 6–8.
10. Hyde, D. Fundamentals of Protective Design for Conventional Weapons. In *User's Guide for Microcomputer Programs ConWep and FunPro, Applications of TM 5-855-1*; U.S. Army Corps of Engineers, UNIFIED FACILITIES CRITERIA (UFC): Washington, DC, USA, 1988.
11. Selivanov, V.; Fedorov, S.; Babkin, A.; Bolotina, I. Using shaped charges with a "magnetic cut-off" for testing anti-meteoroid shields. *Acta Astronaut.* **2021**, *180*, 170–175. [CrossRef]
12. Cole, R. *Underwater Explosions*; Princeton University Press: Princeton, NJ, USA, 1948; pp. 63–78.
13. Stoner, R.; Richard, G.; Bleakney, W. The attenuation of spherical shock waves in air. *J. Appl. Phys.* **1948**, *9*, 670–678. [CrossRef]
14. Knock, C.; Nigel, D. Predicting the peak pressure from the curved surface of detonating cylindrical charges. *Propellants Explos. Pyrotech* **2011**, *3*, 203–209. [CrossRef]
15. Swisdak, M. Explosion effects in air. In *Explosion Effects and Properties: Explosion Effects in Air*; Naval Surface Weapons Center: Maryland, MD, USA, 1975; pp. 120–128.
16. Plooster, M.N. Blast effects from cylindrical explosive charges: Experimental measurement. In *Defense Technical Information Center*; U.S. Departament of Defense: Washington, DC, USA, 1982.
17. Fan, Y.; Chen, L.; Li, Z.; Xiang, X.; Fang, Q. Modeling the blast load induced by a close-in explosion considering cylindrical charge parameters. *Def. Technol.* **2022**. [CrossRef]
18. Gao, C.; Zhen, X.; Fang, Q.; Hong, J.; Wang, J. Numerical investigation on free air blast loads generated from center-initiated cylindrical charges with varied aspect ratio in arbitrary orientation. *Def. Technol.* **2021**. [CrossRef]
19. Rigby, S.; Osborne, C.; Langdon, L.; Cooke, S.; Pope, D. Spherical equivalence of cylindrical explosives: Effect of charge shape on deflection of blast-loaded plates. *Int. J. Impact Eng.* **2021**, *155*, 103892. [CrossRef]
20. Yadav, H.; Gupta, N. Study of collapse of a free surface conical cavity due to a plane or spherical shock wave. *Int. J. Impact Eng.* **1985**, *3*, 217–232. [CrossRef]
21. Xu, S.; Zheng, W.; Shao, X.; Cheng, W. Numerical method for predicting the blast wave in partially confined chamber. *Math. Probl. Eng.* **2018**. [CrossRef]
22. Liu, M.; Liu, G.; Lam, K.; Zong, Z. Meshfree particle simulation of the detonation process for high explosives in shaped charge unlined cavity configurations. *Shock Waves* **2003**, *6*, 509–520. [CrossRef]
23. Pka, D.; Bocian, A.; Bajkowski, M.; Magier, M. Numerical and experimental studies of the ŁK type shaped charge. *Appl. Sci.* **2020**, *10*, 6742. [CrossRef]
24. Wang, Y.; Xu, Z.; Jin, Y.; Zhen, J. The effect of cylindrical liner material on the jet formation and penetration capability of cylinder-cone-shaped charge. *Materials* **2022**, *15*, 3511. [CrossRef]
25. Heuzé, O. General form of the Mie–Grüneisen equation of state. *C. R. Mécanique* **2012**, *340*, 679–687. [CrossRef]
26. Shi, J.; Xiang, Z.; Zu, X.; Xiao, Q. Experimental and numerical investigation of jet performance based on Johnson-Cook model of liner material. *Int. J. Impact Eng.* **2022**, *170*, 104343. [CrossRef]
27. Geum, Y. Numerical simulation of conical and linear-shaped charges using an Eulerian Elasto-Plastic Multi-Material Multi-Phase Flow model with detonation. *Materials* **2022**, *15*, 1700.
28. Sherkar, P.; Shin, P.; Whittaker, A. Influence of Charge Shape and Point of Detonation on Blast-Resistant Design. *J. Struct. Eng.* **2015**, *2*, 04015109. [CrossRef]
29. Hofreiter, L.; Berezutskyi, V.; Figuli, L. Soft Target Protection Theoretical Basis and Practical Measures. *Soft Target Prot.* **2015**. [CrossRef]

30. Hashemia, S.; Bradford, M. Numerical simulation of free-air explosion using LS-DYNA. *Appl. Mech. Mater.* **2014**, *1*, 780–785. [CrossRef]
31. Wang, I. Simulation and experimental validation of the dynamic pressure of shock wave under free-field blast loading. *J. Vibroeng.* **2014**, *7*, 3547–3556.
32. Sohaimi, A.; Arif, S.M.; Ishak, A. Using computational fluid dynamics (CFD) for blast wave propagation under structure. *Procedia Comput. Sci.* **2016**, *1*, 1202–1211. [CrossRef]
33. Fedora, N.; Valge, S. Simulation of blast action on civil structures using ANSYS Autodyn. In Proceedings of the AIP Conference Proceedinge, Moscow, Russia, 3 July 2016.
34. Xue, Q.; Li, S.; Xin, C.; Shi, L. Modeling of the whole process of shock wave overpressure of free-field air explosion. *Def. Technol.* **2016**, *5*, 815–820. [CrossRef]
35. Dobratz, B.M. Physical properties. In *Properties of Chemical Explosives and Explosive Simulants*; Lawrence Livermore Laboratory: Livermore, CA, USA, 1972.
36. Collins, G. (Imperial College London, London, UK). Applied Modelling and Computation Group. Personal communication, 2002.
37. Chang, B.H.; Yin, J.P.; Cui, Z.; Liu, T. Numerical simulation of modified low-density jet penetrating shell charge. *Def. Technol.* **2015**, *3*, 426–437. [CrossRef]
38. Meyers, M. *Dynamic Behavior of Materials;* John Wiley & Sons: Hoboken, NJ, USA, 1994; p. 240.
39. Anderson, D.A.; Tannehill, J.C.; Pletcher, R.H. Mathematical procedure. In *Computational Fluid Mechanics and Heat Transfer;* Taylor & Francis: Abingdon, UK, 2020.
40. Kwasniewski, L. Application of grid convergence index in FE computation. *Bull. Pol. Acad. Sci. Tech. Sci.* **2013**, *1*, 123–128. [CrossRef]
41. Karimi, M.; Akdogan, G.; Dellimore, K.H.; Bradshaw, S.M. Quantification of numerical uncertainty in computational fluid dynamics modelling of hydrocyclones. *Comput. Chem. Eng.* **2012**, *43*, 45–54. [CrossRef]
42. Roach, P. Quantification of Uncertainty in Computational Fluid Dynamics. *Annu. Rev. Fluid Mech.* **1997**, *1*, 123–1260. [CrossRef]
43. Paudel, S.; Saenger, N. Grid refinement study for three dimensional CFD model involving incompressible free surface flow and rotating object. *Comput. Fluids* **2017**, *143*, 123–134. [CrossRef]
44. Mejia, N.; Peralta, R.; Tapia, R.; Duran, R. Damage assessment of RC columns under the combined effects of contact explosion and axial loads by experimental and numerical investigations. *Eng. Struct.* **2022**, *254*, 113776. [CrossRef]

mathematics

MDPI

Article

Mathematical Modeling of the Reliability of Polymer Composite Materials

Madina E. Isametova [1], Rollan Nussipali [1], Nikita V. Martyushev [2,*], Boris V. Malozyomov [3], Egor A. Efremenkov [2] and Aysen Isametov [1]

1 Department of Mechanical Engineering, Institute of Energy and Mechanical Engineering, Satbayev University, Almaty KZ-050000, Kazakhstan
2 Department of Advanced Technologies, Tomsk Polytechnic University, 634050 Tomsk, Russia
3 Department of Electrotechnical Complexes, Novosibirsk State Technical University, 20, Karla Marksa Ave., 630073 Novosibirsk, Russia
* Correspondence: martjushev@tpu.ru

Abstract: An urgent task in creating and using composite materials is the assessment and prediction of their performance properties and reliability. Currently, when studying the reliability of the materials, there is little experimental data, mathematical descriptions, and models for both probabilistic and deterministic methods to assess reliability. Based on the obtained experimental data, this article discusses the development of a methodology for predicting reliability. The article also proposes a statistical model for assessing reliability by the criterion of the structural strength of products made of polymer composite materials. The characteristics of the reliability changes in the materials when in operation are presented. The calculation allowed obtaining graphs showing the dispersion and statistical variability of the characteristics of polypropylene-based polymeric materials at the design, production, and operation stages of the product life cycle. The computational experimental results for determining the influence of the shape of inclusions and mass on the mechanical properties of a polymer composite material aimed at improving the strength characteristics of the products are presented. Based on a computational experiment in the MSC Digimat MF nonlinear solver, equations are provided to demonstrate the regression dependence of the strength of a part made of a polymer composite material on technological factors.

Keywords: modeling; mathematical methods; reliability of materials and structures; statistical characteristics; composite materials; polymeric materials

MSC: 65C20

Citation: Isametova, M.E.; Nussipali, R.; Martyushev, N.V.; Malozyomov, B.V.; Efremenkov, E.A.; Isametov, A. Mathematical Modeling of the Reliability of Polymer Composite Materials. *Mathematics* **2022**, *10*, 3978. https://doi.org/10.3390/math10213978

Academic Editors: Shujin Laima, Yong Cao, Xiaowei Jin and Hehe Ren

Received: 22 September 2022
Accepted: 24 October 2022
Published: 26 October 2022

Publisher's Note: MDPI stays neutral with regard to jurisdictional claims in published maps and institutional affiliations.

Copyright: © 2022 by the authors. Licensee MDPI, Basel, Switzerland. This article is an open access article distributed under the terms and conditions of the Creative Commons Attribution (CC BY) license (https://creativecommons.org/licenses/by/4.0/).

1. Introduction

The main tasks of the reliability theory of products made of polymer composite materials are the establishment of regularities in the occurrence of failures, the determination of quantitative characteristics, and the development of methods for assessing and calculating reliability [1]. These problems are solved in two ways. The first way consists of the study of the statistical regularities of the occurrence of failures of the same type of materials under certain operating conditions. This way is the basis for establishing the laws of distribution of the studied parameters and obtaining numerical characteristics of the operational reliability of the materials and products made from them [2].

The characteristics found in this way are used to calculate the reliability of materials and products.

The second way is aimed at studying the physical nature and the mechanism of failures. It serves as the basis for developing measures to improve the reliability of existing and newly designed technological materials [3].

This way, due to the complexity of obtaining the required initial information, has not yet been widely used in reliability studies, since it is often difficult to take into account all the factors affecting the reliability of systems [4].

Nevertheless, such an approach seems to be more effective in terms of identifying the physical nature of material destruction and the reasons why parameters deviate from acceptable limits. This way is used, despite the operational specifics, when it is still possible to obtain the required initial data, for example, when studying the reliability of polymeric materials and the most critical products manufactured from them [5].

A mathematical model is a set of mathematical objects (numbers, symbols, sets, etc.) and relationships between them, reflecting the most important properties of a technical system. This means taking into account the possible states of the system, path, and intensity of transitions from one state to another, and implies containing tolerance limits to determine parameters and the dependence of these parameters on random disturbances and processes in the elements.

Traditionally, mathematical reliability models can be divided into two groups [1]:

1. Structural models are the models based on the logical interaction schemes of the elements included in the system from the point of view of maintaining the operability of the system as a whole [6]. At the same time, statistical information about the reliability of the elements is used without involving information about the physical properties of the material, parts and connections, external loads and influences, and the mechanisms of interaction between the elements. Structural models are presented in the form of block diagrams and graphs (for example, fault trees and event trees). And the initial information is presented in the form of the known probability values of the failure-free operation of the elements, failure rates, etc.
2. Mathematical models of the reliability theory are the models taking into account mechanical, physical, and other real processes that entail a change in the object properties and object components. These are the models of mechanics widely used in the calculations of machines and structures. Force and kinematic interactions of machine elements and structures are complex. The behavior of these objects essentially depends on their interaction with the environment, nature, and the intensity of the exploitation processes [7].

To predict the behavior of polymeric materials, parts, and structural elements made of them, it is necessary to consider the processes of loading, deformation, wear, damage accumulation, and destruction under variable loads, temperature, and other external influences. It is possible to evaluate the reliability indicators of the systems in a theoretical and computational way, based on the physical models and statistical data regarding the properties of materials, loads, and impacts [8].

In order to compile adequate source mathematical models of the reliability of polymer composite materials and products made from them, it is first necessary to get an idea of the types and groups of such materials and study their mechanical and operational characteristics [9].

A modern technology trend is to increase the share of polymer composite materials. Polymer composite materials (PCMs) are widely used because of their properties. At present, almost no industry can function without PCMs due to their unique properties [10]. Works in the PCM field make it possible to improve material operational properties. Even today, PCMs are resistant to corrosion and oxidation, have good thermal stability, and can be used for thermal, acoustic, and electrical insulation. In addition, due to their manufacturability, PCMs allow the shortening of production processes. They also allow the reduction of material waste during processing [11]. All the processes described above gradually decrease the use of ferrous metals (such as steel alloys, carbon steel, cast iron, and forged iron) and non-ferrous metal alloys (primarily aluminum) when constructing machines and units. This is most evident in the aviation industry. The process of replacing metallic materials has been proceeding for many years [11].

When creating PCM, a bunch of the polymer matrix and fiber is often used to enhance the strength properties of the material in modern technology. Having different matrices and reinforcement mechanisms, composites can be of different types. The most commonly used composite materials are either glass fiber (GF) or reinforced carbon fiber (CF). The share of the studies of such composites is more than 90% of the total number of studies of composites [12]. Composite matrices are most often made from thermoplastic [13] or thermosetting [14] polymers.

The application scope of PCMs in mechanical engineering is quite large. However, the most complete manifestation of the advantages and strengths of PCMs is impossible in a large number of cases. Such cases include impellers, propellers, and impellers for electric centrifugal pumps. In [15], composites from a polymer matrix reinforced with glass fiber were used to manufacture impellers [15]. In general, fiberglass is an inorganic non-metallic material. Heat resistance, high tensile strength, and excellent chemical stability are among the properties of these fibers. Differences in fiber composition vary the properties, making them different. Different Young's moduli can be obtained in the range from 51.7 to 86.9 of the mean score [16].

The main incentive for increasing the economic efficiency of using PCM parts is to reduce the high cost of equipment and increase its reliability. The development and application of the PCM reuse technology by equipment manufacturers will allow companies to reduce the life cycle cost of the equipment operation by increasing its reliability. Increased reliability reduces the number of equipment failures and eliminates the risks of environmental problems [17].

Expanding the application scope of polymeric materials in industry is constrained by the lack of a scientifically-based approach to the choice of performance criteria, methods for assessing the reliability of products, and insufficient experience in their operation under various conditions. Currently, there are very few experimental data and developed methods for assessing the reliability that take into account the behavior of polymeric materials [18]. The review results show that the majority of works are devoted to the study of the PCM mechanical characteristics. A peculiar feature of polymer composite materials is a significant dispersion of strength and deformation characteristics at the initial state, as well as their change and dispersion when in operation. In addition, there are almost no methods for assessing the reliability of the products made of polymeric materials at the stages of design, production, and operation, taking into account the statistical variability of their characteristics. At the same time, the assessment of the reliability and overall mechanical properties of PCMs without mechanical testing is extremely important in the design and manufacture of products made of these materials. The designer must know and consider the material behavior under various loads, changes in material properties over time, and changes in the properties accompanied by scale variations of parts [19].

As to the reliability of polymer composite materials, researchers traditionally try to conduct a series of experiments, process the obtained statistical information, and derive from it the distribution functions of degradation and changes in the reliability of material samples, attributing to them the existing classical distribution functions of a random variable. They are Normal (Gaussian), Lognormal, Gamma distribution, Exponential, Laplace, Rayleigh, Weibull, Wigner, and Pareto. This is convenient from the point of view of the mathematical apparatus that already exists for such distributions. However, as the mathematical apparatus develops, including numerical methods for processing mathematical data, it is much more important to obtain native graphs of the functions of changing the source materials depending on the factors of time, temperature, and other performance indicators. There is no need to attribute these functions (sometimes with large errors) to the existing distribution laws of a random variable. This provides a certain flexibility in research work and allows for results that are more accurate for practical engineers conducting studies on changes occurring in the reliability and degradation of materials depending on changing operational factors in real conditions, as well as on predicting changes in their reliability in the future.

Based on this, it is possible to conclude that there is a lack of experimental data and deterministic methods for assessing reliability, taking into account the behavior of polymer composite materials. There are also no adequate methods for assessing the reliability of products made of polymer composite materials when designing, producing, and operating them, considering the statistical variability of the materials' characteristics. These factors make this topic relevant to the study [20].

The purpose of this work is the development and creation of probabilistic, stochastic source models of both PCMs and products made from them at each stage of the technological processes when treating these materials and products. That would allow revealing the peculiarities of changes in the reliability of materials and products depending on the main parameter (time t). To achieve this goal in the course of research and experimental work, the authors have completed the following tasks:

1. Development of a methodological approach and methodology for predicting the reliability for solving the problem of predicting the reliability of materials for products made of polymer composite materials according to various criteria.
2. Use of the probability theory to process the stochastic information of physical experiments: the information on the statistical variability of deformation–strength, elastic, dilatometric, and shrinkage characteristics.
3. Development of a model for calculating reliability according to the strength criterion.
4. Determination of the statistical characteristics of composite materials and the effective stress concentration factor of the materials.
5. Determination of the mathematical dependence of the failure-free operation probability of the samples on their cross-sectional area.
6. Construction of the dependence of the failure-free operation probability on the holding time at different pressures and temperatures of casting and molding the products from composite materials at different operating temperatures of the products.
7. Experimental studies on the products made of polymer composite materials to improve the strength characteristics of the products and their reliability.
8. Numerical modeling of the strength function of the materials and molded products depending on the cross-sectional area of the samples and the yield strength of thermoplastics based on polypropylene.

2. Materials and Methods

The experimental research in this article was carried out in two main stages. In the first stage, we calculated the reliability parameters of polymeric materials. Since reliability is a complex property of an object, including parameters that largely depend on the mechanical characteristics of the material [21], it is necessary to evaluate it. Therefore, we simulated the mathematical expectation of material degradation, the scattering dispersion of material degradation, the standard deviation of material degradation or scattering, and the coefficient of variation.

First of all, the dependencies were determined and built between the average value of the yield strength and the standard deviation of the yield strength from the logarithm of the cross-sectional area of the samples. Then, based on the obtained statistical model of reliability, the no-failure operation probability was calculated for the samples, and the dependencies of the no-failure operation probability on the cross-sectional area of the samples were plotted [22]. Next, the dependence of the failure-free operation probability on the technological parameters of production, namely, the exposure time under the pressure of the sample and the dependence of the average value, and the standard deviation of the yield strength on the aging time at low temperatures were obtained and plotted [23].

In the second stage of the research, we carried out experimental work to determine the properties of the real samples to compare the calculated parameters for the developed models with the experimental results. The comparison was carried out for one of the materials since this kind of work is extremely laborious and requires a lot of time and resources [24].

2.1. Selection of Research Materials

Polymeric materials of various grades were chosen as the research material. Basically, the choice of materials for the research was based on their wide applicability in modern industries, in particular in the aviation and automotive industries. For the numerical and natural experiments, we chose several groups of common polymeric materials. These were polystyrene, polyamide, polypropylene, and polycarbonate. In general, these materials belonged to the same group of polymeric materials, but their properties differed. This allowed for a more complete construction and testing of the models. In addition, the choice of these materials was also due to the fact that it was quite simple to obtain data on their properties and structure. This sometimes allows for avoiding the need for a large number of full-scale experiments.

One of the promising and topical areas for improving the structure of polymeric materials is the use of fillers. This allows changing their operational properties quite strongly. In the work, we also tested our models on a polymer material with a filler. We took a composite material based on a polycarbonate matrix filled with fiberglass as an experimental material. The choice of this material was due to the fact that it was promising for the purpose of significant improvement of the polymer strength properties. Such composite usage required additional full-scale experiments to confirm the constructed theoretical dependencies.

PP-based thermoplastics were chosen as objects of the study. They were polypropylene homopolymer PP 21060-16; block copolymer of propylene with ethylene BSPE 22007-16; frost-resistant grades of polypropylene MPP 15-04; MPP 15-04-901, asbestos-filled polypropylene PP 21060-A20; glass-filled polypropylene SNP 21060-16-S30; and polycarbonate with short glass fiber, made by injecting 30 pcs of molding for each size. The samples were tensile tested on an Instron 3400 testing machine (Instron Engineering, Norwood, MA, USA) at a tensile rate of 50 mm/min.

2.2. Mechanical Testing

Mechanical tests were carried out in two stages: the first stage was to obtain experimental data for probabilistic modeling of the properties and reliability of CPT, and the second stage was to verify the obtained results and test the developed mathematical models [25]. For this purpose, the calculated properties were compared with the results of mechanical tests. For comparison, the experimental results of testing the samples of PCM (polycarbonate matrix and glass fiber as a reinforcing element) for tension according to the standard method [26] were obtained. The initial data for determining the design properties of the material samples obtained as a result of the full-scale experiments are not given in the article due to the large amount of statistical information. The article presents the results of processing these data in the form of graphs.

The samples were in the form of blades with a cross-sectional area of 2.5, 10, 39, and 200 mm^2, made by injection molding of 30 pcs for each size. The shape of the samples is shown in Figure 1. The length of the symmetrical broadenings at the ends was 34 mm; the length of the inner part between the broadenings was 82 mm. The samples were obtained by casting. Short fiberglass was used as a filler. The short form was chosen based on the technological requirements of foundry technology. The polymer mixtures were prepared on a single-screw extruder with a diameter of 45 mm, L:D = 25 mm, manufactured by Esmos. Electric heating was implemented as follows: The temperature is controlled by thermocouples and a thermostat. The extrusion temperature regime is as follows: Zone I—260 °C; Zone II—265 °C; Zone III—270 °C; and Zone IV—260 °C. The sample testing and stress-strain plotting were performed on an Instron 3400 testing machine (Instron Engineering, Norwood, MA, USA) at a tensile rate of 50 mm/min. The tests were carried out in accordance with "ISO 1268-10:2005 Polymer composites". The production of samples tests the injection molding of long-fiber press materials. The same path geometry of the composite material and the symmetrical arrangement of the cavities ensures the same properties of the test specimens made from the same material batch.

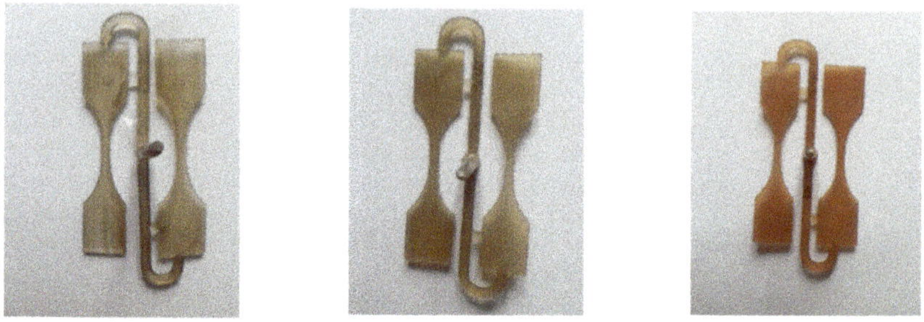

(a) **(b)** **(c)**

Figure 1. Test samples of composites: (**a**) unfilled; (**b**) filled with 20% short glass fibers; (**c**) filled with 30% short glass fibers.

2.3. Methods for Modeling and Calculating Deviations

For the polymeric materials based on PP, the yield point is chosen as the ultimate strength characteristic [17]. It is known that the distribution of random values of stress and strength for structural elements made of polymeric materials can be described by the normal distribution law [27].

The normal distribution of a random variable (Gaussian distribution) is a probability distribution, which in the one-dimensional case is given by a probability density function coinciding with the Gaussian function [28]:

$$f(x) = \frac{1}{\sigma\sqrt{2\pi}}e^{-\frac{1}{2}\left(\frac{x-\mu}{\sigma}\right)^2} \quad (1)$$

where parameter μ is the mathematical expectation (mean), median, and the distribution mode; σ is the standard deviation; σ^2 is the variance of the distribution.

1. Mathematical expectation of the degradation of materials is as follows:

$$L_o = \frac{\sum_{i=1}^{k} L_i \cdot m_i}{\sum_{i=1}^{k} m_i} \quad (2)$$

where L_i is the degradation time in the i-th digit, h; m_i is the number of sample breaks in the i-th digit; k is the number of digits.

2. The dispersion scattering degradation of materials is:

$$D = \sigma^2 = \frac{\sum_{i=1}^{k} (L_i - L_o)^2 \cdot m_i}{\sum_{i=1}^{k} m_i} \quad (3)$$

3. The material degradation standard deviation or scattering:

$$\sigma = \sqrt{D} = \sqrt{\frac{\sum_{i=1}^{k} (L_i - L_o)^2 \cdot m_i}{\sum_{i=1}^{k} m_i}} \quad (4)$$

4. The variation coefficient is:

$$V = \frac{\sigma}{L_o} \tag{5}$$

By processing the statistical information using Formulas (1)–(4), and calculations of the numerical characteristics of the degradation of materials for the obtained samples, it is possible to determine an important characteristic of the degradation of materials when the maximum number of their failures is observed [29].

The mathematical expectation of the degradation L_o characterizes the condition when the number of equipment failures is maximum. Scattering σ and the variation coefficient V show the possible spread of degradations in contrast to their expectation.

It is proposed to evaluate the relative characteristic of the reliability (lack of degradation) of the materials as the main component of their reliability and to determine it through an indicator that characterizes the number of material failures over a certain time, that is, through the failure rate [30]. The failure rate is understood as the ratio of the number of failed samples per unit of time to the average number of objects that are working properly in a given period, provided that the failed objects are not restored and are not replaced by serviceable ones [31]. In other words, the failure rate is numerically equal to the number of failures per unit of time, divided by the number of samples that have worked without fail up to this time. The mathematical description of the failure rate is presented below:

$$\lambda(t) = \frac{n(t)}{N_{av}\Delta t} = \frac{n(t)}{[N - n(t)]\Delta t} = \frac{f(t)}{P(t)} \tag{6}$$

where N is the total number of the samples under consideration;
$f(t)$ is the failure rate or the number of the samples that have failed by the time t per unit time;
$P(t)$ is the number of the samples that have not failed by the time t;
$n(t)$ is the number of the failed samples in the time interval from $t - (\Delta t/2)$ to $t + (\Delta t/2)$;
Δt is the time interval;
N_{av} is the average number of the properly working samples in the interval of $\Delta t : N_{av} = \frac{N_i + N_{i+1}}{2}$;

where N_i is the number of the properly working samples at the end of the interval Δt.

The failure rate dimension is the inverse of time, usually measured in 1/hour.

Based on the proposed structure of material processing, using the statistical reliability model, it is possible to determine the probability of the failure-free operation of the element according to the strength criterion [32].

As the sampling results show, the probability of the failure-free operation of the materials and samples made from them obeys the normal distribution law [33]. Expressing the probability of the failure-free operation R in terms of the normalized normal distribution function, we have:

$$R = 1 - \Phi\left[-\frac{\overline{\sigma}_t - \overline{\sigma}_{eq}}{\sqrt{S_{\sigma_t}^2 + S_{\sigma_{eq}}^2}}\right], \tag{7}$$

where R is the failure probability; Φ is the normalized (standardized) normal distribution function; $\overline{\sigma}_t$, $\overline{\sigma}_{eq}$ are the average tensile yield strength of equivalent voltage; S_{σ_t}, $S_{\sigma_{eq}}$, are the standard deviation of the tensile yield strength of equivalent voltage.

The probabilistic mathematical apparatus presented above is used to determine the reliability parameters of materials.

To assess the reliability of the products made of polymeric materials according to the main criteria (strength, rigidity, climatic resistance, and dimensional accuracy), one must have information on the statistical variability of deformation–strength, elastic, dilatometric, and shrinkage characteristics [34].

The model for calculating the reliability by the strength criterion is based on the analysis of the distributions of acting and ultimate stresses. To assess the strength reliability, it is necessary to know the distribution of random variables, i.e., the maximum equivalent stress and ultimate strength characteristics [35].

At the design stage, factors that affect the variability of equivalent stresses for a complex stress state of a loaded product and the variability of ultimate strength characteristics are taken into account. Factors affecting the variability of equivalent stresses include the dispersion of characteristics, the stress state type, and temperature. The components of the model for calculating the reliability according to the strength criterion in the general case are the characteristics of the polymer material: elastic modulus E, Poisson's ratio μ, coefficients of linear thermal expansion in the glassy α_{st} and highly elastic states, and glass transition temperature T_{st}.

An analysis of the factors affecting the strength shows its dependence on the state or cleanliness of the surface, the scale factor or the influence of the absolute dimensions of the sample, the influence of stress concentrators, and temperature [35].

Reliability was assessed according to the strength criterion for the products made of polymer structural materials operating under load, polymer coatings of the materials with different coefficients of linear thermal expansion, polymer parts reinforced with metal inserts, and metal–polymer products [32].

3. Results and Discussion

Figure 2 shows the mean value and standard deviation of the yield strength as a function of the logarithm of the sample cross-sectional area for PP-based thermoplastics. An increase in the cross-sectional area of the samples causes a decrease in the average value and a change in the standard deviation of the yield strength of the investigated thermoplastics. This is due to the layered structure that is formed in the process of processing the material into a product. In addition, the scale factor has a significant effect on other deformation–strength properties of the materials based on polypropylene [3,4].

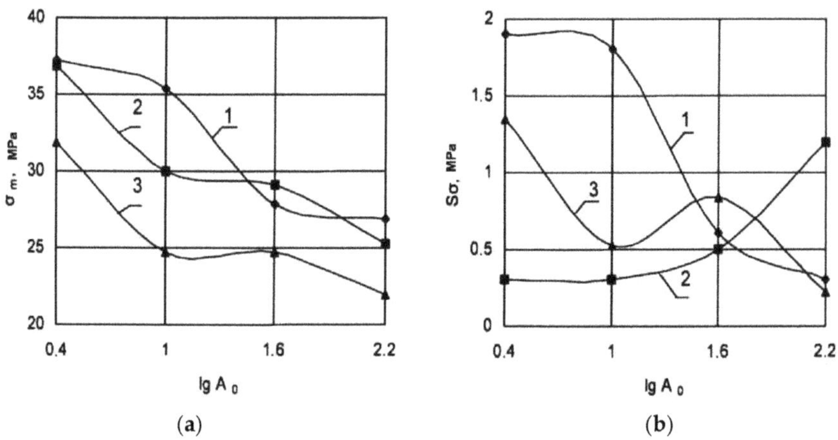

Figure 2. Dependence of (**a**) the average value of the yield strength and (**b**) the standard deviation of the yield strength on the logarithm of the cross-sectional area of the samples A_0. Thermoplastics are based on polypropylene: (1) PP 21060-16, colorless; (2) PP 21060-A20; (3) MPP 15-04 colorless.

The dispersion of the values of equivalent stresses is affected by the dispersion of elastic, deformation, and thermophysical characteristics (Table 1).

Table 1. Statistical characteristics of polypropylene compositions.

Material	Description	E, MPa	μ	A_{st}, 10^{-6}, 1/grad	A_{ve}, 10^{-6}, 1/grad	T_{st}, K
BSPE 22007-16	Compositions of the frost-resistant propylene–ethylene copolymer with increased impact resistance BSPE 22007-16 are used to produce battery monoblocks, technical products, and car bumpers. They have increased impact resistance and can be made on the basis of the propylene–ethylene copolymer with the introduction of special additives that increase the impact strength. Compositions are produced colored and unpainted.	1170/95	0.37/0.020	-	98/12	-
MPP 15-04, colorless	Melt flow index: 1.0 g/10 min. Tensile yield strength: not less than 22.0 MPa. Elongation at break: not less than 130%. Charpy impact strength without notch at minus 50 °C: not less than 25 kJ/m^2. Softening temperature: according to Vicat, at a load of 10 N: not less than 135 °C. Frost resistance: not higher than −50 °C. Frost resistance for painted grades: not higher than −40 °C. Granules of the same color, 2–5 mm in size.	1110/77	0.36/0.018	-	104/14	-
MPP 15-04-901	It is frost-resistant polypropylene. Frost-resistant polypropylene compositions are intended for injection molding of automotive components, battery monoblocks, and technical products.	1100/76	0.36/0.017	-	101/13	-
SNP 21060-16-S30	Melt flow index: 4.1−8.0 g/10 min. Spread of PFR: no more than ±8%. Number of inclusions: no more than 3 pcs. Mass fraction of ash: no more than 0.035%. Mass fraction of volatile substances: no more than 0.09%. Resistance to thermal-oxidative aging: not less than 360 h. Tensile yield strength: not less than 30 MPa. Elongation at break: not less than 500%. Granules of the same color, 2−5 mm in size.	1500/114	0.26/0.016	15/2,7	30/3,2	272/2

Note: the numerator is the average value of the indicator; the denominator is the standard deviation of the indicator.

The experiments showed that there were stress concentration places in products made of polymeric materials at the site of a sharp change in shape, in parts reinforced with metal inserts, and in polymer coatings. The maximum local stresses were determined through stress concentration factors.

We found that with an increase in the cross-sectional area of the samples, the sensitivity of the material to stress concentration increased, but the effective stress concentration coefficient remained less than unity, i.e., in the initial state at a test temperature of 23 ± 2 °C, materials based on PP were insensitive to stress concentrators.

The experimental data on the average values and standard deviations in tensile strength, the strength of the samples with a stress concentrator, and an effective stress concentration factor for polymeric materials based on polystyrene (UPS-825, ABS-2020), polycarbonate PK-2, and glass-filled polyamide PA 610-1-108 are given in Table 2.

When calculating the strength of the parts made of polymeric materials with large cross sections, it is necessary to take into account the influence of the scale factor and stress concentration.

On the basis of the statistical reliability model, the probability of the failure-free operation was calculated for products made of PP 21060-16 and asbestos-filled PP 21060-A20, operating under conditions of a uniaxial stress state (Figure 3). The safety factor for a cross-sectional area of 2.5 mm^2 was 1.5 for both materials.

The safety factor was determined as the ratio of the average value of the yield strength σm to the average value of the equivalent stress σeq. As the cross-sectional area increases, the probability of failure-free operation decreases. For thermoplastic PP 21060-A20, with an increase in the cross-sectional area of the samples from 2.5 to 200 mm^2, the probability of failure-free operation decreases from 0.999 to almost 0.6, while the safety factor remains greater than one.

At the production stage, the technological factors that affect the variability of the mechanical and thermal properties of materials are analyzed. Technological factors include material processing modes, as well as the content of technological and industrial waste.

Table 2. Effective Stress Concentration Factor for Thermoplastics.

Material	Description	σ_{rm}, MPa	$S\sigma_{rm}$, MPa	σ_{rmc}, MPa	$S\sigma_{rmc}$, MPa	K_e
UPS 825 black	High-impact molded polystyrene. Grade 825 is a high impact injection molded polystyrene. The ability of this polymer to be molded with accelerated cycles with minimal stresses gives an exceptional property—the preservation of impact strength.	27.3	0.58	25.9	0.76	1.05
ABS 2020	2020 ABS plastic of the highest grade. Izod impact strength: not less than 24.5 kJ/m^2 (25.0 kgf cm/cm^2). Tensile yield strength: not less than 38.2 MPa (390 kgf/cm^2). Elongation at break: not less than 22%. Vicat heat resistance: not lower than 100 °C. Melt flow index: within 10–12 g/10 min. Bending temperature under load: not less than 100 °C. Mass fraction of water: no more than 0.28%.	40.7	0.65	36.2	0.9	1.12
PA 610-1-108	Polyamide PA 610-1-108 is a reliable and practical material in production. The material is a synthetic polymer product with high physical and chemical properties. The main advantages of the material over similar polyamides are low moisture absorption, excellent electrical insulation, and resistance to petrochemical attacks. When additives are added to the raw material composition of the product during the production process, there is no reaction of foaming, decomposition, and deformation of the original structure. The material perfectly tolerates thermal effects, as well as sudden changes in pressure levels.	134.0	8.62	100.1	3.46	1.34
Polycarbonate PK-2	Melt flow index is within 4–11 g/10 min. Tensile yield strength: not less than 57 MPa. Elongation at break: not less than 60%. Impact strength of the sample with a notch: not less than 30 kJ/m^2. Electrical strength: not less than 19 kV/mm. Polycarbonate is used for casting thin-walled parts of the complex configuration with metal fittings with increased resistance to high temperatures and humidity.	62.2	1.19	52.0	2.46	1.20

where σ_{rm}, $S\sigma_{rm}$, σ_{rmc}, $S\sigma_{rmc}$ are an average value, standard deviation of tensile strength without and with a stress concentrator, and MRA; K_e is the effective stress concentration factor.

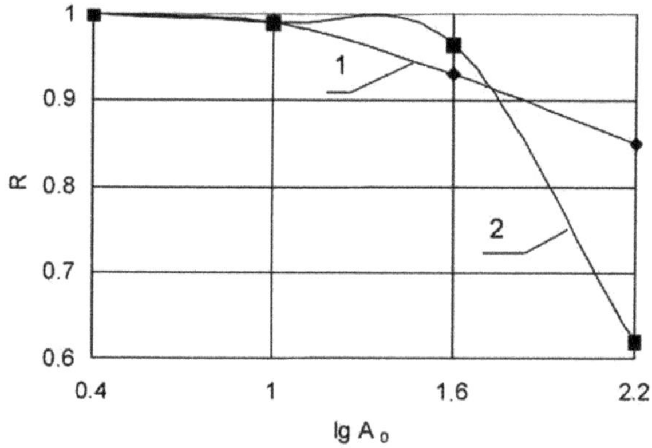

Figure 3. Dependence of the probability of the failure-free operation on lg of the cross-sectional area of the samples for thermoplastics based on polypropylene: (1) PP 21060-16, colorless; (2) PP 21060-A20.

Figure 4 shows the dependence of the probability of the failure-free operation according to the strength criterion on the pressure exposure time for the material PP 21060-16 for various casting temperatures. A decrease in the holding time under pressure and an increase in the casting temperature are shown to entail a decrease in the probability of failure-free operation. This is due to a slight decrease in the average value of the yield strength of the material and an increase in its standard deviation.

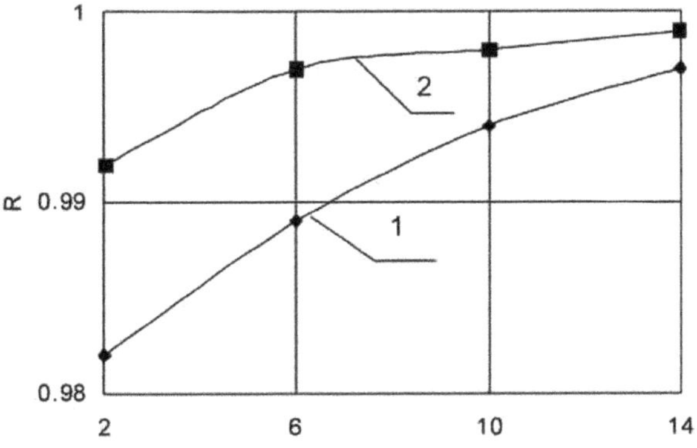

Figure 4. Dependence of the failure-free operation probability on the holding time under pressure PP 21060-16 and the casting temperature at a casting pressure of 80 MPa: (1) 270; (2) 200 °C.

In this way, the real curves of changes in the reliability level of the polymer material were obtained, which depend on two parameters: the holding time under pressure and the material temperature.

The operation stage allows analyzing the external factors that affect the variability of the material science characteristics included in the strength reliability calculation model and the variability of the ultimate strength characteristics. External factors include natural and artificial climatic factors, radiation exposure, and ionizing radiation.

To assess the influence of operational factors on the reliability of products made of polymeric materials operating under load, the influence of natural climatic factors is considered.

Figure 5 shows the mean value and standard deviation of the yield strength versus the aging time for the samples with various cross-sections of the thermoplastic block copolymer of propylene with ethylene BSPE 22007 in cold climates. The material samples were exposed to a cold climate with an average annual temperature of −8–9 °C.

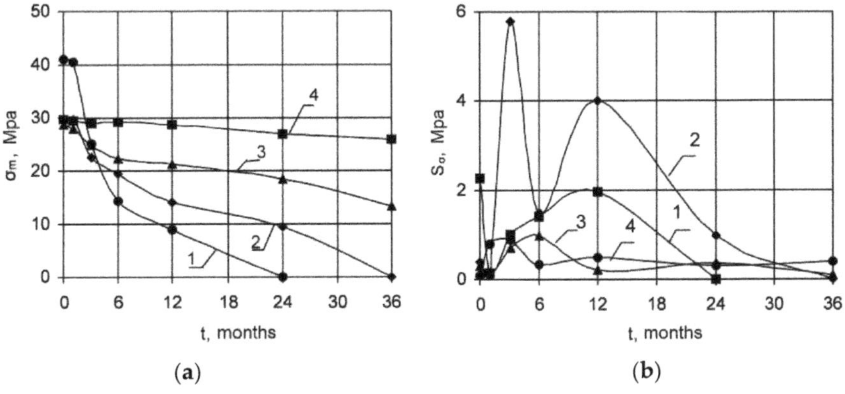

Figure 5. Dependence of (**a**) the average value and (**b**) the standard deviation of the yield strength on the aging time in cold climate conditions for the BSPE 22007-16 material. The cross-sectional areas of the samples: (1) 1 × 2.5; (2) 2 × 5; (3) 3 × 13; (4) 8 × 25 mm^2.

Due to the fact that the solar radiation effect changes the structure in the surface layers of the samples, the effect of this process on the material during natural aging should depend on the thickness of the samples. Indeed, for the colorless materials of the block copolymer of propylene with ethylene BSPE 22007 and frost-resistant polypropylene MPP 15-04, the yield strength of the samples 1 mm thick decreases sharply already after 1 month of exposure. After two years of exposure, the samples of materials MPP 15-04 (colorless) and BSPE 22007-16 (1 mm thick) completely lose their strength. In this case, the samples are scattered at the moment of removal from the stand of the climatic station.

With an increase in the thickness of the samples, the resistance of the material to aging increases. This is due to the fact that in the process of aging, after saturation of the surface layers with oxygen-containing products and closing the channels of free access of oxygen to the deeper layers of the material, a monotonous decrease in strength is observed [5].

The standard deviation of the tensile yield strength initially increases along with increases in the aging time, and then decreases after reaching the limit value.

Polypropylene-based thermoplastics require material modifications, especially in cold climates. Modified materials must be frost-resistant and resistant to solar radiation.

The MPP 15-04-901 material, which is light-stabilized with soot, throughout its entire thickness did not show a significant change in the properties during 3 years of aging in a cold climate.

In view of this, we have obtained dependences for research purposes that can actually increase the reliability of polymeric materials and products made from them, depending on the aging of materials and their strength characteristics. In addition, like all numerical studies, the numerical determination of the reliability provides an excellent opportunity not only to determine the reliability characteristics of individual materials, but to obtain a family of characteristics for different groups of polymers, to compare their aging characteristics, changes in strength and reliability, and to choose the least degradable materials with the same modeling parameters.

Figure 6a shows the dependence of the failure-free operation probability on the aging time of standard samples of thermoplastics 2 mm thick based on polypropylene in a cold climate. The failure-free operation probability is calculated for the case of a uniaxial stress state with an initial safety factor of 1.5 for the materials. The acting stresses during aging were determined for permanent deformation with a change in the elastic modulus.

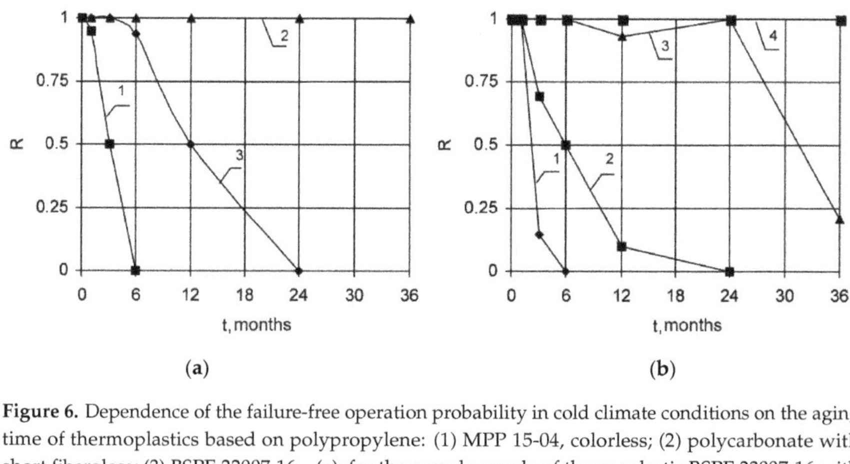

Figure 6. Dependence of the failure-free operation probability in cold climate conditions on the aging time of thermoplastics based on polypropylene: (1) MPP 15-04, colorless; (2) polycarbonate with short fiberglass; (3) BSPE 22007-16—(**a**); for the samples made of thermoplastic BSPE 22007-16 with the following cross-sectional areas: (1) 1 × 2.5; (2) 2 × 5; (3) 3 × 13; (4) 8 × 25 mm—(**b**).

The graph shows that the failure-free operation probability for the considered model depends significantly on the aging time, especially in the case of poorly stabilized colorless thermoplastics. The probability of failure-free operation drops to 0.5 within 3 months for a block copolymer of propylene with ethylene, and within 12 months for frost-resistant polypropylene.

The failure-free operation probability did not change over the studied period of time for thermoplastic MPP 15-04-901.

Polycarbonate with short fiberglass showed the highest resistance to aging in cold climates.

The dependence of the failure-free operation probability on the aging time, considering the scale factor of the BSPE 22007-16 thermoplastic under cold climate conditions is shown in Figure 6b.

Even for a weakly stabilized colorless thermoplastic BSPE 22007-16, with an increase in the thickness of the samples, the failure-free operation probability is shown to increase, and it is close to unity for a sample 8 mm thick during the entire aging time.

In view of this, after analyzing the obtained dependences, we can say that reliability plays an important role in predicting the changes in the properties of materials depending on the time at which critical failures of materials occur. By setting certain optimal levels of the acceptable reliability of the selected composite polymer in the range R from 0 to 1, it is possible to determine the service life of parts made of it. In addition, thanks to the proposed models of changes in the reliability and properties of materials over time, it is possible to evaluate the reliability of a complex system (for example, a centrifugal pump), which consists of several parts based on a composite polymer. At the same time, by setting greater reliability for critical parts and assemblies of the system (for example, centrifugal pump blades), with R from 0.95 and higher, it is possible to significantly increase the technical system reliability as a whole. In addition, it is possible to solve the inverse problem, which is especially important for service engineers, by setting a certain reliability level for a particular part or assembly material. One can gain additional service time for the part, followed by the replacement of this part according to the regulations in order to maintain the required reliability level of the technical system. In this way, in fact, it is possible to form technical regulations for system maintenance with a given guaranteed reliability level depending on time, for almost every unit or part. Speaking about the reliability level, it should be noted that within the framework of this article, the theory of the reliability choice is not specified, but there are two main approaches to this choice:

1. Choosing the reliability level that is optimal in terms of economic expenditures for operation.
2. Choosing the reliability level in terms of the inadmissibility of emergency situations associated with major man-made consequences and human injuries.

It should also be noted that the obtained models of reliability changes in polymer parts and assemblies could be useful not only for operational specialists, but also for developers of technical systems based on composite polymers. Developers, in turn, by setting the reliability of the system parts and determining the reliability of the system as a whole, can determine the system warranty period for consumers, reducing the material costs for additional tests on the aging of materials.

In this way, we were able to obtain specific recommendations for research engineers and manufacturers of the products from the presented polymer composites, depending on the actual performance indicators: operating time, ambient temperature at different material strength factors included in the samples, and effective stresses of the material, taking into account changes in the elastic modulus of the material.

3.1. Study of Composite Material Properties with a Clearly Expressed Inhomogeneous Structure

As an example, let us take the PCM used to manufacture centrifugal pump wheels. It consists of a polycarbonate matrix and fiberglass as a reinforcing element.

If the polymer composite material has a heterogeneous structure and a large number of inclusions that differ greatly in properties, then its properties should be evaluated according to the method described below.

The algorithm for modeling the mechanical characteristics of such two-phase filled composites is based on the theory of J. Eshelby. Based on the theory of Ashebly and the Mori–Tanaka theorem, Tandom and Weng calculated the elastic modulus for fibrous and dispersion-strengthened isotropic matrix composites. The equations below define five independent constants corresponding to Young's modulus, shear and bulk moduli, and Poisson's ratio of the composite material [18,20].

$$\frac{E_{11}}{E_m} = \frac{1}{1 + (c_r(A_1 + 2\nu_m A_2))/(A)} \quad (8)$$

$$\frac{E_{22}}{E_m} = \frac{E_{33}}{E_m} = \frac{1}{1 + (c_r[-2\nu_m A_3 + (1-\nu_m)A_4 + (1+\nu_m)A_5 A])/(2A)} \quad (9)$$

$$\frac{\mu_{12}}{\mu_m} = 1 + \frac{c_r}{2c_m S_{1212} + (\mu_m)/(\mu_r - \mu_m)} \quad (10)$$

$$\frac{\mu_{23}}{\mu_m} = 1 + \frac{c_r}{2c_m S_{2323} + (\mu_m)/(\mu_r - \mu_m)} \quad (11)$$

$$\frac{\kappa_{23}}{\kappa_m} = \frac{(1+\nu_m)(1-2\nu_m)}{1 - \nu_m(1+2\nu_{12}) + c_r[2(\nu_{12} - \nu_m)A_3 + A_4(1 - \nu_m(1+2\nu_{12}))]/A} \quad (12)$$

$$v_{12} = \frac{v_m A - c_r(A_3 - v_m A_4)}{A + c_r(A_1 + 2v_m A_2)} \quad (13)$$

where E_{ig} is the Young's modulus in the direction of the axes; c_r is the volume fraction of the fiberglass filler; A_1, A_2, A_3, A_4, A_5, and A are scale factors; ν_m is the matrix shift module; μ_{ig} is the Poisson's ratio in the direction of axes x, y, z; μ_r is the Poisson's ratio in the direction of the fiberglass filler; μ_m is the matrix Poisson's ratio; S_{igkl} is the Eshebli tensor component; k is the matrix volumetric module; k_{ig} is the volumetric module in the direction of axes x, y, z; ν_{ig} is the shift module in the direction of axes x, y, z.

Expressions for coefficients A_1, A_2,... A A and the Eshebli tensor component S_{igkl}, depending on the shape of the inclusions and the elastic characteristics of the phases can be found in [17]. The elasticity coefficients introduced in this way are effective quantities that determine the macroscopic elastic properties of the material.

The above theories make it possible to determine engineering constants for the designed polymer composite materials. To determine the strength of the structure as a whole, it is necessary to use the equivalent stress criteria, as well as the Tsai–Hill criterion for transversely isotropic bodies (3D), using the setting of the first destroyed FPGF pseudograin [36,37]:

$$\frac{1}{2}\left\{\left(\frac{1}{\sigma_{B11}^2} + \frac{1}{\sigma_{B22}^2} - \frac{1}{\sigma_{B33}^2}\right)(\sigma_{11} - \sigma_{22})^2 + \left(-\frac{1}{\sigma_{B11}^2} + \frac{1}{\sigma_{B22}^2} + \frac{1}{\sigma_{B33}^2}\right)(\sigma_{22} - \sigma_{33})^2 + \left(\frac{1}{\sigma_{B11}^2} - \frac{1}{\sigma_{B22}^2} + \frac{1}{\sigma_{B33}^2}\right)(\sigma_{11} - \sigma_{33})^2\right\} + \frac{1}{\tau_{B12}^2}\tau_{12}^2 + \frac{1}{\tau_{B23}^2}\tau_{23}^2 + \frac{1}{\tau_{B13}^2}\tau_{13}^2 = 1,$$

where σ_{ii} and τ_{ij} are axial and shear components of the Cauchy stress tensor; σ_{Bii} and τ_{Bij} are the ultimate strength along the respective directions [38].

To implement the simulation (Figure 7), the software product MSC Digimat MF (e-Xstream—HEXAGON, Luxembourg, Luxembourg) was used.

The results of modeling the properties of a composite made from a polycarbonate matrix containing glass fibers in the volume are presented in Table 3.

The simulation results show that a content increase in the glass fiber in PCM with a polycarbonate matrix leads to an increase in the ultimate strength, modulus of elasticity, and overall reliability.

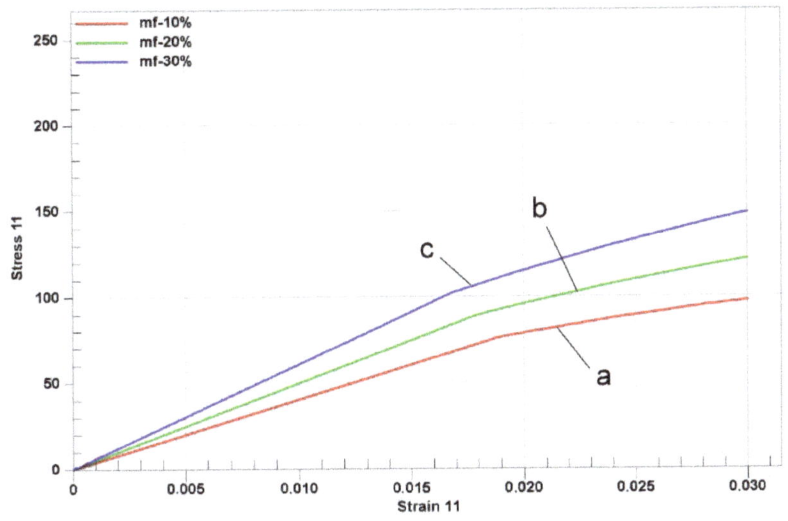

Figure 7. Stress–strain diagrams for a composite material based on a polycarbonate matrix containing: (a) 10% of inclusions (red line), (b) 20% of inclusions (green line), (c) 30% of inclusions (blue line).

Table 3. Computed properties of the studied composite (polycarbonate matrix with the content of glass fibers in the volume).

m_f-Mass Fraction, %	*E, MPA*	*G, MPA*	μ	ρ, g/cm^3	σ_m, MPa
10	3200	1156	0.35	1.26	90
20	4029	1498	0.33	1.33	120
30	5060	1895	0.32	1.415	150

The experimental work on modeling properties has shown that as a result of such calculations, it is possible to choose the optimal compositions of PCM, predict properties, evaluate and predict the reliability of materials in general in the future. In addition, the study carried out made it possible to gain experience in this area and develop a methodology for predicting the properties and reliability of the material.

The reliability prediction methodology includes the following steps:

- selection of a performance criterion based on the analysis of the product, its purpose, mode of operation, operating conditions, and type of expected failures;
- establishment of a set of mechanical and thermophysical characteristics of polymer composite materials based on the criterion of product performance;
- development of new methods and devices for determining mechanical and shrinkage characteristics, taking into account the characteristics of materials;
- development of probabilistic-statistical models for assessing the reliability of products made of polymer composite materials at the stages of design, production, and operation;
- study of the statistical variability of deformation-strength and shrinkage characteristics of the materials at the stages of the product life cycle;
- estimation of the relationships between the reliability and material characteristics included in the reliability model at the stages of design, production, and operation;
- possible reliability prediction, considering fully or partially the determining factors of the design, manufacture, and operation of the product.

This methodology can serve as a recommendation for modeling the properties of new materials.

3.2. Experimental Studies of Products Made of Polymer Composite Materials

The conducted numerical experiments have shown that, for the production of parts, a composite of a polycarbonate matrix and 30% of the mass fraction of glass fiber is optimal. The performed work on the calculation of mechanical properties makes it possible to reduce the number of full-scale tests.

The results obtained with the help of the performed calculations were verified using a full-scale experiment. The authors conducted a tensile test of the samples. We tested the PCM standard samples with a filler content (fiberglass) of 10%, 20%, and 30% (Table 4). The choice of filler content for the full-scale tests was determined by the simulation results. We took values close to the optimal value of 30%. A further increase in the filler content, according to calculations, led to a sharp drop in the properties and material embrittlement. This is also consistent with the literature data. The test results are presented in the form of histograms below (Figure 8).

Table 4. Comparison of numerical and field experiment results.

m_f-Mass Fraction, %	10		20		30	
Type of Experiment	**Field**	**Model**	**Field**	**Model**	**Field**	**Model**
E_t, MPa	5240	3200	5250	4029	6190	5060
σ_m, MPa	125	90	128	120	150	150

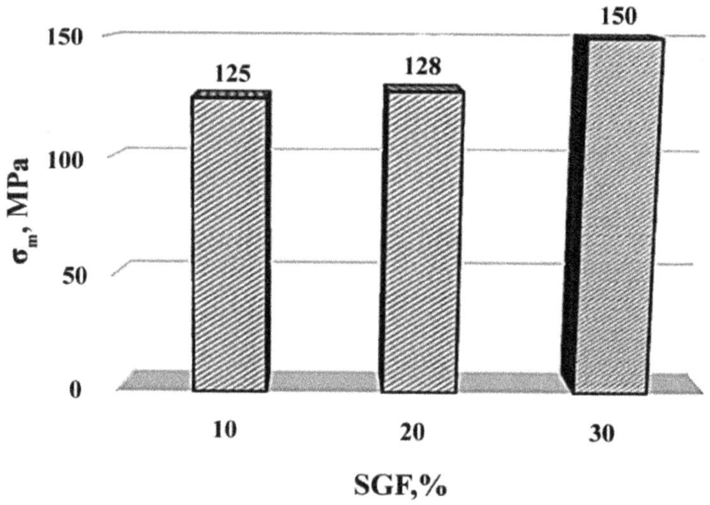

Figure 8. Change in the tensile strength (σm, MPa) of polycarbonate composites filled with different amounts of SGF (%).

The strength data for PCM with the addition of 20% and 30% of the filler practically do not differ from the calculated data. The difference between the data of the computational and full-scale experiments for the 10% filler content is explained by the influence of technological factors. These factors include a significant change in the cooling rate of the workpiece along with a decrease in the amount of filler to 10–12% or less. These technological factors must be taken into account to create a corrected model that allows for providing accurate results for all the filler concentrations. Since the topic of the study is useful for the introduction of PCMs, the authors of the paper will continue their work in this field of study.

4. Conclusions

1. Based on the probabilistic mathematical models, an increase in the cross-sectional area of the samples is shown to cause a decrease in the average value and a change in the standard deviation of the yield strength. At the same time, the failure-free operation probability of the studied thermoplastics decreases.
2. Functional dependences of the influence of technological modes of processing thermoplastics by injection molding on the probability of their trouble-free operation are established and presented.
3. Probabilistic modeling using the normal distribution law allows showing that with an increase in the thickness of the samples, the resistance of the material to aging and degradation increases, and the failure-free operation probability, as the main component of the material reliability, increases.
4. A mathematical algorithm has been developed for modeling the mechanical characteristics of the composite materials based on the Eshebli theory and the Mori–Tanaka theorem by Tandom and Weng, considering the Cauchy stress tensor. The mathematical method that allows obtaining analytical estimates of the effective properties of the materials that affect their reliability has been established on its basis. The results of modeling by the analytical deterministic method and the probabilistic stochastic method are similar to discrepancies of no more than 10% in the region of high filler concentrations in PCM. The discrepancy in low filler concentrations is explained by the insufficient consideration of technological factors.
5. An innovative attempt has been made to use a probabilistic mathematical apparatus not only for analyzing the mechanical properties of materials but also for a comparative assessment of the reliability parameters of these materials. With the development of the mathematical apparatus, including numerical methods for processing mathematical data, it is much more important to obtain native graphs of the functions of changing the source of materials depending on the factors of time, temperature, and other operational indicators, without linking these functions (sometimes with large errors) to the classical distribution laws of random quantities. This gives some flexibility to researchers and allows practical engineers to obtain more accurate results. They study the change in the reliability and degradation of the materials depending on changes in the operating factors in real conditions, as well as make a forecast of changes in the reliability in the future, extrapolating from the results. The authors will devote further study to mathematical and experimental models for predicting the degradation and reliability of composite materials and the creation of a universal mathematical methodology to forecast their sources.

Author Contributions: Conceptualization, B.V.M. and N.V.M.; methodology, M.E.I. and E.A.E.; software, M.E.I. and R.N.; validation, A.I. and B.V.M.; formal analysis, N.V.M.; investigation, E.A.E.; resources, M.E.I.; data curation, R.N.; writing—original draft preparation, B.V.M.; writing—review and editing, N.V.M.; visualization, A.I. All authors have read and agreed to the published version of the manuscript.

Funding: This work was supported by the Ministry of Education and Science of the Republic of Kazakhstan through project AP08857367 "Development of innovative technologies for improving energy efficiency and reliability of centrifugal pumps manufactured in Kazakhstan", for which the authors are very grateful.

Institutional Review Board Statement: Not applicable.

Informed Consent Statement: Not applicable.

Data Availability Statement: The data presented in this study are available from the corresponding authors upon reasonable request.

Conflicts of Interest: The authors declare no conflict of interest.

References

1. Berladir, K.; Zhyhylii, D.; Gaponova, O.; Krmela, J.; Krmelová, V.; Artyukhov, A. Modeling of Polymer Composite Materials Chaotically Reinforced with Spherical and Cylindrical Inclusions. *Polymers* **2022**, *14*, 2087. [CrossRef]
2. Tsivolas, E.; Gergidis, L.N.; Paipetis, A.S. Crack Growth and Delamination Analysis in GFRP Composite Materials. *Appl. Sci.* **2022**, *12*, 1945. [CrossRef]
3. Khodadadi, A.; Golestanian, H.; Aghadavoudi, F. Two modified multiscale modeling approaches for determination of two-phase and hybrid nanocomposite properties. *Proc. Inst. Mech. Eng. Part C J. Mech. Eng. Sci.* **2021**, *236*, 496–510. [CrossRef]
4. Haghighi, M.; Golestanian, H.; Aghadavoudi, F. Determination of mechanical properties of two-phase and hybrid nanocomposites: Experimental determination and multiscale modeling. *J. Polym. Eng.* **2021**, *41*, 356–364. [CrossRef]
5. Jiang, H.; Ren, Y.; Zhang, S.; Liu, Z.; Nie, L. Multi-scale finite element analysis for tension and ballistic penetration damage characterizations of 2D triaxially braided composite. *J. Mater. Sci.* **2018**, *53*, 10071–10094. [CrossRef]
6. Nobeen, N.S.; Zhong, Y.; Francis, B.A.; Ji, X.; Chia, E.S.; Joshi, S.C.; Chen, Z. Constituent materials micro-damage modeling in predicting progressive failure of braided fiber composites. *Compos. Struct.* **2016**, *145*, 194–202. [CrossRef]
7. Hameed, A.Z.; Aravind Raj, S.; Kandasamy, J.; Shahzad, M.A.; Baghdadi, M.A. 3D Printing Parameter Optimization Using Taguchi Approach to Examine Acrylonitrile Styrene Acrylate (ASA) Mechanical Properties. *Polymers* **2022**, *14*, 3256. [CrossRef]
8. Gonçalves, P.T.; Arteiro, A.; Rocha, N.; Pina, L. Numerical Analysis of Micro-Residual Stresses in a Carbon/Epoxy Polymer Matrix Composite during Curing Process. *Polymers* **2022**, *14*, 2653. [CrossRef]
9. Al Kassem, G.; Weichert, D. Micromechanical material models for polymer composites through advanced numerical simulation techniques. In *PAMM: Proceedings in Applied Mathematics and Mechanics*; Wiley Online Library: Hoboken, NJ, USA, 2009. [CrossRef]
10. Chavoshi, S.Z.; Tagarielli, V.L.; Shi, Z.; Lin, J.; Wang, S.; Jiang, J.; Dear, J.P.; Nikbin, K. Predictions of the Mechanical Response of Sintered FGH96 Powder Compacts. *J. Eng. Mater. Technol.* **2019**, *142*, 021003. [CrossRef]
11. Yakimov, S.B.; Ivanovsky, V.N.; Degovtsov, A.V.; Eliseev, D.B.; Aygishev, E.V. On the influence of the fraction composition of abrasive particles in produced fluid on the wear types of the elements of electric centrifugal pumps. *Oil Gas Territ.* **2017**, *11*, 32–38. Available online: https://www.neftegas.info/upload/iblock/4aa/4aa5a548746775ee8051eb0fec24a52b (accessed on 1 September 2022).
12. Fragassa, C. Lightening structures by metal replacement: From traditional gym equipment to an advanced fiber-reinforced composite exoskeleton facta universitatis. *Mech. Eng.* **2021**, *19*, 155–174. [CrossRef]
13. Ahmadifar, A.; Zamani, M.R.; Davar, A.; Jam, J.E.; Beni, M.H. Experimental and numerical buckling analysis of carbon fiber composite lattice conical structure before and after lateral impact. *Appl. Comput. Mech.* **2020**, *6*, 813–822. [CrossRef]
14. Mallick, V. Thermoplastic composite-based processing technologies for high performance turbomachinery components. *Compos. Part A Appl. Sci. Manuf.* **2001**, *32*, 1167–1173. [CrossRef]
15. Li, Q.; Piechna, J.; Mueller, N. Static, dynamic and failure behavior of a novel axial composite impeller for water chiller. *ASME Int. Mech. Eng. Congr. Expo.* **2010**, *44298*, 81–87.
16. Palle, R.R.; Schuster, J.; Shaik Yu, P.; Kazmi, M. Fabrication and characterization of glass fiber with sic reinforced polymer composites. *Open J. Compos. Mater.* **2022**, *12*, 16–29. [CrossRef]
17. Liu, Y.; Guo, Y.; Zhao, J.; Chen, X.; Zhang, H.; Hu, G.; Yu, X.; Zhang, Z. Carbon fiber reinforced shape memory epoxy composites with superior mechanical performances. *Compos. Sci. Technol.* **2019**, *177*, 49–56. [CrossRef]
18. Toshitake, S.; Hiroshi, C.; Tadao, K. Sorption of water by bisphenol-a polycarbonate and polyoxyethylene multiblock copolymers with varying composition and block length. *Polym. J.* **1984**, *16*, 129–138. [CrossRef]
19. Nazarov, S.A. Eshelby's theorem and the optimal pay problem. *Algebra Janaliz* **2009**, *21*, 155–195. [CrossRef]
20. Barralab, M.; Chatzigeorgioua, G.; Meraghnia, F.; Leon, R. Homogenization using modified Mori-Tanaka and TFA framework for elastoplastic-viscoelastic-viscoplastic composites: Theory and numerical validation. *Int. J. Plast.* **2020**, *127*, 102632. [CrossRef]
21. Singh, C.V.; Talreja, R. A multiscale approach to modeling of composite damage. In *Modeling Damage, Fatigue and Failure of Composite Materials*; Woodhead Publishing: Sawston, UK, 2016; pp. 329–345. [CrossRef]
22. Laurin, F.; Carrere, N.; Maire, J.-F. Strength prediction methods for composite structures: Ensuring aeronautical design office requirements. In *Numerical Modelling of Failure in Advanced Composite Materials*; Woodhead Publishing: Sawston, UK, 2015; pp. 507–532. [CrossRef]
23. Oskay, C. Multiscale modeling of the response and life prediction of composite materials. In *Numerical Modelling of Failure in Advanced Composite Materials*; Woodhead Publishing: Sawston, UK, 2015; pp. 351–375. [CrossRef]
24. Beaumont, P.; Soutis, C.; Hodzic, A. Structural integrity and durability of advanced composites: Innovative modelling methods and intelligent design. In *Structural Integrity and Durability of Advanced Composites: Innovative Modelling Methods and Intelligent Design*; Woodhead Publishing: Sawston, UK, 2015; pp. 1–872.
25. Roy, S. Multi-scale modeling of high-temperature polymer matrix composites for aerospace applications. In *Structural Integrity and Durability of Advanced Composites: Innovative Modelling Methods and Intelligent Design*; Woodhead Publishing: Sawston, UK, 2015; pp. 125–142. [CrossRef]
26. Curiel-Sosa, J.L.; Brighenti, R.; Serna Moreno, M.C.; Barbieri, E. Computational techniques for simulation of damage and failure in composite materials. In *Structural Integrity and Durability of Advanced Composites: Innovative Modelling Methods and Intelligent Design*; Woodhead Publishing: Sawston, UK, 2015; pp. 199–219. [CrossRef]

27. Chatzigeorgiou, G.; Meraghni, F.; Charalambakis, N. Multiscale Modeling Approaches for Composites. In *Multiscale Modeling Approaches for Composites*; Elsevier: Amsterdam, The Netherlands, 2021; pp. 1–345. [CrossRef]
28. Liu, P. Damage Modeling of Composite Structures: Strength, Fracture, and Finite Element Analysis. In *Damage Modeling of Composite Structures: Strength, Fracture, and Finite Element Analysis*; Elsevier: Amsterdam, The Netherlands, 2020; pp. 1–384. [CrossRef]
29. Carreras, L.; Guillamet, G.; Quintanas-Corominas, A.; Renart, J.; Turon, A. Mesoscale modelling of delamination using the cohesive zone model approach. In *Multi-Scale Continuum Mechanics Modelling of Fibre-Reinforced Polymer Composites*; Woodhead Publishing: Sawston, UK, 2020; pp. 555–577. [CrossRef]
30. Bouhfid, N.; Raji, M.; Boujmal, R.; Essabir, H.; Bensalah, M.-O.; Bouhfid, R.; Qaiss, A.K. Numerical modeling of hybrid composite materials. In *Modelling of Damage Processes in Biocomposites, Fibre-Reinforced Composites and Hybrid Composites*; Woodhead Publishing: Sawston, UK, 2018; pp. 57–101. [CrossRef]
31. Chokshi, S.; Gohil, P. Experimental Investigation and Mathematical Modeling of Longitudinally Placed Natural Fiber Reinforced Polymeric Composites including Interphase Volume Fraction. *Fibers Polym.* **2022**, *23*, 488–501. [CrossRef]
32. Feoktistov, E.F.; Germashev, I.V.; Derbisher, V.E.; Derbisher, E.V.; Evdokimov, R.A. Selective system analysis tools for identifying the properties of active ingredients in polymer compositions. *ChemChemTech* **2022**, *65*, 6–18. [CrossRef]
33. Kayiran, H.F. Numerical analysis of composite disks based on carbon/aramid-epoxy materials. *Emerg. Mater. Res.* **2021**, *11*, 155–159. [CrossRef]
34. Lubecki, M.; Stosiak, M.; Bocian, M.; Urbanowicz, K. Analysis of selected dynamic properties of the composite hydraulic microhose. *Eng. Fail. Anal.* **2021**, *125*, 105431. [CrossRef]
35. Tassi, N.; Bakkali, A.; Fakri, N.; Azrar, L. Regularized Micromechanical Modeling for the Prediction of Electro-Elastic Behavior of Reinforced Piezoelectric Composites. In Proceedings of the 2021 IEEE International Conference on Recent Advances in Mathematics and Informatics, ICRAMI, Tebessa, Algeria, 21–22 September 2021. [CrossRef]
36. Chantieva, M.; Dzhabrailov, K.; Gematudinov, R.; Suvorov, D. Modern method of computer simulation of structures and physical properties of composite materials. In *Advances in Intelligent Systems and Computing, 1259 AISC*; Springer: Cham, Switzerland, 2005; pp. 553–561. [CrossRef]
37. McCarthy, C.T.; McCarthy, M.A.; Gilchrist, M.D. Predicting Failure in Multi-Bolt Composite Joints Using Finite Element Analysis and Bearing-Bypass Diagrams. *Key Eng. Mater.* **2005**, *293*, 591–598. [CrossRef]
38. Osman, M.A.; Atallah, A. Effect of the particle size on the viscoelastic properties of filled polyethylene. *Polymer* **2006**, *47*, 2357–2368. [CrossRef]

Σ mathematics

MDPI

Article

Numerical Method for System Level Simulation of Long-Distance Pneumatic Conveying Pipelines

Xiaoming Zhou *, Fang Fang and Yadong Li

School of Mechanical and Electrical Engineering, University of Electronic Science and Technology of China, Chengdu 611731, China
* Correspondence: zhouxm@uestc.edu.cn

Abstract: Pneumatic conveying pipelines (PCPs) provide an effective manner for long-distance transport of capsules because of their advantages in high speed, superior safety, and full automation. For better development of PCPs, a system-level simulation tool is desired, but not yet available. In this work, a new 1D model describing systemic dynamics of airflow and capsule movement in PCPs is presented, and 3D simulation is proposed to obtain the characteristic coefficients in the 1D model. The complete model accounts for those phenomena that most profoundly affect the performance of PCPs, such as the 3D layout of the pipeline, the geometry of capsules, as well as the compressibility of air in a long pipeline. A finite volume method is also presented to numerically calculate the model equations, and thereby realize the successful system-level simulation of practical PCPs for the first time. Experimental data were used for validation. For a 550 m-long and small-diameter (27.86 mm) PCP, the errors of predicted conveying times were within 4.43%. For another 30 m-long and large-diameter (125.6 mm) PCP, the errors of predicted conveying time and maximum capsule velocity were within 1%. By enabling readily and accurate prediction of the conveying process, the method provides a feasible tool for the design and application of PCP systems.

Keywords: pneumatic capsule conveying; dynamics model; numerical method; system-level simulation

MSC: 76-10

Citation: Zhou, X.; Fang, F.; Li, Y. Numerical Method for System Level Simulation of Long-Distance Pneumatic Conveying Pipelines. *Mathematics* **2022**, *10*, 4073. https://doi.org/10.3390/math10214073

Academic Editors: Shujin Laima, Yong Cao, Xiaowei Jin and Hehe Ren

Received: 13 September 2022
Accepted: 31 October 2022
Published: 1 November 2022

Publisher's Note: MDPI stays neutral with regard to jurisdictional claims in published maps and institutional affiliations.

Copyright: © 2022 by the authors. Licensee MDPI, Basel, Switzerland. This article is an open access article distributed under the terms and conditions of the Creative Commons Attribution (CC BY) license (https://creativecommons.org/licenses/by/4.0/).

1. Introduction

Transportation of capsules through pipelines has been extensively used in various industries. These capsules are typically hollow containers filled with minerals [1], radioactive materials [2], waste [3,4], or other goods [5–8]. As air is readily available, pneumatic capsule pipelines (PCPs) has drawn substantial attention and have been successfully used in mineral industries, tunnel construction, waste disposal facility and hospitals [2–7,9–17]. Recently, efforts have been paid to develop a high-speed transport system with pneumatic pipelines [10]. Superior characteristics of PCPs have been exhibited, such as high speed, ecological safety, simple structure, handy operation, and the possibility to fully automate the movement [5–10]. Especially for hazardous chemicals or radioactive waste, PCPs provide an effective way to non-contact transportation that avoids most of the potential risks [2].

The performance of a PCP system depends on a series of parameters, such as the size and architecture of the pipeline, the geometry of capsules, the operation pressure, and so on [18,19]. Numerical simulation provides an important and powerful tool for the research and development of PCPs [19,20]. By predicting the performance of a new PCP system at the early stage, optimal design can be more easily achieved, and the development cost can also be significantly reduced.

Currently, there has been a lot of research work focused on developing a numerical method for the pneumatic conveying of granular materials [21–27]. One of the commonly used approaches is the Eulerian/Lagrangian method, where particles are tracked in a Lagrangian frame of reference either individually or as groups with identical properties [28,29].

An alternative approach has been computational fluid dynamics (CFD), with two-fluid continuum models to represent the gas and solid phases as two interpenetrating continua [23,30]. Further, the technique of particle dynamics simulation has also been widely used for investigations of granular and gas-solid systems. In particular, the discrete element method (DEM), has been successfully applied [31]. Several research workers have also applied the approach of combining DEM with CFD [21,25,26].

Despite success in simulating pneumatic conveying of granular materials, the aforementioned methods are not applicable to PCPs, where the solid size is comparable to the feature size of flow and thus their geometry of capsules has a significant impact on the conveying process. Detailed prediction of capsule motion requires the accurate computation of the fluid-structure interaction (FSI), which means fluid forces acting on solid as well as the impact of solid motion on fluid flow need to be calculated simultaneously [32–34]. In a similar situation, i.e., investigation on hydraulic capsule pipelines (HCPs) often involves CFD simulation where both solid and fluid regions are modeled in detail and dynamic mesh/moving mesh techniques are involved to predict the 6 degrees of freedom motion of capsules [35–39]. Such techniques help people to obtain insight into the local processes in PCPs/HCPs, but face big problems when they are used for system-level simulation. The dynamic meshing algorithm will face a serious challenge to maintain mesh validity and quality in case of large-scale motion of capsules, particularly for the pipelines in PCPs that are often as long as several hundred or even thousands of meters [5,9,10]. Moreover, pitching motion may occur and then there will be intensive interaction the between capsule and pipe wall. It is going to be extremely difficult, if not impossible, to directly simulate the overall process with 3D CFD techniques.

A lot of efforts have been made to establish simplified methods to predict the overall performance of PCPs. In the 1980s, Akira and Katsuya derived 1D formulas to describe the pressure loss characteristics of concentric and eccentric capsule pipelines [13–15]. Morikawa et al. established an analytical model based on a series of fundamental experiments, and the characteristics of capsule motion during accelerating and decelerating were analyzed. Tomita simulated capsule movement in a section of a pneumatic pipeline based on a 1D model and the pattern of capsule collision was discussed [20]. Latterly, Kosugi et al. utilized a similar 1D model to evaluate the capsule acceleration and energy consumption characteristics of PCPs [1,2,9,12]. York and Liu derived a theoretical model to predict the drag coefficients of pneumatic capsules [11]. These models played very important roles in the development of industrial PCPs. However, the incompressible flow assumption implied in the models is likely to deviate from the fact significantly for long-distance pipelines. Moreover, the models were all established based on oversimplified pipeline architecture (a single horizontal/vertical tube), although practical PCPs are often composed of multiple horizontal, vertical, and bend segments in which forces applied on capsules may vary a lot. In addition, the pressure difference on both ends of the capsule was considered the only aerodynamic force in the models, which means the viscosity force was neglected [7]. Such an assumption may be correct in case the capsules have regular shapes and are constructed with end plates [8]. Nevertheless, for capsules that have complicated aerodynamic configurations [16], the viscosity force may play an important role in capsule conveying. As a result, the currently available methods are still insufficient to perform accurate system level simulation for practical PCPs. A more effective simulation tool is still desired to support people in determining the optimal design parameters and operation conditions.

In this work, a novel method is presented to evaluate the system-level performance of PCPs with practical pipeline layout, capsule geometry and operating conditions. The method utilizes synergistic simulation based on a new 1D model describing the systemic behavior in cooperation with conventional 3D CFD models reflecting local characteristics. The models are established as simply as possible but still account for those phenomena that most profoundly affect the performance of PCPs. The method has been validated with practical PCPs, and favorable accuracy has been demonstrated. By readily and accurately predicting the overall performance of a PCP, the method provides an effective tool for the early-stage design of pneumatic conveying systems.

2. Mathematical Model

2.1. Air Flow

As mentioned above, the airflow in a PCP tends to be highly unsteady and chaotic, and moreover, the axial dimension is often extremely large relative to the sectional dimensions. Precise modeling and simulation of the three-dimensional flow field in the whole pipeline is practically impossible and unnecessary. Instead, the dynamic distribution of air pressure and flow rate along the pipeline axis i often of greater interest [40]. Therefore, a one-dimensional flow model is established to describe the system-level behaviors in PCPs in this work.

For a one-dimensional transient flow, the continuum equation is given by [41]

$$\frac{\partial \rho}{\partial t} + \frac{1}{A}\frac{\partial Q}{\partial x} = 0 \tag{1}$$

where ρ is the air density, t is time, A is the pipeline cross-sectional area, Q is the mass flow rate of air, and x is the location along the pipeline, respectively.

According to the ideal gas law, along with the hypothesis of the isothermal process, the equation can be modified as

$$\frac{1}{RT}\frac{\partial p}{\partial t} + \frac{1}{A}\frac{\partial Q}{\partial x} = 0 \tag{2}$$

where p denotes the absolute pressure, R is the gas constant (287.053 $m^2/s^2/K$ for dry air) and T is the absolute temperature of air.

Based on Equation (2), together with a momentum equation, p and Q in a PCP could be determined. For the ease of calculation, an explicit form of momentum equation, like the Hagen-Poiseuille equation, would be preferred. However, there is no such equation available corresponding to the turbulent and compressible flow in PCPs. In this study, a simplified manner is proposed. A series of 3D CFD simulations with regard to typical kinds of pipeline segments (straight/bend and with/without capsules) is proposed to be performed in advance, and then model order reduction based on data fitting can be performed to obtain the desired explicit form equation. It has been found that second-order polynomials shown below can be used with favorable goodness of fit.

$$\frac{\partial p}{\partial x} = k_1 Q^2 + k_2 Q \tag{3}$$

where k_1 and k_2 are the fitting coefficients to be determined according to 3D simulation. A previous study also demonstrated such a simple formula is precious enough to describe the flow characteristic of pneumatic pipe with capsules [8]. Based on Equation (3), the axial gradient of flowrate in Equation (2) can be derived as

$$\frac{\partial Q}{\partial x} = \frac{1}{2k_1 Q + k_2}\frac{\partial}{\partial x}(\frac{\partial p}{\partial x}) \tag{4}$$

Substituting Equation (4) into Equation (2), a governing equation describing the dynamic pressure of airflow in PCPs is obtained.

$$\frac{\partial p}{\partial t} + \Gamma\frac{\partial}{\partial x}(\frac{\partial p}{\partial x}) = 0 \tag{5}$$

Similar governing equations in parabolic form have already been used in modeling long-distance gas pipelines where air compressibility needs to be taken into account [41,42]. In the current study, the coefficient Γ is given by

$$\Gamma = \frac{RT}{A(2k_1Q + k_2)} \tag{6}$$

2.2. Capsule Movement

A capsule may be subjected to various forces in PCPs, as shown in Figure 1. Among those forces, the pressure difference on both ends of the capsule usually acts as a main driving force, which can be determined according to the calculated air pressure profile [11,18]

$$F_p = Ac \cdot \Delta p \tag{7}$$

where F_p is the net pressure force acting on a capsule, A_c is the area of capsule end and Δp is the pressure difference.

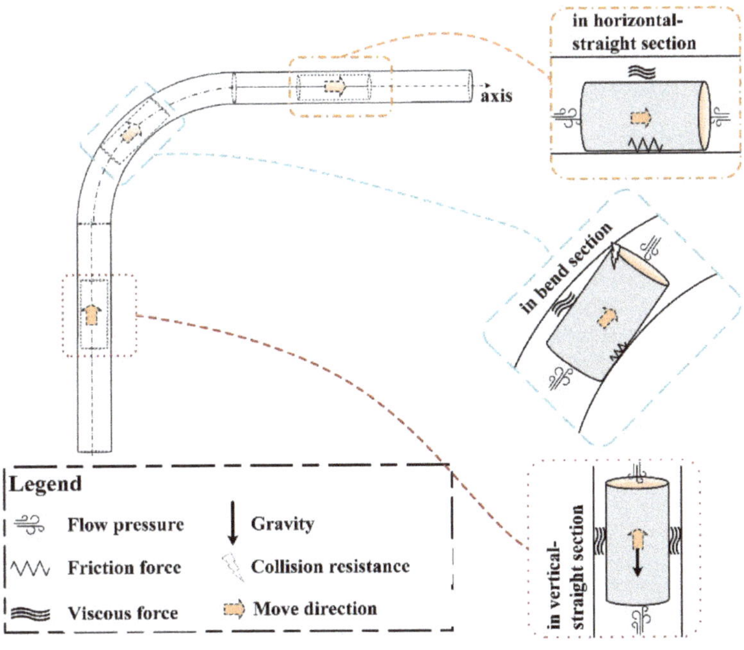

Figure 1. Schematic diagram of force analysis for capsules moving in PCP.

Whatever the configuration and location of the capsule are, there is always a certain gap between the capsule and the pipe wall. When air flows through the gap, a viscous force, F_v, will be produced on the surface of the capsule and provide additional driving or drag force for the capsule. Such force highly depends on the shape of the capsule as well as the relative movement between the capsule and air flow. To account for such an effect in a simple manner, curve-fitting based on three-dimensional CFD simulation is also used. Correspondingly, another second-order polynomial will be obtained, that is,

$$F_v = k_3 Q_l^2 + k_4 Q_l \tag{8}$$

where Q_l is the flow rate of air that flows across the capsule surface (i.e., leakage flow rate), and k_3 and k_4 are the fitting coefficients, respectively.

During the movement of the capsule, the friction force, F_f, between the capsule and the pipe wall acts as a resistance force. It can be evaluated as follows [18]:

$$F_f = -fG \tag{9}$$

where f is the sliding friction coefficient, and G is the capsule weight.

In addition, there may be frequent collisions between the capsule and pipe wall, especially in the bend sections. Such collision consumes the kinetic energy of the capsule and acts as another source of resistance. In this study, such effect is characterized by a collision force, F_c, which is given by

$$F_c = -k_5 v^2 m \tag{10}$$

where k_5 is the kinetic energy loss coefficient, m is the mass of the capsule, and v is the translational velocity of the capsule along the x direction.

Finally, the total force applied to the capsule can be calculated, and the translational motion of the capsule along the direction of the pipe axis (x direction) can be determined by Newton's second law [18,19,35], that is,

$$m\frac{dv}{dt} = F \tag{11}$$

where F is the total force acting on the capsule in the same direction.

3. Numerical Method

To solve the governing equations of airflow, a finite volume method is utilized herein. As shown in Figure 2, the 1D flow domain is discretized with the cell-centered method. A staggered grid technique is applied, that is, the flowrate components are calculated for the points that lie on the faces of control volumes (CVs) [43].

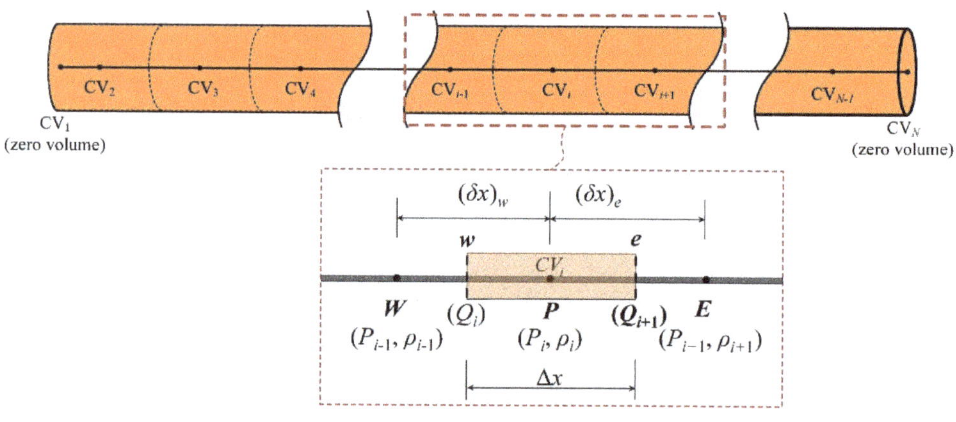

Figure 2. Illustration of the discrete control volumes.

Then, Equation (5) is integrated over the space interval of each CV, resulting

$$\frac{\partial p}{\partial t}\Delta x + \left[\Gamma_e\left(\frac{\partial p}{\partial x}\right)_e - \Gamma_w\left(\frac{\partial p}{\partial x}\right)_w\right] = 0 \tag{12}$$

where Δx is the width of a CV, and the subscripts w and e denote the faces of a CV.

In Equation (12), the pressure gradient terms could be transferred into the nodal form by using the central difference formula, thus

$$\frac{\partial p}{\partial t}\Delta x + \left[\frac{\Gamma_e}{\delta x_e} p_E + \frac{\Gamma_w}{\delta x_w} p_W - \left(\frac{\Gamma_e}{\delta x_e} + \frac{\Gamma_w}{\delta x_e}\right) p_P\right] = 0 \tag{13}$$

where the subscripts P denote the central point of the CV under consideration, and W and E denote the neighbor nodes of P.

Further, to deal with the transient term, the equation is integrated again over the time interval Δt (from t^0 to t). When the implicit formula is used, the nodal form of the equation will be derived as follows

$$(p_P^t - p_P^0)\frac{\Delta x}{\Delta t} + \left[\frac{\Gamma_e}{\delta x_e} p_E^t + \frac{\Gamma_w}{\delta x_w} p_W^t - \left(\frac{\Gamma_e}{\delta x_e} + \frac{\Gamma_w}{\delta x_w}\right) p_P^t\right] = 0 \tag{14}$$

where the superscript t denotes the current time level and the superscript 0 denotes the old values (at the previous time level t^0) of variables.

The equations can be written in a compact form, that is

$$(a_P^0 + a_W + a_E)p_i^t = a_W p_W^t + a_E p_E^t + a_P^0 p_P^0 \tag{15}$$

where the nodal coefficients can be calculated as follows

$$a_w = -\frac{\Gamma_w}{\delta x_w},\ a_e = -\frac{\Gamma_e}{\delta x_e} \text{ and } a_P^0 = \frac{\Delta x}{\Delta t} \tag{16}$$

At each time step, the air flow rates obtained in the previous time step will be used to generate the nodal coefficients. Then the whole-field air pressure is calculated by solving the nodal equations together. Consequently, air flowrate at the current time step can be determined according to Equation (3). As soon as air pressure and flowrate are determined, the forces applied on the capsule can be calculated and the translational motion of the capsule during the time interval can be predicted consequently. During the calculation, several auxiliary variables are defined and updated at each time level to account for the effect of time-varying location of the capsule as well as the 3D layout of the pipeline.

A location index of the capsule, i_c, is defined to map the transient capsule location to the discrete flow domain. At each time level of simulation, the value of the index is updated as follows

For i = 1 to N: if $x_c{}^t \geq x_w(i)$ and $x_c{}^t \leq x_e(i)$, then $i_c{}^t = i$

where $x_w(i)$ and $x_e(i)$ are the x coordinates of the edges of the ith CV, and x_c is the transient capsule location, respectively.

Once $i_c{}^t$ is determined, $F_p{}^t$ can be calculated as

$$F_p^t = A_c\left[p^t\left(i_c^t + 1\right) - p^t\left(i_c^t - 1\right)\right]/2 \tag{17}$$

The leakage flow rate can also be determined according to I^t as follows, and then the viscous force can be calculated correspondingly

$$Q_l^t = Q^t\left(i_c^t\right) - v_c^0 A_c \rho\left(i_c^t\right) \tag{18}$$

To account for the different forces applied on the capsule in various types of pipe segments, two Boolean arrays, **B** and **V**, are defined in the numerical program.

B(i) = 0, denotes the ith CV locates in a straight segment of pipe.

B(i) = 1, denotes the ith CV locates in a bent segment of pipe.

V(i) = 0, denotes the ith CV locates in a horizontal segment of pipe.

V(i) = 1, denotes the ith CV locates in a vertical segment of pipe.

According, the total force applied to the capsule can be determined as

$$F^t = F_p^t + F_v^t + F_f^t + \mathbf{B}(i_c^t) \cdot F_c^t + \mathbf{V}(i_c^t) \cdot G \tag{19}$$

4. Application and Validation

4.1. Case 1

4.1.1. System Configuration

A testing PCP system was newly built in Jiangsu Shengtong Valve Co. Ltd., as shown in Figure 3. The system transports capsules between two capsule launching and receiving units (LRUs, as shown in Figure 3a) with vacuum pipelines. To transport a capsule from LRU-1 to LRU-2, the valve in the air extractor unit 2 (AEU-2) is switched on while all the other valves are switched off. The vacuum pump in AEU-2 is also turned on to extract the air out of the pipeline. Once a desired degree of vacuum has been produced, the valve in air inlet unit 1 (AIU-1) is switched on and the filtrated air rushes into the pipeline and drives the capsule to move forward to LRU-2. A series of velocity sensors were installed on the pipeline. When a capsule passes through a sensor, the transient speed of the capsule will be measured and recorded. Pressure sensors were also installed on the tanks to monitor the dynamic pressure variation during the process.

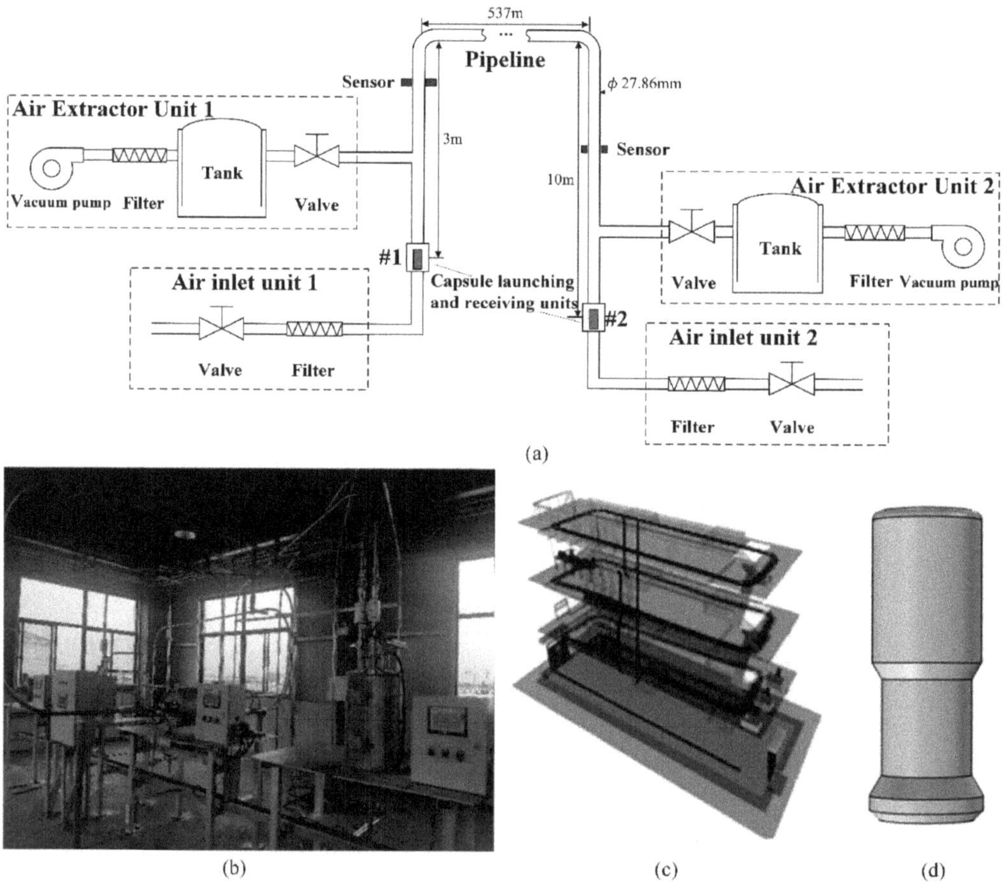

Figure 3. The testing PCP system (**a**) Schematic of the PCP system (**b**) Real view of the PCP system (**c**) 3D architecture of the pipeline (**d**) Configuration of the capsule.

The 3D architecture of the PCP is shown in Figure 3b,c. The pipeline coils up on the three floors of a building and finally returns to the first floor. So, it composes of a series of straight/bent and vertical/horizontal segments. The total length of the pipeline is about 550 m, the inner diameter is $D = 27.86$ mm, and the turning radius of the bend segments is about 500 mm. The tested capsule (shown in Figure 3d), made of polyethylene, has an outer diameter of $d = 22$. The empty weight of the capsule is 20 g. In case a certain organic phase solution is loaded, the total weight can be up to 30 g.

4.1.2. Determination of the Coefficients

Different sections of pipelines with a unit length were modeled in 3D and then static CFD simulations were performed under various air flowrates conditions, as shown in Figure 4. The simulation was conducted on ANSYS Fluent 18.1 (Ansys Inc., Canonsburg, PA, USA) with the shear stress transport (SST) $k-\omega$ viscous model. At the inlets, the mass-flow-inlet boundary condition was used, while the pressure–outlet boundary condition was used at the outlets. Notably, the inlet flowrate is corresponding to the leakage flow rate (Q_l) rather than the total flow rate (Q) in case there is a capsule in the pipe section unit. Discretization of the governing equations was based on the QUICK or second-order upwind schemes. The velocity–pressure coupling was based on the SIMPLE algorithm, and the considered convergence criterion was 10^{-3}.

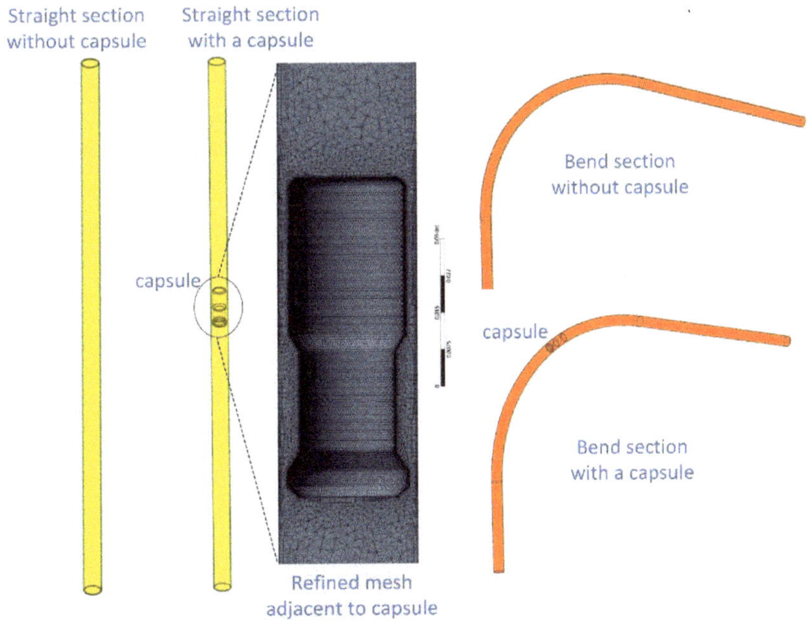

Figure 4. Illustration of the models in 3D CFD simulation.

Unstructured tetrahedral meshing was used to spatial discretize the flow domain. Refined mesh (mesh size s_1) was adopted in the vicinity of the capsule surfaces and coarser mesh (mesh size s_2) elsewhere. Gird independence tests were performed in advance by using gradually refined meshes with the same topology. Test case parameters were the inlet flow rate $Q = 0.05$ kg/s. The finally determined values are $s_1 = 0.6$ mm and $s_2 = 2.0$ mm, as shown in Table 1. The boundary layer mesh consisted of 10 layers with a 1.15 growth rate. The first layer thickness was adjusted depending on the boundary conditions to achieve a dimensionless wall distance y+ value below 5.

Table 1. Grid independence test for the model of a capsule moving in a straight pipeline.

Mesh Size (mm)		No. of Elements	Pressure Drop (Pa)	Viscous FORCE (N)
s_1	s_2			
2.9	0.9	166,097	1480.08	10.14
2.0	0.6	572,800	1823.02	12.50
1.5	0.3	1,539,626	1874.23	12.93

Once convergence was achieved, pressure drops in the pipe section units as well as viscous forces acting on the capsule surface corresponding to different inlet flowrates were extracted from the simulated results, and then the data were curve-fitted with quadratic polynomials. The simulated and curved fitted results regarding pressure drop are shown in Figure 5. The goodness of fit ($R^2 > 0.9997$) indicates the simple quadratic polynomials fit the simulated results very well. The obtained values of k_1 and k_2 are listed in Table 2.

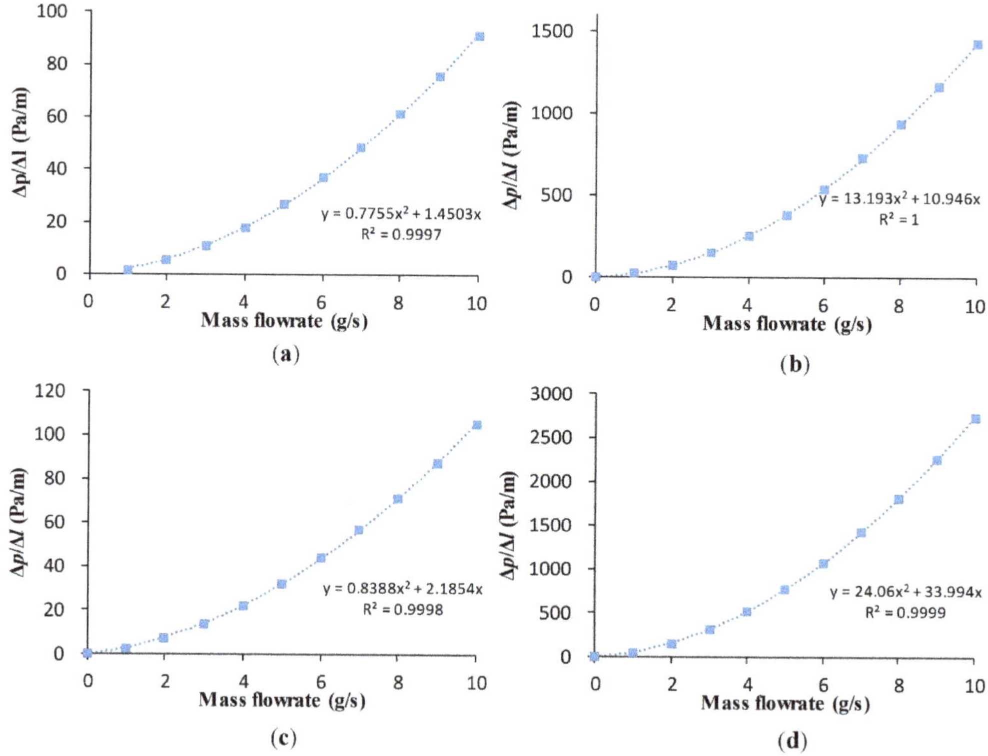

Figure 5. Simulated pressure drop characteristics of various pipe-section units: (**a**) straight-without capsule; (**b**) straight-with a capsule; (**c**) bend-without capsule; (**d**) bend-with a capsule.

Table 2. Obtained values of k_1 and k_2 by 3D simulation and curve fitting.

Pipe Sections Types		k_1 ($\times 10^6$ kg^{-1} m^{-2})	k_2 ($\times 10^3$ m^{-2} s^{-1})
Straight	with a capsule	−13.19	−10.95
	without capsule	−0.78	−1.45
Bend	with a capsule	−24.06	−33.99
	without capsule	−0.84	−2.19

Data with regard to viscous forces were treated in a similar manner. The obtained values of k_3 and k_4 were 4.9×10^3 (m/kg) and 5.1 (m/s), respectively. Due to the air-bearing effect as well as the light weight of the capsule, the friction force was found to be negligible, i.e., $f = 0$. The collision coefficients, k_5, were evaluated by experiments, in which the PCP was operated under a typical condition (initial pressure was 45 kPa) and the overall conveying time (OCT) was measured. The value of k_5 was adjusted from 0 to 1 until the best match of experimental and numerical OCT values was obtained. The finally determined value of k_5 is 0.35 (m^{-1}), which was used all through the following simulation.

4.1.3. Numerical Setting

Corresponding to 3D simulation, control volumes with a unit length were used to discrete the pipeline system in 1D simulation, i.e., the size of each control volume is $\Delta x = 1$ m. In order to obtain a compromise between computational effort and solution accuracy, a variable step size algorithm was applied, i.e.,

$$\Delta t = \lambda \frac{\Delta x}{v} \tag{20}$$

Different values of the coefficients λ had been tested and it was found independent results can be obtained when λ was below 0.005.

The boundary conditions were set corresponding to the actual operating conditions,

$$\begin{array}{lll} t = 0 & p = p_0 & \\ t > 0 & \begin{array}{l} x = 0 \\ x = L \end{array} & \begin{array}{l} p = p_a \\ p = p^t_{\text{tank}} \end{array} \end{array} \tag{21}$$

where p_0 is the initial pressure in the pipeline system, and p_{tank} is the pressure of the tank shown in Figure 3a. According to the configuration of the system, the value of p_{tank} at an arbitrary time can be determined as

$$p^t_{\text{tank}} = \rho^t_{\text{tank}} RT = p_0 + RT \int_0^t Q^t_L dt / V_{\text{tank}} \tag{22}$$

where ${Q_L}^t$ is the transient outlet flow rate of the pipeline and V_{tank} is the volume of the tank.

4.2. Case 2

Data reported by Morikawa et al. [18] were also used for further model validation. The experimental setup consisted of a wheeled capsule which moved in a large-diameter pipeline ($D = 125.6$ mm, $L = 30$ m). Details of the system can be found in the literature [18,19].

Similar to other PCPs for heavy loads, the tested capsule had assembled with various sizes of plates on both ends (so-called end plates) to obtain larger drag force. In this case, viscous forces were found to be neglectable [8,11]. Furthermore, the pipeline is straight and horizontal, thus pressure force and friction force were the only forces contributing to capsule conveying. Pressure drop characteristics in the pipeline and pressure force acted on the capsule were estimated with the same method as illustrated in case 1. In the currently considered situation, the diameter ratio of end plates is 0.93, and the corresponding k_1 and k_2 values were determined as -3.61×10^5 kg^{-1} m^{-2} and -3.04×10^2 m^{-2} s^{-1} for pipe section unit with a capsule, while they were -95 kg^{-1} m^{-2} and -11 m^{-2} s^{-1} for pipe section unit without capsule, respectively. The friction of wheels acting on the capsules had already been determined by experiments, and it can be given as [18]

$$F_f = 0.235m + 1.26 \tag{23}$$

where the capsule weight $m = 2.78$ kg.

The numerical setting for the 1D simulation was all the same as that in case 1, except that a smaller size of CV, $\Delta x = 0.05$ m, was used. Boundary condition was set in accordance with the experimental procedure, i.e.,

$$\begin{array}{ll} t = 0 & p = p_0 \\ t > 0 & \begin{cases} x = 0 & p = \Phi(Q) \\ x = L & p = p_a \end{cases} \end{array} \tag{24}$$

where Φ is a given function describing the characteristic diagram of the blowers used at the inlet [19].

5. Results and Discussion

A series of experiments had been carried out using the testing PCP system shown in Figure 3 under various operation conditions. Each experiment was repeated for at least three times to obtain statistical results. Numerical simulations were performed correspondingly. A typical situation is illustrated herein, for instance, that is, the capsule is empty (m = 20 g), and the initial pressure of the system is p^0 = 35 kPa (absolute pressure).

Capsule velocity results are presented in Figure 6. According to numerical simulation, the capsule is accelerated rapidly at the initial stage, and the transient speed increases by 40 m/s within a short distance (less than 3 m). Then the capsule is generally slowed down to a velocity of around 15 m/s. During the whole process, there are a series of velocity losses when the capsule is passing through the bend or vertical sections of the pipe, and also a series of subsequent procedures of velocity recovery in the following straight and horizontal sections. The simulated velocity profile was compared with the experimentally measured results to validate the model as well as the numerical method. As shown in Figure 6, the simulated and experimental results agree very well. The simulated OCT (35.12 s) is also very close to the experimental result (35.26 $\pm$ 0.92 s)

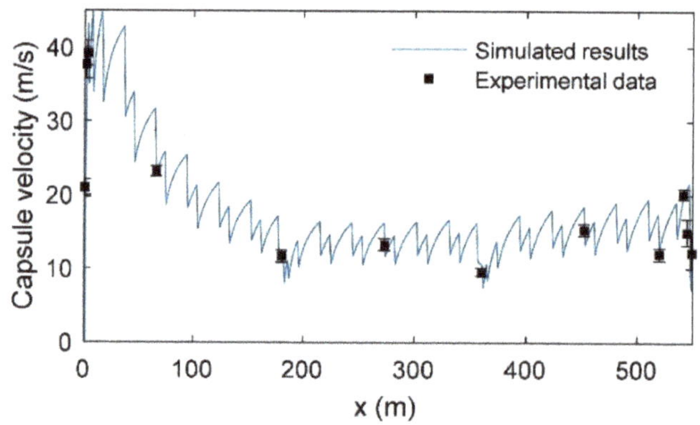

Figure 6. Simulated and experimentally measured velocity profiles of the capsule.

Further analysis with simulation demonstrates viscous force, rather than the pressure force, provides the main driven force at the initial stage due to the significant velocity difference between the airflow and the capsule, as shown in Figure 7. Such a result indicates that the aerodynamic configuration should be one of the main design considerations in developing a PCP system for the purpose of obtaining efficient capsule transportation. Along with the acceleration of the capsule, the viscous force decreases rapidly. As soon as the capsule moves faster than the airflow, viscous force becomes resistant.

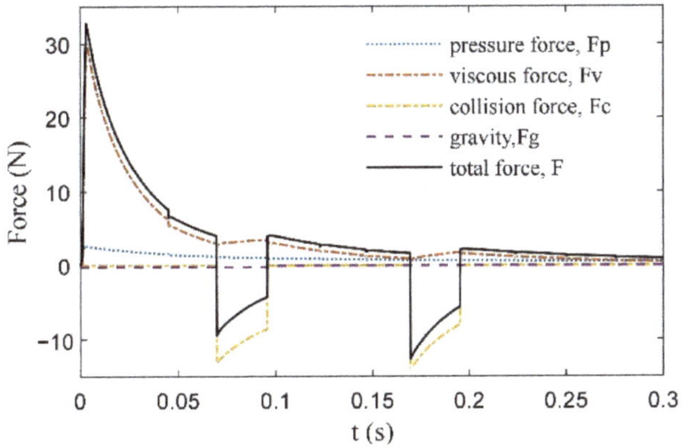

Figure 7. Calculated forces acted on the capsule at the initial stage.

The dynamic pressure distribution in the system was also predicted by simulation and presented in Figure 8. As soon as the process is initiated, the inlet pressure step into the atmosphere. Consequently, the pressure near the inlet increases rapidly while in the rest sections the pressure maintains at the initial level. As air flows forwards to the outlet, the overall pressure distribution evolves from a sharp profile at first to a linear profile generally, as shown in Figure 8a. The simulated dynamic pressure at the outlet (tank pressure) is compared with the experimentally measured results, which demonstrates high agreement again as shown in Figure 8b.

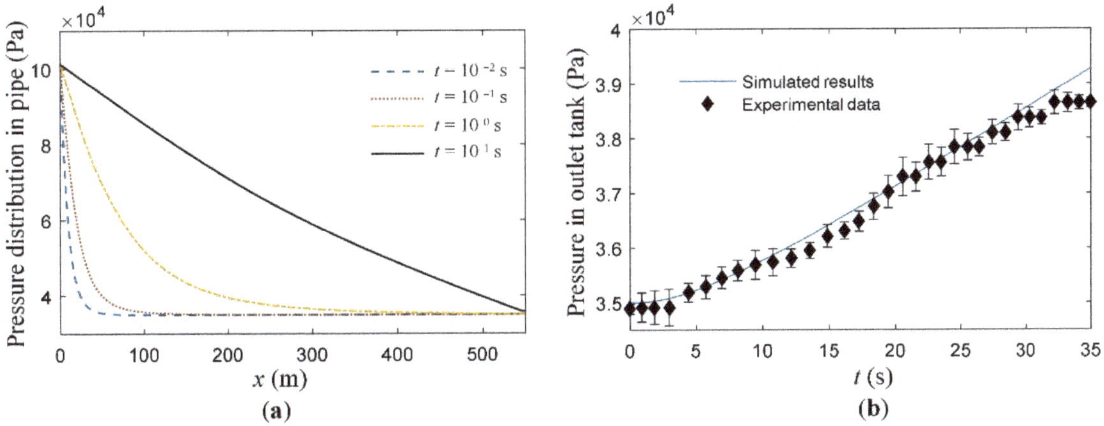

Figure 8. Dynamic of pressure in the pipeline (**a**) and in outlet tank (**b**).

As one of the superiorities over those currently available models, the presented model has taken the compressibility of air into account, which would be significant in case the pipeline is very long [41]. However, the characteristic coefficients, k_1~k_5, were obtained by 3D CFD simulation with an incompressible flow model, which means the coefficients were assumed to be constants although they may vary to some extent under different pressure conditions. In addition, some factors, e.g., capsule weight, have a certain impact on the posture of the capsule in the pipeline. Consequently, the flow profile and conveying process may be impacted. However, an ideal capsule posture was assumed in the 3D simulation. These simplifications may be the most important limitations of the presented method. To evaluate the impact of such simplifications on the accuracy of model prediction, a series of contrast simulations were performed with different pressure levels (from normal pressure to −50 kPa) and capsule postures (concentric and eccentric positions). It was demonstrated the variation of resulted model coefficients was within 10%. Furthermore, experiments had also been conducted under different operation conditions. Simulation with constant coefficient values (given in Section 4.1.2) was performed accordingly and the OCT values were used for comparison. As shown in Figure 9, the simulated values agree with the experimental results very well. The maximum error was only 4.43% among all the considered conditions, demonstrating that errors induced by the simplifications are acceptable in practice. By accurately predicting systemic behavior of PCPs in a relatively simple manner, the presented method can be used to evaluate the effect of every design parameter on system performance in detail, and then the optimal design may be achieved.

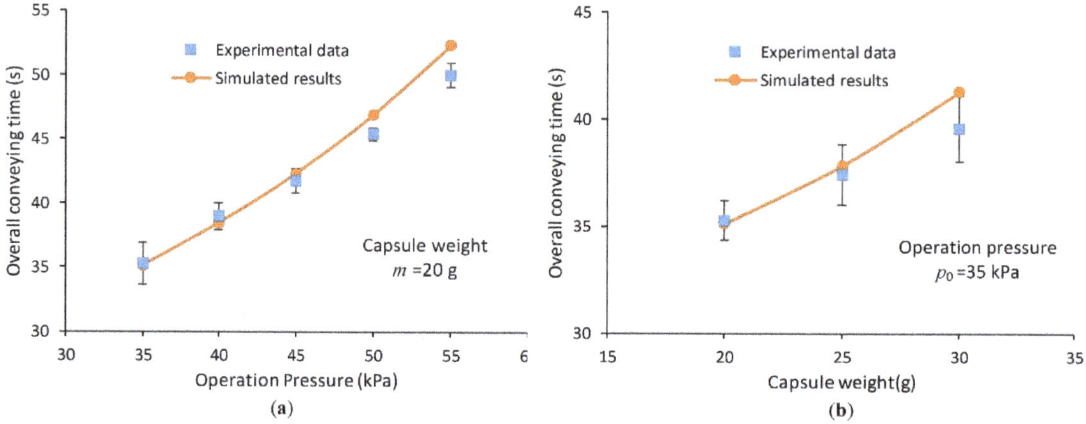

Figure 9. Experimental and simulated overall conveying time with various operation pressure (**a**) and capsule weight (**b**).

In addition to the light-load PCPs (like the testing system in *case* 1), there are also PCPs used for conveying minerals, freight, and other heavy loads in the industry. The pipelines have large diameters, and the capsules have much larger sizes and are usually constructed with wheels and end plates. In order to examine the applicability of the presented method for predicting such PCP systems, a set of experimental data reported in the literature were also used for validation.

As shown in Figure 10, the simulated profiles of velocity and pressure agree well with the experimental data. The predicted OCT (2.68 s) and maximum capsule velocity (9.65 m/s) are very close to the report values (2.7 s and 9.72 m/s), with a relative error of only 0.74% and 0.72%, respectively. Such extremely high accuracy was obtained partly because of the simple (straight only) and short (30 m) pipeline used in the experiments. Another analytical model also gave a comparable prediction in this case [19]. But for the practical systems used in industry, the analytical model, which overlooked the complexity of pipe configuration and air compressibility, will be not applicable anymore.

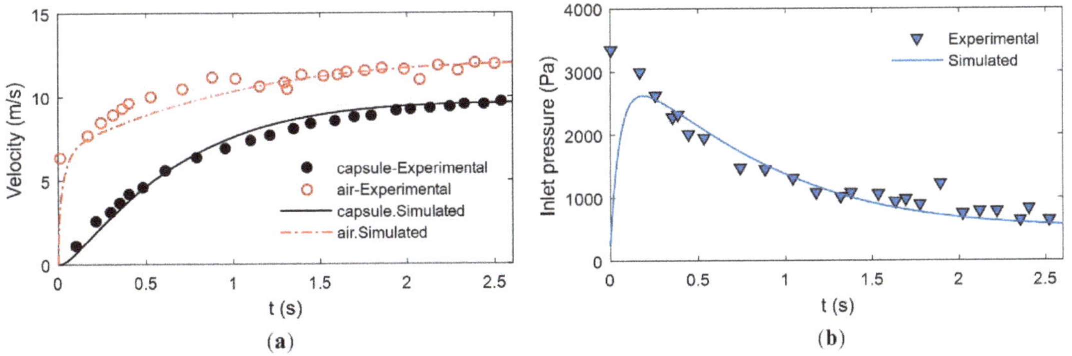

Figure 10. Comparison of simulated results with literature data: (**a**) capsule velocity and air velocity behind the start point of the capsule; (**b**) air pressure at the flow inlet.

6. Conclusions

In this work, a novel method is presented to evaluate the performance of PCPs. A one-dimensional model is established to describe the systemic behavior of PCPs, i.e., the dynamic processes of airflow and capsule motion. The model is simple but still accounts for those phenomena that most profoundly affect the performance of PCPs, such as: the 3D architecture of pipelines, the geometry of capsules, the compressibility of air in long-distance pipelines, as well as the operating conditions of the PCP systems, and so on. Three-dimensional simulation is used to model the local process and obtain the characteristic coefficients in the 1D model. A numerical method is also presented to solve the model equations. With a given pipeline configuration, capsule properties, and operating conditions, the capsule conveying and other related processes can be predicted.

The method has been validated by comparing model predictions with experimental data with respect to two different types of PCPs. The first one has a small diameter (27.86 mm), long-distance (550 m), and 3D-layout pipeline, and the capsule has a relatively complex aerodynamic geometry. Even so, the model prediction achieved favorable accuracy (errors within 4.43%). To our knowledge, it is the first time to report successful simulation of such a complicated but practical PCP system. The second one has a large-diameter (125.6 mm) and a relatively short (30 m) pipeline, and the capsule has been assembled with wheels and end plates. Excellent accuracy was obtained again (errors within 1%), demonstrating the high applicability of the presented method for various PCPs. By rapidly and accurately predicting the overall performance, the presented method provides an effective tool for screening the optimal parameters in the design and application of PCP systems.

Author Contributions: Conceptualization, X.Z.; methodology, X.Z.; software, X.Z. and F.F.; validation, X.Z., F.F. and Y.L.; writing—original draft preparation, X.Z, F.F. and Y.L.; writing—review and editing, X.Z. and F.F.; funding acquisition, X.Z. All authors have read and agreed to the published version of the manuscript.

Funding: This research was funded by National Defense Basic Scientific Research program of China, grant number 91JS211011B.

Institutional Review Board Statement: Not applicable.

Informed Consent Statement: Not applicable.

Data Availability Statement: The experimental data used in validation case 2 are part of the research conducted by Morikawa et al (1984 and 1985). The rest of experimental data presented in this study are available on request from the corresponding author.

Acknowledgments: The authors would like to thank Chen and his group in Jiuangsu Shengtong Valve Co. Ltd., for kindly providing the experimental data.

Conflicts of Interest: The authors declare no conflict of interest.

References

1. Kosugi, S. A Capsule Pipeline System for Limestone Transport. In Proceedings of the 4th International Conference on Bulk Materials, Storage, Handling and Transportation: 7th International Symposium on Freight Pipelines, Wollongong, Australia, 6–8 July 1992; Volume 7, pp. 13–17. [CrossRef]
2. Hane, K.; Okutsu, K.; Matsui, N.; Kosugi, S. Applicability of pneumatic capsule pipeline system to radioactive waste diposal facility. In Proceedings of the WM'02 Conference, Tucson, AZ, USA, 24–28 February 2002.
3. Hidalgo, D.; Martín-Marroquín, J.M.; Corona, F.; Juaristi, J.L. Sustainable vacuum waste collection systems in areas of difficult access. *Tunn. Undergr. Space Technol.* **2018**, *81*, 221–227. [CrossRef]
4. Farré, J.A.; Salgado-Pizarro, R.; Martín, M.; Zsembinszki, G.; Gasia, J.; Cabeza, L.F.; Barreneche, C.; Fernández, A.I. Case study of pipeline failure analysis from two automated vacuum collection system. *Waste Manag.* **2021**, *126*, 643–651. [CrossRef] [PubMed]
5. Liu, H. Pneumatic capsule pipeline-basic concept, practical considerations, and current research. *Mid-Cont. Transp. Symp.* **2000**, *230*, 230–234.
6. Shibani, W.M.; Zulkafli, M.F.; Basuno, B. Methods of transport technologies: A review on using tube/tunnel systems. *IOP Conf. Ser. Mater. Sci. Eng.* **2016**, *160*, 012042. [CrossRef]
7. Okutsu, K.; Esaki, T.; Matsui, N.; Fukunaga, T.; Saito, K. Comprehensive pneumatic transportation system for geological disposal facilities. In Proceedings of the WM'04 Conference, Tucson, AZ, USA, 29 February–4 March 2004.
8. Turkowski, M.; Szudarek, M. Pipeline system for transporting consumer goods, parcels and mail in capsules. *Tunn. Undergr. Space Technol.* **2019**, *93*, 103057. [CrossRef]
9. Kosugi, S. Pneumatic capsule pipelines in Japan and future developments. *Handb. Powder Technol.* **2001**, *10*, 501–511. [CrossRef]
10. Belova, O.V.; Vulf, M.D. Pneumatic capsule transport. *Procedia Eng.* **2016**, *152*, 276–280. [CrossRef]
11. York, K.; Liu, H. Predicting drag coefficient of pneumatic capsule. *J. Transp. Eng.* **2001**, *127*, 390–397. [CrossRef]
12. Kosugi, S. Effect of traveling resistance factor on pneumatic capsule pipeline system. *Powder Technol.* **1999**, *104*, 227–232. [CrossRef]
13. Ohashi, A.; Yanaida, K. The fluid mechanics of capsule pipelines: 1st report, analysis of the required pressure drop for hydraulic and pneumatic capsules. *Bull. JSME* **1986**, *29*, 1719–1725. [CrossRef]
14. Ohashi, A.; Yanaida, K. The fluid mechanics of capsule pipelines: 2nd report, analysis of the pressure loss in concentric capsules, pipelines and annular pipes. *Bull. JSME* **1986**, *29*, 4156–4163. [CrossRef]
15. Ohashi, A.; Yanaida, K. The fluid mechanics of capsule pipelines: 3rd report, analysis of the pressure loss in eccentric capsules pipelines and eccentric annular pipes. *Bull. JSME* **1986**, *29*, 3779–3786. [CrossRef]
16. Liu, H.; Kosugi, S. Use of Pneumatic Capsule Pipeline for Underground Tunneling. In Proceedings of the 12th International Symposium on Freight Pipelines, Prague, Czech Republic, 20–24 September 2004.
17. Liu, H. Feasibility of Using Pneumatic Capsule Pipelines in New York City for Underground Freight Transport. In Proceedings of the ASCE Pipeline Division Specialty Congress, San Diego, CA, USA, 1–4 August 2004; pp. 1–12.
18. Morikawa, Y.; Tsuji, Y.; Chono, S.; Yoshida, H. A Fundamental Investigation of the Capsule Transport: 3rd Report, Friction of Capsule Wheels and Transport Experiment of a Single Capsule. *Bull. JSME* **1984**, *27*, 2181–2187. [CrossRef]
19. Tsuji, Y.; Morikawa, Y.; Chono, S.; Imae, H.; Yoshikawa, T. A Fundamental Investigation of the Capsule Transport: 4th Report, Numerical Analysis of Motion of Accelerating and Decelerating Capsules. *Bull. JSME* **1985**, *28*, 1128–1134. [CrossRef]
20. Tomita, Y. Numerical analysis of pneumatic capsule pipeline system: Continuous loading with short intervals. *Bull. JSME* **1985**, *28*, 2480–2481. [CrossRef]
21. Wee Chuan Lim, E.; Wang, C.-H.; Yu, A.-B. Discrete element simulation for pneumatic conveying of granular material. *AIChE J.* **2006**, *52*, 496–509. [CrossRef]
22. Wang, Y.; Williams, K.; Jones, M.; Chen, B. CFD simulation methodology for gas-solid flow in bypass pneumatic conveying—A review. *Appl. Therm. Eng.* **2017**, *125*, 185–208. [CrossRef]
23. Miao, Z.; Kuang, S.; Zughbi, H.; Yu, A. CFD simulation of dilute-phase pneumatic conveying of powders. *Powder Technol.* **2019**, *349*, 70–83. [CrossRef]
24. Nguyen, D.; Rasmuson, A.; Niklasson Björn, I.; Thalberg, K. CFD simulation of transient particle mixing in a high shear mixer. *Powder Technol.* **2014**, *258*, 324–330. [CrossRef]
25. Kuang, S.; Zhou, M.; Yu, A. CFD-DEM modelling and simulation of pneumatic conveying: A review. *Powder Technol.* **2020**, *365*, 186–207. [CrossRef]
26. Shi, Q.; Sakai, M. Recent progress on the discrete element method simulations for powder transport systems: A review. *Adv. Powder Technol.* **2022**, *33*, 103664. [CrossRef]
27. Towler, G.; Sinnott, R. Chapter 18-Specification and design of solids-handling equipment. In *Chemical Engineering Design*, 3rd ed.; Towler, G., Sinnott, R., Eds.; Butterworth-Heinemann: Oxford, UK, 2022; pp. 735–821.
28. Huber, N.; Sommerfeld, M. Modelling and numerical calculation of dilute-phase pneumatic conveying in pipe systems. *Powder Technol.* **1998**, *99*, 90–101. [CrossRef]
29. Tashiro, H.; Peng, X.; Tomita, Y. Numerical prediction of saltation velocity for gas-solid two-phase flow in a horizontal pipe. *Powder Technol.* **1997**, *91*, 141–146. [CrossRef]

30. Levy, A. Two-fluid approach for plug flow simulations in horizontal pneumatic conveying. *Powder Technol.* **2000**, *112*, 263–272. [CrossRef]
31. Tsuji, Y.; Tanaka, T.; Ishida, T. Lagrangian numerical simulation of plug flow of cohesionless particles in a horizontal pipe. *Powder Technol.* **1992**, *71*, 239–250. [CrossRef]
32. Le, T.T.G.; Jang, K.S.; Lee, K.-S.; Ryu, J. Numerical Investigation of Aerodynamic Drag and Pressure Waves in Hyperloop Systems. *Mathematics* **2020**, *8*, 1973. [CrossRef]
33. Al-Obaidi, A.R. Numerical investigation on effect of various pump rotational speeds on performance of centrifugal pump based on CFD analysis technique. *Int. J. Model. Simul. Sci. Comput.* **2021**, *12*, 2150045. [CrossRef]
34. Al-Obaidi, A.R.; Qubian, A. Effect of outlet impeller diameter on performance prediction of centrifugal pump under single-phase and cavitation flow conditions. *Int. J. Nonlinear Sci. Numer. Simul.* **2022**. [CrossRef]
35. Feng, J.; Huang, P.Y.; Joseph, D.D. Dynamic simulation of the motion of capsules in pipelines. *J. Fluid Mech.* **1995**, *286*, 201–227. [CrossRef]
36. Asim, T.; Mishra, R. Computational fluid dynamics based optimal design of hydraulic capsule pipelines transporting cylindrical capsules. *Powder Technol.* **2016**, *295*, 180–201. [CrossRef]
37. Dupont, C.; Le Tallec, P.; Barthès-Biesel, D.; Vidrascu, M.; Salsac, A.-V. Dynamics of a spherical capsule in a planar hyperbolic flow: Influence of bending resistance. *Procedia IUTAM* **2015**, *16*, 70–79. [CrossRef]
38. Zhang, C.; Sun, X.; Li, Y.; Zhang, X.; Zhang, X.; Yang, X.; Li, F. Hydraulic characteristics of transporting a piped carriage in a horizontal pipe based on the bidirectional fluid-structure interaction. *Math. Probl. Eng.* **2018**, *2018*, 8317843. [CrossRef]
39. Abushaala, S.; Shaneb, A.; Enbais, F.; Abulifa, A. Hydrodynamic analysis of pipelines transporting capsule for onshore applications. *Int. J. Eng. Inf. Technol.* **2018**, *5*, 53–62.
40. Khani, D.; Lim, Y.H.; Malekpour, A. Calculating Column Separation in Liquid Pipelines Using a 1D-CFD Coupled Model. *Mathematics* **2022**, *10*, 1960. [CrossRef]
41. Herrán-González, A.; De La Cruz, J.M.; De Andrés-Toro, B.; Risco-Martín, J.L. Modeling and simulation of a gas distribution pipeline network. *Appl. Math. Model.* **2009**, *33*, 1584–1600. [CrossRef]
42. Yuan, Z.; Deng, Z.; Jiang, M.; Xie, Y.; Wu, Y. A modeling and analytical solution for transient flow in natural gas pipelines with extended partial blockage. *J. Nat. Gas Sci. Eng.* **2015**, *22*, 141–149. [CrossRef]
43. Patankar, S.V. *Numerical Heat Transfer and Fluid Flow*; Hemisphere Publishing Corporation: London, UK, 1980.

mathematics

Article

A Novel Cam-Based Variable Stiffness Actuator: Pitch Curve Synthetic Approach for Reconfiguration Design

Fanghua Mei [2], Shusheng Bi [2] and Bianhong Li [1,*]

[1] School of Mechanical Engineering, Beijing Institute of Technology, Beijing 100081, China
[2] School of Mechanical Engineering and Automation, Beihang University, Beijing 100191, China
* Correspondence: libianhong@bit.edu.cn; Tel.: +86-17801050604

Abstract: Variable stiffness actuators (VSA) have attracted much attention because of their potential for human-like interaction behaviors. This paper devotes to improving the VSA's versatility. VSA with different characteristics can be obtained by shape reconfiguration of its internal driving cams. The proposed VSA mainly includes a variable stiffness module and a cam-based driven module. A common node connects the two modules. It is placed in the common grooves of the dual cams. Kinematically, the radial position of the node can be changed for stiffness adjustment by cam differential motion. Mechanically, the driven force on this node can be resolved into two orthogonal directions by cam groove, one for stiffness adjustment and another for position balance., The paper establishes the analytical relationship between the pressure angle of the cam pitch curve, stiffness adjustment speed and accuracy, and load distribution. Furtherly, the pitch curve synthetic approach for VSA reconfiguration is provided. A special cam shape with a favorable load distribution is proposed to verify the method. The correctness of the design was effectively proved by experiments in the virtual model and physical prototype.

Keywords: reconfiguration; cam pitch curve synthesis; load distribution; stiffness adjustment speed and accuracy

MSC: 37B99

Citation: Mei, F.; Bi, S.; Li, B. A Novel Cam-Based Variable Stiffness Actuator: Pitch Curve Synthetic Approach for Reconfiguration Design. *Mathematics* **2022**, *10*, 4088. https://doi.org/10.3390/math10214088

Academic Editors: Shujin Laima, Xiaowei Jin and Hehe Ren

Received: 1 October 2022
Accepted: 27 October 2022
Published: 2 November 2022

Publisher's Note: MDPI stays neutral with regard to jurisdictional claims in published maps and institutional affiliations.

Copyright: © 2022 by the authors. Licensee MDPI, Basel, Switzerland. This article is an open access article distributed under the terms and conditions of the Creative Commons Attribution (CC BY) license (https://creativecommons.org/licenses/by/4.0/).

1. Introduction

A major difference between compliant actuators and classical rigid actuators is that the former's force-deformation properties are similar to that of human muscle [1,2]. This makes flexible actuators show great promise in human-computer interaction sites, such as assistive exoskeletons and rehabilitation devices [3–6]. In the early stage, Pratt intentionally placed a linear spring in the kinematic chain [7]. It is known as a serial elastic actuator (SEA). This enabled compliant actuators with higher torque robustness and safety, and higher energy efficiency in a cyclic motion [8–11]. In a cyclic movement such as walking behavior, the VSA can help to reduce the impact loss of kinetic energy in the landing process of walking with a low stiffness. Most of the kinetic energy is converted into elastic potential energy of the compliant element. Then the elastic potential energy is released directly to the legs during the take-off phase. System energy flows primarily between the compliant element and the end of the leg. Theoretically, the motors of VSA only need to make small movements, to continuously supplement the impact energy loss and the frictional energy loss to the robot system. This greatly improves the energy efficiency of periodic motion. But the optimal motion frequency is limited by the actuator output stiffness. To overcome the limitation of constant stiffness on actuator performance, the variable stiffness actuator (VSA) introduces a new degree of freedom for stiffness adjustment [12–14].

The VSA's key attributes include output power, stiffness range, efficiency, and accuracy [15]. Unfortunately, these performance indexes are contradictory, requiring compromise designs based on task characteristics [16]. Research scholars have carried out a scientific and detailed classification of these actuators, which provides important guidance for successors [17]. To map a different stiffness from the compliant element to the output of VSA, the adjustment principles include the followings: moving the equilibrium point on the torque-deflection curve of the spring (tuning single-spring preload [18], varying antagonistic-springs preload [19–21]), changing deformation transmission ratio [22–24], and changing the physical properties of the spring [25–27].

The diversity of principles provides a flexible choice for different design intents. Additionally, reconfiguration design is also a frequently-used method, which has better versatility. Its main purpose is to achieve diverse stiffness ranges and behaviors without changing the external interface. Such as the pulley block is reconfigured to change the spring preload for stiffness behaviors similar to human muscle [28–30]. Another popular approach is to obtain different torque-deflection springs. Minacci enhanced the output torque in the whole stiffness range in the agonistic-antagonistic VSA with a combination of a linear and nonlinear spring [31]. Xu provided a symmetry variable stiffness module, allowing convenient reconfiguration of the S-springs for different applications [32]. Qian configures the stiffness profiles offline by changing the spring stiffness or its pre-tension force [33]. However, the other crucial characteristics of the VSA have not been covered enough. In the previous work [34], the two motors can share the external load with a small difference through cam optimal design. It provides an efficient way to fully utilize the performance of dual motors to achieve enhanced torque output capability of the actuator. The work focus on improving the uniformity of load distribution, but the other aspects of the VSA's performance is not considered. Based on the previous work, this new work aims to consider other important performance indexes, including stiffness adjustment speed, and stiffness adjustment accuracy. The paper establishes the analytical relationship between the cam pitch curve's pressure angle and the above key performance indexes for multi-objective optimization design. By an internal adjustment of the cam groove shape, the VSA can be arbitrarily reconfigured depending on its functionality with the external interface unchanged. The versatility of the actuator design can be greatly improved to adapt to different application requirements, only by reconfiguring the internally driven cam shape.

In Section 2, the reconfiguration principle for the proposed problem is present. As well, the cam pitch curve synthetic approach for reconfiguration design was described in Section 3. The cam curve based on a favorable load distribution is provided and verified by virtual model simulation and physical prototype experiment in Section 4. The conclusion is provided in Section 5.

2. Reconfiguration Method of the Cam-Based VSA

2.1. Problem Description

The existing reconfigurability design of the adjustable stiffness actuator takes the stiffness range as the design optimization objective, and the optimization objective is single, which limits the versatility of the actuator. In a robot system, there are usually many degrees of freedom. For example, the Tesla humanoid robot has 28 degrees of freedom. Improving the versatility of the structural design of the actuator is the key to reducing costs. In fact, in addition to the stiffness adjustment range, the key performance indicators of the adjustable stiffness actuator also include output torque, stiffness adjustment time, and stiffness adjustment accuracy. At present, limited by the structural design, there is no model that can cover all the above key performance indicators, and it is impossible to carry out multi-objective design optimization under a unified mathematical model, and the versatile design of the actuator is limited.

2.2. Reconfiguration Method of the Cam-Based VSA for High Versatility

In this paper, a pitch curve synthetic approach for VSA reconfiguration design with the following advantages is provided as follows:

(1) Cam-based VSA with a common driven node. The radial position of the common node can be changed for stiffness adjustment by cam differential motion and its tangential position can be changed for output position control by cam synchronized movement. The cam groove can resolve the driven force into two orthogonal directions: one for stiffness adjustment and another for position balance. Obviously, this common node makes the stiffness adjustment time, accuracy and output torque of the actuator have common structural constraints. Therefore, the system model established in this paper can cover the above key performance indicators.

(2) Feasible solution space of pressure angle, considering the mechanical constraint of the variable stiffness module. The solution space is decided by two solution boundaries: the upper one generated by the stiffness adjustment force and the lower one by the position balance force. The cam can be shaped in a polar coordinate system with the pressure angle function, based on the approximation functions of the two boundaries.

(3) Synthetic approach of pitch curve for reconfiguration design. The paper establishes analytic relationships among the cam pressure angle, stiffness adjustment speed and accuracy, and load distribution. Three cam configurations with different characteristics are given: a bigger pressure angle is helpful to improve the stiffness adjustment speed; a smaller one is beneficial to obtain a more even load on the dual motors; a tradeoff between the above two cases can result in a uniform stiffness adjustment accuracy. By an internal adjustment of the cam groove shape, the VSA can be arbitrarily reconfigured depending on its functionality with the external interface unchanged. This greatly increases the versatility of the actuator design.

The principle of the proposed VSA is illustrated in Figure 1. It is mainly composed of a stiffness adjustment module (VSM) and the cooperative cam-based driving module. In the VSM, the coupler AC and the output link OA are connected by a spring, as shown in Figure 1. Then the rigid guide rod mechanism is transformed into a compliant mechanism. In this mechanism, the spring's torsion angle is just the transmission angle between AC and OA (α in Figure 1). The difference between the input link OB and the output link OA is defined as the deformation angle of the VSA (θ in Figure 1).

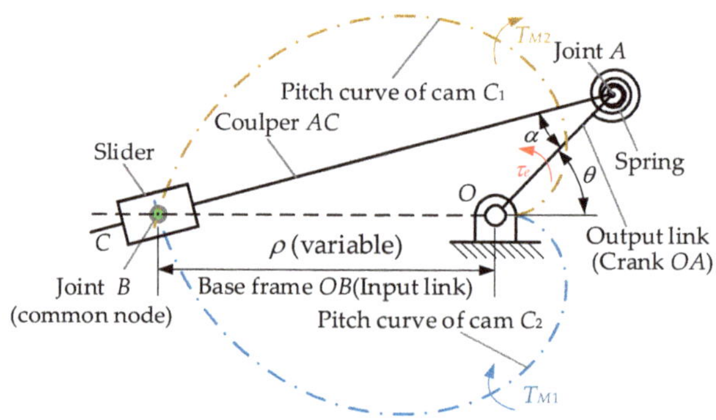

Figure 1. Principle of the cam-based VSA.

τ_e is the load exerted on the output link of the VSA, and can be obtained as

$$\tau_e = \tau_s(\alpha)\frac{d\alpha}{d\theta} \tag{1}$$

where $\tau_s(\alpha)$ is the elastic torque of the spring with respect to deflection α. Thus, the output stiffness K can be

$$K = \frac{d\tau_e}{d\theta} = k_s\left(\frac{d\alpha}{d\theta}\right)^2 + \tau_s(\alpha)\frac{d^2\alpha}{d^2\theta} \tag{2}$$

where k_s is the spring stiffness. $d\alpha/d\theta$ indicates the deformation transmission ratio and can be expressed as

$$d\alpha/d\theta = \rho\cos(\theta-\alpha)/(a\cos\alpha+\rho\cos(\theta-\alpha)) \tag{3}$$

where a and ρ are the length of link OA and link OB. By changing ρ, $d\alpha/d\theta$ can be regulated, and so the stiffness K.

The VSM is driven by two motors through two symmetrical cams (cams C_1, C_2 in Figure 1). Joint B is arranged at the intersection of the symmetrical cam pitch curve, which can realize the adjustment of position and stiffness at the same time. To reduce the internal friction, joint B is composed of two bearing for the two cams, called cam followers. As well, they are placed in the cams' common groove. The stiffness K can be changed with a tunable node B implemented by cams' differential rotation. The speed and accuracy of the stiffness adjustment are decided by the shape of the cam. Furthermore, there is: $\tau_e = T_{M1} + T_{M2}$. At the same time, the cam acts as a force resolver for stiffness adjustment and position balance, and decides the load distribution feature (the ratio of T_{M1}/T_{M2}). The output power of the VSA can be enhanced with optimal load distribution.

So, VSA with different characteristics can be obtained by reconfiguring the cam pitch curve. As well, the cam shape reconfiguration is closely related to the stiffness adjustment module, whose specifications are defined in the previous research work [34].

3. The Cam Pitch Curve Synthetic Approach for Reconfiguration Design

3.1. Cam Pitch Curve Modeling

In this paper, the cam pitch curves are described in a polar coordinate system (Figure 2). The intersection node B is represented by polar coordinate $B(\rho,\kappa(\rho))$. ρ is the radial distance corresponding to certain stiffness ($\rho = OB$) and $\kappa(\rho)$ is the angle mapped to ρ in the polar coordinate system. On node B, the stiffness adjustment pressure angle is defined as the cam curve pressure angle. ($\gamma(\rho)$ in Figure 2). In the part polar coordinate systems, $\gamma(\rho)$ is the key for cam reconfiguration design. It establishes direct mathematical relationships among cam shape, the feasible solution space of cam reconfiguration, and the VSA's primary characteristics.

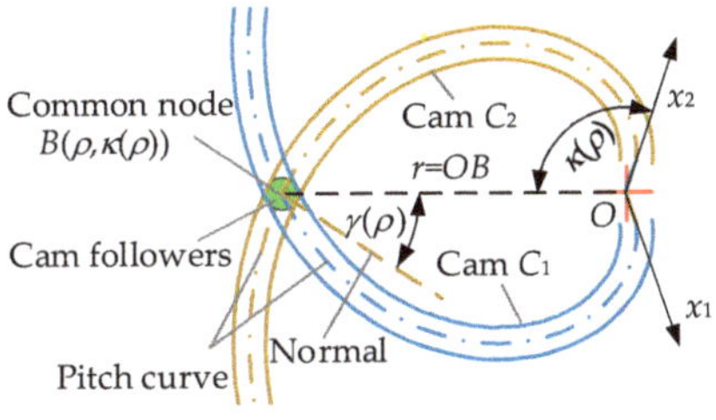

Figure 2. Cam curve described in the polar coordinate system.

The pitch curve can be shaped by the relationship among ρ, $\gamma(\rho)$ and $\kappa(\rho)$ as

$$\kappa(\rho) = \int_{\rho_{\min}}^{\rho} [\rho\tan(\gamma(\rho))]^{-1} d\rho \tag{4}$$

where $\rho_{\min}$ is the minimal length of link OB.

3.2. Feasible Solution Space of Cam Reconfiguration under the Basic Constraints

Benefiting from the symmetry of the structure, only the deformed configuration with a positive direction is discussed. Corresponding to Figures 1 and 2, the balanced forces on node B are shown in Figure 3.

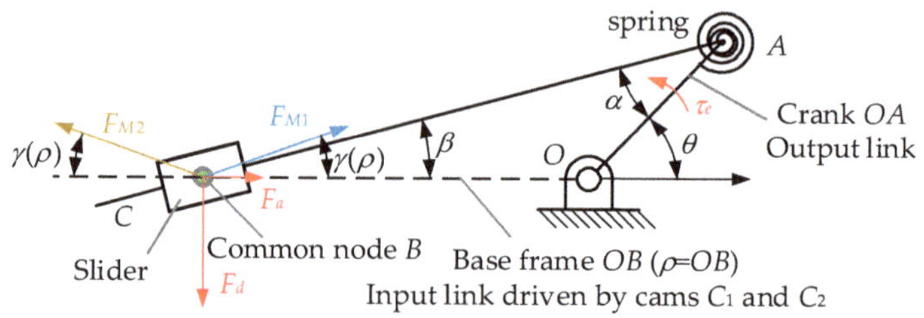

Figure 3. Static forces at the common node *B*.

The force on the followers is resolved into two orthogonal directions (F_d, F_a, red highlight in Figure 3). F_d is called the counter-force for position control and F_a is called the counter-force for stiffness adjustment. The ratio of F_a over F_d can be expressed as

$$F_a/F_d = \tan\beta = a\sin\theta/(\rho + a\cos\theta) \tag{5}$$

where β indicates the angular displacement of the slider relative to OB.

F_{M1}, F_{M2} are the normal force exerted on the common node by cams C_1 and C_2, and there is

$$\begin{cases} (F_{M1} + F_{M2})\sin\gamma(\rho) = F_d \\ (F_{M2} - F_{M1})\cos\gamma(\rho) = F_a \end{cases} \tag{6}$$

Solution space of cam pitch curve. To ensure the bearing followers not be overloaded, $\gamma(\rho)$ should meet the following constraint equation:

$$F_{M2} = \tau_e(1 + \tan\beta\tan\gamma(\rho))\rho^{-1}/2\sin\gamma(\rho) \leq [F_b] \tag{7}$$

Considering the specification constraints in [35], the maximum value of the β, θ, α, τ_e in Equation (7) is obtained according to Equations (1) and (3), and graphed in Figure 4. Correspondingly, the feasible solution space of $\gamma(\rho)$ is calculated numerically and shown by the area enclosed by the solid red line and the dashed red line in Figure 5. The dashed red line and solid red line indicate its lower and upper solution boundary respectively. The former represents the allowable minimum $\gamma(\rho)$ for F_d and the latter represents the allowable maximum $\gamma(\rho)$ for F_a. Beyond this boundary, the overload problem appears on the bearings.

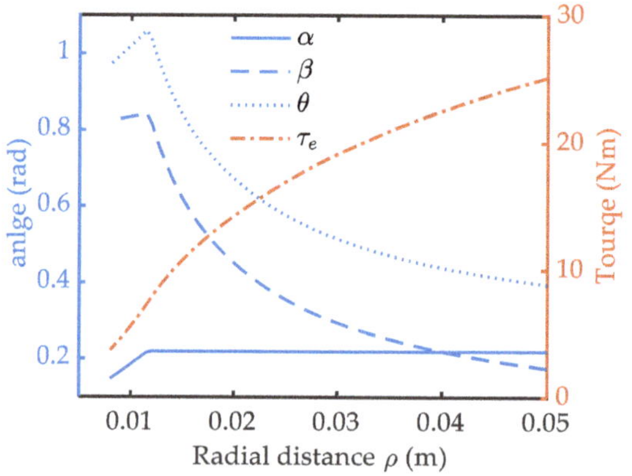

Figure 4. Specification constraints of the variable stiffness module.

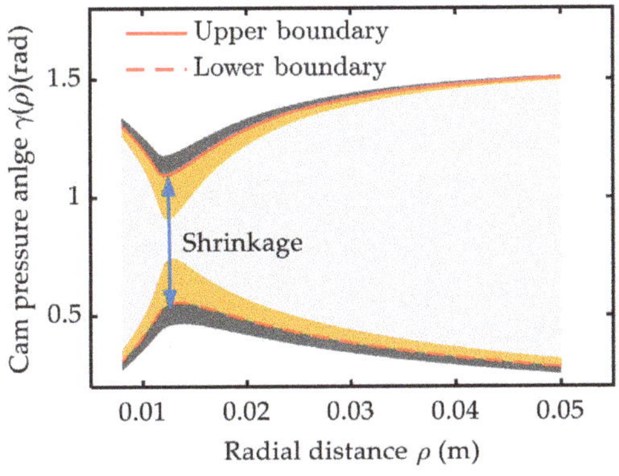

Figure 5. Solution space constrained by bearing's rated load.

There appears a local shrinkage phenomenon near ρ = 0.014 m on the solution space. This is caused by the change of the main factors determining $\gamma(\rho)$. When (ρ < 0.014 m), a small $\gamma(\rho)$ is allowed with low stiffness. Afterward, the stiffness increases quickly and leads to a sharp increase of $\gamma(\rho)$. After the shrinkage point, the decreasing ρ^{-1} and β become the dominant factors and the $\gamma(\rho)$ decreases slowly. The upper boundary curve exhibits an antisymmetric feature as the second solution for Equation (7). The two together generate the shrinkage phenomenon. The degree of the shrinkage is decided by the bearing's rated load. The feasible solution space would broaden outward slightly with a larger bearing ($[F_b]$ = 950 N), indicated by the grey area in Figure 5. But it would shrink inward seriously with a smaller bearing ($[F_b]$ = 750 N), as indicated by the yellow area in Figure 5. The difference is caused by the nonlinearity of the F_{M1} over $\gamma(\rho)$ in Equation (6). This trend is more significant near shrinkage point as the β in this interval is larger, as shown in Figure 4. So, a favorable choice of the cam follower bearing should be based on the mechanical property of the variable stiffness module. Bearing a too small rated load would limit the solution space for the cam reconstruction design and too large one does not help much but increases the curvature radius.

Pressure angle constrained by undercutting. The minimum curvature radius should be large than the radius of the cam followers. So, any feasible $\gamma(\rho)$ in Figure 5 should meet the following undercutting constrained equation:

$$\rho_{\text{pitch}} = \frac{\rho\left[1+\tan^2\gamma(\rho)\right]^{3/2}}{\left|\tan^2\gamma - \rho\gamma'(\rho)\tan\gamma(\rho)\sec^2\gamma(\rho)+1\right|} \geq D/2 \tag{8}$$

where D indicates the diameter of the cam followers, $\gamma'(\rho)$ is the derivative of $\gamma(\rho)$ over ρ.

Expression of the feasible pressure curve in the solution space. The upper solution boundary can be approximately approached by the superposition of the following two pressure angle functions: the main function $\gamma_{fit}(\rho)$ in Equation (9) and the correction function $\gamma_c(\rho)$ in Equation (10). $\gamma_{fit}(\rho)$ devotes to fitting the pressure angle data after the shrinkage point in Figure 5 (ρ = 0.014 m), and $\gamma_c(\rho)$ to compensate for its value in the range before the shrinkage point.

$$\gamma_{fit}(\rho) = 144101\rho^4 + 28797\rho^3 - 2183\rho^2 + 77.1\rho + 0.412 \tag{9}$$

$$\gamma_c(\rho) = a_c + b_c(\rho_{\min}/\rho)^{n_c} \tag{10}$$

Setting $a_c = -0.015$, $b_c = 0.4$, $n_c = 6$ by enumeration method, the upper solution boundary function can be expressed as

$$\gamma_{\text{up}}(\rho) = \gamma_{fit}(\rho) + \gamma_c(\rho) \tag{11}$$

In a likewise fashion, the lower solution boundary function can be approximately approached by

$$\gamma_{\text{low}}(\rho) = 20830\rho^4 - 5303\rho^3 + 531.5\rho^2 - 27.36\rho + 0.864 - 0.25(\rho_{\min}/\rho)^5 \quad (12)$$

Then the pressure angle curve in the solution space can be generally expressed as

$$\begin{cases} \gamma(\rho) = W(\rho)\gamma_{\text{up}}(\rho) + (1-W(\rho))\gamma_{\text{low}} \\ \rho_{\text{pitch}} \geq D/2 \end{cases} \quad (13)$$

where $W(\rho)$ is the function to be determined, and there is $0 \leq W(\rho) \leq 1$.

3.3. *Cam Reconfiguration Synthetic Based on Different Performance Index of the Variable Stiffness Actuator*

Case 1: cam synthetic based on stiffness adjustment speed, such as actuator for wrist joint in a humanoid robot. Usually, it needs to be used for some fine actions, such as grabbing, polishing, and grinding. With a given motor speed, the stiffness adjustment speed can be proportional to angle $\kappa(\rho)$ in Equation (4) and inversely proportional to $\gamma(\rho)$. So, a shorter stiffness adjustment time can be obtained with the pressure angle curve moving toward the upper boundary curve in Figure 5, i.e., $W(\rho) \to 1$.

Case 2: cam synthetic based on output stiffness accuracy, such as actuator for wrist joint in a humanoid robot. Usually, it needs to be used for some fine actions, such as grabbing, polishing, and grinding. A smaller value of the stiffness adjustment resolution is beneficial to obtain a high output stiffness accuracy and is defined as:

$$a_\rho = \Delta p \frac{\partial K}{\partial \kappa} = \Delta p \frac{\partial K}{\partial \rho}\frac{\partial \rho}{\partial \kappa} = \Delta p \frac{\partial K}{\partial \rho} \rho \tan(\gamma(\rho)) \quad (14)$$

where Δp indicates the position resolution of the cam, i.e., the resolution of the polar angle κ. $\partial K/\partial \kappa$ is the partial derivative of K over κ and represents the stiffness resolution related to κ.

To simplify the solution, we ignore the nonlinearity of output stiffness in Equation (2). Then $\partial K/\partial \rho$ can be simplified as

$$\frac{\partial K}{\partial \rho} = \frac{2a\rho}{(a+\rho)^3} \quad (15)$$

For the case with a higher priority of stiffness accuracy, we can predefine the stiffness adjustment function by

$$S(\rho) = \frac{\partial K}{\partial \rho} \rho \tan(\gamma(\rho)) \quad (16)$$

Then the relationship between $W(\rho)$ and $S(\rho)$ can be mapped as

$$S(\rho) = \frac{\partial K}{\partial \rho} \rho \tan(W(\rho)\gamma_{\text{up}}(\rho) + (1-W(\rho))\gamma_{\text{low}}) \quad (17)$$

The local stiffness adjustment accuracy can be arbitrarily set according to the requirements of different tasks by pre-definition of $W(\rho)$. For a certain ρ range with higher stiffness adjustment accuracy, the corresponding $S(\rho)$ can be adjusted to a lower value with a small $W(\rho)$. The cam pressure angle function based on the predefined stiffness adjustment accuracy can be decided by

$$\kappa(\rho) = \int_{\rho_{\min}}^{\rho} \frac{1}{S(\rho)\partial K/\partial \rho} d\rho \quad (18)$$

Case 3: cam synthetic based on load distribution on its dual motors, such as actuator for waist joint in the legged robot. It requires the actuator to have a large driving capacity, but it does not require a high stiffness adjustment time. The torques T_{M1} and T_{M2} on the cams C_1 and C_2 can be derived from F_{M1} and F_{M2} as

$$\begin{cases} T_{M1} = F_{M1} \sin\gamma(\rho)\rho = \tau_e(1 + \tan\beta)\tan\gamma(\rho))/2 \\ T_{M2} = F_{M2} \sin\gamma(\rho)\rho = \tau_e(1 - \tan\beta\tan\gamma(\rho))/2 \end{cases} \quad (19)$$

In this paper, we use ϕ to evaluate the load distribution. It is defined as the smaller torque on the cams over its bigger one. When $\theta > 0$, there is $T_{M\,1} < T_{M\,2}$. Then ϕ can be

$$\phi = \frac{T_{M1}}{T_{M2}} = \frac{1 - \tan\beta \tan\gamma(\rho)}{1 + \tan\beta \tan\gamma(\rho)} \tag{20}$$

When $\theta < 0$, the ϕ can be re-expressed as is

$$\phi = \frac{T_{M2}}{T_{M1}} = \frac{1 - \tan\beta \tan\gamma(\rho)}{1 + \tan\beta \tan\gamma(\rho)} \tag{21}$$

Four different reconfiguration cases can be discussed. First, $\phi = 1$. The motors share the external load evenly. In this case, a serious overload phenomenon happens and the stiffness cannot be tuned. Second, $0 < \phi < 1$. The dual motors synergistically drive an external load. The proximity of the amount is dependent on the $\gamma(\rho)$. The smaller the value of $\gamma(\rho)$, the more uniform the load distribution. Third, $\phi = 0$. Only a single motor takes the load. This is the load distribution status of the existing freestanding VSA. Fourth, $\phi < 0$. The motors work against each other. This reflects the load distribution state of the existing antagonistic VSA.

According to the above discussion, a simple conclusion can be made: for case 1, a bigger $\gamma(\rho)$ is helpful to improve the stiffness adjustment speed; contrary to case 1, a smaller $\gamma(\rho)$ is better to obtain a more even load on the two motors in case 3; case 2 is between the case 1 and case 3.

3.4. Three Cam Reconfiguration Results Based on Three Special Cases

Three special cam reconfigurations based on the above three cases are given and compared in this section. For case 1, the VSA can obtain its maximum stiffness adjustment speed with $W(\rho) = 1$. In this case, the stroke of the polar angle for stiffness adjustment is $\kappa = 0.57$ rad. The pressure angle curve approaches its upper solution boundary (point line in Figure 6). Going back to Equation (4) with Equation (13), the pitch curve for case 1 can be shaped. It is very close to straight line (point line in Figure 7). Obviously, this is more suitable for scenes with requirements for high stiffness adjustment speed. We should note that it does not cover the stiffness adjustment accuracy, as the stiffness resolution is extremely uneven in the whole ρ range. To simplify the comparison, we assume $\Delta p = 1$ rad in Equation (14). With a small ρ value, the adjustment resolution would be very slow and dramatically increase from 10 Nm to 283 Nm with an increasing ρ (solid Figure 8). This is not conducive to improving the accuracy of stiffness adjustment. Another disadvantage is that the VSA works in antagonistic mode with $\phi < -0.2$ (point line in Figure 9). The two driving motors consume each other seriously.

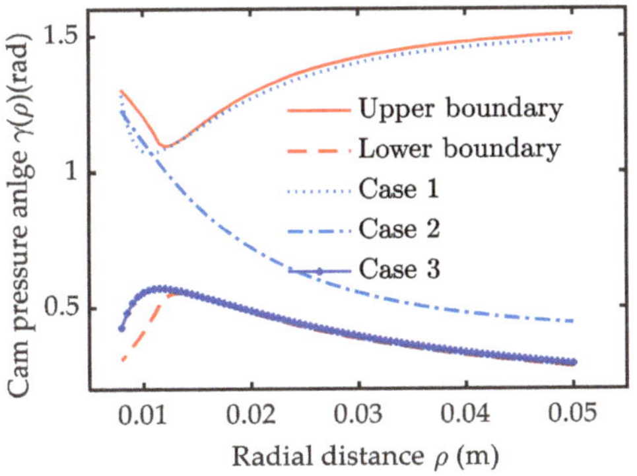

Figure 6. Pressure angle synthetic based on different cases.

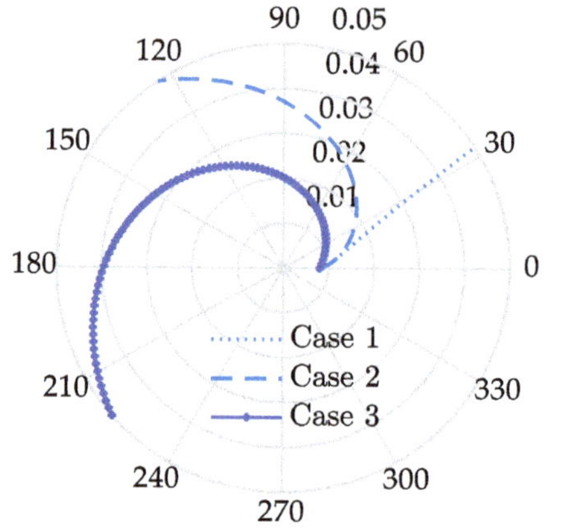

Figure 7. Shape of the pitch curve based on different cases.

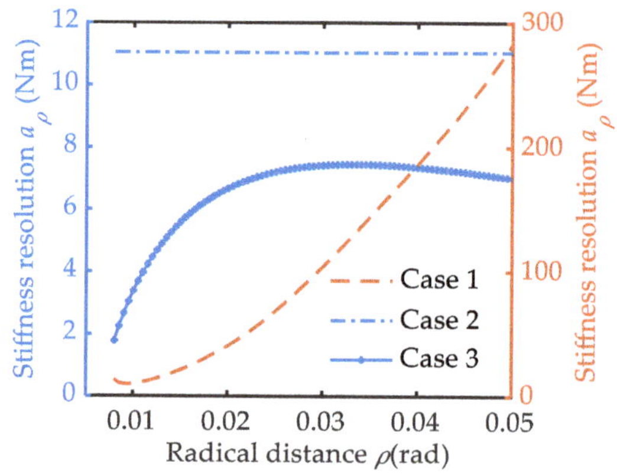

Figure 8. Stiffness resolution based on different cases.

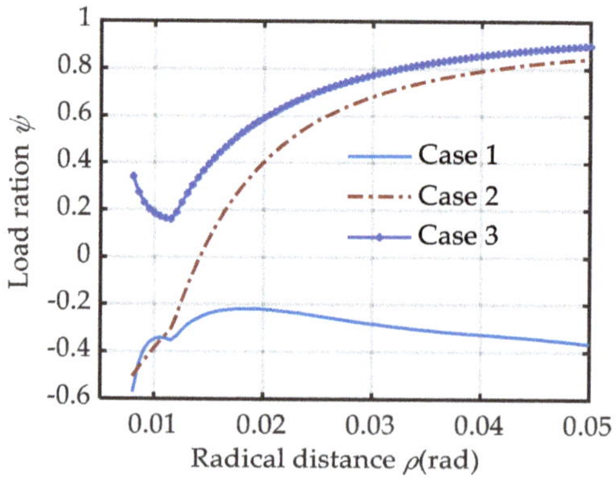

Figure 9. Load ratio based on different cases.

For case 3, an optimal load distribution is obtained with $W(\rho) = 0$. In this case, the pressure angle curve approaches its low solution boundary (asterisk marked in Figure 7).

There is ϕ >0.6 with ρ > 0.02 m. And ϕ would be over 0.8 when ρ > 0.032 m (asterisk marked in Figure 8). It is very useful in full exploitation of the output power of the dual driving motors. Its shape is like that of an Archimedean spiral, but with a variable-pitch (asterisk marked in Figure 6). Obviously, it comes at the cost of stiffness adjustment speed, with a polar angle stroke of κ = 3.86 rad. Trade off can be made between the stiffness adjustment time and the output power (or load distribution). It can be realized by moving the pressure angle curve toward the upper boundary curve with a larger $W(\rho)$. In this way, the output power would decay but the stiffness adjustment speed would be higher.

A special case for case 2 is that: $S(\rho) = C$. C is a constant related to stiffness adjustment accuracy a_ρ. Going back to Equation (18) with Equations (15) and (16), the pressure angle with a uniform stiffness adjustment accuracy can be expressed as

$$\gamma(\rho) = \arctan\left(0.5Ca^{-1}\rho^{-2}(a+\rho)^3\right) \quad (22)$$

By setting C = 0.13, the pressure angle $S(\rho)$ can go through the shrinkage area smoothly (dashed line in Figure 7) and the stiffness resolution remains the same in the whole κ range (dotted line in Figure 9), i.e., a_ρ = 11 Nm. Its value is slightly bigger than that of case 3, for the pressure angle is beyond that of case 3 (dotted line in Figure 7). Except for the uniform stiffness adjustment accuracy, it is also a good embodiment of tradeoff design between the stiffness adjustment time and the output power (or load distribution). The pressure angle curve of case 2 is close to that of case 1 in the low ρ range ($W(\rho) \to 1$ when ρ < 0.014 m) and exhibits a stable offset to that of case 3 in the high ρ range ($W(\rho) \to 0$ when ρ > 0.02 m). It results in a pitch curve between case 1 and case 3 (dashed line in Figure 6). A higher stiffness adjustment speed with a stroke polar angle of κ = 2.16 rad is obtained. At the same time, the load ratio also reaches 0.6 quickly with an increasing ρ. There is good compatibility for stiffness adjustment time and the output power and stiffness adjustment accuracy. The difference and relationships of the three cases are summarized in Table 1.

Table 1. The difference and relationship among the three cam reconfiguration results.

	Case 1	Case 2	Case 3
Stroke of polar angle κ	κ = 0.57 rad	κ = 2.16 rad	κ = 3.86 rad
Stiffness resolution a_ρ	10 Nm < a_ρ <282 Nm	a_ρ = 11 Nm	1.78 Nm < a_ρ < 7.5 Nm
Load ratio ϕ	ϕ < −0.2 in the whole ρ range	ϕ < −0.2 with ρ < 0.014 m; ϕ > 0.6 with ρ > 0.026 m	ϕ > 0.6 with 0.02 < ρ < 0.032 m; ϕ > 0.8 with ρ > 0.032 m.
Pressure angle $\gamma(\rho)$	Maximum $\gamma(\rho)$ close to the upper solution boundary	$\gamma(\rho)$ close to case 1 in low ρ range; $\gamma(\rho)$ close to case 2 in high ρ range.	Minimum $\gamma(\rho)$ close to the lower solution boundary

4. Experiment Verification and Analysis of the Optimal Load Design

The cam shape in case 3 is chosen for the VSA's output power enhancement in a compact joint of the support fund. It focuses on the load distribution design. The load ratio is verified by the Adams simulation and physical prototype experiment from different aspects.

4.1. Load Distribuation Erification by Adams Simulation

Adam's simulation settings. Adam's simulation can provide a fast and exact verification of the design result when the virtual prototype is very close to the theory prototype. It can be regarded as an important supplement to the physical prototype experiment. In cam modeling, the system friction was neglected in the static equilibrium equations of Equations (5) and (19). To avoid the influence of inertia force and friction on the simulation results of cam load ratio, the virtual prototype with non-friction, zero-damping is established, as shown in Figure 10, according to the working principle proposed in Figure 1. The model has the same specifications with that proposed in [34].

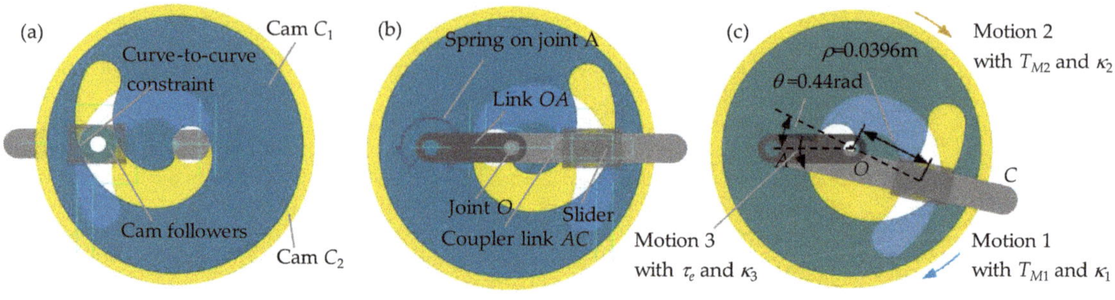

Figure 10. The virtual prototype in ADAMS (**a**) Bottom view; (**b**) Front view; (**c**) Deformed configuration with ρ = 0.0396 m, θ =0.44 rad.

Figure 10a is the bottom view of the virtual prototype. The cam followers are placed in the common grooves of the dual cams with curve-to-curve constraints. Figure 10b is the front view. The cam followers are connected to the linkage mechanism via a slider. Cams C_1 and C_2 rotary around the center O with motion 1 and motion 2. Their angle displacements are indicated by κ_1 and κ_2 respectively. Then the polar angle can be indicated by $\kappa = (\kappa_1 - \kappa_2)/2$ and the corresponding ρ can be obtained by Equations (3) and (12). The output link OA moves around the center O with motion 3 with angular displacement of κ_3. To simplify the simulation, the κ_3 is set to zero. Then the deflection angle of the variable stiffness module can be expressed as $\theta = (\kappa_1 + \kappa_2)/2$.

The simulation steps are as follows:

(1) First, adjust the value of ρ with no deformation by the reverse motion of cams C_1 and C_2. The measurement range varies from ρ = 0.008 m to ρ = 0.05 m, with a step of 0.002 m. The motion angle κ_1 and κ_2 of cams C_1 and C_2 are decided by

$$\begin{cases} \kappa_1(\rho) = -\kappa_2(\rho) = \kappa(\rho) = \int_{\rho_{\min}}^{\rho} [\rho \tan(\gamma(\rho))]^{-1} d\rho \\ \gamma(\rho) = 20830\rho^4 - 5303\rho^3 + 531.5\rho^2 - 27.36\rho + 0.864 - 0.25(\rho_{\min}/\rho)^5 \end{cases} \tag{23}$$

A simple example is demoed in Figure 10b, with $\kappa_1 = -\kappa_2$ = 3.14 rad, ρ = 0.0396 m, θ = 0 rad.

(2) Secondly, deform the variable stiffness module with an angle θ by synchronized motion. The maximum θ corresponding to each ρ is shown in Figure 4. It is mainly constrained by the allowable spring angle. Now the motion angle exerted on the cams C_1 and C_2 become

$$\begin{cases} \kappa_1(\rho) = \int_{\rho_{\min}}^{\rho} [\rho \tan(\gamma(\rho))]^{-1} d\rho + \theta \\ \kappa_2(\rho) = -\int_{\rho_{\min}}^{\rho} [\rho \tan(\gamma(\rho))]^{-1} d\rho + \theta \end{cases}$$

A deformed configuration with κ_1 = 3.58 rad, $\kappa_2 = -2.7$ rad, ρ = 0.0396 m, θ = 0.44 rad is exhibited in Figure 10c.

Adams simulation results. The driving torque T_{M1} and T_{M2} exerted on the two cams can be observed as a characteristic of motion 1 and motion 2 in ADAMS. And the output torque τ_e can be obtained from motion 3. For a clear illustration, τ_e is scaled down by 0.5 times. T_{M1} is indicated by the green mesh, T_{M2} the blue mesh and $\tau_e/2$ the yellow mesh, as shown in Figure 11. There is always $0 < T_{M1} < \tau_e/2/ < T_{M2}$ and $T_{M1} + T_{M2} = \tau_e$, i.e., the VSA works with helping mode in the whole working space. The difference between T_{M1} and T_{M2} decreases notably with an increasing ρ, but increases with an increasing deflection angle θ. For quantitative analysis, the load ratio with maximum θ is graphed in Figure 12 (ϕ_{ADMAS}, solid line).

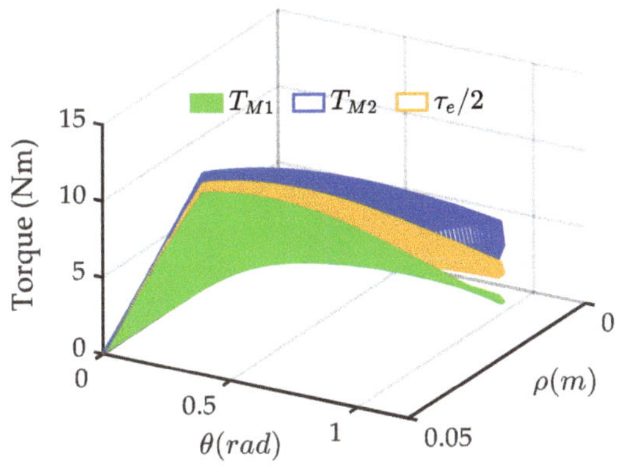

Figure 11. The load distribution observed in ADAMS.

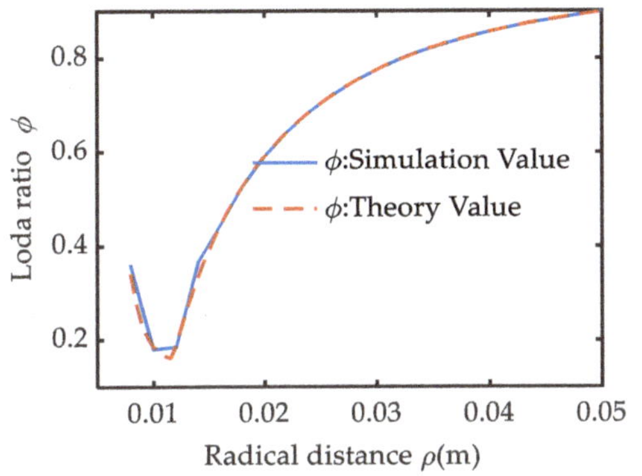

Figure 12. Load ratio comparison between the theory and the ADMAS.

There is a tiny difference between ϕ_{ADMAS} and ϕ_{theory} near $\rho = 0.014$ m. It is caused by the simulation step. For the theory value of load ratio in Equation (20) (ϕ_{theory}), the calculation step is 0.0005 m. And for the ϕ_{ADMAS}, the step is 0.002 m. The influence appears when the ρ-ϕ curve changes sharply in the range of $\rho < 0.016$ m. But its impact becomes very weak in the range of $\rho > 0.016$ m, as the ρ-ϕ curve is gentle in this area. So, we can conclude that the correctness of the cam design method is proved effectively by the load ratio observation in ADAMS. We can conclude that simulation experiments fully verified the correctness of the load distribution design during the deformation process.

4.2. Performance Validation by Physical Prototype

CAD model of a physical prototype. The CAD model is illustrated in Figure 13. The motor M_1 determines the cam C_1 position, and the reduction ratio between the two is 100:29. The motor M_2 devotes to the cam C_2 position and the reduction ratio is 130:47. The cam follower consists of two bearings, the outer rings are respectively arranged in the two cam grooves, and the inner ones are mounted on a common shaft, which is bolted with a slider on guide rod AC. Through the differential movement of the cams, the slider can slide along the guide rod AC to change the radial position and realize the stiffness adjustment. To ensure the compactness of the actuator, the torsion spring at point A is derived from the stiffness adjustment module [35].

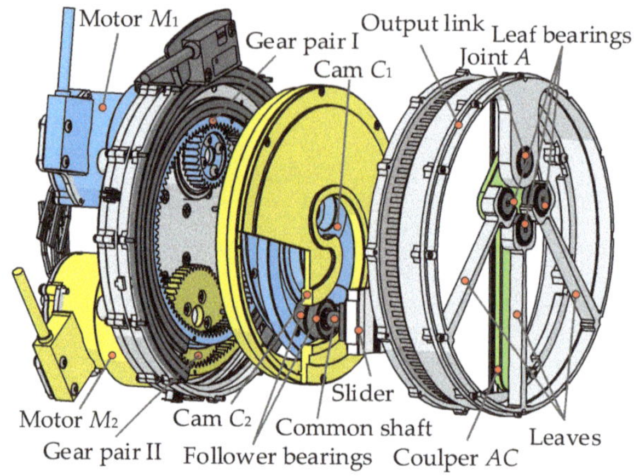

Figure 13. CAD model of the physical prototype.

Physical prototype of reconfigurable cams. The symmetrical cams C_1 and C_2 in Figure 14a,b was machined with the same pitch curve in Figure 10. It focuses on optimal load distribution for output torque enhancement of the VSA. By changing the cam groove shape, the performance of the VSA can be reconfigured, as described in case 1 and case 2.

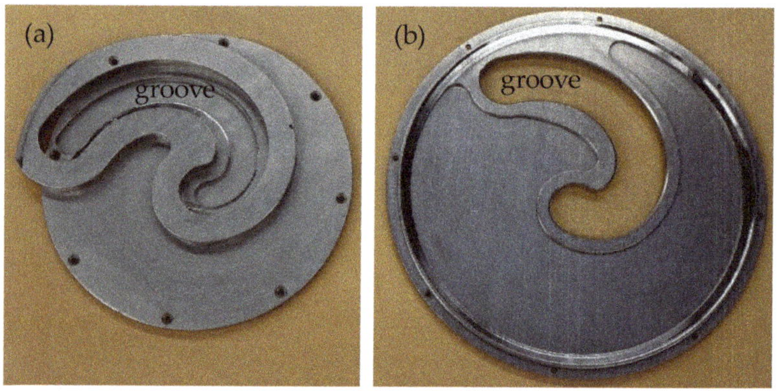

Figure 14. Cam prototype based on optimal load distribution: (**a**) cam C_1; (**b**) cam C_2.

Physical prototype and experiment platform. After the cam group is installed coaxially, a common cam groove is formed. Joint B is set at the common groove through a common shaft (Figure 15a) and its position is decided by the cams' position. By cams differential control, the goal ρ for stiffness adjustment can be set and the stiffness of the VSA would be changed. By cams' synchronous motion, the deformation angle θ changed. To simplify the measurement, both the housing and the output link (Figure 15b) are bolted with the test frame (Figure 15c) Then the ρ and θ can be obtained after reduction ratio calculation with the encoder value of the dual motors. The output torque can be measured through the internal torque sensor between them.

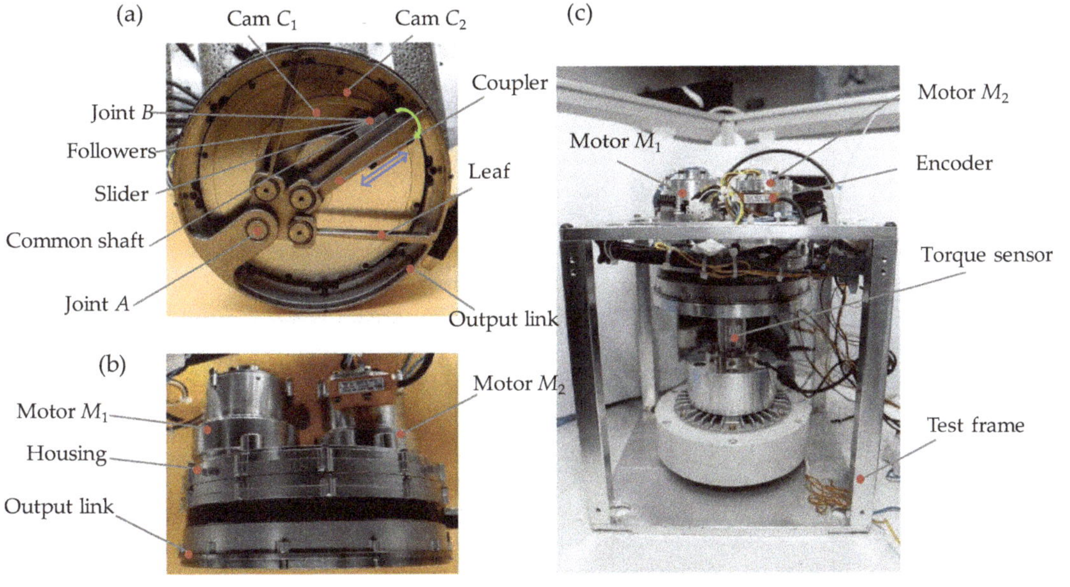

Figure 15. Physical prototype and experiment platform: (**a**) Bottom view of VSA; (**b**) Side view of VSA; (**c**) The test platform.

According to the previous research results [35], the actual stiffness of the manufactured torsion spring is 85 Nm/rad. To avoid overloading the stiffness adjustment module, a matching design of the drive motors is carried out, combined with the load distribution design result in Figure 12. The torque constant of motor M_1 is 36.9 mN/A and that of motor M_2 is 25.1 mN/A. Considering 40% transfer efficiency, the rated driving torque that the motor M_1 can provide to the cam C_1 is 6.12 Nm and the rated torque that M_2 provides to cam C_2 is 6.06 Nm.

Physical prototype performance results. Using a method similar to the ADAMS simulation, the ρ of the VSA is tuned to a certain value by cam differential movement, such as ρ = 0.02 m, ρ = 0.026 m, ρ = 0.032 m, ρ = 0.038 m, ρ = 0.048 m. Then the cams are synchronously driven, and the ρ will remain unchanged in the deformation progress, i.e., the output stiffness remains constant. The force-deformation characteristics of the prototype under different ρ values are shown in Figure 16.

In the direction of the arrow in Figure 16, the output stiffness is respectively 9.4 Nm/rad, 13.19 Nm/rad, 16.89 Nm/rad, 20.17 Nm/rad and 25.28 Nm/rad. For each ρ value, there are two kinds of curves, the loop curve is the actual test result of the output torque, which corresponds to the VSA loading loop; the other curve is the theoretical curve of the force-deformation relationship, which is calibrated according to the force-deformation Equation in (1). The two curves are highly convergent during loading and diverge during unloading. This is mainly due to the elastic hysteresis during unloading, and the elastic hysteresis amplitude is 0.5 Nm. The performance parameters of the prototype are shown in Table 2.

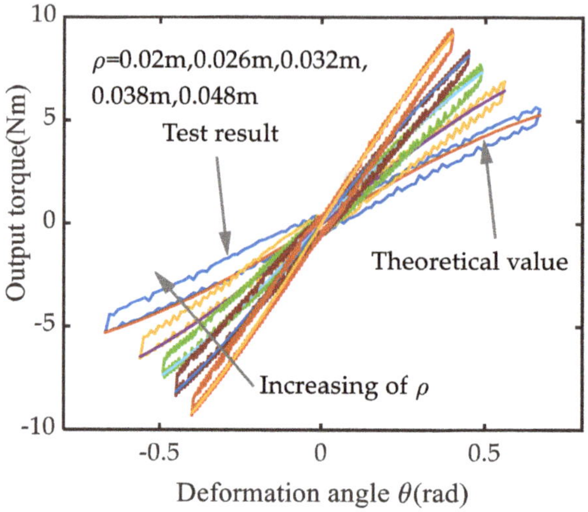

Figure 16. The force-deformation test result in the prototype.

Table 2. Performance of Physical prototype.

Performance (Unit)	Value
Power (W)	60
Radial dimension (mm)	82
Axial dimension (mm)	127
Weight (kg)	2.5
Range of output angle (rad)	-2π~2π
Stiffness adjustment range (Nm/rad)	2.51~26.23
Maximum output torque (Nm)	9.5
Deformability (rad/s)	0.38~1.785
Maximum stiffness adjustment time (s)	1.57

In the direction of the arrow, the value of ρ increases from 0.02 m to 0.048 m. Correspondingly, the deformation is 0.593 rad, 0.523 rad, 0.457 rad and 0.471 rad and the maximum output torque is 5.58 Nm, 6.91 Nm, 7.73 Nm, 8.42 Nm, 9.5 Nm. The changing trend of the maximum output torque corresponds to the load distribution characteristics in Figure 12. When the ρ value is close to 0.048 m, the load ratio is close to 0.82. According to the load distribution Equation in (19), the theoretical maximum output torque is 11 Nm when $\rho = 0.048$ m. The measured maximum output torque is 9.5 Nm. The two are relatively close. The discrepancy between the test results and the theoretical results stems from the fact that the adjustable stiffness module has reached the deformation capacity allowed by its design. It shows that through the optimal design of the load distribution, the torque output performance of the dual motors can be fully utilized, and the output torque of the adjustable stiffness actuator can be enhanced. This verifies the correctness of the load distribution from the aspect of output torque enhancement.

From the obtained results, we can conclude that the proposed VSA interacts with the outside world through the spring and the contact stiffness can be changed from 2.51 Nm/rad to 26.23 Nm/rad. And the deformability verifies from 1.785~0.38 rad correspondingly. This is similar to an artificial muscle, which can be made very soft (2.51 Nm/rad) or very stiff (26.23 Nm/rad), with mechanically controllable flexibility. In a traditional rigid motor, a small contact deformation behavior will generate a huge contact force, which is likely to cause irreversible damage to the person or object in contact with it. However, when VSA performs human-computer interaction, the contact force does not change significantly with the slight change of contact deformation (for example, when the stiffness is 2.51 Nm/rad, the deformation angle changes by 0.1 rad, and the contact force changes only by 0.25 Nm). Besides, it provides enough time for the actuator to respond safely. So, the VSA can improve the safe performance in human-robot interaction.

5. Conclusions

The variable stiffness actuator (VSA) proposed in this paper mainly includes a variable stiffness module and a cam-based actuation module based on two symmetrically arranged cams. The two modules are connected by a common node. And the stiffness is changed by the node's radical distance adjustment. Moreover, the dual cams resolve the contact force into two orthogonal directions, one for stiffness adjustment and another for position balance. By cam reconfiguration, the VSA with different characteristics can be obtained.

A cam shape synthetic approach for VSA reconfiguration has been put forward. The mathematical formulas are established among the VSA's key performance indexes and the key design parameter of the driven cam. It covers the following key factors with a mathematical model for multi-objective optimization, including load distribution, stiffness adjustment speed and accuracy. A bigger pressure angle is helpful to improve the stiffness adjustment speed; a smaller one is better to obtain a favorable load distribution on the dual motors for output power enhancement; the case between the above two can realize a uniform stiffness adjustment accuracy. By reconfiguration of the cam pitch curve, the VSA can be reconfigured depending on its functionality with the external interface unchanged.

Furtherly, the VSA prototype with a favorable load distribution is provided. The design result was verified by the ADAMS simulation and physical prototype experiment effectively. In the ADAMS, the simulation results are highly consistent with the theoretical design results. In the fabricated prototype, the output torque enhancement result verifies the correctness of the load distribution.

At the same time, the proposed new structure also brings challenging problems to the control: the output of the dual motors is cross-coupled, and the load of one motor is a major disturbance term of the dynamic model of the other motor. How to realize the high-precision synchronous control of dual motors under the cross-coupling condition is an important research direction in the future.

Author Contributions: F.M.: conceptualization, methodology, investigation, design, measurement, writing—original draft; S.B.: conceptualization, editing, supervision, funding acquisition review and editing; B.L.: Project administration, Supervision, Writing. All authors have read and agreed to the published version of the manuscript.

Funding: This work was supported by the National Natural Science Foundation of China (Grant No. 52075013) and Fundamental Research Funds for the Central Universities (No. YWF-21-J-913).

Institutional Review Board Statement: The study did not require ethical approval.

Informed Consent Statement: The study did not involve humans.

Data Availability Statement: Not applicable.

Conflicts of Interest: The authors declare no conflict of interest.

References

1. Hong, C.; Tang, D.; Quan, Q.; Cao, Z.; Deng, Z. A combined series-elastic actuator & parallel-elastic leg no-latch bio-inspired jumping robot. *Mech. Mach. Theory* **2020**, *149*, 103814.
2. Liu, L.; Misgeld, B.J.E.; Pomprapa, A.; Leonhardt, S. A Testable Robust Stability Framework for the Variable Impedance Control of 1-DOF Exoskeleton with Variable Stiffness Actuator. *IEEE Trans. Control Syst. Technol.* **2021**, *29*, 2728–2737. [CrossRef]
3. Shao, Y.; Zhang, W.; Su, Y.; Ding, X. Design and optimisation of load-adaptive actuator with variable stiffness for compact ankle exoskeleton. *Mech. Mach. Theory* **2021**, *161*, 104323. [CrossRef]
4. Moltedo, M.; Cavallo, G.; Baček, T.; Lataire, J.; Vanderborght, B.; Lefeber, D.; Rodriguez-Guerrero, C. Variable stiffness ankle actuator for use in robotic-assisted walking: Control strategy and experimental characterization. *Mech. Mach. Theory* **2019**, *134*, 604–624. [CrossRef]

5. Gomez-Vargas, D.; Casas-Bocanegra, D.; Múnera, M.; Roberti, F.; Carelli, R.; Cifuentes, C.A. Variable Stiffness Actuators for Wearable Applications in Gait Rehabilitation. In *Interfacing Humans and Robots for Gait Assistance and Rehabilitation*; Springer: Cham, Switzerland, 2022; pp. 193–212.
6. Li, Z.; Li, W.; Chen, W.H.; Zhang, J.; Wang, J.; Fang, Z.; Yang, G. Mechatronics design and testing of a cable-driven upper limb rehabilitation exoskeleton with variable stiffness. *Rev. Sci. Instrum.* **2021**, *92*, 024101. [CrossRef] [PubMed]
7. Robinson, D.W.; Pratt, J.E.; Paluska, D.J.; Pratt, G.A. Series elastic actuator development for a biomimetic walking robot. In Proceedings of the 1999 IEEE/ASME International Conference on Advanced Intelligent Mechatronics (Cat. No. 99TH8399), Atlanta, GA, USA, 19–23 September 1999; pp. 561–568.
8. de Gaitani, F.H.M.; dos Santos, W.M.; Siqueira, A.A.G. Design and Performance Analysis of a Compact Series Elastic Actuator for Exoskeletons. *J. Control Autom. Electr. Syst.* **2022**, *33*, 1012–1021. [CrossRef]
9. Yang, Z.; Li, X.; Xu, J.; Chen, R.; Yang, H. A new low-energy nonlinear variable stiffness actuator for the knee joint. *Mech. Based Des. Struct. Mach.* **2022**, 1–15. [CrossRef]
10. Christie, M.D.; Sun, S.; Ning, D.H.; Du, H.; Zhang, S.W.; Li, W.H. A highly stiffness-adjustable robot leg for enhancing locomotive performance. *Mech. Syst. Signal Process.* **2019**, *126*, 458–468. [CrossRef]
11. Beckerle, P.; Stuhlenmiller, F.; Rinderknecht, S. Stiffness Control of Variable Serial Elastic Actuators: Energy Efficiency through Exploitation of Natural Dynamics. *Actuators* **2017**, *6*, 28. [CrossRef]
12. Liu, H.; Zhu, D.; Xiao, J. Conceptual design and parameter optimization of a variable stiffness mechanism for producing constant output forces. *Mech. Mach. Theory* **2020**, *154*, 104033. [CrossRef]
13. Albu-Schaffer, A.; Eiberger, O.; Grebenstein, M.; Haddadin, S.; Ott, C.; Wimbock, T.; Wolf, S.; Hirzinger, G. Soft robotics. *IEEE Robot. Autom. Mag.* **2008**, *15*, 20–30. [CrossRef]
14. Li, Z.; Bai, S.; Madsen, O.; Chen, W.; Zhang, J. Design, modeling, and testing of a compact variable stiffness mechanism for exoskeletons. *Mech. Mach. Theory* **2020**, *151*, 103905. [CrossRef]
15. Wolf, S.; Grioli, G.; Eiberger, O.; Friedl, W.; Grebenstein, M.; Höppner, H.; Burdet, E.; Caldwell, D.G.; Carloni, P.; Catalano, M.G.; et al. Variable stiffness actuators: Review on design and components. *IEEE/ASME Trans. Mechatron.* **2015**, *21*, 2418–2430. [CrossRef]
16. Lee, J.H.; Wahrmund, C.; Jafari, A. A Novel Mechanically Overdamped Actuator with Adjustable Stiffness (MOD-AwAS) for Safe Interaction and Accurate Positioning. *Actuators* **2017**, *6*, 22. [CrossRef]
17. Vanderborght, B.; Albu-Schäffer, A.; Bicchi, A.; Burdet, E.; Caldwell, D.G.; Carloni, R.; Catalano, M.; Eiberger, O.; Friedl, W.; Ganesh, G.; et al. Variable impedance actuators: A review. *Robot. Auton. Syst.* **2013**, *61*, 1601–1614. [CrossRef]
18. Li, Z.; Bai, S.; Chen, W.; Zhang, J. Nonlinear Stiffness Analysis of Spring-Loaded Inverted Slider Crank Mechanisms With a Unified Model. *J. Mech. Robot.* **2019**, *12*, 031011. [CrossRef]
19. Moore, R.; Schimmels, J.M. Design of a Quadratic, Antagonistic, Cable-Driven, Variable Stiffness Actuator. *J. Mech. Robot.* **2021**, *13*, 031001. [CrossRef]
20. Li, Z.; Chen, W.; Zhang, J.; Li, Q.; Wang, J.; Fang, Z.; Yang, G. A novel cable-driven antagonistic joint designed with variable stiffness mechanisms. *Mech. Mach. Theory* **2022**, *171*, 104716. [CrossRef]
21. Zhang, M.; Ma, P.; Sun, F.; Sun, X.; Xu, F.; Jin, J.; Fang, L. Dynamic Modeling and Control of Antagonistic Variable Stiffness Joint Actuator. *Actuators* **2021**, *10*, 116. [CrossRef]
22. Govindan, N.; Ramesh, S.; Thondiyath, A. Design of a Variable Stiffness Joint Module to Quickly Change the Stiffness and to Reduce the Power Consumption. *IEEE Access* **2020**, *8*, 138318–138330. [CrossRef]
23. Sun, J.; Guo, Z.; Sun, D.; He, S.; Xiao, X. Design, modeling and control of a novel compact, energy-efficient, and rotational serial variable stiffness actuator (SVSA-II). *Mech. Mach. Theory* **2018**, *130*, 123–136. [CrossRef]
24. Shao, Y.; Zhang, W.; Ding, X. Configuration synthesis of variable stiffness mechanisms based on guide-bar mechanisms with length-adjustable links. *Mech. Mach. Theory* **2021**, *156*, 104153. [CrossRef]
25. Bi, S.S.; Liu, C.; Zhao, H.Z.; Wang, Y.L. Design and analysis of a novel variable stiffness actuator based on parallel-assembled-folded serial leaf springs. *Adv. Robot.* **2017**, *31*, 990–1001. [CrossRef]
26. Li, X.; Zhu, H.; Lin, W.; Chen, W.; Low, K.H. Structure-Controlled Variable Stiffness Robotic Joint Based on Multiple Rotary Flexure Hinges. *IEEE Trans. Ind. Electron.* **2020**, *68*, 12452–12461. [CrossRef]
27. Choi, J.; Hong, S.; Lee, W.; Kang, S.; Kim, M. A Robot Joint with Variable Stiffness Using Leaf Springs. *IEEE Trans. Robot.* **2011**, *27*, 229–238. [CrossRef]
28. Zhu, Y.; Wu, Q.; Chen, B.; Xu, D.; Shao, Z. Design and Evaluation of a Novel Torque-Controllable Variable Stiffness Actuator with Reconfigurability. *IEEE/ASME Trans. Mechatron.* **2021**, *27*, 292–303. [CrossRef]
29. Li, Z.; Bai, S. A novel revolute joint of variable stiffness with reconfigurability. *Mech. Mach. Theory* **2019**, *133*, 720–736. [CrossRef]
30. Mengacci, R.; Garabini, M.; Grioli, G.; Catalano, M.G.; Bicchi, A. Overcoming the torque/stiffness range tradeoff in antagonistic variable stiffness actuators. *IEEE/ASME Trans. Mechatron.* **2021**, *26*, 3186–3197. [CrossRef]
31. Sun, L.; Zhao, W.; Wang, B.; Huang, S.; Li, J. Mechanical design and analysis of a reconfigurable variable stiffness mechanism based on permanent magnetic springs and swing guide mechanism. *Proc. Inst. Mech. Eng. Part C J. Mech. Eng. Sci.* **2022**, 09544062221130205. [CrossRef]
32. Xu, Y.; Guo, K.; Sun, J.; Li, J. Design, modeling and control of a reconfigurable variable stiffness actuator. *Mech. Syst. Signal Process.* **2021**, *160*, 107883. [CrossRef]

33. Qian, Y.; Han, S.; Aguirre-Ollinger, G.; Fu, C.; Yu, H. Design, Modelling, and Control of a Reconfigurable Rotary Series Elastic Actuator with Nonlinear Stiffness for Assistive Robots. *arXiv* **2022**, arXiv:2205.14412.
34. Mei, F.; Bi, S.; Liu, C.; Chang, Q. Optimal Design of Cam Curve Dedicated to Improving Load Uniformity of Bidirectional Antagonistic VSA. In Proceedings of the International Conference on Intelligent Robotics and Applications, Yantai, China, 22–25 October 2021; Springer: Cham, Switzerland; pp. 3–13.
35. Mei, F.; Bi, S.; Chen, L.; Gao, H. A novel design of planar high-compliance joint in variable stiffness module with multiple uniform stress leaf branches on rigid-flexible integral linkage. *Mech. Mach. Theory* **2022**, *174*, 104889. [CrossRef]

mathematics

MDPI

Article

Power Scheduling Optimization Method of Wind-Hydrogen Integrated Energy System Based on the Improved AUKF Algorithm

Yong Wang [1], Xuan Wen [2], Bing Gu [1] and Fengkai Gao [1,*]

[1] Key Laboratory of Modern Power System Simulation and Control & Renewable Energy Technology, Ministry of Education (Northeast Electric Power University), Jilin 132000, China
[2] School of Information Engineering, Nanchang University, Nanchang 330027, China
* Correspondence: fengkaigao@163.com

Abstract: With the proposal of China's green energy strategy, the research and development technologies of green energy such as wind energy and hydrogen energy are becoming more and more mature. However, the phenomenon of wind abandonment and anti-peak shaving characteristics of wind turbines have a great impact on the utilization of wind energy. Therefore, this study firstly builds a distributed wind-hydrogen hybrid energy system model, then proposes the power dispatching optimization technology of a wind-hydrogen integrated energy system. On this basis, a power allocation method based on the AUKF (adaptive unscented Kalman filter) algorithm is proposed. The experiment shows that the power allocation strategy based on the AUKF algorithm can effectively reduce the incidence of battery overcharge and overdischarge. Moreover, it can effectively deal with rapid changes in wind speed. The wind hydrogen integrated energy system proposed in this study is one of the important topics of renewable clean energy technology innovation. Its grid-connected power is stable, with good controllability, and the DC bus is more secure and stable. Compared with previous studies, the system developed in this study has effectively reduced the ratio of abandoned air and its performance is significantly better than the system with separate grid connected fans and single hydrogen energy storage. It is hoped that this research can provide some solutions for the research work on power dispatching optimization of energy systems.

Keywords: AUKF algorithm; integration of wind and hydrogen; UKF; power scheduling

MSC: 68Q25

Citation: Wang, Y.; Wen, X.; Gu, B.; Gao, F. Power Scheduling Optimization Method of Wind-Hydrogen Integrated Energy System Based on the Improved AUKF Algorithm. *Mathematics* **2022**, *10*, 4207. https://doi.org/10.3390/math10224207

Academic Editors: Shujin Laima, Yong Cao, Xiaowei Jin and Hehe Ren

Received: 8 September 2022
Accepted: 2 November 2022
Published: 10 November 2022

Publisher's Note: MDPI stays neutral with regard to jurisdictional claims in published maps and institutional affiliations.

Copyright: © 2022 by the authors. Licensee MDPI, Basel, Switzerland. This article is an open access article distributed under the terms and conditions of the Creative Commons Attribution (CC BY) license (https://creativecommons.org/licenses/by/4.0/).

1. Introduction

With the continuous progress of our society and the development of the economy, the domestic demand for energy is also increasing. The current energy consumption structure has a serious negative impact on environmental protection and the healthy development of the national economy [1]. In particular, coal-based thermal power generation not only causes over-exploitation of coal, but also affects the ecological environment and air quality [2]. Adjusting the existing energy structure is an important measure to promote domestic economic development and improve the ecological environment. At the same time, using renewable energy to replace traditional consumption energy is a way to achieve a safe, economical, and efficient sustainable energy system [3]. The wind-hydrogen integrated energy system is one of the important research directions in the sustainable clean energy system. At present, the utilization method of wind power generation is mainly distributed power generation, which is largely to improve the shortcomings of centralized power generation [4]. Usually, distributed power sources form a micro-grid with multiple systems through topology and act on the main grid. However, there are still many problems in the process of integrating distributed renewable energy into the main power grid, such as reducing the reliability of the power grid and curtailing wind, affecting the reactive power balance of the power grid, and reducing the quality of the power grid. The emergence of key technologies for hydrogen energy storage has effectively promoted the development of distributed power stations and played a key role in the research of distributed energy, especially in the development of fuel cell technology. The hydrogen fuel is supplied to the gas network, which improves the utilization efficiency of wind energy and promotes the development of the wind hydrogen system [5].

At present, the research work of AUKF has become a main direction in the field of energy system power scheduling research; this technology has also attracted the attention of many domestic and foreign scholars. Zhang et al. [6] proposed a robust adaptive UKF (Unscented Kalman Filter) algorithm, based on a fault detection mechanism for estimating the state of distributed-driven electric vehicles, and designed an estimator based on robust adaptive UKF to estimate longitudinal speed, lateral speed, and sideslip angle. Simulation results show that the robust adaptive UKF algorithm can significantly reduce the estimation errors of the three state variables and is superior to the standard UKF algorithm in terms of accuracy and robustness. Ge [7] proposed the information fusion technology based on AUKF and, combined with Markov distance theory, designed a new AUKF scheme to solve the error problem in nonlinear systems. Simulation results show that the proposed method is effective when the process error and measurement noise covariance vary with time. Loukil et al. [8] evaluated the state of charge by means of the Extended Kalman Filter, Unscented Kalman Filter (UKF), and Volumetric Kalman Filter (VKF) online. The open circuit voltage test (OCV) was used to verify the battery model proposed in the study. The results show that the proposed method has better accuracy and robustness and reduces the computational complexity of the traditional algorithm. Yuan et al. [9] proposed a nonlinear internal state observer based on an adaptive volumetric Kalman filter algorithm for estimating the mass of oxygen and nitrogen inside the cathode of an onboard PEMFC system. The performance of the proposed observer is verified, and the results show that the proposed observer has good convergence and accuracy. Yang et al. [10] used a three-axis accelerometer and a three-axis magnetometer measurement system, established a nonlinear model based on quaternion, and proposed an improved adaptive fading square root unscented Kalman filter to eliminate a vibration disturbances signal. The calculation method of the fading factor is optimized, which ensures the adaptability of the algorithm and reduces the computational complexity. The results show that the method can effectively filter out the interference noise in the attitude measurement sensor and improve the solution accuracy of the attitude parameters of the drilling tool in the case of sudden changes in the measurement environment, so as to ensure the dynamic stability of the borehole trajectory. To better describe systems as dynamic entities in dynamic environments and to characterize FLS measurements, Franchi et al. [11] proposed an adaptive unscented Kalman filter (AUKF) based estimator. The results show that the solution passes offline testing and the estimator's predictive validity is validated with navigational sample data.

Therefore, this research first builds a distributed wind hydrogen hybrid energy system model and, on this basis, proposes the power scheduling optimization technology of wind hydrogen integrated energy system based on AUKF and further studies the AUKF power distribution method to better improve the accuracy of the algorithm system and the practicality of application.

2. AUKF Wind-Hydrogen Integrated Energy System Power Scheduling Optimization Method

2.1. Model Construction of Distributed Wind-Hydrogen Hybrid Energy System

A distributed wind-hydrogen hybrid energy system mainly generates electricity through small and medium-sized wind energy and is connected to the grid locally to reduce wind curtailment, thereby improving the utilization rate of battery power storage and hydrogen storage [12]. When the wind energy is connected to the grid and the power is insufficient, the fuel cell will be used to connect the grid. When there is a surplus of wind power, the electrolyzer will be used to absorb and store hydrogen to build a wind-hydrogen integrated energy system [13]. To better study the wind power generation system, the direct drive wind turbine is selected as the research object in this study. Compared with the doubly fed wind turbine, the direct driven wind turbine has a large power density, a wide operating range, and is less affected by the frequency range. In terms of mechanical structure, the direct drive type has a multi-stage structure and does not require a speed increase gearbox. The wind power generation system model in this section is based on the process of wind energy utilization, which includes three parts, physical kinetic energy model, transmission shaft model, and electrical system model. Hydrogen energy storage is an energy storage technology with good development prospects at present. "Hydrogen-electricity" and "electricity-hydrogen" conversion devices are used to control wind power and power supply. The system designed in this study is mainly a distributed common DC bus type. The wind-hydrogen hybrid energy structure is shown in Figure 1.

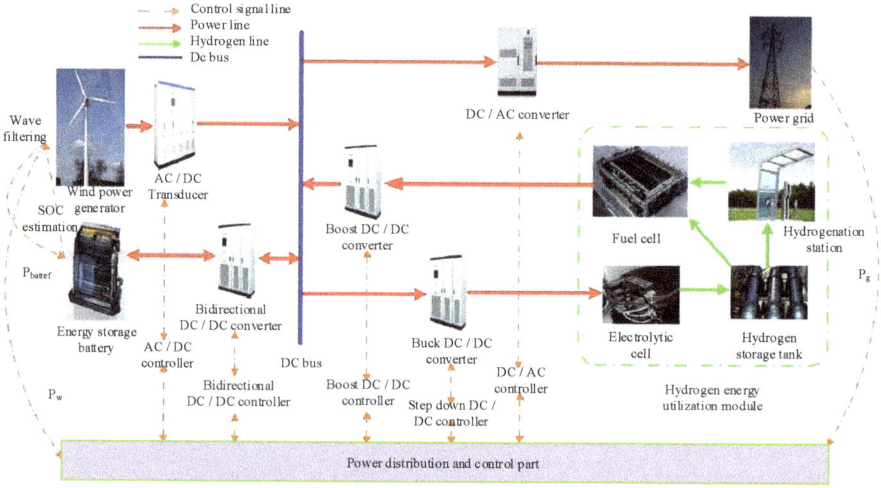

Figure 1. Topology diagram of distributed wind-hydrogen hybrid energy system.

In Figure 1, the Permanent Magent Synchronous Generator (PMSG), Electrolyzer (EL), Fuel Cell (FC), and Battery (Bat) enter the DC bus through the converter. In the energy storage system, the reason for the unbalanced power phenomenon is mainly the dynamic response delay of hydrogen energy storage, which makes the system face the volatility of wind power. This device is used for second-level response operation, assisting EL-FC to perform electric hydrogen-electric cycle operation, so as to ensure that the DC bus can maintain a stable voltage and improve the grid-connected controllability of fans [14]. The stability of the DC bus voltage can only be ensured by keeping the balance of the system's current input and output in the DC capacitor. The calculation of the DC bus capacitor voltage is shown in Formula (1).

$$C_{dc}\frac{dU_{dc}}{dt} = I_{PMSG} + I_{bat} + I_{fc} - I_{el} \tag{1}$$

In Formula (1), C_{dc} represents the DC bus capacitance (F); U_{dc} is DC bus voltage (V); and I_{PMSG}, I_{bat}, I_{fc}, and I_{el} are the currents (A) of PMSG, Bat, FC, and EL, respectively. The system monitors the real-time parameters of each subsystem, allocates power, and operates the control part, so as to judge the current system in real-time and obtain the control signals of each subsystem [15]. When the converter receives the control signal, it assists the system in power distribution to ensure the controllability of the grid-connected power and effectively improve the penetration performance of wind energy.

2.2. Power Dispatching Optimization Technology of Wind-Hydrogen Integrated Energy System

In order to improve the overall accuracy of the model, this study will build the RC link model based on the original Thevenin model, adding the related discipline theory based on polarization resistance and its parallel connection. Set open circuit resistance, polarization internal resistance, and internal resistance as U_{oc}, $R_{pi}(i = 1,2,3)$, and R_o, respectively. The charge and discharge current of the battery, the current on the polarization resistance, and the working voltage of the battery are I, I_p, and Ul. According to the parallel theory of polarization resistance and polarization capacitance, the RC link is formed in parallel. Based on the basic circuit laws and BMS design requirements, the circuit formulas (Ul, R_{pi}) of the RC link of the Thevenin model are obtained, as shown in Formula (2).

$$\begin{cases} Ul = U_{oc} + IR_o + U_{pi} \\ U_{pi} = \frac{1}{C_{pi}R_{pi}}U_{pi} + \frac{1}{C_{pi}}I \end{cases} \quad (2)$$

Assume that the on-time calculation formula of BMS is BMS_k, where k is the time constant, and the state quantity of the BMS system is BMS_0; see Formula (3).

$$BMS_k = BMS_0 + \int_0^t \frac{I(t)}{C_N}dt \quad (3)$$

Set the polarization resistance as U_{p1}, U_{p2}, U_{p3}, and select the constant voltage at the battery end in the BMS system as the observation to obtain the observation equation, as shown in Formula (4).

$$[U_{I,k}] = [1\ 1\ 1\ 0]\left[U_{p1,k}, U_{p2,k}, U_{p3,k}, BMS_k\right] + [R_o][I_{I,k}] + [U_{oc}] + [v_k] \quad (4)$$

In Formula (4), T_s is the sampling time, C_N is the rated capacity of the battery, $v_k \sim (0, R)$ is the observation noise, and $w_{i,k} \sim (0, Q_i)$ is the system noise, where I in the system noise can be 1–4. The battery data is mostly completed under a different battery state of charge (State of charge, SOC) [16]. Therefore, in order to accurately identify the parameters of different models, the Ultimate Tensile Strength (UTS) sub-capacity cabinet was used for research and analysis; the object was a 3.2 Ah 18,650 lithium battery at a room temperature of 25 °C. The third order Thevenin model is used to analyze the constant current charge and discharge parameters. The model design is shown in Figure 2. Wherein, Figure 2a is the third-order Thevenin model, and Figure 2b is the sampling point diagram of the complete pulse discharge process.

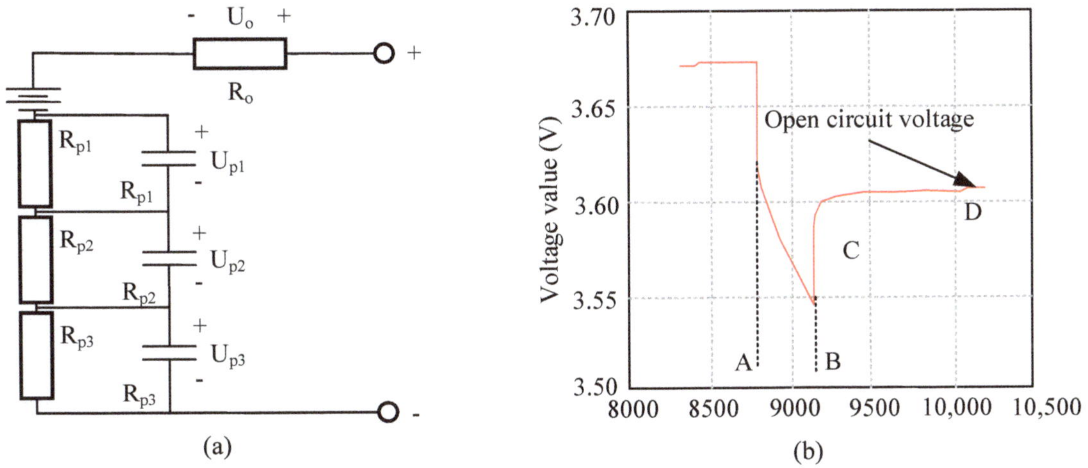

Figure 2. Model and sampling.

The battery charging state of the BMS system is 100.00%. The UTS sub-container set on the UTS sub-capacitor is set to discharge for 6 min (360 s) and then stand for 18 min (1080 s). The discharge pulse current is 0.5 C to ensure that the SOC of the battery decreases by 0.1 each time when it is charged. The experiment was repeated a total of 7 times. Finally, find the functional relationship between open circuit voltage and BMS (SOC) fitted by 7th degree polynomial, as shown in Formula (5). The polynomial fitting functions are all carried out on the basis of Matrix Laboratory (MATLAB) theory [17].

$$\begin{aligned} U_{oc} = & -92.4 \cdot BMS^7 + 267.6 \cdot BMS^6 \\ & -436.1 \cdot BMS^5 + 342.9 \cdot BMS^4 \\ & -140.8 \cdot BMS^3 + 26.7 \cdot BMS^2 \\ & -1.78 \cdot BMS^1 + 3.363 \end{aligned} \tag{5}$$

In Figure 2, A to B is regarded as the corresponding process of discharge of the polynomial fitting function, and B to D is regarded as the corresponding process of its resting. The BMS at a certain time node of the intercepted 7 polynomial fitting functions is 0.5. In this model, the corresponding active range of the RC network in the zero state is mainly in the A to B area. The starting point is point A. Therefore, according to the equivalent circuit model of the battery, the calculation formula of the voltage (U_{RCi}) in the A–B region can be obtained:

$$U_{RCi} = IR_p(1 - e^{-\frac{t}{R_{pi}C_{pi}}}) \tag{6}$$

In Formula (6), the value of RC links of different orders is $i = 1,2,3$. Similarly, if the parameters of the B–D static area are fitted according to the curve fitting function under the MATLAB theory, the voltage calculation method is shown in Formula (7).

$$Ut = b_1 \exp[-c_1(t - t_B)] + b_2 \exp[-c_2(t - t_B)] + b_3 \exp[-c_3(t - t_B)] + U_D + b \tag{7}$$

However, it should be noted that if it is needed to solve the resistance, capacitance, and internal resistance of the RC link, the calculation formulas of R_{pi} and R_0 should be combined to achieve the parameter fitting, as shown in Formula (8).

$$\begin{cases} R_{pi} = \frac{b_1}{I\{1-\exp[-c_1(t_B-t_A)]\}} \\ R_0 = \frac{b}{I} \end{cases} \tag{8}$$

Finally, R_0, the parameter fitting calculation formula related to the BMS function is obtained, as shown in Formula (9).

$$\begin{aligned} R_0 = & -142.46 \cdot BMS^7 + 573.74 \cdot BMS^6 \\ & -826.54 \cdot BMS^5 + 634.99 \cdot BMS^4 \\ & -217.25 \cdot BMS^3 + 90.26 \cdot BMS^2 \\ & -12.56 \cdot BMS^1 + 0.7162 \end{aligned} \tag{9}$$

Figure 3a shows the polarization resistance of RC link, and Figure 3b shows the polarization capacitance of RC link. Formula (9) is used as the parameter fitting calculation formula for the function relationship between R_0 and BMS; finally the polarization resistance and capacitance of the RC link under the third order Thevenin model of the constant current charge-discharge experiment can be obtained. From the above Figure 3a,b, the polarization resistance and capacitance $R_{p1}, C_{p1}, R_{p2}, C_{p2}$ of the RC link under the third order Thevenin model are relatively stable from 0.1 to 0.9. However, the R_{p3}, C_{p3} polarization resistance is relatively stable between 0.1 and 0.9, while the polarization capacitance has a relatively large variation in this area. The reason is that the capacitor is a series-mixed structure, which is affected by factors such as leakage and breakdown. It leads to the abnormality of the equivalent circuit and increases the capacitance loss [18]. In addition, the resistance value of capacitor and DC is infinite, so when leakage or breakdown occur, the DC resistance will decrease.

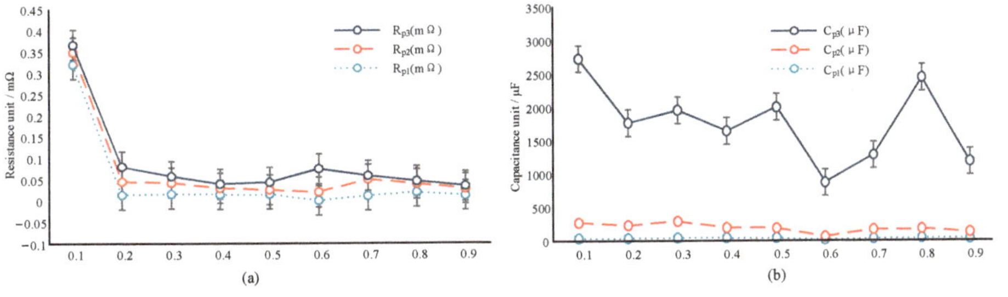

Figure 3. Polarization resistance and capacitance of RC link under the third order Thevenin model.

2.3. *Adaptive Kalman Filtering (AUKF) Power Allocation Method*

In order to improve the power distribution effect of the model proposed in this study, an unscented Kalman filter (UKF) algorithm is firstly proposed, which is a minimum mean square error estimation algorithm based on unscented transform (UT). UKF improves the adaptive performance of traditional Kalman filtering, ensures the accuracy of sampling, and makes known variables consistent with the distribution of probability density. For real-time estimation of battery SOC, charge and discharge monitoring is required during battery operation. Due to the complex electrochemical reaction causing the estimation error of the SOC value, the error will accumulate. The UKF can be adjusted by SOC and various parameters to reduce the influence of the error, and finally calculate the accurate minimum root mean square estimation result. Therefore, a dynamic equivalent circuit model is constructed according to the UKF principle, and error terms ζ and ξ are introduced at the same time, as shown in Formula (10).

$$\begin{cases} soc_{j+1} = h(soc_k, i_k) \\ U_{j+1} = g(soc_k, i_k) \end{cases} \quad (10)$$

where i_k represents three-phase power supply current. Formula (10) is used as the state measurement formula of UKF, and the UKF gain also plays a decisive role in SOC correction. In order to improve the anti-interference of non-Gaussian nature. The errors of SOC and terminal voltage exist in the state vector. Therefore, x_{k-1} is set as the extended state vector and $P^x_{k-1}$is the covariance, so the SOC estimation method is shown in Formula (11).

$$\begin{cases} x_{k-1} = \begin{bmatrix} soc_{k-1} & 0 & 0 \end{bmatrix} \\ P^x_{k-1} = \begin{bmatrix} P_{k-1} & 0 & 0 \\ 0 & \zeta' & 0 \\ 0 & 0 & \xi' \end{bmatrix} \end{cases} \quad (11)$$

In Formula (11), $k = 1, 2, \ldots, \infty$, ξ' and ζ'represent the covariance of the error terms ζ and ξ.

The application of UKF in SOC estimation is the capacity waveform of a fully charged battery discharged at a rate of 1 C. The whole discharge time is 4150 s, with four discharges of 1000 s successively and an interval of 50 s. The SOC estimation algorithm proposed by the model is used to estimate the experimental data. Extended Kalman filter (EKF) is widely used in battery estimation. The initial SOC is based on the UKF algorithm and the standard covariance of the actual value and the initial SOC is 0.1. At the beginning of discharge, a UKF-based algorithm can well estimate the real SOC curve but an EKF-based method cannot estimate the real value of SOC. This shows that EKF is more dependent on the initial value and UKF's algorithm converges faster. In the middle of discharge, the estimation effect of EKF and UKF algorithm is similar. However, at the end of discharge, the EKF algorithm fluctuates greatly and cannot estimate the battery SOC value very well. The same problem does not exist in the UKF algorithm. The fast convergence rate of UKF shows that it is more suitable for nonlinear systems than EKF.

Because the filtering technology in the current project can only perform the power distribution of a specific frequency band, it has certain limitations in application. Additionally, the power input value also has a certain influence on the phase delay and is difficult to meet the grid connection requirements in the application project. Therefore, this study proposes a power allocation method based on AUKF, as shown in Figure 4.

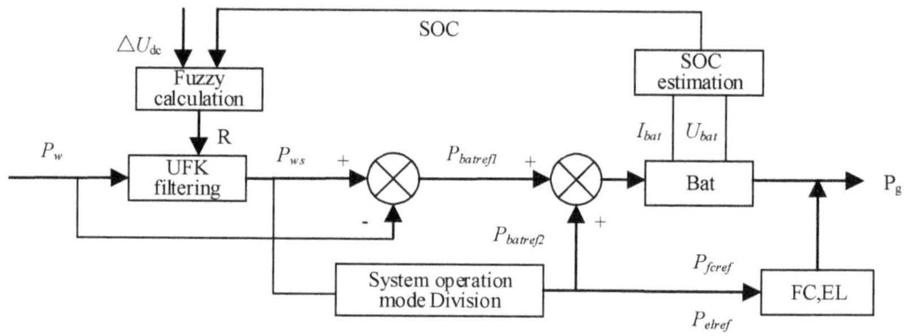

Figure 4. AUKF filter control diagram.

The output power of the fan without the intervention of the energy storage system is expressed as P_w and the smoothed output power after filtering is expressed as P_{ws}. The output power of the wind turbine is obtained after the intervention of the AUKF and represented by P_{ws}. The difference between the output power and the smoothed power is expressed as the fluctuating power of the battery $P_{batref1}$. P_{ws} obtains the power values of EL, FC, and Bat through system operation, which are P_{elref}, P_{fcref}, and $P_{batref2}$, respectively. Among them, $P_{batref2}$ represents the power imbalance caused by the delayed response of FC and EL in the process of hydrogen energy storage, i.e., $P_{batref} = P_{batref1} + P_{batref2}$. When the SOC value is close to the limit, the SOC estimation and the change of the DC bus voltage can indicate the filtering ability of the UKF, so that the SOC value is within the safe range to meet the grid-connected power P_g requirements of the grid.

In practical engineering, if the grid-connected power is not properly limited, when the wind speed is too large, fluctuations in the DC bus voltage will occur, which easily lead to deep charge and discharge. Therefore, the fuzzy control is integrated into the UKF to monitor the SOC and DC bus voltage changes in real time and achieve the power distribution effect based on the AUKF. The SOC is selected as the fuzzy variable, and the input of the model control quantity is selected as the change of the bus voltage relative to the reference value, so as to ensure the stability of the DC bus and ensure the power smoothing performance of the hydrogen energy storage device. The target value calculation of the extension smooth output is shown in Formula (12).

$$\begin{cases} p_k^{y-} = \sum\limits_{i=0}^{2L} w_i^{(c)} (Pw_{i,k|k-1} - P_{wk}^{-})(Pw_{i,k|k-1} - p_{wk}^{-}) + \varphi R(k+1) \\ K_k = p_k^{xy} \left(p_k^{y-}\right)^{-1} \\ (P_{ws})_{k|k} = (\hat{P}_w)_{k|k-1} + K_k[(P_w)_k - (\hat{P}_w)_{k|k-1}] \end{cases} \quad (12)$$

The value of the measured covariance R in UKF affects the smoothing effect of the wind power, that is, when the value of R is small, the change of the measurement equation will have a significant impact on the filtering effect. When R is large, it can cope with wind speed and sudden change of bus voltage. When the change of DC bus is positive, the energy storage system should be in the charging state; otherwise, it should be in the discharging state. The range of battery SOC is considered through fuzzy logic control. When the battery SOC is high and in the charging state or the battery SOC is low and in the discharging state, the target output power of the battery can be changed by reducing R, the difference between the smooth value and the wind power; thus, the power borne by the battery can be reduced. When the SOC of the battery is high and in the discharge state or the SOC of the battery is low and in the charge state, increase R; thus, the power borne by the battery is increased. This can slow down the overcharge and overdischarge of the battery under extreme conditions and can effectively improve the battery life. The difference between the filtered smooth power and the grid load is borne by EL and FC.

As a whole, the distributed wind-hydrogen hybrid system decomposes and coordinates different energy forms in production, transmission, consumption, etc. At the same time, it takes time, space, multiple constraints, and utilization efficiency into account, including the overall coordination and power distribution of the system. In this paper, the grid load is used as the objective function of the system, as shown in Formula (13), to change the nonadjustable generation characteristics of renewable energy.

$$\min f = \sum_{t=t_0}^{T} \left| P_{ws} - P_g + P_{fc} - P_{e1} + P_{bat} \right| \tag{13}$$

In Formula (13), $P_{w\min} \leq P_w \leq P_{w\max}$, $0 \leq P_{fc} \leq P_{fc\max}$, $0 \leq P_{el} \leq P_{el\max}$, $p_{t\min} \leq p_t \leq p_{t\max}$, $U_{dc\min} \leq U_{dc} \leq U_{dc\max}$. $P_{w\min}$, $P_{w\max}$ respectively represent the lower limit and upper limit of the extension power P_w (W). $U_{dc\min}$ and $U_{dc\max}$ represent the lower limit and upper limit of DC bus voltage U_{dc} (V), respectively. $p_{t\min}$ and $p_{t\max}$, represent the lower limit and upper limit of the hydrogen storage tank pressure P_t (kpa). $P_{el\max}$ represents the fuel cell power (W). $U_{dc\max}$ represents the power of the electrolyzer (W).

For the battery energy storage constraint, in addition to considering the SOC operating range, the constraint of charging and discharging times is added. Although the operating range of the battery SOC has been optimized, the limit value of SOC is still a constraint for the safe operation of the battery. The main constraints of the energy storage battery are shown in Formula (14).

$$\begin{cases} P_{bat} \leq Pbatrate \\ SOC_{\min} \leq SOC \leq SOC_{\max} \\ \sum\limits_{t=0}^{n\Delta T} U_{kch} < K_{ch} \\ \sum\limits_{t=0}^{n\Delta T} U_{dis} < K_{dis} \end{cases} \tag{14}$$

In Formula (14), $\Delta T$is the period long term and $n$is the number of periods. K_{dis}, K_{ch}, U_{kch}, and U_{dis} respectively represent the limit value of battery charge and discharge times and the battery charge and discharge times in a certain period of time.

The system model is further divided into different modes to allow the battery to compensate for the delay characteristics of hydrogen energy. According to the grid-connected power and load requirements, let the net power be P_{se}, then $P_{se} = P_{ws} - P_g$. If $P_{ws} < P_g$, then $P_{se} < 0$, it means low wind speed; if $P_{ws} > P_g$ so $P_{se} > 0$, means high wind speed. For the P_{ws} allocation in the energy storage system model, the pressure of the hydrogen storage tank is used as the mode division basis, four modes can be obtained and the final output power of FC, EL, and Bat can be calculated.

When $P_{se} < 0$, the electrolyzer was out of operation and the model was the lack of power. The operating state of FC and Bat was selected by the pressure of the hydrogen storage tank. Mode 1: When the battery is completely supplied with the insufficient power, the SOC is too low and in extreme conditions the battery can be decommissioned. The reference power calculation is shown in Formula (15).

$$\begin{cases} P_{elref} = 0 \\ P_{fcref} = 0, \ p_t \leq p_{t\min} \\ P_{batref2} = \begin{cases} P_{se}, SOC \geq SOC_{\min} \\ 0, SOC \geq SOC_{\min} \end{cases} \end{cases} \quad (15)$$

Mode 2: If $P_{se}$is equal to the FC power, that is, P_{se}less than the maximum power of the FC, then the Bat is affected by the FC delay, which will cause the unbalanced power of the system. See Formula (16) for the reference power calculation.

$$\begin{cases} P_{elref} = 0 \\ P_{fcref} = \begin{cases} P_{fc\max}, P_{t\min} < p_t \cap |P_{se}| \geq P_{fc\max} \\ |P_{se}|, p_{t\min} < \cap |P_{se}| < P_{fc\max} \end{cases} \\ P_{batref2} = \begin{cases} P_{se} + P_{fc}, SOC_{\min} \leq SOC \leq SOC_{\max} \\ 0, SOC < SOC_{\min} \cup SOC > SOC_{\max} \end{cases} \end{cases} \quad (16)$$

When $P_{se} > 0$, the fuel cell was out of operation, the system model still had residual power, and the operating state of FC and Bat was selected by the pressure of the hydrogen storage tank.

Mode 3: When the EL operation is affected by the high pressure of the hydrogen storage tank, the Bat absorbs all the remaining power. When the SOC is too high, and in extreme conditions, the battery can be de-operated. The reference power calculation is shown in Formula (17).

$$\begin{cases} P_{fcref} = 0 \\ P_{elref} = 0, \ p_t \leq p_{t\max} \\ P_{batref2} = \begin{cases} P_{se}, SOC \leq SOC_{\max} \\ 0, SOC > SOC_{\max} \end{cases} \end{cases} \quad (17)$$

Mode 4: If $P_{se}$is less than the EL power, that is, P_{se} is less than the maximum power of the EL, then the Bat is affected by the EL delay, which will cause the unbalanced power of the system. See Formula (18) for the reference power calculation.

$$\begin{cases} P_{fcref} = 0 \\ P_{elref} = \begin{cases} P_{el\max}, P_t < p_{t\max} \cap P_{se} \geq P_{el\max} \\ P_{se}, p_t < p_{t\max} \cap P_{se} < P_{el\max} \end{cases} \\ P_{batref2} = \begin{cases} P_{se} + P_{el}, SOC_{\min} \leq SOC \leq SOC_{\max} \\ 0, SOC < SOC_{\min} \cup SOC > SOC_{\max} \end{cases} \end{cases} \quad (18)$$

3. Verification and Analysis of Power Dispatching Optimization of Wind Hydrogen Integrated Energy System

3.1. Grid-Connected Simulation When the Wind Turbine Is Connected to the Grid Alone and the Battery Is Only Filtered

In order to verify the AUKF power allocation strategy, this section establishes the above system model based on the MATLAB/simulink platform. The simulation uses the real wind speed data and average load data of a wind farm. In order to meet the repeatability and accuracy of the results, the simulation arrangements are as follows: (1) First, conduct the simulation when the fan is connected to the grid separately and provide the tracking of other parameters of the fan. (2) In order to verify the compensation effect of the battery on the delay characteristics of the hydrogen energy device, the simulation is carried out for the case that the battery only filters and does not bear the unbalanced power generated by hydrogen storage. (3) In order to verify the effectiveness of the strategy in this paper, in the simulation, in order to extend the battery life, the operating range of the battery SOC is set to 0.2–0.8. Therefore, the initial value SOC0 of the battery SOC is set to 0.2 and 0.8 to compare the results. Finally, the voltage fluctuation of DC bus is given.

First, the estimated and reference values of battery terminal voltage and SOC are analyzed, as shown in Figure 5. Wherein, Figure 5a shows the estimated value and reference value of battery terminal voltage, and Figure 5b shows the estimated value and reference value of SOC. Under the influence of noise, the accuracy of the voltage prediction values under the above three algorithms during battery operation fluctuates slightly. The estimated value of the improved AUKF algorithm is very close to the estimated value of the UKF algorithm and is relatively far from the estimated value of the PF algorithm, suggesting that the BMS estimation model based on the improved AUKF algorithm is more accurate. From the perspective of SOC estimation, compared with the UKF algorithm and PF algorithm, the improved AUKF algorithm has higher prediction accuracy for SOC estimation.

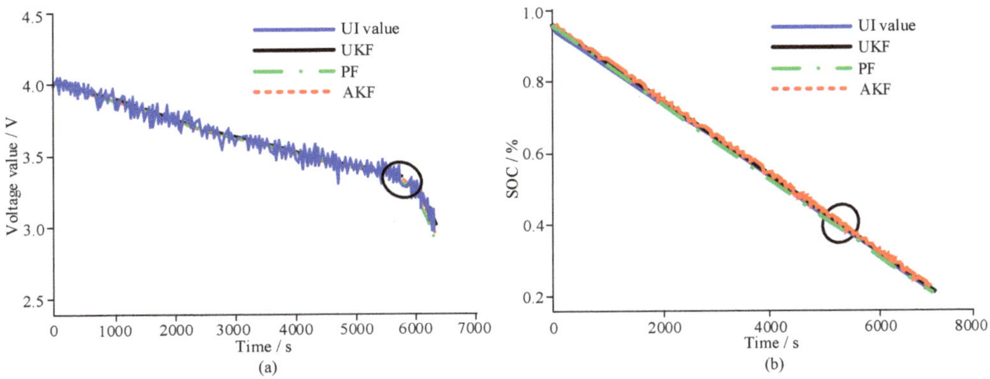

Figure 5. Estimated and reference values of battery terminal voltage and SOC

A separate grid-connected simulation is carried out through the fan parameters. The grid load demand power and grid-connected power are shown in Figure 6. It can be seen from Figure 6 that there is a big difference between the power demanded by the grid load and the grid-connected power. Additionally, the requirements for the system distribution control performance are high. These two curves can judge the stability and security of the system effectively. In 0–2.0 min, 2.2–4.6 min, 11.7–14.1 min, and some other time periods, high-power loads were put into use without energy storage equipment, and the phenomenon of power shortage occurred. At 7.1–8.2 min, the wind speed changed greatly but the load power did not fluctuate. At this time, there was a large residual power in the system. After 13.9 min, the system load demand is less, and there is also a large residual power. Therefore, load changes and sudden changes in wind speed seriously affect the stability of the system power, resulting in unstable operation of the power grid. When the wind turbine is connected to the grid alone, the tracking results of parameters such as dq-axis current and torque show that the wind turbine has a better operation effect.

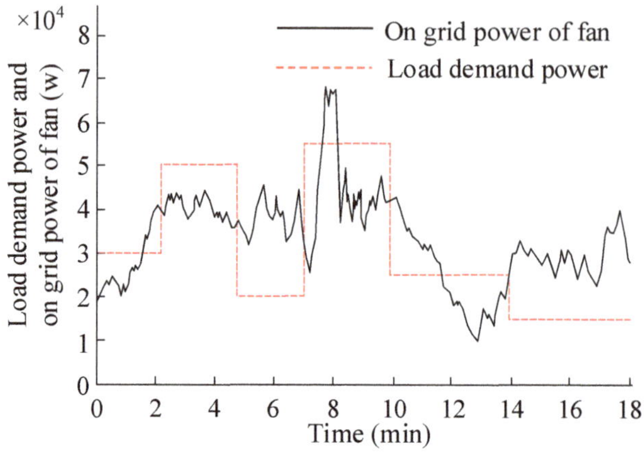

Figure 6. Comparison diagram of load demand and grid connected power of wind turbine.

When the same load demand and wind speed are the same, the grid-connected power of the system after the hydrogen energy device is added to the system as Figure 7. Wherein, Figure 7a shows SOC_0 are 0.2 and Figure 7b shows SOC_0 are 0.8. The battery only needs to bear the fluctuating power of AUKF and does not compensate the delay strategy of FC and EL. When the values of SOC_0 are 0.2 and 0.8, the grid-connected power of the system is much smaller than the individual grid-connected power of the fans. When the value of SOC_0 is 0.8, the stability of grid-connected power is poor, mainly because the system discharge and battery capacity are limited, so that the system absorbs less fluctuating power, thus improving the instability of grid connected power (>0.2). Usually, the system is affected by the pressure of the hydrogen storage tank and the response delay of the hydrogen energy storage, so that the grid-connected power of the system is continuously affected. From the results in Figure 7, it can be seen that the difference between the on-grid power of the wind turbine and the load demand of the grid can be effectively compensated by the battery, and the delay characteristic causes that when the SOC_0 is 0.8 and 0.2, there are surplus power (7.1min) and shortage power (7.9min) respectively, reflecting the weak ability of EL and FC to respond to changes in wind speed.

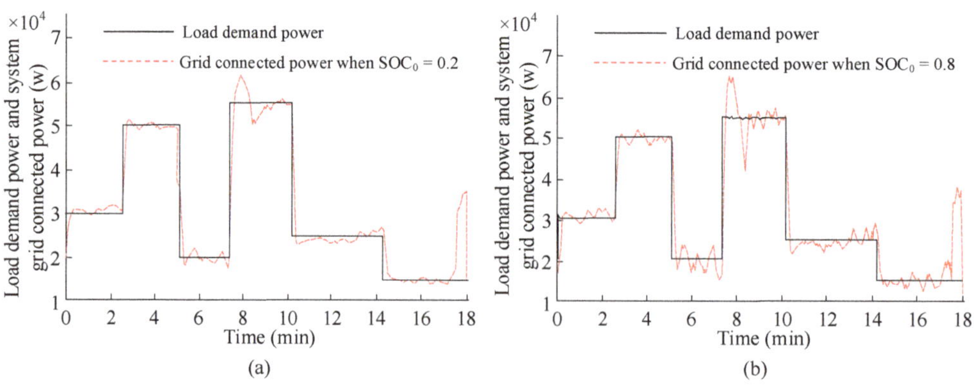

Figure 7. Grid connection of hydrogen energy storage under different conditions.

3.2. Grid-Connected Simulation of Battery Filtering and Delay Compensation

To verify the ability of the adaptive UKF power allocation strategy, this section establishes the above system model based on the MATLAB/simulink platform. The simulation uses the real wind speed data and average load data of a wind farm. In the same simulation environment, the grid-connected power time curve of the system is shown in Figure 8. The results show that, when the SOC_0 is 0.8 and 0.2, the system can continuously and stably track the load demand of the grid connected power, so that the system operates in dynamic balance. Additionally, the power distribution meets the load demand of the grid connected power, with strong stability, which is better than the independent hydrogen storage system.

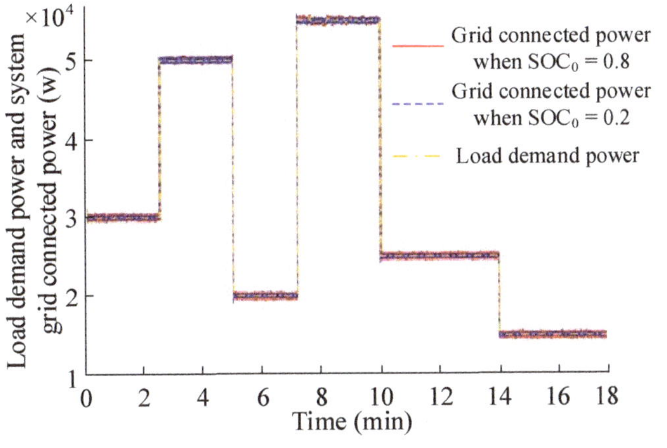

Figure 8. Load demand power and system grid connected power.

The FC and EL power change curves in the whole simulation time period are shown in Figure 9. Wherein, Figure 9a shows FC SOC_0 are 0.2, Figure 9b shows FC SOC_0 are 0.8, Figure 9c shows EL SOC_0 are 0.2, Figure 9d shows EL SOC_0 are 0.8. In Figure 9a, when the SOC_0 is 0.2, the FC start-up is lower than the required time limit. The fuel cell is operated at 0 min, 2.49 min, 7.21 min, etc. Due to the large density of hydrogen, the throughput time of the power grid is extended, so that the FC delays. In Figure 9b, when the SOC_0 is 0.8, the fuel cell is operated at 0 min, 2.49 min, 7.21 min, etc., and the SOC is high; the battery needs to bear more power shortage to reduce the SOC. So, FC is burdened with lower vacancy power. Within 2 min after the system is running, the battery power is lower than Figure 9a and the slope is too large. Figure 9a is consistent with the highest power in Figure 9b, indicating that the system is in a safe operating state when the system is operating to an intermediate period. In Figure 9c, when the SOC_0 is 0.2, at 1.95 min, 5.04 min, 7.89 min, etc., there is residual power in the system. The electrolytic cell cannot track in real time, resulting in unbalanced power. At 17.4–18.1 min, the pressure of the hydrogen storage tank is the highest and the EL return delay is delayed. In Figure 9d, when the SOC_0 is 0.8, the power absorbed by the battery is relatively low, so the power burden of the electrolytic cell is relatively large during this period. When SOC_0 is 0.8, the electrolytic cell has been put into operation for 1.8 min, which is affected by the fuel cell operation delay. At this time, the EL power increases from 0 to 1.02 kW, which is higher than the corresponding position (0.84 kw) in Figure 9c. At the same time, the power values are higher than the corresponding position power in Figure 9c at 5.8 min, 7.8 min, 10.0 min, and 13.9 min. The change of electrolytic cell power at other times is affected by SOC and bus voltage state.

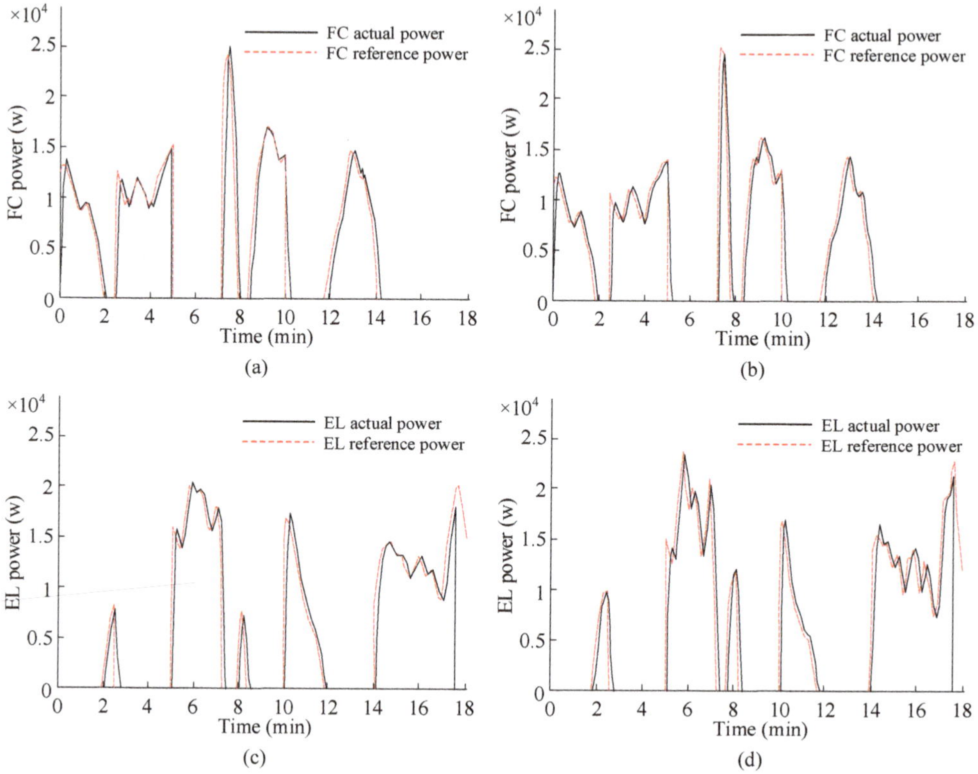

Figure 9. FC and EL power change curve.

The power borne by FC and EL is relatively smooth after filtering, which can prolong the service life of system equipment. The research and analysis show that when the SOC_0 is 0.2, the hydrogen storage tank pressure of the system is too large after 4.8 min, which will cause the battery to return; the SOC will return in about 17.6 min in any case. This shows that the fuel cell plays a role in the system's remaining power and shortage power; however, the gap between the minimum and maximum power is small, so the allocation strategy proposed in this study will not further increase the equipment capacity.

The SOC curve of the energy storage battery changes, as shown in Figure 10. Wherein, Figure 10a shows SOC_0 are 0.2, Figure 10b shows SOC_0 are 0.8. When the SOC_0 is 0.2, the battery is charged and discharged only through the system's remaining and lacking power. The overdischarge phenomenon occurs in 7.2–10.3 min, when SOC is 0.179. After adopting the security strategy, the SOC value remains above 0.2. When the SOC_0 is 0.8, the battery is at the upper limit critical value, the SOC rises rapidly, and the SOC value reaches 0.85 after 18 min. After adjustment by the security policy, the SOC value remains below 0.8.

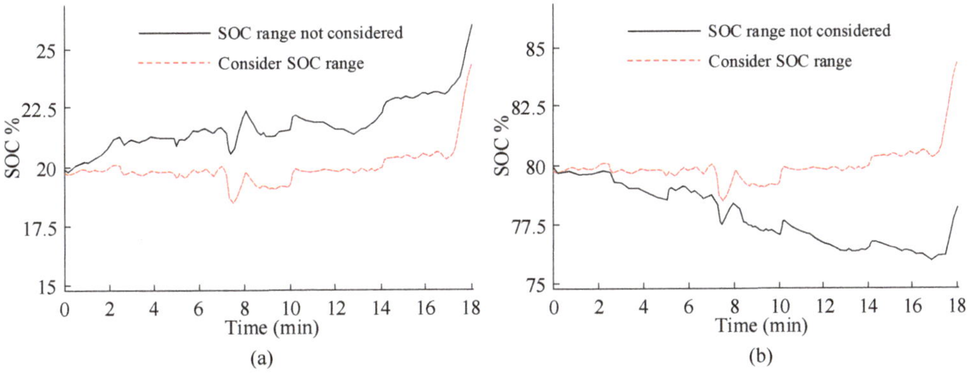

Figure 10. Battery SOC change curve.

Then, the influence of the method proposed in this study on the DC bus voltage of the system is analyzed, as shown in Figure 11. Wherein, Figure 11a represents the change curve of DC bus, Figure 11b represents the change curve of reactive power, and Figure 11c represents the change of DC bus under different algorithms. The results show that under the action of the PI controller, the DC bus voltage and reactive power curves are basically consistent with the reference values. When the SOC_0 is 0.8 and 0.2 and the wind speed changes greatly, the DC bus voltage of the system can be stabilized at 800 V, which has strong stability, reflecting that the proposed distribution strategy can slow down the overcharge and discharge of the battery and also stabilize the voltage of the DC bus. Figure 11c shows the voltage curve of the DC bus obtained by different algorithms. The stability in the period of 7.1–9.7 min is small. Therefore, if the adaptive control method is not used, the performance of the KF filter and the first-order low-pass filter algorithm is poor. This leads to the large fluctuation of the DC bus, which has a great impact on the safe operation of the power grid.

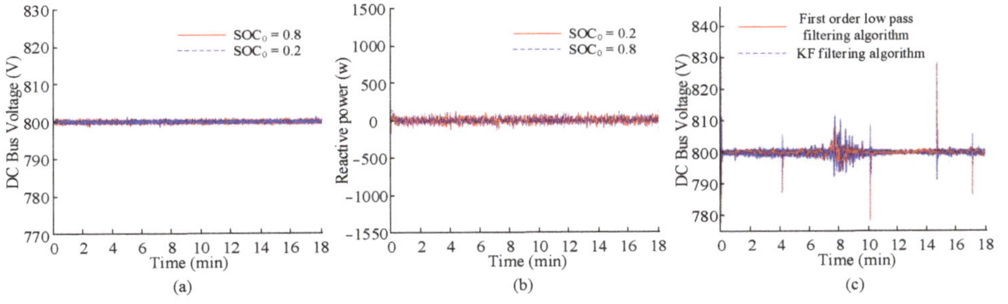

Figure 11. FC and EL power change curve.

4. Conclusions

To solve the power dispatching optimization problem of the wind-hydrogen integrated energy system, this research constructs a distributed wind-hydrogen hybrid energy system model, proposes the power dispatching optimization technology of the wind-hydrogen integrated energy system, and finally constructs a power allocation strategy based on the AUKF algorithm. The results show that when SOC_0 is 0.8 and 0.2, when the wind speed changes greatly, the DC bus voltage of the system can be stabilized at 800 V. The system can obtain continuous and stable tracking of grid connected power on load demand, which makes the system operate in dynamic balance, and the power distribution meets the load demand of grid connected power; reflecting that the proposed distribution strategy can slow down the overcharge and overdischarge of the battery and also stabilize the DC bus voltage. It is superior to the independent hydrogen energy storage system. When the SOC_0 is 0.2, the battery is charged and discharged only through the system's remaining and lacking power. The overdischarge phenomenon occurs between 7.2 and 10.3 min, when the SOC is 0.179. After adopting the security strategy, the SOC value remains above 0.2. When the SOC_0 is 0.8, the battery is at the upper limit critical value, the SOC rises rapidly, and the SOC value reaches 0.85 after 18 min. After the adjustment of the safety strategy, the SOC value is kept below 0.8. The DC bus voltage curve obtained by using different algorithms is less stable in the 7.1–9.7 min period, so the method proposed in this study can meet the grid connection power requirements and the expected goal of smoothing the power of hydrogen energy devices. However, this paper only conducts simulation, lacks hardware support, and directly determines the system configuration based on the difference between wind power and load. The capacity optimization simulation verification of the simulation system will become a new topic in the next step.

Author Contributions: Conceptualization, Y.W.; methodology, Y.W.; software, Y.W. and X.W.; validation, Y.W., X.W. and B.G.; formal analysis, Y.W. and B.G.; investigation, Y.W. and B.G.; resources, F.G.; data curation, X.W. and F.G.; writing—original draft preparation, Y.W.; writing—review and editing, Y.W. and X.W.; visualization, X.W.; supervision, B.G.; funding acquisition, X.W. All authors have read and agreed to the published version of the manuscript.

Funding: This research was funded by 2022 Open Fund Project of Beijing Key Laboratory of Demand Side Multi-Energy Carriers Optimization and Interaction Technique, (Research on Optimal Operation of Integrated Energy Systems with Hydrogen Storage System Considering Source-load Uncertainty, YDB51202201360).

Data Availability Statement: The data used to support the findings of this study are available from the corresponding author upon request.

Conflicts of Interest: The authors declare no conflict of interest.

References

1. Gallego, A.J.; Sánchez, A.J.; Berenguel, M.; Camachoa, E.F. Adaptive UKF-based model predictive control of a Fresnel collector field. *J. Process Control.* **2020**, *85*, 76–90. [CrossRef]
2. Liu, G.; Xu, F. Application of robustly adaptive UKF algorithm in ground-based bearings-only tracking for space targets. *Xi Tong Gong Cheng Yu Dian Zi Ji Shu/Syst. Eng. Electron.* **2018**, *40*, 623–629.
3. Bing, Z.; Xu, J.; Miao, W.; Bian, H.; Li, J. Robust adaptive UKF approach for underwater moving base initial alignment. *Yi Qi Yi Biao Xue Bao/Chin. J. Sci. Instrum.* **2018**, *39*, 73–80.
4. Wang, N.; Li, L.; Wang, Q. Adaptive UKF-Based Parameter Estimation for Bouc-Wen Model of Magnetorheological Elastomer Materials. *J. Aerosp. Eng.* **2019**, *32*, 04018130. [CrossRef]
5. Zhang, M.D.; Dai, H.F.; Hu, B.Q.; Chen, C. Robust adaptive UKF based on SVR for inertial based integrated navigation. *Def. Technol.* **2020**, *16*, 846–855. [CrossRef]
6. Li, Y.; Qiao, X.; Wu, H.; Zheng, L.; Zhang, Z. State estimation of distributed electric vehicle based on robust adaptive UKF. *Sci. Sin. Technol.* **2020**, *50*, 1461–1473. [CrossRef]
7. Wang, D.; Zhang, H.; Ge, B. Adaptive Unscented Kalman Filter for Target Tacking with Time-Varying Noise Covariance Based on Multi-Sensor Information Fusion. *Sensors* **2021**, *21*, 5808. [CrossRef] [PubMed]
8. Loukil, J.; Masmoudi, F.; Derbel, N. A real-time estimator for model parameters and state of charge of lead acid batteries in photovoltaic applications. *J. Energy Storage* **2021**, *34*, 102184. [CrossRef]
9. Yuan, H.; Dai, H.; Wei, X.; Ming, P. A novel model-based internal state observer of a fuel cell system for electric vehicles using improved Kalman filter approach. *Appl. Energy* **2020**, *268*, 115009. [CrossRef]
10. Yang, Y.; Li, F.; Gao, Y.; Mao, Y. Multi-Sensor Combined Measurement While Drilling Based on the Improved Adaptive Fading Square Root Unscented Kalman Filter. *Sensors* **2020**, *20*, 1897. [CrossRef] [PubMed]
11. Franchi, M.; Ridolfi, A.; Zacchini, L. 2D Forward Looking SONAR in Underwater Navigation Aiding: An AUKF-based strategy for AUVs. *IFAC-PapersOnLine* **2020**, *53*, 14570–14575. [CrossRef]
12. Hu, G.G.; Gao, B.B.; Zhong, Y.M.; Gu, C. Unscented Kalman filter with process noise covariance estimation for vehicular INS/GPS integration system. *Inf. Fusion* **2020**, *64*, 194–204. [CrossRef]
13. Gan, X.S.; Gao, W.M.; Dai, Z.; Liu, W.D. Research on WNN soft fault diagnosis for analog circuit based on adaptive UKF algorithm. *Appl. Soft Comput.* **2017**, *50*, 252–259.
14. Cheng, J.; Wang, T.; Wang, L.; Wang, Z. A New Polar Transfer Alignment Algorithm with the Aid of a Star Sensor and Based on an Adaptive Unscented Kalman Filter. *Sensors* **2017**, *17*, 2417. [CrossRef] [PubMed]

15. Han, C.; Yang, Y.; Yang, T.; Qin, Y.; Che, Y. Parameter estimation of slow potassium dynamics in a neuron model for seizure-like activity via adaptive lag synchronization and unscented Kalman filter. *Int. J. Mod. Phys. B* **2019**, *33*, 1950159. [CrossRef]
16. Lee, X.Y.; Gao, G.W. An improved algorithm of UKF-SLAM based on RBF neural network adaptive robot. *J. Phys. Conf. Ser.* **2019**, *1325*, 012017. [CrossRef]
17. Peng, S.; Zhu, X.; Xing, Y.; Shi, H.; Cai, X.; Pecht, M. An adaptive state of charge estimation approach for lithium-ion series-connected battery system. *J. Power Sources* **2018**, *392*, 48–59. [CrossRef]
18. Asl, R.M.; Hagh, Y.S.; Palm, R. Robust control by adaptive non-singular terminal sliding mode. *Eng. Appl. Artif. Intell.* **2017**, *59*, 205–217.

Σ mathematics

MDPI

Article

Gain-Switched Short Pulse Generation from 1.55 μm InAs/InP/(113)B Quantum Dot Laser Modeled Using Multi-Population Rate Equations

Hilal S. Duranoglu Tunc [1], Nuran Dogru [2,*] and Erkan Cengiz [2]

[1] Radio Frequency and Photonics Engineering, Dresden University of Technology, 01069 Dresden, Germany
[2] Electrical and Electronics Engineering, University of Gaziantep, 27310 Gaziantep, Turkey
* Correspondence: dogru@gantep.edu.tr; Tel.: +90-342-3172132

Abstract: The gain-switching properties of an InAs-InP (113)B quantum dot laser based on multi-population rate equations are examined theoretically in detail to generate shorter pulses with the application of a Gaussian pulse beam to the laser excited state. The numerical results demonstrated that as the homogeneous and the inhomogeneous broadening increase, the differential gain, the gain compression factor, and the threshold current of the excited state decrease while the threshold current of the ground state increases. It was also observed that the contribution of the excited state to gain-switched output pulses depend on not only the value of the inhomogeneous broadening but also the magnitude of the applied current. Additionally, it was found that without an optical beam, the output pulse has a long pulse width due to ground state emissions and the change in the parameters strongly affecting the output. However, under the optical beam, narrow pulses around 26 ps have high peak power owing to the excited state emission generated even at low currents and also the change in the laser parameters having a negligible effect. Finally, the gain-switching characteristics with and without a Gaussian pulse beam are shown to be similar for liner-gain and nonlinear-gain cases except that higher peak power and narrower output pulses are obtained for the linear-gain case.

Keywords: gain-switching; semiconductor laser; quantum-dot; homogeneous-broadening; inhomogeneous-broadening; pulse generation

MSC: 78M99; 65M99

Citation: Tunc, H.S.D.; Dogru, N.; Cengiz, E. Gain-Switched Short Pulse Generation from 1.55 μm InAs/InP/(113)B Quantum Dot Laser Modeled Using Multi-Population Rate Equations. *Mathematics* **2022**, *10*, 4316. https://doi.org/10.3390/math10224316

Academic Editors: Shujin Laima, Yong Cao, Xiaowei Jin and Hehe Ren

Received: 22 September 2022
Accepted: 24 October 2022
Published: 17 November 2022

Publisher's Note: MDPI stays neutral with regard to jurisdictional claims in published maps and institutional affiliations.

Copyright: © 2022 by the authors. Licensee MDPI, Basel, Switzerland. This article is an open access article distributed under the terms and conditions of the Creative Commons Attribution (CC BY) license (https://creativecommons.org/licenses/by/4.0/).

1. Introduction

Quantum dot lasers have superior features compared to quantum well counterparts [1–4] such as temperature independence, a low threshold current [5], they can be operated with low chirp for both ground state (Grs) and excited state (Exs) lasing [4], and have better resistance values for optical feedback [6]. The feature of being relatively insensitive to temperature makes quantum dot (Q-Dot) lasers avoid the need for thermoelectric coolers [7]. Since these mentioned features mean that Q-Dot lasers are compact, cheap, lightweight, and low power systems, they are appropriate candidates for applications in optical communications [7].

Low-cost directly adjustable lasers will play an important role in next-generation telecommunication links for developing uncooled and non-insulating communication devices. As a result, Q-Dot lasers are very promising for such applications. In optical communication systems, a 1.55 μm light source is required because of the low loss in transmission. InGaAs-GaAs Q-Dot devices do not allow laser emissions over 1.45 μm, which causes information loss in long-distance transmissions. For this reason, to achieve standard long-distance transmission, one uses long-haul optical transmission at a wavelength of up to 1.55 μm. Consequently, one chooses the InAs-InP(113)B Q-Dot lasers with the InAs Q-Dot laser grown on an InP substrate that emits at a wavelength of 1.55 μm [3,8,9]. Owing to their simple fabrication methods and low manufacturing costs, the gain-switched semiconductor laser diodes are preferred over their counterparts. Therefore, in this study, we used the gain-switching method to obtain short pulses. To date, although several studies have been performed to investigate 1.55 μm InAs-InP Q-Dot lasers, to the best of our knowledge, no detailed work has been performed under the gain-switching condition for InAs-InP Q-Dot lasers based on multi-population rate equations involving nonlinear gain. For this, an external optical Gaussian beam (EOGB) was applied to the excited state (Exs) of the Q-Dot laser with current injection to the wetting layer (Wly) to investigate the properties of the gain-switched pulses. Although, Q-Dot lasers have superior performance, they cannot always satisfy the expected features in reality due to the homogeneous and inhomogeneous broadenings and the gain compression factor [10–12]. To obtain an appropriate and suitable approach to experimental results theoretically, as many aspects of real experiments as possible should be taken into account when performing the simulation. For this, the effect of the homogeneous and the inhomogeneous broadening with the effect of the gain compression were taken into consideration in this study. Therefore, this paper is organized as follows: Section 2 introduces the theoretical description of multi-population rate equations for the direct relaxation model considering the nonlinear-gain case. The obtained results discussed in Section 3 show that by applying an EOGB into the Exs, very short pulses, with a pulse width of around 26 ps and high peak power, are generated due to the Exs emissions at low currents. In addition, it was shown that the contribution of excited state to gain-switched output pulses does not depend on only the value of the inhomogeneous broadening but also on the magnitude of the applied current. Furthermore, the effect of homogeneous and inhomogeneous broadening on the differential gain, the gain compression factor, and the threshold current is also investigated. Finally, our results are summarized and concluded in Section 4.

2. Materials and Methods

The laser model used in this study for InAs-InP(113)B Q-Dot is based on the multi population rate equations for the direct relaxation model described in [2,11,13]. The laser carrier and photon density equations were solved by the fourth order Runge–Kutta method using MATLAB software to investigate the carrier dynamics in the two lowest energy levels, Grs and Exs. The initial values of carrier and photon densities were taken to be a zero. A stimulated emission term was also added to the Exs to allow lasing from both states. The effect of temperature and carrier loss were neglected in the study. We assumed that the carriers were directly injected from the contacts to the Wly; therefore, the carrier dynamics were not considered in the barrier. Direct transition from the Wly to the Grs was introduced to reproduce the experimental results [2,11,13]. The Q-Dot active region consists of the Q-Dots ensemble having different sizes. In the model, in order to consider the effect of the inhomogeneous broadening (Γ_{ihom}), the Q-Dot ensemble is divided into 2X + 1 groups, depending on their resonant energies for the interband transition [14,15]. Figure 1 shows the relaxation mechanisms in the xth Q-Dot subgroup. Energies of Exs and Grs of xth Q-Dot are represented as E_{Exs_x} and E_{Grs_x}, respectively. As a result, the longitudinal cavity photon modes of up to 2P + 1 are constructed in the cavity [13]. When the index x is equal to X, this situation corresponds to the central Q-Dot group. When index p is equal to P, this case corresponds to the central mode with the transitional energies of E_{Exs0} and E_{Grs0} for Exs and Grs, respectively. Each Q-Dot group energy width (ΔE) and mode energy separation (ΔE_p) are assumed to be equal and taken to be as 1 meV [13]. The xth Q-Dot group energy and pth mode energies are indicated by:

$$E_{Exs\_x,Grs\_x} = E_{Exs0,Grs0} - (X - x)\Delta \mathrm{E} \quad x = 1, 2, \ldots, 2X + 1, \tag{1}$$

$$E_{Exs\_p\,,\ Grs\_p} = E_{Exs0,Grs0} - (P - p)\Delta E_p \quad p = 1, 2, \ldots, 2P + 1, \tag{2}$$

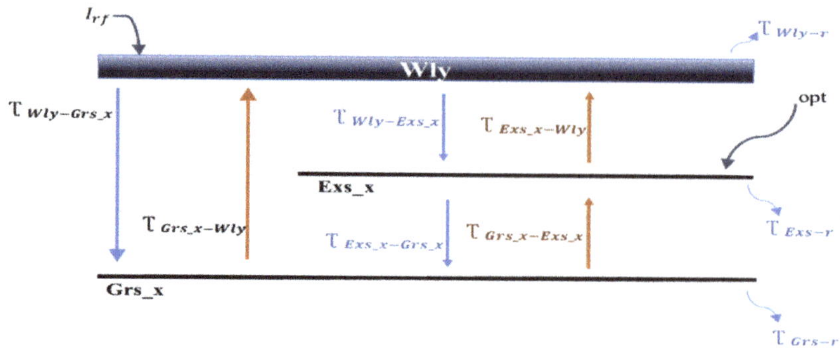

Figure 1. Schematic representation of carrier dynamics for xth QD subgroup.

When injection current I is applied to the Wly of the Q-Dot laser, some carriers move to the lower state E_{Exs-x} and E_{Grs-x} with a capture time of $\tau_{Wly-Exs\_x}$ for the transition from the Wly to E_{Exs_x} and a relaxation time of $\tau_{Wly-Grs\_x}$ for the Wly to the E_{Grs_x} transition. Some photons are emitted from the Wly due to spontaneous emission over a time τ_{Wly-r}. However, in the Exs, some carriers are relaxed into the E_{Grs_x} with a relaxation time $\tau_{\text{Exs\_x}-\text{Grs\_x}}$. Furthermore, the more energetic carriers are thermally transferred to the Wly with a time $\tau_{\text{Exs\_x}-\text{Wly}}$. The other carriers recombine spontaneously with an emission time $\tau_{\text{Exs}-\text{r}}$ or by the stimulated emission of photons. The same mechanism for the carrier dynamics transitions is applied at the Grs level. The same processes occur for the carrier population in the Grs level with regard to the Exs.

The capture and relaxation times can be calculated [13] as:

$$\tau_{Wly-Exs\_x} = \frac{1}{(A_{Wly} + C_{Wly}N_{Wly})(1 - f_{Exs\_x})(G_{xExs})}, \quad (3)$$

$$\tau_{Exs\_x-Grs\_x} = \frac{1}{(A_{Exs} + C_{Exs}N_{Wly})(1 - f_{Grs\_x})}, \quad (4)$$

$$\tau_{Wly-Grs\_x} = \frac{1}{(A_{Wly} + C_{Wly}N_{Wly})(1 - f_{Grs\_x})(G_{xGrs})}, \quad (5)$$

Here, N_{Wly} is the carrier density in the Wly, $A_{Wly,Exs}$, $C_{Wly,Exs}$ are the phonon and Auger coefficients in the Wly and Exs, respectively. Their values are estimated experimentally [16]. $f_{Exs\_x,\ Grs\_x}$ is the occupation probabilities in xth group of Q-Dot in the Exs and Grs.

$$f_{Exs\_x} = \frac{N_{Exs\_x}}{\mu_{Exs}N_oG_{xExs}}, f_{Grs\_x} = \frac{N_{Grs\_x}}{\mu_{Grs}N_oG_{xGrs}}, \quad (6)$$

$\mu_{Exs,\ Grs}$ is the degeneracy of the Exs and Grs,
N_o is the Q-Dot density and
$N_{Exs\_x,\ Grs\_x}$ is the carrier density in the Exs and Grs of xth Q-Dot.
$G_{xExs,\ xGrs}$ is the density rate of xth Q-Dot in the Exs and Grs.

To calculate $G_{xExs,\ xGrs}$, the Q-Dot size distribution is assumed to be a Gaussian function given as:

$$G_{xExs,xGrs} = G_{inh,Exs,Grs}(E_{Exs\_x,Grs\_x} - E_{Exs0,Grs0})\Delta E, \quad (7)$$

$$G_{inh,Exs,Grs}(E_{Exs\_x,Grs\_x} - E_{Exs0,Grs0}) = \frac{1}{\sqrt{2\pi}\sigma} exp\left(-\frac{(E_{Exs\_x,Grs\_x} - E_{Exs0,Grs0})^2}{2\sigma^2}\right), \quad (8)$$

The full-width half-maximum of the Gaussian function is given as Γ_{inh} = 2.35 σ. In other words, Γ_{inh} is described as inhomogeneous broadening. The carrier escape time is related to the carrier capture time [17] and given as:

$$\tau_{Exs\_x-Wly} = \tau_{Wly-Exs\_x}\frac{\mu_{Exs}}{\mu_{Wly}}e^{(E_{Wly}-E_{Exs\_x})/k_BT}, \tag{9}$$

$$\tau_{Grs\_x-Wly} = \tau_{Wly-Grs\_x}\frac{\mu_{Grs}}{\mu_{Wly}}e^{(E_{Wly}-E_{Grs\_x})/k_BT}, \tag{10}$$

$$\tau_{Grs\_x-Exs\_x} = \tau_{Exs\_x-Grs\_x}\frac{\mu_{Grs}}{\mu_{Exs}}e^{(E_{Exs\_x}-E_{Grs\_x})/k_BT}, \tag{11}$$

where μ_{Wly} is the degeneracy of the Wly, k_B is the Boltzmann constant, T is the temperature, and E_{Wly} is the energy of the Wly.

Change in the carrier density in the Wly, Exs, and Grs and change in the photon density in the Exs and Grs for the multi-modes rate equations are given as:

$$\frac{dN_{Wly}}{dt} = \frac{I}{qV} + \sum_x \frac{N_{Exs\_x}}{\tau_{Exs\_x-Wly}} + \sum_x \frac{N_{Grs\_x}}{\tau_{Grs\_x-Wly}} - \frac{N_{Wly}}{\overline{\tau_{Wly-Exs}}} - \frac{N_{Wly}}{\overline{\tau_{Wly-Grs}}} - \frac{N_{Wly}}{\tau_{Wly-r}}, \tag{12}$$

$$\begin{aligned}\frac{dN_{Exs\_x}}{dt} &= \frac{N_{Wly}}{\overline{\tau_{Wly-Exs\_x}}} + \frac{N_{Grs\_x}(1-f_{Exs\_x})}{\tau_{Grs\_x-Exs\_x}} - \frac{N_{Exs_x}}{\tau_{Exs_x-Grs_x}} - \frac{N_{Exs_x}}{\tau_{Exs_x-Wly}} - \frac{N_{Exs_x}}{\tau_{Exs-r}} - \\ &\Gamma v_g \sum_p g_{pxExs}S_{Exsp} + \Gamma v_g \frac{(1-f_{Exs_x})g_{pxExs}}{(2f_{Exs_x}-1)}opt,\end{aligned} \tag{13}$$

$$\frac{dN_{Grs\_x}}{dt} = \frac{N_{Wly}}{\overline{\tau_{Wly-Grs}}} + \frac{N_{Exs\_x}}{\tau_{Exs\_x-Grs\_x}} - \frac{N_{Grs_x}(1-f_{Exs_x})}{\tau_{Grs_x-Exs_x}} - \frac{N_{Grs_x}}{\tau_{Grs_x-Wly}} - \frac{N_{Grs_x}}{\tau_{Grs-r}} - \Gamma v_g \sum_p g_{pxGrs}S_{Grsp}, \tag{14}$$

V is the volume, q is the charge, Γ is the confinement factor, and v_g is the group velocity. $\overline{\tau_{Wly-Exs}}$, and $\overline{\tau_{Wly-Grs}}$ indicate the average capture times from the Wly to Exs and from the Wly to Grs in Q-Dot ensemble. They are defined as follows:

$$\overline{\tau_{Wly-Exs}} = \sum_x \frac{1}{\left(A_{Wly} + C_{Wly}N_{Wly}\right)(1-f_{Exs\_x})(G_{xExs})}, \tag{15}$$

$$\overline{\tau_{Wly-Grs}} = \sum_x \frac{1}{\left(A_{Wly} + C_{Wly}N_{Wly}\right)(1-f_{Grs\_x})(G_{xGrs})}, \tag{16}$$

Nonlinear gain in Exs and Grs is given as:

$$g_{pxExs} = \mu_{Exs}\frac{\pi q^2\hbar}{cn_r\varepsilon_0 m_0^2}N_o\frac{\left|P^{\sigma}_{Exs}\right|^2}{E_{Exs\_x}}(2f_{Exs\_x}-1)G_{xExs}L_{Exs}\left(E_{Exs\_p}-E_{Exs\_x}\right)\frac{1}{1+\varepsilon_{Exsp}S_{Exsp}}, \tag{17}$$

$$g_{pxGrs} = \mu_{Grs}\frac{\pi q^2\hbar}{cn_r\varepsilon_0 m_0^2}N_o\frac{\left|P^{\sigma}_{Grs}\right|^2}{E_{Grs_x}}(2f_{Grs\_x}-1)G_{xGrs}L_{Grs}\left(E_{Grs\_p}-E_{Grs\_x}\right)\frac{1}{1+\varepsilon_{\ Grsp}S_{Grsp}}, \tag{18}$$

c, ε_o, $\hbar$, n_r, and m_o are the speed of light, dielectric constant in free space, Planck constant, refractive index of active medium, and free mass of electron, respectively. $\left|P^{\sigma}_{Exs,\ Grs}\right|^2$, is the transition matrix element [10] and it is estimated approximately at $2m_oE_{Exs0,Grs0}$ for InAs [17]. $S_{Exs\_p,\ Grs\_p}$ is the photon density of the pth mode emitted from Exs and Grs. The homogeneous broadening of the stimulated emission process is assumed to be Lorentzian such that $L_{Exs,Grs}\left(E_{Grs\_p}-E_{Grs\_x}\right)$,

$$L_{Exs,Grs}\left(E_{Exs\_p,\ Grs\_p}-E_{Exs\_x,\ Grs\_x}\right) = \frac{\Gamma_{hom}/\pi}{\left(E_{Exs\_p,\ Grs\_p}-E_{Exs\_x,\ Grs\_x}\right)^2 + \left(\Gamma_{hom}\right)^2}, \tag{19}$$

Γ_{hom} is the full-width half-maximum of homogeneous broadening.

The gain saturation parameter, $\varepsilon_{Exsp,Grsp}$ of the Exs and Grs, is given as:

$$\varepsilon_{Exsp,\ Grsp} = \frac{hq^2\tau_p \left|P^{\partial}_{Exs,\ Grs}\right|^2}{2n_r^2\epsilon_0 m_0^2\ E_{Exs\_p,\ Grs\_p}} L_{Exs,\ Grs}\left(E_{Exs\_p,\ Grs\_p} - E_{Exs0,\ Grs0}\right), \quad (20)$$

where τ_p is the photon lifetime and it is computed from the following equations:

$$\frac{1}{\tau_p} = v_g[\alpha_{int} + \frac{1}{2L}\ln(\frac{1}{R1R2})], \quad (21)$$

where R1 and R2 are the reflectivities of the mirrors and L is the length of the laser. α_{int} is the internal loss, while the mirror loss is calculated using to the equation: $\ln(1/R1R2)/(2Ln_r)$.

$L_{Exs,Grs}\left(E_{Exs\_p,Grs\_p} - E_{Exs0,Grs0}\right)$ in Equation (20) is the Lorentzian function and given as:

$$L_{Exs,Grs}\left(E_{Exs\_p,\ Grs\_p} - E_{Exs0,\ Grs0}\right) = \frac{\Gamma_{hom}/\pi}{\left(E_{Exs\_p,\ Grs\_p} - E_{Exs0,\ Grs0}\right)^2 + (\Gamma_{hom})^2}, \quad (22)$$

The photon density in Exs and Grs is expressed as:

$$\frac{dS_{Exsp}}{dt} = \Gamma v_g \sum\nolimits_x g_{pxExs} S_{Exsp} - \frac{S_{Exsp}}{\tau_p} + \beta \sum\nolimits_x \left(L_{Exs}\left(E_{Exs_p} - E_{Exs_x}\right) \frac{N_{Exs}}{\tau_{Exs-r}} \right) \Delta E_p, \quad (23)$$

$$\frac{dS_{Grsp}}{dt} = \Gamma v_g \sum\nolimits_p g_{pxGrs} S_{Grsp} - \frac{S_{Grsp}}{\tau_p} + \beta \sum\nolimits_x \left(L_{Grs}\left(E_{Grs\_p} - E_{Grs\_x}\right) \frac{N_{Grs}}{\tau_{Grs-r}} \right) \Delta E_p, \quad (24)$$

where β is the spontaneous coupling factor. opt in Equation (13) is the photon density due to the applied EOGB to Exs in a round-trip time $\tau_{RT} = 2\ L/v_g$. This term is equal to the number of photons per second per volume irradiating the Exs level in a single round-trip.

$$opt = \frac{P_i(2L/v_g)}{qE_{Exs\_x}V}, \quad (25)$$

P_i indicates the applied peak power of the Gaussian pulse to Exs.

The parameters used in the simulations are given in Table 1. The values of these parameters were obtained from [13,18–20].

In the algorithm, firstly the constant values and parameters of the laser are determined from Table 1. After that, since the process repeats for every Q-Dot and every mode, the number of modes (i.e., p) and number of Q-Dots (i.e., x) are defined. As a result, the created simulation consists of three intertwined loops. Before starting all loops, the current is applied to the Wly of the laser. The outermost loop returns as many as the number of quantum dots we have determined (here, our results are relevant to three Q-Dots). In this loop, the energy differences are found with Equation (1). Inside the quantum dot loop, there is a second loop that is repeated according to the mode number. Within the mode loop, the energy differences between the modes are calculated by Equation (2). After these steps are completed, the homogeneous and inhomogeneous broadenings are calculated using Equations (8) and (19). By using the calculated homogeneous and inhomogeneous broadenings and the equations that are numbered as Equations (17), (18) and (20), the material gain and gain compression factor of Exs and Grs are calculated. After that, the third loop that provides the calculation of carrier and photon densities of Exs and Grs is started. In this loop, the rate equations defined as Equations (12)–(14), (23) and (24) are solved using fourth order Runge–Kutta Method. When this loop is completed, the photon and carrier density values of the relevant mode of the related quantum dot is reached. Then, the loops repeated by the number of modes and repeated by the number of quantum dots are finished, respectively. In our study, three Q-Dots and three modes were examined and, according to this algorithm, there are three modes for each Q-Dot. Since there are three Q-Dots, the center Q-Dot corresponds to the second Q-Dot. Similar to other Q-Dots, there are three modes for the second Q-Dot. Additionally, the results are written using the modes of the center Q-Dot (it is the second Q-Dot for our simulation). The sum of the modes can be calculated by summing the three modes taken from the second Q-Dot.

Table 1. Q-Dot laser parameters.

Cavity length, L 0.245 cm
Cavity width, w 12 μm
Confinement factor, Γ 0.025
Quantum dot density, No 6 × 10^{16} cm^{-3}
Refractive index, nr 3.27
Cavity internal loss, αint 6 cm^{-1}
Mirror reflectivity, R1, R2 0.95, 0.05
Spontaneous emission ofWly, τwr 500ps
Spontaneous emission of Exs, τer 500ps
Spontaneous emission of Grs, τp 1.2ns
Photon lifetime, τr 8.92 ps
Spontaneous coupling factor, β 1 × 10^{-4}
Emission energy of Wly, Ewly 1.05 eV
Emission energy of Exs, Eexs 0.840 eV
Emission energy of GS, Egrs 0.792 eV
Phonon relaxation of Wly, Awly 1.35 × 10^{10} s^{-1}
Auger coefficient of Wly, Cwly 5 × 10^{-9} cm^3s^{-1}
Phonon relaxation of Wly, Aexs 1.5 × 10^{10} s^{-1}
Auger coefficient of Exs, Cexs 9 × 10^{-8} cm^3s^{-1}
Degeneracy of Grs, Exs, Wly, μgrs, exs, wly 2,4,10
Operating frequency, f 1 GHz
Wavelength, λ 1.55 μm
Homogeneous broadening, Γhom 15 meV
Inhomogeneous broadening, Γihom 45 meV

3. Discussion and Results

A 1.55 μm InAs-InP (113)B Q-Dot laser was used in the simulation. The following equation was used to calculate the applied AC current I, with frequency f, and amplitude $I_{\rm rf}$ [21,22].:

$$I(t) = \frac{I_{rf}}{2}(|\cos(2\Pi ft)| - \cos(2\Pi ft)),$$

Unlike previous studies, here, the nonlinear gain was included in multi-population rate equations.

X and P are taken as X = P = 1 (i.e., it was assumed that there are three Q-Dot ensembles) and an $\Gamma_{\rm hom}$ of 15 meV and $\Gamma_{\rm ihom}$ of 45 meV has been used in the following results unless stated otherwise. For these values the gain compression factor, $\varepsilon_{Exsp,\ Grsp}$ is calculated as 7.8 × 10^{-16} cm^3 for Exs and Grs. To observe the radiation simultaneously from both Exs and Grs, the I_{rf} was taken to be 40 mA in the simulations.

Since $\Gamma_{\rm hom}$ and $\Gamma_{\rm ihom}$ affect the threshold current ($I_{\rm th}$), the differential gain and the gain compression factor [10,12], first without EOGB, and the effect of $\Gamma_{\rm hom}$ and $\Gamma_{\rm ihom}$ on these mentioned parameters were investigated. Subsequently, an EOGB was applied to the Exs to observe how the optical beam illumination affects the gain-switching output pulses.

The $I_{\rm th}$ was calculated as 30 mA for Exs and 2 mA for Grs for the linear-gain case ($\varepsilon_{\rm Exs,Grs} = 0$) (see Figure 2a); 21 mA for Exs and 2 mA for Grs for the nonlinear-gain case ($\varepsilon_{\rm Exs,Grs} \neq 0$) were obtained (see Figure 2b). The total threshold current (Grs + Exs) for both cases was calculated as 2 mA. As seen in Figure 2b, deviation from Figure 2a due to $\varepsilon_{\rm Exs,Grs}$ is because of the direct relaxation from the Wly to Grs.

$\Gamma_{\rm ihom}$ changes between 30 and 80 meV at room temperature [23,24], therefore, we changed it from 30 meV to 80 meV. In this case, $\Gamma_{\rm hom}$ is taken as to be 15 meV at room temperature [11]. Similarly, since the range of Γ_{hom} is between 10 and 30 meV [2], Γ_{hom} is changed from 10 to 30 meV and Γ_{ihom} is taken to be 45 meV.

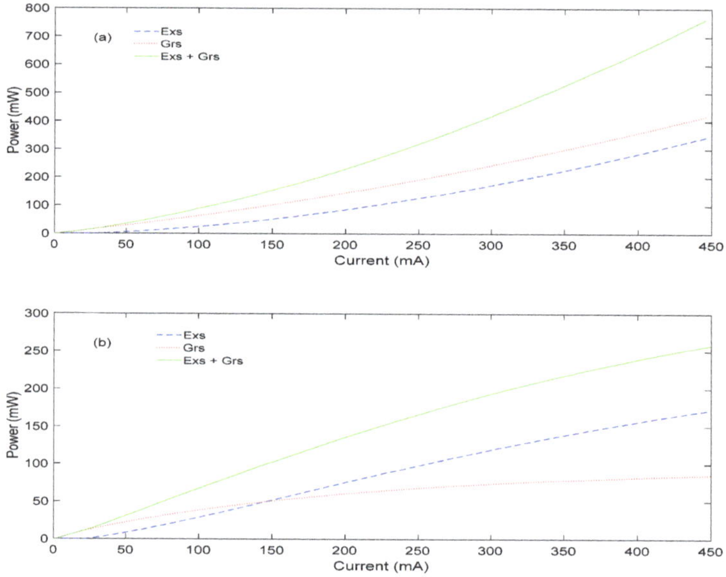

Figure 2. Output power vs. dc current without applying EOGB to the Exs, (**a**) $\varepsilon_{Exs,Grs} = 0$ (**b**) $\varepsilon_{Exs,Grs} \neq 0$.

For the center subgroup of the Q-Dot (second subgroup), when Γ_{ihom} is changed from 30 meV to 80 meV, as the I_{th} of Exs drops from 27 mA to 10 mA the I_{th} of Grs increases from 1 mA to 6 mA (see Figure 3). If Γ_{ihom} is greater than 70 meV, the threshold current increases as the photon density of Grs decreases and finally the threshold currents of Grs and Exs become the same at 11 mA. The effect of Γ_{ihom} on the differential gain is shown in Figure 4. As seen in the figure, as Γ_{ihom} increases, the differential gain of Exs and Grs decreases. Similar results were also observed in [12].

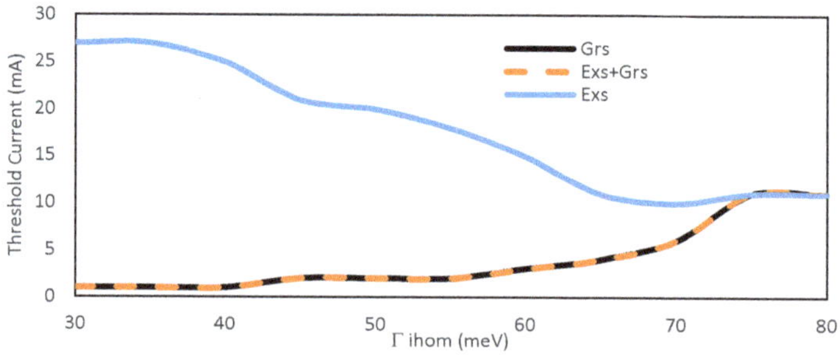

Figure 3. Variation of the threshold current as a function of Γ_{ihom}.

The behavior of Γ_{hom} on I_{th} and on differential gain is similar to that of Γ_{ihom}, providing similar differential gain characteristics as in Figure 4 when Γ_{hom} is increased from 10 meV to 30 meV. For the center subgroup of the Q-Dot, as Γ_{hom} is increased from 10 meV to 30 meV, I_{th} of Exs decreases up to 22.5 meV (dropping from 26 mA to 10 mA) and after that point it slightly increases. I_{th} of Grs increases from 1 mA to 6 mA (see Figure 5). When Γ_{hom} is greater than 22.5 meV the photon density of Grs decreases, whereas the threshold current increases, yielding a threshold current of 14 mA, which is equal to that of the Exs. Figure 6 indicates the effect of Γ_{hom} on the gain compression factors of Exs and Grs. As seen in the figure, the gain compression factor decreases with the increasing Γ_{hom}.

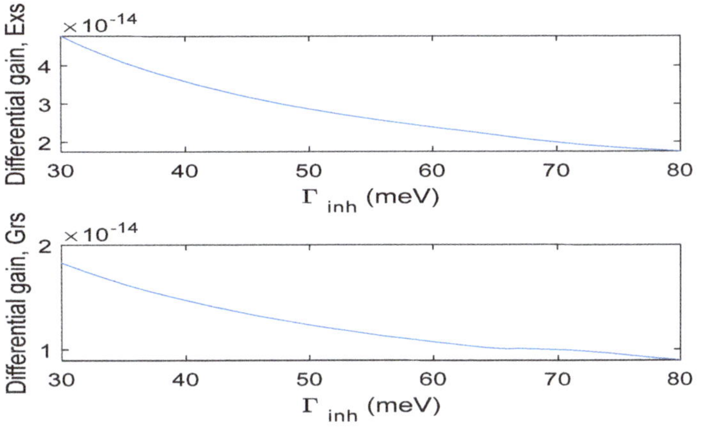

Figure 4. Variation of differential gain as a function of the Γ_{ihom} for I_{rf} = 40 mA.

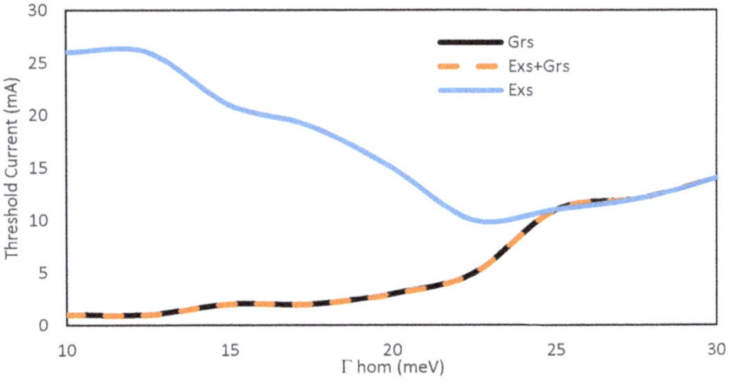

Figure 5. Variation of the threshold current as a function of Γ_{hom}.

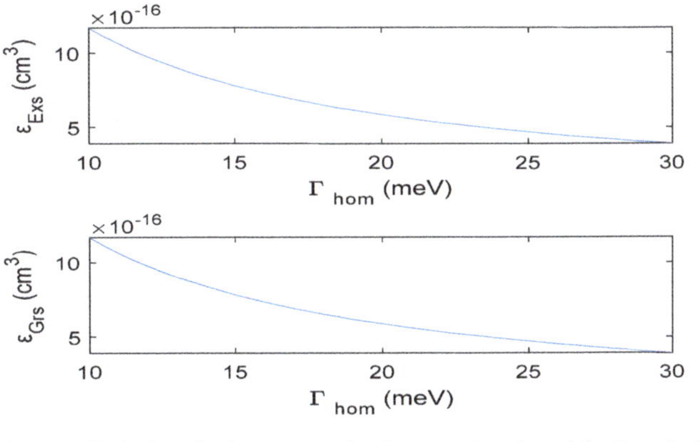

Figure 6. Variation of gain compression factor as function of the Γ_{hom} for I_{rf} = 40 mA.

As seen in the results, the differential gain of Exs is greater than that of the Grs because degeneracy of the Exs is twice that of the Grs. However, the gain compression factor is the same for Grs and Exs. Our results also showed that the output power decreases with the increasing Γ_{hom} and Γ_{ihom}.

As mentioned before, the threshold current was obtained at 2 mA for the Grs and 24 mA for the Exs for the nonlinear-gain case. Therefore, to observe the gain-switched output pulses and also the simultaneous emission from both the Grs and the Exs, we applied I_{rf} of 40 mA. Figure 7 indicates the gain-switched output pulses for an I_{rf} of 40 mA. As shown in the figures, the Grs pulse width is longer (370 ps), while the Exs pulse width is narrow (43 ps). It can be also observed from the figure that the Exs and Grs together contribute to the output pulses since the applied current magnitude is greater than the threshold currents of both states. Therefore, the generated pulses are due to both Exs and Grs emission. The total (Exs + Grs) pulse width is 255 ps and the peak power is 28 mW. As seen in the results, the pulse width of the gain-switched output pulses are long. We also observed that increasing the injection current leads to both the peak power and pulse width increasing. The reason for the increase in the output pulse width with the current is that, although the photon density of the Grs increases with the current, the Grs photon density decreases slowly after reaching the maximum value, as seen in Figure 7. However, the Exs photon density decreases rapidly compared to that of the Grs, yielding a shorter output pulse. It can be said that the long pulses in the InAs-InP (113)B lasers are emitted from the InP ground state.

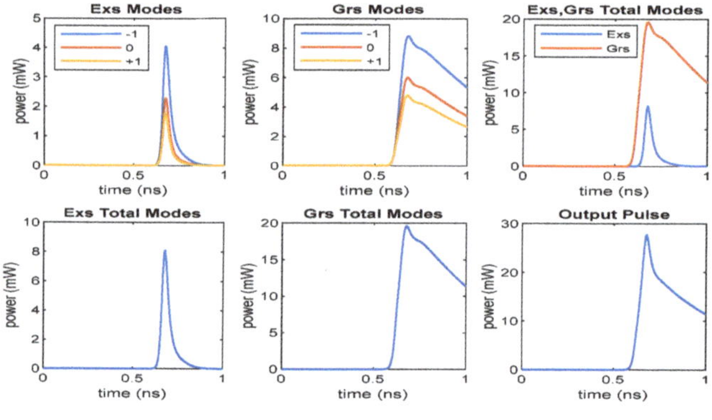

Figure 7. Output pulses for an I_{rf} current of 40 mA.

For InGaAs-GaAs lasers, it was shown that [22] Grs emission is completely saturated in the light-current characteristics, while the Exs emission increases with the increasing current. As a result, if the injection current is increased, the Exs radiation becomes dominant over that of Grs, yielding shorter pulses owing to Exs radiation. Investigation on the InAs-GaAs monolithic Q-Dot lasers revealed that, when the applied injection current increases, the width of the gain-switched pulse decreases [25]. However, in the case of InAs-InP (113)B lasers, the Grs emission does not go to saturation completely (see Figure 2) with the increasing injection current, instead both Grs and Exs emissions increase with the increasing current. Therefore, as mentioned before, the output pulse width of InAs-InP lasers increases with the increasing injection current as compared to that of InAs-GaAs lasers.

Furthermore, our results showed that as Γ_{hom} and Γ_{ihom} increase the I_{th} of Exs decreases, whereas I_{th} of Grs increases (see Figures 3 and 5). Therefore, according to the magnitude of the applied current, even with a smaller value of Γ_{ihom}, the contribution of Exs to output pulses is possible. In order to show this, 25 mA of I_{rf} current is applied and the gain-switched output pulses were obtained for Γ_{ihom} = 30 meV ($\Gamma_{ihom} < \Delta E_{dif}$ = E_{Exs0}-E_{Grs0} =48 meV) and Γ_{ihom} = 55 meV ($\Gamma_{ihom} > \Delta E_{dif}$ = 48 meV). As seen in Figures 8 and 9, the output pulse with a full-width half-maximum (FWHM) of 386 ps and peak power of 26 mW for Γ_{ihom} = 30 meV is generated from Grs emission only. However, since I_{th} of Exs decreased for Γ_{ihom} = 55 meV, both Grs and Exs contribute the output pulse providing an FWHM of 233 ps and peak power of 10 mW. If we apply a current greater than the peak current of 25 mA, for example 60 mA for Γ_{ihom} = 30 meV, both Grs and Exs contribute to the lasing process simultaneously, as shown in Figure 10 producing an FWHM of 478 ps and peak power of 53 mW. Briefly, we can say that the contribution of Exs to gain-switched output pulses depend on not only the value of Γ_{ihom}, which is smaller or greater than the energy difference between Exs and Grs, but also on the magnitude of the applied current. In addition, it can be also observed from the results that the width of pulses are long due to dominant effect of the Grs emission as mentioned before. Wang et al. [12] showed that if Γ_{ihom} is smaller than the energy difference between Exs and Grs ($\Delta E_{dif} = E_{Exs0}\text{-}E_{Grs0}$), lasing occurs only due to Grs if Γ_{ihom} is greater than the ΔE_{dif}; both Grs and Exs contribute to the lasing process. However, as seen from our results, Exs lasing depends on the magnitude of current as well as on the value of Γ_{ihom}.

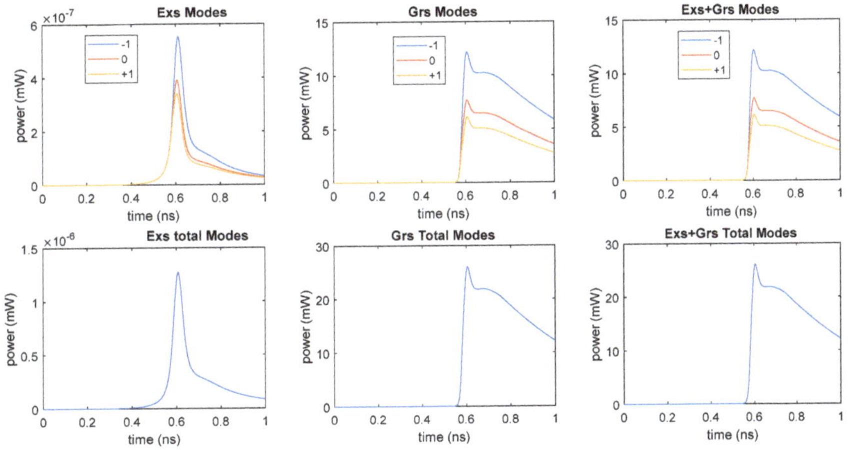

Figure 8. Output pulses for an I_{rf} current of 25 mA for Γ_{ihom} = 30 meV.

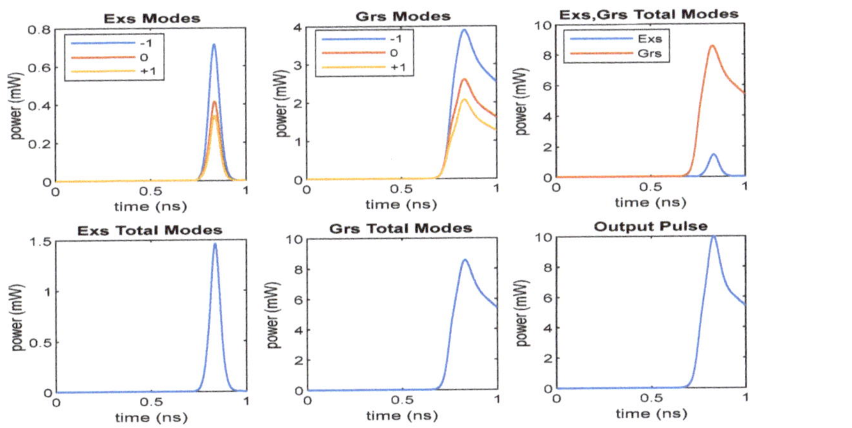

Figure 9. Output pulses for an I_{rf} current of 25 mA for Γ_{ihom} = 55 meV.

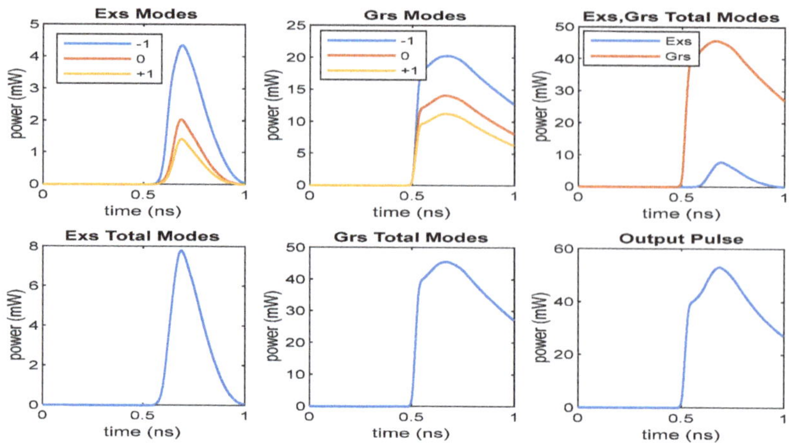

Figure 10. Output pulses for an I_{rf} current of 60 mA for Γ_{ihom} = 30 meV.

According to obtained results, we can say that it is impossible to generate gain-switched short pulses with a high peak power as long as the Grs emission is dominant over the Exs emission for InAs-InP QD lasers. Since the threshold current of Exs is much higher than that of Grs and increasing the injection current makes both Grs and Exs emissions increase, Exs emissions cannot be dominant over Grs emissions. Therefore, in order to obtain gain-switched short pulses with high peak power at low currents, the Exs emission must be sustained while Grs emission must be suppressed. For this reason, an external Gaussian pulse beam to the Exs was applied. When an optical beam is applied to the Exs, depending on the peak value of the applied optical beam, the threshold currents of Grs and Exs can become zero (see Figure 11). Furthermore, the photon density of the Exs can exceed that of the Grs up to a certain current range. This yields gain-switched short pulses exhibiting high power at low currents. Figure 11 shows light vs. dc current characteristics obtained by applying an EOGB with a peak power of 10 mW and a width of 10 ps. In order to see the zero-threshold current for both the states, the dc current was applied up to 50 mA. As seen in the figure, the power of Exs is greater than that of the Grs up to some current value with the application of optical beam and the threshold currents become zero for both states as explained before.

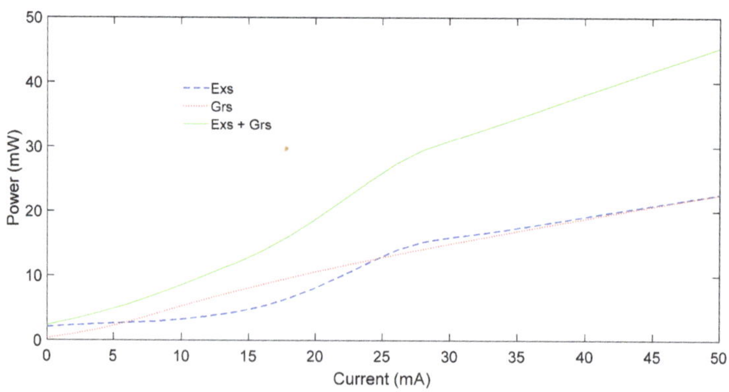

Figure 11. Output power vs. dc current under the EOGB illumination of 10 mW.

Figure 12 indicates the gain-switched output pulses under the optical beam having a peak power of 10 mW and a width of 10 ps for I_{rf} of 12 mA. As seen in the figure, Exs emission is dominant over Grs emission, which means the output pulse is generated due to Exs emission. Therefore, the width of the output pulse is narrow (26 ps) and the peak power is high (82 mW) even though the applied current is low. Additionally, the peak power of EOGB must be increased to further increase the peak power of the output pulse. Figure 13 shows output pulses for an optical beam peak power of 20 mW for I_{rf} of 12 mA. As seen in the figure, while the peak power of the output increases, the width of the output pulse slightly increases and provides a value of 27 ps. Furthermore, according to the applied current, we can adjust the magnitude of the optical beam to obtain short pulses.

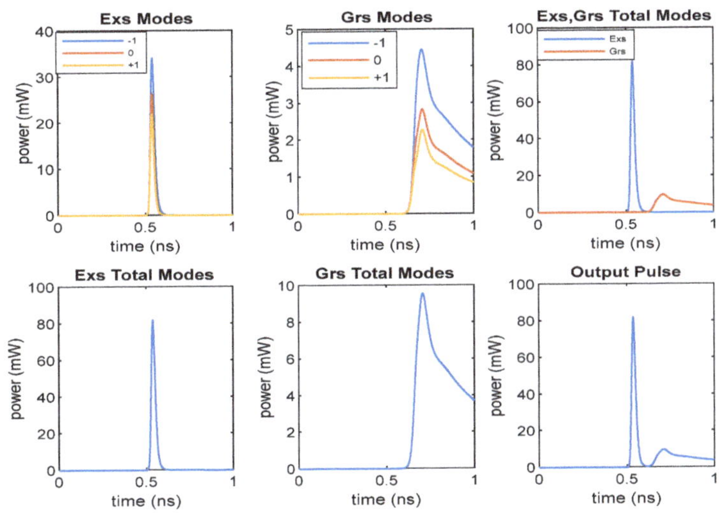

Figure 12. Output pulse under the illumination of an EOGB of 10 mW for I_{rf} = 12 mA.

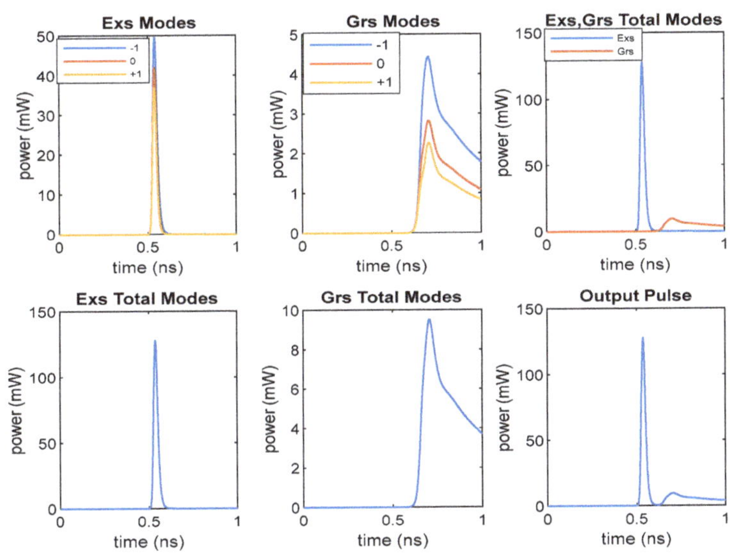

Figure 13. Output pulse under the illumination of an EOGB of 20 mW for I_{rf} = 12 mA.

It was also found that changes in the laser parameters do not affect the output pulse width and peak power significantly in the presence of the optical beam. However, without

EOGB, the output pulses are strongly affected by the change in the laser parameters. Similar results were also obtained for the InAs-InP (113)B quantum dot laser based on single mode rate equations [26].

Regarding the zero-gain compression factor, our results demonstrated that the behavior of gain-switching characteristics with and without EOGB are similar for liner-gain and nonlinear-gain cases except that higher peak power and narrower output pulses are obtained for the linear-gain case.

As a conclusion, when an EOGB is applied to the Exs, the photon emission of Exs becomes dominant over the Grs, providing shorter output pulses with a high peak power. The Exs emission can be tuned for the C-band optical communication window with proper band energy engineering and growth optimization, such as the double cap procedure [27,28].

4. Conclusions

In this study, for the first time, the gain-switching properties have been theoretically investigated in detail in the absence and presence of optical beam illumination for direct the relaxation model of InAs-InP (113)B Q-dot lasers. The model is based on multi-population rate equations involving nonlinear gain. The first effect of the homogeneous and the inhomogeneous broadenings on the differential gain, the gain compression factor, and the threshold current was examined in the absence of the optical beam. Subsequently, the gain-switched output pulses were studied in the absence and presence of optical beam illumination. Our results indicated the following:

(1) The differential gain and the gain compression factor decrease with the increasing homogeneous and inhomogeneous broadenings. However, while the threshold current of the ground state increases, that of the excited state decreases as the broadenings are increased.

(2) While gain-switched pulses are produced only due to ground state emission at small currents, the Exs and Grs emissions contribute to the output pulses at greater currents values (greater than the threshold currents of both excited state and ground state). Since the photon density of the ground state decreases gradually after reaching its maximum value, the output pulses originating from ground state emission have long pulse widths. On the other hand, the photon density of the excited state decreases rapidly after reaching its maximum value, yielding a narrower pulse width. Therefore, when an optical Gaussian pulse beam is applied to the quantum dot laser, gain-switching shorter pulses with high peak power are obtained since excite state emissions dominate ground state emissions.

(3) The contribution of excited state to gain-switched output pulses depend on the magnitude of the applied current as well as on the value of the inhomogeneous broadening.

(4) In the absence of the optical beam, the laser output is strongly affected by the change in the laser parameters, whereas in the presence of the optical beam, this effect is negligible.

(5) The behavior of gain-switching characteristics with and without a Gaussian pulse beam are similar for liner-gain and nonlinear-gain cases except that higher peak power and narrower output pulses are obtained for the linear-gain case.

As a result, short pulses with a width of around 26 ps with a high peak power can be generated at low currents by applying an external optical beam to the Exs. These results showed that InAs-InP (113)B quantum dot lasers are a candidate source for many applications as well as optical communication systems.

A more sophisticated model such as the investigation of the electron-hole model for multi-population rate equations would be the subject of future work.

Author Contributions: Methodology, N.D.; software, H.S.D.T. and E.C.; investigation, N.D., H.S.D.T. and E.C.; writing—original draft preparation, N.D.; supervision, N.D.; project administration, N.D. All authors have read and agreed to the published version of the manuscript.

Funding: This research was funded by The Scientific and Technological Research Council of Turkey (TUBITAK), grant number 119F099.

Data Availability Statement: Not applicable.

Conflicts of Interest: The authors declare no conflict of interest.

References

1. Shimizu, M.; Suzuki, Y.; Watanabe, M. Characteristics of Cavity Round-Trip Time Pulses in Short-Cavity Q-Switched AlGaAs Multiple-Quantum-Well Semiconductor Lasers. *Jpn. J. Appl. Phys.* **1998**, *37*, 1040. [CrossRef]
2. Grillot, F.; Veselinov, K.; Gioannini, M.; Montrosset, I.; Even, J.; Piron, R.; Homeyer, E.; Louaiche, S. Spectral Analysis of 1.55-m InAs–InP(113)B Quantum-Dot Lasers Based on a Multipopulation Rate Equations Mode. *IEEE J. Quantum Electron.* **2009**, *45*, 872. [CrossRef]
3. Caroff, P.; Paranthoen, C.; Platz, C.; Dehaese, O.; Folliot, H.; Bertru, N.; Labbe, C.; Piron, R.; Homeyer, E.; Le Corre, A.; et al. High gain and low-threshold InAs QD lasers on InP. *J. Appl. Phys.* **2005**, *87*, 243107.
4. Saito, H.; Nishi, K.; Kamei, A.; Sugou, S. Low chirp observed in directly modulated quantum dot lasers. *IEEE Photon. Technol. Lett.* **2000**, *12*, 1298. [CrossRef]
5. Reithmaier, J.P.; Forchel, A. Recent advances in semiconductor quantum-dot lasers. *C. R. Phys.* **2003**, *4*, 611. [CrossRef]
6. Huang, H.; Duan, J.; Jung, D.; Liu, A.Y.; Zhang, Z.; Norman, J.; Bowers, J.E.; Frédéric, G. Analysis of the optical feedback dynamics in InAs/GaAs quantum dot lasers directly grown on silicon. *J. Opt. Soc. Am. B* **2018**, *35*, 2780. [CrossRef]
7. Rafailov, E.U.; Cataluna, M.A.; Sibbett, W. Mode-locked quantum-dot lasers. *Nat. Photonics* **2007**, *1*, 395–401. [CrossRef]
8. Sritirawisarn, N.; Otten FW, M.; van Eijkemans, T.J.; Nötzelet, R. Surface morphology induced InAs quantum dot or dash formation on InGaAs/InP(100). *J. Cryst. Growth* **2007**, *305*, 63. [CrossRef]
9. Heck, S.C.; Osborne, S.; Healy, S.B.; O'Reilly, E.P.; Lealarge, F.; Pointgt, F.; Le Gouezigou, O.; Accard, A. Experimental and theoretical study of InAs/InGaAs/InP quantum dash laser. *IEEE J. Quantum Electron.* **2009**, *45*, 1508. [CrossRef]
10. Sugawara, M.; Mukai, K.; Nakata, Y.; Ishikawa, H. Effect of homogeneous broadening of optical gain on lasing spectra in self-assemled $In_xGa_{1-x}As/GaAs$ quantum dot lasers. *Phys. Rev.* **2000**, *61*, 7595. [CrossRef]
11. Grillot, F.; Veselinov, K.; Gioannini, M.; Piron, R.; Homeyer, E.; Even, J.; Loualiche, S.; Montrosset, I. Theoretical analysis of 1.55-μm InAs/InP (113)B quantum dot lasers based on a multi-population rate equation model. In Proceedings of the Physics and Simulation of Optoelectronic Devices XVII, San Jose, CA, USA, 24 February 2009; Volume 7211.
12. Wang, C.; Gionnini, M.; Montrosset, I.; Even, J.; Grillot, F. Influence of inhomogeneous broadening on the dynamics of quantum dot lasers. In Proceedings of the SPIE OPTO, Physics and Simulation of Optoelectronic Devices XXIII, San Francisco, CA, USA, 28 April 2015; Volume 9357.
13. Aleem, M.N.A.; Huessein, K.F.A.; Ammar, A.A. Semiconductor quantum dot lasers as pulse sources for high bit rate data transmission. *PIER* **2013**, *28*, 185. [CrossRef]
14. Gioannini, M.; Rossetti, M. Time-domain traveling wave model of quamtum dot DFB lasers. *IEEE J. Sel. Top. Quantum Electron.* **2011**, *17*, 1318. [CrossRef]
15. Gioannini, M.; Bardella, P.; Montrosset, I. Time-domain traveling-wave analysis of multimode dynamics of quantum dot Fabry-Perot lasers. *IEEE J. Sel. Top. Quantum Electron.* **2015**, *21*, 1900811. [CrossRef]
16. Veselinov, K.; Grillot, F.; Miska, P.; Homeyer, E.; Caroff, P.; Platz, C.; Even, J.; Dehaese, O.; Loualiche, S.; Marie, X.; et al. Carrier dynamics and saturation effects in (311)B InAs-InP quantum dot lasers. *Opt. Quantum Electron.* **2006**, *38*, 369. [CrossRef]
17. Xu, D.V.; Yoon, S.F.; Tong, C.Z. Self-consistent analysis of carrier confinement and output power in 1.3-μm InAs-GaAs quantum dot VCSELs. *IEEE J. Quantum Electron.* **2008**, *44*, 879. [CrossRef]
18. Dogru, N.; Adams, M.J. Intensity noise of actively mode-locked quantum dot external cavity laser. *J. Light. Technol.* **2014**, *32*, 3215. [CrossRef]
19. Dogru, N.; Adams, M.J. Numerical simulation of a mode-locked quantum dot external cavity laser. *IET Optoelectron.* **2014**, *8*, 44. [CrossRef]
20. Veselinov, K.; Grillot, F.; Cornet, C.; Even, J.; Bekaiarski, A.; Gioannini, M.; Loualiche, S. Analysis of the double laser emission occurring in 1.55-μm InAs-InP(113)B quantum-dot lasers. *IEEE J. Quantum Electron.* **2007**, *43*, 810. [CrossRef]
21. Avrutin, E.; Ryvkin, B.; Kostamovaara, J.; Kuksenkov, D. Strongly asymmetric waveguide laser diodes for high brightness picosecond optical pulses generation by gain switching at GHz repetition rates. *Semicond. Sci. Technol.* **2015**, *30*, 055006. [CrossRef]
22. Avrutin, E.A.; Dogru, N.; Ryvkin, B.; Kostamovaara, J.T. Spectral control of asymmetric-waveguide large signal modulated diode lasers for non-linear applications. *IET Optoelectron.* **2016**, *10*, 57. [CrossRef]
23. Bhattacharya, P.; Klotzkin, D.; Qasaimeh, O.; Zhou, W.; Krishna, S.; Zhu, D. High-speed modulation and switching characteristics of In(Ga)As-Al(Ga)As self-organized quantum-dot lasers. *IEEE J. Sel. Top. Quantum Electron.* **2000**, *6*, 426. [CrossRef]

24. Cornet, C.; Labbe, C.; Folliot, H.; Bertru, N.; Dehaese, O.; Even, J.; Le Corre, A.; Paranthoen, C.; Platz, C.; Loualiche, S. Quantitative investigation of optical absorption in InAs/InP (311)B quantum dots emitting at 1.55 µm wavelength. *Appl. Phys. Lett.* **2004**, *85*, 5685. [CrossRef]
25. Hantschmann, C.; Vasil'ev, P.P.; Chen, S.; Liao, M.; Seeds, A.J.; Liu, H.; Penty, R.V.; White, I.H. Gain switching of monolithic 1.3 µm InAs/GaAs quantum dot lasers on silicon. *J. Light. Technol.* **2018**, *36*, 3837. [CrossRef]
26. Dogru, N.; Duranoglu Tunc, H.S.; Al-Dabbagh, A.M. Gain-switched short pulse generation from InAs-InP(113)B quantum dot laser excited state. *Opt. Laser Technol.* **2022**, *148*, 107709. [CrossRef]
27. Paranthoen, C.; Bertru, N.; Dehaese, O.; Loualiche, S.; Lmabert, B. Height dispersion control of InAs/InP(113)B quantum dots emitting at 1.55 µm. *Appl. Phys. Lett.* **2001**, *78*, 1751. [CrossRef]
28. Koenraad, P.M.; Bertru, N.; Bimberg, D.; Loualiche, S. Electronic and optical properties of InAs/InP quantumdots on InP(100) and InP(311)B substrates: Theory and experiment. *Phys. Rev. B* **2006**, *74*, 035312.

mathematics

MDPI

Article

Modern Physical-Mathematical Models and Methods for Design Surface Acoustic Wave Devices: COM Based P-Matrices and FEM in COMSOL

Aleksey S. Koigerov

Department of Micro- and Nanoelectronics, Faculty of Electronics, Saint Petersburg Electrotechnical University "LETI", Popova Str., 5, 197376 Saint Petersburg, Russia; askoigerov@etu.ru or a.koigerov@gmail.com

Abstract: Comparative results of calculation and measurement of the frequency responses of the surface acoustic waves filter on a piezoelectric substrate of 64°YX-cut lithium niobate and delay line on a piezoelectric substrate of 128°YX-cut lithium niobate is presented. The calculation was performed on the basis of two approaches—the finite element method in the COMSOL Multiphysics software and using the model of coupling of modes based on P-matrices. A brief overview and features of each approach are presented. The calculation results based on the two approaches are in good agreement with each other and with the experimental results of measurements of the characteristics of the bandpass filter. The delay line operating with the use of the third harmonic frequency is calculated by FEM. The results showed a good match between numerical simulation and experiment. The considered approaches for designing SAW devices allow us to relatively quickly and accurately predict the frequency responses at the simulation stage, thereby reducing the number of experimental iterations and increasing the efficiency of development.

Keywords: surface acoustic wave; LSAW; piezoelectric substrate; coupling of modes model; finite element method; delay line; bandpass filter; lithium niobate; COM

MSC: 74J15; 65Y10; 15B99

Citation: Koigerov, A.S. Modern Physical-Mathematical Models and Methods for Design Surface Acoustic Wave Devices: COM Based P-Matrices and FEM in COMSOL. *Mathematics* **2022**, *10*, 4353. https://doi.org/10.3390/math10224353

Academic Editors: Shujin Laima, Yong Cao, Xiaowei Jin and Hehe Ren

Received: 26 October 2022
Accepted: 16 November 2022
Published: 19 November 2022

Publisher's Note: MDPI stays neutral with regard to jurisdictional claims in published maps and institutional affiliations.

Copyright: © 2022 by the author. Licensee MDPI, Basel, Switzerland. This article is an open access article distributed under the terms and conditions of the Creative Commons Attribution (CC BY) license (https://creativecommons.org/licenses/by/4.0/).

1. Introduction

In recent decades, devices based on surface acoustic waves (SAW) have become an integral part of modern radio electronics [1,2]. They are massively used both in household electronic equipment and in communication systems, military and special equipment with special operating conditions. SAW devices carve out a niche in the frequency range from tens of megahertz to 2.5 ... 3 GHz due to the advantages of mass-dimensional indicators, high reliability, low cost and excellent electrical characteristics [1,2]. Research and development of new SAW devices are relevant due to the increasing need for such components for modernization and the creation of new equipment for telecommunication systems.

One of the important stages in the design of SAW filters is mathematical modeling. The reduction in design time and simultaneous reduction in filter development costs is an urgent task, which can be solved both by applying modern computational soft and by improving and developing already-known modeling tools. The modeling stage allows you to reduce the time of the device's entry into the market and increase the efficiency of development, both by increasing accuracy and by minimizing experimental iterations.

A comparison of the simulation and measurements for SAW devices shows good agreement for different approaches [3–7]. Analytical [3–5] and numerical [6,7] approaches are equally popular with developers. The priority is determined by the specific task. For example, analytical methods are required for the initial synthesis and optimization of SAW device topology; numerical methods are suitable for the SAW parameter extraction [8].

Finally, the numerical approach is suitable for verification of development at the final stage, because the real experiment can be replaced by a very accurate multiphysics simulation.

Therefore, the topic of developing SAW devices is relevant today.

The presence of periodic multi-element topological structures (electrodes) is one of the features of SAW devices. The principle of operation is based on the effects of multiple reflections and transformations of SAW in such structures. The SAW filter (Figure 1a) and SAW delay line (DL) (Figure 1b) consist of a piezoelectric substrate with input and output inter-digital transducers (IDT) applied to it for the excitation and reception of acoustic waves. The operating frequency is determined by the velocity of the SAW and the step of the arrangement of the electrodes of the IDT ($f = V/\lambda$, where V is the velocity of the wave, λ is the wavelength).

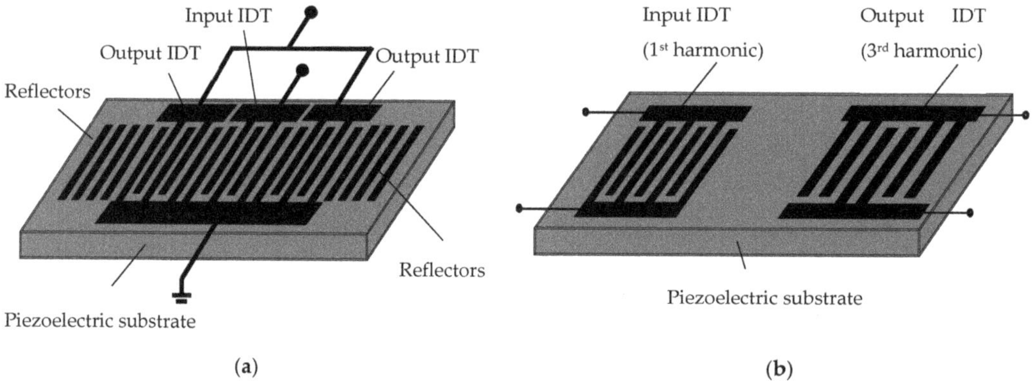

Figure 1. SAW devices: (**a**) resonator filter; (**b**) delay line.

The aim of the work is to demonstrate the capabilities of modern approaches for modeling SAW devices by the example of calculating a bandpass filter on a piezoelectric substrate of 64°YX-cut lithium niobate and a test SAW DL on 128°YX-cut lithium niobate. The calculation is based on two approaches—the finite element method (FEM) in the COMSOL Multiphysics software and the model of the coupling of modes (COM-model) based on P-matrices.

2. Physical-Mathematical Models

Today, there are various models [9–13] and methods for modeling SAW devices that allow predicting the frequency responses of devices with varying degrees of accuracy. These are the delta sources method, the method of equivalent circuits [11], the COM model [9,10], P-matrices [9,10], Green's functions, some discrete analysis approaches [12,13], hierarchical cascading based on B-matrices [14] and the finite element method (FEM) [15].

The analytical approach based on the COM model and its formalization based on the P-matrices is most widely used among developers for designing SAW devices. The COM model requires a small number of key COM parameters and a relatively short calculation time, which allows the synthesis and optimization of parameters of the topology of a SAW device.

The rapid progress of computing technologies and the development of software have made it possible to solve many problems with multiphysical communication. Recently, numerical methods of analysis involving standard computer packages, such as COMSOL and ANSYS, have become widespread [16–23]. The main advantage of numerical approaches based on FEM is that their use requires only knowledge of the constants of the material and the geometry of the device. Therefore, it is possible to calculate devices entirely in 3-D and 2-D dimensions. In addition, these methods allow, based on the analysis of simple test cells, to determine the values of key COM parameters for fast analytical approaches based on COM and P-matrices. However, it should be understood that taking into account many parameters in 3-D modeling of real full-aperture devices leads to a very large increase in the requirements for computing resources and an increase in the analysis time.

Figure 2 shows schematically two modern approaches to modeling SAW devices. The first approach is to calculate the device as a whole using FEM. The second is a preliminary analysis of simple test cells using FEM in order to obtain key COM parameters [24–26], and then based on these parameters, calculations are performed using a fast P-matrix approach. The purpose of each approach is to calculate a complete set of Y-parameters, from which they are converted to S-parameters by recalculation.

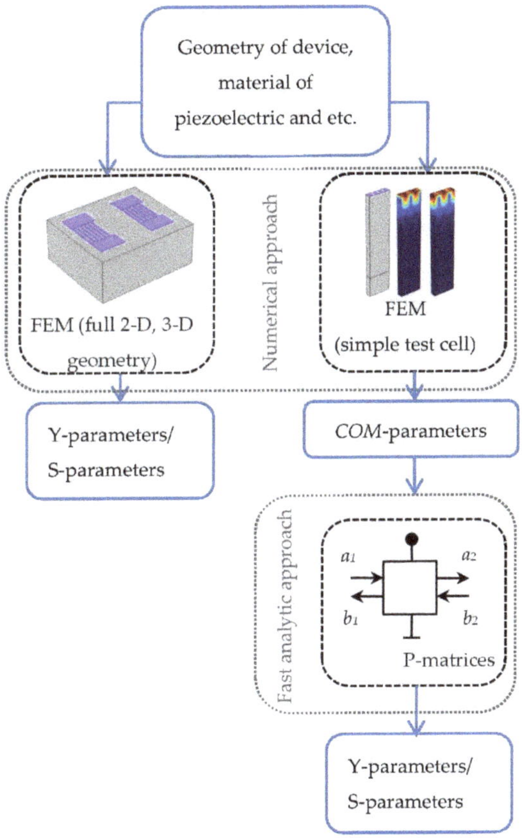

Figure 2. The modern approaches for calculating the frequency responses of SAW devices.

2.1. COM-Model

The model [27] is based on the consideration of two homogeneous plane waves propagating in opposite directions in the structure of the device:

$$R(x,k) = R(k)\exp(-jkx);\ S(x,k) = S(k)\exp(+jkx), \tag{1}$$

where $R(k)$, $S(k)$—the amplitudes of the corresponding waves,

j—imaginary unit,

x—coordinate along which the wave propagates,

$k = \omega/V$—the wave number,

$\omega = 2\pi f$—the circular frequency,

f—the frequency,

V—the velocity in the structure.

Processes of reflection and transformation of SAW take place when the wave propagates in the periodic electrode structure. The presence of electrodes on the surface changes the velocity of wave propagation and causes mutual communication between the waves. Note, two reasons: the first is the partial reflection of SAW from the electrodes and the second is the excitation of SAW by current flowing in metal electrodes. For example, you can write equations linking the complex amplitudes of waves at the input $R_1(x,k)$, $S_1(x,k)$ and the output $R_2(x,k)$, $S_2(x,k)$ of the input IDT and the equation for the current through the input IDT I (Figure 3a). To formalize the calculation process, it is convenient to present the coupled wave equations in matrix form in the form of P-matrices elements connecting the amplitudes of acoustic waves at the input and output of acoustic ports, as well as the current and applied potential at the electrical port.

$$\begin{bmatrix} b_1 \\ a_2 \\ I \end{bmatrix} = \begin{bmatrix} P_{11} & P_{12} & P_{13} \\ P_{21} & P_{22} & P_{23} \\ P_{31} & P_{32} & P_{33} \end{bmatrix} \begin{bmatrix} a_1 \\ b_2 \\ U \end{bmatrix}, \tag{2}$$

where b_1, b_2, a_1, a_2 are the amplitudes of the waves at the input and output of the acoustic ports of a single IDT,

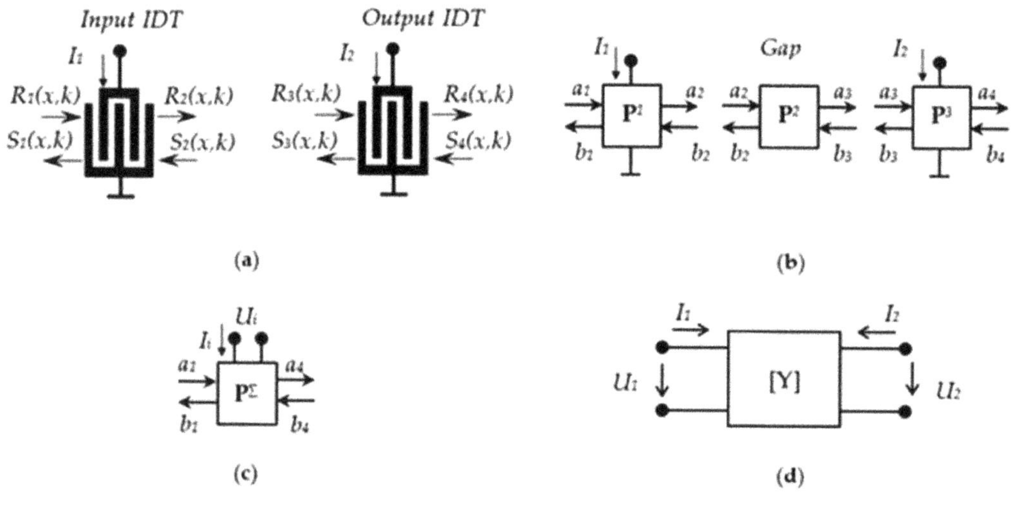

Figure 3. SAW DL as: (**a**) topology; (**b**) blocks for P-matrix; (**c**) final P-matrix and (**d**) two port device.

I and U—the current and voltage at the electrical port.

Consider the topology of the SAW DL from the positions of the COM model (Figure 3a). Each IDT is considered an element with two acoustic inputs and one electric. Following the ideology of the P-matrix method, the topology of the DL can be formally represented in the form of three elements of P-matrices, shown in Figure 3b. The first element displays the input IDT and is connected to the input port. The second element is the free surface of the piezoelectric material or the gap between the transducers. The third element is the output IDT connected to the output port. The acoustic ports of the units are connected in series with each other in accordance with the topological description. The potential U_1 is applied to the input port, U_2 is applied to the output port, and currents I_1 and I_2 flow through them, respectively.

The sequence of actions when using the P-matrices method is as follows:

- an equivalent acoustoelectric circuit is drawn up (Figure 3b);
- the P-matrices of all elements of the device are calculated;

- the total P-matrix (P^{Σ}) is calculated (Figure 3c), which determines the relationship of complex wave amplitudes at the input and output of the device as a whole.

The components of the total P-matrix of the acoustic channel (P^{Σ}) can be calculated by multiplying the corresponding components. Conditionally write down:

$$P^{\Sigma} = P^{IDT-1} \times P^{gap} \times P^{IDT-2}. \tag{3}$$

The total matrix determines the relationship of the complex amplitudes of the waves at the input and output of the SAW device. It can be used to form a matrix of admittances. Moreover, it is necessary to calculate the total matrices relative to the input and output ports from the following physical considerations:

$$\begin{bmatrix} b_1 \\ a_4 \\ I_i \end{bmatrix} = \begin{bmatrix} P_{11}^{\Sigma} & P_{12}^{\Sigma} & P_{13}^{\Sigma} \\ P_{21}^{\Sigma} & P_{22}^{\Sigma} & P_{23}^{\Sigma} \\ P_{31}^{\Sigma} & P_{32}^{\Sigma} & \left(P_{33}^{\Sigma}\right)_{ik} \end{bmatrix} \begin{bmatrix} a_1 \\ b_4 \\ U_k \end{bmatrix}_{U_j=0}, \tag{4}$$

where b_1, b_4, a_1, a_4—the amplitudes of the waves at the input and output of the acoustic ports of the DL,

I_i, U_k, i, k, j = 1, 2 ($k \neq j$)—the currents and voltages at the input and output electrical ports,

$(P^{\Sigma}{}_{33})_{ik}$—an element of the total matrix is the admittance Y_{ik}, depending on the state of the electrical ports.

In matrices form, the SAW DL under consideration, as a two-port device, shown in Figure 3d, can be described using the admittance matrix of interest to us:

$$\begin{bmatrix} I_1 \\ I_2 \end{bmatrix} = \begin{bmatrix} Y_{11} & Y_{12} \\ Y_{21} & Y_{22} \end{bmatrix} \begin{bmatrix} U_1 \\ U_2 \end{bmatrix}, \tag{5}$$

where I_i и U_i, i = 1, 2 currents and voltages at the input and output electrical ports, respectively, elements $Y_{11}, Y_{12}, Y_{21}, Y_{22}$—$Y$-parameters, must be determined.

For the successful implementation of COM based on P-matrices, it is necessary to know:

1. The physical interpretation of all components of the P-matrices [9,10]. Acoustic components P_{11}, P_{12}, P_{21}, and P_{22} describe the transmission and reflection coefficients over the acoustic ports. The components P_{13} and P_{23} show the efficiency of excitation of surface acoustic waves by applying voltage U to the bus bars of the IDT. The components P_{31} and P_{32} characterize the efficiency of conversion of SAW into the electric current I in the IDT. P_{13}, P_{23}, P_{31}, and P_{32} are directly proportional to the effective value of the electromechanical coupling coefficient. The element P_{33} of the total matrix determines the desired admittance of the device. To analyze the devices, it is necessary to determine all the components of the P-matrices;
2. Rules for cascading P-matrices [9]. So, for example, the element P_{33} of the total P-matrix of two "neighboring" blocks is calculated by the formula:

$$P_{33}^{\Sigma} = P_{33}^{1} + P_{33}^{2} + P_{32}^{1}\frac{P_{13}^{2} + P_{11}^{2}P_{23}^{1}}{1 - P_{11}^{2}P_{22}^{1}} + P_{31}^{2}\frac{P_{23}^{1} + P_{22}^{1}P_{13}^{2}}{1 - P_{22}^{1}P_{11}^{2}}; \tag{6}$$

3. The transition from a set of Y-parameters to S-parameters. Example of recalculation for the transmission coefficient:

$$S_{21} = \frac{-2Y_{21}Y_0}{(Y_0 + Y_{11})(Y_0 + Y_{22}) - Y_{12}Y_{21}} \tag{7}$$

Most often, the S-parameters are determined with a characteristic impedance value equal to Z_0 = 50 ohms. The physical meaning of S_{11} is the reflection coefficient at the input, and S_{21} is the complex transmission coefficient. $Y_0 = 1/Z_0$.

4. A method for determining COM parameters [8,24–26]. A set of key COM parameters is necessary to find all the components of the P-matrices. The most common ways to obtain COM parameters are the following:

- Analytical solutions;
- Extraction of parameters from experimental data with subsequent construction of empirical dependencies;
- Numerical solutions based on FEM.

It should be noted that analytical solutions, as a rule, are limited to either simple geometries and the case of isotropic materials, or to special cases for which these solutions are valid. In general, a large number of corrections and empirical coefficients are needed, taking into account the features of the topology and manufacturing technology, as well as the materials used. Thus, the method of obtaining the necessary coefficients based on numerical modeling is seen by the author as a good alternative to additional experimental studies. In the approach described here (FEM + COM), the author adheres to the technique of extracting key COM parameters based on the numerical approach in the COMSOL.

2.2. FEM in COMSOL

The COMSOL Multiphysics software based on the finite element method allows the modeling of SAW devices. The problem of SAW propagation is determined by differential equations and solved considering the complex geometry of the device, the properties of materials (substrate, electrodes, reflectors) and boundary conditions.

It is known that the presence of a wave of mechanical displacements and an associated wave of electric potential propagating at the same phase velocity is a feature of the propagation of SAW in piezoelectric substrates. Moreover, in the general case of acoustic waves (Rayleigh and leaky SAW), three orthogonal components of mechanical displacement (two shear and one longitudinal) must be taken into account. Taking into account all these physical features, it is possible by analyzing the propagation of SAW only by numerical method.

Piezoelectric equations in tensor form have the following form:

$$\begin{aligned} T &= C \cdot S - e \cdot E \\ D &= \varepsilon \cdot E + e \cdot S \end{aligned} \tag{8}$$

where T, S—stress and strain tensors;

E, D—electric field intensity and induction vectors;

C, e, ε—tensors of elastic modulus, piezomodules and permittivity, respectively. These tensors and the density of the material are constants that fully describe the piezoelectric substrate.

The FEM-based approach makes it possible to obtain the necessary parameters and characteristics in 3-D dimension, including estimating the leaky of a useful acoustic mode into the depth of the substrate and obtaining information about all acoustic modes excited in a particular topology, in contrast to the one-dimensional consideration of the problem using COM-model. At its core, such 3-D modeling will be the most accurate, since it more adequately takes into account wave processes in real devices. However, at the same time, this calculation requires large computational and time resources.

Reducing and optimizing the model, consider several assumptions:

(1) The transducer must have no apodization by amplitude weighting;
(2) The transducer aperture must not be less than 15 wavelengths; otherwise, the waveguide effect must be taken into account [28];
(3) The distance between neighboring transducers should be small, then it is possible not to take diffraction into account;

(4) The solution for a small aperture extends to the full transducer aperture with the accuracy of the aperture coefficient;
(5) We do not consider the influence of contact bus bars.

It is clear that these assumptions significantly narrow the range of analyzed SAW devices, but at the same time, this approach is applicable to the Double Mode SAW filter (DMS) [29] and the DL.

Figure 4 shows the principle of design (DMS-filter) optimization for FEM in COMSOL. For example, a topology with a small number of IDT electrodes and reflectors is considered.

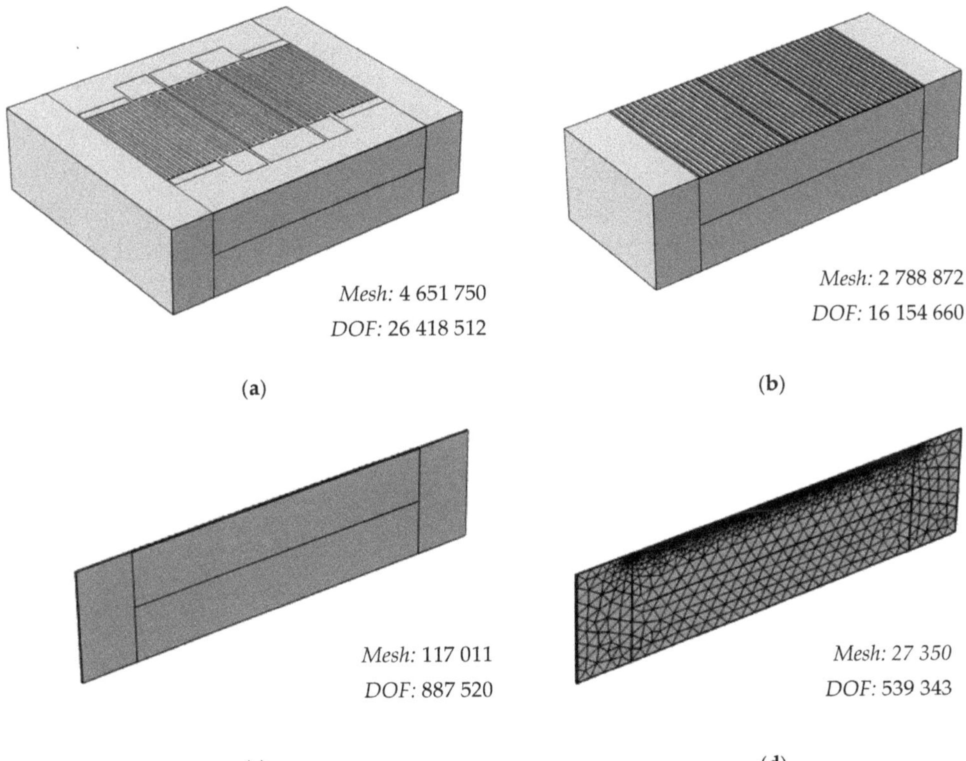

Figure 4. Optimization of the design number of the mesh elements and DOF: (**a**) 3-D DMS filter geometry with bus bars and full aperture; (**b**) filter geometry with full aperture and without bus bars; (**c**) transfer to a small-aperture variant; (**d**) mesh optimization due to SAW physics features.

As can be seen from Figure 4, a full 3D design, together with bus bars, requires a fairly large number of finite elements or mesh elements for a discretized model. Figure 4 presents an approach to reduce and simplify the design in question. It should be understood that each node will have four unknowns (three components of mechanical displacement and potential), which depend on the physics of the problem to be solved (in our case-piezoelectric), then the number of degrees of freedom (DOF) for the entire structure will also be large. Therefore, by reducing ("narrowing") the geometry and optimizing the mesh, the number of DOF can also be reduced quite significantly. In the real design of the considered filter, the total number of electrodes of IDT and reflectors is more than 150 pieces.

COMSOL allows performing analysis of SAW devices in the Eigenfrequency domain, time analysis (Time Dependent), and calculation of the frequency domain and stationary.

In our case, it is necessary to calculate the admittance of the SAW device, that is, to find the real and imaginary parts of the admittances Y_{11}, Y_{21}, Y_{12}, and Y_{22} in the frequency domain. The calculation sequence in COMSOL is as follows:

1. Defining the workspace and setting the geometry;
2. The input of initial data (material, aperture, etc.);
3. Setting the initial and boundary conditions (potentials on the electrodes, a perfectly matched layer (PML), etc.);
4. Building a mesh;
5. Determination of the parameters of the solver and calculation.

Finally, we obtain a large set of decisions on the number of DOF. We can go to the necessary characteristics of the device, in our case it is a set of Y-parameters from the built-in COMSOL tools. Then, to determine the transfer coefficient, go from the Y-parameters to the S-parameters.

3. Results

3.1. DMS Filter

Let us present the results of the calculation of the output admittance and frequency response of one section of the DMS filter, performed on the basis of two presented approaches: analytical-COM and numerical-FEM.

Figure 1a shows the topology of the resonator filter on longitudinal resonant modes or DMS filter, for which the responses are calculated. In the simulation, the frequency dependencies of admittances (Y_{11}, Y_{12}, Y_{21}, Y_{22}) are calculated, and then the S-parameters can be determined.

Figure 5 shows an example of the display of the constructed mesh and the solution in the form of a mechanical displacement for a model based on the FEM.

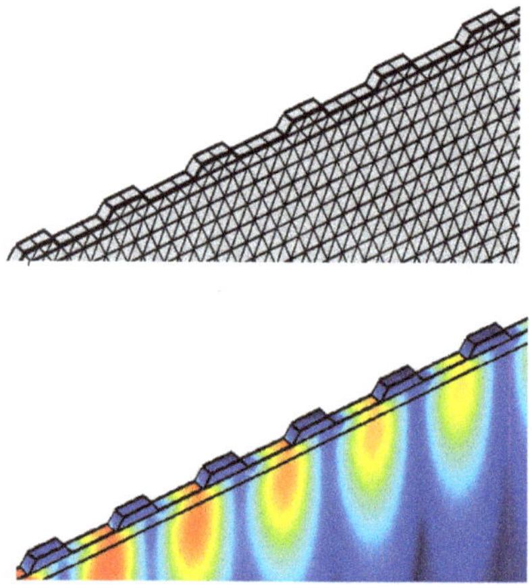

Figure 5. Example of mesh construction and solution in the form of mechanical displacement components for a fragment of topology.

In the responses to the output admittance (Figure 6), calculated by two methods, there is a small discrepancy in the area of the rightmost resonant mode, which seems to be associated with a greater value of acoustic energy leakage at the upper frequencies, inherent in the leaky SAW. Despite this, the results of the bandwidth analysis on the frequency response (Figure 7a) show that this discrepancy is not so significant. In the process of simulation of one section of DMS using the FEM, the following effects were not taken into account: resistive losses in IDT electrodes, acoustic wave diffraction, and losses due to the viscous properties of the material. This is conducted for the following reasons. Firstly, it is possible to fully take into account diffraction and resistive losses, but then it will be necessary to draw a complete 3D model, which will require a large number of mesh elements and DOF, and, as a result, large computational resources and calculation times. Secondly, taking into account propagation losses is associated with the need to introduce appropriate coefficients into the model, the erroneous values of which will lead to additional errors in the calculations.

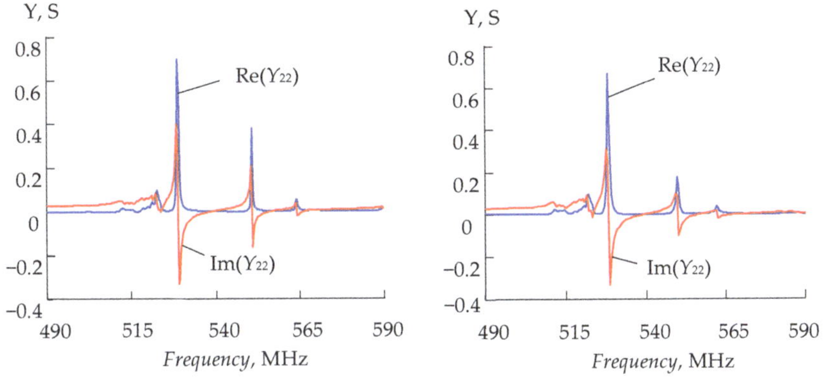

(**a**) (**b**)

Figure 6. Admittance for one section DMS filter: (**a**) calculated by COM; (**b**) calculated by FEM.

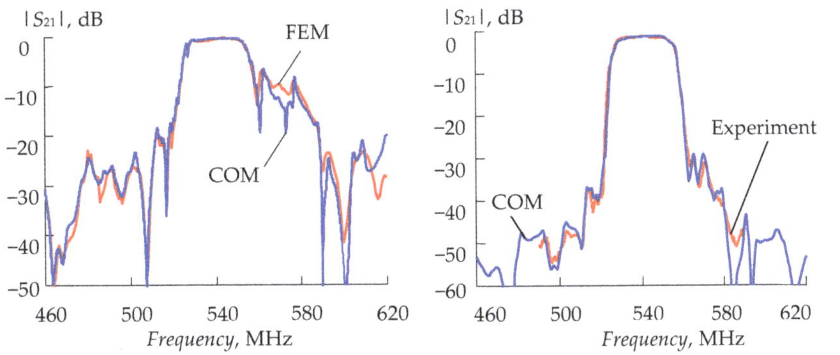

(**a**) (**b**)

Figure 7. Frequency response: (**a**) calculated by COM and FEM for one section DMS filter; (**b**) calculated by COM and experimental for two section DMS filter.

Then let us compare the calculation results with the available experimental results for the filter obtained on the basis of the cascade inclusion of two sections of DMS. Such inclusion is quite typical for this class of DMS filters and is popular among manufacturers of acoustoelectric SAW products. In the basis of calculation let us take COM but connect to the calculation some types of sources of losses, namely resistive losses, propagation losses, losses on the leakage of the main acoustic mode into the substrate depth and taking into account the excitation of SAW after a certain cutoff frequency.

Figure 7a shows the calculated frequency response of one section of the DMS-filter without losses on a 64°YX cut lithium niobate substrate. Figure 7b shows a comparison of the frequency response of the filter based on the simulation by COM and experiment results for cascade inclusion of two section DMS.

The main results and peculiarities of calculation are summarized in the Table 1.

Table 1. Comparison of the result of calculating one section DMS filter based on two approaches: FEM in COMSOL and COM based P-matrices.

Parameter	FEM	COM
Mesh discretization, wavelengths	1/12	-
Number of elements (mesh statistics)	157,738	-
Required RAM, GB	29.23	-
Number of degrees of freedom (DOF)	3,105,240	-
Number of frequency points	201	201
Computation time	~16 h 30 min	2 s
Bandpass at level of −1 dB, MHz	24.4	24.6
Insertion loss, dB	−0.29	−0.32
Passband ripple, dB	0.6	0.45
Central frequency, MHz	540.25	540.45

The FEM calculations did not have the task of optimizing the calculation time, so a direct solver was used, the number of mesh elements was about 157,738, and the density of the mesh was 12 elements per wavelength. In general, both calculations showed approximately the same result, which is a good indicator for a preliminary evaluation of the output characteristics. The greatest discrepancy in the response is observed in the high-frequency region, where "parasitic" bulk acoustic waves (BAW) predominate, where, although it is possible to take them into account in the COM, is still approximate. However, and most importantly, the difference is that the FEM-based calculation took about 16 h, while the COM-based calculation took about 2 s.

A comparison of the results of calculating the transmission coefficient obtained on the basis of the COM with the experimental data for the two-section DMS filter is shown in Figure 7b. The filter has a center frequency of 540 MHz and a bandpass (at a level of −1 dB) of 24.3 MHz or 4.5%. Insertion loss—1.3 dB. Differences in the frequency responses in the passband do not exceed 0.15 dB, in the stopband −5 dB. The greatest calculation accuracy is found in the passband of the filter. The accuracy in the stopband is less due to the presence of the parasitic LC elements and "secondary effects" in the real devices.

3.2. Delay Line

Despite the fact that FEM is inferior in calculation speed, it is a very effective tool for calculation devices with a small number of electrodes, because of many secondary effects, such as leakage of the wave into the substrate volume, the presence of parasitic BAW modes and harmonic frequencies, are automatically taken into account.

Transducers can operate not only at main, but at harmonic frequencies [30,31]. The intensity of excitation high harmonics depends on different parameters: the metallization coefficient, the thickness of the metallization, the shape of the electrode and the type of transducer.

Figure 8a shows the principle of operation of the transducers at harmonics. It can be seen that the IDT with $\lambda/4$ operates only in fundamental mode to a frequency of 1.5 GHz, while for the IDT with split electrodes: 1.5 GHz—the third harmonic, the main mode is at a frequency of 0.5 GHz. The combination of IDTs as the input and output IDTs—is the base of our SAW DL, we calculate the admittance parameters for the DL.

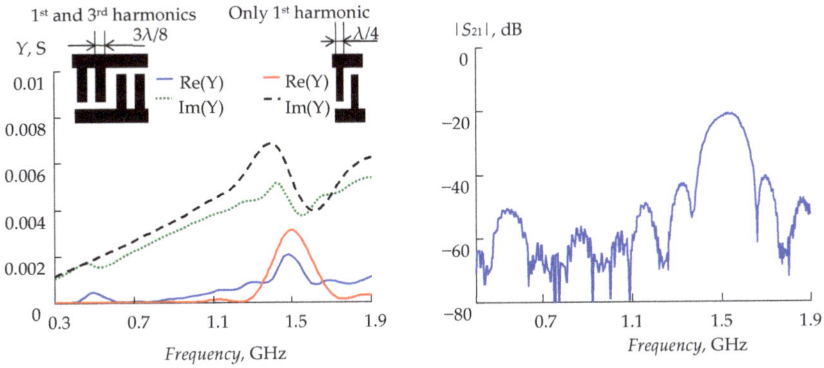

(**a**) (**b**)

Figure 8. SAW DL: (**a**) principle of operation of the transducers at harmonics (main and 3rd harmonic excitation for IDT with split electrodes and only main for IDT with λ/4); (**b**) frequency response calculated by FEM for scheme without "parasitic" LC elements.

The DL topology consists of two bidirectional transducers. The input of the transducer is IDT with λ/4 electrodes operating in the main mode, the output is a split-electrode transducer with a 3λ/8 electrode width. The center frequency of the delay line is 1.5 GHz. The substrate is 128° YX cut lithium niobate. The input IDT is six pairs. The output is four. The relative value of the metallization thickness is H_m/λ = 2.9%, the absolute value is H_m = 75 nm.

Figure 9a shows a schematic with "parasitic" LC elements. Taking into account the LC elements allows us to compare the simulation and measurement results shown in Figure 9b. The center frequency of the DL is 1.5 GHz and the bandpass (at a level of −3 dB) is 112 MHz or 7.46%. The insertion loss is 22.2 dB. The results showed good agreement between the numerical simulation and experiment.

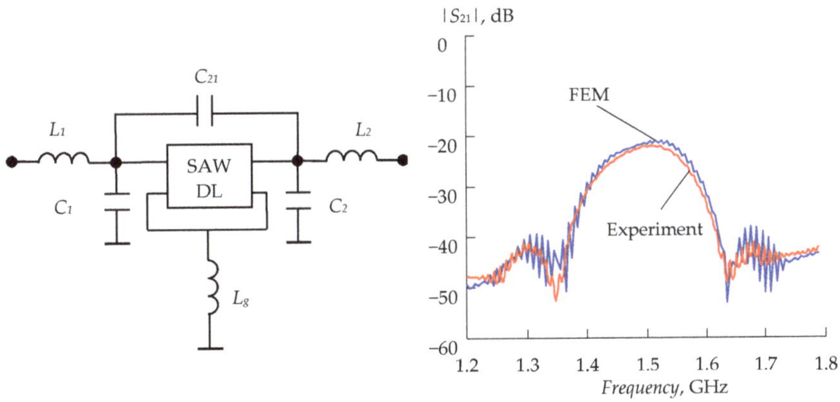

(**a**) (**b**)

Figure 9. SAW DL: (**a**) scheme with "parasitic" LC elements; (**b**) frequency response calculated by FEM and experiment for scheme with "parasitic" LC elements.

4. Discussion

The accumulated experience in the use of different approaches to the modeling of SAW devices allows us to draw conclusions.

The COM-based analytical approach and the numerical approach (FEM in COMSOL) are in demand in the design of SAW devices. Both approaches are comparable in accuracy in bandpass calculations. In the stopband, FEM is more accurate because it automatically takes into account several secondary effects, such as wave leakage into the substrate depth. The main disadvantages of FEM are high computational resource requirements and long computation time. Therefore, FEM is more suitable for analysis at the final stage of development where we can replace the real experiment with a qualitative multiphysics simulation. In addition, FEM is well suited for preliminary analysis of acoustic wave parameters based on simple test cells.

The COM-based analytical approach allows us to obtain results significantly faster. It is reasonable to use COM for preliminary characterization during the synthesis and topology optimization stage. Optimization is also one of the important stages of development. We can proceed to it when the adequacy of the model is proved. Since one iteration for COM takes a couple of seconds, it is very convenient to do topology optimization based on the analytical approach. The issue of optimization of SAW devices should be considered separately.

One of the features of COM is the need to find the model parameters beforehand. The parameters can be extracted from simple test cells [24] using FEM. Such a combined approach (FEM + COM) includes all the advantages of a fast analytical model with the accuracy provided by FEM only.

The full calculation algorithm using FEM in COMSOL is presented in [31]. The experiment was carried out in accordance with the manufacturing process of SAW devices. More details about the manufacturing process can be found, for example, in [32].

5. Conclusions

A comparative analysis of the results of numerical simulation and calculations based on the COM model is carried out. The calculation results are in good agreement with each other and with the experimental results of measurements of the characteristics of a bandpass filter. It shows the adequacy of both approaches, which are based on fundamentally different provisions. Practical recommendations for reducing the calculation time of SAW devices in modeling based on the FEM in COMSOL have been proposed. The use of different approaches allows us to approach the experiment with a high probability of successful results. Finally, analytical models still for fast and effective synthesis and optimization of filter parameters are necessary.

Funding: This research received no external funding.

Data Availability Statement: The data presented in this study are available on request from the corresponding author.

Acknowledgments: The author expresses their gratitude to the Microsaw OY for the experimental data provided.

Conflicts of Interest: The author declares no conflict of interest.

References

1. Warder, P.; Link, A. Golden Age for Filter Design: Innovative and Proven Approaches for Acoustic Filter, Duplexer, and Multiplexer Design. *IEEE Microw. Mag.* **2015**, *16*, 60–72. [CrossRef]
2. Bauer, T.; Eggs, C.; Wagner, K.; Hagn, P. A Bright Outlook for Acoustic Filtering: A New Generation of Very Low-Profile SAW, TC SAW, and BAW Devices for Module Integration. *IEEE Microw. Mag.* **2015**, *16*, 73–81. [CrossRef]
3. Hashimoto, K.-Y.; Omori, T.; Yamaguchi, M. Design considerations on wideband longitudinally-coupled double-mode SAW filters. In Proceedings of the 2002 IEEE Ultrasonics Symposium, Munich, Germany, 8–11 October 2002; pp. 153–157. [CrossRef]
4. Loseu, A.S. Novel LSAW DMS filter structure for narrow duplex gap SE->Bal RX filter application. In Proceedings of the 2016 IEEE International Ultrasonics Symposium (IUS), San Diego, CA, USA, 11–14 October 2010; pp. 1258–1262. [CrossRef]

5. Malocha, S.; Gamble, K.J.; Dong, H.; Dharmalingam, A. Automated COM parameter extraction for $SiO_2/LiNbO_3$ and SiO2/LiTaO3 substrates. In Proceedings of the 2016 IEEE International Ultrasonics Symposium (IUS), Tours, France, 18–21 September 2016; pp. 1–4. [CrossRef]
6. Plessky, V.; Koskela, J.; Willemsen, B.A.; Turner, P.J.; Iliev, F.; Hammond, R.B.; Fenzi, N.O. FEM modeling of an entire 5-IDT CRF/DMS filter. In Proceedings of the 2017 IEEE International Ultrasonics Symposium (IUS), Washington, DC, USA, 6–9 September 2017; pp. 1–5. [CrossRef]
7. Iyama, A.; Li, X.; Bao, J.; Matsuoka, N.; Omori, T.; Hashimoto, K.-Y. Full 3D FEM Analysis of Scattering at a Border Between IDT and Reflector in SAW Resonators. In Proceedings of the 2019 IEEE International Ultrasonics Symposium (IUS), Glasgow, UK, 6–9 October 2019; pp. 1235–1238. [CrossRef]
8. Zhang, Y.-M.; Jin, J.; Li, H.-L.; Hu, H.-P. A Novel Method to Extract COM Parameters for SAW Based on FEM. In Proceedings of the 2019 13th Symposium on Piezoelectrcity, Acoustic Waves and Device Applications (SPAWDA), Harbin, China, 11–14 January 2019; pp. 1–5. [CrossRef]
9. Plessky, V.; Koskela, J. COUPLING-OF-MODES ANALYSIS OF SAW DEVICES. *Int. J. High Speed Electron. Syst.* **2000**, *10*, 867–947. [CrossRef]
10. Dmitriev, V.F. Modified equations of coupled surface acoustic waves. *Journal of Communications Technology and Electronics* **2009**, *54*, 1134–1143. [CrossRef]
11. Orlov, V.S. Wideband Two-Mode Leaky Surface Acoustic Wave Filter with Non-Equdistant Elecrodes of Transducers and Reflecting Gratings. *T-Comm.* **2019**, *13*, 36–45.
12. Sveshnikov, B. Discrete analysis of regular systems. In Proceedings of the IEEE International Ultrasonics Symposium, San Diego, CA, USA, 11–14 October 2010; pp. 1890–1893. [CrossRef]
13. Rukhlenko, A.S. Nodal analysis of multitransducer SAW devices. In Proceedings of the 1995 IEEE Ultrasonics Symposium, Seattle, WA, USA, 7–10 November 2002; pp. 297–300. [CrossRef]
14. Shimko, A.; Plessky, V. Fast SAW Device Simulation in COMSOL Using the Hierarchical Cascading Method. In Proceedings of the 2018 IEEE International Ultrasonics Symposium, Kobe, Japan, 22–25 October 2018; pp. 1–3. [CrossRef]
15. Koigerov, A.S.; Korlyakov, A.V. Finite Element Modeling of Surface Acoustic Wave Devices Using COMSOL. *Russ. Microelectron.* **2022**, *51*, 226–235. [CrossRef]
16. Zhgoon, S.; Shvetsov, A.; Patel, M.; Bhattacharjee, K. In-situ monitored deposition of SiO_2 on longitudinal wave based resonator. In Proceedings of the 2009 IEEE International Ultrasonics Symposium, Roma, Italy, 21 September 2009; pp. 2647–2650. [CrossRef]
17. Tang, G.; Goto, R.; Nakamura, H. Modeling and Suppression Method for Guided Mode in TC-SAW Devices. In Proceedings of the 2019 IEEE International Ultrasonics Symposium (IUS), Glasgow, UK, 6–9 October 2019; pp. 2087–2090. [CrossRef]
18. Zhang, Q.; Chen, Z.; Chen, Y.; Dong, J.; Tang, P.; Fu, S.; Wu, H.; Ma, J.; Zhao, X. Periodic Analysis of Surface Acoustic Wave Resonator with Dimensionally Reduced PDE Model Using COMSOL Code. *Micromachines* **2021**, *12*, 141. [CrossRef] [PubMed]
19. Hao, W.C.; Wei LU, O.; Zhao, G.H.; Jiao, H.L.; Yin, Y.G. FEM analysis of response mechanism for temperature sensors based on surface acoustic wave resonators. In Proceedings of the 2019 13th Symposium on Piezoelectricity, Acoustic Waves and Device Applications (SPAWDA), Harbin, China, 11–14 January 2019; pp. 1–5. [CrossRef]
20. Shen, J.; Fu, S.; Su, R.; Xu, H.; Zeng, F.; Song, C.; Pan, F. Systematical Study of the Basic Properties of Surface Acoustic Wave Devices Based on ZnO and GaN Multilayers. *Electronics* **2020**, *10*, 23. [CrossRef]
21. Jean Claude, A.O.; Eloi Jean Jacques, B.; Gaston, N.M.; Adoum, T.N.; Elysée, O.N.; Omar, E. Modeling and Electrical Characterization of a Bilayer Pt/AlN/Sapphire One Port Resonator for Sensor Applications. *Electronics* **2021**, *10*, 370. [CrossRef]
22. Ma, R.; Liu, W.; Sun, X.; Zhou, S.; Lin, D. FEM Simulation of a High-Performance 128 Y–XLiNbO3/SiO2/Si Functional Sub-strate for Surface Acoustic Wave Gyroscopes. *Micromachines* **2022**, *13*, 202. [CrossRef] [PubMed]
23. Shevchenko, S.Y.; Mikhailenko, D.A. Topological Optimization of Circular SAW Resonators: Overcoming the Discreteness Effects. *Sensors* **2022**, *22*, 1172. [CrossRef] [PubMed]
24. Koigerov, A.S.; Balysheva, O.L. Numerical Analysis of Parameters of Pseudosurface Acoustic Waves in Lithium Niobate and Tantalate Crystals. *J. Commun. Technol. Electron.* **2021**, *66*, 1388–1395. [CrossRef]
25. Dvoesherstov, M.Y.; Cherednik, V.I.; Bosov, S.I.; Orlov, I.Y.; Rudenko, O.V. Numerical and experimental analysis of the parameters of an electroacoustic thin-film microwave resonator. *Acoust. Phys.* **2013**, *59*, 513–520. [CrossRef]
26. Sun, X.; Ma, R.; Zhou, S.; Shao, X.; Cheng, J.; Lin, D.; Wang, W.; Liu, W. Fast, Accurate and Full Extraction of Coupling-of-Modes Parameters by Finite Element Method. *Crystals* **2022**, *12*, 706. [CrossRef]
27. Dmitriev, V.F.; Koigerov, A.S. Study of Surface Acoustic Wave ID Tags with Specified Correlation Propertieces. *J. Commun. Technol. Electron.* **2011**, *56*, 1256–1265. [CrossRef]
28. Sveshnikov, B.V.; Bagdasaryan, A.S. The Main Principles of Formation of the Transverse Modes in the Multilayered Wave-guides of Surface Acoustic Waves. *Radiophys Quantum* **2016**, *59*, 97–110. [CrossRef]
29. Morita, T.; Watanabe, Y.; Tanaka, M.; Nakazawa, Y. Wideband low loss double mode SAW filters. In Proceedings of the IEEE 1992 Ultrasonics Symposium, Tucson, AZ, USA, 20–23 October 1992; Volume 1, pp. 95–104. [CrossRef]
30. Campbell, C. Obtaining the fundamental and harmonic radiation conductances of a reflective SAW interdigital transducer. In Proceedings of the IEEE Ultrasonics Symposium, Sendai, Japan, 05–08 October 1998; Volume 1, pp. 169–173. [CrossRef]

31. Koigerov, A.S.; Balysheva, O.L. Finite element simulation of SAW delay line operating with the use of third harmonic frequency. *Comput. Telecommun. Control.* **2022**, *15*, 40–50. [CrossRef]
32. Available online: https://www.ndk.com/catalog/AN-SD_GG_e.pdf (accessed on 13 November 2022).

mathematics

MDPI

Article

A Fully Coupled Thermomechanical Phase Field Method for Modeling Cracks with Frictional Contact

Wan Wan and Pinlei Chen *

Department of Civil and Environmental Engineering, University Park, The Pennsylvania State University, 215c Sackett Building, State College, PA 16802, USA
* Correspondence: pzc216@psu.edu

Abstract: In this paper, a thermomechanical coupled phase field method is developed to model cracks with frictional contact. Compared to discrete methods, the phase field method can represent arbitrary crack geometry without an explicit representation of the crack surface. The two distinguishable features of the proposed phase field method are: (1) for the mechanical phase, no specific algorithm is needed for imposing contact constraints on the fracture surfaces; (2) for the thermal phase, formulations are proposed for incorporating the phase field damage parameter so that different thermal conductance conditions are accommodated. While the stress is updated explicitly in the regularized interface regions under different contact conditions, the thermal conductivity is determined under different conductance conditions. In particular, we consider a pressure-dependent thermal conductance model (PDM) that is fully coupled with the mechanical phase, along with the other three thermal conductance models, i.e., the fully conductive model (FCM), the adiabatic model (ACM), and the uncoupled model (UCM). The potential of this formulation is showcased by several benchmark problems. We gain insights into the role of the temperature field affecting the mechanical field. Several 2D boundary value problems are addressed, demonstrating the model's ability to capture cracking phenomena with the effect of the thermal field. We compare our results with the discrete methods as well as other phase field methods, and a very good agreement is achieved.

Keywords: coupled thermomechanical problem; frictional contact; phase field method; cracks and fractures

MSC: 70-08; 82M36; 82M37

Citation: Wan, W.; Chen, P. A Fully Coupled Thermomechanical Phase Field Method for Modeling Cracks with Frictional Contact. *Mathematics* **2022**, *10*, 4416. https://doi.org/10.3390/math10234416

Academic Editors: Shujin Laima, Yong Cao, Xiaowei Jin and Hehe Ren

Received: 20 October 2022
Accepted: 16 November 2022
Published: 23 November 2022

Publisher's Note: MDPI stays neutral with regard to jurisdictional claims in published maps and institutional affiliations.

Copyright: © 2022 by the authors. Licensee MDPI, Basel, Switzerland. This article is an open access article distributed under the terms and conditions of the Creative Commons Attribution (CC BY) license (https://creativecommons.org/licenses/by/4.0/).

1. Introduction

Thermomechanical contact cracks are ubiquitous in engineering applications, ranging from metal forming and powder compaction processes [1] to heat conduction across the contact interfaces in cooling systems of microelectronics [2]. It is essential yet challenging to accurately model the frictional crack phenomena, including fracture onset, propagation, and branching, particularly in a multi-physical environment [1,3,4]. To tackle the aforementioned complex physical phenomena with regard to cracks and fractures that cannot be resolved using analytical methods, developments within the context of computational mechanics and numerical simulations have been a matter of intensive research in recent years.

In general, thermomechanical contact constraints are treated using methods such as the Lagrange multiplier method and augmented Lagrange multiplier method [5–8], or the penalty method [9], which are inherited from the discontinuous Galerkin (DG) method. In these methods, the contact constraints are either enforced through the Lagrange multipliers or by penalty regularization. When using the Lagrange multiplier method, an inf–sup stability requirement needs to be satisfied with the additional unknown degree of freedom [6,7]. On the other hand, for the penalty method, while it remains primal and is easy to implement, a carefully chosen penalty parameter is crucial to avoiding the loss of coercivity [10] and ill-conditioned systems with too many constraints [11]. The Nitsche-type method, originally proposed to enforce element boundaries in a weak sense [12,13], is another method used to model contact and frictional conditions [2,10,14,15]. Different from the Penalty-type method, the Nitsche-type method is generally consistent without penetration. One advantage of the Nitsche-type method over the Lagrange multiplier method is that it contains appropriate and consistent terms that only involve the primary fields, i.e., there is no need to fulfill the inf–sup condition [10]. Despite all the advantages of the Nitsche-type method, the interface weighting parameters and stability parameters are user-defined with special treatments. To resolve this issue in Nitsche's method with regard to user-defined parameters, the variational multiscale discontinuous Galerkin (VMDG) method [16,17] has been proposed to provide a primal formulation with interfacial stabilization for both weak and strong discontinuities using the variational multiscale (VMS) technique. In the VMDG method, the formulation is naturally derived, and no ad hoc parameters are appended. Nevertheless, in all these interfacial element formulations, continuity restrictions are imposed at the junction of overlapping finite element grids, and all methods exhibit element-wise conservative approximations [14,18] for cracks. Moreover, the discontinuities are aligned with element boundaries. Due to the complexity of the crack patterns, meshes should be fine enough around the crack region to ensure arbitrary crack branching [18]. On the other hand, allow the discontinuity to be embedded inside elements, local remeshing techniques, such as the advanced methods based on X-FEM [19–21] or E-FEM [22–24], are used near crack regions for sharp crack propagation. However, these local enrichment strategies suffer in three-dimensional (3D) applications [3,25,26] and present limitations when predicting crack initiation, branching, and coalescence for multiple crack fronts [27]. In addition, in the context of fracture mechanics, modeling the structural behavior of multiaxial fatigue problems is challenging. The experimental results show that it is essential to model the fracture surface based on qualitative fractography [28] and to understand the fracture surface response based on fracture surface topography parameters [29]. In the work recently published by Lanwer et al. [30], a combined experimental and computational method is proposed to investigate the fatigue and degradation behavior of the fiber-matrix composite. In their work, a mechanism-oriented bonding model on the inserted fiber–matrix interfaces is developed for FE analysis. However, to better understand the fiber–matrix bond mechanism and the possibility of cracks propagating in the matrix, it is desired to have a numerical method where the crack path is not defined a priori.

The phase field method is a feasible algorithm proposed in recent years that provides a new perspective toward simulating complex crack topologies [3]. Different from the discrete methods such as the above-mentioned VMDG, Nitsche's, penalty, or Lagrange multiplier methods, the phase field method is rooted in classical energy-based Griffith's theory [26,31]. The sharp crack surface is regularized within a thin band of a diffusive crack zone governed by a scale variable, called the damage parameter, that distinguishes the damaged and undamaged domains [3,25]. This nonlocal damage variable is governed by a Poisson-type partial differential equation (PDE) and evolves with crack propagation. Compared to discrete methods, the phase field method has decisive advantages; the explicit crack interface tracking is unveiled by this scale variable [32], and the numerical implementation is straightforward [3]. This method has gained extensive attention in recent years, making remarkable contributions to modeling quasi-static and dynamic brittle fractures [4,26,33,34], ductile fractures [35,36], fatigue [37–43], and multi-physics applications [32,44–46]. For modeling frictional cracks, because preexisting phase field models for fractures only consider non-contact or stick contact conditions without incorporating a frictional slip condition, Fei and Choo [47,48] proposed a stress decomposition scheme within the context of the phase field method to model frictional slip condition. In their approach, unlike discrete methods, there is no need to implement specific tracking strategies for the interface/cracking surface and for the evolution of the gap function along the contact surface. Their approach, although very promising, only works for pure mechanical problems. Other phase field methods for multi-physics applications [32,44–46] only degrade or maintain the effect of thermal conductivity based on the damage variable, which is not sufficient to accommodate different thermal conductance conditions at the contact surfaces. In discrete modeling, the contact heat flux is characterized by a pressure-dependent thermal contact conductance as well as by the temperature jump across the contact interface [49,50]. A similar treatment should be developed within the context of the phase field method. To the best of the authors' knowledge, there is no such phase field model that accommodates different scenarios for thermal conductance.

In the present work, following the work done by Fei and Choo [47,48], we extend the pure mechanical phase field formulation to a thermomechanically coupled formulation for frictional contact problems. The proposed framework has the following features: (1) the contact constraints at the interfaces are represented without any explicit functions or algorithms, and (2) different thermal conductance conditions, including the pressure-dependent thermal conductance, are accommodated via the existence of the contact pressure and the phase field damage parameter. In other words, the key idea of the proposed method is to incorporate the thermal conductance constraints through the suitable calculation of the thermal conductivity in the fracture surface region. In addition to the proper calculations of the stress tensor for different contact behaviors and constraints for the mechanical phase [47], a fully coupled thermomechanical formulation for frictional contact problems is derived in the current work. The proposed phase field method is able to handle the complex crack geometry and the contact condition in the mechanical phase while coping with the different thermal conductance conditions in the thermal phase.

In the following sections, we first briefly introduce of the phase field method for coupled thermomechanical problems in Section 2. In Section 3, we develop the governing equations and corresponding weak forms for coupled thermomechanical problems that involve frictional contact. In Section 4, following a summary of the approach used to explicitly generate the stress tensor at the contact interfaces based on the different contact conditions, we introduce a new strategy to calculate the thermal conductivity within the interface region. A set of numerical simulations verifying the proposed algorithm is shown in Section 5, followed by concluding remarks in Section 6.

2. Phase Field Method for Coupled Thermomechanical Problems

The purpose of this section is to develop a new phase field formulation that accommodates both thermal and mechanical constraints within the fracture surface region. The formulation is derived along the same lines as [48] to model general frictional interfaces in solids, which we extend to incorporate thermal conductance constraints. This formulation is useful for modeling frictional contact problems in a thermomechanical setting.

2.1. Regularized Variational Framework

We first establish the regularized variational framework for thermomechanical problems in developing governing equations for the phase field problem. As shown in Figure 1, let Ω be the open domain and Γ_I the curve for the possible cracks. In a regularized framework, the scalar parameter d in the fracture surface energy equation is used to approximate the crack geometry, while l_c is interpolated to control the thickness of the crack in its regularized form. The scalar parameter $d \in [0,1]$ is incorporated to denote the damage crack region ($d = 1$) and the intact bulk domain ($d = 0$).

The variational approach for fracture mechanics proposed by Francfort and Marigo [18] states the energy function for the cracked body [25]. Based on the energy functions from [18], the regularized form of the energy describing the cracked structure induced by the thermomechanical effects can be expressed as follows:

$$E(\boldsymbol{u}, \theta, d, \nabla d) = E_e(\boldsymbol{u}, \theta, d) + E_d(d, \nabla d) \tag{1}$$

where $E_e(\boldsymbol{u}, \theta, d)$ is the elastic energy stored in the cracked body, $E_d(d, \nabla d)$ is the fracture surface energy, $\boldsymbol{u}$ is the displacement field, and $\theta = T - T_{\text{ref}}$ is the relative temperature field of the current temperature T with respect to the reference temperature T_{ref}.

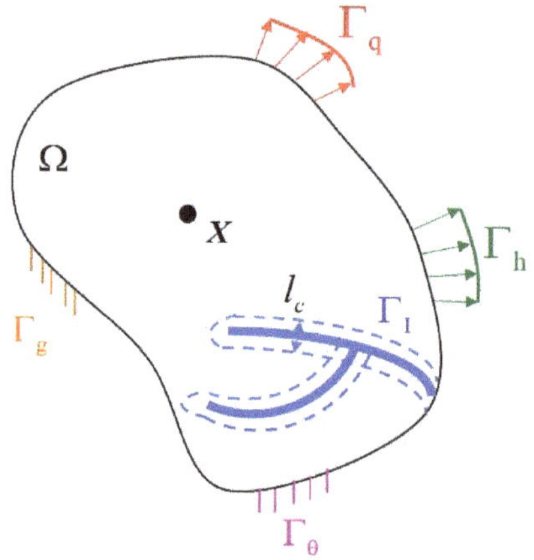

Figure 1. Schematic representation of a domain with its boundary conditions and a strong discontinuity at Γ_{I}.

In the standard linear theory of elasticity for isotropic solids, the global energy storage functional is the sum of the elastic energy and the fracture energy:

$$E(\boldsymbol{u}, \theta, d, \nabla d) = \int_{\Omega} \Psi(\boldsymbol{\varepsilon}, \theta, d)\, d\Omega + \int_{\Gamma_{\text{I}}} \mathcal{G}_c d\Gamma_{\text{I}} \tag{2}$$

where $\Psi(\boldsymbol{\varepsilon}, \theta, d)$ is the energy density of the bulk and $\mathcal{G}_c$ is the Griffth's critical energy release. Assuming the quadratic free energy functional, the undamaged strain energy functional $\Psi(\boldsymbol{\varepsilon}, \theta)$ can be expressed as

$$\Psi(\boldsymbol{\varepsilon}, \theta) = \frac{1}{2}\boldsymbol{\varepsilon} : \mathbb{C} : \boldsymbol{\varepsilon} - \theta \boldsymbol{m} : \boldsymbol{\varepsilon} - \frac{1}{2}\frac{c_v}{T_{\text{ref}}}\theta^2 \tag{3}$$

where $\boldsymbol{\varepsilon}$ is the strain, $\mathbb{C}$ is the fourth-order tensor representing the material moduli for the bulk domain, $c_v = \rho_0 c_p$ is the volumetric heat capacity (with ρ_0 being the density and c_p the specific heat capacity), and $\boldsymbol{m}$ is the second-order thermomechanical coupling tensor, which is discussed in detail in Section 3.

In Equation (2), $\mathcal{G}_c$ is the Griffth's critical energy release, with $\int_{\Gamma_{\text{I}}} \mathcal{G}_c d\Gamma_{\text{I}} = \int_{\Omega} \mathcal{G}_c \gamma(d, \nabla d)\, d\Omega$ measuring the critical fracture energy; $\gamma(d, \nabla d)$ is the crack surface density functional, and we adopt the most common one, which is written as the convex function

$$\gamma(d, \nabla d) = \frac{1}{2l_c} d^2 + \frac{l_c}{2}(\nabla d)^2 \tag{4}$$

2.2. Phase Field Approximation

It is noted that the crack surface behavior is governed by the unilateral conditions of stress carrying capacity, depending on whether the solid is in tension or compression [1,51]. In the present work, we follow the idea from Miehe [3]. Considering the unilateral contact, the damage is assumed to only modify the positive part of the strain energy, with the positive part defined in terms of the principal strains at which spectral decomposition of the strain tensor is required. Based on this, the free energy density function in Equation (3) can be rewritten as $\Psi(\boldsymbol{\varepsilon},\theta,d)$ in the bulk to accommodate the damage parameter d, then decomposed to the positive part and negative part, as shown in Equation (5).

$$\Psi(\boldsymbol{\varepsilon},\theta,d) = [g(d)+k]\Psi^{+}(\boldsymbol{\varepsilon},\theta) + \Psi^{-}(\boldsymbol{\varepsilon},\theta) \tag{5}$$

The existence of the small positive variable k is used to ensure that the partly broken systems are well-posed when numerical discretization is applied [3]. In the following applications, we set $k = 10^{-8}$. A simple degradation function that describes the degradation of the tensile part of the stored energy evolving damage is interpolated as $g(d) = (1-d)^2$. It is assumed to have the following properties: (1) $g(d=0) = 1$ represents the undamaged phase; (2) $g(d=1) = 0$ represents the fully damaged phase; (3) $g'(d=1) = 0$ guarantees that the energetic fracture force converges to a finite value when the fully damaged phase is reached [3]. Here, $\Psi^{+}(\boldsymbol{\varepsilon})$ and $\Psi^{-}(\boldsymbol{\varepsilon})$ are the strain energies decomposed from the positive and negative components of the strain tensor.

In order to define the positive and negative parts of the stored energy, the strain field is decomposed into the tensile and compressive modes, as follows:

$$\boldsymbol{\varepsilon} = \boldsymbol{\varepsilon}^{+} + \boldsymbol{\varepsilon}^{-} \tag{6}$$

where $\boldsymbol{\varepsilon}^{\pm} = \sum_{i=1}^{n_{el}} \langle \varepsilon^i \rangle \pm \boldsymbol{n}^i \otimes \boldsymbol{n}^i$, with $\boldsymbol{\varepsilon}^i$ defined as the principal strain, and $\boldsymbol{n}^i$ as the principal strain direction, and where $\langle x \rangle_{\pm} = (x \pm |x|)/2$. Using the definitions above, the positive (tensile) part $\Psi^{+}(\boldsymbol{\varepsilon})$ and the negative (compressive) part $\Psi^{-}(\boldsymbol{\varepsilon})$ of the stored energy due to the mechanical loadings are decomposed as follows:

$$\Psi^{\pm}(\boldsymbol{\varepsilon}) = \frac{\lambda}{2}(\langle tr(\boldsymbol{\varepsilon})\rangle^{\pm})^2 + \mu tr\{(\boldsymbol{\varepsilon}^{\pm})^2\} = \frac{\kappa}{2}(\langle tr(\boldsymbol{\varepsilon})\rangle^{\pm})^2 + \mu tr\{(\boldsymbol{\varepsilon}^{\pm}_{dev})^2\} \tag{7}$$

By substituting Equation (4) and Equation (5) into Equation (2) and taking the variational derivative with respect to the damage parameter d, the governing equation for the phase field problem to be solved by evaluating the phase field $d(\boldsymbol{x},t)$ at time t is summarized as follows:

$$g'(d)\mathcal{H} - \mathcal{G}_c(\frac{d}{l_c} - l_c \Delta d) = 0 \ \text{ in } \ \Omega \tag{8}$$

$$d(\boldsymbol{x},t) = 1 \ \text{ on } \ \Gamma_{\mathrm{I}} \tag{9}$$

$$\nabla d(\boldsymbol{x},t) \cdot \boldsymbol{n} = 0 \ \text{ on } \ \partial\Omega \tag{10}$$

where $\mathcal{H}$ is the strain history function, $\mathcal{G}_c$ is the fracture energy, and $\boldsymbol{n}$ is the outward unit normal to $\partial\Omega$.

As stated in [48], $\mathcal{H}$ can be arbitrarily defined as a constant for models with stationary cracks, meaning that the phase field equation only needs to be solved once in order to find the distribution of the phase field parameter. When dealing with crack propagation, $\mathcal{H}$ needs to be calculated based on the updated stress tensor and the phase field parameter. For the calculation of the strain history functional $\mathcal{H}$, we adopt the idea from Miehe et al. [3], as follows:

$$\mathcal{H}(\boldsymbol{x},t_{n+1}) = \max_{\o \in [0,t_n]} \{\Psi^{+}(\boldsymbol{x},\tau)\}. \tag{11}$$

3. Governing Equations and Corresponding Weak Forms

The balance of the linear momentum, as well as the balance of the energy of the problem, are provided below:

$$\boldsymbol{0} = \nabla \cdot \boldsymbol{\sigma} + \rho \boldsymbol{b} \tag{12}$$

$$\rho c_p \dot{\theta} = -\nabla \cdot \boldsymbol{q} - T_{\mathrm{ref}} \boldsymbol{m} : \nabla \boldsymbol{v} + r \tag{13}$$

where σ is the Cauchy stress tensor, $\nabla \cdot (\cdot) = \text{tr}[\text{grad}(\cdot)]$ is the divergence operator, $\rho > 0$ is the density, $\boldsymbol{b}$ is the mass-specific body force, c_p is the specific heat capacity, $\theta = T - T_{\text{ref}}$ is the temperature difference of the current temperature T with respect to the reference temperature T_{ref}, $\dot{\theta}$ is the time derivative of the temperature field, $\boldsymbol{q}$ is the heat flux vector, $\boldsymbol{v}$ is the velocity of the mechanical field, r is the heat source, and $\boldsymbol{m} = 3\kappa\beta \mathrm{I}$ is the second-order thermomechanical coupling tensor, where κ is the bulk modulus and β is the coefficient of thermal expansion. Using Fourier's relation, the heat flux vector is defined as $\boldsymbol{q} = -\boldsymbol{k}\nabla\theta$; by assuming isotropic, $\boldsymbol{k} = k\mathrm{I}$ is defined as the thermal conductivity.

Remark 1. *It should be noted that Equations (12) and (13) are fully coupled through the existence of the second-order thermomechanical coupling tensor* $\boldsymbol{m}$.

The boundary conditions of this coupled problem are provided by

$$\boldsymbol{u} = \bar{\boldsymbol{u}} \text{ on } \Gamma_{\text{g}} \tag{14}$$

$$\sigma \cdot \boldsymbol{n} = \bar{\boldsymbol{t}} \text{ on } \Gamma_{\text{h}} \tag{15}$$

$$\theta = \bar{\theta} \text{ on } \Gamma_{\theta} \tag{16}$$

$$\boldsymbol{q} \cdot \boldsymbol{n} = -\bar{q} \text{ on } \Gamma_{\text{q}} \tag{17}$$

where $\bar{\boldsymbol{u}}$, $\bar{\boldsymbol{t}}$, $\bar{\theta}$, and $\bar{q}$ are the prescribed displacement, traction, temperature, and heat flux, respectively, and $\boldsymbol{n}$ is the unit normal vector pointing outwards at the boundaries shown in Figure 1.

The corresponding weak forms are summarized as follows by multiplying the test functions $\{\eta, \delta\theta, \delta d\}$, integrating by part, and applying the divergence theorem. The formal statement of the weak forms is as follows: given $\{\mathcal{G}_c, \mathcal{H}, l_c, \rho, \boldsymbol{b}, r, \bar{\boldsymbol{u}}, \bar{\boldsymbol{t}}, c_p, \boldsymbol{k}, T_{\text{ref}}, \bar{\theta}, \bar{q}\}$, find $\{\boldsymbol{u}, \theta, d\}$ such that Equations (18)–(20) are satisfied for all $\{\eta, \delta\theta, \delta d\}$.

Weak form of the phase field:

$$\int_{\Omega} \delta d \cdot \{g'(d)\mathcal{H} - \frac{\mathcal{G}_c}{l_c} d\} d\Omega - \int_{\Omega} \mathcal{G}_c l_c (\nabla \delta d) \cdot (\nabla d) d\Omega = 0 \tag{18}$$

Weak form of the balance of momentum:

$$\int_{\Omega} (\nabla \boldsymbol{\eta} : \sigma - \boldsymbol{\eta} \cdot \rho \boldsymbol{b}) dV - \int_{\Gamma_{\text{h}}} \bar{\boldsymbol{t}} \cdot \boldsymbol{\eta} d\Gamma_{\text{h}} = 0 \tag{19}$$

Weak form of the balance of energy:

$$\begin{aligned} \int_{\Omega} [-\rho c_p \dot{\theta} \cdot \delta\theta - \nabla\delta \cdot (\boldsymbol{k}\nabla\theta)] dV + \int_{\Omega} [-T_{\text{ref}}(\boldsymbol{m} : \nabla \boldsymbol{v}) \cdot \delta\theta + r \cdot \delta\theta] dV \\ + \int_{\Gamma_{\text{q}}} \bar{q} \cdot \delta\theta d\Gamma_{\text{q}} = 0 \end{aligned} \tag{20}$$

In the context of phase field modeling with the expression of $g(d)$ mentioned in the previous section, in Equation (19) we can express the stress tensor in the domain as a combination of the stress for the bulk and the interface [48], as follows:

$$\sigma = g(d)\sigma_{\text{bulk}} + [1 - g(d)]\sigma_{\text{interface}} \tag{21}$$

where σ_{bulk} and $\sigma_{\text{interface}}$ are the stresses in the interior and on the interface, respectively. Equation (21) is considered a generalized expression of the stress in the phase field model for the frictional contact problem [47].

The bulk Cauchy stress tensor σ_{bulk} is represented as $\sigma = \mathbb{C} : \epsilon - \boldsymbol{m}\theta$, where $\mathbb{C}$ is the fourth-order tensor representing the elastic modulus of the bulk material and ϵ is the strain as defined in Section 2.1. The calculation of the interface stress $\sigma_{\text{interface}}$ is discussed in Section 4 under different contact conditions.

In a similar fashion, we propose a generalized expression of the thermal conductivity $\boldsymbol{k}$ in Equation (20) for the coupled thermomechanical problem as

$$\boldsymbol{k} = (1 - A)\boldsymbol{k}_{\text{bulk}} + A\boldsymbol{k}_{\text{interface}} \tag{22}$$

where $\boldsymbol{k}_{\text{bulk}} = k_{\text{bulk}}\mathrm{I}$ is the thermal conductivity of the interior domain, $\boldsymbol{k}_{\text{interface}} = k_{\text{interface}}\mathrm{I}$ is the thermal conductivity of the interface domain, and A is a triggering value that distinguishes the bulk from the interface domain. We discuss how to decide this triggering parameter A and provide the expressions for the bulk and interface thermal conductivity $\boldsymbol{k}_{\text{bulk}}$ and $\boldsymbol{k}_{\text{interface}}$ in Section 4.

4. Stress Tensor and Thermal Conductivity Calculation for Different Contact Conditions

4.1. Stress Tensor σ Updates in the Phase Field Modeling

For the mechanical phase, following [47], updates to the Cauchy stress are made to incorporate the contact-dependent mechanical response of the interface based on different contact conditions.

We first summarize the stress tensor updates of $\sigma_{\text{interface}}$ in Equation (21) based on the different contact conditions. The normal strain is calculated to determine the following debonding/contact conditions:

$$\varepsilon_N = \boldsymbol{\varepsilon} : (\boldsymbol{n} \otimes \boldsymbol{n}) \begin{cases} > 0 : & \text{non-contact} \\ \leq 0 : & \text{in contact} \end{cases} \tag{23}$$

For the non-contact condition with $\varepsilon_N > 0$, the stress free state results in the interface stress tensor $\sigma_{\text{interface}} = \mathbf{0}$, and there is an open crack between two surfaces. Therefore, the stress tensor in Equation (21) is expressed as $\sigma = g(d)\sigma_{\text{bulk}}$.

For the in contact condition with $\varepsilon_N \leq 0$, the yield function $f(\boldsymbol{t}_T, t_N)$ is introduced to distinguish the stick and slip conditions. The yield function $f(\boldsymbol{t}_T, t_N)$ with a frictional coefficient μ_f for the frictional Coulomb model is defined as

$$f(\boldsymbol{t}_T, t_N) = \|\boldsymbol{t}_T\| + \mu_f t_N \begin{cases} < 0 : & \text{stick} \\ \geq 0 : & \text{slip} \end{cases} \tag{24}$$

where $\boldsymbol{t}_T = (\mathrm{I} - \boldsymbol{n} \otimes \boldsymbol{n})\sigma_{\text{bulk}}$ and $t_N = \sigma_{\text{bulk}} : (\boldsymbol{n} \otimes \boldsymbol{n})$.

When the interface is considered in the stick condition, there is no relative motion between the bulk and interface domains [47], and $\sigma_{\text{bulk}} = \sigma_{\text{interface}}$ yields the stress tensor in Equation (21) as $\sigma = \sigma_{\text{bulk}}$. On the other hand, when the interface is considered in the slip condition with $f(\boldsymbol{t}_T, t_N) \leq 0$, the interface stress tensor is calculated by decomposing into a frictional part σ_{friction} and a no-penetration part $\sigma_{\text{no-penetration}}$, as proposed by Fei and Choo [47], with the expressions as follows:

$$\sigma_{\text{friction}} = \mu_f t_N \text{sign}(\boldsymbol{t}_T)(\boldsymbol{n} \otimes \boldsymbol{m} + \boldsymbol{m} \otimes \boldsymbol{n}) \tag{25}$$

$$\sigma_{\text{no-penetration}} = \sigma_{\text{bulk}} - \|\boldsymbol{t}_T\|(\boldsymbol{n} \otimes \boldsymbol{m} + \boldsymbol{m} \otimes \boldsymbol{n}) \tag{26}$$

When substituting Equations (25) and (26) into Equation (21), the overall stress tensor under the slip condition is obtained as

$$\sigma = \sigma_{\text{bulk}} + (1 - g(d))(\mu_f t_N \text{sign}(\boldsymbol{t}_T) - \|\boldsymbol{t}_T\|)(\boldsymbol{n} \otimes \boldsymbol{m} + \boldsymbol{m} \otimes \boldsymbol{n}) \tag{27}$$

The procedures for updating the interface stress tensor $\sigma_{\text{interface}}$ and the overall stress tensor σ are summarized in Box 1, where x_{int} represents the geometry description of an integration point.

Box 1. Stress update algorithm for phase field modeling of the frictional contact problem.

Step 1: Inputs at $\boldsymbol{x}_{int}$: strain $\boldsymbol{\varepsilon}$, phase field variable d, the normal unit vector $\boldsymbol{n}$,
and the tangential unit vector $\boldsymbol{m}$.
Step 2: If the phase field variable $d = 0$, THEN
Bulk domain,
Set $\boldsymbol{\sigma} = \boldsymbol{\sigma}_{bulk} = \mathbb{C} : \boldsymbol{\varepsilon} - \boldsymbol{m}\theta$,
EXIT
Step 3: ELSE Interface domain. Calculate the normal strain $\varepsilon_N = \boldsymbol{\varepsilon} : (\boldsymbol{n} \otimes \boldsymbol{n})$
If $\varepsilon_N > 0$, THEN
Non−contact condition, $\boldsymbol{\sigma}_{\text{interface}} = \boldsymbol{0}$,
Set $\boldsymbol{\sigma} = g(d)\boldsymbol{\sigma}_{\text{bulk}}$,
EXIT
ELSE $t_N \leq 0$,
Contact condition,
Calculate frictional yield function $f = \|\boldsymbol{t}_T\| + \mu_f t_N$,
THEN go to Step 4.
Step 4: Contact condition.
IF $f < 0$ THEN
Stick condition, $\boldsymbol{\sigma}_{\text{interface}} = \boldsymbol{\sigma}_{\text{bulk}}$,
Set $\boldsymbol{\sigma} = g(d)\boldsymbol{\sigma}_{\text{bulk}} + [1 - g(d)]\boldsymbol{\sigma}_{\text{interface}} = \boldsymbol{\sigma}_{\text{bulk}}$,
EXIT
ELSE,
Slip condition, $\boldsymbol{\sigma}_{\text{interface}} = \boldsymbol{\sigma}_{\text{friction}} + \boldsymbol{\sigma}_{\text{no-penetration}}$,
Set $\boldsymbol{\sigma} = \boldsymbol{\sigma}_{\text{bulk}} + (1 - g(d))(\mu_f t_N)\text{sign}(\boldsymbol{t}_T) - \|\boldsymbol{t}_T\|(\boldsymbol{n} \otimes \boldsymbol{m} + \boldsymbol{m} \otimes \boldsymbol{n})$,
EXIT
END

4.2. *Thermal Conductivity Tensor* **k** *Updates in Phase Field Modeling*

To the best of our knowledge, there is no specific formulation of thermal conductivity in the existing literature on the phase field method for coupled thermomechanical problems when considering frictional contact. In most existing phase field models, the thermal conductivity $\boldsymbol{k}$ is degraded as $g(d)\boldsymbol{k}$ when considering the damage effect. To accommodate frictional contact in the thermal field, we consider the heat transfer associated with the fracture damage as well as different types of thermal contact conditions. To this end, we present thermal conductivity $\boldsymbol{k}$ updates based on four thermal conductance contact models.

As shown in the Figure 2, we enlarge the domain near the crack region in Figure 1, and the crack is shown in Figure 2a. Using the phase field method, the crack is modeled by the thin diffusive damage band shown in Figure 2b. As provided in Equation (22), the trigger parameter A is used to distinguish the bulk and interface domains. By setting the threshold to the damage value, the distribution of the trigger parameter A is shown in Figure 2c. The procedure for updating the thermal conductivity for different regions is explained in Box 2; the value of A is determined by comparing the phase field variable d with the threshold, then jumping into the corresponding thermal conductivity updates.

Remark 2. *Recalling the phase field governing equation Equation (8), the analytical solution can be written as $d = e^{-|x|/l_c}$, where x is the distance from the current location to the nearest $d = 1$ point. This argument is strong evidence for defining the damage threshold. From this equation, the width of the diffusive band is determined by the length parameter l_c. We set the threshold as $d = e^{-1} \approx 0.378$, where $x = l_c$, to divide the bulk and interface regions. When the damage value at the integration point surpasses this value, we assume that the interface area is entered.*

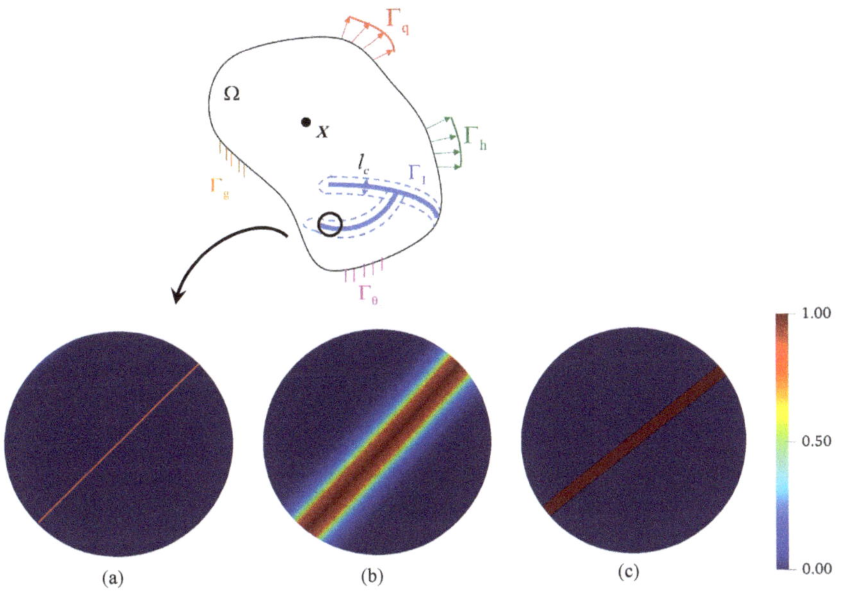

Figure 2. Crack evolution of proposed phase field method in the thermal field: (**a**) actual crack; (**b**) crack description in the phase field method; (**c**) crack description under trigger parameter A.

With Box 2, different thermal situations can be monitored in the phase field method. In this section, we introduce four different thermal models and demonstrate how to define $\boldsymbol{k}_{\text{bulk}}$ and $\boldsymbol{k}_{\text{interface}}$ for the respective models.

Box 2. Thermal conductivity update algorithm for phase field modeling.

Step 1: Inputs at $\boldsymbol{x}_{\text{int}}$: phase field variable d,
thermal conductivity $\boldsymbol{k}_{\text{bulk}}$ and $\boldsymbol{k}_{\text{interface}}$.
Step 2: Set $\boldsymbol{k} = (1-A)\boldsymbol{k}_{\text{bulk}} + A\boldsymbol{k}_{\text{interface}}$
Step 3: If $d >$ threshold, Interface domain
$A = 1$, THEN $\boldsymbol{k} = \boldsymbol{k}_{\text{interface}}$
ELSE, Bulk domain
$A = 0$, THEN $\boldsymbol{k} = \boldsymbol{k}_{\text{bulk}}$
END

Four Thermal Conductance Contact Models

Four different thermal conductance models are introduced in this section and implemented in the following applications. The definitions of $\boldsymbol{k}_{\text{bulk}}$ and $\boldsymbol{k}_{\text{interface}}$ in different thermal scenarios are displayed in Table 1. For the fully conductive model (FCM), the thermal conductivity is kept as a constant, assuming the whole model is in the undamaged region with $\boldsymbol{k} = \boldsymbol{k}_0$. For the adiabatic model (ADM), a small enough value for the $\boldsymbol{k}_{\text{interface}}$ avoids heat interaction through the crack region. Normal contact stress is utilized for both the pressure-dependent (PDM) and uncoupled (UCM) models, meaning that the capability of heat transfer is dominated by both the mechanical loading and the damage effect. It is noted that the thermal expansion coefficient β is set to be very small in the UCM in order to eliminate the coupling effect from the mechanical and thermal field.

Table 1. Four different thermal conductance models with different settings of thermal conductivity k and thermal expansion coefficient β.

Thermal Conductance Models	k_{bulk}	$k_{\text{interface}}$	Thermal Expansion Coefficient
Pressure dependent model (PDM)	$k_0 g(d)$	$k_0 g(d)(\frac{t_n}{H_e})^{\varepsilon_c}$	$\beta = 2.386 \times 10^{-3}/°\text{C}$
Uncoupled model (UCM)	$k_0 g(d)$	$k_0 g(d)(\frac{t_n}{H_e})^{\varepsilon_c}$	$\beta = 2.386 \times 10^{-24}/°\text{C}$
Fully conductive model (FCM)	k_0	k_0	$\beta = 2.386 \times 10^{-3}/°\text{C}$
Adiabatic contact model (ACM)	$k_0 g(d)$	10^{-7}	$\beta = 2.386 \times 10^{-3}/°\text{C}$

Here, we use the pressure-dependent thermal contact model as an example to show how the process of thermal conductivity updating works. Instead of having a thermal contact conductance formulation at the contact surface, in the phase field formulation, for the first time, we develop a formulation for the interfacial thermal conductivity that is a function of the phase-field variable and the contact pressure, which accounts for the normal stress-related heat exchange through the spots. Inspired by the thermal conductance expression from discrete methods [52], we propose the following formulation for the pressure-dependent thermal conductivity:

$$k_{\text{interface}} = g(d)\left(\frac{t_{\text{N,bulk}}}{H_e}\right)^{\varepsilon_c} k_{\text{bulk}} \tag{28}$$

where $t_{\text{N,bulk}}$ is the contact traction in the normal direction, H_e is the Vickers hardness coefficient, and ε_c is the thermal constant. The updates for the thermal conductivity based on the pressure-dependent contact conditions are summarized in Box 3. The bulk and interface thermal domains are separated by the phase field variable d with the threshold setting. When $d <$ threshold, we consider the bulk domain with $A = 0$, and employ the expression of k_{bulk} for the thermal conductivity. Otherwise, we consider the interface domain with $A = 1$ and $k_{\text{interface}}$. For the pressure-dependent model, we use the norm of the normal strain to differentiate the contact and debonding conditions. When $\varepsilon_N \leq 0$, we apply the pressure-dependent model to calculate $k_{\text{interface}}$.

Box 3. Thermal conductivity update algorithm for phase field modeling of the pressure-dependent contact model.

Step 1: Inputs at $\boldsymbol{x}_{\text{int}}$: the strain $\boldsymbol{\varepsilon}$, the thermal conductivity $\boldsymbol{k}_0$, the phase field variable d, the normal unit vector $\boldsymbol{n}$, and the tangential unit vector $\boldsymbol{m}$, the threshold value: $e^{-1} \approx 0.378$.
Step 2: Set $\boldsymbol{k} = (1 - A)\boldsymbol{k}_{\text{bulk}} + A\boldsymbol{k}_{\text{interface}}$
Step 3: If the phase field variable $d <$ threshold, Bulk domain
  $A = 0$, THEN $\boldsymbol{k} = \boldsymbol{k}_{\text{bulk}}$
  Set $\boldsymbol{k}_{\text{bulk}} = g(d)\boldsymbol{k}_0$
  EXIT
Step 4: ELSE, the phase field variable $d \geq$ threshold, Interface domain
  $A = 1$, THEN $\boldsymbol{k} = \boldsymbol{k}_{\text{interface}}$
  Calculate the normal strain $\varepsilon_N = \boldsymbol{\varepsilon} : (\boldsymbol{n} \otimes \boldsymbol{n})$
  If $\varepsilon_N > 0$, THEN
    Non−contact condition,
    $\boldsymbol{k}_{\text{interface}} = g(d)\boldsymbol{k}_0$,
    EXIT
  ELSE,
    Contact condition,
    $\boldsymbol{k}_{\text{interface}} = g(d)\left(\frac{t_{\text{N,bulk}}}{H_e}\right)^{\varepsilon_c}\boldsymbol{k}_0$
  EXIT
  END

5. Numerical Examples

In this numerical simulation section, we investigate the performance of the proposed method by means of representative numerical examples. Here, we aim to: (1) demonstrate our novel thermal formulation for the thermomechanical contact problem within the context of the phase field framework; (2) verify the proposed thermomechanical phase field formulation for frictional contact problems where the fracture surfaces are stationary; and (3) validate the efficiency of the proposed method for possible crack propagation under frictional contact modeling. The coupling effect between thermal and mechanical fields is considered under different thermal contact conductance conditions. Throughout this section, all simulations are exploited in two dimensions (2D) with linear quadrilateral elements (Q4). No heat sources or body forces are introduced, and plane strain conditions are employed for all examples. For time integration, the implicit backward Euler scheme is used for the transient heat transfer and the quasi-static assumption is applied for the mechanical equilibrium equation. While the whole framework works for the transient temperature problems, all numerical examples in this section are simulated at a steady state with a large enough Δt value to clearly observe the temperature distribution contours under different thermal scenarios.

In the following sections, we demonstrate the feasibility of the thermal formulation through two pure heat conduction problems, then compare our results with the numerical solutions from the X-FEM method in Section 5.1. Two different boundary conditions are explored, namely, the isothermal and the adiabatic situations. Then, the fully coupled thermomechanical frictional contact model is investigated, with an inner crack in Section 5.2 and a prescribed interface in Section 5.3 used to illustrate the accuracy of the proposed method. Comparisons with the literature for the mechanical phase (Section 5.2) and the coupled thermomechanical phase (Section 5.3) are presented under four different thermal contact conductance conditions. Lastly, we study a frictional crack propagation problem in Section 5.4 to show the ability of the proposed method to capture cracking phenomena using the thermomechanical coupled setting.

5.1. *Square Plate with (a) Central Horizontal and (b) Inclined Cracks*

In the first numerical example, we demonstrate the feasibility of the proposed thermomechanical coupled phase field formulation in a pure thermal setting. Two different inner cracks are utilized, namely, a horizontal crack and a slanting crack. As shown in Figure 3a,b, we first consider a square domain with a horizontal center crack that is subjected to two different thermal boundary conditions [53] for the adiabatic (Figure 3a) and isothermal (Figure 3b) cases. For the adiabatic case, temperatures of $T = 1$ °C and $T = -1$ °C are imposed on the top and bottom surfaces, respectively, with no heat flux transferring across the crack [49]. For the isothermal case, the temperature is maintained at $T = 1$ °C for all edge surfaces, while the temperature field of the inner crack is different from the boundaries, with $T = -1$ °C. Figure 4 depicts the results for the model with a slant center crack using the same thermal boundary settings.

For the horizontal center crack model shown in Figure 3, the block size is 2 m × 2 m, with the red line depicting the inner crack. The inner crack is located in the middle, with crack length a of 1.2 m, meaning that $a/L = 0.6$, where L is the side length of the domain. The mesh size of this simulation is 50 × 50, as shown in Figure 5a, with the length parameter set to $l_c = 0.16$ m. For the adiabatic case, in order to guarantee that the heat transferring through the crack is small enough to be ignored, the interface thermal conductance $k_{\text{interface}}$ is set to 10^{-7} W/mm °C.

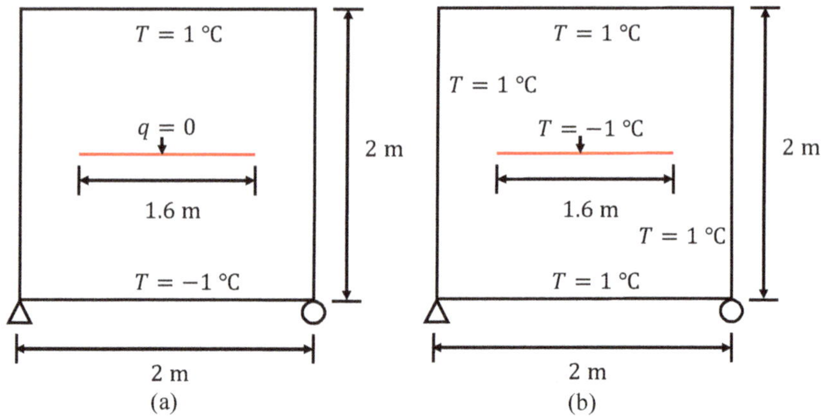

Figure 3. Geometry and boundary conditions of a square plate with a horizontal center crack: (**a**) adiabatic case; (**b**) isothermal case.

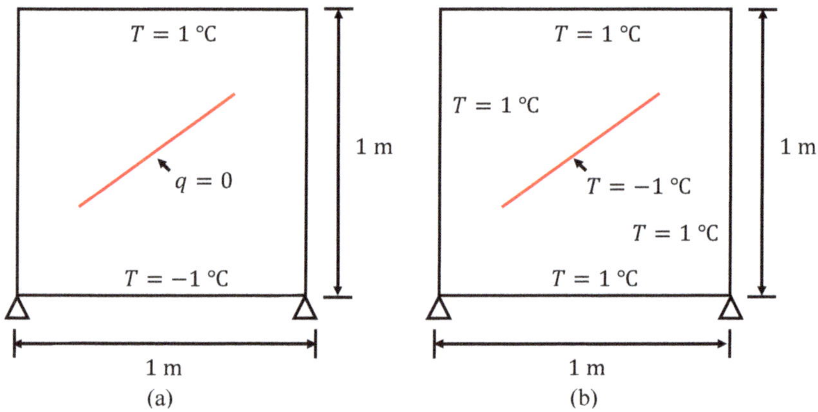

Figure 4. Geometry and boundary conditions of a square plate with a slant center crack: (**a**) adiabatic case; (**b**) isothermal case.

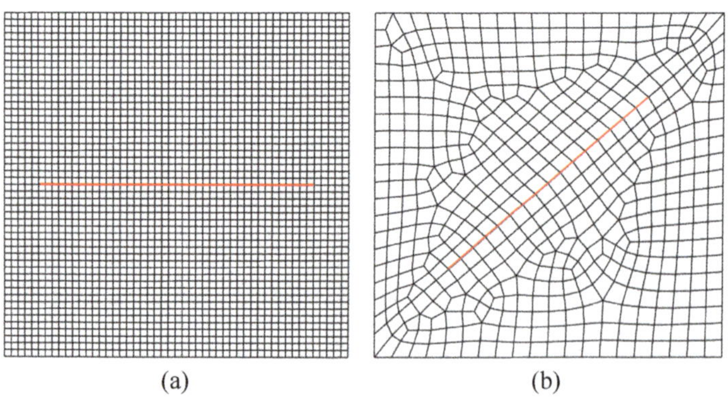

Figure 5. Mesh distribution of the square plate: (**a**) horizontal crack; (**b**) inclined crack.

For the slant center crack, as illustrated in Figure 4, the domain size is 1 m × 1 m, with a stationary crack starting from (0.3 m, 0.33 m) to (0.7 m, 0.68 m). The problem domain is discretized by unstructured meshes, as shown in Figure 5b, with an approximated mesh size of $h = 0.05$ m and with $l_c = 0.2$ m. Detailed material properties for these two crack models are summarized in Table 2.

Table 2. Detailed material properties for the square plate with cracks.

Bulk Material		
Young's modulus	E	10,000 MPa
Poisson's ratio	ν	0.3
Density	ρ	2.7×10^{-9} kg/mm^3
Thermal expansion coefficient	β	2.386×10^{-24}/°C
Bulk thermal conductivity	k_{bulk}	150 W/mm°C
Interface thermal conductivity (for adiabatic case)	$k_{\text{interface}}$	10^{-7} W/mm°C

The resulting contour plots of the temperature distribution for the models with horizontal and slant center cracks under two different thermal conditions (the adiabatic and isothermal cases) are exhibited in Figure 6. For the adiabatic case, shown in Figure 6a,c, the discontinuities in the thermal field are clearly shown near the fracture region, as the two sides of the crack are supposed to be insulated from each other. The width of the observed crack is controlled by the length parameter l_c, which is the width of the diffusive damage band. On the other hand, for the isothermal case, shown in Figure 6b,d, the thermal contours are uniformly distributed. Compared to the analysis in [49,53], where the X-FEM method is used, we observe that the results match remarkably well with the reference. This agreement demonstrates that the proposed thermomechanical coupled phase field formulation is able to correctly identify and reproduce the temperature discontinuity and continuity profile near the crack regions for both the isothermal and adiabatic cases.

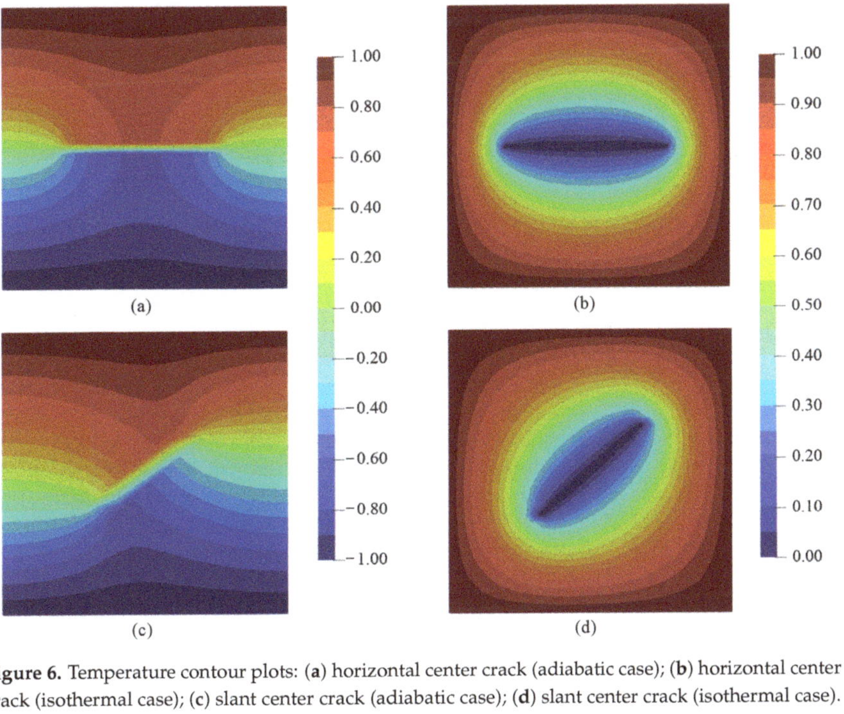

Figure 6. Temperature contour plots: (**a**) horizontal center crack (adiabatic case); (**b**) horizontal center crack (isothermal case); (**c**) slant center crack (adiabatic case); (**d**) slant center crack (isothermal case).

Remark 3. *For the adiabatic case, as shown in Table 2,* $\mathbf{k}_{interface}$ *should be set with a sufficiently small value rather than 0 in order to avoid any singularity in the matrix calculation.*

5.2. Squared Domain with an Internal Slant Frictional Crack

After validating the pure thermal problem, we extend the model with the slant center crack in Section 5.1 to model a thermomechanical coupled problem with a frictional contact crack. The purpose of the second example is to investigate the ability of the proposed phase field method for thermomechanical problems with frictional contact. The problem was initially proposed by Dolbow et al. [20], and was later elaborated in [48] to verify the phase field method for frictional contact cracks in purely mechanical problems. As shown in Figure 7a, the geometry of the domain is a 1 m $\times$ 1 m square with an existing crack located from $(0.3\ \mathrm{m}, 0.33\ \mathrm{m})$ to $(0.7\ \mathrm{m}, 0.68\ \mathrm{m})$ [48]. A uniform displacement loading $d = -0.1$ m in total is applied on the top surface in 10 steps. We adopt the same material properties used in [48], with elastic modulus $E = 10,000$ MPa, Poisson's ratio $\nu = 0.3$, and the frictional coefficient of the crack surface $\mu_f = 0.1$. The two fractional mesh distributions are shown in Figure 7, in (b) with coarse mesh size $h = 0.008$ m, $l_c = 0.032$ m and in (c) with the finest mesh size $h = 0.002$ m, $l_c = 0.008$ m are investigated in this section. In this simulation, the crack driving force parameter $\mathcal{H}$ is calculated following the same strategy as in Appendix A of Borden et al. [4], and the critical fracture energy is set to $\mathcal{G}_c = 50\ \mathrm{N/m^2}$.

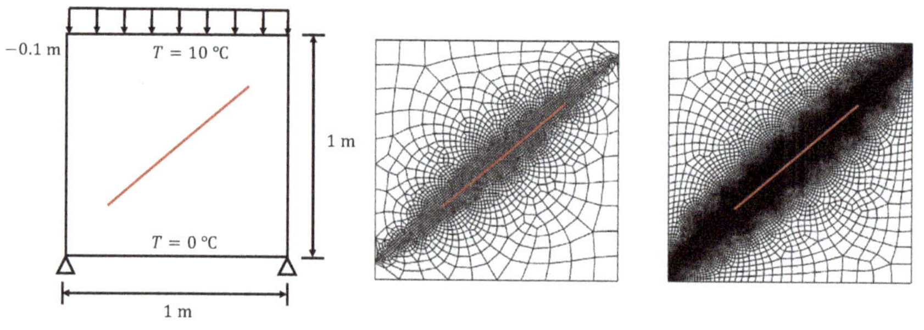

Figure 7. Description of the inclined crack problem: (**a**) boundary conditions and geometries; (**b**) coarse mesh distribution; (**c**) fine mesh distribution.

As the main focus of this paper, we investigate the effect of the different thermal conductance conditions on the mechanical phase. In addition to mechanical loading, we apply the thermal boundary conditions shown in Figure 7a, with 10 °C prescribed to the top surface and 0 °C to the bottom surface, for further exploration.

In Table 1, we display different thermal conductance models with different thermal conductivity $\boldsymbol{k}$ as provided in Equation (22). The thermal expansion coefficients are presented in Table 1. The four different thermal conductivity models discussed in Section 4.2, namely, the pressure-dependent model (PDM), uncoupled model (UCM), fully conductive model (FCM), and adiabatic contact model (ACM), are employed. First, we compare the normal contact stress along the crack with [47] using the uncoupled model (Figure 8). The comparison shows that with mesh refinement, the proposed method approaches the reference solution with good agreement.

The results of the displacement and temperature contours at the last step using the fine mesh are shown in Figure 9. It can be noted that for the uncoupled case (UCM), we set the thermal expansion coefficient to be small enough that the coupling effect can be ignored. Comparing our results with the purely mechanical simulation presented in Fei and Choo's work [48], excellent agreement on the displacement contours is achieved. For the other three cases with thermal effects, displacements in the x direction are more significant compared to the UCM case due to coupled thermomechanical effects. Because the displacement in the y direction is fixed, there is not much difference shown on contour plots in Figure 9.

As for the thermal field, the temperature distribution is uniform in the fully conductive model with the same thermal conductivity for the bulk (k_{bulk}) and the interface ($k_{\text{interface}}$) domains. Thus, in the fully conductive case shown in Figure 9 (3), the location of the inclined crack is not visible. For the other three models, the fracture crack in the temperature contours can be clearly observed. As shown in Table 1, sharing the same $k_{\text{interface}}$, which is determined by the contact pressure and damage parameter, the difference in the temperature distribution for the PDM and UCM case is dominated by the coupling term between the thermal and mechanical field. As shown in Figure 9 (3), the PDM case with a stronger coupling effect exhibits a more continuous temperature distribution around the crack region. In the adiabatic model (ACM), with $k_{\text{interface}}$ set to be a small enough constant, there is almost no heat transference in that area, and strong discontinuity in the temperature field is visible.

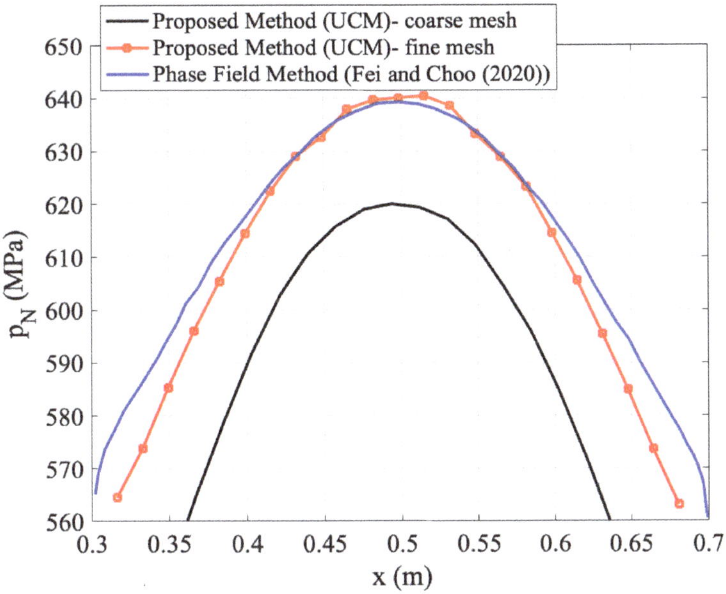

Figure 8. Normal contact stress along the crack at the final step for the uncoupled model (UCM) in comparison with Fei and Choo [48].

5.3. The Frictional Sliding Problem under Different Thermomechanical Coupled Conditions

In this section, we use the proposed frictional contact model to solve a frictional sliding problem. The problem was simulated in our previous paper, where a discrete VMDG method was used [50]. The detailed geometry is shown in Figure 10, where the 1 m × 1 m domain is subjected to two prescribed displacement loadings on the top surface. In addition, a heat flux $\bar{q}_n = 1200\ \text{W/m}^2$ is applied on the top surface pointing inward, with 0 °C fixed on the bottom surface. The total displacement is applied in 10 steps, while the time increment Δt is set to be $\Delta t = 2.8 \times 10^{16}$ s to ensure that the thermal phase is in the quasi-static state. As stated in Section 4.2, four different thermal conductivity conditions are considered, as provided in Table 1. For the adiabatic contact model (ACM), as mentioned in [52], it should be noted that the heat flux boundary condition must be replaced by the temperature boundary condition $T = 10$ °C on the top surface to avoid the singularity in the equations of the thermal system. The detailed material properties are provided in Table 3.

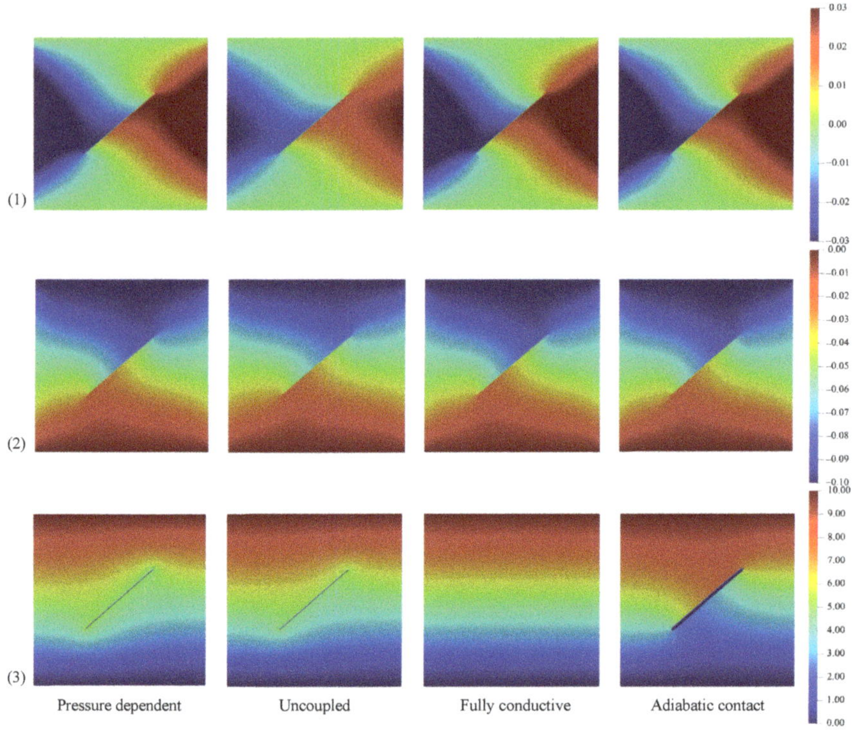

Figure 9. Contour plots of (**1**) Displacement in the X direction; (**2**) displacement in the Y direction; (**3**) temperature contours at the last step for four different thermal conditions.

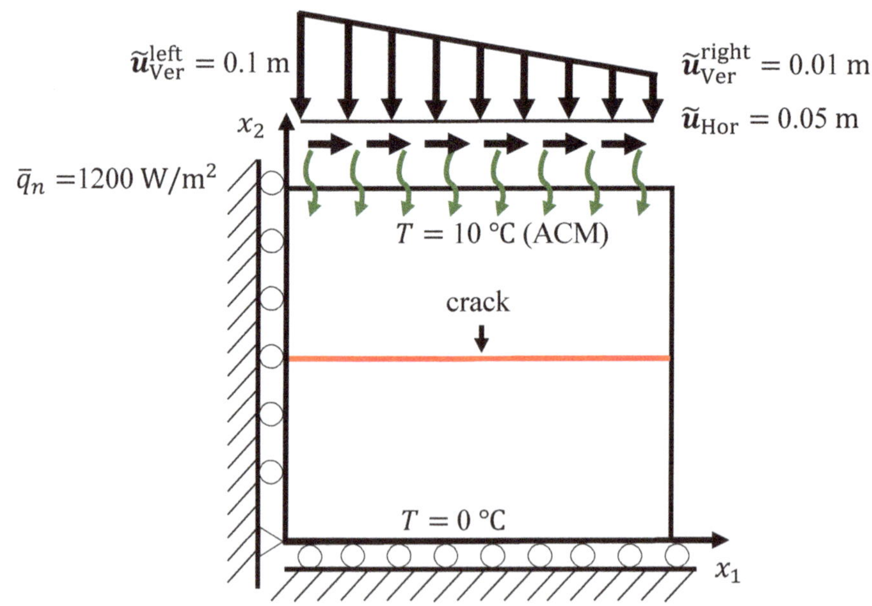

Figure 10. Geometry illustration of the frictional sliding problem.

Table 3. Detailed material properties of the frictional sliding problem.

Poisson's ratio	$\nu = 0.3$
Young's modulus	$E = 1.0 \times 10^4$ MPa
Thermal conductivity	$k = 150$ W/m °C
Thermal conductance coefficient	$h_{c0} = 6.5 \times 10^{-5}$ W/m °C
Vickers hardness	$H_e = 100$ MPa
Thermal constant	$\varepsilon_c = 1$
Frictional coefficient	$\mu = 0.1$

In Figure 11, the contours of temperature distribution are shown in their deformed configurations. A comparison is performed in this figure among the different thermal contact conductivity models, i.e., PDM, UCM, FCM, and ADM. In addition, we compare the results with our previous work [50], where the VMDG method was used. Very good agreement is achieved between the proposed phase field method and the previous VMDG method. It is noted that a slight difference in the temperature contour between the VMDG and the proposed phase field method can be observed in the adiabatic case, as shown in Figure 11. Because the discontinuity is controlled by the length parameter l_c in the phase field method, when s smaller length parameter is applied the sharper discontinuity is captured in the temperature as well as the displacement. The VMDG method is a discrete method with duplicated nodes at the fracture surface; thus, the sharp discontinuity in the displacement is captured exactly. In contrast, in the proposed phase field method, discontinuity is captured in a diffuse fashion influenced by the mesh size and the length parameter l_c.

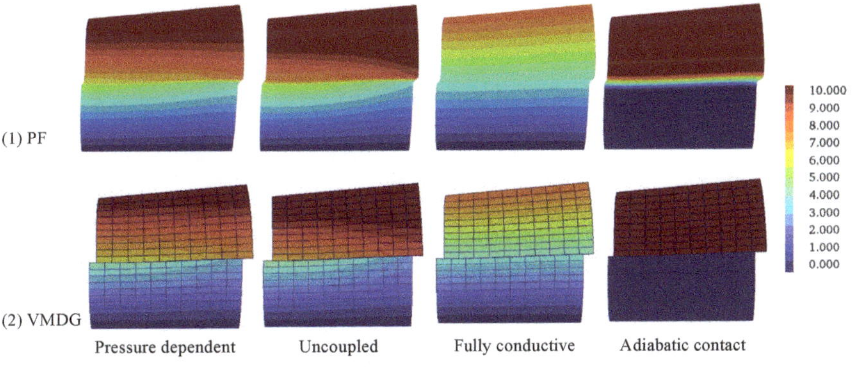

Figure 11. Temperature contours of four different thermal models for **(1)** the proposed phase field method and **(2)** the VMDG method in the deformed configuration.

To further assess the performance and accuracy of the proposed phase field model for the frictional sliding problem, we compare the normal contact stress results with Khoei and Bahmani's [52] analysis, where the X-FEM method was used. As in [52], we use a uniform structured FE mesh of 75×75 quadrilateral elements, and the penalty parameters are used to constrain the tangential and normal stick conditions. As shown in Figure 12, a strong agreement is achieved when comparing the proposed phase field method to the X-FEM method. As stated in the previous sections, the proposed phase field method does not require a specific treatment or algorithm at the contact surface and is easier to implement compared to discrete methods.

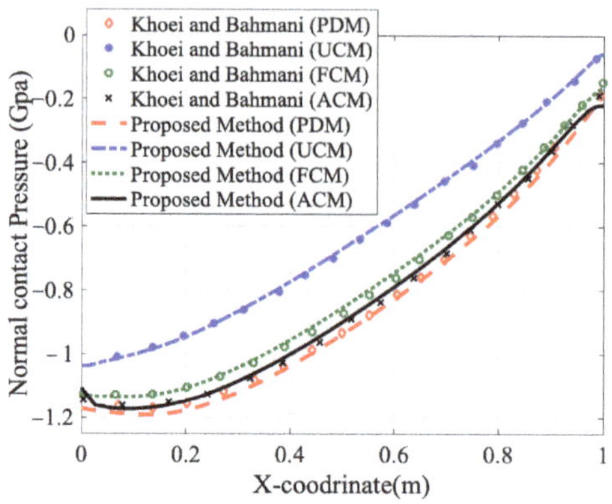

Figure 12. Normal contact pressure for four different thermal models in comparison with Kohei and Bahmani [52].

5.4. Propagation of an Inclined Crack in a Rectangular Plate

To enrich the applications of the proposed method, in this example we simulate the crack propagation to demonstrate the capacity of the framework following the verification of the stationary interface problems. As shown in Figure 13a, a rectangular domain with geometry 2 m × 4 m has a 45° inclined crack located between (0.0 m, 0.7 m) and (1.3 m, 2.0 m). Proportional displacement loading $\hat{u}_y = -2 \times 10^{-4}$ m is prescribed on the top surface in 100 load steps. For the thermal phase, the temperature on the top surface is set to 10 °C while it is 0 °C for the bottom surface. The material parameters used in this example are $E = 10{,}000$ MPa, $\nu = 0.3$, $\mu_f = 0.01$, and $\mathcal{G}_c = 50$ kJ/m^2. The mesh size of this problem is approximately 0.05 m. as shown in Figure 13b, with the length parameter set to $l_c = 0.2$ m.

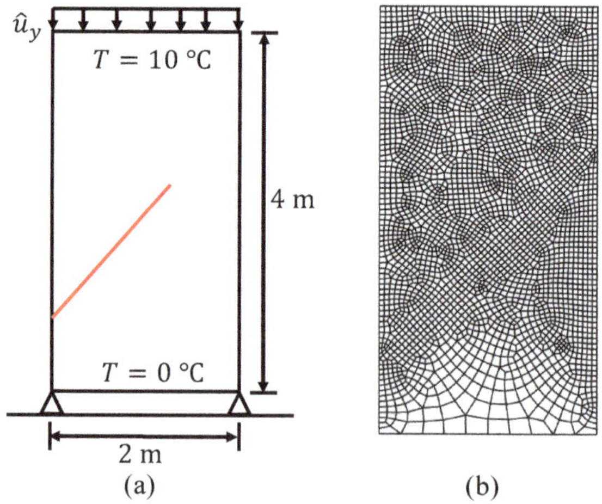

Figure 13. Problem description of the rectangle plate with an inclined crack: (**a**) geometry and boundary conditions; (**b**) unstructured FE mesh.

Following the algorithm proposed by Amor [54], the strain history energy $\mathcal{H}$ should be updated and employed in the calculation at each load step, rather than arbitrarily defined as for stationary cracks, owing to the dynamic crack propagation. This means that the evolution of the phase field damage parameter d is dependent on the displacement from previous steps. The thermal expansion coefficient β is chosen to be a relatively small number in this simulation.

The evolution of the phase field parameter d and the temperature contour plots are shown in Figure 14 at three different load steps and with three different thermal contact conductance models. The propagation of the crack and the evolution of the temperature are clearly captured using the proposed phase field method. For the fully conductive case (FCM), the temperature is uniformly distributed, as the heat is free to transfer between the upper and lower parts of the domain. For the adiabatic case (ACM), the temperature field exhibits a sharp discontinuity across the damaged crack. As the crack propagates, the temperature distribution shows a stronger discontinuity, while the damage region expands. At the last load step, when the crack is fully developed, and the whole domain is separated into two parts, and the temperature fields of the upper and lower parts are completely discontinuous. For the pressure-dependent model (PDM), when compared to the ACM case, heat transfer is more obvious at the beginning of the crack propagation process, as it is dependent on the magnitude of the contact stress at the crack region. During the crack initiation and propagation stage, the temperature discontinuity becomes less distinguishable as the crack propagates, because $k_{\text{interface}}$ is dominated by increasing displacement loading rather than the phase field damage variable d. After the crack is fully developed, the damage variable is dominated by the conductivity, and there is no thermal interaction between the two subdomains.

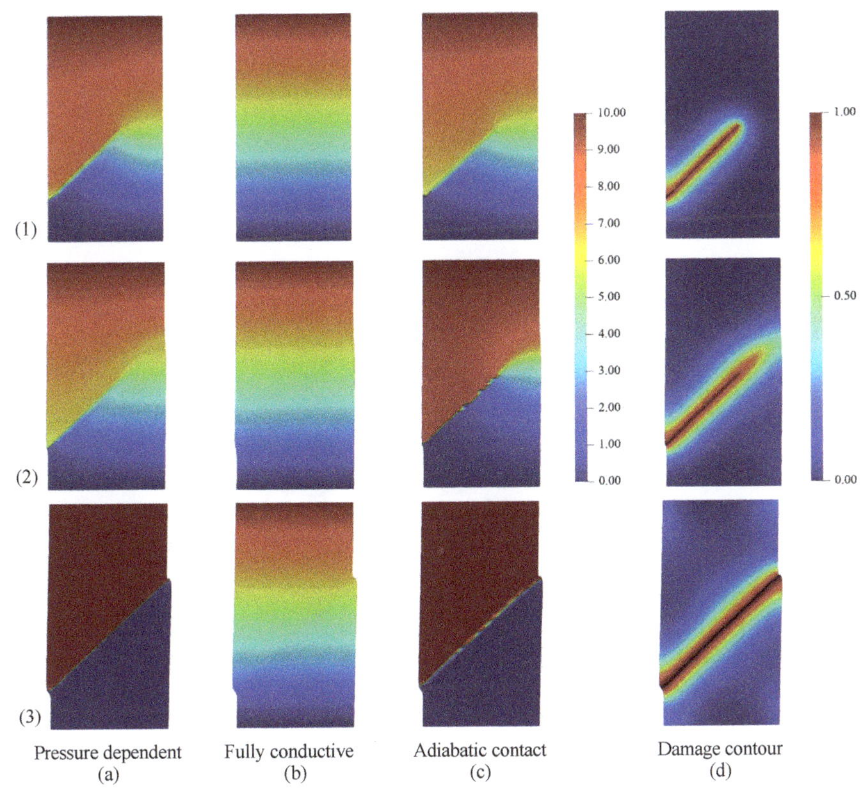

Figure 14. Temperature evolution in three different thermal models: (**a**) PDM, (**b**) FCM, and (**c**) ADM, with (**d**) damage contours at three load steps: (1) $\hat{u}_y = -2 \times 10^{-4}$ m, (2) $\hat{u}_y = -1 \times 10^{-2}$ m, and (3) $\hat{u}_y = -2 \times 10^{-2}$ m.

6. Concluding Remarks

In this paper, a thermomechanical coupled phase field method has been developed for modeling cracks with frictional contact. In the mechanical phase, the proposed method follows the work of Fei and Choo [48], regularizing the stress tensor at contact regions under different contact conditions, with a specific focus on frictional contact to accommodate the no-penetration constraints. For the thermal phase, we propose a novel formulation for thermal conductivity in a regularized contact region by accommodating different thermal conductance conditions and the phase field damage parameter. We investigate several benchmark examples to assess the proposed computational method. First, we verify the proposed thermal algorithm using different pure thermal models. Then, we simulate a problem with an internal slant frictional crack and extend the model into thermomechanical coupled fields. In the third example, we study the thermomechanical coupled frictional sliding problem and compare the results with the X-FEM and the VMDG methods, finding good agreement, which demonstrates the capacity of the proposed phase field framework in simulating coupled thermomechanical problems with frictional sliding. Lastly, we demonstrate that the proposed method can simulate crack propagation with thermal effects. Based on the above conclusions, the proposed method has potential applications in various areas, including modeling of thermomechanical coupled crack propagation of composite structures, deposition processes in friction stir welding, and metal forming processes.

There are several key features in this paper, including (i) the formulation accommodates no-penetration constraints of the contact behavior in the phase field method and (ii) the formulation accommodates different thermal conductance conditions without the need for a sophisticated algorithm to impose thermal contact constraints on crack surfaces. The proposed phase field method can be implemented easily in comparison to the existing discrete methods for frictional cracks. The proposed model can be applied in the future for complex geometry and crack branching, and merging in coupled multi-physics settings. Although the proposed thermomechanical coupled phase field method is promising, it has a number of deficiencies. The main limitations are threefold. First, the inertial effect in the mechanical field is not considered. Second, in terms of accuracy, the phase field method does not show superior performance for stationary cracks compared to discrete methods. Third, without duplicating nodes at the cracking interfaces it is difficult to capture the sharp discontinuity along the cracking surfaces. With all these considerations, our future work will focus on advancing the model in order to (1) accommodate dynamic effects in the mechanical field, (2) adopt a discrete method for predefined crack regions to capture the sharp discontinuities, and (3) track both stationary interface cracks and propagating cracks simultaneously. Work is underway to adopt the VMDG method [50] to model stationary interfaces and combine it with the present phase field model for crack propagation.

Author Contributions: Conceptualization, W.W. and P.C.; methodology, W.W. and P.C; software, W.W.; validation, W.W. and P.C.; formal analysis, W.W.; investigation, W.W. and P.C.; writing—original draft preparation, W.W.; writing—review and editing, P.C.; visualization, W.W.; supervision, P.C.; project administration, P.C.; funding acquisition, P.C. All authors have read and agreed to the published version of the manuscript.

Funding: This research was supported in part by a Seed Grant award from the Institute for Computational and Data Sciences at the Pennsylvania State University.

Institutional Review Board Statement: Ethical review and approval were waived for this study, due to the reason that the studies are not involving humans or animals.

Conflicts of Interest: The authors declare no conflict of interest.

Nomenclature

Symbol	Description	Unit
T	Temperature	°C
E	Young's modulus	MPa
k	Thermal conductivity	W/m°C
c_p	Specific heat capacity	J/kg°C
ρ	Density	kg/m^3
$h_{\mathbf{hcont}}$	Heat conductivity	W/m^2°C
β	Thermal expansion coefficient	/°C
h_{c0}	Coefficient of thermal contact conductivity	W/m°C
H_e	Vickers hardness	N/m^2
$q_{\mathbf{hont}}$	Heat flux on the contact surface	W/m^2
σ_c	Critical stress	N/m^2
h_c	Softening stiffness.	N/m^3
δ_c	Critical separation	m
h_s	Chemical bonding conductance	W/m^2°C
h_p	Surface contact conductance	W/m^3°C
h_{air}	Gas conductance	W/m^2°C
$\bar{q}_n$	Applied heat flux	W/m^2
l_c	Damage length parameter	m
$\mathcal{G}_c$	Griffth's critical energy	N/m
$\mathcal{H}$	Strain energy history	MPa
E_e	Stored elastic energy	
E_d	Fractured surface energy	
Ψ	Bulk energy density	
γ	Crack energy density	

Abbreviations

Abbreviation	Description
PF	Phase Field
VMDG	Variational Multiscale Discontinuous Galerkin
FCM	Fully Coupled Model
ADM	Adiabatic Model
PDM	Pressure Dependent Model
UCM	Uncoupled Model

References

1. Chaboche, J.L. Development of continuum damage mechanics for elastic solids sustaining anisotropic and unilateral damage. *Int. J. Damage Mech.* **1993**, *2*, 311–329. [CrossRef]
2. Seitz, A.; Wall, W.A.; Popp, A. Nitsche's method for finite deformation thermomechanical contact problems. *Comput. Mech.* **2019**, *63*, 1091–1110. [CrossRef]
3. Miehe, C.; Hofacker, M.; Welschinger, F. A phase field model for rate-independent crack propagation: Robust algorithmic implementation based on operator splits. *Comput. Methods Appl. Mech. Eng.* **2010**, *199*, 2765–2778. [CrossRef]
4. Borden, M.J.; Verhoosel, C.V.; Scott, M.A.; Hughes, T.J.; Landis, C.M. A phase-field description of dynamic brittle fracture. *Comput. Methods Appl. Mech. Eng.* **2012**, *217*, 77–95. [CrossRef]
5. Hansbo, P.; Lovadina, C.; Perugia, I.; Sangalli, G. A Lagrange multiplier method for the finite element solution of elliptic interface problems using non-matching meshes. *Numer. Math.* **2005**, *100*, 91–115. [CrossRef]
6. Hirmand, M.; Vahab, M.; Khoei, A. An augmented Lagrangian contact formulation for frictional discontinuities with the extended finite element method. *Finite Elem. Anal. Des.* **2015**, *107*, 28–43. [CrossRef]
7. Simo, J.C.; Laursen, T. An augmented Lagrangian treatment of contact problems involving friction. *Comput. Struct.* **1992**, *42*, 97–116. [CrossRef]
8. Dittmann, M.; Franke, M.; Temizer, I.; Hesch, C. Isogeometric analysis and thermomechanical mortar contact problems. *Comput. Methods Appl. Mech. Eng.* **2014**, *274*, 192–212. [CrossRef]
9. Cardiff, P.; Karač, A.; Ivanković, A. Development of a finite volume contact solver based on the penalty method. *Comput. Mater. Sci.* **2012**, *64*, 283–284. [CrossRef]

10. Chouly, F.; Fabre, M.; Hild, P.; Mlika, R.; Pousin, J.; Renard, Y. An overview of recent results on Nitsche's method for contact problems. In *Geometrically Unfitted Finite Element Methods and Applications*; Springer: Berlin/Heidelberg, Germany, 2017; pp. 93–141.
11. Wriggers, P.; Zavarise, G. A formulation for frictionless contact problems using a weak form introduced by Nitsche. *Comput. Mech.* **2008**, *41*, 407–420. [CrossRef]
12. Arnold, D.N. An interior penalty finite element method with discontinuous elements. *SIAM J. Numer. Anal.* **1982**, *19*, 742–760. [CrossRef]
13. Nitsche, J. Über ein Variationsprinzip zur Lösung von Dirichlet-Problemen bei Verwendung von Teilräumen, die keinen Randbedingungen unterworfen sind. *Abh. Math. Semin. Univ. Hambg.* **1971**, *36*, 9–15. [CrossRef]
14. Sanders, J.D.; Laursen, T.A.; Puso, M.A. A Nitsche embedded mesh method. *Comput. Mech.* **2012**, *49*, 243–257. [CrossRef]
15. Annavarapu, C.; Hautefeuille, M.; Dolbow, J.E. A robust Nitsche's formulation for interface problems. *Comput. Methods Appl. Mech. Eng.* **2012**, *225*, 44–54. [CrossRef]
16. Truster, T.J.; Chen, P.; Masud, A. Finite strain primal interface formulation with consistently evolving stabilization. *Int. J. Numer. Methods Eng.* **2015**, *102*, 278–315. [CrossRef]
17. Masud, A.; Chen, P. Thermoelasticity at finite strains with weak and strong discontinuities. *Comput. Methods Appl. Mech. Eng.* **2019**, *347*, 1050–1084. [CrossRef]
18. Francfort, G.A.; Marigo, J.J. Revisiting brittle fracture as an energy minimization problem. *J. Mech. Phys. Solids* **1998**, *46*, 1319–1342. [CrossRef]
19. Moës, N.; Dolbow, J.; Belytschko, T. A finite element method for crack growth without remeshing. *Int. J. Numer. Methods Eng.* **1999**, *46*, 131–150. [CrossRef]
20. Dolbow, J.; Moës, N.; Belytschko, T. An extended finite element method for modeling crack growth with frictional contact. *Comput. Methods Appl. Mech. Eng.* **2001**, *190*, 6825–6846. [CrossRef]
21. Fries, T.P.; Belytschko, T. The extended/generalized finite element method: An overview of the method and its applications. *Int. J. Numer. Methods Eng.* **2010**, *84*, 253–304. [CrossRef]
22. Armero, F.; Garikipati, K. An analysis of strong discontinuities in multiplicative finite strain plasticity and their relation with the numerical simulation of strain localization in solids. *Int. J. Solids Struct.* **1996**, *33*, 2863–2885. [CrossRef]
23. Oliver, J. Modelling strong discontinuities in solid mechanics via strain softening constitutive equations. Part 1: Fundamentals. *Int. J. Numer. Methods Eng.* **1996**, *39*, 3575–3600. [CrossRef]
24. Armero, F.; Linder, C. New finite elements with embedded strong discontinuities in the finite deformation range. *Comput. Methods Appl. Mech. Eng.* **2008**, *197*, 3138–3170. [CrossRef]
25. Nguyen, T.T.; Yvonnet, J.; Zhu, Q.Z.; Bornert, M.; Chateau, C. A phase field method to simulate crack nucleation and propagation in strongly heterogeneous materials from direct imaging of their microstructure. *Eng. Fract. Mech.* **2015**, *139*, 18–39. [CrossRef]
26. Ehlers, W.; Luo, C. A phase-field approach embedded in the theory of porous media for the description of dynamic hydraulic fracturing. *Comput. Methods Appl. Mech. Eng.* **2017**, *315*, 348–368. [CrossRef]
27. Paggi, M.; Reinoso, J. Revisiting the problem of a crack impinging on an interface: A modeling framework for the interaction between the phase field approach for brittle fracture and the interface cohesive zone model. *Comput. Methods Appl. Mech. Eng.* **2017**, *321*, 145–172. [CrossRef]
28. Macek, W. Fracture surface formation of notched 2017A-T4 aluminium alloy under bending fatigue. *Int. J. Fract.* **2022**, *234*, 141–157. [CrossRef]
29. Macek, W.; Branco, R.; Costa, J.D.; Trembacz, J. Fracture Surface Behavior of 34CrNiMo6 High-Strength Steel Bars with Blind Holes under Bending-Torsion Fatigue. *Materials* **2021**, *15*, 80. [CrossRef]
30. Lanwer, J.P.; Höper, S.; Gietz, L.; Kowalsky, U.; Empelmann, M.; Dinkler, D. Fundamental Investigations of Bond Behaviour of High-Strength Micro Steel Fibres in Ultra-High Performance Concrete under Cyclic Tensile Loading. *Materials* **2021**, *15*, 120. [CrossRef]
31. Griffith, A. The phenomena of rupture and flow in solids. In Proceedings of the First International Congress for Applied Mechanics, Delft, The Netherlands, 22–26 April 1924; pp. 53–63.
32. Schneider, D.; Schoof, E.; Huang, Y.; Selzer, M.; Nestler, B. Phase-field modeling of crack propagation in multiphase systems. *Comput. Methods Appl. Mech. Eng.* **2016**, *312*, 186–195. [CrossRef]
33. Bourdin, B.; Francfort, G.A.; Marigo, J.J. Numerical experiments in revisited brittle fracture. *J. Mech. Phys. Solids* **2000**, *48*, 797–826. [CrossRef]
34. Bourdin, B.; Francfort, G.A.; Marigo, J.J. The variational approach to fracture. *J. Elast.* **2008**, *91*, 5–148. [CrossRef]
35. Ulmer, H.; Hofacker, M.; Miehe, C. Phase field modeling of brittle and ductile fracture. *PAMM* **2013**, *13*, 533–536. [CrossRef]
36. Ambati, M.; Gerasimov, T.; De Lorenzis, L. Phase-field modeling of ductile fracture. *Comput. Mech.* **2015**, *55*, 1017–1040. [CrossRef]
37. Carrara, P.; Ambati, M.; Alessi, R.; De Lorenzis, L. A framework to model the fatigue behavior of brittle materials based on a variational phase-field approach. *Comput. Methods Appl. Mech. Eng.* **2020**, *361*, 112731. [CrossRef]
38. Schreiber, C.; Kuhn, C.; Müller, R.; Zohdi, T. A phase field modeling approach of cyclic fatigue crack growth. *Int. J. Fract.* **2020**, *225*, 89–100. [CrossRef]

39. Schreiber, C.; Müller, R.; Kuhn, C. Phase field simulation of fatigue crack propagation under complex load situations. *Arch. Appl. Mech.* **2021**, *91*, 563–577. [CrossRef]
40. Seiler, M.; Linse, T.; Hantschke, P.; Kästner, M. An efficient phase-field model for fatigue fracture in ductile materials. *Eng. Fract. Mech.* **2020**, *224*, 106807. [CrossRef]
41. Loew, P.J.; Poh, L.H.; Peters, B.; Beex, L.A. Accelerating fatigue simulations of a phase-field damage model for rubber. *Comput. Methods Appl. Mech. Eng.* **2020**, *370*, 113247. [CrossRef]
42. Tan, Y.; He, Y.; Li, X.; Kang, G. A phase field model for fatigue fracture in piezoelectric solids: A residual controlled staggered scheme. *Comput. Methods Appl. Mech. Eng.* **2022**, *399*, 115459. [CrossRef]
43. Schröder, J.; Pise, M.; Brands, D.; Gebuhr, G.; Anders, S. Phase-field modeling of fracture in high performance concrete during low-cycle fatigue: Numerical calibration and experimental validation. *Comput. Methods Appl. Mech. Eng.* **2022**, *398*, 115181. [CrossRef]
44. Miehe, C.; Schaenzel, L.M.; Ulmer, H. Phase field modeling of fracture in multi-physics problems. Part I. Balance of crack surface and failure criteria for brittle crack propagation in thermo-elastic solids. *Comput. Methods Appl. Mech. Eng.* **2015**, *294*, 449–485. [CrossRef]
45. Miehe, C.; Hofacker, M.; Schänzel, L.M.; Aldakheel, F. Phase field modeling of fracture in multi-physics problems. Part II. Coupled brittle-to-ductile failure criteria and crack propagation in thermo-elastic–plastic solids. *Comput. Methods Appl. Mech. Eng.* **2015**, *294*, 486–522. [CrossRef]
46. Tangella, R.G.; Kumbhar, P.; Annabattula, R.K. Hybrid phase-field modeling of thermo-elastic crack propagation. *Int. J. Comput. Methods Eng. Sci. Mech.* **2022**, *23*, 29–44. [CrossRef]
47. Fei, F.; Choo, J. A phase-field model of frictional shear fracture in geologic materials. *Comput. Methods Appl. Mech. Eng.* **2020**, *369*, 113265. [CrossRef]
48. Fei, F.; Choo, J. A phase-field method for modeling cracks with frictional contact. *Int. J. Numer. Methods Eng.* **2020**, *121*, 740–762. [CrossRef]
49. Nguyen, M.N.; Bui, T.Q.; Nguyen, N.T.; Truong, T.T. Simulation of dynamic and static thermoelastic fracture problems by extended nodal gradient finite elements. *Int. J. Mech. Sci.* **2017**, *134*, 370–386. [CrossRef]
50. Wan, W.; Chen, P. Variational multiscale method for fully coupled thermomechanical interface contact and debonding problems. *Int. J. Solids Struct.* **2021**, *210*, 119–135. [CrossRef]
51. Shahba, A.; Ghosh, S. Coupled phase field finite element model for crack propagation in elastic polycrystalline microstructures. *Int. J. Fract.* **2019**, *219*, 31–64. [CrossRef]
52. Khoei, A.; Bahmani, B. Application of an enriched FEM technique in thermo-mechanical contact problems. *Comput. Mech.* **2018**, *62*, 1127–1154. [CrossRef]
53. Duflot, M. The extended finite element method in thermoelastic fracture mechanics. *Int. J. Numer. Methods Eng.* **2008**, *74*, 827–847. [CrossRef]
54. Amor, H.; Marigo, J.J.; Maurini, C. Regularized formulation of the variational brittle fracture with unilateral contact: Numerical experiments. *J. Mech. Phys. Solids* **2009**, *57*, 1209–1229. [CrossRef]

mathematics

MDPI

Article

Interaction of Variable Fluid Properties with Electrokinetically Modulated Peristaltic Flow of Reactive Nanofluid: A Thermodynamical Analysis

Yasir Akbar [1,2], Shiping Huang [1,2,*] and Hammad Alotaibi [3]

1 China-Singapore International Joint Research Institute, Guangzhou 510700, China
2 School of Civil Engineering and Transportation, South China University of Technology, Guangzhou 510640, China
3 Department of Mathematics and Statistics, College of Science, Taif University, P.O. Box 11099, Taif 21944, Saudi Arabia
* Correspondence: ctasihuang@scut.edu.cn

Abstract: In the present study, the interaction of variable fluid properties with electrokinetically regulated peristaltic transportation of a reactive nanofluid embedded in a porous space is studied. The nanofluid saturates the porous space/medium with inhomogeneous porosity, which changes with distance from the channel boundary. It is assumed that nanofluids are accompanied by variable thermal conductivity and viscosity. The impacts of magnetic field, Brownian motion, electric field, viscous dissipation, chemical reaction, mixed convection, and thermophoresis are incorporated. Moreover, the contribution of zero mass flux boundary condition is executed. The complexity of the equations describing the flow of a nanofluid is reduced by applying the lubrication theory. The fully non-linear equations are solved by utilizing a numerical technique. Particular attention is paid to the analysis of entropy optimization, since its minimization is the best measure to enhance the efficiency of thermal systems. These results demonstrate that a positively oriented external electric field contributes to an increase in nanofluid velocity. Temperature of nanofluid increases more rapidly due to an augmentation in Joule heating parameter. It is noticed that the temperature of water is comparatively lower than that of kerosene. The system's energy loss can be reduced when the thermal conductivity parameter enhance. The magnitude of Bejan number is enhanced by increasing electroosmotic parameter. Further, a substantial decrement in concentration profile is perceived when the Schmidt number is augmented.

Keywords: variable fluid properties; variable porosity; electrokinetic forces; zero mass flux; heat transfer

MSC: 80A19; 35Q79; 76S05

Citation: Akbar, Y.; Huang, S.; Alotaibi, H. Interaction of Variable Fluid Properties with Electrokinetically Modulated Peristaltic Flow of Reactive Nanofluid: A Thermodynamical Analysis. *Mathematics* **2022**, *10*, 4452. https://doi.org/10.3390/math10234452

Academic Editors: Shujin Laima, Yong Cao, Xiaowei Jin and Hehe Ren

Received: 27 October 2022
Accepted: 22 November 2022
Published: 25 November 2022

Publisher's Note: MDPI stays neutral with regard to jurisdictional claims in published maps and institutional affiliations.

Copyright: © 2022 by the authors. Licensee MDPI, Basel, Switzerland. This article is an open access article distributed under the terms and conditions of the Creative Commons Attribution (CC BY) license (https://creativecommons.org/licenses/by/4.0/).

1. Introduction

The importance of peristaltic mechanisms in numerous physiological and industrial processes has rendered this concept convincingly trendy in research. Peristaltic motion is a type of wave motion that occurs within tubular systems that spread out along their length. Peristaltic motion is observed in tiny blood vessel vasomotion, bile in the bile duct, valveless movement of the cardiovascular system, transport of cilia etc. This process has crucial functions in the health industry involving noxious fluid transfer, heart lung units, rotary pumps, warm locomotion etc. Engineers used peristaltic activity, which has many industrial applications. Roller and finger motors, in fact, work according to this mechanism. Historically, Latham [1] and Shapiro et al. [2] initially conducted the analysis on peristaltic movement of viscous liquid. They conducted their investigation under creeping flow phenomena. Srinivas et al. [3] presented a thermal analysis with slip conditions on MHD peristaltic motion. Khan et al. [4] illustrated the impacts of magnetic field on Walter's B liquid through an inclined channel. Impact of heterogeneous-homogeneous reactions on peristaltic movement of Bingham fluid via channel is reported by Tanveer et al. [5].

The rapid progress of nanoscience has revolutionized every area of life, i.e., information technology, energy, food safety, national security, industry, transportation, medicine, and environmental discipline. The use of nanotechnology in medicine/drugs has led to significant improvements through the restructuring of outdated treatments. Nowadays, operations are performed without involving any cuts and prunes for brain tumors, cancer treatment and lithotripsy that were once thought to be incredibly challenging and menacing. Apart from countless applications of nanofluids in industrial and practical settings, the primary goal of nanoparticles is to improve heat transfer phenomena. Choi and Eastman [6,7] were the first who discussed the concept of nanofluids. Shehzad et al. [8] addressed peristaltic transportation of nanoliquid with MHD effects. The numerical results were acquired in this study. Peristaltic transport of ionic nanofluids with double diffusive convection were discussed by Prakash et al. [9]. Recently, analytical results for peristaltic transportation of non-Newtonian Bingham blood liquid via divergent channels were highlighted by Eldabe et al. [10]. Additional research can be seen in references [11–13] on improving heat transmission.

Fluid movement across porous material has been of enormous concern over the last few years owing to its multiple uses in medicine and industry. Flow through porous material takes place in human lungs, rye bread, bile ducts and movement of underground water etc. Fluid flow via porous material has an effective role in the field of food industries, petroleum engineering, biological systems, and hydrology. Such uses can be found in production of oil, fossil fuels, bio films, heat pipes, pebble-type heat exchanger, catalytic reactors, thin glass bead packs etc. The preliminary analysis on porous media was executed by Darcy [14]. An investigation of variants in porous space motion models is presented by Alazmi et al. [15]. A detailed study of fluctuating porosity, local thermal non equilibrium and thermal dispersion on free surface flow in porous space were checked by Alazmi et al. [16]. Pal et al. [17] explored the aspects of radiation and porous space having variable porosity over a vertical plate. Flows of the boundary layer saturated by nanoliquid in a porous space were debated by Kuznetsov et al. [18]. Asghar et al. [19] illustrated both numerical and analytical results for peristaltic transport of mixed convective flows of viscoelastic liquid.

The main requirements of microfluidic systems are efficient pumping, accurate mixing, and flow command. Electroosmotic pumps (EOPs), built on the principle of electroosmosis, are more ordinary micropumps and are controlled by an external electric field adjacent to the liquid-solid interface. Within the charged layer, an electric double layer (EDL) is developed and linked to the outside diffuse layer. The molecules in the scattered area of the EDL migrate when an external force field is applied, leading to mass dislocation of the fluid caused by the density effect, also referred as electroosmotic flow (EOF). This phenomenon informs implementation in medical diagnostic plans, as well as the development of microchips for transporting small volumes and accurately mixing chemicals. Due to the improved electroosmotic layout, instantaneous yield, and large financial advantages, simulation of electroosmotic nanofluid flows has sparked a great deal of interest. Numerous mathematical models consider how fluid flow behaves in diverse geometries [20–25].

The study of entropy generation is extremely important for evaluating the performance of various industrial and engineering systems. The term entropy comes from the Greek letter Entropia, meaning change or transition to it. Entropy computes the quantity of energy in any system that cannot generate any output. The amount of energy produced in any irreversible phase is called entropy generation. The entropy of reversible processes remains unchanged. For irreversible processes, entropy always increases. Entropy is used to improve system performance. Higher entropy production in a system increases irreversibility, which reduces the efficiency of the system. Therefore, machines require a small amount of entropy for better performance. The principle of entropy generation for thermodynamic systems was originally introduced by Bejan [26]. Rashidi et al. [27]

presented the irreversibility rate for peristaltically driven nanoliquid with blood as a base fluid. Recently, Akbar et al. [28] highlighted the aspects of radiative heat flux and Hall currents in peristaltic transportation of nanoliquid with irreversibility rate. Thereafter, many researchers discuss the study of entropy generation for nanoliquids (see refs. [29–31]).

The novelty of the present communication is to study the interaction of variable fluid properties with electrokinetically regulated peristaltic transportation of a reactive nanofluid through an inhomogeneous porous medium. Aspects of variable thermal conductivity, mixed convection, electric field, thermophoresis, variable viscosity, chemical reaction, viscous dissipation, magnetic field, and Brownian movement are brought into contemplation. The mathematical formulation is constructed subject to zero mass flux boundary condition. Numerical results are computed by using NDSolve in Mathematica. Salient properties of different integrated parameters on flow quantities are addressed via graphs and tables.

2. Problem Description

Here we considered the 2D peristaltic carriage of an aqueous solution, which varies through an external electric field along the length of the channel. The combined effects of peristaltic pumping and applied electric field cause fluid to flow in a symmetric channel. The process of peristalsis occurs because sinusoidal waves passing along the channel boundaries with a constant velocity c. The surface of the channel barrier develops a negative charge as a result of the ions present in the fluid medium, pulling counterions to it. This produces an EDL, a layer of counterions close to the channel boundary. The counterions in the EDL migrate towards their respective electrodes when an electrical source is provided through the channel's ends, exerting a driving force on the liquid particles. Further, it is supposed that the electric field E_x has imposed axially, and magnetic field B_0 is transversely of the fluid flow. The geometry of the problem is presented via Figure 1. Mathematically, the boundaries of the channel walls are described as [8]:

$$\pm H(\overline{X},\bar{t}) = \pm a_1 \cos\left(\frac{2\pi}{\lambda}(\overline{X} - c\bar{t})\right) \pm d_1. \tag{1}$$

Here d_1 and λ are respectively the half width of the channel and wavelength. The function of the electric potential in the electrolyte satisfies the Poisson equation. In accordance with it, the electric potential Ω is expressed as [20]:

$$\nabla^2\Omega = -\frac{\rho_e}{\varepsilon}. \tag{2}$$

where ρ_e is the net charge density of the mixture at present and is defined as:

$$\rho_e = ez(\overline{n}_+ - \overline{n}_-). \tag{3}$$

The Boltzmann distribution function for local ionic density is given as:

$$\overline{n}_\pm = \overline{n}_0 \mathrm{e}^{\left(\pm \frac{ez}{T_{av}K_B}\Omega\right)}. \tag{4}$$

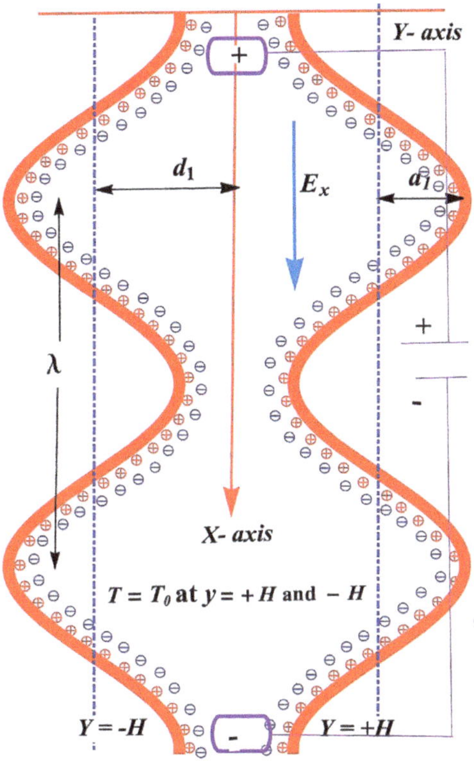

Figure 1. Geometric representation of the problem.

Three important aspects are considered here: convection, diffusion, and chemical reaction. The diffusion-convection reaction illustrates how these three mechanisms affect a substance's concentration as it is dispersed throughout a medium. Numerous industrial applications exist for reactive convective diffusion. The variable viscosity, porosity, and thermal conductivity (changeable liquid characteristics) of the fluid are considered in the analysis. Further, the aspects of mixed convection, electric field, thermophoresis, viscous dissipation, magnetic field, chemical reaction, and Brownian movement are carried out. Utilizing the Oberbeck-Boussinesq approximation and considering the most suitable practical case when the concentration of nanoparticles is diluted, and choosing an appropriate reference pressure, the basic governing equations are specified as [11,22,29,31]:

$$\frac{\partial \overline{U}}{\partial \overline{X}} + \frac{\partial \overline{V}}{\partial \overline{Y}} = 0, \tag{5}$$

$$\begin{aligned} \rho_f\left(\frac{\partial \overline{U}}{\partial \overline{t}} + \overline{U}\frac{\partial \overline{U}}{\partial \overline{X}} + \overline{V}\frac{\partial \overline{U}}{\partial \overline{Y}}\right) = & -\frac{\partial \overline{P}}{\partial \overline{X}} + \frac{\partial}{\partial \overline{Y}}\left[\mu_f(T)\left(\frac{\partial \overline{U}}{\partial \overline{Y}} + \frac{\partial \overline{V}}{\partial \overline{X}}\right)\right] + 2\frac{\partial}{\partial \overline{X}}\left[\mu_f(T)\frac{\partial \overline{U}}{\partial \overline{X}}\right] - \overline{U}{B_0}^2\sigma_f \\ & + \frac{\mu_f(T)}{\widetilde{k_1}(\overline{Y})}\overline{U} + \alpha\rho_f g(T - T_0) + \alpha^*\rho_f g(C - C_0) + \rho_e E_x, \end{aligned} \tag{6}$$

$$\begin{aligned} \rho_f\left(\frac{\partial \overline{V}}{\partial \overline{t}} + \overline{U}\frac{\partial \overline{V}}{\partial \overline{X}} + \overline{V}\frac{\partial \overline{V}}{\partial \overline{Y}}\right) = & -\frac{\partial \overline{P}}{\partial \overline{Y}} + \frac{\partial}{\partial \overline{X}}\left[\mu_f(T)\left(\frac{\partial \overline{V}}{\partial \overline{X}} + \frac{\partial \overline{U}}{\partial \overline{Y}}\right)\right] + 2\frac{\partial}{\partial \overline{Y}}\left[\mu_f(T)\frac{\partial \overline{V}}{\partial \overline{Y}}\right] \\ & + \frac{\mu_f(T)}{\widetilde{k_1}(\overline{Y})}\overline{V} + E_x B_0 \sigma_f, \end{aligned} \tag{7}$$

$$(\rho C)_f\left(\overline{U}\frac{\partial T}{\partial \overline{X}}+\overline{V}\frac{\partial T}{\partial \overline{Y}}+\frac{\partial T}{\partial \overline{t}}\right) = \left(\frac{\partial T}{\partial \overline{Y}}+\frac{\partial T}{\partial \overline{X}}\right)\left[K_f(T)\left(\frac{\partial T}{\partial \overline{X}}+\frac{\partial T}{\partial \overline{Y}}\right)\right]+\frac{\mu_f(T)}{\widetilde{k_1}(\overline{Y})}\left(\overline{V}^2+\overline{U}^2\right)+\sigma_f {B_0}^2\overline{U}^2$$
$$+\tau(\rho C)_f\left[\frac{D_T}{T_m}\left\{\left(\frac{\partial T}{\partial \overline{X}}\right)+\left(\frac{\partial T}{\partial \overline{Y}}\right)\right\}^2+D_B\left(\frac{\partial T}{\partial \overline{X}}\frac{\partial C}{\partial \overline{X}}+\frac{\partial C}{\partial \overline{Y}}\frac{\partial T}{\partial \overline{Y}}\right)\right] \tag{8}$$
$$+\mu_f(T)\left[\left(\frac{\partial \overline{V}}{\partial \overline{X}}+\frac{\partial \overline{U}}{\partial \overline{Y}}\right)^2+2\left(\frac{\partial \overline{U}}{\partial \overline{X}}\right)^2+2\left(\frac{\partial \overline{V}}{\partial \overline{Y}}\right)^2\right]+\sigma_f(E_x)^2,$$

$$\left(\frac{\partial C}{\partial \overline{t}}+\overline{U}\frac{\partial C}{\partial \overline{X}}+\overline{V}\frac{\partial C}{\partial \overline{Y}}\right)=D_B\left(\frac{\partial^2 C}{\partial \overline{Y}^2}+\frac{\partial^2 C}{\partial \overline{X}^2}\right)+\frac{D_T}{T_m}\left(\frac{\partial^2 T}{\partial \overline{X}^2}+\frac{\partial^2 T}{\partial \overline{Y}^2}\right)-\widehat{\gamma}_c(C-C_0). \tag{9}$$

where $\overline{P}(\overline{X},\overline{Y},\overline{t})$, T, ρ_f and K_f are the pressure, temperature, density, and thermal conductivity, respectively. Fixed frame to wave frame transformation is described as [22]:

$$\overline{x}=\overline{X}-c\overline{t}, \overline{v}(\overline{x},\overline{y})=\overline{V}(\overline{X},\overline{t},\overline{Y}),\ \overline{p}(\overline{x},\overline{y})=\overline{P}(\overline{X},\overline{t},\overline{Y}),\ \overline{u}(\overline{x},\overline{y})=\overline{U}(\overline{Y},\overline{t},\overline{X})-c. \tag{10}$$

In wave frame, Equations (5)–(9) become:

$$\frac{\partial \overline{u}}{\partial \overline{x}}+\frac{\partial \overline{v}}{\partial \overline{y}}=0, \tag{11}$$

$$\rho_f\left((c+\overline{u})\frac{\partial \overline{u}}{\partial \overline{x}}+\overline{v}\frac{\partial \overline{u}}{\partial \overline{y}}\right) = -\frac{\partial \overline{P}}{\partial \overline{x}}+\frac{\partial}{\partial \overline{y}}\left[\mu_f(T)\left\{\frac{\partial \overline{v}}{\partial \overline{x}}+\frac{\partial \overline{u}}{\partial \overline{y}}\right\}\right]+2\frac{\partial}{\partial \overline{x}}\left[\mu_f(T)\frac{\partial \overline{u}}{\partial \overline{x}}\right]-(\overline{u}+c){B_0}^2\sigma_f$$
$$+\frac{\mu_f(T)}{\widetilde{k_1}(\overline{y})}\overline{U}+g(T-T_0)\alpha\rho_f++\rho_f\alpha^* g(C-C_0)+\rho_e E_x, \tag{12}$$

$$\rho_f\left((\overline{u}+c)\frac{\partial \overline{v}}{\partial \overline{x}}+\overline{v}\frac{\partial \overline{v}}{\partial \overline{y}}\right) = -\frac{\partial \overline{P}}{\partial \overline{y}}+\frac{\partial}{\partial \overline{x}}\left[\mu_f(T)\left\{\frac{\partial \overline{v}}{\partial \overline{x}}+\frac{\partial \overline{u}}{\partial \overline{y}}\right\}\right]+2\frac{\partial}{\partial \overline{y}}\left[\mu_f(T)\frac{\partial \overline{v}}{\partial \overline{y}}\right]$$
$$+\frac{\mu_f(T)}{\widetilde{k_1}(\overline{y})}\overline{v}+E_x B_0\sigma_f, \tag{13}$$

$$(\rho C)_f\left((\overline{u}+c)\frac{\partial T}{\partial \overline{x}}+\overline{v}\frac{\partial T}{\partial \overline{y}}\right) = \left(\frac{\partial T}{\partial \overline{y}}+\frac{\partial T}{\partial \overline{x}}\right)\left[K_f(T)\left(\frac{\partial T}{\partial \overline{y}}+\frac{\partial T}{\partial \overline{x}}\right)\right]+\frac{\mu_f(T)}{\widetilde{k_1}(\overline{y})}\left((\overline{u}+c)^2+\overline{v}^2\right)+\sigma_f {B_0}^2\overline{U}^2$$
$$+\tau(\rho C)_f\left[\frac{D_T}{T_m}\left\{\left(\frac{\partial T}{\partial \overline{x}}\right)+\left(\frac{\partial T}{\partial \overline{y}}\right)\right\}^2+D_B\left(\frac{\partial C}{\partial \overline{x}}\frac{\partial T}{\partial \overline{x}}+\frac{\partial C}{\partial \overline{y}}\frac{\partial T}{\partial \overline{y}}\right)\right] \tag{14}$$
$$+\mu_f(T)\left[\left(\frac{\partial \overline{v}}{\partial \overline{x}}+\frac{\partial \overline{u}}{\partial \overline{y}}\right)^2+2\left(\frac{\partial \overline{u}}{\partial \overline{x}}\right)^2+2\left(\frac{\partial \overline{v}}{\partial \overline{y}}\right)^2\right]+\sigma_f(E_x)^2,$$

$$\left(\overline{v}\frac{\partial C}{\partial \overline{y}}+(\overline{u}+c)\frac{\partial C}{\partial \overline{x}}\right)=D_B\left(\frac{\partial^2 C}{\partial \overline{y}^2}+\frac{\partial^2 C}{\partial \overline{x}^2}\right)+\frac{D_T}{T_m}\left(\frac{\partial^2 T}{\partial \overline{x}^2}+\frac{\partial^2 T}{\partial \overline{y}^2}\right)-\widehat{\gamma}_c(C-C_0). \tag{15}$$

Reynold's model of viscosity was intimated as a [29]:

$$\mu_f(T)=\mu_0 e^{-\alpha_0(T-T_0)},\ \text{for}\ \alpha_0 \ll 1, \tag{16}$$

which, after performing Maclaurin's series, can be recorded as:

$$\mu_f(T)=\mu_0(1-\alpha_0(T-T_0)),\ \text{for}\ \alpha_0 \ll 1, \tag{17}$$

where α_0 is the dimensional viscosity parameter. Further, the temperature-depending thermal conductivity [31] is classified as:

$$K_f(T)=K_0(1+\xi_0(T-T_0)), \tag{18}$$

where ξ_0 is the dimensional thermal conductivity parameter.

Equations (3) and (4) in (2) and the Debye-Hückel estimation [21]:

$$\frac{d^2\Omega}{dy^2} = \omega^2\Omega. \tag{19}$$

Equation (19) is subject to the assumption that the potential is fixed at the wall surface and that the potential distribution is symmetrical about the center line.

$$\begin{aligned} \Omega(y) &= 1, \text{ at } y = h, \\ \Omega'(y) &= 0, \text{ at } y = 0. \end{aligned} \tag{20}$$

where the electroosmotic parameter is represented by ω. It is given as:

$$\omega = \frac{d}{\lambda_D}, \tag{21}$$

where,

$$\lambda_D = \frac{1}{ez}\left(\frac{\varepsilon K_B T_{av}}{2n_0}\right)^{\frac{1}{2}}. \tag{22}$$

The potential function is calculated from Equation (19) subject to boundary conditions (20) in the following manner:

$$\Omega(y) = \frac{\cosh(\omega y)}{\cosh(\omega h)}. \tag{23}$$

In view of "low Reynolds and long wavelength approximations", Equations (12)–(15) become:

$$0 = -\frac{\partial p}{\partial x} + \frac{\partial}{\partial y}\left((1-\alpha\theta)\frac{\partial^2\psi}{\partial y^2}\right) + G_t\theta + G_c\phi - M^2\left(1 + \frac{\partial\psi}{\partial y}\right) + \frac{1}{k(y)}\left(\frac{\partial\psi}{\partial y} + 1\right) + U_{hs}\Omega''(y), \tag{24}$$

$$0 = \frac{\partial p}{\partial y}, \tag{25}$$

$$\begin{aligned} 0 \; &= \frac{\partial}{\partial y}\left[(1+\xi\theta)\frac{\partial\theta}{\partial y}\right] + Br(1-\alpha\theta)\left(\frac{\partial^2\psi}{\partial y^2}\right)^2 + BrM^2\left(1+\frac{\partial\psi}{\partial y}\right)^2 + S + \Pr N_b\left(\frac{\partial\theta}{\partial y}\frac{\partial\phi}{\partial y}\right) \\ &+ \frac{Br(1-\alpha\theta)}{k(y)}\left(\frac{\partial\psi}{\partial y} + 1\right)^2 + \Pr N_t\left(\frac{\partial\theta}{\partial y}\right)^2, \end{aligned} \tag{26}$$

$$0 = \frac{\partial^2\phi}{\partial y^2} + \frac{N_t}{N_b}\left(\frac{\partial^2\theta}{\partial y^2}\right) - S_c\gamma_c\phi. \tag{27}$$

The non-dimensional quantities used in the aforementioned calculations are:

$$\begin{aligned} & x = \frac{\overline{x}}{\lambda},\ t = \frac{c\overline{t}}{\lambda},\ h = \frac{\overline{H}_1}{d_1},\ a = \frac{a_1}{d_1},\ p = \frac{d_1^2\overline{p}}{c\lambda\mu_0},\ v = \frac{\mu_0}{\rho_f},\ y = \frac{\overline{y}}{d_1},\ v = \frac{\overline{v}}{c\delta},\ \delta = \frac{d_1}{\lambda},\ \xi = \xi_0 T_0, \\ & K(\theta) = \frac{\overline{K}(T)}{K_0},\ M^2 = \frac{\sigma_f}{\mu_0}B_0^2 {d_1}^2,\ u = \frac{\overline{u}}{c},\ \mathrm{Re} = \frac{\rho_f c d_1}{\mu_0},\ \Pr = \frac{\mu_0 C_f}{K_0},\ Ec = \frac{c^2}{C_f T_0},\ \alpha = \alpha_0 T_0 \\ & \phi = \frac{C - C_0}{C_0},\ \theta = \frac{T - T_0}{T_0},\ Br = \Pr.Ec,\ N_t = \frac{\tau D_T T_0}{v T_m},\ N_b = \frac{\tau D_B C_0}{v},\ S = \frac{{d_1}^2\sigma_f E_x^2}{K_0 T_0},\ v = -\psi_x, \\ & S_c = \frac{\mu_0}{\rho_f D_B},\ G_t = \frac{\rho_f g\alpha {d_1}^2 T_0}{\mu_0 c},\ G_c = \frac{\rho_f g\alpha^* {d_1}^2 C_0}{\mu_0 c},\ u = \psi_y,\ U_{hs} = -\frac{\varepsilon E_x}{\mu_0 c},\ \gamma_c = \frac{\widehat{\gamma_c} d_1^2}{v}, \\ & k(y) = \frac{\widetilde{k_1}(\overline{y})}{d_1^2}. \end{aligned} \tag{28}$$

Also, the continuity Equation (11) is identically satisfied. In given equations, Re, Ec, θ, Pr, M, G_c, U_{hs}, S, γ_c, N_t, S_c, G_t and N_b are the dimensionless Reynolds number, Eckert number, temperature, Prandtl number, Hartman number, concentration Grashoff number, Helmholtz–Smoluchowski velocity, Joule heating parameter, chemical reaction parameter, thermophoresis parameter, Schmidt number, thermal Grashoff number and Brownian motion parameter, respectively.

The relation between porosity and permeability is given as [11]:

$$k(y) = \frac{{d_p}^2 \varsigma^2}{150(1-\varsigma)^2}. \tag{29}$$

where d_p is the diameter of the pore. Alazmi and Wafai [15,16] showed that porosity depends on the normal distance from the boundary, given as:

$$\varsigma = C_0\left(1 + C_1 \exp\left(-\frac{C_2 y}{d_p}\right)\right). \tag{30}$$

The values of C_1, C_2, and C_0 are respectively chosen to be 1, 2 and 0.37 [11]. The mean flows η and F in laboratory and wave frames are defined as:

$$\eta = F + 1. \tag{31}$$

Kuznetsov and Nield [18] suggested that it is more appropriate to take thermophoresis at the boundaries instead of assessing constant nanomaterials concentration at the walls. Mathematically it is defined as:

$$D_B \frac{\partial C}{\partial \overline{Y}} + \frac{D_T}{T_m}\frac{\partial T}{\partial \overline{Y}} = 0, \text{ at } \overline{Y} = \pm H. \tag{32}$$

The dimensionless boundary conditions in moving frame are:

$$\begin{aligned} \psi = 0,\ \frac{\partial^2 \psi}{\partial y^2} = 0,\ \frac{\partial \theta}{\partial y} = 0,\ \frac{\partial \phi}{\partial y} = 0 \quad \text{at } y = 0, \\ \psi = F,\ \frac{\partial \psi}{\partial y} = -1,\ \theta = 0,\ N_b \frac{\partial \phi}{\partial y} + N_t \frac{\partial \theta}{\partial y} = 0 \text{ at } y = h. \end{aligned} \tag{33}$$

3. Entropy Generation

It is well known from thermodynamics that the loss of energy in a system contributes to thermodynamic irreversibility, and this produces entropy. Entropy generation is a degree of chaos in a thermodynamic system. In the present study, entropy production comes from various sources such as viscous dissipation, variable porosity, diffusion and EMHD irreversibility. The strength of entropy production (N_S) is defined as:

$$\begin{aligned} N_S &= (1+\xi\theta)\left(\frac{\partial \theta}{\partial y}\right)^2 + Br(1-\alpha\theta)\left(\frac{\partial^2 \psi}{\partial y^2}\right)^2 + BrM^2\left(1 + \frac{\partial \psi}{\partial y}\right)^2 + S + \mathrm{Pr}N_b\left(\frac{\partial \theta}{\partial y}\frac{\partial \phi}{\partial y}\right) \\ &+ \frac{Br(1-\alpha\theta)}{k(y)}\left(1+\frac{\partial \psi}{\partial y}\right)^2 + \mathrm{Pr}N_t\left(\frac{\partial \theta}{\partial y}\right)^2. \end{aligned} \tag{34}$$

Bejan number is assigned as the proportion of entropy produced by thermal irreversibility to total entropy:

$$B_e = \frac{(1+\xi\theta)\left(\frac{\partial \theta}{\partial y}\right)^2}{\left[\begin{array}{c} (1+\xi\theta)\left(\frac{\partial \theta}{\partial y}\right)^2 + Br(1-\alpha\theta)\left(\frac{\partial^2 \psi}{\partial y^2}\right)^2 + BrM^2\left(1+\frac{\partial \psi}{\partial y}\right)^2 + S \\ +\mathrm{Pr}N_b\left(\frac{\partial \theta}{\partial y}\frac{\partial \phi}{\partial y}\right) + \frac{Br(1-\alpha\theta)}{k(y)}\left(1+\frac{\partial \psi}{\partial y}\right)^2 + \mathrm{Pr}N_t\left(\frac{\partial \theta}{\partial y}\right)^2 \end{array}\right]}. \tag{35}$$

The Bejan number (B_e) is a parameter that reflects the significance of thermal irreversibility in the domain.

The analytical solution of the Equations (24)–(27) in these settings is not an easy job. Findings are graphically interpreted in the next segment. Therefore, the set of differential Equations (24)–(27) subject to boundary conditions (33) are numerically resolved by utilizing NDSolve in Mathematica 13.1. This approach is very effective and beneficial for boundary value problems. Additionally, a step size of 0.01 allows for consistent adjustments of both x and y. The accuracy of this methodology is remarkable and is stable unconditionally.

4. Results and Discussion

Numerical findings are discussed in this section. Graphs for heat transfer, irreversibility rate, Bejan number, concentration and velocity profiles are gained and evaluated. Numerical values of HMT rate at the boundary are displayed via tables.

4.1. Temperature Profile

Figure 2a–f are devoted to estimate the alteration in temperature profile subject to variation in S, ω, N_t, N_b, ξ and M. Figure 2a reports that temperature profile becomes higher by enhancing S. An electrolyte solution's resistance to the flow of an electric current is measured by the Joule heating parameter. When S is high, heat production increases as a result of the extraordinarily high drag forces. From Figure 2b, temperature is larger and more progressive on increasing the electroosmotic parameter. Figure 2b reflects that the stronger ω raises the nanofluid temperature. This behavior is expected because higher values of ω cause a thin EDL, so the mass of the liquid proceeds toward the central part of the pump, which raises the temperature of the nanofluid due to significant convection. Figure 2c displays that temperature increases by enhancing the values of N_t. Similarly, an expansion in nanoliquid temperature is seen by expanding the values of N_b (see Figure 2d). This is mainly because an improvement in Brownian motion parameter enhances the kinetic energy that converts into internal energy and thereby improves the temperature. A similar inclination was uncovered by Shehzad et al. [8]. Figure 2e shows that the temperature declines by increasing the thermal conductivity parameter. However, a maximum temperature is obtained for constant thermal conductivity. The reason for this is that the liquid's capability to retain or radiate heat to its vicinity can be regulated by a fluid's thermal conductivity. When ξ increases, the thermal conductivity of the system is also growing. Therefore, the temperature profile declines. Figure 2f portrays that a stronger magnetic field significantly raises the temperature of nanofluid. This is due to the Joule heating effects. Figure 2g is outlined to assess and measure the temperature of different basic fluids (water and kerosene). It is noticed that the temperature of water is comparatively lower than that of kerosene.

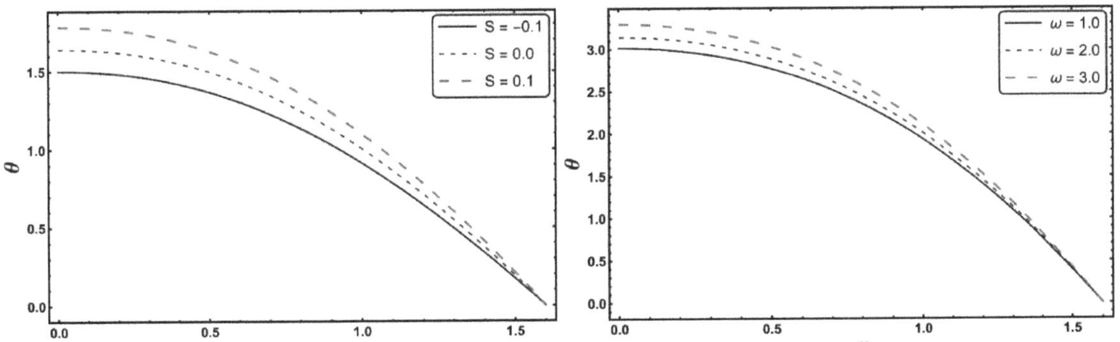

(a) (b)

Figure 2. *Cont.*

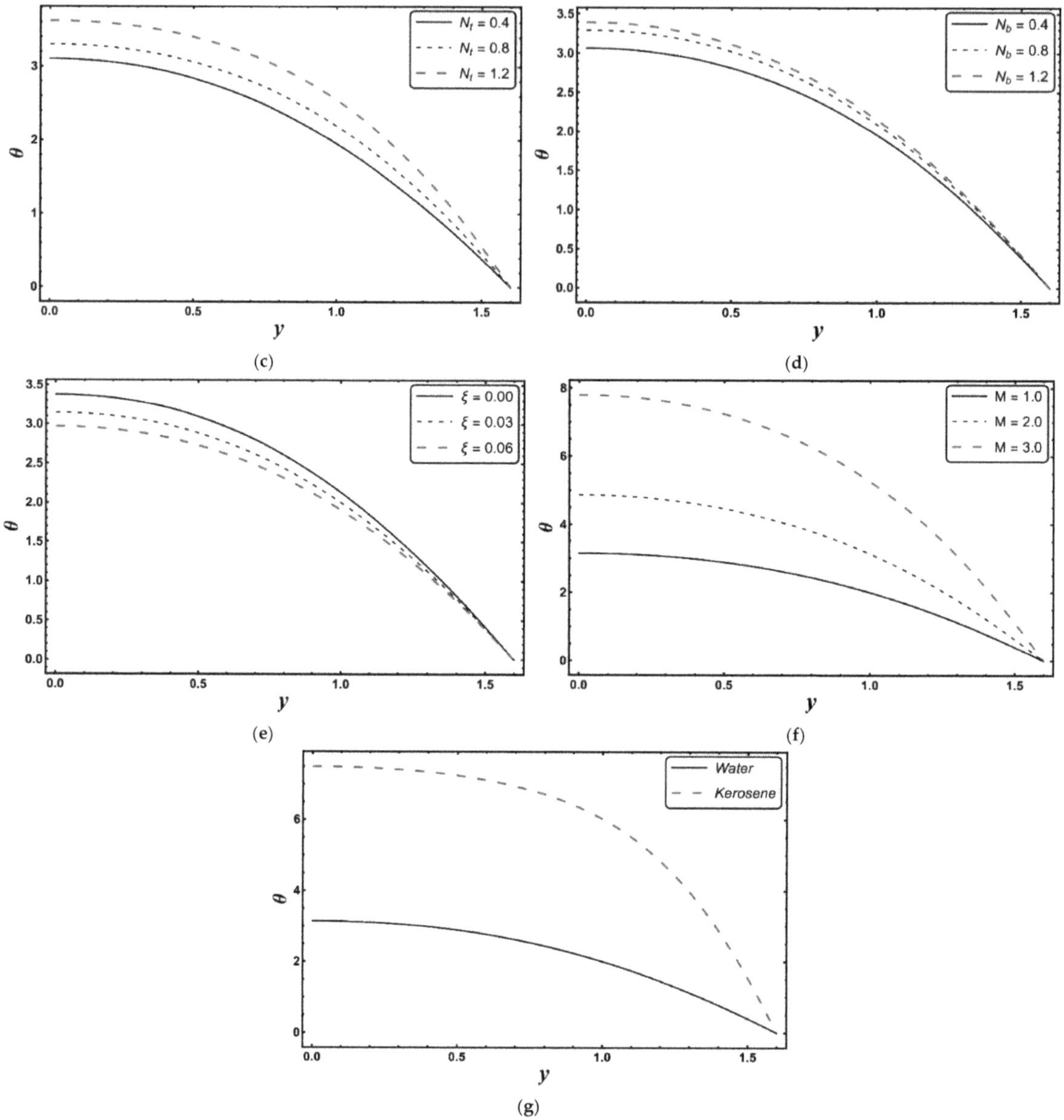

Figure 2. (**a–g**): Temperature profile against different parameters.

4.2. Heat Transfer Rate at the Wall

Bar charts in Figure 3a–d are prepared to examine the behavior of rate of heat transfer at the wall $-\theta'(h)$ versus various flow parameters. Bar chart in Figure 3a reflects that addition in S develops the $\theta'(h)$. S is related to a square of solidity of the electric field, so an expansion in S is physically correlated with an intense electric field, which in turn accelerates fluids faster and improves convective heat transmission. Therefore, there is a notable increase in the rate of heat transfer. ω with it rising values raises the heat transfer rate (see bar chart in Figure 3b). Since the electroosmotic parameter is inversely proportional to the Debye length, an augmentation in electroosmotic factor reduces the characteristic

Debye length, which results in a growth of $-\theta'(h)$. A similar effect was documented in the research of Hussain et al. [25]. However, the situation is reversed for ξ. From bar chart in Figure 3c, a reduction in $-\theta'(h)$ is witnessed by increasing ξ. Bar chart in Figure 3d exhibits that heat transfer rate significantly improves for higher M. Figure 3e is acquired to measure $-\theta'(h)$ for two different base liquids (kerosene and water). It is assessed that an excessive value of $-\theta'(h)$ is achieved by kerosene as compared to water.

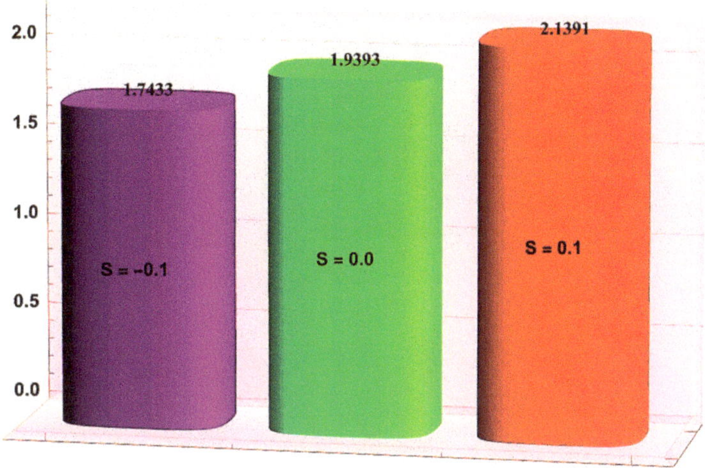

(a)

(b)

Figure 3. *Cont.*

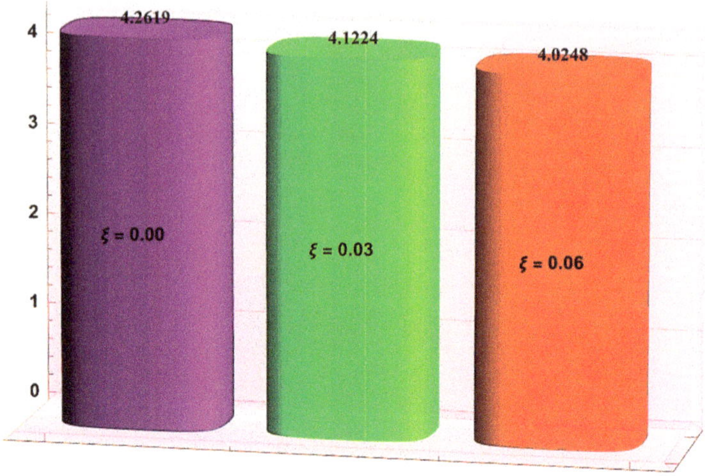

(c)

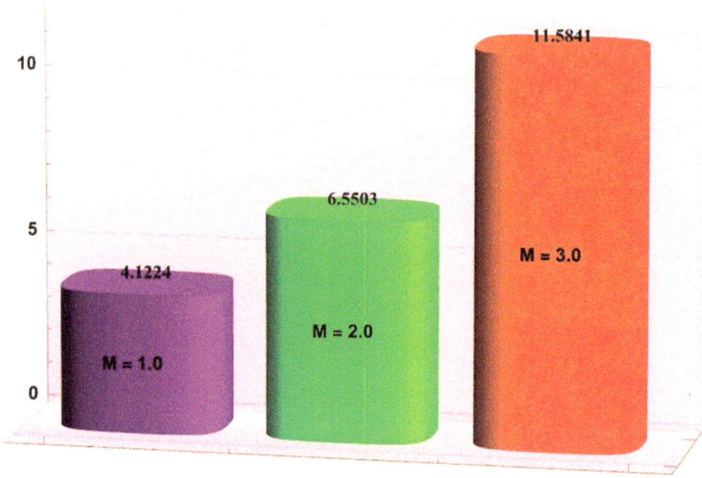

(d)

Figure 3. *Cont.*

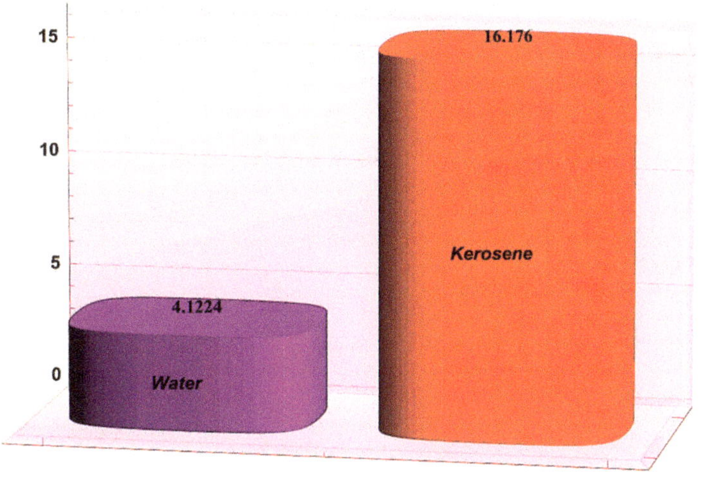

(e)

Figure 3. (**a–e**): Effects of different relevant parameters on heat transfer rate at the channel wall $-\theta'(h)$.

4.3. Entropy Analysis

The physical impacts of S, ω, ξ and G_t on entropy generation number (N_s) are shown through Figure 4a–d. Notably, the entropy generation curves exhibit a parabolic tendency with the lowest value close to the channel's center. The involvement of a Joule heating parameter further amplified the irreversibility process (see Figure 4a). Nanofluid temperature is high due to Joule heating parameter, and then the entropy also increases. This is consistent with the results of Akbar and Alotaibi [22]. It can be perceived from a Figure 4b that an augmentation in the electroosmotic parameter causes a notable increase in entropy generation. Figure 4c elucidates that entropy generation suppresses for higher ξ. Since a larger amount of ξ led to a reduction in temperature and, consequently, less disturbance. From this analysis, we conclude that for thermal management of biomedical instruments, the variable thermal conductivity must be taken into consideration. However, a reverse fashion is detected for larger G_t (see Figure 4d). The process of irreversibility is even more intensified in the presence of mixed convection.

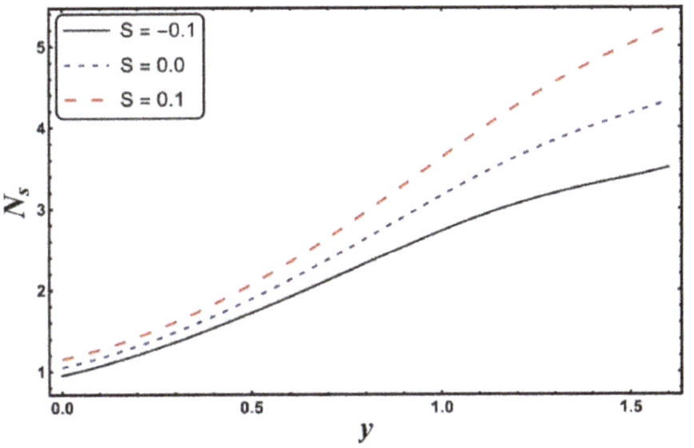

(a)

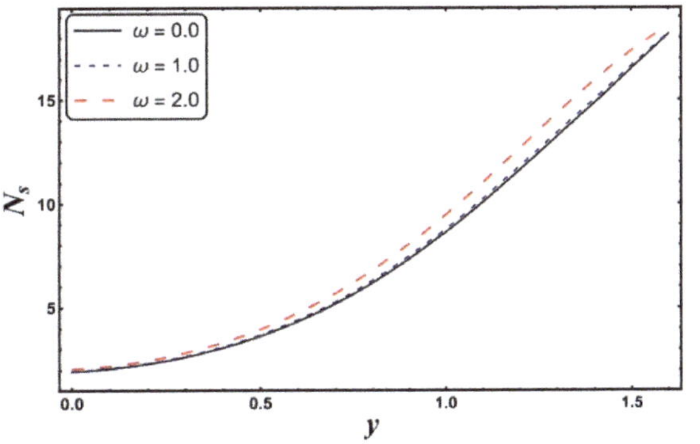

(b)

Figure 4. *Cont.*

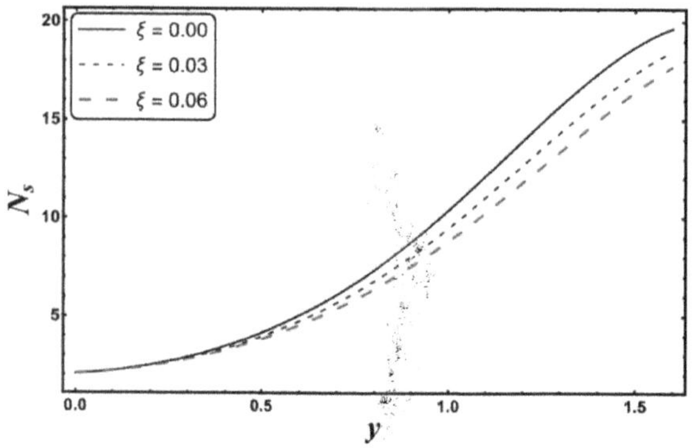

(c)

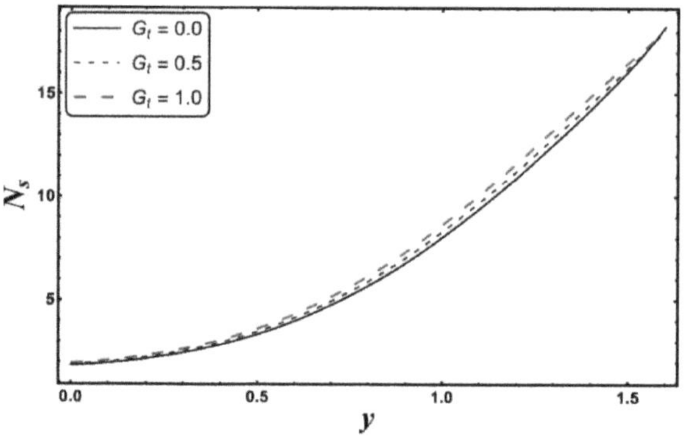

(d)

Figure 4. (**a–d**): Effects of different relevant parameters on entropy generation.

4.4. Bejan Number

Figure 5a–c gives the effects of S, ω and ξ on Bejan number (B_e). In all plots, Bejan number has a supreme value at the wall of the channel ($y = h$). The interval of B_e lies between 0 and 1. In certain cases, if $B_e \to 1$, in physical terms it indicates that the entropy generation due to heat conduction (HE) is much greater than total entropy generation (TE). While, $B_e \to 0$, this represents that HE is much less than TE. Figure 5a reflects that the strength of Bejan number is intensified by highlighting S. An increase in S reduces the overall irreversibility, which leads to an increase in the Bejan number. Analogous behavior is also encountered for greater ω. Figure 5c expresses that by mounting the thermal conductivity parameter, Bejan number is weakening.

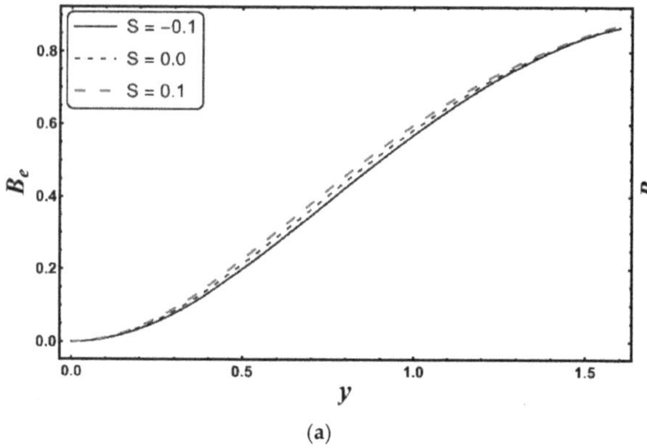

(a)

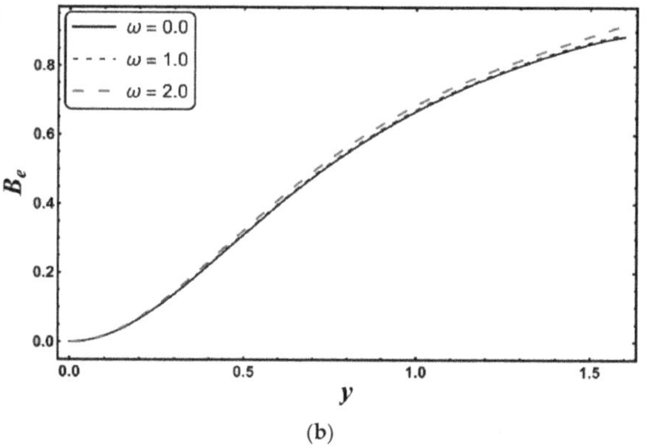

(b)

Figure 5. *Cont.*

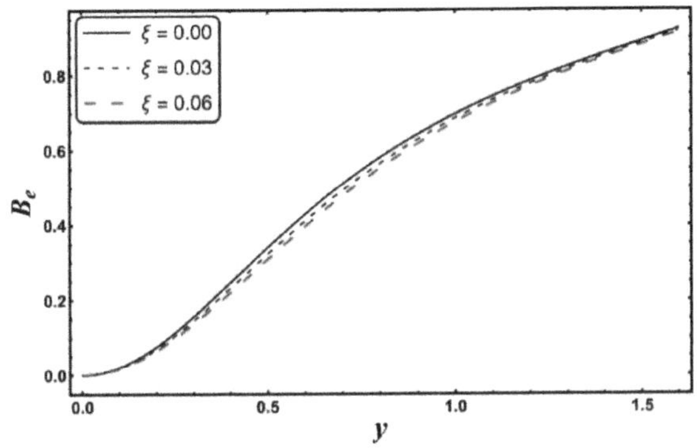

(c)

Figure 5. (**a–c**): Effects of different relevant parameters on Bejan number.

4.5. Nanoparticles Concentration

Impacts of S_c, γ, N_t and N_b on nanoparticles concentration are examined through Figure 6a–d. The resulting sketches manifest that the concentration profile near the walls of the channel is influenced by the parameters contained in the transition. This is primarily due to zero mass flux conditions for the concentration being regarded. Figure 6a portrays that nanoparticles concentration suppresses for larger S_c. Since S_c is inversely proportional to mass diffusion, therefore higher S_c causes a decrease in the mass diffusion rate, which ultimately reduces the concentration of nanoparticles. Figure 6b articulates that nanoparticles concentration is reduced for larger γ. Physical support is provided by the fact that the interfacial mass transfer rate is consolidated as a result of γ, which lowers the concentration profile. Figure 6c describes that a substantial decrease in concentration profile is perceived when N_t is being augmented. Figure 6d indicates that the concentration rises through improved values of N_b. However, the situation is reversed near the channel wall. The progression of N_b enhances the random motion of nanomaterials, which leads to an elevated concentration of nanomaterials.

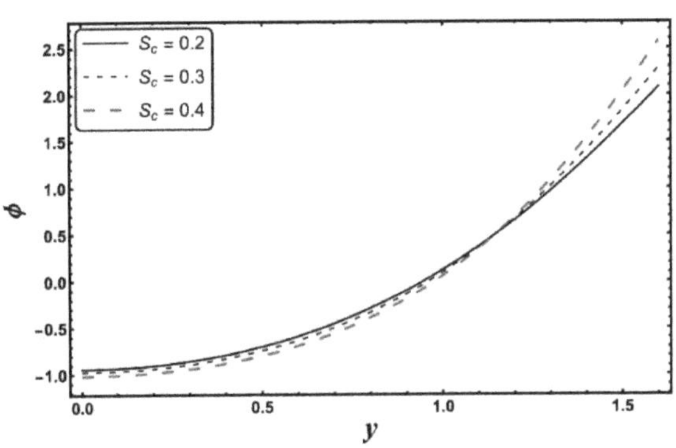

(a)

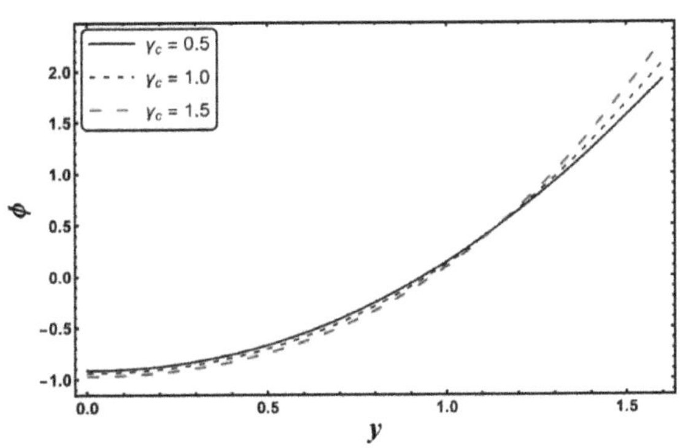

(b)

Figure 6. *Cont.*

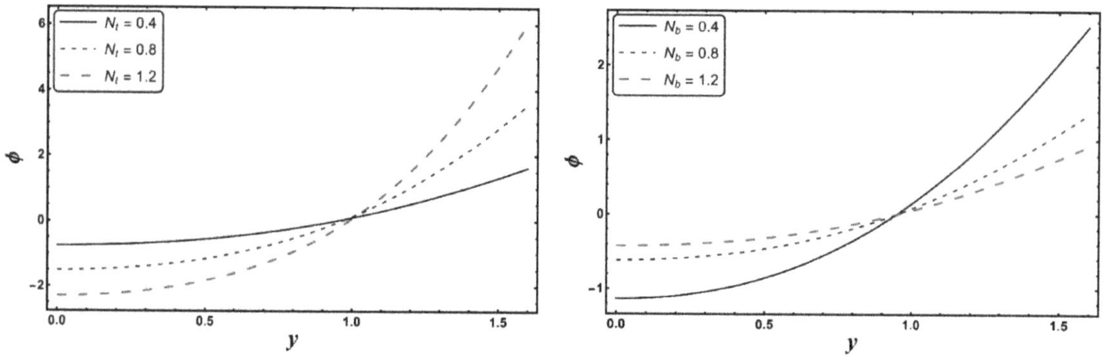

(c) (d)

Figure 6. (**a–d**): Effects of different parameters on concentration profile.

4.6. *Rate of Mass Transfer at the Boundary*

Table 1 is arranged to see the behavior of various parameters on mass transfer rate at boundary $\phi'(h)$. This table signifies that $\phi'(h)$ rises by expanding the values of S_c, γ and N_t whereas it shows decreasing behavior by increasing N_b.

Table 1. Mass transfer rate at the channel wall against different flow parameters.

S_c	γ_c	N_b	N_t	$\phi'(h)$
0.1	1.0	0.03	0.5	3.6417
0.2				4.1224
0.3				4.7646
0.2	0.0			3.2667
	0.5			3.6417
	1.0			4.1224
		0.1		21.3819
		0.2		9.8702
		0.3		6.6527
			0.1	0.7094
			0.2	1.4692
			0.3	2.2861

4.7. *Velocity Profile*

Figure 7a–e are sketched to investigate the behavior of Helmholtz Smoluchowski velocity/electroosmotic velocity (U_{hs}), electroosmotic parameter (ω), variable viscosity parameter (α), Hartman number (M) and concentration Grashof number (G_c) on velocity profile. According to Figure 7a, a higher U_{hs} causes a decline in velocity in the middle of channel, while the reverse trend is observed at the boundaries. A positively oriented external electric field can be obtained when U_{hs} is negative. The reverse axial electric field can be archived when U_{hs} is positive, and there is no electric field when $U_{hs} = 0$. For negative U_{hs}, the electroosmotic velocity adds to the peristaltic motion's velocity, increasing the final axial velocity. The only source of fluid acceleration when $U_{hs} = 0$ is peristalsis, so the velocity is significantly lower than it would be for negative values. However, at positive values, the electroosmotic velocity opposes peristaltic pumping; as a result, the least acceleration of the liquid is observed in this situation. As a result, the direction inside the channel and the electric field's direction plays a crucial role in determining the characteristics of the velocity distribution. Figure 7b shows that the nanofluid flow increases with increasing electroosmotic parameter. A higher value of the electroosmotic parameter indicates the presence of a higher concentration of ions (in the base fluid), which is responsible for the formation of a thinner EDL layer, thereby creating a lower velocity resistance force, and hence the fluid flow is increased. It is necessary to state that the magnetohydrodynamic body force is inferior to the electrokinetic effect in terms of hydrodynamic control, and this is crucial for the precise design of micropumps. From Figure 7c, an increment in α yields to an increase in nanofluid velocity. This means that the nanofluid has a higher velocity near the middle of the channel than a nanoliquid with a constant viscosity ($\alpha = 0$) depending on the temperature. Strengthening the viscosity parameter α lowers the viscosity of the nanofluid and therefore resistance to flow, which enhances the nanofluid velocity. A stronger magnetic field results in a lower velocity (see Figure 7d). This is due to the emergence of Lorentz forces. Such trends have been reported in Abbasi et al. [11]. Figure 7e elucidates that velocity retards by increasing the values of G_c. This is primarily because with an increase in G_c the viscosity of nanoliquid increases which lessens the movement of nanoliquid.

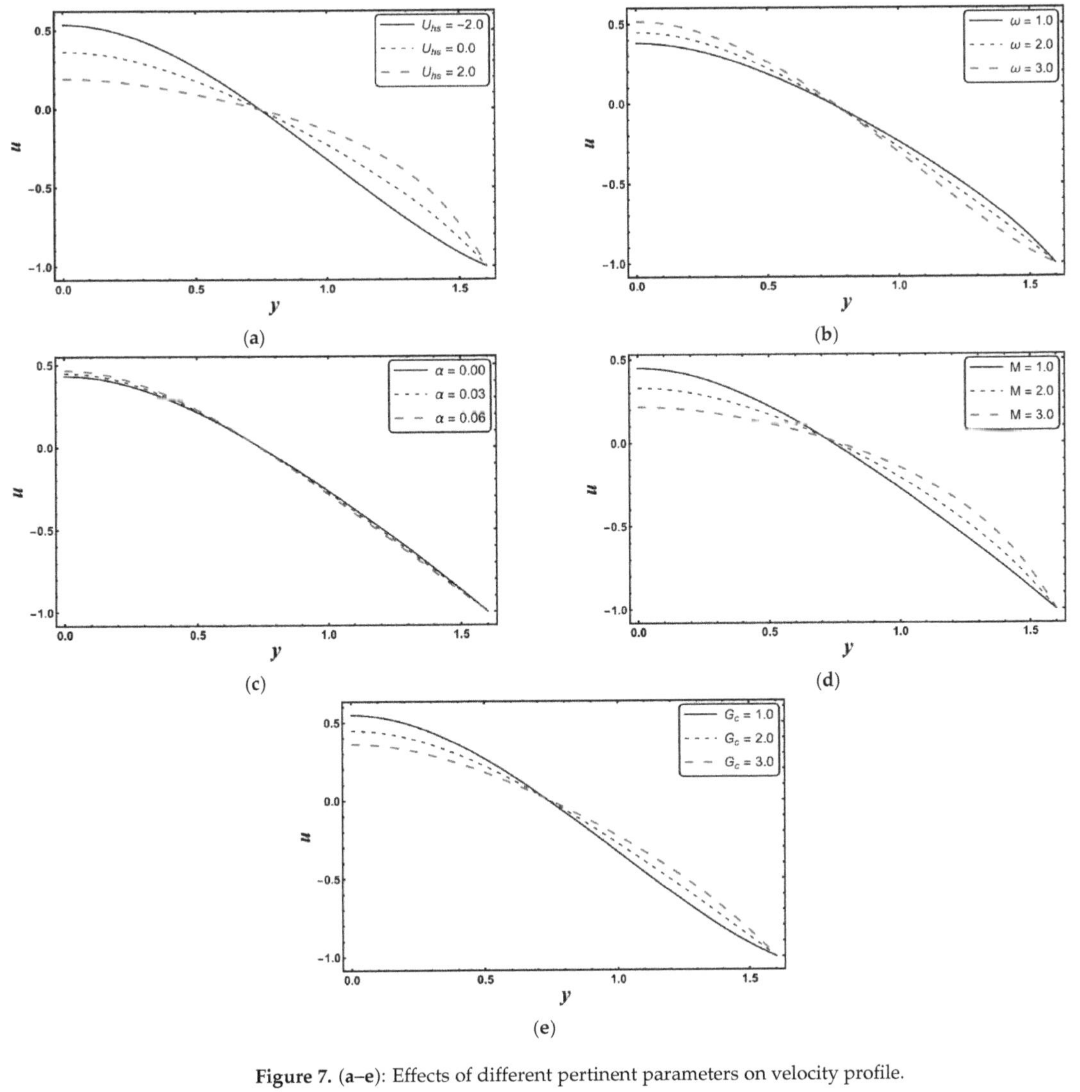

Figure 7. (**a**–**e**): Effects of different pertinent parameters on velocity profile.

5. Conclusions

The present study examines the interaction of variable fluid properties with electrokinetically regulated peristaltic transportation of a reactive nanofluid embedded in a porous space. The ensuing key facts have been produced from the above investigation:

- More energy is contributed to the nanofluid system in response of the Joule heating parameter.
- An inclining change in heat transfer rate at the wall associated with the larger Electroosmotic parameter is exhibited.
- It is noticed that the temperature of water is comparatively lower than that of kerosene.
- Entropy generation suppresses for higher variable thermal conductivity parameter.
- The process of irreversibility is even more intensified in the presence of mixed convection.
- The magnitude of Bejan number is enhanced by increasing electroosmotic parameter.
- A substantial decrease in nanoparticles concentration is perceived when chemical reaction parameter is being augmented.
- A significant increase in mass transfer rate at the wall is found at a higher Schmidt number.
- A positively oriented external electric field contributes to the velocity of nanofluid.

Author Contributions: Conceptualization, S.H.; Methodology, Y.A. and H.A.; Software, H.A.; Validation, H.A.; Formal analysis, Y.A.; Investigation, Y.A.; Resources, S.H.; Writing—original draft, Y.A. and H.A.; Writing—review & editing, S.H.; Supervision, S.H.; Project administration, S.H.; Funding acquisition, H.A. All authors have read and agreed to the published version of the manuscript."

Funding: This research received no external funding.

Data Availability Statement: Not applicable.

Acknowledgments: H. Alotaibi is thankful for the Taif University research supporting project number (TURSP-2020/304), Taif University, Taif, Saudi Arabia.

Conflicts of Interest: The authors declare no conflict of interest.

Nomenclature

$(\vec{x}, \vec{y})$:	Coordinates in wave frame
$(\vec{U}, \vec{V})$:	Velocity components in lab frame
$(\vec{u}, \vec{v})$:	Velocity components in wave frame
n_0:	Concentration of ions at the bulk
e:	Electronic charge
c:	Speed of peristaltic wave
$\vec{J}$:	Current density
$\vec{B}$:	Applied magnetic field
K_B:	Boltzmann constant
$\vec{E}$:	Applied electric field
C_f:	Specific heat of fluid
μ_f:	Viscosity of fluid
T:	Dimensional temperature
δ:	Wave number
z:	Charge balance
σ_f:	Electric conductivity of fluid
g:	Acceleration due to gravity
$(\vec{X}, \vec{Y})$:	Coordinates in lab frame
P:	Dimensional pressure
T_w:	Temperature at channel wall
p:	Dimensionless pressure

T_0:	Temperature of wall
F:	Dimensionless flow rate in wave frame
θ:	Dimensionless temperature
ψ:	Stream function
η:	Dimensionless flow rate in laboratory frame
Pr:	Prandtl number
K_f:	Thermal conductivity of fluid
Re:	Reynolds number
Br:	Brinkman number
T_{av}:	Average temperature of the electrolytic solution
Ec:	Eckert number
ρ_f:	Density of fluid
G_t:	Temperature Grashoff number
M:	Hartman number
λ:	Wavelength
d_1:	Half width of the channel
n^+ and n^-:	Number of densities of cations and anions

References

1. Latham, T.W. Fluid Motions in a Peristaltic Pump. Master's Thesis, Massachusetts Institute of Technology, Cambridge, MA, USA, 1966.
2. Shapiro, A.H.; Jaffrin, M.Y.; Weinberg, S.L. Peristaltic pumping with long wavelengths at low Reynolds number. *J. Fluid Mech.* **1969**, *37*, 799–825. [CrossRef]
3. Srinivas, S.; Gayathri, R.; Kothandapani, M. The influence of slip conditions, wall properties and heat transfer on MHD peristaltic transport. *Comput. Phys. Commun.* **2009**, *180*, 2115–2122. [CrossRef]
4. Khan, A.A.; Usman, H.; Vafai, K.; Ellahi, R. Study of peristaltic flow of magnetohydrodynamics Walter's B fluid with slip and heat transfer. *Sci. Iran.* **2016**, *23*, 2650–2662. [CrossRef]
5. Tanveer, A.; Khan, M.; Salahuddin, T.; Malik, M.Y.; Khan, F. Theoretical investigation of peristaltic activity in MHD based blood flow of non-Newtonian material. *Comput. Methods Programs Biomed.* **2020**, *187*, 105225. [CrossRef] [PubMed]
6. Choi, S.U.; Eastman, J.A. *Enhancing Thermal Conductivity of Fluids with Nanoparticles*; (No. ANL/MSD/CP-84938; CONF-951135–29); Argonne National Lab (ANL): Argonne, IL, USA, 1995.
7. Eastman, J.A.; Choi, U.S.; Li, S.; Thompson, L.J.; Lee, S. Enhanced thermal conductivity through the development of nanofluids. *MRS Online Proc. Libr. OPL* **1996**, *457*, 3. [CrossRef]
8. Shehzad, S.A.; Abbasi, F.M.; Hayat, T.; Alsaadi, F. MHD mixed convective peristaltic motion of nanofluid with Joule heating and thermophoresis effects. *PLoS ONE* **2014**, *9*, e111417. [CrossRef] [PubMed]
9. Prakash, J.; Sharma, A.; Tripathi, D. Convective heat transfer and double diffusive convection in ionic nanofluids flow driven by peristalsis and electromagnetohydrodynamics. *Pramana* **2020**, *94*, 4. [CrossRef]
10. Eldabe, N.T.; Abouzeid, M.; Shawky, H.A. MHD peristaltic transport of Bingham blood fluid with heat and mass transfer through a non-uniform channel. *J. Adv. Res. Fluid Mech. Therm. Sci.* **2021**, *77*, 145–159. [CrossRef]
11. Abbasi, F.M.; Hayat, T.; Alsaadi, F.; Dobai, A.M.; Gao, H. MHD peristaltic transport of spherical and cylindrical magneto-nanoparticles suspended in water. *AIP Adv.* **2015**, *5*, 077104. [CrossRef]
12. Sajid, T.; Tanveer, S.; Munsab, M.; Sabir, Z. Impact of oxytactic microorganisms and variable species diffusivity on blood-gold Reiner–Philippoff nanofluid. *Appl. Nanosci.* **2021**, *11*, 321–333. [CrossRef]
13. Gasmi, H.; Khan, U.; Zaib, A.; Ishak, A.; Eldin, S.M.; Raizah, Z. Analysis of Mixed Convection on Two-Phase Nanofluid Flow Past a Vertical Plate in Brinkman-Extended Darcy Porous Medium with Nield Conditions. *Mathematics* **2022**, *10*, 3918. [CrossRef]
14. Darcy, H. *Les Fontaines Publiques de la Volle de Dijon*; Vector Dalmont: Paris, France, 1856.
15. Alazmi, K.; Vafai, K. Analysis of variants within the porous transport models. *J. Heat Transf.* **2004**, *122*, 303–326. [CrossRef]
16. Alazmi, K.; Vafai, K. Analysis of variable porosity, thermal dispersion and local thermal non-equilibrium on free surface flows through porous media. *J. Heat Transf.* **2004**, *126*, 389–399. [CrossRef]
17. Pal, D.; Mondal, H. Radiation effects on combined convection over a vertical flat plate embedded in a porous medium of variable porosity. *Meccanica* **2009**, *44*, 133–144. [CrossRef]
18. Kuznetsov, A.V.; Nield, D.A. The Cheng—Minkowycz problem for natural convective boundary layer flow in a porous medium saturated by a nanofluid: A revised model. *Int. J. Heat Mass Transf.* **2013**, *65*, 682–685. [CrossRef]
19. Asghar, Z.; Ali, N. Mixed convective heat transfer analysis for the peristaltic transport of viscoplastic fluid: Perturbation and numerical study. *AIP Adv.* **2019**, *9*, 095001. [CrossRef]
20. Rice, C.L.; Whitehead, R. Electrokinetic flow in a narrow cylindrical capillary. *J. Phys. Chem.* **1965**, *69*, 4017–4024. [CrossRef]
21. Tang, G.H.; Li, X.F.; He, Y.L.; Tao, W.Q. Electroosmotic flow of non-Newtonian fluid in microchannels. *J. Non-Newton. Fluid Mech.* **2009**, *157*, 133–137. [CrossRef]

22. Akbar, Y.; Alotaibi, H. Electroosmosis-Optimized Thermal Model for Peristaltic Transportation of Thermally Radiative Magnetized Liquid with Nonlinear Convection. *Entropy* **2022**, *24*, 530. [CrossRef]
23. Siryk, S.V.; Bendandi, A.; Diaspro, A.; Rocchia, W. Charged dielectric spheres interacting in electrolytic solution: A linearized Poisson–Boltzmann equation model. *J. Chem. Phys.* **2021**, *155*, 114114. [CrossRef]
24. Obolensky, O.I.; Doerr, T.P.; Yu, Y.K. Rigorous treatment of pairwise and many-body electrostatic interactions among dielectric spheres at the Debye–Hückel level. *Eur. Phys. J. E* **2021**, *44*, 129. [CrossRef] [PubMed]
25. Hussain, A.; Wang, J.; Akbar, Y.; Shah, R. Enhanced thermal effectiveness for electroosmosis modulated peristaltic flow of modified hybrid nanofluid with chemical reactions. *Sci. Rep.* **2022**, *12*, 13756. [CrossRef] [PubMed]
26. Bejan, A. A study of entropy generation in fundamental convective heat transfer. *ASME J. Heat Transf.* **1979**, *101*, 718–725. [CrossRef]
27. Rashidi, M.; Bhatti, M.; Abbas, M.; Ali, M. Entropy generation on MHD blood flow of nanofluid due to peristaltic waves. *Entropy* **2016**, *18*, 117. [CrossRef]
28. Akbar, Y.; Shanakhat, I.; Abbasi, F.M.; Shehzad, S.A. Entropy generation analysis for radiative peristaltic motion of silver-water nanomaterial with temperature dependent heat sink/source. *Phys. Scr.* **2020**, *95*, 115201. [CrossRef]
29. Akbar, Y.; Abbasi, F.M. Impact of variable viscosity on peristaltic motion with entropy generation. *Int. Commun. Heat Mass Transf.* **2020**, *118*, 104826. [CrossRef]
30. Sneha, K.N.; Mahabaleshwar, U.S.; Sharifpur, M.; Ahmadi, M.H.; Al-Bahrani, M. Entropy Analysis in MHD CNTS Flow Due to a Stretching Surface with Thermal Radiation and Heat Source/Sink. *Mathematics* **2022**, *10*, 3404. [CrossRef]
31. Akbar, Y.; Huang, S. Enhanced Thermal Effectiveness for Electrokinetically Driven Peristaltic Flow of Motile Gyrotactic Microorganisms in a Thermally Radiative Powell Eyring Nanofluid Flow with Mass Transfer. *Chem. Phys. Lett.* **2022**, *808*, 140120. [CrossRef]

mathematics

MDPI

Article

The Effect of Diameter and Position of Transverse Cylindrical Vortex Generators on Heat Transfer Improvement in a Wavy Channel

Stanislav Kotšmíd and Zuzana Brodnianská *

Faculty of Technology, Technical University in Zvolen, Studentska 26, 960 01 Zvolen, Slovakia
* Correspondence: zuzana.brodnianska@tuzvo.sk

Abstract: The present study investigates the effect of outer diameter (10 mm and 15 mm) and 5 positions of cylindrical vortex generators (CVGs) installed to the wavy channel in order to improve heat transfer parameters in conjunction with low-pressure drops. The wavy channels with and without CVGs are compared in terms of the local heat transfer coefficient, mean Nusselt number, Colburn factor, friction, and thermal performance for *Re* in the range of 857 to 8001. Furthermore, the effect of the cooling air flow direction (forward and backward) is assessed. Inserting the CVGs to the channel causes the enhancement of Nusselt numbers and Colburn factors for all CVGs positions and *Re* in comparison with the channels without CVGs. The maximum thermal performance factor $TPF_B = 0.8229$ was achieved for the channel with CVGs position '5' and 15 mm diameter, backward air flow, and *Re* = 1677. The backward air flow is more efficient compared with forward air flow since the cooling air gets into the valleys to a greater extent, and thus, better mixing of the fluid occurs. The numerical investigation, conducted with Ansys Fluent software, is compared with the experimental one acquired by holographic interferometry at good agreement of the local heat transfer coefficients. Finally, new correlating equations for the mean Nusselt number were created.

Keywords: wavy channel; cylindrical vortex generator; heat transfer; thermal performance; numerical simulation

MSC: 65D10; 76M12; 80M12

Citation: Kotšmíd, S.; Brodnianská, Z. The Effect of Diameter and Position of Transverse Cylindrical Vortex Generators on Heat Transfer Improvement in a Wavy Channel. *Mathematics* **2022**, *10*, 4546. https://doi.org/10.3390/math10234546

Academic Editors: Shujin Laima, Yong Cao, Xiaowei Jin and Hehe Ren

Received: 9 November 2022
Accepted: 25 November 2022
Published: 1 December 2022

Publisher's Note: MDPI stays neutral with regard to jurisdictional claims in published maps and institutional affiliations.

Copyright: © 2022 by the authors. Licensee MDPI, Basel, Switzerland. This article is an open access article distributed under the terms and conditions of the Creative Commons Attribution (CC BY) license (https://creativecommons.org/licenses/by/4.0/).

1. Introduction

Plenty of experimental and numerical studies have been devoted to the enhanced heat transfer of rectangular corrugated channels that are widely employed as heat exchangers, recovery units, electronic devices, solar air heater, and different heaters and coolers in the field of energy, mechanical and chemical engineering, aerospace technology, laser equipment and automotive. The corrugation of heat exchange surfaces leads to the flow deviation and acceleration adjacent to the wavy protrusions, which results in intensifying the convective rate of heat transfer [1]. In many studies, the insertion of various vortex generators (VGs) into the flowing medium has been confirmed as effective in terms of thermal performance improvement; however, certain pressure losses always appear there.

The advantage of wavy channels is the creation of recirculation or/and swirl flows in the corrugation valleys. The onset and growth of recirculation zones promote the mixing of air in the boundary layer. Therefore, the wavy surface has a significant effect on the enhancement of heat transfer [2]. Naphon [2] experimentally studied the channel with height of 12.5 mm and V inline corrugated lower and upper heated surfaces with the corrugation tile angle of 20°, 40°, and 60° for heat flux q = 0.5–1.2 kW/m^2 and *Re* = 500–1400. The Nusselt numbers at higher corrugated tile angles were higher than those at lower ones. Consequently, Naphon [3] also studied the channel height of 20 and 25 mm with the length of channel 300 mm for staggered arrangement and *Re* in the range of 2000–9000. The heat transfer and pressure drop for the corrugated channel are 3.51 and 1.96 times higher than those for the smooth channel. Three wavy channels applied as solar air heaters for the mass flow rate in the range from 0.01 kg/s to 0.04 kg/s were experimentally studied by Singh et al. [4]. The maximum thermal performance was achieved for mass flow rate of 0.04 kg/s. The thermal performance increased from 47% to 66% with increased mass flow rate from 0.01 kg/s to 0.04 kg/s, respectively. The solar air heaters with a different shape of VGs were explored experimentally and numerically by several authors. Conical VGs in a staggered arrangement used by Bezbaruah et al. [5] achieved 257% enhancement in thermal performance. According to Silva et al. [6], the VG shape and angle of attack affect the heat transfer more than *Re* number. In the paper by Zhao [7], the V-shaped ribs and the delta winglet VG pair were studied to investigate the mixing effect in the solar air heater channel. The delta-winglet VGs combined with the 60° V-shaped ribs achieved the enhanced heat transfer by 39.4% compared with the only delta-winglet VG case. The combination of a sinusoidal wavy channel and VGs brought an increase in terms of thermal performance factor in several studies. Caliskan et al. [8] achieved the improvement of 2.2 times due to VG, sinusoidal structure, and punched hole. To mix the flow and enhance the convection, Nassab et al. [9] attached the inclined thin elastic porous winglet on the heated wall as the VG in the solar air heater. The porous VG significantly improved the outlet bulk temperature difference up to 500%. Particle image velocimetry (PIV) was used by Kurtulmus et al. [10] to investigate the flow physics in the wavy converging-diverging channel for *Re* in the range of 4×10^3 to 1×10^4. They conducted the numerical simulations to confirm the experimental results for the same parameters. The shear stress transport k-ω turbulence model was used to perform numerical analyses. The highest $TPF = 1.46$ was obtained for the ratio of maximum channel height to minimum channel height of 0.5 and $Re = 4 \times 10^3$.

Enhancing the efficiency of channel/microchannel heat exchangers is important from the standpoint of the cooled electronic/microelectronic component proper functioning. Liu et al. [11] achieved the critical *Re* numbers from 600 to 700 using the longitudinal VGs in a microchannel and improved the heat transfer performance (9–21% higher for the laminar flow and 39–90% for the turbulent flow). Due to this, the pressure drops increase as well (34–83% for the laminar flow and 61–169% for the turbulent flow). Moreover, the empirical correlations for Nusselt numbers and friction factors were developed. Chen et al. [12] presented an increase in heat transfer performance by 12.3–73.8% and 3.4–45.4% for the microchannels with longitudinal VGs and the aspect ratios of 0.0667 and 0.25, respectively, while the pressure drops were increased by 40.3–158.6% and 6.5–47.7%. The VGs help to achieve the critical *Re* numbers lower than 1000, which is below the generally accepted value of 2300. A single-phase laminar flow in the rectangular microchannel equipped with longitudinal VGs was numerically studied by Ebrahimi et al. [13]. When comparing the channel with longitudinal VGs and the smooth microchannel for *Re* in the range of 100 to 1100, the increase of 2–25% in the mean Nusselt number was observed for the former one. Higher *Re* numbers caused higher heat transfer enhancement; however, VGs caused higher-pressure drops. Raihan et al. [14] placed the CVGs to the heat sinks where the lowest thermal resistance was achieved for the VGs at the front of the minichannels with the radius 300 μm and no distance between them and found that pressure drop increased with a larger VG radius. To increase heat transfer, the simultaneous use of transverse VGs and porous media in the microchannel was investigated by Moosavi et al. [15]. The convective heat transfer coefficient increased with the height and number of VGs. There was an enhancement of 260–1200% in terms of *Re* number in the range of 125 to 1000. The VGs caused better overall performance in the microchannel than the porous medium. Compared with the empty microchannel, the heat transfer coefficient is 2.6 times higher when using 8 VGs with 12.5% of the channel height. Amini and Habibi [16] used the flexible splitters for enhanced heat transfer capability and higher hydrothermal performance of heat sink. The flexible splitters achieved better heat transfer capability and higher hydrothermal performance compared with the rigid ones. In comparison with the channel without splitters, the flexible splitters achieved 10% less total hydrothermal efficiency and 190% higher rejected heat.

Al-Asadi et al. [17] numerically explored the cylindrical vortex generators (CVGs) of radii up to 400 μm with a half-circle and quarter-circle cross section in a microchannel in terms of thermal resistance, pressure drop, and performance evaluation criteria index (pressure drop vs. thermal resistance). The uniform heat flux and *Re* number in the range of 100 to 2300 represented the conditions for microelectronic cooling. The research confirmed the significant potential of using VGs. Based on the performance evaluation criteria index, small-radius centered VGs offer a good potential for the efficiency improvement at lower *Re* number. Subsequently, Al-Asadi et al. [18] studied various gaps along the CVGs' length placed transversely over the microchannel span to reduce the pressure drop and enhance heat transfer performance. The gaps between each end of the VGs and the channel side wall offer enhanced performance. Cylinders of a circular, square, or possibly oval shape are inserted into the rectangular channels for the purpose of breaking up the air and creating vortices. Leu et al. [19] inserted the inclined block-shape VGs behind the tubes of a plate-fin and tube heat exchanger. The VGs' span angle of 45° provides the best heat transfer augmentation since the longitudinal vortices are generated and the heat transfer performance in the wake regions is improved. The adiabatic circular cylinder in the uniformly heated mini-channel was numerically investigated by Cheraghi et al. [20]. It was found that the maximum heat transfer enhancement from channel walls is achieved when the cylinder is placed in the middle of the channel. An important conclusion is that the displacement of cylinder towards the bottom wall leads to the suppression of the vortex shedding, establishment of a steady flow, and reduction of both wall heat transfer and pressure drop. The improvement in thermal performance of a rectangular channel with small-scale CVGs was achieved by Wang [21] where the circular cylinder was located in a fully developed turbulent boundary layer of a rectangular channel. The interaction between the cylinder wake and the wall boundary layer altered the flow structure of the turbulent boundary layer. Consequently, Wang [22] used the small-scale slit-vent circular cylinder in the mentioned channel. When the gap ratio (distance from the cylinder to channel bottom/cylinder diameter) was more than 2, the overall thermal performance of a rectangular channel with the slit-vent cylinder was improved. Han et al. [23] inserted a half-cylinder as the VG to the rectangular channel; consequently, the effects of the height, length, and spacing of the VGs were studied by Han et al. [24].

The channel fitted with a circular cylinder was researched experimentally by Vyas [25]. The interferometry method showed the effect of the cylinder in generating the flow instabilities and alterations in the thermal boundary layer along the heated channel wall. Moreover, the vortex shedding behind the cylinder was captured and a gradual increase in the vortex shedding frequency was observed with increasing *Re* number. Dey [26] varied the axial and transverse location of an adiabatic square cylinder in the channel to analyze the effect of the parameters on the wall heat transfer performance and the channel flow characteristics. Particle swarm optimization was used to find out that the ratio $L_2/D = 33$ and $H/D = 10$ can provide the maximum thermal performance ($\eta = 1.063$) when the cylinder is placed at $s/D = 5$ and $H/D = 3$ for $Re = 100$. The effect of the round, oval, and diamond shape of the pins in combination with the VGs in a microchannel on the heat transfer enhancement was investigated in the paper by Wang [27]. The VGs intensified the fluid mixing and increased the secondary flow by 30%. For the purpose of increasing the average heat transfer, the punched delta winglet pair as a longitudinal VG was used by Wu [28]. The average Nusselt number increased with the attack angle of the delta winglet pair. Zhang [29] studied the heat transfer performances and flow characteristics of VGs in the high aspect ratio rectangular ribbed channel. Liquid crystal thermography and CFD simulations with the SST k-ω model in a transition state were used for the experimentally and numerically studies. The flow characteristics revealed that longitudinal VGs generated the vortices to disturb the boundary layers, which enhanced the flow mixing and augmented the heat transfer performance. In the paper by Ibrahim [30], the winglet VGs (delta and rectangular) in the bank of oval tubes were used. On the basis of the experimental results, it was found that the delta winglets give the best performance in the single-phase and two-phase flow tube bank of oval tubes.

In this study, the examined asymmetric wavy geometry of the heated channel is the novel geometry, and in combination with the appropriate placement and outer diameter of CVGs, it improves heat transfer processes due to the direction and pressing of cooling air into the valleys and the creation of recirculation zones. The direction of inlet cooling air also plays an important role in heat transfer intensification due to different flow characteristics in the channel. In the previous literature, the channels with symmetric wavy protrusions were investigated mainly that did not achieve such a significant improvement in heat transfer characteristics. This fact motivated us to design and investigate a new geometric shape of heat exchange surfaces. Moreover, with the addition of CVGs, the possibilities of further increases in thermal performance have been expanded.

2. Numerical Background

2.1. Physical Model

The geometric dimensions of the examined configurations are shown in Figure 1. The length of 400 mm, the height of 40 mm, spacing between protrusions peaks of 40 mm, and the shape of the wavy channel protrusions were identical for all configurations. The cylindrical vortex generators (CVGs) with the diameter of 10 and 15 mm were inserted to the wavy channel in five different horizontal positions (Figure 1b,c). Overall, eight CVGs were centered relative to the channel height. The air flowed forward (air inlet A) and backward (air inlet B) through the channel for all examined configurations. The wavy channels with the CVGs diameter of 10 mm (Figure 1b) and 15 mm (Figure 1c) were compared with the wavy channel without CVGs (Figure 1a). The surface temperature of wavy surfaces was kept to T_s = 318.15 K while the air flow through the wavy channel was changed in the range of 5 to 50 m^3/h.

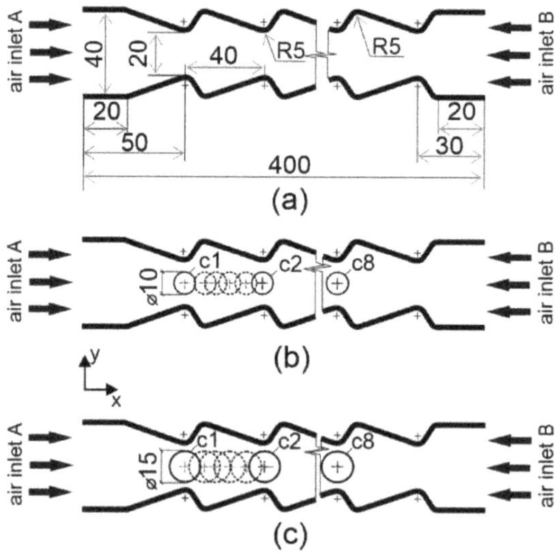

Figure 1. Geometric dimensions of the examined configurations (**a**) wavy channel A (WCA) and wavy channel B (WCB), (**b**) wavy channel A with CVGs diameter of 10 mm (WCCA10) and wavy channel B with CVGs diameter of 10 mm (WCCB10), (**c**) wavy channel A with CVGs diameter of 15 mm (WCCA15) and wavy channel B with CVGs diameter of 15 mm (WCCB15).

The configurations of the examined channels are shown in Table 1. For the sake of clarity, the investigated configurations are defined by the abbreviations. The wavy channel with forward air flow (WCA) and the wavy channel with backward air flow (WCB) do not include the CVGs. In the wavy channels with the CVG diameter of 10 mm (WCCA10) and 15 mm (WCCA15) with forward air flow, the CVGs' horizontal position in the range of $x_0/s = 0$ to $x_4/s = 0.79$ was considered. The same conditions were set for backward air flow (WCCB10, WCCB15).

Table 1. Examined configurations and positions of the cylindrical vortex generators (CVGs).

Configuration	Q (m^3/h)	Cylindrical Vortex Generators
Wavy channel A (WCA)	5, 10, 15, 20, 30, 40, 50	none
Wavy channel B (WCB)		none
Wavy channel A with CVGs ø 10 mm (WCCA10)		horizontal change position: $x_0/s = 0$, $x_1/s = 0.27$, $x_2/s = 0.38$, $x_3/s = 0.58$, $x_4/s = 0.79$
Wavy channel A with CVGs ø 15 mm (WCCA15)		
Wavy channel B with CVGs ø 10 mm (WCCB10)		
Wavy channel B with CVGs ø 15 mm (WCCB15)		

2.2. Data Reduction

The local heat transfer coefficients from numerical simulations are calculated by Sui [31]:

$$h_x = \frac{q_x}{\frac{(T_s - T_{a,in,m}) - (T_s - T_{a,out,m})}{\ln\left[\frac{(T_s - T_{a,in,m})}{(T_s - T_{a,out,m})}\right]}} \tag{1}$$

The mean Nusselt number of the whole channel is defined as [32]:

$$Nu_m = \frac{h_m \cdot D_{hyd}}{k_a} \tag{2}$$

Hence, the hydraulic diameter was defined as $D_{hyd} = (2 \cdot W \cdot H)/(W + H)$ [33]. The mean heat transfer coefficient for the whole channel is defined as [32]:

$$h_m = \frac{\int_0^L (h_{x,l} + h_{x,u})dx}{2L} \tag{3}$$

where L is the contour length of wavy surfaces in the test section.

The Colburn factor j and friction factor f of the whole channel are defined as [34]:

$$j = \frac{Nu_m}{Re \cdot Pr^{\frac{1}{3}}} \tag{4}$$

and [35]:

$$f = \frac{\Delta p}{\frac{L_2}{D_{hyd}} \cdot \frac{\rho_a \cdot v_{a,m}^2}{2}} \tag{5}$$

The thermal performance factor of the wavy channel with CVGs vs. wavy channel without CVGs for forward air flow (air inlet A) is defined as [5]:

$$TPF_A = \left(\frac{Nu_{WCCA}}{Nu_{WCA}}\right)\left(\frac{f_{WCCA}}{f_{WCA}}\right)^{-\frac{1}{3}} \tag{6}$$

while for backward air flow (air inlet B), it is defined as [5]:

$$TPF_B = \left(\frac{Nu_{WCCB}}{Nu_{WCB}}\right)\left(\frac{f_{WCCB}}{f_{WCB}}\right)^{-\frac{1}{3}} \tag{7}$$

2.3. Boundary Conditions

A preliminary study of the mesh grid size was carried out where quadrilateral elements were used. Overall, five different numbers of elements were created in the wall adjacent area, and the average heat transfer coefficient for the channel was being evaluated. Each mesh variant has a different number and bias of elements in perpendicular direction to the wall. On the basis of the study, the mesh with 2970 elements in the wall adjacent area was sufficient from the accuracy point of view. When refining the domain, maximum 0.4% improvement could be achieved. The average element height on the wall 0.082 mm continuously increased to 0.162 mm in the middle of the channel. Furthermore, the y^+ values were controlled as another quality criterion. Considering the element quality (aspect ratio, angles, etc.), the element widths were appropriately adjusted. The blue line of the mesh dependency test represents the change in the mean heat transfer coefficient h_m depending on the number of elements (Figure 2). The percentage discrepancy of h_m between two consecutive numbers is represented by the green line. The maximum limit of 2% for a sufficient number of elements is represented by the red dotted line.

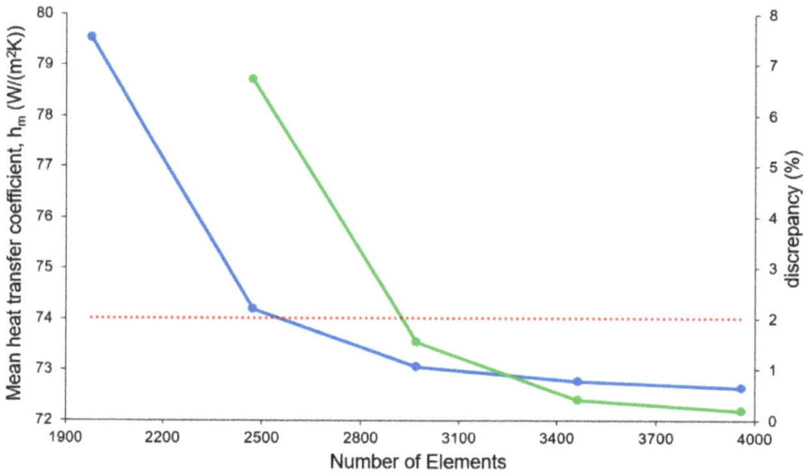

Figure 2. Mesh dependency test.

The governing equations of mass, momentum, and energy conservation were solved by the Ansys Fluent software in the following form [18]:

Continuity equation:

$$\nabla\cdot(\rho\mathbf{v}) = 0 \tag{8}$$

Momentum equation:

$$\nabla\cdot\left(\rho\mathbf{v}\mathbf{v}^T\right) = -\nabla p + \nabla\cdot\left\{\mu\left[\nabla\mathbf{v} + (\nabla\mathbf{v})^T - \frac{2}{3}(\nabla\cdot\mathbf{v})\mathbf{I}\right]\right\} + \rho\mathbf{g} \tag{9}$$

Energy equation:

$$\nabla\cdot(\rho c_p\mathbf{v}T) = \nabla\cdot(k\nabla T) \tag{10}$$

The turbulent flow was solved by the k-ω SST model using the incompressible ideal gas density. The pressure–velocity coupling was handled by the coupled scheme with the pseudo transient formulation while the second–order upwind schemes were used as a spatial discretization. The solution was considered to be fully converged when the residuals of continuity, velocity, energy, k, and ω reached the criterion 10^{-6}.

The flow is considered to be steady two-dimensional with the air variable properties as follows:

$$k(T) = -2.48{\cdot}10^{-8}T^2 + 8.92{\cdot}10^{-5}T + 1.12{\cdot}10^{-3} \tag{11}$$

$$\mu(T) = -3.76{\cdot}10^{-11}T^2 + 6.95{\cdot}10^{-8}T + 1.12{\cdot}10^{-6} \tag{12}$$

$$c_p(T) = 3.34{\cdot}10^{-4}T^2 - 0.156T + 1023.53 \tag{13}$$

The boundary conditions according to Figure 3 are described as follows:

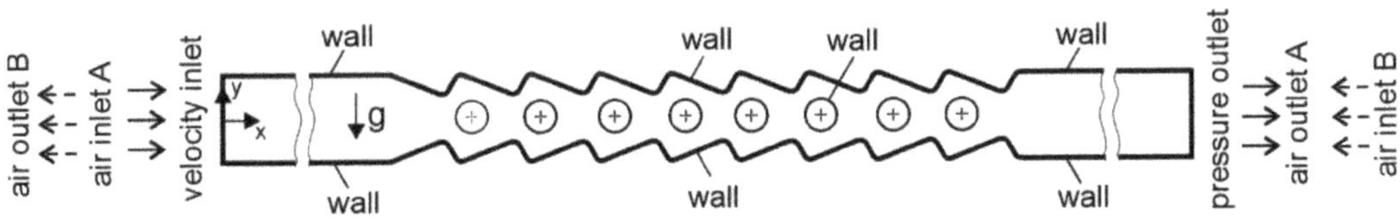

Figure 3. Boundary conditions for forward and backward air flow in the wavy channel.

- velocity inlet—air inlet A, B:

$$v_x = v_{in,a} = const., \qquad v_y = 0, \qquad T = T_{in,a} = const. \tag{14}$$

- pressure outlet—air outlet A, B:

$$\frac{\partial v_x}{\partial x} = \frac{\partial v_y}{\partial x} = \frac{\partial T}{\partial x} = 0 \tag{15}$$

- wall—tubes, inlet and outlet section:

$$v_x = v_y = 0, \qquad \frac{\partial T}{\partial n} = 0 \tag{16}$$

- wall—test section:

$$v_x = v_y = 0, \qquad T = T_s = const. \tag{17}$$

3. Experimental Validation

The holographic interferometry method was used to obtain the local heat transfer coefficients for the wavy channel without CVGs and forward air flow (WCA) and the wavy channel with CVGs of 15 mm diameter for forward air flow (WCCA15) [32,36]. Two coherent waves interacted with each other where one wave deformed when passing through the temperature field and the other one passed outside. The variant of Mach–Zehnder interferometer was used to visualize the temperature fields in the vicinity of wavy protrusions. The resulting interference fringes on the interferograms represented the isotherms in the vicinity of the heated wavy surfaces. The experimental local heat transfer coefficients h_{xexp} for the WCA and WCCA15 at the local sections '1' to '5' were compared with the local heat transfer coefficients h_{xnum} obtained by numerical simulations (Figure 4). The discrepancies in the local heat transfer coefficient between the numerical and experimental results for all local sections were below 19.67%.

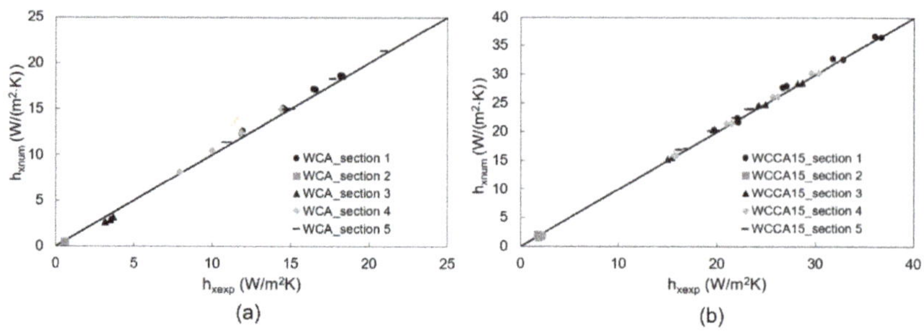

Figure 4. Comparison between the experimental and numerical local heat transfer coefficients for H = 40 mm, T_s = 318.15 K, Q = 5–20 m^3/h, (**a**) wavy channel without CVGs, (**b**) wavy channel with CVGs of 15 mm diameter.

4. Results and Discussion

The courses of the mean Nusselt numbers Nu_m for all investigated wavy channels are shown in Figure 8. An increase of Nu_m with Re was confirmed for all investigated configurations, while the size of the recirculation zone and the vortex strength in the valleys formed an increase in heat transfer. When evaluating the wavy channels without CVGs, the values of Nu_m for WCB were higher in the range of 1.28% to 5.09% compared with WCA for Q = 10–50 m^3/h. On the contrary, the WCA achieved higher Nu_m by 4.78% compared with the WCB for Q = 5 m^3/h. The Nu_m values increased with Re in the range of 11.06 to 58.48 and 10.53 to 61.16 for the configuration WCA and WCB, respectively.

The local heat transfer coefficients h_x along the lower and upper heated surfaces for the WCA and WCB configurations and Q = 50 m^3/h are compared in Figure 5. It is shown that the distribution of h_x did not change significantly. The maximum h_x was achieved on the 2nd protrusion of the WCA at the local section of 0.288 m (h_x = 65.42 W/(m^2·K) and on the 8th protrusion of the WCB at the local section of 0.532 m (h_x = 89.70 W/(m^2·K). The fundamental difference between the compared configurations is that the peaks of WCB protrusions gradually increase along the channel; on the other hand, the peaks of WCA protrusions gradually decrease. This fact has a significant effect on the overall heat transfer through the wavy channel. It was found that the backward air flow improved the local and mean heat transfer parameters compared with the forward one. The backward air flow changes the flow characteristics in the channel, i.e., the distribution of velocity and pressure parameters. The flowing air is slowed down more when hitting the peaks of the protrusions and does not flow smoothly in the vicinity of the protrusions as in the case of forward air flow. The better mixing of air in the valleys leads to an increase in h_x.

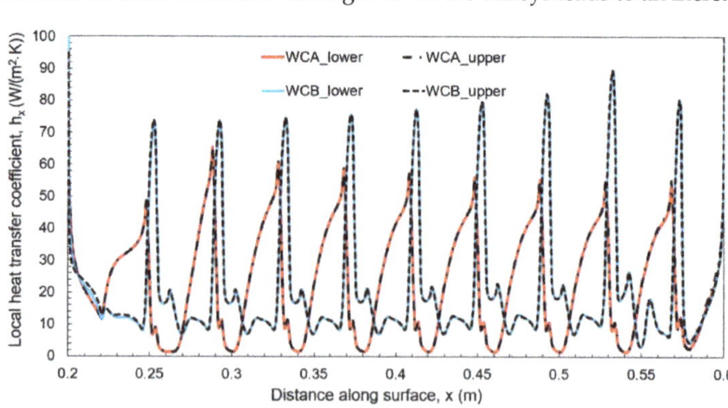

Figure 5. The comparison of the local heat transfer coefficients along the lower and upper heated surfaces of WCA and WCB configurations for Q = 50 m^3/h.

The distribution of the temperature fields along the WCA and WCB length for Q = 50 m^3/h are shown in Figures 6 and 7. The detailed distribution of the temperature fields and velocity vectors in the vicinity of the 2nd protrusion (WCA) and the 8th protrusion (WCB) is shown in Figure 6b,c and Figure 7b,c, respectively. In the both cases, the thermal boundary layer thickness increases with the channel length. For the WCB configuration, the cooling air causes better mixing in valleys, which leads to more efficient heat transfer in the valleys and subsequently higher h_x compared with the WCA configuration (Figures 5–7). For the WCA configuration, the minimum h_x = 1.39 W/(m^2·K) and maximum h_x = 65.42 W/(m^2·K) are achieved on the 2nd protrusion at the local sections 0.261 m and 0.288 m (Figure 6b), respectively. For the other protrusions, there are minimum h_x values in the valleys and maximum h_x values at the leading edge before reaching the protrusion top; however, h_x gradually decreases with the channel length. The effect of the air recirculation appears in the valleys while two recirculation zones are formed for the WCA configuration (Figure 6c). In the valleys, the air flow slows down and its recirculation occurs there (Figures 6c and 7c). For the WCB configuration, the minimum h_x = 3.11 W/(m^2·K) and maximum h_x = 89.70 W/(m^2·K) are achieved on the 8th protrusion at the local sections 0.549 m and 0.532 m (Figure 7b), respectively. Only one recirculation zone is formed in the valleys; however, the flow rate is intensive enough to improve heat transfer there (Figure 7c). More intense flow of cooling air in the valleys leads to an increase in both local and mean heat transfer parameters for the WCB configuration.

When comparing the WCA, WCB, and wavy channels with CVGs (10 mm, 15 mm), the first mentioned configuration achieved lower Nu_m for all investigated CVGs positions (Figure 8). It was found that Nu_m decreases with CVGs position (1 to 4) for all wavy channels; however, there is an increase at the position '5'. The maximum Nu_m in the range of 40.21 to 163.74 (Re = 857 to 6383) was achieved for the configuration of WCCA15 and CVGs position '1' (Figure 8a). On the other hand, the maximum Nu_m = 196.00 was obtained for the configuration of WCCB15 (position '1') and Re = 8000. The Nu_m increased 3.35 times for the WCCA15 (position '1') compared with the WCA for the maximum flow rate of 50 m^3/h. When changing the CVGs positions from '1' to '4', the difference between Nu_m values decreased while Nu_m for the WCCA15 (position '4') was only 1.81 times higher compared with the WCA. On the contrary, the difference between Nu_m of the mentioned configurations increased for the position '5' (2.31 times in favor of the WCCA15). The Prandtl number of the air inlet temperature 296.15 K represents the value of 0.729 for all examined configurations.

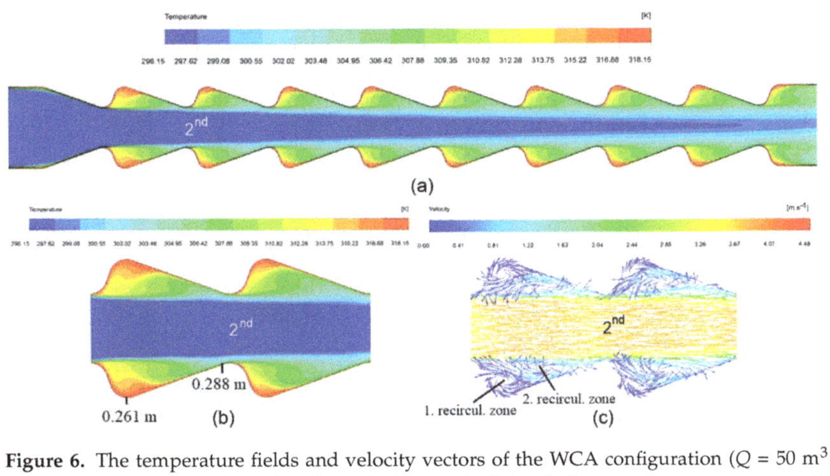

Figure 6. The temperature fields and velocity vectors of the WCA configuration (Q = 50 m^3/h), (**a**) temperature fields along the channel, (**b**) detail of the 2nd protrusion—temperature fields, (**c**) detail of the 2nd protrusion—velocity vectors.

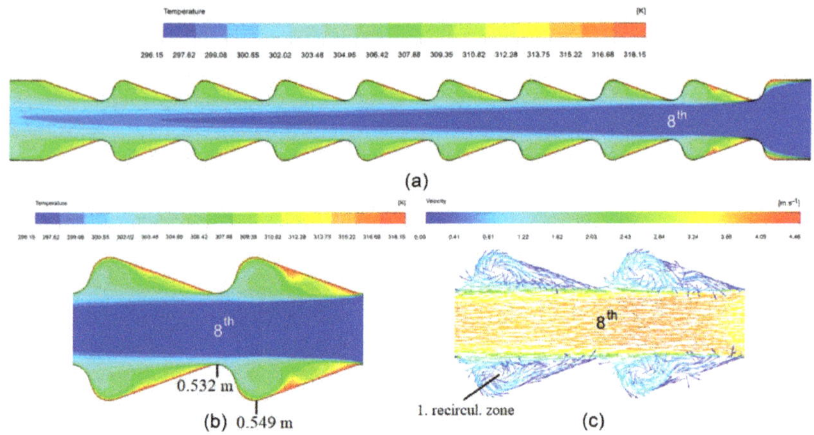

Figure 7. The temperature fields and velocity vectors of the WCB configuration (Q = 50 m^3/h), (**a**) temperature fields along the channel, (**b**) detail of the 8th protrusion—temperature fields, (**c**) detail of the 8th protrusion—velocity vectors.

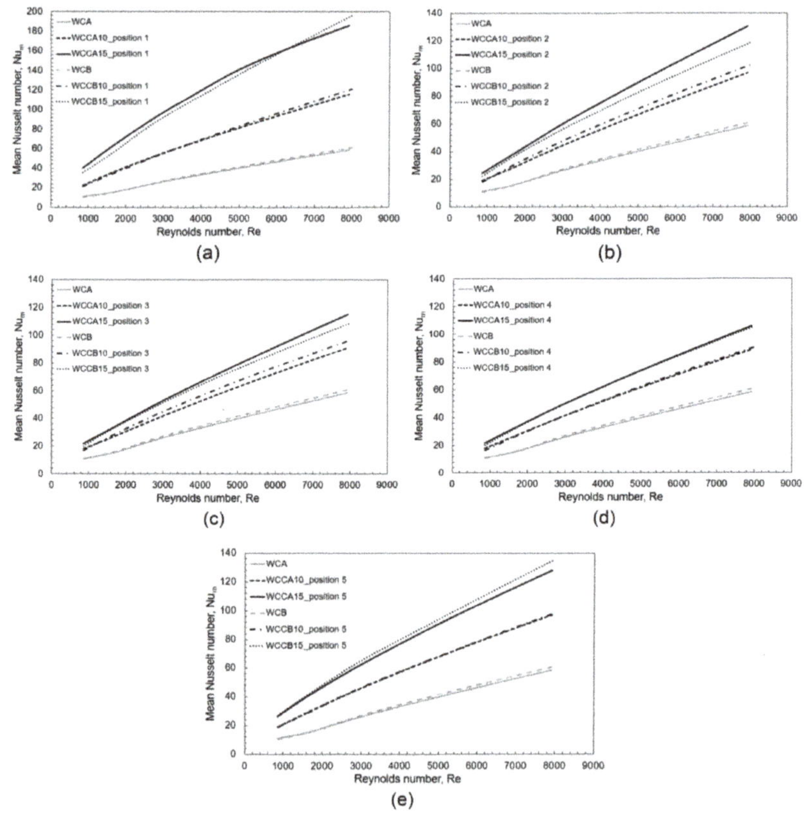

Figure 8. The effect of configuration and position of CVGs on the mean Nusselt number when changing the Reynolds number, (**a**) WC vs. WCC at the position '1', (**b**) WC vs. WCC at the position '2', (**c**) WC vs. WCC at the position '3', (**d**) WC vs. WCC at the position '4', (**e**) WC vs. WCC at the position '5'.

When investigating the CVGs diameter effect, the CVGs of 15 mm diameter achieved higher Nu_m values compared with 10 mm for all investigated positions (Figure 8). The Nu_m of the WCCA15 configuration is higher by 61.48% compared with the WCCA10 while the value for the WCCB15 is higher by 62.24% compared with the WCCB10 for position '1' and the flow rate of 50 m^3/h (Figure 8a). At position '4' (Figure 8d), there is a decrease in differences between the CVGs of 10 and 15 mm where the WCCA15 achieved higher values only by 18.76% compared with the WCCA10, while the WCCB15 obtained higher values only by 16.68% compared with the WCCB10. Air flow direction (inlet air A, B) does not significantly affect the change of Nu_m. The differences between Nu_m for the WCCA10–WCCB10 and WCCA15–WCCB15 represent the value of 5.69 and 10.10 for the position '1' and maximum flow rate of 50 m^3/h (Figure 8a). The positions '4' and '5' achieved differences ΔNu_m = 1.41 and 1.26 (Figure 8d,e).

The highest values of Nu_m were achieved for the configuration WCCA15, flow rate 5–30 m^3/h, and CVGs position '1' together with the configuration WCCB15, flow rate 40–50 m^3/h, and CVGs position '1' (Figure 8a). The comparison of h_x along lower and upper surfaces of the WCCA15 (Q = 5 m^3/h and 30 m^3/h) and WCCB15 (Q = 50 m^3/h) configurations for CVGs position '1' is shown in Figure 9. Based on the distribution of h_x values along the WCCB15 configuration, it can be clearly observed the increase of h_x peaks from the 3rd to 9th protrusions for the lower and upper surfaces. When increasing the flow rate Q, higher h_x values were achieved. With an increase in the flow rate, the thermal boundary layer is pressed against the heated surface and becomes thinner, and thus the heat transfer is improved. Higher air flow velocities also lead to more intense swirls in the valleys. From the distribution of h_x peaks of the WCCA15 (Q = 5 m^3/h and 30 m^3/h) is clearly observed the decrease along the channels. On the contrary, an increase of h_x peaks along the channel can be observed for backward air flow (WCCB15).

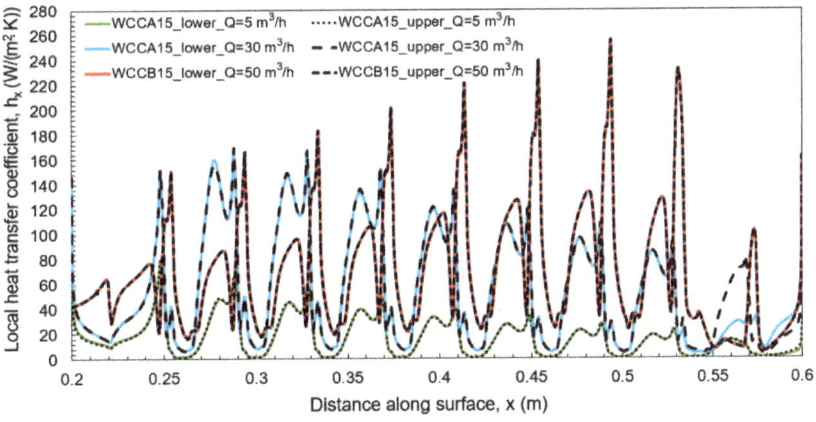

Figure 9. The comparison of the local heat transfer coefficients along lower and upper surfaces of the WCCA15 and WCCB15 configurations for CVGs position '1' when changing the flow rate.

The distributions of temperature fields and velocity vectors along the WCCB15 length for Re = 8001 (Q = 50 m^3/h) are shown in Figure 10. The CVGs position '1' caused maximum h_x values along the channel due to the efficient distribution of cooling air into the valleys (Figure 10a). The CVGs position '1' causes a significant compression of the thermal boundary layer, especially in front of the fifth to eighth peak of the protrusions, and a significant recirculation of air behind the CVGs, which leads to an important intensification of heat transfer. In the protrusion valleys, two recirculation zones are formed where higher air velocity improved the heat transfer (Figure 10b).

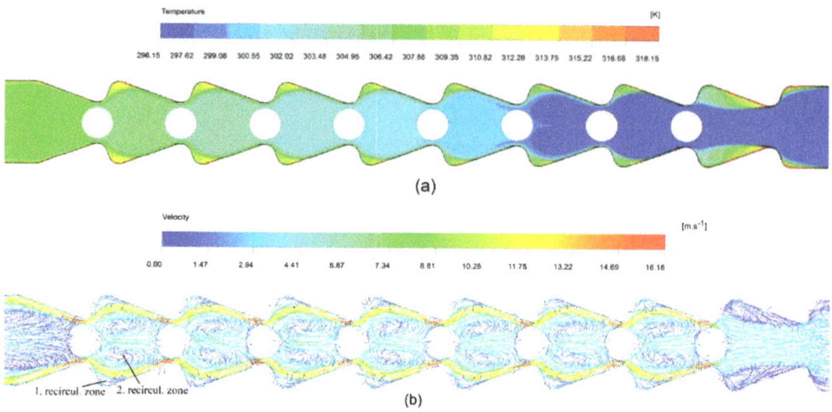

Figure 10. The temperature fields and velocity vectors of the WCCB15 for $Q = 50\ m^3/h$ and CVGs position '1', (**a**) temperature fields along the channel, (**b**) velocity vectors along the channel.

To assess the overall effectiveness of the examined wavy channels with/without CVGs, it is necessary to consider not only heat transfer parameters, but pressure drops as well. Generally, convective heat transfer and pressure drops are considered together to design the corrugated channels. On the basis of Equations (4) and (5), the Colburn factors j and friction factors f were calculated and their dependence on the Re is shown in Figure 11. The Colburn factor j is a dimensionless heat transfer parameter to represent the convection movement of heat. It decreases with Re for all investigated configurations. The maximum j was achieved for the WCCA15 configuration at CVGs position '1' and $Re = 857$ ($j = 0.05208$). With an increase of Re to 7927, the value of j decreased to 0.02604 (Figure 11a). At the same time, the friction factor f achieved the maximum value of 54.673 for the WCCA15 (CVGs position '1', $Re = 857$) and only slightly decreased with increased Re to 7927 ($f = 50.511$). The Colburn factor j decreased with CVGs position and for the position '5' it achieved the value $j = 0.03414$ for $Re = 857$.

The WCCA15 (position '1') reached 3.64 and 3.84 times higher values of j compared with the WCA and WCB configurations for $Re = 857$, respectively. The differences in j between the mentioned channels decreased with increased Re. Simultaneously, the friction factor f of the WCA and WCB configurations achieved the minimum values in the range of 0.483 to 0.514 for the WCA and 0.466 to 0.527 for the WCB depending on Re. When changing the CVGs position, the j values decreased to the position '4'; however, they increased at the position '5' for the whole range of Re. The values of f were significantly affected by the CVGs position (Figure 11f–j). For the WCCA15 configuration, CVGs at the position '2' caused a drop in f values in the range of 79.71% to 77.49% compared with the position '1'. A drop in f values in the range of 31.29% to 29.45% and 3.42% to 17.7% was noticed for the position '3' and '4', respectively. On the contrary, the position '5' caused an increase above the f values of the position '2' to '4', whereas the values were lower in the range of 68.99% to 72.42% compared with the position '1'.

From the standpoint of CVGs diameter, higher values of j together with f were achieved for the diameter of 15 mm compared with 10 mm for all investigated positions and Re. The WCCA15 and WCCB15 configurations showed higher j in the range of 80.58% to 61.54% and 66.15% to 62.19% compared with the WCCA10 and WCCB10 for CVGs position '1' and all Re. When changing the CVGs position ('1' to '4'), the differences between the mentioned configurations decreased. For the position '5', the different j values between the configurations with 15 mm and 10 mm CVGs diameter increased. Due to the CVGs diameter, lower values of the friction factor f were achieved for the WCCA10 and WCCB10 configurations compared with the WCCA15 and WCCB15, respectively. The WCCA15 and WCCB15 configurations showed higher f in the range of 5.75 to 5.68 times and 5.05 to 3.94 times compared with the WCCA10 and WCCB10 for CVGs position '1' and all *Re*. The differences between the mentioned configurations decreased for the position '2' to '4', while an increase in the f value difference was achieved for the position '5'.

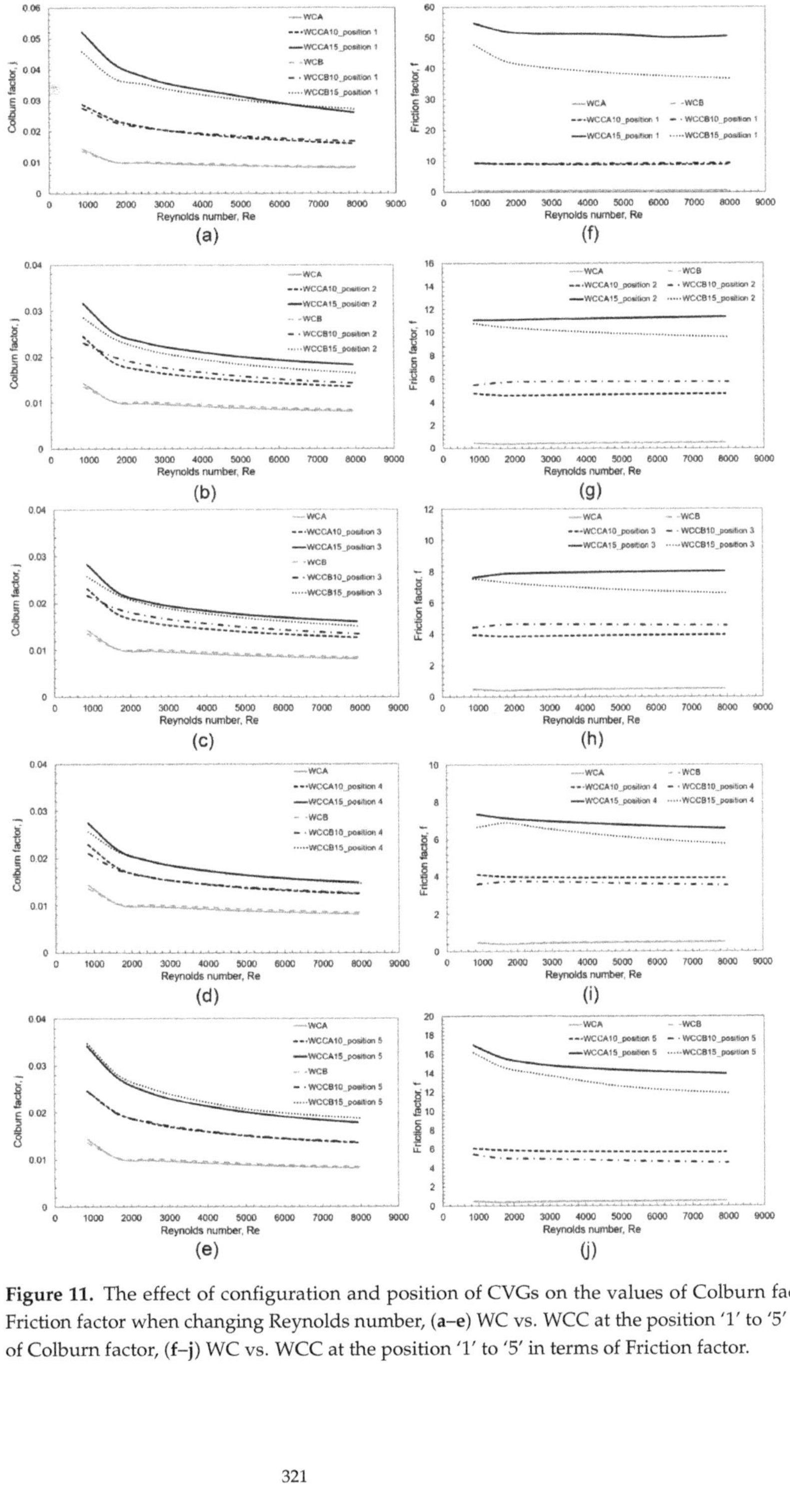

Figure 11. The effect of configuration and position of CVGs on the values of Colburn factor and Friction factor when changing Reynolds number, (**a–e**) WC vs. WCC at the position '1' to '5' in terms of Colburn factor, (**f–j**) WC vs. WCC at the position '1' to '5' in terms of Friction factor.

The comparison of h_x values for lower surfaces of the WCCA15 and WCCB15 configuration with CVGs position '1' to '5' and Re = 857 (Q = 5 m^3/h) is shown in Figures 12 and 13. Due to the change in the direction of the air flow (forward and backward), different h_x distributions along lower surfaces were achieved. While the peaks of the protrusions have a decreasing course with the channel length for the WCCA15 configuration, the WCCB15 has the opposite character. The maximum value of h_x = 79.70 W/(m^2·K) was noticed on the 1st peak for the position '1'. The positions '2' to '3' showed the decreasing course along the channel. The position '5' achieved maximum h_x = 30.14 W/(m^2·K) on the 3rd peak and gradually decreased (Figure 12). The maximum value of h_x = 77.72 W/(m^2·K) was noticed on the 8th peak of the WCCB15, while the 9th peak had a decreasing course for the position '1' (Figure 13). For the position '2' (WCCB15), there is a decreasing trend of peaks along the channel. The position '3' shows an increasing trend to the 6th peak with a subsequent decrease. The position '4' and '5' shows an increasing trend along the whole channel.

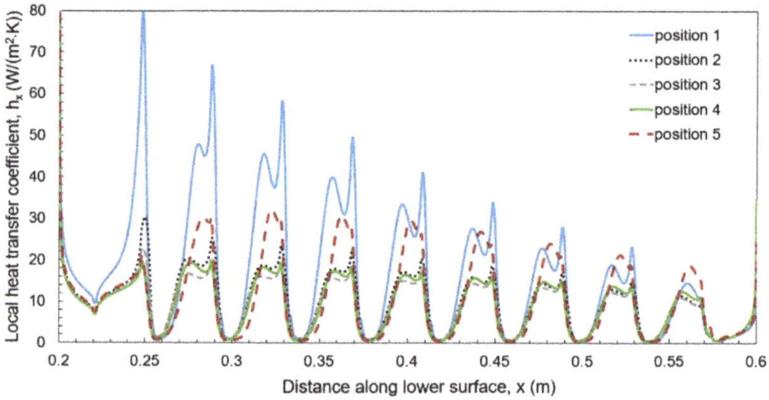

Figure 12. The comparison of local heat transfer coefficients along lower surfaces of the WCCA15 for CVGs position '1' to '5' and Re = 857.

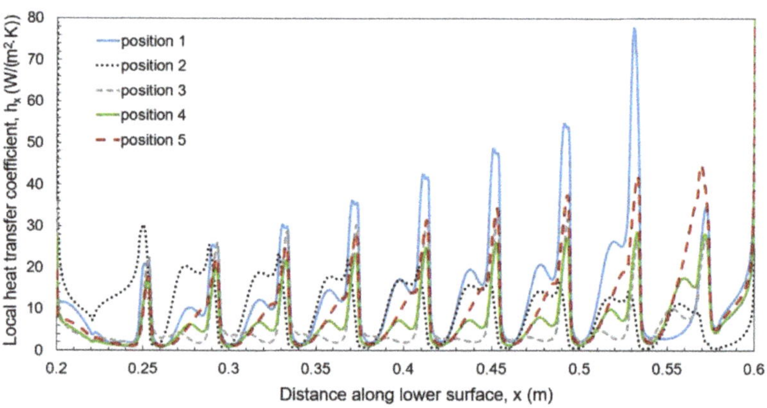

Figure 13. The comparison of local heat transfer coefficients along lower surfaces of the WCCB15 for CVGs position '1' to '5' and Re = 857.

The distributions of temperature fields and velocity vectors along the channel of the WCCA15 configuration for Re = 857 (Q = 5 m^3/h) and CVGs position '1' is shown in Figure 14. On the basis of the temperature fields (Figure 14a), it is clear that maximum h_x was achieved on the leading edge of the first protrusion (CVGs position '1') at the local section 0.248 m. The low air velocity caused an accumulation of heat in the valleys and at the same time the CVGs position '1' caused an accumulation of heat behind them. Nevertheless, the position '1' caused better pressing of the thermal boundary layer compared with the other positions and it is the most effective in terms of the Colburn factor j. Three recirculation zones are formed in the valleys that enhanced the fluid mixing (Figure 14b). The distributions of temperature fields and velocity vectors along the channel of the WCCB15 configuration for Re = 857 (Q = 5 m^3/h) and CVGs position '1' is shown in Figure 15. Due to the backward air flow, maximum h_x is achieved on the 8th protrusion at the local section 0.530 m where the highest pressure of the thermal boundary layer to the wavy surface occurs. Two recirculation zones are formed in the individual valleys for lower and upper wavy surface (Figure 15b).

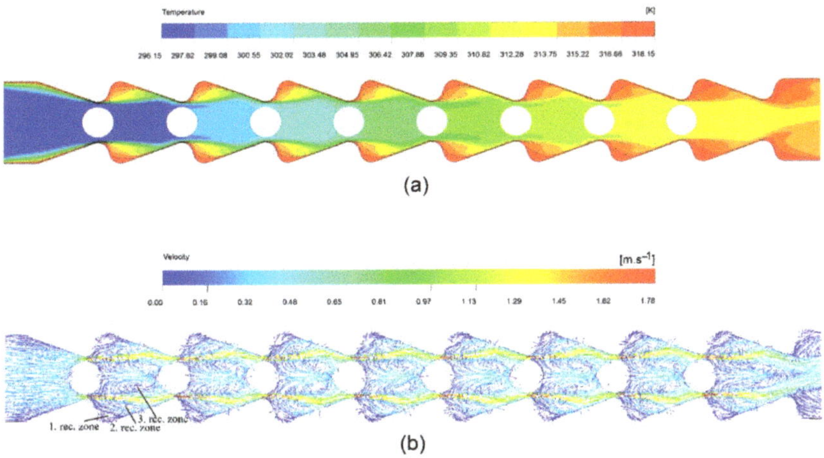

Figure 14. The temperature fields and velocity vectors of the WCCA15 (position '1') for Re = 857 (Q = 5 m^3/h), (**a**) temperature fields along the channel, (**b**) velocity vectors along the channel.

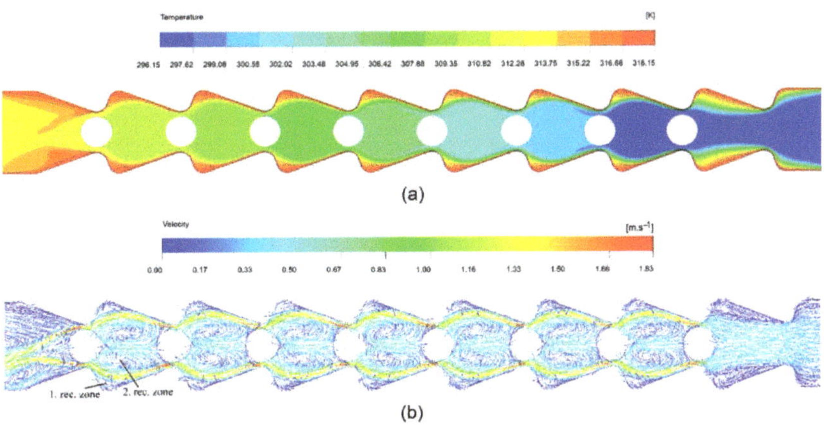

Figure 15. The temperature fields and velocity vectors of the WCCB15 (position '1') for Re = 857 (Q = 5 m^3/h), (**a**) temperature fields along the channel, (**b**) velocity vectors along the channel.

The thermal performance factor for forward and backward air flow were calculated by Equations (6) and (7). The distributions of thermal performance factor TPF_A for the air inlet A and CVGs diameter of 10 mm and 15 mm are shown depending on Re in Figure 16a,b. When considering heat transfer parameters of the investigated configurations together with pressure drops, the maximum TPF_A values in the range of 0.8170 to 0.7999 were achieved for the WCCA15 and the position '2' with Re = 1669–7930 (Figure 16b). For Re = 858 (Q = 5 m^3/h), the second highest value (TPF_A = 0.7769) was reached. For the WCCA10 and Re in the range of 2467 to 7930, the CVGs position '2' is efficient, while the position '1' and '3' are more appropriate for Re = 1669 (TPF_A = 0.8199) and Re = 858 (TPF_A = 0.8040), respectively.

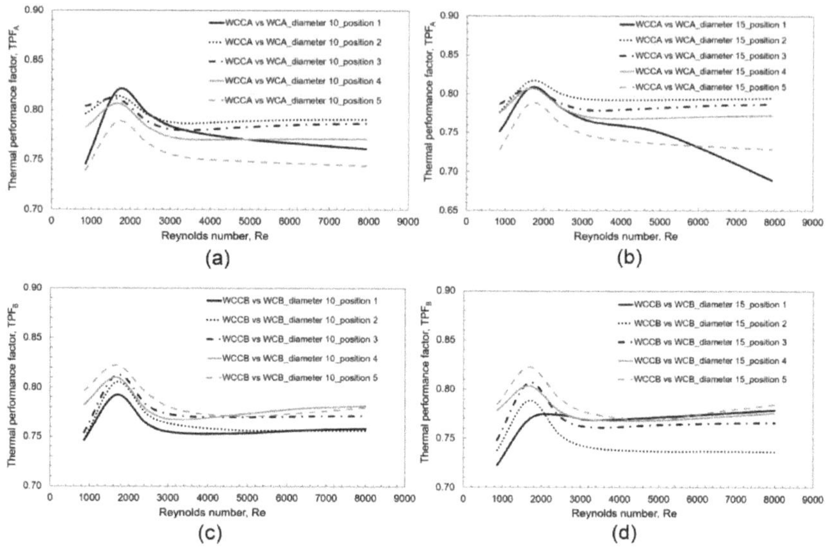

Figure 16. Thermal performance factor for different diameter and CVGs position 1–5, (**a**) WCCA vs. WCA for diameter of 10 mm, (**b**) WCCA vs. WCA for diameter of 15 mm, (**c**) WCCB vs. WCB for diameter of 10 mm, (**d**) WCCB vs. WCB for diameter of 15 mm.

The distributions of thermal performance factor TPF_B for the air inlet B depending on Re is shown in Figure 16c,d for 10 and 15 mm diameter. The maximum TPF_B values in the range of 0.8229 to 0.7684 were achieved for the WCCB15 and the position '5' in the range of Re = 861 to 3279 and 6432 to 7989 (Figure 16d). For 10 mm diameter, the maximum TPF_B values in the range of 0.7769 to 0.8222 (Re = 862 to 3282) were achieved for the WCCB10 configuration and the position '5' (Figure 16c). The WCCB10 configuration and the position '4' is more efficient one for Re in the range of 4869 to 7999 where TPF_B = 0.7733–0.7816. The maximum thermal performance factor TPF_B = 0.8229 was noticed for the WCCB15, CVGs position '5' and Re = 1677 (Q = 10 m^3/h). The temperature field, pressure field, and velocity vectors are shown in Figure 17.

The highest thermal performance factor was achieved for the configuration WCCB15 and Q = 10 m^3/h at CVGs position '5'. The temperature field (Figure 17a) shows that the backward air flow is effective since the cooling air gets to a greater extent into the valleys and thus better fluid mixing occurs. At the same time, CVGs position '5' is also effective in terms of pressure drops in this flow direction. Two recirculation zones are formed in the valleys of individual protrusions (Figure 17b). The CVGs significantly help to compress the thermal boundary layer to the wavy surface and to direct the flowing air into the protrusion valleys. From the distribution of pressure fields along the channel of WCCA15 configuration (Figure 17c), it can be observed that total pressure increase with the channel length. A higher total pressure occurs in the valleys compared with the area behind the CVGs. Due to the CVGs' location close to the top of the protrusions, a greater compression of the cooling air into the valleys appears there; consequently, the air must overcome greater resistance when passing through the next protrusions. The distribution of the turbulence kinetic energy is shown in Figure 17d. The maximum turbulence kinetic energy in the range of 0.148 to 0.181 m^2/s^2 is found on the leading side of '3'–'8' CVGs and between the 9th protrusions. The CVGs location behind each other and narrowed space between the protrusion peaks caused an increase in the turbulence kinetic energy.

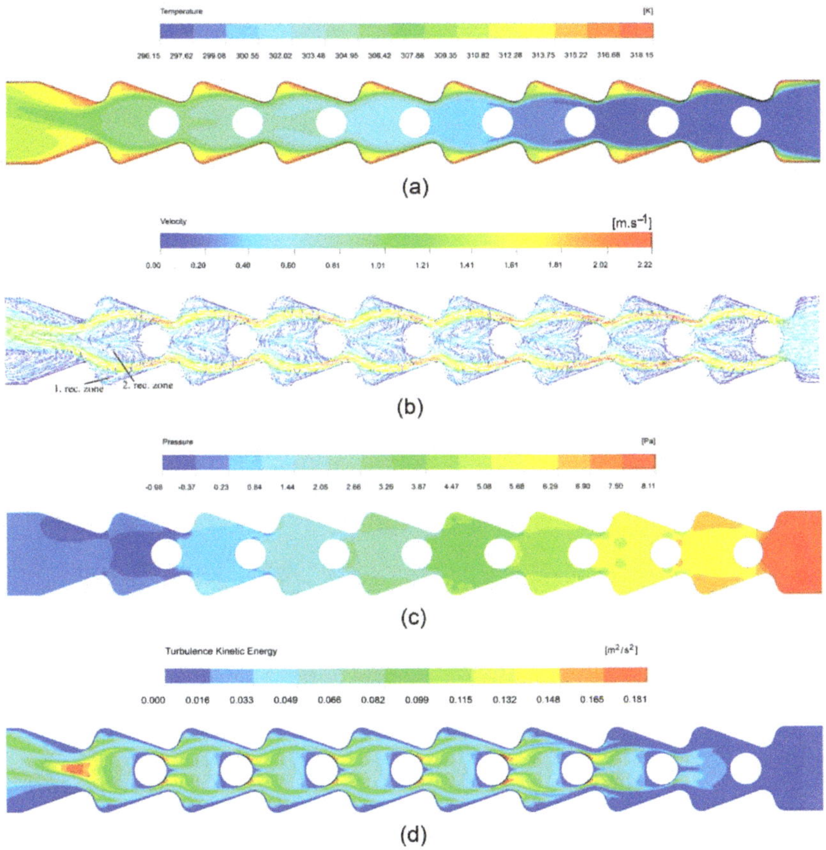

Figure 17. WCCB15 configuration for CVGs position '5' for *Re* = 1677 (*Q* = 10 m3/h), (**a**) temperature field, (**b**) velocity vectors, (**c**) pressure field, (**d**) turbulence kinetic energy.

The distribution of x-velocities for the WCCB15 configuration (CVGs position '5') for $Q = 10\ m^3/h$ is shown in Figure 18. The values of x-velocities for the 1st to 8th valley are shown at the local sections from 0.26 m to 0.54 m with the spacing 0.04 m (Figure 18a) and for the 1st to 9th peak at the local sections from 0.25 m to 0.57 m with the same spacing (Figure 18b). The distribution of x-velocities at the local sections of the valleys V1 to V8 acquired a similar character in the range of 0.535 m/s to −1.945 m/s. The local sections in the valleys V7 and V6 achieved the maximum velocity of −1.945 m/s and −1.799 m/s in y-position of −0.011 m. The cooling air (in backflow) hits the CVG directly and surrounds it, while thanks to the narrow gap between the CVG and the protrusion, the effect of intense air pressure on the protrusion is created, which also has a positive effect on behavior in valleys. In the middle of the wavy channel (y-position of 0 m), x-velocities in the range of 0.439 m/s to 0.535 m/s were achieved. Gradually with the increase of y-position, the x-velocities increased to negative values (backflow) to y-position of 0.011 m (respectively −0.011 m) and subsequently the velocity decreased again and reached the 0 m/s in y-position of 0.016 m (respectively −0.016 m). The distribution of x-velocities at the local sections of the peaks P2 to P8 acquired a similar character; the peaks P1 and P9 were affected by the inlet and outlet section of the channel. In the middle of the wavy channel between the peaks of protrusions, the minimum x-velocities approaching 0 m/s were achieved. Gradually with the increase of y-position, the x-velocities increased to velocities 0.238 m/s and subsequently to −2.174 m/s in y-position of 0.009 m (respectively −0.009 m) and decreased towards 0 m/s again. The maximum x-velocities achieved in y-position of 0.009 m is the result of air pressing and at the same time also pressing of the thermal boundary layer.

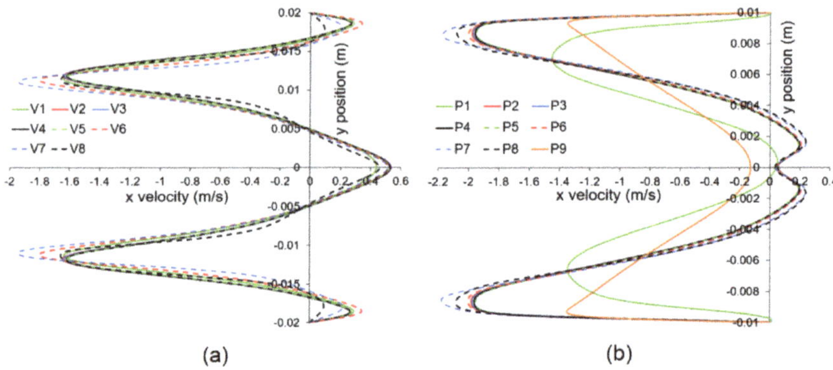

Figure 18. Distribution of x-velocities of the WCCB15 configuration for CVGs position '5' for Re = 1677 (Q = 10 m^3/h), (**a**) sections of the 1st to 8th valley, (**b**) sections of the 1st to 9th peak.

New correlating equations for the mean Nusselt number Nu_m were created for the WCCA and WCCB configurations and CVGs position of '1' to '5' for the flow rate Q in the range of 10 m^3/h to 50 m^3/h, CVGs diameter of D = 10 mm and 15 mm, and the channel height H = 40 mm.

WCCA15 configuration (CVGs position '1' to '5'):

$$\begin{aligned} Nu_m &= Re^{-0.494(D/H)+0.872}.(D/H)^{-3.860(D/H)+2.390} \\ Nu_m &= Re^{-0.017(D/H)+0.801}.(D/H)^{3.567(D/H)+0.970} \\ Nu_m &= Re^{-0.001(D/H)+0.798}.(D/H)^{4.396(D/H)+0.817} \\ Nu_m &= Re^{-0.115(D/H)+0.808}.(D/H)^{3.533(D/H)+0.926} \\ Nu_m &= Re^{-0.224(D/H)+0.819}.(D/H)^{1.124(D/H)+1.363} \end{aligned} \quad (18)$$

with the percent standard deviation of the error E_{SD} = 0.77%, and the error E ranged from −2.34% to +2.69%.

WCCB15 configuration (CVGs position '1' to '5'):

$$\begin{aligned} Nu_m &= Re^{-0.129(D/H)+0.831}.(D/H)^{0.559(D/H)+1.583} \\ Nu_m &= Re^{-0.156(D/H)+0.820}.(D/H)^{3.078(D/H)+0.953} \\ Nu_m &= Re^{-0.120(D/H)+0.814}.(D/H)^{3.844(D/H)+0.824} \\ Nu_m &= Re^{-0.269(D/H)+0.859}.(D/H)^{2.511(D/H)+1.255} \\ Nu_m &= Re^{-0.139(D/H)+0.801}.(D/H)^{1.592(D/H)+1.259} \end{aligned} \quad (19)$$

with the percent standard deviation of the error E_{SD} = 0.52%, and the error E ranged from −1.06% to +2.18%. The correctness of the correlating equations is shown in Figure 19 where the values of Nu_m from the correlating equations and numerical simulations were compared.

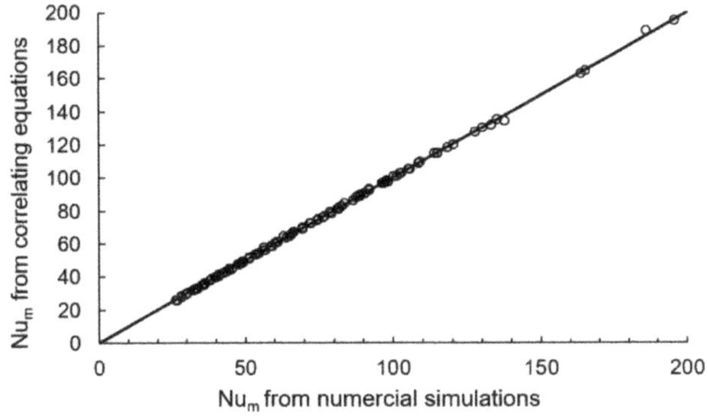

Figure 19. Comparison between new correlating equations and numerical results.

5. Conclusions

Today, it is necessary to put even more emphasis on saving energy and efficient heat transfer in heat exchanger types. The improvement in heat transfer characteristics was achieved by the novel asymmetric wavy geometry of the heated channel. Inserting the CVGs to the channel led to directing and pressing of cooling air into the valleys and to better air recirculation. On the basis of this, there was the enhancement of Nusselt numbers and Colburn factors for all positions of CVGs and *Re* compared with the channels without CVGs. The backward flow of cooling air brought an improvement in terms of thermal-hydraulic characteristics compared with the forward flow.

The configuration of wavy channel with CVGs of 15 mm at the position '5' for $Re = 1677$ and backward flow air is the most effective in terms of heat transfer and pressure drops. The new correlating equations for the mean Nusselt number Nu_m were created for the WCCA and WCCB configurations for CVGs position '1' to '5', flow rate in the range of 10 m^3/h to 50 m^3/h, CVGs diameter of 10 mm and 15 mm, and the channel height 40 mm.

The specifically following conclusions can be made from the current study:

1. The experimentally and numerically obtained local heat transfer coefficients h_{xexp} and h_{num} are in good agreement for the WCA and WCCA15 configurations for the channel height 40 mm and flow rate in the range of 5 to 20 m^3/h.
2. In terms of comparing the wavy channels without CVGs:
   - The Nu_m increased with *Re* for all investigated configurations.
   - The Nu_m for the WCB were higher in the range of 1.28% to 5.09% compared with the WCA for $Q = 10$ to 50 m^3/h. On the contrary, the WCA for $Q = 5$ m^3/h achieved higher Nu_m by 4.78% with to the WCB.
   - The backward air flow improved the local and mean heat transfer parameters compared with the forward one. The cooling air causes better mixing in valleys for the WCB configuration, which leads to more efficient heat transfer in the valleys and subsequently to higher h_x compared with the WCA configuration.
3. In terms of comparing the wavy channels with CVGs:
   - The wavy channels with CVGs achieved the higher Nu_m for all investigated positions compared with the WCA and WCB configurations. The Nu_m increased 3.35 times for the WCCA15 (position '1') compared with the WCA for maximum flow rate of 50 m^3/h.
   - The values of Nu_m decreases with CVGs position ('1' to '4'); however, there is an increase at the position '5'.
   - The maximum Nu_m in the range of 40.21 to 163.74 ($Re = 857$ to 6383) was achieved for the configuration of the WCCA15 and CVGs position '1'; the maximum

Nu_m = 196.00 was achieved for the configuration of WCCB15 (position '1') for Re = 8000.

- The CVGs of 15 mm diameter achieved higher Nu_m compared with 10 mm for all investigated positions. The Nu_m of the WCCA15 configuration is higher by 61.48% compared with the WCCA10, while the WCCB15 configuration is higher by 62.24% compared with the WCCB10 for the position '1' and flow rate of 50 m^3/h.
- The differences between Nu_m of the WCCA10 – WCCB10 and WCCA15–WCCB15 for the position '1' and flow rate of 50 m^3/h represent the value 5.69 and 10.10, respectively. The highest values of Nu_m were achieved for the configuration WCCA15 for flow rate 5 to 30 m^3/h, position '1' and the configuration WCCB15 for flow rate 40 to 50 m^3/h, position '1'.
- The Colburn factor j decreased with Re for all investigated configurations. The value of j = 0.05208 achieved the maximum for the WCCA15, position '1' and Re = 857. The mentioned configuration reached 3.64 and 3.84 times higher values of j compared with the WCA and WCB. The values of j, f were significantly affected by the position and diameter of CVGs. The WCCA15 (position '2') caused a drop in f values up to the 79.71% compared with the position '1'. The diameter of 15 mm caused higher j and f values for all Re compared with 10 mm.
- The maximum TPF_A in the range of 0.8170 to 0.7999 were achieved for the WCCA15, position '2' and Re = 1669–7930. The maximum TPF_B in the range of 0.8229 to 0.7684 were achieved for the WCCB15, position '5' and Re = 861–3279 and 6432–7989. Specifically, TPF_B = 0.8229 was achieved the WCCB15, position '5' and Re = 1677 (Q = 10 m^3/h).

The conclusions of the presented work can be the basis for further research, e.g., other surface temperatures, cooling air temperatures, channel height, spacing of protrusions, inline and offset protrusions configuration, and shape and position of CVGs in the channel.

Author Contributions: Conceptualization, Z.B.; methodology, S.K.; software, S.K.; validation, Z.B.; formal analysis, S.K.; investigation, Z.B.; resources, Z.B.; data curation, S.K.; writing—original draft preparation, Z.B.; writing—review and editing, S.K.; visualization, S.K.; supervision, Z.B.; project administration, Z.B.; funding acquisition, S.K. All authors have read and agreed to the published version of the manuscript.

Funding: The paper has been written on the basis of the research intention and solution of the research grant project "Progressive Research into Utility Properties of Materials and Products Based on Wood (LignoPro)", ITMS 313011T720, supported by the Operational Programme Integrated Infrastructure (OPII), funded by the ERDF.

Data Availability Statement: Not applicable.

Conflicts of Interest: The authors declare no conflict of interest.

Nomenclature

Roman Symbols:

c_p	specific heat capacity at constant pressure, J/(kg·K)
D	outer diameter of vortex generator, m
D_{hyd}	hydraulic diameter, m
f	friction factor
g	gravity vector
h	heat transfer coefficient, W/(m^2·K)
H	channel height, m
j	Colburn factor
k	thermal conductivity coefficient, W/(m·K)
L	contour length of wavy surfaces in the test section, m
L_2	length of the heated test section, m

Nu	Nusselt number
p	pressure of air, Pa
Pr	Prandtl number
q	heat flux, W/m^2
Q	flow rate, m^3/h
Re	Reynolds number
s	spacing, m
T	temperature, K
TPF	thermal performance factor
v	velocity of air, m/s
v	velocity vector
Greek Symbols:	
Δ	difference values
η	thermal performance
μ	dynamic viscosity, kg/(m·s)
ρ	density of air, kg/m^3
Subscripts:	
a	air
A	forward flow
B	backward flow
exp	experimental
in	inlet
l	lower
out	outlet
m	mean values
num	numerical
s	surface
u	upper
x	local value

References

1. Kolsi, L.; Selimefendigil, F.; Ghachem, K.; Alqahtani, T.; Algarni, S. Multiple Impinging Jet Cooling of a Wavy Surface by Using Double Porous Fins under Non-Uniform Magnetic Field. *Mathematics* **2022**, *10*, 638. [CrossRef]
2. Naphon, P. Heat transfer characteristics and pressure drop in channel with V corrugated upper and lower plates. *Energy Convers. Manag.* **2007**, *48*, 1516–1524. [CrossRef]
3. Naphon, P. Laminar convective heat transfer and pressure drop in the corrugated channels. *Int. Commun. Heat Mass Transf.* **2007**, *34*, 62–71. [CrossRef]
4. Singh, S.; Singh, A.; Chander, S. Thermal performance of a fully developed serpentine wavy channel solar air heater. *J. Energy Storage* **2019**, *25*, 100896. [CrossRef]
5. Bezbaruah, P.J.; Das, R.S.; Sarkar, B.K. Experimental and numerical analysis of solar air heater accoutered with modified conical vortex generators in a staggered fashion. *Renew. Energ.* **2021**, *180*, 109–131. [CrossRef]
6. Silva, F.A.S.; Dezan, D.J.; Pantaleão, A.V.; Salviano, L.O. Longitudinal vortex generator applied to heat transfer enhancement of a flat plate solar water heater. *Appl. Therm. Eng.* **2019**, *158*, 10. [CrossRef]
7. Zhao, Z.; Luo, L.; Qiu, D.; Wang, Z.; Sundén, B. On the solar air heater thermal enhancement and flow topology using differently shaped ribs combined with delta-winglet vortex generators. *Energy* **2021**, *224*, 17. [CrossRef]
8. Caliskan, S.; Şevik, S.; Özdilli, Ö. Heat transfer enhancement by a sinusoidal wavy plate having punched triangular vortex generators. *Int. J. Therm. Sci.* **2022**, *181*, 17. [CrossRef]
9. Nassab, S.A.G.; Sheikhnejad, Y.; Nia, M.F. Novel design of natural solar air heat for higher thermal performance utilizing porous vortex generator. *Therm. Sci. Eng. Prog.* **2022**, *33*, 11. [CrossRef]
10. Kurtulmus, N.; Zontul, H.; Sahin, B. Heat transfer and flow characteristics in a sinusoidally curved converging-diverging channel. *Int. J. Therm. Sci.* **2020**, *148*, 106163. [CrossRef]
11. Liu, C.; Teng, J.T.; Chu, J.C.; Chiu, Y.L.; Huang, S.; Jin, S.; Dang, T.; Greif, R.; Pan, H.H. Experimental investigations on liquid flow and heat transfer in rectangular microchannel with longitudinal vortex generators. *Int. J. Heat Mass Transf.* **2011**, *54*, 3069–3080. [CrossRef]
12. Chen, C.; Teng, J.T.; Cheng, C.H.; Jin, S.; Huang, S.; Liu, C.; Lee, M.T.; Pan, H.H.; Greif, R. A study on fluid flow and heat transfer in rectangular microchannels with various longitudinal vortex generators. *Int. J. Heat Mass Transf.* **2014**, *69*, 203–214. [CrossRef]
13. Ebrahimi, E.; Roohi, S.; Kheradmand, S. Numerical study of liquid flow and heat transfer in rectangular microchannel with longitudinal vortex generators. *Appl. Therm. Eng.* **2015**, *78*, 576–583. [CrossRef]

14. Raihan, M.F.B.; Al-Asadi, M.T.; Thompson, H.M. Management of conjugate heat transfer using various arrangements of cylindrical vortex generators in micro-channels. *Appl. Therm. Eng.* **2021**, *182*, 15. [CrossRef]
15. Moosavi, R.; Banihashemi, M.; Lin, C.X.; Abel Chuang, P.Y. Combined effects of a microchannel with porous media and transverse vortex generators (TVG) on convective heat transfer performance. *Int. J. Therm. Sci.* **2021**, *166*, 15. [CrossRef]
16. Amini, Y.; Habibi, S.E. Effects of multiple flexible vortex generators on the hydrothermal characteristics of a rectangular channel. *Int. J. Therm. Sci.* **2022**, *175*, 14. [CrossRef]
17. Al-Asadi, M.T.; Alkasmoul, F.S.; Wilson, M.C.T. Heat transfer enhancement in a micro-channel cooling system using cylindrical vortex generators. *Int. Commun. Heat Mass Transf.* **2016**, *74*, 40–47. [CrossRef]
18. Al-Asadi, M.T.; Alkasmoul, F.S.; Wilson, M.C.T. Benefits of spanwise gaps in cylindrical vortex generators for conjugate heat transfer enhancement in micro-channels. *Appl. Therm. Eng.* **2018**, *130*, 571–586. [CrossRef]
19. Leu, J.S.; Wu, Y.H.; Jang, J.Y. Heat transfer and fluid flow analysis in plate-fin and tube heat exchangers with a pair of block shape vortex generators. *Int. J. Heat Mass Transf.* **2004**, *47*, 4327–4338. [CrossRef]
20. Cheraghi, M.; Raisee, M.; Moghaddami, M. Effect of cylinder proximity to the wall on channel flow heat transfer enhancement. *Comptes Rendus Mécanique* **2014**, *342*, 63–72. [CrossRef]
21. Wang, J.; Zhao, Y. Heat and fluid flow characteristics of a rectangular channel with a small diameter circular cylinder as vortex generator. *Int. J. Therm. Sci.* **2015**, *92*, 1–13. [CrossRef]
22. Wang, J.; Wang, C. Heat transfer and flow characteristics of a rectangular channel with a small circular cylinder having slit-vent vortex generator. *Int. J. Therm. Sci.* **2016**, *104*, 158–171. [CrossRef]
23. Han, Z.; Xu, Z.; Wang, J. $CaSO_4$ fouling characteristics on the rectangular channel with half-cylinder vortex generators. *Appl. Therm. Eng.* **2018**, *128*, 1456–1463. [CrossRef]
24. Han, Z.; Xu, Z.; Qu, H. Parametric study of the particulate fouling characteristics of vortex generators in a heat exchanger. *Appl. Therm. Eng.* **2020**, *167*, 10. [CrossRef]
25. Vyas, A.; Mishra, B.; Agrawal, A.; Srivastava, A. Non-intrusive investigation of flow and heat transfer characteristics of a channel with a built-in circular cylinder. *Phys. Fluids* **2018**, *30*, 22. [CrossRef]
26. Dey, P. Optimal position of square cylinder vortex generator in channel is not a function of ordinate only—A heat transfer and optimization study. *Eng. Sci. Technol.* **2022**, *28*, 11. [CrossRef]
27. Wang, J.; Yu, K.; Ye, M.; Wang, E.; Wang, W.; Sundén, B. Effects of pin fins and vortex generators on thermal performance in a microchannel with Al2O3 nanofluids. *Energy* **2022**, *239*, 14. [CrossRef]
28. Wu, J.M.; Tao, W.Q. Effect of longitudinal vortex generator on heat transfer in rectangular channels. *Appl. Therm. Eng.* **2012**, *37*, 67–72. [CrossRef]
29. Zhang, G.; Liu, J.; Sundén, B.; Xie, G. Combined experimental and numerical studies on flow characteristic and heat transfer in ribbed channels with vortex generators of various types and arrangements. *Int. J. Therm. Sci.* **2021**, *167*, 14. [CrossRef]
30. Ibrahim, A.Q.; Alturaihi, R.S. Experimental work for single-phase and two-phase flow in duct banks with vortex generators. *Results Eng.* **2022**, *15*, 16. [CrossRef]
31. Sui, Y.; Teo, C.J.; Lee, P.S. Direct numerical simulation of fluid flow and heat transfer in periodic wavy channels with rectangular cross-sections. *Int. J. Heat Mass Transf.* **2012**, *55*, 73–88. [CrossRef]
32. Brodnianská, Z.; Kotšmíd, S. Intensification of convective heat transfer in new shaped wavy channel configurations. *Int. J. Therm. Sci.* **2021**, *162*, 17. [CrossRef]
33. Menni, Y.; Ameur, H.; Sharifpur, M.; Ahmadi, M.H. Effects of in-line deflectors on the overall performance of a channel heat exchanger. *Eng. Appl. Comput. Fluid Mech.* **2021**, *15*, 512–529. [CrossRef]
34. Islamoglu, Y.; Parmaksizoglu, C. The effect of channel height on the enhanced heat transfer characteristics in a corrugated heat exchanger channel. *Appl. Therm. Eng.* **2003**, *23*, 979–987. [CrossRef]
35. Elshafei, E.A.M.; Awad, M.M.; Negiry, E.; Ali, A.G. Heat transfer and pressure drop in corrugated channels. *Energy* **2010**, *35*, 101–110. [CrossRef]
36. Cernecky, J.; Koniar, J.; Brodnianska, Z. The effect of regulating elements on convective heat transfer along shaped heat exchange surfaces. *Chem. Process Eng.* **2013**, *34*, 5–16. [CrossRef]

mathematics MDPI

Article

Numerical Analysis of Fourier Finite Volume Element Method for Dirichlet Boundary Optimal Control Problems Governed by Elliptic PDEs on Complex Connected Domains

Mengya Su, Liuqing Xie and Zhiyue Zhang *

School of Mathematical Sciences, Jiangsu Provincial Key Laboratory for Numerical Simulation of Large Scale Complex Systems, Nanjing Normal University, Nanjing 210023, China

* Correspondence: zhangzhiyue@njnu.edu.cn

Abstract: In this research, we investigate an optimal control problem governed by elliptic PDEs with Dirichlet boundary conditions on complex connected domains, which can be utilized to model the cooling process of concrete dam pouring. A new convergence result for two-dimensional Dirichlet boundary control is proven with the Fourier finite volume element method. The Lagrange multiplier approach is employed to find the optimality systems of the Dirichlet boundary optimal control problem. The discrete optimal control problem is then obtained by applying the Fourier finite volume element method based on Galerkin variational formulation for optimality systems, that is, using Fourier expansion in the azimuthal direction and the finite volume element method in the radial direction, respectively. In this way, the original two-dimensional problem is reduced to a sequence of one-dimensional problems, with the Dirichlet boundary acting as an interval endpoint at which a quadratic interpolation scheme can be implemented. The convergence order of state, adjoint state, and Dirichlet boundary control are therefore proved. The effectiveness of the method is demonstrated numerically, and numerical data is provided to support the theoretical analysis.

Keywords: dirichlet boundary control; complex connected domain; fourier finite volume element method; error estimates; L^2 norm

MSC: 65N12; 65N22; 35J67; 49M25

Citation: Su, M.; Xie, L.; Zhang, Z. Numerical Analysis of Fourier Finite Volume Element Method for Dirichlet Boundary Optimal Control Problems Governed by Elliptic PDEs on Complex Connected Domains. *Mathematics* **2022**, *10*, 4779. https://doi.org/10.3390/math10244779

Academic Editors: Shujin Laima, Yong Cao, Xiaowei Jin, Hehe Ren and Ioannis K. Argyros

Received: 10 November 2022
Accepted: 12 December 2022
Published: 15 December 2022

Publisher's Note: MDPI stays neutral with regard to jurisdictional claims in published maps and institutional affiliations.

Copyright: © 2022 by the authors. Licensee MDPI, Basel, Switzerland. This article is an open access article distributed under the terms and conditions of the Creative Commons Attribution (CC BY) license (https://creativecommons.org/licenses/by/4.0/).

1. Introduction

Partial differential equations are commonly used to describe two-dimensional plane stable field equations like steady concentration distributions, stable temperature distributions, electrostatic field equations, steady current field equations without rotation, and steady flow equations without rotation [1–4]. The optimal control problems governed by elliptic partial differential equations also play an important role in physical engineering, biological engineering, and social sciences areas, see [5–10]. Since the 1970s, the numerical approximation methods for optimal control problems have all received increasing attention. The main research methods are the finite difference method [11], finite element method [12–15], finite volume element method [16], and spectral method [17–19].

The optimal control problem [6,7] is a mathematical problem in which the minimum value of an objective function is determined under differential equation constraints. Finding a numerical solution is essential because it is challenging to find an analytical solution to a problem of this nature. In this paper, we look at a Dirichlet boundary optimal control problem on a complex connected domain that is governed by elliptic equations. The form is as follows:

$$\min_{u \in U_{ad}} J(y,u) := \frac{1}{2}\|y - y_d\|^2_{L^2(\Omega)} + \frac{\alpha}{2}\|u\|^2_{L^2(\partial\Omega_1)}, \quad (1)$$

subject to

$$\begin{cases} -\Delta y = f, & \text{in } \Omega, \\ y = u, & \text{on } \partial\Omega_1, \\ \frac{\partial y}{\partial n_2} = 0, & \text{on } \partial\Omega_2. \end{cases} \tag{2}$$

The set $\Omega \subset R^2$ denotes a bounded complex connected domain with boundary $\Gamma = \partial\Omega_1 \cup \partial\Omega_2$. Equation (2) is a state equation, y is the state variable, $u \in \partial\Omega_1$ is the Dirichlet boundary control variable, $\alpha > 0$ is a regularization parameter, and $y_d \in H^1(\Omega)$, $f \in H^1(\Omega)$. n_2 is the outer unit normal of the boundary $\partial\Omega_2$. U_{ad} is the admissible control set which is assumed to be of box type

$$u \in U_{ad} := \left\{ u \in H^{1/2}(\partial\Omega_1) : u_a \leq u \leq u_b \right\}$$

with $u_a < u_b$ denoting constants. The domain is shown as Figure 1.

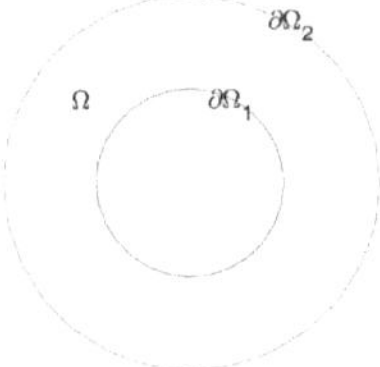

Figure 1. Domain.

This optimal Dirichlet boundary control problem can be used to describe the cooling process of concrete dam pouring [20]. $\partial\Omega_1$ is the pipe boundary on which the cold water enters and is therefore a Dirichlet boundary control condition. Ω indicates the region where the cold water acts, and y_d is the ideal state; the goal is to control the temperature of the cold water so that the temperature $y \in \Omega$ is infinitely close to y_d. Note that there is no heat exchange on $\partial\Omega_2$ and hence a homogeneous Neumann boundary condition.

Dirichlet boundary control problems are more challenging than Neumann control or distributed control problems in general, both theoretically and numerically. However, the Dirichlet situation is attracting an increasing number of researchers. For example, the semilinear elliptic Dirichlet boundary control problem with pointwise control constraints in a convex, polygonal, open domain is studied and the $1 - 1/p$ convergence order of control is derived in [21]. The authors in [22] considered Dirichlet boundary control problems posed on smooth domains and obtained that the error order of control is $h|lnh|^{1/2}$. Based on a mixed variation scheme, the authors in [23] used a mixed finite element method to approximate the optimal control problem posed on both polygonal and general smooth domains. The authors in [24] used local mesh refinement toward the boundary by standard finite element discretizations and arrived second-order convergence. [25] also derived second-order convergence for elliptic Dirichlet boundary control but in finite dimensional control space. Numerical analysis for elliptic control problems can be found in [21,26–28]. For more details, one may refer to [12,29,30] and the references therein. In addition, for finite element approximations of distributed and Neumann boundary optimal control problems one can see [31–35], and for other numerical methods, one may refer to [36–39].

The finite volume element method (FVEM) is a discretization technique for partial differential equations. It is widely employed in the numerical approximation of some problems for partial differential equations because of its local conservative property and other appealing properties, such as robustness with unstructured meshes. For instance, the authors in [40] analyzed the spatially semidiscrete piecewise linear finite volume element method for parabolic equations in a convex polygonal domain in the plane. Two-grid finite volume element discretization techniques were presented for the two-dimensional second-order nonself-adjoint and indefinite linear elliptic problems and the two-dimensional second-order nonlinear elliptic problems in [41]. A priori error estimates for a semidiscrete piecewise linear finite volume element approximation to a second-order wave equation in a two-dimensional convex polygonal domain is discussed in [42]. More applications of the finite volume element method can be referred to [43–50] and the references therein.

The combination of the finite volume element method with other numerical methods can generate competitive numerical methods for solving partial differential equation problems. For example, an immersed finite volume element method was used to solve the elliptic interface problems in [51]. A one-parameter family of discontinuous Galerkin finite volume element methods was applied to approximate the solution of a class of second-order linear elliptic problems in [52]. The Fourier finite volume element method was employed to study two-dimensional quasigeostrophic equations on a sphere in [53]. The authors in [54] utilized the Fourier finite volume element method to give the numerical experiments of two classes of Dirichlet and distributed optimal control problems driven by elliptic PDEs on complex connected domains. The main concept behind the Fourier finite volume element approach is to employ the finite volume element method in the radial direction while applying the Fourier expansion in the azimuthal direction. In the radial direction, choose linear finite element and piecewise constant function spaces for the trial and test function spaces, respectively. The control for the variational inequality is generated employing a variational discretization technique (see [55]). As a result, the two-dimensional optimal control problem can be simplified to a sequence of one-dimension problems. A desired result can be obtained by this procedure.

Generally, the Dirichlet boundary optimal control problem is typically challenging to achieve a high order in two-dimensional environments. The purpose of this article is to provide a related theoretical explanation of this problem, as a prior work on numerical simulation [54] demonstrates that the Fourier finite element approach can reduce the error order of Dirichlet boundary control on complex connected domains. In addition, it is worth noting that, in contrast to [25], the Dirichlet boundary control space in this work possesses infinite dimensions.

To the best of our knowledge, this is the first study to estimate the convergence order of the Dirichlet boundary control problem using the Fourier finite volume element approach on complex connected domains. The error of Dirichlet boundary control consists of two parts: the Fourier truncation error and the one-dimensional finite volume element error. The Fourier finite volume element approach is applied to reduce a two-dimensional optimal control problem to a group of one-dimensional problems, with the Dirichlet boundary acting as an interval endpoint at which a quadratic interpolation scheme can be implemented so that Dirichlet boundary control can be reached to higher order convergence. It is pointed out here that this proving method can also be extended to the parabolic problem.

The outline for this paper is provided below. In Section 2, we deduce the optimal control problem and corresponding optimality conditions. In order to solve the elliptic problem, the Fourier finite volume element method is introduced in Section 3. In Section 4, the Fourier finite volume element method is used to demonstrate the convergence order of the Dirichlet boundary control. A few examples are given in Section 5 to help illustrate the theoretical analysis. Some recommendations are made toward the end of Section 6.

2. Optimality System

For $m \geq 0$ and $1 \leq s \leq \infty$, applying the standard notation $W^{m,s}$ for Sobolev space on Ω with $||\cdot||_{m,s,\Omega}$ and denoting by $H^m(\Omega)$ with norm $||\cdot||_{m,\Omega}$ and seminorm $|\cdot|_{m,\Omega}$ for $s = 2$. That is,

$$W^{m,s}(\Omega) := \{v \in L^s(\Omega), |D^\alpha v \in L^s(\Omega), \forall \alpha \in \mathbb{Z}_+^n, |\alpha| \leq m\},$$

and

$$\|v\|_{W^{m,s}(\Omega)} = \left(\sum_{|\alpha| \leq m} \int_\Omega |D^\alpha v|^s dx \right)^{\frac{1}{s}}, \qquad |v|_{W^{m,s}(\Omega)} = \left(\sum_{|\alpha| = m} \int_\Omega |D^\alpha v|^s dx \right)^{\frac{1}{s}},$$

where $D^\alpha v$ denotes the α-th order weak derivative of v.

We use $(\cdot,\cdot)$ for the $L^2(\Omega)$-inner product, $\langle\cdot,\cdot\rangle_{\partial\Omega_1}$ for the $L^2(\partial\Omega_1)$-inner product, $(\cdot,\cdot)_Q$ for the $L^2(Q)$-inner product, $\langle\cdot,\cdot\rangle_{\Gamma_1}$ for the $L^2(\Gamma_1)$-inner product, and $(\cdot,\cdot)_I$ for the $L^2(I)$-inner product.

Let $Y := \{v \in H^1(\Omega), v|_{\partial\Omega_1} = u\}$ and $V := \{v \in H^1(\Omega), v|_{\partial\Omega_1} = 0\}$; the weak formulation of the state Equation (2) reads: find $y \in Y$ such that

$$a(y,v) = (f,v), \forall\, v \in V, \tag{3}$$

where the bilinear form $a(\cdot,\cdot)$ is given by

$$a(y,v) = \int_\Omega \nabla y \cdot \nabla v dx.$$

Then, the optimal control problem (1) and (2) can be described as: Find $(y,u) \in Y \times U_{ad}$

$$(P) \begin{cases} \min\limits_{u \in U_{ad}} J(y,u) := \frac{1}{2}\|y - y_d\|^2_{L^2(\Omega)} + \frac{\alpha}{2}\|u\|^2_{L^2(\partial\Omega_1)}, \\ s.t. \;\; a(y,v) = (f,v), \forall\, v \in V. \end{cases} \tag{4}$$

Suppose that $(\bar{y},\bar{u})$ is the optimal solution. This is due to the fact that the control problem is strictly convex and satisfies the existence and uniqueness requirements of the solution in the constrained state Equation (2). Then, using the Lagrange multiplier method [5,7] to construct Lagrange function

$$L(y,u,p) = J(y,u) - \int_\Omega (-\Delta y - f) p dx - \int_{\partial\Omega_1} (y - u) p ds - \int_{\partial\Omega_2} \left(\frac{\partial y}{\partial n_2}\right) p ds.$$

We take the Fréchet derivative with respect to the state y and choose a special $p(u)$, such that

$$L_y(y(u),u,p) = 0. \tag{5}$$

The adjoint state equation can be obtained as follows:

$$\begin{cases} -\Delta p = \bar{y} - y_d, & \text{in } \Omega, \\ p = 0, & \text{on } \partial\Omega_1, \\ \frac{\partial p}{\partial n_2} = 0, & \text{on } \partial\Omega_2. \end{cases} \tag{6}$$

The weak form of the adjoint state equation reads:

$$a(p,v) = (\bar{y} - y_d, v), \; \forall\, v \in V. \tag{7}$$

We take the Fréchet derivative with respect to u. Then, the variation inequality, that is, the optimality condition is obtained:

$$\left\langle \alpha\bar{u} - \frac{\partial \bar{p}}{\partial n_1}, u - \bar{u} \right\rangle_{\partial\Omega_1} \geq 0, \; \forall\, u \in U_{ad}, \tag{8}$$

where $\bar{p}$ is the solution of adjoint state Equation (6) and n_1 is the outer unit normal of the boundary $\partial\Omega_1$.

That is, the necessary and sufficient condition for control $\bar{u} \in U_{ad}$ to be optimal is that it satisfies the variation inequality (8).

Taken together, the following theorem holds.

Theorem 1 ([56]). *Assuming that the objective functional is in the form of* (1), *the optimal control of the problem* (P) *exists and is unique, and the control* $u \in U_{ad}$ *is determined by the solution* $\{\bar{y}, \bar{p}, \bar{u}\}$ *of the optimality system, that is,*

$$a(\bar{y}, v) = (f, v),\ \forall v \in V, \tag{9a}$$
$$a(\bar{p}, w) = (\bar{y} - y_d, w),\ \forall w \in V, \tag{9b}$$
$$\left\langle \alpha\bar{u} - \frac{\partial \bar{p}}{\partial n_1}, u - \bar{u} \right\rangle_{\partial\Omega_1} \geq 0,\ \forall u \in U_{ad}. \tag{9c}$$

If $y \in H^2(\Omega)$ *and* $p \in H^2(\Omega)$, *then the optimality systems* (9) *can be written by*

$$\begin{cases} -\Delta\bar{y} = f,\ -\Delta\bar{p} = \bar{y} - y_d, & \text{in } \Omega, \\ \bar{y} = \bar{u},\ \bar{p} = 0, & \text{on } \partial\Omega_1, \\ \frac{\partial \bar{y}}{\partial n_2} = 0,\ \frac{\partial \bar{p}}{\partial n_2} = 0, & \text{on } \partial\Omega_2, \\ \int_{\partial\Omega_1} \left(\alpha\bar{u} - \frac{\partial \bar{p}}{\partial n_1}\right)(u - \bar{u})ds \geq 0, & \forall u \in U_{ad}. \end{cases}$$

The variation inequality (8) *is equivalent to*

$$\bar{u} = P_{U_{ad}}\left(\frac{1}{\alpha}\frac{\partial \bar{p}}{\partial n_1}\right)|_{\partial\Omega_1},$$

and the action of the orthogonal projection $P_{U_{ad}}$: $H^{1/2}(\partial\Omega_1) \mapsto U_{ad}$ *is given by*

$$P_{U_{ad}}(g(x)) = \max\{u_a, \min\{g(x), u_b\}\}.$$

Then, the optimality system (9) *can be written as*

$$a(\bar{y}, v) = (f, v),\ \forall v \in V, \tag{10a}$$
$$a(\bar{p}, w) = (\bar{y} - y_d, w),\ \forall w \in V, \tag{10b}$$
$$\bar{u} = P_{U_{ad}}\left(\frac{1}{\alpha}\frac{\partial \bar{p}}{\partial n_1}\right)|_{\partial\Omega_1}. \tag{10c}$$

3. Fourier Finite Volume Element Method

3.1. Polar Coordinates Transform

Given the definition of the arbitrary bounded annular domain

$$\Omega = \left\{(x_1, x_2) : g_1(x_1, x_2) \leq x_1^2 + x_2^2 \leq g_2(x_1, x_2)\right\},$$

where g_1 and g_2 are the functions defined on $\bar{\Omega}$ satisfying

$$\partial\Omega_1 = \left\{(x_1, x_2) : x_1^2 + x_2^2 = g_1(x_1, x_2)\right\},\ \partial\Omega_2 = \left\{(x_1, x_2) : x_1^2 + x_2^2 = g_2(x_1, x_2)\right\},$$

let $x_1 = r\cos\theta$ and $x_2 = r\sin\theta$, then, in the polar coordinates (r, θ),

$$\partial\Omega_1 \to \Gamma_1 : r = R_1(\theta),\ \partial\Omega_2 \to \Gamma_2 : r = R_2(\theta),\ \theta \in [0, 2\pi),$$

$$\frac{\partial}{\partial x_1} = \cos\theta\frac{\partial}{\partial r} - \frac{\sin\theta}{r}\frac{\partial}{\partial\theta},\ \frac{\partial}{\partial x_2} = \sin\theta\frac{\partial}{\partial r} + \frac{\cos\theta}{r}\frac{\partial}{\partial\theta}.$$

The Laplacian operator Δ in the polar coordinates is

$$\Delta = \frac{\partial^2}{\partial r^2} + \frac{1}{r}\frac{\partial}{\partial r} + \frac{1}{r^2}\frac{\partial^2}{\partial \theta^2},$$

and

$$n_1 = -\left(\frac{\cos\theta + \frac{R_1'(\theta)}{R_1(\theta)}\sin\theta}{\sqrt{1+\left(\frac{R_1'(\theta)}{R_1(\theta)}\right)^2}}, \frac{\sin\theta - \frac{R_1'(\theta)}{R_1(\theta)}\cos\theta}{\sqrt{1+\left(\frac{R_1'(\theta)}{R_1(\theta)}\right)^2}} \right),\ n_2 = \left(\frac{\cos\theta + \frac{R_2'(\theta)}{R_2(\theta)}\sin\theta}{\sqrt{1+\left(\frac{R_2'(\theta)}{R_2(\theta)}\right)^2}}, \frac{\sin\theta - \frac{R_2'(\theta)}{R_2(\theta)}\cos\theta}{\sqrt{1+\left(\frac{R_2'(\theta)}{R_2(\theta)}\right)^2}} \right),$$

$$\frac{\partial y(x_1,x_2)}{\partial n_1} = \left(\frac{\partial y(x_1,x_2)}{\partial x_1}, \frac{\partial y(x_1,x_2)}{\partial x_2}\right)\cdot n_1 = -\frac{\frac{\partial y(r\cos\theta, r\sin\theta)}{\partial r} - \frac{R_1'(\theta)}{R_1^2(\theta)}\frac{\partial y(r\cos\theta, r\sin\theta)}{\partial \theta}}{\sqrt{1+\left(\frac{R_1'(\theta)}{R_1(\theta)}\right)^2}},$$

where n_1 denotes the outer unit normal of the boundary Γ_1.

Assumption 1. *There exist positive constants γ_1, γ_2, γ_3 and γ_4 such that*

$$0 < \gamma_1 \le R_1(\theta) < R_2(\theta) \le \gamma_2 < \infty,$$

$$\left|R_1'(\theta)\right| \le \gamma_3 < \infty,\ \left|R_2'(\theta)\right| \le \gamma_4 < \infty.$$

Setting $y := y(r,\theta)$, $f := f(r,\theta)$, $y_d := y_d(r,\theta)$, on the boundary $u = u(\theta)|_{\Gamma_1}$. The form of (2) in polar coordinates is

$$\begin{cases} -\left(\frac{\partial^2 y}{\partial r^2} + \frac{1}{r}\frac{\partial y}{\partial r} + \frac{1}{r^2}\frac{\partial^2 y}{\partial \theta^2}\right) = f, & \text{in } Q, \\ y = u, & \text{on } \Gamma_1, \\ \frac{\frac{\partial y}{\partial r} - \frac{R_2'(\theta)}{R_2^2(\theta)}\frac{\partial y}{\partial \theta}}{\sqrt{1+\left(\frac{R_2'(\theta)}{R_2(\theta)}\right)^2}} = 0, & \text{on } \Gamma_2, \end{cases} \tag{11}$$

where $Q = (R_1(\theta), R_2(\theta)) \times (0, 2\pi)$.

Remark 1. *The boundary condition on Γ_2 of (11) can be written as $\frac{\partial y}{\partial r} = 0$, $\frac{R_2'(\theta)}{R_2^2(\theta)}\frac{\partial y}{\partial \theta} = 0$, the derivation process will be given later.*

Let $Y_f := \{v \in H^1(Q), v|_{\Gamma_1} = u(\theta)\}$, $U_{adf} := \left\{u \in H^{1/2}(\Gamma_1) : u_a \le u \le u_b\right\}$, $V_f := \{v \in H^1(Q), v|_{\Gamma_1} = 0\}$. Define that

$$\|v\|_{L^2(Q)} = (v,v)_Q^{\frac{1}{2}} := \left(\int_0^{2\pi}\int_{R_1(\theta)}^{R_2(\theta)} r|v(r,\theta)|^2 dr d\theta\right)^{\frac{1}{2}}, \forall v \in V_f,$$

$$\|u\|_{L^2(\Gamma_1)} = (u,u)_{\Gamma_1}^{\frac{1}{2}} := \left(\int_0^{2\pi} R_1(\theta)|u(R_1(\theta),\theta)|^2 d\theta\right)^{\frac{1}{2}}, \forall u \in U_{adf}.$$

Obviously, there holds that $\|v(r,\theta)\|_{L^2(Q)} = \|v(x_1,x_2)\|_{L^2(\Omega)}$, $\|u(R_1(\theta),\theta)\|_{L^2(\Gamma_1)} = \|u(x_1,x_2)\|_{L^2(\partial\Omega_1)}$.

In the polar coordinates, the optimal control problem (4) can be redescribed as: Find $(y,u) \in Y_f \times U_{adf}$ such that

$$(P(r,\theta))\begin{cases} \min\limits_{u\in U_{adf}} J(y,u) := \frac{1}{2}\|y-y_d\|^2_{L^2(Q)} + \frac{\alpha}{2}\|u\|^2_{L^2(\Gamma_1)}, \\ s.t. \;\; A(y,v) = (f,v)_Q, \forall\, v \in V_f, \end{cases} \tag{12}$$

where the bilinear form $A(\cdot,\cdot)$ and $(f,v)_Q$ are given by

$$A(y,v) = \int_Q r\frac{\partial y}{\partial r}\frac{\partial v}{\partial r}drd\theta - \int_Q \frac{1}{r}\frac{\partial^2 y}{\partial \theta^2}vdrd\theta,$$

$$(f,v)_Q = \int_Q fvrdrd\theta,$$

respectively.

The optimality system (9) can be written as

$$A(\bar{y},v) = (f,v)_Q, \forall v \in V_f, \tag{13a}$$

$$A(\bar{p},w) = ((\bar{y}-y_d),w)_Q, \forall w \in V_f, \tag{13b}$$

$$\left\langle \alpha\bar{u}\sqrt{R_1'(\theta)^2 + R_1^2(\theta)} + \left(\frac{\partial \bar{p}}{\partial r} - \frac{R_1'(\theta)}{R_1^2(\theta)}\frac{\partial \bar{p}}{\partial \theta}\right)R_1(\theta), u-\bar{u}\right\rangle_{\Gamma_1} \geq 0, \forall u \in U_{adf}. \tag{13c}$$

3.2. Fourier Expansion and Truncation

Since the solution $y(r,\theta)$ of (11) is periodic in θ, it can be written as:

$$y(r,\theta) = \sum_{|m|=0}^{\infty} y_m(r)e^{im\theta}, \tag{14}$$

where $y_m(r) = \frac{1}{2\pi}\int_0^{2\pi} y(r,\theta)e^{-im\theta}d\theta$.

Taking an truncation [57] to (14),

$$y_f(r,\theta) = \sum_{|m|=0}^{M} y_m(r)e^{im\theta}. \tag{15}$$

Substitute (15) into (11), we can obtain

$$\begin{cases} -\left(\frac{\partial^2 y_f}{\partial r^2} + \frac{1}{r}\frac{\partial y_f}{\partial r} + \frac{1}{r^2}\frac{\partial^2 y_f}{\partial \theta^2}\right) = f_f, & \text{in } Q, \\ y_f = u_f, & \text{on } \Gamma_1, \\ \frac{\partial y_f}{\partial r} = 0, \; \frac{R_2'(\theta)}{R_2^2(\theta)}\frac{\partial y_f}{\partial \theta} = 0, & \text{on } \Gamma_2, \end{cases} \tag{16}$$

with $f_f = \sum\limits_{|m|=0}^{M} f_m(r)e^{im\theta}$ and $u_f = \sum\limits_{|m|=0}^{M} u_m(r)e^{im\theta}$.

The optimal control problem (P) can be redescribed as: Find $\left(y_f,u_f\right) \in Y_f \times U_{adf}$ such that

$$\left(P_f\right)\begin{cases} \min\limits_{u_f\in U_{adm}} J\left(y_f,u_f\right) := \frac{1}{2}\left\|y_f - y_{d_f}\right\|^2_{L^2(Q)} + \frac{\alpha}{2}\left\|u_f\right\|^2_{L^2(\Gamma_1)}, \\ s.t. \;\; A\left(y_f,v_f\right) = \left(f_f,v_f\right)_Q, \forall\, v_f \in V_f, \end{cases} \tag{17}$$

where $y_{d_f} = \sum_{|m|=0}^{M} y_{d_m}(r)e^{im\theta}$.

Obviously, (16) can be rewritten as:

$$\begin{cases} -\left(\frac{d^2 y_m}{dr^2} + \frac{1}{r}\frac{dy_m}{dr} - \frac{m^2}{r^2}y_m\right) = f_m, & \text{in } Q, \\ y_m = u_m, & \text{on } \Gamma_1, \\ \frac{dy_m}{dr} = 0,\ \frac{R_2'(\theta)}{R_2^2(\theta)}y_m = 0, & \text{on } \Gamma_2, \end{cases} \tag{18}$$

where $m = 0, \pm 1, \pm 2, \ldots, \pm M$.

We now give the process of deriving the boundary conditions on Γ_2 of (11), (16) and (18):

Proof. The initial form of the boundary condition on $\partial\Omega_2$ of the Cartesian coordinate system is

$$\frac{\partial y}{\partial n_2} = 0, \quad \text{on } \partial\Omega_2.$$

After a polar coordinate transformation, it becomes

$$\frac{\frac{\partial y}{\partial r} - \frac{R_2'(\theta)}{R_2^2(\theta)}\frac{\partial y}{\partial \theta}}{\sqrt{1 + \left(\frac{R_2'(\theta)}{R_2(\theta)}\right)^2}} = 0, \quad \text{on } \Gamma_2.$$

According to Assumption 1, it is the equivalent to

$$\frac{\partial y}{\partial r} - \frac{R_2'(\theta)}{R_2^2(\theta)}\frac{\partial y}{\partial \theta} = 0, \quad \text{on } \Gamma_2.$$

Expanded and truncated by Fourier series, then, we have

$$\frac{\partial y_f}{\partial r} - \frac{R_2'(\theta)}{R_2^2(\theta)}\frac{\partial y_f}{\partial \theta} = 0, \quad \text{on } \Gamma_2,$$

namely

$$\sum_{|m|=0}^{M}\left(\frac{dy_m}{dr} - im\frac{R_2'(\theta)}{R_2^2(\theta)}y_m\right)e^{im\theta} = 0, \quad \text{on } \Gamma_2.$$

According to the orthogonality of the trigonometric system and Assumption 1, we derive

$$0 = -2\pi\frac{\gamma_4}{\gamma_2}\int_0^{2\pi} e^{im\theta}e^{-in\theta}d\theta \le \int_0^{2\pi}\frac{R_2'(\theta)}{R_2^2(\theta)}e^{im\theta}e^{-in\theta}d\theta \le 2\pi\frac{\gamma_4}{\gamma_1}\int_0^{2\pi} e^{im\theta}e^{-in\theta}d\theta = 0,\ n \ne m,$$

then, we have

$$\int_0^{2\pi}\left(\frac{dy_m}{dr} - im\frac{R_2'(\theta)}{R_2^2(\theta)}y_m\right)e^{im\theta}e^{-im\theta}d\theta = \int_0^{2\pi}\left(\frac{dy_m}{dr} - im\frac{R_2'(\theta)}{R_2^2(\theta)}y_m\right)d\theta = 0, \quad \text{on } \Gamma_2.$$

From $R_2(2\pi) = R_2(0) \ne 0$, we get

$$\frac{dy_m}{dr} = 0,\ \frac{R_2'(\theta)}{R_2^2(\theta)}y_m = 0, \quad \text{on } \Gamma_2.$$

Thus, we have

$$\frac{\partial y_f}{\partial r} = 0,\ \frac{R_2'(\theta)}{R_2^2(\theta)}\frac{\partial y_f}{\partial \theta} = 0, \quad \text{on } \Gamma_2,$$

and

$$\frac{\partial y}{\partial r} = 0, \ \frac{R_2'(\theta)}{R_2^2(\theta)}\frac{\partial y}{\partial \theta} = 0, \quad \text{on } \Gamma_2.$$

□

Correspondingly, the adjoint state equation of (18) is

$$\begin{cases} -\left(\frac{d^2 p_m}{dr^2} + \frac{1}{r}\frac{dp_m}{dr} - \frac{m^2}{r^2}p_m\right) = f_m, & \text{in } Q, \\ p_m = 0, & \text{on } \Gamma_1, \\ \frac{dp_m}{dr} = 0, \ \frac{R_2'(\theta)}{R_2^2(\theta)}p_m = 0, & \text{on } \Gamma_2, \end{cases} \tag{19}$$

where $m = 0, \pm1, \pm2, \ldots, \pm M$.

The weak forms of (18) and (19) are as follows:

$$A_m(\bar{y}_m, v_m) = (f_m, v_m)_Q, \forall v_m \in V_f, \tag{20a}$$

$$A_m(\bar{p}_m, w_m) = ((\bar{y}_m - y_{d_m}), w_m)_Q, \forall w_m \in V_f, \tag{20b}$$

where $f_m, v_m, w_m, p_m, y_{d_m}$ are defined like y_m with $m = 0, \pm1, \pm2, \ldots, \pm M$ and the bilinear form $A_m(\cdot,\cdot)$ is given by

$$A_m(y_m, v_m) = \int_Q r\frac{dy_m}{dr}\frac{dv_m}{dr}drd\theta + \int_Q \frac{m^2}{r}y_m v_m drd\theta.$$

From the above, $\theta \in [0, 2\pi)$, and $y_m(r) = \frac{1}{2\pi}\int_0^{2\pi} y(r,\theta)e^{-im\theta}d\theta$. Consider the Fourier interpolation at point $\theta_k = \frac{2\pi\cdot k}{M}$ $(k = 1, 2, 3, \cdots, M)$:

$$y_m(r) = \frac{1}{2\pi}\int_0^{2\pi} y(r,\theta)e^{-im\theta}d\theta \sim \frac{1}{M}\sum_{k=1}^{M} y_m(r,\theta_k)e^{-im\theta_k}, \tag{21}$$

where M is the number of grid lines in the θ direction. It applies to $f_m, y_{d_m}, v_m, w_m, p_m, u_m$.

Denoting $y_{m_k}(r) = y_m(r,\theta_k)$, correspondingly, (15) becomes

$$y_{f_\tau} = \sum_{|m|=0}^{M}\left(\frac{1}{M}\sum_{k=1}^{M} y_{m_k}(r)e^{-im\theta_k}\right)e^{im\theta}, \tag{22}$$

where y_{f_τ} is the approximation of y_f and the definition of f_{f_τ} and $y_{d_{f_\tau}}$ are similar.

3.3. Finite Volume Element Method

For any fixed $k = 1, 2, \cdots, M$, $\Gamma_1 = R_1(\theta) \times (0, 2\pi)$ becomes to $\Gamma_{1_k} = R_1(\theta_k)$, $\Gamma_2 = R_2(\theta) \times (0, 2\pi)$ to $\Gamma_{2_k} = R_2(\theta_k)$, and $I = (R_1(\theta), R_2(\theta))$ to $I_k = (R_1(\theta_k), R_2(\theta_k))$. Let $Y_{m_k} := \{v \in H^1(I_k), v = u_{m_k} \ on \ \Gamma_{1_k}\}$, $U_{adm_k} := \left\{u \in H^{1/2}(\Gamma_{1_k}) : u_a \le u \le u_b\right\}$, $V_{m_k} := \{v \in H^1(I_k), v = 0 \ on \ \Gamma_{1_k}\}$, and $Y_{f_\tau} := \bigotimes_{k=1}^{M} Y_{m_k}$, $U_{adf_\tau} := \bigotimes_{k=1}^{M} U_{adm_k}$, $V_{f_\tau} := \bigotimes_{k=1}^{M} V_{m_k}$. Define some norms and seminorm as follows:

$$\|v\|_{L^2(I_k)} = (v,v)_{I_k}^{\frac{1}{2}} := \left(\int_{R_1(\theta_k)}^{R_2(\theta_k)} r|v|^2 dr\right)^{\frac{1}{2}}, \forall v \in V_{m_k},$$

$$|v|_{H^1(I_k)} = \left(\frac{\partial v}{\partial r}, \frac{\partial v}{\partial r}\right)_{I_k}^{\frac{1}{2}} := \left(\int_{R_1(\theta_k)}^{R_2(\theta_k)} r\left|\frac{\partial v}{\partial r}\right|^2 dr\right)^{\frac{1}{2}}, \forall v \in V_{m_k},$$

respectively, and $\|v\|^2_{H^1(I_k)} = \|v\|^2_{L^2(I_k)} + |v|^2_{H^1(I_k)}, \forall v \in V_{m_k}$.

$$\|u\|_{L^2\left(\Gamma_{1_k}\right)} = (u,u)^{\frac{1}{2}}_{\Gamma_{1_k}} := \left(R_1(\theta_k)|u(R_1(\theta_k),(\theta_k))|^2\right)^{\frac{1}{2}}, \forall u \in U_{adm_k}.$$

It is easy to prove that these norms are well defined. There holds:

$$\left\|v_{f_\tau}\right\|_{L^2(Q),\tau} = \left(\frac{1}{M}\sum_{k=1}^{M}\|v\|^2_{L^2(I_k)}\right)^{\frac{1}{2}}, \forall v_{f_\tau} \in Y_{f_\tau},$$

$$\left\|u_{f_\tau}\right\|_{L^2(\Gamma_1),\tau} = \left(\frac{1}{M}\sum_{k=1}^{M}\|u\|^2_{L^2\left(\Gamma_{1_k}\right)}\right)^{\frac{1}{2}}, \forall u_{f_\tau} \in U_{adf_\tau}.$$

The corresponding discrete norms are defined as follows:

$$\|v_h\|_{L^2(I_k)} = (v_h,v_h)^{\frac{1}{2}}_{I_k} := \left(\sum_{i=1}^{N}\int_{r_{i-1}(\theta_k)}^{r_i(\theta_k)} r|v_h|^2 dr\right)^{\frac{1}{2}}, \forall v_h \in Y^h_{m_k},$$

$$\|u_h\|_{L^2\left(\Gamma_{1_k}\right)} = (u_h,u_h)^{\frac{1}{2}}_{\Gamma_{1_k}} := \left(R_1(\theta_k)|u_h(|R_1(\theta_k),(\theta_k))|^2\right)^{\frac{1}{2}}, \forall u_h \in U_{adm_k}.$$

There holds:

$$\left\|v_{f_h}\right\|_{L^2(Q),\tau} = \left(\frac{1}{M}\sum_{k=1}^{M}\|v_h\|^2_{L^2(I_k)}\right)^{\frac{1}{2}}, \forall v_{f_h} \in Y^h_{f_\tau},$$

$$\left\|u_{f_h}\right\|_{L^2(\Gamma_1),\tau} = \left(\frac{1}{M}\sum_{k=1}^{M}\|u_h\|^2_{L^2\left(\Gamma_{1_k}\right)}\right)^{\frac{1}{2}}, \forall u_{f_h} \in U^h_{ad}.$$

The definition of discrete functions and discrete spaces will be given later.

The cost functional with state Equation (18) becomes an optimal control problem over a one-dimensional fixed interval. From (18), it can be inferred that:

$$\begin{cases} -\left(\frac{d^2 y_{m_k}}{dr^2} + \frac{1}{r}\frac{dy_{m_k}}{dr} - \frac{m^2}{r^2}y_{m_k}\right) = f_{m_k}, & \text{in } I_k = (R_1(\theta_k), R_2(\theta_k)), \\ y_{m_k} = u_{m_k}, & \text{on } \Gamma_{1_k}, \\ \frac{dy_{m_k}}{dr} = 0,\ \frac{R_2'(\theta_k)}{R_2^2(\theta_k)}y_{m_k} = 0, & \text{on } \Gamma_{2_k}, \end{cases} \tag{23}$$

where $m = 0, \pm1, \pm2, \ldots, \pm M$.

The optimality system can be rewritten as:

$$A_{m_k}(\bar{y}_{m_k}, v_{m_k}) = (f_{m_k}, v_{m_k})_{I_k}, \forall v_{m_k} \in V_{m_k}, \tag{24a}$$

$$A_{m_k}(\bar{p}_{m_k}, w_{m_k}) = \left(\left(\bar{y}_{m_k} - y_{d_{m_k}}\right), w_{m_k}\right)_{I_k}, \forall w_{m_k} \in V_{m_k}, \tag{24b}$$

$$\left\langle \alpha\bar{u}_{m_k}\sqrt{R_1'(\theta_k)^2 + R_1^2(\theta_k)} + \frac{d\bar{p}_{m_k}}{dr}R_1(\theta_k), u_{m_k} - \bar{u}_{m_k}\right\rangle_{\Gamma_{1_k}} \geq 0, \forall u_{m_k} \in U_{adm_k}, \tag{24c}$$

where the bilinear form $A_{m_k}(\cdot,\cdot)$ is given by

$$A_{m_k}(y_{m_k}, v_{m_k}) = \int_{I_k} r\frac{dy_{m_k}}{dr}\frac{dv_{m_k}}{dr}dr + m^2\int_{I_k}\frac{1}{r}y_{m_k}v_{m_k}dr.$$

The optimal control problem $\left(P_f\right)$ can be redescribed as: Find $\left(y_{f_\tau}, u_{f_\tau}\right) \in Y_{f_\tau} \times U_{adf_\tau}$ such that

$$\left(P_{f_\tau}\right)\begin{cases} \min\limits_{u_{f_\tau} \in U_{adf_\tau}} J\left(y_{f_\tau}, u_{f_\tau}\right) := \frac{1}{2}\left\|y_{f_\tau} - y_{d_{f_\tau}}\right\|^2_{L^2(Q),\tau} + \frac{\alpha}{2}\left\|u_{f_\tau}\right\|^2_{L^2(\Gamma_1),\tau}, \\ s.t.\ \ A_{f_\tau}\left(y_{f_\tau}, v_{f_\tau}\right) = \left(f_{f_\tau}, v_{f_\tau}\right)_{Q,\tau}, \forall\, v_{f_\tau} \in V_{f_\tau}, \end{cases} \tag{25}$$

where $y_{f_\tau} := \sum\limits_{|m|=0}^{M} \left(\frac{1}{M} \sum\limits_{k=1}^{M} y_{m_k}(r) e^{-im\theta_k}\right) e^{im\theta}$, the definition of $u_{f_\tau}, y_{d_{f_\tau}}, v_{f_\tau}, f_{f_\tau}$ are similar.

For the purpose of finite volume element approximation of (24a), discretizing the interval $[R_1(\theta_k), R_2(\theta_k)]$ into a grid T_h with nodes

$$R_1(\theta_k) = r_0(\theta_k) < r_1(\theta_k) < r_2(\theta_k) < \ldots < r_{N-1}(\theta_k) < r_N(\theta_k) = R_2(\theta_k).$$

Denoting the mesh size $h_i(\theta_k) = r_i(\theta_k) - r_{i-1}(\theta_k)$, and writing $I_{k_i} = [r_{i-1}(\theta_k), r_i(\theta_k)]$. Placing a dual grid T_h^* with nodes

$$R_1(\theta_k) = r_0(\theta_k) < r_{1/2}(\theta_k) < r_{3/2}(\theta_k) < \ldots < r_{N-1/2}(\theta_k) < r_N(\theta_k) = R_2(\theta_k),$$

write $I_{k_i}^* = [r_{i-1/2}(\theta_k), r_{i+1/2}(\theta_k)]$, $I_{k_0}^* = [r_0(\theta_k), r_{1/2}(\theta_k)]$ and $I_{k_N}^* = [r_{N-1/2}(\theta_k), r_N(\theta_k)]$.

Typical basis function $\phi_i(r)$ on I_{k_i} and $\psi_j(r)$ on $I_{k_j}^*$ are shown below

$$\phi_i(r) = \begin{cases} 1 - h_i^{-1}|r - r_i(\theta_k)|, & r_{i-1}(\theta_k) \le r \le r_i(\theta_k), \\ 1 - h_{i+1}^{-1}|r - r_i(\theta_k)|, & r_i(\theta_k) \le r \le r_{i+1}(\theta_k), \\ 0. & elsewhere. \end{cases} \tag{26}$$

$$\psi_j(r) = \begin{cases} 1, & r \in I_j^*, \\ 0. & r \notin I_j^*. \end{cases} \tag{27}$$

Now, let $Y_{m_k}^h$ be the standard linear finite element space defined on the T_h:

$$Y_{m_k}^h = \{v \in C(I_k) : v|_{I_k} \text{ is piecewise linear function for all } I_k \in T_h\}$$

and its dual volume element space $Y_{m_k}^{h*}$

$$Y_{m_k}^{h*} = \left\{v \in L^2(I_k) : v|_{I_k^*} \text{ is piecewise constant function for all } I_k^* \in T_h^*\right\}.$$

Obviously, $Y_{m_k}^h = span\{\phi_j(r)\}_{j=0}^N$ and $Y_{m_k}^{h*} = span\{\psi_j(r)\}_{j=0}^N$.

Two interpolation projection operators $\Pi_h : Y_{m_k} \to Y_{m_k}^h$ and $\Pi_h^* : Y_{m_k} \to Y_{m_k}^{h*}$ are defined and satisfy $\Pi_h^* Y_{m_k}^h = Y_{m_k}^{h*}$,

$$\Pi_h y_{m_k} = \sum_{i=0}^{N} y_{m_k,i}\phi_i(r), \quad \Pi_h^* v_{m_k} = \sum_{j=0}^{N} v_{m_k,j}\psi_j(r),$$

where $y_{m_k,i} = y_{m_k}(r_i(\theta_k))$ and $v_{m_k,j} = v_{m_k}(r_j(\theta_k))$. Denoting $y_{m_k}^h := y_{m_k}^h(u_{m_k})$, the finite volume element approximation corresponding to the state equation in problem (P_{m_k}) is defined by the function $y_{m_k}^h \in Y_{m_k}^h$ such that

$$A_{m_k}\left(y_{m_k}^h, \Pi_h^* v_{m_k}\right) = \left(f_{m_k}, \Pi_h^* v_{m_k}\right)_{I_k}, y_{m_k}^h|_{\Gamma_{1_k}} = u_{m_k}, \forall \Pi_h^* v_{m_k} \in Y_{m_k}^{h*}, \tag{28}$$

where

$$\begin{cases} A_{m_k}\left(y^h_{m_k},\psi_j(r)\right) & = \int_{r_{j-1/2}(\theta_k)}^{r_{j+1/2}(\theta_k)} r\frac{dy^h_{m_k}}{dr}\frac{d\psi_j(r)}{dr}dr + m^2\int_{r_{j-1/2}(\theta_k)}^{r^{j+1/2}(\theta_k)}\frac{1}{r}y^h_{m_k}dr \\ & = r_{j-1/2}(\theta_k)\frac{y_{m_k,j}-y_{m_k,j-1}}{h_j} - r_{j+1/2}(\theta_k)\frac{y_{m_k,j+1}-y_{m_k,j}}{h_{j+1}} \\ & \quad + m^2\left(\ln\left(r_{j+1/2}(\theta_k)\right) - \ln\left(r_{j-1/2}(\theta_k)\right)\right)y_{m_k,j} \\ & = -\frac{r_{j-1/2}(\theta_k)}{h_j}y_{m_k,j-1} - \frac{r_{j+1/2}(\theta_k)}{h_{j+1}}y_{m_k,j+1} \\ & \quad + \left(\frac{r_{j-1/2}(\theta_k)}{h_j} - \frac{r_{j+1/2}(\theta_k)}{h_{j+1}} + m^2\left(\ln\left(r_{j+1/2}(\theta_k)\right) - \ln\left(r_{j-1/2}(\theta_k)\right)\right)\right)y_{m_k,j}. \\ \left(f_{m_k},\psi_j(r)\right)_{I_k} & = \int_{r_{j-1/2}(\theta_k)}^{r_{j+1/2}(\theta_k)} f_{m_k}(r)rdr. \end{cases} \quad (29)$$

The formulation (28) is reduced to the linear system

$$K_{m_k}y^h_{m_k} = f_{m_k},$$

the elements of K_{m_k} with

$$\begin{cases} a_{j,j} = \frac{r_{j-1/2}(\theta_k)}{h_j} + \frac{r_{j+1/2}(\theta_k)}{h_{j+1}} + m^2\left(\ln\left(r_{j+1/2}(\theta_k)\right) - \ln\left(r_{j-1/2}(\theta_k)\right)\right), & j = 1,2,\ldots,N-1, \\ a_{0,0} = \frac{r_{1/2}(\theta_k)}{h_1} + m^2(\ln(r_{1/2}(\theta_k)) - \ln(r_0(\theta_k))), & \\ a_{N,N} = \frac{r_{N-1/2}(\theta_k)}{h_N} + m^2(\ln(r_N(\theta_k)) - \ln(r_{N-1/2}(\theta_k))), & \\ a_{j,j-1} = -\frac{r_{j-1/2}(\theta_k)}{h_j}, & j = 1,2,\ldots,N, \\ a_{j,j+1} = -\frac{r_{j+1/2}(\theta_k)}{h_{j+1}}, & j = 0,1,2,\ldots,N-1, \end{cases}$$

where $y^h_{m_k} = \left(y^h_{m_k,0}, y^h_{m_k,1},\ldots,y^h_{m_k,N}\right)^T$, $f_{m_k} = (f_{m_k,0}, f_{m_k,1},\ldots,f_{m_k,N})^T$. The numerical solution of the Equation (23) is obtained by solving this linear system.

Now, the optimality system is:

$$A_{m_k}\left(\bar{y}^h_{m_k},\Pi^*_h v_{m_k}\right) = \left(f_{m_k},\Pi^*_h v_{m_k}\right)_{I_k}, \forall\Pi^*_h v_{m_k} \in Y^{h*}_{m_k}, \quad (30a)$$

$$A_{m_k}\left(\bar{p}^h_{m_k},\Pi^*_h w_{m_k}\right) = \left(\left(\bar{y}^h_{m_k} - y_{d_{m_k}}\right),\Pi^*_h w_{m_k}\right)_{I_k}, \forall\Pi^*_h w_{m_k} \in Y^{h*}_{m_k}, \quad (30b)$$

$$\left\langle \alpha\bar{u}_{m_k}\sqrt{R_1'(\theta_k)^2 + R_1^2(\theta_k)} + \frac{d\bar{p}^h_{m_k}}{dr}R_1(\theta_k), u_{m_k} - \bar{u}_{m_k}\right\rangle_{\Gamma_{1_k}} \geq 0, \forall u_{m_k} \in U_{ad m_k}. \quad (30c)$$

Let $Y^h_{f_\tau} := \bigotimes_{k=1}^{M} Y^h_{m_k}$, $Y^{h*}_{f_\tau} := \bigotimes_{k=1}^{M} Y^{h*}_{m_k}$. The semidiscrete optimal control problem can be described as: Find $\left(y^h_{f_\tau}, u_{f_\tau}\right) \in Y^h_{f_\tau} \times U_{adf_\tau}$ such that

$$\left(P^h_{f_\tau}\right)\begin{cases} \min\limits_{u_{f_\tau}\in U_{adf_\tau}} J\left(y^h_{f_\tau},u_{f_\tau}\right) := \frac{1}{2}\left\|y^h_{f_\tau} - y_{d_{f_\tau}}\right\|^2_{L^2(Q),\tau} + \frac{\alpha}{2}\left\|u_{f_\tau}\right\|^2_{L^2(\Gamma_1),\tau}, \\ s.t.\ \ A_{f_\tau}\left(y^h_{f_\tau},\Pi^*_h v_{f_\tau}\right) = \left(f_{f_\tau},\Pi^*_h v_{f_\tau}\right)_{Q,\tau}, \forall\Pi^*_h v_{f_\tau} \in Y^{h*}_{f_\tau}, \end{cases} \quad (31)$$

where $y^h_{f_\tau} := \sum\limits_{|m|=0}^{M}\left(\frac{1}{M}\sum\limits_{k=1}^{M} y^h_{m_k}e^{-im\theta_k}\right)e^{im\theta}$, $A_{f_\tau}\left(y^h_{f_\tau},\Pi^*_h v_{f_\tau}\right) := \sum\limits_{|m|=0}^{M}(\frac{1}{M}\sum\limits_{k=1}^{M}(A_{m_k}(\bar{y}^h_{m_k}, \Pi^*_h v_{m_k}))e^{-im\theta_k})e^{im\theta}$.

Last, the variational discretization method is used to discretize u_{m_k}, denoting $u_h := u^h_{m_k}, y_h := y^h_{m_k}\left(u^h_{m_k}\right)$; then, the optimality system is

$$A_{m_k}(\bar{y}_h, \Pi^*_h v_{m_k}) = (f_{m_k}, \Pi^*_h v_{m_k})_{I_k}, \forall \Pi^*_h v_{m_k} \in Y^{h*}_{m_k}, \tag{32a}$$

$$A_{m_k}(\bar{p}_h, \Pi^*_h w_{m_k}) = \left(\left(\bar{y}_h - y_{d_{m_k}}\right), \Pi^*_h w_{m_k}\right)_{I_k}, \forall \Pi^*_h w_{m_k} \in Y^{h*}_{m_k}, \tag{32b}$$

$$\left\langle \alpha \bar{u}_h \sqrt{R_1'(\theta_k)^2 + R_1^2(\theta_k)} + \frac{d\bar{p}_h}{dr} R_1(\theta_k), u_h - \bar{u}_h \right\rangle_{\Gamma_{1_k}} \geq 0, \forall u_h \in U_{adm_k}. \tag{32c}$$

The full-discrete optimal control problem can be described as: Find $\left(y_{f_h}, u_{f_h}\right) \in Y^h_{f_k} \times U^h_{ad}$ such that

$$\left(P_{f_h}\right) \begin{cases} \min\limits_{u_{f_h} \in U^h_{ad}} J_h\left(y_{f_h}, u_{f_h}\right) := \frac{1}{2}\left\|y_{f_h} - y_{d_{f_\tau}}\right\|^2_{L^2(Q),\tau} + \frac{\alpha}{2}\left\|u_{f_h}\right\|^2_{L^2(\Gamma_1,\tau)}, \\ s.t. \;\; A_{f_\tau}\left(y_{f_h}, \Pi^*_h v_{f_\tau}\right) = \left(f_{f_\tau}, \Pi^*_h v_{f_\tau}\right)_{Q,\tau}, \forall \Pi^*_h v_{f_\tau} \in Y^{h*}_{f_k}, \end{cases} \tag{33}$$

where $U^h_{ad} := U_{adf_k}, y_{f_h} := \sum\limits_{|m|=0}^{M} \left(\frac{1}{M}\sum\limits_{k=1}^{M} y_h e^{-im\theta_k}\right) e^{im\theta}$ and the definition of p_{f_h}, u_{f_h} are similar.

Theorem 2. *The discrete optimal control of the problem $\left(P_{f_h}\right)$ exists and is unique, and the control $u_{f_h} \in U^h_{ad}$ is determined by the solution $\left\{\bar{y}_{f_h}, \bar{p}_{f_h}, \bar{u}_{f_h}\right\}$ of the optimality system, that is,*

$$A_{f_\tau}\left(\bar{y}_{f_h}, \Pi^*_h v_{f_\tau}\right) = \left(f_{f_\tau}, \Pi^*_h v_{f_\tau}\right)_{Q,\tau}, \forall \Pi^*_h v_{f_\tau} \in Y^{h*}_{f_\tau}, \tag{34a}$$

$$A_{f_k}\left(\bar{p}_{f_h}, \Pi^*_h w_{f_\tau}\right) = \left(\left(\bar{y}_{f_h} - y_{d_{f_\tau}}\right), \Pi^*_h w_{f_\tau}\right)_{Q,\tau}, \forall \Pi^*_h w_{f_\tau} \in Y^{h*}_{f_\tau}, \tag{34b}$$

$$\left\langle \alpha \bar{u}_{f_h} \sqrt{R_1'(\theta_k)^2 + R_1^2(\theta_k)} + \frac{\partial \bar{p}_{f_h}}{\partial r} R_1(\theta_k), u_{f_h} - \bar{u}_{f_h} \right\rangle_{\Gamma_1,\tau} \geq 0, \forall u_{f_h} \in U^h_{ad}. \tag{34c}$$

4. A Priori Error Estimates

In this section, the error estimate between continuous optimal control problem (P) and discrete optimal control problem $\left(P_{f_h}\right)$ are obtained.

Here and in what follows, we use "$a \lesssim b$" to denote that there exists a positive generic constant C, which is independent of M and h, such that "$a \leq Cb$". "$a \approx b$" means that "$a \lesssim b \lesssim a$".

Before giving the main result, some Lemmas need to be listed.

Lemma 1 ([17]). *For arbitrary $v \in H^l((0, 2\pi)), l \geq \frac{1}{2}$,*

$$\left\|v - v_{f_\tau}\right\| \lesssim M^{-l}|v|_l, \tag{35}$$

where $v_{f_\tau} = \sum\limits_{|m|=0}^{M} \left(\frac{1}{M}\sum\limits_{k=1}^{M} v_{m_k}(r) e^{-im\theta_k}\right) e^{im\theta}$.

From the results of [16], we can derive the next two Lemmas similarly.

Lemma 2. *It holds*

$$A_{m_k}\left(y^h_{m_k}, \Pi^*_h v^h_{m_k}\right) \lesssim \left\|y^h_{m_k}\right\|_{H^1(I_k)} \left\|v^h_{m_k}\right\|_{H^1(I_k)}, \forall y^h_{m_k}, v^h_{m_k} \in Y^h_{m_k}. \tag{36}$$

$$A_{m_k}\left(y^h_{m_k},\Pi^*_h y^h_{m_k}\right) \gtrsim \left|y^h_{m_k}\right|^2_{H^1(I_k)}, \ \forall y^h_{m_k} \in Y^h_{m_k}. \tag{37}$$

Lemma 3. *It holds*

$$\left(y^h_{m_k},\Pi^*_h v^h_{m_k}\right)_{I_k} = \left(v^h_{m_k},\Pi^*_h y^h_{m_k}\right)_{I_k}, \ \forall y^h_{m_k}, v^h_{m_k} \in Y^h_{m_k}. \tag{38}$$

$$A_{m_k}\left(y^h_{m_k},\Pi^*_h v^h_{m_k}\right) = A_{m_k}\left(v^h_{m_k},\Pi^*_h y^h_{m_k}\right), \ \forall y^h_{m_k}, v^h_{m_k} \in Y^h_{m_k}. \tag{39}$$

Set $\left|\left|\left|y^h_{m_k}\right|\right|\right| = \left(y^h_{m_k},\Pi^*_h y^h_{m_k}\right)^{1/2}_{L^2(I_k)}$, *then* $|||\cdot|||$ *is equivalent to* $\|\cdot\|_{I_k}$ *on* $Y^h_{m_k}$, *that is*

$$\left\|y^h_{m_k}\right\|_{L^2(I_k)} \lesssim \left|\left|\left|y^h_{m_k}\right|\right|\right| \lesssim \left\|y^h_{m_k}\right\|_{L^2(I_k)}, \ \forall y^h_{m_k} \in Y^h_{m_k}. \tag{40}$$

Lemma 4. *Let* $\bar{y}_{m_k} \in H^2(I_k)$ *be the solution of Equation* (23) *and* $\bar{y}^h_{m_k} \in Y^h_{m_k}$ *be the solution of Equation* (28); *then, the following estimate holds:*

$$\left|\bar{y}_{m_k} - \bar{y}^h_{m_k}\right|_{H^1(I_k)} \lesssim h|\bar{y}_{m_k}|_{H^2(I_k)}. \tag{41}$$

The proof refers to [16].

Lemma 5 ([58])**.** *Let* $\bar{y}^h_{m_k} \in Y^h_{m_k}$ *be the solution of Equation* (28), *and* $\bar{y}_{m_k}$ *be the solution of Equation* (23) *with* $\bar{y}_{m_k} \in Y_{m_k} \cap H^2(I_k)$, *and* $\bar{y}_{m_k} \in H^2(I_k)$, $f_{m_k} \in H^1(I_k)$; *then, the following estimate holds:*

$$\left\|\bar{y}_{m_k} - \bar{y}^h_{m_k}\right\|_{L^2(I_k)} \lesssim h^2\left(\|\bar{y}_{m_k}\|_{H^2(I_k)} + \|f_{m_k}\|_{H^1(I_k)}\right). \tag{42}$$

The proof refers to Theorem 3.5 *in [58].*

Remark 2. *Similarly, for* $\bar{p}^h_{m_k} \in Y^h_{m_k}$ *and* $\bar{p}_{m_k} \in Y_{m_k} \cap H^2(I_k)$ *as the solution of corresponding adjoint state equation of* (28) *and* (23), *respectively, and* $y_{d_{m_k}} \in H^1(I_k)$, *it holds*

$$\left\|\bar{p}_{m_k} - \bar{p}^h_{m_k}\right\|_{L^2(I_k)} \lesssim h^2\left(\|\bar{p}_{m_k}\|_{H^2(I_k)} + \left\|\bar{y}_{m_k} - y_{d_{m_k}}\right\|_{H^1(I_k)}\right). \tag{43}$$

Lemma 6 ([7])**.** *Let* $(\bar{y}_{m_k}, \bar{u}_{m_k}, \bar{p}_{m_k}) \in (Y_{m_k} \times U_{adm_k} \times V_{m_k})$ *be the solutions of* (24), $(\bar{y}_h,\ \bar{u}_h,\ \bar{p}_h) \in \left(Y^h_{m_k} \times U_{adm_k} \times Y^h_{m_k}\right)$ *be the solutions of* (32) *and* $\left(\bar{y}^h_{m_k},\ \bar{p}^h_{m_k}\right) \in \left(Y^h_{m_k} \times Y^h_{m_k}\right)$ *be the solution of* (30), *respectively. Then, the following estimates hold*

$$\left\langle R_1(\theta_k)\left(\frac{d\bar{p}_h}{dr} - \frac{d\bar{p}_{m_k}}{dr}\right), \bar{u}_{m_k} - \bar{u}_h\right\rangle_{\Gamma_{1_k}} \lesssim -\left\|\bar{y}^h_{m_k} - \bar{y}_h\right\|^2_{L^2(I_k)} + \left\|\bar{y}^h_{m_k} - \bar{y}_{m_k}\right\|^2_{L^2(I_k)}, \tag{44}$$

$$\begin{aligned} &\alpha c_0\|\bar{u}_{m_k} - \bar{u}_h\|^2_{L^2\left(\Gamma_{1_k}\right)} + \left\|\bar{y}^h_{m_k} - \bar{y}_h\right\|^2_{L^2(I_k)} \\ \lesssim\ &\|\bar{u}_{m_k} - \bar{u}_h\|_{L^2\left(\Gamma_{1_k}\right)}\left\|\frac{d\bar{p}_{m_k}}{dr} - \frac{d\bar{p}^h_{m_k}}{dr}\right\|_{L^2\left(\Gamma_{1_k}\right)} + \left\|\bar{y}_{m_k} - \bar{y}^h_{m_k}\right\|^2_{L^2(I_k)}, \end{aligned} \tag{45}$$

where $c_0 = \min\limits_{k=1,2,3,\ldots,L} \sqrt{\left(R'_1(\theta_k)\right)^2 + R^2_1(\theta_k)}$.

Proof. We first show (44). Using $\Pi_h^*\left(\bar{p}_{m_k}^h\right)$ and $\Pi_h^*(\bar{p}_h)$ time the state equations about $\bar{y}_{m_k}^h$ and $\bar{y}_h$, $\Pi_h^*\left(\bar{y}_{m_k}^h\right)$ and $\Pi_h^*(\bar{y}_h)$ time the adjoint state equations about $\bar{p}_{m_k}^h$ and $\bar{p}_h$ and integrate on interval I_k, respectively, we can obtion that

$$\begin{aligned} A_{m_k}\left(\bar{y}_{m_k}^h,\Pi_h^*\left(\bar{p}_{m_k}^h\right)\right) &= \left(f_{m_k},\Pi_h^*\left(\bar{p}_{m_k}^h\right)\right)_{I_k}, \\ A_{m_k}\left(\bar{p}_{m_k}^h,\Pi_h^*\left(\bar{y}_{m_k}^h\right)\right) &= \left(\bar{y}_{m_k}-y_{d_{m_k}},\Pi_h^*\left(\bar{y}_{m_k}^h\right)\right)_{I_k} - \left\langle \left(\frac{d\bar{p}_{m_k}^h}{dr}\right),\bar{u}_{m_k}R_1(\theta_k)\right\rangle_{\Gamma_{1_k}}, \end{aligned} \tag{46}$$

$$\begin{aligned} A_{m_k}\left(\bar{y}_{m_k}^h,\Pi_h^*(\bar{p}_h)\right) &= \left(f_{m_k},\Pi_h^*(\bar{p}_h)\right)_{I_k}, \\ A_{m_k}\left(\bar{p}_h,\Pi_h^*\left(\bar{y}_{m_k}^h\right)\right) &= \left(\bar{y}_h-y_{d_{m_k}},\Pi_h^*\left(\bar{y}_{m_k}^h\right)\right)_{I_k} - \left\langle \left(\frac{d\bar{p}_h}{dr}\right),\bar{u}_{m_k}R_1(\theta_k)\right\rangle_{\Gamma_{1_k}}, \end{aligned} \tag{47}$$

$$\begin{aligned} A_{m_k}\left(\bar{y}_h,\Pi_h^*\left(\bar{p}_{m_k}^h\right)\right) &= \left(f_{m_k},\Pi_h^*\left(\bar{p}_{m_k}^h\right)\right)_{I_k}, \\ A_{m_k}\left(\bar{p}_{m_k}^h,\Pi_h^*(\bar{y}_h)\right) &= \left(\bar{y}_{m_k}-y_{d_{m_k}},\Pi_h^*(\bar{y}_h)\right)_{I_k} - \left\langle \left(\frac{d\bar{p}_{m_k}^h}{dr}\right),\bar{u}_hR_1(\theta_k)\right\rangle_{\Gamma_{1_k}}, \end{aligned} \tag{48}$$

$$\begin{aligned} A_{m_k}\left(\bar{y}_h,\Pi_h^*(\bar{p}_h)\right) &= \left(f_{m_k},\Pi_h^*(\bar{p}_h)\right)_{I_k}, \\ A_{m_k}\left(\bar{p}_h,\Pi_h^*(\bar{y}_h)\right) &= \left(\bar{y}_h-y_{d_{m_k}},\Pi_h^*(\bar{y}_h)\right)_{I_k} - \left\langle \left(\frac{d\bar{p}_h}{dr}\right),\bar{u}_hR_1(\theta_k)\right\rangle_{\Gamma_{1_k}}. \end{aligned} \tag{49}$$

From Lemma 3 and the above four formulas, it can be deduced that

$$\begin{aligned} \left(f_{m_k},\Pi_h^*\left(\bar{p}_{m_k}^h\right)\right)_{I_k} - \left(\bar{y}_{m_k}-y_{d_{m_k}},\Pi_h^*\left(\bar{y}_{m_k}^h\right)\right)_{I_k} + \left\langle \left(\frac{d\bar{p}_{m_k}^h}{dr}\right),\bar{u}_{m_k}R_1(\theta_k)\right\rangle_{\Gamma_{1_k}} &= 0, \\ \left(f_{m_k},\Pi_h^*(\bar{p}_h)\right)_{I_k} - \left(\bar{y}_h-y_{d_{m_k}},\Pi_h^*\left(\bar{y}_{m_k}^h\right)\right)_{I_k} + \left\langle \left(\frac{d\bar{p}_h}{dr}\right),\bar{u}_{m_k}R_1(\theta_k)\right\rangle_{\Gamma_{1_k}} &= 0, \end{aligned} \tag{50}$$

$$\begin{aligned} \left(f_{m_k},\Pi_h^*\left(\bar{p}_{m_k}^h\right)\right)_{I_k} - \left(\bar{y}_{m_k}-y_{d_{m_k}},\Pi_h^*(\bar{y}_h)\right)_{I_k} + \left\langle \left(\frac{d\bar{p}_{m_k}^h}{dr}\right),\bar{u}_hR_1(\theta_k)\right\rangle_{\Gamma_{1_k}} &= 0, \\ \left(f_{m_k},\Pi_h^*(\bar{p}_h)\right)_{I_k} - \left(\bar{y}_h-y_{d_{m_k}},\Pi_h^*(\bar{y}_h)\right)_{I_k} + \left\langle \left(\frac{d\bar{p}_h}{dr}\right),\bar{u}_hR_1(\theta_k)\right\rangle_{\Gamma_{1_k}} &= 0. \end{aligned} \tag{51}$$

Then, from the above two formulas, we have

$$\begin{aligned} \left(f_{m_k},\Pi_h^*\left(\bar{p}_{m_k}^h-\bar{p}_h\right)\right)_{I_k} - \left(\bar{y}_{m_k}-\bar{y}_h,\Pi_h^*\left(\bar{y}_{m_k}^h\right)\right)_{I_k} + \left\langle \left(\frac{d\bar{p}_{m_k}^h}{dr}-\frac{d\bar{p}_h}{dr}\right),\bar{u}_{m_k}R_1(\theta_k)\right\rangle_{\Gamma_{1_k}} &= 0, \\ \left(f_{m_k},\Pi_h^*\left(\bar{p}_{m_k}^h-\bar{p}_h\right)\right)_{I_k} - \left(\bar{y}_{m_k}-\bar{y}_h,\Pi_h^*(\bar{y}_h)\right)_{I_k} + \left\langle \left(\frac{d\bar{p}_{m_k}^h}{dr}-\frac{d\bar{p}_h}{dr}\right),\bar{u}_hR_1(\theta_k)\right\rangle_{\Gamma_{1_k}} &= 0. \end{aligned} \tag{52}$$

Subtracting the two equations in (52), we can derive that

$$\left(\bar{y}_{m_k}-\bar{y}_h,\Pi_h^*\left(\bar{y}_{m_k}^h-\bar{y}_h\right)\right)_{I_k} + \left\langle \left(\frac{d\bar{p}_h}{dr}-\frac{d\bar{p}_{m_k}^h}{dr}\right),(\bar{u}_{m_k}-\bar{u}_h)R_1(\theta_k)\right\rangle_{\Gamma_{1_k}} = 0. \tag{53}$$

Hence, using Young's inequality and the definition of $|||\cdot|||$, we have

$$\begin{aligned}
&\left\langle R_1(\theta_k)\left(\frac{d\bar{p}_h}{dr}-\frac{d\bar{p}^h_{m_k}}{dr}\right),\bar{u}_{m_k}-\bar{u}_h\right\rangle_{\Gamma_{1_k}}\\
&=\left(\bar{y}_h-\bar{y}_{m_k},\Pi_h^*\left(\bar{y}^h_{m_k}-\bar{y}_h\right)\right)_{I_k}\\
&=\left(\bar{y}_h-\bar{y}^h_{m_k},\Pi_h^*\left(\bar{y}^h_{m_k}-\bar{y}_h\right)\right)_{I_k}+\left(\bar{y}^h_{m_k}-\bar{y}_{m_k},\Pi_h^*\left(\bar{y}^h_{m_k}-\bar{y}_h\right)\right)_{I_k}\\
&\leq \varepsilon\cdot c\left\|\Pi_h^*\left(\bar{y}^h_{m_k}-\bar{y}_h\right)\right\|^2_{L^2(I_k)}+C(\varepsilon)\left\|\bar{y}_{m_k}-\bar{y}^h_{m_k}\right\|^2_{L^2(I_k)}-\left|\left|\left|\bar{y}_h-\bar{y}^h_{m_k}\right|\right|\right|^2\\
&\leq \varepsilon\cdot c\left\|\Pi_h^*\left(\bar{y}^h_{m_k}-\bar{y}_h\right)\right\|^2_{L^2(I_k)}+C(\varepsilon)\left\|\bar{y}_{m_k}-\bar{y}^h_{m_k}\right\|^2_{L^2(I_k)}-\left\|\bar{y}_h-\bar{y}^h_{m_k}\right\|^2_{L^2(I_k)},
\end{aligned}\tag{54}$$

where $c > 0$ is a bounded constant. Let $\varepsilon \to 0$, we complete the proof of (44).

Next, we show (45). Let $u_{m_k} = \bar{u}_h$ in (24c) and $u_h = \bar{u}_{m_k}$ in (32c), respectively. Then, adding the two inequalities, we obtain

$$\alpha\sqrt{\left(R_1'(\theta_k)\right)^2+R_1^2(\theta_k)}\left\|\bar{u}_{m_k}-\bar{u}_h\right\|^2_{L^2\left(\Gamma_{1_k}\right)}\leq\left\langle R_1(\theta_k)\left(\frac{d\bar{p}_h}{dr}-\frac{d\bar{p}_{m_k}}{dr}\right),\bar{u}_{m_k}-\bar{u}_h\right\rangle_{\Gamma_{1_k}}.\tag{55}$$

According to (44) and Cauchy inequality, we get

$$\begin{aligned}
&\left\langle R_1(\theta_k)\left(\frac{d\bar{p}_h}{dr}-\frac{d\bar{p}_{m_k}}{dr}\right),\bar{u}_{m_k}-\bar{u}_h\right\rangle_{\Gamma_{1_k}}\\
&=\left\langle R_1(\theta_k)\left(\frac{d\bar{p}_h}{dr}-\frac{d\bar{p}^h_{m_k}}{dr}\right),\bar{u}_{m_k}-\bar{u}_h\right\rangle_{\Gamma_{1_k}}+\left\langle R_1(\theta_k)\left(\frac{d\bar{p}^h_{m_k}}{dr}-\frac{d\bar{p}_{m_k}}{dr}\right),\bar{u}_{m_k}-\bar{u}_h\right\rangle_{\Gamma_{1_k}}\\
&\lesssim\left\|\bar{y}_{m_k}-\bar{y}^h_{m_k}\right\|^2_{L^2(I_k)}-\left\|\bar{y}_h-\bar{y}^h_{m_k}\right\|^2_{L^2(I_k)}+\left\|\bar{u}_{m_k}-\bar{u}_h\right\|_{L^2\left(\Gamma_{1_k}\right)}\left\|\frac{d\bar{p}^h_{m_k}}{dr}-\frac{d\bar{p}_{m_k}}{dr}\right\|_{L^2\left(\Gamma_{1_k}\right)}.
\end{aligned}\tag{56}$$

Combining (55) and (56), we complete the proof. □

Lemma 7. *Let the conditions of Lemma 6 be fulfilled, also, $\bar{p}_{m_k} \in H^{2+\beta}(I_k)$, $\frac{1}{2} < \beta < 1$. Then, there holds*

$$\left\|\frac{d\bar{p}_{m_k}}{dr}-\frac{d\bar{p}^h_{m_k}}{dr}\right\|_{L^2\left(\Gamma_{1_k}\right)}\lesssim h^2.$$

Proof. For any fixed $k = 1,2,3,\ldots,M$, $R_1(\theta_k)$ is a fixed point. From the Sobolev embedding theorem [16]: $H^{2+\beta}(I_k) \hookrightarrow C^2(\bar{I}_k)$ for $\frac{1}{2} < \beta < 1$. Then, using quadratic interpolation scheme, we have

$$\frac{d\bar{p}^h_{m_k}}{dr}(R_1(\theta_k))=-\frac{3\bar{p}_{m_k}(R_1(\theta_k))-4\bar{p}_{m_k}(R_1(\theta_k)+h)+\bar{p}_{m_k}(R_1(\theta_k)+2h)}{2h},$$

by the Taylor expansion,

$$\left\|\frac{d\bar{p}_{m_k}}{dr}-\frac{d\bar{p}^h_{m_k}}{dr}\right\|_{L^2\left(\Gamma_{1_k}\right)}=\left|\frac{d\bar{p}_{m_k}}{dr}(R_1(\theta_k))-\frac{d\bar{p}^h_{m_k}}{dr}(R_1(\theta_k))\right|\lesssim h^2.$$

□

Remark 3. *Based on the regularity of the right-hand side of the adjoint Equation (24b), we assume that $\bar{p}_{m_k} \in H^{2+\beta}(I_k)$, $\frac{1}{2} < \beta < 1$ is reasonable.*

Proof. Since $f_{m_k} \in H^1(I_k)$, we have $\bar{y}_{m_k} \in H^2(I_k)$. From $\bar{y}_{m_k} - y_{d_{m_k}} \in H^1(I_k)$ and elliptic regularity, it implies that $\bar{p} \in H^3(I) \cap V_{m_k} \subset H^{2+\beta}(I_k) \cap V_{m_k}$, $\frac{1}{2} < \beta < 1$, using the trace theorem with this together, and the relation of $\bar{u}_{m_k}$ and $\bar{p}_{m_k}$, we obtain $\bar{u}_{m_k} \in H^1(I_k) \subset H^{\frac{1}{2}}(I_k)$, which combining with $f_{m_k} \in H^1(I_k)$ in turns gives $\bar{y}_{m_k} \in H^2(I_k) \cap Y_{m_k}$. □

Lemma 8. *Let $(\bar{y}_{m_k}, \bar{p}_{m_k}) \in (Y_{m_k} \times V_{m_k})$ be the solutions of (24) and $(\bar{y}_h, \text{and} \bar{p}_h) \in \left(Y^h_{m_k} \times Y^h_{m_k}\right)$ be the solution of (32), respectively. Then, there holds*

$$\|\bar{p}_{m_k} - \bar{p}_h\|_{L^2(I_k)} \lesssim \|\bar{y}_{m_k} - \bar{y}_h\|_{L^2(I_k)} + \left\|\bar{p}_{m_k} - \bar{p}^h_{m_k}\right\|_{L^2(I_k)}. \tag{57}$$

Proof. Combined with (30b) and (32b), then

$$A_{m_k}\left(\bar{p}^h_{m_k} - \bar{p}_h, \Pi^*_h w\right) = (\bar{y}_{m_k} - \bar{y}_h, \Pi^*_h w)_{I_k}, \forall w \in Y^h_{m_k}. \tag{58}$$

Taking $w = \bar{p}^h_{m_k} - \bar{p}_h$ in (58) to get

$$A_{m_k}\left(\bar{p}^h_{m_k} - \bar{p}_h, \Pi^*_h(\bar{p}_{m_k} - \bar{p}_h)\right) = \left(\bar{y}_{m_k} - \bar{y}_h, \Pi^*_h\left(\bar{p}^h_{m_k} - \bar{p}_h\right)\right)_{I_k}, \forall w \in Y^h_{m_k}. \tag{59}$$

By Lemma 2 and Young's inequality,

$$A_{m_k}\left(\bar{p}^h_{m_k} - \bar{p}_h, \Pi^*_h\left(\bar{p}^h_{m_k} - \bar{p}_h\right)\right) \gtrsim \left|\bar{p}^h_{m_k} - \bar{p}_h\right|^2_{H^1(I_k)} \gtrsim \left\|\bar{p}^h_{m_k} - \bar{p}_h\right\|^2_{L^2(I_k)}, \tag{60}$$

$$\begin{aligned}\left(\bar{y}_{m_k} - \bar{y}_h, \Pi^*_h\left(\bar{p}^h_{m_k} - \bar{p}_h\right)\right)_{I_k} &\leq \frac{1}{2}\left|\left|\left|\bar{y}_{m_k} - \bar{y}_h\right|\right|\right|^2 + \frac{1}{2}\left|\left|\left|\bar{p}^h_{m_k} - \bar{p}_h\right|\right|\right|^2 \\ &\lesssim \|\bar{y}_{m_k} - \bar{y}_h\|^2_{L^2(I_k)} + \left\|\bar{p}^h_{m_k} - \bar{p}_h\right\|^2_{L^2(I_k)},\end{aligned} \tag{61}$$

which, together with the triangle inequality, leads to the estimate (57). □

Based on the above Lemmas, we can immediately obtain the following main results of optimal error estimates.

Theorem 3. *Let $(\bar{y}, \bar{p}, \bar{u}) \in (H^2(\Omega) \cap Y) \times (H^{2+\beta}(\Omega) \cap V) \times U_{ad}$ and $\left(\bar{y}_{f_h}, \bar{p}_{f_h}, \bar{u}_{f_h}\right) \in \left(H^2(Q) \cap Y^h_{f_k}\right) \times \left(H^{2+\beta}(Q) \cap Y^h_{f_k}\right) \times U^h_{ad}$, $\left(\frac{1}{2} < \beta < 1\right)$ be the solutions of the problems (P) and $\left(P_{f_h}\right)$ respectively. Then we have*

$$\left\|\bar{u} - \bar{u}_{f_h}\right\|_{L^2(\partial\Omega_1)} \lesssim M^{-\frac{1}{2}} + Mh^2, \tag{62}$$

$$\left\|\bar{y} - \bar{y}_{f_h}\right\|_{L^2(\Omega)} \lesssim M^{-\frac{1}{2}} + Mh^2, \tag{63}$$

$$\left\|\bar{p} - \bar{p}_{f_h}\right\|_{L^2(\Omega)} \lesssim M^{-\frac{1}{2}} + Mh^2. \tag{64}$$

Proof. Combined with the above Lemmas, there holds:

$$
\begin{aligned}
\left\|\bar{u}-\bar{u}_{f_h}\right\|_{L^2(\partial\Omega_1)} &\leq \left\|\bar{u}-\bar{u}_{f_\tau}\right\|_{L^2(\Gamma_1)}+\left\|\bar{u}_{f_\tau}-\bar{u}_{f_h}\right\|_{L^2(\Gamma_1)} \\
&\lesssim M^{-\frac{1}{2}}|\bar{u}|_{H^{\frac{1}{2}}(\Gamma_1)}+\sum_{|m|=0}^{M}\left\|\frac{1}{M}\sum_{k=1}^{M}(\bar{u}_{m_k}-\bar{u}_h)e^{-im\theta_k}\right\|_{L^2(\Gamma_1)} \\
&\lesssim M^{-\frac{1}{2}}+\sum_{|m|=0}^{M}\left\|\frac{1}{M}\sum_{k=1}^{M}\left(\frac{d\bar{p}_{m_k}}{dr}-\frac{d\bar{p}^h_{m_k}}{dr}\right)e^{-im\theta_k}\right\|_{L^2(\Gamma_1)} \\
&+\sum_{|m|=0}^{M}\left\|\frac{1}{M}\sum_{k=1}^{M}\left(\bar{y}_{m_k}-\bar{y}^h_{m_k}\right)e^{-im\theta_k}\right\|_{L^2(Q)} \\
&\lesssim M^{-\frac{1}{2}}+Mh^2,
\end{aligned}
\tag{65}
$$

$$
\begin{aligned}
\left\|\bar{y}-\bar{y}_{f_h}\right\|_{L^2(\Omega)} &\leq \left\|\bar{y}-\bar{y}_{f_\tau}\right\|_{L^2(Q)}+\left\|\bar{y}_{f_\tau}-\bar{y}_{f_h}\right\|_{L^2(Q)} \\
&\lesssim M^{-\frac{1}{2}}|\bar{y}|_{H^{\frac{1}{2}}(I_k)}+\sum_{|m|=0}^{M}\left\|\frac{1}{M}\sum_{k=1}^{M}(\bar{y}_{m_k}-\bar{y}_h)e^{-im\theta_k}\right\|_{L^2(Q)} \\
&\lesssim M^{-\frac{1}{2}}+\sum_{|m|=0}^{M}\left\|\frac{1}{M}\sum_{k=1}^{M}\left(\bar{y}_{m_k}-\bar{y}^h_{m_k}\right)e^{-im\theta_k}\right\|_{L^2(Q)} \\
&\lesssim M^{-\frac{1}{2}}+\frac{1}{M}\sum_{|m|=0}^{M}\sum_{k=1}^{M}h^2 \\
&\lesssim M^{-\frac{1}{2}}+Mh^2,
\end{aligned}
\tag{66}
$$

$$
\begin{aligned}
\left\|\bar{p}-\bar{p}_{f_h}\right\|_{L^2(\Omega)} &\leq \left\|\bar{p}-\bar{p}_{f_\tau}\right\|_{L^2(Q)}+\left\|\bar{p}_{f_\tau}-\bar{p}_{f_h}\right\|_{L^2(Q)} \\
&\lesssim M^{-\frac{1}{2}}|\bar{p}|_{H^{\frac{1}{2}}(I_k)}+\sum_{|m|=0}^{M}\left\|\frac{1}{M}\sum_{k=1}^{M}(\bar{p}_{m_k}-\bar{p}_h)e^{-im\theta_k}\right\|_{L^2(Q)} \\
&\lesssim M^{-\frac{1}{2}}+\sum_{|m|=0}^{M}\left\|\frac{1}{M}\sum_{k=1}^{M}(\bar{y}_{m_k}-\bar{y}_h)e^{-im\theta_k}\right\|_{L^2(Q)}+\sum_{|m|=0}^{M}\left\|\frac{1}{M}\sum_{k=1}^{M}\left(\bar{p}_{m_k}-\bar{p}^h_{m_k}\right)e^{-im\theta_k}\right\|_{L^2(Q)} \\
&\lesssim M^{-\frac{1}{2}}+\frac{1}{M}\sum_{|m|=0}^{M}\sum_{k=1}^{M}h^2+\frac{1}{M}\sum_{|m|=0}^{M}\sum_{k=1}^{M}h^2 \\
&\lesssim M^{-\frac{1}{2}}+Mh^2,
\end{aligned}
\tag{67}
$$

where M can be controlled artificially so as not to affect the error order. □

5. Numerical Experiments

In this section, numerical experiments are presented for the Fourier finite volume element method to confirm the theoretical results. The numbers of grid points are $N+1$ and L in the radial and azimuthal direction, respectively. So the total number of computational nodes is $NL=(N+1)\times L$. Here, fixed $M=L=64$. In the numerical experiments, L^2 and L^∞ norms are defined as follows (see [59]):

$$
E_2=\sqrt{\frac{1}{NL}\sum_{i=1}^{NL}\left|\left(u_{f_h}\right)_i-(u_{exa})_i\right|^2},\ E_2^b=\sqrt{\frac{1}{L}\sum_{i=1}^{L}\left|\left(u_{f_h}\right)_i-(u_{exa})_i\right|^2},
$$

$$E_{\infty} = \max\{\left|\left(u_{f_h}\right)_i - (u_{exa})_i\right|, i = 1, 2, \ldots, NL\},$$
$$E^b_{\infty} = \max\{\left|\left(u_{f_h}\right)_i - (u_{exa})_i\right|, i = 1, 2, \ldots, L\}.$$

For the error functional, the experimental order of convergence is defined by

$$\text{Order} = \frac{\log E(h_1) - \log E(h_2)}{\log h_1 - \log h_2}.$$

The Algorithm 1 is as follows:

Algorithm 1: Algorithm for the solution of optimal control problem.

1: Provide an initial u_0 of the control function u;
2: Solve the equation of state in y using the above u_0;
3: Solve the adjoint equation for p, being known y and y_d;
4: Compute the new control function u_1 using the above p;
5: If $|u_0 - u_1| \leq 1.0 \times 10^{-10}$, setting $u_{f_h} = u_1$, else setting $u_0 = u_1$ and goto step 2;
6: Take the last computed control function u_{f_h} to compute the y_{f_h} and p_{f_h}.

5.1. Experiment 1

The first experiment is an unconstrained problem defined on the domain $\Omega = \{1 < x_1^2 + x_2^2 < 2\}$ with

$$f = \left(\frac{\pi^2}{16} + \frac{1}{r^2}\right) \sin\left(\frac{\pi}{4} r\right) \sin\theta - \frac{\pi}{4r} \cos\left(\frac{\pi}{4} r\right) \sin\theta,$$
$$y_d = \sin\left(\frac{\pi}{4} r\right) \sin\theta - \sqrt{2}\alpha \left[\left(\frac{\pi}{4} - \frac{1}{\pi r^2}\right) \cos\left(\frac{\pi}{2} r\right) \sin\theta - \frac{1}{2r} \sin\left(\frac{\pi}{4} r\right) \sin\theta\right].$$

The optimal solution is given by

$$y = \sin\left(\frac{\pi}{4} r\right) \sin\theta,$$
$$p = \alpha \frac{\sqrt{2}}{\pi} \cos\left(\frac{\pi}{2} r\right) \sin\theta,$$
$$u = \frac{\sqrt{2}}{2} \sin\theta,$$

where $\alpha = 1.3$ is selected.

The corresponding numerical results of grid refinement analysis for experiment 1 are presented in Table 1, which contains the error and convergence order of the control u, the state y and the adjoint state p in the sense of both L^2-norm and L^{∞}-norm. Figure 2 depicts the convergence orders by slopes. It is apparent that the second order convergence rates of u, y, p are achieved with this methods.

The numerical solution u_{f_h} versus exact solution u with $N = 64$ is shown in Figure 3a, and the error of control u is plotted in Figure 3b. Figures 4–6 show the numerical solution and the exact solution for the state and adjoint the error between them, respectively. From Figure 6, we find that both errors are of the scale of 10^{-4} at $N = 64$, which indicates that the numerical method has a good approximation.

Table 1. Error of control u, state y, and adjoint state p for experiment 1 with fixed L.

(**a**) L^2-norm

N	$\|\|u_{f_h} - u\|\|_{L^2(\partial\Omega_1)}$	Order	$\|\|y_{f_h} - y\|\|_{L^2(\Omega)}$	Order	$\|\|p_{f_h} - p\|\|_{L^2(\Omega)}$	Order
8	1.2641×10^{-2}		1.0022×10^{-2}		6.1839×10^{-3}	
16	2.9821×10^{-3}	2.12	2.3802×10^{-3}	2.11	1.4400×10^{-3}	2.15
32	7.2104×10^{-4}	2.07	5.7755×10^{-4}	2.06	3.4628×10^{-4}	2.08
64	1.7706×10^{-4}	2.04	1.4208×10^{-4}	2.03	8.4826×10^{-5}	2.04
128	4.3852×10^{-5}	2.02	3.5227×10^{-5}	2.02	2.0988×10^{-5}	2.02
256	1.0914×10^{-5}	2.01	8.7656×10^{-6}	2.01	5.2182×10^{-6}	2.01
512	2.7245×10^{-6}	2.00	2.1842×10^{-6}	2.01	1.3001×10^{-6}	2.01

(**b**) L^∞-norm

N	$\|\|u_{f_h} - u\|\|_{L^\infty(\partial\Omega_1)}$	Order	$\|\|y_{f_h} - y\|\|_{L^\infty(\Omega)}$	Order	$\|\|p_{f_h} - p\|\|_{L^\infty(\Omega)}$	Order
8	1.7877×10^{-2}		1.6492×10^{-2}		1.1750×10^{-2}	
16	4.2173×10^{-3}	2.12	4.0400×10^{-3}	2.04	2.8245×10^{-3}	2.08
32	1.0197×10^{-3}	2.07	9.9734×10^{-4}	2.03	6.9079×10^{-4}	2.04
64	2.5040×10^{-4}	2.04	2.4758×10^{-4}	2.01	1.7070×10^{-4}	2.02
128	6.2016×10^{-5}	2.02	6.1673×10^{-5}	2.01	4.2423×10^{-5}	2.01
256	1.5435×10^{-5}	2.01	1.5383×10^{-5}	2.00	1.0571×10^{-5}	2.01
512	3.8531×10^{-6}	2.00	3.8379×10^{-6}	2.00	2.6369×10^{-6}	2.00

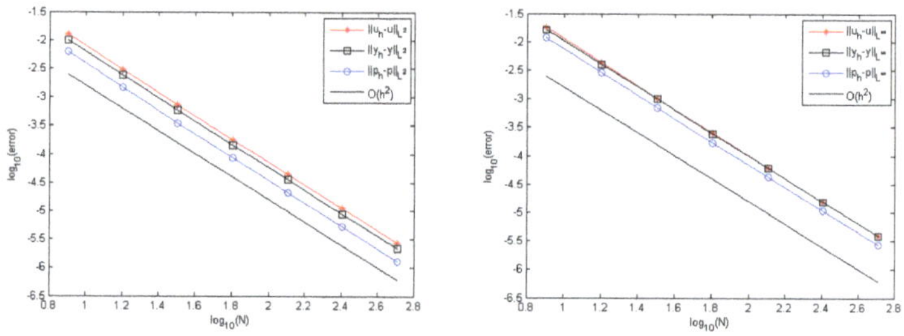

Figure 2. Convergence orders of $u_{f_h} - u$, $y_{f_h} - y$, and $p_{f_h} - p$ in different norms.

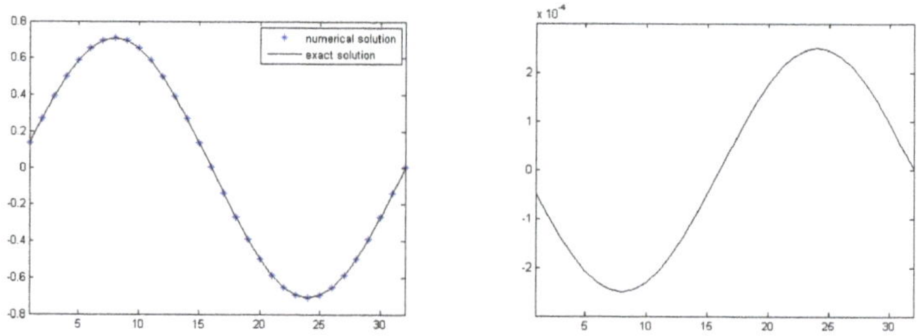

(**a**) (**b**)

Figure 3. The numerical solution u_{f_h} versus exact solution u (**a**), error $u_{f_h} - u$ (**b**) for experiment 1 with $N = 64$.

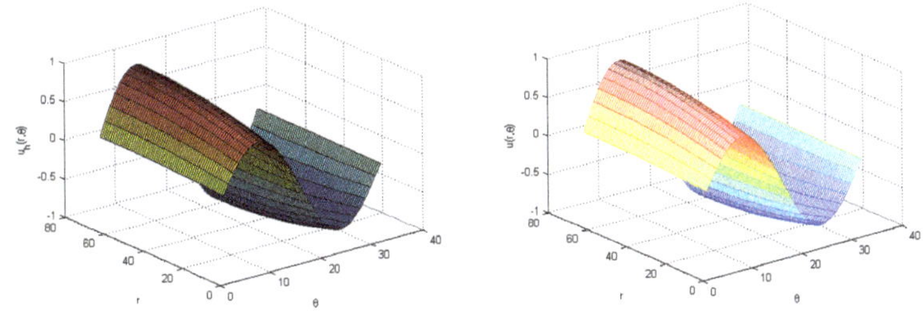

(a) (b)

Figure 4. Numerical solution y_{f_h} (**a**) and exact solution y (**b**) with $N = 64$.

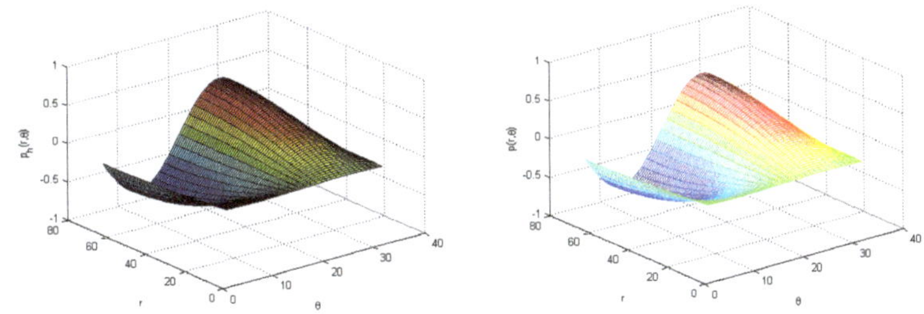

(a) (b)

Figure 5. Numerical solution p_{f_h} (**a**) and exact solution p (**b**) with $N = 64$.

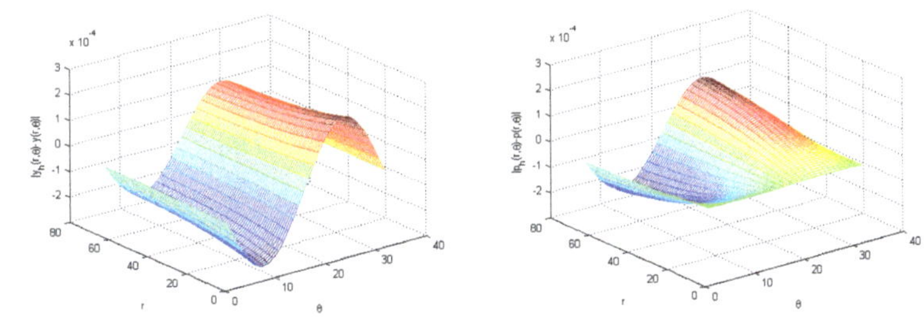

(a) (b)

Figure 6. Error for state y (**a**) and adjoint state p (**b**) with $N = 64$.

5.2. Experiment 2

The second experiment is an constrained control problem defined on the $\Omega = \{1 < x_1^2 + x_2^2 < 2\}$ with

$$f = \frac{1}{\alpha}\left(\frac{5}{r^2} - 3\right)\max(0, \sin\theta),$$
$$y_d = \left(\frac{1}{\alpha}r^2 - \frac{4}{\alpha}r - \frac{3}{r^2} + \frac{5}{\alpha} + 3\right)\max(0, \sin\theta),$$

the optimal solution is given by

$$y = \frac{1}{\alpha}\left(r^2 - 4r + 5\right)\max(0, \sin\theta),$$
$$p = \left(r^2 - 4r + 3\right)\max(0, \sin\theta),$$
$$u = \frac{2}{\alpha}\max(0, \sin\theta),$$

where $\alpha = 1.3$ is selected.

Table 2 presents the error and convergence order of the control u, the state y, and the adjoint state p in the sense of both L^2-norm and L^∞-norm, the corresponding profiles of their convergence order are shown in Figure 7. From them, we derive that the convergence order of these three variables are second.

Table 2. Error of control u, state y and adjoint state p for experiment 2 with fixed L.

(a) L^2-norm						
N	$\|\|u_{f_h} - u\|\|_{L^2(\partial\Omega_1)}$	Order	$\|\|y_{f_h} - y\|\|_{L^2(\Omega)}$	Order	$\|\|p_{f_h} - p\|\|_{L^2(\Omega)}$	Order
8	1.8638×10^{-3}		7.5762×10^{-4}		1.4328×10^{-3}	
16	4.6715×10^{-4}	1.99	2.0419×10^{-4}	1.86	3.4342×10^{-4}	2.09
32	1.1707×10^{-4}	2.00	5.2882×10^{-5}	1.93	8.4040×10^{-5}	2.04
64	2.9414×10^{-5}	1.99	1.3358×10^{-5}	1.98	2.0831×10^{-5}	2.02
128	7.5096×10^{-6}	1.96	3.2515×10^{-6}	2.05	5.2401×10^{-6}	1.99
256	2.0341×10^{-6}	1.85	7.1071×10^{-7}	2.29	1.3680×10^{-6}	1.92

(b) L^∞-norm						
N	$\|\|u_{f_h} - u\|\|_{L^\infty(\partial\Omega_1)}$	Order	$\|\|y_{f_h} - y\|\|_{L^\infty(\Omega)}$	Order	$\|\|p_{f_h} - p\|\|_{L^\infty(\Omega)}$	Order
8	3.7278×10^{-3}		2.9252×10^{-3}		4.4435×10^{-3}	
16	9.3417×10^{-4}	2.00	8.2853×10^{-4}	1.77	1.1098×10^{-3}	2.00
32	2.3401×10^{-4}	2.00	2.2003×10^{-4}	1.88	2.7740×10^{-4}	2.00
64	5.8703×10^{-5}	1.99	5.6482×10^{-5}	1.95	6.9430×10^{-5}	2.00
128	1.4881×10^{-5}	1.97	1.4089×10^{-5}	2.00	1.7464×10^{-5}	1.99
256	3.9240×10^{-6}	1.90	3.3027×10^{-6}	2.13	4.4741×10^{-6}	1.95

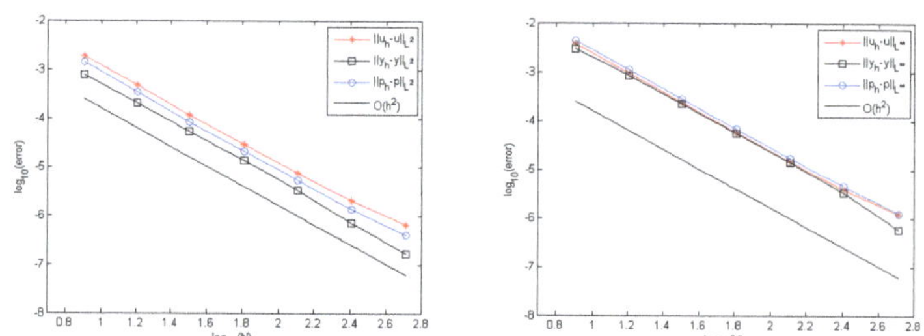

Figure 7. Convergence orders of $u_{f_h} - u$, $y_{f_h} - y$, and $p_{f_h} - p$ in different norms.

Figure 8a,c describe the profile of the exact and numerical solution of control u, while Figure 8b,d display its numerical error with $N = 64$ and $N = 128$, respectively. From this figure, we can also observe that the convergence order is second. The numerical solution and the exact solution of the state and adjoint are presented in Figures 9–11 and error between them is showed in Figure 11. Figure 12 depicts the continuous Dirichlet boundary control u and discrete Dirichlet boundary control u_{f_h} together with their active sets, it is clear to see that the discrete active set is approximate to active set. These numerical results demonstrate the efficiency of our proposed method.

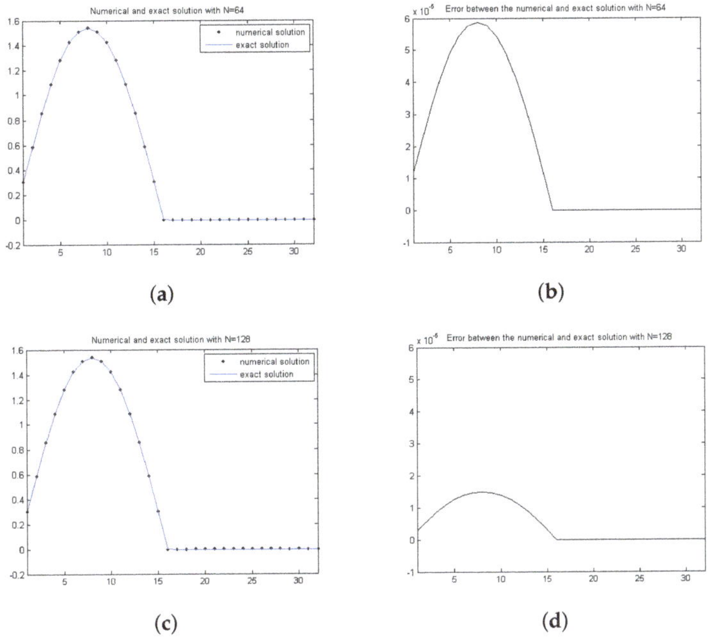

Figure 8. The numerical solution u_{f_h} versus exact solution u (**a**,**c**), error $u_{f_h} - u$ (**b**,**d**) for experiment 2.

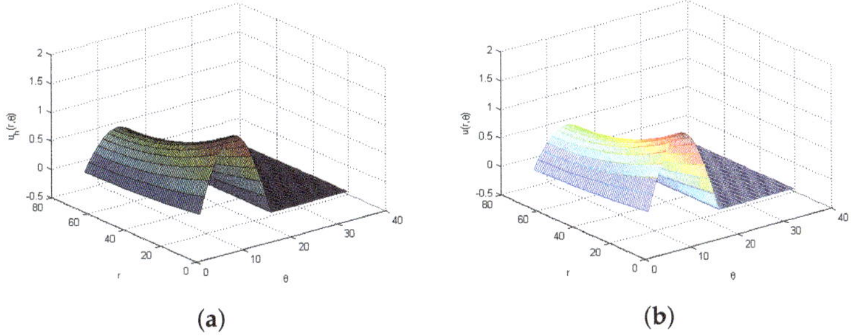

Figure 9. Numerical solution y_{f_h} (**a**) and exact solution y (**b**) with $N = 64$.

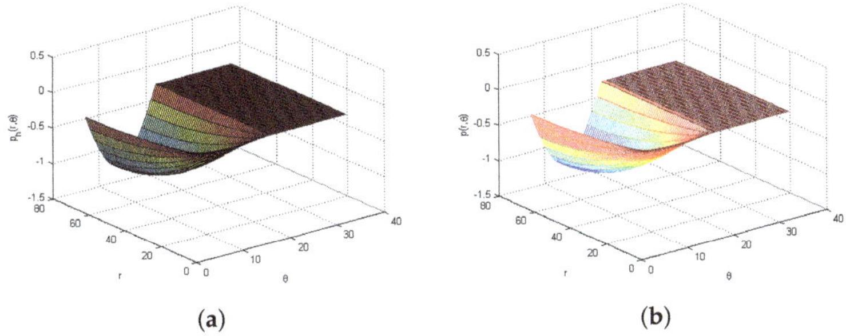

Figure 10. Numerical solution p_{f_h} (**a**) and exact solution p (**b**) with $N = 64$.

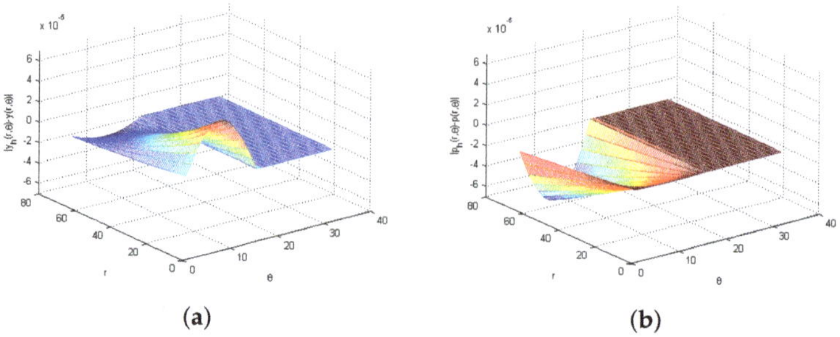

Figure 11. Error for state y (**a**) and adjoint state p (**b**) with $N = 64$.

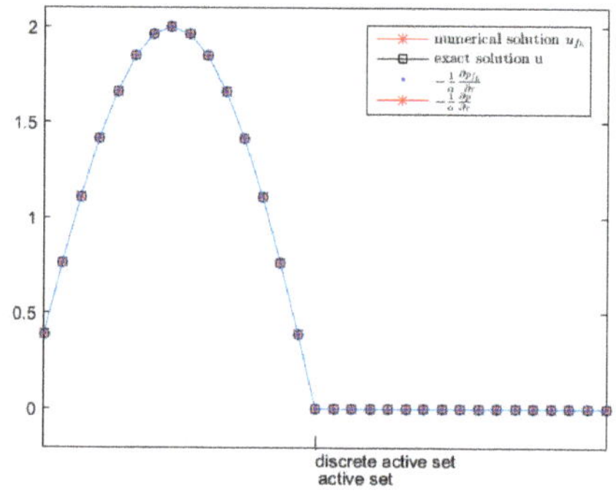

Figure 12. Discrete active set and active set of Dirichlet boundary control u.

6. Concluding Remarks

This research explored an optimal control problem on a complex connected domain governed by elliptic PDEs with Dirichlet boundary conditions. First, the optimality system for the optimal control problem is determined. Then, using the Fourier finite volume element approach to convert this problem into polar coordinates and discretize the optimal control problem. Next, the convergence order of the Dirichlet boundary control, the state, and the adjoint state are proven. This error estimate contains two components: the Fourier truncation error and the one-dimensional finite volume element error. Finally, numerical experiments are shown to back up the theoretical findings.

Author Contributions: Conceptualization, L.X.; Methodology, Z.Z.; Formal analysis, M.S.; Investigation, M.S.; Data curation, L.X.; Supervision, Z.Z. All authors have read and agreed to the published version of the manuscript.

Funding: This work was funded by the National Natural Science Foundation of China grant number 11971241, the first author also funded by Postgraduate Research and Practice Innovation Program in Jiangsu Province grant number KYCX21-1317.

Data Availability Statement: The data used to support the findings of this study are available from the corresponding author upon request.

Conflicts of Interest: The authors declare no conflict of interest.

References

1. Han, Q.; Lin, F. *Elliptic Partial Differential Equations*; American Mathematical Soc.: Providence, RI, USA, 2011; Volume 1.
2. Nirenberg, L. On elliptic partial differential equations. In *Il Principio di Minimo e sue Applicazioni alle Equazioni Funzionali*; Springer: Berlin/Heidelberg, Germany, 2011; pp. 1–48.

3. Boureghda, A. Solution of an ice melting problem using a fixed domain method with a moving boundary. *Bull. Math. Soc. Sci. Math. Roum.* **2019**, *62*, 341–353.
4. Gefen, A.; Weihs, D. *Computer Methods in Biomechanics and Biomedical Engineering: Proceedings of the 14th International Symposium CMBBE, Tel Aviv, Israel, 2016*; Springer: Cham, Switzerland, 2018. [CrossRef]
5. Tröltzsch, F. *Optimal Control of Partial Differential Equations: Theory, Methods, and Applications*; American Mathematical Soc.: Providence, RI, USA, 2010; Volume 112.
6. Lions, J.L. *Optimal Control of Systems Governed by Partial Differential Equations*; Springer: Berlin/Heidelberg, Germany, 1971.
7. Hinze, M.; Pinnau, R.; Ulbrich, M.; Ulbrich, S. *Optimization with PDE Constraints*; Springer: Berlin/Heidelberg, Germany, 2008; Volume 23.
8. Zamani, N.; Chuang, J. Optimal control of current in a cathodic protection system: A numerical investigation. *Optim. Control Appl. Methods* **1987**, *8*, 339–350. [CrossRef]
9. Zhong, W.; Zhong, X. Elliptic partial differential equation and optimal control. *Numer. Methods Partial Differ. Equ.* **1992**, *8*, 149–169.
10. Yousept, I. Optimal control of quasilinear H(curl)-elliptic partial differential equations in magnetostatic field problems. *SIAM J. Control Optim.* **2013**, *51*, 3624–3651. [CrossRef]
11. Khursheed, A. *The Finite Element Method in Charged Particle Optics*; Springer: Boston, MA, USA, 1999.
12. French, D.A.; Thomas King, J. Approximation of an elliptic control problem by the finite element method. *Numer. Funct. Anal. Optim.* **1991**, *12*, 299–314. [CrossRef]
13. Yan, M.; Gong, W.; Yan, N. Finite element methods for elliptic optimal control problems with boundary observations. *Appl. Numer. Math.* **2015**, *90*, 190–207. [CrossRef]
14. Christof, C.; Vexler, B. New regularity results and finite element error estimates for a class of parabolic optimal control problems with pointwise state constraints. *ESAIM Control Optim. Calc. Var.* **2021**, *27*, 4. [CrossRef]
15. Liu, J.; Zhou, Z. Finite element approximation of time fractional optimal control problem with integral state constraint. *AIMS Math.* **2021**, *6*, 979–997. [CrossRef]
16. Li, R.; Chen, Z.; Wu, W. *Generalized Difference Methods for Differential Equations: Numerical Analysis of Finite Volume Methods*; CRC Press: New York, NY, USA, 2000.
17. Shen, J.; Tang, T.; Wang, L. *Spectral Methods: Algorithms, Analysis and Applications*; Springer: Berlin/Heidelberg, Germany, 2011; Volume 41.
18. Pfeiffer, H.P.; Kidder, L.E.; Scheel, M.A.; Teukolsky, S.A. A multidomain spectral method for solving elliptic equations. *Comput. Phys. Commun.* **2003**, *152*, 253–273. [CrossRef]
19. Tao, Z.Z.; Sun, B. Galerkin spectral method for elliptic optimal control problem with L^2-norm control constraint. *Discret. Contin. Dyn. Syst.-B* **2022**, *27*, 4121. [CrossRef]
20. Chen, R. On optimal boundary control of a class of system governed by parabolic partial differential equation. *Sci. China Ser. A-Math. Phys. Astron. Technol. Sci.* **1982**, *25*, 1205–1218.
21. Casas, E.; Raymond, J.P. Error estimates for the numerical approximation of Dirichlet boundary control for semilinear elliptic equations. *SIAM J. Control Optim.* **2006**, *45*, 1586–1611. [CrossRef]
22. Deckelnick, K.; Günther, A.; Hinze, M. Finite element approximation of Dirichlet boundary control for elliptic PDEs on two-and three-dimensional curved domains. *SIAM J. Control Optim.* **2009**, *48*, 2798–2819. [CrossRef]
23. Gong, W.; Yan, N. Mixed finite element method for Dirichlet boundary control problem governed by elliptic PDEs. *SIAM J. Control Optim.* **2011**, *49*, 984–1014. [CrossRef]
24. Pfefferer, J.; Winkler, M. Finite element error estimates for normal derivatives on boundary concentrated meshes. *SIAM J. Control Optim.* **2019**, *57*, 2043–2073. [CrossRef]
25. Vexler, B. Finite element approximation of elliptic Dirichlet optimal control problems. *Numer. Funct. Anal. Optim.* **2007**, *28*, 957–973. [CrossRef]
26. May, S.; Rannacher, R.; Vexler, B. Error analysis for a finite element approximation of elliptic Dirichlet boundary control problems. *SIAM J. Control Optim.* **2013**, *51*, 2585–2611. [CrossRef]
27. Chang, L.; Gong, W.; Yan, N. Weak boundary penalization for Dirichlet boundary control problems governed by elliptic equations. *J. Math. Anal. Appl.* **2017**, *453*, 529–557. [CrossRef]
28. Hu, W.; Shen, J.; Singler, J.R.; Zhang, Y.; Zheng, X. A superconvergent hybridizable discontinuous Galerkin method for Dirichlet boundary control of elliptic PDEs. *Numer. Math.* **2020**, *144*, 375–411. [CrossRef]
29. Geveci, T. On the approximation of the solution of an optimal control problem governed by an elliptic equation. *RAIRO. Anal. Numérique* **1979**, *13*, 313–328. [CrossRef]
30. Karkulik, M. A finite element method for elliptic Dirichlet boundary control problems. *Comput. Methods Appl. Math.* **2020**, *20*, 827–843. [CrossRef]
31. Hinze, M.; Matthes, U. A note on variational discretization of elliptic Neumann boundary control. *Control Cybern.* **2009**, *38*, 577–591.
32. Casas, E.; Dhamo, V. Error estimates for the numerical approximation of Neumann control problems governed by a class of quasilinear elliptic equations. *Comput. Optim. Appl.* **2012**, *52*, 719–756. [CrossRef]
33. Gunzburger, M.D.; Lee, H.C.; Lee, J. Error estimates of stochastic optimal Neumann boundary control problems. *SIAM J. Numer. Anal.* **2011**, *49*, 1532–1552. [CrossRef]

34. Krumbiegel, K.; Meyer, C.; Rösch, A. A priori error analysis for linear quadratic elliptic Neumann boundary control problems with control and state constraints. *SIAM J. Control Optim.* **2010**, *48*, 5108–5142. [CrossRef]
35. Brenner, S.; Oh, M.; Sung, L.Y. P1 finite element methods for an elliptic state-constrained distributed optimal control problem with Neumann boundary conditions. *Results Appl. Math.* **2020**, *8*, 100090. [CrossRef]
36. Akman, T.; Yücel, H.; Karasözen, B. A priori error analysis of the upwind symmetric interior penalty Galerkin (SIPG) method for the optimal control problems governed by unsteady convection diffusion equations. *Comput. Optim. Appl.* **2014**, *57*, 703–729. [CrossRef]
37. Luo, X.; Chen, Y.; Huang, Y.; Hou, T. Some error estimates of finite volume element method for parabolic optimal control problems. *Optim. Control Appl. Methods* **2014**, *35*, 145–165. [CrossRef]
38. Chen, Y.; Yi, N.; Liu, W. A Legendre–Galerkin spectral method for optimal control problems governed by elliptic equations. *SIAM J. Numer. Anal.* **2008**, *46*, 2254–2275. [CrossRef]
39. Ravindran, S.S. Penalization of Dirichlet Boundary Control for Nonstationary Magneto-Hydrodynamics. *SIAM J. Control Optim.* **2020**, *58*, 2354–2382. [CrossRef]
40. Chatzipantelidis, P.; Lazarov, R.; Thomée, V. Error estimates for a finite volume element method for parabolic equations in convex polygonal domains. *Numer. Methods Partial. Differ. Equ. Int. J.* **2004**, *20*, 650–674. [CrossRef]
41. Bi, C.; Ginting, V. Two-grid finite volume element method for linear and nonlinear elliptic problems. *Numer. Math.* **2007**, *108*, 177–198. [CrossRef]
42. Kumar, S.; Nataraj, N.; Pani, A.K. Finite volume element method for second order hyperbolic equations. *Int. J. Numer. Anal. Model.* **2008**, *5*, 132–151.
43. Luo, X.; Chen, Y.; Huang, Y. Some Error Estimates of Finite Volume Element Approximation for Elliptic Optimal Control Problems. *Int. J. Numer. Anal. Model.* **2013**, *10*, 697–711.
44. Cai, Z.; McCormick, S. On the accuracy of the finite volume element method for diffusion equations on composite grids. *SIAM J. Numer. Anal.* **1990**, *27*, 636–655. [CrossRef]
45. Ewing, R.; Lazarov, R.; Lin, Y. Finite volume element approximations of nonlocal reactive flows in porous media. *Numer. Methods Partial. Differ. Equ. Int. J.* **2000**, *16*, 285–311. [CrossRef]
46. Karaa, S.; Mustapha, K.; Pani, A.K. Finite volume element method for two-dimensional fractional subdiffusion problems. *IMA J. Numer. Anal.* **2017**, *37*, 945–964. [CrossRef]
47. Li, R.; Gao, Y.; Chen, J.; Zhang, L.; He, X.; Chen, Z. Discontinuous finite volume element method for a coupled Navier-Stokes-Cahn-Hilliard phase field model. *Adv. Comput. Math.* **2020**, *46*, 1–35. [CrossRef]
48. Lin, Y.; Liu, J.; Yang, M. Finite volume element methods: An overview on recent developments. *Int. J. Numer. Anal. Model. Ser. B* **2013**, *4*, 14–34.
49. Gan, X.; Xu, D. An efficient symmetric finite volume element method for second-order variable coefficient parabolic integro-differential equations. *Comput. Appl. Math.* **2020**, *39*, 1–24. [CrossRef]
50. Lou, Y.; Chen, C.; Xue, G. Two-grid finite volume element method combined with Crank-Nicolson scheme for semilinear parabolic equations. *Adv. Appl. Math. Mech.* **2021**, *13*, 892–913.
51. Ewing, R.E.; Li, Z.; Lin, T.; Lin, Y. The immersed finite volume element methods for the elliptic interface problems. *Math. Comput. Simul.* **1999**, *50*, 63–76. [CrossRef]
52. Kumar, S.; Nataraj, N.; Pani, A.K. Discontinuous Galerkin finite volume element methods for second-order linear elliptic problems. *Numer. Methods Partial. Differ. Equ. Int. J.* **2009**, *25*, 1402–1424. [CrossRef]
53. Wang, Q.; Zhang, Z.; Li, Z. A Fourier finite volume element method for solving two-dimensional quasi-geostrophic equations on a sphere. *Appl. Numer. Math.* **2013**, *71*, 1–13.
54. Lin, X.; Su, M.; Zhang, Z. Fourier Finite Volume Element Method for Two Classes of Optimal Control Problems Governed by Elliptic PDEs on Complex Connected Domain. *Numer. Funct. Anal. Optim.* **2020**, *41*, 379–412. [CrossRef]
55. Hinze, M. A variational discretization concept in control constrained optimization: The linear-quadratic case. *Comput. Optim. Appl.* **2005**, *30*, 45–61. [CrossRef]
56. Chen, R. Optimal boundary control of parabolic system on doubly connected region in new space. *Sci. China (Sci. Sin.) Ser. A* **1995**, *8*, 933–944.
57. Djellab, N. Résolution Numérique de Problèmes D'équations aux Dérivées Partielles Issus de la Biologie et la Médecine. Ph.D. Thesis, Ferhat ABBAS University, Setif, Algeria, 2022.
58. Ewing, R.E.; Lin, T.; Lin, Y. On the accuracy of the finite volume element method based on piecewise linear polynomials. *SIAM J. Numer. Anal.* **2002**, *39*, 1865–1888. [CrossRef]
59. Qiu, Z.; Zeng, Z.; Mei, H.; Li, L.; Yao, L.; Zhang, L. A Fourier–Legendre spectral element method in polar coordinates. *J. Comput. Phys.* **2012**, *231*, 666–675. [CrossRef]

mathematics MDPI

Article

Numerical Formulation of Anisotropic Elastoplastic Behavior Coupled with Damage Model in Forming Processes

Lotfi Ben Said [1,2,*], Marwa Allouch [2], Mondher Wali [2] and Fakhreddine Dammak [2]

1 Department of Mechanical Engineering, College of Engineering, Ha'il University, Ha'il City 81451, Saudi Arabia
2 Laboratory of Electrochemistry and Environment (LEE), National Engineering School of Sfax, (ENIS), University of Sfax, Sfax 3038, Tunisia
* Correspondence: bensaid_rmq@yahoo.fr

Abstract: The present paper proposes a mathematical development of the plasticity and damage approaches to simulate sheet metal forming processes. It focuses on the numerical prediction of the deformation of the sheet metal during the deep drawing process when a crack appears. Anisotropic plasticity constitutive equations are proposed. A fully implicit integration of the coupling constitutive equations is used and leads to two nonlinear local scalar equations that are solved by Newton's method. The developed model allows predicting the onset of cracks in sheet metals during cold forming operations. The numerical model is implemented in ABAQUS software using user-defined subroutines, which are VUMAT and UMAT. The accuracy of the anisotropic elastoplastic model fully coupled with ductile damage is evaluated using numerical examples.

Keywords: mathematical formulation; anisotropic plasticity; coupled plastic damage; Lemaitre damage model; metal forming

MSC: 74K20

Citation: Ben Said, L.; Allouch, M.; Wali, M.; Dammak, F. Numerical Formulation of Anisotropic Elastoplastic Behavior Coupled with Damage Model in Forming Processes. *Mathematics* **2023**, *11*, 204. https://doi.org/10.3390/math11010204

Academic Editors: Hongyu Liu and Davide Valenti

Received: 24 November 2022
Revised: 19 December 2022
Accepted: 28 December 2022
Published: 30 December 2022

Copyright: © 2022 by the authors. Licensee MDPI, Basel, Switzerland. This article is an open access article distributed under the terms and conditions of the Creative Commons Attribution (CC BY) license (https://creativecommons.org/licenses/by/4.0/).

1. Introduction

Cold forming processes are widely used in industrial engineering. They allow for the production of principally sheet workpieces of various domains such as automotive and aeronautic parts. These processes are generally characterized by a high degree of permanent deformation of the blank under the action of the punch and die. Many approaches have been developed to predict the mechanical behavior of sheet materials [1,2]. In addition, several numerical approaches have been developed and applied in the simulations of sheet metal forming processes such as deep drawing and stamping operations. The study of any sheet forming process requires a knowledge of mechanical behavior evolution until the damage of the blank [3,4]—the large irreversible deformation leading to high strain localization zones and then cracks due to the ductile damage. Indeed, the sheets present anisotropy, which must be considered in the simulations of sheet shaping [5,6]. However, one of the most used plasticity models is the classical Hill 1948 yield criterion. This criterion represents a generalized plasticity yield function for anisotropic materials when compared to J2 plasticity. In sheet metal forming, the workpiece tends to have discontinuities due to the large plastic deformations causing nucleation and the void's growth. Then, cracks propagate until failure.

A wide variety of models for the failure mechanism is discussed in the literature [7,8]. They are divided principally into two types. The first type of models are developed in the context of fracture mechanics [9]. The second type are defined by Continuum Damage Mechanics (CDM) formulation, in which the damage field is characterized by an internal variable [10]. Recently, models incorporating damage and anisotropic yield functions have attracted the attention of many authors due to the high demand of accurate numerical models in metal forming industries. Damage models are mainly based either on the Gurson approach [11], or on CDM [10,12], among others. These approaches were developed to accurately simulate forming processes and predict damage in sheet workpieces. For the uncoupled approach, the damage field is calculated without considering its effect on the mechanical behavior model. However, in the coupled approach, the damage affects the overall constitutive equations of mechanical fields.

The Gurson model [11] is based on the localization of deformation in a specific necking zone. The constitutive relation related to the Gurson theory consists of micro structural criterion in porous materials. The variation of the void's volume during failure evolution is considered and added to the yield function expression by using the void density parameter. In the same context, the Gurson, Needleman, and Tvergaard (GNT) model [13,14] takes into account the effect of the void's coalescence on the acceleration of the failure process. In the literature, many researchers are interested in the analysis of the growth and coalescence of voids during ductile damage [15–18].

Furthermore, CDM describes the evolution of the damage variable from a continuum mechanics approach. The implementation of the CDM model combined with the anisotropic elastoplastic constitutive equations require the use of advanced resolution schemes. Moreover, the elastoplastic models fully coupled with CDM include the effects of isotropic/kinematic hardening. The nonlinear isotropic/kinematic hardening and the consistent elastoplastic tangent modulus were acquired by [19]. In this work, the nonlinear material behavior is the result of the plasticity and the ductile damage phenomena. Indeed, numerical integration leads to four equations, which are two scalars and two tensors. De Souza et al. [20,21] used the finite strain extensions of this model. Nonlinear kinematic hardening is taken into account; however, the resulting return mapping schemes demand the same number of equations [22]. The backward Euler scheme is used to integrate the rate of constitutive relations. The consistent tangent operator was derived using the exact linearization of the algorithm.

In the literature, many formulations of the damage dissipation potential are proposed For ductile damage [10,12]. The continuum ductile damage model of Lemaitre [23] was usually used [19,22,24]. In the same context, a damage model was proposed [25] and used as a function of the accumulated plastic strain. In this model, a general nonlinear law of damage evolution is applied. In addition, Badreddine et al. [26] and Saanouni et al. [27] have proposed a modified Lemaitre damage model. They defined a threshold on the rate of release of the strain energy density. Khelifa et al. [28] evaluated a coupling between anisotropic elastoplastic behavior with mixed nonlinear isotropic and kinematic hardening and an isotropic ductile damage. A deep drawing test shows the efficiency of this model.

This paper discusses an improved elastoplastic model that is strongly coupled to the effect of damage in the yield function and plastic potential. The plastic flow anisotropy was enhanced by using quadratic Hill 1948 criterion based on plastic strain evolution. A mathematical formulation of the plasticity fully coupled with the damage model is developed in order to study stress changes and damage during forming operations. Moreover, the fully coupled anisotropic elastoplastic/damage model presented in this paper leads to only two nonlinear local scalar equations that are solved by the using Newton method. The constitutive equations are related to anisotropic plastic formulation, taking into account the isotropic/kinematic hardening and coupled to ductile damage model. After that, a numerical simulation of the forming process is presented. The developed model is applied in the context of the deep drawing operation using ABAQUS software via VUMAT and UMAT subroutines.

2. Plasticity Coupled with Damage

In this section, a thermodynamic model is developed to correctly describe the performances of the materials in forming processes and to develop the consistent user-friendly numerical tools. In addition, numerical models are able to capture numerous phenomena that arise through plastic deformation such as anisotropic yielding, nonlinear isotropic hardening, kinematic hardening, and damage. In this context, the elastoplastic equations defined below take into account the anisotropic plasticity and the mixed isotropic/kinematic hardening and damage.

2.1. State Variables

The simplest practice used to define the thermodynamic state of the material is the use of measured variables capable at a given point to describe the state of the material and to expect its evolution. These variables are the effective state variables that define the fictitious undamaged state of the material. From a phenomenological point of view, the concept underlying the present model is related to the subsequent pairs of effective state variables:

- The effective stress tensors and elastic strain $(\tilde{\sigma}, \tilde{\varepsilon}^e)$;
- The effective isotropic hardening parameters $\left(\tilde{r}, \tilde{R}\right)$;
- The effective kinematics hardening parameters $\left(\tilde{\boldsymbol{\alpha}}, \tilde{\boldsymbol{X}}\right)$.

These variables can be expressed as follows

$$\tilde{\varepsilon}^e = \sqrt{1-d}\,\varepsilon^e,\ \tilde{\sigma} = \sigma/\sqrt{1-d} \tag{1}$$

$$\tilde{r} = \sqrt{1-d}\,r,\ \tilde{R} = R/\sqrt{1-d} \tag{2}$$

$$\tilde{\boldsymbol{\alpha}} = \sqrt{1-d}\,\boldsymbol{\alpha},\ \tilde{\boldsymbol{X}} = \boldsymbol{X}/\sqrt{1-d} \tag{3}$$

where d is the isotropic ductile damage variable, R is the drag stress in isotropic hardening, $\boldsymbol{\alpha}$ and r are internal variables corresponding to kinematic and isotropic hardening, respectively.

2.2. Fundamental Equations

In the incremental plasticity theory, the strain tensor can be expressed in the additive form of the elastic-damage ε^e and the plastic-damage ε^p

$$\varepsilon = \varepsilon^e + \varepsilon^p \tag{4}$$

The Helmholtz free energy is obtained using the following form

$$\psi(\varepsilon^e, \boldsymbol{\alpha}_k, r, d) = \psi^e(\varepsilon^e, d) + \psi^p(\boldsymbol{\alpha}_k, r, d) \tag{5}$$

In which the elastic and plastic parts are defined by

$$\begin{gathered} \psi^e(\varepsilon^e, d) = \tfrac{1-d}{2}\,\varepsilon^e : \boldsymbol{D} : \varepsilon^e, \\ \psi^p(\boldsymbol{\alpha}_k, r_k, d) = \tfrac{1-d}{2}\left(\sum_{k=1}^{N} Q_k r_k^2 + \sum_{k=1}^{M} a_k \boldsymbol{\alpha}_k : \boldsymbol{\alpha}_k\right) \end{gathered} \tag{6}$$

where N and M are the number of variables corresponding to isotropic and kinematic hardening, respectively, Q_k and a_k are material parameters, and $\boldsymbol{D}$ is the general elastic operator of the undamaged material. The associated thermodynamic variables can be formulated from the following relationships

$$\sigma = \frac{\partial \psi^e}{\partial \varepsilon^e},\ \boldsymbol{X}_k = \frac{\partial \psi^p}{\partial \boldsymbol{\alpha}_k},\ R = \frac{\partial \psi^p}{\partial r},\ Y = -\frac{\partial \psi}{\partial d} \tag{7}$$

where Y is the associated damage variable. Using Equations (6) and (7), the variables of type stress are expressed as

$$\sigma = (1-d)\boldsymbol{D} : \varepsilon^e,\ \boldsymbol{X} = \sum_{k=1}^{M} \boldsymbol{X}_k = (1-d)\sum_{k=1}^{M} a_k \boldsymbol{\alpha}_k \tag{8}$$

$$
\begin{aligned}
R &= \sum_{k=1}^{N} R_k = (1-d) \sum_{k=1}^{N} Q_k r_k, \\
Y &= \tfrac{1}{2}\boldsymbol{\varepsilon}^e : \boldsymbol{D} : \boldsymbol{\varepsilon}^e + \tfrac{1}{2}\left(\sum_{k=1}^{N} Q_k r_k^2 + \sum_{k=1}^{M} a_k \boldsymbol{\alpha}_k : \boldsymbol{\alpha}_k \right)
\end{aligned}
\tag{9}
$$

2.3. Hill Anisotropy Criterion

The Hill 1948 model is specially suggested for anisotropic sheet metal produced using the rolling process [29]. Numerous other criteria exist in the literature [3,30] to describe the anisotropic performance of sheet metal using either quadratic or non-quadratic yield functions. The Hill criterion is the most useful in the literature due to its reduced number of parameters to be determined experimentally. The quadratic Hill 1948 criterion expresses the equivalent stress with an anisotropy operator of six parameters (F, G, H, N, M and L) as

$$
\sigma_{eq}^{H}(\boldsymbol{\xi}) = \left[H(\xi_1-\xi_2)^2 + F(\xi_2-\xi_3)^2 + G(\xi_3-\xi_1)^2 + 2N\xi_{12}^2 + 2L\xi_{23}^2 + 2M\xi_{31}^2 \right]^{1/2} \tag{10}
$$

where F, G, H, N, M and L are material constants obtained by tests of the material in different orientations and $\boldsymbol{\xi}$ is the effective stress tensor, given by

$$
\boldsymbol{\xi} = \boldsymbol{\sigma} - \boldsymbol{X} \tag{11}
$$

The quadratic criterion of Hill 1948 is integrated into the model using the fourth rank tensor $\boldsymbol{P}$ defined by:

$$
\sigma_{eq}^{H}(\boldsymbol{\xi}) = \varphi_f(\boldsymbol{\xi}) = \|\boldsymbol{\xi}\|_{\boldsymbol{P}} = \sqrt{\boldsymbol{\xi}^t \boldsymbol{P} \boldsymbol{\xi}} \tag{12}
$$

$$
\boldsymbol{P} = \begin{bmatrix}
H+G & -H & -G & 0 & 0 & 0 \\
 & H+F & -F & 0 & 0 & 0 \\
 & & F+G & 0 & 0 & 0 \\
 & & & 2N & 0 & 0 \\
 & Sym & & & 2M & 0 \\
 & & & & & 2L
\end{bmatrix} \tag{13}
$$

The yield and the plastic potential functions, f and F, are given in terms of the associated thermodynamic variables, as follows

$$
f = \frac{\varphi_f(\boldsymbol{\xi}) - R}{\sqrt{1-d}} - \sigma_Y \tag{14}
$$

$$
F = f + \frac{1}{2(1-d)}\left[\sum_{k=1}^{N} \frac{\beta_k}{Q_k} R_k^2 + \sum_{k=1}^{M} \frac{b_k}{a_k} \boldsymbol{X}_k : \boldsymbol{X}_k \right] + F_d(Y,d) \tag{15}
$$

where σ_Y is the initial yield stress, β_k and b_k denote the isotropic and kinematic hardening material parameters, respectively, and $F_d(Y,d)$ can be any damage model. The evolution equations can be obtained using the generalized normal rule as follows

$$
\dot{\boldsymbol{\varepsilon}}^p = \dot{\gamma}\frac{\partial F}{\partial \boldsymbol{\sigma}} = \frac{\dot{\gamma}}{\sqrt{1-d}}\boldsymbol{n},\ \boldsymbol{n} = \frac{1}{\varphi_f}\boldsymbol{P}\boldsymbol{\xi} \tag{16}
$$

$$
\dot{\boldsymbol{\alpha}}_k = -\dot{\gamma}\frac{\partial F}{\partial \boldsymbol{X}_k} = \dot{\boldsymbol{\varepsilon}}^p - \frac{\dot{\gamma}}{(1-d)}\frac{b_k}{a_k}\boldsymbol{X}_k = \dot{\boldsymbol{\varepsilon}}^p - \dot{\gamma} b_k \boldsymbol{\alpha}_k \tag{17}
$$

$$
\dot{r}_k = -\dot{\gamma}\frac{\partial F}{\partial R_k} = \dot{\gamma}\left[\frac{1}{\sqrt{1-d}} - \frac{\beta_k R_k}{Q_k(1-d)} \right] = \dot{\gamma}\, h_k,\ h_k = \frac{1}{\sqrt{1-d}} - \beta_k r_k \tag{18}
$$

$$
\dot{d} = \dot{\gamma}\frac{\partial F}{\partial Y} = \dot{\gamma}\overline{Y},\ \overline{Y} = \frac{\partial F_d}{\partial Y} \tag{19}
$$

where $\dot{\gamma}$ designates the plastic multiplier which is consistent with the Kuhn–Tucker conditions for loading and unloading

$$\dot{\gamma} \geq 0,\ f \leq 0,\ \dot{\gamma} f = 0 \tag{20}$$

Using Equations (8) and (17)–(19), the evolution equation of the back stress $\boldsymbol{X}_k$ is given as below:

$$\dot{\boldsymbol{X}}_k = (1-d)a_k\dot{\boldsymbol{\alpha}}_k - a_k\boldsymbol{\alpha}_k\dot{d} = (1-d)a_k\left[\dot{\boldsymbol{\varepsilon}}^p - \frac{\dot{\gamma}}{(1-d)}\frac{b_k}{a_k}\boldsymbol{X}_k\right] - \frac{\dot{d}}{1-d}\boldsymbol{X}_k \tag{21}$$

$$\dot{\boldsymbol{X}}_k = a_k\dot{\gamma}\sqrt{1-d}\,\boldsymbol{n} - \dot{\gamma}\left(b_k + \frac{\overline{Y}}{1-d}\right)\boldsymbol{X}_k \tag{22}$$

$$\dot{\boldsymbol{X}} = \sum_{k=1}^{M}\dot{\boldsymbol{X}}_k = \dot{\gamma}\boldsymbol{H}_X,\ \boldsymbol{H}_X = a\sqrt{1-d}\,\boldsymbol{n} - \frac{\overline{Y}}{1-d}\boldsymbol{X} - \sum_{k=1}^{M} b_k\boldsymbol{X}_k,\ a = \sum_{k=1}^{M} a_k \tag{23}$$

3. Numerical Integration Schema

An algorithm is developed to simulate the present plasticity model. It is based on the fully implicit backward Euler integration. Indeed, for elastoplastic numerical problems, this integration scheme is usually used because of its unconditional stability. With this numerical integration procedure, it is crucial to develop the algorithmic tangent module. The main objective of using this module is to preserve the quadratic rate of the asymptotic convergence of the Newton method.

It can be followed that the enforcement of the consistency condition and the damage equation is reduced to two scalar equations. The unknowns of this system of equations are the plastic multiplier $\Delta\gamma$ and the damage variable $d_{n+1} = d$. The Newton–Raphson method is used to solve this system of equations. Appendix A summarizes the one-step to answer the couple $(\Delta\gamma, d_{n+1} = d)$.

The derivation of the consistent tangent modulus follows only the standard application of consistent linearization concepts. In Appendix B, we illustrate its final expression. The tangents modulus for the present coupled anisotropic plasticity-ductile damage is appropriate for plane strain, plane stress, and axisymmetric and 3D problems. Only two terms are modified, which are $\boldsymbol{D}$ and $\boldsymbol{P}$.

Finally, the complete and fully implicit integration scheme of the coupled plastic-damage with nonlinear isotropic/kinematic hardening is shown in Table 1.

Table 1. Integration scheme of the coupled plastic-damage (UMAT).

Compute trial elastic stress (Elastic predictor)
$\Delta\gamma = 0$
$\sigma^{trial} = \sigma_n + (1-d_n)\boldsymbol{D}\Delta\boldsymbol{\varepsilon},\ \overline{\boldsymbol{X}}_{k,n} = \boldsymbol{X}_{k,n}\ \overline{\boldsymbol{\xi}} = \sigma^{trial} - \sum_{k=1}^{M}\overline{\boldsymbol{X}}_{k,n}$
(i) Check plastic condition
IF $\frac{1}{(1-d)^{0.5}}[\varphi_{n+1} - R] - \sigma_Y \leq 0$ THEN (Elastic)
Set $(\ )_{n+1} = (\ )_n,\ \boldsymbol{D}^{ep} = \boldsymbol{D}$ and RETURN
ELSE (Plastic correction)
(ii) Find $(\Delta\gamma, d)$ by local iteration (Appendix A)
(iii) Update variables
$\boldsymbol{\xi}_{n+1} = \boldsymbol{I}_c^{-1}.\overline{\boldsymbol{\xi}},\ \boldsymbol{n}_{n+1} = \frac{1}{\varphi_{n+1}}\boldsymbol{H}\boldsymbol{\xi}_{n+1}$
$\boldsymbol{X}_{k,n+1} = \frac{1-d_{n+1}}{1-d_n}\overline{\boldsymbol{X}}_{k,n} + \omega_k\boldsymbol{n}_{n+1},\ \boldsymbol{X}_{n+1} = \sum_{k=1}^{M}\boldsymbol{X}_{k,n+1},\ \sigma_{n+1} = \boldsymbol{\xi}_{n+1} + \boldsymbol{X}_{n+1}$
(iv) Consistent elastoplastic modulus (Appendix B)
$\boldsymbol{D}^{ep} = (1-d_{n+1})\left[\boldsymbol{D}^* - \frac{1}{q}\boldsymbol{V}_1 \otimes \boldsymbol{V}_2\right]$
ENDIF

Damage Model

For the coupled anisotropic plasticity damage models, the damage potential, F_d should be considered in the derivation of the diverse equations. In this present work, the modified Lemaitre damage model is adopted and written as follows

$$F_d = \frac{S}{(s+1)(1-d)^{\beta}}\left\langle \frac{Y-Y_0}{S} \right\rangle^{s+1}, \overline{Y} = \frac{1}{(1-d)^{\beta}}\left\langle \frac{Y-Y_0}{S} \right\rangle^{s} \tag{24}$$

where β, s, S and Y_0 are material parameters. The strain density release rate Y, defined in Equation (14), can be derived using

$$Y = Y(\widetilde{\sigma}_{n+1}, r_k, \boldsymbol{\alpha}_k) = \frac{\widetilde{q}^2}{6G} + \frac{\widetilde{p}^2}{2K} + \frac{1}{2}\left(\sum_{k=1}^{N} Q_k r_k^2 + \sum_{k=1}^{M} a_k \boldsymbol{\alpha}_k : \boldsymbol{\alpha}_k \right) \tag{25}$$

where K and G are the bulk and shear modulus, respectively, and $\widetilde{p}$ and $\widetilde{q}$ are expressed as

$$\widetilde{p} = \frac{1}{3} tr(\widetilde{\sigma}_{n+1}), \ \widetilde{q} = \sqrt{3J_2(\widetilde{\sigma}_{n+1})} \tag{26}$$

4. Numerical Results of Coupled Anisotropic Plasticity and Damage Models

The main objective of this section is to develop a numerical analysis in order to validate the coupled anisotropic plasticity and damage models. The isotropic hardening describes the sheet material's behavior during a cold forming operation. It determines the size of the yield surface. The isotropic hardening law depends on the initial value of yield stress σ_y and material constants Q and β, which represent the isotropic hardening parameters. This law is given in Equation (27).

$$\sigma = \sigma_y + Q(1 - e^{-\beta.\varepsilon^p}) \tag{27}$$

Previous sections describe the developed numerical models, which are implemented in the finite element software Abaqus/Explicit through UMAT and VUMAT subroutines. Four numerical examples are analyzed in the next parts.

4.1. Perforated Square Plate under Biaxial Extension

As shown in Figure 1a, the square plate has as a thickness of $t = 1.0$ mm and a central circular hole. The damage field is illustrated with different values of anisotropic parameter α.

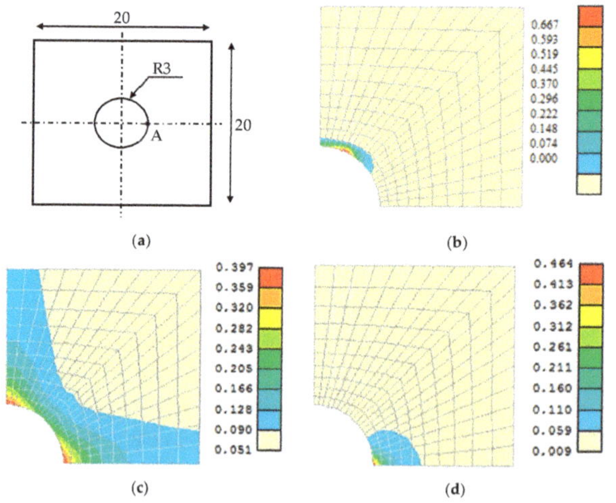

Figure 1. Square plate with a circular hole, (**a**) geometry, (**b**) $\alpha = 0.5$, (**c**) $\alpha = 1$, (**d**) $\alpha = 1.5$.

The material properties are given in Table 2. Only isotropic hardening is considered in this example. α is a parameter that controls the anisotropy.

Table 2. Material properties of perforated square steel plate.

Elasticity	$E = 210\,\text{GPa}, \nu = 0.3$
Isotropic Hardening (MPa)	$Q = 3300\,\text{MPa}; \sigma_y = 620\,\text{MPa}; \beta = 0.4$
Damage	$\delta = 1, \beta = 1, s = 1, S = 3.5\,\text{MPa}, Y_0 = 0\,\text{MPa}$

Anisotropic Hill criterion is considered with the following material properties.

$$R_{11} = 1,\ R_{22} = \alpha R_{11},\ R_{33} = R_{12} = R_{13} = R_{23} = 1 \tag{28}$$

Subsequently, the classical Hill 1948 coefficients are obtained using Equation (29).

$$\begin{bmatrix} F \\ G \\ H \end{bmatrix} = \frac{1}{2}\begin{bmatrix} -1 & 1 & 1 \\ 1 & -1 & 1 \\ 1 & 1 & -1 \end{bmatrix}\begin{bmatrix} 1/R_{11}^2 \\ 1/R_{22}^2 \\ 1/R_{33}^2 \end{bmatrix},\ N = M = L = 1.5 \tag{29}$$

By noting the symmetry, only a quarter part of the plate is considered in the simulation. In this example, a biaxial extension is considered and applied on the top and right boundaries of the quarter plate. This plate is discretized using 4-node quadrilateral plane stress element. The finite element mesh employed is shown in Figure 1. Appropriate symmetry boundary conditions are applied. Loading is performed by controlling the same displacement on the top and right boundaries of the square plate, $u_1 = u_2 = u$. Depending on the choice of anisotropic parameter α, different values of the prescribed displacement u are to be interpreted as ensuring that the damage does not reach an excessive value. The damage at point A (d_A) and maximum damage in the plate (d_{max}) are listed in Table 3 for different values of the parameter α.

Table 3. Specified displacement and damage for different value of α.

$\alpha = R_{22}/R_{11}$	u (mm)	d_A	d_{max}
0.5	0.115	0.00278	0.667
1	1.415	0.397	0.397
1.5	0.38	0.464	0.464

Damage contour plots at the final state for each value of parameter α are illustrated in Figure 1. The isotropic J_2 elastoplasticity corresponds to $\alpha = 1.0$. The damage contours obtained using numerical analysis are in agreement with those expected. As the parameters α increase, the damage at point A increase. For the three values of the parameter α, damage evolution at point A (d_A) versus displacement u are illustrated in Figure 2.

4.2. Numerical Simulations of Bulge Test

As a second numerical test, a sheet metal forming process is analyzed in this part. In fact, the bulge test is considered. It is usually used to characterize the formability of thin sheets. This process is schematized in Figure 3.

During the bulge test, the blank lies on a rigid die and its edged is clamped. Only one quarter is modeled due to symmetry. The fully coupled anisotropic plasticity/damage model is implemented using ABAQUS/Explicit software by using the user interface subroutine VUMAT. The sheet has a thickness of 1 mm. It is meshed using 588 thin shell elements with a reduced integration of type S4R. The matrix is considered as a rigid body. It is discretized with the rigid elements of type R3D4. A hydraulic pressure is applied on the bottom surface of the circular blank sheet. The maximum value of the ramped pressure evolution is 7.2 MPa.

The material properties are listed in Table 4, according to [31]. Simulations were carried out considering an isotropic material model ($r_0 = r_{45} = r_{90} = 1$).

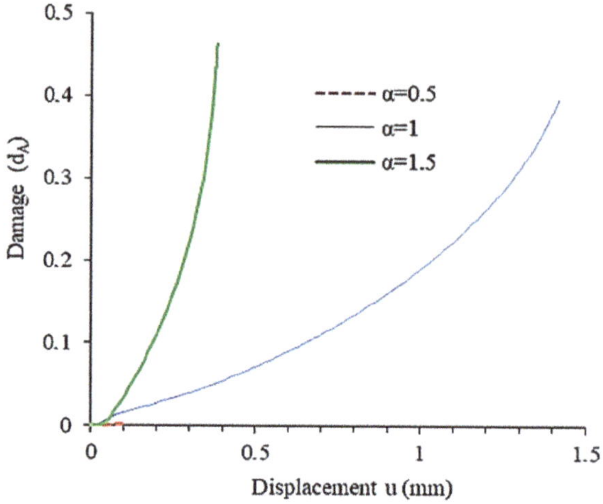

Figure 2. d_A versus u curves.

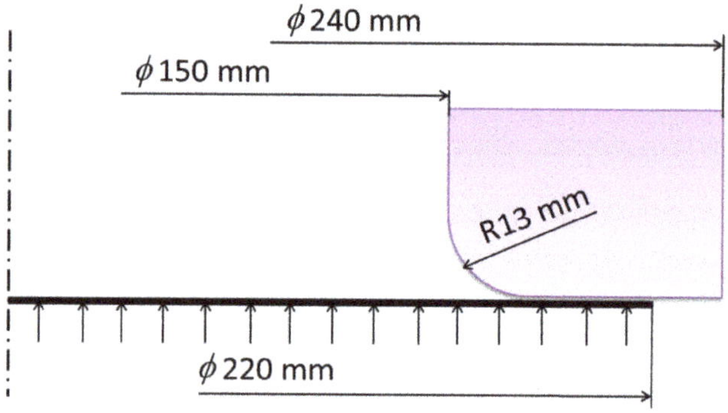

Figure 3. Geometry tool of the bulge test.

Table 4. Material properties considered in bulge test.

Elasticity	$E = 210\,\text{GPa}, \nu = 0.3$
Isotropic Hardening (MPa)	$\sigma_p = 488.35(0.001 + \varepsilon^p)^{0.2427}$
Initial yield stress, σ_{y_0} (MPa)	175
Damage	$\delta = 1, \beta = 1, s = 1, S = 1.25\,\text{MPa}, Y_0 = 0\,\text{MPa}$

The damage distribution in the studied bulge test is presented in Figure 4. Based on the numerical results (Figure 4), the isotropic model shows that the maximum value of damage (SDV4) is located in the bulge center. The damaged element deletion method is activated in the simulation of bulge test using ABAQUS/Explicit. Figure 4 shows that, if the ductile damage reaches a critical value (0.98), then elements are supposed fully damaged and detached from the structure. In the same context, Figure 5 illustrates the damage evolution for the isotropic case.

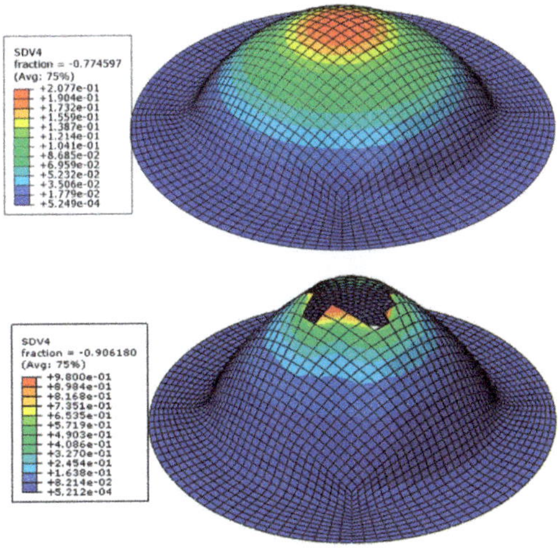

Figure 4. Bulge test damage distribution (isotropic damage model).

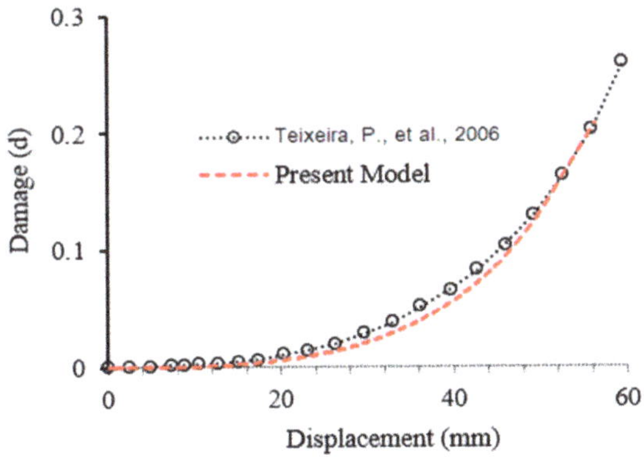

Figure 5. Damage evolution [31].

The numerical damage evolutions are examined by using the nodes situated in the middle layer. Therefore, and as shown is Figure 5, the result obtained by the present model was compared with that developed by [31]. A good agreement between both results is showed.

4.3. Model Evaluation Using Uniaxial Tensile Test

In this section, the predictive model capability is examined by comparing the numerical and experimental results obtained from the uniaxial tensile test. The anisotropic elastoplastic mechanical model of DD13 sheet steel is considered in the simulation of the tensile test. The DD13 steel material is hot rolled sheet metal. This sheet metal has a ferritic microstructure. The chemical composition of the blank is presented in Table 5. The material properties of the blank sheet are provided in Tables 6 and 7. A double exponential law is adopted for the anisotropic elastoplastic mechanical model. The expression of the stress evolution is written as

$$\sigma(p) = \sigma_Y + A_1\left(1 - e^{\beta_1 \varepsilon^p}\right) + A_2\left(1 - e^{\beta_2 \varepsilon^p}\right) \tag{30}$$

where ε_p represents the equivalent plastic strain, σ_Y is the yield stress, and $A_k = \frac{Q_k}{\beta_k}$, β_k , $k = 1,2$ are the material parameters.

Table 5. Chemical composition of the DD13 sheet material.

C	S_{max}	Mn_{max}	P_{max}
0.08	0.03	0.4	0.03

Table 6. Mechanical properties of the DD13 material [32].

Elastic Prop.			Hill 1948 Coefficients			
E(GPa)	ν	σ_Y (MPa)	F	G	H	N
220	0.3	278	0.43	0.47	0.53	1.49

Table 7. Hardening and damage parameters for DD13 [32].

Isotropic hardening parameters	Q_1 (MPa)	Q_2 (MPa)	β_1	β_2
	490	50	1.35	30
Damage parameters	β	s	S (MPa)	Y_0 (MPa)
	5	1.5	200	15

The eight nodes hexahedral elements (C3D8) mesh is adopted for the simulation of the tensile test, the results of which is illustrated in Figure 6a. An imposed displacement was applied in the axial direction. Numerical and experimental results of the force–displacement curves of the tensile test along the rolling direction (RD) are obtained using the VUMAT subroutine and are illustrated in Figure 7.

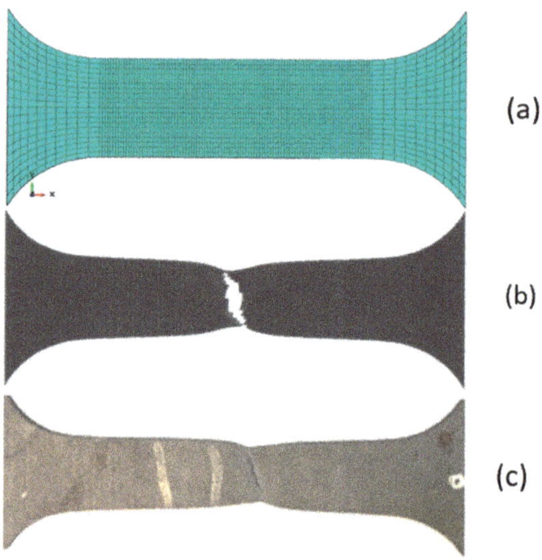

Figure 6. Specimens: (**a**) mesh with 7480 C3D8 elements, (**b**) numerical fracture in the rolling direction RD (0°) for displacement 21 mm, (**c**) experimental fracture in the RD.

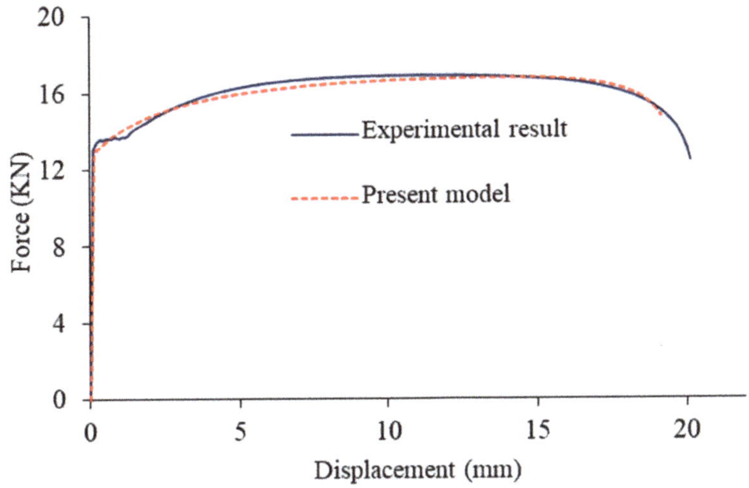

Figure 7. Experimental and numerical force–displacement curves.

Figure 6b presents the specimen damage for 21 mm displacement in the RD using the present model. The experimental specimen final fracture in the RD is given in Figure 6c. As depicted experimentally, the numerical damage takes place at the central zone, and the rupture facies are not perpendicular to the loading axis. Results in terms of the load–displacement curves are presented in Figure 7. By using the presented anisotropic plasticity/damage model, Figure 7 shows an acceptable fit of the numerical result when compared to experimental one. Next, the efficiency of the presented model will be evaluated in the case of the cross-die deep drawing test.

4.4. Numerical Simulation of Cross-Die Deep Drawing Test

Cross-die deep drawing simulation is carried out in this section. This test is used to cover a wide range of stress states and to reproduce most significant strain paths that can be found in deep drawing, i.e., tensile, shear, plane strain, and biaxial loading modes. An improved elastoplastic model strongly coupled with damage effect in the yield function and plastic potential is used. The developed model is implemented in ABAQUS software via the VUMAT subroutine. For the simulation, a 3D finite element model is performed in Abaqus software to analyze the cross-die test. The die, punch, and blank holder are defined as discrete rigid parts, and the sheet was assigned as a deformable homogenous shell. The initial dimensions of the square blank sheet were equal to $260 \times 260 \times 1$ mm^3. A four nodes quadrilateral shell element S4R with a size of 5×5 mm^2 and with five integration points through the thickness was employed for meshing the sheet. Penalty contact is used in forming simulations. The Coulomb friction coefficient of 0.05 was considered between sheet and tools surfaces. The blank holding force during forming was 450 kN. The punch stroke of 60 mm was considered in the simulation. Figure 8 shows the main geometrical parameters of the tools. The die and punch radii are 20 mm and 14 mm, respectively. In all cases, the blank sheet orientation with respect to the tools is shown in Figure 8. In the simulation of cross-die deep drawing, the blank is made of DD13 sheet metal.

After the simulation, the blank sheet thinning was determined along three directions (i.e., rolling direction (RD), transverse direction (TD), and diagonal direction (DD)) as illustrated in Figure 9. From this figure, it is noticed that the thinning of the simulated workpiece is more important in DD (0.49 mm-thickness) compared to RD and TD ($\approx$0.7 mm-thickness).

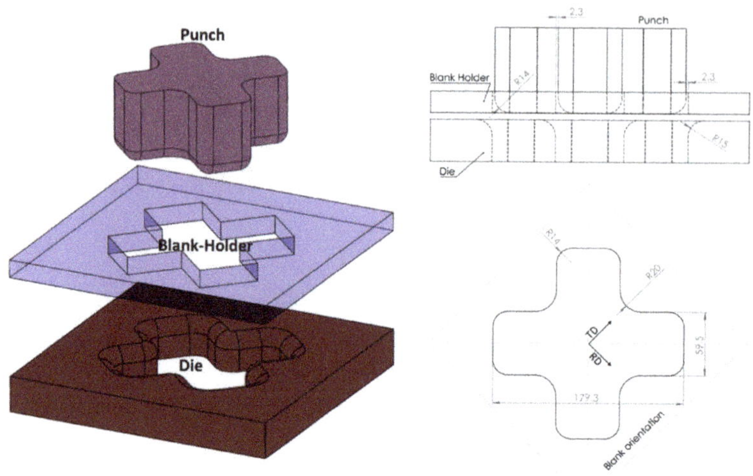

Figure 8. Cross-die deep drawing test.

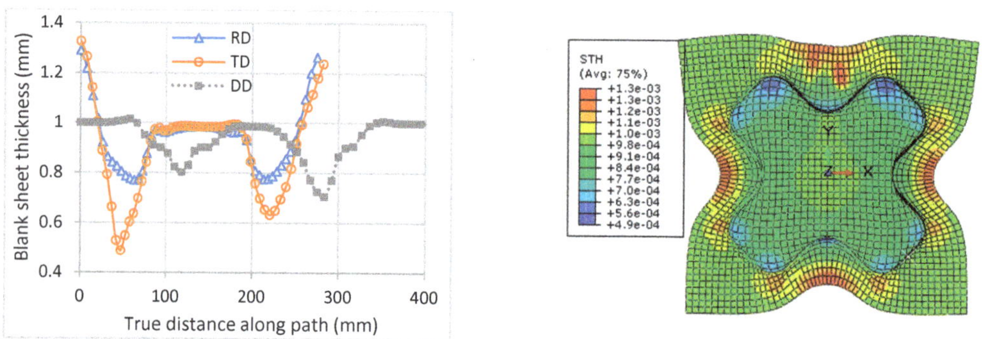

(a) (b)

Figure 9. (**a**) Evolution of sheet thickness: along RD, TD, and DD; (**b**) distribution of the thickness in the simulated part.

Figures 10 and 11 show the simulation results of the cross-die test. The damage location and the force–displacement response were predicted precisely, as presented in the work of [33,34].

The minor and major strains of the 60 mm-height of the cross-die are illustrated in Figure 12. The strain path analysis of the cross-die simulation reveals the complex forming process. In the simulated part, the strain distributions of some points are near or above the experimental forming limit diagram (FLD) curve. The location of the damage is the same as that presented in the experimental work of [33]. In other words, the figure can illustrate the capability of the proposed model in the damage prediction of a cross-die deep drawing test.

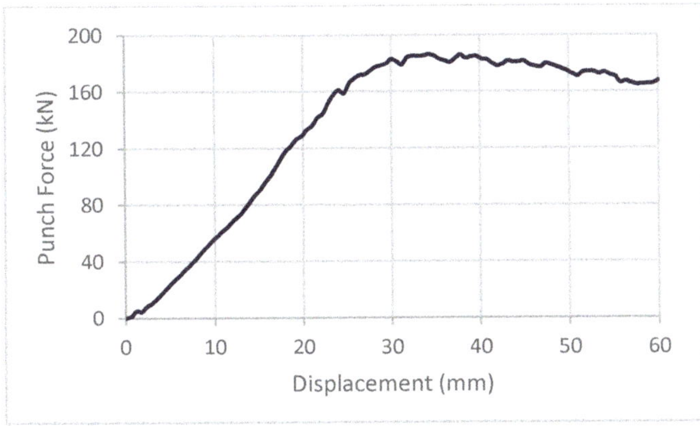

Figure 10. Punch force during forming process.

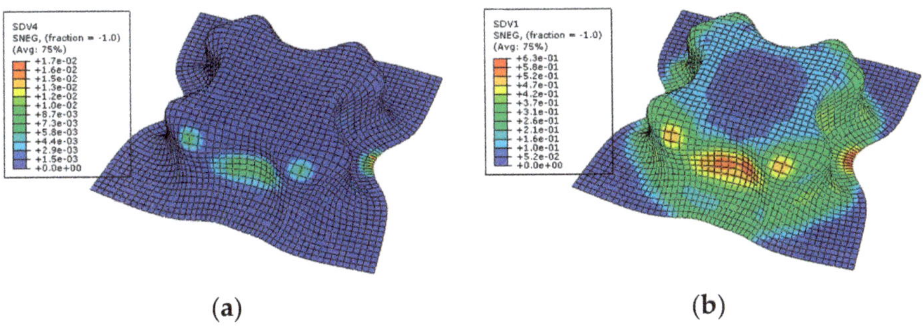

Figure 11. Simulated results of cross-die deep drawing test (**a**) distribution of damage; (**b**) distribution of equivalent plastic stain.

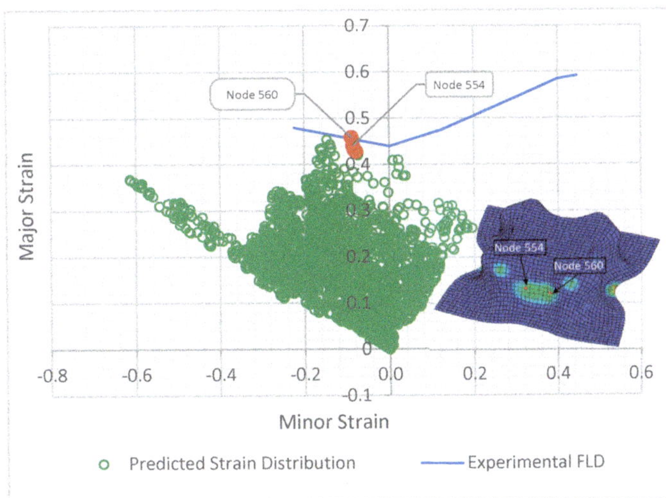

Figure 12. Distribution of strains at different locations.

5. Conclusions

In this paper, a coupled model of anisotropic plasticity and continuous ductile damage is proposed. A generalized quadratic yield function is considered to exhibit isotropic and nonlinear kinematic hardening. According to the literature, more than two local equations are required in coupled elastoplastic damage models. However, in our work, only two scalar equations are required to solve the developed numerical algorithm. The unknowns in this system of equations are the plastic multiplier and the damage variables. Using the implicit solver, and in order to preserve the quadratic rate of asymptotic convergence of Newton's method, the algorithmic tangent modulus is developed. It is given in closed form using exact linearization. The mathematical models are implemented using the ABAQUS/ Explicit software and the UMAT and VUMAT subroutines of the user interface. The results of DD13 sheet metal in cross-die deep drawing show the effect of anisotropic coefficients and hardening and damage parameters on the distribution of thickness and damage in the obtained workpiece. Numerical examples are developed which show the efficiency and ability of the proposed model to predict ductile damage growth in the sheet forming process.

Author Contributions: L.B.S.: Conceptualization, Methodology, Writing—Original draft preparation. M.A.: Software, visualization, Data curation, investigation. M.W.: Visualization, Writing—Review and Editing, Investigation. F.D.: Supervision, Conceptualization, Methodology, Writing—Review and Editing. All authors have read and agreed to the published version of the manuscript.

Funding: This research received no external funding.

Institutional Review Board Statement: Not applicable.

Informed Consent Statement: Not applicable.

Data Availability Statement: Not applicable.

Conflicts of Interest: The authors declare no competing interest.

Appendix A. Local Iteration: Resolve of ($\Delta\gamma$,d_{n+1}=d) by Newton's Method

Set: $\Delta\gamma = 0,\ d = d_n,\ \sigma^{trial} = \sigma_n + (1 - d_n)\boldsymbol{D}\Delta\boldsymbol{\varepsilon}$

(i) Check convergence

$$\boldsymbol{R}_i = \begin{bmatrix} f_1 \\ f_2 \end{bmatrix}_i = \begin{bmatrix} \frac{\varphi - R}{(1-d)^{0.5}} - \sigma_Y \\ d - d_n - \Delta\gamma\,\overline{Y} \end{bmatrix}_i,\ \varphi = \left[\overline{\xi}^T.\boldsymbol{I}_c^{-T}.\boldsymbol{H}.\boldsymbol{I}_c^{-1}.\overline{\xi}\right]^{1/2}$$

$$\overline{\xi} = \tfrac{1-d}{1-d_n}\left(\sigma^{trial} - \sum_{k=1}^{M}\exp(-b_k\Delta\gamma)\boldsymbol{X}_{k,n}\right)$$

$$\boldsymbol{I}_c = \boldsymbol{I} + \frac{1}{\varphi_{n+1}(1-d)^{-0.5}}[\Delta\gamma\boldsymbol{D} + a_\omega\boldsymbol{I}]\boldsymbol{H},\ a_\omega = \sum_{k=1}^{M}\tfrac{a_k}{b_k}[1 - \exp(-b_k\Delta\gamma)]$$

IF $|\boldsymbol{R}_i| < Tol$ **THEN** End Loop

(ii) Compute Jacobian

$$J_i = \begin{bmatrix} f_{1,1} & f_{1,2} \\ f_{2,1} & f_{2,2} \end{bmatrix}_i$$

(iii) Evaluate solution

$$\begin{bmatrix} \Delta\gamma \\ d \end{bmatrix}_{i+1} = \begin{bmatrix} \Delta\gamma \\ d \end{bmatrix}_i - J_i^{-1}\boldsymbol{R}_i$$

(iv) Set $i = i + 1$ go to (i)

Appendix B. Consistent Tangent Modulus ($d = d_{n+1}$, $\varphi = \varphi_{n+1}$)

$$Q_a = QH,\ Q = \frac{1}{\varphi_{n+1}} \sum_{k=1}^{M} \omega_k,\ I_X = I + Q_a$$

$$I_D = I_X I_c^{-1},\ D^* = I_D D,\ V_1 = I_D x$$

$$x = DH x_1 + \frac{Z}{(1-d)} \sigma_{n+1},\ x_1 = \frac{1}{(1-d)^{-0.5}} \left[T\, \xi_{n+1} - u\, I_X^{-1} h\right]$$

$$Z = -\frac{\partial f_2/\partial(\Delta\gamma)}{\partial f_2/\partial d},\ T = u_{,1} + \frac{\delta u\, Z}{1-d},\ u = \frac{\Delta\gamma}{\varphi}$$

$$h = \sum_{k=1}^{M} h_k,\ h_k = \frac{-1}{1-d_n}(Z + b_k(1-d_{n+1}))\overline{X}_{k,n} + \left[d\omega_k + \frac{\omega_k}{u}\left(u_{,1} + Zu_{,2} - \frac{1}{\varphi_{n+1}}\right)\right] n_{n+1}$$

$$u_{,1} = \frac{\varphi - \varphi_{,1}\Delta\gamma}{\varphi^2},\ \varphi_{,1} = \partial R/\partial(\Delta\gamma),\ u_{,2} = -u\frac{\varphi_{,2}}{\varphi},\ \varphi_{,2} = \frac{\partial R}{\partial d} - \delta\sigma_Y(1-d)^{\delta-1}$$

$$d\omega_k = \frac{a_k}{(1-d_{n+1})^{-0.5}} \left[\exp(-b_k\Delta\gamma) + \frac{1-\exp(-b_k\Delta\gamma)}{b_k} T_1\right],\ T_1 = \frac{(\delta-1)\,Z}{1-d_{n+1}}$$

$$q = \alpha + n_{n+1}^T . z,\ \alpha = \frac{\partial R}{\partial\Delta\gamma} + \frac{\partial R}{\partial d} Z - \frac{\delta Z(\varphi - R)}{1-d_{n+1}},\ V_2 = D_c^t n_{n+1}$$

$$D_c = I_X^{-1} D^* = I_c^{-1} D,\ z = V_1 + I_X^{-1} y,\ y = h - Q_a V_1$$

References

1. Karafillis, A.P.; Boyce, M. A general anisotropic yield criterion using bounds and a transformation weighting tensor. *J. Mech. Phys. Solids* **1993**, *41*, 1859–1886. [CrossRef]
2. Barlat, F.; Maeda, Y.; Chung, K.; Yanagawa, M.; Brem, J.C.; Hayashida, Y.; Lege, D.J.; Matsui, K.; Murtha, S.J.; Hattori, S.; et al. Yield function development for aluminum alloy sheets. *J. Mech. Phys. Solids* **1997**, *45*, 1727–1763. [CrossRef]
3. Ben Said, L.; Wali, M. Accuracy of Variational Formulation to Model the Thermomechanical Problem and to Predict Failure in Metallic Materials. *Mathematics* **2022**, *10*, 3555. [CrossRef]
4. Murugesan, M.; Jung, D.W. Johnson Cook Material and Failure Model Parameters Estimation of AISI-1045 Medium Carbon Steel for Metal Forming Applications. *Materials* **2009**, *12*, 609. [CrossRef]
5. Ben Said, L.; Wali, M.; Khedher, N.; Kessentini, A.; Algahtani, A.; Dammak, F. Efficiency of rubber-pad cushion in bending process of a thin aluminum sheet. *J. Rubber Res.* **2020**, *23*, 89–99. [CrossRef]
6. Bouhamed, A.; Mars, J.; Jrad, H.; Ben Said, L.; Wali, M.; Dammak, F.; Torchani, A. Identification of fully coupled non-associated-Ductile damage constitutive equations for thin sheet metal applications: Numerical feasibility and experimental validation. *Thin-Walled Struct.* **2022**, *176*, 109365. [CrossRef]
7. Liu, K.; Jin, S.; Rui, Y.; Huang, J.; Zhou, Z. Effect of Lithology on Mechanical and Damage Behaviors of Concrete in Concrete-Rock Combined Specimen. *Mathematics* **2022**, *10*, 727. [CrossRef]
8. Bonora, N.; Majzoobi, G.H.; Khademi, E. Numerical implementation of a new coupled cyclic plasticity and continum damage model. *Comput. Mater. Sci.* **2014**, *81*, 538–547. [CrossRef]
9. Rodriguez, P.; Ulloa, J.; Samaniego, C.; Samaniego, E. A variational approach to the phase field modeling of brittle and ductile fracture. *Int. J. Mech. Sci.* **2018**, *144*, 502–517. [CrossRef]
10. Chaboche, J.L. Anisotropic creep damage in the framework of the continuum damage mechanics. *Nucl. Eng. Des.* **1984**, *79*, 309–319. [CrossRef]
11. Gurson, A.L. Continuum theory of ductile rupture by void nucleation and growth: Part I—Yield criteria and flow rules for porous ductile media. *J. Eng. Mater. Technol.* **1977**, *99*, 2–15. [CrossRef]
12. Lemaitre, J.; Chaboche, J.L. *Mechanics of Solid Materials*; University Press: Cambridge, UK, 1990.
13. Needleman, A.; Tvergaard, V. An analysis of ductile rupture in notched bars. *J. Mech. Phys. Solids* **1984**, *32*, 461. [CrossRef]
14. Needleman, A.; Tvergaard, V. An analysis of ductile rupture modes at a crack tip. *J. Mech. Phys. Solids* **1987**, *35*, 151. [CrossRef]
15. Gao, X.; Wang, T.; Kim, J. On Ductile Fracture Initiation Toughness: Effects of Void Volume Fraction, Void Shape and Void Distribution. *Int. J. Solids Struct.* **2005**, *42*, 5097–5117. [CrossRef]
16. Zhang, Z.; Skallerud, B. Void Coalescence with and without Prestrain History. *Int. J. Damage Mech.* **2010**, *19*, 153–174. [CrossRef]
17. Wciślik, W.; Lipiec, S. Void-Induced Ductile Fracture of Metals: Experimental Observations. *Materials* **2022**, *15*, 6473. [CrossRef] [PubMed]
18. Abbassi, F.; Belhadj, T.; Mistou, S.; Zghal, A. Parameter identification of a mechanical ductile damage using Artificial Neural Networks in sheet metal forming. *Mater. Des.* **2013**, *45*, 605–615. [CrossRef]
19. Benallal, A.; Billardon, R.; Doghri, I. An integration algorithm and the corresponding consistent tangent operator for fully coupled elastoplastic and damage equations. *Appl. Numer. Methods* **1988**, *4*, 731–740. [CrossRef]

20. De Souza Neto, E.A.; Peric, D. A computational framework for a class of models for fully coupled elastoplastic damage at finite strains with reference to the linearization aspects. *Comput. Methods Appl. Mech. Eng.* **1996**, *130*, 179–193. [CrossRef]
21. De Souza Neto, E.A.; Peric, D.; Owen, D.R.J. Continuum modelling and numerical simulation of material damage at finite strains. *Arch. Comput. Methods Eng.* **1998**, *5*, 311–384. [CrossRef]
22. Doghri, I. Numerical implementation and analysis of a class of metal plasticity models coupled with ductile damage. *Int. J. Numer. Methods Eng.* **1995**, *38*, 3403–3431. [CrossRef]
23. Lemaitre, J. A continuous damage mechanics model for ductile fracture. *J. Eng. Mater. Technol.* **1985**, *107*, 83–89. [CrossRef]
24. Krairi, K.; Doghri, I. A thermodynamically based constitutive model for thermoplastic polymers coupling viscoelasticity, viscoplasticity and ductile damage. *Int. J. Plast.* **2014**, *60*, 163–181. [CrossRef]
25. Bonora, N. A nonlinear CDM model for ductile failure. *Eng. Fract. Mech.* **1997**, *58*, 11–28. [CrossRef]
26. Badreddine, H.; Saanouni, K.; Dogui, A. On non-associative anisotropic finite plasticity fully coupled with isotropic ductile damage for metal forming. *Int. J. Plast.* **2010**, *26*, 1541–1575. [CrossRef]
27. Saanouni, K. On the numerical prediction of the ductile fracture in metal forming. *Eng. Fract. Mech.* **2008**, *75*, 3545–3559. [CrossRef]
28. Khelifa, M.; Oudjene, M.; Khennane, A. Fracture in sheet metal forming: Effect of ductile damage evolution. *Comput. Struct.* **2007**, *85*, 205–212. [CrossRef]
29. Hill, R. A theory of the yielding and plastic flow of anisotropic metals. *Proc. R. Soc. London Ser. A Math. Phys. Sci.* **1948**, *193*, 281–297.
30. Hosford, W.F. A Generalized Isotropic Yield Criterion. *J. Appl. Mech.* **1972**, *39*, 607–609. [CrossRef]
31. Teixeira, P.; Santos, A.D.; Andrade Pires, F.M.; César de Sa, J.M.A. Finite element prediction of ductile fracture in sheet metal forming processes. *J. Mater. Process. Technol.* **2006**, *177*, 278–281. [CrossRef]
32. Ghorbel, O.; Mars, J.; Koubaa, S.; Wali, M.; Dammak, F. Coupled anisotropic plasticity-ductile damage; modeling, experimental verification, and application to sheet metal forming simulation. *Int. J. Mech. Sci.* **2019**, *150*, 548–560. [CrossRef]
33. Habibi, N.; Sundararaghavan, V.; Prahl, U.; Ramazani, A. Experimental and Numerical Investigations into the Failure Mechanisms of TRIP700 Steel Sheets. *Metals* **2018**, *8*, 1073. [CrossRef]
34. Carvalho-Resende, T.; Balan, T.; Bouvier, S.; Abed-Meraim, F.; Sablin, S.-S. Numerical investigation and experimental validation of a plasticity model for sheet steel forming. *Model. Simul. Mater. Sci. Eng.* **2013**, *21*, 015008. [CrossRef]

Disclaimer/Publisher's Note: The statements, opinions and data contained in all publications are solely those of the individual author(s) and contributor(s) and not of MDPI and/or the editor(s). MDPI and/or the editor(s) disclaim responsibility for any injury to people or property resulting from any ideas, methods, instructions or products referred to in the content.

mathematics

MDPI

Article

Design Optimisation of Bi-Cruciate Retaining Total Knee Arthroplasty (TKA) Prosthesis via Taguchi Methods

Natrisya Qistina Mohd Mukhtar [1], Solehuddin Shuib [1], Muhamad Azhan Anuar [1], Mohd Fairudz Mohd Miswan [2] and Mohd Afzan Mohd Anuar [1,*]

1 School of Mechanical Engineering, College of Engineering, Universiti Teknologi MARA, Shah Alam 40450, Malaysia
2 Department of Orthopaedics and Traumatology, Faculty of Medicine, Universiti Teknologi MARA, Sungai Buloh 47000, Malaysia
* Correspondence: afzan341@uitm.edu.my

Abstract: Total knee replacement has become a viable option for treating severe knee arthritis. The demand for more kinematically functional implants that better replicate natural knee kinematics led to the development of total knee arthroplasty (TKA), including bi-cruciate-retaining (BCR) TKA. However, optimised design parameters of BCR TKA knee implants that can help achieve a long-term prosthetic survival rate remain unknown. Therefore, this study aimed to investigate the effect of the design parameters of BCR TKA knee implants on the mechanics of knee joints and optimise and individualise the knee implant design parameters using the Taguchi method incorporating finite element analysis. Herein, experimental factors and levels were selected and nine finite element models of BCR TKA knee implants were developed to optimise the design of the following parameters: the curvature ratio on the sagittal plane, curvature ratio on the coronal plane, and tibial slope. In addition, finite element analysis was used to determine the effect of the design parameters on the peak contact stress on ultra-high-molecular-weight polyethylene (UHMWPE) and its deformation. Consequently, among the three parameters that affect the peak contact stress and its deformation, the curvature ratio on the sagittal plane had the greatest effect (range = 10.96), followed by the curvature ratio on the coronal plane (range = 3.54), and the tibial slope (range = 2.56). The optimal design parameters for the BCR TKA knee implant were a curvature ratio of 1.5 on both the sagittal and coronal planes and a tibial slope of 5°. Under these conditions, the peak contact stress and deformation were 25.80 MPa and 0.0835 mm, respectively. The optimisation method based on finite element analysis and the Taguchi method can produce one of the highest-performing BCR TKA knee implant designs, thereby reducing the peak contact stress and deformation. This method sheds fresh light on the development of the BCR TKA knee implant as well as biomechanical decision-making to implant the TKA prosthesis correctly.

Keywords: joint mechanics; total knee replacement; bi-cruciate retaining; finite element analysis; optimisation; Taguchi methods

MSC: 74S05; 05B15

Citation: Mohd Mukhtar, N.Q.; Shuib, S.; Anuar, M.A.; Mohd Miswan, M.F.; Mohd Anuar, M.A. Design Optimisation of Bi-Cruciate Retaining Total Knee Arthroplasty (TKA) Prosthesis via Taguchi Methods. *Mathematics* **2023**, *11*, 312. https://doi.org/10.3390/math11020312

Academic Editors: Fernando Simoes and Yang Liu

Received: 15 November 2022
Revised: 20 December 2022
Accepted: 4 January 2023
Published: 7 January 2023

Copyright: © 2023 by the authors. Licensee MDPI, Basel, Switzerland. This article is an open access article distributed under the terms and conditions of the Creative Commons Attribution (CC BY) license (https://creativecommons.org/licenses/by/4.0/).

1. Introduction

Knee implants have existed since the early 1880s in the biomedical engineering industry. The initial notion for knee joint replacement was proposed in Berlin by the German surgeon Themistocles Gluck, who presented a revolutionary system of joint replacement with an ivory element in a series of lectures [1]. Over the years, modern implants have been explored to imitate natural knee kinematics to potentially enhance a return to great levels of activity and satisfaction [2]. Nevertheless, this enthusiasm for those findings is not necessarily consistent with scientific validation, and consequently, there are many unanswered issues. Thus, every different concept of the design has been conceived to solve and help the special needs, such as reaching the highest range of motion, reducing pain and debris, articular geometry, the type of fixation, the modularity of augments and stems, the types of constraints, knee kinematics, as well as the costs [3].

Total knee arthroplasty (TKA) is well-known as the ultimate solution for end-stage knee osteoarthritis [4]. A typical TKA implant consists of three components, namely the femoral component, tibial insert, and tibial component, as shown in Figure 1a. Femoral and tibial components are both made of metal alloy; meanwhile, the tibial insert is made of polyethylene to imitate the function of soft tissues surrounding the bones as an absorber. The femoral component is implanted in the femoral bone to reproduce the anatomical landmark of the femur at the knee joint. Meanwhile, the tibial component reproduces the tibial bone at the knee joint, and it looks like a platform for the tibial insert to be secured [5]. The desire for more kinematically functional implants that better replicate natural knee kinematics led to the development of bi-cruciate-retaining (BCR) TKA. In theory, BCR TKA could improve implant longevity by reducing the stress transmitted through the prosthesis, as BCR TKA is a unique prosthetic implant that keeps both the anterior cruciate ligament (ACL) and posterior cruciate ligament (PCL) [6]. Moreover, Pritchett et al. discovered that patients who received a BCR TKA implant had good survival and function after more than 20 years of use and that sacrificing ACL is unnecessary [7]. The TKA implant's durability or survivability are critical issues because the goals of the knee replacement procedure are long-term pain relief and the patient's knee function restoration [8]. After a certain duration, knee implants will fail, and revision surgery needs to be performed. However, revision is a relatively expensive procedure and causes worse results than the primary surgery [9,10].

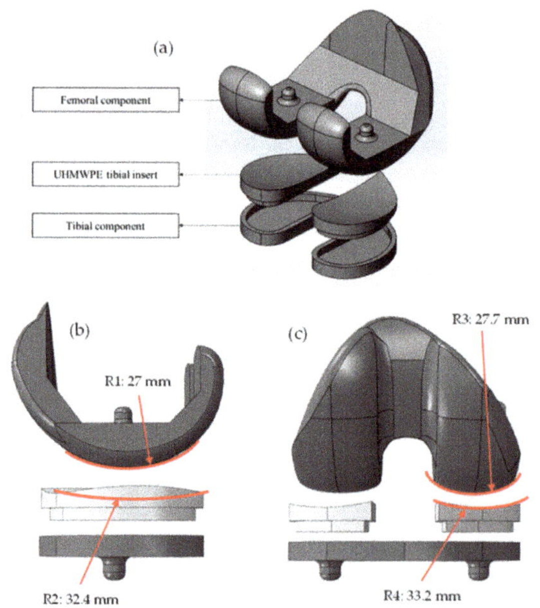

Figure 1. (**a**) Components of BCR TKA knee implant model. (**b**) The radius of curvature of femoral and tibial inserts on sagittal plane. (**c**) The radius of curvature of femoral and tibial inserts on coronal plane. The curvature ratio is defined as the ratio of the tibial insert radius of curvature to the femoral radius of curvature.

Knee arthritis is a significant condition that affects around 70 million people globally, and total knee replacement has become a viable option for treating severe knee arthritis.

In 2020, Zhang et al. showed that 8–25% of conventional TKA patients are not satisfied with their implant, whilst a greater satisfaction of patients who underwent the BCR TKA process has been reported [6]. Based on the report, it is necessary to construct mechanical studies to create biocompatible implants to optimise the design of knee implants; however, it is difficult to perform this on the structural mechanics of the human body, which involves bones, tissues, and other organs. Therefore, this study proposed the reduction of the peak value of the contact stress on the upper surface of the implant's ultra-high-molecular-weight polyethylene (UHMWPE) tibial insert and its wear and to extend the life of the prosthesis by using the finite element (FE) model.

In designing a knee implant, considerations for its materials are needed because its design as well as the materials it is made of play critical roles in the effort to limit the stress level in the implant component [11]. The stresses accumulate at a faster rate when there is a greater load, and the contact stress that acts over the femoral component becomes more intense as the weight increases. Aseptic loosening is the most common type of knee implant failure, and this is because of UHMWPE wear [12–14]. Based on Archard wear law, volumetric wear is directly proportional to contact stress and sliding distance [15,16]. A retrieval study was performed that found that abrasive wear is initiated by third bodies and is determined by sliding distance and shear force. Meanwhile, surface wear, such as delamination and pitting, is affected by contact stress [17]. Thus, increasing the tibiofemoral conformity, which is defined as the femoral to tibial contact radii ratio [18], can reduce the contact stress and sliding distance, subsequently decreasing the occurrence of surface fatigue wear [19–21].

Taguchi's orthogonal array method was initially developed by Genichi Taguchi; it is a statistical approach to optimise the selected experimental factor to improve the quality of the manufactured products [22,23]. The application of this method has been extended to chemistry, pharmaceuticals, and engineering [24,25]. The orthogonal array can efficiently decrease the number of computational simulations, thus leading to shorter preoperative planning time for TKA surgery. However, the application of the Taguchi orthogonal array in TKA finite element analysis was less pronounced by previous researchers. Recently, a study was conducted by Dong et al. to optimise the TKA implantation parameters using an orthogonal array based on finite element analysis [26]. Besides that, a very limited number of studies on the optimisation of tibiofemoral contact geometry have been performed. Previous researchers only conducted comparative studies to investigate the effect of tibiofemoral conformity of different implant designs on knee mechanics, i.e., knee kinematics and wear [27–30]. The optimisation of TKA implants was performed in recent studies to optimise the implantation parameters, i.e., varus–valgus angle and tibial rotation [26,31]; however, the optimisation of contact geometry at the tibiofemoral interface was not discussed.

Therefore, this study primarily aimed to investigate the effect of the design parameters of the BCR TKA knee implant on the mechanics of knee joints and optimise and individualise the knee implant design parameters using the Taguchi method incorporating finite element analysis (FEA). FEA is a powerful computational tool that has been applied in numerous structural analyses [26,32,33]. In this study, the design optimisation aimed to reduce wear at the tibial insert, hence improving the survival rate of the implant. In addition, clinical scores of the modern universal total knee arthroplasty system have been proven in studies to be of tremendous value not only to the surgeon but also to the healthcare system as a whole, thus making them an absolute necessity in the context of contemporary medical practice [34].

The scope of the study was to optimise and individualise the BCR TKA knee implant design parameters using FEA combined with the Taguchi technique. The significant design parameters that were taken into account were the curvature ratio of the sagittal plane, curvature ratio of the coronal plane, and tibial slope. The results of the peak contact stress and deformation of the developed designs were subsequently investigated to determine the best combination of design parameters. Nine FE models of BCR TKA knee joints were developed and then analysed using SIMULIA Abaqus to optimise the design parameters.

ASTM F75 cobalt chromium molybdenum (Co-Cr-Mo) and UHMWPE were the materials used for the femoral component and tibial insert, respectively. They were used because, based on a study by Kohli et al. and static structural data, Co-Cr-Mo experienced the least amount of deformation as compared with titanium alloy and stainless steel [35]. Meanwhile, according to Bhandarkar et al., the stress behaviour of one of their material models with a tibial cushion constructed of UHMWPE material was superior to that of the other material models in terms of generating the least amount of stress [36].

2. Materials and Methods

An orthogonal array of the s element, denoted by L_N (s^m), was an $N \times m$ matrix. The number of rows, N of L_N (s^m), could be seen as a subset of the s^m number of experiments for a complete factorial plan in the m experimental factor, each having s number of levels [37]. In this study, three different experimental factors were selected as the optimisation parameters of the BCR TKA UHMWPE tibial insert. The design parameters that were selected as experimental factors were A (curvature ratio of the UHMWPE tibial insert on the sagittal plane), B (curvature ratio of the UHMWPE tibial insert on the coronal plane), and C (tibial slope), as presented in Table 1. Taguchi's orthogonal array, L9 (3^3), was utilised to estimate the factors that influence the contact stress and deformation of BCR TKA knee implants and to determine which factors were more important than others. Three levels were chosen for each factor, and these levels were used in the optimisation process. The curvature ratios of the UHMWPE tibial insert for both the sagittal and coronal planes were 1.0, 1.2, and 1.5, whilst the levels used for the tibial slope were 0°, 5°, and 10° [38]. Nine groups of experimental level combinations (the combinations of design parameters) were constructed based on the orthogonal experimental design proposed by Taguchi, as well as nine different BCR TKA knee implant models.

Table 1. Knee implant experimental factors and design levels.

Experimental Factors	Level 1	Level 2	Level 3
A: Curvature ratio on sagittal plane	1.5	1.2	1.0
B: Curvature ratio on coronal plane	1.5	1.2	1.0
C: Tibial slope	0°	5°	10°

The combination of design parameters led to the development of nine different models of the BCR TKA knee implant, each of which featured nine different variations of the UHMWPE tibial insert. The base 3D model of BCR TKA was constructed based on the anatomical landmark of the knee joint of a female subject (age 29, mass = 70 kg, height = 170 cm) taken from a previous study [39]. Multiple assembled models with different parameters of the BCR TKA knee implant were established by altering this base model and reconstructing the UHMWPE tibial insert using SOLIDWORKS, thus meeting the requirements of factor combinations in Taguchi's orthogonal experimental design. As shown in Figure 1a, each of these models was made up of a femoral component, a set of UHMWPE tibial inserts, and a tibial component. These three major components made up the entire model. Figure 1b,c show the radius of the curvature of the femoral component and the tibial insert on both the sagittal and coronal planes.

Herein, the FE model of this BCR TKA knee implant was developed using SIMULIA Abaqus. A validated FE model developed in our previous study was used [40,41]. Similar material properties, boundary conditions, and loads were set for each of the nine models to perform the FEA. The materials used for the femoral component and tibial insert were Co-Cr-Mo and UHMWPE, respectively. All materials were assumed to be homogeneous, isotropic, and linearly elastic [42]. The mechanical properties of the materials are presented in Table 2.

Table 2. Mechanical properties of materials used in this study [43–46].

Material	Ultimate Tensile Strength (Megapascals)	Young's Modulus (Megapascals)	Yield Strength (Megapascals)	Poisson's Ratio	Elongation (Percent)
Ultra-high molecular weight polyethylene (UHMWPE)	27	800	23	0.4	7.0
ASTM F75 cobalt chromium molybdenum (Co-Cr-Mo)	920	210,000	540	0.29	16.5

Then, to define the contact, the 'hard' contact model was used to prevent the transfer of tensile stress across the interface and decrease the penetration of the slave (femoral component) surface into the master (UHMWPE tibial insert) surface at the constraint points. A coefficient of friction of 0.04 was considered for the interaction between the femoral component and the UHMWPE tibial insert [47]. Surfaces on top of the femoral component and below the UHMWPE tibial insert were constrained to their reference points, as shown in Figure 2a. The UHMWPE tibial insert was set to be structurally fixed by prohibiting all translation degrees of freedom and by applying the boundary condition to their reference points. Meanwhile, the boundary condition for the femoral component was applied on its reference point to allow rotation and displacement on the vertical axis. Afterwards, each configuration of the models underwent the same load conditions. A vertical compressive load of 1000 N corresponding to the 100 kg mass of the subject was applied onto the midpoint of the transepicondylar axis of the femur along the y-axis to simulate the load, as shown in Figure 2 [48]. Subsequently, tetrahedral elements with an approximate element size of 1.2 mm [40,41,49–52] were used to mesh all models, and the number of elements of each component is presented in Table 3. Figure 2b shows the FE model of the knee implant. Finally, the FE simulations were performed.

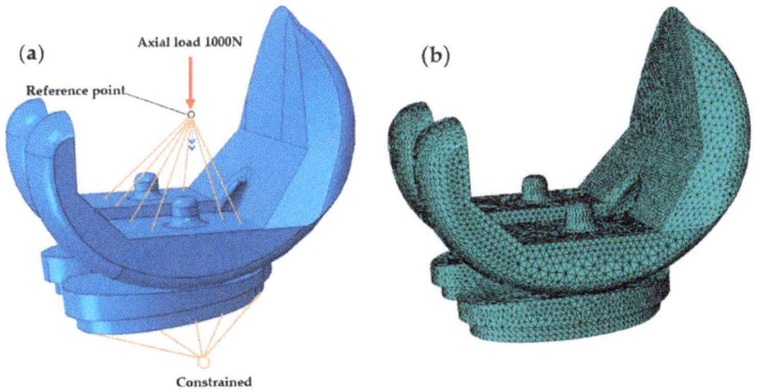

Figure 2. (**a**) The boundary and loading conditions of the FE model. (**b**) FE model of the knee implant.

Table 3. Mesh parameters of the BCR TKA knee implant model for each component.

Component	Type of Mesh	Element Size (Millimeters)	Number of Elements
Femoral	Tetahedral	1.2	182,186
Right tibial insert	Tetahedral	1.2	23,838
Left tibial insert	Tetahedral	1.2	23,703

An analysis of the range of the peak value of contact stress on the UHMWPE tibial insert was carried out to optimise the design. The range was determined using Equation (1):

$$R_j = \max K_{ji} - \min K_{ji},\ 1 \le i \le m \tag{1}$$

where K is the mean of the peak values of contact stress, j is the experimental factor, i is the level, R_j is the range of experimental factor j, and m is the number of levels that were chosen based on a factor. The parameter that was most effective for the peak contact stress and deformation of the BCR TKA knee implant design can be determined from this equation. The greater range of factors indicates that the experimental factor gives a more significant influence on the results [26].

3. Results and Discussion

Each of the designs of the UHMWPE tibial insert affected different contact areas and stresses because of the variation of the BCR TKA knee design parameters. The values of deformation and the peak contact stress on the upper surface of the UHMWPE tibial insert of each model are shown in Table 4. The distribution of the contact stress on the UHMWPE tibial insert is shown in Figure 3. Meanwhile, the deformation of the UHMWPE tibial insert is shown in Figure 4. Stress and deformation were observed with an oval-shape that occurred in the region of the UHMWPE tibial insert.

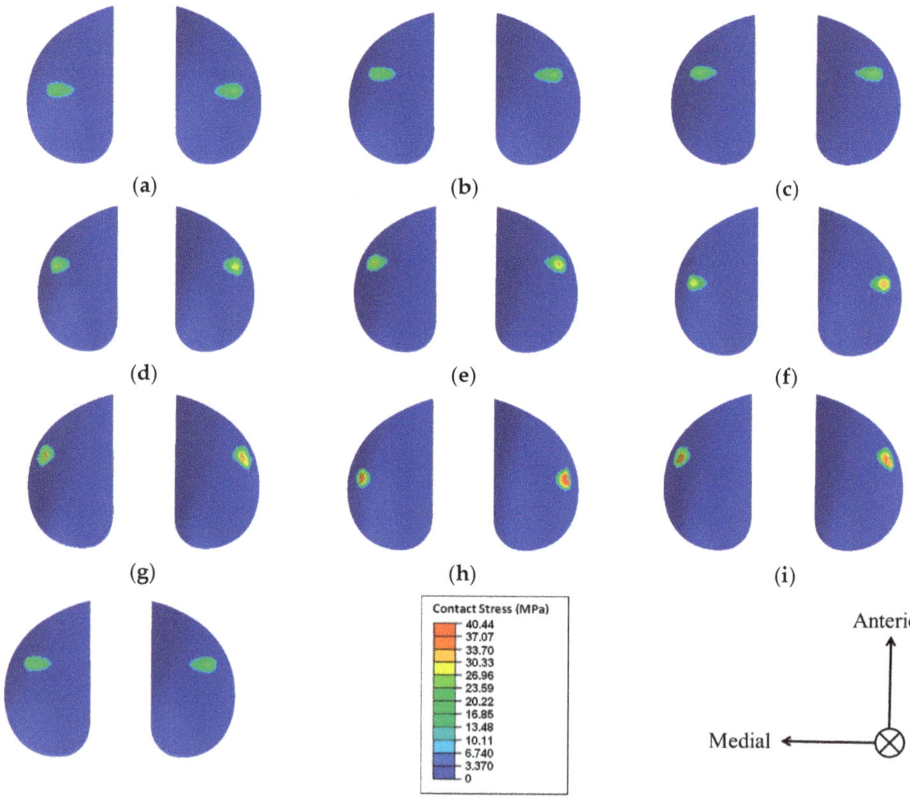

Figure 3. Distribution of the contact stress on the UHMWPE tibial insert. (**a**) Model of the $A_1B_1C_1$ group; (**b**) model of the $A_1B_2C_2$ group; (**c**) model of the $A_1B_3C_3$ group; (**d**) model of the $A_2B_1C_2$ group; (**e**) model of the $A_2B_2C_3$ group; (**f**) model of the $A_2B_3C_1$ group; (**g**) model of the $A_3B_1C_3$ group; (**h**) model of the $A_3B_2C_1$ group; (**i**) model of the $A_3B_3C_2$ group; and (**j**) model of the $A_1B_1C_2$ group (optimised).

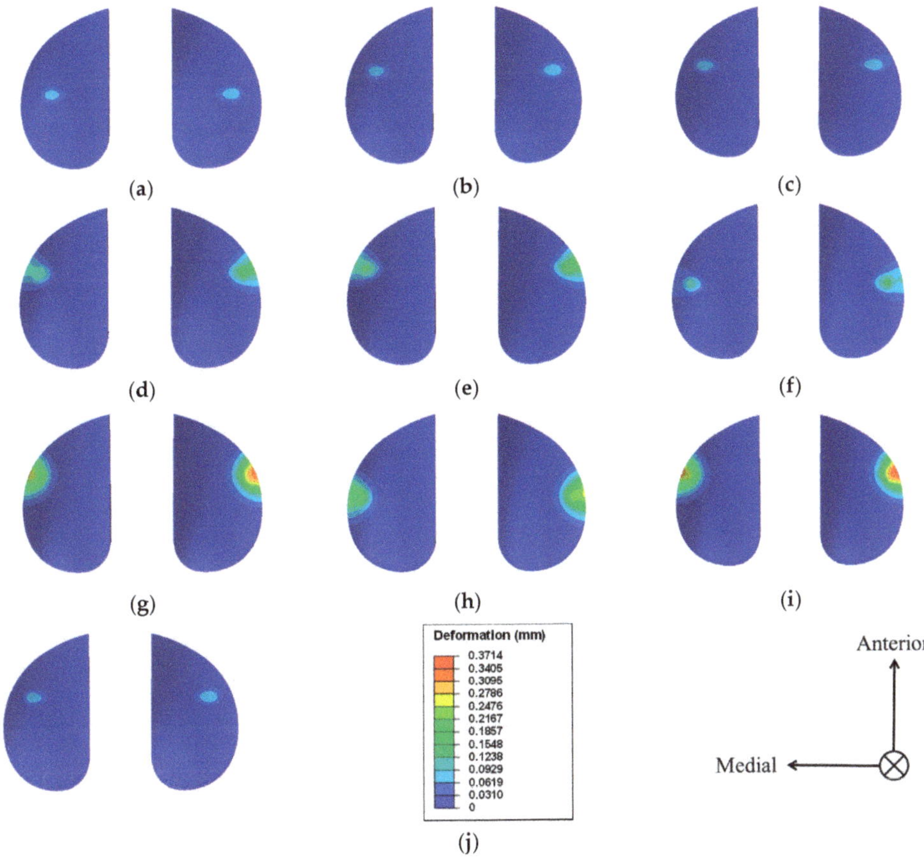

Figure 4. Deformation of the UHMWPE tibial insert. (**a**) Model of the $A_1B_1C_1$ group; (**b**) model of the $A_1B_2C_2$ group; (**c**) model of the $A_1B_3C_3$ group; (**d**) model of the $A_2B_1C_2$ group; (**e**) model of the $A_2B_2C_3$ group; (**f**) model of the $A_2B_3C_1$ group; (**g**) model of the $A_3B_1C_3$ group; (**h**) model of the $A_3B_2C_1$ group; (**i**) model of the $A_3B_3C_2$ group; and (**j**) model of the $A_1B_1C_2$ group (optimised).

Table 4. Experimental level combinations of orthogonal experimental design.

Model	Experimental Level Combination	Curvature Ratio on Saggital Plane	Curvature Ratio on Coronal Plane	Tibial Slope (Degrees)	Peak Value of Contact Stress (Megapascals)	Deformation (Millimeters)
1	$A_1B_1C_1$	1.5	1.5	0	24.89	0.0822
2	$A_1B_2C_2$	1.5	1.2	5	25.69	0.0851
3	$A_1B_3C_3$	1.5	1.0	10	26.78	0.0885
4	$A_2B_1C_2$	1.2	1.5	5	29.39	0.1533
5	$A_2B_2C_3$	1.2	1.2	10	32.53	0.1710
6	$A_2B_3C_1$	1.2	1.0	0	33.49	0.1371
7	$A_3B_1C_3$	1.0	1.5	10	33.75	0.3506
8	$A_3B_2C_1$	1.0	1.2	0	40.44	0.2595
9	$A_3B_3C_2$	1.0	1.0	5	36.05	0.3714

Observing the peak value of the contact stress, the highest peak value of the contact stress among the nine models was 40.44 MPa (group $A_3B_2C_1$, Figure 3h), and it was found in the lateral compartment. The lowest value was 24.89 MPa (group $A_1B_1C_1$, Figure 3a), which was also located in the lateral compartment. According to [42], every varus or valgus alignment causes a change in the medial and lateral contact stresses in comparison with the neutral-aligned model. The effect was stronger for more severe alignment configurations than it was for neutral alignment. However, the distribution of stress was mostly influenced by the design of the knee implant as well as the force that was delivered because of the static analysis that was performed and the absence of any alignment configurations. Given this, the maximum contact stress in each model was mostly on the lateral component. In addition to this, the maximal difference in the peak value of the contact stresses between the lateral and medial compartments was 6.32 MPa (group $A_3B_2C_1$, Figure 3h). Based on these results, even minute alterations in the design parameters of the BCR TKA knee implant could lead to a relatively large change in contact stress (with a maximum change value of 15.55 MPa), thereby indicating the significance of an individualised and accurate design of the BCR TKA knee implant.

Observing the deformation of the UHMWPE tibial insert, the highest deformation among the nine models was 0.3714 mm (group $A_3B_3C_2$, Figure 4i), which was found in the lateral compartment. The lowest value was 0.0822 mm (group $A_1B_1C_1$, Figure 4a), which was also found in the lateral compartment. The deformation on the UHMWPE tibial insert surface was asymmetric on both sides, caused by the different contact stress distributions. In addition to this, the maximal difference in the deformation of the UHMWPE tibial insert between the lateral and medial compartments was 0.0718 mm (group $A_3B_2C_1$, Figure 4h).

An analysis of the range of the peak values of the contact stress on UHMWPE was carried out for each of the nine different knee models using Equation (1). Moreover, the findings of the orthogonal experiment are provided in Table 5. As shown in the table, K_{ji} denotes the mean of the peak values of the contact stress for the experimental factor j at level i. Based on the results of the calculation and the range analysis of the orthogonal experimental design, the curvature ratio on the sagittal plane had the greatest effect on the peak value of the contact stress, followed by the curvature ratio on the coronal plane, whilst the tibial slope had the smallest effect. The trend chart on the influence of various BCR TKA design parameters on the peak value of the contact stress was obtained through the range analysis and is depicted in Figure 5. The optimal design parameters for the BCR TKA UHMWPE tibial insert were obtained as $A_1B_1C_2$, which had curvature ratios of 1.5 on both the sagittal and coronal planes, respectively, and a tibial slope of 5°.

Individualised BCR TKA knee implant design parameters can be optimised to restore the mechanical alignment of the lower extremities, as well as promote consistent load distributions of both the medial and lateral compartments of the knee implant joint to reduce wear and extend prosthesis survival [53]. In this study, the result of the contact stress distribution of TKA models described was compatible with the previously published literature, particularly in terms of the tibial slope. The 3D model of the BCR TKA knee implant was reconstructed based on the optimised design parameters to verify the optimisation results of the orthogonal experimental design. For this optimised design, the number of elements in the meshing of the femoral component was 182,186, and the number of elements in the right and left tibia were 23,838 and 23,703 elements, respectively. The results showed that the peak value of contact stress on the UHMWPE tibial insert was 25.80 MPa (group $A_1B_1C_2$, Figure 3j), which was located in the lateral compartment of the BCR TKA knee implant. The peak value of the contact stress was slightly higher than that of the lowest contact stress model, $A_1B_1C_1$, by 0.91 MPa; however, it was reduced by 14.64 MPa from the highest value of 40.44 MPa (36.20%). The difference in the peak values of contact stress between the medial and the lateral compartments was only 0.48 MPa, and the load was more uniformly distributed than that of most of the other models. As for the deformation, the maximum deformation of this optimised model was 0.0835 mm, and the maximal difference in the deformation of the UHMWPE tibial insert between the lateral and medial compartments was only 0.0058 mm. In addition to this, the deformation was reduced by 0.2879 mm from the highest value of 0.3714 mm (77.52%).

Table 5. Optimisation of the results of the orthogonal experimental design.

Model	Experimental Factor j (j = 1,2,3)			Peak Value of Contact Stress (Megapascals)
	A	B	C	
1	1	1	1	24.89
2	1	2	2	25.69
3	1	3	3	26.78
4	2	1	2	29.39
5	2	2	3	32.53
6	2	3	1	33.49
7	3	1	3	33.75
8	3	2	1	40.44
9	3	3	2	36.05
K_{j1}	25.79	29.34	32.94	
K_{j2}	31.80	32.89	30.38	
K_{j3}	36.75	32.11	31.02	
Range R_j	10.96	3.54	2.56	
Ranking	A > B > C			
Optimal level	A_1	B_1	C_2	

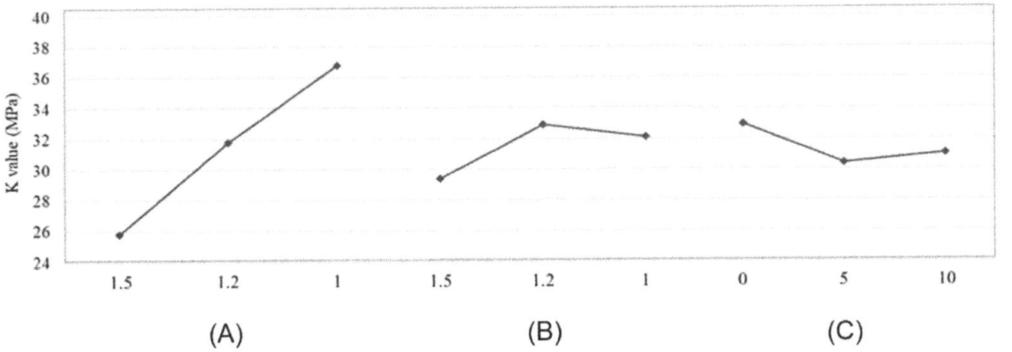

Figure 5. Trend influence of implant design parameters at the peak value of the contact stress on the UHMWPE tibial insert. (**A**) Curvature ratio in sagittal plane. (**B**) Curvature ratio in coronal plane. (**C**) Tibial slope (°).

This optimised implant design had a curvature ratio of 1.5 on the sagittal plane, a curvature ratio of 1.5 on the coronal plane, and a tibial slope of 5°. According to Shen et al., among four different posterior tibial slopes (0°, 3°, 6°, and 9°), the 3° and 6° posterior slopes showed more uniform distributions of contact stress in the medial and lateral compartments with the least polyethylene wear [54]. This was compatible with the findings of this study wherein the optimised design, model $A_1B_1C_2$, also showed a uniform distribution of contact stress in both compartments. However, comparing it to the other models, the peak contact stress of the optimised design was slightly higher than in the models that had the lowest contact stress, $A_1B_1C_1$ (with a curvature ratio of 1.5 on both the sagittal and coronal planes, respectively, and a 0° tibial slope) and $A_1B_2C_2$ (with a curvature ratio of 1.5 and 1.2 on the sagittal and coronal planes, respectively, and a 5° tibial slope). This was caused by edge loading that induced a critical stress area on the tibial insert. According to Dhaka et al., the completeness and conformality of the contact are both directly impacted by the geometry of the contact [55]. It was found that the likelihood of crack initiation increased (because of the increase of contact stress) as the contact geometry became less flat and less conformal in the centre. The increase in crack length leads to a decrease in component fatigue life [33]. This indicates that the stress initiation increases as the corner becomes sharper at the tibiofemoral interfaces. From this, as the UHMWPE tibial insert was tilted

5° to fulfil the optimal design parameters, the UHMWPE tibial insert might have come in contact with a more acute geometry of the femoral component, thereby leading to a slightly higher contact stress than that of the other two models. Previous researchers [56,57] have investigated the effect that the radii of corners in a partially flat pad had on the fretting fatigue life and concluded that, in general, fretting fatigue life decreases with an increase in corner radii. This was attributed to increased stress caused by rounding the corners at the tibiofemoral contact.

However, this study had several limitations. We only simulated the variation of contact pressure on the plastic tibial insert under static conditions. The contact mechanics between the femoral component and the plastic insert under moving conditions, that is, flexional motion or under dynamic conditions, must be further studied to obtain more reliable data for optimisation purposes. To the best of our knowledge and according to the literature, these three parameters, which are the radius of curvature ratio on the sagittal plane, radius of curvature ratio on the coronal plane, and tibial slope, are important geometrical parameters that greatly affect the mechanics of knee implants including the contact stress distribution on the plastic insert as well as the kinematics (mobility) of the implanted knee joint. We selected three levels for each parameter to quantitatively represent the conformity of the tibial and femoral interface. Thus, more levels should be selected to perform more rigorous optimisation to study the effects of these parameters and investigate the effects of parameter variation on contact stress.

4. Conclusions

This study used the FEA method combined with Taguchi's orthogonal experimental design to optimise the design parameters of the BCR TKA knee implant. This was to minimise the peak value of the contact stress and deformation of the UHMWPE tibial insert to reduce wear and extend the life of the implant. Even minute adjustments to the parameters of the design could result in large shifts in the peak value of the contact stress exerted on the UHMWPE, and this could negatively affect the implant's ability to withstand wear over time. This method may be adopted for all patients undergoing TKA knee implants, and it can also be a new investigation for preoperative TKA planning. In addition, this study can offer a basis for the biomechanical decision of proper BCR TKA or other TKA knee implant designs. From this study, it was revealed that among the three parameters that affect the UHMWPE tibial insert's peak contact stress and deformation, the curvature ratio on the sagittal plane had the greatest effect (range = 10.96), followed by the curvature ratio on the coronal plane (range = 3.54), and the tibial slope (range = 2.56). Finally, the optimal design parameters for the BCR TKA knee implant were a curvature ratio of 1.5 on both the sagittal and coronal planes and a tibial slope of 5°. Under these conditions, the peak contact stress and deformation were 25.80 MPa and 0.0835 mm, respectively.

Author Contributions: Conceptualisation, M.A.M.A. and M.F.M.M.; methodology, S.S. and M.A.A.; software, N.Q.M.M.; validation, S.S., M.A.M.A. and M.F.M.M.; formal analysis, N.Q.M.M.; investigation, N.Q.M.M.; resources, M.A.M.A.; data curation, S.S. and N.Q.M.M.; writing—original draft preparation, N.Q.M.M.; writing—review and editing, N.Q.M.M. and M.A.M.A.; visualization, N.Q.M.M.; supervision, M.A.M.A. and M.F.M.M.; project administration, M.A.A.; funding acquisition, M.A.M.A. All authors have read and agreed to the published version of the manuscript.

Funding: This research was funded by the Universiti Teknologi MARA, grant number 600-RMC/GPK 5/3 (098/2020).

Data Availability Statement: Not applicable.

Acknowledgments: The authors are pleased to acknowledge our undergraduate student, Muhammad Azim Mat Raffei, for the excellent assistance and technical support in the computational-aided drawing (CAD) model development.

Conflicts of Interest: The authors declare no conflict of interest.

References

1. Comitini, S.; Tigani, D.; Leonetti, D.; Commessatti, M.; Cuoghi, F.; Barca, P.; Martucci, A.; Bettuzzi, C.; Amendola, L. Evolution in Knee Replacement Implant. *Single Cell Biol.* **2015**, *4*, 109. [CrossRef]
2. Osmani, F.A.; Thakkar, S.C.; Collins, K.; Schwarzkopf, R. The utility of bicruciate-retaining total knee arthroplasty. *Arthroplast Today* **2017**, *3*, 61–66. [CrossRef]
3. Dall'Oca, C.; Ricci, M.; Vecchini, E.; Giannini, N.; Lamberti, D.; Tromponi, C.; Magnan, B. Evolution of TKA design. *Acta Biomed.* **2017**, *88*, 17–31. [CrossRef]
4. Mahomed, N.N.; Barrett, J.; Katz, J.N.; Baron, J.A.; Wright, J.; Losina, E. Epidemiology of Total Knee Replacement in the United States Medicare Population. *J. Bone Jt. Surg.* **2005**, *87*, 1222. [CrossRef]
5. Traina, F.; De Fine, M.; Affatato, S. 5—Anatomy of the knee and suitable prostheses. In *Wear of Orthopaedic Implants and Artificial Joints*; Affatato, S., Ed.; Woodhead Publishing Series in Biomaterials; Woodhead Publishing: Sawston, UK, 2013; pp. 115–132. ISBN 978-0-85709-128-4.
6. Zhang, Q.; Chen, Z.; Zhang, Z.; Jin, Z.; Muratoglu, O.K.; Varadarajan, K.M. Leveraging subject-specific musculoskeletal modeling to assess effect of anterior cruciate ligament retaining total knee arthroplasty during walking gait. *Proc. Inst. Mech. Eng. Part H J. Eng. Med.* **2020**, *234*, 1445–1456. [CrossRef]
7. Pritchett, J.W. Bicruciate-retaining Total Knee Replacement Provides Satisfactory Function and Implant Survivorship at 23 Years. *Clin. Orthop. Relat. Res.* **2015**, *473*, 2327–2333. [CrossRef]
8. Evans, J.T.; Walker, R.W.; Evans, J.P.; Blom, A.W.; Sayers, A.; Whitehouse, M.R. How long does a knee replacement last? A systematic review and meta-analysis of case series and national registry reports with more than 15 years of follow-up. *Lancet* **2019**, *393*, 655–663. [CrossRef]
9. Kassam, A.-A.; Dieppe, P.; Toms, A. An analysis of time and money spent on investigating painful total knee replacements. *Orthop. Proc.* **2012**, *94*, 234. [CrossRef]
10. Kallala, R.F.; Vanhegan, I.S.; Ibrahim, M.S.; Sarmah, S.; Haddad, F.S. Financial analysis of revision knee surgery based on NHS tariffs and hospital costs. *Bone Jt. J.* **2015**, *97*, 197–201. [CrossRef]
11. Jackson Irudhayam, S.; Antony Prabu, D.; Jayakumar, K.S.; Hariram, V.; Sankaralingam, T. Stress distribution in knee Implant: A FEA study. *Mater. Today Proc.* **2022**, *62*, 977–980. [CrossRef]
12. Haijie, L.; Dasen, L.; Tao, J.; Yi, Y.; Xiaodong, T.; Wei, G. Implant Survival and Complication Profiles of Endoprostheses for Treating Tumor Around the Knee in Adults: A Systematic Review of the Literature Over the Past 30 Years. *J. Arthroplast.* **2018**, *33*, 1275–1287.e3. [CrossRef] [PubMed]
13. Henderson, E.R.; Groundland, J.S.; Pala, E.; Dennis, J.A.; Wooten, R.; Cheong, D.; Windhager, R.; Kotz, R.I.; Mercuri, M.; Funovics, P.T.; et al. Failure mode classification for tumor endoprostheses: Retrospective review of five institutions and a literature review. *J. Bone Jt. Surg. Am.* **2011**, *93*, 418–429. [CrossRef]
14. Flannery, M.; McGloughlin, T.; Jones, E.; Birkinshaw, C. Analysis of wear and friction of total knee replacements: Part I. Wear assessment on a three station wear simulator. *Wear* **2008**, *265*, 999–1008. [CrossRef]
15. Archard, J.F. Contact and Rubbing of Flat Surfaces. *J. Appl. Phys.* **1953**, *24*, 981–988. [CrossRef]
16. Kauzlarich, J.J.; Williams, J.A. Archard wear and component geometry. *Proc. Inst. Mech. Eng. Part J J. Eng. Tribol.* **2001**, *215*, 387–403. [CrossRef]
17. Wimmer, M.A.; Laurent, M.P.; Haman, J.D.; Jacobs, J.J.; Galante, J.O. Surface Damage Versus Tibial Polyethylene Insert Conformity: A Retrieval Study. *Clin. Orthop. Relat. Res.* **2012**, *470*, 1814–1825. [CrossRef]
18. Pascau, A.; Guardia, B.; Puertolas, J.A.; Gómez-Barrena, E. Knee model of hydrodynamic lubrication during the gait cycle and the influence of prosthetic joint conformity. *J. Orthop. Sci.* **2009**, *14*, 68–75. [CrossRef]
19. Bartel, D.L.; Bicknell, V.L.; Wright, T.M. The effect of conformity, thickness, and material on stresses in ultra-high molecular weight components for total joint replacement. *J. Bone Jt. Surg. Am.* **1986**, *68*, 1041–1051. [CrossRef]
20. Huang, Z.; Ouyang, G.; Xiao, L. Rotating-platform knee arthroplasty: A review and update. *Orthop. Surg.* **2011**, *3*, 224–228. [CrossRef]
21. Kurtz, S.M.; Bartel, D.L.; Rimnac, C.M. Postirradiation aging affects stress and strain in polyethylene components. *Clin. Orthop. Relat. Res.* **1998**, *350*, 209–220. [CrossRef]
22. Sabarish, K.V.; Pratheeba, P. An experimental analysis on structural beam with Taguchi orthogonal array. *Mater. Today Proc.* **2020**, *22*, 874–878. [CrossRef]
23. Tekade, R.K.; Chougule, M.B. Formulation Development and Evaluation of Hybrid Nanocarrier for Cancer Therapy: Taguchi Orthogonal Array Based Design. *BioMed Res. Int.* **2013**, *2013*, e712678. [CrossRef]
24. Nagarjun, P.A.; Rao, R.S.; Rajesham, S.; Rao, L.V. Optimization of lactic acid production in SSF by Lactobacillus amylovorus NRRL B-4542 using Taguchi methodology. *J. Microbiol.* **2005**, *43*, 38–43.
25. Varshosaz, J.; Eskandari, S.; Tabakhian, M. Production and optimization of valproic acid nanostructured lipid carriers by the Taguchi design. *Pharm. Dev. Technol.* **2010**, *15*, 89–96. [CrossRef]
26. Dong, Y.; Zhang, Z.; Dong, W.; Hu, G.; Wang, B.; Mou, Z. An optimization method for implantation parameters of individualized TKA tibial prosthesis based on finite element analysis and orthogonal experimental design. *BMC Musculoskelet. Disord.* **2020**, *21*, 165. [CrossRef]

27. Brockett, C.; Carbone, S.; Fisher, J.; Jennings, L. Influence of conformity on the wear of total knee replacement: An experimental study. *Proc. Inst. Mech. Eng. Part H J. Eng. Med.* **2017**, *232*, 127–134. [CrossRef]
28. Koh, Y.-G.; Park, K.-M.; Kang, K.-T. The biomechanical effect of tibiofemoral conformity design for patient-specific cruciate retainging total knee arthroplasty using computational simulation. *J. Exp. Orthop.* **2019**, *6*, 23. [CrossRef]
29. Khasian, M.; Meccia, B.A.; LaCour, M.T.; Komistek, R.D. Effects of the Medial Plateau Bearing Insert Conformity on Mid-Flexion Paradoxical Motion in a Posterior-Stabilized Total Knee Arthroplasty Design. *J. Arthroplast.* **2021**, *36*, 2386–2392. [CrossRef]
30. Indelli, P.F.; Risitano, S.; Hall, K.E.; Leonardi, E.; Migliore, E. Effect of polyethylene conformity on total knee arthroplasty early clinical outcomes. *Knee Surg. Sport. Traumatol. Arthrosc.* **2019**, *27*, 1028–1034. [CrossRef]
31. Mou, Z.; Dong, W.; Zhang, Z.; Wang, A.; Hu, G.; Wang, B.; Dong, Y. Optimization of parameters for femoral component implantation during TKA using finite element analysis and orthogonal array testing. *J. Orthop. Surg. Res.* **2018**, *13*, 179. [CrossRef]
32. Tang, Q.; Twumasi, J.O.; Hu, J.; Wang, X.; Yu, T. Finite element simulation of photoacoustic fiber optic sensors for surface corrosion detection on a steel rod. In Proceedings of the Nondestructive Characterization and Monitoring of Advanced Materials, Aerospace, Civil Infrastructure, and Transportation XII, Denver, CO, USA, 5–8 March 2018; SPIE: Paris, France, 2018; Volume 10599, pp. 341–353.
33. Masoudi Nejad, R.; Noroozian Rizi, P.; Zoei, M.S.; Aliakbari, K.; Ghasemi, H. Failure Analysis of a Working Roll Under the Influence of the Stress Field Due to Hot Rolling Process. *J. Fail. Anal. Preven.* **2021**, *21*, 870–879. [CrossRef]
34. Bonner, B.; Law, J.I.; Dacus, E.; Hofmann, E. The Modern Universal Total Knee Arthroplasty: Maximized Value, Streamlined Efficiency. Available online: https://econpapers.repec.org/bookchap/itopchaps/226804.htm (accessed on 14 December 2022).
35. Kohli, A.; Mathad, M.; V Hosamani, S.; Adagimath, M.K.; Kotturshettar, B.B. Finite element analysis of knee joint implant for varying bio material using ANSYS. *Mater. Today Proc.* **2022**, *59*, 941–950. [CrossRef]
36. Bhandarkar, S.; Dhatrak, P. Optimization of a knee implant with different biomaterials using finite element analysis. *Mater. Today Proc.* **2022**, *59*, 459–467. [CrossRef]
37. Kacker, R.N.; Lagergren, E.S.; Filliben, J.J. Taguchi's Orthogonal Arrays Are Classical Designs of Experiments. *J. Res. Natl. Inst. Stand. Technol.* **1991**, *96*, 577–591. [CrossRef]
38. Singerman, R.; Dean, J.C.; Pagan, H.D.; Goldberg, V.M. Decreased posterior tibial slope increases strain in the posterior cruciate ligament following total knee arthroplasty. *J. Arthroplast.* **1996**, *11*, 99–103. [CrossRef]
39. Guess, T.M.; Razu, S. Loading of the medial meniscus in the ACL deficient knee: A multibody computational study. *Med. Eng. Phys.* **2017**, *41*, 26–34. [CrossRef]
40. Mohd Anuar, M.A.; Todo, M.; Nagamine, R.; Hirokawa, S. Dynamic Finite Element Analysis of Mobile Bearing Type Knee Prosthesis under Deep Flexional Motion. *Sci. World J.* **2014**, *2014*, 586921. [CrossRef]
41. Anuar, M.A.M.; Todo, M.; Nagamine, R. Computational Model for Mechanics of Total Knee Replacement: Effect of Tibial Rotation during Deep Flexion in Relation to Post-Cam Design. *Int. J. Biosci. Biochem. Bioinform.* **2014**. [CrossRef]
42. Innocenti, B.; Bellemans, J.; Catani, F. Deviations from Optimal Alignment in TKA: Is There a Biomechanical Difference Between Femoral or Tibial Component Alignment? *J. Arthroplast.* **2016**, *31*, 295–301. [CrossRef]
43. Dayyoub, T.; Maksimkin, A.V.; Kaloshkin, S.; Kolesnikov, E.; Chukov, D.; Dyachkova, T.P.; Gutnik, I. The Structure and Mechanical Properties of the UHMWPE Films Modified by the Mixture of Graphene Nanoplates with Polyaniline. *Polymers* **2018**, *11*, 23. [CrossRef]
44. Baron, S.; Desmond, D.; Ahearne, E. The fundamental mechanisms of wear of cemented carbide in continuous cutting of medical grade cobalt chromium alloy (ASTM F75). *Wear* **2019**, *424–425*, 89–96. [CrossRef]
45. Wang, A.; Yau, S.-S.; Essner, A.; Herrera, L.; Manley, M.; Dumbleton, J. A Highly Crosslinked UHMWPE for CR and PS Total Knee Arthroplasties. *J. Arthroplast.* **2008**, *23*, 559–566. [CrossRef] [PubMed]
46. Fleming, T.J.; Kavanagh, A.; Duggan, G. The effect of melt temperature on the mechanical properties of cast ASTM F75 CoCrMo alloy as explained by nitrogen and oxygen content. *J. Mater. Res. Technol.* **2020**, *9*, 9479–9486. [CrossRef]
47. Takian, W.; Rooppakhun, S.; Ariyarit, A.; Sucharitpwatskul, S. Optimal Conformity Design of Tibial Insert Component Based on ISO Standard Wear Test Using Finite Element Analysis and Surrogate Model. *Symmetry* **2021**, *13*, 2377. [CrossRef]
48. D'Lima, D.D.; Fregly, B.J.; Patil, S.; Steklov, N.; Colwell, C.W. Knee joint forces: Prediction, measurement, and significance. *Proc. Inst. Mech. Eng. H* **2012**, *226*, 95–102. [CrossRef]
49. Kang, K.-T.; Son, J.; Kwon, S.K.; Kwon, O.-R.; Park, J.-H.; Koh, Y.-G. Finite element analysis for the biomechanical effect of tibial insert materials in total knee arthroplasty. *Compos. Struct.* **2018**, *201*, 141–150. [CrossRef]
50. Kwon, O.-R.; Kang, K.-T.; Son, J.; Kwon, S.-K.; Jo, S.-B.; Suh, D.-S.; Choi, Y.-J.; Kim, H.-J.; Koh, Y.-G. Biomechanical comparison of fixed- and mobile-bearing for unicomparmental knee arthroplasty using finite element analysis. *J. Orthop. Res.* **2014**, *32*, 338–345. [CrossRef]
51. Koh, Y.-G.; Park, K.-M.; Lee, H.-Y.; Kang, K.-T. Influence of tibiofemoral congruency design on the wear of patient-specific unicompartmental knee arthroplasty using finite element analysis. *Bone Jt. Res.* **2019**, *8*, 156–164. [CrossRef]
52. Kang, K.-T.; Son, J.; Kim, H.-J.; Baek, C.; Kwon, O.-R.; Koh, Y.-G. Wear predictions for UHMWPE material with various surface properties used on the femoral component in total knee arthroplasty: A computational simulation study. *J. Mater. Sci. Mater. Med.* **2017**, *28*, 105. [CrossRef]
53. Fang, D.M.; Ritter, M.A.; Davis, K.E. Coronal alignment in total knee arthroplasty: Just how important is it? *J. Arthroplast.* **2009**, *24*, 39–43. [CrossRef]

54. Shen, Y.; Li, X.; Fu, X.; Wang, W. A 3D finite element model to investigate prosthetic interface stresses of different posterior tibial slope. *Knee Surg. Sport. Traumatol. Arthrosc.* **2015**, *23*, 3330–3336. [CrossRef] [PubMed]
55. Dhaka, P.; Prakash, R.V. Effect of Contact Geometry on the Contact Stresses in a Flat with Round Edge Contact. *Frat. Ed Integrità Strutt.* **2019**, *13*, 630–638. [CrossRef]
56. Mall, S.; Naboulsi, S.; Namjoshi, S.A. Contact geometry effects on fretting fatigue crack initiation behaviour of Ti–6Al–4V. *Tribol. Mater. Surf. Interfaces* **2008**, *2*, 25–32. [CrossRef]
57. Juoksukangas, J.; Lehtovaara, A.; Mäntylä, A. The effect of contact edge geometry on fretting fatigue behavior in complete contacts. *Wear* **2013**, *308*, 206–212. [CrossRef]

Disclaimer/Publisher's Note: The statements, opinions and data contained in all publications are solely those of the individual author(s) and contributor(s) and not of MDPI and/or the editor(s). MDPI and/or the editor(s) disclaim responsibility for any injury to people or property resulting from any ideas, methods, instructions or products referred to in the content.

mathematics

MDPI

Article

Analytical and Numerical Model of Sloshing in a Rectangular Tank Subjected to a Braking

Oana-Maria Balaş [1,*], Cristian Vasile Doicin [1] and Elena Corina Cipu [2,3]

1 Department of Machine Building, University Politehnica of Bucharest, 060042 Bucharest, Romania
2 Department of Applied Mathematics, University Politehnica of Bucharest, 060042 Bucharest, Romania
3 CiTi, Faculty of Applied Sciences, University Politehnica of Bucharest, 060042 Bucharest, Romania
* Correspondence: oanamariamanta@gmail.com

Abstract: This paper examines the movement of waves that occur in a fuel tank—both with and without a wave breaker—when a car is travelling at a constant speed and then suddenly brakes. This phenomenon is known as slosh noise, and the paper presents an analysis of the movement of free surfaces in relation to the level of noise generated. The paper focuses on mathematical models of the fluid flow for both tanks—one without any technical solutions for breaking waves, and the other with a solution for breaking waves. The model is constructed based on a set of initial hypotheses about the fluid flow within the tank, by developing the speed potential in a series of fundamental solutions and considering the main variables that affect the phenomenon of sloshing, such as the depth of the liquid, the tank's geometry, and the frequency and amplitude of the initial external force acting on the tank. The analysis of free surface movement is used to find the correlation with the sound generated in the tank. Nonlinearities that arise from the sudden braking are also modelled and numerically studied using MATLAB software. Following the mathematical model, a technical wave-breaking solution was implemented and tested, and it was shown that the amplitude of the movement of the free surface is reduced by half. Further research on the correspondence between the free surface movement based on the behaviour of potential energies in the two cases may be developed.

Keywords: slosh noise; rectangular tank; mathematical modelling; potential flow; spectral methods; fundamental solutions

MSC: 76-10; 76B07; 76M22; 35A08

Citation: Balaş, O.-M.; Doicin, C.V.; Cipu, E.C. Analytical and Numerical Model of Sloshing in a Rectangular Tank Subjected to a Braking. *Mathematics* **2023**, *11*, 949. https://doi.org/10.3390/math11040949

Academic Editor: Lihua Wang

Received: 24 December 2022
Revised: 31 January 2023
Accepted: 7 February 2023
Published: 13 February 2023

Copyright: © 2023 by the authors. Licensee MDPI, Basel, Switzerland. This article is an open access article distributed under the terms and conditions of the Creative Commons Attribution (CC BY) license (https://creativecommons.org/licenses/by/4.0/).

1. Introduction

Many researchers have investigated the phenomenon of sloshing using various methods: analytical [1,2], numerical or experimental. They have observed that different types of baffles, inserted in tanks [3], can reduce the natural sloshing frequencies. For example, analytical studies, numerical experiments and moving particle semi-implicit computation have been carried out using porous baffles for sloshing reduction in a swaying rectangular tank by Cho and Kim [4], and Poguluri Sunny Kumar [5], using the Galerkin method and Chebyshev polynomials for modelling and simulating the sloshing phenomenon in a porous screen-equipped tank.

It is assumed that the fuel in the tank is an incompressible fluid, and the potential formulation can be used to describe its free surface. The determination of the free surface inside the tank is closely related to the correct approximation of the sound generated by the ripple. However, the potential formulation may not always accurately express the reality [6], and numerical modelling might be necessary to produce more realistic results. The nonlinearities generated by sudden braking can also be numerically studied.

The main methods used in numerical analysis include: MAC (Marker and Cell) approximation, VOF (Volume of Fluid Method) approximation, LSM method (Level Set

Method) or a combination of these methods. More recently, the SPH (Smoothed Particle Hydrodynamics) approximation [7] has been used in 2D numerical modelling to simulate sound propagation [8]. The slosh noise that occurs in a fuel tank can be a hit noise due to a wave hitting the walls of the tank, or a splash noise due to turbulence and the agglomeration of small waves inside the fuel tank. These can be studied through the oscillatory movement of the free surface of the liquid inside the fuel tank. A vertical baffle is more effective in reducing the sloshing amplitude than a horizontal one.

An improved MPS method and numerical simulation under an initial rotational excitation are made in [9], and it is proved that when the baffle is flush with the surface, the damping effect is optimal. An improved ALE technique (Arbitrary Langrangian Eulerian finite element method) was used in [10] to improve the tank design to reduce noise levels. With the same optimization goal, Frosina et al. in [11] use a CFD (Computational Fluid Dynamics) modelling approach to study the correct fuel suction under all driving conditions.

In this paper, the main variables that affect the ripple phenomenon are considered: liquid depth, tank geometry, and the frequency and amplitude of the initial external force acting on the tank. To reduce the wave nonlinearities and noise, various types of breakers can be installed in the tank. These breakers aim to reduce the pressure on the ceiling or walls, as well as to reduce extreme fluid phenomena, including ripples.

This paper is organized as follows: the problem description, general principles and hypotheses are considered in the next section. Section 3 is dedicated to the mathematical model of the fluid flow in the tank without a slosh noise reduction baffle. The fluid flow is determined by the potential of the velocity, using the method of fundamental solutions and describing the amplitude evolution of the free surface. In Section 4, the noise reduction baffle is introduced into the model. The solution of the potential function in the two areas delimited by the baffle is obtained, and the evolution of the free surface is graphically represented. The effects of using a suitable baffle are investigated. Finally, some conclusions are made.

2. Problem Description and Assumptions

We investigate the movement of waves created within a fuel tank, with and without a wave breaker, when a car is travelling at a constant speed and suddenly brakes. The aim of this study is to evaluate the effectiveness of incorporating a slosh noise buffer in a tank, both analytically and experimentally. A simplified tank shape is considered, in line with the patented technical solution for baffles proposed by the author (EP3296136A1 Dispositif Anti Clapot d'un Reservoir de Carburant d'un Vehicule Automobile, Applied By RENAULT SAS [FR], Inventor BALAS OANA MARIA [RO]).

We apply the general principles to our specific problem, taking into account boundary and initial conditions, to arrive at a well-posed problem:

$$\text{Mass conservation:} \quad \int_D \rho(\mathbf{x},t)d\,V = 0, \forall D \in \mathcal{M} \tag{1}$$

$$\text{Impulse variation:} \quad \frac{d}{d\,t}\int_D \rho\mathbf{a}\,d\,V = \int_{\partial D} \mathbf{t}d\,\sigma + \int_D \rho\mathbf{f}\,d\,V \tag{2}$$

$$\text{Kinetic moment variation:} \quad \frac{d}{d\,t}\int_D \rho\mathbf{x}\times\mathbf{v}\,d\,V = \int_{\partial D} \mathbf{x}\times\mathbf{t}d\,\sigma + \int_D \mathbf{x}\times\rho\mathbf{f}\,d\,V \tag{3}$$

In addition to the general assumptions related to fluid motion, we add the following hypotheses:

- The effects of liquid compressibility, viscosity and surface tension could be neglected. According with the the first principle, we can write

$$\text{div}\mathbf{v} = 0. \tag{4}$$

- The flow is potential, meaning that the velocity potential $\phi(x, y, t)$ exists such that

$$u = \frac{\partial \phi}{\partial x}, v = \frac{\partial \phi}{\partial y} \tag{5}$$

- The movement of the fluid is laminar in the z direction, and the movement is flat [12].
- Boundary conditions are imposed such that

$$\frac{d\phi}{dn} = \mathbf{v}_t \cdot \mathbf{n} \text{ on the tank walls.} \tag{6}$$

3. Mathematical Model of the Fluid Flow in the Tank without a Slosh Noise Reduction Baffle

The fluid flow is determined by the potential ϕ of the fluid velocity that verifies the Laplace equation

$$\Delta\phi = 0 \tag{7}$$

and boundary conditions:

$$\frac{\partial \phi}{\partial x}(-l, y, t) = \frac{\partial \phi}{\partial x}(l, y, t) = 0 \tag{8}$$

on the side walls, and on the floor

$$\frac{\partial \phi}{\partial y}(x, 0, t) = 0 \tag{9}$$

according with the geometry of the tank as in Figure 1.

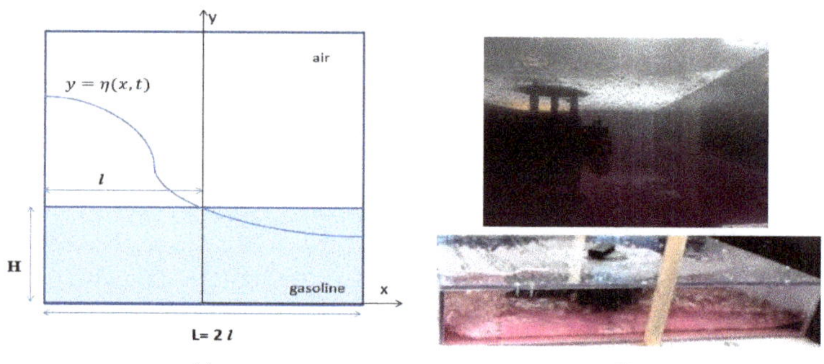

(a) (b)

Figure 1. Tank geometry. (**a**) Geometry of a non-stop tank used for the analytical model. (**b**) Geometry of a non-stop tank for the experimental study.

The width of the tank is considered in the x direction (520 mm), the length in the z direction (1000 mm) and the height in the y direction (160 mm). The origin is considered in the middle of the bottom of the surface of the tank. Additionally, H is the height of the liquid in the tank.

The boundary condition (6) expressed for passing from the inertial coordinate system to the tank fixed coordinate system leads to the conditions imposed upon the free surface $y = \eta(x, t)$, see [13], that are the cinematic condition:

$$\frac{\partial \eta}{\partial t} - \mathbf{v} \cdot \nabla \eta - \frac{\partial \eta}{\partial y} + \frac{\partial \eta}{\partial x} \cdot \frac{\partial \phi}{\partial x} = 0 \tag{10}$$

and dynamic condition

$$\frac{\partial \phi}{\partial t} - \mathbf{v} \cdot \nabla \phi + \frac{1}{2}(\nabla \phi)^2 + g\,\eta = 0. \tag{11}$$

As the liquid is incompressible, the potential energy of a liquid element is given only by the potential gravitational energy [3,14–16]:

$$U^e = \frac{1}{2}\rho g b \int_0^L \eta^2(x,t)\mathrm{d}\,x \tag{12}$$

and the kinetic energy of the liquid element is given by [3,16]:

$$T^e = \frac{1}{2}\rho g \int_V (\nabla \phi)^2 \mathrm{d}\,V. \tag{13}$$

When the tank is subjected to a horizontal acceleration, $\ddot{X}_0(t)$ lateral sounds of the contained fluid will appear, where:

$$\dot{X}_0(t) = \begin{cases} U_0 - a\,t, & t \in [0, t_1] \\ -a\,t_1, & t \in [t_1, t_s] \end{cases} \tag{14}$$

t_s is the total stop time of the tank ($t_s = 5\,\mathrm{s}$), $t_1 = 0.4\,\mathrm{s}$, $a = U_0/t_1$, and constant a represents the average value of the acceleration (of braking, in this case). Based on the state of the art of the topic developed by the authors, the optimal timing for the braking event that generates the slosh noise phenomena is 5 s. This duration it is used for the analytical model and experimental tests [17–22].

Movement in the tank is described by the potential ϕ that is decomposed into two functions:

$$\phi = \varphi + \psi, \tag{15}$$

where φ is the solution of the Laplace's equation with static conditions on the walls:

$$\varphi = x\,u + y\,v, \tag{16}$$

and ψ also satisfies the Laplace's equation in D and the following boundary conditions:

$$\text{on the side walls: } \frac{\partial \psi}{\partial x}(-\frac{L}{2}, y, t) = 0 = \frac{\partial \psi}{\partial x}(\frac{L}{2}, y, t) \tag{17}$$

$$\text{on the floor of the tank: } \frac{\partial \psi}{\partial y}|_{y=0} = 0 \tag{18}$$

$$\text{on the free surface: } \frac{\partial \eta}{\partial t} - \frac{\partial \psi}{\partial y} + \frac{\partial \eta}{\partial x} \cdot \frac{\partial \phi}{\partial x} = 0 \tag{19}$$

Analytical Model (Ma) for Determining the Potential

The potential will be determined using the superposition method of the liquid's own functions in the tank, based on the linearized theory of potentials, compared to the nonlinear Boussinesq model [12].

We use the method of fundamental solutions (MFS), also described in [12,13], and consider that the potential has the form

$$\psi(x,y,t) = \psi_0(x,y,t) + \sum_n \psi_n(x,y,t) \tag{20}$$

where

$$\psi_n(x,y,t) = f_n(x,y)\,A_n(t),\ n \geq 1 \tag{21}$$

are the fundamental solutions that verify the Laplace equation, $\Delta\psi = 0$ with the conditions (17)–(19). One finds, for the functions f_n, the problem

$$\Delta f_n = 0, \frac{\partial f_n}{\partial x}\left(-\frac{L}{2}, y\right) = 0 = \frac{\partial f_n}{\partial x}(\frac{L}{2}, y), \frac{\partial f_n}{\partial y}|_{y=0} = 0 \tag{22}$$

with the boundary conditions (considered linear, in the first approximation)

$$\frac{\partial \eta}{\partial t} - \frac{\partial \psi}{\partial y} = 0, \frac{\partial \psi}{\partial t} + g\eta = 0 \tag{23}$$

and where the first potential ψ_0 is a particular solution that takes into account the movement of the tank, verifies the Laplace equation and non-homogeneous boundary conditions

$$\Delta\psi_0 = 0, \frac{\partial \psi_0}{\partial x}(-\frac{L}{2}, y, t) = \dot{X}(t) = \frac{\partial \psi_0}{\partial x}(\frac{L}{2}, y, t), \frac{\partial \psi_0}{\partial y}|_{y=0} = 0. \tag{24}$$

For the free surface of the fuel, we have

$$\frac{\partial \eta_0}{\partial t} - \frac{\partial \psi}{\partial y} = 0, \frac{\partial \psi_0}{\partial t} + g\eta_0 + \epsilon\psi_0 = 0, \text{for } y = \eta_0(x,t). \tag{25}$$

with $\epsilon = 0$ in linear theory. Considering the derivative according with t in (23), respectively, in (25) we obtain

$$\frac{\partial^2 \psi_0}{\partial t^2} = -g\frac{\partial \eta_0}{\partial t} = \frac{\partial \psi_0}{\partial y}, \frac{\partial^2 \psi}{\partial t^2} = -g\frac{\partial \eta}{\partial t} = \frac{\partial \psi}{\partial y}. \tag{26}$$

$f_n(x,y)$ and A_n have separate variables, and one obtains:

$$-\frac{\ddot{A}_n(t)}{A_n(t)} = \frac{g\frac{\partial f_n}{\partial y}}{f_n(x,y)} = \omega_n^2 \tag{27}$$

from where

$$g\frac{\partial f_n}{\partial y} - \omega_n^2 f_n(x,y) = 0, \ddot{A}_n(t) + \omega_n^2 A_n(t) = 0. \tag{28}$$

Using the solutions for (28), the fundamental solution for the potential is

$$\psi_n(x,y,t) = f_n(x,y)\sin(\omega_n t), \omega_n^2 = g\lambda_n \tanh(\lambda_n H) \tag{29}$$

$$f_n(x,y) = -K_n \cos(\lambda_n(x+l))\cosh(\lambda_n y), \lambda_n = \frac{n\pi}{L} \tag{30}$$

checking the boundary conditions

$$\frac{\partial \eta_n}{\partial t} - \frac{\partial \psi_n}{\partial y}(x, \eta_n(x,t)) = 0, \frac{\partial \psi_n}{\partial t}(x, \eta_n(x,t)) + g\eta_n = 0. \tag{31}$$

From the condition $\eta_n(-l,0) = H$, where H is the height of the fuel in the tank, the constants $K_n = \dfrac{gH}{\omega_n \cosh(\lambda_n H)}$ are determined. For η_n, we have the solution

$$\eta_n(x,t) = H\cos(\lambda_n(x+l))\cos(\omega_n t) \tag{32}$$

and the amplitude of the free surface is:

$$\eta(x,y,t) = \eta_0(x,y,t) + \sum_n \eta_n(x,t). \tag{33}$$

To determine the potential $\psi_0(x,y,t)$ and amplitude $\eta_0(x,t)$, we solve the problem (22)–(23), where $\dot{X}_0(t) = U_0 - a\,t, a \neq 0$ corresponding to braking.

$$\psi_0 = A_0(t) + (U_0 - a\,t)\,x,\ \eta_0(l,0) = H,\ \eta_0(x,t) = -\frac{1}{g}\frac{\partial \psi_0}{\partial t}. \tag{34}$$

For calculating the amplitude $A_0(t)$, a pendulum equation is used (see [12]).

$$\ddot{A}_0(t) + B_1\dot{A}_0(t) + \omega_1^2 A_0 = \ddot{X}, \tag{35}$$

with $B_1 = \frac{\sqrt{2\omega_1 \nu}}{Lb}\left(b + L + b\frac{\lambda_1(L-2H)}{\sinh 2\lambda_1 H}\right)$. Under the given problem, the value $\Delta = B_1^2 - 4\omega_1^2$ is positive and for $\delta = \sqrt{\Delta}$ and $r_{1,2} = (-B_1 \pm \delta)/2$, $r_1 - r_2 = \delta$, the solution of the Equation (35) has the form

$$A_0(t) = \begin{cases} A_{01}(t) = c_{11}\exp(r_1 t) + c_{12}\exp(r_2 t) - \dfrac{a}{\omega_1^2}, & t \in [0, t_1] \\ A_{02}(t) = c_{21}\exp(r_1 t) + c_{22}\exp(r_2 t), & t \in [t_1, t_s] \end{cases} \tag{36}$$

constants $c_{11}, c_{12}, c_{21}, c_{22}$ being determined from the initial conditions as

$$c_{11} = \frac{\dot{A}_0^1(0) - (A_0(0) + \frac{a}{\omega_1^2})r_2}{\delta},\ c_{12} = \frac{(A_0^1(0) + \frac{a}{\omega_1^2})r_1 - \dot{A}_0^1(0)}{\delta}$$

$$c_{21} = \frac{\dot{A}_0^2(0) - A_0^2(0)r_2}{\delta},\ c_{22} = \frac{(A_0^2(0))r_1 - \dot{A}_0^2(0)}{\delta}$$

For the given issue, we consider conditions compatible with relationships (25) and (31).

$$A_{01}(0) = 0, \dot{A}_{01}(0) = al - gH, A_{02}(0) = A_{01}(t_1), \dot{A}_{02}(0) = \dot{A}_{01}(t_1). \tag{37}$$

meaning that

$$A_{01}(t_1) = c_{11}e^{r_1 t_1} + c_{12}e^{r_2 t_1} - \frac{a}{\omega_1^2},\ \dot{A}_{01}(t_1) = c_{11}r_1 e^{r_1 t_1} + c_{12}r_2 e^{r_2 t_1}. \tag{38}$$

The amplitude $A_0(t)$ analytically obtained in (36) and numerically computed using a Runge–Kutta method in MatLab was plotted on the same graph in Figure 2a. Because of the accuracy of the calculus, only one method was used in Figure 2b.

The maximum amplitude is measured a short time after braking ([0, 0.4] to [0, 0.8] seconds). As seen in Figure 2a, for a time interval of [0, 0.4], the free surface follows a slight climb and stagnation. Additionally, as seen in Figure 2b, the "quietness" of the waves inside the tank is observed.

If a fuel tank does not contain wave breakers, a large wave is generated followed by successive smaller waves that will hit each other (Figure 3). The noise generated in this case represents the phenomenon of slosh noise, which is unpleasant for the user.

According to relation (36), when the time increases after t_1, the amplitude will be larger then the case $t < t_1$ if the term $\frac{a}{\omega_1^2}$ is bigger then the sum of the first two terms. That fact leads to the change of wave shape expressed in Figure 3.

As a remark, for Boussinesq's non-linear model with a slight disturbance of amplitude, the linear conditions on the free surface will change [23]. Using cinematic condition (25) for any η, $\frac{\partial \psi}{\partial t} + g\eta + \epsilon\psi = 0$ and the dynamic condition for the free surface $\frac{\partial \eta}{\partial t} - \frac{\partial \psi}{\partial y} = 0$, one finds the governing equation for the potential: $\frac{\partial^2 \psi}{\partial t^2} + \epsilon\frac{\partial \psi}{\partial t} + g\frac{\partial \psi}{\partial y} = 0$.

In [12], the free surface elevation is made precise, the expression of the velocity potential of the first sloshing mode is given and the coefficient ϵ was described by an approximation. The relative free surface elevations at the left wall with different excitation frequencies were numerically computed. We have analytically defined the time variation of the amplitude and the free surface inside the tank. Additionally, in [16], only numerical results were obtained.

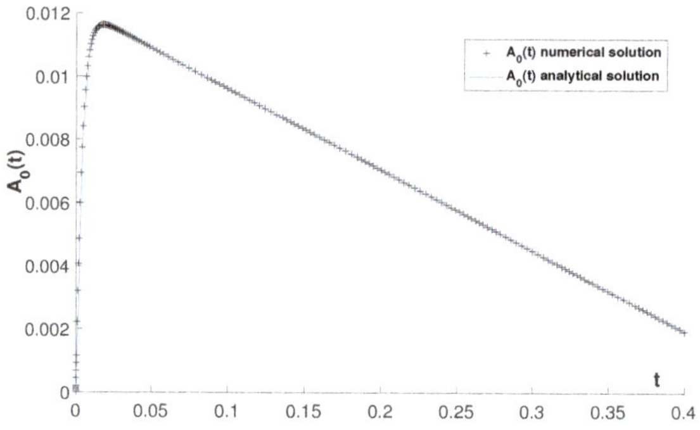

(**a**) time interval 0.4 s

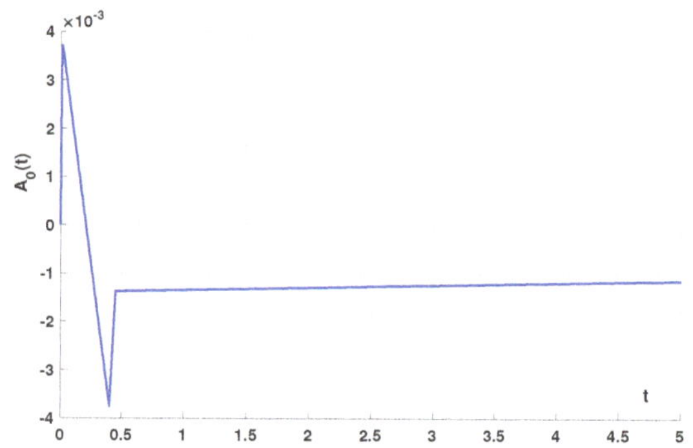

(**b**) time interval 5 s

Figure 2. Evolution of amplitude (A0 [m]) (**a**) time $t \in [0, 0.4]$ s, (**b**) time $t \in [0, 5]$ s.

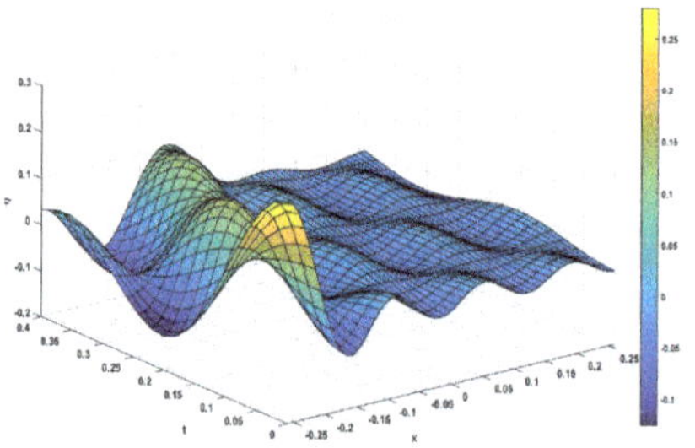

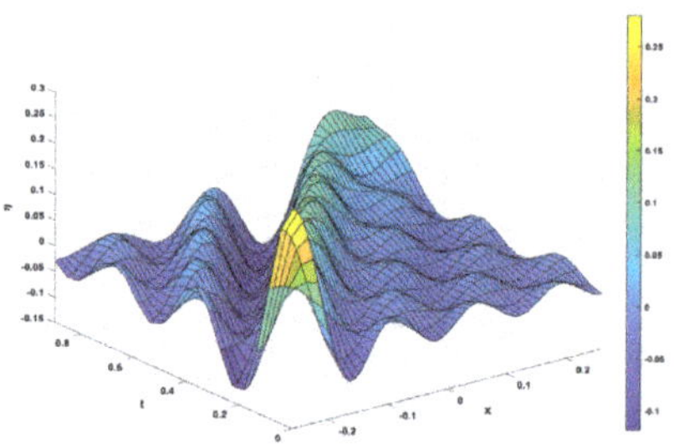

(**a**) time interval 0.4 s (**b**) time interval 0.8 s

Figure 3. Evolution of the free surface (**a**) $t \in [0, 0.4]$ s, (**b**) time $t \in [0, 0.8]$ s.

4. Mathematical Model of the Fluid Flow in the Tank with a Slosh Noise Reduction Baffle

The initial status of a tank that includes a wave breaker is outlined in the Figure 4, where: h = 30 mm, tank length = 1000 mm, tank width (L) = 520 mm, and tank height = 160 mm.

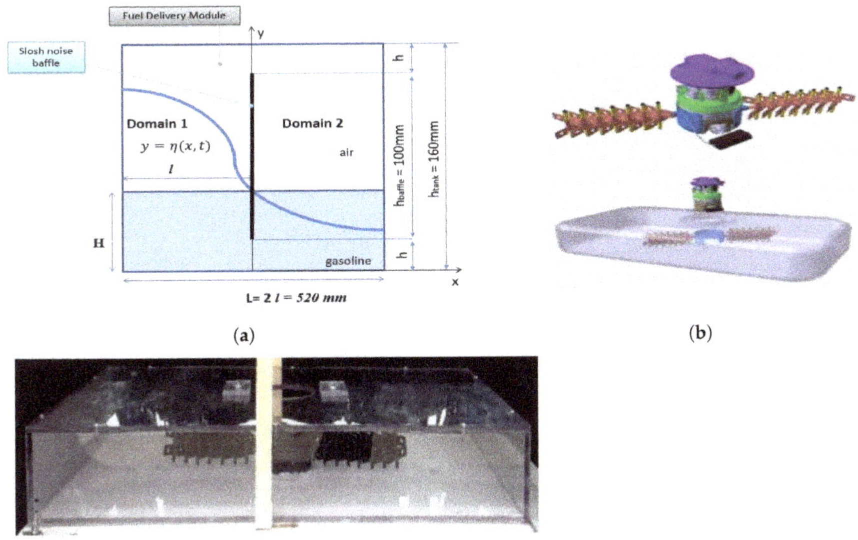

(a) (b)

(c)

Figure 4. Geometry of a slosh noise baffle integrated in the tank. (**a**) The geometry of the baffle tank used for (MA). (**b**) Assembly of the baffle in the tank. (**c**) The geometry of the baffle tank used for experimental study.

We consider the movement of the free surface on the width of the tank as flat movement in the xOy plane (in the transverse plane) and with the same values of the amplitude at any section along the length of the tank. According to the geometry shown in Figure 4a, with sp = notation for the presence of a slosh noise baffle inside the tank and fsp = notation for the case without the presence of a slosh noise baffle inside the tank, the movement in the tank is broken down into two areas: $\mathcal{D} = D_1 \cup D_2$ with $D_1 = [h, h + h_{sp}] \times [-l, 0]$, $D_2 = [h, h + h_{sp}] \times [0, l]$. The description of the geometry of the baffle for the experimental study (Figure 4b,c) is found in the patent, which is referenced within the paper at the beginning of Section 2.

The potential $\phi = \varphi + \psi$ check the Laplace equation with the shape (16) for φ and (20) for ψ in both areas.

Taking into account the initial speed U_0 and the volume of liquid in the tank, one obtains an average value for the mass forces $f(t) = \int \frac{F}{m} dt = f_0(t)$, which will be used in the boundary conditions. According to the experimental approach and data, see [20], below are presented the values for the forces associated to the initial speed U_0.

The data from Table 1 show the values for the forces, f_0, associated with different initial speeds, U_0 (10 km/h, 30 km/h, and 50 km/h) for three different volumes (15 L, 25 L, and 35 L) and corresponding masses (12.5 kg, 20.9 kg, and 29.2 kg) of a liquid. The forces are consistent across different speeds for the same volume and mass. The data show that the force decreases with increasing volume and mass of the liquid and that the force increases with increasing initial speed.

The boundary conditions on the D_1 side walls are:

$$\frac{\partial \psi}{\partial x}(-\frac{L}{2}, y, t) = \dot{X}(t), \ \frac{\partial \psi}{\partial x}(0_-, y, t) = f(t), y \in [h, h + h_{sp}], \tag{39}$$

and on the D_2 side walls are

$$\frac{\partial \psi}{\partial x}(0_+, y, t) = 0, \ \frac{\partial \psi}{\partial x}(\frac{L}{2}, y, t) = \dot{X}(t), y \in [h, h + h_{sp}], \tag{40}$$

also, on the floor of the tank, the condition imposed is:

$$\left.\frac{\partial \psi}{\partial y}\right|_{y=0} = 0. \tag{41}$$

The first condition in (39) and the last condition in (40) expressed for $\frac{\partial \psi}{\partial x}$ express the condition on the wall of the tank, in which case the fluid will have the velocity of the tank described by $\dot{X}(t)$. On the left side of the baffle, the mass forces are considered identically distributed on the baffle using $f_0(t)$.

Table 1. Parameter values of f_0 [N/kg] relative to the initial speed U_0.

Volume Liquid [L]	Mass [kg]	f_0 [N/kg] at $U_0 = 10$ km/h	f_0 [N/kg] at $U_0 = 30$ km/h	f_0 [N/kg] at $U_0 = 50$ km/h
15	12.5	2.00800	2.28800	2.57600
25	20.9	2.00800	2.00000	2.27751
35	29.2	2.00342	2.28082	2.57192
45	37.6	2.0000	2.27926	2.56915

Using the inertia coefficient C and the drag coefficient $\alpha = \left(\frac{1}{P C_c} - 1\right)^2$ described through the porosity of the breaker (see [5]) and the discharge coefficient C_c, the jump condition on the sides of the breaker is:

$$\left[\frac{\partial \psi}{\partial t}(x,y,t)\right]_-^+ = \frac{\alpha}{2}\frac{\partial \psi}{\partial x}\left|\frac{\partial \psi}{\partial x}\right| + 2C\frac{\partial^2 \psi}{\partial x \partial t}. \tag{42}$$

and C is negligible if the thickness of the wave breaker is neglected.

On the other hand, the condition of the speed continuity at the level of $y = h$ expressing that the speed is continuous when passing from the level $y < h$ to $y = h$. For $y < h$, the liquid is without a wave breaker and the speed solution is known at the free surface $y = h$, in each domain (D_1 and D_2) determined by the separation of the baffle:

$$\frac{\partial \psi}{\partial x} = u_{fsp}(x,y,t)\Big|_{y=h},\ x \in [-l, 0],\ \text{for determining the solution in } D_1, \tag{43}$$

$$\frac{\partial \psi}{\partial x} = u_{fsp}(x,y,t)\Big|_{y=h},\ x \in [0, l],\ \text{for determining the solution in} D_2, \tag{44}$$

where $u^{fsp}(x,t) = \frac{\partial \psi^{fsp}}{\partial x}(x,h,t)$, ψ^{fsp} being the potential solution of the form (20) for the problem of the motion without a breaker.

According to the previously determined solution, we find that:

$$\begin{aligned} u^{fsp}(x,t) &= -a\,t + \sum_n u_n^{fsp}(x,t), t \in [0,t_1], \\ u^{fsp}(x,t) &= -a\,t_1 + \sum_n u_n^{fsp}(x,t), t \in [t_1,t_s], \end{aligned} \tag{45}$$

where

$$u_{n\,fsp}(x,y,t) = \frac{\partial \psi_n^{fsp}}{\partial x}(x,y,t) = \frac{\partial f_n^{fsp}}{\partial x}(x,y)\sin(\omega_n^{fsp} t), t \in [0,t_s]. \tag{46}$$

and for any $t \in [0,t_s]$, we have

$$u_n^{fsp}(x,t) = u_{n\,fsp}(x,y,t)\Big|_{y=h} = K_n\lambda_n\cosh(\lambda_n H)\sin(\lambda_n(x+l))\sin(\omega_n^{fsp} t). \tag{47}$$

(see [4]).

Additionally, the hydrostatic pressure and free surface can be described by:

$$p = -g\frac{\partial\psi}{\partial t}, \eta = \frac{p}{\rho g}. \tag{48}$$

The solutions of the potential function in the two areas are:

$$\psi^1 = \psi_0^1 + \psi_f, x \in [-l, 0], \text{respectively}, \psi^2 = \psi_0^2 + \psi_f, x \in [0, l], \tag{49}$$

with $\psi_f = \sum_{n-1}^{\infty} \psi_n$, where $\psi_n = f_n^1(x, y)\sin(\omega_n^{sp} t)$ has solution type (21), $n \geq 1$,

$$f_n^1(x, y) = -C_n \cos(\lambda_n^{sp}(x + l))\cosh(\lambda_n^{sp} H), \tag{50}$$

f_n^1 is a fundamental solution that verifies:

$$\Delta f_n^1 = 0, \frac{\partial f_n^1}{\partial x}(-l, y) = 0 = \frac{\partial f_n^1}{\partial x}(0, y), \frac{\partial f_n^1}{\partial y}|_{y=0} = 0 \tag{51}$$

For the functions ψ_0^1 in the D_1 domain and ψ_0^2 in the D_2 domain, we have obtained for $\forall y \in [h, h + h_{sp}]$, $t \in [0, t_1]$ the solutions

$$\psi_0^1 = A_{01}^1(t) + \int_0^1 \frac{1}{\omega_1^{sp}}[-a(1-\theta) + f_0\theta]\,\mathrm{d}\theta + x((U_0 - at)(1-\theta) + f_0 t\theta), \tag{52}$$

when $x \in [-l, 0]$ and

$$\psi_0^2 = A_{01}^2(t) + \int_0^1 \frac{1}{\omega_1^{sp}}[f_0(1-\theta) - a\theta]\,\mathrm{d}\theta + x(f_0 t(1-\theta) + (U_0 - at)\theta) \tag{53}$$

when $x \in [0, l]$, for $\theta = \dfrac{t}{t_1}$.

For $t \in [t_1, t_s]$ and denoting $\theta = \dfrac{t - t_1}{t_s - t_1}$, the functions ψ_0^1 and ψ_0^2 have the shape

$$\begin{aligned} \psi_0^1 &= A_{02}^1(t) + x((U_0 - at)(1-\theta) + f_0 t\theta), \forall x \in [-l, 0], \\ \psi_0^2 &= A_{02}^2(t) + x(f_0 t(1-\theta) + (U_0 - at)\theta), \forall x \in [0, l], \end{aligned} \tag{54}$$

where $A_{01}^2(t) = A_{01}^1(t) = c_{11}e^{r_1 t} + c_{12}e^{r_2 t}$; $A_{02}^2(t) = A_{02}^1(t) = c_{21}e^{r_1 t} + c_{22}e^{r_2 t}$.

The free surface, depicted in Figure 5 for $t \in [0, 0.4]$ s and $t \in [0, 0.9]$ s, is determined by the relationship $\dfrac{\partial\eta}{\partial t} + g\eta = 0$ for $y = \eta(x, t)$, with $\eta^i = \eta_0^i + \sum_n \eta_n^i(x, t)$ and $i = 1, 2$ the free surfaces in the two domains D_1 and D_2.

According with the method of fundamental solutions used in (20), we obtain:

$$\eta_0^i = -\frac{1}{g}\frac{\partial\psi_0^i}{\partial t} - \frac{1}{g}\frac{\partial\psi_f}{\partial t}, i = 1, 2. \tag{55}$$

where

$$-\frac{1}{g}\frac{\partial\psi_f}{\partial t} = \sum_{n=0}^{\infty} H\cos(\lambda_n^{sp}(x + l))\cos(\omega_n^{sp} t) \tag{56}$$

Additionally, for $t \in [0, t_1]$, we have

$$\begin{aligned} -\frac{1}{g}\frac{\partial\psi_0^1}{\partial t} &= -\frac{1}{g}\left[\dot{A}_{01}^1(t) + x\left(-a + 2(f_0 + a)\frac{t}{t_1} - \frac{U_0}{t_1}\right)\right], \forall x \in [-l, 0], \\ -\frac{1}{g}\frac{\partial\psi_0^2}{\partial t} &= -\frac{1}{g}\left[\dot{A}_{01}^2(t) + x\left(f_0 + \frac{U_0}{t_1} - 2(f_0 + a)\frac{t}{t_1}\right)\right], \forall x \in [0, l], \end{aligned} \tag{57}$$

and for $t \in [t_1, t_s]$, one obtains

$$-\frac{1}{g}\frac{\partial \psi_0^1}{\partial t} = -\frac{1}{g}\left[\dot{A}_{02}^1(t) + x\left(-a + 2(f_0 + a)\frac{t}{t_s - t_1} - \frac{U_0}{t_1}\right)\right], \forall x \in [-l, 0],$$
$$-\frac{1}{g}\frac{\partial \psi_0^2}{\partial t} = -\frac{1}{g}\left[\dot{A}_{02}^2(t) + x\left(f_0 + \frac{U_0}{t_1} - 2(f_0 + a)\frac{t}{t_s - t_1}\right)\right], \forall x \in [0, l]. \quad (58)$$

The relationships developed, (57) and (58), indicate a dependency of the height and number of waves created within a vehicle tank on the presence or absence of a wave breaker, its geometry also being important. The same dependency was also determined experimentally, following the measurement of the noise level recorded under different running conditions, according to the data in Table 2.

In [24,25], a correlation between the sound intensity due to sloshing and the pressure fluctuation dp/dt has been found, and connecting to (49), $\frac{\partial \eta}{\partial t} = \frac{1}{\rho g}\frac{\partial p}{\partial t}$, the variation in time and space was depicted in Figure 5.

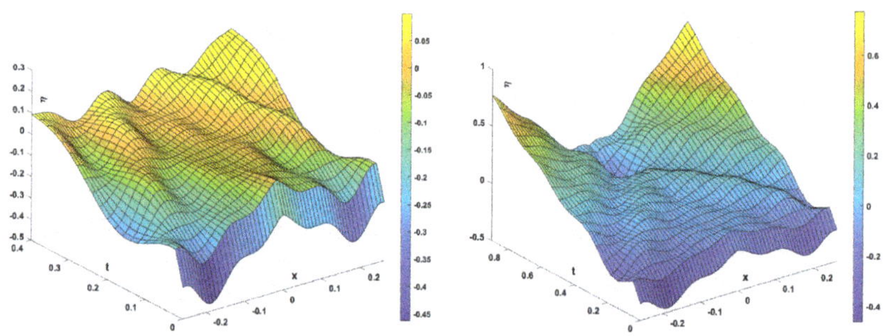

(**a**) with baffle in the two areas of integration, time interval 0.4 s. (**b**) with baffle in the two areas of integration, time interval 0.9 s.

Figure 5. Evolution of the free surface (**a**) $t \in [0, 0.4]$ s, (**b**) time $t \in [0, 0.9]$ s.

Table 2. Initial conditions for the cases considered during acoustic measurements.

No.	Case	Presence of Baffle	Volum of Liquid [L]	Speed before Braking [km/h]
1	S1	no baffle	15	10
2	S2	no baffle	15	30
3	S3	no baffle	25	10
4	S4	no baffle	25	30
5	S5	no baffle	35	10
6	S6	no baffle	35	30
7	S7	no baffle	45	10
8	S8	no baffle	45	30
9	F1	Baffle included	15	10
10	F2	Baffle included	15	30
11	F3	Baffle included	25	10
12	F4	Baffle included	25	30
13	F5	Baffle included	35	10
14	F6	Baffle included	35	30
15	F7	Baffle included	45	10
16	F8	Baffle included	45	30

According to Figure 5, when a tank has a wave breaker, a single large wave is observed and the liquid tends to move towards the sides. Theoretically, by incorporating a wave breaker into a tank, the noise caused by the sloshing phenomenon is reduced due to the lack of waves. By analysing Figures 6 and 7, it can be seen that the free surface behaves differently, with a significant reduction in the number of waves in the case of a wave breaker being integrated. This results in a reduction in the discomfort caused by the sloshing phenomenon. Negative values on the X-axis are a result of the chosen axis system, where -0.25 m and $+0.25$ m represent the tank walls.

The reference level is set to the level of the liquid at rest (H level, as seen in Figures 1b and 4b) and positive and negative variations from this level are observed after braking.

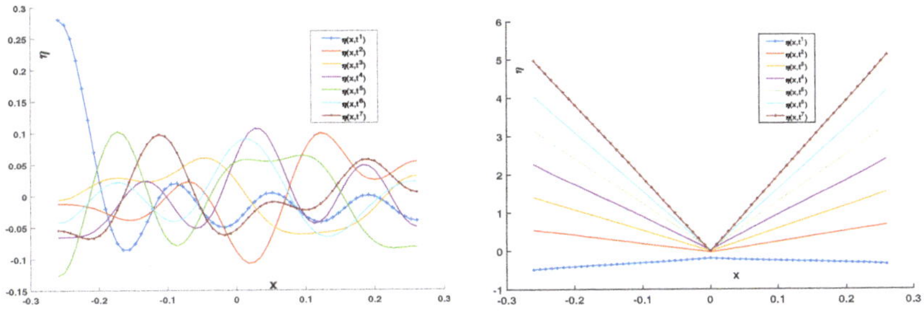

(a) (b)

Figure 6. Evolution of wave amplitude (free surface section in direction X). (**a**) Evolution of wave amplitude for a tank without a baffle. (**b**) Evolution of wave amplitude for a tank with a breaker included.

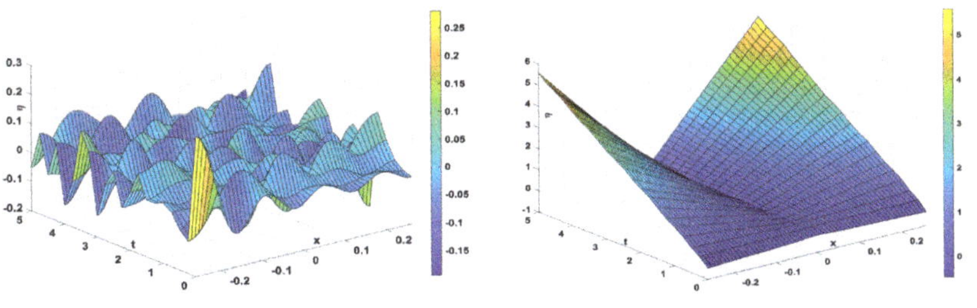

(a) (b)

Figure 7. Evolution of wave amplitude. (**a**) Behaviour of the free surface for a slosh noise baffle-free tank. (**b**) Behaviour of the free surface for a slosh noise baffle in the tank.

As can be seen in Figure 7a, there are ripples on the free surface, these being unfractionated surfaces (the gradient on the curves does not change its convexity), which are smoother, and thus no noise is generated by the collision of small waves. The greater the distance between two peaks of the amplitude, the flatter the free surface is, and thus non-noisy.

In the considered model, the study is carried out in the centre of the tank, not taking into account that the vehicle tanks have an upper limit, given by the tank ceiling. For future research, it is an advanced study taking into account the model's upper limitation, considering that when the wave returns, the potential movement becomes turbulent.

All the graphics in the paper were created by the authors, and the computations were made using MatlabR2022b codes.

5. Conclusions and Future Researches

For people travelling in a car with a stop-start system, the slosh noise caused by the movement of fuel in the tank is considered to be an annoyance. The intensity of this phenomenon increases during braking and accelerating.

The paper studies the movement of fuel in the tank, analysing both the waves and the sound generated during the accelerating and braking of the car. The associated phenomenon, called the slosh noise effect, is studied through analytical and approximate models. The analytical mathematical model of the free surface of the fluid during movement includes the determination of the potential function and the velocity components, in two different variants, with and without wave breakers. The model of the fuel movement in a tank containing wave breakers (baffles) was developed by dividing the fuel volume into two regions, separated by the baffle surfaces and defining both boundary and jump conditions on the baffle surfaces.

Based on the analytical models (for tanks with and without baffles), graphical representations of the free surface movement were made in both variants, with and without baffles. Comparing the graphs of the waves in each case, it is observed that the introduction of the baffles reduces the phenomenon by half (see Section 4). Thus, it is found that the amplitude of the movement of the free surface of the fluid in the case of the implementation of a wave breaker solution of the type of baffle is reduced by half compared to the movement of the free surface of the fluid contained in a fuel tank that does not present anti-blinking technical solutions.

The theme represents the creation of a new baffle design for fuel tanks in the automotive industry that can be adapted to already existing fuel tanks without modifying the original design. The baffle is needed to decrease noise generated by the fuel waves inside the fuel tank. Its effect is shown in Figure 8, confirmed by physical experimental tests [20].

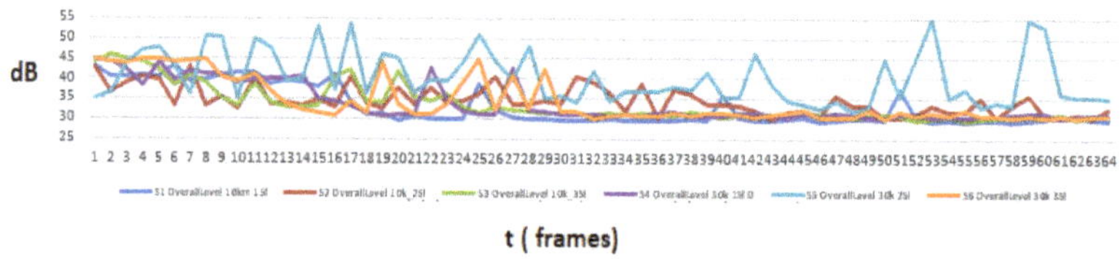

(**a**)

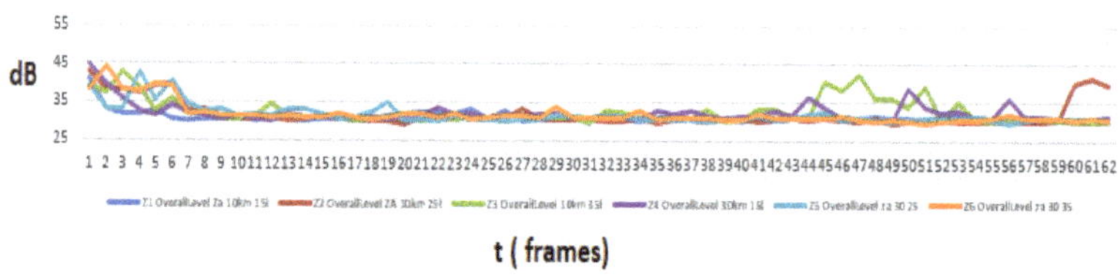

(**b**)

Figure 8. Noise variation based on a technical solution implemented inside the tank. (**a**) Fuel tank without any slosh noise solution. (**b**) Patented slosh noise baffle integrated in the tank.

The comparative analysis by the amplitude and free surface leads to new future research directions on the correspondence between free surface movement and the noise level generated through the module of the velocity, and the nondimensional simplified form of the Bernoulli integral for incompressible flows:

$$\frac{1}{2}(\mathbf{v}^{fsp})^2 + \frac{(c^{fsp})^2}{\gamma - 1} = \frac{1}{2}(\mathbf{v}^{sp})^2 + \frac{(c^{sp})^2}{\gamma - 1},$$

with γ being the ratio between specific heat at constant pressure and specific heat at constant volume [1,26]. The Bernoulli integral allows us to make the connection between the velocity of the fuel and the level of the sound due to the waves in the tank. As one observes from the previous formula, for a smaller module of the velocity $\mathbf{v}^{fsp} = \sqrt{u_{fsp}^2 + v_{fsp}^2}$ results in a larger value for the sound speed and also in a larger value of the velocity module when the wave breaker is introduced, meaning $\mathbf{v}^{sp} = \sqrt{u_{sp}^2 + v_{sp}^2}$, then the speed sound becomes smaller.

According with our notations, $\mathbf{v}^{sp} = (u_{sp}, v_{sp})$ and $\mathbf{v}^{isp} = (u_{sp}^i, v_{sp}^i)$ with $i = 1, 2$, is the velocity corresponding to the two domains D_1 and D_2 (see Section 4). For $t \in [0, t_1]$ and any $y \in [h, h + h_{sp}]$, we have

$$\begin{aligned}
u_{sp}^1 &= \frac{\partial \psi_0^1}{\partial x} = (U_0 - a\,t)(1-\theta) + f_0 t\theta \\
&\quad + \sum_{n=1}^{\infty} \frac{C_n}{\lambda_n^{sp}} \sin(\lambda_n^{sp}(x+l)) \cosh(\lambda_n^{sp} y) \sin(\omega_n^{sp} t), \theta = \frac{t}{t_1} \\
v_{sp}^1 &= \frac{\partial \psi_0^1}{\partial y} = -\sum_{n=1}^{\infty} \frac{C_n}{\lambda_n^{sp}} \cos(\lambda_n^{sp}(x+l)) \sinh(\lambda_n^{sp} y) \sin(\omega_n^{sp} t),
\end{aligned} \tag{59}$$

and also for $t \in [t_1, t_s]$ and any $y \in [h, h + h_{sp}]$, the velocity components are

$$\begin{aligned}
u_{sp}^2 &= \frac{\partial \psi_0^2}{\partial x} = (U_0 - a\,t)\theta + f_0 t(1-\theta) \\
&\quad + \sum_{n=1}^{\infty} \frac{C_n}{\lambda_n^{sp}} \sin(\lambda_n^{sp}(x+l)) \cosh(\lambda_n^{sp} y) \sin(\omega_n^{sp} t), \theta = \frac{t - t_1}{t_s - t_1} \\
v_{sp}^2 &= \frac{\partial \psi_0^2}{\partial y} = -\sum_{n=1}^{\infty} \frac{C_n}{\lambda_n^{sp}} \cos(\lambda_n^{sp}(x+l)) \sinh(\lambda_n^{sp} y) \sin(\omega_n^{sp} t).
\end{aligned} \tag{60}$$

Figure 8, expressing the result of the experimental study, and Figures 3, 5–7, describing the results of the analytical study, lead to the conclusion that the use of the baffle reduces the slosh noise, improving the efficiency of the tank usage. Figure 3a is compared with Figure 5a, and Figure 3b is compared with Figure 5b.

For future studies, we aim to analyse the energy behaviour of the system through potential energy defined in (12) and kinetic energy defined in (13) that, for the case with the breaker solution implemented, becomes

$$\begin{aligned}
U_{sp}^e &= \frac{1}{2}\rho g b\Big(\int_{-l}^{0} (\eta_0^1)^2(x,t) + \int_0^l (\eta_0^1)^2(x,t)\Big)\mathrm{d}\,x, \\
T_{sp}^e &= \frac{1}{2}\rho g \int_V (\nabla \psi_{sp})^2 \mathrm{d}\,V.
\end{aligned} \tag{61}$$

and compare the two solutions from this point of view.

Author Contributions: Conceptualization, O.-M.B.; Methodology, E.C.C.; Validation, O.-M.B., C.V.D. and E.C.C.; Formal analysis, E.C.C.; Resources, O.-M.B. and C.V.D.; Writing—original draft, E.C.C.; Writing—review & editing, O.-M.B. and E.C.C.; Supervision, C.V.D.; Project administration, O.-M.B.; Funding acquisition, O.-M.B. All authors have read and agreed to the published version of the manuscript.

Funding: The work has been founded through the European Social Fund (FSE-POCU 2014-2020, contract nr. 13530/16.06.2022- cod SMIS: 153734), within the project "Preparation of doctoral students and postdoctoral researchers in order to acquire applied research skills—SMART".

Data Availability Statement: Not applicable.

Acknowledgments: The work has been founded through the European Social Fund (FSE-POCU 2014-2020, contract nr. 13530/16.06.2022- cod SMIS: 153734), within the project "Preparation of doctoral students and postdoctoral researchers in order to acquire applied research skills—SMART".

Conflicts of Interest: The authors declare no conflict of interest.

Abbreviations

The notations used all over the paper are the following:

m	mass of the material system $\mathcal{M}$ and $\rho(\mathbf{x}, t)$ the mass density
ν, g	molecular viscosity in [kg m^{-1} s^{-1}] and gravitational acceleration
L , b	tank width [mm] and tank length [mm]
η	amplitude of the free surface of the fluid inside the tank
x, v, a	position, velocity and acceleration of the material point
$\mathbf{v}_t$	velocity of the tank
n, f	normal exterior and external forces acting on the surface ∂D

References

1. Dragos, L. *Introducere Matemation in Mecanica Fluidelor/Mathematical Introduction in Fluid Mechanics*; Romanian Academy Press: Bucharest, Romania, 2000.
2. Fox, R.W.; McDonald, A.T.; Pritchard, P.J. *Introduction in Fluid Mechanics*, 6th ed.; John Wiley Sons: New York, NY, USA, 2004; ISBN 0-471-37653-1.
3. Chu, C.R.; Wu, Y.R.; Wu, T.R.; Wang, C.Y. Slosh -induced hydrodynamic force in a water tank with multiple baffles. *Ocean Engineering* **2018**, *167*, 282–292. [CrossRef]
4. Cho, I.H.; Kim, M.H. Effect of dual porous baffles on sloshing reduction in a swaying rectangular tank. *Ocean Eng.* **2016**, *126*, 364–373. [CrossRef]
5. Poguluri, S.K.; Cho, I.H. Liquid sloshing in a rectangular tank with vertical slotted porous screen: Bassed on analytical, numerical and experimental approach. *Ocean Eng.* **2019**, *189*, 106–373–173. [CrossRef]
6. Lu, L.; Jiang, S.C.; Zhao, M.; Tang, G.Q. Two-dimensional viscous numerical simulation of liquid sloshing in rectangular tank with/ without baffles and comparison with potential flow solutions. *Ocean Eng.* **2015**, *108*, 662–667. [CrossRef]
7. Shao, J.R.; Li, H.Q.; Liu, G.R.; Liu, M.B. An improved sph method for modeling liquid sloshing dynamics. *Comput. Struct.* **2012**, *100–101*, 18–26. [CrossRef]
8. Hassan, H.A.S. Muti dimensional nurbs model for predicting maximum free surface oscilation in swaying rectangular storage tanks. *Comput. Math. Appl.* **2018**, *76*, 2496–2513. [CrossRef]
9. Wang, L.; Xu, M.; Zhang, Q. Numerical Investigation of Shallow Liquid Sloshing in a Baffled Tank and the Associated Damping Effect by BM-MPS Method. *J. Mar. Sci. Eng.* **2021**, *9*, 1110. [CrossRef]
10. Koli, G.C.; Kulkarni, V.V. *Simulation of Fluid Sloshing in a Tank, World Congress on Engineering (WCE 2010)*; Imperial Coll London: London, UK, 2010; Volume II, pp. 1028–1033, LECT NOTES ENG COMP, INT ASSOC ENGINEERS-IAENG, ISSN 2078-0958, ISBN 978-988-18210-7-2.
11. Frosina, E.; Senatore, A.; Andreozzi, A.; Marinaro, G.; Buono, D.; Bianco, G.; Auriemma, D.; Fortunato, F.; Damiano, F.; Giliberti, P. Study of the sloshing in a fuel tank using CFD and EFD approaches. In Proceedings of the ASME/BATH 2017 Symposium on Fluid Power and Motion Control (FPMC2017), Sarasota, FL, USA, 16–19 October 2017; ISSN 2475-7004, ISBN 978-0-7918-5833-2.
12. Yan, S.; Liu, Z.Y. Numerical model of sloshing in rectangular tank based on boussinesq type equations. *Ocesn Eng.* **2016**, *121*, 166–173. [CrossRef]
13. Lin, B.H.; Chen, B.F.; Tsai, C.C. Method of fundamental solutions on simulating sloshing liquids in a 2d tank. *Comput. Math. Appl.* **2019**, *88*, 52–69. [CrossRef]
14. Matsson, J. *Ansys 19.1 Relesse Notes, SAS IP*; Version 19.1; SDC Publications: Mission, KS, USA, 2018.
15. Arafa, M. Finite element snalysis of sloshing in rectangular liquid-filled tanks. *J. Vib. Control* **2007**, *13*, 883–903. [CrossRef]
16. Demirel, E.; Aral, M.M. Liquid sloshing damping in an accelerated tank using a novel slot baffle design. *Water* **2018**, *10*, 1565. [CrossRef]
17. Hallez, R.l.; McGann, I.F.; Sibal, S.D.; Li, F. *Radiated Fuel Tank Slosh Noise Simulation*; SAE Internationa: Warrendale PA, USA, 2011. [CrossRef]
18. Charpentier, A.; Kim, H.; Hwang, Y.; Noh, J.; Caro, S. Validation of Fuel Tank Slosh Noise and Vibration Predictions. In Proceedings of the INTER-NOISE and NOISE-CON Congress and Conference Proceedings, Hamburg, Germany, 21–24 August 2016.
19. Frosina, E.; Senatore, A.; Andreozzi, A.; Fortunato, F.; Giliberti, P. Experimental and Numerical Analyses of the Sloshing in a Fuel Tank. *Energies* **2018**, *11*, 682. [CrossRef]
20. Manta, O.M.; Balas, R.; Ulmeanu, M.E.; Murzac, R.; Doicin, C.V. Construction and testing of the wave breaking prototype—Slosh noise baffle. *UPB Sci. Bull.* **2022**, *84*, 103–116. ISSN 1454-2358.
21. Manta, O.M.; Balas, R.; Murzac, R.; Ulmeanu, M.; Doicin, C.V. Statical Analysis of Slosh Noise Baffle, Macromolecular Symposia. In Proceedings of the International Conference on Design and Technologies for Polymeric and Composite Products (POLCOM), Bucharest, Romania, 10–11 October 2019; WILEY-V C H VERLAG GMBH: Weinheim, Germany, 2020; ISSN 1022-1360. [CrossRef]
22. Manta, M.; Balas, R.; Doicin, C.V. Research and constructive solutions on the reduction of slosh noise, 20th Innovative Manufacturing Engineering and Energy Conference (IMANEE 2016). In Proceedings of the IOP Conference Series-Materials Science and Engineering, Kallithea, Greece, 23–25 September 2016; IOP Publishing Ltd.: Bristol, UK, 2016; ISSN 1757-8981.
23. Matsson, J. *ANSYS Software User's Guide 15.0, SAS IP*; Version 15.0; SDC Publications: Mission, KS, USA, 2013.

24. Wiesche, S.A.D. Noise due to sloshing within automotive fuel tanks. *Forschung im Ingenieurwesen* **2006**, *70*, 13–24. [CrossRef]
25. Agawane, G.; Jadon, V.; Balide, V.; Banerjee, R. An Experimental Study of Sloshing Noise in a Partially Filled Rectangular Tank. *SAE Int. J. Passeng. Cars-Mech. Syst.* **2017**, *10*. ISSN 1946-3995. [CrossRef]
26. Milne-Thomson, L.M. *Theoretical Hydrodynamics*, 4th ed.; MacMillan Co., Ltd.: London, UK, 1962.

Disclaimer/Publisher's Note: The statements, opinions and data contained in all publications are solely those of the individual author(s) and contributor(s) and not of MDPI and/or the editor(s). MDPI and/or the editor(s) disclaim responsibility for any injury to people or property resulting from any ideas, methods, instructions or products referred to in the content.

mathematics

MDPI

Article

Faults Modeling in Networked Environment and Its Tolerant Control with Multiple Simultaneous Faults

Atif Mahmood [1,*], Abdul Qayyum Khan [2], Nasim Ullah [3,†], Adil Sarwar Khan [2], Muhammad Asim Abbasi [2], Alsharef Mohammad [3,†] and Abdulfattah Noorwali [4,†]

1 Grafton College, No. 6 Park Road, Chak Shahzad, Islamabad 45600, Pakistan
2 Pakistan Institute of Engineering and Applied Sciences, Nilore, Islamabad 45650, Pakistan
3 Department of Electrical Engineering, College of Engineering, Taif University, Taif 21944, Saudi Arabia
4 Department of Electrical Engineering, Umm Al-Qura University, Makkah 24221, Saudi Arabia
* Correspondence: engg.khaki@gmail.com or atif.m@pk.graftoncollege.org
† These authors contributed equally to this work.

Abstract: This paper presents two new fault models for networked systems. These fault models are more realistic and generalized for networked systems in the sense that they can represent the effects of fault at the node and network levels. At the network layer, the uncertain effects of the network lines are modeled using a Markov chain with complex transition probabilities simultaneously with the stochastic behavior of the network using a Bernoulli process. A new output feedback-based controller, which is two-mode dependent and considers network uncertainties and output measurements for gain calculation, is presented. Using the tools of robust control and stochastic stability, linear matrix inequality-based sufficient conditions are derived. The proposed controller successfully maintains the system's performance by tolerating the effects of simultaneous sensor and actuator faults, ensuring the stability of networked loops. Simulation results verify the applicability of the presented fault-tolerant control against multiple simultaneous faults.

Keywords: fault modeling; networked systems; fault-tolerant control; stochastic stability; Markovian jump system

MSC: 97M50

Citation: Mahmood, A.; Khan, A.Q.; Ullah, N.; Khan, A.S.; Abbasi, M.A.; Mohammad, A.; Noorwali, A. Faults Modeling in Networked Environment and Its Tolerant Control with Multiple Simultaneous Faults. *Mathematics* **2023**, *11*, 996. https://doi.org/10.3390/math11040996

Academic Editors: Shujin Laima, Yong Cao, Xiaowei Jin and Hehe Ren

Received: 8 January 2023
Revised: 4 February 2023
Accepted: 8 February 2023
Published: 15 February 2023

Copyright: © 2023 by the authors. Licensee MDPI, Basel, Switzerland. This article is an open access article distributed under the terms and conditions of the Creative Commons Attribution (CC BY) license (https://creativecommons.org/licenses/by/4.0/).

1. Introduction

We encounter Networked Control Systems (NCSs) in several applications, for instance, in the automobile and manufacturing industries, airplanes, and tele-health monitoring. In these applications, NCSs offer many benefits such as cost reduction, easy installation, reduced maintenance, and maximum efficiency with reliability. Along with these benefits, NCSs include many challenging issues due to limited bandwidth and the utilization of shared resources by NCS components. These issues include network-induced random time delays due to queuing, processing, transmission, and propagation time at different nodes and links. The packets may also suffer from uncertain data packet dropouts due to network traffic. These uncertainties can significantly degrade the performance of systems if not addressed adequately. To address these issues, researchers have focused their efforts on this in the last few years [1–4].

To model these network-induced uncertainties, researchers have used the Markov chain and Bernoulli process [2–5]. The Markov chain, used in the most of the literature, requires complete knowledge of Transition Probabilities (TPs). In practical applications, these are costly and very hard to obtain, in some cases, even impossible. It is, therefore, very important to consider partly known TPs in the Markov chain. This is why stability criteria are proposed for Markovian jump systems (MJSs) with partially known TPs in [6,7], and results with less conservative outcomes are presented in [8–10]. The conditions for the stability and stabilization of NCSs with partially known TPs are presented in [11]. Markov-based modeling of time-delay with partly known TPs is important when all the data packets reach the destination. In practical applications, data packets may drop out due to the network traffic in the shared network links. It is worthwhile to mention that in the literature, researchers only addressed either the time-delay or the packet drop out in networked systems. The inadequate modeling of network uncertainties during the controller design process makes the controller strategies very limited in practical engineering. We address both the network's main impurities simultaneously.

In addition to the communication network impurities, faults may occur in sensors, actuators, and/or process components [12–18], making the control of networked systems more challenging. These faults can degrade performance, lead to instability, and even cause fatalities [18]. In networked systems, the effects of faults may propagate from one node to other nodes. These propagated effects of faults increase the severity of local node faults [19]. To the authors' knowledge, in the literature on networked systems, the propagated effects of faults at the network level, along with network's main uncertainties, must still be addressed. For this purpose, we proposed two new fault models that are more generalized for networked systems. These fault models mathematically represent the magnitude of node-level and network-level faults simultaneously with their propagated effects and the network's main impurities. Immediate maintenance and repair are not always available, so fault tolerance has received great attention both in academia and practice [20,21]. Motivated by these challenges, researchers have reported Fault-Tolerant Control (FTC) strategies for sensor or actuator faults [17,18,22,23]. In the aforementioned literature, researchers have addressed a single fault or a single type of fault at a time; that is, either multiple sensor faults or multiple actuator faults with either time-delay or packet loss. Assuming the occurrence of a single fault or single type of multiple faults at a time makes the diagnostic and tolerance algorithm very limited in use. In practice, actuator and sensor faults may develop simultaneously due to poor networked environments. To the best of our knowledge, very few researchers have addressed the issue of multiple types of simultaneous fault tolerance in networked systems. Excellent work is done in [20] on double-fault, investigating the guaranteed cost FTC in networked systems using the piecewise delay method. The authors modeled the system with a constant time-delay, which is a conservative approach from a practical point of view. Secondly, the state feedback control requires the information of all states of the system, which are, in practice, very difficult to obtain.

Driven by the mentioned challenges in the literature survey, an FTC is proposed for the tolerance of faults at the node and network levels, along with network-induced uncertain effects. Contributions in the article can be summarized as follows: (1) We propose two new fault models for networked systems that cover the effects and magnitude of faults at the node and network levels, simultaneously with propagated faulty effects and the network's major impurities. (2) To adequately model the major network-induced time delay, we use the Markov chain with partially known TPs, simultaneously with the packet dropouts using the Bernoulli process. In the literature, time-delay with partial TPs and packet loss is not addressed with simultaneous multiple types of faults. (3) A two-mode dependent controller is proposed, which considers network-induced effects along with sensor measurements for a gain calculation to address multiple types of simultaneous generalized faults. (4) In comparison with work in the literature, simultaneous sensor and actuator faults are addressed for networked systems, using an LMI with the help of the proposed two-mode dependent output feedback controller.

The subsequent sections of the script are organized as follows. Section 2 is dedicated to problem formulation, first presenting the fault models for networked systems, and then modeling uncertain network-induced imperfections. Section 3 is dedicated to presenting the proposed FTC design for NCSs based on the Markov jump system and Bernoulli process. Lastly, Section 4 presents the simulated study of the proposed FTC discussed for the DC motor to ensure its effectiveness and the applicability of the system.

Notation: The occurrence probabilities are defined as $P(\cdot)$. The notation $(\cdots)$ denotes ψ wherever we show quadratic forms $\psi^T P(\cdots)$. All the used symbols are defined in the respective sections, and I represents an identity matrix. We provided a key table (Table 1) for symbols and notation at the end of the manuscript for better understanding.

Table 1. Notation used throughout the manuscript.

Notations Used	
Notation	**Description**
Φ	Actuator Faults
Ψ	Sensor Faults
ρ	Partially Known TPM of Markov Chain
τ_k	Time-Delay
τ_1	Maximum Time-Delay
I	Identity Matrix of Compatible Dimensions
τ_{kca}	Time-Delay from Controller-to-Actuator link
τ_{ksc}	Time-Delay from Actuator-to-Controller link
$\alpha(k)$	Binary Random Vector for Packet Dropout in S/C link
$\bar{\alpha}(k)$	Expected Binary Random Vector for Packet Dropout in S/C link
$\beta(k)$	Binary Random Vector for Packet Dropout in C/A link
$\bar{\beta}(k)$	Expected Binary Random Vector for Packet Dropout in C/A link
ζ_k	Solution of Augmented State equation
$\zeta(k)$	Augmented State Vector
$K(\tau_k, \bar{\alpha})$	Controller's Gain

2. Problem Formulation

Consider a networked environment, as shown in Figure 1, where six nodes are connected in a network. There is one faulty node that affects the neighboring connected nodes as the faulty effects propagate via network links. Each node of the network is a complete process, i.e., a plant with sensors and actuators. This process can be controlled over networks, as demonstrated in Figure 2. The controller controls the plant from a remote location in the presence of faults and disturbances via a communication network. Plant dynamics are given as described in Equation (1).

$$\begin{aligned} x(k+1) &= Ax(k) + Bu^F(k) + Hw(k) \\ y(t) &= Cx(k) \end{aligned} \tag{1}$$

Here, the state vector is $x(k) \in \mathbb{R}^n$, the control input is $u^F(k) \in \mathbb{R}^m$, and the external disturbance is $w(k) \in \mathbb{R}^n$, which belong to $l_2[0,\infty)$, where $l_2[0,\infty)$ is the space of finite-energy discrete-time signals. The output is $y(k) \in \mathbb{R}^p$, where the constant matrices A, B, H, and C are of compatible dimensions. Additionally, the output matrix has a full-row rank.

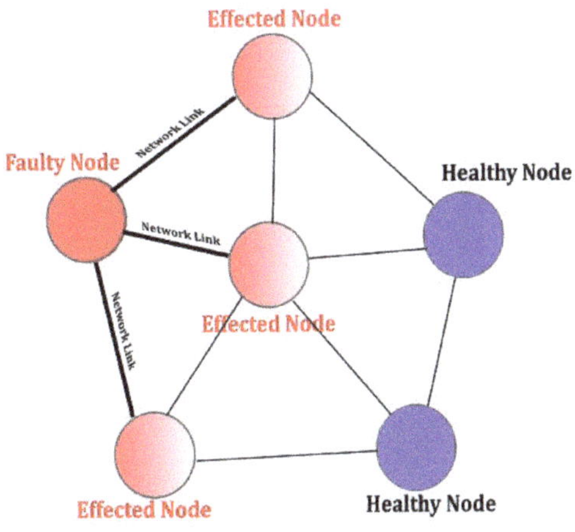

Figure 1. Control over communication network.

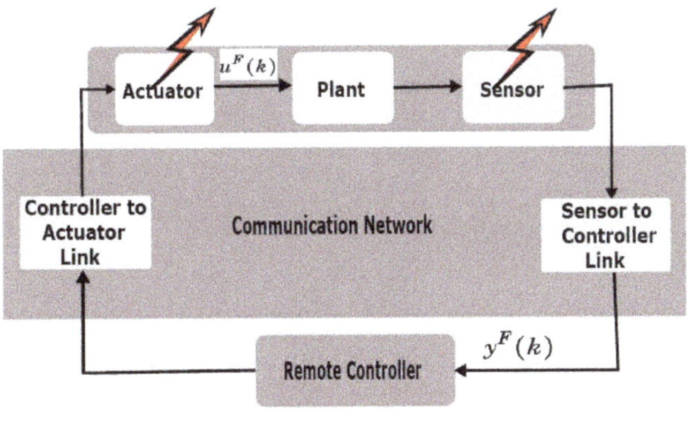

Figure 2. Control over communication network.

2.1. Proposed Fault Models for Networked Systems

The fault models used in the existing research are either the constant faults model, probabilistic fault model, or generalized fault model. Only in the generalized fault model is time-delay considered for networked systems [20]. In a practical networked environment, packet dropout can not be ignored. Additionally, the propagated effects of fault from the neighboring connected node are also required to be incorporated into the fault models. To incorporate the faulty effects into the fault models at the node and network levels, we proposed two fault models for sensors and actuators in a networked environment. The sensor fault model is presented as:

$$y^F(k) = \Psi\hat{\alpha}(k)y(k-\tau_k) + f(\cdot) \tag{2}$$

where

$$\Psi = \mathrm{diag}(\psi_1, \psi_2, \cdots, \psi_m) \tag{3}$$

is the faults matrix such that $\psi_l \in [0,1]$. The l given in subscript indicates the status of each individual sensor as

$$\psi_l = \begin{cases} 1, & \text{Normal operation of lth sensor} \\ 0, & \text{complete failure of lth sensor} \\ \text{else}, & \text{Partial operation of lth sensor} \end{cases} \tag{4}$$

The range of l is from 1 to m. The network-induced uncertainties are $\hat{\alpha}(k)$ and τ_{ksc}; these are the random variables for data packets dropout and random time-delays, respectively.

$$\hat{\alpha}(k) = \text{diag}(\hat{\alpha_1}(k), \hat{\alpha_2}(k), \cdots, \hat{\alpha_m}(k)) \tag{5}$$

where every $\hat{\alpha_1}(k)$, $\hat{\alpha_2}(k)$, up to $\hat{\alpha_m}(k)$, is a binary random variable. τ_{ksc} is the time-delay in the sensor-to-controller network links. The function $f(\cdot)$ represents the faulty effects that propagate from the neighboring connected nodes.

Similarly, the proposed actuator fault model is given as:

$$u^F(k) = \Phi\hat{\beta}(k)u(k - \tau_{kca}) + g(\cdot) \tag{6}$$

where

$$\Phi = \text{diag}(\bar{\phi_1}, \bar{\phi_2}, \cdots, \bar{\phi_m}) \tag{7}$$

is the faults matrix for the actuator such that $\bar{\phi_l} \in [0,1]$. The l given in subscript indicates the status of each individual actuator as

$$\phi_l = \begin{cases} 1, & \text{Normal operation of lth actuator} \\ 0, & \text{complete failure of the lth actuator} \\ \text{else}, & \text{Partial operation of lth actuator} \end{cases} \tag{8}$$

The range of l is from 1 to m. The network-induced uncertainties are $\bar{\beta}(k)$ and τ_{kca}; these are the random variables for data packets dropout and random time-delays, respectively.

$$\hat{\beta}(k) = \text{diag}(\hat{\beta_1}(k), \hat{\beta_2}(k), \cdots, \hat{\beta_m}(k)) \tag{9}$$

where every $\hat{\beta_1}$, $\hat{\beta_2}$, up to $\hat{\beta_m}$, is a binary random variable and τ_{kca} is the time-delay in the controller-to-actuator network links. The function $g(.)$ represents the faulty effects that propagate from the neighboring connected nodes.

Remark 1. *The overall network-induced uncertainties $\tau_k = \tau_{kca} + \tau_{ksc}$, $\bar{\alpha}(k) = \hat{\alpha}(k) + \hat{\beta}(k)$ are considered here, instead of the separate induction of uncertainties from sensor-to-controller links and controller-to-actuator links. Similarly, for the calculation of the controller's gain, the propagated effects are neglected to avoid computational complexity.*

2.2. Network-Induced Uncertainties Modeling

The lump delay $\tau_k = \tau_{kca} + \tau_{ksc}$ and the packet loss $\bar{\alpha}(k)$ are mathematically modeled as below.

2.2.1. Time-Delay Modeling

The exchange of measurement and control data between the plant and the controller occurred via a shared communication network, as shown in Figure 2. The data packets may experience random time-delays or even drop while traversing through the network. We consider random variation in τ_k in the range

$$\tau_k \in \{0, 1, \cdots, \tau_1\} \tag{10}$$

The time-delays τ_k are modeled with a Markov chain θ with a partially known Transition Probabilities Matrix (TPM) ρ. There are N number of delay states, i.e, $\theta \in \{1, 2, \cdots, N\}$, where $\theta = 1$ corresponds to $\tau_k = 0$, $\theta = 2$ corresponds to $\tau_k = 1$, and so on. Let ρ denote the partially known TPM of the Markov chain, given as:

$$\rho = [\rho_{ij}] \tag{11}$$

where $\rho_{ij} = \mathbb{P}(\tau_{k+1} = j|\tau_k = i)$ for all $i, j \in \theta$ and $\Sigma_{j=1}^{\tau_1}\rho_{ij} = 1, \rho_{ij} \geq 0$. For example, if $\tau_1 = 3$, the partial known TPM ρ is given as below.

$$\rho = \begin{bmatrix} \rho_{00} & \rho_{01} & ? & \rho_{03} \\ ? & \rho_{11} & \rho_{12} & ? \\ \rho_{20} & \rho_{21} & ? & \rho_{23} \\ \rho_{30} & ? & \rho_{32} & ? \end{bmatrix} \tag{12}$$

where the ? in the matrix are the unknown time-delay states' transition probabilities, and the remaining entries are known TPs. Let $\theta^i_{uk}, \theta^i_k$ represent the column indices that are used for the unknown and known values in the i_{th} row of the above matrix, respectively. Here, $\theta = \theta_k + \theta_{uk}$ for all $i \in \theta$. The known entries, θ_k, of TPM can be rewritten as:

$$\theta_k = (k^i_1, \cdots, k^i_m) \tag{13}$$

where $1 \leq m \leq \tau_1$.

The $k^i_m \in N^+$ represents the m_{th} known TP with the index k^i_m in the i_{th} row of the TPM. The restriction of complete knowledge of TPs for practical applications is often difficult to satisfy. Furthermore, the TP matrix covers the two different cases: completely known and completely unknown TPs in the Markov chain.

2.2.2. Packet Dropout Modeling

To adequately model the network-induced uncertainties, we model the packet dropout along with time-delay while using complex TPs. We model the packet dropouts with a binary random vector $\hat{\alpha}(k)$, where $\hat{\alpha}(k)$ denotes the packet dropouts in the communication link. $\hat{\alpha}_i(k) = 1$ implies that the packet is successfully delivered via the i_{th} link, and $\hat{\alpha}_i(k) = 1$ denotes that the packet has dropped out, where i ranges from 1 to m. The following probabilities are assumed for $\hat{\alpha}_i(k)$:

$$E[\hat{\alpha}_i(k)] = Pr(\hat{\alpha}_i(k)) = \bar{\alpha}(k) \tag{14}$$

where E is the expected value and $Pr(\hat{\alpha}_i(k))$ is the probability of packet propagation in the channels. $Pr(\hat{\alpha}_i(k)) = 1$ implies that the packet has a maximum chance of successful propagation, while the other case means that the packet is lost. The missing parameter is described via the Bernoulli process.

Remark 2. *Time-delay tk is taken into account for the case where $Pr(\hat{\alpha}_i(k)) = 1$, which means the controller can only use the delayed version of the output if the data packet is successfully transmitted and propagated over the network link. We assume zero time-delays for the case of $Pr(\hat{\alpha}_i(k)) = 0$, which means that the packet has dropped out. It is very important to note that in most of the literature, the time-delay is only addressed if complex transition probabilities are used. In practical engineering, the packet dropout cannot be ignored in the network links, as the components of NCSs utilize shared communication channels, which may result in packet loss. This packet dropout leads to performance degradation.*

2.3. Output Feedback-Based Controller Design

The remotely located controller was chosen to be the output feedback and is based, static, and two-mode-dependent, as given below.

$$u(k) = K(\tau_k, \bar{\alpha}(k))y^F(k) \tag{15}$$

$$u(k) = K(\tau_k, \bar{\alpha}(k))\Psi\bar{\alpha}(k)Cx(k - \tau_k) \tag{16}$$

$K(\tau_k, \bar{\alpha}(k))$ is the gain of the controller.

Remark 3. *The control law u(k) given in Equation (7) clearly demonstrates that it depends on the sensor's measured output, network-induced time-delay, packet dropout, and the fault matrix* Ψ. *The controller's gain K tolerates the effects of fault.*

The augmented vector for states is $\zeta(k) = [x^T(k), x^T(k-1), x^T(k-2), ..., x^T(k-\tau_k)]^T \in R^{(\tau+1)n}$. Substituting 2, 6, and 16 in 1, the model of the closed-loop system with sensor and actuator faults, communication delays, and packet dropouts is obtained as:

$$\zeta(k+1) = (\bar{A} + \bar{B}\Phi K(\tau_k, \bar{\alpha}(k))\Psi\bar{\alpha}(k)C)\zeta(k) + \hat{H}w(k) \tag{17}$$

The above derived system in Equation (17) is a close-loop stochastic system with multiple types of faults that are sensor and actuator faults, one data packet dropout mode $\bar{\alpha}(k)$, and one time-delay mode τ_k, where the probabilities of transitions are described using the Markov chain with partially known TPs and the stochastic parameter $\bar{\alpha}(k)$ using the Bernoulli process. In the above Equation (17),

$$\bar{A} = \begin{bmatrix} A & 0 & \cdots & 0 & 0 \\ I & 0 & \cdots & 0 & 0 \\ 0 & I & \cdots & 0 & 0 \\ \vdots & \vdots & \ddots & \vdots & \vdots \\ 0 & 0 & \cdots & I & 0 \end{bmatrix}, \bar{B} = \begin{bmatrix} B \\ 0 \\ 0 \\ \vdots \\ 0 \end{bmatrix}$$

$$\bar{C} = \begin{bmatrix} 0 & \cdots & C_{\tau_{k+1}} & 0 & \cdots & 0 \end{bmatrix}, \bar{H} = \begin{bmatrix} H \\ 0 \\ 0 \\ \vdots \\ 0 \end{bmatrix}$$

I is the identity matrix of completable dimensions.

3. Fault-Tolerant Control for Networked System

Definition 1. *The stochastic Markovian jump system given in Equation (17) is stable with any initial condition* $\zeta(0)$, τ_0, $\hat{\alpha}(0)$ *if the following inequality is fulfilled.*

$$E\{\Sigma_{k=0}^{\infty}||\zeta_k||^2|\zeta(0), \tau_0, \hat{\alpha}(0)\} \leq \infty \tag{18}$$

here, ζ_k *is the solution of the augmented state equation given in Equation (17) at time k under the initial conditions* $\zeta(0)$, τ_0, $\hat{\alpha}(0)$.

Theorem 1. *For a closed-loop system, as in (17), there exists an output-based feedback control of the form given in Equation (16), if there exist matrices* $X_i > 0$, R_i, G_i, Q_i, *satisfying*

$$\begin{bmatrix} -G_i^T X_i G_i & 0 & \Xi_{13} \\ 0 & -I & \Xi_{23} \\ \Xi_{13}^T & \Xi_{23}^T & \Xi_{33} \end{bmatrix} < 0$$

where

$$\Xi_{31} = \begin{Bmatrix} \sqrt{\rho_{ik_1^i}}\{\bar{A}G_i + \bar{B}\Phi K_i(\tau_k, \bar{\alpha}(k))\Psi\bar{\alpha}(k)R_i\bar{C}\} \\ \vdots \\ \sqrt{\rho_{ik_m^i}}\{\bar{A}G_i + \bar{B}\Phi K_i(\tau_k, \bar{\alpha}(k))\Psi\bar{\alpha}(k)R_i\bar{C}\} \\ \sqrt{1-\rho_k^i}\{\bar{A}G_i + \bar{B}\Phi K_i(\tau_k, \bar{\alpha}(k))\Psi\bar{\alpha}(k)R_i\bar{C}\} \end{Bmatrix},$$

$$\Xi_{23} = \left\{ \begin{array}{c} \sqrt{\rho_{ik_1^i}}\{\bar{H}\} \\ \vdots \\ \sqrt{\rho_{ik_m^i}}\{\bar{H}\} \\ \sqrt{1-\rho_k^i}\{\bar{H}\} \end{array} \right\},$$

$\Xi_{33} = diag\{X_{k_1^i}, \cdots, -X_{k_m^i}, -X_j\}$

According to the definition, $K_i(\tau_k, \bar{\alpha}(k))\bar{C}G_i = R_i\bar{C}$, it is derived, so that

$$K_i(\tau_k, \bar{\alpha}(k)) = R_i Q^{-1}$$

Proof. For proof, we chose the Lyapunov candidate as

$$V(\tau_k, \alpha(k)) = \zeta^T(k) P_i(\tau_k, \alpha(k)) \zeta(k) \tag{19}$$

$$\begin{aligned} &\mathrm{E}[\Delta V(\tau_k, \alpha(k))] \\ &= \mathrm{E}[\zeta^T(k+1)\{\Sigma_{k=0}^N \rho_{ij} \bar{P}_j(\tau_k+1, \bar{\alpha}(k+1))\}\zeta(k+1)] \\ &- \zeta^T(k) P_i(\tau_k, \alpha(k))\zeta(k) \\ &\bar{P}_j = \{\Sigma_{k=0}^N \rho_{ij} P_j(\tau_k+1, \alpha(k+1))\} \end{aligned} \tag{20}$$

then,

$$\begin{aligned} &\mathrm{E}[\Delta V(\tau_k, \alpha(k))] \le \zeta^T(k)\{(\bar{A}G_i + \bar{B}\Phi K(\tau_k, \bar{\alpha}(k))\Psi\bar{\alpha}(k)R_i\bar{C})^T \bar{P}_j(\cdots)\}\zeta(k) \\ &+ \zeta^T(k)\{(\bar{A}G_i + \bar{B}\Phi K(\tau_k, \bar{\alpha}(k))\Psi\bar{\alpha}(k)R_i\bar{C})^T \bar{P}_j \bar{H}\}w(k) + w(k)^T\{\bar{H}^T \bar{P}_j(\bar{A}G_i \\ &+ \bar{B}\Phi K(\tau_k, \bar{\alpha}(k))\Psi\bar{\alpha}(k)R_i\bar{C})\}\zeta(k) w(k)^T \bar{H}^T \bar{P}_j \bar{H} w(k) - \zeta^T(k) P_i \zeta(k) \end{aligned} \tag{21}$$

It can be verified that $\Delta V \le 0$, which implies $\mathrm{E}\{\Sigma_{k=0}^{\infty} ||\zeta_k||^2 | \zeta(0), \tau_k 0, \alpha(0)\} \le \infty$. This inequality ensures the stochastic stability for the close-loop Equation (9). We defined the main augmented states vector as $\xi = \begin{bmatrix} \zeta(k) \\ w(k) \end{bmatrix}$ and wrote Equation (10) as

$$\Xi_0 = \begin{bmatrix} \hat{\Xi_{11}} - P_i & \hat{\Xi_{12}} \\ \hat{\Xi_{12}}^T & \bar{H}^T \bar{P}_j \bar{H} \end{bmatrix}$$

$$\hat{\Xi_{11}} = \{(\bar{A}G_i + \bar{B}\Phi K_i(\tau_k, \bar{\alpha}(k))\Psi\bar{\alpha}(k)R_i\bar{C})^T \bar{P}_j(\cdots)\}$$

$$\hat{\Xi_{21}} = \{(\bar{A}G_i + \bar{B}\Phi K_i(\tau_k, \bar{\alpha}(k))\Psi\bar{\alpha}(k)R_i\bar{C})^T \bar{P}_j \bar{H}\}$$

We conducted pre- and post-multiplication of $\mathrm{diag}(G_i^T, I)$ to Ξ_0 and defining $X_i = P_i^{-1}$, $K(\tau_k, \alpha(k))\bar{C}G_i = R_i\bar{C}$, and then used the Schur complement. Next, network-induced uncertain impurities were introduced to Ξ_0, which resulted in the following inequality that is given in the theorem.

$$\begin{bmatrix} -G_i^T X_i G_i & 0 & \star \\ 0 & -I & \star \\ \Xi_{31} & \Xi_{32} & \Xi_{33} \end{bmatrix} < 0$$

The controller gain is derived from the definition $Ki(\tau_k, \alpha(k))\bar{C}G_i = R_i\bar{C}$, and it is derived that

$$K_i(\tau_k, \bar{\alpha}(k)) = R_i Q_i^{-1}$$

Lemma 1. *There exist nonsingular matrices Q_i for the output matrix $\bar{C}$ with rank p such that $Q_i\bar{C} = \bar{C}G_i$. For this, there exist full-rank matrices G_i that satisfy the condition given below as*

$$G_i = V_i \begin{bmatrix} G_{i1} & 0 \\ G_{i2} & G_{i3} \end{bmatrix} V_i^T = V_{i1} G_{i1} V_{i1}^T + V_{i2} G_{i2} V_{i1}^T + V_{i2} G_{i3} V_{i2}^T$$

where $Q_i = U^T \sigma G_{i1}^{-1} \sigma^{-1} U$. *The* U *is calculated using the SVD of* $\bar{C}$ *matrix.* $\bar{C} = U\bar{C}V_i = U\bar{C}[V_{i1} V_{i2}] = U\bar{C}[\sigma \quad 0]$, *where* σ *are the singular nonzero values of* $\bar{C}$.

Corollary 1. *Let* $\epsilon_1 > 0$, $\epsilon_2 > 0$, $\gamma > 0$, *and* $\nu > 0$ *be the known scalars. Then, the system given in (17) is a fault-tolerant, stochastically stable system if there exist* $X_i > 0$, R_i, G_{i1}, G_{i2}, G_{i3}, Q_i, *and* $L_i(\tau_k)$ *such that the LMI hold, and the desired FTC* $K(\tau_k, \alpha(k))$ *can be achieved by* $K(\tau_k, \alpha(k)) = R_i U^T \Sigma G_i^{-1} \Sigma^{-1} U$.

Proof. If there exist matrices G_{i1}, G_{i2}, and G_{i3} satisfying the equation given in Lemma 1 and there exist nonsingular matrices Q_i that satisfy $Q_i\bar{C} = \bar{C}G_i$, then, consequently, it is equivalent to:

$$Q_i U^T [\sigma \quad 0] V_i^T = U^T [\sigma \quad 0] V_i^T G_i$$

The post-multiplication of V_i, ($V_i^T V_i = I$ to orthogonal matrix V_i) results in:

$$Q_i U^T [\sigma \quad 0] = U^T [\sigma \quad 0] V_i^T G_i V_i$$

It can be readily derived that

$$[Q_i U^T \sigma \quad 0] = [U^T \sigma G_{i1} \quad 0]$$

and $Q_i = U^T \sigma G_{i1} \sigma^{-1} U$. The controller equation is $K_i(\tau_k, \bar{\alpha}(k)) = R_i Q_i^{-1}$. The desired gain is equal to:

$$K_i(\tau_k, \bar{\alpha}(k)) = R_i U^T \sigma G_{i1} \sigma^{-1} U$$

□

□

4. Simulation Results

A numerical example is given below with simulation results to validate the applicability of the proposed FTC design.

A DC motor system is shown in Figure 3 in a networked environment, where the state-space representation for the DC motor system is given below. The state variable $I_a(t)$ is the armature winding current and $\omega(t)$ is the motor rotational speed. The inputs are armature winding input voltage $e_a(t)$ and load torque $T_l(t)$, where the physical parameters are in Table 2. The signal chosen for external disturbance is $w(k) = [1/(1+k^2)] \in l_2[0,\infty)]$.

$$\frac{d}{dt}\begin{bmatrix} I_a(t) \\ \omega(t) \end{bmatrix} = \begin{bmatrix} -\frac{R}{L} & -\frac{K_b}{L} \\ \frac{K}{J} & -\frac{B}{J} \end{bmatrix} \begin{bmatrix} I_a(t) \\ \omega(t) \end{bmatrix} + \begin{bmatrix} -\frac{1}{L} & 0 \\ 0 & -\frac{1}{J} \end{bmatrix} \begin{bmatrix} e_a(t) \\ T_l(t) \end{bmatrix}$$

by using the physical parameters of Table 2 and the application of the zero-order hold method of discretization on the inputs with a sampling period of 0.05, the discrete-time system with the initial conditions is described as:

$$A = \begin{bmatrix} 0.2379 & -0.0022 \\ 8.96 & 0.9223 \end{bmatrix}, B = \begin{bmatrix} 0.158 & 1.642 \\ 1.643 & -1131 \end{bmatrix}, C = \begin{bmatrix} 0 & 1 \end{bmatrix}, x_0 = \begin{bmatrix} 0.7 & -0.7 \end{bmatrix}$$

to demonstrate the simultaneous sensors and actuator faults in the networked environment, we considered the following sensor and actuator faults.

$$y^F(k) = \mathrm{diag}(1, 0.7)\bar{\alpha}(k) y(k - \tau_k),$$
$$u^F(k) = \mathrm{diag}(1, 0.7) u(k)$$

the value 0.7 denotes that the sensor and actuator are 30 percent faulty, meaning they are working at 70 percent. Probabilities of the stochastic variable $\bar{\alpha}(k)$ for data packet dropouts are given in Figure 4 with the probability $E[a(k)] = \bar{\alpha}(k) = 0.7$. $\tau_1 = 3$ is the maximum time-delay in the network links that are shown in the same Figure 4. The transition probability matrix ρ for the time-delays τ_k using the Markov chain is given as

$$\rho = \begin{bmatrix} 0.3 & 0.54 & ? & 0.25 \\ ? & 0.17 & 0.98 & ? \\ 0.65 & 0.36 & ? & 0.29 \\ 0.3 & ? & 0.85 & ? \end{bmatrix}, \hat{\alpha}_i(0) = I(2)$$

where the "?" in the matrix are unknown transition probabilities. The Markov evolution of control mode is shown in Figure 5.

Table 2. Numerical values for the state space equation of DC motor.

DC Motor Parameter		
Parameter	**Description**	**Value**
J	Inertia of the rotor	42.6×10^{-6} kgm^2
R	Electrical resistance	0.170 ohm
L	Electrical inductance	4.67H
B	Damping coefficient	47.3×10^{-8}
K	Torque constant	14.7×10^{-3} Nm/A
Kb	Back-EMF constant	14.7×10^{-3} V_s/rad

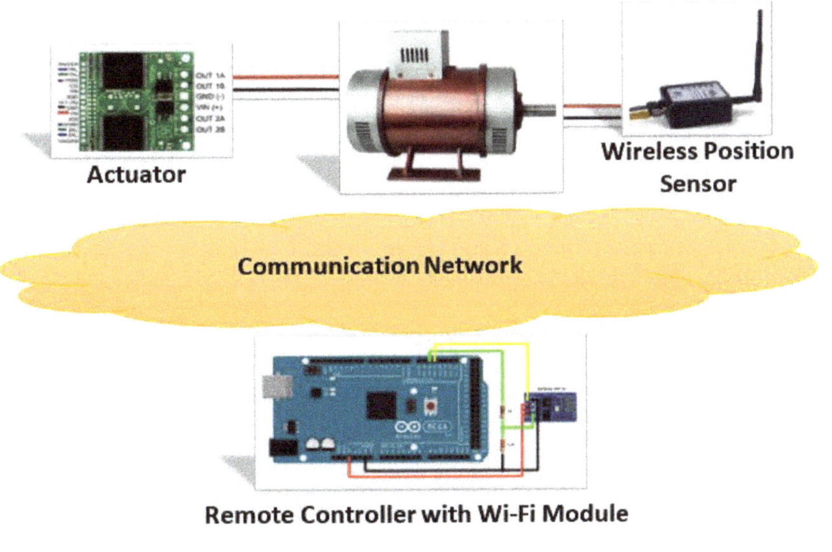

Figure 3. Networked DC motor control system.

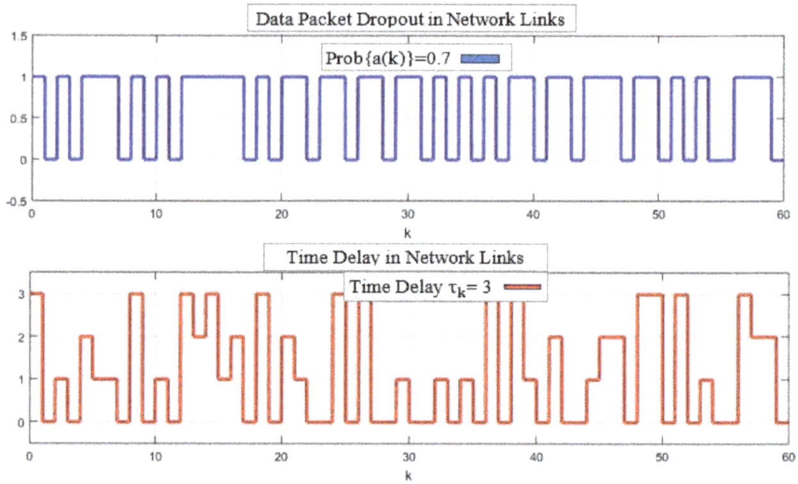

Figure 4. Network-induced stochastic faults $\alpha(k)$ with $\bar{\alpha}(k) = 0.6$ and time-delay $\tau_k = 3$.

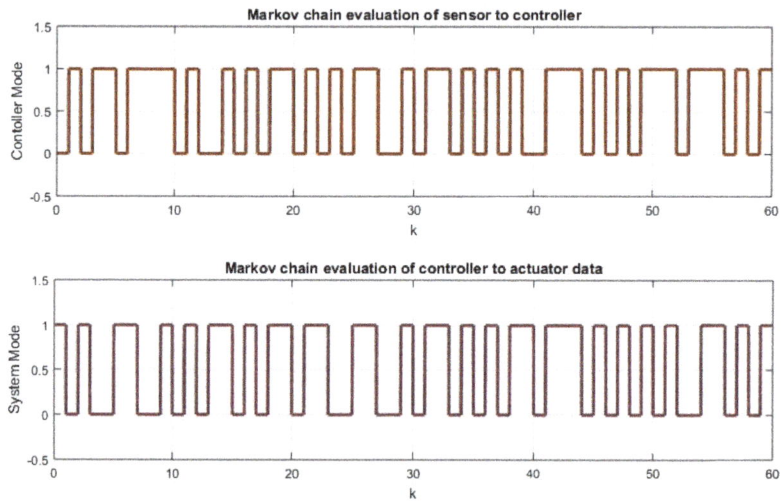

Figure 5. Evolution of Markov chain.

This 30 percent sensor fault is applied at $k = 7$, as shown in Figure 6. The proposed FTC technique successfully tolerates its effects and stabilizes the states. The 70 percent actuator fault is applied at $k = 15$ simultaneously with the sensor fault. The states are still stable, even in the presence of simultaneous sensor and actuator faults. To show the applicability of the proposed FTC, we increased the magnitude of sensor and actuator faults up to 70 percent. The proposed FTC tolerates the simultaneous effects of 70 faults, as shown in Figure 7.

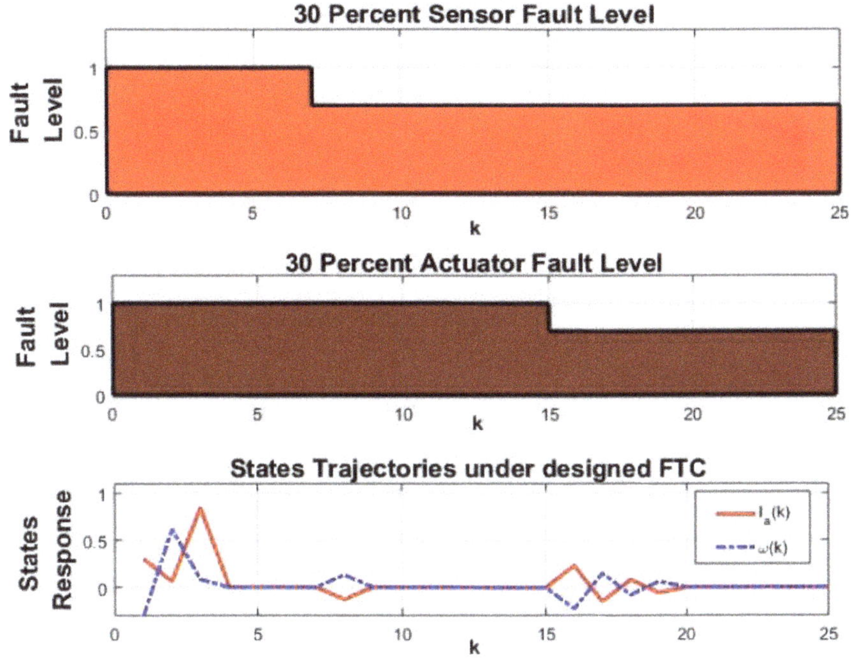

Figure 6. Tolerance of 30 percent sensor and actuator simultaneous faults.

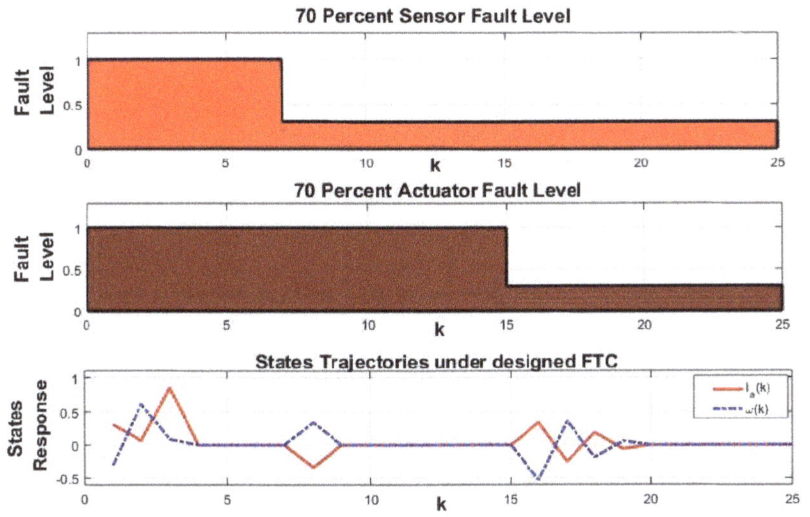

Figure 7. Case 2: Multiple (sensor and actuator) types of simultaneous faults. Fault level is 70 percent.

Comparative Analysis: To compare the results of the proposed FTC with conventional controllers, we simulated the aforementioned data as they were, with a conventional controller. The results are given in Figure 8, which demonstrates that the conventional controller is unable to tolerate the effects of faults and cannot stabilize the states of the DC motor in the presence of faults in a networked environment. Gain matrices are given for the case when we consider 70 percent simultaneous sensor and actuator faults under the proposed FTC in a networked environment.

$$K1 = \begin{bmatrix} -0.0587 \\ -0.0199 \end{bmatrix}, K2 = \begin{bmatrix} -0.0587 \\ -0.0199 \end{bmatrix}, K3 = \begin{bmatrix} -0.0150 \\ -0.0242 \end{bmatrix}, K4 = \begin{bmatrix} -0.1857 \\ -0.1912 \end{bmatrix}$$

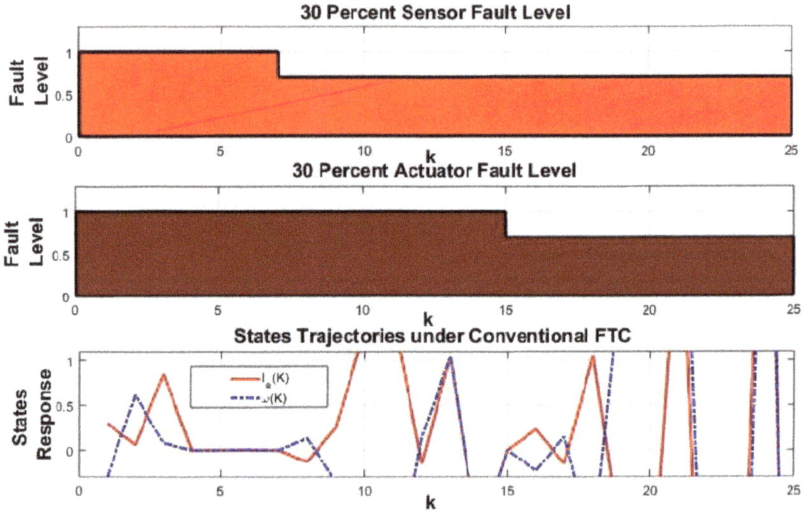

Figure 8. State response of the networked DC motor system under normal FTC.

5. Conclusions

This research proposed two new fault models for sensors and actuators in a networked environment, along with a new FT-NCS scheme. The proposed fault models adequately address the faulty effects at the node and network levels. In these fault models, network-induced time-delay and packet dropouts are modeled simultaneously using the Markov chain with complex TPs and Bernoulli process, respectively. The FT-NCS scheme is an output feedback-based strategy where the controller depends on the networked affected output of the system. The proposed scheme successfully tolerates the effects of simultaneous sensor and actuator faults. A numerical example together with simulation results verifies the performance and stochastic stability of the networked systems. Designing a dynamic controller gain can further improve the tolerance capability of the proposed FTC design for practical applications.

Author Contributions: Conceptualization, M.A.A.; Methodology, A.M. (Atif Mahmood); Software, A.S.K.; Formal analysis, A.M. (Atif Mahmood) and A.Q.K.; Resources, N.U., A.M. (Alsharef Mohammad) and A.N.; Writing—original draft, A.M. (Atif Mahmood); Writing—review & editing, A.M. (Atif Mahmood). All authors have read and agreed to the published version of the manuscript.

Funding: This research was funded by Deanship for Research and Innovation, Ministry of Education in Saudi Arabia through the project number: IFP22UQU4290235DSR217.

Data Availability Statement: Not applicable.

Acknowledgments: The authors extend their appreciation to the Deanship for Research and Innovation, Ministry of Education in Saudi Arabia for funding this research work through the project number: IFP22UQU4290235DSR217.

Conflicts of Interest: The authors declare no conflict of interest.

Abbreviations

The following abbreviations are used in this manuscript:

NCS	Networked Control System
FTC	Fault-Tolerant Control
TP	Transition Probabilities

References

1. Kang, W.; Cheng, J.; Wang, B.; Park, J.; Fardoun, H.M. Event-triggered reliable control for Markovian jump systems subject to nonuniform sampled data. *J. Frankl. Inst.* **2017**, *354*, 5877–5894. [CrossRef]
2. Zhang, T.; Gao, J.; Li, J. Event-triggered H_{inf} filtering for discrete-time Markov jump delayed neural networks with quantizations. *Syst. Sci. Control. Eng.* **2018**, *6*, 74–84. [CrossRef]
3. Qu, H.; Wei, N.; Li, M.; Li, Y. Observer-based guaranteed cost control for networked control systems with packet dropout and nonlinear disturbance. *Trans. Inst. Meas. Control* **2020**, *30*, 3039–3053. [CrossRef]
4. Bahreini, M.; Farsangi, M.M.; Lee, K.Y. Output feedback stabilization of networked brushless dc motor with random delay via Markovian jump systems. *IFAC-Pap. Line* **2015**, *30*, 55–60. [CrossRef]
5. Xu, Z.; Ni, H.; Reza Karimi, H.; Zhang, D. A Markovian jump system approach to consensus of heterogeneous multiagent systems with partially unknown and uncertain attack strategies. *Int. J. Robust Nonlinear Control* **2020**, *30*, 3039–3053. [CrossRef]
6. Li, Y.; Yu, Z.; Liu, Y.; Ren, J. Stochastic Stabilization for Discrete-Time Markovian Jump Systems With Time-Varying Delay and Two Markov Chains Under Partly Known Transition Probabilities. *IEEE Access* **2021**, *9*, 26937–26947. [CrossRef]
7. Zhang, X.; Lu, W. Stability and stabilization analysis of Markovian jump systems with generally bounded transition probabilities. *IEEE Access* **2020**, *13*, 8416–8434.
8. Sun, H.-J.; Zhangp, Y.; Wu, A.-G. Stochastic stability analysis of Markovian jump linear systems with incomplete transition descriptions. *IEEE Access* **2018**, *12*, 1974–1982. [CrossRef]
9. Zhang, Y.; He, Y.; Wu, M.; Zhang, J. Stabilization for Markovian jump systems with partial information on transition probability based on free-connection weighting matrices. *IEEE Access* **2011**, *47*, 79–84. [CrossRef]
10. Qiu, L.; Shi, Y.; Xu, B.; Yao, F. Robust stochastic stability and delayed-state-feedback stabilisation of uncertain Markovian jump linear systems with random time delays. *IET Control Theory Appl.* **2015**, *9*, 1878–1886. [CrossRef]
11. Zhang, J.; Peng, C.; Fei, M.-R.; Tian, Y.-C. Output feedback control of networked systems with a stochastic communication protocol. *J. Frankl. Inst.* **2017**, *9*, 3838–3853. [CrossRef]
12. Tan, C.; Li, L.; Zhang, H. Stabilization of networked control systems with both network-induced delay and packet dropout. *Automatica* **2015**, *59*, 194–199. [CrossRef]
13. Nazir, M.; Khan, A.Q.; Mustafa, G.; Abid, M. Robust fault detection for wind turbines using reference model-based approach. *J. King Saud Univ.-Eng. Sci.* **2017**, *29*, 244–252. [CrossRef]
14. Bahreini, M.; Zarei, J. Robust finite-time fault-tolerant control for networked control systems with random delays: A Markovian jump system approach. *Nonlinear Anal. Hybrid Syst.* **2020**, *36*, 100873. [CrossRef]
15. Khan, A.S.; Khan, A.Q.; Iqbal, N.; Sarwar, M.; Mahmood, A.; Shoaib, M.A. Distributed fault detection and isolation in second order networked systems in a cyber–physical environment. *ISA Trans.* **2020**, *103*, 131–142. [CrossRef]
16. Mahmood, A.; Khan, A.Q.; Mustafa, G.; Ullah, N.; Abid, M.; Khan, A.S. Remote Fault-Tolerant Control for Industrial Smart Surveillance System. *Math. Probl. Eng.* **2021**, *2021*, 1–12. [CrossRef]
17. Shen, M.; Yan, S.; Zhang, G. A new approach to event-triggered static output feedback control of networked control systems. *ISA Trans.* **2016**, *65*, 468–474. [CrossRef] [PubMed]
18. Liu, X.; Ma, G.; Pagilla, P.R.; Ge, S.S. Dynamic output feedback asynchronous control of networked Markovian jump systems. *IEEE Trans. Syst. Man Cybern. Syst.* **2018**, *50*, 2705–2715. [CrossRef]
19. Ye, Z.; Zhang, D.; Cheng, J.; Wu, Z.-G. Event-Triggering and Quantized Sliding Mode Control of UMV Systems Under DoS Attack. *IEEE Trans. Veh. Technol.* **2022**, *71*, 8199–8211. [CrossRef]
20. Mohsen, B.; Jafar, Z. Robust fault-tolerant control for networked control systems subject to random delays via static-output feedback. *ISA Trans.* **2019**, 153–162.
21. Bahreini, M.; Zarei, J.; Razavi-Far, R.; Saif, M. Robust fault-tolerant control of uncertain networked control systems subject to random delays and data packet dropouts. In Proceedings of the 2017 IEEE International Conference on Systems, Man, and Cybernetics (SMC), Banff, AB, Canada, 5–8 October 2017; Volume 9, pp. 2459–2464.
22. Zhu, Q.; Lu, K.; Zhu, Y. Guaranteed Cost Fault-Tolerant Control of Double-Fault Networked Control Systems: 304 Piecewise Delay Method. *IEEE Trans. Syst. Man Cybern. Syst.* **2019**, *2019*. [CrossRef]
23. Zhu, Q.; Lu, K.; Zhu, Y. Observer-based feedback control of networked control systems with delays and packet dropouts, Automatica. *J. Dyn. Syst. Meas. Control* **2016**, *59*, 194–199.

Disclaimer/Publisher's Note: The statements, opinions and data contained in all publications are solely those of the individual author(s) and contributor(s) and not of MDPI and/or the editor(s). MDPI and/or the editor(s) disclaim responsibility for any injury to people or property resulting from any ideas, methods, instructions or products referred to in the content.

mathematics

MDPI

Article

The Use of Trigonometric Series for the Study of Isotropic Beam Deflection

Adrian Ioan Botean

Mechanical Engineering Department, Faculty of Road Vehicles, Mechatronics and Mechanics, Technical University of Cluj-Napoca, 28 Memorandumului, 400114 Cluj-Napoca, Romania; adrian.ioan.botean@rezi.utcluj.ro

Abstract: The average deformed fiber is a continuous and smooth function of the fourth order. The deflection and rotation of beams can be determined by various methods available in the literature. Thus, in this paper, the expression of the average deformed fiber is defined in advance, then it is considered an infinite sum of sinusoidal functions that are successively evaluated using sinusoidal trigonometric series if it is considered a periodic function, or using Fourier series if it is considered a non-periodic function. The method is examined by solving several beam problems. The results indicate that the method can be used with confidence for solving any bending beam problem.

Keywords: beam; bending; static load; average deformed fiber; deformations; sinusoid; trigonometric series; Fourier series method

MSC: 74A05; 74A10

Citation: Botean, A.I. The Use of Trigonometric Series for the Study of Isotropic Beam Deflection. *Mathematics* **2023**, *11*, 1426. https://doi.org/10.3390/math11061426

Academic Editors: Shujin Laima, Yong Cao, Xiaowei Jin and Hehe Ren

Received: 23 February 2023
Revised: 10 March 2023
Accepted: 14 March 2023
Published: 15 March 2023

Copyright: © 2023 by the author. Licensee MDPI, Basel, Switzerland. This article is an open access article distributed under the terms and conditions of the Creative Commons Attribution (CC BY) license (https://creativecommons.org/licenses/by/4.0/).

1. Introduction

Bars subjected to bending are structural elements that take loads applied in the transverse plane. These loads act on a unit of reduced length (forces and/or moments of nodal forces), or on the entire length of the bar (loads whose distribution is governed by a constant, linear, or parabolic function). After the operating time, the loads can be static loads or dynamic loads. In the case of static loads, it is assumed that the velocities and accelerations are zero. Dynamic loads are the result of the action of masses in motion or the variation over time—according to some laws—of the loads applied directly to the bodies. Here, we can discuss inertia forces (high, constant, or continuously variable accelerations), shock loads (sudden–discontinuous–variations of speeds and accelerations) and periodic (sometimes random) variable loads of a very large number of repeated tasks times.

Under the action of these loads, the bar deforms, according to Figure 1. The deformed axis of the bar is called the deformed average fiber or elastic line because the study of beam deformations is generally carried out within the limit of small deformations, which do not exceed the elastic stress limit of the material from which this bar is made. The size of the deformations of the straight bars, under simple bending stress, is estimated using the following quantities: the displacement of the center of mass of the considered cross-section, which represents the ordinate of the cross-section, denoted by y; the angle of rotation of the cross-section φ_x; and the radius of curvature ρ_x or the curvature $1/\rho_x$ next to the section corresponding to the elevation x [1–3].

In the case of the periodic variation of the stress, a periodic variation of the deformations is obtained, giving rise to vibrations.

Thus, both in the case of static and dynamic stresses, the study of the displacement of the center of gravity of the cross-section of the bar is the central parameter because the rotation of the cross-section of the bar, in the field of elastic deformations, has low values.

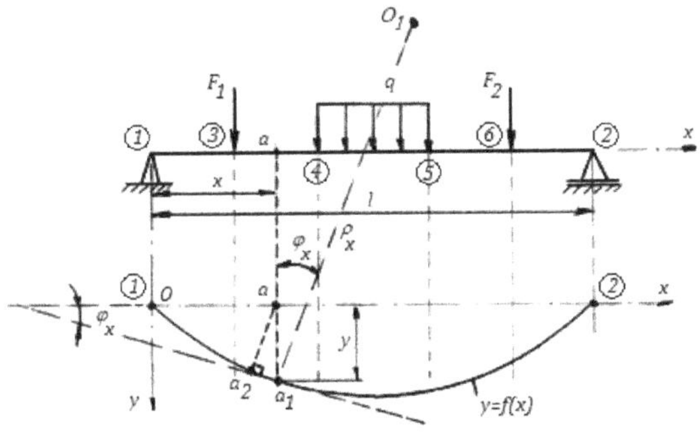

Figure 1. Plane deformation of a straight beam subjected to simple bending [1].

For static loads deflection of beams can be determined by various approaches, some of which are: the direct integration method, Clebsch method for calculating integration constants, moment-area approach (Mohr method), energy method, which includes Castigliano's theorems and unit load technique, stiffness and flexibility methods, principal superposition, three bending moments technique and singularity functions method, and Taylor's expansion series [1–7].

An interesting radiograph of the different methods used to calculate the deformations of straight bars statically stressed in bending can be found in the reference [8].

This study aims to analyze the average deformed fiber in the case of a bar, simply supported, statically stressed in simple bending, using trigonometric series (Fourier series), appreciating the fact that the average deformed fiber is a periodic function that can be represented by a sum infinity of sine and cosine terms. The first application of the Fourier method to the solution of isotropic beam problems was given by Filon (a sinusoidal series) [9] and Ribiere (a cosinusoidal series) in 1889 [10].

The method of ordinary Fourier series in its classical form makes it possible to satisfy the boundary conditions on two opposite faces, and on the other two, up to self-balanced loads. The superposition of Fourier series on the other variable to remove the loads that arise reduces to an infinite system of algebraic equations to find the coefficients of the Fourier series of the required solutions. The exact solution of such a system has been obtained for only one case: when two of the opposite faces of the beam are clamped and the other two are subject to a prescribed load [11].

Thus, the Fourier series, for such applications, can be used to obtain optimal shape solution for a non-prismatic planar beam [12,13].

In the case of beams (straight or curved) made of composite materials the deflection functions, the Lagrange multiplier functions, and the loads are expressed as trigonometric series to satisfy the governing equations and the simply supported constraints at both ends [14–16].

Other studies on this topic can be found in the references [17–21].

In this paper, the expression of the average deformed fiber (the continuous and smooth function of the fourth order) is defined in advance for a straight bar subjected to plane bending because the plane of loads coincides with the main axes of inertia. The deformed average fiber is considered to represent an infinite sum of sinusoidal functions, which are successively evaluated through sinusoidal trigonometric series (if this is considered to be a periodic function) or using the Fourier series if this is considered to be a non-periodic function.

Thus, the displacement in the vertical plane of the center of gravity of the cross-section for a straight bar, simply supported, is studied for two loading cases: in the first case, a concentrated force acting in the vertical plane (in the direction of the y axis, according to Figure 1), positioned asymmetrically or symmetrically to the support points; in the second case of loading, a uniformly distributed load is considered over the entire length unit and which also acts in the direction of the y axis.

The calculation relations of the displacement obtained with the help of the trigonometric series and the Fourier series are compared with those offered by the specialized literature (obtained by direct integration of the differential equation of the deformed average fiber) to check the convergence of the obtained results [1–6].

In the final part of this paper, a case study is made for a simply supported bar loaded on the entire length unit through a distributed load, whose variation law is a linear function.

2. The Deformed Average Fiber of the Beam

The beam is subjected to simple bending using a system of external forces (nodal forces F_1 and F_2 and the uniformly distributed load q), perpendicular to the longitudinal axis, which act in a main plane of inertia. Under the action of these loads, the bar bends, its longitudinal axis deforming in the same plane as that of the external loads, producing plane bending.

Thus, according to Figure 1, in node "a" located at a distance x from the articulated support (from node 1) a linear deformation will be recorded, represented by the arrow aa_1 = y and an angular deformation represented by the rotation angle (or slope) of the cross-section φ_x. In Figure 1, the points (nodes) where either the supports are defined, or the different types of loads act are marked with 1–6.

Nodes "a" and a_1 define the position of the center of gravity of the cross-section in the undeformed position, respectively, in the deformed position of the straight bar before and after bending. In other words, the deformation aa_1 represents the displacement of the center of gravity of the cross-section in a direction perpendicular (normal) to the axis of the bar. After bending, the axis of the bar will not change its length, and the center of gravity of the cross-section will move laterally about the normal position on the undeformed axis, going through arc a_1a_2. This displacement represents an infinitely small higher-order about the length l of the bar. Consequently, this displacement can be neglected and the center of gravity of the cross-section, from the deformed position of the bar, will be in the direction of the normal to the undeformed axis.

The rotation angle or slope φ_x is an angular deformation and represents the angle by which the cross section corresponding to the x-axis rotates to its initial position.

The radius of curvature ρ_x, line O_1a_1, is normal to the tangent to the deformed axis next to the section corresponding to the x-axis.

The average deformed fiber, in the orthogonal system of axes xOy, is a shape function:

$$y = f(x) \tag{1}$$

If this function is assumed to be known, displacements, rotations, and curves can be determined. The rotations are obtained from the first derivative of the function $f(x)$:

$$\frac{dy}{dx} = tg\varphi_x \cong \varphi_x \tag{2}$$

The curves are given by the expression:

$$\frac{1}{\rho_x} = \pm \frac{\frac{d^2y}{dx^2}}{\left[1 + \left(\frac{dy}{dx}\right)^2\right]^{\frac{3}{2}}} \tag{3}$$

In the case of bars subjected to simple bending in the elastic domain, the rotations are small, and the term $(dy/dx)^2$ is neglected, relation (3) becoming:

$$\frac{1}{\rho_x} = \pm \frac{d^2y}{dx^2} \tag{4}$$

In conclusion, to calculate the curvature of the average deformed fiber, in a certain cross section, the rotation expression is derived from the respective section, or the second derivative of the displacement will be performed.

The problem can be solved the other way around. If the expression of the curves along the axis of the beam is known:

$$\pm\frac{d^2y}{dx^2} = \frac{1}{\rho_x} \tag{5}$$

the expression of rotations $\varphi_x = dy/dx$ and displacements $y = f(x)$ can be determined by successive integration.

The resulting integration constants will be determined from the condition of continuity and smoothness of the curve of the average deformed fiber along its entire length, because, by its physical nature, the deformed axis of the bar is a continuous and smooth curve.

The curve $y = f(x)$ is continuous when a given value of the abscissa x corresponds to a single value of the ordinate y.

The term smoothness defines a curve that does not present breaks along its length. In other words, only one tangent can be taken at each point of the curve.

In conclusion, for a curve to be continuous and smooth (in the case of the average deformed fiber) the function $y = f(x)$, and it is first derivative $dy/dx = \varphi x = f'(x) = y'$, must be continuous throughout the length of the beam.

The relation:

$$\frac{1}{\rho_x} = \frac{M_i}{E \cdot I_z} \tag{6}$$

expresses the connection between the curvature of the bar and the bending moment function.

Relation (4) expresses the mathematical formula of curvature:

$$\frac{1}{\rho_x} = \pm\frac{d^2y}{dx^2}$$

From the two expressions that define the curvature, the following relation is obtained:

$$\frac{d^2y}{dx^2} = \pm\frac{M_i}{E \cdot I_z} \tag{7}$$

which is called the differential equation of the deformed average fiber.

From the analysis of this expression, the following observations can be highlighted: The sign of relation (7) is established by choosing an orthogonal system of reference axes. In particular, the origin of the orthogonal system of axes is defined in the center of gravity of a corresponding transverse section whose displacement is zero (in simple support, articulated or embedment); but, in general, it can be chosen in the center of gravity of any cross-section. The longitudinal axis of the bar before deformation coincides with the x-axis, with the positive sign oriented to the right. The axis of the ordinates y, with the positive direction down, will be perpendicular to the abscissa x, according to Figure 2, where the curve Oab represents the average deformed fiber. Points a and b are points of inflection of the deformed average fiber. On the portion Oa the deformed average fiber shows a positive curvature because its concavity is directed in the direction of the positive axis Oy, and on the portion ab, the curvature is negative. The bending moments corresponding to these curves have opposite signs.

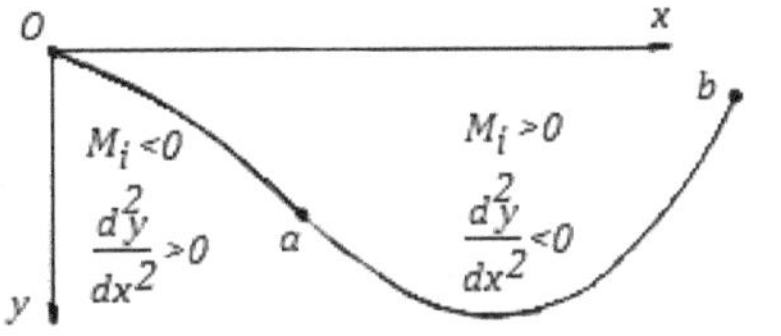

Figure 2. Establishing the sign of the differential equation of the average deformed fiber.

According to Figure 2, where the y-axis is oriented downwards, relation (7) will be of the form:

$$\frac{d^2y}{dx^2} = -\frac{M_i}{E \cdot I_z} \tag{8}$$

If the y-axis is oriented upwards, expression (7) will be of the form:

$$\frac{d^2y}{dx^2} = +\frac{M_i}{E \cdot I_z} \tag{9}$$

If the beam is of the constant section, it follows that the bending stiffness modulus $E \cdot I_z$ is constant. By deriving expression (8) and considering the differential relations between efforts:

$$\frac{dM_i}{dx} = T_y \text{ și } \frac{dT_y}{dx} = -q(x) \tag{10}$$

the expression of the average deformed fiber can also be written in the following forms:

$$\frac{d^3y}{dx^3} = -\frac{T_y}{E \cdot I_z} \text{ și } \frac{d^4y}{dx^4} = \frac{q(x)}{E \cdot I_z} \tag{11}$$

In the node where the bending moment M_i is zero, the deformed average fiber presents an inflection point.

3. Trigonometric Series Applied in the Study of the Average Deformed Fiber

It is considered that the average deformed fiber can have a sinusoidal variation, and it is expressed mathematically in the following form:

$$y(x) = A \cdot sin\left(\frac{2 \cdot \pi}{T} \cdot x + \varphi\right) \tag{12}$$

where A is the oscillation amplitude, φ represents the initial phase, and T is the oscillation period.

The deformed mean fiber is a function that can be expressed as an infinite sum of sinusoidal functions, according to the example in Figure 3. In Figure 3, the points (nodes) where either the supports are defined, or the different types of loads act are marked with 1–3.

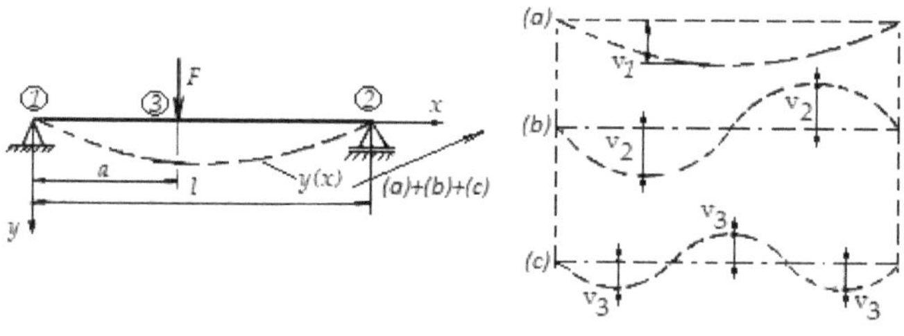

Figure 3. Representation of the deformed average fiber as a sum of "n" sinusoids.

The relation (12) can be expressed, in the most general case (considering the example in Figure 3), as follows:

$$y(x) = v_n \cdot sin\frac{n \cdot \pi \cdot x}{l} \tag{13}$$

where: $n = 1, 2, 3, \ldots$

For case (a) from Figure 3, relation (13) has the following form:

$$y(x)_{(a)} = v_1 \cdot sin\frac{1 \cdot \pi \cdot x}{l} \tag{14}$$

For case (*b*) from Figure 3, relation (13) has the following form:

$$y(x)_{(b)} = v_2 \cdot sin\frac{2 \cdot \pi \cdot x}{l} \tag{15}$$

For case (*c*) from Figure 3, relation (13) has the following form:

$$y(x)_{(c)} = v_3 \cdot sin\frac{3 \cdot \pi \cdot x}{l} \tag{16}$$

By summing relations (14)–(16) we obtain:

$$y(x) = \sum_{n=1}^{\infty} v_n \cdot sin\frac{n \cdot \pi \cdot x}{l} = v_1 \cdot sin\frac{\pi \cdot x}{l} + v_2 \cdot sin\frac{2 \cdot \pi \cdot x}{l} + v_3 \cdot sin\frac{3 \cdot \pi \cdot x}{l} + \ldots \tag{17}$$

The coefficients $v_1, v_2, v_3, \ldots$, represent the maximum ordinates of the sinusoids (oscillation amplitude), and indices (1,2,3, ...) represent the number of half-waves on the length l of the bar (oscillation period).

The expression of the potential energy of elastic deformation for the bar subjected to bending is of the form:

$$U_d = \int_0^l \frac{M_i^2}{2 \cdot E \cdot I_z} \cdot dx = \frac{E \cdot I_z}{2} \cdot \int_0^l \left(\frac{d^2y}{dx^2}\right)^2 \cdot dx \tag{18}$$

where:

$$M_i = -E \cdot I_z \cdot \frac{d^2y}{dx^2} \tag{19}$$

To calculate the potential energy of elastic deformation depending on the coefficients $v_1, v_2, v_3, \ldots$, the trigonometric series (17) is derived twice, and the obtained expression is inserted into the relation (18):

$$\frac{dy}{dx} = \frac{\pi \cdot v_1}{l} \cdot cos\frac{\pi \cdot x}{l} + \frac{2 \cdot \pi \cdot v_2}{l} \cdot cos\frac{2 \cdot \pi \cdot x}{l} + \frac{3 \cdot \pi \cdot v_3}{l} \cdot cos\frac{3 \cdot \pi \cdot x}{l} + \ldots \tag{20}$$

$$\frac{d^2y}{dx^2} = -\frac{1^2 \cdot \pi^2 \cdot v_1}{l^2} \cdot sin\frac{\pi \cdot x}{l} - \frac{2^2 \cdot \pi^2 \cdot v_2}{l^2} \cdot sin\frac{2 \cdot \pi \cdot x}{l} - \frac{3^2 \cdot \pi^2 \cdot v_3}{l^2} \cdot sin\frac{3 \cdot \pi \cdot x}{l} - \ldots \tag{21}$$

$$\begin{gathered}\left(\frac{d^2y}{dx^2}\right)^2 = \left(\frac{1 \cdot \pi}{l}\right)^4 \cdot v_1^2 \cdot sin^2\frac{\pi \cdot x}{l} + \left(\frac{2 \cdot \pi}{l}\right)^4 \cdot v_2^2 \cdot sin^2\frac{2 \cdot \pi \cdot x}{l} + \left(\frac{3 \cdot \pi}{l}\right)^4 \cdot v_3^2 \cdot sin^2\frac{3 \cdot \pi \cdot x}{l} + \ldots + \\ +2 \cdot v_1 \cdot v_2 \cdot \frac{1^2 \cdot 2^2 \cdot \pi^4}{l^4} \cdot sin\frac{\pi \cdot x}{l} \cdot sin\frac{2 \cdot \pi \cdot x}{l} + 2 \cdot v_2 \cdot v_3 \cdot \frac{2^2 \cdot 3^2 \cdot \pi^4}{l^4} \cdot sin\frac{2 \cdot \pi \cdot x}{l} \cdot sin\frac{3 \cdot \pi \cdot x}{l} + \\ +2 \cdot v_1 \cdot v_3 \cdot \frac{1^2 \cdot 3^2 \cdot \pi^4}{l^4} \cdot sin\frac{\pi \cdot x}{l} \cdot sin\frac{3 \cdot \pi \cdot x}{l} + \ldots\end{gathered} \tag{22}$$

The expression of the potential energy of elastic deformation becomes a sum of terms, generalized in the following form:

$$\left(\frac{n \cdot \pi}{l}\right)^4 \cdot v^2 \cdot sin^2\frac{n \cdot \pi \cdot x}{l} \tag{23}$$

and

$$2 \cdot v_n \cdot v_m \cdot \frac{n^2 \cdot m^2 \cdot \pi^4}{l^4} \cdot sin\frac{n \cdot \pi \cdot x}{l} \cdot sin\frac{m \cdot \pi \cdot x}{l} \tag{24}$$

where indices n and m are integers.

By integrating these terms, it results:

$$\int_0^l sin^2\frac{n \cdot \pi \cdot x}{l} \cdot dx = \frac{l}{n \cdot \pi} \cdot \left[-\frac{1}{4} \cdot sin\frac{2 \cdot n \cdot \pi \cdot x}{l} + \frac{1}{2} \cdot \frac{n \cdot \pi \cdot x}{l}\right]_0^l = \frac{l}{2} \tag{25}$$

$$\int_0^l sin\frac{n\cdot\pi\cdot x}{l}\cdot sin\frac{m\cdot\pi\cdot x}{l}\cdot dx = \frac{l}{\pi}\cdot\left[\frac{1}{2\cdot(n-m)}\cdot sin(n-m)\cdot\frac{\pi\cdot x}{l} - \frac{1}{2\cdot(n+m)}\cdot sin(n+m)\cdot\frac{\pi\cdot x}{l}\right]_0^l = 0 \quad (26)$$

Thus, relation (18) will be of the form:

$$U_d = \frac{E\cdot I_z}{2}\cdot\frac{\pi^4}{l^4}\cdot\frac{l}{2}\cdot\left(1^4\cdot v_1^2 + 2^4\cdot v_2^2 + 3^4\cdot v_3^2 + \ldots\right) = \frac{E\cdot I_z\cdot\pi^4}{4\cdot l^3}\cdot\sum_{n=1}^{\infty} n^4\cdot v_n^4 \quad (27)$$

It is known that, at a reduced deformation of an elastic system, starting from the equilibrium position, the deformation potential energy is equal to the mechanical work produced by the external forces during this deformation. In other words, according to relation (17), a small deformation is equivalent to a small change in the coefficients v_1, v_2, v_3, which represent the arrows of the beam in different nodes. Thus, dv_n is considered the variation of the coefficient v_n. With this variation, the term:

$$v_n\cdot sin\frac{n\cdot\pi\cdot x}{l} \quad (28)$$

turns into:

$$(v_n + dv_n)\cdot sin\frac{n\cdot\pi\cdot x}{l} \quad (29)$$

This increase is equivalent to the introduction of a new sinusoid in the trigonometric series (17), of the form:

$$dv_n\cdot sin\frac{n\cdot\pi\cdot x}{l} \quad (30)$$

Through this additional deformation, the point of application of force F, located at an elevation a with the origin of the orthogonal system of reference axes (node 1 in Figure 3), moves with:

$$dv_n\cdot sin\frac{n\cdot\pi\cdot x}{l}$$

To determine the amplitude v_n, the condition is imposed that the external mechanical work (dL_{ext}) produced by the loads applied to the bar is transformed into potential energy of deformation (dL_{int}) as a result of moving to a new equilibrium position (dv_n). The magnitude dv_n is produced by a small static increase dF of the applied concentrated force (according to Figure 4).

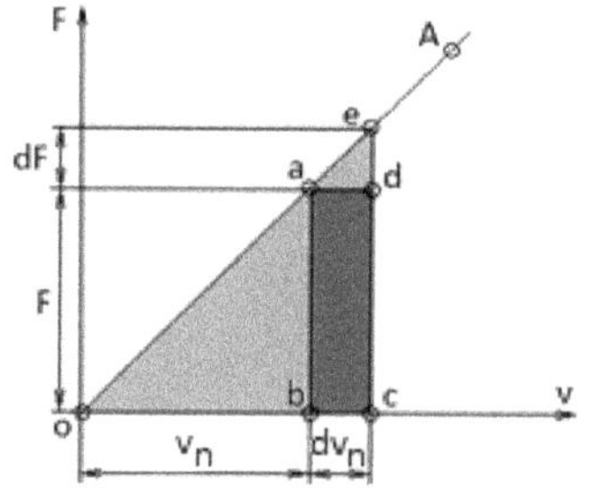

Figure 4. Representation of the external mechanical work (dL_{ext}) produced by the loads applied to the beam.

In Figure 4, the straight-line OA represents the characteristic curve of the material from which the bar is made for the range of elastic deformations. The external mechanical work represents the area of the surface *abcde* under the characteristic curve, and is expressed as follows:

$$dL_{ext} = A_{abcde} = A_{abcd} + A_{ade}$$

or

$$dL_{ext} = F \cdot dv_n + \frac{dF \cdot dv_n}{2} \cong F \cdot dv_n$$

The $\frac{dF \cdot dv_n}{2}$ term is neglected considering that it is an infinitesimal of higher order. The external mechanical work produced by the force F is of the form:

$$dL_{ext} = F \cdot dv_n \cdot sin \frac{n \cdot \pi \cdot a}{l} \quad (31)$$

The internal mechanical work, expressed as a function of $v_1, v_2, v_3, \ldots$, through the variation of a single coefficient, will present an increase in the form:

$$\begin{gathered} dL_{int} = \frac{\partial U_d}{\partial v_n} \cdot dv_n = \frac{\partial}{\partial v_n} \cdot \left(\frac{E \cdot I_z \cdot \pi^4}{4 \cdot l^3} \cdot \sum_{n=1}^{\infty} n^4 \cdot v_n^4 \right) \cdot dv_n \Rightarrow \\ dL_{int} = \frac{E \cdot I_z \cdot \pi^4}{2 \cdot l^3} \cdot n^4 \cdot v_n \cdot dv_n \end{gathered} \quad (32)$$

Applying the principle of conservation of energy, from the equality of the internal mechanical work, relation (32) with the external mechanical work, relation (31), results:

$$F \cdot dv_n \cdot sin \frac{n \cdot \pi \cdot a}{l} = \frac{E \cdot I_z \cdot \pi^4}{2 \cdot l^3} \cdot n^4 \cdot v_n \cdot dv_n \quad (33)$$

From relation (33), we obtain:

$$v_n = \frac{2 \cdot F \cdot l^3 \cdot sin \frac{n \cdot \pi \cdot a}{l}}{E \cdot I_z \cdot \pi^4 \cdot n^4} \quad (34)$$

By replacing the v_n coefficients in relation (17), it results:

$$y(x) = \frac{2 \cdot F \cdot l^3}{E \cdot I_z \cdot \pi^4} \cdot \left(\frac{1}{1^4} \cdot sin \frac{\pi \cdot a}{l} \cdot sin \frac{\pi \cdot x}{l} + \frac{1}{2^4} \cdot sin \frac{2 \cdot \pi \cdot a}{l} \cdot sin \frac{2 \cdot \pi \cdot x}{l} + \frac{1}{3^4} \cdot sin \frac{3 \cdot \pi \cdot a}{l} \cdot sin \frac{3 \cdot \pi \cdot x}{l} \right) \quad (35)$$

or

$$y(x) = \frac{2 \cdot F \cdot l^3}{E \cdot I_z \cdot \pi^4} \cdot \sum_{n=1}^{\infty} \frac{1}{n^4} \cdot sin \frac{n \cdot \pi \cdot a}{l} \cdot sin \frac{n \cdot \pi \cdot x}{l} \quad (36)$$

Relation (36) allows the calculation of the arrow y in any section of the considered beam. Thus, considering $a = l/2$ (according to Figure 5), the displacement of point 3 is evaluated as follows:

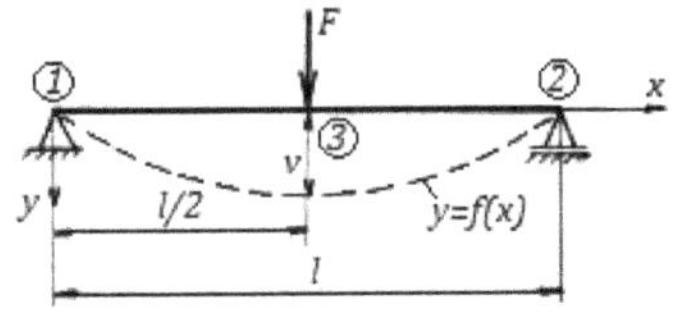

Figure 5. Simply supported bar, subjected to bending using a concentrated force, F.

From relation (36), it follows:

$$\begin{gathered} v = \frac{2 \cdot F \cdot l^3}{E \cdot I_z \cdot \pi^4} \cdot \left(\frac{1}{1^4} \cdot sin \frac{1 \cdot \pi \cdot \frac{l}{2}}{l} \cdot sin \frac{1 \cdot \pi \cdot \frac{l}{2}}{l} + \frac{1}{2^4} \cdot sin \frac{2 \cdot \pi \cdot \frac{l}{2}}{2} \cdot sin \frac{2 \cdot \pi \cdot \frac{l}{2}}{l} + \frac{1}{3^4} \cdot sin \frac{3 \cdot \pi \cdot \frac{l}{2}}{l} \cdot sin \frac{3 \cdot \pi \cdot \frac{l}{2}}{l} + \ldots \right) \Rightarrow \\ v = \frac{2 \cdot F \cdot l^3}{E \cdot I_z \cdot \pi^4} \cdot \left(\frac{1}{1^4} \cdot sin^2 \frac{\pi}{2} + \frac{1}{2^4} \cdot sin^2 \pi + \frac{1}{3^4} \cdot sin^2 \frac{3 \cdot \pi}{2} + \ldots \right) \Rightarrow \\ v = \frac{2 \cdot F \cdot l^3}{E \cdot I_z \cdot \pi^4} \cdot \left(\frac{1}{1^4} + \frac{1}{3^4} + \frac{1}{5^4} + \ldots \right) \end{gathered} \quad (37)$$

In Figure 5, the points (nodes), where either the supports are defined or the different types of loads act, are marked with 1–3.

If we consider, sequentially, the first term, then the first two terms, and finally the first three terms in the parenthesis, we get:

$$v = \frac{2 \cdot F \cdot l^3}{E \cdot I_z \cdot \pi^4} \cdot \frac{1}{1^4} = \frac{2 \cdot F \cdot l^3}{97.211 \cdot E \cdot I_z} = \frac{F \cdot l^3}{48.605 \cdot E \cdot I_z} = 0.020574 \cdot \frac{F \cdot l^3}{E \cdot I_z} \quad (38)$$

$$v = \frac{F \cdot l^3}{48.013 \cdot E \cdot I_z} = 0.020827 \cdot \frac{F \cdot l^3}{E \cdot I_z} \quad (39)$$

$$v = \frac{F \cdot l^3}{47.937 \cdot E \cdot I_z} = 0.02086 \cdot \frac{F \cdot l^3}{E \cdot I_z} \quad (40)$$

The exact relation of the maximum displacement is expressed by the relation [1–6]:

$$v = \frac{F \cdot l^3}{48 \cdot E \cdot I_z} = 0.020833 \frac{F \cdot l^3}{E \cdot I_z} \quad (41)$$

The relative deviation between the data obtained from relations (38) and (41) is 1.243%, the data obtained from relations (39) and (41) is 0.028%, and the data obtained from relations (40) and (41) is 0.129%.

For the case where the bar is supported and subjected to bending using a uniformly distributed load, as in Figure 6, the concentrated force F, from relation (36), can be replaced using the expression:

$$F = \int_0^l q \cdot dx \quad (42)$$

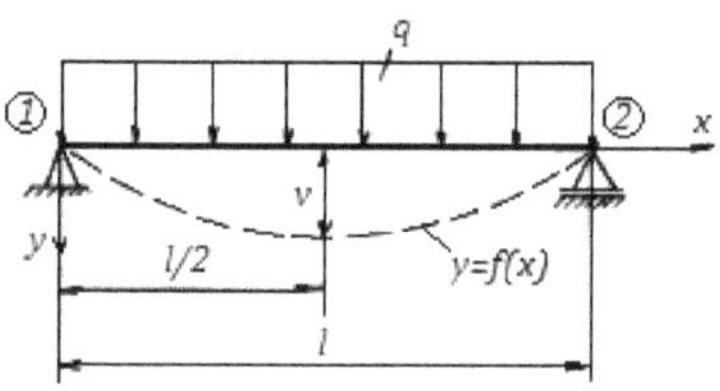

Figure 6. Simply supported beam, stressed using a uniformly distributed load, q.

In Figure 6, the points (nodes) where either the supports are defined or the different types of loads act are marked with 1–2.

Thus, the variation of the external mechanical work becomes:

$$\frac{dL_{ext}}{dv_n} = \int_0^l q \cdot dx \cdot sin \frac{n \cdot \pi \cdot x}{l} = \left[q \cdot \left(-\frac{l}{n \cdot \pi} \right) \cdot cos \frac{n \cdot \pi \cdot x}{l} \right]_0^l = -\frac{q \cdot l}{n \cdot \pi} \cdot (cosn \cdot \pi - 1) \quad (43)$$

Equating this expression with the increase in internal mechanical work results:

$$\frac{E \cdot I_z \cdot \pi^4}{2 \cdot l^3} \cdot n^4 \cdot v_n = -\frac{q \cdot l}{n \cdot \pi} \cdot (cosn \cdot \pi - 1) \Rightarrow v_n = \frac{-2 \cdot q \cdot l^4}{E \cdot I_z \cdot \pi^5 \cdot n^5} \cdot (cosn \cdot \pi - 1) \quad (44)$$

Thus, the equation of the average deformed fiber will be of the form:

$$y(x) = -\sum_{n=1}^{\infty} \frac{2 \cdot q \cdot l^4}{E \cdot I_z \cdot \pi^5 \cdot n^5} \cdot (cosn \cdot \pi - 1) \cdot sin \frac{n \cdot \pi \cdot x}{l} \quad (45)$$

For $n = 1, 3, 5, \ldots$

$$v_n = \frac{4 \cdot q \cdot l^4}{E \cdot I_z \cdot \pi^5 \cdot n^5} \quad (46)$$

and for $n = 2, 4, 6, \ldots$

$$v_n = 0 \quad (47)$$

In this situation, the expression of the average deformed fiber will be of the form:

$$y(x) = \frac{4 \cdot q \cdot l^4}{E \cdot I_z \cdot \pi^5} \cdot \left(\frac{1}{1^5} \cdot sin \frac{1 \cdot \pi \cdot x}{l} + \frac{1}{3^5} \cdot sin \frac{3 \cdot \pi \cdot x}{l} + \frac{1}{5^5} \cdot sin \frac{5 \cdot \pi \cdot x}{l} + \ldots \right) \tag{48}$$

The maximum displacement will be recorded in the middle of the distance between the two supports, for which $x = l/2$:

$$v = \frac{4 \cdot q \cdot l^4}{E \cdot I_z \cdot \pi^5} \cdot \left(\frac{1}{1^5} - \frac{1}{3^5} + \frac{1}{5^5} - \frac{1}{7^5} + \ldots \right) \tag{49}$$

If we consider, sequentially, the first term, then the first two terms, and finally, the first three terms in the parenthesis, we receive:

$$v = \frac{4 \cdot q \cdot l^4}{306.019 \cdot E \cdot I_z} = 0.013071 \cdot \frac{q \cdot l^4}{E \cdot I_z} \tag{50}$$

$$v = 0.0130172 \cdot \frac{q \cdot l^4}{E \cdot I_z} \tag{51}$$

$$v = 0.0130214 \cdot \frac{q \cdot l^4}{E \cdot I_z} \tag{52}$$

The exact relation of the maximum displacement is expressed by the relation [1–6]:

$$v = \frac{5 \cdot q \cdot l^4}{384 \cdot E \cdot I_z} = 0.0130208 \cdot \frac{q \cdot l^4}{E \cdot I_z} \tag{53}$$

The relative deviation between the data obtained from relations (49) and (52) is 0.384%, the data obtained from relations (50) and (52) is 0.027%, and the data obtained from relations (51) and (52) is 0.004%.

4. Fourier Series Applied to the Study of the Average Deformed Fiber

Fourier series are expressed through the following mathematical relationship:

$$y(x) = \frac{a_o}{2} + \sum_{n=1}^{\infty} \left[a_n \cdot cos\left(\frac{n \cdot \pi \cdot x}{l} \right) + b_n \cdot sin\left(\frac{n \cdot \pi \cdot x}{l} \right) \right] \tag{54}$$

where a_o, a_n, and b_n are the Fourier coefficients of the function $f(x)$, and are expressed through the following relations (Euler's formulas):

$$a_o = \frac{1}{l} \cdot \int_{-l}^{l} y(x) \cdot dx \tag{55}$$

$$a_n = \frac{1}{l} \cdot \int_{-l}^{l} y(x) \cdot cos \frac{n \cdot \pi \cdot x}{l} \cdot dx \tag{56}$$

$$b_n = \frac{1}{l} \cdot \int_{-l}^{l} y(x) \cdot sin \frac{n \cdot \pi \cdot x}{l} \cdot dx \tag{57}$$

Since the average deformed fiber is a continuous and odd function, the terms a_o and a_n are zero.

Thus:

$$b_n = \frac{2}{l} \cdot \int_{0}^{l} y(x) \cdot sin \frac{n \cdot \pi \cdot x}{l} \cdot dx \tag{58}$$

Therefore, the Fourier series of an odd function, defined on the interval (0, l), is a sinusoidal series and relation (53) will be of the form:

$$y(x) = \sum_{n=1}^{\infty}\left[b_n \cdot sin\left(\frac{n\cdot\pi\cdot x}{l}\right)\right] \tag{59}$$

For the case of support and request in Figure 6, a function of the form is defined:

$$y(x) = \sum_{n=1}^{\infty} C_n \cdot sin\frac{n\cdot\pi\cdot x}{l} \tag{60}$$

which satisfies the condition $y(x) = 0$ for $x = 0$ and $x = l$.

Thus:

$$x = 0 \rightarrow y(0) = \sum_{n=1}^{\infty} C_n \cdot sin\frac{n\cdot\pi\cdot(0)}{l} = 0 \tag{61}$$

$$x = l \rightarrow y(l) = \sum_{n=1}^{\infty} C_n \cdot sin\frac{n\cdot\pi\cdot(l)}{l} = 0 \tag{62}$$

If, from Figure 6, we consider $q = q(x) = y(x)$, from relation (53) it follows:

$$q(x) = \sum_{n=1}^{\infty}\left[b_n \cdot sin\left(\frac{n\cdot\pi\cdot x}{l}\right)\right] \tag{63}$$

From relation (62), we obtain:

$$b_n = \frac{2}{l}\cdot\int_0^l q(x)\cdot sin\frac{n\cdot\pi\cdot x}{l}\cdot dx \tag{64}$$

From relations (11) and (62), it follows:

$$\frac{d^4y(x)}{dx^4} = \frac{\sum_{n=1}^{\infty}\left[b_n \cdot sin\left(\frac{n\cdot\pi\cdot x}{l}\right)\right]}{E\cdot I_z} \tag{65}$$

Successively deriving relation (59) results in:

$$\frac{d^4y(x)}{dx^4} = \sum_{n=1}^{\infty} C_n\cdot\left(\frac{n\cdot\pi}{l}\right)^4\cdot sin\frac{n\cdot\pi\cdot x}{l} \tag{66}$$

From relations (64) and (65), we obtain:

$$\begin{gathered}\sum_{n=1}^{\infty} C_n\cdot\left(\frac{n\cdot\pi}{l}\right)^4\cdot sin\frac{n\cdot\pi\cdot x}{l} = \frac{\sum_{n=1}^{\infty}\left[b_n\cdot sin\left(\frac{n\cdot\pi\cdot x}{l}\right)\right]}{E\cdot I_z} \Rightarrow C_n\cdot\left(\frac{n\cdot\pi}{l}\right)^4 = \frac{b_n}{E\cdot I} \Rightarrow \\ C_n = \frac{b_n}{E\cdot I}\cdot\left(\frac{l}{n\cdot\pi}\right)^4\end{gathered} \tag{67}$$

Thus, from relation (63), it follows:

$$\begin{gathered}b_n = \frac{2\cdot q(x)}{l}\cdot\int_0^l sin\frac{n\cdot\pi\cdot x}{l}\cdot dx = \frac{2\cdot q(x)}{l}\cdot\left(-\frac{l}{n\cdot\pi}\cdot cos\frac{n\cdot\pi\cdot x}{l}\right)\Big|_0^l = \\ = -\frac{2\cdot q(x)}{n\cdot\pi}\cdot\left(cos\frac{n\cdot\pi\cdot l}{l} - cos\frac{n\cdot\pi\cdot 0}{l}\right) = -\frac{2\cdot q(x)}{n\cdot\pi}\cdot(cosn\cdot\pi - cos0) \\ = \frac{2\cdot q(x)}{n\cdot\pi}\cdot(1 - cosn\cdot\pi) = \frac{2\cdot q(x)}{n\cdot\pi}\cdot[1-(-1)] \Rightarrow \\ b_n = \frac{4\cdot q(x)}{n\cdot\pi}\end{gathered} \tag{68}$$

where: $n = 1, 3, 5, 7, 9, \ldots, \infty$—odd function.

From relation (66), it follows:

$$C_n = \frac{4 \cdot q(x)}{E \cdot I} \cdot \frac{l^4}{(n \cdot \pi)^5} \tag{69}$$

Substituting relation (68) into relation (59) results in:

$$y(x) = \frac{4 \cdot q(x) \cdot l^4}{\pi^5 \cdot E \cdot I} \sum_{n=1}^{\infty} \frac{1}{n^5} \cdot sin \frac{n \cdot \pi \cdot x}{l} \tag{70}$$

For $x = l/2$, from relation (69), we obtain:

$$y(x) = v = \frac{4 \cdot q(x) \cdot l^4}{\pi^5 \cdot E \cdot I} \sum_{n=1}^{\infty} \frac{1}{n^5} \cdot sin \frac{n \cdot \pi \cdot \left(\frac{l}{2}\right)}{l} = \frac{4 \cdot q(x) \cdot l^4}{\pi^5 \cdot E \cdot I} \sum_{n=1}^{\infty} \frac{1}{n^5} \cdot sin \frac{n \cdot \pi}{2} \tag{71}$$

For $n = 1$ from relation (70), it follows:

$$v = \frac{4 \cdot q(x) \cdot l^4}{\pi^5 \cdot E \cdot I} \cdot \frac{1}{1^5} \cdot sin \frac{1 \cdot \pi}{2} = \frac{4 \cdot q(x) \cdot l^4}{\pi^5 \cdot E \cdot I} = 0.013071 \cdot \frac{q \cdot l^4}{E \cdot I_z} \tag{72}$$

It is observed that relation (71) is identically equal to relation (49).

For the case of support and load in Figure 7a, relation (57) is of the form:

$$\begin{aligned} b_n &= \tfrac{2}{l} \cdot \int_a^{a+c} \tfrac{F}{c} \cdot sin \tfrac{n \cdot \pi \cdot x}{l} \cdot dx = \tfrac{2 \cdot F}{l} \cdot \left(-\tfrac{l}{n \cdot \pi \cdot c} \cdot cos \tfrac{n \cdot \pi \cdot x}{l} \right) \Big|_a^{a+c} \\ &= -\tfrac{2 \cdot F}{n \cdot \pi \cdot c} \cdot \left[cos \tfrac{n \cdot \pi \cdot (a+c)}{l} - cos \tfrac{n \cdot \pi \cdot a}{l} \right] \\ b_n &= -\tfrac{2 \cdot F}{n \cdot \pi \cdot c} \cdot \left(cos \tfrac{n \cdot \pi \cdot a}{l} \cdot cos \tfrac{n \cdot \pi \cdot c}{l} - sin \tfrac{n \cdot \pi \cdot a}{l} \cdot sin \tfrac{n \cdot \pi \cdot c}{l} - cos \tfrac{n \cdot \pi \cdot a}{l} \right) \end{aligned} \tag{73}$$

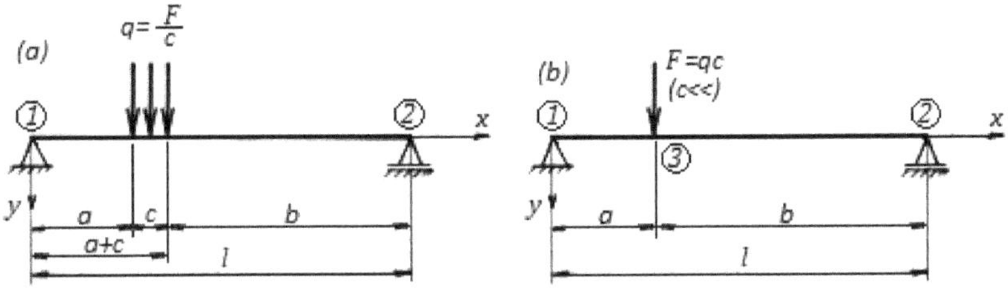

Figure 7. Simply supported bar and subjected to bending.

If c tends to zero [according to Figure 7b], it follows:

$$cos \frac{n \cdot \pi \cdot c}{l} = 1; sin \frac{n \cdot \pi \cdot c}{l} = \frac{n \cdot \pi \cdot c}{l}$$

Thus, from relation (72), we obtain:

$$\begin{aligned} b_n = -\tfrac{2 \cdot F}{n \cdot \pi \cdot c} \cdot \left(cos \tfrac{n \cdot \pi \cdot a}{l} - \tfrac{n \cdot \pi \cdot c}{l} \cdot sin \tfrac{n \cdot \pi \cdot a}{l} - cos \tfrac{n \cdot \pi \cdot a}{l} \right) &= \tfrac{2 \cdot F}{n \cdot \pi \cdot c} \cdot \left(-\tfrac{n \cdot \pi \cdot c}{l} \cdot sin \tfrac{n \cdot \pi \cdot a}{l} \right) \Rightarrow \\ b_n = \tfrac{2 \cdot F}{l} \cdot sin \tfrac{n \cdot \pi \cdot a}{l} \end{aligned} \tag{74}$$

Substituting relation (73) into relation (66) yields:

$$C_n = \frac{b_n}{E \cdot I} \cdot \left(\frac{l}{n \cdot \pi} \right)^4 = \frac{2 \cdot F}{E \cdot I} \cdot \frac{l^3}{(n \cdot \pi)^4} \cdot sin \frac{n \cdot \pi \cdot a}{l} \tag{75}$$

Substituting relation (74) into relation (59) results in:

$$y(x) = \sum_{n=1}^{\infty} C_n \cdot sin\frac{n \cdot \pi \cdot x}{l} = \frac{2 \cdot F \cdot l^3}{\pi^4 \cdot E \cdot I} \cdot \sum_{n=1}^{\infty} \frac{1}{n^4} \cdot sin\frac{n \cdot \pi \cdot a}{l} \cdot sin\frac{n \cdot \pi \cdot x}{l} \tag{76}$$

For $x = l/2$, from relation (75), it follows:

$$y(x) = v = \frac{2 \cdot F \cdot l^3}{\pi^4 \cdot E \cdot I} \cdot \sum_{n=1}^{\infty} \frac{1}{n^4} \cdot sin\frac{n \cdot \pi \cdot \frac{l}{2}}{l} \cdot sin\frac{n \cdot \pi \cdot \frac{l}{2}}{l} = \frac{2 \cdot F \cdot l^3}{\pi^4 \cdot E \cdot I} \cdot \sum_{n=1}^{\infty} \frac{1}{n^4} \cdot sin^2\frac{n \cdot \pi}{2} \tag{77}$$

For $n = 1$, from relation (76), we obtain:

$$v = \frac{2 \cdot F \cdot l^3}{\pi^4 \cdot E \cdot I} \cdot \frac{1}{1^4} \cdot sin^2\frac{1 \cdot \pi}{2} = 0.020531 \cdot \frac{F \cdot l^3}{E \cdot I} \tag{78}$$

The relative deviation between the data obtained from relations (41) and (77) is 1.449%.

5. Case Study Using the Fourier Series

It is defined as a simply supported bar loaded on the entire length unit (l) through a distributed load whose variation law is a linear function (q), according to Figure 8.

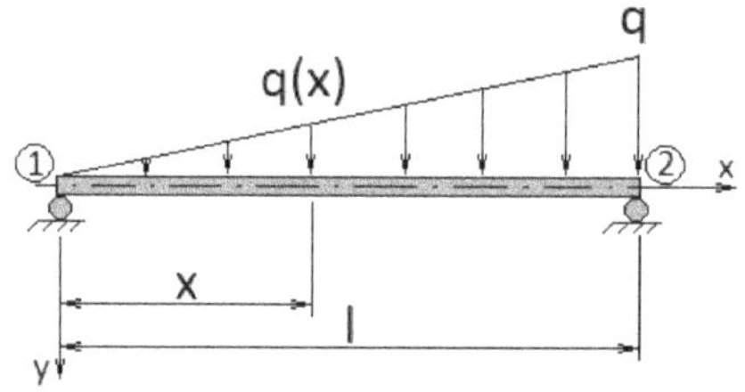

Figure 8. Simply supported bar and subjected to bending.

In a certain cross-section x, the magnitude of the distributed load $q(x)$ is expressed through the following relationship:

$$q(x) = q \cdot \frac{x}{l} \tag{79}$$

For the case of support and request in Figure 8, a function of the form is defined:

$$y(x) = \sum_{n=1}^{\infty} C_n \cdot sin\frac{n \cdot \pi \cdot x}{l}$$

where:

$$C_n = \frac{b_n}{E \cdot I} \cdot \left(\frac{l}{n \cdot \pi}\right)^4$$

If, from Figure 8, we consider $q = q(x) = y(x)$, from relation (53), it follows:

$$q(x) = \sum_{n=1}^{\infty} \left[b_n \cdot sin\left(\frac{n \cdot \pi \cdot x}{l}\right)\right] \tag{80}$$

From relation (79), we obtain:

$$b_n = \frac{2}{l} \cdot \int_0^l q(x) \cdot sin\frac{n \cdot \pi \cdot x}{l} \cdot dx \tag{81}$$

In relation (80), replacing $q(x)$ with the expression from formula (78) results:

$$b_n = \frac{2}{l}\cdot\int_0^l q\cdot\frac{x}{l}\cdot sin\frac{n\cdot\pi\cdot x}{l}\cdot dx = \frac{2\cdot q}{l^2}\cdot\int_0^l x\cdot sin\frac{n\cdot\pi\cdot x}{l}\cdot dx =$$
$$= \frac{2\cdot q}{l^2}\cdot\left[\left(\frac{l}{n\cdot\pi}\right)^2\cdot sin\frac{n\cdot\pi\cdot x}{l} - \frac{l}{n\cdot\pi}\cdot x\cdot cos\frac{n\cdot\pi\cdot x}{l}\right]\Bigg|_0^l = 2\cdot q\cdot(-n\cdot\pi\cdot cosn\cdot\pi)$$

Thus:

$$b_n = \frac{2\cdot q}{n\cdot\pi}\cdot(-1)^{n+1} \tag{82}$$

for $n = 1, 2, 3, 4, 5, \ldots, \infty$.

$$C_n = \frac{b_n}{E\cdot I_z}\cdot\left(\frac{l}{n\cdot\pi}\right)^4 = \frac{2\cdot q\cdot l^4}{\pi^5\cdot E\cdot I_z}\cdot\frac{(-1)^{n+1}}{n^5} \tag{83}$$

Thus:

$$y(x) = \sum_{n=1}^{\infty} C_n\cdot sin\frac{n\cdot\pi\cdot x}{l} = \frac{2\cdot q\cdot l^4}{\pi^5\cdot E\cdot I_z}\cdot\sum_{n=1}^{\infty}\frac{(-1)^{n+1}}{n^5}\cdot sin\frac{n\cdot\pi\cdot x}{l} \tag{84}$$

Since for this case of support and loading $y(x)$ for $x = l/2$, the calculation relation is of the form [1–6]:

$$y(x) = \frac{5\cdot q\cdot l^4}{768\cdot E\cdot I_z} = 0.00651\cdot\frac{q\cdot l^4}{E\cdot I_z} \tag{85}$$

For $n = 1$ from relation (83), it follows:

$$y(x) = \frac{2\cdot q\cdot l^4}{\pi^5\cdot E\cdot I_z}\cdot\sum_{n=1}^{\infty}\frac{(-1)^{n+1}}{n^5}\cdot sin\frac{n\cdot\pi\cdot\left(\frac{l}{2}\right)}{l} = \frac{2\cdot q\cdot l^4}{\pi^5\cdot E\cdot I_z}\cdot\sum_{n=1}^{\infty}\frac{(-1)^{n+1}}{n^5}\cdot sin\frac{n\cdot\pi}{2} \Rightarrow$$
$$y(x) = 0.00653\cdot\frac{q\cdot l^4}{E\cdot I_z} \tag{86}$$

The relative deviation between the data obtained from relations (84) and (85) is 0.306%.

6. Conclusions

The Fourier series method is used to obtain the solutions for the unknown transverse displacement $y(x)$ as infinite series, both in the case of static and dynamic loads. In this work, the concept of the average deformed fiber was defined in advance, highlighting the fact that this is a continuous periodic or non-periodic function. In this work, the concept of the average deformed fiber was defined in advance, highlighting the fact that this is a continuous periodic or non-periodic function. This can be expressed through trigonometric series and Fourier series.

The following cases were defined: simple right beam, supported on its ends, loaded in the transverse plane using a concentrated force (F); in the second case, it is considered a simple right beam, supported on its ends, loaded in the transverse plane using a uniformly distributed load (q); and in the third case, it is considered a simple right beam, supported on the ends, loaded in the transverse plane using a linear load distributed $q(x)$. All these types of loads are applied statically.

The determination of the displacement of the center of gravity of the cross-section is established using trigonometric series and Fourier series and the results obtained are compared with those provided by the specialized literature (the displacement of the center of gravity being determined by direct integration of the differential equation of the average deformed fiber).

For the first case of support and loading, using trigonometric series, the relative deviation between the data obtained from relations (38) and (41) is 1.243%, the data obtained from relations (39) and (41) is 0.028%, and the data obtained from relations (40) and (41) is 0.129%.

In the second case of support and loading, using trigonometric series, the relative deviation between the data obtained from relations (49) and (52) is 0.384%, the data obtained from relations (50) and (52) is 0.027%, and the data obtained from relations (51) and (52) is 0.004%.

For the first case of support and loading using Fourier series, it is observed that relation (71) is identically equal to relation (49).

In the second case of support and loading using Fourier series, the relative deviation between the data obtained from relations (41) and (77) is 1.449%.

In the third case of support and loading using Fourier series, the relative deviation between the data obtained from relations (84) and (85) is 0.306%.

The displacements are found as single series of infinite terms with good convergence.

The trigonometric series and Fourier series method has been successfully applied in this work to solve flexural problems.

Even though the method of trigonometric series and Fourier series is known and applied in many fields of science in the current applications of mechanics of materials, it is not currently used. For this reason, this work intends to popularize these methods by presenting them in an exhaustive and comprehensive form, starting from the presentation of the concept of medium deformed fiber to the solution of some current applications.

Thus, it can be concluded that the use of the trigonometric series and the Fourier series presents a series of advantages: they are well studied and have a solid theory, there are a variety of theorems and properties that can be used to understand the behavior of Fourier series and to perform calculations with them; they have a wide range of practical applications; offers an elegant and simple method that leads to fast and accurate solutions that can be easily implemented in a wide range of programs, such as MATLAB or Mathematica.

Funding: This research received no external funding.

Data Availability Statement: Not applicable.

Conflicts of Interest: The author declares no conflict of interest.

References

1. Botean, A.I. *Rezistența Materialelor. Solicitări Simple, Ediția a II-a Revizuită Și Adăugită*; Editura UTPRESS: Cluj-Napoca, Romania, 2019.
2. Hibbeler, R.C. *Mechanics of Materials*, 6th ed.; Pearson Education International: London, UK, 2005.
3. Gere, J.M.; Goodno, B.J. *Mechanics of Materials*, 8th ed.; Cengage Learning: Boston, MA, USA, 2013.
4. Beer, F.P.; Johnston, E.R. *Mechanics of Materials*; McGraw-Hill: Singapore, 1985.
5. Gere, J.M.; Timoshenko, S.P. *Mechanics of Materials*; PWS: Boise, ID, USA, 1997.
6. Popov, E.P. *Engineering Mechanics of Solids*; Prentice-Hall: Hoboken, NJ, USA, 1990.
7. Fariba, F. A new method for analysis of beam deflection using Taylor's expansion series. *Comput. Res. Prog. Appl. Sci. Eng.* **2015**, *3*, 178–181.
8. Grandin, H.T.; Rencis, J. A New Approach to Solving Beam Deflection Problems Using the Method of Segments. In Proceedings of the 2006 Annual Conference & Exposition, Chicago, IL, USA, 19–21 June 2006; pp. 11.79.1–11.79.21. [CrossRef]
9. Filonenko Borodich, M.M. *Elasticity Theory*; Gos. Izd. Fiz. Mat. Lit.: Moscow, Russia, 1959. (In Russian)
10. Ribiere, M.C. Sur divers cas de la flexion des prismes rectangles. *Compt. Rend.* **1889**, *126*, 1190–1192.
11. Shevlyakov, Y.A.; Ivanov, Y.B. A study of the bending of a short beam. *J. Math. Sci.* **1996**, *82*, 3447–3453. [CrossRef]
12. Cucuzza, R.; Rosso, M.M.; Marano, G.C. Optimal preliminary design of variable section beams criterion. *SN Appl. Sci.* **2021**, *3*, 745. [CrossRef]
13. Karamanos, S.A. Bending instabilities of elastic tubes. *Int. J. Solids Struct.* **2002**, *39*, 2059–2085. [CrossRef]
14. Bui, X.B.; Nguyen, T.K.; Le, Q.C.; Nguyen, T.T.P. A novel two-variable model for bending analysis of laminated composite beams. In Proceedings of the 5th International Conference on Green Technology and Sustainable Development (GTSD), IEEE Xplore, Ho Chi Minh City, Vietnam, 27–28 November 2020. [CrossRef]
15. Qiu, X.X.; Liu, H.B.; Wu, C.L.; Gu, Z.W. A trigonometric analytical solution of simply supported horizontally curved composite I-beam considering tangential slips. *Math. Probl. Eng.* **2016**, *2016*, 2465025. [CrossRef]
16. Kovalchuk, S.B. Exact solution of the problem on elastic bending of the segment of a narrow multilayer beam by an arbitrary normal load. *Mech. Compos. Mater.* **2020**, *56*, 55–74. [CrossRef]
17. Tang, R.C.; Jayne, B.A. Solution of an orthotropic beam problem by Fourier series. *Wood Fiber* **1971**, *3*, 84–89.
18. Wang, J.T.-S.; Lin, C.-C. Dynamic analysis of generally supported beams using Fourier series. *J. Sound Vib.* **1996**, *196*, 285–293. [CrossRef]

19. Zhu, H.; Sankar, B.V. A Combined Fourier Series—Galerkin Method for the Analysis of Functionally Graded Beams. *J. Appl. Mech.* **2004**, *71*, 421–424. [CrossRef]
20. Ike, C.C. Fourier series method for finding displacements and stress fields in hyperbolic shear deformable thick beams subjected to distributed transverse loads. *J. Comput. Appl. Mech.* **2022**, *53*, 126–141. [CrossRef]
21. Carrera, E.; Filippi, M.; Zappino, E. Free vibration analysis of laminated beam by polynomial, trigonometric, exponential and zig-zag theories. *J. Compos. Mater.* **2013**, *48*, 2299–2316. [CrossRef]

Disclaimer/Publisher's Note: The statements, opinions and data contained in all publications are solely those of the individual author(s) and contributor(s) and not of MDPI and/or the editor(s). MDPI and/or the editor(s) disclaim responsibility for any injury to people or property resulting from any ideas, methods, instructions or products referred to in the content.

mathematics

MDPI

Article

A Continuum Damage-Based Anisotropic Hyperelastic Fatigue Model for Short Glass Fiber Reinforced Polyamide 66

Elouni Chebbi [2], Lotfi Ben Said [1,2,*], Badreddine Ayadi [1] and Fakhreddine Dammak [2]

[1] Department of Mechanical Engineering, College of Engineering, University of Ha'il, Ha'il City 2440, Saudi Arabia
[2] Laboratory of Electrochemistry and Environment (LEE), National Engineering School of Sfax, University of Sfax, Sfax 3038, Tunisia
* Correspondence: bensaid_rmq@yahoo.fr

Abstract: A phenomenological 3D anisotropic nonlinear fatigue damage model has been developed for a short glass fiber-reinforced polyamide. The model is formulated within the framework of continuum damage mechanics and is based on a proposed anisotropic hyperelastic strain energy function. The proposed model accounts for the effects of fiber content and nonlinear material behavior. The mechanical behavior of polyamide reinforced with 20% and 30% wt short glass fiber has been experimentally investigated under quasi-static and fatigue loading. Fatigue tests under bending loading are carried out on rectangular specimens cut in the parallel and perpendicular direction to the mold flow direction. The proposed fatigue damage model allows predicting the fatigue damage of composite materials reinforced with short fiberglass, considering fiber orientation and fiber content. The model is used to predict the damage evolution and the number of cycles to failure, and good agreement between predicted values and experimental data is observed.

Keywords: fatigue analysis; polyamides; failure; degradation; fatigue model; short glass fiber

MSC: 74-10

Citation: Chebbi, E.; Ben Said, L.; Ayadi, B.; Dammak, F. A Continuum Damage-Based Anisotropic Hyperelastic Fatigue Model for Short Glass Fiber Reinforced Polyamide 66. *Mathematics* **2023**, *11*, 1508. https://doi.org/10.3390/math11061508

Academic Editors: Andrey Jivkov, Whye-Teong Ang and Lihua Wang

Received: 27 January 2023
Revised: 3 March 2023
Accepted: 16 March 2023
Published: 20 March 2023

Copyright: © 2023 by the authors. Licensee MDPI, Basel, Switzerland. This article is an open access article distributed under the terms and conditions of the Creative Commons Attribution (CC BY) license (https://creativecommons.org/licenses/by/4.0/).

1. Introduction

Numerous industries, including automotive, aeronautics, aerospace, construction, military, and sports equipment, are currently witnessing significant technological advancements in the use of composite materials. Composite materials are preferred due to their ability to reduce weight and, as a result, minimize energy consumption. They are also valued for their resistance to various environmental factors and their flexibility, which allows them to be shaped in different ways compared to metals [1]. Among the various types of composites, thermoplastic matrix composites have gained popularity and continue to experience rapid growth. Despite their many advantages, however, it is often challenging to obtain parts that meet the expectations of manufacturers. Extreme precision is required during the implementation of composites, and the slightest defect in impregnation or manufacturing can cause significant deformations within the material [2,3]. As a result, its mechanical characteristics are weakened, making it imperative to reduce the deformations within the material. Many factors influence the properties of composite materials, such as the type of fibers and matrix used or the processing method. However, it is widely acknowledged that the fiber–matrix interface plays a critical role because stress transfer occurs through this interface, and good compatibility between the two parts is necessary. The quality of the interface is closely linked to the presence of a specific surface treatment known as sizing. The impact of sizing on the properties of glass fiber-reinforced composite materials has been extensively studied, and it is evident that the quality of the interface significantly affects the properties of the material. Currently, short carbon fiber-reinforced thermoplastic matrix composites have the best adhesion properties, while glass fiber composites still require improved adhesion properties.

The use of short fiber reinforced thermoplastic composites has gained significant attention in various industrial fields and applications, including transportation, sports, aerospace, and automotive industries. These materials must have superior mechanical and chemical properties, be malleable to form complex shapes and be lightweight. Many authors have investigated the mechanical behavior of polyamide 66 (PA66GFs) reinforced with glass fibers in previous studies [4–12]. The properties of composite material are influenced by various factors, such as fiber type, matrix type, fiber volume fraction and orientation, interface, and fabrication process. Injection molding is a highly efficient and productive method for processing PA66GFs, and its mechanical properties depend heavily on this processing technique.

In addition, it has been shown that the mechanical properties of PA66GFs are primarily governed by three main variables: fiber characteristics (diameter, length, orientation, and content), molding conditions (temperature, pressure, and molding speed), and mechanical testing conditions (deformation speed, test temperature, and hygrothermal condition). Polyamide 66 reinforced by short glass fiber composites (PA66GFs) display anisotropic properties, and it has been found that the material properties such as Young's modulus, fatigue strength, and tensile strength are significantly higher in the flow direction than perpendicular to the polymer flow direction when considering the material as a three-dimensional solid. This orientation dependency of PA66GFs mechanical properties makes it an anisotropic material, as highlighted by several studies [13–18]. Haut du formulaire.

Composite materials are known to experience damage accumulation, with stiffness reduction often beginning early in the fatigue life due to various types of damage (matrix cracking, fiber fracture, fiber pullout, and matrix fiber delamination). The type of failure that occurs is dependent on the material variables and test conditions. Moreover, the damage mechanisms can interact differently and have different predominance depending on these factors. In the case of short fiber reinforced PA66GF subjected to cyclic loading, the damage evolution occurs in three stages [19–23]. The first stage corresponds to material softening and damage initiation, characterized by a significant reduction in stiffness during the initial cycles. The second stage involves coalescence and the propagation of micro-cracks that occurred during the first stage. This phase is characterized by interfacial fiber–matrix damage, and a relatively steady reduction in stiffness is observed, corresponding to the behavior accommodation of the material. In the final stage, fiber fractures occur with the appearance of macroscopic cracks, leading to the total failure of the material. Degradation mechanisms result in a rapid reduction in stiffness.

Mechanical components made of PA66GFs are frequently subjected to random or cyclic loading during their service life, which can result in irreversible damage [24]. To ensure that these components meet the necessary requirements of safety, economy, and reliability, it is critical to evaluate their cyclic behavior and the evolution of fatigue damage. However, these properties are usually determined through expensive, complex, and time-consuming experimental tests. Therefore, numerical simulations should be employed to predict the evolution of damage and to provide a reliable estimate of fatigue life. Nevertheless, to enable numerical simulations, the development of simple and accurate fatigue damage models is essential.

The fatigue damage of composite materials has been extensively investigated and documented in the literature. In their work, Amjadi and Fatemi [25] introduced a fatigue damage model that focuses on the critical plane approach for predicting the fatigue life of SGFR thermoplastics under tension-tension or tension-compression loading. Their model takes into account the effects of fiber orientation and mean stress, as well as temperature and frequency. They applied this damage model to a general fatigue model in order to incorporate these additional effects.

Several researchers have proposed different fatigue damage models for short glass fiber-reinforced polyamide composites. Toubal et al. [21] developed an analytical model based on cumulative damage to predict damage evolution. The model used a new damage parameter determined via the final Young's modulus [20]. Chebbi et al. [9,26] also proposed a 1D fatigue damage model based on young modulus degradation for predicting damage evolution in short glass fiber reinforced PA66GFs composite materials, using a similar approach and modifying the phenomenological model proposed by Chaboche [27]. Poursartip et al. [28] developed a phenomenological model where the unidirectional damage growth rate is a power function of mean stress and stress magnitude, independent of damage when cycle loading reaches constant stress magnitude. Recently, Chen et al. [29] proposed a novel damage model that integrates multiple deformation mechanisms using the modified Mori–Tanaka model and Transformation Field Analysis (MT–TFA) approach for predicting monotonic and cyclic stress–strain responses applied on short fibers reinforced polyamide composites. Liu et al. [30] and Kawai [31] used an expression for damage that varies with the compression and tension regime and is related to the damage itself and the amount of strain applied. Van Paepegem et al. [32] proposed a fatigue damage model that uses the amplitude of stress instead of the strain amplitude, which was validated by experimental results prepared on a flat woven glass/epoxy composite. Taheri-Behrooz et al. [33] presented multiple damage models, including four previously studied models for unidirectional stiffness degradation, upon which they based their own proposed models.

The use of Continuum Damage Mechanics (CDM) in conjunction with a fatigue predictor has been a common approach in the development of fatigue-damage formalism. Kachanov [34] was the first to introduce the CDM theory to explain the process of material degradation, and it was later extended to include fatigue damage due to its effectiveness in modeling the behavior of composite materials.

In the formulation of fatigue damage models, the small strain assumption is often used instead of the hyperelastic approach. The assumptions can be integrated with single or multiple damage variables corresponding to isotropic or anisotropic damage models, respectively. Ladevèze et al. [35] formulated a new phenomenological fatigue damage model using an anisotropic damage formulation and the CDM theory for laminate composite sheets in the plane stress assumptions. This model was later reformulated by Sedrakian et al. [36] to account for the strain energy and facilitate finite element implementation.

Nouri et al. [37] extended this method for predicting nonlinear cumulative fatigue damage in short glass fiber reinforced polyamide 66 under mechanical loading. The damage rate was assumed to be the sum of an exponential law and a power function to capture the three stages of damage typically observed in this material. Avanzini et al. [38] used a simplified version of the model to predict the fatigue behavior of a PEEK-based short fiber reinforced composite, considering isotropic fatigue damage with one damage variable. In related work, the authors [39] used a similar approach to model fatigue damage in short fiber reinforced PEEK, modifying the damage state variable to accurately describe the damage behavior. The fatigue damage model was implemented into a finite element code. Payan et al. [40] modeled the behavior of laminated carbon/epoxy composites under static and cyclic loading with plane stress assumptions and an orthotropic elastic potential. This model was later used by Hochard et al. [41] to develop a nonlinear cumulative damage model for woven-ply laminates in the framework of CDM subjected to cyclic and static loadings.

Wang et al. [42] employed the CDM theory in combination with a hyperelastic approach to describe the fatigue life of carbon-filled natural rubbers as a function of nominal strain amplitude under cyclic loading. They derived the damage evolution using Ogden strain energy density (SED) [43]. Ayoub et al. [44,45] improved upon the Continuum Damage Mechanics model proposed by Wang et al. [42] by utilizing a generalized form of Ogden SED and developing the theoretical framework for multiaxial loading. They tested the model using fatigue tests on a styrene–butadiene rubber (SBR) material under both constant and variable amplitude loading conditions to validate its applicability. The proposed model requires three damage parameters in addition to the constitutive law parameters.

Calvo et al. [46] proposed an uncoupled directional continuum damage model for biological soft tissues with fiber reinforcement using a hyperelastic approach. Their model considers two damage variables, one for the matrix and one for the fibers. Several damage models have been proposed recently [47–50] for metallic materials that can be extended for thermoplastic-based composites.

The objective of this paper is to investigate the fatigue damage behavior of glass fiber-reinforced polyamide 66 under both small and large deformations. To this end, a 3D anisotropic damage model is proposed for short glass fiber-reinforced polyamide based on the CDM theory. The model is developed using a hyperelastic finite deformation description of the elastic response and is an extension of the results reported by Chebbi et al. [8] for transversely anisotropic hyperelasticity where only the quasi-static uniaxial tensile and bending material behavior is considered. In addition, it is also an extension of the results illustrated in Chebbi et al. [9,26] for 3D anisotropic fatigue damage, where only a 1D elastic fatigue damage model is considered based on the degradation of the elastic modulus to predict the damage growth in composite materials.

The proposed 3D anisotropic fatigue damage model for short glass fiber-reinforced polyamide is developed in the framework of CDM theory and includes internal variables that introduce scalar variables for the fibers and matrix damages. The model takes into account the orientation of fibers due to the injection process of composite materials and is used to study the orthotropic material behavior under fatigue loading. To validate the model, material parameters are first determined through tensile tests on PA66GF in longitudinal and transverse directions. The fatigue damage of the PA66GF composite is then studied through both numerical simulations and experimental tests. The numerical simulations are performed via the developed finite element code and are used for sensitivity analysis of the effect of model parameters on damage evolution. The fatigue experimental tests are used to validate the proposed fatigue damage model.

2. Fatigue Damage Model Formulation

2.1. Constitutive Equations for Hyperelastic Material Model

Consider a continuum body with a reference placement $\Omega \subset R^3$ and a material particle defined by its position $\boldsymbol{X} \in R^3$ in the reference configuration. Denote by $\varphi(\boldsymbol{X}, t) : \Omega \times R \rightarrow R^3$ the mapping function between the reference configuration and the deformed configuration and $\boldsymbol{F}(\boldsymbol{X}, t)$ is the deformation gradient.

$$\boldsymbol{F} = \frac{\partial \varphi}{\partial \mathbf{X}},\ J = det(\boldsymbol{F}) \quad (1)$$

where $J > 0$ is the local volume ratio. As a measure of strain, the right symmetric Cauchy–Green strain tensor is considered and defined as follows:

$$\boldsymbol{C} = \boldsymbol{F}^T \boldsymbol{F} \quad (2)$$

The fully elastic constitutive response is applicable for an extremely slow deformation and is expressed via a free energy. In the case of short glass fiber reinforced polyamide, the free energy is assumed to be composed of two separate terms, as described below.

$$\psi = \eta_m\ \psi_m + \psi_f(c, \eta_k), k = 1, \ldots, n \quad (3)$$

Subscripts m and f are for matrix and fiber, c denotes the fibers volume fraction, $\eta_m \in [0, 1]$ is normalized scalar considered for the matrix damage variable, $\eta_i \in [0, 1]$, $i = 1, \ldots, n$ are normalized scalars considered for fibers damage variables. These damage variables give an account of the evolution of the damage within the family of fibers or variables responsible for the damage, which can occur on the interface of the fiber–matrix.

ψ_m, the matrix energy, is the isotropic part of the ground matrix. This strain energy potential is formulated considering the invariants terms and the incompressibility assumption. It is expressed as follows:

$$\psi_m = \psi_m(I_1, I_2),\ I_3 = J^2 = 1 \tag{4}$$

where

$$I_1 = tr(C),\ I_2 = \frac{1}{2}\left[(tr(C))^2 - tr\left(C^2\right)\right] \tag{5}$$

For the fiber energy ψ_f, N favored fiber directions are studied and characterized by unit vectors defined in the reference configuration by $\boldsymbol{A}_\alpha$ ($\alpha = 1, \ldots N$). Upon deformation, the unit vectors $\boldsymbol{A}_\alpha$ ($\alpha = 1, \ldots N$) are transformed into $\lambda_\alpha \boldsymbol{a}_\alpha$ ($\alpha = 1, \ldots N$), where $\boldsymbol{a}_\alpha$ ($\alpha = 1, \ldots N$) are unit vectors in the deformed configuration, and λ_α are the stretches along the fibers directions

$$\lambda_\alpha^2 = \boldsymbol{A}_\alpha \cdot \boldsymbol{C}\, \boldsymbol{A}_\alpha,\ \lambda_\alpha \boldsymbol{a}_\alpha = \boldsymbol{F}\, \boldsymbol{A}_\alpha \tag{6}$$

The energy function ψ_f should be an even function of $\boldsymbol{A}_\alpha$ ($\alpha = 1, \ldots N$), expressed as follows:

$$\psi_f = \psi_f(c,\ C, A_\alpha, \eta_k),\ \alpha = 1, \ldots N,\ k = 1, \ldots, n \tag{7}$$

According to Spencer [51], the energy function ψ_f can be formulated as a function of a set of pseudo invariants as follows:

$$\psi_f = \psi_f\left(c,\ I_{4(\alpha\beta)}, I_{5(\alpha\beta)}, \zeta_{\alpha\beta}, \eta_k\right),\ \alpha = 1, \ldots \beta\,;\ \beta = 1, \ldots N,\ k = 1, \ldots, n \tag{8}$$

where $I_{4(\alpha\beta)}$ and $I_{5(\alpha\beta)}$ are defined as

$$I_{4(\alpha\beta)} = \boldsymbol{A}_\alpha \cdot \boldsymbol{C} \cdot \boldsymbol{A}_\beta,\ I_{5(\alpha\beta)} = \boldsymbol{A}_\alpha \cdot \boldsymbol{C}^2 \cdot \boldsymbol{A}_\beta \tag{9}$$

and

$$\zeta_{\alpha\beta} = \boldsymbol{A}_\alpha \cdot \boldsymbol{A}_\beta \tag{10}$$

In order to obtain the stress tensor, we differentiate Equation (3) with respect to time

$$\dot{\psi} = \left[\eta_m \frac{\partial \psi_m}{\partial \boldsymbol{C}} + \frac{\partial \psi_f}{\partial \boldsymbol{C}}\right] : \dot{\boldsymbol{C}} + \psi_m\, \dot{\eta}_m + \sum_{k=1}^{n} \frac{\partial \psi_f}{\partial \eta_k} \dot{\eta}_k \tag{11}$$

The internal dissipation D_{int} is given by the second principle of thermodynamics and is expressed as follows:

$$D_{int} = \frac{1}{2} \boldsymbol{S} : \dot{\boldsymbol{C}} - \dot{\psi} \geq 0 \tag{12}$$

$$D_{int} = \left[\boldsymbol{S} - 2\eta_m \frac{\partial \psi_m}{\partial \boldsymbol{C}} - 2\frac{\partial \psi_f}{\partial \boldsymbol{C}}\right] : \frac{\dot{\boldsymbol{C}}}{2} - \psi_m \dot{\eta}_m - \sum_{k=1}^{n} \frac{\partial \psi_f}{\partial \eta_k} \dot{\eta}_k \tag{13}$$

Therefore, the second Piola–Kirchhoff stress tensor may be written as the sum of the matrix and fiber contributions:

$$\boldsymbol{S} = \eta_m \boldsymbol{S}_m + \boldsymbol{S}_f \tag{14}$$

where

$$\boldsymbol{S}_m = 2\frac{\partial \psi_m}{\partial \boldsymbol{C}},\ \boldsymbol{S}_f = 2\frac{\partial \psi_f}{\partial \boldsymbol{C}} \tag{15}$$

2.2. Energy Function

For the matrix isotropic free energy function, ψ_m, the incompressible Yeoh model [52] is considered as in [8]. This free energy is written as

$$\psi_m = \psi_m(I_1) = C_1(I_1 - 3) + C_2(I_1 - 3)^2 + C_3(I_1 - 3)^3 \tag{16}$$

where C_1, C_2, and C_3 are material properties. The second Piola–Kirchhoff stress tensor of matrix contribution is then

$$S_m = 2\frac{\partial \psi_m}{\partial I_1}\frac{\partial I_1}{\partial C} \tag{17}$$

where the first derivatives of the two first invariants, with respect to C tensor, are given in [53,54].

$$\frac{\partial I_1}{\partial C} = I - C_{33}C^{-1} \tag{18}$$

$$\frac{\partial I_2}{\partial C} = I_1 I - C - C_{33}(I_1 - C_{33})C^{-1} \tag{19}$$

where C_{33} is the (3,3) components of the right Cauchy–Green strain tensor, Equation (2). For the fibers, the energy function is supposed as follows:

$$\psi_f = \sum_{k=1}^{3} \eta_k \psi_{fk} + A_4(c)\left(I_{4,(11)} - 1\right)\left(I_{4,(22)} - 1\right) \tag{20}$$

$$\begin{cases} \psi_{fk} = A_k(c)\left(I_{4,(kk)} - 1\right)^2, \ k = 1,2 \\ \psi_{f3} = A_3(c)\left(I_{4,(12)} - \zeta_{12}\right)^2 \end{cases} \tag{21}$$

where A_k $(k = 1, \dots, 4)$ are material properties. These materiel properties must satisfy the following conditions which are required by the fact that the fiber energy ψ_f vanishes at zero volume fraction of glass fibers

$$A_k(0) = 0, \ k = 1, \dots, 4 \tag{22}$$

The second Piola–Kirchhoff stress tensor relative to fibers. Equation (15)b is deduced from Equation (20) as

$$S_f = \sum_{k=1}^{3} \eta_k S_{fk} + S_{f4} \tag{23}$$

$$S_{f1} = 4A_1(c)\left(I_{4,(11)} - 1\right)\frac{\partial I_{4(11)}}{\partial C}, \ S_{f2} = 4A_2(c)\left(I_{4,(22)} - 1\right)\frac{\partial I_{4(22)}}{\partial C} \tag{24}$$

$$S_{f3} = 4A_3(c)\left(I_{4,(12)} - \zeta_{12}\right)\frac{\partial I_{4(12)}}{\partial C}, \ S_{f4} = 2A_4(c)\left[\left(I_{4,(11)} - 1\right)\frac{\partial I_{4(22)}}{\partial C} + \left(I_{4,(22)} - 1\right)\frac{\partial I_{4(11)}}{\partial C}\right] \tag{25}$$

where the first derivatives of the invariants $I_{4(\alpha\beta)}$, Equation (9) with respect to tensor C, is

$$\frac{\partial I_{4(\alpha\beta)}}{\partial C} = \frac{1}{2}(A_\alpha \otimes A_\beta + A_\beta \otimes A_\alpha) \ \alpha = 1,2\,; \ \beta = 1,2 \tag{26}$$

2.3. Damage Evolution Equations

Using Equation (14), the internal dissipation, Equation (13), can be rewritten as

$$D_{int} = D_{int,m} + D_{int,f} \tag{27}$$

where

$$D_{int,m} = -Y_m \dot{\eta}_m \geq 0 \tag{28}$$

$$D_{int,f} = -\sum_{k=1}^{3} Y_k \dot{\eta}_k \geq 0, \ Y_k = \frac{\partial \psi_f}{\partial \eta_k}, \ k = 1, \dots, 3 \tag{29}$$

Y_m and Y_k ($k = 1, ..., 3$) are the thermodynamic dual variables associated with the damage variables η_m and η_k $(k = 1, \ldots, 3)$, respectively. Using Equations (13) and (20), they are given by

$$\begin{cases} Y_m = \psi_m \\ Y_k = \psi_{fk}, \; k = 1,3 \end{cases} \tag{30}$$

Therefore, the evolution equation of the thermodynamic force variables Y_m and Y_k $(k = 1, ..., 3)$ are

$$\begin{cases} \dot{Y}_m = 2\frac{\partial \psi_m}{\partial C} : \frac{\dot{C}}{2} = S_m : \frac{\dot{C}}{2} \\ \dot{Y}_k = 2\frac{\partial \psi_f}{\partial C} : \frac{\dot{C}}{2} = S_{fk} : \frac{\dot{C}}{2} \end{cases} \tag{31}$$

The evolution of damage variables η_m and $(\eta_k, \; k = 1, ..., 3)$ are obtained from an irreversible equation as follows. Let Ξ_m and Ξ_k $(k = 1, \ldots, 3)$ defined by the following expressions [54]

$$\Xi_m = \sqrt{2Y_m}, \; \Xi_k = \sqrt{2Y_k} \tag{32}$$

and let $\Xi_{m,t}$ and $\Xi_{k,t}$ $(k = 1, ..., 3)$ be the maximum value of Ξ_m and $(k = 1, ..., 3)$, respectively, over the closed time interval $[0, t]$ [55].

$$\Xi_{m,t} = \max_{s \in (-\infty, t)} \sqrt{2Y_m(s)}, \; \Xi_{k,t} = \max_{s \in (-\infty, t)} \sqrt{2Y_k(s)} \tag{33}$$

The damage criteria in strain space are defined by the following expressions:

$$\varphi_m = \Xi_m - \Xi_{m,t} \leq 0, \; \varphi_k = \Xi_k - \Xi_{k,t} \leq 0, \; k = 1, ..., 3 \tag{34}$$

For $\varphi_m < 0$ no evolution of damage variable η_m occurs. For $\varphi_k < 0$ no evolution of damage variable η_k occurs. The equations $\varphi_m = 0$ and $(\varphi_k = 0, \; k = 1, ..., 3)$ define the damaged surfaces with normals:

$$N_m = \frac{\partial \varphi_m}{\partial C}, \; N_k = \frac{\partial \varphi_k}{\partial C}, \; k = 1, ..., 3 \tag{35}$$

Loading conditions are

$$\begin{cases} \varphi_m = 0 \; and \; N_m : \dot{C} > 0 \\ \varphi_k = 0 \; and \; N_k : \dot{C} > 0, \; k = 1, ..., 3 \end{cases} \tag{36}$$

Finally, the evolution equation of damage variables η_m and $\eta_k (k = 1, ..., 3)$ are given by [56,57]

$$\dot{\eta}_m = \begin{cases} h_m(\Xi_m, \eta_m)\dot{\Xi}_m & if \quad \varphi_m = 0 \; et \; N_m \cdot \dot{E} > 0 \\ 0 & otherwise \end{cases} \tag{37}$$

$$\dot{\eta}_k = \begin{cases} h_k(\Xi_k, \eta_k)\dot{\Xi}_k & if \quad \varphi_k = 0 \; et \; N_k \cdot \dot{E} > 0 \\ 0 & otherwise \end{cases}, \; k = 1, ..., 3 \tag{38}$$

where h_m and h_k are functions that describe the damages evolutions. From Equation (39), it can be deduced that the evolution equations $\dot{\Xi}_m$ and $\dot{\Xi}_k$ are related to $\dot{Y}_m$ and $\dot{Y}_k$, respectively, as follows:

$$\dot{\Xi}_m = \frac{1}{\Xi_m}\dot{Y}_m, \; \dot{\Xi}_k = \frac{1}{\Xi_k}\dot{Y}_k \tag{39}$$

Under a cyclic loading condition, displacement, or loading controls, the damage will accumulate with the cycle's number. The time rate change of damage variables, $\dot{\eta}_m$ and $\dot{\eta}_k$, can be expressed in terms of η_m and η_k, respectively, with respect to the cycle's number.

Based on this consideration, the damage fatigue rate could be linked to the number of cycles N and written as follows:

$$\frac{d\eta_m}{dN} = h_m(\Xi_m, \eta_m) \,, \; \frac{d\eta_k}{dN} = h_k(\Xi_m, \eta_k) \tag{40}$$

The power law function is commonly utilized in numerous fatigue models for predicting the degradation of mechanical properties. Nevertheless, these models incorporate distinct effective quantities for damage evolution and characterization of material properties. Thus, the evolution equation that will be considered in this paper is as follows:$(D = 1 - \eta)$

$$\frac{dD_m}{dN} = \frac{a_m \, Y_m^{b_m}}{\left[\varepsilon + \left(D_m - D_{m0}\right)^{c_m}\right](1 - D_m)^{d_m}}, \; \frac{dD_k}{dN} = \frac{a_k \, Y_k^{b_k}}{\left[\varepsilon + \left(D_k - D_{k0}\right)^{c_k}\right](1 - D_k)^{d_k}} \tag{41}$$

Where $\varepsilon = 10^{-4}$, a_k, b_k, c_k, and d_k are material constants and D_{k0} is the initial damage.

Next, we use the assumption that the damage of the whole composite PA66GFs is related to the damage variable D_1 as the experimental tests are bending tests in the longitudinal direction. Then, we can write

$$D_m = D_1 \,, \; D_k = D_1 \tag{42}$$

2.4. Elasticity Tensor

Starting from Equation (14) yields

$$\dot{S} = \mathbb{C} : \frac{1}{2}\dot{C} \,, \; \mathbb{C} = \mathbb{C}_m + \sum_{k=1}^{3} \mathbb{C}_{fk} + \mathbb{C}_{f4} \tag{43}$$

where $\mathbb{C}_m$ is the matrix contribution to the material tangent moduli. However, $\mathbb{C}_{fk}$, $k = 1{,}4$ are the fibers contribution to the material tangent moduli. The $\mathbb{C}_m$ is given by [58]

$$\mathbb{C}_m = \begin{cases} \eta_m \mathbb{C}_{m0} + \frac{\partial \eta_m}{\partial \psi_m} \mathbf{S}_m \otimes \mathbf{S}_m & if \quad \varphi_m = 0 \; and \; \mathbf{N}_m \cdot \dot{\mathbf{C}} > 0 \\ \eta_m \mathbb{C}_{m0} & otherwise \end{cases} \tag{44}$$

with

$$\mathbb{C}_{m0} = 4 \frac{\partial^2 \psi_m}{\partial C \partial C} \tag{45}$$

and $\mathbb{C}_{fk}$ is given by

$$\mathbb{C}_{fk} = \begin{cases} \eta_k \mathbb{C}_{fk0} + \frac{\partial \eta_k}{\partial \psi_{fk}} \mathbf{S}_{fk} \otimes \mathbf{S}_{fk} & if \quad \varphi_k = 0 \; and \; \mathbf{N}_k \cdot \dot{\mathbf{C}} > 0 \\ \eta_k \mathbb{C}_{fk0} & otherwise \end{cases} \tag{46}$$

with

$$\mathbb{C}_{fk0} = 8A_k(c) \left[\frac{\partial I_{4(kk)}}{\partial C} \otimes \frac{\partial I_{4(kk)}}{\partial C} \right] k = 1, 2 \tag{47}$$

$$\mathbb{C}_{f30} = 8A_3(c) \left[\frac{\partial I_{4(12)}}{\partial C} \otimes \frac{\partial I_{4(12)}}{\partial C} \right] \tag{48}$$

and finally $\mathbb{C}_{f4}$ is given by

$$\mathbb{C}_{f4} = 4A_4(c) \left[\frac{\partial I_{4(11)}}{\partial C} \otimes \frac{\partial I_{4(22)}}{\partial C} + \frac{\partial I_{4(22)}}{\partial C} \otimes \frac{\partial I_{4(11)}}{\partial C} \right] \tag{49}$$

3. Experimental Study

The experimental investigation involved the use of polyamide 66, which was reinforced with short glass fibers at weight percentages of 10%, 20%, and 30%. The molding injection process was utilized to manufacture four grades of composites, namely, PA66GF00, PA66GF10, PA66GF20, and PA66GF30, with glass contents of 0%, 10%, 20%, and 30% based on polyamide 66. Rectangular plates with specific dimensions and ISO 527-2 tensile specimens were produced, as detailed in Chebbi et al. [9]. The mechanical properties were characterized via tensile tests in accordance with the ISO 527-2 standard specification. The specimens were cut along both the longitudinal and transverse directions, which are parallel and perpendicular, respectively, to the direction of mold flow. Room temperature tensile tests were conducted using a 10 kN INSTRON testing machine equipped with a RUDLPH laser extensometer, with a crosshead speed of 1 mm/min.

The specimens were subjected to cyclic loading using a fatigue-testing machine that was constructed in-house, as described in Chebbi et al. [9]. The adjustable crank-linkage mechanism was utilized to apply the alternating displacement ($u(t)$) to one end of the specimen (point B) while the other end was clamped (point A). Consequently, the specimen was loaded as a clamped–clamped beam with one moving clamp (as shown in Figure 1). The amplitude of the displacement ($u_{\max}$) and the displacement ratio ($R_d = u_{\min}/u_{Max}$) were adjustable parameters. The force acting on the composite sample was measured using a force gauge connected to the sample fixture.

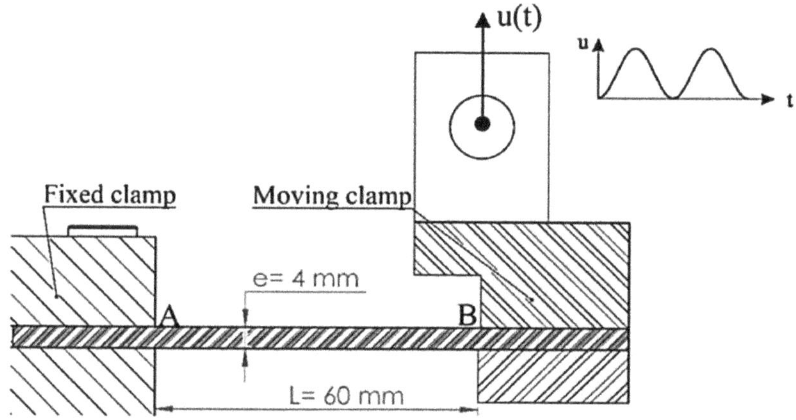

Figure 1. Specimen clamping.

The fatigue tests were conducted at room temperature with a constant alternating displacement, using a cyclic frequency of 2 Hz for load cycles. The aim was to minimize the increase in temperature due to the self-heating phenomenon, as proposed by Handa et al. [59]. The variation of the displacement applied to the specimen during the test, as well as the resultant force, were recorded instantaneously. Three minimum tests were performed for each variation of displacement between 8 mm and 12.5 mm.

4. Identification of the Anisotropic Hyperelastic Behavior of PA66GFs

The parameters of the energy potential (defined in Equations (16) and (20)), including $C_1, C_2, C_3, A_1(c)$, and $A_2(c)$, were identified via an inverse method with three experimental tests. Two tensile tests were conducted in the longitudinal and transverse directions for PA66GFs, and a tensile test was conducted for the pure matrix. A finite element (FE) model was developed based on the specimens used in the tensile tests. Load control was employed, and an error function was expressed as follows:

$$f = \left[\sum_{k=1}^{n} \left(U_k^{FE} - U_k^{Exp} \right)^2 \right]^{1/2} \tag{50}$$

This error function is the sum of different contributions from loaded nodes estimated at different load levels. U_k^{FE}, U_k^{Exp} are, respectively, the nodal displacements from the Finite Element simulation and from the experiments. The non-linear least squares minimization problems Equation (50) is solved via the Levenberg–Marquardt algorithm. The FE model uses a four-node quadrilateral shell element proposed by Dammak et al. [60].

The material properties for the matrix, relative to the Yeoh model, are obtained in Ref. [8] as $C_1 = 128$Mpa, $C_2 = -4670$Mpa, and $C_3 = 1.5237 \times 10^5$Mpa.

With C_1, C_2, and C_3 obtained, the experimental results of uniaxial tensile tests of PA66GFs along the longitudinal direction are used to obtain the material parameter $A_1(c)$. The predicted composite responses are plotted in Figure 2. A good agreement with the experimental data is observed under moderate deformation.

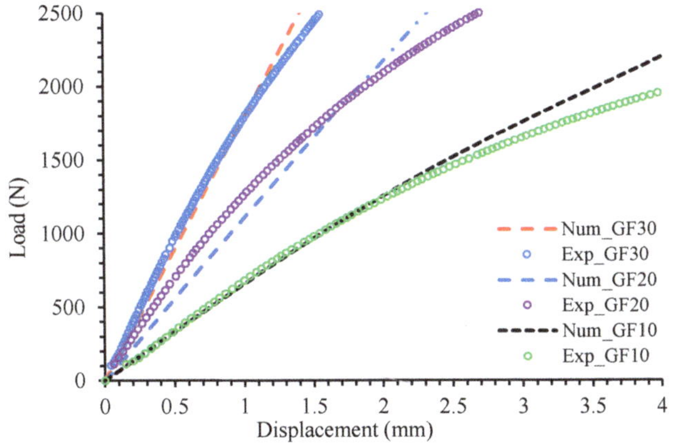

Figure 2. Load-displacement curves of tensile tests on PA66GFs: longitudinal direction.

Finally, the material parameter $A_2(c)$ for the studied material was obtained by fitting the transverse uniaxial tensile test data as plotted in Figure 3. The experimental data are in good agreement with predicted results within the applicable domain of the presented model.

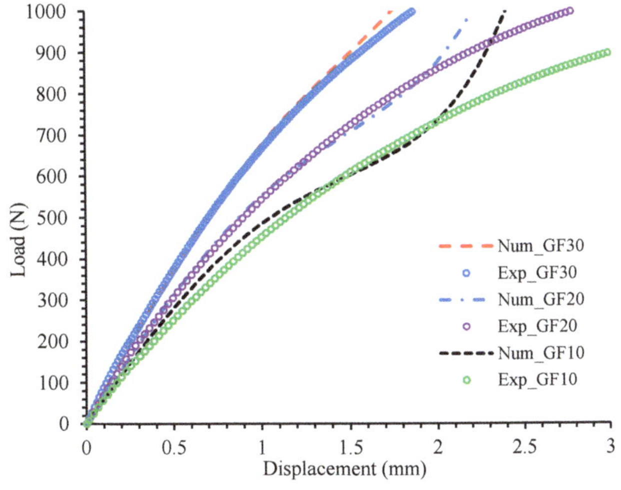

Figure 3. Load-displacement curves of tensile tests on PA66GFs: transverse direction.

The other two material parameters, $A_3(c)$ and $A_4(c)$, in the anisotropic hyperelastic model cannot be determined without additional experimental tests, such as shear tests. As these tests have not yet been conducted, the material parameters are currently considered to be valueless.

$$A_3(c) = A_4(c) = 0.0 \tag{51}$$

The material properties for the longitudinal and transverse directions, $A_1(c)$ and $A_2(c)$, were determined via a nonlinear least squares method and are summarized in Table 1 for three different volume fractions.

Table 1. Identification of the material parameter $A_1(c)$ and $A_2(c)$.

	wt%	c	$A_1(c)$[**Mpa**]	$A_2(c)$[**Mpa**]
PA66GF10	10	0.04489	62.04	3.915
PA66GF20	20	0.09565	192.1	16.12
PA66GF30	30	0.15349	347.3	34.21

The evolution of $A_1(c)$ and $A_2(c)$ can be calculated by second-order polynomial functions with a good correlation factor.

$$\begin{cases} A_1(c) = c(A_{10} + A_{11}c) \\ A_2(c) = c(A_{20} + A_{21}c) \end{cases} \tag{52}$$

The values of the material properties $A_1(c)$ and $A_2(c)$ identified for the three different materials are plotted as a function of the fiber volume fraction, c, in Figure 4. It is worthwhile to notice the difference between the longitudinal and transverse directions.

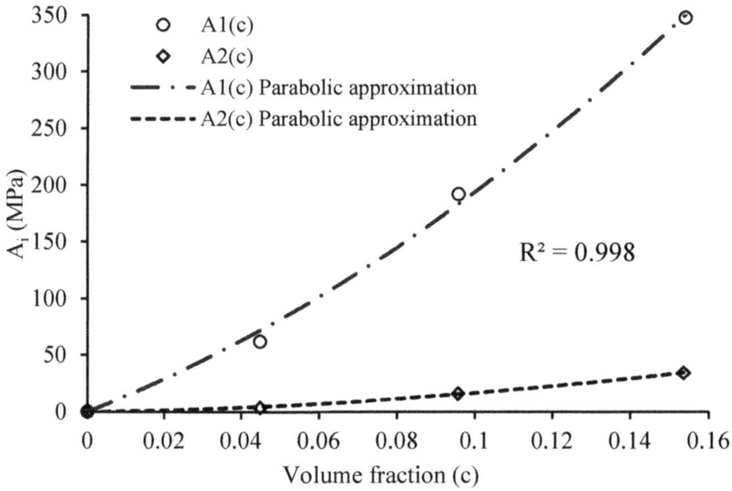

Figure 4. Function $A_1(c)$ and $A_2(c)$ as function of the volume fraction c.

The final whole model parameters are summarized in Table 2.

Table 2. Set of anisotropic model parameters.

C_1[**Mpa**]	C_2[**Mpa**]	C_3[**Mpa**]	A_{10}[**Mpa**]	A_{11}[**Mpa**]	A_{20}[**Mpa**]	A_{21}[**Mpa**]
128	−4570	$1.5237\ 10^5$	1320	6245	56.4	1194

Young modulus in longitudinal and transverse directions can be expressed as follows:

$$\begin{cases} E_L = 6C_1 + 8c(A_{10} + cA_{11}) \\ E_T = 6C_1 + 8c(A_{20} + cA_{21}) \end{cases} \tag{53}$$

These moduli are given in Table 3 for PA66, PA66GF10, PA66GF 20, and PA66GF 30. The results obtained are in good agreement with those obtained through experimental characterization [8]. It is interesting to note the difference between Young's modulus in the longitudinal and transverse directions. This difference is induced by the orientation of the fibers in these directions.

Table 3. Young's modulus in longitudinal and transverse directions.

wt%	0	0.1	0.2	0.3
E_L	768	1342	2235	3565
E_T	768	807.5	898.5	1062

5. Fatigue Damage Model

5.1. Numerical Implementation

The flowchart in Figure 5 outlines the looping scheme used for the fatigue damage model implemented in the in-house finite element code. The cycle jump procedure is used to integrate the damage growth rate equation (Equation (41)) by extrapolation, which allows for a computationally efficient simulation. The incremental method is used to calculate the increment of the cyclic internal variables at all Gauss points. The evolutionary variables are then extrapolated and used to calculate the next cycle jump. After a certain number of increments (ΔN cycles), the total damage is estimated via the fourth-order Runge–Kutta integration method (Equation (54)) [61]. This damage estimate can be used to predict new material properties, and the simulation is repeated iteratively until total failure ($D = 1$).

$$D_{N+\Delta N} = D_N + \frac{1}{6}(K_1 + 2K_2 + 2K_3 + K_4)\Delta N \tag{54}$$

where

$$\begin{aligned} K_1 &= f(N,\ D_N) \\ K_2 &= f\left(N + \tfrac{1}{2}\Delta N,\ D_N + \tfrac{1}{2}\Delta N \cdot K_1\right) \\ K_3 &= f\left(N + \tfrac{1}{2}\Delta N,\ D_N + \tfrac{1}{2}\Delta N \cdot K_2\right) \\ K_4 &= f(N + \Delta N,\ D_N + \Delta N \cdot K_3) \end{aligned} \tag{55}$$

where ΔN is the discretization step size, and $f(N,\ D_N) = \frac{dD}{dN}$.

5.2. Sensitivity Study

The following paragraph provides a sensitivity analysis of the damage fatigue model (Equation (48)) on its four parameters, namely, a, b, c, and d. This analysis aims to examine the impact of each parameter on the evolution and kinetics of damage, as well as the number of cycles until failure. Additionally, the study aims to optimize the process of identifying the damage model parameters. The structure being modeled is a rectangular plate with the dimensions of $60 \times 15 \times 4$ mm. The first edge of the structure is fixed, and a sinusoidal displacement is applied to the second edge, as illustrated in Figure 6. The simulation utilizes material properties acquired through quasi-static identification, as indicated in Table 2. The modeled structure is meshed using four-node shell elements.

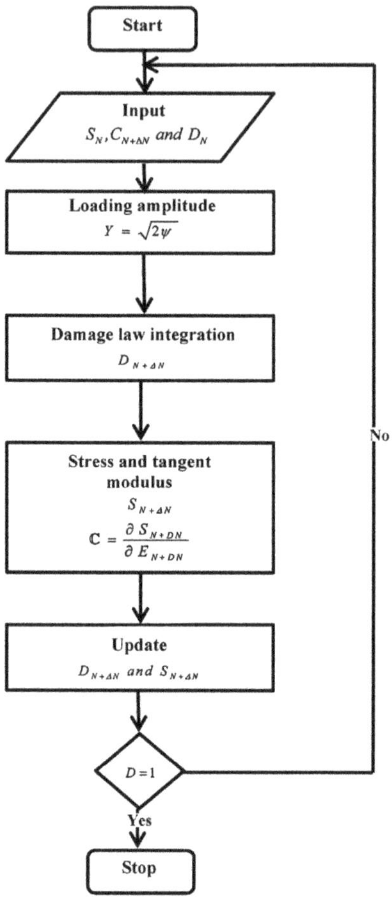

Figure 5. Flowchart of the implementation.

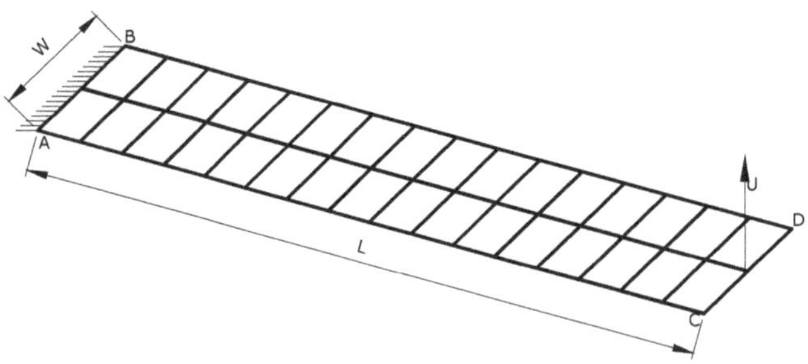

$$AB : \begin{cases} u = v = w = 0 \\ \theta_x = \theta_y = \theta_z = 0 \end{cases}$$

$$CD : \{\theta_x = \theta_y = \theta_z = 0$$

Figure 6. Finite element model and boundary conditions.

A numerical sensitivity analysis was carried out on the PA66GF20 sample with a prescribed displacement of 10 mm. In each test, one parameter was modified while the others remained constant. Table 4 shows the initial values of the damage model parameters. For the remainder of the study, the initial damage value, D_{f0}, (Equation (48)), was set to zero. The damage evolution curves at the outer layer fixed extremes of the specimen are illustrated in Figures 7–10.

Table 4. Initial values of damage fatigue model parameters.

a	*b*	*c*	*d*
2.3×10^{-8}	8.32	0.99	3.33

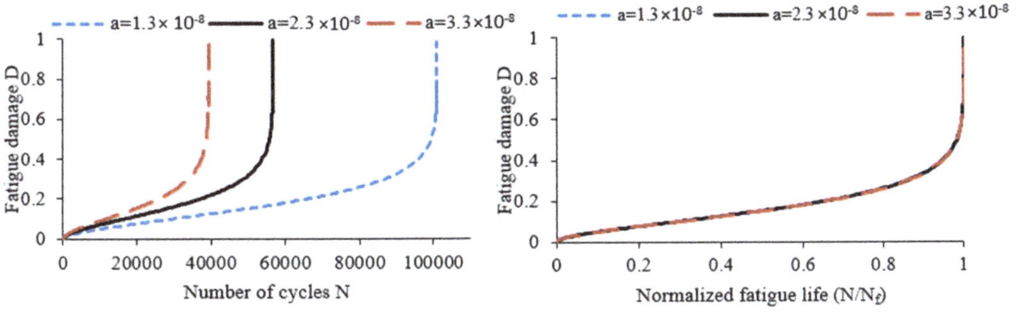

Figure 7. Influence of parameter (a) on damage evolution.

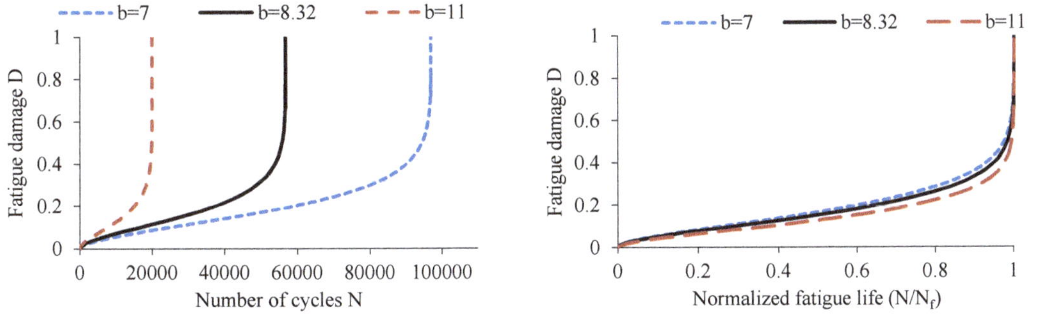

Figure 8. Influence of parameter (b) on damage evolution.

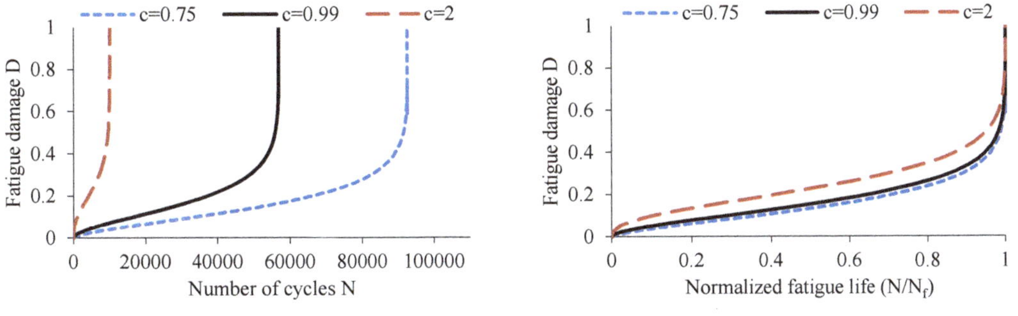

Figure 9. Influence of parameter (c) on damage evolution.

As depicted in Figure 7, which shows fatigue damage evolution in relation to normalized fatigue life, the parameter (a) does not affect the kinetics of damage. However, it significantly impacts the damage rate of the second stage. As a result, increasing the value of the parameter (a) reduces the number of cycles required for failure to occur.

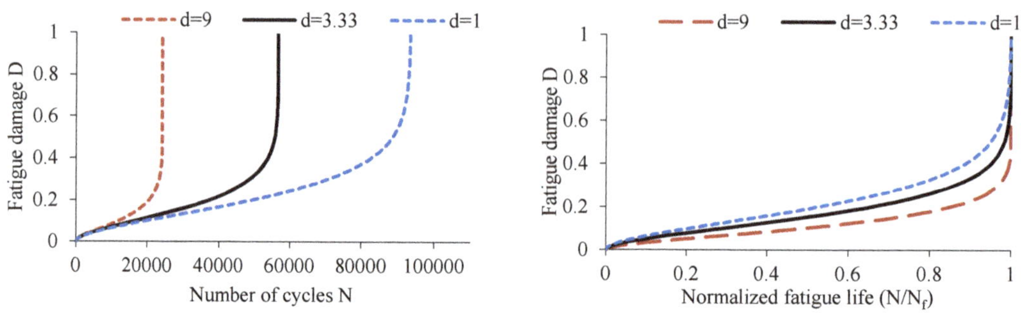

Figure 10. Influence of parameter "d" on the damage evolution.

Figure 8 demonstrates that the parameter (b) has a notable impact on the kinetics of damage. This parameter is responsible for initiating damage during the third stage. However, increasing its value decreases the number of cycles needed to reach failure.

Modifying the parameter (c) alters the evolution and kinetics of fatigue damage, as depicted in Figure 9. Increasing this parameter causes a rapid evolution of damage during the first stage, resulting in a decrease in the fatigue life of the composite specimen.

Figure 10 displays the impact of the parameter (d) on the evolution and kinetics of damage. This parameter has a significant impact on the damage slope of the second stage and the onset of the third stage. As the value of the parameter (d) increases, the rate of damage evolution accelerates, leading to a considerable decrease in the fatigue life of the structure. This may result in rapid degradation of the material. However, the parameter (d) has no impact on the first stage of damage evolution.

5.3. Validation of the Fatigue Damage Model

The fatigue model proposed in this paper was used to investigate the fatigue behavior of PA66GF20 and PA66GF30 specimens under bending tests. First, the materials parameters were identified via a nonlinear least squares method. An objective function representing the difference between the values of the numerical and experimental results was determined and minimized using the Levenberg–Marquart algorithm [62]. For each material, four constants are obtained, and the results are summarized in Table 5. Experimentally measured force-cycle history for PA66GF20 and PA66GF0 specimens are presented in Figures 11 and 12, respectively. The higher the applied displacement, the higher the initial force acting in the composite specimen. The curves show three stages. The first stage is characterized by a rapid decrease in material stiffness. In the second stage, the force acting in the composite specimen decreases in a relatively steady manner. The last stage corresponds to the propagation and the coalescence of cracks until the brutal rupture. In addition, increasing the amplitude of the applied displacement reduces the fatigue life without changing the damage kinetics. Numerical results for the force degradation are presented in Figures 13 and 14, respectively. The three stages of damage evolution are well established. It is interesting to note the good agreement between the experimental and the numerical results, which proves the accuracy of the damage model used in these simulations and its efficiency in reproducing the fatigue behavior of the studied composites. Furthermore, simulated the number of cycles until failure is in good agreement with experimental ones, as shown in Tables 6 and 7.

Table 5. Material parameters of the fatigue damage model for PA66GF20 and PA66GF2030.

Composite	a	b	c	d
PA66GF20	2.3×10^{-8}	8.32	0.99	3.33
PA66GF30	1.05×10^{-8}	8.9	1.0	3.33

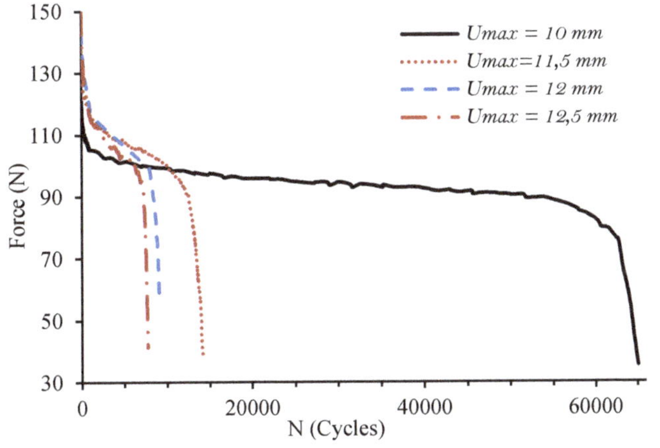

Figure 11. Experimentally measured force-cycle history for PA66GF20 specimens.

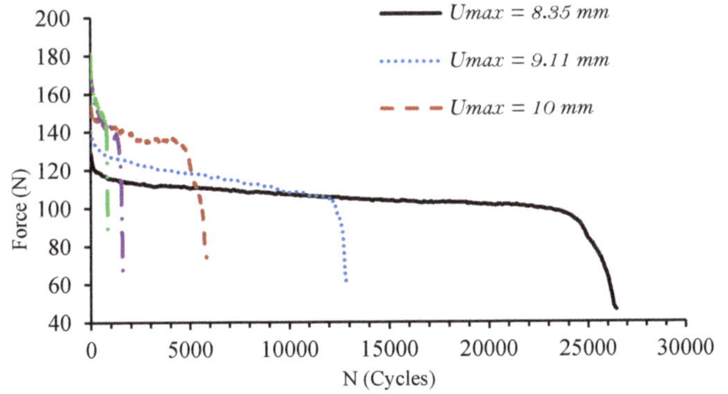

Figure 12. Experimentally measured force-cycle history for PA66GF30 specimens.

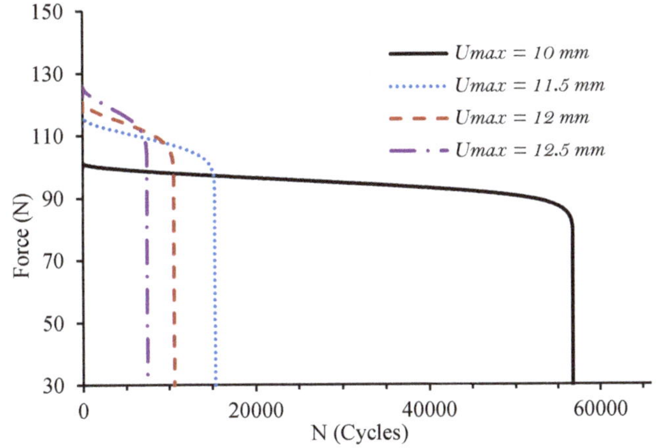

Figure 13. Simulated force-cycle history for PA66GF20 specimens.

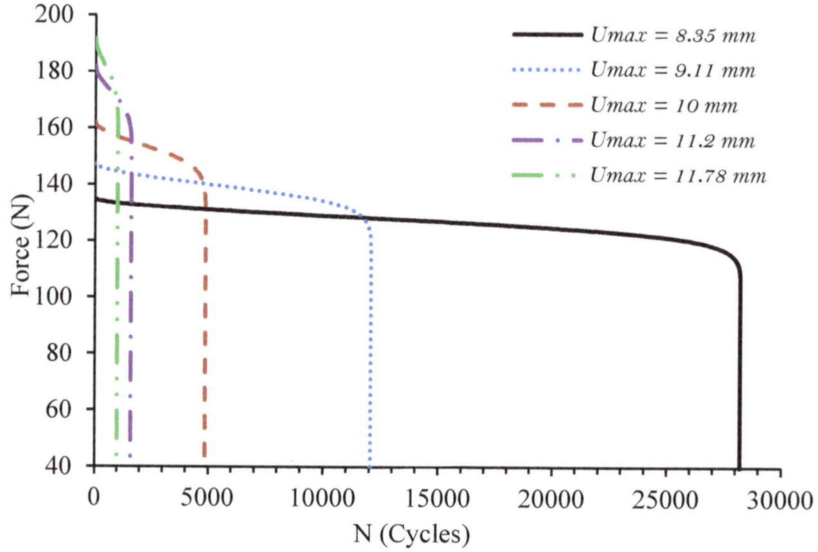

Figure 14. Simulated force-cycle history for PA66GF30 specimens.

Table 6. Experiment and numerical number of cycles to failure of PA66GF20.

Imposed Displacement	10	11.5	12	12.5
Exp results	65,000	14,200	9060	7740
Num results	57,000	15,330	10,580	7461
Error %	12.3	7.9	16.7	3.6

Table 7. Experimental and numerical number of cycle to failure of PA66GF30.

Imposed Displacement	8.35	9.11	10	11.2	11.78
Experimental results	26,000	12,850	5830	1582	855
Numerical results	28,200	12,047	4857	1617	1000
Error %	8.4	6.2	16.6	2.2	16.9

Figures 15 and 16 depict the damage evolution as a function of the number of cycles at the extreme fixed outer layer of the PA66GF20 and PA66GF30 specimens, respectively. The simulated curves exhibit the three stages of damage evolution that are typical of these materials. The numerical results demonstrate the model's capability to accurately replicate the behavior of the composites under investigation.

In Figure 17, the damage contours in the deformed configuration are illustrated for the PA66GF30 specimen under a bending test with an imposed displacement of 8.35 mm. It is evident that the maximum value of damage is concentrated at the clamped cross-section. However, it is also important to note a substantial level of damage at the moving section where the imposed displacement was applied. These findings were verified through experimental observations, where most of the tested specimens were found to have failed at the fixed section.

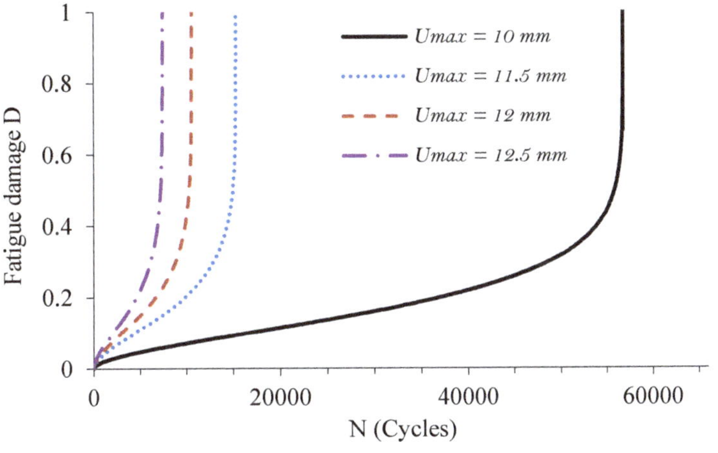

Figure 15. Simulated damage evolution at the extreme fixed outer layer of PA66GF20 specimens.

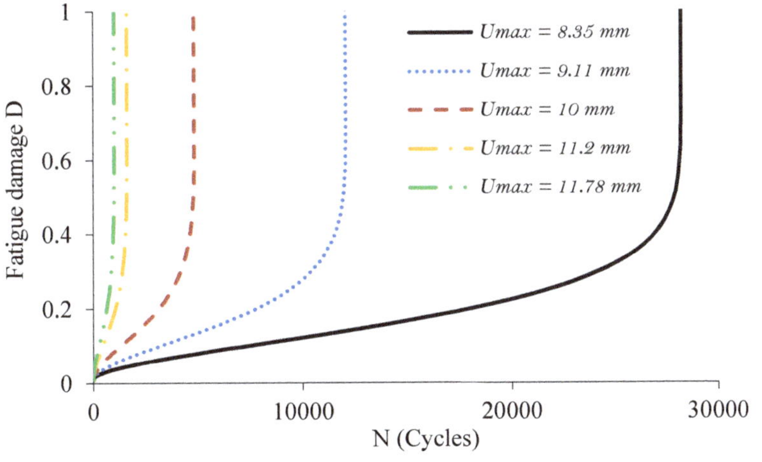

Figure 16. Simulated damage evolution at the extreme fixed outer layer of PA66GF30 specimens.

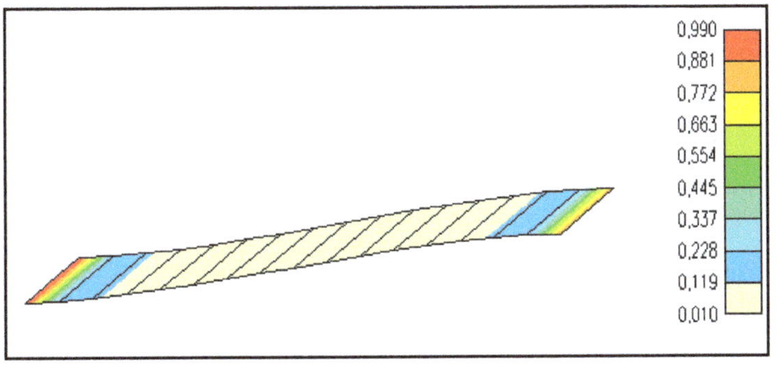

Figure 17. Damage contour plot in the deformed configuration of the PA66GF30 specimen.

6. Conclusions

The present paper introduced a new 3D anisotropic fatigue damage model that is based on phenomenological principles. The model is used to predict the mechanical behavior of short glass fiber-reinforced polyamide 66 when subjected to fatigue tests. The model merges both the hyperelastic approach and continuum damage mechanics in the same framework. This model allows taking into account the orientation of the fibers by considering the different fiber contents. To determine the hyperelastic constitutive model, tensile tests were conducted in both the longitudinal and transverse directions. The fatigue damage model was incorporated into an in-house finite element code, and a parametric study was conducted to examine how the model's evolution and kinetics were affected by the model parameters. This sensitivity analysis enabled us to enhance the procedure for determining the parameters of the fatigue damage model. The accuracy of the proposed model was tested against experimental results, which demonstrated its effectiveness. The simulated results accurately predicted the evolution of damage and captured the specific damage kinetics related to PA66GFs. Furthermore, it was revealed that the developed model's performance was satisfactory compared to the experimental findings.

Author Contributions: E.C.: Conceptualization, methodology, experimental investigation, writing—original draft preparation, review, and editing. L.B.S.: software, visualization, data curation, investigation. B.A.: visualization, writing—review and editing, investigation. F.D.: supervision, conceptualization, methodology, writing—review and editing. All authors have read and agreed to the published version of the manuscript.

Funding: This research has been funded by Deputy for Research & Innovation, Ministry of Education, through Initiative of Institutional Funding at University of Ha'il—Saudi Arabia, through project number IFP-22 165.

Institutional Review Board Statement: Not applicable.

Informed Consent Statement: Not applicable.

Data Availability Statement: Not applicable.

Conflicts of Interest: The authors declare no conflict of interest.

References

1. Hriberšek, M.; Kulovec, S. Study of the glass fibres and internal lubricants influence in a polyamide 66 matrix on the wear evolution of polyacetal and polyamide 66 based gears in a meshing process. *Eng. Fail. Anal.* **2022**, *134*, 106071. [CrossRef]
2. Han, W.; Zhou, J.; Shi, Q. Research progress on enhancement mechanism and mechanical properties of FRP composites reinforced with graphene and carbon nanotubes. *Alex. Eng. J.* **2022**, *64*, 541–579. [CrossRef]
3. Khan, Z.I.; Habib, U.; Mohamad, Z.B.; Rahmat, A.R.; Abdullah, N.A. Mechanical and thermal properties of sepiolite strengthened thermoplastic polymer nanocomposites: A comprehensive review. *Alex. Eng. J.* **2022**, *61*, 975–990. [CrossRef]
4. Güllü, A.; Özdemir, A.; Özdemir, E. Experimental investigation of the effect of glass fibres on the mechanical properties of polypropylene (PP) and polyamide 6 (PA6) plastics. *Mater. Des.* **2006**, *27*, 316–323. [CrossRef]
5. Mouhmid, B.; Imad, A.; Benseddiq, N.; Benmedakhène, S.; Maazouz, A. A study of the mechanical behaviour of a glass fibre reinforced polyamide 6,6: Experimental investigation. *Polym. Test.* **2006**, *25*, 544–552. [CrossRef]
6. Benaceur, I.; Othman, R.; Guegan, P.; Dhieb, A.; Damek, F. Sensitivity of the flow stress of nylon 6 and nylon 66 to strain-rate. *Int. J. Mod. Phys. B* **2008**, *22*, 1249–1254. [CrossRef]
7. Ghorbel, A.; Saintier, N.; Dhiab, A.; Dammak, F. Étude du comportement mécanique d'un polyamide 66 chargé de fibres de verre courtes. *Mécanique Ind.* **2011**, *12*, 333–342.
8. Chebbi, E.; Wali, M.; Dammak, F. An anisotropic hyperelastic constitutive model for short glass fiber reinforced polyamide. *Int. J. Eng. Sci.* **2016**, *106*, 262–272. [CrossRef]
9. Chebbi, E.; Mars, J.; Wali, M.; Dammak, F. Fatigue behavior of short glass fiber reinforced polyamide 66: Experimental study and fatigue damage modeling. *Period. Polytech. Mech. Eng.* **2016**, *60*, 247–255. [CrossRef]
10. Ramazani, S.; Morshed, M.; Ghane, M. Effect of service temperature on structure and mechanical properties of polyamide 6 & 66 tyre cords. *J. Polym. Res.* **2011**, *18*, 781–792.
11. Arif, M.F.; Saintier, N.; Meraghni, F.; Fitoussi, J.; Chemisky, Y.; Robert, G. Multiscale fatigue damage characterization in short glass fiber reinforced polyamide-66. *Compos. Part B* **2014**, *61*, 55–65. [CrossRef]
12. Ibáñez-Gutiérrez, F.T.; Cicero, S.; Carrascal, I.A. On the influence of moisture content on the fracture behaviour of notched short glass fibre reinforced polyamide 6. *Compos. Part B* **2019**, *159*, 62–71. [CrossRef]

13. Zhou, Y.; Mallick, P.K. Fatigue performance of an injection-molded short E-glass fiber-reinforced polyamide 6,6. I. Effects of orientation, holes, and weld line. *Polym. Compos.* **2006**, *27*, 230–237. [CrossRef]
14. Bernasconi, A.; Davoli, P.; Basile, A.; Filippi, A. Effect of fibre orientation on the fatigue behaviour of a short glass fibre reinforced polyamide-6. *Int. J. Fatigue* **2007**, *29*, 199–208. [CrossRef]
15. Brunbauer, J.; Mösenbacher, A.; Guster, C.; Pinter, G. Fundamental influences on quasistatic and cyclic material behavior of short glass fiber reinforced polyamide illustrated on microscopic scale. *J. Appl. Polym. Sci.* **2014**, *131*, 40842. [CrossRef]
16. Benaarbia, A.; Chrysochoos, A.; Robert, G. Thermomechanical behavior of PA6.6 composites subjected to low cycle fatigue. *Compos. Part B* **2015**, *76*, 52–64. [CrossRef]
17. Li, X.P.; Zhao, G.Q.; Yang, C. Effect of mold temperature on motion behavior of short glass fibers in injection molding process. *Int. J. Adv. Manuf. Technol.* **2014**, *73*, 639–645. [CrossRef]
18. Stadlera, G.; Primetzhoferc, A.; Pinterb, G.; Grüna, F. Investigation of fibre orientation and notch support of short glass fibre reinforced thermoplastics. *Int. J. Fatigue* **2020**, *131*, 105284. [CrossRef]
19. Reifsnider, K.L.; Henneke, E.G.; Stinchcomb, W.W.; Duke, J.C. Damage mechanics and NDE of composite laminates. In *Mechanics of Composite Materials-Recent Advances*; Hashin, Z., Herakovich, C.T., Eds.; Pergamon Press: New York, NY, USA, 1983; pp. 399–420.
20. Mao, H.; Mahadevan, S. Fatigue damage modelling of composite materials. *Compos. Struct.* **2002**, *58*, 405–410. [CrossRef]
21. Toubal, L.; Karama, M.; Lorrain, B. Damage evolution and infrared thermography in woven composite laminates under fatigue loading. *Int. J. Fatigue* **2006**, *28*, 1867–1872. [CrossRef]
22. Belmonte, E.; De Monte, M.; Hoffmann, C.J.; Quaresimin, M. Damage mechanisms in a short glass fiber reinforced polyamide under fatigue loading. *Int. J. Fatigue* **2017**, *94*, 145–157. [CrossRef]
23. Mejri, M.; Toubal, L.; Cuilliere, J.C.; François, V. Fatigue life and residual strength of a short- natural-fiber-reinforced plastic vs Nylon. *Compos. Part B* **2017**, *110*, 429–441. [CrossRef]
24. Mortazavian, S.; Fatemi, A. Fatigue behavior and modeling of short fiber reinforced polymer composites: A literature review. *Int. J. Fatigue* **2015**, *70*, 297–321. [CrossRef]
25. Amjadi, M.; Fatemi, A. A Fatigue damage model for Life prediction of Injection-Molded short glass fiber-reinforced Thermoplastic composites. *Polymers* **2021**, *13*, 2250. [CrossRef]
26. Chebbi, E.; Mars, J.; Hentati, H.; Wali, M.; Dammak, F. A New Cumulative Fatigue Damage Model for Short Glass Fiber-Reinforced Polyamide 66. In *Design and Modeling of Mechanical Systems—III*; Haddar, M., Chaari, F., Benamara, A., Chouchane, M., Karra, C., Aifaoui, N., Eds.; Lecture Notes in Mechanical Engineering; Springer: Berlin/Heidelberg, Germany, 2018; pp. 227–234.
27. Chaboche, J.L. Une loi differentielle d'endommagement de fatigue avec cumulation non linéaire. *Rev. Française Mécanique* **1974**, *51*, 71–82.
28. Poursartip, A.; Ashby, M.F.; Beaumont, P.W.R. The fatigue damage mechanics of a carbon fiber composite laminate: I–Development of the model. *Compos. Sci. Technol.* **1986**, *25*, 193–218. [CrossRef]
29. Chen, Q.; Chatzigeorgiou, G.; Robert, G.; Meraghni, F. Viscoelastic-viscoplastic homogenization of short glass-fiber reinforced polyamide composites (PA66/GF) with progressive interphase and matrix damage: New developments and experimental validation. *Mech. Mater.* **2022**, *164*, 104081. [CrossRef]
30. Liu, B.; Lessard, L.B. Fatigue and damage tolerance analysis of composite laminates: Stiffness loss damage modeling and life prediction. *Compos. Sci. Technol.* **1994**, *51*, 43–51. [CrossRef]
31. Kawai, M. A phenomenological model for off-axis fatigue behavior of unidirectional polymer matrix composites under different stress ratios. *Compos. Part A* **2004**, *35*, 955–963. [CrossRef]
32. Van Paepegem, W.; Degrieck, J.; De Baets, P. Finite Element Approach for Modelling Fatigue Damage in Fibre-reinforced Composite Materials. *Compos. Part B* **2001**, *32*, 575–588. [CrossRef]
33. Taheri-Behrooz, F.; Shokrieh, M.M.; Lessard, L.B. Residual Stiffness in Cross-ply Laminates Subjected to Cyclic Loading. *Compos. Struct.* **2008**, *85*, 205–212. [CrossRef]
34. Kachanov, M.L. Time of the rupture process under creep conditions, Izy Akad. *Nauk. SSR Otd. Tech. Nauk.* **1958**, *8*, 26–31.
35. Ladevèze, P.; Le Dantec, E. Damage modelling of the elementary ply for laminated composites. *Compos. Sci. Technol.* **1992**, *43*, 257–267. [CrossRef]
36. Sedrakian, A.; Ben Zineb, T.; Billoet, J.L. Contribution of industrial composite parts to fatigue behaviour simulation. *Int. J. Fatigue* **2002**, *24*, 307–318. [CrossRef]
37. Nouri, H.; Meraghni, F.; Lory, P. Fatigue damage model for injection-molded short glass fibre reinforced thermoplastics. *Int. J. Fatigue* **2009**, *31*, 934–942. [CrossRef]
38. Avanzini, A.; Donzella, G.; Gallina, D. Fatigue damage modelling of PEEK short fibre composites. *Procedia Eng.* **2011**, *10*, 2052–2057. [CrossRef]
39. Avanzini, A.; Donzella, G.; Gallina, D.; Pandini, S.; Petrogalli, C. Fatigue behavior and cyclic damage of peek short fiber reinforced composites. *Compos. Part B* **2013**, *45*, 397–406. [CrossRef]
40. Payan, J.; Hochard, C. Damage modelling of laminated carbon/epoxy composites under static and fatigue loads. *Int. J. Fatigue* **2002**, *24*, 299–306. [CrossRef]
41. Hochard, C.; Payan, J.; Bordreuil, C. A progressive first ply failure model for woven ply CFRP laminates under static and fatigue loads. *Int. J. Fatigue* **2006**, *28*, 1270–1276. [CrossRef]

42. Wang, B.; Lu, H.; Kim, G.H. A damage model for the fatigue life of elastomeric materials. *Mech. Mater.* **2002**, *34*, 475–483. [CrossRef]
43. Ogden, R.W. *Non-Linear Elastic Deformation*; Ellis Horwood Limited: New York, NY, USA, 1984.
44. Ayoub, G.; Naït-Abdelaziz, M.; Zaïri, F.; Gloaguen, J.M. Multiaxial fatigue life prediction of rubber-like materials using the continuum damage mechanics approach. *Proc. Eng.* **2011**, *2*, 985–993. [CrossRef]
45. Ayoub, G.; Nait-Abdelaziz, M.; Zairi, F.; Gloaguen, J.M.; Charrier, P. A continuum damage model for the high-cycle fatigue life prediction of styrene-butadiene rubber under multiaxial loading. *Int. J. Solids Struct.* **2011**, *48*, 2458–2466. [CrossRef]
46. Calvo, B.; Pena, E.; Martinez, M.A.; Doblaré, M. An uncoupled directional damage model for fibred biological soft tissues. Formulation and computational aspects. *Int. J. Numer. Meth Eng.* **2007**, *69*, 2036–2057. [CrossRef]
47. Ben Said, L.; Wali, M. Accuracy of Variational Formulation to Model the Thermomechanical Problem and to Predict Failure in Metallic Materials. *Mathematics* **2022**, *10*, 3555. [CrossRef]
48. Ben Said, L.; Allouch, M.; Wali, M.; Dammak, F. Numerical Formulation of Anisotropic Elastoplastic Behavior Coupled with Damage Model in Forming Processes. *Mathematics* **2023**, *11*, 204. [CrossRef]
49. Long, X.; Guo, Y.; Su, Y.; Siow, K.S.; Chen, C. Unveiling the damage evolution of SAC305 during fatigue by entropy generation. *Int. J. Mech. Sci.* **2023**, *244*, 108087. [CrossRef]
50. Niu, X.; Zhu, S.P.; He, J.C.; Liao, D.; Correia, J.A.; Berto, F.; Wang, Q. Defect tolerant fatigue assessment of AM materials: Size effect and probabilistic prospects. *Int. J. Fatigue* **2022**, *160*, 106884. [CrossRef]
51. Spencer, A.J.M. *Continuum Theory of the Mechanics of Fibre-Reinforced Composites*; Springer: New York, NY, USA, 1984.
52. Yeoh, O.H. Characterization of elastic properties of carbon black filled rubber vulcanizates. *Rubber Chem. Technol.* **1990**, *63*, 792–805. [CrossRef]
53. Dammak, F.; Regaieg, A.; Kallel, I.K.; Dhieb, A. Modeling the law of transversely isotropic hyperelastic behavior of elastomers. *Eur. J. Comput. Mech.* **2007**, *16*, 103–126. [CrossRef]
54. Abdessalem, J.; Kallel, I.K.; Fakhreddine, D. Theory and finite element implementation of orthotropic and transversely isotropic incompressible hyperelastic membrane. *Multidiscip. Model. Mater. Struct.* **2011**, *7*, 424–439. [CrossRef]
55. Simo, J.C. On a fully three-dimensional finite-strain viscoelastic damage model: Formulation and computational aspects. *Comput. Methods Appl. Mech.* **1987**, *60*, 153–173. [CrossRef]
56. Naghdi, P.M.; Trapp, J.A. The significance of formulating plasticity theory with reference to loading surfaces in strain space. *Int. J. Eng. Sci.* **1975**, *13*, 785–797. [CrossRef]
57. Simo, J.C.; Hughes, T.J.R. *Computational Inelasticity*; Springer: New York, NY, USA, 1998.
58. Holzapfel, G.A. *Nonlinear Solid Mechanics*; Wiley: New York, NY, USA, 2000.
59. Handa, K.; Kato, A.; Narisawa, I. Fatigue characteristics of a glass-fiber-reinforced polyamide. *J. Appl. Polym. Sci.* **1999**, *72*, 1783–1793. [CrossRef]
60. Dammak, F.; Abid, S.; Gakwaya, A.; Dhatt, G. A formulation of the non linear discrete Kirchhoff quadrilateral shell element with finite rotations and enhanced strains. *Rev. Eur. Des Eléments* **2005**, *14*, 7–31. [CrossRef]
61. Chebbi El Jarraya, A.; Dammak, F. A comparative study for two-damage modelling models using composite material. *Int. J. Comput. Mater. Sci. Eng.* **2012**, *1*, 1250014.
62. Meraghni, F.; Nouri, H.; Bourgeois, N.; Czarnota, C.; Lory, P. Parameters identification of fatigue damage model for short glass fiber reinforced polyamide (PA6-GF30) using digital image correlation. *Procedia Eng.* **2011**, *10*, 2110–2116. [CrossRef]

Disclaimer/Publisher's Note: The statements, opinions and data contained in all publications are solely those of the individual author(s) and contributor(s) and not of MDPI and/or the editor(s). MDPI and/or the editor(s) disclaim responsibility for any injury to people or property resulting from any ideas, methods, instructions or products referred to in the content.

mathematics

MDPI

Article

Numerical Simulation of Long-Span Bridge Response under Downburst: Parameter Optimization Using a Surrogate Model

Yu Feng [1], Lingfeng Xin [1], Jianming Hao [1,2,*], Nan Ding [3,*] and Feng Wang [1]

1 School of Highway, Chang'an University, Xi'an 710064, China; rainingfeng@chd.edu.cn (Y.F.)
2 Department of Civil, Structural and Environmental Engineering, University at Buffalo, Buffalo, NY 14260, USA
3 School of Automobile, Chang'an University, Xi'an 710064, China
* Correspondence: jianminghao@chd.edu.cn (J.H.); nanding@chd.edu.cn (N.D.)

Abstract: Long-span bridges located in thunderstorm-prone areas can potentially be struck by downburst transient winds. In this study, the downburst time-varying mean wind was simulated by an impinging jet model based on computational fluid dynamics (CFD). To make the simulation results fit well with the measurements, a parameter optimization method was developed. The objective function was established based on the errors between the simulated characteristic points and the target values from the measurement data. To increase the effectiveness, a Kriging surrogate model that was trained using data from numerical simulations was used. The parameter optimization method and the Kriging model were verified using five groups of test samples. The optimization efficiency was significantly increased by replacing the numerical model with a surrogate model during the optimization iteration. The simulation accuracy was clearly improved by the numerical modeling of a downburst based on optimized parameters. Subsequently, the nonstationary turbulent downburst wind was obtained by the combination of the Hilbert-based nonstationary fluctuations and the CFD-based time-varying trend. Finally, the dynamic response of a long-span bridge subjected to the moving downburst was presented. The results based on the simulation validate the optimized downburst wind field and highlight the significant influence on the bridge's aerodynamics and buffeting response.

Keywords: downbursts; parameter optimization; surrogate model; long-span bridges; computational fluid dynamics; numerical simulation; finite element model

MSC: 74F10

Citation: Feng, Y.; Xin, L.; Hao, J.; Ding, N.; Wang, F. Numerical Simulation of Long-Span Bridge Response under Downburst: Parameter Optimization Using a Surrogate Model. *Mathematics* **2023**, *11*, 3150. https://doi.org/10.3390/math11143150

Academic Editors: Shujin Laima, Yong Cao, Xiaowei Jin and Hehe Ren

Received: 5 July 2023
Revised: 14 July 2023
Accepted: 15 July 2023
Published: 17 July 2023

Copyright: © 2023 by the authors. Licensee MDPI, Basel, Switzerland. This article is an open access article distributed under the terms and conditions of the Creative Commons Attribution (CC BY) license (https://creativecommons.org/licenses/by/4.0/).

1. Introduction

Downbursts, induced by intense downdrafts, are the most destructive thunderstorms near the ground, which can exert violent impacts on engineering structures. Recently, thunderstorm downbursts have been constantly observed in coastal and mountainous areas [1], where the design wind velocity is usually determined by such non-synoptic wind events [2,3]. Unfortunately, long-span bridges are often located in coastal and mountainous areas to cross over straits and valleys, causing them to be significantly threatened by thunderstorm downbursts. Hence, the wind-induced responses of long-span bridges should be highlighted for their safety and reliability under downburst events.

The buffeting response analysis of long-span bridges under downbursts requires accurate wind field inputs. Field measurements are the most effective method to investigate downburst flows. The early programs of NIMROD [4] and JAWS [5] were implemented to investigate the downburst structures, and the recent programs of WP and WPS [6,7] were also implemented for the safety assessment of ports. But the field measurements are challenging because of the randomness of downbursts' occurrence. Therefore, experimental and numerical simulations based on flow features of downdrafts have become an alternative to study downburst-like wind fields. The impinging jet model is widely applied to the simulation of downburst-like winds, due to its high efficiency and acceptable accuracy. The impinging jet experiment was first implemented by Bakke in 1957 [8], where the flow supplied by the blower impinged a smooth plate, and the experimental flow velocity profile was consistent with the theoretical solution by Glauert [9] within the test range. Later, Proeh et al. [10] investigated the relationship between the flow velocity profile and the simulation parameters (e.g., jet velocity, turbulence intensity, Reynolds stress, etc.) with a similar impinging jet experiment. Today, updated versions of the impinging jet simulators have been successively established to investigate the influence of the translation effects [11], transient ring vortex [12], and ambient boundary-layer wind [13] on the downburst wind field. On the other hand, the CFD-based impinging jet simulation was also implemented to capture the flow characteristics of the downburst wind field [14–18]. However, the simulation based on the impinging jet model is only the approximation of the flow of field-measured downburst, derived from the different formation mechanisms. Furthermore, the mapping relationship is vague between the field measurements and the parameters employed in the experimental and numerical simulations. Hence, the field measurements could not provide direct guidance on the simulation parameters.

Alternatively, the optimization of the parameters with sparse field-measurement data would be a promising method to improve the accuracy of downburst simulations. The parameter optimization strategy would be developed to determine the optimal parameters, through which the simulation could be consistent with the field measurements (target). However, many iterations are required in the optimization to ascertain the global optimal parameters, and the efficiency is limited by the time-consuming CFD simulation. Therefore, the Kriging surrogate model, providing an approximation of a CFD-based model with extremely low computational demand, was introduced in the optimization. Currently, the surrogate model has been widely applied in the aerodynamic shape optimization of airfoils [19,20], buildings [21,22], and bridge decks [23,24]. Inspired by the aerodynamic optimization described above, the surrogate-model-based parameter optimization method was extended to the simulation of downburst in this study.

In this study, the buffeting response analysis of long-span bridges under downburst was implemented to examine transient effects on the bridge aerodynamics, where the Kriging-based optimization was introduced for high-fidelity downburst wind field reconstitution. Section 2 depicts the method to numerically simulate the downburst based on the CFD scheme. Section 3 describes the Kriging-based optimization method of downburst simulation, where five numerical downburst examples are employed to validate the accuracy of the optimization strategy and highlight its efficiency. Section 4 discusses the buffeting response of a long-span bridge under downburst, where a 2D indicial function is introduced to highlight the downburst wind-induced transient effects on the buffeting response.

2. Downburst Based on CFD Scheme

2.1. Stationary Downburst Simulation

(1) Computational domain and mesh

The stationary downburst was numerically simulated using the impinging jet model, where the downdraft impinges on the ground and the accelerating effects occur at the near-ground region. Considering the symmetrical flow of stationary downbursts, one-half of the computational domain was considered to save computational time. As shown in Figure 1, a cuboid computational domain with the size of $12D_j \times 6D_j \times 4D_j$ was used in the simulation, and the semicircular jet inlet with diameter D_j was located $2D_j$ from the ground. For typical downbursts, the diameter of the downdraft is approximately 1000 m [25], and the geometric scale of 1:1000 was selected in this model.

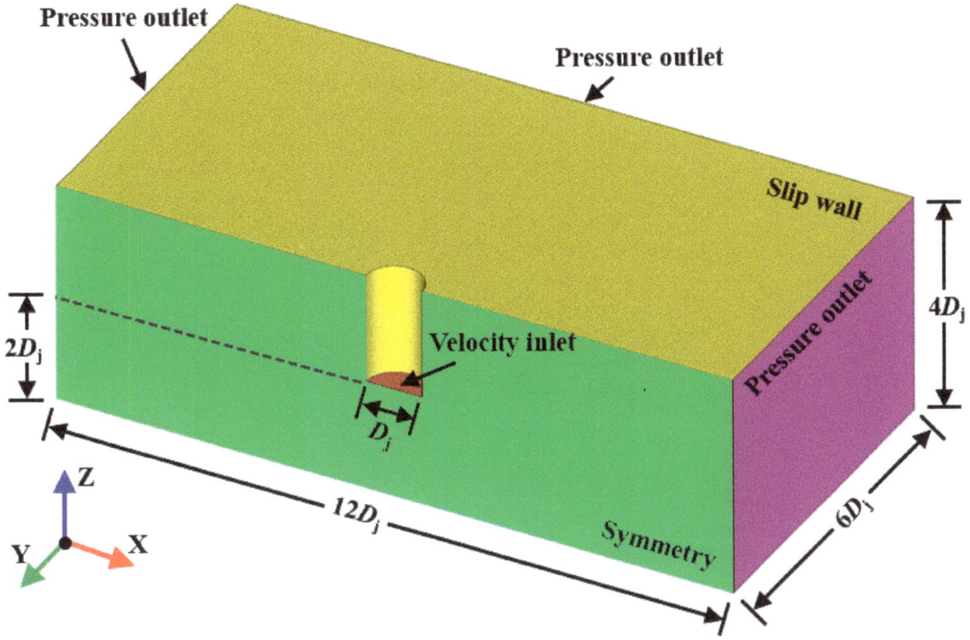

Figure 1. Schematic diagram of the numerical model for stationary downburst.

Since only one-half of the computational domain is considered in the model, the symmetry boundary was introduced, where the normal velocity and gradient of fluxes were assigned as 0. The velocity inlet boundary was used in the jet, with a velocity of 8 m/s. The no-slip wall boundary was utilized for the bottom floor, while the slip wall was employed at the top, with shear stress ignored. Moreover, the pressure outlet boundary was selected inside the computational domain, with pressure of 0, because flows were fully developed in the outlet boundary. The mesh of the numerical model is presented in Figure 2. The smaller mesh size was applied to the bottom of the computational domain, where buildings and bridges are usually located, while a relatively coarser mesh was used at the top. Such a hybrid mesh strategy has been widely applied to non-synoptic wind simulation due to its better balance between accuracy and efficiency [1,26]. The detailed grid configurations of the numerical model are summarized in Table 1, where two grid configurations are compared for the grid independence test.

Table 1. Grids' information.

	Zones	Grid 1	Grid 2
Vertical discretization	$0 \leq z < 0.15D_j$ $0.15D_j \leq z < 2.0D_j$ $2.0D_j \leq z \leq 4.0D_j$	$\delta_{z\_max} = 0.005D_j$ $\delta_{z\_max} = 0.05D_j$ $\delta_{z\_max} = 0.2D_j$	$\delta_{z\_max} = 0.003D_j$ $\delta_{z\_max} = 0.05D_j$ $\delta_{z\_max} = 0.2D_j$
Horizontal discretization	Zone1($0 \leq R < 0.5D_j$) Zone1 ($0.5D_j \leq R < 2.1D_j$)	$\delta_{h\_max} = 0.025D_j$ $\delta_{h\_max} = 0.1D_j$	$\delta_{h\_max} = 0.025D_j$ $\delta_{h\_max} = 0.1D_j$
	Zone2	$\delta_{h\_max} = 0.15D_j$	$\delta_{h\_max} = 0.15D_j$
Cell number	/	4.8×10^5	6.2×10^5

Note: δ_{z_max} and δ_{h_max} represent the mesh size in the vertical and horizontal directions, respectively.

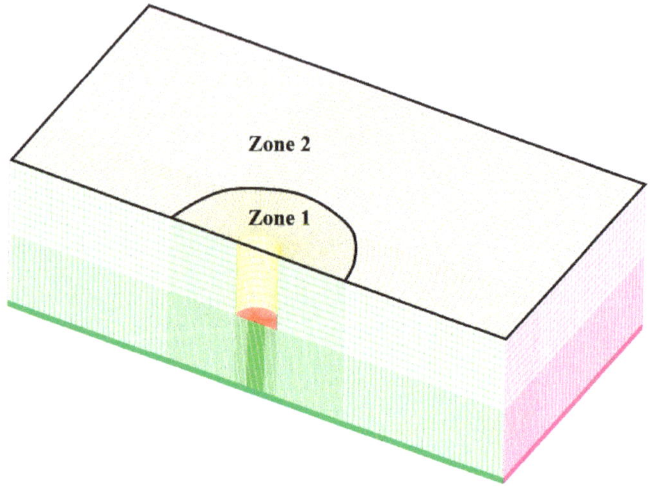

Figure 2. Mesh of the numerical model. Zone 1 indicates central zone of downburst with radius of $2.1D_{\mathrm{j}}$ and Zone 2 indicates other zone.

(2) Solution scheme

The numerical model was discretized using the finite volume scheme, and SIMPLEC was employed for the solution with $dt = 1.6\mathrm{e}^{-2} \times D_{\mathrm{j}}/U_{\mathrm{jet}}$. Moreover, the gradient, convective, and Laplacian terms were discretized using second-order discretization schemes. The turbulence was modeled by the SST $\mathrm{k} - \omega$ scheme [27], due to its better performance in impinging jet simulations [28]. The numerical simulation of the downburst was set to run for $16D_{\mathrm{j}}/U_{\mathrm{jet}}$ to ensure that the initial transient effects disappear, and then another $8D_{\mathrm{j}}/U_{\mathrm{jet}}$ of simulation was used for the estimation of mean quantities.

(3) Validation

The grid independence test was implemented based on the comparison of the velocity profiles at $r = D_{\mathrm{j}}$. As shown in Figure 3, only slight differences could be observed in the velocity profiles obtained by Grid 1 and Grid 2, and the maximum wind velocity difference was less than 2%. Hence, Grid 1, with fewer cells, was chosen for the subsequent simulation.

Figure 4 presents the velocity contour of the downburst at the $Y = 0$ plane (coordinate origin located in the center of the ground). The downdraft from the jet inlet impinged on the ground and generated the maximum wind velocity in the near-ground region with approximately $r = D_{\mathrm{j}}$, where the maximum wind velocity could be up to $U_{\mathrm{max}} = 0.974U_{\mathrm{jet}}$ occurring at the height $Z_{\mathrm{max}} = 0.03D_{\mathrm{j}}$ from the ground. Moreover, obvious symmetrical flow could be observed in the downburst's wind field, which means that one-half of the computational domain considered in the simulation is reasonable.

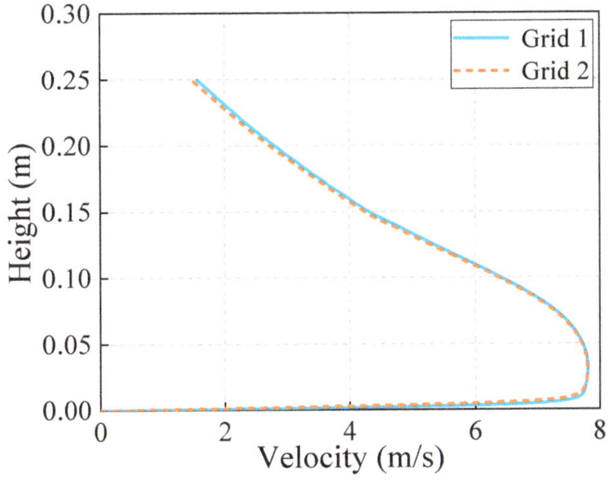

Figure 3. Grid independence test.

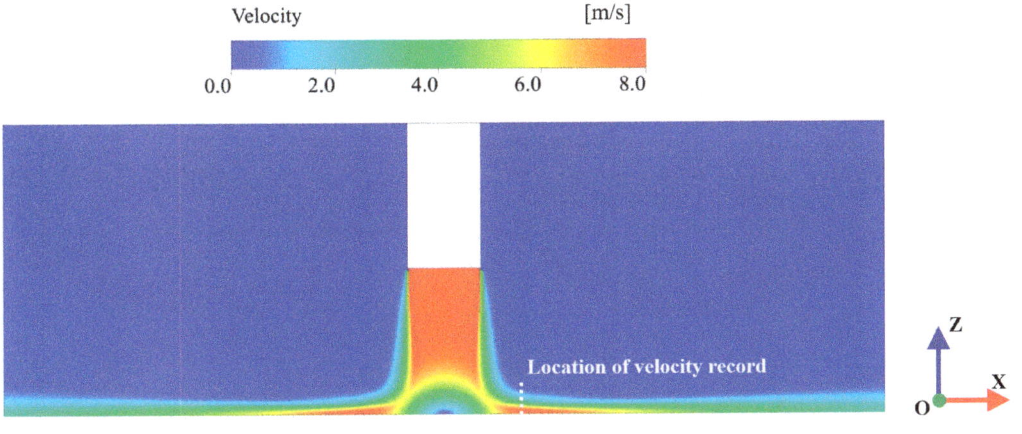

Figure 4. Velocity contour for stationary downburst.

Figure 5a shows the simulated downburst wind velocity profiles, along with measurements from NIMROD [4] and JAWS [5]. The velocity and the height are normalized by the maximum velocity ($U_{\max}$) and according height ($Z_{\max}$), respectively. As shown in the figure, the wind profile from the simulation shows a reasonable match to the measurements, and the slight deviation could be partially attributed to the limited resolution of the measurements. Moreover, the comparison of the simulations and experiments [29] is also plotted in 0b. The velocity and the height are normalized by the jet velocity and diameter, respectively. The wind profile from the numerical simulation presents good agreement with the experiment results, especially in the near-ground region, where it could reproduce the features of the downburst wind field well.

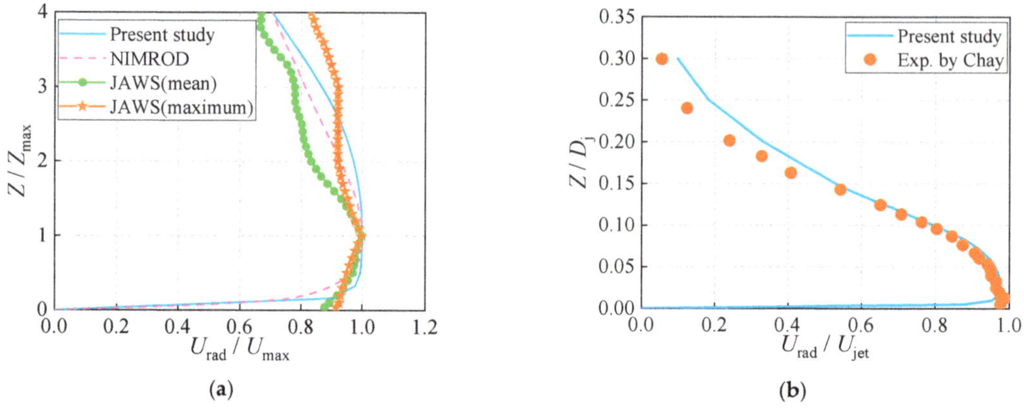

Figure 5. Comparison of wind velocity profiles with numerical simulations and (**a**) field measurement data; (**b**) experimental data.

2.2. *Moving Downburst Simulation*

(1) Numerical set-up

The downburst simulation was extended from the validated stationary case to the moving one. As shown in Figure 6, the numerical model of the moving downburst is similar to the stationary case presented in Figure 1, but the jet inlet could move with the introduction of the sliding-mesh technique [30,31]. The computational domain was divided into two regions: the moving-jet region and the stationary wind field region. Both regions were connected by the interface, allowing the two regions to move relatively and transfer fluxes. Moreover, the velocity inlet boundary was employed to model the ambient boundary-layer wind and actually drive the downdraft motion. The jet translation velocity and the ambient boundary-layer wind were set to $0.3/U_{\text{jet}}$, referring to the numerical simulation by Li et al. [32].

The mesh of the numerical model for moving downburst is presented in Figure 7, where the grid configurations are similar to those of Grid 1 in Table 1, with a total cell number of about 8.7×10^5. The SIMPLEC scheme was also employed in the solution of the moving downburst case with a timestep size of $dt = 1.6\text{e}^{-2} \times D_j/U_{\text{jet}}$, and the SST $\text{k} - \omega$ scheme [27] was used for turbulence modeling.

(2) Numerical results

Figure 8 presents the wind velocity contour of the moving downburst at the $Y = 0$ and $Z = 0.03D_j$ plane. Significant asymmetry in the flow of the downbursts was observed in the velocity contour due to the translation effects of the downdraft. The accelerating regions were generated in the front and trailing edges, but the wind velocity peak at the front edge was obviously higher than that at the trailing edge. In addition, the wind velocity outside the downdraft-affected region was approximately equal to the ambient wind speed (2.4 m/s).

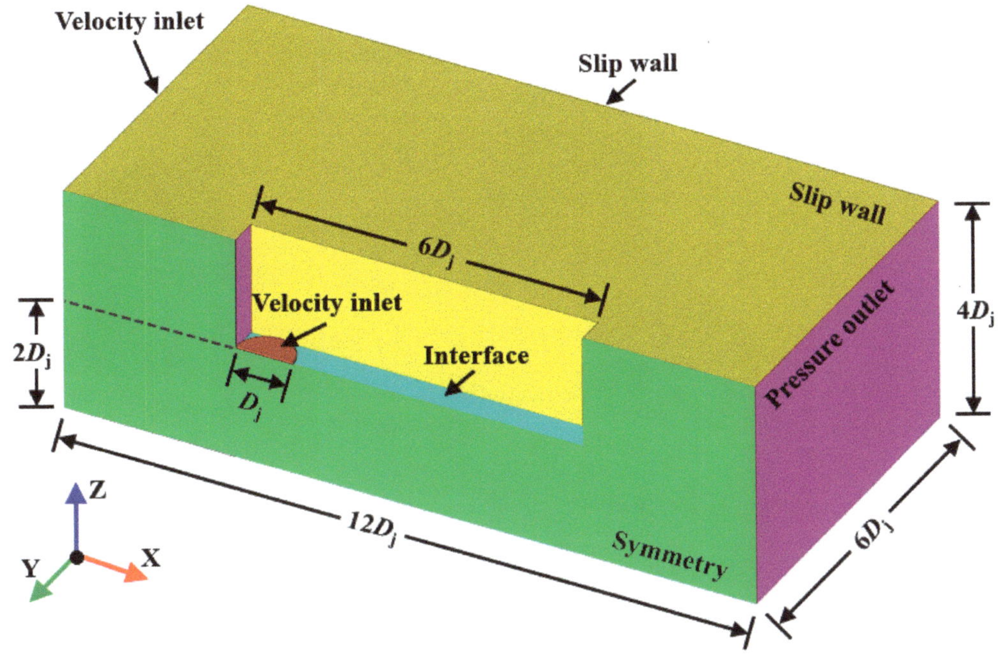

Figure 6. Schematic diagram of the numerical model for moving downburst.

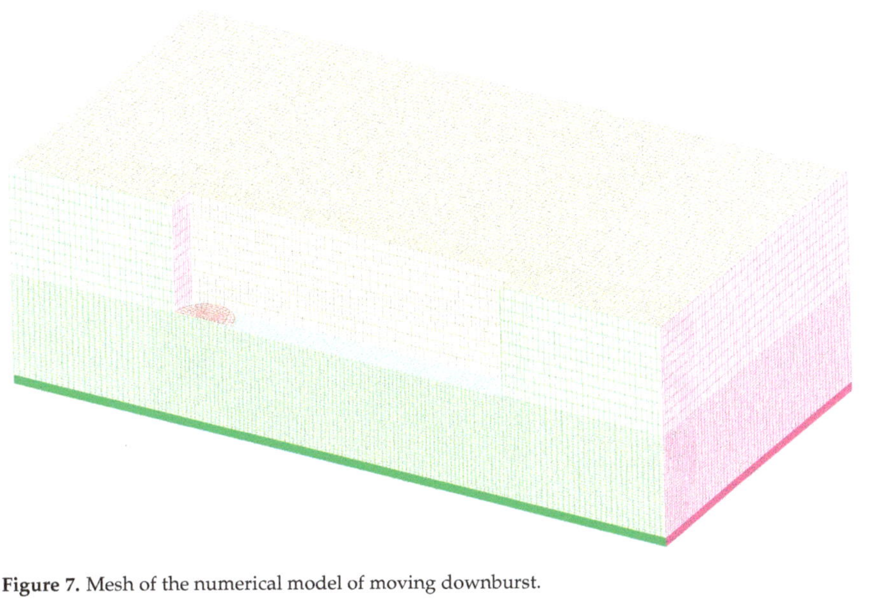

Figure 7. Mesh of the numerical model of moving downburst.

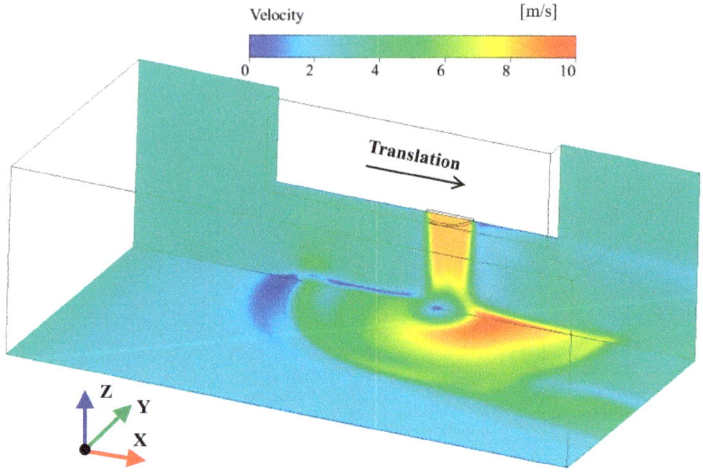

Figure 8. Velocity contour of moving downburst.

The wind velocity time history at $P(0, 0, 0.05D_j)$ is shown in Figure 9, where the measurements of the AAFB downburst [33] are also presented. Considering the differences in the velocity and time scales between the simulations and the measurements, two sets of coordinates were used in the comparison. The numerical simulation shows a similar wind velocity time history to the measured AAFB downburst, but notable deviations can be observed in the wind velocity peaks and valleys between the simulations and the measurements. This may be attributed to the estimation error of the simulation parameters (e.g., jet translation velocity) limited by the field measurement technique. Hence, an optimization strategy needs to be developed to obtain the best parameters and reduce the deviation.

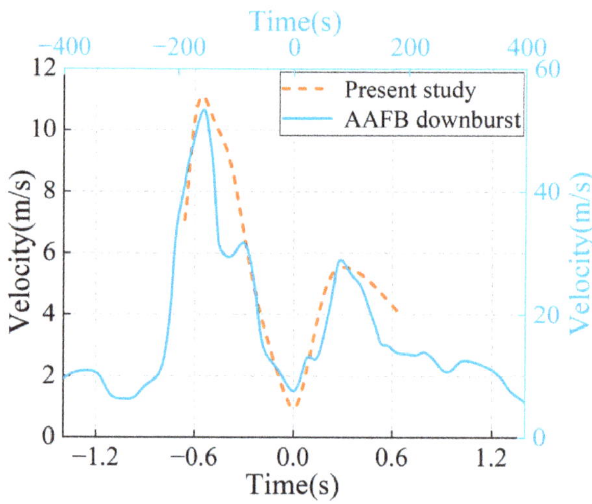

Figure 9. Wind velocity time history based on CFD and measurements. The black axis indicates the simulation and the blue axis indicates the measured AAFB downburst.

3. Kriging-Based Optimization of Downburst

3.1. Kriging Surrogate Modeling

The parameter optimization was computationally challenging due to the time-consuming CFD simulation required for each iteration. Therefore, the surrogate model was applied to each optimization iteration in this study to enhance the efficiency. The Kriging model is a regression model characterized by local and global statistical information, and it presents better surrogate accuracy for nonlinear problems, expressed as follows:

$$\boldsymbol{Y}(\boldsymbol{x}) = \boldsymbol{F}(\boldsymbol{x})^{\mathrm{T}}\boldsymbol{\beta} + \boldsymbol{Z}(\boldsymbol{x}) \tag{1}$$

where $\boldsymbol{F}(\boldsymbol{x})$ is the chosen regression function with respect to point $\boldsymbol{x}$; $\boldsymbol{\beta}$ is the regression parameter; and $\boldsymbol{Z}(\boldsymbol{x})$ is random process, which is assumed to have mean zero and covariance.

$$\mathrm{cov}[\boldsymbol{Z}(\boldsymbol{x}^i), \boldsymbol{Z}(\boldsymbol{x}^j)] = \sigma^2[R(\theta, \boldsymbol{x}^i, \boldsymbol{x}^j)] \tag{2}$$

where σ^2 is the variance; $R(\theta, \boldsymbol{x}^i, \boldsymbol{x}^j)$ is the correlation function with respect to training points $\boldsymbol{x}^i$ and $\boldsymbol{x}^j$; and the parameter θ can be obtained by maximum likelihood estimation.

The Kriging predictor $\hat{y}$ at point $\boldsymbol{x}^*$ can be given as follows:

$$\hat{y} = \boldsymbol{F}(\boldsymbol{x}^*)\boldsymbol{\beta}^* + \boldsymbol{r}^{\mathrm{T}}\boldsymbol{R}^{-1}(\boldsymbol{Y} - \boldsymbol{F}\boldsymbol{\beta}^*) \tag{3}$$

where $\boldsymbol{\beta}^* = (\boldsymbol{F}^{\mathrm{T}}\boldsymbol{R}^{-1}\boldsymbol{F})^{-1}(\boldsymbol{F}^{\mathrm{T}}\boldsymbol{R}^{-1}\boldsymbol{Y})$; $\boldsymbol{R}$ is the correlation matrix of training points $\boldsymbol{x}^i$; and $\boldsymbol{r}$ is the vector correlation indicating correlation between $\boldsymbol{x}^*$ and training points $\boldsymbol{x}^i$.

3.2. Experimental Design

In downburst events, the downdraft usually moves with the ambient boundary-layer wind [32], and the maximum wind velocity tends to occur combined with ambient wind [34]. Therefore, the jet inlet velocity, ambient boundary-layer wind velocity, and jet translation velocity exert significant influence on downburst simulations, but the ambient boundary-layer wind velocity and jet translation velocity are usually normalized by the jet inlet velocity. Hence, the ambient boundary-layer wind velocity (U_b) and jet translation velocity (U_T) were selected as parameters to be optimized in this study, and the allowable variations were set as $U_b \in [0.3U_{jet}\ 0.4U_{jet}]$ and $U_T \in [0.2U_{jet}\ 0.3U_{jet}]$, respectively.

A uniform design was employed to effectively determine the mapping relationship between the downburst simulations and the parameters (U_b and U_T). As demonstrated in Figure 10, 21 design points were uniformly arranged in the parameter space, where 20 design points were treated as a training set for the construction of the surrogate model, and 1 design point was considered as a test set for the validation. The validation was implemented five times with different test sets, namely, Case 4, Case 8, Case 11, Case 14, and Case 18 (see Figure 10).

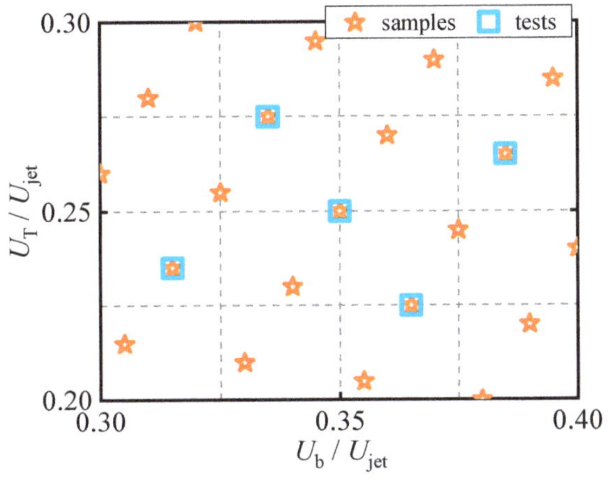

Figure 10. Sampling plan.

3.3. Optimization Strategy

The downburst characterized by significant time-varying mean wind (TVMW), such as the double wind velocity peak in AAFB downburst, exerts non-negligible transient effects on bridges' aerodynamics [35,36]. Therefore, the TVMW of the downburst was chosen as a target to be matched between simulations and measurements. As shown in 0, the difference between measurements and simulations could be quantized by the wind velocity peaks and valleys, and the objective function could be formulated as follows (see Figure 11):

$$f(x) = \sum_{i=1}^{3} \left[\omega^{\mathrm{U}} |U_i^s(x) - U_i^m| + \omega^{\mathrm{t}} |t_i^s(x) - t_i^m| \right] \tag{4}$$

where U_i and t_i are the velocity peak (or valley) and the corresponding time, respectively; the superscripts s and m represent simulations and measurements, respectively. Considering the disparity in magnitude between the wind velocity (U_i) and the time (t_i), the weight coefficients ω^{U} and ω^{t} were introduced, as follows:

$$\omega^{\mathrm{U}} = \frac{\Delta t}{3(\Delta U + \Delta t)} \tag{5}$$

$$\omega^{\mathrm{t}} = \frac{\Delta U}{3(\Delta U + \Delta t)} \tag{6}$$

where $\Delta t = t_3^{\mathrm{m}} - t_1^{\mathrm{m}}$ is the time scale and $\Delta U = \max[U_1^{\mathrm{m}}, U_2^{\mathrm{m}}, U_3^{\mathrm{m}}]$ is the velocity scale.

The optimal parameters could be acquired by minimizing the objective function, enabling CFD-based simulations to agree well with the measurements. Figure 12 schematically presents the flowchart of the parameter optimization. The initial parameters were first selected for the simulation of the downburst. The objective function was then constructed with simulations and measurements according to Equation (4). Finally, the genetic algorithm (GA) was used to determine the optimal parameters for downburst simulation.

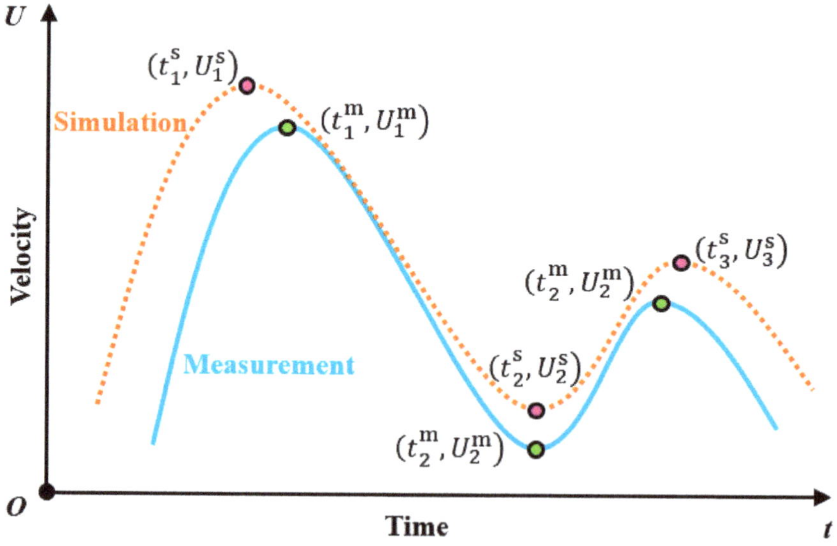

Figure 11. Schematic diagram of the objective function. The blue solid line indicates the measurements and the orange dashed line indicates the simulations.

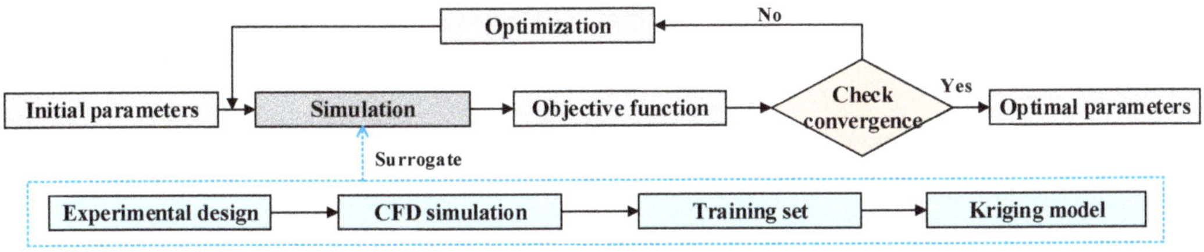

Figure 12. Flowchart of parameter optimization.

However, the CFD simulation was required in every iteration of the parameter optimization, which was computationally challenging. Therefore, the Kriging model was introduced to participate in the parameter optimization instead of the CFD simulation, for high efficiency. The first step in the construction of the Kriging model was the experimental design, where a uniform design was employed for sampling. The CFD numerical simulation was then implemented to generate the training set, and the Kriging surrogate model was finally constructed. Once the surrogate model had been established, it was employed to predict downburst wind with arbitrary parameters.

3.4. Validation

The simulation of a hypothetical downburst was implemented with the "real" parameter $x_{rea} = [U_b\ U_T]$ for validation, and the feature parameters (U_i and t_i) of the downburst TVMW were also obtained. The CFD-based feature parameters could be considered as the target for the validation of the Kriging model's accuracy. Subsequently, the "real" parameter was chosen as the target for the validation of the parameter optimization with "real" parameters unknown. If the optimized parameter x_{opt} is convergent, coinciding with the "real" parameter x_{rea}, the optimization method developed is valid.

Figure 13 presents the validation of the Kriging model's accuracy, where five successive cases are treated as test sets for the validation. The surrogate results of t_2 are not discussed, due to the t_2^s required being equal to the t_2^m for synchronization in the optimization. As shown in Figure 13, the Kriging-based feature parameters U_1, U_2, U_3, t_1, and t_3, are almost consistent with the CFD simulation results, and the error between the them is less than 2%.

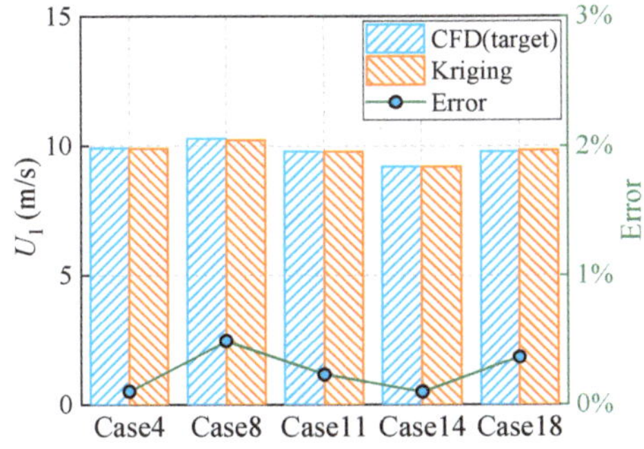

(a)

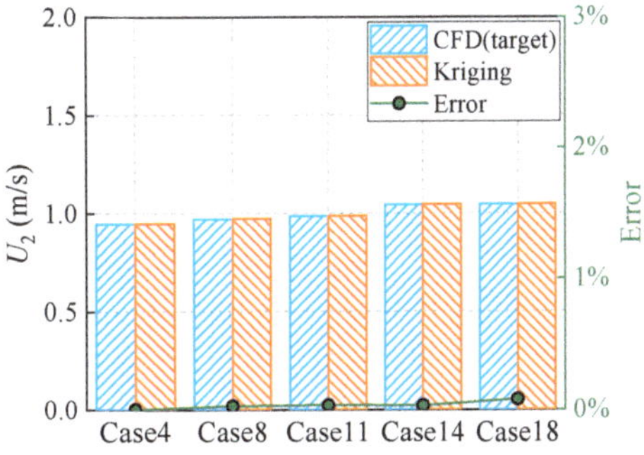

(b)

Figure 13. *Cont.*

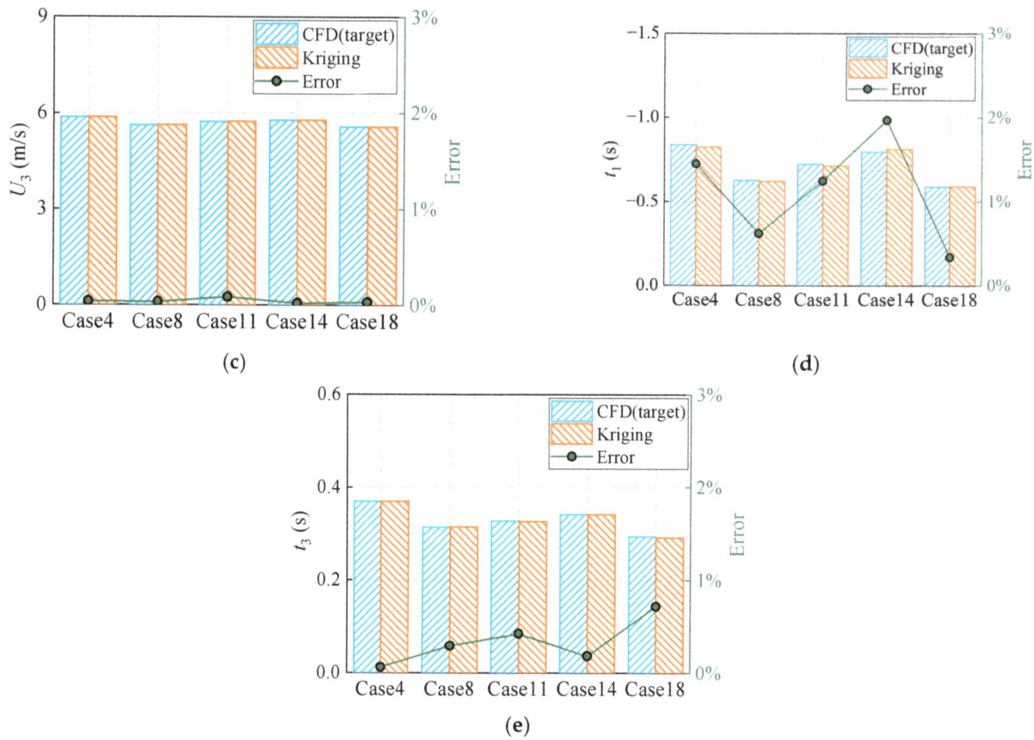

Figure 13. Validation of the Kriging scheme: (**a**) U_1; (**b**) U_2; (**c**) U_3; (**d**) t_1; (**e**) t_3.

The comparison between the "real" parameters and the optimized parameters is plotted in Figure 14, where the error between them is less than 3%. The observation suggests that the proposed parameter optimization method based on the Kriging surrogate model is an effective way to improve CFD-based simulations for special downbursts.

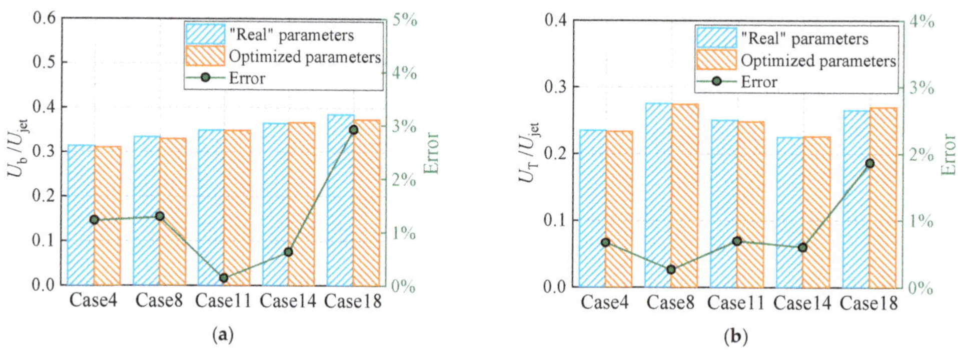

Figure 14. Validation of optimized parameters: (**a**) ambient boundary-layer wind velocity; (**b**) jet translation velocity.

In addition, the contribution of the introduced Kriging model to the optimization efficiency should be discussed. The CFD simulation and the parameter optimization were implemented based on a computation platform with Intel Xeon E5-2630 20-core processors and system memory of 64 GB. Figure 15 presents the distributions of the computational time of the CFD- and Kriging-based simulations. The mean time for the CFD-based simulation was 5736 s, but that for the Kriging-based simulation was 0.00085 s, which is almost negligible compared with the CFD model. On the other hand, a number of the parameter combinations were generated by a GA to obtain the global optimal solution of the objective function, e.g., an average of 792 parameter combinations are required to obtain the optimal parameters (see Figure 16), which means that 792 simulations must be implemented in the optimization. Clearly, the CFD-based parameter optimization would be computationally challenging. However, the Kriging-based parameter optimization would be highly efficient due to its negligible time consumption compared with the CFD simulation. The main computational cost of Kriging-based parameter optimization is the construction of the surrogate model, but only 21 CFD simulations are required to generate the training set. The above discussion indicates that the introduction of a surrogate model in parameter optimization could significantly improve the optimization efficiency.

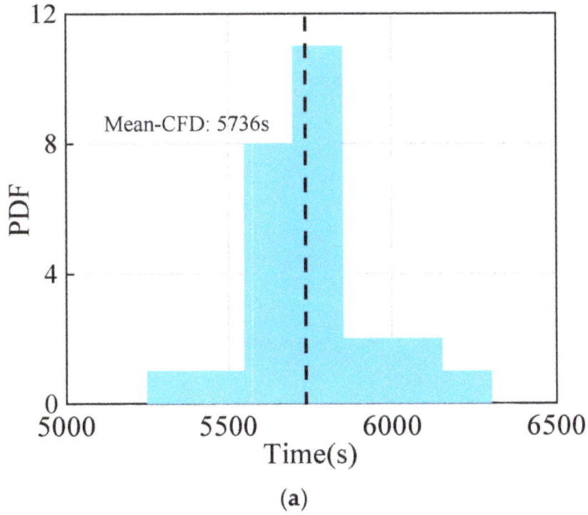

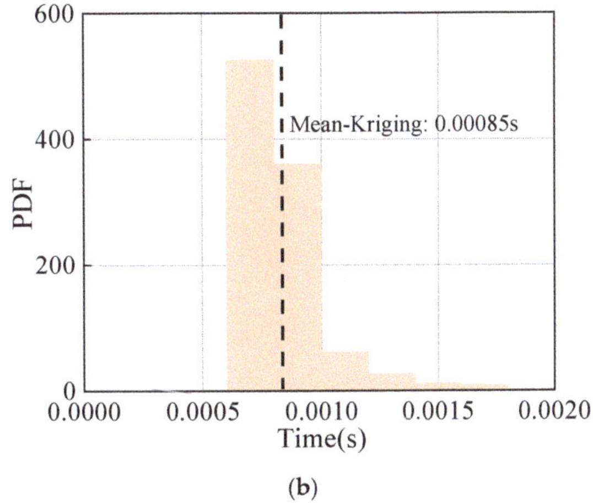

Figure 15. Simulation time based on the (**a**) CFD model and (**b**) Kriging model. The blue and orange bars indicate the distributions of the computational time of the CFD- and Kriging-based simulations, respectively.

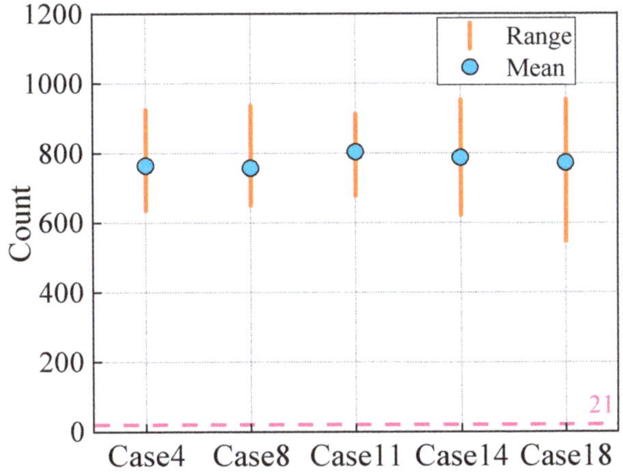

Figure 16. Number of parameter combinations.

4. Downburst-Induced Long-Span Bridge Response

4.1. Long-Span Bridge Model

A long-span suspension bridge with a main span of 1490 m was selected as an example bridge for examining the downburst wind-induced bridge buffeting response (see Figure 17). A spine-beam scheme was employed to establish the bridge's finite element (FE) model, through which the bridge's global behaviors under downburst could be efficiently obtained with acceptable precision. Moreover, the sagging effects of the suspension cable were also considered in the FE model, using the Ernst equation. The FE model of the example bridge was validated in the authors' previous work [26,37] by comparing the first 10 modal properties.

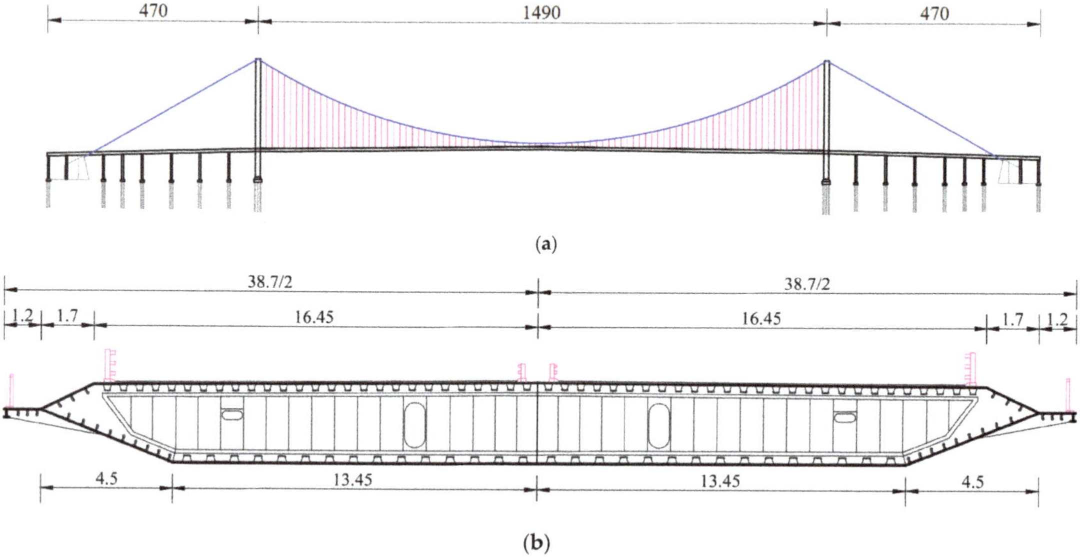

Figure 17. Configurations of the example bridge (unit: m): (**a**) elevation; (**b**) bridge deck.

The main girder was divided into 92 elements with an interval of 16.1 m. The wind loads were assumed to be uniform for each element, and then they were transferred to the node through the beam element shape function in the buffeting response analysis.

4.2. Modeling of the Downburst Wind Field

(1) Time-varying mean wind

The AAFB downburst, as an example, was chosen as a target for simulation in this study [33]. Following the downburst parameter optimization method presented in Section 3.3, the optimal simulation parameters of AAFB downburst were obtained, where the optimized ambient boundary-layer wind velocity U_b and the jet translation velocity U_T were $0.395U_{jet}$ and $0.269U_{jet}$, respectively. It should be noted that the length scale ($\lambda_L = 1/1199$) and the velocity scale ($\lambda_U = 1/5.55$) are required in the optimization to relate the CFD-based simulations to the field measurement data [38]. As shown in Figure 18, the CFD-based TVMW with optimal parameters agrees well with the AAFB downburst records, especially the wind velocity peaks and valleys. This observation suggests that optimized downburst wind simulators can adequately replicate the transient nature of AAFB downburst, through which the downburst wind field at the elevation of the bridge deck ($h = 69.3$m) can be acquired.

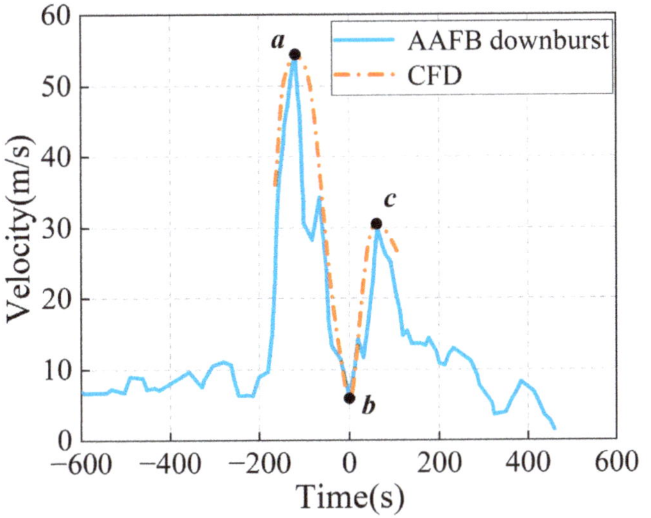

Figure 18. CFD-based simulation and AAFB downburst record. Point a, b and c represent the wind velocity peak and valley.

The downburst is assumed to move in a straight line and pass across the mid-span of the bridge perpendicularly. Figure 19 shows the TVMW velocity along the span during the downburst translation. As presented in the figure, the downburst wind velocities change significantly with the time, but only slightly with the span. Furthermore, CFD-based non-turbulent downburst can be synthesized with nonstationary fluctuations to provide accurate input for the bridge buffeting response analysis.

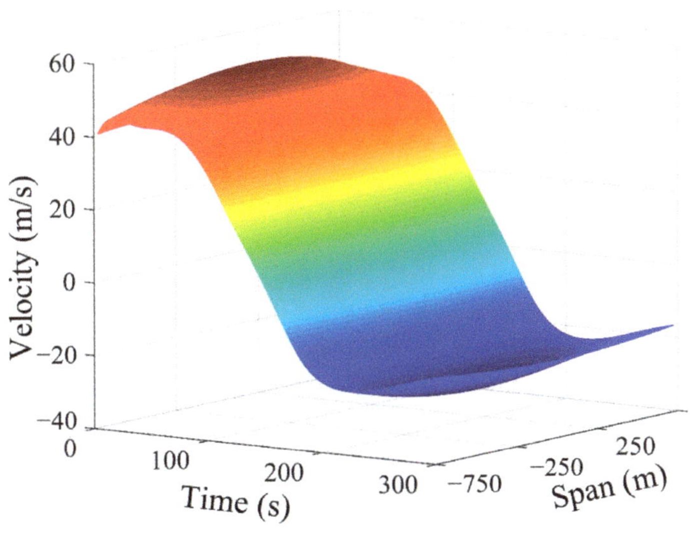

Figure 19. Time-varying mean wind velocity along the bridge span.

(2) Nonstationary fluctuating wind

Considering the time-dependent spectrum of downburst wind velocity, the nonstationary fluctuating wind could be simulated using a recently developed Hilbert-based scheme [39,40]. The nonstationary fluctuating measurements could be decomposed into subcomponents with wavelet packet transform.

$$x(t) = \sum_{j=2}^{2^J} x_j(t) + x_1(t) \tag{7}$$

where $x_1(t)$ is the time-variant trend (mean wind), and $x_j(t)$ is the zero-mean subcomponent, which can be considered to be a monocomponent when the decomposition level is high enough.

The Hilbert transform was employed to acquire the instantaneous information for each subcomponent based on the complex analytic signal [41]:

$$z(t) = x(t) + iH[x(t)] = a(t)e^{i\theta(t)} \tag{8}$$

where $i = \sqrt{-1}$; $a(t)$ and $\theta(t)$ are the instantaneous amplitude and phase, respectively;$H[\cdot]$ represents the Hilbert transform, defined as follows:

$$H[x(t)] = P\int_{-\infty}^{+\infty} \frac{x(\tau)}{\pi(t-\tau)} d\tau \tag{9}$$

where P is the Cauchy principal value. The instantaneous frequency can be given as follows:

$$\omega(t) = \frac{\mathrm{d}\theta(t)}{\mathrm{d}t} \tag{10}$$

Based on the instantaneous frequency sequence extracted from the measurements, the simulated instantaneous frequency $\widetilde{\omega}_j^l(t)$ of scale j at point l could be artificially generated with discrete wavelet transform (DWT) [39,40], and the simulated frequency-modulated subcomponents would also be obtained.

$$\widetilde{f}_j^l(t) = \sqrt{2}\cos[\widetilde{\theta}_j^l(t)] \tag{11}$$

where $\widetilde{\theta}_j^l(t)$ is the simulated instantaneous phase, obtained by the integrations with respect to $\widetilde{\omega}_j^l(t)$.

On the other hand, the Cholesky decomposition was introduced to simulate the nonstationary wind field with consideration of the spatial correlation, and the uncorrelated frequency-modulated subcomponents could be transformed into correlated subcomponents:

$$\widetilde{\mathbf{F}}_j^{\mathrm{cor}}(t) = \mathbf{\Phi}_j(t)\widetilde{\mathbf{F}}_j^{\mathrm{unc}}(t) \tag{12}$$

where $\widetilde{\mathbf{F}}_j^{\mathrm{cor}}(t) = [\widetilde{f}_j^{l_1,\mathrm{cor}}(t)\ \widetilde{f}_j^{l_2,\mathrm{cor}}(t)\ \cdots\ \widetilde{f}_j^{l_L,\mathrm{cor}}(t)]^{\mathrm{T}}$ and $\widetilde{\mathbf{F}}_j^{\mathrm{unc}}(t) = [\widetilde{f}_j^{l_1,\mathrm{unc}}(t)\ \widetilde{f}_j^{l_2,\mathrm{unc}}(t)\ \cdots\ \widetilde{f}_j^{l_L,\mathrm{unc}}(t)]^{\mathrm{T}}$ are the vectors of the correlated and uncorrelated frequency-modulated subcomponents of scale j, respectively, and $\mathbf{\Phi}_j(t)$ can be obtained through the Cholesky decomposition.

$$\mathbf{R}_j^{\mathrm{tar}}(t) = \mathbf{\Phi}_j(t)\mathbf{\Phi}_j^T(t) \tag{13}$$

where $\mathbf{R}_j^{\mathrm{tar}}(t)$ is the target spatial correlation matrix at scale j, which can be obtained by the coherence function [42]:

$$\mathrm{coh}(\Delta,\omega) = \rho(\Delta)\exp(-K(\Delta)\omega\Delta) \tag{14}$$

where $\rho(\Delta)$ and $K(\Delta)$ can be fitted by the least-squares method:

$$\rho(\Delta) = \exp(-\alpha\Delta) \tag{15}$$

$$K(\Delta) = -k_1 \times \ln(\Delta) + k_0 \tag{16}$$

where α, k_0, and k_1 are the parameters to be fitted. The procedure of nonstationary wind simulation is summarized in Figure 20.

To ensure the reasonable superposition of the Hilbert-based nonstationary fluctuations and CFD-based time-varying mean wind, several normalization manipulations were employed. Consequently, the maximum and minimum of the measured trend are coincident with the CFD simulations, as shown in Figure 21. The field-measurement fluctuations were accordingly scaled, and they were employed for the simulation of nonstationary fluctuation wind. Figure 22 presents the scaled measurements of the fluctuating wind velocity time history and a sample simulation, where the simulation shows close similarity with the measurement. Moreover, the Hilbert spectrum of the simulation exhibits a similar pattern to that of the measurement (see Figure 23), indicating that the energy distribution of the field-measured nonstationary fluctuation wind was well reproduced in the simulations.

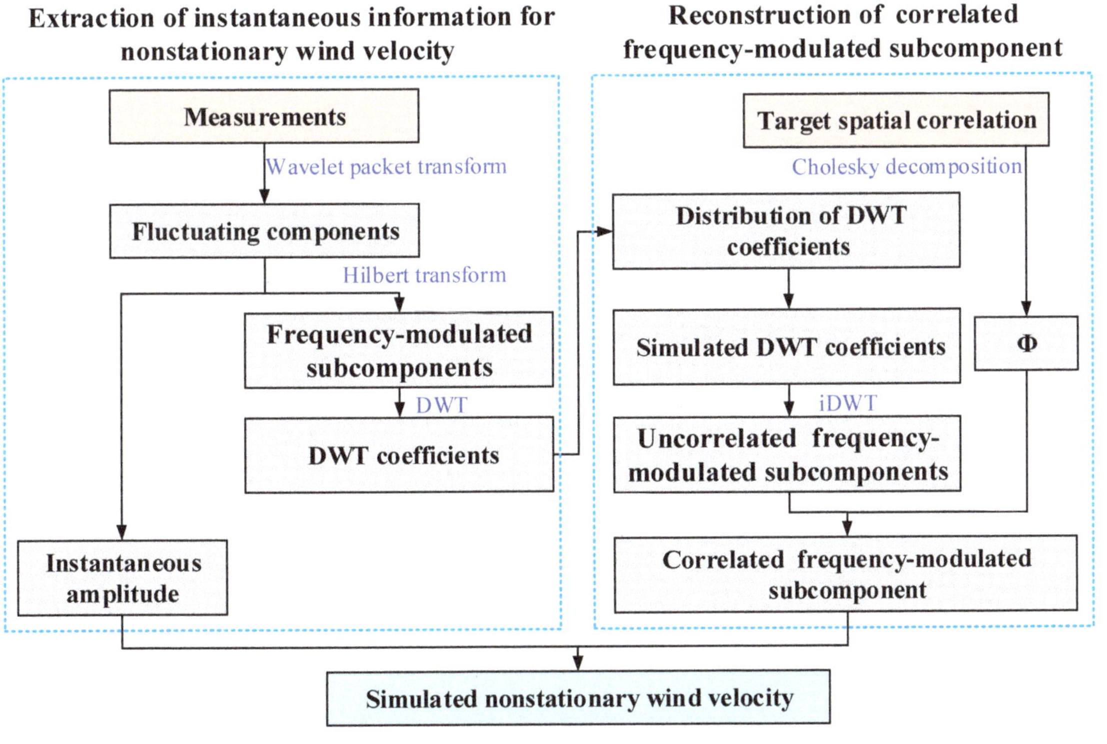

Figure 20. Procedure of nonstationary wind simulation.

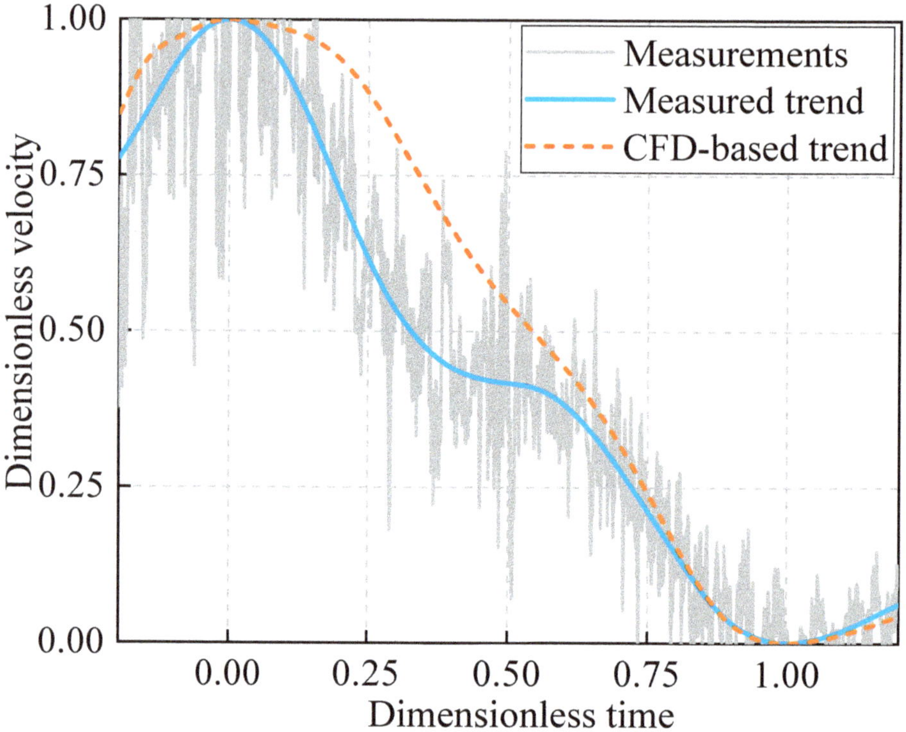

Figure 21. Measurements and CFD-based results.

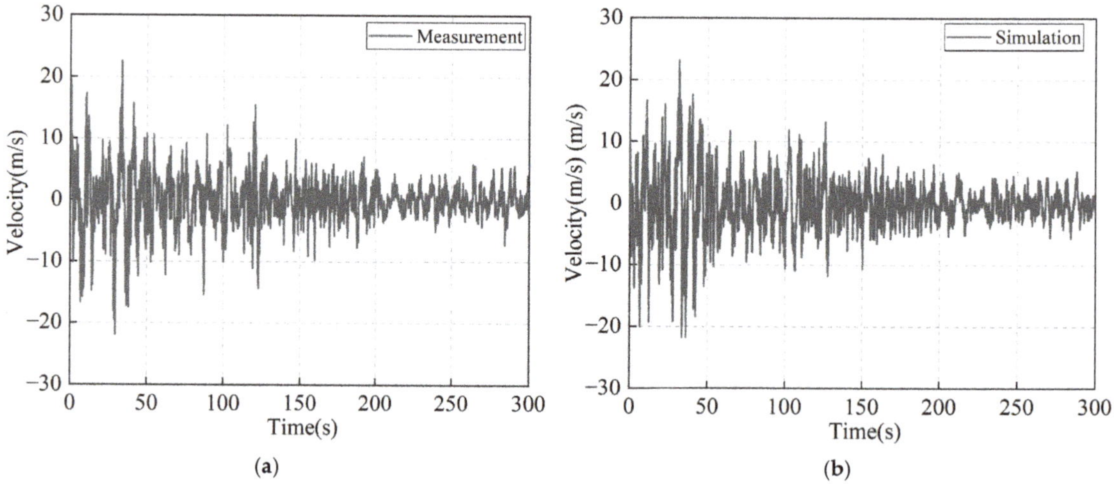

Figure 22. Nonstationary fluctuating wind: (**a**) measurement; (**b**) simulation.

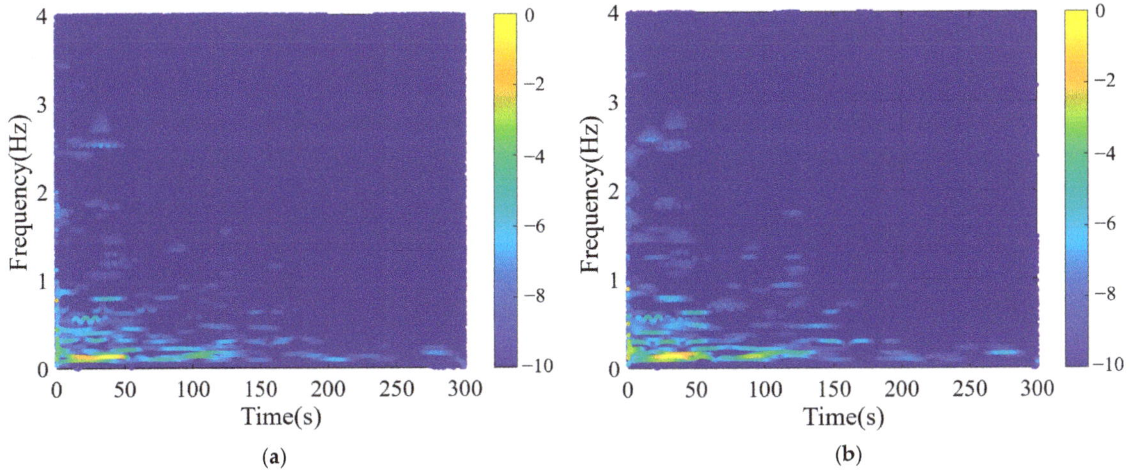

Figure 23. Hilbert spectra: (**a**) measurement; (**b**) simulation.

4.3. Transient Aerodynamics

The semi-empirical analysis framework has been extensively used for the simulation of aeroelastic/aerodynamic loads [43]. The motion-induced aeroelastic loads in the time domain are generally described using the indicial function, due to its clear physical interpretation of wind-induced effects on the bluff-body [44]. For the bluff body's cross-section, it is intractable to obtain the theoretical representation of the elementary response components, because of the intensive flow separation. Scanlan et al. [43] found the semi-empirical model with aeroelastic IRF (referred to as the 1D indicial function) as follows:

$$\varphi_{yx}(t) = 1 - \sum_{i=1}^{N} a_{iyx} e^{-d_{iyx} Ut/B} \tag{17}$$

where B is the width of the bridge deck; U is the incoming velocity; the subscripts y $(y = D, L, M)$ and x $(x = p, h, \alpha)$ represent aeroelastic loads and motion, respectively; a and d can be fitted with the flutter derivatives; N is a parameter determined from the aerodynamic properties of the bridge deck, and $N = 3$ is used for the bridge deck.

Considering the downburst-induced transient effects on the bridge, the 2D indicial function was employed to model the aerodynamics. In the wind–bridge interaction system, the 2D indicial function can be defined as follows [1]:

$$\varphi_{yx}[t, U(\tau)] = 1 - \sum_{i=1}^{N} a_{iyx} e^{-d_{iyx} U(\tau)t/B} \tag{18}$$

where $U(\tau)$ is the time-varying incoming velocity. The scale t indicates the flow wake convection, and the scale τ relates to the aeroelastic system variation. The 2D aeroelastic indicial function $\varphi_{yx}[t, U(\tau)]$ is degenerated to the 1D indicial function $\varphi_{yx}[t]$ when the incoming wind velocity $U(\tau)$ is constant.

In this study, the aeroelastic system was assumed to vary slowly due to the slowly varying mean wind, and the same set of aerodynamic parameters were utilized to identify the indicial function at each mean wind speed [45]. In other words, the flutter derivatives experimentally measured under stationary winds were used to obtain the 2D indicial function in the time-variant aeroelastic system [1]. Also, the 2D indicial function would be improved if more advanced experimental identification schemes were available.

For the example bridge deck, the parameters of the aeroelastic indicial function could be fitted with the flutter derivatives [46], but the aerodynamic indicial function is referred to the Küssner function due to the challenge in measuring the aerodynamic admittance function by the wind tunnel test [47]. It should be noted that the flutter derivatives involved in drag force and horizontal motion were obtained based on quasi-steady theory because of a lack of experimental data [48].

Consequently, the aeroelastic loads can be determined as follows:

$$D_{se}(t) = \tfrac{1}{2}\rho U(t)^2 BC'_D \quad \begin{aligned} \Big\{ &\Big[\varphi_{Dp}[t,U(0)]\dot{p}(0)/U(0) + \textstyle\int_0^t \varphi_{Dp}[t-\tau,U(\tau)]\ddot{p}(\tau)/U(\tau)d\tau\Big] \\ &+\Big[\varphi_{Dh}[t,U(0)]\dot{h}(0)/U(0) + \textstyle\int_0^t \varphi_{Dh}[t-\tau,U(\tau)]\ddot{h}(\tau)/U(\tau)d\tau\Big] \\ &+\Big[\varphi_{D\alpha}[t,U(0)]\alpha(0) + \textstyle\int_0^t \varphi_{D\alpha}[t-\tau,U(\tau)]\dot{\alpha}(\tau)d\tau\Big]\Big\} \end{aligned} \tag{19}$$

$$L_{se}(t) = \tfrac{1}{2}\rho U(t)^2 BC'_L \quad \begin{aligned} \Big\{ &\Big[\varphi_{Lp}[t,U(0)]\dot{p}(0)/U(0) + \textstyle\int_0^t \varphi_{Lp}[t-\tau,U(\tau)]\ddot{p}(\tau)/U(\tau)d\tau\Big] \\ &+\Big[\varphi_{Lh}[t,U(0)]\dot{h}(0)/U(0) + \textstyle\int_0^t \varphi_{Lh}[t-\tau,U(\tau)]\ddot{h}(\tau)/U(\tau)d\tau\Big] \\ &+\Big[\varphi_{L\alpha}[t,U(0)]\alpha(0) + \textstyle\int_0^t \varphi_{L\alpha}[t-\tau,U(\tau)]\dot{\alpha}(\tau)d\tau\Big]\Big\} \end{aligned} \tag{20}$$

$$M_{se}(t) = \tfrac{1}{2}\rho U(t)^2 B^2 C'_M \quad \begin{aligned} \Big\{ &\Big[\varphi_{Mp}[t,U(0)]\dot{p}(0)/U(0) + \textstyle\int_0^t \varphi_{Mp}[t-\tau,U(\tau)]\ddot{p}(\tau)/U(\tau)d\tau\Big] \\ &+\Big[\varphi_{Mh}[t,U(0)]\dot{h}(0)/U(0) + \textstyle\int_0^t \varphi_{Mh}[t-\tau,U(\tau)]\ddot{h}(\tau)/U(\tau)d\tau\Big] \\ &+\Big[\varphi_{M\alpha}[t,U(0)]\alpha(0) + \textstyle\int_0^t \varphi_{M\alpha}[t-\tau,U(\tau)]\dot{\alpha}(\tau)d\tau\Big]\Big\} \end{aligned} \tag{21}$$

where ρ is the air density; $C'_D = \mathrm{d}C_D/\mathrm{d}\alpha$; $C'_L = \mathrm{d}C_L/\mathrm{d}\alpha$; $C'_M = \mathrm{d}C_M/\mathrm{d}\alpha$; C_D, C_L, and C_M are the steady-state force coefficients; p, h, and α are the horizontal, vertical, and torsional motion, respectively. Similarly, the aerodynamic loads can be determined as follows:

$$\begin{aligned} D_{bu}(t) = \; & \tfrac{1}{2}\rho U(t)^2 B\{2C_D\Big[\psi_{D(u/U)}[t,U(0)]\tfrac{u(0)}{U(t)} + \textstyle\int_0^t \psi_{D(u/U)}[t-\tau,U(\tau)]\tfrac{\dot{u}(\tau)}{U(\tau)}d\tau\Big] \\ & +(C'_D - C_L)\Big[\psi_{D(w/U)}[t,U(0)]\tfrac{w(0)}{U(t)} + \textstyle\int_0^t \psi_{D(w/U)}[t-\tau,U(\tau)]\tfrac{\dot{w}(\tau)}{U(\tau)}d\tau\Big]\Big\} \end{aligned} \tag{22}$$

$$\begin{aligned} L_{bu}(t) = \tfrac{1}{2}\rho U(t)^2 B \quad & \{2C_L\Big[\psi_{L(u/U)}[t,U(0)]\tfrac{u(0)}{U(t)} + \textstyle\int_0^t \psi_{L(u/U)}[t-\tau,U(\tau)]\tfrac{\dot{u}(\tau)}{U(\tau)}d\tau\Big] \\ & +(C_D + C'_L)\Big[\psi_{L(w/U)}[t,U(0)]\tfrac{w(0)}{U(t)} + \textstyle\int_0^t \psi_{L(w/U)}[t-\tau,U(\tau)]\tfrac{\dot{w}(\tau)}{U(\tau)}d\tau\Big]\Big\} \end{aligned} \tag{23}$$

$$\begin{aligned} M_{bu}(t) = \tfrac{1}{2}\rho U(t)^2 B^2 \quad & \Big\{2C_M\Big[\psi_{M(u/U)}[t,U(0)]\tfrac{u(0)}{U(t)} + \textstyle\int_0^t \psi_{M(u/U)}[t-\tau,U(\tau)]\tfrac{\dot{u}(\tau)}{U(\tau)}d\tau\Big] \\ & +C'_M\Big[\psi_{M(w/U)}[t,U(0)]\tfrac{w(0)}{U(t)} + \textstyle\int_0^t \psi_{M(w/U)}[t-\tau,U(\tau)]\tfrac{\dot{w}(\tau)}{U(\tau)}d\tau\Big]\Big\} \end{aligned} \tag{24}$$

where u and w are the horizontal and vertical fluctuating wind, respectively; $\psi[t, U(\tau)]$ is the 2D aerodynamic indicial function. It should be noted that the strip-theory assumption is adopted in the buffeting analysis, and the effects of turbulence intensity [49] and angle of attack [50] on the unsteady aerodynamic loading may be considered further when advanced theory is available.

4.4. Transient Wind-Induced Response

The downburst wind-induced buffeting analysis of the example bridge was carried out in the time domain. The turbulent downburst wind field was obtained by superimposing the CFD-based TVMW and Hilbert-based nonstationary fluctuations, and 1D and 2D indicial functions were employed to model the bridge's aerodynamics. Ten simulations were generated to acquire the time-varying buffeting response root-mean-square (RMS) to examine the downburst-induced transient effects on the buffeting response.

Significant differences could be observed in the RMS buffeting response of the example suspension bridge from the 1D and 2D indicial functions, as shown in Figure 24. Specifically, the maximum differences in the vertical, torsional, and lateral RMS were 31.35%, 34.15%, and 44.29%, respectively, which could be attributed to the exclusion of the downburst-induced transient effects on the aerodynamics in the 1D indicial function. The RMS bridge buffeting response acquired by the 2D indicial function was smaller than that acquired by the 1D indicial function, which suggests that the downburst wind-induced buffeting response would be overestimated without the consideration of transient effects on the bridge's aerodynamics.

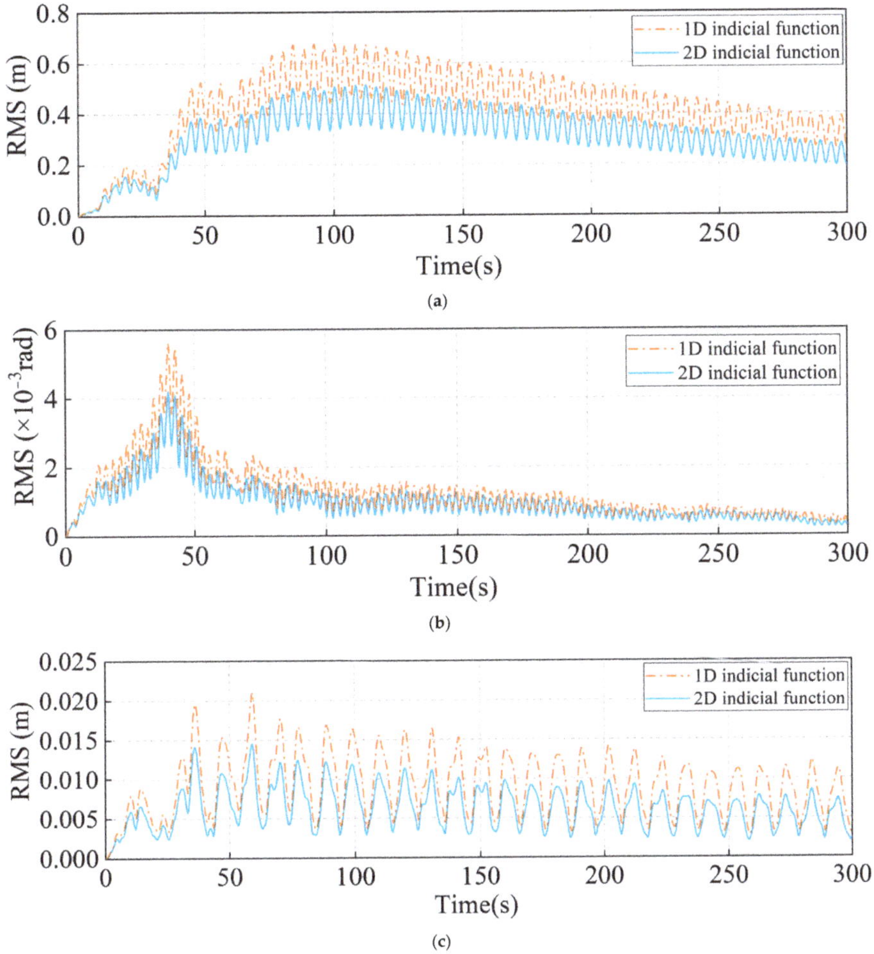

Figure 24. RMS time-varying buffeting response: (**a**) vertical direction; (**b**) torsional directions; (**c**) horizontal directions.

5. Conclusions

The buffeting response analysis of a long-span bridge under downburst was implemented in this study to investigate the transient effects on the bridge's aerodynamics. The time-varying mean wind was acquired with the CFD-based impinging jet model, where an optimization strategy conjunct with the available field measurement data was developed to provide guidance on parameter selection for more accurate simulations. Moreover, the Kriging surrogate model was introduced in the parameter optimization, through which significant improvements were observed in the optimization efficiency. The turbulent downburst wind was generated by combining the Hilbert-based nonstationary fluctuating wind and the CFD-based time-varying mean wind. Subsequently, the 1D and 2D indicial functions were employed to model the aerodynamics acting on the long-span bridge, and the downburst-induced transient effects on the buffeting response were investigated. The results for the example bridge present significant differences in the bridge buffeting response acquired from the 1D and 2D indicial functions, highlighting the non-negligible transient effects on the aerodynamics and the buffeting response in downburst events. Additionally, the downburst-induced transient effects exerted negative impacts on the aerodynamics, which could result in the overestimation of the bridge buffeting response if overlooked.

Author Contributions: Conceptualization, Y.F. and J.H.; methodology, Y.F., L.X. and N.D.; software, L.X.; validation, N.D. and F.W.; formal analysis, Y.F. and N.D.; writing—original draft preparation, Y.F., L.X. and F.W.; supervision, J.H.; funding acquisition, J.H. and F.W. All authors have read and agreed to the published version of the manuscript.

Funding: This research was funded by the National Key R&D Program of China (grant numbers 2021YFB2600600) and the Shaanxi Province Natural Science Foundation (grant number 2023-JC-QN-0597 and 2023-JC-QN-0526).

Data Availability Statement: The authors declare that the data presented in this study are available upon request.

Acknowledgments: The High-Performance Computing Center of Chang'an University and the Center for Computational Research at the University at Buffalo are gratefully acknowledged.

Conflicts of Interest: The authors declare no conflict of interest.

References

1. Hao, J.; Wu, T. Downburst-induced transient response of a long-span bridge: A CFD-CSD-based hybrid approach. *J. Wind Eng. Ind. Aerodyn.* **2018**, *179*, 273–286. [CrossRef]
2. Twisdale, L.A.; Vickery, P.J. Research on thunderstorm wind design parameters. *J. Wind Eng. Ind. Aerodyn.* **1992**, *41*, 545–556. [CrossRef]
3. Solari, G.; Burlando, M.; De Gaetano, P.; Repetto, M.P. Characteristics of thunderstorms relevant to the wind loading of structures. *Wind Struct.* **2015**, *20*, 763–791. [CrossRef]
4. Fujita, T.T. Tornadoes and downbursts in the context of generalized planetary scales. *J. Atmos. Sci.* **1981**, *38*, 1511–1534. [CrossRef]
5. Hjelmfelt, M.R. Structure and life cycle of microburst outflows observed in Colorado. *J. Appl. Meteorol. Climatol.* **1988**, *27*, 900–927. [CrossRef]
6. Solari, G.; Repetto, M.P.; Burlando, M.; De Gaetano, P.; Pizzo, M.; Tizzi, M.; Parodi, M. The wind forecast for safety management of port areas. *J. Wind Eng. Ind. Aerodyn.* **2012**, *104*, 266–277. [CrossRef]
7. Solari, G. Thunderstorm response spectrum technique: Theory and applications. *Eng. Struct.* **2016**, *108*, 28–46. [CrossRef]
8. Bakke, P. An experimental investigation of a wall jet. *J. Fluid Mech.* **1957**, *2*, 467–472. [CrossRef]
9. Glauert, M. The wall jet. *J. Fluid Mech.* **1956**, *1*, 625–643. [CrossRef]
10. Poreh, M.; Tsuei, Y.; Cermak, J.E. Investigation of a turbulent radial wall jet. *J. Appl. Mech.* **1967**, *34*, 457–463. [CrossRef]
11. Letchford, C.; Chay, M. Pressure distributions on a cube in a simulated thunderstorm downburst. Part B: Moving downburst observations. *J. Wind Eng. Ind. Aerodyn.* **2002**, *90*, 733–753. [CrossRef]
12. Mason, M.; Letchford, C.; James, D. Pulsed wall jet simulation of a stationary thunderstorm downburst, Part A: Physical structure and flow field characterization. *J. Wind Eng. Ind. Aerodyn.* **2005**, *93*, 557–580. [CrossRef]
13. Richter, A.; Ruck, B.; Mohr, S.; Kunz, M. Interaction of severe convective gusts with a street canyon. *Urban Clim.* **2018**, *23*, 71–90. [CrossRef]
14. Selvam, R.P.; Holmes, J. Numerical simulation of thunderstorm downdrafts. *J. Wind Eng. Ind. Aerodyn.* **1992**, *44*, 2817–2825. [CrossRef]
15. Kim, J.; Hangan, H. Numerical simulations of impinging jets with application to downbursts. *J. Wind Eng. Ind. Aerodyn.* **2007**, *95*, 279–298. [CrossRef]
16. Sengupta, A.; Sarkar, P.P. Experimental measurement and numerical simulation of an impinging jet with application to thunderstorm microburst winds. *J. Wind Eng. Ind. Aerodyn.* **2008**, *96*, 345–365. [CrossRef]
17. Aboshosha, H.; Bitsuamlak, G.; El Damatty, A. Turbulence characterization of downbursts using LES. *J. Wind Eng. Ind. Aerodyn.* **2015**, *136*, 44–61. [CrossRef]
18. Abd-Elaal, E.-S.; Mills, J.E.; Ma, X. Numerical simulation of downburst wind flow over real topography. *J. Wind Eng. Ind. Aerodyn.* **2018**, *172*, 85–95. [CrossRef]
19. Tang, J.; Hu, Y.; Song, B.; Yang, H. Unsteady aerodynamic optimization of airfoil for cycloidal propellers based on surrogate model. *J. Aircr.* **2017**, *54*, 1241–1256. [CrossRef]
20. Raul, V.; Leifsson, L. Surrogate-based aerodynamic shape optimization for delaying airfoil dynamic stall using Kriging regression and infill criteria. *Aerosp. Sci. Technol.* **2021**, *111*, 106555. [CrossRef]
21. Bernardini, E.; Spence, S.M.; Wei, D.; Kareem, A. Aerodynamic shape optimization of civil structures: A CFD-enabled Kriging-based approach. *J. Wind Eng. Ind. Aerodyn. J. Int. Assoc. Wind Eng.* **2015**, *144*, 154–164. [CrossRef]

22. Ding, F.; Kareem, A. A multi-fidelity shape optimization via surrogate modeling for civil structures. *J. Wind Eng. Ind. Aerodyn.* **2018**, *178*, 49–56. [CrossRef]
23. Montoya, M.C.; Nieto, F.; Hernández, S.; Kusano, I.; Álvarez, A.; Jurado, J. CFD-based aeroelastic characterization of streamlined bridge deck cross-sections subject to shape modifications using surrogate models. *J. Wind Eng. Ind. Aerodyn.* **2018**, *177*, 405–428. [CrossRef]
24. Jaouadi, Z.; Abbas, T.; Morgenthal, G.; Lahmer, T. Single and multi-objective shape optimization of streamlined bridge decks. *Struct. Multidiscip. Optim.* **2020**, *61*, 1495–1514. [CrossRef]
25. Holmes, J.D.; Hangan, H.M.; Schroeder, J.L.; Letchford, C.W.; Orwig, K.D. A forensic study of the Lubbock-Reese downdraft of 2002. *Wind Struct.* **2008**, *11*, 137–152. [CrossRef]
26. Feng, Y.; Hao, J.; Han, W.; Su, Q.; Wu, T. An optimized numerical tornado simulator and its application to transient wind-induced response of a long-span bridge. *J. Wind Eng. Ind. Aerodyn.* **2022**, *227*, 105072. [CrossRef]
27. Menter, F.R. Two-equation eddy-viscosity turbulence models for engineering applications. *AIAA J.* **1994**, *32*, 1598–1605. [CrossRef]
28. Mason, M.; Wood, G.; Fletcher, D. Impinging jet simulation of stationary downburst flow over topography. *Wind Struct.* **2007**, *10*, 437–462. [CrossRef]
29. Chay, M.; Letchford, C. Pressure distributions on a cube in a simulated thunderstorm downburst-Part A: Stationary downburst observations. *J. Wind Eng. Ind. Aerodyn.* **2002**, *90*, 711–732. [CrossRef]
30. Howell, R.; Qin, N.; Edwards, J.; Durrani, N. Wind tunnel and numerical study of a small vertical axis wind turbine. *Renew. Energy* **2010**, *35*, 412–422. [CrossRef]
31. Khayrullina, A.; Blocken, B.; Janssen, W.; Straathof, J. CFD simulation of train aerodynamics: Train-induced wind conditions at an underground railroad passenger platform. *J. Wind Eng. Ind. Aerodyn.* **2015**, *139*, 100–110. [CrossRef]
32. Li, C.; Li, Q.; Xiao, Y.; Ou, J. Simulations of moving downbursts using CFD. In Proceedings of the Seventh Asia-Pacific Conference on Wind Engineering, Taipei, Taiwan, 8–12 November 2009.
33. Fujita, T.T. *Andrews AFB Microburst, SMRP Research Paper 205*; University of Chicago: Chicago, IL, USA, 1985.
34. Fujita, T.T.; Byers, H.R. Spearhead echo and downburst in the crash of an airliner. *Mon. Weather Rev.* **1977**, *105*, 129–146. [CrossRef]
35. Butler, K.; Cao, S.; Kareem, A.; Tamura, Y.; Ozono, S. Surface pressure and wind load characteristics on prisms immersed in a simulated transient gust front flow field. *J. Wind Eng. Ind. Aerodyn.* **2010**, *98*, 299–316. [CrossRef]
36. Shirato, H.; Maeta, K.; Kato, Y.; Takasugi, Y. Transient drag force on 2-D bluff bodies under gusty wind condition. In Proceedings of the 7th Asia-Pacific Conference on Wind Engineering, Taipei, Taiwan, 8–12 November 2009.
37. Hao, J.; Wu, T. Numerical analysis of a long-span bridge response to tornado-like winds. *Wind Struct.* **2020**, *31*, 459–472.
38. Aboutabikh, M.; Ghazal, T.; Chen, J.; Elgamal, S.; Aboshosha, H. Designing a blade-system to generate downburst outflows at boundary layer wind tunnel. *J. Wind Eng. Ind. Aerodyn.* **2019**, *186*, 169–191. [CrossRef]
39. Wang, H.; Wu, T. Hilbert-wavelet-based nonstationary wind field simulation: A multiscale spatial correlation scheme. *J. Eng. Mech.* **2018**, *144*, 04018063. [CrossRef]
40. Feng, Y.; Su, Q.; Hao, J.; Han, W.; Wang, H. A comparative study on the transient wind-induced response of long-span bridges subject to downbursts and typhoons. *Eng. Struct.* **2023**, *280*, 115649. [CrossRef]
41. Gabor, D. Theory of communication. Part 1: The analysis of information. *J. Inst. Electr. Eng.-Part III Radio Commun. Eng.* **1946**, *93*, 429–441. [CrossRef]
42. Chen, L.; Letchford, C. Numerical simulation of extreme winds from thunderstorm downbursts. *J. Wind Eng. Ind. Aerodyn.* **2007**, *95*, 977–990. [CrossRef]
43. Scanlan, R.H.; Béliveau, J.; Budlong, K.S. Indicial aerodynamic functions for bridge decks. *J. Eng. Mech. Div.* **1974**, *100*, 657–672. [CrossRef]
44. Wu, T.; Kareem, A. Revisiting convolution scheme in bridge aerodynamics: Comparison of step and impulse response functions. *J. Eng. Mech.* **2014**, *140*, 04014008. [CrossRef]
45. Chen, X. Analysis of multimode coupled buffeting response of long-span bridges to nonstationary winds with force parameters from stationary wind. *J. Struct. Eng.* **2015**, *141*, 04014131. [CrossRef]
46. Chen, A. *Study of Aerodynamic Performance of Runyang Bridge*; Technical Report WT200218; Tongji University: Shanghai, China, 2002.
47. Jones, R.T. *The Unsteady Lift of a Wing of Finite Aspect Ratio*; National Advisory Committee for Aeronautics: Boston, MA, USA, 1940.
48. Chen, X.; Matsumoto, M.; Kareem, A. Aerodynamic coupling effects on flutter and buffeting of bridges. *J. Eng. Mech.* **2000**, *126*, 17–26. [CrossRef]
49. Li, S.; Liu, Y.; Li, M.; Zeng, W.; Gu, S.; Gao, Y. The effect of turbulence intensity on the unsteady gust loading on a 5: 1 rectangular cylinder. *J. Wind Eng. Ind. Aerodyn.* **2022**, *225*, 104994. [CrossRef]
50. Li, S.; Li, M.; Wu, B.; Li, K.; Yang, Y. Three-dimensional aerodynamic lift on a rectangular cylinder in turbulent flow at an angle of attack. *J. Fluids Struct.* **2023**, *118*, 103859. [CrossRef]

Disclaimer/Publisher's Note: The statements, opinions and data contained in all publications are solely those of the individual author(s) and contributor(s) and not of MDPI and/or the editor(s). MDPI and/or the editor(s) disclaim responsibility for any injury to people or property resulting from any ideas, methods, instructions or products referred to in the content.

mathematics

MDPI

Article

An Improved Incremental Procedure for the Ground Reaction Based on Hoek-Brown Failure Criterion in the Tunnel Convergence-Confinement Method

Yu-Lin Lee [1,*], Chi-Huang Ma [1] and Chi-Min Lee [2]

1 Department of Civil Engineering, Chung Hua University, Hsinchu 300110, Taiwan; d11004001@chu.edu.tw
2 Department of Civil Engineering, National Central University, Taoyuan City 320953, Taiwan; francislee0129@g.ncu.edu.tw
* Correspondence: rosalee@chu.edu.tw

Abstract: The purpose of this study is to introduce the Hoek–Brown nonlinear failure criterion into the convergence–confinement method (CCM), which is based on the linear failure criterion, and implant it into the ground reaction curve (GRC) in this theory. Based on consistent and rigorous theoretical analysis and according to the mechanical relationships, the principle of equilibrium, the material constitutive law, and the strain/displacement compatibility equation are used to deduce the closed-form analytical solution of the stress/displacement of the rock mass in the plastic region and to complete the simulation and interpretation of the nonlinear behavior of surrounding rock due to the advancing excavation of a circular tunnel. In this paper, confinement loss is regarded as the concept of increment in numerical analysis, and the calculation process and analysis steps of the explicit analysis method (EAM) are proposed. This method can not only realize the calculation of analytical solutions but can also be performed using simple spreadsheets. In addition, to verify the feasibility of this calculation method, this study uses published data to verify the validity of the analytical solution implemented by the incremental procedure and to study the influence of nonlinear failure criteria on the GRC, especially the mechanical behavior at the intrados of the tunnel and the distributions of tress/displacement on the cross-section of the tunnel. A comparison between the published results and the proposed solution in this study reveals consistent and favorable trends.

Keywords: convergence–confinement method; non-linear failure criterion; closed-form solution; incremental procedure

MSC: 74C05

Citation: Lee, Y.-L.; Ma, C.-H.; Lee, C.-M. An Improved Incremental Procedure for the Ground Reaction Based on Hoek-Brown Failure Criterion in the Tunnel Convergence-Confinement Method. *Mathematics* **2023**, *11*, 3389. https://doi.org/10.3390/math11153389

Academic Editor: Fernando Simoes

Received: 1 July 2023
Revised: 27 July 2023
Accepted: 31 July 2023
Published: 3 August 2023

Copyright: © 2023 by the authors. Licensee MDPI, Basel, Switzerland. This article is an open access article distributed under the terms and conditions of the Creative Commons Attribution (CC BY) license (https://creativecommons.org/licenses/by/4.0/).

1. Introduction

The convergence–confinement method (CCM) is a systematic approach used in the design and construction of tunnels in rock masses. It recognizes that rock masses tend to deform and converge around an excavated tunnel due to the redistribution of stress. The method aims to control and manage this convergence by providing adequate confinement or support to ensure the stability and safety of the tunnel [1–3]. The method provides a framework for understanding and managing the convergence behavior of the rock mass, while the support design translates this understanding into practical measures to enhance tunnel stability [4,5]. The fundamental concept of the CCM is based on the interaction between the primary and secondary stress fields induced by tunnel excavation. When a tunnel is excavated, the primary stress in the rock mass is redistributed, causing the rock to deform and converge toward the opening. This convergence can lead to displacements, deformations, and potentially unstable conditions if not properly controlled [6–9].

The CCM focuses on achieving three main objectives, as shown in Figure 1: (1) The ground reaction curve (GRC) aims to limit the amount of convergence and control the rate at which it occurs. By controlling convergence, the risk of tunnel deformation and failure is reduced. The level of acceptable convergence depends on factors such as the tunnel purpose, ground conditions, support system, and safety requirements. Much of the research literature is devoted to this approach to developing mathematical and empirical expressions for ground reaction curves under different behavioral assumptions [10–15]. (2) Support confining curve (SCC) refers to the application of external support to the tunnel walls to counteract the inward movement and maintain stability. This is achieved through the installation of various support systems such as rock bolts, shotcrete, steel ribs, or other reinforcement elements. The support elements help confine the rock mass and distribute the stresses, reducing convergence and enhancing tunnel stability. Many studies on SCC have dealt with the limitations of nonlinearity of structural support, time dependence, progressive hardening, and transient conditions. Under different assumptions, the current research results have achieved a solution for the support design between SCC and GRC in the final equilibrium state (as shown at point E in Figure 1) [16–23].

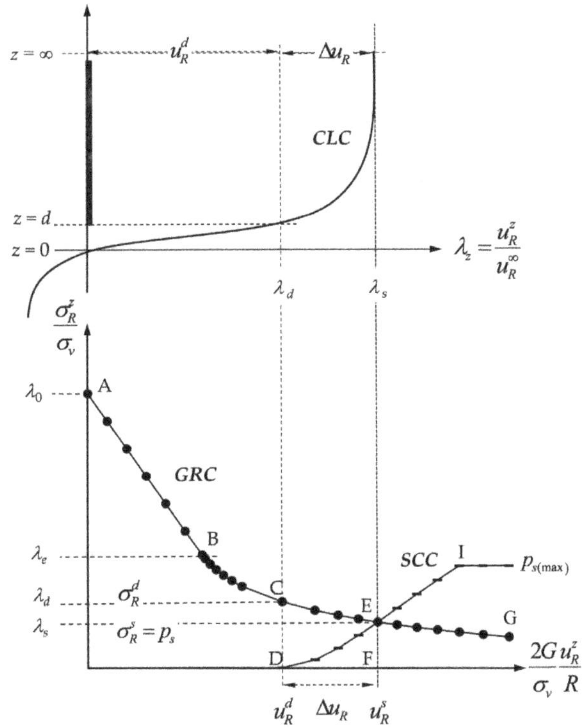

Figure 1. A conceptual diagram of the interaction between ground convergence and support confinement caused by tunnel advancing excavation in the convergence–confinement method (CCM) analysis, including three curves: confinement loss curve (CLC), support confining curve (SCC), and ground reaction curve (GRC).

(3) The confinement loss curve (CLC) emphasizes the importance of an observational approach during tunnel construction. This means continuously monitoring the behavior of the rock mass and adjusting the support measures accordingly. The value of the confinement loss can be obtained through the relationship between the unsupported distance from the tunnel face and the convergence measurement data of the tunnel. This value can be an incremental value, a positive scalar, or a function that takes into account the effect of advancing excavation on the tunnel face. This CLC principle shows that during the continuous advancement of the tunnel face, the confinement loss increases, resulting in a

decrease in the radial stress around the tunnel and an increase in the radial displacement. Recently, much research literature has mentioned the effect of confinement losses around tunnels and constitutive models using numerical procedures to improve the accuracy of CCM analysis [24–28]. By implementing the convergence–confinement method, engineers can effectively manage the convergence behavior of rock masses in tunneling projects. It provides a systematic and proactive approach to ensuring the stability and safety of underground excavations [29,30]. In recent years, many scholars have proposed related numerical simulation research, such as the hybridized FSM and DDM stress analysis of the discontinuous surrounding rock of the tunnel, the mixed indirect boundary element method, and the numerical simulation of rock failure analysis in the crushing zone [31–33].

The ground reaction curve (GRC) is a concept used in the convergence–confinement method to understand the response of the rock mass and support system to tunnel excavation. It represents the relationship between the convergence (displacement) of the tunnel wall and the applied support pressure. In addition, the failure criterion provides insight into the strength and behavior of the rock mass, which influences the shape and characteristics of the ground reaction curve. In this study, the characteristics of the GRC are investigated and implemented by using the non-linear failure criterion of generalized Hoek–Brown [34–36]. The criterion allows engineers to assess the stability of rock slopes or tunnels under different stress conditions, taking into account the strength and quality of the rock mass. This criterion helps engineers evaluate the stability of the rock mass and determine the support requirements during tunneling [37–40]. By using the generalized Hoek-Brown failure criterion, engineers can estimate the rock mass strength and predict the potential failure mechanisms that may occur during tunneling. This information is crucial in selecting appropriate support systems and determining the required support pressure to control convergence and maintain tunnel stability [41–44]. Finally, the generalized Hoek–Brown failure criterion provides a basis for understanding the strength and failure behavior of the rock mass, while the ground reaction curve provides a means to evaluate the actual response of the rock mass and support system during tunneling. The failure criterion informs the design of the support system, and the ground reaction curve validates its effectiveness. Together, these concepts contribute to the overall assessment and management of convergence and confinement in the convergence-confinement method for tunneling projects.

The novelty and improvement of the GRC in this paper is to adopt the Hoek–Brown nonlinear failure criterion and insert it into the CCM theoretical analysis to replace the traditional Mohr–Coulomb linear failure criterion. Its advantage is that it can more realistically reflect the nonlinear mechanical behavior of the rock mass in the failure stage, especially in response to the plastic behavior of the surrounding rock. The purpose of this study is to use the theoretical analysis and basic principles of the convergence–confinement method to comprehensively discuss the mechanical behavior of tunnel excavation-induced ground reaction by considering the generalized Hoek–Brown nonlinear failure criterion. It not only provides a complete set of equations and details of their derivation, verification, and comparison but also illustrates the influence and availability of this nonlinear failure criterion based on the analysis results of the stress/displacement distribution on the cross-section and at the intrados of the tunnel.

2. Related Problem Description

2.1. Relationship between Tunnel Advancing Excavation Effect and Confinement Loss

Due to the advancing excavation of the tunnel face, the surrounding rock converges and the stress redistributes. That is to say, the impact of the unsupported distance on the advancing excavation of the working face is to consider the changes in stress and displacement caused by a certain observation section in the front after the continuous excavation of the tunnel. Based on the relevant basic research [6,7], using the tunnel convergence measurement data, a statistical regression analysis is used to establish a function related to the effect of tunnel face advancing excavation and to estimate the confinement loss. The function of this confinement loss curve (CLC) is shown in Figure 2. At a certain distance (z) from the working face, the definition of confinement loss (λ_z) can be given as

$$\lambda_z = \lambda_0 + (1 - \lambda_0) f\left(\frac{z}{R}\right) \tag{1}$$

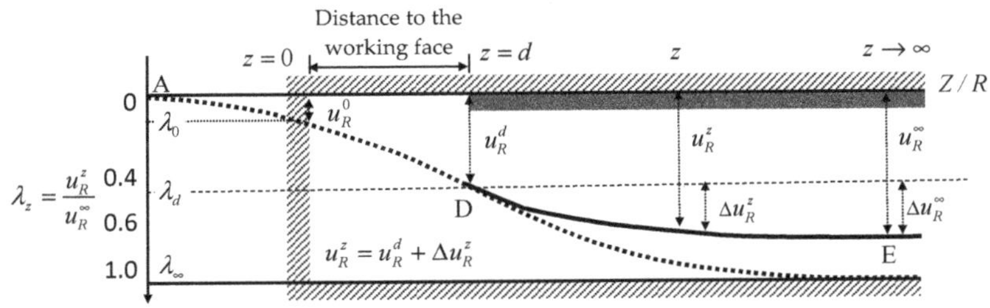

Figure 2. Schematic representation of the confinement loss curve (CLC) without support (dashed line) or with support (solid line).

For the assumption of the effect function of advancing excavation in the tunnel face, $f(z/R)$ can also be called the advancing effect function, which can be expressed by the following:

$$f\left(\frac{z}{R}\right) = 1 - \left(\frac{m}{m + \frac{z}{R}}\right)^2 \tag{2}$$

where R is the tunnel excavation radius, λ_0 is a confinement loss at the working face ($z = 0$, point A in Figure 1), and can be given as:

$$\lambda_0 = 1 - \left(\frac{m}{m + \frac{d}{R}}\right)^2 \tag{3}$$

2.2. Stress Variation around a Circular Tunnel

In the analysis of the convergence–confinement method, the stress changes in the surrounding rock are generated due to the advancing excavation of the tunnel. The change in this stress can be described by the concept of stress gradient, which is expressed as the difference between the far-field stress and the near-field stress around the tunnel. The assumption of increment in numerical analysis is to treat the confinement loss as part of an increment or as a fraction of the stress gradient. This is an important principle and concept used in the theory of the convergence-confinement method. The change in this stress can be described by the following expression [6,7]:

(1) The stress state of the far-field ($r \rightarrow \infty$): Before the excavation of the tunnel, the stress of the surrounding rock is the initial in situ stress or the initial isotropic stress (as shown in Figure 3). Its stress can be expressed as follows:

$$\sigma_r^i = \sigma_\theta^i = \sigma_v \tag{4}$$

where σ_r^i, σ_θ^i, and σ_v are the initial radial stress, the initial tangential stress, and the vertical stress.

(2) The stress state of the near-field ($R \leq r < \infty$): After the tunnel is excavated, the stress change of the surrounding rock can be obtained through Kirsch's solution, as shown in the following:

$$\sigma_r^f = \left(1 - \frac{R^2}{r^2}\right)\sigma_v \tag{5}$$

$$\sigma_\theta^f = \left(1 + \frac{R^2}{r^2}\right)\sigma_v \tag{6}$$

where σ_θ^f and σ_r^f are the final tangential stress and the final radial stress around the tunnel proximity, respectively.

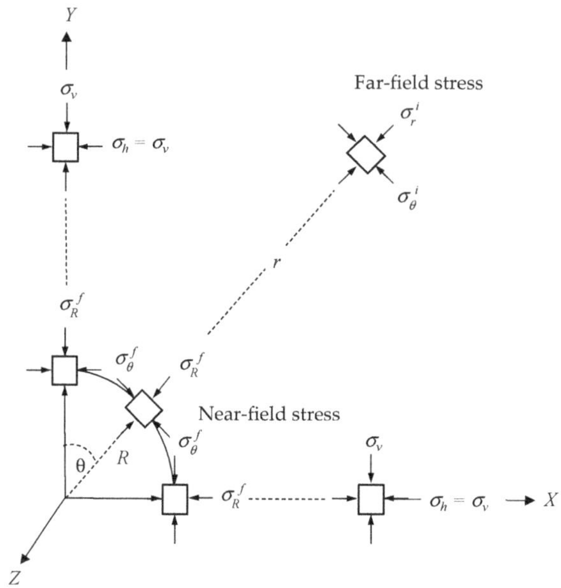

Figure 3. Stress variation around the tunnel from far-field to near-field in an isotropic stress field.

Assuming that the stress gradient produced by the advancing excavation of the tunnel face is the difference between the far-field stress and the near-field stress, the changes in the tangential stress and radial stress can be expressed as follows:

$$\overline{\sigma}_r = \sigma_r^f - \sigma_r^i = \left(1 - \frac{R^2}{r^2}\right)\sigma_v - \sigma_v \tag{7}$$

$$\overline{\sigma}_\theta = \sigma_\theta^f - \sigma_\theta^i = \left(1 + \frac{R^2}{r^2}\right)\sigma_v - \sigma_v \tag{8}$$

Regarding the assumption of increment in numerical analysis, the stress increment can be expressed by multiplying the stress gradient by the confinement loss, and its relationship can be expressed as follows:

$$\Delta\sigma_r = \lambda\overline{\sigma}_r = -\lambda\frac{R^2}{r^2}\sigma_v \tag{9}$$

$$\Delta\sigma_\theta = \lambda\overline{\sigma}_\theta = +\lambda\frac{R^2}{r^2}\sigma_v \tag{10}$$

Therefore, at a certain point around the tunnel, the stress change due to the advancing excavation of the tunnel can be obtained, as shown in the following equations:

$$\sigma_r = \sigma_r^i + \Delta\sigma_r = \left(1 - \lambda\frac{R^2}{r^2}\right)\sigma_v \tag{11}$$

$$\sigma_\theta = \sigma_\theta^i + \Delta\sigma_\theta = \left(1 + \lambda\frac{R^2}{r^2}\right)\sigma_v \tag{12}$$

In addition, from the results obtained by Kirsch's solution, the radial displacement (u_r) in the elastic region can be given as the following:

$$\frac{2G}{\sigma_v}\frac{u_r}{R} = \lambda\left(\frac{R}{r}\right) \tag{13}$$

where G is the shear modulus of the rock mass.

It is worth noting here that these equations must satisfy the boundary conditions and can be verified by the following instructions: (1) if $\lambda = 0$, it means that the tunnel has not been excavated, and the stress state of its surrounding rock is the same as the initial in-situ stress in the far-field; (2) if $\lambda = 1$, it indicates that the unsupported tunnel has been completely excavated, and the stress of its surrounding rock is the same as Kirsch's stress in the near-field.

3. Derivation of Stress/Displacement Equations in the Plastic Regions

3.1. Derivation of the Confinement Loss in Elastic Limit with the Non-Linear Failure Criteria

Assuming that the mechanical behavior of the rock mass is elastic-perfectly-plastic, when the stress of the surrounding rock of the tunnel meets the limit conditions defined by the failure criterion, a disturbance zone, or the so-called plastic radius, gradually appears around the tunnel. It is not only a function of the peak strength parameter of the surrounding rock but also a function of the confinement loss in the elastic limit situation. When the value of confinement loss increases, the plastic radius increases, but the radial stress in the plastic zone decreases. Therefore, the radial stress is a function of the plastic radius.

The generalized Hoek–Brown failure criterion [34] is a widely used non-linear criterion in geotechnical engineering to assess the rock mass strength and predict its failure behavior. This failure criterion considers the influence of several parameters to capture the complex behavior of rock masses. These parameters include the uniaxial compressive strength (UCS), the geological strength index (GSI), and other geotechnical parameters. The UCS is the strength of the intact rock material, and the GSI represents the quality and condition of the rock mass. This criterion is used in various geotechnical applications, including tunneling, slope stability analysis, and rock engineering design. It provides a more realistic representation of the strength and failure behavior of rock masses compared to linear failure criteria such as the Mohr–Coulomb criterion shown in Figure 4. The mathematical expression for the generalized Hoek–Brown failure criterion is as follows,

$$f(\sigma_3, \sigma_1) = \sigma_1 - \sigma_3 - \sigma_{ci}\left(m_b\frac{\sigma_3}{\sigma_{ci}} + s\right)^a \tag{14}$$

where the empirical constants m_b and s are determined based on laboratory testing, field observations, and experience, and σ_{ci} is the uniaxial compression strength (UCS) of the intact rock. These constants vary depending on the rock type and the condition of the rock mass. The constants can be obtained from published charts or tables specific to the rock types and rock mass classifications. This equation describes the relationship between the stress state and the strength of the rock mass, and the parameters can be expressed as:

$$m_b = m_i exp\left(\frac{GSI - 100}{28 - 14D}\right) \tag{15}$$

$$s = exp\left(\frac{GSI - 100}{9 - 3D}\right) \tag{16}$$

where m_b is a reduced value of the material constant. m_i, s, and a are constants for the rock mass. D is a factor that depends upon the degree of disturbance to which the rock mass has been subjected by blast damage and stress relaxation. It varies from 0 for undisturbed, in situ rock masses to 1 for very disturbed rock masses. Since the parameter a is variable and must be obtained from the experimental data by statistical regression analysis, in order to facilitate the calculation and derivation of the closed-form analytical solution of the differential equation, it is recommended to use $a = 0.5$ in this study. Then the representation of the equation can be given as follows:

$$f(\sigma_3, \sigma_1) = \sigma_1 - \sigma_3 - \sqrt{m_b \sigma_3 \sigma_{ci} + s\sigma_{ci}^2} \tag{17}$$

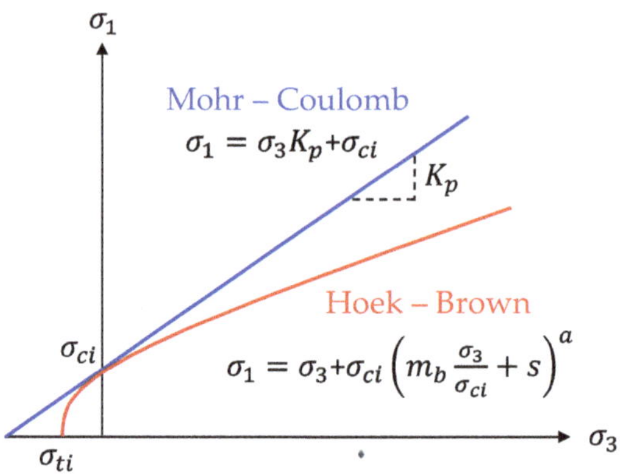

Figure 4. Schematic illustration of linear (Mohr-Coulomb) and non-linear (Hoek-Brown) failure criteria.

In addition, the above equation can be normalized by the vertical stress (σ_v) for dimensionless, therefore:

$$f\left(\frac{\sigma_3}{\sigma_v}, \frac{\sigma_1}{\sigma_v}\right) = \frac{\sigma_1}{\sigma_v} - \frac{\sigma_3}{\sigma_v} - \sqrt{m_b\left(\frac{\sigma_3}{\sigma_v}\right)\left(\frac{\sigma_{ci}}{\sigma_v}\right) + s\left(\frac{\sigma_{ci}^2}{\sigma_v^2}\right)} \tag{18}$$

Moreover, with consideration of the effect of stability, this equation can be redefined by the following:

$$f\left(\frac{\sigma_3}{\sigma_v}, \frac{\sigma_1}{\sigma_v}\right) = \frac{\sigma_1}{\sigma_v} - \frac{\sigma_3}{\sigma_v} - \sqrt{2Nm_b\left(\frac{\sigma_3}{\sigma_v}\right) + 4sN^2} \tag{19}$$

where the stability number N can be defined and given as:

$$N = \frac{\sigma_{ci}}{2\sigma_v} \tag{20}$$

In the previous description of the stresses at the intrados of the tunnel ($r = R$), one can obtain the radial and tangential stresses as follows:

$$\sigma_3 = \sigma_r = (1 - \lambda_e)\sigma_v \tag{21}$$

$$\sigma_1 = \sigma_\theta = (1 + \lambda_e)\sigma_v \tag{22}$$

Substituting Equations (23) and (24) into the Hoek–Brown strength criterion Equation (21), the relationship can be shown as follows:

$$f\left(\frac{\sigma_3}{\sigma_v}, \frac{\sigma_1}{\sigma_v}\right) = 2\lambda_e - \sqrt{2Nm_b(1 - \lambda_e) + 4sN^2} \tag{23}$$

Finally, the confinement loss in the elastic limit situation (λ_e) can be obtained as follows:

$$\lambda_e = \frac{N}{4}\left(\sqrt{m_b^2 + 8\frac{m_b}{N} + 16s} - m_b\right) \tag{24}$$

It is worth noting that the confinement loss in the elastic limit situation (λ_e) is a function of the initial vertical stress (σ_v) and the peak strength parameters of the rock mass (σ_{ci}, m_b, s).

3.2. Derivation of the Plastic Radius

To study the calculation of the plastic radius in the plastic zone, this paper adopts the assumption of axisymmetry, and its differential equation in the equilibrium state can be expressed as:

$$\frac{d\sigma_r}{dr} + \frac{\sigma_r - \sigma_\theta}{r} = 0 \tag{25}$$

By substituting the Hoek–Brown failure criterion, Equation (19) into this Equation (25), one can obtain the relationship as follows:

$$\int_{\sigma_r^-}^{\sigma_r^+} \frac{d\sigma_r}{\sqrt{2Nm_b\sigma_r + 4sN^2}} = \int_{R}^{R_p} \frac{dr}{r} \tag{26}$$

By integrating the above equation, the plastic radius around a tunnel can be obtained as follows:

$$\left(\frac{R_p}{R}\right) = exp\left\{\frac{1}{Nm_b}\left[(2\lambda_e) - \sqrt{2Nm_b(1-\lambda) + 4sN^2}\right]\right\} \tag{27}$$

where R_p is the radius of the elastic-plastic interface, or so-called plastic radius, and is also a function of the initial vertical stress (σ_v) and the peak strength parameters of the rock mass (σ_{ci}, m_b, s). In particular, it is also dependent on the confinement loss (λ) which is an important factor in the incremental procedure to simulate the effect of advancing excavation of the tunnel face in the convergence–confinement method. In addition, the condition of the elastic-plastic interface needs to be satisfied, and it is verified by setting $\lambda = \lambda_e$, therefore $R_p/R = 1$. At the same time, the radial and tangential stresses are also satisfied by the Hoek-Brown non-linear failure criterion.

3.3. Derivation of Stress in the Plastic Region

To study the radial stress in the plastic region by substituting the Hoek-Brown failure criterion, Equation (19), into Equation (25), it can be expressed as follows:

$$\int_{\sigma_r^+}^{\sigma_r^-} \frac{d\sigma_r}{\sqrt{2Nm_b\sigma_r + 4sN^2}} = \int_{R_p}^{r} \frac{dr}{r} \tag{28}$$

Thus, the radial stress in the plastic region can be obtained as follows:

$$\frac{\sigma_r}{\sigma_v} = (1 - \lambda_e) + (2\lambda_e)ln\left(\frac{r}{R_p}\right) + \frac{Nm_b}{2}ln^2\left(\frac{r}{R_p}\right) \tag{29}$$

In addition, the tangential stress can also be given as:

$$\frac{\sigma_\theta}{\sigma_v} = (1 + \lambda_e) + (2\lambda_e + Nm_b)ln\left(\frac{r}{R_p}\right) + \frac{Nm_b}{2}ln^2\left(\frac{r}{R_p}\right) \tag{30}$$

Therefore, the above stress can also be expressed as a function of $\sigma = f(r, \theta, \lambda)$ or $\sigma = f(r, \theta, Z)$. In addition, the condition of the elastic-plastic interface needs to be satisfied, and if it is verified by setting $r = R_p$, then the above equations become Equations (20) and (21).

3.4. Derivation of Displacement in the Plastic Region

In the elastic region, the tangential and radial strains, ε_θ^e and ε_r^e, can be expressed by the equations of constitutive law as:

$$\begin{Bmatrix} \varepsilon_\theta^e \\ \varepsilon_r^e \end{Bmatrix} = \frac{1}{2G}\begin{bmatrix} 1-\nu & \nu \\ \nu & 1-\nu \end{bmatrix}\begin{Bmatrix} \sigma_\theta \\ \sigma_r \end{Bmatrix} \tag{31}$$

where ν is the Poisson's ratio and G is the shear modulus of the rock mass.

Regarding the assumption of the small strain problem, the relationship between displacement and strain at any point in the surrounding rock of the tunnel can be expressed by a compatibility equation as follows:

$$\varepsilon_r = \frac{\partial u_r}{\partial r} \tag{32}$$

$$\varepsilon_\theta = \frac{\partial u_\theta}{r\partial\theta} + \frac{u_r}{r} \cong \frac{u_r}{r} \tag{33}$$

In this study, the non-associated plastic flow rule and the normality rule are used to determine the flow amount and direction of the displacement in the plastic region, as shown in Figure 5. Via the assumption that the plane strain and the elastic strain are relatively smaller than the plastic strain, the plastic parts of the radial and tangential strains can therefore be expressed as follows:

$$\varepsilon_r^p + K_\psi \varepsilon_\theta^p = 0 \tag{34}$$

where the coefficient of passive pressure, K_p, can be expressed as:

$$K_\psi = tan^2\left(45 + \frac{\psi}{2}\right) \tag{35}$$

where ψ is the dilation angle of the intact rock. The above equation in another form can be expressed as the following,

$$(\varepsilon_r - \varepsilon_r^e) + K_\psi(\varepsilon_\theta - \varepsilon_\theta^e) = 0 \tag{36}$$

where the subscripts p and e represent the plastic and elastic parts, respectively. Using Equations (32), (33), and (36) leads to the following differential equation:

$$f(r) = \varepsilon_r^e + K_\psi \varepsilon_\theta^e = \frac{\partial u_r}{\partial r} + K_\psi \frac{u_r}{r} \tag{37}$$

By substituting the equation of constitutive law, Equation (31), into the above equation, then:

$$f(r) = \frac{\partial u_r}{\partial r} + K_\psi \frac{u_r}{r} = \frac{1}{2G}\{[(1-v)K_\psi - v](\sigma_\theta) + [(1-v) - \nu K_\psi](\sigma_r)\} \tag{38}$$

To obtain the analytical solution of the radial displacement (u_r) in the plastic region, the homogeneous solution and the particular solution can be obtained by using the engineering mathematics method in consideration of the boundary conditions. This differential equation can be expressed as:

(1) Homogeneous solution ($f(r) = 0$):

$$f(r) = \frac{\partial u_r}{\partial r} + K_\psi \frac{u_r}{r} = 0 \tag{39}$$

Integrating the above equation with the boundary conditions ($r = R_p$ and $u_r = u_{R_p}$), it can be expressed as:

$$\int_{u_r}^{u_{R_p}} \frac{\partial u_r}{\partial r} = -K_\psi \int_r^{R_p} \frac{\partial r}{r} \tag{40}$$

Therefore, the homogeneous solution of the radial displacement can be expressed as:

$$\frac{u_r}{r} = \frac{1}{r^{K_\psi+1}} u_{R_p} (R_p)^{K_\psi} \tag{41}$$

where u_{R_p} is the radial displacement at the elastic-plastic interface ($r = R_p$) and can be given as:

$$u_{R_p} = \lambda_e \left(\frac{\sigma_v}{2G}\right)(R_p) \tag{42}$$

To consider it in its normalized form, it can be obtained as:

$$\frac{2G}{\sigma_v}\frac{u_r}{R} = \lambda_e \left(\frac{r}{R}\right)\left(\frac{R_p}{r}\right)^{K_\psi+1} \tag{43}$$

(2) Particular solution ($f(r) = \frac{\partial u_r}{\partial r} + K_\psi \frac{u_r}{r}$):

According to the stresses obtained in the plastic region, Equations (29) and (30), can be written in a new form as:

$$f(r) = \frac{\partial u_r}{\partial r} + K_\psi \frac{u_r}{r} = \frac{1}{2G}\left[(1 - v - vK_\psi)(\sigma_r) + (K_\psi - vK_\psi - v)(\sigma_\theta)\right] \tag{44}$$

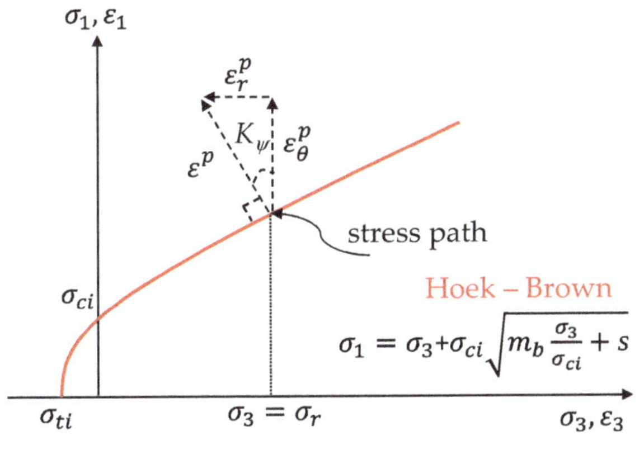

Figure 5. Plastic potential function with non-associated flow rule.

By rearranging the above equation, it can be represented as follows:

$$f(r) = \frac{1}{2G}\left[D_1 + D_2 ln\left(\frac{r}{R_p}\right) + D_3 ln^2\left(\frac{r}{R_p}\right)\right] \tag{45}$$

where the coefficients D_1, D_2, and D_3 can be given as:

$$D_1 = (K_\psi - 1)(\lambda_e) \tag{46}$$

$$D_2 = (1 + K_\psi)(1 - 2v)(2\lambda_e) + (K_\psi - vK_\psi - v)Nm_b \tag{47}$$

$$D_3 = (1 + K_\psi)(1 - 2v)\left(\frac{Nm_b}{2}\right) \tag{48}$$

By combining the homogeneous solution Equation (41) and the particular solution Equation (45), the radial displacement in the plastic region can be expressed as:

$$\frac{u}{r} = \frac{1}{r^{K_\psi+1}}\int_{R_p}^{r} r^{K_\psi} f(r)dr + \frac{u_r}{r} \quad (49)$$

In addition, the radial displacement in the plastic region can be obtained as:

$$\frac{u}{r} = \frac{1}{2G}\frac{1}{r^{K_\psi+1}}\left[D_1 f_1(r) + D_2 f_2(r) + D_3 f_3(r) + 2Gu_{R_p}(R_p)^{K_\psi} - D_1 f_1(R_p) - D_2 f_2(R_p) - D_3 f_3(R_p)\right] \quad (50)$$

where $f_1(r)$, $f_2(r)$ and $f_3(r)$ can be given as:

$$f_1(r) = \int r^{K_\psi} dr = \frac{r^{K_\psi+1}}{K_\psi+1} \quad (51)$$

$$f_2(r) = \int r^{K_\psi} ln\left(\frac{r}{R_p}\right)dr = \frac{r^{K_\psi+1}}{K_\psi+1}\left[ln\left(\frac{r}{R_p}\right) - \frac{1}{K_\psi+1}\right] \quad (52)$$

$$f_3(r) = \int r^{K_\psi} ln^2\left(\frac{r}{R_p}\right)dr = \frac{r^{K_\psi+1}}{K_\psi+1}\left[ln^2\left(\frac{r}{R_p}\right) - \frac{2}{K_\psi+1}ln\left(\frac{r}{R_p}\right) + \frac{2}{(K_\psi+1)^2}\right] \quad (53)$$

From the above series of mathematical operations, the closed-form analytical solution of the radial displacement in the plastic zone is finally obtained. For validation of this equation, one can examine the radial displacement at the elastic-plastic interface ($r = R_p$), and the same result is obtained as shown by Equation (42).

4. Implementation of Incremental Procedure for the Analytical Solution

Calculation Steps and Analysis Process of the Incremental Method

The calculation steps and analysis process of the incremental method used in this study can be called an explicit calculation program. It can realize the calculation of the analytical solution obtained above and convert it into an executable calculation program, such as using a simple calculation spreadsheet to perform direct calculation, and the results can be shown in Figure 6. Therefore, the procedure proposed in this paper can be called an explicit analysis method (EAM), which can consider the confinement loss as an incremental step, thereby simulating the effect of tunnel advancing excavation, calculating the stress/displacement in each step, and drawing the ground reaction curve, the stress path of the intrados of the tunnel, and the stress/displacement distribution on the cross-section of the tunnel. The results can be seen in Figure 7.

The calculation steps and analysis process of the explicit analysis method (EAM) can be interpreted one by one through the following analysis steps:

(1) Data input stage: This stage is the input action of calculation data, including data such as tunnel excavation radius, unsupported distance, overburden depth, physical and mechanical parameters of surrounding rock, etc.

(2) Calculation stage of confinement loss: To estimate the confinement loss λ_z at a certain distance z from the tunnel working face, it can be calculated by Equation (1).

(3) Calculation stage of the incremental step: Dividing the confinement loss by n segments yields the incremental step, which can be expressed as follows:

$$\Delta\lambda = \frac{1}{n}(1 - \lambda_z) \quad (54)$$

(4) Calculating each step value of λ as

$$\begin{aligned} \lambda_{i+1} &= \lambda_z & i &= 0 \\ \lambda_{i+1} &= \lambda_i + i\Delta\lambda & i &= 1 \sim (n-1) \end{aligned} \tag{55}$$

(5) Attaining the final value $\lambda_n = \lambda_{i+1}$

(6) According to Equation (24), it estimates the confinement loss in the elastic limit situation (λ_e).

(7) Calculation stage of stress/displacement in the elastic zone: If $\lambda_{i+1} < \lambda_e$, it indicates that the stress state is in the elastic zone, and the radial stress, tangential stress, and radial displacement can be calculated according to Equations (11), (12), and (13), respectively.

(8) Calculation stage of stress/displacement in the plastic zone: If $\lambda_{i+1} \geq \lambda_e$, it indicates that the stress state is in the plastic zone, and the plastic radius can be calculated according to Equation (27). Once this value is obtained, the program will automatically substitute Equations (29), (30), and (50) to calculate the radial stress, tangential stress, and radial displacement, respectively.

(9) Data recording stage: In this stage, the stress/displacement are recorded respectively, which can be expressed as the representation of the distribution of stresses/displacements $(\frac{r}{R}, \frac{\sigma_r}{\sigma_v})$, $(\frac{r}{R}, \frac{\sigma_\theta}{\sigma_v})$, and $(\frac{r}{R}, \frac{2Gu_r}{R\sigma_v})$ on the cross-section of the tunnel and $(\frac{2Gu_r}{R\sigma_v}, \frac{\sigma_r}{\sigma_v})$ at the intrados of the tunnel.

(10) Judgment stage 1 of the calculation ends: When $i < n - 1$, repeat steps (4) through (10).

(11) Judgment stage 2 of the calculation ends: When $i = n - 1$, stop performing calculations and record all the obtained data.

(12) Drawing production stage: Drawing the distribution diagram of stress/displacement on the cross-section and at the intrados of the tunnel.

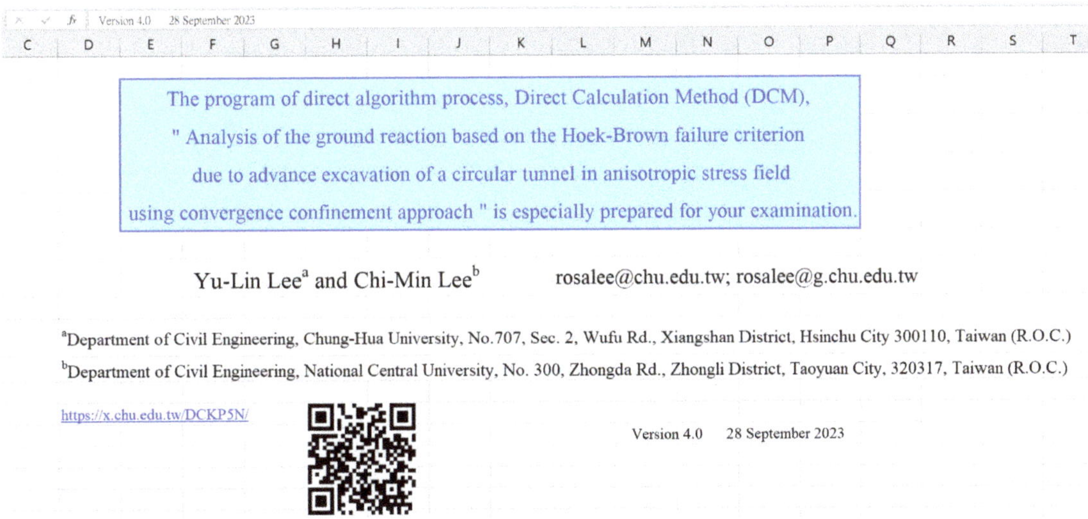

Figure 6. A spreadsheet of calculations presented by the explicit analysis methods (EAM).

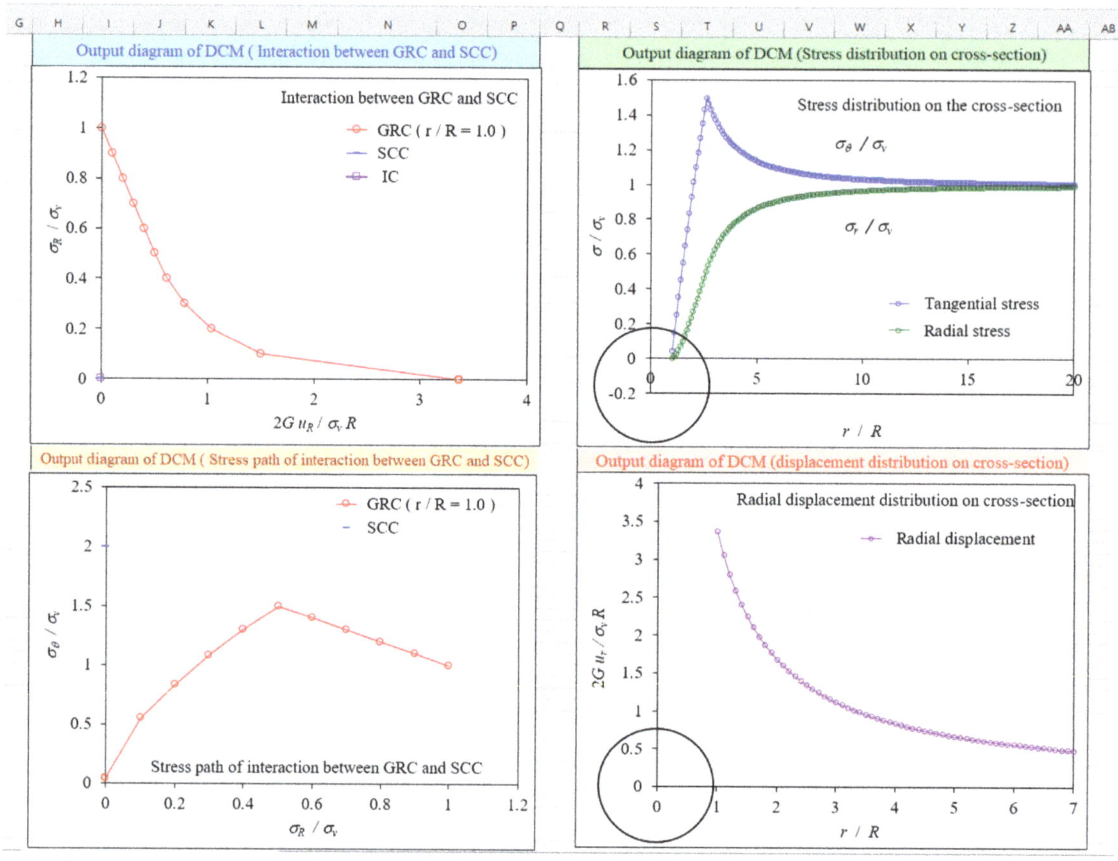

Figure 7. Plotting results presented by the explicit analysis method (EAM).

5. Comparison of Results Obtained between Published Data and This Study

Case studies comparing this study with the EAM calculations include published research such as Sharan (2003) [44] and Rocksupport (2004) [16]. First, to analyze the ground reaction caused by tunnel-advancing excavation under unsupported conditions, the input data required for numerical calculation are shown in Table 1. To investigate the effect of parameters used by the different case studies on the stress/displacement, the dimensionless radial and tangential stresses and the dimensionless radial displacement in the elastic region and the plastic region are compared using the typical cases of hard rock (Case I) and soft rock (Cases II–IV) [16,44]. Table 1 shows the properties of the rocks, and it can be observed that the dilation angle (K_ψ) and the degree of disturbance (D) of the rocks are assumed to be zero in this study. In addition, the values of GSI and UCS of the hard rock used in the calculation are much larger than those of the soft rock.

5.1. Stress/Displacement at the Intrados of the Tunnel

Due to the advancing excavation of the tunnel face, the mechanical behavior of the surrounding rock is altered. This behavior can be explained by the ground reaction curve and stress path at any point on the interior of the tunnel. For the presentation of stress/displacement in the elastic and plastic regions, the radial displacement is expressed in a dimensionless ($2Gu_r/R\sigma_v$) manner, while the radial and tangential stresses are expressed in a normalized vertical stress (σ_v) manner. The obtained results are shown in Figures 8–15.

Table 1. Input data of the computation of EAM by using the published data [16,44].

Reference	Sharan (2003) [44]		Rocksupport (2004) [16]	
Parameter	Case I	Case II	Case III	Case IV
E (MPa)	40,000	5500	3530	2100
ν	0.20	0.25	0.3	0.3
m_i	7.5	7.5	10	12
GIS	100	80	22	17
D	0	0	0	0
σ_{ci} (MPa)	300	30	5	4
K_ψ	0	0	0	0
σ_v (MPa)	108	30	1.62	2.02
R (m)	4.0	5.0	6.0	5.0

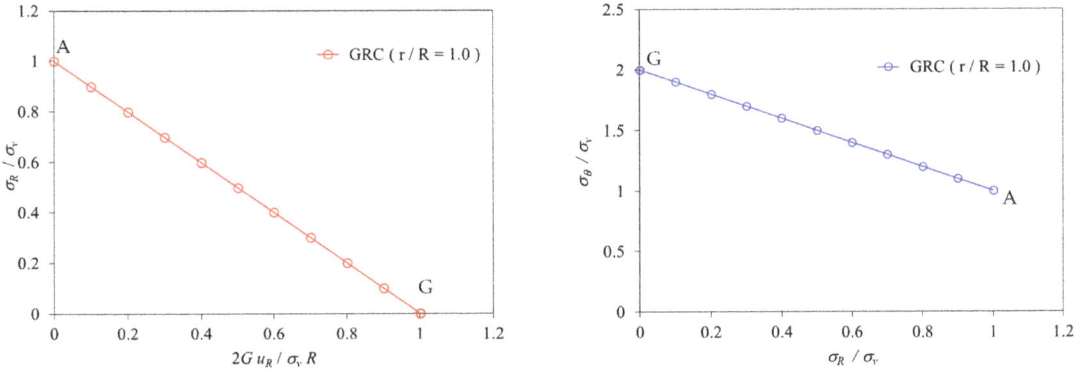

(a) (b)

Figure 8. Results obtained by the EAM using the data of Case I: (**a**) the ground reaction curve and (**b**) the stress path at the intrados of the tunnel (R_p/R = 1.0).

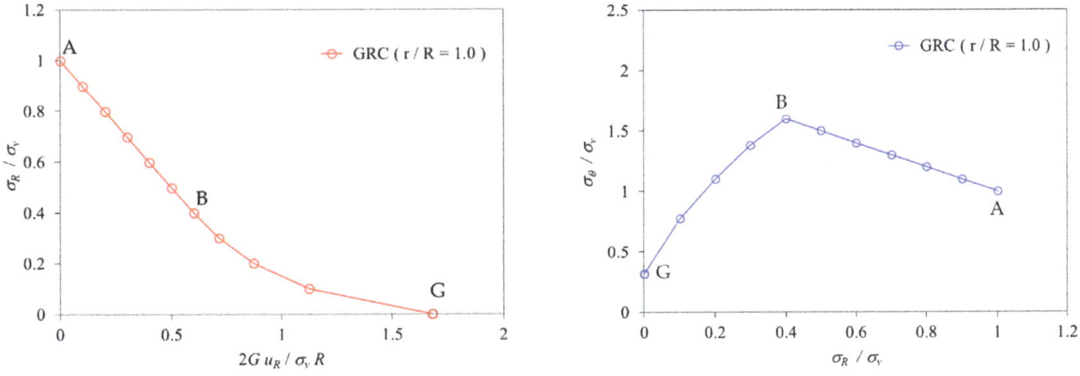

(a) (b)

Figure 9. Results obtained by the EAM using the data from Case II: (**a**) the ground reaction curve; and (**b**) the stress path at the intrados of the tunnel (R_p/R = 1.65).

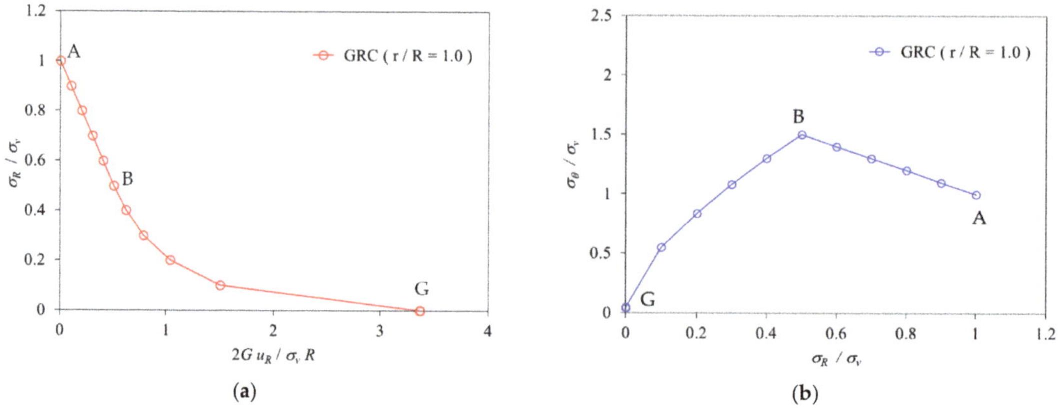

Figure 10. Results obtained by the EAM using the data from Case III: (**a**) the ground reaction curve; and (**b**) the stress path at the intrados of the tunnel (R_p/R = 2.59).

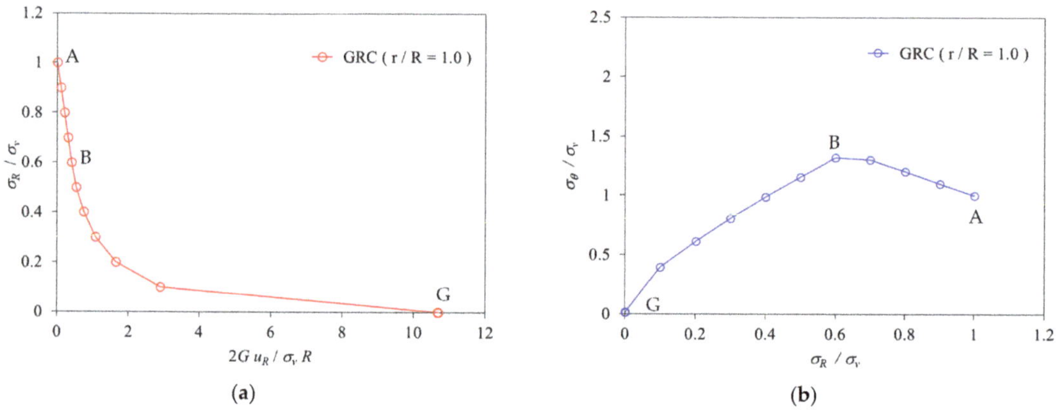

Figure 11. Results obtained by the EAM using the data of Case IV: (**a**) the ground reaction curve and, (**b**) the stress path at the intrados of the tunnel (R_p/R = 5.38).

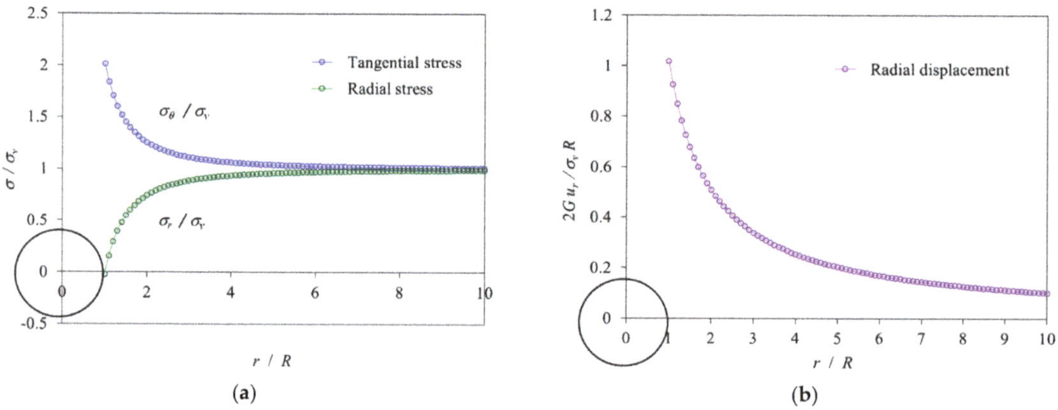

Figure 12. Results obtained by the EAM using the data from Case I: (**a**) stress distribution; and (**b**) radial displacement distribution on the cross-section of the tunnel (R_p/R = 1.0).

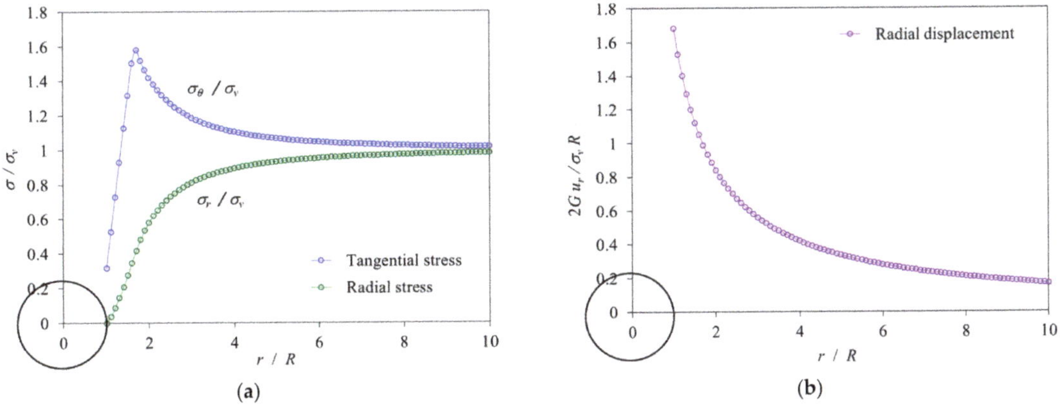

Figure 13. Results obtained by the EAM using the data of Case II: (**a**) stress distribution and (**b**) radial displacement distribution on the cross-section of the tunnel (R_p/R = 1.65).

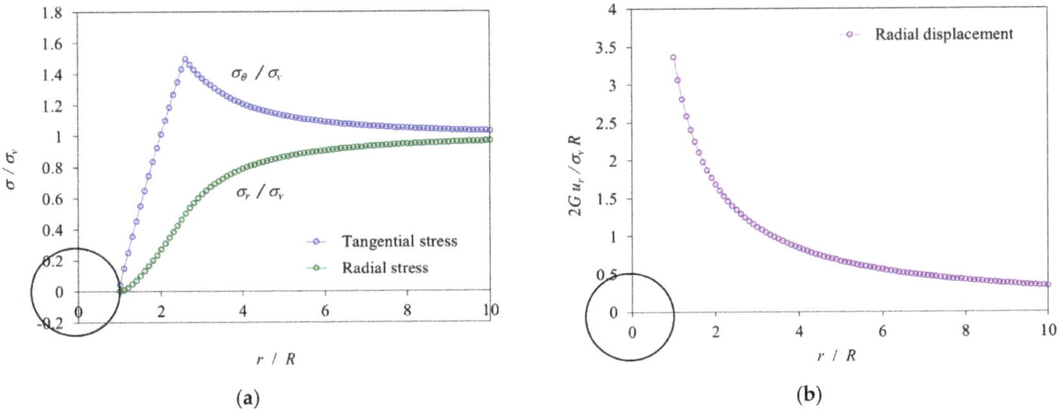

Figure 14. Results obtained by the EAM using the data of Case III: (**a**) stress distribution and (**b**) radial displacement distribution on the cross-section of the tunnel (R_p/R = 2.59).

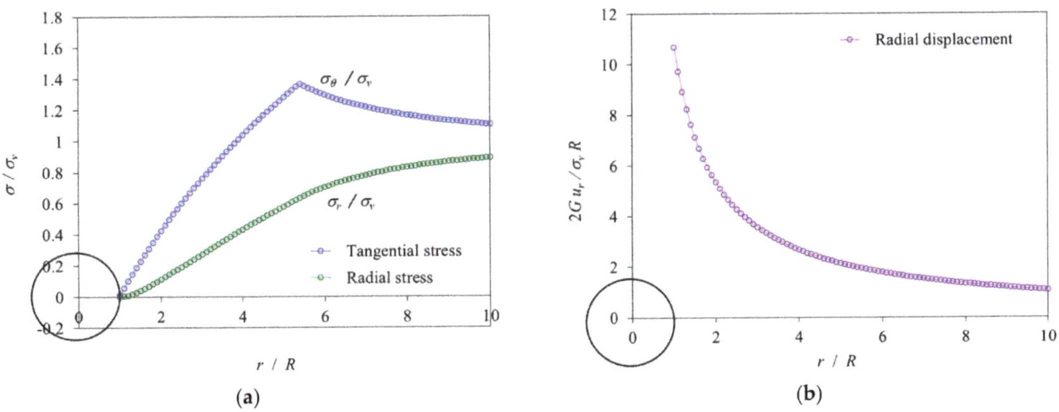

Figure 15. Results obtained by the EAM using the data of Case IV: (**a**) stress distribution and (**b**) radial displacement distribution on the cross-section of the tunnel (R_p/R = 5.38).

As shown in Figure 8, the results obtained by the EAM using the data from Case I [44] indicate that the behavior of the hard rock presents linear elasticity in the ground reaction curve and the stress path. The calculated result is in agreement with the theoretical value that the dimensionless radial displacement is equal to 1.0 (Figure 8a), and the dimensionless radial and tangential stresses are equal to 0 and 2, respectively (Figure 8b).

In addition, the characteristic behavior of the soft rocks (Cases II–IV) is described in Figures 9–11. It indicates that the behavior of the soft rocks presents non-linear elastic-perfectly-plasticity in the ground reaction curve. The interface between the elastic region (line AB) and the plastic region (curve BC) is represented by point B. For the stress path, the Hoek-Brown failure criterion is obviously shown to have characteristic non-linearity by the curve BG in Figures 9b, 10b and 11b.

According to the analysis results between EAM and the listed articles (shown in Table 2), the percentage error of the radial displacement is from 0.5% to 3.51% for the hard and soft rocks. The results obtained by the calculation of EAM in this study show a consistent trend with the data in the references.

Table 2. Comparison of results between EAM and published studies.

Published Studies	Radial Displacement, u_R (mm)	Plastic Zone Radius, R_p (m)	EAM Radial Displacement, u_R (mm) (Error * %)	EAM Plastic Zone Radius, R_p (m) (Error * %)
Case I	12.52	N/A	12.96 (3.51%)	N/A
Case II	56.05	8.12	57.30 (2.23%)	8.25 (1.67%)
Case III	12.0	13.77	12.06 (0.5%)	15.55 (12.93%)
Case IV	65.5	26.30	66.80 (1.98%)	26.9 (2.28%)

* Error (%) = |(published data − EAM)/published data| × 100%.

5.2. Distribution of Stress/Displacement on the Cross-Section of the Tunnel

Under the isotropic stress condition, the distribution of stress/displacement on the cross-section of the tunnel caused by the excavation of the circular tunnel is investigated in this study. According to the stress distribution results of the tunnel, the following five stress states can be used to describe and verify the stress changes caused by the advancing excavation of the tunnel face: (1) When $\lambda = 0$ ($r \to \infty$), it indicates that the stresses are in the initial stress state as shown by the horizontal line on the right side in Figure 12a; (2) When $0 \leq \lambda \leq \lambda_e$ ($R_p \leq r \leq \infty$), it indicates that the stress state is in the elastic region, and at this time the tangential stress and radial stress increase with the increase of the confinement loss, and the two stresses are symmetrically separated up and down along the horizontal axis (r/R); (3) When $\lambda = \lambda_e$ ($r = R_p$), the plastic radius appears, and two stresses are at the elastic-plastic interface. The radial stress begins to change the curvature, and the tangential stress attains the maximum value as shown in Figures 13a, 14a and 15a; (4) When $\lambda_e \leq \lambda \leq 1$ ($R \leq r \leq R_p$), it indicates that the stresses are in the plastic region, and this leads to both the tangential stress and radial stress being decreased steeply; and (5) When $\lambda = 1$ ($r = R$), the radial stress becomes zero and the tangential stress is equal to the coefficient $\sqrt{4sN^2}$ proposed by the Hoek–Brown failure criterion.

According to results obtained by the explicit analysis method (EAM) and the analysis results provided by the listed literature (as shown in Table 2), the percentage error of the plastic zone radius is from 1.67% to 2.28% for the soft rocks. However, the plastic radius obtained in Case III shows an error value of up to 12%, which may occur during the recursive process of the plastic radius solution.

6. Conclusions

Through the nonlinear mechanical behavior (Hoek–Brown model) caused by the advancing excavation of a circular tunnel, this study conducts rigorous theoretical analysis (CCM), derivation of mechanical differential equations, establishment and practice of incremental calculation programs (EAM), as well as a comparison with published literature results. The following conclusions can be drawn: (1) The closed-form analytical solution for the behavior of ground based on the Hoek–Brown nonlinear failure criterion due to the advancing excavation of a circular tunnel in an isotropic stress state is investigated. (2) The method of judging whether the stress state is in the elastic region or the plastic region depends on the calculation of the confinement loss in the elastic limit situation, which is affected by the peak strength parameters of the rock mass and the initial vertical stress. (3) It is found that when the confinement loss increases, the plastic radius also increases, resulting in a gradual decrease in the radial stress and tangential stress while the radial displacement increases. The plastic radius is also affected by factors such as confinement losses at the elastic limit and rock mass peak strength parameters. (4) In particular, this study proposes an incremental procedure of the explicit analysis method (EAM), which takes the confinement loss as an incremental step to simulate the effect of advancing excavation on the tunnel face, calculates the stress and displacement at each step, and plots the ground reaction curves, stress paths at the intrados of the tunnel, and the distributions of stress/displacement on the cross-section of the tunnel. (5) The comparison results between the analytical solution of the explicit program and the published literature show a consistent trend in elastoplastic media. (6) The stress change caused by the advancing excavation of the tunnel face can be explained by the stress gradient, which is the difference between the far-field stress and the near-field stress around the tunnel. The increase in stress can be accounted for as part of the stress gradient using confinement losses. (7) The proposed incremental procedure can deal with the influence of the nonlinear failure criterion of rock mass and can not only be a useful tool for the analysis of circular tunnels in an isotropic stress state but may also be applied to the simulation of the ground behavior of the tunnel under anisotropic stress conditions in the next stage of research. However, this method also has its limitations; namely, the CCM analysis can only be used for the excavation of circular deep tunnels. As for the analysis of non-circular shallow tunnels, it cannot meet the assumptions of this theory.

Author Contributions: Methodology, supervision, writing—original draft, Y.-L.L.; formula derivation, verification, C.-H.M. and C.-M.L.; software programming, computation, C.-M.L. All authors have read and agreed to the published version of the manuscript.

Funding: This research received no external funding.

Data Availability Statement: The data is unavailable due to privacy.

Conflicts of Interest: The authors declare no conflict of interest.

References

1. Panet, M. Calcul du souténement des tunnels à section circulaire par la method convergence-confinement avec un champ de contraintes initiales anisotrope. *Tunn. Et Ouvrages Souterr.* **1986**, *77*, 228–232.
2. Panet, M. *Le Calcul des Tunnels par la Méthode de Convergence-Confinement*; Presses de l'Ecole Nationale des Ponts et Chaussées: Paris, France, 1995.
3. Hoek, E.; Brown, E.T. *Underground Excavations in Rock*; The Institution of Mining and Metallurgy: London, UK, 1980. Available online: http://faculty.tafreshu.ac.ir/file/download/course/1571250904-2underground-excavations-in-rock.pdf (accessed on 1 September 1980).
4. Panet, M. *Recommendations on the Convergence-Confinement Method*; Association Française des Tunnels et de l'Espace Souterrain (AFTES): Paris, France, 2001; pp. 1–11. Available online: https://tunnel.ita-aites.org/media/k2/attachments/public/Convergence-confinement%20AFTES.pdf (accessed on 1 January 2021).
5. Panet, M.; Sulem, J. *Convergence-Confinement Method for Tunnel Design*; Springer: Berlin/Heidelberg, Germany, 2022. Available online: https://link.springer.com/book/10.1007/978-3-030-93193-3 (accessed on 1 January 2022).
6. Lee, Y.-L.; Hsu, W.-K.; Lee, C.-M.; Xin, Y.-X.; Zhou, B.-Y. Direct Calculation Method for the Analysis of Non-linear Behavior of Ground-Support Interaction of a Circular Tunnel Using Convergence Confinement Approach. *Geotech. Geol. Eng.* **2020**, *39*, 973–990. [CrossRef]
7. Lee, Y.-L.; Hsu, W.-K.; Chou, P.-Y.; Hsieh, P.-W.; Ma, C.-H.; Kao, W.-C. Verification and Comparison of Direct Calculation Method for the Analysis of Support–Ground Interaction of a Circular Tunnel Excavation. *Appl. Sci.* **2022**, *12*, 1929. [CrossRef]
8. Oreste, P.P. Analysis of structural interaction in tunnels using the convergence-confinement approach. *Tunnell Undergr. Space Technol.* **2003**, *18*, 347–363. [CrossRef]

9. Oreste, P. The convergence–confinement method: Roles and limits in modern geomechanical tunnel design. *Am. J. Appl. Sci.* **2009**, *6*, 757–771. [CrossRef]
10. Brown, E.T.; Bray, J.W.; Ladanyi, B.; Hoek, E. Ground Response Curves for Rock Tunnels. *J. Geotech. Eng.* **1983**, *109*, 15–39. [CrossRef]
11. Brady, B.; Brown, E. *Rock Mechanics for Underground Mining*; Chapman & Hall: London, UK, 1993.
12. Wang, Y. Ground Response of Circular Tunnel in Poorly Consolidated Rock. *J. Geotech. Eng.* **1996**, *122*, 703–708. [CrossRef]
13. Guan, Z.; Jiang, Y.; Tanabasi, Y. Ground reaction analyses in conventional tunnelling excavation. *Tunn. Undergr. Space Technol.* **2007**, *22*, 230–237. [CrossRef]
14. Alejano, L.; Rodriguez-Dono, A.; Alonso, E.; Manín, G.F. Ground reaction curves for tunnels excavated in different quality rock masses showing several types of post-failure behaviour. *Tunn. Undergr. Space Technol.* **2011**, *24*, 689–705. [CrossRef]
15. Mousivand, M.; Maleki, M.; Nekooei, M.; Mansoori, M.R. Application of Convergence–Confinement Method in Analysis of Shallow Non-circular Tunnels. *Geotech. Geol. Eng.* **2017**, *35*, 1185–1198. [CrossRef]
16. Rocksupport. *Rock Support Interaction and Deformation Analysis for Tunnels in Weak Rock*; Tutorial Manual of Rocscience Inc./Rocscience Inc.: Toronto, ON, USA, 2004; pp. 1–76. Available online: https://www.rocscience.com/downloads/rocsupport/RocSupport%20Tutorial.pdf (accessed on 1 January 2004).
17. Rodríguez, R.; Díaz-Aguado, M.B. Deduction and use of an analytical expression for the characteristic curve of a support based on yielding steel ribs. *Tunn. Undergr. Space Technol.* **2013**, *33*, 159–170. [CrossRef]
18. Cui, L.; Zheng, J.-J.; Zhang, R.-J.; Lai, H.-J. A numerical procedure for the fictitious support pressure in the application of the convergence–confinement method for circular tunnel design. *Int. J. Rock Mech. Min. Sci.* **2015**, *78*, 336–349. [CrossRef]
19. Carranza-Torres, C.; Engen, M. The support characteristic curve for blocked steel sets in the convergence-confinement method of tunnel support design. *Tunn. Undergr. Space Technol.* **2017**, *69*, 233–244. [CrossRef]
20. Oke, J.; Vlachopoulos, N.; Diederichs, M. Improvement to the Convergence-Confinement Method: Inclusion of Support Installation Proximity and Stiffness. *Rock Mech. Rock Eng.* **2018**, *51*, 1495–1519. [CrossRef]
21. Lee, Y.L. Explicit procedure and analytical solution for the ground reaction due to advance excavation of a circular tunnel in an anisotropic stress field. *Geotech. Geol. Eng.* **2018**, *36*, 3281–3309. [CrossRef]
22. De La Fuente, M.; Taherzadeh, R.; Sulem, J.; Nguyen, X.S.; Subrin, D. Applicability of the convergence-confinement method to full-face excavation of circular tunnels with stiff support system. *Rock Mech. Rock Eng.* **2019**, *52*, 2361–2376. [CrossRef]
23. Lee, Y.-L. Explicit analysis for the ground-support interaction of a circular tunnel excavation in anisotropic stress fields. *J. Chin. Inst. Eng.* **2020**, *43*, 13–26. [CrossRef]
24. Bernaud, D.; Rousset, G. The 'New Implicit Method' For Tunnel Analysis. *Int. J. Numer. Anal. Methods Géoméch.* **1996**, *20*, 673–690. [CrossRef]
25. Humbert, P.; Dubouchet, A.; Fezans, G.; Remaud, D. CESAR-LCPC, un progiciel de calcul dédié au génie civil. *Bull. Lab. Ponts Chaussées* **2005**, *256*, 7–37. Available online: https://www.ifsttar.fr/collections/BLPCpdfs/blpc_256-257_7-37.pdf (accessed on 1 July 2005).
26. González-Nicieza, C.; Álvarez-Vigil, A.; Menéndez-Díaz, A.; González-Palacio, C. Influence of the depth and shape of a tunnel in the application of the convergence–confinement method. *Tunn. Undergr. Space Technol.* **2008**, *23*, 25–37. [CrossRef]
27. Vlachopoulos, N.; Diederichs, M.S. Improved Longitudinal Displacement Profiles for Convergence Confinement Analysis of Deep Tunnels. *Rock Mech. Rock Eng.* **2009**, *42*, 131–146. [CrossRef]
28. Mousivand, M.; Maleki, M. Constitutive Models and Determining Methods Effects on Application of Convergence–Confinement Method in Underground Excavation. *Geotech. Geol. Eng.* **2017**, *36*, 1707–1722. [CrossRef]
29. Zhao, K.; Bonini, M.; Debernardi, D.; Janutolo, M.; Barla, G.; Chen, G. Computational modelling of the mechanised excavation of deep tunnels in weak rock. *Comput. Geotech.* **2015**, *66*, 158–171. [CrossRef]
30. Lee, Y.L. Establishment of the confinement loss curve using the tunnel convergence data. *J. Chin. Inst. Eng.* **2020**, *43*, 613–627. [CrossRef]
31. Nikadat, N.; Marji, M.F. Analysis of stress distribution around tunnels by hybridized FSM and DDM considering the influences of joints parameters. *Géoméch. Eng.* **2016**, *11*, 269–288. [CrossRef]
32. Nikadat, N.; Fatehi, M.; Abdollahipour, A. Numerical modelling of stress analysis around rectangular tunnels with large discontinuities (fault) by a hybridized indirect BEM. *J. Central South Univ.* **2015**, *22*, 4291–4299. [CrossRef]
33. Lazemi, H.A.; Marji, M.F.; Bafghi, A.R.Y.; Goshtasbi, K. Rock Failure Analysis of the Broken Zone Around a Circular Opening. *Arch. Min. Sci.* **2013**, *58*, 165–188. [CrossRef]
34. Hoek, E.; Brown, E.T. Empirical Strength Criterion for Rock Masses. *J. Geotech. Eng. Div.* **1980**, *106*, 1013–1035. [CrossRef]
35. Hoek, E.; Brown, E.T. Practical estimates or rock mass strength. *Int. J. Rock Mech. Min. Sci. & Geomech. Abstr.* **1997**, *34*, 1165–1186. [CrossRef]
36. Hoek, E.; Carranza-Torres, C.; Corkum, B. Hoek–Brown Failure Criterion—2002 Edition. *Proc. NARMS-Tac* **2020**, *1*, 267–273. Available online: https://static.rocscience.cloud/assets/verification-and-theory/RSData/Hoek-Brown-Failure-Criterion-2002-Edition.pdf (accessed on 1 August 2002).
37. Carranza-Torres, C.; Fairhurst, C. The elasto-plastic response of underground excavations in rock masses that satisfy the Hoek–Brown failure criterion. *Int. J. Rock Mech. Min. Sci.* **1999**, *36*, 777–809. [CrossRef]

38. Carranza-Torres, C.; Fairhurst, C. Application of the Convergence-Confinement method of tunnel design to rock masses that satisfy the Hoek-Brown failure criterion. *Tunn. Undergr. Space Technol.* **2000**, *15*, 187–213. [CrossRef]
39. Carranza-Torres, C. Elasto-plastic solution of tunnel problems using the generalized form of the hoek-brown failure criterion. *Int. J. Rock Mech. Min. Sci.* **2004**, *41*, 480–491. [CrossRef]
40. Sharan, S. Exact and approximate solutions for displacements around circular openings in elastic–brittle–plastic Hoek–Brown rock. *Int. J. Rock Mech. Min. Sci.* **2005**, *42*, 542–549. [CrossRef]
41. Park, K.-H.; Kim, Y.-J. Analytical solution for a circular opening in an elastic–brittle–plastic rock. *Int. J. Rock Mech. Min. Sci.* **2005**, *43*, 616–622. [CrossRef]
42. Serrano, A.; Olalla, C.; Reig, I. Convergence of circular tunnels in elastoplastic rock masses with non-linear failure criteria and non-associated flow laws. *Int. J. Rock Mech. Min. Sci.* **2011**, *48*, 878–887. [CrossRef]
43. Shen, B.; Barton, N. The disturbed zone around tunnels in jointed rock Masses. *Int. J. Rock Mech. Min. Sci.* **1997**, *34*, 117–125. [CrossRef]
44. Sharan, S. Elastic–brittle–plastic analysis of circular openings in Hoek–Brown media. *Int. J. Rock Mech. Min. Sci.* **2003**, *40*, 817–824. [CrossRef]

Disclaimer/Publisher's Note: The statements, opinions and data contained in all publications are solely those of the individual author(s) and contributor(s) and not of MDPI and/or the editor(s). MDPI and/or the editor(s) disclaim responsibility for any injury to people or property resulting from any ideas, methods, instructions or products referred to in the content.

mathematics MDPI

Article

A Hybrid Large Eddy Simulation Algorithm Based on the Implicit Domain Decomposition

Amir E. Fard and Sergey Utyuzhnikov *

School of Engineering, University of Manchester, Manchester M13 9PL, UK; amir.fard@manchester.ac.uk
* Correspondence: s.utyuzhnikov@manchester.ac.uk

Abstract: The resolution of small near-wall eddies encountered in high-Reynolds number flows using large eddy simulation (LES) requires very fine meshes that may be computationally prohibitive. As a result, the use of wall-modeled LES as an alternative is becoming more popular. In this paper, the near-wall domain decomposition (NDD) approach that was originally developed for Reynolds-averaged Navier–Stokes simulations (RANSs) is extended to the hybrid RANS/LES zonal decomposition. The algorithm is implemented in two stages. First, the solution is computed everywhere with LES on a coarse grid using a new non-local slip boundary condition for the instantaneous velocity at the wall. The solution is then recomputed in the near-wall region with RANS. The slip boundary conditions used in the first stage guarantee that the composite solution is smooth at the inner/outer region interface. Another advantage of the model is that the turbulent viscosity in the inner region is computed based on the corresponding RANS velocity. This shows improvement over those hybrid models that have only one velocity field in the whole domain obtained from LES. The model is realized in the open source code OpenFOAM with different approximations of turbulent viscosity and is applied to the planar channel flow at frictional Reynolds numbers of $\mathrm{Re}_\tau = 950$, 2000, and 4200. Mean streamwise velocity and Reynolds stress intensities are predicted reasonably well in comparison to the solutions obtained with unresolved LES and available DNS benchmarks. No additional forcing at the interface is required, while the log–layer mismatch is essentially reduced in all cases.

Keywords: hybrid RANS/LES; turbulence; channel flow; log–layer mismatch; implicit near-wall domain decomposition

MSC: 76F65

Citation: E. Fard, A.; Utyuzhnikov, S. A Hybrid Large Eddy Simulation Algorithm Based on the Implicit Domain Decomposition. *Mathematics* **2023**, *11*, 4340. https://doi.org/10.3390/math11204340

Academic Editors: Shujin Laima, Yong Cao, Xiaowei Jin and Hehe Ren

Received: 24 August 2023
Revised: 16 October 2023
Accepted: 17 October 2023
Published: 19 October 2023

Copyright: © 2023 by the authors. Licensee MDPI, Basel, Switzerland. This article is an open access article distributed under the terms and conditions of the Creative Commons Attribution (CC BY) license (https://creativecommons.org/licenses/by/4.0/).

1. Introduction

Numerical simulation of turbulent flows has been widely used over recent decades thanks to the advancement of computational power and resources. The direct numerical simulation (DNS) for large-Reynolds-number flows is still limited to simple geometries due to the very large number of grid points required to capture all eddies up to the Kolmogorov scale [1]. In DNS, the grid size required to resolve all structures varies as $N \approx O(\mathrm{Re}^{2.64})$ [2]. In the large eddy simulation (LES) of free-streaming flows, the required grid density increases only modestly with the growth of Re as $N \approx O(\mathrm{Re}^{0.4})$ [3]. Therefore, LES has evolved as an advanced engineering tool in the analysis of turbulent flows.

The so-called resolved LES, i.e., direct resolution of all energetic scales, is a powerful tool for free shear flows such as jets, mixing layers, and wakes. However, its application to wall-bounded flows is still limited due to the presence of fine eddies encountered in the near-wall area, which necessitates the use of fine meshes for LES [4]. In close proximity to walls, the length scale of dynamically important motions decreases, and energetic eddies are not large any more [5]. It is shown in [2] that the grid resolution requirement for a resolved LES in the boundary layer flows is proportional to $\mathrm{Re}^{1.85}$, which is almost as costly as DNS. For a moderate frictional Reynolds number of $Re_\tau = 2000$, Temmerman et al. [6] showed that the unresolved LES produces a large discrepancy of around 40% from the DNS benchmark and that only resolved LES with a grid more than an order of magnitude finer in each direction can produce acceptable results. Such fine meshes are still a significant computational burden for real engineering applications.

In recent years, the use of wall-modelled LES (WMLES) [7] instead of resolved LES has received more attention. WMLES employs near-wall approximations that permit a much coarser resolution to be used close to the walls without a significant loss of accuracy. The idea is to model the near-wall turbulent structures rather than to resolve them. In WMLES, two approaches are widely used: wall-stress and RANS/LES models. It should be noted that the classification and names of the methods in the literature may vary.

The wall-stress models (WSMs) can be classified as equilibrium or non-equilibrium models [8]. The equilibrium WSM approximates the wall-shear stress (WSS) based on the logarithmic law or power law and applies this approximation in the form of a Neumann velocity boundary condition to the wall. The use of equilibrium WSMs dates back to the papers by Deardorff [9] and Schumann [10]. This approximation disregards convection and pressure-gradient terms in the boundary layer and is therefore primarily valid for simple configurations but is inaccurate with separated flows or recirculating zones. The deficiency of wall laws and the importance of streamwise grid resolution in predicting separation zones are already addressed by Temmerman et al. [11].

In the two-layer WSM (non-equilibrium), an auxiliary fine one-dimensional (1D) grid is embedded between an LES grid point and the wall. Then, a simplified set of the Reynolds-averaged Navier–Stokes equations (RANS) based on the thin boundary layer equations (TBLEs) is solved on the embedded mesh [12–15]. The outer-layer LES provides the velocity boundary condition for the inner-layer RANS model. In return, the inner-layer wall-model predicts the wall shear stress required by the LES at the wall. Non-equilibrium effects, such as unsteady advection and pressure gradient, can be accounted for using the TBLE model. Nonetheless, the coupling between the LES and RANS models is rather weak and only occurs through the boundary conditions at the wall ($y = 0$) and the interface boundary ($y = y_{int}$). Cabot and Moin [14] demonstrated the importance of the pressure gradient and advection terms in the simulation of a backward-facing step. Several modifications have been made to the model over the course of recent years (see, e.g., [8,16,17]).

In the other approach, often referred to as hybrid RANS/LES models, RANS and LES solutions are usually (although not always) blended [7,18,19]. For this purpose, a blending function is introduced [20] for the modeled turbulent viscosity [7] or the length scale as in detached eddy simulations (DESs) [21–23]. DES has shown very good efficacy for separated flows but not for attached flows [22]. In addition, blending RANS and LES models always has an intermediate region where the blended model is not justified.

In the user-defined-interface hybrid methods, the inner region is covered by RANS and separated from the LES area by an interface. The influence of near-wall turbulent structures is modeled by RANS. In this way, the near-wall RANS region can be superimposed onto the LES domain [6,24]. Then, the boundary conditions (BCs) for RANS are obtained from LES. Alternatively, switching from LES to RANS can be undertaken by selecting the turbulent viscosity ν_T and kinetic energy k from either LES or RANS models [25,26]. A detailed description of BCs at the RANS/LES interface is provided in [27]. In all cases, attention is needed to maintain turbulence during the transition between RANS and LES.

Despite recent advancements in hybrid RANS/LES methods, there are still issues that must be resolved. This is a result of the difficulties associated with managing interface boundary conditions (IBCs). LES equations predict fluctuations, whereas RANS equations do not. The addition of artificial fluctuations introduces its own uncertainties [18]. The log–layer mismatch (LLM) is another significant issue in hybrid RANS/LES simulations. This is evident even in planar channel flow simulations [20,28,29] and leads to overestimation or underestimation of the skin friction. The formation of an artificial buffer layer and consequently unrealistic physical structures can contaminate the LES area.

To avoid the LLM, Keating and Piomelli [30] recommend stochastic forcing at the interface area. This can expedite the formation of resolved eddies and lead to improved outcomes. Hamba [20] introduces additional filtering. Zhong and Tucker [31] use the $k - l$ method to approximate the eddy viscosity. Davidson and Peng [25] utilize the $k - \omega$ for their eddy viscosity model in the RANS region. Davidson and Dahlström [32] increase the resolved shear stress by introducing fluctuations at the interface. Temmerman et al. [6] determine the eddy viscosity in the RANS region using the $k - l$ or $k - \omega$ method; the eddy viscosity of the RANS interface is matched with the LES subgrid viscosity. Davidson and Billson [26] add fluctuations at the interface to increase the resolved shear stress. Larsson et al. [5] use additional forcing to induce resolved motions in the LES region. They discuss that matching the turbulent viscosity at the interface has a minimal effect on the final solution.

However, these solutions require additional data from a preliminary benchmark solution or contain user-defined parameters (such as the forcing amplitude) to increase resolved turbulent fluctuations at the interface. The model accuracy varies considerably based on the values of these free parameters, and robust selection criteria for the forcing-method parameters are unavailable, to the best of our knowledge. Consequently, LLM still occurs for the majority of channel flow simulations when hybrid RANS/LES models are used. This illustrates the importance of accurate enough modeling the inner region and the connection between the inner and outer regions. According to Piomelli [7], the RANS/LES methods are least accurate when applied to attached and thin shear layers. They are seemingly better suited for separated flows over curved surfaces and with adverse pressure gradients.

Even with a near-wall model, the grid resolution in the outer LES region should be good enough. Kawai and Larsson [33] highlight the importance of grid independence studies in WSMs or hybrid models with an auxiliary RANS model. LES must be well-resolved at the interface point to provide accurate enough information to the RANS model. They also show that the auxiliary RANS model should not necessarily be located between the first off-wall grid point and the wall because the LES model is under-resolved in the near-wall region and is therefore contaminated by truncation and subgrid-scale (SGS) model errors [34]. The effect of decreasing the interface boundary height on reducing accuracy also occurs in [28]. Keating and Piomelli [30] obtain better results by setting the interface far enough after the buffer region. This helps them generate the RANS logarithmic layer before the start of the LES region.

The near-wall domain decomposition (NDD) was first developed for high-Reynolds RANS [35–37]. The original approach to NDD presumes the computation domain to be split into the inner and outer regions. In the inner region, a simplified locally one-dimensional TBLE model with a prescribed turbulent viscosity can be used [38]. For the outer region, the effect of the inner region is replaced by nonlocal IBCs, which are obtained by the transfer of the original BCs from the wall to the interface boundary [37]. As demonstrated in [39], the NDD can be realized with the full set of RANS equations, although this affects the rate of convergence. A principally new approach called the implicit NDD is proposed in [40]. In this case, the problem can be solved on a relatively coarse grid in the entire region with specially derived computational slip BCs at the wall. Then, the solution is recomputed in the inner region with the use of the TBLE model. The derived slip BCs at the wall guarantee that the composite solution is smooth up to the first derivative. A significant advantage of this approach is that it does not require any explicit split of the computational domain into two sub-domains.

In the current paper, the implicit NDD (INDD) [40] is extended to the RANS/LES zonal decomposition. As a result, in the first (predictor) stage, only LES is used with the slip BCs at the wall. Then, in the second (corrector) stage, the solution in the inner region is recomputed. In this way, the RANS region is embedded onto the LES domain. The computing time needed for the RANS solution is almost negligible since a one-dimensional

(TBLE) model is considered in the inner region. In this work, in contrast to the original NDD, the turbulent viscosity is determined from the $k-l$ model rather than prescribed.

The remainder of this paper is structured as follows. Section 2 describes the model used in the inner region, including the slip BCs. Then, in Section 3, the INDD algorithm is provided. In turn, the configuration and characteristics of the channel flow test case are described in Section 4. The obtained results are presented there and compared with other approaches, including DNS, unresolved LES, and conventional hybrid methods. Finally, conclusions are drawn, and recommendations and future prospects are discussed in Section 5.

2. Near-Wall Model

2.1. Slip Boundary Conditions

In the implicit NDD, the solution is initially obtained on a relatively coarse mesh using LES and slip BCs at the wall. Then, a TBLE is solved in the inner region on a one-dimensional mesh to obtain the velocity with the no-slip BC at the wall and the velocity taken from the LES at the opposite end. In this way, the grid used for RANS is independent from the grid used for LES. At the end, the complete solution consists of the RANS solution in the inner region and the LES solution beyond the interface (see Figure 1). The red dashed line represents the preliminary velocity profile in the inner region resulting from the slip boundary condition. The slip BCs for LES guarantee that the composite time-averaged solution is smooth at the interface. The same procedure is applied to both tangential components of the velocity.

Let us consider a one-dimensional RANS region embedded into the LES mesh between $y=0$ and $y=y^*$ and follow the TBLE format of the boundary-layer equation:

$$\frac{\partial}{\partial y}\left(\mu\frac{\partial u}{\partial y}\right)=R_u(y), \tag{1}$$

where u is the streamwise (wall-parallel) velocity, $\mu(y)$ is the total viscosity as the sum of the laminar (μ_l) and turbulent (μ_T) viscosities, and $R_u(y)$ includes non-equilibrium terms such as the pressure gradient and convective terms. As shown in [40], for a small enough y^* the convective terms can be neglected with low effect on the accuracy. Thus, in the current study, R_u corresponds to the inverse pressure gradient along the wall taken at y^*.

For Equation (1), the Dirichlet BCs are set:

$$\begin{cases} u=0 & \text{at } y=0, \\ u=u^* & \text{at } y=y^*. \end{cases}$$

According to [35–37], the BC can be exactly transferred from the wall $y=0$ to the interface boundary $y=y^*$:

$$u(y^*)=f_1\left.\frac{du}{dy}\right|_{y^*}-\tilde{f}_2, \tag{2}$$

where

$$f_1=\int_0^{y^*}\frac{\mu(y^*)}{\mu(y)}dy,\quad \tilde{f}_2=\int_0^{y^*}\frac{1}{\mu(y)}\left(\int_y^{y^*}R_u d\xi\right)dy. \tag{3}$$

It is worth noting that (2) cannot be obtained by double-integrating the governing Equation (1) from the wall since the derivative of the solution at the wall is unknown.

For the outer region, Equation (2) is fully equivalent to the governing Equation (1) and the no-slip BC at the wall [36]. To simplify the decomposition algorithm, at the implicit NDD [40] it is proposed to transfer the IBC (2) back to the wall with μ and R_u taken at y^*. This leads to the computational slip BC at the wall [40]:

$$u(0)=f_{w1}\left.\frac{du}{dy}\right|_{y=0}+f_{w2}, \tag{4}$$

with

$$f_{w1} = f_1 - y^*, \quad \text{and} \quad f_{w2} = \tilde{f}_2 + \frac{y^* R_u^*}{\mu^*}\left(f_1 - \frac{y^*}{2}\right), \tag{5}$$

where symbol $*$ corresponds to the values taken at y^*.

The aim of the slip BC (4) is two-fold. It allows the LES solution to be formally obtained up to the wall on a relatively coarse grid. In addition, it guarantees that the time-averaged composite RANS/LES solution is smooth up to the first derivative [40]. The solution obtained in the preliminary (LES) stage is schematically shown in the inner region by the red curve in Figure 1.

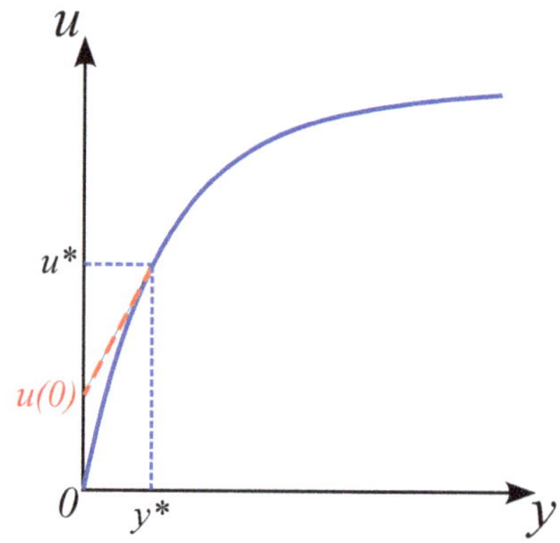

Figure 1. Sketch of the implicit NDD.

As soon as the LES solution with the slip BC has been obtained, the RANS solution in the inner region can be updated. To update the shear stress (τ_w), Equation (1) is integrated twice using the velocity at y^* (already known from LES) which leads to

$$\tau_w = \frac{u(y^*) - \int_0^{y^*} \frac{\int_0^y R_u d\xi}{\mu} dy}{\int_0^{y^*} \frac{dy}{\mu}}. \tag{6}$$

It is to be noted here that $u(y^*)$ corresponds to an instantaneous velocity from LES. Next, the RANS velocity in the entire inner region is updated from the exact solution of the governing Equation (1):

$$u(y_i) = \tau_w \int_0^{y_i} \frac{dy}{\mu} + \int_0^{y_i} \frac{\int_0^y R_u d\xi}{\mu} dy. \tag{7}$$

2.2. Turbulent Viscosity Estimation

In the aforementioned equations, the turbulent viscosity must be evaluated. It can be estimated from algebraic correlations or from k-based methods. In this work, we examine three approaches, namely the mixing length model, the $k-\omega$ method, and the $k-l$ method by Wolfshtein [41,42]. In further consideration, by default, we imply the Cartesian coordinate system and Einstein notation for repeated indices, which are supposed to vary from 1 to 3.

Model 1: The mixing length model by Cabot [43] including a damping function is used to estimate the turbulent viscosity:

$$\nu_T = \kappa y u_\tau D^2, \quad D = 1 - \exp(-y u_\tau / \nu A^+), \tag{8}$$

where $\kappa = 0.41$, $A^+ = 19$, $u_\tau = \sqrt{|\tau_w|/\rho}$, and $\nu_T = \mu_T/\rho$.

Model 2: We use the two-equation $k-\omega$ model by Wilcox [44]. The k equation in this model is given by

$$\frac{\partial k}{\partial t}+\frac{\partial u_j k}{\partial x_j}=\frac{\partial}{\partial x_j}\left[(\nu_l+\sigma_k\nu_T)\left(\frac{\partial k}{\partial x_j}\right)\right]+P_k-\beta^* k\omega, \tag{9}$$

where $\sigma_k=1/2$ is the diffusion Prandtl number, $\beta^*=0.09$, and u_j is the RANS velocity, while P_k is the turbulence production term that reads

$$P_k=\tau_{ij}^{turb}\frac{\partial u_i}{\partial x_j}. \tag{10}$$

Here, τ_{ij}^{turb} corresponds to the Reynolds stress tensor:

$$\tau_{ij}^{turb}=\frac{\nu_T}{2}\left(\frac{\partial u_i}{\partial x_j}+\frac{\partial u_i}{\partial x_j}\right),\quad (i,j=1,2,3).$$

The transport equation for ω reads

$$\frac{\partial \omega}{\partial t}+\frac{\partial u_j\omega}{\partial x_j}=\frac{\partial}{\partial x_j}\left[(\nu_l+\sigma_\omega\nu_T)\frac{\partial \omega}{\partial x_j}\right]+P_\omega-\beta\omega^2. \tag{11}$$

Here, $\beta=3/40$, $\sigma_\omega=1/2$, $\epsilon=\beta^*\omega k$ and the production term P_ω reads

$$P_\omega=\alpha\frac{\omega}{k}\tau_{ij}^{turb}\frac{\partial u_i}{\partial x_j}, \tag{12}$$

where $\alpha=5/9$. Turbulent viscosity is then evaluated as

$$\nu_T=\frac{k}{\omega}. \tag{13}$$

As discussed below, k and ω equations are solved in the approximation of TBLE.

Model 3: We also adapt the $k-l$ method [45] based on the transport of turbulent kinetic energy. In this case, we have a slightly different form of the k equation:

$$\frac{\partial k}{\partial t}+\frac{\partial u_j k}{\partial x_j}=\frac{\partial}{\partial x_j}\left[\left(\nu_l+\frac{\nu_T}{\sigma_k}\right)\frac{\partial k}{\partial x_j}\right]+P_k-\epsilon. \tag{14}$$

Here, $\sigma_k=1$. The boundary value for k at the interface (y^*) is equal to $k^*=k^{res}+k^{sgs}$, where k^{res} is the time-averaged resolved and dominant part of the turbulent kinetic energy in LES, and k^{sgs} is its sub-grid scale part; $k^{res}=0.5\overline{u_i'u_i'}$, where u_i' $(i=1,2,3)$ are turbulent pulsations.

Under the TBLE assumption, Equation (14) can be rewritten in the 1D form along the wall normal direction (y) as

$$\frac{\partial}{\partial y}\left[\left(\nu_l+\frac{\nu_T}{\sigma_k}\right)\frac{\partial k}{\partial y}\right]+\nu_T\left(\frac{\partial u}{\partial y}\right)^2-\epsilon=0. \tag{15}$$

This is a reasonable approximation for a low enough y. As noted in [24], low-Re RANS models often yield acceptable solutions when the normal to the wall direction is predominant. Therefore, high aspect ratio cells (order of 100–1000) can be used in the wall vicinity. This gives a superiority over resolved LESs, where fine streamwise meshes are required. It is worth noting that the embedded mesh for any fixed coordinate x along the wall is entirely local. In the aforementioned $k-l$ equation, we have

$$\epsilon=C_\epsilon k^{3/2}/l_\epsilon, \tag{16}$$

and turbulent viscosity is evaluated through

$$\nu_T = C_\mu l_\mu k^{1/2}, \tag{17}$$

where $C_\epsilon = 1$ and $C_\mu = 0.09$. The length scales in this RANS model are defined as

$$l_\epsilon = 2.4y(1 - \exp(-0.263y^\times)), \tag{18}$$

$$l_\mu = 2.4y(1 - \exp(-0.016y^\times)), \tag{19}$$

where $y^\times = y\rho k^{1/2}/\mu$.

It is clear that the $k - l$ method is computationally less expensive than the $k - \omega$ model. We use the $k - l$ model in all cases, unless otherwise stated.

3. Implicit Near-Wall Domain Decomposition

3.1. Algorithm

To summarize, the implicit NDD algorithm for the zonal RANS/LES model is implemented as follows:

1. Initialize the coarse grid for LES.
2. Initialize the interface boundary y^* and a sub-grid for RANS.
3. Initialize the flow fields for both the unresolved LES grid and RANS sub-grid.
4. Compute the turbulent viscosity.
5. Compute f_1 and $\tilde{f}_2$ (Equation (3)) based on the chosen turbulent viscosity model of Section 2.2.
6. Compute the coefficients f_{w1} and f_{w2} (Equation (5)) to impose the slip boundary condition at the wall.
7. Solve the LES governing equations on the coarse grid with the slip boundary condition (Equation (4)).
8. Transfer the LES streamwise velocity and turbulent kinetic energy at y^* (i.e., u^* and k^*_{tot}) to the embedded RANS model.
9. Compute the wall shear stress in the inner region using u^* value (Equation (6)).
10. Compute the RANS velocity solution in the inner region (Equation (7)) with the updated τ_w.
11. Compute the turbulent kinetic energy (Equation (14)), if needed.
12. Repeat the procedure from step 4.

3.2. Discussion

The INDD effectively combines the zonal and wall-stress approaches and has some advantages over conventional methods, as discussed below.

(I) The solution at the interface is smooth because the slip boundary condition is transferred to the wall. In addition, the composite time-averaged solution is also smooth. This follows from the design of the computational slip BCs [40].

(II) Since we use RANS equations in the inner region, we avoid the issues regarding the selection of a proper k^* value as a BC for the RANS region (see, e.g., [6]). If u^{LES} is used in the inner region for the evaluation of k from Equation (14), the contribution of resolved turbulent kinetic energy (k_{res}) into the inner region is already taken into account; therefore, k^* should only include the modeled part, i.e., k_{sgs}. However, Temmerman et al. [6] argued that the issue is not that simple and other assumptions are needed regarding the correct k^* value. In the current work, we take $k^* = k_{sgs} + k_{res}$ at the boundary of the RANS region because u^{RANS} is used in the inner region to predict k.

(III) In the current approach, since both the RANS velocity and turbulent kinetic energy are obtained on a fine 1D mesh in the inner region, the grid independence of the RANS solution can be easily ensured. Moreover, using u from the RANS solution in the inner region can help prevent the formation of an "artificial buffer layer", that is, a transition zone between modeled and resolved turbulence. Larsson et al. [5] discussed that the artificial buffer layer is an effect of the merging of two different modeling regions. We additionally show that the current algorithm does not need any enforcement of external force or synthetic turbulence at the interface.

(IV) In comparison to WSMs, according to Larsson et al. [8], while LESs can impart flow structures onto the wall-model, it is problematic for the flow structures in the wall-model to penetrate into the LES region. Therefore, in WSMs, the RANS/LES coupling is rather weak. In the INDD, this coupling is enhanced via the RANS solution in the entire inner region and non-local IBCs.

(V) One shortcoming of the current approach against WSMs is that it is computationally more expensive.

4. Test Cases

4.1. Setup

Simulations are carried out with the open source and finite-volume-based CFD software OpenFOAM distributed by the OpenFOAM Foundation [46]. Planar channel flow at three frictional Reynolds numbers, namely $\mathrm{Re}_\tau = 950$, 2000, and 4200, is considered, where the friction Reynolds number is defined as

$$\mathrm{Re}_\tau = \frac{u_\tau h}{\nu}. \tag{20}$$

Here, h is the half channel height, ν is the fluid kinematic viscosity, and $u_\tau = \sqrt{|\tau_w|/\rho}$ is the friction velocity.

Domain size, grid resolution, and the interface location y^* are listed in Table 1, where x, y, and z represent the streamwise, wall-normal, and spanwise directions, respectively. The streamwise and spanwise directions have periodic boundary conditions. At the wall, $y = 0$, we originally set the no-flux and no-slip BCs. The channel half-height is $h = 1$ m. The channel flow is driven by a driving force determined from the DNS-computed bulk velocity.

Table 1. Characteristics of studied test cases.

Case	Re_τ	$L_x \times L_y \times L_z$	Resolution	Δx^+	Δy^+	Δz^+	$\Delta y_{j+1}/\Delta y_j$	y^*/h	y^{*+}
C950	950	$2\pi h \times 2h \times \pi h$	$40 \times 64 \times 36$	148	$1.57 \to 126$	83	1.15	0.063	60
C2000	2000	$2\pi h \times 2h \times \pi h$	$40 \times 72 \times 36$	312	$1.78 \to 267$	174	1.15	0.065	129
C4200	4200	$3\pi h \times 2h \times \pi h$	$60 \times 84 \times 42$	659	$1.82 \to 547$	314	1.15	0.0476	200

The mesh is uniform in the x and z directions, and refined in the y direction with a specified stretch factor. In the inner region, the embedded mesh usually consists of 20−30 nodes.

The results of different approaches, including unresolved LES, implicit NDD, and benchmark DNS are compared. The first two models are implemented in the current study and compared to the available benchmark DNS data. In each test case, all studied models (except for DNS) have identical time and space resolutions. In addition, the effects of three turbulent viscosity models of Section 2.2 are compared with each other.

The WALE model [47] is used for the subgrid-scale stress modeling in the LES. The model is originally implemented in OpenFOAM. Each simulation starts with a fully developed turbulent channel flow and allows for enough running time before capturing the output values.

The interface boundary in the simulations is situated at $0.05h \lesssim y^* \lesssim 0.1h$ as recommended in [30], where h is the channel half-height.

4.2. Simulation Results

In this section, the simulation results for the mean streamwise velocity and Reynolds normal stress intensities obtained by INDD are compared to DNS and unresolved LES (i.e., LES computed on a relatively coarse grid without any special near-wall modeling). In the inner region, the $k - l$ eddy viscosity model is used.

The normalised mean streamwise velocity $u^+ = \overline{u}/u_\tau$ for $\mathrm{Re}_\tau = 950$ is plotted in Figure 2 against the normalised distance from the wall $y^+ = yu_\tau/\nu$ and compared to the DNS data from Hoyas and Jiménez [48]. It is evident that the unresolved LES simulation significantly overestimates the mean streamwise velocity. The unresolved LES can only predict well enough the velocity profile near the viscous sub-layer ($y^+ < 10$), whereas in the logarithmic region the velocity exhibits a strong upward lift. This situation is substantially improved by using the INDD, as the agreement with DNS in both the inner and outer regions is satisfactory. Here and further, the location of the interface is indicated by a vertical dashed line. Intriguingly, no LLM occurs with the current approach, despite avoiding additional force terms in the momentum equation. That can be attributed to the appropriate exchange of flow physics between the RANS and LES regions. With the TBLE approximation and focus on the wall-normal gradients, we are able to use wall-parallel cells, which are much coarser than the local eddies. They cannot be appropriately resolved with the conventional SGS models.

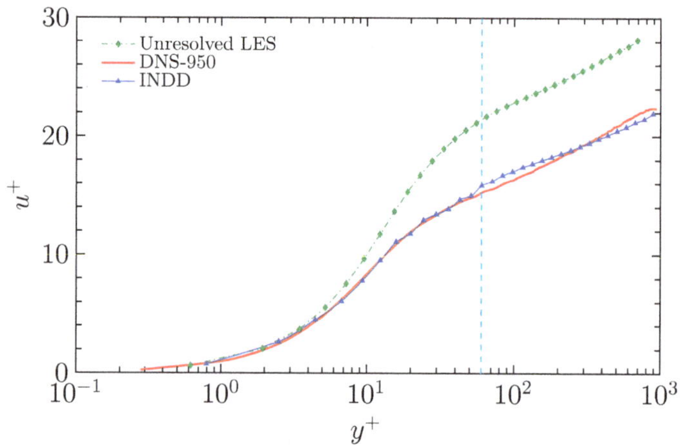

Figure 2. Mean streamwise velocity for C950 compared to DNS [48].

The normalised Reynolds stress intensities ($\overline{u'u'}^+$, $\overline{v'v'}^+$, and $\overline{w'w'}^+$) for $\mathrm{Re}_\tau = 950$ are depicted in Figure 3. In turn, Figure 4 illustrates the normalized Reynolds shear stress for C950. The overall agreement with the DNS is rather good. It is to be noted that the prediction of the Reynolds stress intensities with INDD in the inner region is rather formal. It corresponds to LES with the slip boundary conditions in the preliminary stage. The LES is not intended to be resolved in this region. The overall prediction of INDD is rather accurate, with the exception of the interface region. Near the RANS region, we cannot expect a high accurate prediction of the Reynolds stress intensities. A similar issue also occurs in other works related to RANS/LES models (see, e.g., [30]). This happens because RANS cannot predict turbulent velocity fluctuations. As a result, the Reynolds stresses in the interface area cannot be well predicted.

The results for the mean streamwise velocity at $\mathrm{Re}_\tau = 2000$ are displayed in Figure 5. They are compared to DNS, unresolved LES, and those from Davidson and Dahlström [32] (shown as DD2005) both without and with a force term. The mean velocity of the unresolved LES is significantly overpredicted, which is due to the substantial underprediction of the friction velocity (around 40%). Without incorporating additional force terms into the momentum equation, the results obtained with INDD are in a rather good agreement with the DNS data. Our prediction almost coincides with that obtained by Davidson and Dahlström [32] when they included a force term. However, the nature and magnitude of the added force term can change their profile considerably. As depicted in the figure, when no forcing is applied in [32], a large deviation from the DNS data occurs.

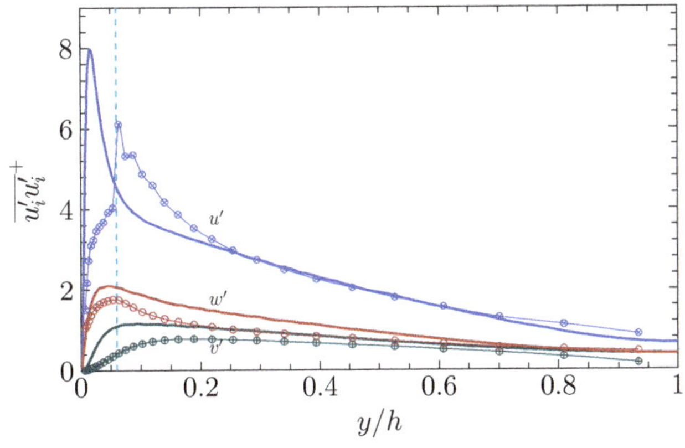

Figure 3. Reynolds normal stress intensities for C950. lines: DNS [48]; circles: INDD.

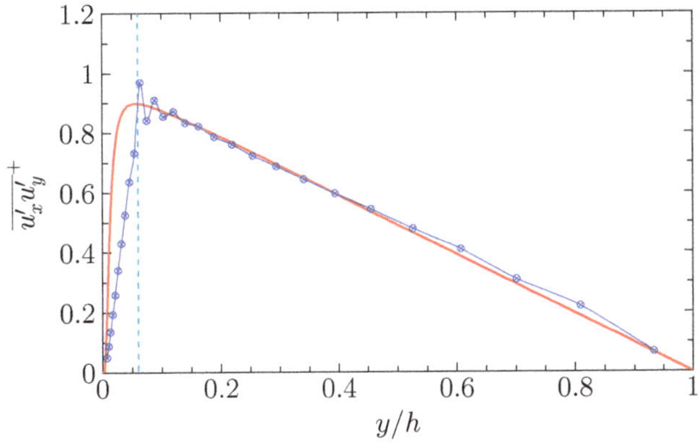

Figure 4. Reynolds shear stress for C950. Red line: DNS [48]; blue circles: INDD.

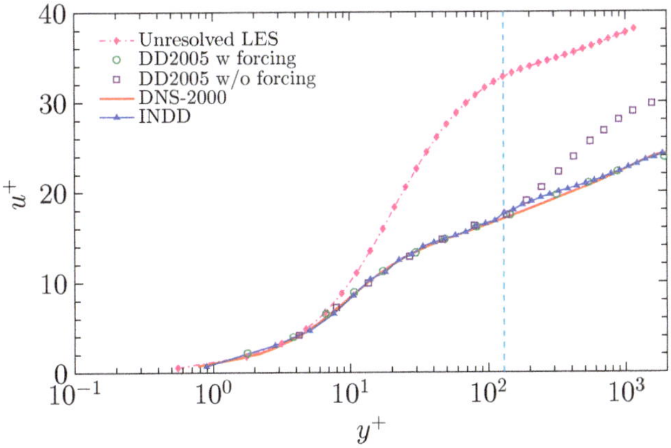

Figure 5. Mean streamwise velocity for C2000 compared to DNS [48] and hybrid LES-RANS (DD2005) [32].

The Reynolds normal stress intensities for $\mathrm{Re}_\tau = 2000$ are shown in Figure 6. The INDD results correspond to $y^{*+} = 129$, while $y^{*+} = 62$ in [32]. Again, away from the interface, the agreement of INDD with the DNS data is rather good. Despite taking a larger y^* value than DD2005, INDD demonstrates superior agreement with the benchmark data for all components. The velocity fluctuations at $y^{*+} = 129$ are not available in [32] but we anticipate for DD2005 a larger shift to the right and, thus, a greater difference from DNS in this case. In turn, Figure 7 shows the relative values of $INDD - DNS$. The main difference is near the interface area and it fades away when approaching the channel center. The hybrid model predicts the maximum normal stress to be at the interface, while in DNS it is essentially closer to the wall. This happens because LES is under-resolved in the inner region. As a result, the pulsations u' sharply drop there.

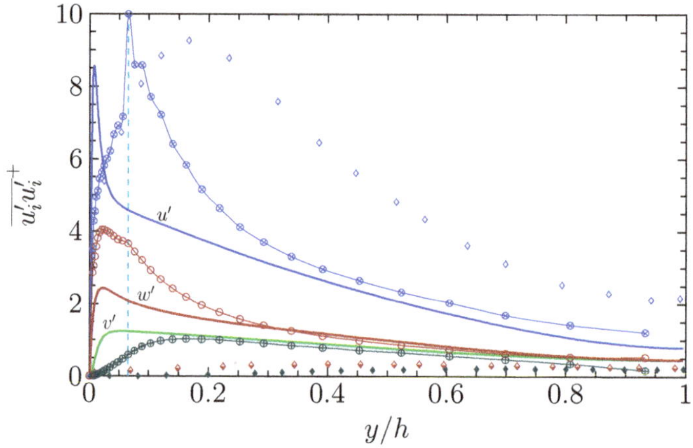

Figure 6. Reynolds normal stress intensities for C2000. Lines: DNS [48]; circles: INDD with $y^{*+} = 129$; diamonds: DD2005 from Ref. [32] with $y^{*+} = 62$, without forcing.

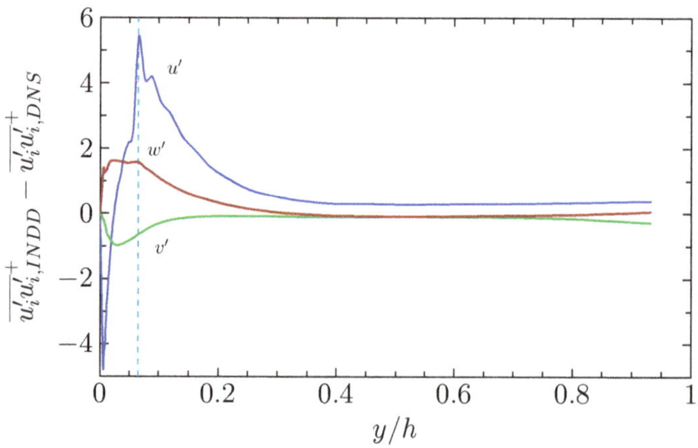

Figure 7. Relative Reynolds normal stress intensities for C2000.

The shear stress profile is plotted in Figure 8. Considering the coarse mesh used here and the deficiency of the RANS model in predicting fluctuations, the overall agreement with DNS is reasonably good. The hybrid model predicts the maximum point close to the interface.

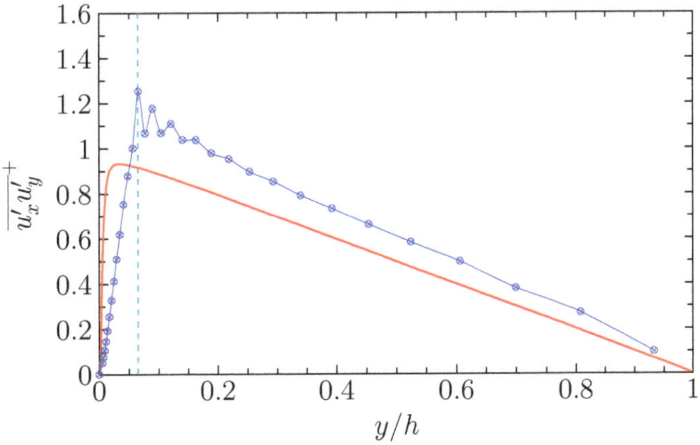

Figure 8. Reynolds shear stress for C2000. Red line: DNS [48]; blue circles: INDD.

Figure 9 demonstrates the results obtained with the INDD and our conventional hybrid RANS/LES simulation without forcing (like [5]) on the same mesh. With the hybrid approach, the LES solution is computed in the entire region in such a way that, in the inner region, the subgrid eddy viscosity is replaced by the eddy viscosity predicted from Model 3. It can be seen that a mismatch at the interface is reproduced with this approach. As noted in [49], the implementation of a blending function for the eddy viscosity is able to reduce the mismatch at the interface, although it does not remove it beyond the interface. In contrast, the INDD profile is more in line with the DNS benchmark, and the velocity profile is smoother even without the use of any blending function. INDD significantly mitigates the LLM and does not have a velocity jump.

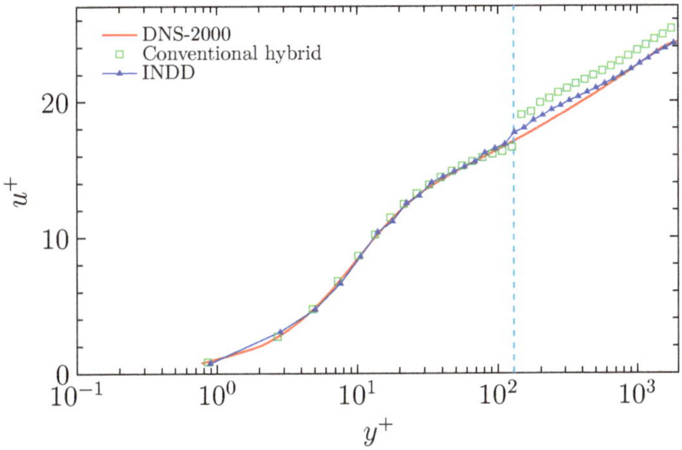

Figure 9. Mean streamwise velocity for C2000. Comparison of INDD (blue triangles) and conventional hybrid methods without a blending function (green squares).

The mean streamwise velocity for $Re_\tau = 4200$ is illustrated in Figure 10. Overall, the agreement between the current study and the DNS [50] for both inner and outer regions is rather good. The results of Keating and Piomelli [30] (shown as KP2006), when no forcing is applied, are overpredicted. The addition of the force term improves the KP2006 results, but it requires the selection of free forcing parameters that are not known a priori. This issue is addressed in a recent review by Larsson et al. [8]. They note that the log–layer mismatch is a linear function of the forcing amplitude. Finally, it is concluded that, since there is no robust general method to determine the forcing amplitude, the concept of adding force terms to initiate the transition from RANS to LES is not a comprehensive strategy.

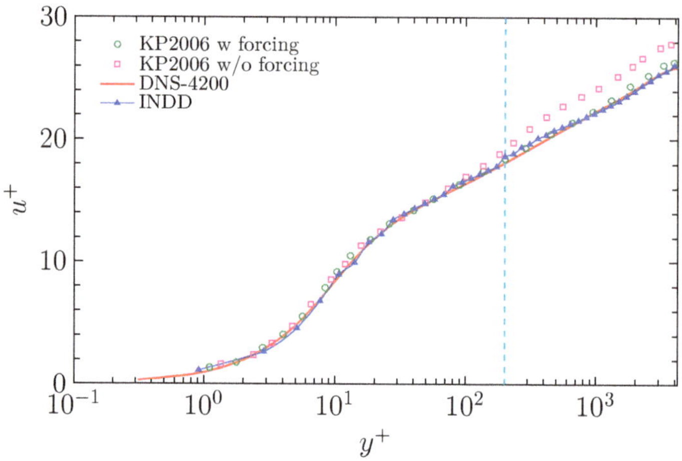

Figure 10. Mean streamwise velocity for C4200 compared to DNS [50] and hybrid LES-RANS (KP2006) [30].

As shown in Figure 11, the Reynolds stress intensities predicted by INDD are closer to the benchmark data with the increase in the distance from the interface. Specifically with regard to the streamwise component, the prediction with the INDD is comparable with that of KP2006, where a force term is used. The result of INDD for the shear stress in Figure 12 shows a reasonable agreement with the benchmark data considering the coarse mesh utilized in the current study.

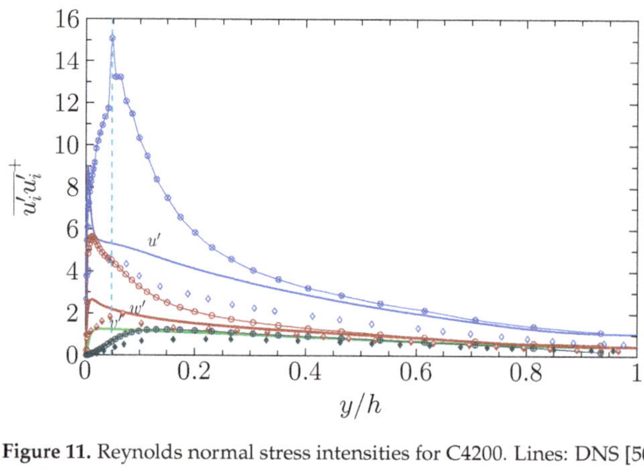

Figure 11. Reynolds normal stress intensities for C4200. Lines: DNS [50]; circles: INDD; diamonds: Ref. [30] (KP2006) with forcing.

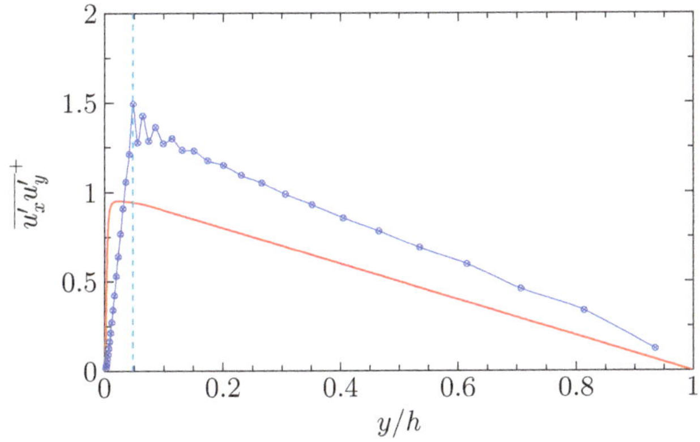

Figure 12. Reynolds shear stress intensities for C4200. Red line: DNS [50]; blue circles: INDD.

As known, the LLM results in streak-like areas in the regions in the vicinity of the interface [30,51]. This is different from the low-speed streaks that trigger the turbulence generation cycle. Figure 13 depicts a snapshot of the streamwise velocity at $y/H = 0.04$. Clearly, the "super-streaks" that are distinct to the LLM in the conventional RANS/LES model are not observed here.

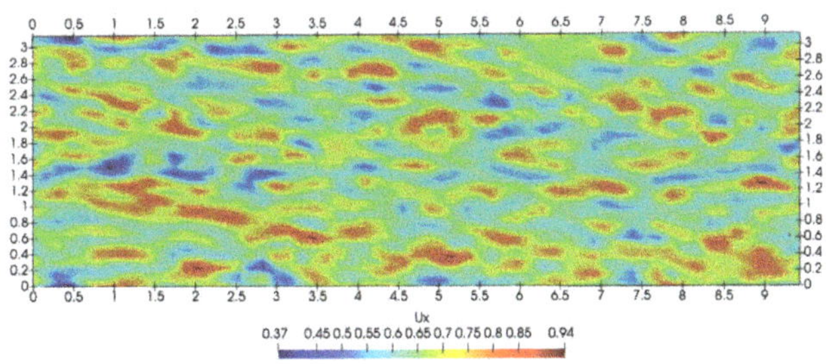

Figure 13. Contours of instantaneous streamwise velocity on a $x - z$ plane at $y/h = 0.04$ for C4200.

Overall, for all Reynolds numbers considered, either minor or negligible LLM has been observed in cases where INDD is used.

4.3. *Effect of Eddy Viscosity Model*

Next, the influence of the eddy viscosity model on the mean velocity profile for $\mathrm{Re}_\tau = 4200$ is studied. Comparisons are made in Figure 14. The results obtained with the $k - l$ method, $k - \omega$, and mixing length models are compared against the DNS data. As can be seen, the $k - l$ model has a clear superiority. The mixing length and $k - \omega$ models significantly underestimate the mean velocity in the core region. This result is consistent with the statement by Temmerman et al. [6], who argue that unresolved LES cannot provide a reliable prediction for ϵ or ω because the appropriate evaluation of the dissipation rate requires a fine-enough mesh as dissipation occurs at small scales.

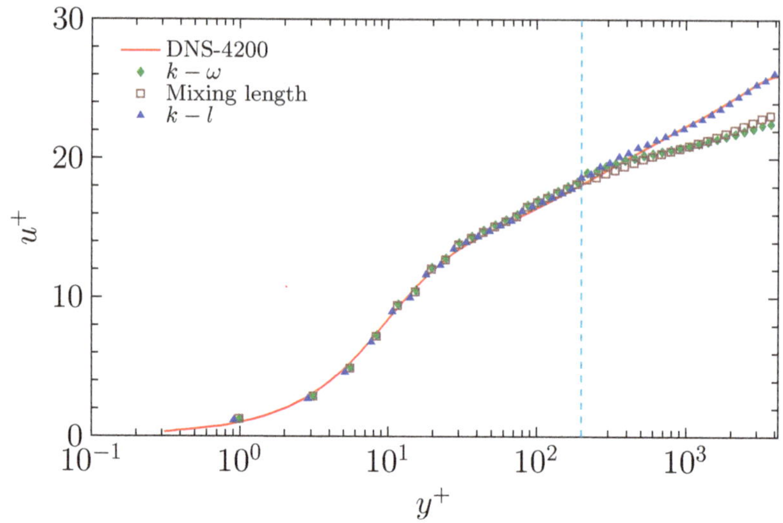

Figure 14. Effect of eddy viscosity model on mean streamwise velocity for C4200.

5. Conclusions

In this paper, the implicit near-wall domain decomposition approach has been extended to hybrid RANS/LES simulations. In the approach, the solution is obtained in two stages. First, an LES solution is computed for the entire region with specially derived non-local slip boundary conditions at the wall. Then, in the second stage, the solution is recomputed in an inner region near the wall based on a TBLE approximation. The slip BCs at the wall guarantee that the time-averaged composite solution is smooth. To evaluate the eddy viscosity in the inner region, it is recommended to use the $k-l$ turbulence model. The obtained results demonstrate that the approach is able to provide rather accurate predictions in a wide range of Reynolds numbers without the implementation of any additional forcing term at the interface. The velocity profile corresponds to the DNS data reasonably well, such that the LLM effect is practically negligible. The conventional hybrid models often suffer from a large LLM. They may include extra force terms or synthetic turbulence fluctuations at the interface. The amplitude of the force term is case-dependent and there is not a universal approach to determine it. In contrast, INDD does not need any additional force term. In the current study, we applied the model to frictional Reynolds numbers of 950, 2000, and 4200. In all cases, the mean velocity profile is well predicted. However, better results are obtained for higher Reynolds numbers. The current work demonstrates that the developed approach can be successfully used to reduce or eliminate LLM. In future work, the approach will be tested on flows around complex geometries.

Author Contributions: Software, validation, investigation, writing—original draft preparation, A.E.F.; conceptualization, methodology, writing—review and editing, supervision, project administration, funding acquisition, S.U. All authors have read and agreed to the published version of the manuscript.

Funding: This work was supported by EPSRC grant, UK EP/V038249/1.

Data Availability Statement: The authors can share some algorithms.

Acknowledgments: This work was supported by EPSRC grant, UK EP/V038249/1. The authors acknowledge the use of CSF HPC cluster at the University of Manchester. In addition, the authors are grateful to the unknown referees for useful remarks which improved the quality of the paper.

Conflicts of Interest: The authors declare no conflict of interest.

Nomenclature

The following abbreviations are used in this manuscript:

Roman symbols

t	time (s)
u_τ	friction velocity (m/s)
k	turbulent kinetic energy (m^2/s^2)
Re	Reynolds number (-)
u	flow velocity (m/s]
C_μ	model constant = 0.09 (-)
x	streamwise direction (-)
y	wall-normal direction (-)
z	spanwise direction (-)
D	damping function (-)
P	turbulence production term
Greek symbols	
τ_w	wall shear stress (N/m^2)
ρ	density (kg/m^3)
μ	dynamic viscosity (Pa·s)
ν	kinematic viscosity (Pa·s)
ϵ	turbulent kinetic energy dissipation (m^2/s^3)
ω	specific dissipation rate (1/s)
α	model constant (-)
β	model constant (-)
σ	model constant (-)
Subscripts and superscripts	
res	resolved
sgs	subgrid scale
u	velocity
l	laminar
T	turbulent
int	interface
*	interface location
w	wall
τ	friction-related parameter
Abbreviations	
LES	large eddy simulation
WMLES	wall-modeled LES
DNS	direct numerical simulation
TBLE	thin boundary layer equation
RANS	Reynolds-averaged Navier–Stokes
WSM	wall-stress model
LLM	log–layer mismatch
DES	detached eddy simulation
NDD	near-wall domain decomposition
BC	boundary condition
IBC	interface boundary condition

References

1. Heinz, S. A Mathematical Solution to the Computational Fluid Dynamics (CFD) Dilemma. *Mathematics* **2023**, *11*, 3199. [CrossRef]
2. Choi, H.; Moin, P. Grid-point requirements for large eddy simulation: Chapman's estimates revisited. *Phys. Fluids* **2012**, *24*, 011702. [CrossRef]
3. Chapman, D.R. Computational aerodynamics development and outlook. *AIAA J.* **1979**, *17*, 1293–1313. [CrossRef]
4. Sagaut, P. *Large Eddy Simulation for Incompressible Flows*; Springer: Berlin/Heidelberg, Germany, 2006.
5. Larsson, J.; Lien, F.; Yee, E. The artificial buffer layer and the effects of forcing in hybrid LES/RANS. *Int. J. Heat Fluid Flow* **2007**, *28*, 1443–1459. [CrossRef]
6. Temmerman, L.; Hadžiabdić, M.; Leschziner, M.; Hanjalić, K. A hybrid two-layer URANS–LES approach for large eddy simulation at high Reynolds numbers. *Int. J. Heat Fluid Flow* **2005**, *26*, 173–190. [CrossRef]

7. Piomelli, U. Wall-layer models for large-eddy simulations. *Prog. Aerosp. Sci.* **2008**, *44*, 437–446. [CrossRef]
8. Larsson, J.; Kawai, S.; Bodart, J.; Bermejo-Moreno, I. Large eddy simulation with modeled wall-stress: Recent progress and future directions. *Mech. Eng. Rev.* **2016**, *3*, 15-00418. [CrossRef]
9. Deardorff, J.W. A numerical study of three-dimensional turbulent channel flow at large Reynolds numbers. *J. Fluid Mech.* **1970**, *41*, 453–480. [CrossRef]
10. Schumann, U. Subgrid scale model for finite difference simulations of turbulent flows in plane channels and annuli. *J. Comput. Phys.* **1975**, *18*, 376–404. [CrossRef]
11. Temmerman, L.; Leschziner, M.A.; Mellen, C.P.; Fröhlich, J. Investigation of wall-function approximations and subgrid-scale models in large eddy simulation of separated flow in a channel with streamwise periodic constrictions. *Int. J. Heat Fluid Flow* **2003**, *24*, 157–180. [CrossRef]
12. Balaras, E.; Benocci, C. Subgrid-scale models in finite-difference simulations of complex wall bounded flows. In Proceedings of the 74th Fluid Dynamics Symposium on "Application of Direct and Large Eddy Simulation to Transition and Turbulence", Chania, Greece, 18–21 April 1994.
13. Balaras, E.; Benocci, C.; Piomelli, U. Two-layer approximate boundary conditions for large-eddy simulations. *AIAA J.* **1996**, *34*, 1111–1119. [CrossRef]
14. Cabot, W.; Moin, P. Approximate wall boundary conditions in the large-eddy simulation of high Reynolds number flow. *Flow Turbul. Combust.* **2000**, *63*, 269–291. [CrossRef]
15. Wang, M.; Moin, P. Dynamic wall modeling for large-eddy simulation of complex turbulent flows. *Phys. Fluids* **2002**, *14*, 2043–2051. [CrossRef]
16. Moin, P.; Bodart, J.; Bose, S.; Park, G.I. Wall-modeling in complex turbulent flows. In *Advances in Fluid-Structure Interaction: Updated Contributions Reflecting New Findings, Presented at the ERCOFTAC Symposium on Unsteady Separation in Fluid-Structure Interaction, St John Resort, Mykonos, Greece, 17–21 June 2013*; Springer International Publishing: Cham, Switzerland, 2016; pp. 207–219.
17. Bose, S.T.; Park, G.I. Wall-modeled large-eddy simulation for complex turbulent flows. *Annu. Rev. Fluid Mech.* **2018**, *50*, 535–561. [CrossRef] [PubMed]
18. Heinz, S. A review of hybrid RANS-LES methods for turbulent flows: Concepts and applications. *Prog. Aerosp. Sci.* **2020**, *114*, 100597. [CrossRef]
19. Drikakis, D.; Geurts, B. *Turbulent Flow Computation*; Kluwer Academic Publishers: Dordrecht, The Netherlands, 2002.
20. Hamba, F. An approach to hybrid RANS/LES calculation of channel flows. In *Engineering Turbulence Modelling and Experiments 5*; Elsevier: Amsterdam, The Netherlands, 2002; pp. 297–305.
21. Spalart, P.R. Comments on the Feasibility of LES for Wings and on the Hybrid RANS/LES Approach. In Proceedings of the First AFOSR International Conference on DNS/LES, Ruston, LA, USA, 4–8 August 1997; pp. 137–147.
22. Nikitin, N.; Nicoud, F.; Wasistho, B.; Squires, K.; Spalart, P.R. An approach to wall modeling in large-eddy simulations. *Phys. Fluids* **2000**, *12*, 1629–1632. [CrossRef]
23. Spalart, P.R. Detached-eddy simulation. *Annu. Rev. Fluid Mech.* **2009**, *41*, 181–202. [CrossRef]
24. Temmerman, L.; Leschziner, M.; Hanjalic, K. A-priori studies of a near-wall RANS model within a hybrid LES/RANS scheme. In *Engineering Turbulence Modelling and Experiments 5*; Elsevier: Amsterdam, The Netherlands, 2002; pp. 317–326.
25. Davidson, L.; Peng, S.H. Hybrid LES-RANS modelling: A one-equation SGS model combined with a $k-\omega$ model for predicting recirculating flows. *Int. J. Numer. Methods Fluids* **2003**, *43*, 1003–1018. [CrossRef]
26. Davidson, L.; Billson, M. Hybrid LES-RANS using synthesized turbulent fluctuations for forcing in the interface region. *Int. J. Heat Fluid Flow* **2006**, *27*, 1028–1042. [CrossRef]
27. Quómóró, P.; Sagaut, P. Zonal multi-domain RANS–LES simulations of turbulent flows. *Int. J. Numer. Methods Fluids* **2002**, *40*, 903–925.
28. Piomelli, U.; Balaras, E.; Pasinato, H.; Squires, K.D.; Spalart, P.R. The inner–outer layer interface in large-eddy simulations with wall-layer models. *Int. J. Heat Fluid Flow* **2003**, *24*, 538–550. [CrossRef]
29. Tessicini, F.; Temmerman, L.; Leschziner, M. Approximate near-wall treatments based on zonal and hybrid RANS–LES methods for LES at high Reynolds numbers. *Int. J. Heat Fluid Flow* **2006**, *27*, 789–799. [CrossRef]
30. Keating, A.; Piomelli, U. A dynamic stochastic forcing method as a wall-layer model for large-eddy simulation. *J. Turbul.* **2006**, *7*, N12. [CrossRef]
31. Zhong, B.; Tucker, P.G. $k-l$ based hybrid LES/RANS approach and its application to heat transfer simulation. *Int. J. Numer. Methods Fluids* **2004**, *46*, 983–1005. [CrossRef]
32. Davidson, L.; Dahlström, S. Hybrid LES-RANS: An approach to make LES applicable at high Reynolds number. *Int. J. Comput. Fluid Dyn.* **2005**, *19*, 415–427. [CrossRef]
33. Kawai, S.; Larsson, J. Wall-modeling in large eddy simulation: Length scales, grid resolution, and accuracy. *Phys. Fluids* **2012**, *24*, 015105. [CrossRef]
34. Jimenez, J.; Moser, R.D. Large-eddy simulations: Where are we and what can we expect? *AIAA J.* **2000**, *38*, 605–612. [CrossRef]
35. Utyuzhnikov, S. The method of boundary condition transfer in application to modeling near-wall turbulent flows. *Comput. Fluids* **2006**, *35*, 1193–1204. [CrossRef]
36. Utyuzhnikov, S. Robin-type wall functions and their numerical implementation. *Appl. Numer. Math.* **2008**, *58*, 1521–1533. [CrossRef]
37. Utyuzhnikov, S. Domain decomposition for near-wall turbulent flows. *Comput. Fluids* **2009**, *38*, 1710–1717. [CrossRef]

38. Jones, A.; Utyuzhnikov, S. A near-wall domain decomposition approach in application to turbulent flow in a diffuser. *Appl. Math. Model.* **2016**, *40*, 329–342. [CrossRef]
39. Petrov, M.; Utyuzhnikov, S.; Chikitkin, A.; Titarev, V. On extension of near-wall domain decomposition to turbulent compressible flows. *Comput. Fluids* **2016**, *210*, 104629. [CrossRef]
40. Lyu, S.; Utyuzhnikov, S. A computational slip boundary condition for near-wall turbulence modelling. *Comput. Fluids* **2022**, *246*, 105628. [CrossRef]
41. Davidson, L. *An Introduction to Turbulence Models*; Chalmers University of Technology: Gothenburg, Sweden, 2022.
42. Breuer, M.; Jaffrézic, B.; Arora, K. Hybrid LES–RANS technique based on a one-equation near-wall model. *Theor. Comput. Fluid Dyn.* **2016**, *22*, 157–187. [CrossRef]
43. Cabot, W. Large-Eddy Simulations with Wall Models. Center for Turbulence Research Annual Research Briefs. 1995. Available online: https://ntrs.nasa.gov/citations/19960022297 (accessed on 13 October 2023).
44. Wilcox, D.C. Reassessment of the scale-determining equation for advanced turbulence models. *AIAA J.* **1988**, *26*, 1299–1310. [CrossRef]
45. Wolfshtein, M. The velocity and temperature distribution in one-dimensional flow with turbulence augmentation and pressure gradient. *Int. J. Heat Mass Transf.* **1969**, *12*, 301–318. [CrossRef]
46. OpenFOAM 10. Available online: https://openfoam.org/version/10/ (accessed on 13 October 2023).
47. Nicoud, F.; Ducros, F. Subgrid-scale stress modelling based on the square of the velocity gradient tensor. *Flow Turbul. Combust.* **1999**, *62*, 183–200. [CrossRef]
48. Hoyas, S.; Jiménez, J. Scaling of the velocity fluctuations in turbulent channels up to $Re_\tau = 2003$. *Phys. Fluids* **2006**, *18*, 011702. [CrossRef]
49. Hamba, F. A Hybrid RANS/LES Simulation of Turbulent Channel Flow. *Theor. Comput. Fluid Dyn.* **2003**, *16*, 387–403. [CrossRef]
50. Lozano-Durán, A.; Jiménez, J. Effect of the computational domain on direct simulations of turbulent channels up to $Re_\tau = 4200$. *Phys. Fluids* **2014**, *26*, 011702. [CrossRef]
51. Baggett, J.S. On the Feasibility of Merging LES with RANS for the Near-Wall Region of Attached Turbulent Flows. Annual Research Briefs. 1998; pp. 267–277. Available online: https://ntrs.nasa.gov/api/citations/19990068442/downloads/19990068442.pdf#page=271 (accessed on 13 October 2023).

Disclaimer/Publisher's Note: The statements, opinions and data contained in all publications are solely those of the individual author(s) and contributor(s) and not of MDPI and/or the editor(s). MDPI and/or the editor(s) disclaim responsibility for any injury to people or property resulting from any ideas, methods, instructions or products referred to in the content.

mathematics

Article

Trajectory Smoothing Planning of Delta Parallel Robot Combining Cartesian and Joint Space

Dachang Zhu *, Yonglong He, Xuezhe Yu and Fangyi Li *

School of Mechanical and Electrical Engineering, Guangzhou University, Guangzhou 510006, China; heyonglong@e.gzhu.edu.cn (Y.H.); 2112307093@e.gzhu.edu.cn (X.Y.)
* Correspondence: zdc98998@gzhu.edu.cn (D.Z.); fangyi_li@gzhu.edu.cn (F.L.)

Abstract: Delta parallel robots have been widely used in precision processing, handling, sorting, and the assembly of parts, and their high efficiency and motion stability are important indexes of their performance.Corners created by small line segments in trajectory planning cause abrupt changes in a tangential discontinuous trajectory, and the vibration and shock caused by such changes seriously affect the robot's high-speed and high-precision performance. In this study, a trajectory-planning method combining Cartesian space and joint space is proposed. Firstly, the vector method and microelement integration method were used to establish the complete kinematic and dynamic equations of a delta parallel robot, and an inverse kinematic/dynamic model-solving program was written based on the MATLAB software R2020a. Secondly, the end-effector trajectory of the delta parallel robot was planned in Cartesian space, and the data points and inverse control points of the end effector's trajectory were obtained using the normalization method. Finally, the data points and control points were mapped to the joint space through the inverse kinematic equation, and the fifth-order B-spline curve was adopted for quadratic trajectory planning, which allowed the high-order continuous smoothing of the trajectory planning to be realized. The simulated and experimental results showed that the trajectory-smoothing performance in continuous high-order curvature changes could be improved with the proposed method. The peak trajectory tracking error was reduced by 10.53%, 41.18%, and 44.44%, respectively, and the peak torque change of the three joints was reduced by 3.5%, 11.6%, and 1.6%, respectively.

Keywords: delta parallel robot; kinematic and dynamic modelling; trajectory smoothing planning; combining Cartesian space with joint space

MSC: 34M25

Citation: Zhu, D.; He, Y.; Yu, X.; Li, F. Trajectory Smoothing Planning of Delta Parallel Robot Combining Cartesian and Joint Space. *Mathematics* **2023**, *11*, 4509. https://doi.org/10.3390/math11214509

Academic Editors: Shujin Laima, Yong Cao, Xiaowei Jin and Hehe Ren

Received: 1 October 2023
Revised: 28 October 2023
Accepted: 30 October 2023
Published: 1 November 2023

Copyright: © 2023 by the authors. Licensee MDPI, Basel, Switzerland. This article is an open access article distributed under the terms and conditions of the Creative Commons Attribution (CC BY) license (https://creativecommons.org/licenses/by/4.0/).

1. Introduction

The delta parallel robot has been widely used in precision parts processing, hanling, sorting, and assembly because of its high speed and high precision [1]. When a straight line or an arc approaches a target curve, the acceleration of the trajectory of the end effector is abrupt due to tangential discontinuity at the connecting corner of the fitted line segment, which makes the vibration of the delta parallel robot inevitable during high-speed operation and even causes production safety accidents [2]. Polynomial functions and interpolation methods are often used for robot trajectory planning and optimization by giving constraints on the starting and ending points, as well as constraints on the displacement, velocity, and acceleration. Boryga [3] presented a smooth trajectory planning method using higher-degree polynomial functions of acceleration to determine accurate dependencies derived for the calculation of polynomial coefficients and motion time in the case of velocity, acceleration, and jerk constraints, thus ensuring the continuity and smoothness of the trajectory. A seventh-order polynomial was applied to the trajectory planning to achieve the position, velocity, acceleration, and jerk of the actuating joints, and the positions/orientations of the parallel mechanism modules were interpolated to obtain a smooth trajectory without impact [4]. To achieve a smooth and precise trajectory while minimizing the jerk, Damasevicius et al. [5] proposed natural cubic splines for finding a Pareto-optimal set of robot arm trajectories. When a robot is required to machine a complex curved workpiece with high precision and speed, the path is generally dispersed into a series of points and transmitted to the robot, which not only reduces the precision, but also causes damage to the motors and robot. To improve the dynamic performance of the delta parallel pickup robot in high-speed pick-and-place processes, taking time and acceleration as optimization objectives, a trajectory optimization method based on the improved butterfly optimization algorithm (IBOA) was proposed [6]. Zhang et al. [7] inserted a quintic Bezier curve between small adjacent line segments to achieve velocity and acceleration continuity at the connecting points, and a quartic polynomial was adopted to achieve a constant velocity at the velocity limitation. To solve the problem of trajectory continuity, some fitting curves were presented, such as quintic and cubic nonuniform rational NURBS curves [8,9], the quintic Pythagorean hodograph (PH) curve [10], combining cubic splines with a linear segment with parabolic blends [11], and the S-curve [12]. However, since the trajectory of the end effector in Cartesian space needs to be mapped to the joint space through the inverse kinematic equation, it is realized by the joint actuator through the torque control according to the calculated joint variable values. Therefore, the end-effector position, joint variables, and the precise modeling of the robot kinematics and dynamics equations impact trajectory smoothing planning and become a very challenging subject in robotics [13,14].

Should surfaces such as sharp corners, holes, or protrusions be considered in trajectory planning [15]? Considering the execution characteristics of joint actuators, most trajectory smoothing planning considers the planning method in joint space. This takes joint velocity, acceleration, and jerk continuity as the trajectory smoothing targets [16,17]. Considering the Gaussian interpolation of the boundary conditions, a radial basis function method was proposed by Chettibi [18] to generate point-to-point smooth trajectories of robot arms. A multiaxis real-time synchronous look-ahead trajectory planning algorithm was proposed by Liang et al. [19] based on dynamically given position and velocity sequences under the constraint of maximum velocity and the acceleration of each joint axis. Shrivastava et al. [20] used the cuckoo search algorithm to suppress the linear motion equation to avoid the directional singularity in Cartesian space. Then, the Bezier curve was used to depict the shape of the joint trajectory by interpolating the linear polynomials with the parabolic blend. In the joint space, the joint movement was divided into acceleration, uniform speed, and deceleration parts; the fourth-order polynomial formed by the root weight was used to plan the acceleration to ensure the continuity of the displacement, speed, acceleration, and jerk of each joint and end effector of the robot [21].

On the other hand, some of the literature has studied the trajectory planning of robot end effectors in Cartesian space [22–27]. However, trajectory smoothing planning in a single space cannot guarantee trajectory smoothness in other spaces. Moreover, in the process of high-speed reciprocating motion of a high-speed parallel robot, the influence of its nonlinear dynamic characteristics on the dynamic response and stable operation of the system cannot be ignored, especially when the smooth trajectory is mapped from Cartesian space (or joint space) to joint space (or Cartesian space) [28]. The comprehensive kinematics and dynamics characteristics of the three DoF parallel manipulator were analyzed under the accepted Jacobian link matrices and proverbial virtual work principle, and the discretized piecewise quintic polynomials were employed in order to interpolate the angular positions of the sequence of joints; these were transformed from predefined via points in Cartesian space [29]. Dupac [30] proposed quintic Hermite piecewise interpolants having functional continuity, and the smoothness of the end effector path was guaranteed. At the same time, inverse kinematics and inverse dynamics were used to compute the coordinates of the joints. The smoothness of the trajectory of the robot's end effector was not only smoothly planned in the Cartesian space, but the kinematic and dynamic changes in the robot joints and the torque generated by the joint actuators were also obtained [31]. This study places a focus on the shock and vibration caused by abrupt trajectory changes, and trajectory-smoothing planning by combining Cartesian and joint space was proposed. The main contributions of this study are summarized in the following:

(1) The delta parallel robot's complete kinematics/dynamics model was established using vector decomposition and the elementary kinematic energy method. The inverse kinematics/dynamics model of the delta parallel robot was solved using the pseudoinverse matrix solution method, and the mapping relationship between Cartesian space and joint space was constructed.

(2) The trajectory in Cartesian space (end effector) was planned using the normalization method, and data points and inverse points were used to control the mapping accuracy from Cartesian space to joint space.

(3) Using a quintic B-spline curve, combined with the data points and inverse control points, the trajectory planning in the joint space was smoothed.

The rest of this paper is structured as follows: In Section 2, the kinematic and dynamic model of the Delta parallel robot is presented. The trajectory smoothing planning combining Cartesian and joint space is proposed in Section 3. The experimental results are shown in Section 4. Finally, conclusions are drawn in Section 5.

2. Kinematic and Dynamic Model of the Delta Parallel Robot

2.1. Kinematic Model of the Delta Parallel Robot

The origin O of the fixed coordinate system $\{O - XYZ\}$ is located in the geometric center of the equilateral triangle. The center point A_i $(i = 1 - 3)$ of the three sides of the equilateral triangle is connected to the active link and the fixed platform by revolute joints. The outer tangent circle radius of the equilateral triangle is R, the axis of X is along the direction of $\overrightarrow{OA_1}$, and the axis of Y is parallel to the axis of the revolute joint A_1. The origin o' of the moving coordinate system $\{o' - xyz\}$ is located in the geometric center of the equilateral triangle. The center point C_i $(i = 1 - 3)$ of the three sides of the equilateral triangle is connected to the passive link and the moving platform through a fixed connection. The outer tangent circle radius of the equilateral triangle is r. The length of the active links A_iB_i and passive links B_iC_i are the constant values l_a and l_b, respectively. The variable parameters in joint space are θ_i, $i = 1, 2, 3$, and the three output displacements in the Cartesian space of the moving platform are x, y, and z. The geometric configuration of the delta parallel robot is shown in Figure 1.

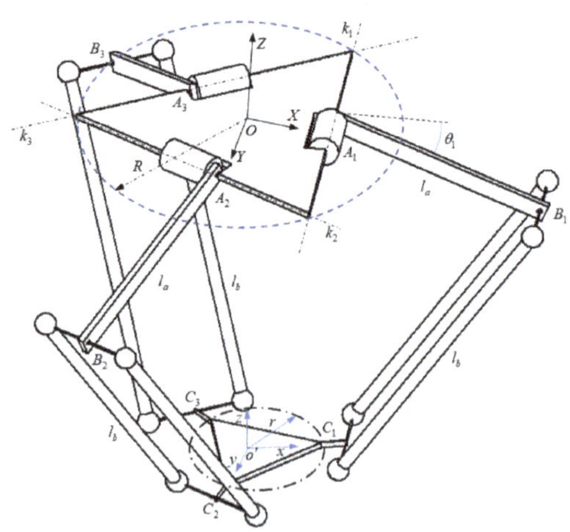

Figure 1. The geometric configuration of delta parallel robot with three DoFs.

Assume that the origin of the moving platform o' is $\begin{bmatrix} x & y & z \end{bmatrix}^T$ with respect to the fixed coordinate system. The inverse positional kinematic of the delta parallel robot can be given by

$$\overrightarrow{B_iC_i} = \overrightarrow{Oo} - \overrightarrow{OA_i} - \overrightarrow{A_iB_i} \text{ and } \left\| \overrightarrow{B_iC_i} \right\| = l_b \tag{1}$$

The axis vectors of the revolute joint R_i are k_i $\left(k_i = \begin{bmatrix} k_{xi} & k_{yi} & k_{zi} \end{bmatrix}^T, \quad i = 1,2,3\right)$. According to the geometric composition characteristics of the Delta parallel robot, k_i can be derived as follows:

$$k_1 = \begin{bmatrix} 0 & 1 & 0 \end{bmatrix}^T, \quad k_2 = \begin{bmatrix} \sqrt{3}/2 & 1/2 & 0 \end{bmatrix}^T, \quad k_3 = \begin{bmatrix} \sqrt{3}/2 & -1/2 & 0 \end{bmatrix}^T \tag{2}$$

The homogeneous transformation matrix of rotation θ about any axis $k = \begin{bmatrix} k_x & k_y & k_z \end{bmatrix}^T$ is satisfied with

$$\mathrm{Rot}(k,\theta) = \begin{bmatrix} k_xk_x(1-c\theta)+c\theta & k_yk_x(1-c\theta)-k_zs\theta & k_zk_x(1-c\theta)+k_ys\theta & 0 \\ k_xk_y(1-c\theta)+k_zs\theta & k_yk_y(1-c\theta)+c\theta & k_zk_y(1-c\theta)-k_xs\theta & 0 \\ k_xk_z(1-c\theta)-k_ys\theta & k_yk_z(1-c\theta)+k_xs\theta & k_zk_z(1-c\theta)+c\theta & 0 \\ 0 & 0 & 0 & 1 \end{bmatrix} \tag{3}$$

${}^oP_{B'}$ is the changed position of point B in the $\{o - xyz\}$ coordinate system, which can be obtained by translation and rotation based on the initial position ${}^oP_B$, which yields to

$${}^oP_{B'} = \mathrm{Rot}(k_i,\theta_i)^oP_B + \mathrm{Trans}\left(\overrightarrow{OA_i}\right) \tag{4}$$

${}^oP_{C'}$ is the changed position of point C in the $\{o - xyz\}$ coordinate system, which can be obtained according to the motion characteristics of the moving platform, which yields to

$${}^oP_{C'} = \mathrm{Trans}(\overrightarrow{Oo})^oP_C \tag{5}$$

By substituting (4) and (5) into (1), we obtain

$$(x - m\cos\alpha_i)^2 + (y - m\sin\alpha_i)^2 + (z + l_a\sin\theta_i)^2 = l_b^2 \tag{6}$$

where $m = R - r + l_a\cos\theta_i$ and $\alpha_i = \frac{2(i-1)\pi}{3}$ are the angles between the OA_i and X axis, respectively, where $i = 1,2,3$.

Assume that $\sin(\theta_i) = \frac{2t_i}{1+t_i^2}$ and $\cos(\theta_i) = \frac{1-t_i^2}{1+t_i^2}$.

Equation (6) can then be calculated as follows

$$\theta_i = 2\arctan\left(\frac{-U_i \pm \sqrt{U_i^2 - 4K_iV_i}}{2K_i}\right) \tag{7}$$

where

$$K_i = l_b^2 - l_a^2 - x^2 - y^2 - z^2 - (R-r)^2 + 2(x\cos\alpha_i + y\sin\alpha_i)(R - r - l_a) + 2(R-r)l_a$$

$$U_i = -4zl_a$$

$$V_i = l_b^2 - l_a^2 - x^2 - y^2 - z^2 - (R-r)^2 + 2(x\cos\alpha_i + y\sin\alpha_i)(R - r + l_a) - 2(R-r)l_a$$

Assume that $b_i = B_iC_i$ and take the derivative of both sides with respect to the time; thus, we obtain

$$Q\dot{X} + B\dot{\theta} = 0 \tag{8}$$

where $B = \text{diag}(b_1^T c_1, b_2^T c_2, b_3^T c_3)$ is a diagonal matrix, $Q = \begin{bmatrix} b_1^T & b_2^T & b_3^T \end{bmatrix}^T$, and $c_i = \begin{bmatrix} l_a \sin\theta_i \cos\alpha_i & l_a \sin\theta_i \sin\alpha_i & l_a \cos\theta_i \end{bmatrix}^T$, $\dot{X} = \begin{bmatrix} \dot{x} & \dot{y} & \dot{z} \end{bmatrix}^T$ is the velocity vector of the end effector of the delta parallel robot, $\dot{\theta} = \begin{bmatrix} \dot{\theta}_1 & \dot{\theta}_2 & \dot{\theta}_3 \end{bmatrix}^T$ is the velocity vector of the joints, and $0 \in R^{3\times1}$ is the zero matrix.

Equation (8) can then be rewritten with

$$\dot{\theta} = -B^{-1}Q\dot{X} = J\dot{X} \tag{9}$$

where J is the kinematic Jacobian matrix of the delta parallel robot.

By taking the derivative of (9) with respect to the time, we obtain

$$\ddot{\theta} = J^{-1}(\ddot{X} - \dot{J}\dot{\theta}) \tag{10}$$

where $\dot{J} = Q^{-1}\dot{Q}Q^{-1}B - Q^{-1}\dot{B}$ and $\dot{Q}$, $\dot{B}$ are satisfied with

$$\dot{Q} = l_a \begin{bmatrix} \cos\alpha_1 \sin\theta_1 & \sin\alpha_1 \sin\theta_1 & \cos\theta_1 \\ \cos\alpha_2 \sin\theta_2 & \sin\alpha_2 \sin\theta_2 & \cos\theta_2 \\ \cos\alpha_3 \sin\theta_3 & \sin\alpha_3 \sin\theta_3 & \cos\theta_3 \end{bmatrix} \dot{\theta}^T + \dot{X}^T \tag{11}$$

and

$$\dot{B} = \text{diag}\left(\dot{b}_1^T c_1 + b_1^T \dot{c}_1, \dot{b}_2^T c_2 + b_2^T \dot{c}_2, \dot{b}_3^T c_3 + b_3^T \dot{c}_3\right) \tag{12}$$

2.2. Dynamic Model of the Delta Parallel Robot

The dynamic model of the delta parallel robot with three DoFs is given by

$$M(\theta)\ddot{\theta} + C(\theta,\dot{\theta})\dot{\theta} + G(\theta) = \tau \tag{13}$$

where $M(\theta) \in R^{3\times3}$ is the inertial mass matrix, $C(\theta,\dot{\theta}) \in R^{3\times3}$ is the Coriolis and centripetal force, $\tau \in R^{3\times1}$ is the moment, $G(\theta) \in R^{3\times1}$ is the gravity matrix. The dynamic equation of the delta parallel robot has the following properties:

Remark 1. *The inertial mass matrix $M(\theta)$ is a positive symmetric matrix and is bounded; it is satisfied by*

$$mI < M(\theta) = M^T(\theta) \leqslant \bar{m}I \tag{14}$$

where m and $\bar{m}$ are constants that are more than zero, and $I \in R^{3\times3}$ is the identity matrix.

The mass of the active link is m_b, the mass of the passive link is m_p, and the mass of the moving platform is m_m. The mass matrix $M(\theta)$ of the delta parallel robot consists of three parts: an active link $M_{m_b}(\theta)$, a passive link $M_{m_p}(\theta)$ and a moving platform $M_{m_m}(\theta)$.

Considering the motion characteristics of the Delta parallel robot, the mass matrix of the moving platform can be expressed as

$$M_{m_m}(\theta) = m_{pl}J^T J \tag{15}$$

where m_{pl} is the mass of the moving platform and load, and J is the Jacobian matrix.

The mass matrix of the active link is given by

$$M_{m_b}(\theta) = \begin{bmatrix} I_{b1} & 0 & 0 \\ 0 & I_{b2} & 0 \\ 0 & 0 & I_{b3} \end{bmatrix} \tag{16}$$

where $I_{b1} = I_{b2} = I_{b3} = I_m + (\frac{m_b}{3} + m_c)l_a^2$, I_m is the moment of inertia of the actuator, and m_c is the mass of the spherical hinge. The linear velocity at any point along the link B_iC_i can be expressed as

$$v_{B_iC_i}(x) = \left(1 - \frac{x}{l_b}\right)v_1 + \frac{x}{l_b}v_2 \tag{17}$$

where v_1 is the velocity at the connection between the B_iC_i, and A_iB_i, v_2 is the velocity at the connection between the B_iC_i and the moving platform. The elementary kinematic energy can be given by

$$dT = \frac{1}{2}v_{B_iC_i}^2 dm = \frac{1}{2}v_{B_iC_i}^2 \rho s dx \tag{18}$$

where ρ is the material density of the link, and s is the cross-sectional area.

By integrating (17), we obtain

$$T = \int_0^{l_b} dT = \frac{1}{2}\rho s \int_0^{l_b} v_{B_iC_i}^2 dx = \frac{1}{2}\left(\frac{1}{3}m_l\left(v_1^2 + v_2^2 + v_1v_2\right)\right) \tag{19}$$

The Jacobian matrix of the joint B_i is defined as $J_{u,i}$, $M_{m_p}(\theta)$ and can be derived as

$$M_{m_p}(\theta) = \sum_{i=1}^{3} \frac{1}{3}m_l\left(J^TJ + J_{u,i}^TJ_{u,i} + J_{u,i}^TJ\right) \tag{20}$$

Assuming that the equivalent mass of the moving platform is $m_{eq} = m_{pf} + m_l$, we have the following matrix:

$$\sum_{i=1}^{3} \frac{1}{3}m_l\left(J_{u,i}^TJ_{u,i}\right) = \frac{1}{3}m_l\begin{bmatrix} l_a^2 & 0 & 0 \\ 0 & l_a^2 & 0 \\ 0 & 0 & l_a^2 \end{bmatrix} \tag{21}$$

The mass matrix of the delta parallel robot can be expressed completely as

$$M(\theta) = I_{bt} + m_{eq}J^TJ \tag{22}$$

where $I_{bt} = \begin{bmatrix} I_{eq} & 0 & 0 \\ 0 & I_{eq} & 0 \\ 0 & 0 & I_{eq} \end{bmatrix}$, and $I_{eq} = I_m + \left(\frac{m_b}{3} + \frac{2m_l}{3} + m_c\right)l_a^2$.

3. Trajectory Smoothing Planing Combining Cartesian and Jiont Space

Trajectory smoothing planning of the delta parallel robot combining Cartesian and joint space is mainly conducted to solve the problem of process vibration caused by acceleration and jerk changes, which are caused by discontinuity at the inflection point of the small line segment.

3.1. Trajectory Planning in Cartesian Space

Assume that the end effector of the delta parallel robot passes through the set point $p_i = (x_i, y_i, z_i)$ $(i = 0, 1, \cdots, n)$, and the complex trajectory consists of multiple microline segments that are connected. The coordinates of each interpolation point are expressed as

$$x = x_0 + \lambda\Delta x, \quad y = y_0 + \lambda\Delta y, \quad z = z_0 + \lambda\Delta z \tag{23}$$

where λ is a normalized factor, (x_0, y_0, z_0) is the initial point position, Δx, Δy, and Δz are increments on the x, y and z, respectively, and they are satisfied with

$$\Delta x = x_{i+1} - x_i, \quad \Delta y = y_{i+1} - y_i, \quad \Delta z = z_{i+1} - z_i \tag{24}$$

Assume that the velocity of the line in the middle section is v, and the acceleration of the parabola segment is a; the movement time and distance of the parabola segment are satisfied with

$$T_p = \frac{v}{a}, \quad L_p = \frac{1}{2}aT_p^2 \tag{25}$$

where T_p is the run time of the parabola segment, and L_p is the displacement of the parabola segment.

Considering Equation (24), the time, displacement, and acceleration of the parabola segment after normalization can be expressed as

$$T_{p\lambda i} = T_p/T_i, \quad L_{p\lambda i} = L_p/L_i, \quad a_{p\lambda i} = 2L_{p\lambda i}/T_{p\lambda i}^2 \tag{26}$$

where L_i and T_i are the displacement and time of two adjacent data points, respectively, which are given by

$$L_i = \sqrt{(x_{i+1} - x_i)^2 + (y_{i+1} - y_i)^2 + (z_{i+1} - z_i)^2}$$

$$T_i = 2T_p + (L_i - 2L_p)/v$$

The normalized factor λ is given by

$$\lambda = \begin{cases} \frac{1}{2}a_{\lambda i}t^2 & 0 \leqslant t \leqslant T_{p\lambda i} \\ \frac{1}{2}a_{\lambda i}T_{p\lambda i}^2 + a_{\lambda i}T_{p\lambda i}(t - T_{p\lambda i}) & T_{p\lambda i} < t \leqslant 1 - T_{p\lambda i} \\ \frac{1}{2}a_{\lambda i}T_{p\lambda i}^2 - a_{\lambda i}T_{p\lambda i}(t - 1 + T_{p\lambda i}) + \frac{1}{2}a_{\lambda i}(t + T_{p\lambda i} - 1)^2 & 1 - T_{p\lambda i} < t \leqslant 1 \end{cases} \tag{27}$$

where $t = i/n, i = 0, 1, \cdots, n$. $\lambda = 0$ is the starting point of the line segment, and $\lambda = 1$ is the end point of the line segment.

3.2. Trajectory Planning in Joint Space

By using Equations (7)–(22), the interpolation points obtained from Cartesian space are inversely mapped to joint space and used as the critical points of trajectory planning in joint space for quadratic interpolation using the quintic B-spline curve, which is expressed as

$$\theta_{i,k}(t) = \sum_{i=0}^{k} P_{i+l}B_{l,k}(t) \tag{28}$$

where $t \in [0, 1]$, $\theta_{i,k}(t)$ is the B-spline curve of kth, $P_{i+l}(l = 0, \cdots, k)$ are the control points, and $B_{l,k}(t)$ is the B-spline basis function, which can be given by

$$B_{l,k}(t) = \frac{1}{k!}\sum_{j=0}^{k-l}(-1)^j C_{k+1}^j (t + k - l - j)^k \tag{29}$$

where $C_{k+1}^j = \frac{(k+1)!}{j!(k+1-j)!}$, and $k = 5$.

By substituting (29) into (28), we obtain

$$\theta_{i,5}(t) = \frac{1}{120}\begin{bmatrix} 1 & t & t^2 & t^3 & t^4 & t^5 \end{bmatrix} = M\begin{bmatrix} P_i & P_{i+1} & P_{i+2} & P_{i+3} & P_{i+4} & P_{i+5} \end{bmatrix}^T \tag{30}$$

where

$$M = \begin{bmatrix} 1 & 26 & 66 & 26 & 1 & 0 \\ -5 & -50 & 0 & 50 & 5 & 0 \\ 10 & 20 & -60 & 20 & 10 & 0 \\ -10 & 20 & 0 & -20 & 10 & 0 \\ 5 & -20 & 30 & -20 & 5 & 0 \\ -1 & 5 & -10 & 10 & -5 & 1 \end{bmatrix}$$

When $t = 0$, the end point of the B-spline curve of the fifth dimension is given by

$$\theta_{i,5}(0) = \frac{1}{120}(P_i + 26P_{i+1} + 66P_{i+2} + 26P_{i+3} + P_{i+4}) \tag{31}$$

Given $m+1$ data points in joint space $\theta_i(i = 0, 1, \cdots, m)$, we inverse calculate the control point P_i. Since the number of the control points is $m + 5$, four initial constraint equations are selected as follows:

$$\begin{cases} \ddot{\theta}_0(0) = 20P_0 + 40P_1 - 120P_2 + 40P_3 + 20P_4 = 0 \\ \dddot{\theta}_0(0) = -60P_0 + 120P_1 - 120P_3 + 60P_4 = 0 \\ \ddot{\theta}_m(1) = 20P_m + 40P_{m+1} - 120P_{m+2} + 40P_{m+3} + 20P_{m+4} = 0 \\ \dddot{\theta}_m(1) = -60P_m + 120P_{m+1} - 120P_{m+3} + 60P_{m+4} = 0 \end{cases} \tag{32}$$

By combining (30) and (31), we obtain

$$120\begin{bmatrix} 0 \\ 0 \\ \theta_0 \\ \theta_1 \\ \vdots \\ \theta_m \\ 0 \\ 0 \end{bmatrix} = \begin{bmatrix} -5 & -50 & 0 & 50 & 5 & & & & \\ 20 & 40 & -120 & 40 & 20 & & & & \\ 1 & 26 & 66 & 26 & 1 & & & & \\ & 1 & 26 & 66 & 26 & 1 & & & \\ & & \ddots & \ddots & \ddots & \ddots & \ddots & & \\ & & & 1 & 26 & 66 & 26 & 1 \\ & & & 20 & 40 & -120 & 40 & 20 \\ & & & -5 & -50 & 0 & 50 & -5 \end{bmatrix}\begin{bmatrix} P_0 \\ P_1 \\ \vdots \\ P_m \\ P_{m+1} \\ P_{m+2} \\ P_{m+3} \\ P_{m+4} \end{bmatrix} \tag{33}$$

The method of the inverse control vertex is used to calculate the B-spline curve, and the B-spline curve of degree k is defined as

$$p(t) = \frac{\sum_{i=0}^{n} d_i \omega_i B_{i,k}(t)}{\sum_{i=0}^{n} \omega_i B_{i,k}(t)} = \frac{TB_{i,k}(t)D_i}{TB_{i,k}(t)W_i}, 0 \leqslant t \leqslant 1 \tag{34}$$

where $d_i(i = 0, 1, \cdots, n)$ is the control vertex of the curve $p(t)$, and ω_i is the weight factor whose number is equal to the number of control vertices.

$$t = \frac{u - u_{i+k}}{u_{i+k+1} - u_{i+k}}$$

$$D_i = \begin{bmatrix} \omega_i d_i & \omega_{i+1} d_{i+1} & \omega_{i+2} d_{i+2} & \omega_{i+3} d_{i+3} \end{bmatrix}^T$$

$$W_i = \begin{bmatrix} \omega_i & \omega_{i+1} & \omega_{i+2} & \omega_{i+3} \end{bmatrix}^T$$

where u is a set of node vectors, which are satisfied with $[u_0, u_1 \cdots, u_{n+k+1}] \in [0, 1]$ and $\boldsymbol{T}=\begin{bmatrix} t^3 & t^2 & t & 1 \end{bmatrix}$.

4. Simulations and Experiments

The parameters of the delta parallel robot are shown in Table 1.

Table 1. Parameters of the delta parallel robot.

Parameters	Values	Parameters	Values
Length of active link l_a	0.1800 m	Radius of the fixed platform R	0.1350 m
Length of passive link l_b	0.5000 m	Radius of the moving platform r	0.0400 m
Mass of the moving platform m_p	0.2231 kg	Mass of the active link m_b	0.3392 kg
Mass of the passive link m_l	0.1412 kg	Moment of inertia of the motor I_m	0.000073 kg·m^2

The test time was set to 10 s, and the sampling number was set to 20,001. The traditional PID controller was used to verify the single-space (Cartesian space) trajectory smoothing planning, and the proposed trajectory method was compared. The PID controller parameters were set to $K_I = \text{diag}[3.05, 4.05, 3.05]^T$, $K_P = \text{diag}[75, 75, 70]^T$, and $K_D = \text{diag}[10, 15, 10]^T$.

4.1. Simulations

In accordance with Equations (20)–(22), SolidWorks software was used to establish the fixed platform, motor, active link, positive link, and other part models of the delta parallel robot, and after assembly, Adams software was imported to build a multibody dynamic system. We created the interface file with MATLAB in the Adams/Controls module and called the system model established by the Adams software in the MATLAB programming environment. The specific process is as follows:

(1) Save the 3D solid graphics in the SolidWorks software in the $*.X_T$ format by reading the assembly file of this format inthe Adams software; the delta parallel robot model is imported into the Adams multibody dynamic simulation environment.

(2) Define the material and quality attributes of each part in the Adams environment and add the influence factors of gravity to improve the multibody dynamic system model of the delta parallel robot in the Adams software, as shown in Figure 2a.

(3) Define the system's state variables (angle/velocity) and create a torque association between the input variables of the system and the single components.

(4) Set up the Adams/Controls module to realize data exchange between the Adams and the MATLAB/Simulink,R2020a and generate the *.m* file. The control block diagram of the Adams and MATLAB united simulation is shown in Figure 2b.

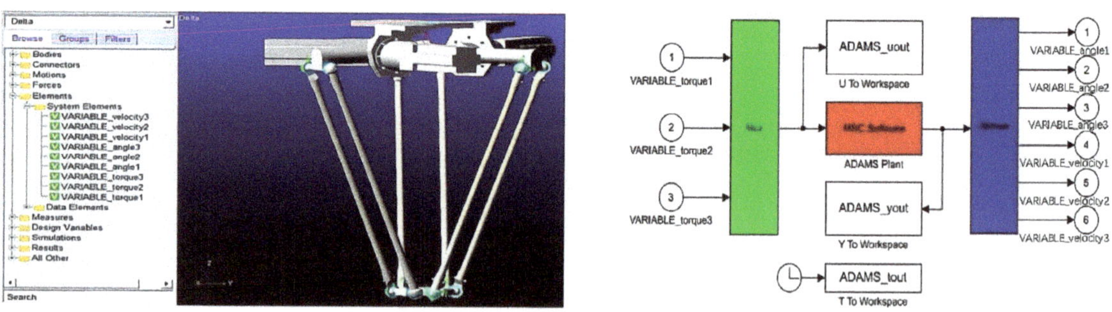

(*a*) (*b*)

Figure 2. Simulation platform of the delta parallel robot. (**a**) The multibody dynamic system model of the delta parallel robot in Adams software. (**b**) The control block diagram of Adams and MATLAB software united simulation.

Two trajectory comparison methods have been adopted in this paper: one is to map the trajectory planned in Cartesian space to joint space through inverse kinematics (without quadratic trajectory planning), and the other is to map the trajectory planned in Cartesian space to joint space through inverse kinematics and the quintic B-spline curve proposed in Section 2.2 for quadratic trajectory planning.

The end-effector motion trajectory of the delta parallel robot was selected as a five-pointed star curve. A total of 11 data points of the curve were given, and the start and end weight factors were selected as 1.0, respectively; the rest were 0.9. The trajectory of the end effector in Cartesian space is shown in Figure 3.

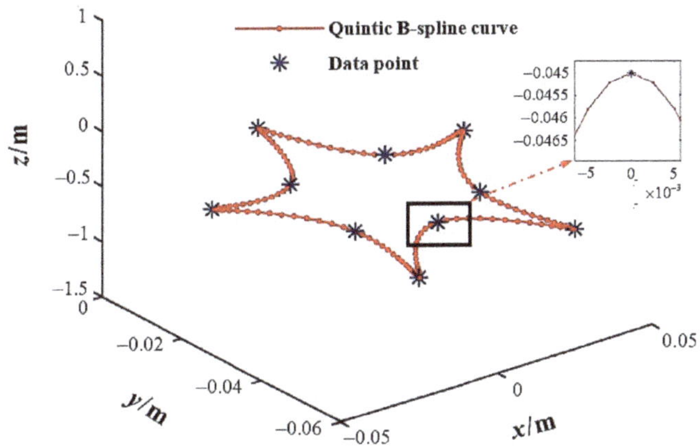

Figure 3. End-effector trajectory of the delta parallel robot in Cartesian space.

The trajectory planned in the Cartesian space can be mapped to the joint space through the inverse kinematic transformation of the delta parallel robot. If the trajectory of each joint runs according to the mapped trajectory, process vibrations will be generated, which are usually suppressed by the control method. In this paper, the mapped trajectories were quadratically planned so that the trajectories could be smoothed in joint space. When the same PID control was adopted, the trajectory tracking curves of each joint for quadratic planning and nonquadratic planning were derived and are shown in Figure 4. The joint torque is shown in Figure 5. After the process vibrations were suppressed by quadratic trajectory planning, the comparison of quadratic planning trajectory tracking errors as found and is shown in Figure 6.

Figures 3 and 4 show that the PID controller could effectively track the desired trajectory of the Cartesian space trajectory planning and the quadratic trajectory planning in the joint space, and its steady-state error was kept within 2×10^{-3} rad. Figures 5 and 6 show that quadratic trajectory planning in joint space could effectively improve the process vibration phenomenon caused by corner discontinuity of the adjacent straight segments. The torque curve was smooth, and the root-mean-square value was reduced. The value pairs of the trace tracking error and control moment root mean square are shown in Table 2.

Table 2. Comparison of the root mean square of the control moment.

Joint	Torque Moment ($\|\tau\|_{RMSE}$ (N·m))		
	Without Quadratic Planning	With Quadratic Planning	Reduction Rate
1st	0.7309	0.7308	0.014%
2nd	0.5716	0.5707	0.015%
3rd	0.8822	0.8817	0.057%

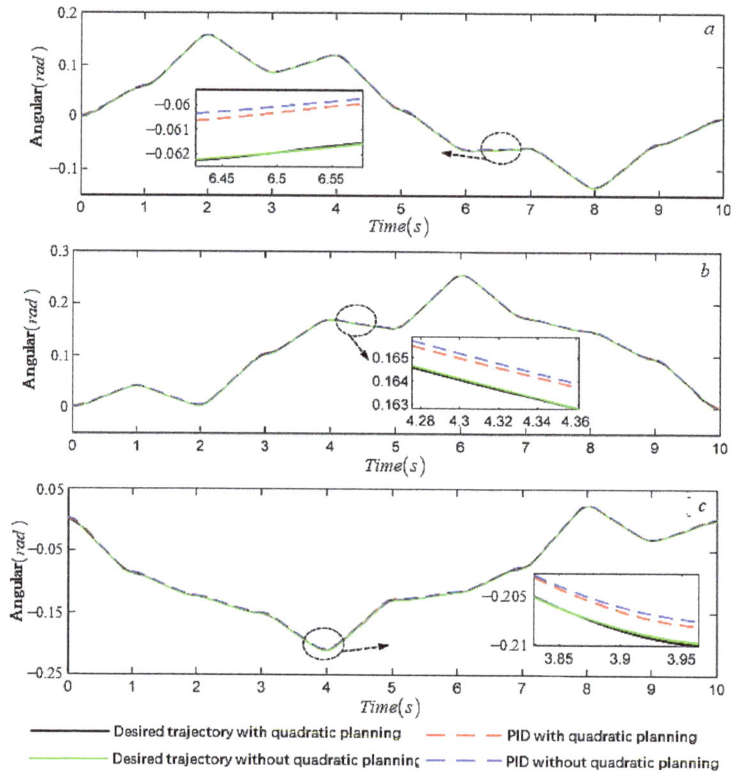

Figure 4. Trajectory tracking curves of each joint for quadratic planning and nonquadratic planning. (**a**) Ioint $1^{\#}$. (**b**) Ioint $2^{\#}$. (**c**) Ioint $3^{\#}$.

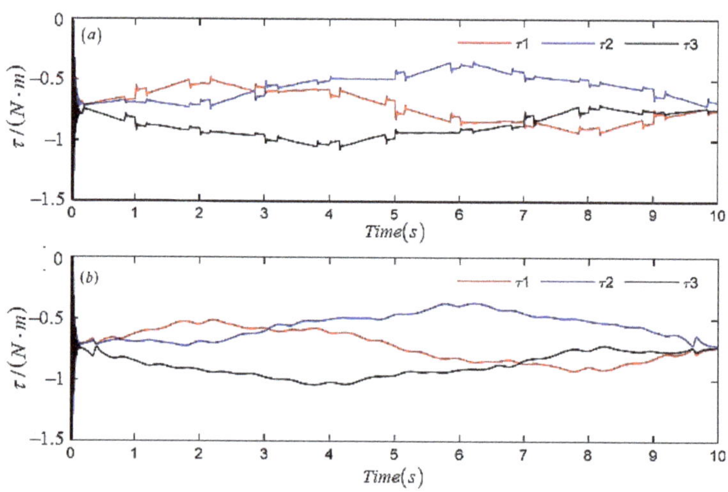

Figure 5. Joint torque with quadratic planning and nonquadratic planning. (**a**) Without quadratic planning. (**b**) With quadratic planning.

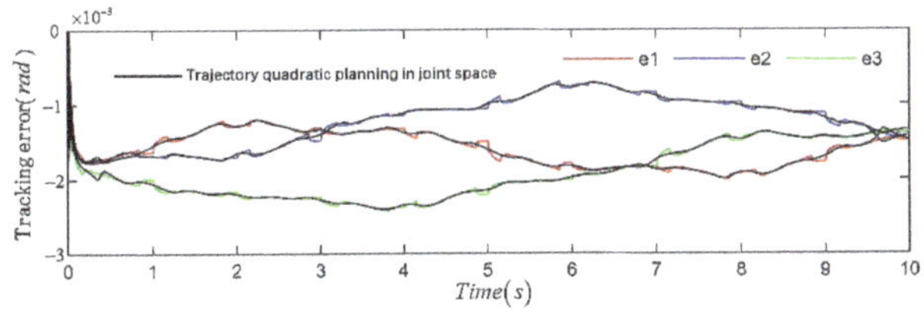

Figure 6. Trajectory tracking error with quadratic planning in joint space.

4.2. Experiments

The experimental platform of the delta parallel robot based on the EtherCAT communication mode was constructed. The motion control card was selected from the Googo GEN-009-00 series, which is EtherCAT's distributed clock device that ensures synchronous movement between the various axes, thus avoiding position deviation in the time response due to the strong coupling characteristics between the various axes. Based on the EtherCAT master–slave architecture, three slave stations were configured on the experimental platform. The model number is JSDG2S-15A-E, and the connection cables are CAT5E-STP RJ45 industrial ethernet cables. The motor model is JSMA-PBC04AAKB, the speed of the motor is 3000 rpm, the rated power is 400 W, the moment of inertia is 0.000073 kg·m^2, and the reduction ratio of the motor reducer is 1:25. The experimental platform of the delta parallel robot is shown in Figure 7.

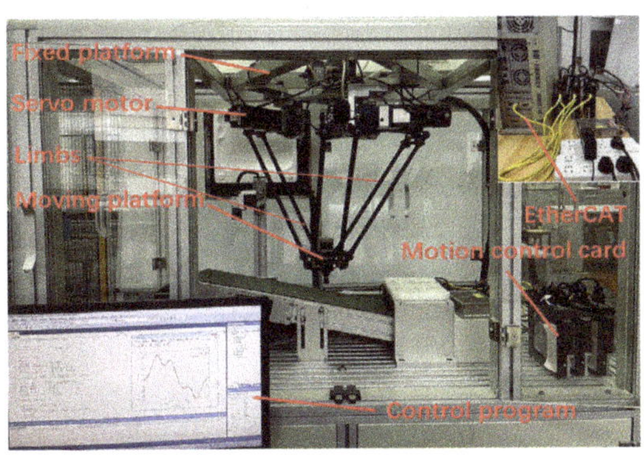

Figure 7. The experimental platform of the Delta parallel robot.

The interpolation points obtained from Cartesian space were mapped to joint space through inverse kinematics, and the fifth dimension uniform B-spline curve was used as the input data for the second interpolation and trajectory smoothing planning of the angle. The angular velocity, angular acceleration, and angular jerk were obtained in joint space, which are shown in Figures 8–10, respectively.

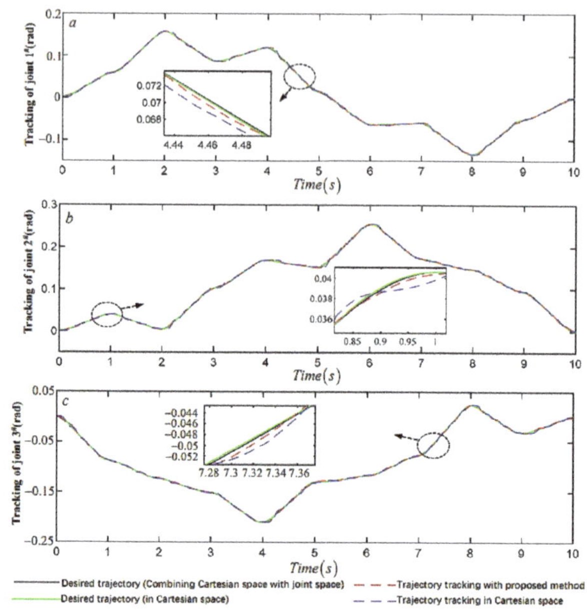

Figure 8. Trajectory tracking of each joint with proposed method and in Cartesian space. (**a**) Joint 1. (**b**) Joint 2. (**c**) Joint 3.

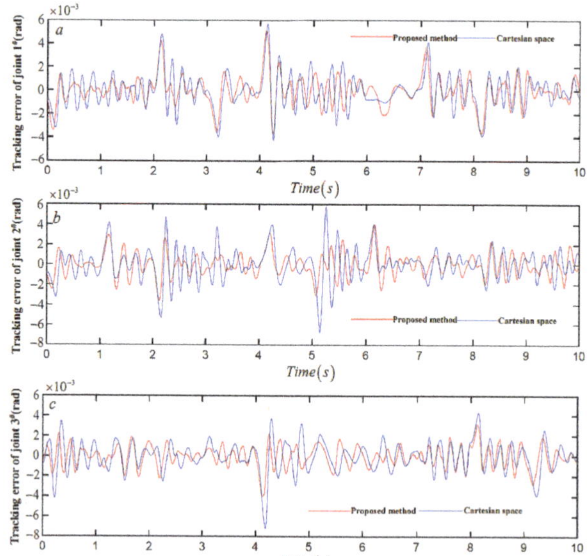

Figure 9. Tracking error of each joint with proposed method and in Cartesian space. Comparison of joint velocity trajectories in joint space. (**a**) Joint 1. (**b**) Joint 2. (**c**) Joint 3.

The control torque of the three joints is shown in Figure 10.

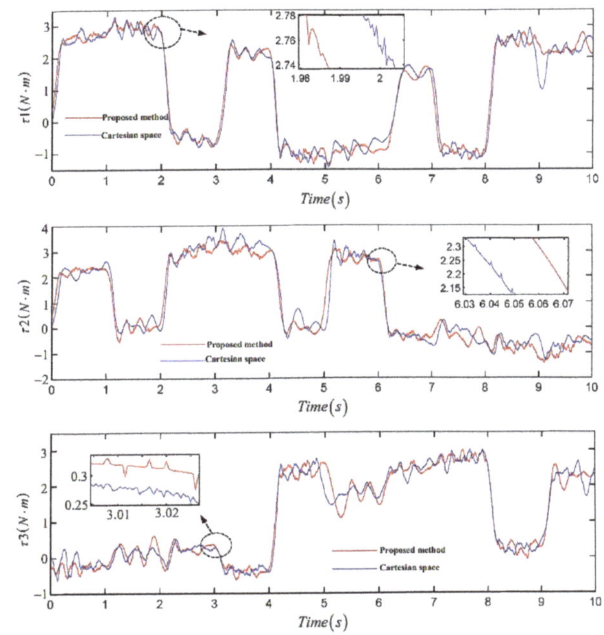

Figure 10. Comparison of joint acceleration trajectories in joint space.

Figures 8 and 9 show that, compared to the single-space (Cartesian space) trajectory planning, the trajectory planning algorithm combining joint space could obtain a smoothing trajectory, and the discontinuity of the jerk curve and trajectory mutation could be effectively improved under the same controller (a traditional PID). Among them, the peak tracking errors of joint 2 and 3 were 29% and 44% lower, respectively, than that of the single-space trajectory planning, and the error value of joint 2 was smaller in the 5 s transition stage. The errors rapidly converged at the initial stage of the three joints.

The comparison of the peak values of the trajectory tracking errors is shown in Table 3.

Table 3. Comparison of the peak values of trajectory tracking errors.

Joint	The Peak Value of Trajectory Tracking Error (rad)		
	Cartesian Space	Combining Cartesian and Joint Space	Reduction Rate
1st	0.0057	0.0051	10.53%
2nd	0.0068	0.0040	41.18%
3rd	0.0072	0.0040	44.44%

Figure 10 shows that the peak torque reduction rate of joint 2 of the trajectory obtained by the proposed trajectory planning algorithm was 11.6%, and the torque change trend was gentle. Although the peak torque reduction rates of joints 1 and 3 were 3.5% and 1.6%, respectively, it can be seen from the torque amplification diagram that the torque vibration and shock phenomena at the transition of the adjacent line segments, such as 2 s, 3 s, and 6 s, were effectively reduced when the acceleration chattering was improved. A comparison of the peak values of the control torque is shown in Table 4.

Table 4. Comparison of the peak values of control torque.

Joint	Peak Value of Control Torque τ_{max}/(N·m)		
	Cartesian Space	Combining Cartesian and Joint Space	Reduction Rate
1st	3.2909	3.1743	3.54%
2nd	3.9193	3.4657	11.65%
3rd	3.0056	2.9584	1.57%

5. Conclusions

In order to solve the problem of process shocks and vibrations caused by tangential discontinuity at the corner of small line segments in the trajectory planning of the delta parallel robot end effector, a smooth trajectory planning method based on the combination of the cubic trajectory planning in Cartesian space and the quintic uniform B-spline curve in joint space has been proposed in this paper. (1) The trajectory smoothing planning method combined with Cartesian space and joint space effectively solves the trajectory smoothing problem with the continuous high-order curves' derivatives, and the obtained joint jerk is continuously smooth. (2) The proposed method can make the robot's end effector move precisely along a smooth trajectory while making the angular velocity, acceleration, and jerk of the joint continuously smooth without impact. (3) Smooth trajectory planning was carried out from the two aspects of robot kinematics and dynamics, wherein the peak tracking error for joint 1, joint 2, and joint 3 reduced by 10.53%, 41.18% and 44.44%, respectively, and the maximum joint torque reduction was 11.65%, thereby effectively reducing the vibration and impact during the movement.

Author Contributions: Conceptualization, D.Z. and F.L.; methodology, Y.H.; software, X.Y.; validation, Y.H.; writing—original draft preparation, D.Z.; writing—review and editing, F.L. All authors have read and agreed to the published version of the manuscript.

Funding: This research received no external funding.

Data Availability Statement: The data used to support the findings of this study are available from the corresponding author upon request.

Conflicts of Interest: The authors declare no conflict of interest.

References

1. Simionescu, I.; Ciupitu, L.; Ionita, L.C. Static balancing with elastic systems of DELTA parallel robots. *Mech. Mach. Theory* **2015**, *87*, 150–162. [CrossRef]
2. Liu, C.; Cao, G.H.; Qu, Y.Y. Safety analysis via forward kinematics of delta parallel robot using maching learning. *Saf. Sci.* **2019**, *117*, 243–249. [CrossRef]
3. Boryga, M. The use of higher-degree polynomials for trajectory planning with jerk, acceleration and velocity constraints. *Int. J. Comput. Appl. Technol.* **2020**, *63*, 337–347. [CrossRef]
4. Zhao, Y.J.; Yuan, F.F.; Chen, C.W.; Jin, L.; Li, J.Y.; Zhang, X.W.; Lu, X.J. Inverse kinematics and trajectory planning for a hyper-redundant bionic trunklink robot. *Int. J. Robot. Autom.* **2020**, *35*, 229–241.
5. Damasevicius, R.; Maskeliunas, R.; Narvydas, G.; Narbutaite, R.; Polap, D.; Wozniak, W. Intelligent automation of dental material analysis using robotic arm with Jerk optimized trajectory. *J. Ambient Intell. Hum. Comput.* **2020**, *11*, 6223–6234. [CrossRef]
6. Wu, P.; Wang, Z.Y; Jing, H.X.; Zhao, P.F. Optimal time-jerk trajectory planning for Delta parallel robot based on improved butterfly optimization algorithm. *Appl. Sci.* **2022**, *12*, 8145. [CrossRef]
7. Zhang, S.; Liu, X.J.; Yan, B.K.; Bi, J.; Han, X.D. A real-time look-ahead trajectory planning methodology for multi small line segments path. *Chin. J. Mech. Eng.* **2023**, *36*, 59. [CrossRef]
8. Wu, G.L.; Zhao, W.K.; Zhang, X.P. Optimum time-energy-jerk trajectory planning for serial robotic manipulators by reparameterized quintic NURBS curves. *Proc. Inst. Mech. Eng. Part C J. Mech. Eng. Sci.* **2021**, *235*, 4382–4393. [CrossRef]
9. Xu, G.P.; Zhang, H.; Meng, Z.; Sun, Y.Z. Automatic interpolation algorithm for NURBS trajectory of shoe spraying based on 7-DOF robot. *Int. J. Cloth. Sci. Technol.* **2021**, *34*, 434–450. [CrossRef]
10. Liang, X.; Su, T.T. Quintic Pythagorean-Hodograph curves based trajectory planning for Delta robot with a prescribed geometrical constaint. *Appl. Sci.* **2019**, *9*, 4491. [CrossRef]

11. Bilal, H.; Yin, B.Q.; Kuma, A.; Ali, M.; Zhang, J.; Yao, J.F. Jerk-bounded trajectory planning for rotary flexible joint manipulator: An experimental approach. *Soft Comput.* **2023**, *27*, 4029–4039. [CrossRef]
12. Fang, Y.; Hu, J.; Liu, W.H.; Shao, Q.Q.; Qi, J.; Peng, Y.H. Smooth and time-optimal S-curve trajectory planning for automated robots and machines. *Mech. Mach. Theory* **2019**, *137*, 127–153. [CrossRef]
13. Singh, G.; Banga, V.K. Kinematics and trajectory planning analysis based on hybrid optimization algorithm for an industrial robotic manipulators. *Mech. Mach. Theory* **2022**, *26*, 11339–11372. [CrossRef]
14. Dong, H.; Cong, M.; Chen, H.P. Effective algorithms to find a minimum-time yet high smooth robot joint trajectory. *Int. J. Robot. Autom.* **2019**, *34*, 331–343. [CrossRef]
15. Brown, S.; Pierson, H.A. Adaptive path planning of novel complex parts for industrial spraying operations. *Prod. Manuf. Res.* **2020**, *8*, 335–368. [CrossRef]
16. Wang, F.; Wu, Z.J.; Bao, T.T. Time-jerk optimal trajectory planning of industrial robots based on a hybrid WOA-GA algorithm. *Processes* **2022**, *10*, 1014. [CrossRef]
17. Nadir, B.; Mohammed, O.; Minh-Tuan, N.; Abderrezak, S. Optimal trajectory generation method to find a smooth robot joint trajectory based on multiquadric radial basis functions. *Int. J. Adv. Manuf. Technol.* **2022**, *120*, 297–312. [CrossRef]
18. Chettibi, T. Smooth point-to-point trajectory planning for robot manipulators by using radial basis functions. *Robotica* **2019**, *37*, 539–559. [CrossRef]
19. Liang, Y.Y.; Yao, C.Z.; Wu, W.; Wang, L.; Wang, Q.Y. Design and implementation of multi-axis real-time synchronous look-ahead trajectory planning algorithm. *Int. J. Adv. Manuf. Technol.* **2022**, *119*, 4991–5009. [CrossRef]
20. Shrivastava, A.; Dalla, V.K. Multi-segment trajectory tracking of the redundant space robot for smooth motion planning based on interpolation of linear polynomials with parabolic blend. *Proc. Inst. Mech. Eng. Part C J. Mech. Eng. Sci.* **2022**, *236*, 9255–9269. [CrossRef]
21. Wang, H.; Wang, H.; Huang, J.H.; Zhao, B.; Quan, L. Smooth point-to-point trajectory planning for industrial robots with kinematical constraints based on high-order polynomial curve. *Mech. Mach. Theory* **2019**, *139*, 284–293. [CrossRef]
22. Wang, G.R.; Xu, F.; Zhou, K.; Pang, Z.H. S-velocity profile of industrial robot based on NURBS curve and slerp interpolation. *Processes* **2022**, *10*, 2195. [CrossRef]
23. Grassmann, R.M.; Burgner-Kahrs, J. Quaternion-based smooth trajectory generator for via poses in SE(3) considering kinematic limits in Cartesian space. *IEEE Robot. Autom. Lett.* **2019**, *4*, 4192–4199. [CrossRef]
24. Singh, G.; Banga, V.R. Combinations of novel hybrid optimization algorithms-based trajectory planning analysis for an industrial robotic manipulators. *J. Field Robot.* **2022**, *39*, 650–674. [CrossRef]
25. Zhao, Y.Q.; Mei, J.P.; Niu, M.T. Vibration error-based trajectory planning of a 5-dof hybrid machine tool. *Robot. Comput.-Integr. Manuf.* **2021**, *69*, 102095. [CrossRef]
26. Wang, Q.; Wang, Z.B.; Shuai, M. Trajectory planning for a 6-DoF manipulator used for orthopaedic surgery. *Int. J. Intell. Robot. Appl.* **2020**, *4*, 82–94. [CrossRef]
27. Kelaiaia, R. Improving the pose accuracy of the Delta robot in machining operations. *Int. J. Adv. Manuf. Technol.* **2017**, *91*, 2205–2215. [CrossRef]
28. Yang, D.; Xie, F.G.; Liu, X.J. Velocity constraints based approach for online trajectory planning of high-speed parallel robots. *Chin. J. Mech. Eng.* **2022**, *35*, 127. [CrossRef]
29. Lu, S.; Ding, B.X.; Li, Y.M. Minimum-jerk trajectory planning pertaining to a translational 3-degree-of-freedom parallel manipulator through piecewise quintic polynomials interpolation. *Adv. Mech. Eng.* **2020**, *12*, 1687814020913667. [CrossRef]
30. Dupac, M. Mathematical modeling and simulation of the inverse kinematic of a redundant robotic manipulator using azimuthal angles and spherical polar piecewise interpolation. *Math. Comput. Simul.* **2023**, *209*, 282–298. [CrossRef]
31. Rout, A.; Deepak, B.B.V.L.; Biswal, B.B.; Mahanta, G.B. Trajectory generation of an industrial robot with constrained kinematic and dynamic variations for improving positional accuracy. *Int. J. Appl. Metaheuristic Comput.* **2021**, *12*, 163–179. [CrossRef]

Disclaimer/Publisher's Note: The statements, opinions and data contained in all publications are solely those of the individual author(s) and contributor(s) and not of MDPI and/or the editor(s). MDPI and/or the editor(s) disclaim responsibility for any injury to people or property resulting from any ideas, methods, instructions or products referred to in the content.

MDPI
St. Alban-Anlage 66
4052 Basel
Switzerland
www.mdpi.com

Mathematics Editorial Office
E-mail: mathematics@mdpi.com
www.mdpi.com/journal/mathematics

Disclaimer/Publisher's Note: The statements, opinions and data contained in all publications are solely those of the individual author(s) and contributor(s) and not of MDPI and/or the editor(s). MDPI and/or the editor(s) disclaim responsibility for any injury to people or property resulting from any ideas, methods, instructions or products referred to in the content.

www.ingramcontent.com/pod-product-compliance
Lightning Source LLC
Chambersburg PA
CBHW061458220926
51850CB00004B/116
9783725802197